AF850024

Ernst Karner and Barbara C Steininger (eds)

European Tort Law 2024

European Tort Law Yearbook

Edited by the
European Centre of Tort
and Insurance Law

together with the
Institute for European Tort Law
of the Austrian Academy of Sciences
and the University of Graz

European Tort Law 2024

Ernst Karner
Barbara C Steininger (eds)

With Contributions by

Ewa Bagińska • Marko Baretić • Elena Bargelli • Søren Bergenser • Agris Bitāns • Lucian Bojin • Sergiu Căileanu • Giannino Caruana Demajo • Rui Cascão • Michael Chatzipanagiotis • Sébastien De Rey • Emanuel GD van Dongen • Anton Dulak • Andreas Bloch Ehlers • Sandra Friberg • Lukas Glöckner • Martin Hogg • Jiří Hrádek •Zoé Jacquemin • Anne LM Keirse • Jens Kleinschmidt • Jonas Knetsch • Bernhard A Koch • Päivi Korpisaari • Irene Kull • Janno Lahe • Peter Loser • Inês Oliveira Martins • Colm Peter McGrath • Filip Melzer • Attila Menyhárd • David Messner-Kreuzbauer • Barbara Novak • André Pereira • Ronen Perry • Giulia Puleio • Eoin Quill • Lawrence Quintano • Albert Ruda • Loreta Šaltinytė • Barbara C Steininger • Hristina Tancheva • Knut Martin Tande • Thomas Thiede • Viktor Tokushev • Zafeirios Tsolakidis • Paulina Wyszyńska-Ślufińska

DE GRUYTER

European Centre of Tort and Insurance Law
Reichsratsstraße 17/2
1010 Vienna
Austria
Tel: +43 1 4277-29650
Fax: +43 1 4277-29670
E-Mail: ectil@ectil.org

Institute for European Tort Law
of the Austrian Academy of Sciences
and the University of Graz
Reichsratsstraße 17/2
1010 Vienna
Austria
Tel: +43 1 4277-29651
Fax: +43 1 4277-29670
E-Mail: etl@oeaw.ac.at

ÖAW

UNI GRAZ

ISBN 978-3-11-138904-2
e-ISBN (PDF) 978-3-11-138927-1
e-ISBN (EPUB) 978-3-11-138939-4

Library of Congress Control Number: 2025943847

Bibliographic information published by the Deutsche Nationalbibliothek
The Deutsche Nationalbibliothek lists this publication in the Deutsche Nationalbibliografie; detailed bibliographic data are available on the internet at http://dnb.dnb.de.

© 2025 Walter de Gruyter GmbH, Berlin/Boston, Genthiner Straße 13, 10785 Berlin
Printing and binding: CPI books GmbH, Leck

www.degruyterbrill.com
Questions about General Product Safety Regulation:
productsafety@degruyterbrill.com

FSC www.fsc.org
MIX
Papier | Fördert gute Waldnutzung
FSC® C083411

This book is dedicated to
Miquel Martín-Casals
and to
Bénédict Winiger
who both celebrated their 70th birthday in 2025

Preface

Published jointly by the European Centre of Tort and Insurance Law (ECTIL) and the Institute for European Tort Law (ETL), this Yearbook provides information and analysis about tort law developments in Europe in 2024. It contains reports from all EU Member States except Luxembourg. Additionally, reports from Norway, England and Wales, Scotland and Switzerland, and an overview of developments in the field of EU law are included. Moreover, the Yearbook contains a report on developments in Israeli tort law. In conclusion, a comparative analysis evaluates selected highlights and identifies emerging trends.

The Yearbook is associated with the Annual Conference on European Tort Law, which is held each year in the week after Easter. The 24th Annual Conference took place in Vienna from 24 to 25 April 2025. The next Annual Conference on European Tort Law is scheduled for 8 to 10 April 2026. Papers from the Special Session of the Conference appear each year in a special issue of the Journal of European Tort Law. This year, the theme was 'PFAS and Tort Law'. The papers can be found in vol 16 no 2 of the Journal.

The editors express their gratitude to their colleagues on the ECTIL-ETL staff for their help with the Yearbook and Conference in myriad ways. Special thanks go to Lisa Zeiler for organising the Conference in a way that made meeting in Vienna so enjoyable, Julian Pehm and Samuel Loibl for taking care of technical aspects, Donna Stockenhuber for proof-reading the entire manuscript with expertise, fervour and sensitivity, Kathrin Karner-Strobach for handling the copy-editing in the same manner, Samuel Loibl and Adyasha Samal for formatting and coordinating the publication process and Adyasha Samal for compiling the Index.

Ernst Karner
Barbara C Steininger
Vienna, July 2025

https://doi.org/10.1515/9783111389271-001

Contents

David Messner-Kreuzbauer and Barbara C Steininger

I. Austria

A. Legislation

1. Act Accompanying the Digital Services Act (DSA-Begleitgesetz, DSA-BegG) Bundesgesetzblatt (BGBl) I 182/2023

In cases of violations of honour, § 1330 of the Austrian Civil Code (*Allgemeines Bürgerliches Gesetzbuch*, ABGB) foresees compensation for actual harm and lost profits, but not for non-pecuniary loss. The current Act, which aims to adapt Austrian law to the Digital Services Act,[1] introduces a new § 16 E-Commerce-Act (*E-Commerce-Gesetz*, ECG)[2] providing for a compensation claim for non-pecuniary loss suffered due to online hate speech. It entered into force on 17 February 2024.[3] 1

According to this new § 16 ECG, a natural person who suffered significant defamation in an electronic communications network[4] is entitled to claim compensation for the personal encroachment suffered from the user who provided the offending content. This will typically be the person who posted the defamatory 2

Note: The authors would like to thank Nick Mutterer for his assistance in preparing the literature overview.

1 Regulation (EU) 2022/2065 of the European Parliament and of the Council of 19 October 2022 on a Single Market For Digital Services and amending Directive 2000/31/EC (Digital Services Act) [2022] Official Journal (OJ) L 277/1.
2 The rule formerly contained in § 16 ECG regulated the exclusion of liability of host providers. As the exclusion of liability of providers of intermediary services is now included directly in the DSA, § 16 was available for the new rule. See preparatory materials on the DSA-BegG, ErläutRV 2309 BlgNR 28 GP, 27; available online via <https://www.parlament.gv.at/dokument/XXVII/I/2309/fname_1595816.pdf>.
3 See on this provision *H Wittmann*, Das DSA-Begleitgesetz: Neue Instrumente zur Bekämpfung von "Hass im Netz", Medien und Recht (MR) 2023, 298; *D Dokalik*, Immaterieller Schadenersatz für Hasspostings. Der neue § 16 ECG idF des DSA-BegleitG BGBl I 2023/182, Österreichische Jurist: innen-Zeitung (ÖJZ) 2024, 589; *C Handig*, Ehrensache? Immaterieller Schaden und Ehrenbeleidigung, ecolex 2024, 232; *P Zöchbauer*, Zum Ersatz ideeller Schäden nach § 16 ECG idF BGBl I 2023/182, MR 2024, 3.
4 The term refers to art 3 g DSA and art 2 (1) of Directive 2018/1972/EU.

https://doi.org/10.1515/9783111389271-002

content[5] but it could also be someone who shared or otherwise actively disseminated the content.[6] The materiality threshold (only *significant* defamation justifies compensation) aims to ensure that the courts will not have to deal with trivial questions.[7] Compensation for non-pecuniary loss provided for by other provisions (the preparatory materials refer to §§ 1328, 1328a ABGB, § 29 Data Protection Act, *Datenschutzgesetz*, DSG, §§ 78, 87 Copyright Act, *Urheberrechtsgesetz*, UrhG)[8] remains unaffected. If a media owner intervenes, liability will be channelled to the latter (who will only be responsible according to the Media Act), while the journalist or author writing the text cannot be held liable.[9] Finally, it should be mentioned that the Act also repeals § 1490 ABGB, which provided for a special short prescription period of only one year for defamation through words, writing or gestures. Consequently, the general rule of § 1489 ABGB is now applicable in such cases (three years after the injured becomes aware of the harm and the wrongdoer).[10]

3 In our view, the current exclusion of compensation for non-pecuniary loss for all cases of defamation is problematic. Academics have argued that at least for violations of human dignity, compensation for non-pecuniary loss should be available, even under the current § 1330 ABGB.[11] The introduction of a provision expressly providing for compensation for non-pecuniary loss for significant defamation therefore merits approval, though it is hard to see why this should be limited to defamation occurring via electronic communications networks.[12] Methodologically, there is now even a risk that the courts see the new § 16 ECG as a conscious decision against providing redress in other cases, rather than as the expression of a more general (and in our view, sound) principle.

5 Preparatory materials, ErläutRV 2309 BlgNR 28 GP 27.

6 *Dokalik*, ÖJZ 2024, 591.

7 *Dokalik*, ÖJZ 2024, 590.

8 Preparatory materials, ErläutRV 2309 BlgNR 28 GP 28.

9 *Dokalik*, ÖJZ 2024, 591.

10 See preparatory materials, ErläutRV 2309 BlgNR 28 GP 29.

11 *F Bydlinski*, Der Ersatz ideellen Schadens als sachliches und methodisches Problem, Juristische Blätter (JBl) 1965, 253 f; *idem*, Der immaterielle Schaden in der österreichischen Rechtsentwicklung, Festschrift von Caemmerer (1978) 798; *E Karner/H Koziol*, Der Ersatz ideellen Schadens im österreichischen Recht und seine Reform. 15. Österreichischer Juristentag II/1 (2003) 98 f; *H Koziol*, Österreichisches Haftpflichtrecht II (3rd edn 2018) no A/5/278.

12 In this sense also *Zöchbauer*, MR 2024, 4. Cf also *Dokalik*, ÖJZ 2024, 590.

2. Act Modifying Liability 2024 (*Haftungsrechtsänderungsgesetz* 2024) BGBl I 33/2024

This Act introduces a new § 1319b into the ABGB, regulating liability for the maintenance of trees.[13] Although § 176 Forestry Act (*Forstgesetz*, ForstG) already contained provisions regulating and limiting the liability of forest keepers for the condition of forests and forest paths, this is the first general provision in Austrian law in this matter. Politically, it aims to reassure tree keepers that they need not cut their trees down in fear of liability. 4

Broadly, § 1319b ABGB stipulates that: 1) the keeper of a tree is liable for personal injury and property damage if caused by negligent check-ups or securing of the tree; 2) that the standard of care depends on the location and the danger connected to the tree, the size, the growth and the condition of the tree, as well as the feasibility of examinations and securing, while the interest in the natural setting (park, biosphere…) must also be taken into account; and finally, that 3) the 'general rules' on the burden of proof are applicable to such a claim. 5

The first two sections in effect reproduce the general test for a duty to secure and the ensuing standard of care in relation to others' general rights under Austrian law.[14] Their general effect is not a fundamental change, but rather makes the general test more concrete for keeping trees and defines the interests that speak for and against a duty to secure.[15] The legislator also resisted the temptation to reduce relevant fault to gross negligence. 6

Yet, there are some substantial changes as well. The third section attempts to make clear that in a tort claim against a person in control of a tree, the burden of proof falls on the claimant. The background that motivated the legislator to become active is the following. Before the 2024 Act, the courts extended the provi- 7

---

13 *B Borkowski*, Das HaftRÄG 2022: Eine Neuordnung der Haftung für Bäume, Zeitschrift für Verkehrsrecht (ZVR) 2023, 57; *C Diesenreither*, Neue Wurzeln für die Baumhaftung: § 1319b ABGB, ZVR 2024, 319; *E Karner*, Die Neuregelung der Baumhaftung in § 1319b ABGB, ÖJZ 2024, 727; *F Kerschner*, Keine Angstschnitte mehr – zur neuen Baumhaftung, RFG (Recht & Finanzen für Gemeinden) 2024, 43; *J Stabentheiner/MC Wieser*, Gesetzliche Neuregelung der Haftung für Bäume – das Haftungsrechts-Änderungsgesetz 2024, Zivilrecht Aktuell (Zak) 2024, 124; *E Wagner*, Hurra – Ministerialentwurf zur Baumhaftung (endlich) da! Recht der Umwelt (RdU) 2024, 4. Many of these authors also shaped the draft of the law.

14 On the standard, see *E Karner* in: B Winiger/E Karner/K Oliphant (eds), Digest of European Tort Law: Essential Cases on Misconduct (2018) 2/3 no 3 (citing 'the value of the endangered right, how severe the impending damage is, the degree of danger, the interests of the parties involved and whether a person could, within the bounds of reasonableness, be expected to act differently').

15 See in-depth *Karner*, ÖJZ 2024, 730 ff.

sion on buildings, § 1319 ABGB, to trees.[16] § 1319 ABGB sets an objective standard of care and reverses the burden of proof concerning misconduct. Thus, the analogy meant that, like the keeper of a building, the defendant had to prove that they had acted according to the objective standard of care expected of a tree keeper. But the preparatory documents to the draft strongly emphasise that the 'ordinary rules', rather than the rules for buildings, should apply to trees. This may mean a standard that is generally subjective, as is the basic rule of the ABGB. Also, the reference to 'ordinary rules' on the burden of proof results in an end to the judge-made shift of the burden to the keeper.[17] Reference to 'general rules' means that by default, a claimant bears the burden of proof regarding all elements of a case, in particular for the misconduct of the alleged tortfeasor.[18] This is likely what the law aims to achieve, although a very literal reading of the text could still leave some doubts. Besides applying § 1319 to trees, the courts have developed a general shift of the burden of proof for duties to secure a risk, to which the keeping of trees belongs.[19] Is this an 'ordinary rule' that remains applicable, or does § 1319b (3) ABGB now prevent such a shift in the burden of proof? The answer must probably be the latter, since the legislator intended to relieve tree keepers, and since the justification for a general shift in the burden of proof in all cases concerning a duty to secure seems doubtful in any case.[20]

3. Act Implementing the Collective Redress Directive (*Verbandsklagen-Richtlinie-Umsetzungs-Novelle*, VRUN) BGBl I 85/2024

8 This Act implements the Collective Redress Directive with delay, by adding provisions in §§ 619 ff of the Civil Procedure Ordinance (*Zivilprozessordnung*, ZPO) and a new Statute on Qualified Entities (*Qualifizierte-Einrichtungen-Gesetz*, QUEG). As this is a procedural matter and European law provides for the general rules of the procedure, we will not discuss it extensively here but limit ourselves to two re-

16 Austrian Supreme Court (Oberster Gerichtshof, OGH) 1 Ob 50/70 Evidenzblatt der Rechtsmittelentscheidungen (EvBl) in ÖJZ 1970/294; RS0029932.
17 ErläutRV 2462 BlgNR 27 GP 1, 8. The document can be found under <https://www.parlament.gv.at/dokument/XXVII/I/2462/fname_1613464.pdf>.
18 ErläutRV 2462 BlgNR 27 GP 8.
19 OGH 7 Ob 132/64 Sammlung für Zivilrecht (SZ) 41/146; RS0022476.
20 *Karner*, ÖJZ 2024, 733 f.

markable features of the Austrian implementation. First, Austria used its discretion under art 9 (2) of the Directive to choose an 'opt-in procedure', meaning that consumers have to join a collective redress claim rather than declaring no participation (§ 628 ZPO). Second, for this reason and others, academics are sceptical as to whether the collective claim for redress will be more effective than the domestic instrument used for collective claims in Austria so far,[21] namely an assignment of all claims to one entity, which then pursues them in their own name.

B. Cases

1. Oberster Gerichtshof (Austrian Supreme Court, OGH) 23 January 2024, 1 Ob 189/23k:[22] Liability for a Judge's Failure to Declare Partiality

a) Brief Summary of the Facts

The claimant was a party to proceedings before a local court in several issues, including one concerning his capacity. He filed numerous complaints and appeals alleging the partiality of the judge sitting on the court of protection ('protection judge') as well as the partiality of the president of the court who decided on the complaints about the protection judge. Among these complaints was one raised in 2017 alleging a relationship between the protection judge and the president of the court. This complaint was denied as were the others. However, a friendly relationship between the judges later transpired to exist since some point in 2015, the precise beginning of which remained unclear. Later in 2017, the entire court finally recused itself for a different reason, namely that the claimant had physically threatened the judge of protection. In the case that ultimately came before the OGH, the claimant filed a tort suit under the Public Authority Liability Act (*Amtshaftungsgesetz*, AHG) against the federal state as the entity responsible for the civil courts and adjudication on civil matters. In this claim, he alleges that the denial of his complaint was wilful and that the judges would have been obligated to reveal their relationship. This, he claims, has cost him € 110,590 on further procedural complaints to effect the recusal that was guaran- 9

21 See eg, *F Scholz-Berger*, Kollektive Durchsetzung von Abhilfeansprüchen nach Umsetzung der VerbandsklagenRL in Österreich, ecolex 2024, 583, 588, with an assessment of the Act and further references to the extensive discussion.

22 ECLI:AT:OGH0002:2024:0010OB00189.23K.0123.000; EvBl 2024/219 with cmt by *D Schindl*.

teed by his procedural rights, which he would not have incurred if the judges had properly recused themselves.

10 Before the case reached the Supreme Court, the lower courts had already declared a part of the claim unsubstantiated or otherwise defective. Concerning one part, the lower courts had said that the burden of proof concerning the start of the relationship was on the claimant, and that he had failed to discharge it. The trial court only upheld a small part of the sum, whereas the appellate court ordered the taking of further evidence regarding a broadly overlapping sum (€ 17,059). This was necessary, the court said, because from whence the relationship was proven to exist, the judges would indeed have had to file notice of their relationship under § 22 (1), (2) Court Management Act (*Gerichtsorganisationsgesetz*, GOG). From this time on, the appellate court assumed, how the procedure would have played out if the judges had acted properly was a significant issue.

b) Judgment of the Court

11 The Supreme Court upholds this decision demanding further evidence. However, it denies that the claimant benefits from any facilitation of proof concerning the beginning of the relationship. According to the OGH, a reversal of the burden of proof would require 'entirely specific, disproportionate difficulties of proof', whereas the other party has access to the relevant insights and it is 'not only easily possible but also feasible without further ado according to good faith and fair dealing to make the relevant disclosure', and, the OGH claimed, this was not true for the federal state concerning the private behaviour of judges. Accepting a 'proof of first impression' (*Anscheinsbeweis*, prima facie case) would require a typical course of events, and there was no typical course of events relating to when a relationship starts.

12 The second and longer part of the OGH's reasoning concerns the question of how the claimant's loss would have to be assessed from the time the judges' obligation to report their relationship and recuse themselves was proven. The Supreme Court treats this as a case of an omission and applies the but-for test. This would mean that the trial court would have to add the required action to the actual facts, and then see whether the loss would fall away. The lower courts had not established whether an impartial judge would have decided in the same way in substance or differently. The Supreme Court further discusses an established doctrine to the effect that, when a defendant has breached a statutory duty, the claimant has a prima facie case that their loss would have ensued (if it corresponds with the protective purpose of the statute). However, according to the OGH, the availability of this prima facie case depends on the circumstances.

It is again not a typical course of events that a judge deemed partial for external factors takes a wrong decision, because this does not necessarily mean that the judge is also 'subjectively' partial. Thus, the defendant would have to prove that the proceedings would have arrived at a different conclusion if the judges had recused themselves. The OGH finally recalls a specific rule for assessing how the procedure would hypothetically have unfolded absent the alleged wrongdoing of the authorities. A trial court has to assume that the officials or judges who would then have heard the case would have made legally correct decisions, rather than taking evidence on how the actual judges then in charge would have decided.

c) Commentary

Tuning the proverb on its head, it could be asked whether a bad case makes hard 13 law. The claimant generated an avalanche of complaints and threatened a judge, whereas the judges' offence seems minor and potentially irrelevant. This borders on abuse of procedural mechanisms and it would be understandable if the courts had used their margins of interpretation against them. This said, let us walk through the application of familiar rules by the OGH under these difficult circumstances.

Concerning the time when the relationship started and therefore when 14 wrongful conduct first occurred, it seems justified to say that there is no typical connection as necessary for a prima facie case. The reasoning on what the Supreme Court calls a reversal of the objective burden of proof (burden of persuasion) is less convincing. The OGH actually does not even consider the mechanism that is properly so called.[23] An actual shift of the burden of proof is triggered by certain facts of the case, not by difficulties in gathering evidence in the trial.[24] Still, in substance, the court was right to allow no reversal. Although the relation between court and party is a special relation in which it would be available in general (§ 1298 ABGB), triggering this reversal requires the judge's conviction that a very abstract norm of conduct has been breached,[25] meaning that only from there the courts may place the burden on the defendant of proving that they did not act wrongfully (negligently) properly speaking. It was open whether

23 On which, see *E Karner*, The Function of the Burden of Proof in Tort Law, in: H Koziol/ BC Steininger (eds), European Tort Law 2008 (2009) 68.

24 *BC Steininger*, Art 4:201 PETL: Revisiting the Grey Areas between Fault-Based and Strict Liability (2023) 14 Journal of European Tort Law (JETL) 89, 93 f.

25 See *F Bydlinski*, Zur Haftung der Dienstleistungsberufe in Österreich und nach dem EG-Richtlinienvorschlag, JBl 1992, 341, 347 ff; Karner (fn 23) no 9 ff.

such a norm had been breached at the right time. Thus, what the claimant wanted to do in this case was to use later misconduct as reversing the burden of proof that such misconduct had already existed earlier. But a rule allowing this does not exist under Austrian law.

15 The proof rule the Supreme Court actually contemplated was the sanction for a failure of a party to adduce facts and assist the court in fact-finding. This responsibility does not reverse the burden of proof, but it can have consequences in evidence, namely adverse inferences against the uncooperative party when the courts establish their 'free conviction' about the facts (§ 272 [1] Civil Procedure Ordinance, *Zivilprozessordnung*, ZPO).[26] Stating this more clearly could have supported the OGH's conclusions, because whatever the federal state did or did not know, this arguably did not change much about the possibilities and probabilities in play when the relationship began. An assessment of this should, however, have been left to the trial judge. Instead, the court stated that evidence concerning the private relationship is not under the federal state's control and, for this reason, there should be no shifts in the burden of proof. This argument is unfortunately unconvincing. Under general rules, the knowledge of judges is arguably attributable to the employer (ie, the federal state), and therefore legally under their control.[27]

16 Now to the second significant issue: the problem of how to establish whether an earlier recusal would have left the claimant better off. The OGH appears to set strict standards again by assuming that the claimant has to prove their case completely.

17 However, perhaps because the case file was very unclear, the Court did not distinguish between two types of harm a claimant may complain of in cases turning on the wrongful decision of a court or authority. The first one is the 'judgment damage' (*Urteilsschaden*) produced by a substantially wrong decision. In the case at hand, the claimant may have demanded compensation for the damage caused by decisions concerning his capacity. In assessing this damage, it is hard to see why the trial court would have to do much more fact-finding or that proof rules matter very much. Let us explain why. In determining whether a false de-

---

26 OGH 11 May 2005, 9 Ob 1 2/05p; *T Klicka*, Aufklärungspflichten der Prozessparteien im österreichischen Zivilprozessrecht, JBl 1992, 231, 233 f; *JCT Rassi*, Die Aufklärungs- und Mitwirkungspflichten der nicht beweisbelasteten Partei im Zivilprozess aus österreichischer Sicht (2008) 121 Zeitschrift für Zivilprozess (ZZP) 165, 197 ff.

27 According to the seminal article on attributing knowledge to superiors, this would depend on the qualification of the judges as general representatives of the federal state, or their specific assignment to the relevant task. *G Iro*, Banken und Wissenszurechnung, Österreichisches Bank-Archiv (ÖBA) 2001, 3 and 112.

cision was a cause of the claimant's harm, the law simplifies the task of the court hearing the tort claim ('the secondary procedure'). While it has to take actual wrongdoing of the authorities (in the 'primary procedure') as it happened, it may reconstruct the hypothetical proceedings of another court or authority that are relevant to the causal chain under the assumption that other authorities – such as the court competent in the case of lawful recusal – would have made *right* decisions.[28] They need not guess whether, besides the wrongdoing authority, other authorities would have (also) decided wrongly. Therefore, whether the claimant would receive anything in this regard only depends on whether a diligent judge would have decided differently than the one that should have recused herself in the present case. There is no indication in the accessible data that this would have been so.

The claimant, however, appears to have (only or mainly?) demanded the pro- 18
cedural costs he incurred when trying to achieve a different substantive result in the primary procedure: the cost of his various appeals and complaints. However, even there we see little need for further evidence. Although the OGH does not cite this rule, there is a test for the reimbursement of procedural costs via a public authority liability claim,[29] which the claimant arguably fails to satisfy. The court or other authority must not only have caused the claimant's need to react against the wrong decision; the reaction must also have been a reasonable pursual of one's procedural rights. It is hard to see how the claimant's actions could be described as reasonable.[30] As far as the facts are known, the first complaint against the protection judge was entirely unsubstantiated. And complaining about the external partiality of a judge within (!) this otherwise unsubstantiated complaint does not seem any more reasonable, even if there happened to be an objective (external) ground for partiality. If we analyse this correctly, the claimant had no right to any compensation of his procedural efforts.

In short, the circumstances of the case surely made the decision difficult, but 19
we submit here that an easier route out of the problem would have been available to the Supreme Court.

---

28 On this rule, see *D Messner-Kreuzbauer*, Rechtsunkenntnis und fehlerhafte Behördenauskunft, wirtschaftsrechtliche blätter (wbl) 2025, 1, 11.

29 Eg, OGH 14 July 2022, 1 Ob 115/22 EvBl 2023/35 with cmt *AL Nikolay*.

30 *Schindl*, EvBl 2024/219 also doubts whether it was caused.

2. OGH 26 April 2024, 6 Ob 210/23k:[31] Torrent of Abuse on Social Media ('Shitstorm'); Causation; Non-Pecuniary Loss

a) Brief Summary of the Facts

20 The claimant in this case is a police officer who was filmed and photographed during a police operation in the context of a demonstration against the government's COVID-19 measures. Someone other than the defendant had published the video on Facebook accompanied with the following text: 'Let this face of the policeman go around the world. This policeman escalated at the demonstration in I*. An 82-year-old innocent man was pulled to the ground, arrested and interrogated for hours. This policeman is guilty.' In reality, the claimant had only been part of a police cordon and had not taken part in the operation against the 82-year-old man. The defendant saw the post, identified the claimant as a police officer and shared a screenshot of the post including both a picture on which the claimant was recognisable (although he had been wearing a protective mask) and the text, on his own Facebook profile without checking the original post for its truthfulness. The defendant later deleted the post himself but it had been online for at least six days. The claimant identified 406 persons who had taken part in the torrent of abuse on social media that emerged, a phenomenon referred to as a 'shitstorm' in German. Various posts were accompanied by disparaging comments which the claimant found very degrading and embarrassing. Friends and colleagues and a former superior addressed the posting and even the claimant's family members were approached about it. The situation was very stressful for the claimant, who constantly felt the need to justify himself.

21 In the current proceedings, the claimant, amongst others, sought revocation and publication of this revocation as well as compensation for the non-pecuniary loss suffered due to the violation of image and data protection, amounting to € 3,000 in total. The Court of First Instance ordered the defendant to revoke and publish this revocation and granted the claimant compensation amounting to € 450 in total. The Court of Appeal rejected the appeal of both parties. As the

---

31 ECLI:AT:OGH0002:2024:0060OB00210.23K.0426.000; Kommunikation und Recht (K&R) 2024, 542 with cmt by *A Kezer* = Medien und Recht (MR) 2024, 114 = Recht der Wirtschaft (RdW) 2024/457 = Zeitschrift für IT-Recht und Digitalisierung (MMR) 2024, 853 = ecolex 2024/462 with cmt by *P Zöchbauer* = Zeitschrift für Urheber- und Medienrecht (ZUM) 2024, 817 with cmt *C Gomille* = EvBl 2024/255 = Zeitschrift für Informationsrecht (ZIIR) 2024, 402 with cmt *Thiele* = JBl 2024, 660 = jusIT 2024/112 with cmt by *M Kröpfl*. See also *S Adametz/A Kezer*, MR 2024, 108; *B Burtscher*, Haftung für "Shitstorm", ÖJZ 2024, 848.

defendant's appeal had not included the part of the decision concerning revocation and its publication, these parts became final.

b) Judgment of the Court

They key issue of the OGH's decision was the question whether and to what extent the defendant, as an individual poster participating in the torrent of abuse on social media, is liable to pay compensation for the damage incurred. 22

The OGH's 6th panel held that the defendant had acted in violation of the rules on data and image protection and stressed that non-pecuniary harm suffered as a consequence of such violations is in principle compensable. While the UrhG (Copyright Act), which in its art 87 para 2 provides for compensation of non-pecuniary harm suffered as a consequence of the violation of the right to one's image, requires a serious encroachment to justify compensation, there is no threshold of seriousness under the General Data Protection Regulation (GDPR). The OGH further sets out that compensation also requires culpable behaviour and then identifies the question of causation as the most problematic aspect in the context of the current case: 23

According to the OGH, a single person can set a 'shitstorm' in the sense of a storm of indignation in the virtual world in motion and can contribute to it but cannot bring it about alone, as only the public abuse by a large number of persons will make the victim experience an unjustified condemnation by the general public. Based on this assumption, the OGH outlines different concepts discussed in scenarios of uncertain causation in the past, namely alternative causation (where each of several possible, specifically dangerous actions could in itself have caused the entire damage or a certain part thereof and, while only one of these actually caused the damage, it remains unclear which one did), cumulative causation (where each tortfeasor brought about a real and simultaneously effective ground for the harm and each of these grounds alone would have caused the entire harm) and, finally, combined impact scenarios (so-called 'summierte Einwirkungen', where the harm was only caused through the combined impact of several events). 24

The OGH then argues that, in the case at hand, all contributors to the torrent of abuse on social media clearly violated image and data protection and therefore all of them caused the concrete loss related to this individual violation. However, only the involvement of several persons acting at least negligently brought about a different and greater harm, as the victim experienced an unjustified condemnation by the general public. The OGH further states that the posts cannot be understood to be completely separate and the behaviour of the tortfeasors sharing the 25 'original post' therefore cannot be qualified as either alternatively or cumulatively causal or as a case of combined impact, but will have to be categorised as 'mixed' and 'overlapping' in this respect.

26 In the view of the OGH, the unclarity as to whether individual consequences were caused by specific (re-)posts, which is typical for a torrent of abuse on social media, must be borne by the tortfeasors. All posters of the torrent of abuse, as a rule, act at least negligently. If all of them engage in misconduct which is specifically dangerous[32] and therefore entails a suspicion of causality, and if this misconduct contains all elements of liability except for the strict proof of causation of the entire damage, the risk that causation cannot be clarified is to be borne by the posters and not by the injured party. Consequently, the OGH concludes that in such scenarios, the tortfeasors contributorily caused the entire damage and will be jointly and severally liable for such damage in analogy to § 1302 ABGB, a result also reached in cases of alternative and cumulative causation. Consequently, a claimant will only have to claim and prove that they are or were the victim of a torrent of abuse on social media in which the tortfeasor in question participated unlawfully and culpably. Due to the inability to clarify the damage shares of individual posters, the victim can usually claim the entire damage from such a tortfeasor.

27 The OGH then refers to damage caused in the course of demonstrations, where partial liability instead of joint and several liability is assumed based on the argument of 'minimal causation'. In such scenarios, damage is caused by a large number of persons, none of whom causes the entire damage. Instead, each of the tortfeasors only minimally contributes to the damage. In the view of the OGH there can, however, be no question of such minimal causation in the case at hand as the posters – including the defendant – were actively involved by sharing the image and the accompanying text and consequently not only participated in the dissemination as such, but also called for further dissemination, ie for the torrent of abuse.

28 The fact that the claimant in the case at hand had based his claim on several legal grounds can, according to the OGH, not lead to him being awarded more than the harm suffered. Consequently, the € 650 the plaintiff had already been awarded based on the Media Act has to be taken into account. In the view of the 9th panel of the OGH, the core of the damage suffered is the harm to the claimant's reputation, the insult he had suffered and the fear and anxiety brought

32 According to the OGH, any sharing of the post in combination with the call for dissemination is such a concretely dangerous action, as it brings about additional risk of dissemination and hence damage.

about by this. When awarding compensation for this harm, the OGH considered it – if at all possible – unnecessary to precisely allocate individual parts of the compensation to individual legal bases (GDPR, Data Protection Act, Copyright Act and Media Act) because of the claim being justified even when prior compensation is taken into account.

The plaintiff had already received € 650 from the defendant and € 550 from 29
another poster and he had been awarded compensation based on the Media Act amounting to € 650. In the view of the OGH, it would have been up to the defendant to prove payment of any compensation beyond this amount. It comes to the conclusion that it is not necessary to precisely determine the entire loss as even an (additional) award of € 3,000 as claimed in the current proceedings would lead to the claimant receiving not even € 5,000 as compensation, an amount which, in the view of the OGH, is undoubtedly justified when taking into account the seriousness of the allegations against the claimant in the post, the massive public decry and the stress brought about by this for the claimant.

c) Commentary

In the present case, the substantial non-pecuniary harm suffered by the claimant 30
emanates from numerous posts violating his personality rights. It is evident that the original post was causal in the sense of a *conditio sine qua non* for the entire harm suffered[33] and it is, as stressed by the OGH, also clear that each of the many other posts caused at least some small part of the damage. Except for the original one, the posts were, however, not a 'but-for cause' for the *entire* harm. If we assume that one of these posts had not been published, the total harm suffered by the claimant would have changed only marginally.[34] Moreover, it is hardly possible to ascertain which posts led to other posts. In this sense, the defendant had argued that it was unclear whether even a single person had seen his post.

This undoubtedly complicated scenario leads the OGH to assume a combina- 31
tion of alternative and cumulative causation and combined impact, although these categories are mutually exclusive,[35] and on this basis decides for joint and several liability. While the OGH's argument that the unclarity whether individual consequences were caused by specific posts must be borne by the tortfeasors is convincing, this result cannot simply be based on such a mixed category. Moreover, such a

33 *B Burtscher*, ÖJZ 2024, 849; *C Gomille*, ZUM 2024, 828.
34 Cf *F Bydlinski*, Schadensverursachung im deutschen und österreichischen Recht (1964) 109 ff.
35 This is rightly stressed by *Burtscher*, ÖJZ 2024, 849.

'mixture' is, in our view, not necessary; even though the phenomenon of a torrent of abuse on social media is a recent one, the problems of causation it entails are not entirely new and have largely been addressed under the notion of 'minimal causation'[36] eg in the context of damage brought about in the course of strikes or demonstrations.[37] In these cases, it cannot be ascertained whether an event caused a certain harm while it is clear that several comparable events together did indeed cause harm.[38] Although strike and demonstration cases refer to pecuniary loss, the concept also fits for the present non-pecuniary loss case: due to the large number of posts, only a small contribution to the entire non-pecuniary loss suffered can be ascertained for individual posts, not however a but-for condition for the entire harm. While court practice in minimal causation cases is in favour of joint and several liability,[39] doctrine favours partial liability in equal shares.[40] According to the convincing intermediary view put forward by *Koziol*, joint and several liability according to §§ 1301 and 1302 ABGB will (only) apply if the tortfeasors acted jointly and intentionally.[41]

32 As is convincingly argued by *Burtscher*[42] acting jointly includes the torrent of abuse scenario of the present case of posts requesting others to let the face of the claimant go around the world, which, from the start, aims to harm the claimant by way of posters acting in concert. Consequently, holding the defendant jointly and severally liable for the claimant's entire harm is convincing although the reasoning behind this result is not. In scenarios in which posters acted either unintentionally or not jointly, only partial liability in equal shares can be justified in our view.[43]

33 While we consider minimal causation to be decisive for this case, the OGH only referred to this concept and the partial liability favoured in doctrine as a way to escape joint and several liability in the case of a minimal contribution to the damage. The Supreme Court does not decide whether minimal causation

36 *F Bydlinski* (fn 34) 108 ff; *H Koziol*, Österreichisches Haftpflichtrecht I (4th edn 2020) no B/2/120 ff. For cases in which someone links or likes contents of someone else, *E Karner/J Pehm*, Zivilrechtliche Verantwortlichkeit von (Online-)Medien, in: H Koziol (ed), Tatsachenmitteilungen und Werturteile (2018) 122, expressly refer to minimal causation.

37 See *Koziol* (fn 36) no B/2/120.

38 *Koziol* (fn 36) no B/2/120; *E Karner* in: P Bydlinski/S Perner/M Spitzer (eds), Kommentar zum ABGB (KBB) (7th edn 2023) § 1302 no 11.

39 OGH Sammlung zivilrechtlicher Entscheidungen des k.k. Obersten Gerichtshofes; neue Folge (GlUNF) 3873; JBl 1931, 81.

40 *F Bydlinski* (fn 34) 110; KBB/*Karner* (fn 38) § 1302 no 11 with further refs.

41 *Koziol* (fn 36) no B/2/121 f.

42 ÖJZ 2024, 850 f.

43 *F Bydlinski* (fn 34) 110.

would indeed lead to partial liability as it denies a minimal contribution for the case at hand due to the active behaviour of the posters who also called for dissemination of the post. When doing so, the OGH focuses on the quality of the behaviour – the weight of an action in concert – rather than the causation problem related to the marginal difference made for the entire harm suffered through that behaviour and the unclarity as to whether the defendant's post led to any other posts. But we consider the causation aspect decisive in this respect.

It should be added that, according to prevailing opinion, tortfeasors who acted jointly and intentionally can escape liability if they prove that they did not cause the entire harm,[44] for instance because they only took part in the torrent of abuse on social media at a very late stage.[45] *Koziol* convincingly argues that, in such scenarios, a safeguard liability (*Sicherstellungshaftung*) applies: as tortfeasors who, by taking part in a joint and wrongful act, increased the risk that the situation cannot be clarified and thereby make it harder to enforce a victim's compensation claim, they should bear this risk.[46] Even if they can prove that they did not cause the entire damage, they remain liable but will have a right of recourse against other tortfeasors. 34

Finally, it should be stated that it is unfortunate that there was no assessment of the entire harm suffered in the case at hand. The claimant himself assessed it at € 2,000 per post which means more than € 800,000. This is quite out of proportion when one compares this to awards in personal injury cases,[47] where the highest award is currently € 350,000.[48] 35

---

44 *F Bydlinski*, Archiv für die civilistische Praxis (AcP) 158, 430; *P Gruber*, Kausalität bei Mittätern und Pflicht zur Schadensverhinderung, JBl 2017, 612; KBB/*Karner* (fn 38) § 1301 no 5; *R Reischauer* in: Rummel, ABGB (3rd edn 2007) § 1302 no 1; OGH 5 Ob 39/11p, EvBl 2012/80 = ecolex 2012/170 with cmt by *G Wilhelm* = RdW 2012/569, see also *C Bamberger/C Kriechbaumer*, RdW 2012, 504; 2 Ob 97/16b, SZ 2016/879; Zak 2016/712 = EvBl 2017/104 with cmt by *M Spitzer* = JBl 2017, 592; 9 Ob 52/18i, Zak 2018/686 = Österreichisches Anwaltsblatt (AnwBl) 2019/13 = JBl 2019, 113 = Zeitschrift für Gesundheitsrecht (ZfG) 2018, 175 = ecolex 2019/245; 1 Ob 178/18k, Zak 2018/820 = Zeitschrift für Verbraucherrecht (VbR) 2019/7 = AnwBl 2019/65 = ZfG 2019, 22.

45 Cf *Burtscher*, ÖJZ 2024, 851 f.

46 *H Koziol*, Die Sicherstellungshaftung – eine weitere Spur im Haftungsrecht, AcP 219 (2019) 397.

47 This was stressed by *E Karner* when presenting the case at Vienna University of Economics and Business on 15 January 2025.

48 OLG Innsbruck 18.7.2024, 10 R 34/24 m, see below no 78.

3. OGH 15 May 2024, 6 Ob 70/24y:[49] Art 82 GDPR and Scope of Protection

a) Brief Summary of the Facts

36 After a wine festival, the heavily intoxicated claimant tried to park his car on the grounds of the defendant, where the claimant was a tenant. He damaged his car in the process. The incident was captured on CCTV that the defendant had installed due to previous instances of vandalism. When the claimant demanded insurance pay-outs from his motor vehicle coverage, the insurer's employees duly noted the camera, asked for the video material, and concluded that they could deny coverage by reference to the claimant's obvious intoxication. The dispute between the claimant and the insurer ended in a settlement.[50] The claimant, unabashed, filed a claim for financial compensation[51] for the 'lost' insurance coverage against the defendant, claiming that the CCTV violated his right to data protection and that he was entitled to damages under art 82 GDPR.

b) Judgment of the Court

37 The OGH declared the appeal 'inadmissible' (*unzulässig*), which means it is not significant enough for treatment on the merits at the highest level. (That in itself is, however, often a significant statement, and the Court does give some reasons, which warrant the inclusion in this Year's report.) In substance, the Court confirms that the insurer was under no obligation to pay under such circumstances. As far as the claimant is concerned, the Court further indicates that harm such as this falls outside the protective purpose (*Schutzbereich der Norm*, also *Schutzzweckzusammenhang, Rechtswidrigkeitszusammenhang*) of the norm that was breached. The OGH takes this as so clear that, under the *CILFIT* criteria, no reference to the CJEU is necessary.

---

49 ECLI:AT:OGH0002:2024:0060OB00070.24Y.0515.000; EvBl 2025/7 with cmt by *N Herscovici* = ZIIR 2024, 287 with cmt *C Thiele* = ZVR 2025/11 with cmt by *M Cepic*.

50 Perhaps because the claimant could have argued against the insurer that the evidence was illegally obtained; but even under the most exclusion-friendly Austrian view, this would probably not have mattered for a scenario like this. See *Hersovici*, EvBl 2025/7.

51 He also claimed compensation of non-pecuniary losses, but the lower courts declared the claim prescribed.

c) Commentary

In terms of the result, this decision is hardly debatable – as the Supreme Court nicely puts it, liability under the GDPR for the coverage would amount to 'compensation in tort law for (unsuccessfully) attempting to fraudulently obtain money'. The interesting questions are methodological and procedural. 38

First, the Austrian courts acknowledged that the issue was one of autonomous EU law, but at the same time resorted to a key Germanic concept, the scope of protection. They can point to the CJEU and § 29 (1) (Austrian) Data Protection Act (*Datenschutzgesetz*) for this result. In *Österreichische Post,* the CJEU said that '[a]s regards the assessment of any damages payable under art 82 of the GDPR, in the absence of a provision having such a purpose in that regulation, national courts must apply the domestic rules of each Member State relating to the extent of financial compensation'[52] and the Data Protection Act leaves the details of a claim to the 'common provisions of private law'. However, it is difficult to say whether the scope of protection is part of the (autonomous European) cause of action or the assessment of damages. Theoretically speaking, it is perhaps best described as a characteristic Germanic mechanism bridging both.[53] Would the courts of other Member States be at liberty to deal with this problem under their functional equivalents, such as causation, illegality or perhaps under the heading of public policy? In academic literature, this question is sometimes answered in the negative: the issue at hand would presumably have to be assessed according to European standards of 'causation', with all its admitted idiosyncrasies.[54] 39

Second, this methodological difficulty certainly raises the question of whether the *CILFIT* criteria really applied. It would have been a clear-cut case to deepen the contours of autonomous EU tort law. Perhaps it could nonetheless be argued that, regardless of the legal heading, it was so clear for everyone with some experience in private law that the case should not turn out differently even under autonomous concepts of EU tort law, that the involvement of the CJEU was not necessary here. 40

---

52 CJEU 4.5.2023, Österreichische Post (Non-material damage in connection with the processing of personal data), C-300/21, EU:C:2023:370, paras 53, 54 and 59.

53 *Hans Stoll*, Haftungsfolgen im bürgerlichen Recht (1993) 6 f, 7 ff, 35 ff; *D Messner-Kreuzbauer*, Zentrale Unterschiede im Schadensrecht der Mitgliedstaaten, in: T Bauermeister/S Schwamberger (eds), Private Enforcement im Recht des Digitalen Binnenmarkts (2025) 59, 65 ff.

54 See *W Wurmnest/M Gömann*, Comparing Private Enforcement of EU Competition and Data Protection Law (2022) 13 JETL 168 ff, 174 f, with refs. In the same sense for the case at hand *Cepic*, ZVR 2025, 30.

4. OGH 22 October 2024, 4 Ob 109/24v:[55] Fear of Injury; Product Liability

a) Brief Summary of the Facts

41 The claimant, who suffered from sleep apnoea, used a non-continuous ventilator device whenever he was sleeping. In 2021, he received an urgent safety message from the producer, according to which, the polyester-based polyurethane (PEPUR) sound abatement foam in its ventilators may 1) degrade into particles which may enter the device's air pathway and be ingested or inhaled by the user; and 2) release certain chemicals. According to the producer, these problems can result in permanent, even life-threatening harm. After checking the website indicated in the message, the claimant was informed that his serial number was affected. He was asked to register his unit and his device was replaced.

42 Based on product liability, the claimant sued the defendant who imported the device into the EEA, and claimed damages for pain and suffering for the bodily pain and the mental harm suffered amounting to € 7,000. Moreover, he filed an application for a declaratory judgment. Both the Court of First Instance as well as the Court of Appeal concluded that the claimant had not (yet) suffered any compensable harm but held that the product was defective and granted the requested declaratory judgment.

b) Judgment of the Court

43 The OGH confirms the decision reached by the lower courts. The 4th panel of the Supreme Court first refers to the decision of the Court of First Instance which concluded that the claimant's device contained the potentially harmful foam, a result reached by applying the normal standard of proof of high probability. As this finding was confirmed by the Court of Appeal, the question can no longer be addressed in the proceedings before the Supreme Court.

44 In a next step, the OGH sets out that if a device like the one in question contains material that may degrade and reach the user's lungs and/or release chemicals, and either of these alternatives may lead to health impairments, the device does not provide the safety which an average user is entitled to expect. Thereby, the OGH argues, the claimant has already proven a product defect in the sense of § 5 of the Product Liability Act (*Produkthaftungsgesetz*, PHG). In the view of the

55 ECLI:AT:OGH0002:2024:0040OB00109.24V.1022.000; Zak 2024, 358 = JBl 2024, 799.

Court, it is not decisive whether the device did indeed decompose and reach the claimant's lungs or release chemicals. Consequently, according to the OGH, the product is defective and it is not merely a case of a risk of defectiveness so that the OGH sees no need to refer to the CJEU's decision in C-503/13, C-504/13, *Boston Scientific v AOK Sachsen-Anhalt* in this respect.

The OGH then concludes that the decision of the lower courts to affirm the request for a declaratory judgment even though they had denied the existence of damage was in line with recent court practice, as future damage could not be ruled out. 45

Finally, the OGH deals in more detail with the question of harm suffered by the claimant. It stresses that the Product Liability Directive does not deal with compensation for non-pecuniary loss. According to the OGH's 4th panel, product liability aims to provide a no-fault minimum protection for bodily harm and property damage but does not have to compensate all detrimental consequences. In accordance with its past practice, the OGH stresses that mental harm not resulting from bodily injury will only be compensable exceptionally, eg in the case of serious interference with the mental sphere in product liability cases. Mere annoyance or feelings of anxiety or fear do not suffice. In the view of the OGH, an encroachment upon the mental sphere (not in itself reaching the level of an injury to health – *Krankheitswert*) consisting merely of discomfort and feelings of displeasure are not sufficient to be considered as bodily injury or an equivalent thereof. 46

According to the fact-finding, the claimant to date has neither suffered a disease of the lungs or respiratory tract nor a reduction in performance. Although the claimant feared harmful foam emissions due to the safety notice and had 'an uneasy feeling or fear that he could fall ill as a result' when putting on the mask, there was no psychiatric health disorder reaching the level of an injury to health at any time and he continued to use the device without enquiring about alternatives. Pollutant emissions from the device could not be ruled out, but the penetration of particles into the respiratory tract or lungs or the release of chemicals could – to date – not be determined either. 47

Consequently, the OGH concludes that the claimant is not entitled to compensation for non-pecuniary loss. 48

c) Commentary

Under Austrian law, mental suffering can, according to general rules, be compensated if the person suffered bodily injury. If a claimant's feelings of anxiety and fear reach the level of an injury to health, compensation for non-pecuniary loss is therefore possible. In a case from 2016, the OGH also awarded compensation 49 to a claimant who feared negative consequences after a 1 cm long tip of dissecting scissors broke off during heart surgery, and ended up in the claimant's pulmonary vein, where it could not be retrieved and consequently grew in completely.[56] Although with a probability bordering on certainty no negative physical consequences were to be expected, the fact of the scissors remaining in the claimant's body was considered to be bodily injury and therefore compensation was justified.

50 In the case at hand, however, the claimant had (at least to date) not suffered any bodily injury. While other countries have seen court practice on fear of developing a disease in the future due to, for instance, exposure to asbestos or PFAS, there seem to have been no such specific cases under Austrian law. There was, however, a case in the early 20th century in which the claimant drank milk from a dairy, discovered glass splinters in his mouth and thought he might also have swallowed such splinters, in which the claimant was awarded compensation for his fear.[57]

51 In Austrian doctrine,[58] it has been argued that compensation for mere fear can only be justified if the tortfeasor brought about a massive endangerment of the victim's bodily integrity through gross negligence or intent and only if the endangerment of the victim's bodily integrity made bodily injury highly probable from the perspective of the person endangered and therefore triggered serious fear. This solution is based on an analogy to §§ 1323 and 1324 ABGB but should also apply if there are serious reasons to attribute the harm to the tortfeasor other than gross negligence or intent.[59] While no fault is required for product liability to be established, a severe defectiveness should therefore also suffice for justifying liability.

52 In the case at hand, the OGH did not have to deal with these questions in further detail as it – in our view rightly – considered the fear suffered by the claimant not to be serious enough as he continued to use the device without even enquiring about alternatives. One should also take into account that compensation for fear of death will, even according to doctrine, only be available in cases of a massive endangerment of a person's life or bodily integrity which makes injury or death highly probable as such endangerment provides at least some objective

56 OGH 4 Ob 48/16m, JBl 2016, 385 = ecolex 2016/249 = Zak 2016/296 = AnwBl 2016, 382 = RdM-LS 2016/55 = ZfG 2016, 56 = Haftung und Versicherung/Responsabilité et Assurances 2017, 202 with cmt by *C Huber*.

57 OGH GlUNF 3983 and 4243.

58 *E Karner*, Ersatz ideeller Schäden bei Körperverletzung (1999) 106 ff; *Karner/Koziol* (fn 11) 64 ff; *H Koziol*, Die Bedeutung des Zeitfaktors bei der Bemessung ideeller Schäden, in: FS Hausheer (2002) 607 ff; *H Koziol*, Österreichisches Haftpflichtrecht II (3rd edn 2018) no A/5/107.

59 *Koziol* (fn 58) no A/5/107.

clues for the mental harm suffered.[60] Again, it is doubtful whether such a massive endangerment and high probability of harm were indeed present in the case at hand.

5. OGH 23 October 2024, 9 Ob 12/24s:[61] Bereavement; Protective Purpose of the Medical Treatment Contract

a) Brief Summary of the Facts

On the afternoon of 16 March 2021, the claimant's 87-year-old mother was brought to the defendant's hospital by an ambulance and received outpatient treatment in the orthopaedic department. Although she had shown symptoms of a coronary illness, she was then sent home, where she died on the same evening. Discharging her from hospital care without further clarifying her symptoms was medically wrong. 53

The 65-year-old claimant argued that he had had a very close emotional relationship with his mother all his life. At least since the death of his father in 2014, he – on average – spent three days a week in his mother's house where he stayed overnight, assisted with household and other tasks and kept his mother company. He claimed compensation for funeral costs (approximately € 4,000) and, moreover, bereavement damages amounting to € 25,000. 54

According to the Court of First Instance, discharging the claimant's mother amounted to gross negligence. While there was no contract between the claimant and the defendant hospital, the Court of First Instance held that the claimant was included in the scope of protection of the treatment contract between his mother and the hospital and it awarded the claimant compensation for the funeral costs as well as bereavement damages amounting to € 10,000. The Court of Appeal increased this bereavement damages award by another € 5,000. 55

b) Judgment of the Court

The OGH confirms the finding of gross negligence on the part of the defendant hospital. 56

60 *Koziol* (fn 58) no A/5/107.
61 ECLI:AT:OGH0002:2024:0090OB00012.24S.1023.000; Zak 2024/671 = RZ 2024/28 = ZVR 2025/77 with cmty by *BC Steininger* = ZfG 2025, 32.

57 Apart from that, the decision focuses on the question of whether the claimant is included in the scope of protection of his mother's treatment contract with the defendant. In the view of the 9th panel of the OGH, this is only justified if an interpretation of the contract allows the conclusion that duties of care were taken over in relation to third parties (ie the claimant). According to the decision of the OGH, a generalising objective assessment ensuring foreseeability of the proximity between the third party and the contractual performance is required. For the treatment contract at hand, the decisive factor is whether a striking intimate family relationship between the claimant and his mother was to be expected on the basis of normal social structures, while special circumstances deviating from the usual social structures are not relevant.

58 The OGH refers to its past practice, according to which, spouses, cohabitants and minor children are included in the protective scope of the treatment contract, not however, grown-up siblings. For the present case, the Supreme Court holds that, from a generalising perspective and on the basis of normal social structures, an intimate family relationship is to be expected even between adult children and their parents. Therefore, the OGH holds that the claimant is included in the scope of protection of his mother's treatment contract with the defendant and confirms the Court of Appeal's decision.

c) Commentary

59 Under Austrian law, close relatives of a deceased primary victim can claim compensation for their non-pecuniary loss under § 1325 ABGB, the Austrian Civil Code's provision on bodily injury, if they suffer mental shock, ie an injury to their mental health. If their suffering does not reach the level of an injury to (mental) health, compensation is only possible provided that the tortfeasor acted with gross negligence or intent, a condition fulfilled in the case at hand.[62]

60 Starting point for the award of compensation in cases of 'mere' bereavement is the existence of an intense emotional relationship between the claimant and the deceased primary victim[63] as it typically exists between members of the nuclear family (*Kernfamilie*)[64]. Because bereavement cases lack the objective indication provided by the health impairment suffered in mental shock cases, the formal

62 *K-H Danzl*, Handbuch Schmerzengeld (2019) no 3.73 ff; *E Karner*, Zur Ersatzfähigkeit von Schock- und Trauerschäden, in: FS Danzl (2017) 97 f.

63 *Karner* (fn 58) 99 ff.

64 See *K-H Danzl*, Handbuch Schmerzengeld (2019) no 3.70; *T Schoditsch*, Die schadenersatzrechtliche "Kernfamilie" im Licht des Art 8 MRK, ÖJZ 2024, 283.

family relation is of high importance here.[65] It has, however, convincingly been argued in literature that proof of a sufficiently close emotional relationship will justify compensation even if there is no formal family relationship.[66] These principles were developed by court practice in the area of tortious liability but later extended to cases in which the defendant's liability was based on a contract with protective effect for third parties[67] – often medical malpractice claims against hospitals which are held liable for their staff.[68]

As the claimant in the case at hand clearly had an intense emotional relationship with his mother, the result reached by the OGH merits full approval. The OGH's reasoning is less convincing in our view: first, the OGH does not deal with the relationship between the claimant and his mother in any further detail but only refers to the existence of a parent-child relationship and a generalising perspective on the basis of normal social structures. This reference and the argument that circumstances deviating from normal structures are not relevant goes back to an earlier decision. In that case, which was also based on a treatment contract with protective effect towards third persons, the OGH denied a grown-up sibling who had a particularly close emotional relationship with his deceased brother compensation for bereavement even though, in tort cases, grown-up siblings are awarded compensation if they can prove a sufficiently close emotional relationship with the deceased in the individual case. Applying a more abstract concept of family in contractual cases than in tort seems rather strange as, according to the general rules, a higher level of protection applies in contractual liability than in tort.[69] 61

---

65 See *Karner* (fn 58) 99 ff.

66 *E Karner*, cmt on OGH 8 Ob 127/02p, ZVR 2002, 393, who provides the example of a distant relative who took in a child without formally adopting it. Cf also OGH 2 Ob 126/23b, reported on by *D Messner-Kreuzbauer/BC Steininger*, Austria, in: E Karner/BC Steininger (eds), European Tort Law 2023 (2024) 1, no 39 ff.

67 Cf OGH 9 Ob 83/09k, 7 Ob 105/17t and 4 Ob 176/19i. See also *E Karner*, cmt on OGH 7 Ob 105/17t, Recht der Medizin (RdM) 2018, 148 f; *M Spitzer*, cmt on OGH 7 Ob 105/17t, EvBl 2018/105, 731 f; *C Huber*, cmt on OGH 4 Ob 176/19i, ZVR 2020/210, 379; *S Nitsch*, Schock- und Trauerschadenersatzansprüche nach österreichischem und deutschem Recht, Zeitschrift für Rechtsvergleichung (ZfRV) 2019, 30; *J Pehm*, Austria, in: E Karner/BC Steininger (Hrsg), European Tort Law (ETL) 2017 (2018) 1, no 59. Cf also *C Huber*, cmt on OGH 7 Ob 105/17t, ZVR 2018/103, 197.

68 In such cases, tortious claims may be available against the doctor or nurse in question, but the hospital can regularly only be held vicariously liable on the basis of the treatment contract.

69 *M Spitzer*, cmt on OGH 7 Ob 105/17t, EvBl 2018/105, 731 f; *Steininger*, ZVR 2025, 202.

62 In our view, even in the contractual context, the decisive factor can only be whether it is foreseeable for the doctor or hospital operator that culpably causing the death of a patient may trigger grief for people who had a close emotional relationship with the deceased.[70] Normal social structures may facilitate proof of a close emotional relationship, but cannot be a prerequisite for compensation. As the OGH itself holds in the present decision, it is not important whether the hospital was aware of the patient having a spouse or children. The decisive question merely is the foreseeability for the contractual partner that a close emotional relationship may exist. As such foreseeability does not depend on the typicality of a situation, a restriction to typical constellations or usual social structures cannot be justified.[71]

6. OGH 19 November 2024, 1 Ob 167/24a:[72] Liability of a Town for a Mayor's Sexual Violence

a) Brief Summary of the Facts

63 The facts of this case relate to an incident widely reported in the Austrian media. Between December 2015 and July 2016, the mayor of a small town in Upper Austria repeatedly raped the claimant, who was then the head of the town's office (*Amtsleiterin*). This caused his victim to develop a returning depression. After the claimant finally filed a disciplinary complaint in May 2019, the town assembly voted not to retain her as head of office after her period of function, following which, the mayor assigned her the post of an ordinary official, and in 2021, her competence to perform marriage ceremonies was also discontinued. Finally, after public opinion had already turned against the town politicians responsible for handling the case, a new mayor placed the claimant in early retirement, citing her health-related incapacity to work. She then filed a tort claim under the AHG against the town[73], claiming damages for the difference between her actual earnings

70 See *Karner*, RdM 2018, 148 f; *Spitzer*, EvBl 2018, 732; *C Huber*, cmt on OGH 7 Ob 105/17t, ZVR 2018/103, 197; *idem*, ZVR 2020, 379; *Nitsch*, ZfRV 2019, 32; *Pehm* (fn 67) no 60. Cf OGH 9 Ob 83/09k, 7 Ob 105/17t and 4 Ob 176/19i.

71 *Steininger*, ZVR 2025, 202.

72 ECLI:AT:OGH0002:2024:0010OB00167.24 A.1119.000.

73 Under Austrian law, towns and cities are independent legal persons with access to some public powers, as well as capacity in private law 'within the boundaries of federal and state law' conferred by art 116 (2) Federal Constitution (Bundes-Verfassungsgesetz, B-VG).

and the income she would have had had she continued as head of the town office (€ 73,373).

b) Judgment of the Court

There were two main issues before the Supreme Court. The first was whether the mayor's behaviour could constitute an action 'in enforcement of the law' (*in Vollziehung der Gesetze*) that is necessary for attribution of an official's behaviour to a public body under § 1 (1) AHG. At the appellate stage, the Court of Appeal in Linz had denied this, citing the lack of a relation between the mayor's crimes and the exercise of public functions. But the Supreme Court disagrees. It argues that the relation between town and claimant was situated in public law (citing the relevant statutes on town organisation and town officials). Consequently, since the town had a duty of care to promote the welfare of its officials (*Fürsorgepflicht*), this duty was also of a public law nature. Public law assigned the mayor powers to order specific behaviour of the claimant on behalf of the public. What matters is a relevant 'outer and inner connection' between the official's behaviour and the enforcement of law, and abuse of power does not necessarily disrupt this connection. The OGH admits that settling the scope of an official's functions is 'at times a difficult issue of demarcation' and considers some memorable precedents on public and vicarious liability (abuse at a boarding school within strict education scheme – liability confirmed[74]; conscripted soldier shot by colleague with service weapon for personal motives – liability denied;[75] abuse by a vicar more generally – liability denied[76]). In the present case, the Supreme Court underlines the physical and temporal proximity to public power and concludes that the mayor had done exactly the opposite of his duty to promote the claimant's welfare. The mayor's behaviour in itself, the Court held, was enough to attribute his harmdoing to the defendant. There was no need to even consider whether the omission of other officials to act against the abuse could also serve as a basis for liability. 64

The second issue related to causation and contributory negligence. On the facts, it was established that the sexual violence was at least one cause of the claimant's health issues, but not that it was also a *conditio sine qua non* for the town's decision not to reinstate her as head of the town office. The defendant claimed that this decision had nothing to do with her health and was due to 65

74 27 March 2014, 1 Ob 29/14t.

75 24 September 2020, 1 Ob 123/20z EvBl 2021/1 with cmt by *J Zarari*.

76 26 January 2022, 7 Ob 25/21h ecolex 2022, 361 with cmt by *N Brandstätter*.

her inappropriate behaviour. The OGH held that it was up to the claimant to prove otherwise.

c) Commentary

66 Where officials do wrong, there are three important options. The vicarious liability of public entities for their officials is subject to no further condition as long as the officials do wrong 'in enforcement of the law', that is, in exercise of their public function.[77] Otherwise, it is still possible that they are acting on behalf of the public entity in the latter's private capacity (for instance, directing a business directly owned by the public entity). In this case, the public entity can also be liable, but only under the narrower conditions of private law (as general representative of the public body, or under §§ 1313a, 1315 Austrian Civil Code, *Allgemeines Bürgerliches Gesetzbuch*, ABGB). If, finally, the actions of the official are entirely unrelated to the public body, then it is their own private act, and only the official is responsible. The behaviour exhibited in the case could conceivably have fallen in all three categories, but the Supreme Court only discussed the division between public function and acts in a purely personal capacity. The reason is that Austrian law traditionally considers the relation between public entities and appointed public servants such as the claimant to fall squarely into public law and any acts relating to it as an exercise of public functions. Cases such as this show that this is a highly formal approach: the public functions exercised by towns in the Austrian constitutional system have very little to do with this case, considering that combatting sexual violence is generally a federal task and not a task for the towns. This case rather turns on the essential problems of power within a hierarchical organisation, which are broadly similar no matter whether public servants or private officials are concerned.

67 Considering the traditional setup, it is more comprehensible why the Supreme Court in this case considered rape and its concealment as an 'enforcement of the laws' in spite of the obvious linguistic oddity. However, even granting that Austrian law imports central employers' duties into public law, much remains to be explained. In (more) ordinary contexts, Austrian law seems to attribute sexual violence to the perpetrators but not to the entities for which the perpetrator fulfils (legitimate) tasks. For example, if the mayor had committed his hideous crimes at

77 For discussion of, and examples for, the rather broad scope of this concept, see *BA Koch*, Austria, in: K Oliphant (ed), The Liability of Public Authorities in Comparative Perspective (2016) nos 21 ff, 52 ff.

private meetings far from the town office and without any relation to it and the public powers vested there, the relation to his office would not have been strong enough. It therefore seems that the case at hand turned strongly on the idea that the offender was, at the same time, responsible for fulfilling the duties of a public employer within the town hall,[78] and that the rapes and their concealment were sufficiently connected to this task to warrant attribution to the town.

Both for public authority liability ('enforcement of the laws') as well as private **68** employers, a 'functional approach' determines the proximity of the relation.[79] But how can it be tested that the mayor's acts were 'functioning' for the public body? Did he not precisely *fail* to function in every possible way? This would appear to be the necessary conclusion under any theory that equates the relevant 'function' with furthering the public or governmental interest. Even some standard moves to extend the concept of public interest (typical aptitude is sufficient, appearances are sufficient) do not help in the extreme case at hand. For what possible sense could committing and concealing sexual violence have for the public authority in a normal state?

The foundation for this decision is that we expect public authorities (and em- **69** ployers) to do something by virtue of their status, and that the mayor was the person responsible for 'functioning' in this way. He served as a resource for the town to monitor abuse within its sphere of influence and even if he failed completely in this, his designation for the task at least relieved the town of having someone else do it. In the present case, the reason we expect protective actions by authorities from the outset is that the general power structure makes abuse easier. The OGH cites temporal and spatial proximity to the exercise of actual, positive functions of the town as important factors. This is convincing since it is an indication that we must expect this structure to have had an influence. In the present case, that is in fact quite obvious, since the mayor's powers to assign and oversee work clearly facilitated his crimes, and made their concealment possible. If anything, this is also the factor distinguishing the present case from the recent case where one militia recruit shot another with his service weapon,[80] since there the risk posed by the organisational structure was more generic and fleeting rather than structural. What the present case means is that a community is responsible for the structural power in the hands of a mayor it elected, whereas the general public is not responsible for the crimes of a recruit slightly facilitated

78 The employment relation between town hall as official is understood as one of public law, due to the formal source of rights and duties in an appointment.

79 *A Kahl* in: A Fenyves/F Kerschner/A Vonkilch, Klang-Kommentar zum ABGB: AHG (2024) § 1 no 90 ff.

80 1 Ob 123/20z.

by its compulsory service policies and distribution of weapons among servicemen. This result appears not necessary, but at least defensible.

70 On damages, however, the decision merits critique. Why should the claimant have to prove that her post would have been continued absent the crime? This ruling gives far too much credit to the defendant's suggestion that her alleged 'inappropriate behaviour' is unrelated to the crimes and that the burden falls on the claimant to prove otherwise. This *may* be the case, but it is far more likely that no fact-finding exercise will ever conclusively establish the causal relation in such psychological matters. Should the claimant really bear the burden of proof for this uncertainty, which is after all only due to the crimes attributable to the defendant? The court overlooks that, as soon as the claimant was successful in proving 'initial harm' or, in a more convincing version, a sufficient violation of protected interests, § 273 (1) Civil Procedure Ordinance (*Zivilprozessordnung*, ZPO) relieves the claimant of providing specific proof in favour of a probabilistic assessment, based on the likelihood of the claimant's continuation in her post.[81]

7. OGH 17 December 2024, 10 Ob 22/24v:[82] Assessment of Damages for a Real Estate Agent's Failure to Perform

a) Brief Summary of the Facts

71 The claimant submitted an offer of € 325,000 to the defendant real estate agent, for a piece of land in the latter's commission. The defendant failed to forward it to the property owner. Unaware of the offer, the owner concluded a contract with someone else, who had offered the same price as the claimant, but subject to conditions. If the land owner had been aware of the claimant's offer, he would have accepted it, rather than the conditional agreement actually concluded with the other offeror. The claimant pursued an action for damages against the estate agent, amounting to the difference between the offer and the value of the land, an estimated € 369,500 – thus, for € 44,500, claiming that he would have been better off without the defendant's failure to perform her duties.

---

81 More generally, *D Messner-Kreuzbauer*, Quantifying or Avoiding the Unknown, in: A Bell/ J McCunn (eds), Uncertainty in Comparative Law and Legal History (2025) 153, 174 ff.
82 ECLI:AT:OGH0002:2024:0100OB00022.24 V.1217.000.

b) Judgment of the Court

The question before the Supreme Court was whether the claimant was entitled to this difference although it was admitted that, had the owner concluded the contract with him, he would have incurred further costs (the commission for the agent, a tax on land transfer, stamp fee, drafting the contract, etc). The case turned on difficult questions regarding a contractual liability claim for non-performance under § 921 ABGB. The OGH reminds that such a claim entitles a party to the difference between the harm the claimant suffered because performance did not take place, and what they saved because they did not have to perform themselves. It then goes on to discuss how the two 'methods' accepted for calculating the award under Austrian law (*Berechnungsmethoden*) relate to such a claim under the given circumstances. These are a 'subjective-concrete assessment' (*subjektiv-konkrete Schadensberechnung*, a concrete assessment, tracking the net worth for a person) and an 'objective-abstract assessment' (*objektiv-abstrakte Schadensberechnung*, objective assessment, tracking the worth of a specific asset). 72

The OGH first mentions in passing that the claimant would in any case have been entitled to damages for the higher costs of concluding a different but equivalent bargain, but that he had failed to substantiate such losses. Turning to the financial loss, the claimant also did not lose any net worth when the extra costs for the bargain are taken into account, meaning that there is no harm under a concrete assessment. As far as an abstract assessment is concerned, the OGH assumes that the claimant can, in general, choose it for contractual claims under § 921 ABGB and that it would, in principle, exclude consideration of benefits. However, the Supreme Court cites an established exception for benefits that are 'rooted in the same nexus of facts, because the harming incident has, according to the normal course of events, also produced a benefit in the assets of the injured which is vested in the damaged thing (the affected entitlement) itself'. Where a claimant relies on an abstract assessment under § 921 ABGB, the OGH assumes this exception includes saved expenditure that would have been incurred 'exclusively because the contract had to be implemented'. 73

Although this already means that the claimant was not entitled to damages, the Supreme Court further offers a brief analysis to the effect that, although an abstract assessment is usually applied to contractual claims under § 921 ABGB, such an assessment would, on closer inspection, not be appropriate for the case at hand. The OGH reminds that an abstract assessment requires a clearly defined entitlement or legal position. Although this is not strictly reserved for entitlements to basic rights (health, property, privacy, etc) and can include contractual claims for performance or non-performance (as § 921 ABGB), the present case does not fit the pattern of cases where abstract assessments are allowed for contractual 74 claims. Such an assessment is only allowed for damages claims which 'continue' (or embody) a prior claim right to contractual performance or other secured legal position which existed before the violation. The Supreme Court assumed the claimant did not have a claim of this nature against the real estate agent in the case.

c) Commentary

75 The present case concerns what many legal systems would classify as a claim in contract rather than in tort. Nonetheless, such claims are understood as part of an overarching branch of law, the law of damages (*Schadenersatzrecht*), in Austria. And the reasoning of the OGH in this case nicely shows how principles that Austrian law considers identical for contract and tort can be at issue in a contractual liability case. Here, this concerns overarching principles of the abstract assessment of loss (in essence, focusing on the market value of a legal position).

76 It is noteworthy in substance for two central conclusions on abstract assessments. The first is a continued commitment to abstract assessments for contractual claims,[83] although this commitment did not turn out to be significant in the present case. While proponents say that the ABGB plainly prescribes abstract assessments for all cases of slight negligence in § 1332 and that this is based in the time-honoured Austrian conception of legal entitlements and the continuity thesis (*Rechtsfortwirkungsgedanke*),[84] it is notoriously embattled in academic literature.[85] The decision is also interesting because it distinguishes the case against the real estate agent at hand from the more exemplary cases of contractual liability (claims of performance against a seller). It bases this distinction on an unusually profound theoretical consideration: that only some prior entitlements are

---

83 On which, see *E Karner*, Fragen der objektiv-abstrakten Schadensberechnung in: S Perner/S Rubin/M Spitzer/A Vonkilch (eds), Festschrift für Attila Fenyves (2013) 189, 201 f; *C Rabl*, Schadenersatz wegen Nichterfüllung (1998) 61 ff.

84 *H Koziol*, Objektiv-abstrakte und subjektiv-konkrete Schadensberechnung, JBl 2023, 758, 766 ff. The underlying theory was developed by *R Neuner*, Interesse und Vermögensschaden, AcP 133 (1931) 277, 290 ff and *W Wilburg*, Zur Lehre von der Vorteilsausgleichung (1932) 82 Jherings Jahrbücher für die Dogmatik des bürgerlichen Rechts 51, 125 ff.

85 A radical critique prefers the German and Swiss view, according to which, any and all economic damage must by conceptual necessity be a difference between the assets of the claimant in reality and in the alternative world where the damage had not happened. Others would limit the role of abstract assessments. For a nuanced overview and a suggestion for a compromise, see *M Leitner*, Objektiv-abstrakt berechneter Schadenersatz auch bei subjektiv-konkret geringerem Schaden? Neue Gedanken zu einem ewigen Streit, JBl 2023, 69.

strong enough to be 'continued' or embodied in a claim for damages after harm has been done. Although the Supreme Court does not say explicitly why the claim against a real estate agent is not capable of this, it is rather clear. The exemplary case is an unconditional claim right for performance. The claimant typically obtains the right to such a performance when they form a bargain with the other party, at the expense of committing to a performance of their own. The *synallagma* (mutuality) of the contract foreseen by the parties is what justifies the reinforcement of the legal relation between them, to the effect that each claimant can demand unrelated criteria to be screened out, at least as a matter of default. But the *synallagma* in a real estate agency contract did not consist in an exchange between money and land. Rather, the agent only undertook to facilitate the claimant's negotiations with others and to provide him with respective chances and was to be paid for this by the hope of a commission. Chances, as such, are normally not stable enough to be the proper object of entitlements.

The Supreme Court also develops the rules for deduction of benefits under 77
the abstract assessment track further. In general, it is well known that an abstract assessment does not allow deduction subject to the specific exception cited by the Supreme Court (which is nicely illustrated by a case where the claimant's land increased in value after a building is set on fire[86]). This is due to the logic of this kind of assessment, which focuses on the object of a legal entitlement and leaves out other considerations.[87] The question though of how this plays out in contractual claims, where the basis for the abstract assessment is the claim for performance to a specific object, has caused problems.[88] In the present decision, the OGH transposes the exception to those claims due 'exclusively because the contract had to be implemented.' This is reasonable because expenditures that any ordinary purchaser would incur can be considered as taken into account by the parties when they create the legal position of the claimant. But the boundaries of this exception will be more difficult to draw. For instance, it is less clear why avoiding taxes or costs that only a particular claimant would have had to pay should be taken as a deductible benefit even if 'exclusively because the contract had to be implemented' from the claimant's point of view. More clearly, it would be absurd

---

86 OGH 29 May 2008, 2 Ob 176/07 ZVR 2008/241 with cmt by *C Huber.*

87 *C Wendehorst,* Schadensfeststellung und Vorteilsausgleichung, in: E Gitschthaler/J Pierer/B Zöchling-Jud (eds), FS Fischer-Czermak (2023) 919, 922 f.

88 Inter alia, it was controversial whether a claim for specific performance in contractual liability (rather than on a warranty) that ends up leaving the claimant better off (eg, with a new product or better service than owed) must be deducted. This is affirmed for concrete assessments (OGH 31 January 2023, 4 Ob 185/22t) subject to some limits, but the position on abstract assessments was less clear before the present decision.

to deduct costs such as a foreign defendant travelling to Austria, their overcareful hiring of expensive lawyers for meticulously checking contract drafts, or their celebration of the contract with expensive champagne. It seems to matter what costs are included in the contractual *synallagma.*[89]

8. Personal Injury

78 2024 saw a new highest award of compensation for pain and suffering. The Higher Regional Court of Innsbruck awarded € 350,000 to a child who suffered most severe brain damage as a consequence of lack of oxygen due to a delayed caesarean section. The boy's condition is permanent without prospect of improvement.[90]

C. Literature

Data Protection, Personal Rights, IT and Technology:

79 *B Burtscher*, Der EuGH und Art 82 DSGVO, ÖJZ 2024, 584; *B Burtscher*, Haftung für "Shitstorm", ÖJZ 2024, 848; *M Cepic*, Von der Rechtmäßigkeit über die Zulässigkeit zum Schadenersatz – Art 6, Art 9 und Art 82 DSGVO nun geklärt? Zugleich eine Besprechung von EuGH 21.12.2023, C-667/21 (Krankenversicherung Nordrhein), jusIT 2024, 60; *D Dokalik*, Immaterieller Schadenersatz für Hasspostings, ÖJZ 2024, 589; *A Foglar-Deinhardstein*, OGH zum Schutzzweck des Datenschutzrechts, ecolex 2024, 811; *C Handig*, Ehrensache? Immaterieller Schaden und Ehrenbeleidi-

89 By contrast, a further related decision of 2024 concerning the diesel emissions scandal litigation (more generally reported in last year's Yearbook) did not sufficiently consider this. OGH 28 October 2024, 3 Ob 122/24y EvBl 2025/108 with cmt by *D Messner-Kreuzbauer* discussed a deduction of benefits for a claim at the borderlines of tort and contract, namely the direct claim of a car buyer against the producer. Since the 2023 cases, the OGH deducts benefits such as the use of the car if the buyer demands reimbursement of the full price, in return for the car; see *Messner-Kreuzbauer/Steininger* (fn 66) no 2 ff. In the 2024 decision, however, the Court denied such a deduction in cases where the buyer limits their claim to the difference between what they really paid and what they would have paid absent the car's manipulation or other emissions problem. The OGH partly based this on the idea that the assessment of damages was abstract. But the exception the OGH aptly transposed to contracts in the present case would have applied, considering that the benefit of use indeed occurs 'exclusively because the contract had to be implemented.' Still, the result reached there is justified considering that the benefit received was not *unjustified.*

90 OLG Innsbruck 18.7.2024, 10 R 34/24m, ECLI:AT:OLG0819:2024:01000R00034.24M.0718.000.

gung, ecolex 2024, 232; *S Humer*, KI-Trainingsdaten – eine haftungsrechtliche Einordnung, ZIIR 2024, 144; *D Jahnel/A Pallwein-Prettner*, Rechtsbehelfe, Haftung und Sanktionen, in: D Jahnel/A Pallwein-Prettner (eds), Datenschutzrecht (4th edn 2024); *H Koziol*, Die Ehre Verstorbener und ihr Schutz (2024); *M Löw*, Ziviler Rechtsschutz bei Hass im Netz, ZIIR 2024, 388; *P Zöchbauer*, Zum Ersatz ideeller Schäden nach § 16 ECG idF BGBl I 2023/182, MR 2024, 3

Environment:

D Ecker, Zivilrechtliche Verantwortlichkeit für fehlerhafte Nachhaltigkeits- 80
berichterstattung – mit Fokus auf die Außenhaftung (2024); *B Kraml*, Die Haftung des Managements bei Greenwashing, CFOaktuell 2024, 64

CSDDD/Supply Chains:

A Baumgartner, Einbettung der CS3D-Aktivitätskettenhaftung in die Schadener- 81
satzdogmatik des ABGB, GesRZ 2024, 361; *F Ettmayer/S Kapferer*, Zivilrechtliche Aspekte des Lieferkettenmanagements, in: F Ruhmannseder (ed), Compliance in der Lieferkette (2024) 369; *M Fuchs*, Die Verantwortung von Unternehmen für Körperschäden von Arbeitnehmern im Rahmen von Lieferketten, in: S Auer-Mayer et al (eds), Festschrift Mosler (2024) 71; *H Hayden*, Haftung für fremdes Verhalten am Beispiel der CSDDD, JBl 2024, 429; *A-M Heil*, Lieferkettenrichtlinie – ein erster Überblick, ÖJZ 2024, 720; *S Nitsch*, Lieferkettenverantwortung nach geltendem österreichischen Recht in: Kalss/Torggler (Hrsg), Lieferkettenverantwortung. Beiträge zum 11. Wiener Unternehmensrechtstag (2024) 1

General:

R Ber, Die Hundeattacke – Vorbeugung und Rechtsfolgen (2024); *K-H Danzl*, Be- 82
merkenswerte schadenersatzrechtliche Entscheidungen des OGH aus dem Jahr 2023, ZVR 2024, 139; *K-H Danzl*, Das Schmerzengeld – Herausforderung für medizinische Sachverständige, Österreichische Zeitschrift für das Ärztliche Gutachten (DAG) 2024, 23; *JW Flume*, Naturalrestitution und Wertersatz, in: A Konecny/G Musger et al (eds), Festschrift Lovrek (2024) 145; *J Fromherz/S Loibl*, Schadenersatzrecht im Fokus: Entwicklungen in Europa 2023 – Bericht über die 23rd Annual Conference on European Tort Law (ACET), ZVR 2024, 431; *A Geroldinger/J Lehner*, Dreißigjährige Verjährung von Ersatzansprüchen bei Entstehung des Schadens aus qualifiziert strafbarer Handlung, wbl 2024, 57; *C Huber*, Schockschaden bei qualifizierter Beteiligung am Unfallgeschehen, ÖJZ 2024, 550; *E Karner*, Zur deliktsrechtlichen Funktion der Beweislast aus rechtsvergleichender Perspektive, in: A Konecny/G Musger et al (eds), Festschrift Lovrek (2024) 391; E Karner/D Messn-

er-Kreuzbauer (eds), Fault-Based and Strict Liability – Chinese and European Perspectives (2024); L Kolbitsch-Franz/B Schima (eds), Praxishandbuch Schadenersatzrecht (2024); *H Koziol*, Die Bedeutung des Selbstbestimmungsrechts der Eltern für die Schadenersatzansprüche wegen unerwünschter Elternschaft, JBl 2024, 553; *H Koziol*, Rechtszuweisung, Güterzuordnung und deren Schutz (2024); *C Kriechbaumer*, Reform des (Kartell-)Schadenersatzrechts als Folge der Rechtsprechung in den "Abgas-Verfahren"? Der OGH und die Büchse der Pandora, RdW 2024, 242; *R Madl*, § 1489 Satz 2 ABGB: Auf den Zeitpunkt des Schadenseintritts kommt es doch an! – Neuerlicher Appell an den OGH aus Anlass der jüngsten EGMR-Judikatur in Asbestfällen, ÖJZ 2024, 751; *K Markowetz*, Die Anwendbarkeit des schadenersatzrechtlichen Grundsatzes "neu für alt" auf Tiere. Zugleich ein Beitrag zum Verhältnis von "neu für alt" und § 1332a ABGB, ZVR 2024, 358; *D Messner-Kreuzbauer*, Tracing the Permission to Act in Necessity in the Germanic Tradition. From 'Alleged Right' to 'Absolutely Ascertained Principle of Our Law', Vienna Law Review (VLR) 8 (2024) 1; *K Pochmarski/K Stipic*, Haftung und Regress (Teil I), Sachverständige 2024, 133; *D Prisching/B Sommer*, Schadenersatzrechtliche Gleichstellung von "wrongful birth" und "wrongful conception", Zak 2024, 104; *R Reischauer*, Substanzwert/Nutzungsausfall und konkrete Schadensberechnung – eine Antwort auf Koziol, JBl 2024, 349; *M Schickmair*, Ersatz des immateriellen Schadens bei Unterbindung des Kontaktes zum Kind, in: E Gitschthaler/J Pierer/B Zöchling-Jud (eds), Festschrift Fischer-Czermak (2024) 741; *T Schoditsch*, Die schadenersatzrechtliche "Kernfamilie" im Licht des Art 8 MRK, ÖJZ 2024, 283; *W Schrammel*, Die Koordinierung von Schadenersatzrecht und Sozialversicherungsrecht bei Schädigungen mit Auslandsberührung, in: S Auer-Mayer et al (eds), Festschrift Mosler (2024) 471; *BC Steininger*, Schockschadenschmerzengeld für Stiefvater nach Tod seines mj Stiefsohns, ZVR 2024, 20; *R Trabe/M Pfeifer*, Wessen Vermögenssphäre ist im Schadensfall des Leasingobjekts betroffen?, ZFR 2024, 17; *C Wendehorst*, Schadensfeststellung und Vorteilsausgleichung, in: E Gitschthaler/J Pierer/B Zöchling-Jud (eds), Festschrift Fischer-Czermak (2024) 919

Investors and Banking:

83 *P Bydlinski*, Überhöhte Bewertung von Sacheinlagen: Haftung der Gründungsprüfer nach § 42 AktG auf die Differenz? GesRZ 2024, 85; *J Mitterecker*, Die Haftung des Vorsitzenden in der (streitigen) Generalversammlung, GES 2024, 17; *S Perner*, (Neue) Verbandsklagen am Finanzmarkt, in: C Kronthaler/S Laimer (eds), Innsbrucker Forum für Bank- und Versicherungsrecht 2024, 137; *J Reich-Rohrwig*, Einpersonen-GmbH – grundsätzlich keine Haftung des Alleingesellschafters – Glosse zu OGH 2 Ob 67/22z, ecolex 2024, 60

Medical Liability:

C Huber, Wrongful conception infolge einer fehlerhaften Spirale, ÖJZ 2024, 460; 84
GW Huber/J Dietrich, Rechtsmäßiges Alternativverhalten bei ÄsthOpG-Aufklärungsmändeln, RdM 2024, 271; *E Keinert*, Grenzen der ärztlichen Aufklärungspflicht bei typischen Operationsrisiken, Zak 2024, 264; *BA Koch*, Medizinhaftung im digitalen Zeitalter, in: E Gitschthaler/J Pierer/B Zöchling-Jud (eds), Festschrift Fischer-Czermak (2024) 329; *P Schwarzenegger*, Wrongful birth und wrongful conception – weiterführende Überlegungen zu OGH (verstärkter Senat) 3 Ob 9/23d, JBl 2024, 366; *M Schickmair*, wrongful birth – wrongful conception, Zeitschrift für Familien- und Erbrecht (EF-Z) 2024, 114; *M-K Steiner*, Der Einsatz von Placebos in der Medizin aus juristischer Sicht (2024); *BC Steininger*, Verstärkter Senat zur Gleichbehandlung von "wrongful birth" und "wrongful conception", RdM 2024, 110; *BC Steininger*, Schutzzweck des Behandlungsvertrags, ÖJZ 2024, 361; *A Tanczos/D Tanczos*, Arzthaftung (3rd edn 2024)

Procedural Law:

M Woller, EuGH "rettet" verschuldensunabhängige Haftung nach § 394 EO – 85
Glosse zu EuGH C-473/22, ecolex 2024, 783; *M Lutschounig*, Zur Entscheidung über Haftungsansprüche gegen den Insolvenzverwalter im Zivilprozess – Ein Beitrag über die Beurteilung strittiger Rechte im Insolvenzverfahren, in: A Konecny et al (eds), Festschrift Lovrek (2024) 487

Product Liability:

M Karollus, Sonderschadenersatzrecht für die Diesel-Fälle? wbl 2024, 689; 86
M Lutschounig, Neue Haftungs- und Beweisfragen in Dieselmassenverfahren, ZVR 2024, 103; *M Spitzer*, Schadenersatz ohne Schaden bei Dieselmotoren, ÖJZ 2024, 260

Professional and Liability of Public Authorities:

H Koziol, Die Haftung des Staates bei Schädigung durch den Beginn von Strafver- 87
fahren – Eine Skizze, in: A Konecny/G Musger et al (eds), Festschrift Lovrek (2024) 447; *M Paar*, COVID-19 Ausbruch in Ischgl im März 2020 und die Frage der Amtshaftung, RdM 2024, 15 and 60; *H Sailer*, Amtshaftung wegen unvertretbarer Rechtsanwendung, in: A Konecny et al (eds), Festschrift Lovrek (2024) 661

Transportation, Traffic and Infrastructure:

P Bydlinski, Kollision mit einem Fußgänger aus einer Betreuungseinrichtung, ÖJZ 88
2024, 428; *V Cap/J Stabentheiner/M Weber*, Aktuelle Judikatur zur Pisten-

sicherungspflicht – und was bleibt nach dem abendlichen Pistenschluss? ZVR 2024, 461; *C Diesenreither*, Neue Wurzeln für die Baumhaftung: § 1319b ABGB, ZVR 2024, 319; *R Fucik*, Die Entschädigung von Verkehrsopfern, ÖJZ 2024, 979; *M Ganner*, Baumhalterhaftung in Österreich, in: E Gitschthaler/J Pierer/B Zöchling-Jud (eds), Festschrift Fischer-Czermak (2024) 195; *S Gleirscher*, Bergsport und Haftung im Angesicht des Klimawandels, ZVR 2024, 74; *M Gschöpf*, Sicherungspflichten von Pistenhaltern – Eine Betrachtung ausgewählter Risikobereiche auf der Skipiste unter dem Aspekt des Klimawandels, ZVR 2024, 63; *M Hinteregger*, Verkehrsunfall durch Behinderten aus Betreuungseinrichtung im Rahmen eines sog "Einkaufstrainings", ZVR 2024, 27; *E Karner*, Die Neuregelung der Baumhaftung in § 1319b ABGB, ÖJZ 2024, 727; *G Kathrein*, Ein Schutz vor dem Einklemmen eines Fahrgasts muss auch bei nicht automatisch schließenden Türen gegeben sein, ZVR 2024, 443; *F Kerschner*, Keine Angstschnitte mehr – zur neuen Baumhaftung, RFG 2024, 43; *U Knibbe*, Durch neue Wetterphänomene bedingte Pistensicherungspflichten, ZVR 2024, 469; *F Laher*, Hackerangriff und Haftung nach EKHG, ZVR 2024, 191; *F Laher*, Unfall ohne physische Berührung oder mechanische Gewalteinwirkung, ÖJZ 2024, 365; *D Messner-Kreuzbauer*, Haftung für autonome Fahrzeuge – Innovationsdruck und Technikneutralität, ZVR 2024, 79; *S Pechtl*, Zur verschuldensunabhängigen Gefährdungshaftung von Seilbahnbetreibern, RdW 2024, 304; *J Stabentheiner/MC Wieser*, Gesetzliche Neuregelung der Haftung für Bäume – das Haftungsrechts-Änderungsgesetz 2024, Zak 2024, 124; *I Vonkilch*, Ergänzende Erwägungen für eine nachbarrechtliche Gefährdungshaftung nach § 364a ABGB analog, RdU 2024, 235; *E Wagner*, Hurra – Ministerialentwurf zur Baumhaftung (endlich) da! RdU 2024, 4; *E Wagner*, Neue Baumhaftung – HaftRÄG 2024, RdW 2024, 524

Sébastien De Rey

II. Belgium

A. Legislation
Act of 7 February 2024 containing Book 6 'Tort Law' of the Civil Code (Belgian Official Gazette 1 July 2024, 79, 393)

On 1 January 2025, following a period of more than 200 years, a new tort law came into force in Belgium as part of a new Belgian Civil Code. This reform, set forth in Book 6 'Tort Law' of the new Civil Code[1], replaces arts 1382–1386 of the Civil Code of 1804, which continued to govern tort law in Belgium until recently. Due to the considerable impact on the field, the present report focuses on this reform. Following an explanation of the rationale and objectives of the reform (part 1), a presentation of the structure of the new tort law (part 2) and its general provisions (part 3), an overview of the new Belgian tort law is provided, focusing on its key innovations and identifying the most notable changes related to the facts generating liability (part 4), causation (part 5), damage (part 6), and the consequences of liability and remedies (part 7). 1

1. Objectives of the Reform

Tort law in Belgium remained largely untouched by the legislator for more than 200 years, with the provisions of the Civil Code of 1804, promulgated by Napoleon, remaining in force. The Code of 1804 consolidated the entire law of torts into five general provisions only (arts 1382–1386). Over the course of two centuries, the Belgian legislature only added one further provision, dealing with the liability for those suffering from mental illness (art 1386*bis*). Formulated as very general provisions, it was up to case law to translate these articles into concrete legal rules. For instance, in the absence of any concretisation by the legislature, case law was 2

Note: This report was finalised in February 2025. With special thanks to Bernard Dubuisson and Jan Wassink.

1 See Act 7 February 2024 containing Book 6 'Tort Law' of the Civil Code, Belgian Official Gazette 1 July 2024, 79, 393.

https://doi.org/10.1515/9783111389271-003

required to translate the generally worded arts 1382 and 1383 – referred to as some of the most general tort provisions ever drafted[2] – into concrete rules to determine when there is personal misconduct, what damage allows for compensation, and from what point it can be established that there is causation leading to liability.

Nevertheless, as a result of the considerable body of case law that accumulated over the past two hundred years, the gap between the text of the Civil Code of 1804 and the law as applied by the courts had become almost untenable. While the general wording and flexibility of the Code – thanks to the genius of its drafters – were initially considered its greatest strengths, allowing for significant judicial development, the text had ultimately been eroded by the substantial body of case law. This erosion, in turn, jeopardised legal certainty, accessibility, and predictability of tort law. Moreover, in certain instances, the wording of the Code was so definitive that there was no room for evolution by case law, necessitating legislative intervention.

3 The reform of Belgian tort law, however, is not a standalone initiative; rather, it is part of a comprehensive reform of private law in general, leading to a new Belgian Civil Code. This new Code, which will finally contain ten books, is being introduced gradually, with new books being added to the code since 2019. This new Civil Code is thus a work in progress, with new books being added to the code as it progresses. On 1 February 2024, Book 6 'Tort Law' was passed by Parliament.[3] It entered into force on 1 January 2025.[4] As with all other books of the new Code,[5] it was prepared by a Commission of experts in the field, chaired by Bernard Dubuisson (UCLouvain) and Hubert Bocken (UGent),[6] the latter, at a later stage, being replaced by Geert Jocqué (KU Leuven).[7] By opting for *evolution* rather than *revolution*, the reform does not represent a radical departure from the preceding legal framework. Indeed, the overarching objective of the reform is to codify case law and solutions found in legal scholarship, make precise adjustments, and supplement or refine where necessary, based on solutions drawn from for-

---

2 *C Van Dam*, European Tort Law (2013) 56.

3 Bill 1 February 2024 containing Book 6 'Tort Law' of the Civil Code, DocParl Chamber 2023–24, no 55–3213/013.

4 Act 7 February 2024 containing Book 6 'Tort Law' of the Civil Code, Belgian Official Gazette 1 July 2024, 79,393.

5 On this methodology followed by the Belgian legislator, see *S De Rey*, The Reform of Belgian Tort Law: Overview, Methodology, and Why it Succeeded, European Review of Private Law (ERPL) 2025, 135–172; *D Heirbaut*, Blitzkrieg Codification: The 2020 Belgian Civil Code, in: M Graziadei/L Zhang (eds), The Making of the Civil Codes: A Twenty-First Century Perspective (2022) 127–148.

6 Ministerial Decree 30 September 2017, Belgian Official Gazette 9 October 2017, 91, 600.

7 Ministerial Decree 14 September 2023, Belgian Official Gazette 12 October 2023, 92, 229.

eign codifications and harmonisation projects (such as the Draft Common Frame of Reference [DCFR] and the Principles of European Tort Law [PETL]), while respecting the Belgian legal tradition. Hence, the recodification of Belgian tort law seems to boil down to the following three overarching objectives: (a) restoring legal certainty, (b) enhancing accessibility, and (c) modernisation and innovation.

a) Restoring Legal Certainty

The first objective of the tort law reform is to restore legal certainty by aligning 4 the text of the Code with the law in action. This goal is shared by all recent reforms in Western Europe.[8] In the case of the Belgian tort law reform, this is particularly evident, since the Civil Code of 1804 regulated the law of torts with six provisions only. In the new Civil Code, however, the matter is now addressed in 40 articles (arts 6.1–6.40), supplemented by 15 additional provisions that transfer the rules on product liability from a separate piece of legislation to the Civil Code (see arts 6.41–6.55).

In order to achieve this objective, it was necessary for the legislature to *codify* 5 legal principles and doctrines that were put forward in case law and legal scholarship since 1804. In this context, one can consider the confirmation of fault as the foundation for personal misconduct (art 6.5), the equal treatment of natural persons and legal persons (art 6.4), and the possibility of State liability (art 6.14 § 2 and art 6.15 para 2). With regard to the rules on damages, examples include the codification of the principle of full compensation (art 6.30), the assessment of damages *in concreto* (art 6.30), the various modes of compensation (art 6.31), the moment of assessment of damages (art 6.32), and the freedom of the injured party to dispose of the compensation without being obliged to use the awarded compensation to repair the damage incurred (art 6.39).

The objective to restore legal certainty also requires that where the law does 6 not provide a clear solution, the legislator *resolves uncertainties*. However, some questions were not yet ripe for codification.

For instance, the question of compensation for *environmental damage* and the mechanisms for organising this compensation, although emerging as an increasingly important issue, were not yet deemed to be sufficiently developed for codification. The complexity of the problem, including 'the selection of appropriate

8 *R Schulze*, Changes in the Law of Obligations in Europe, in: R Schulze/F Zoll (eds), The Law of Obligations in Europe. A New Wave of Codifications (2013) 3, 4.

legal instruments', has resulted in the postponement of the debate.[9] In preparation of this, a Commission of experts was established and tasked with 'the elaboration of a proposal for the regulation of liability for damage to collective environmental interests, including ecological damage to unappropriated environmental resources, the climate, and other components of the ecosystem'.[10]

Another area of development that could necessitate a reassessment of tort law, is the phenomenon of *artificial intelligence* (AI). Although this may eventually demand a re-evaluation of tort law legislation, the Belgian legislature did not accord it a significant degree of attention during its reform. More so, the rules on strict liability for defective objects are limited to tangible goods (art 6.16), which raises the question of whether this liability also extends to damage caused by AI systems. It is evident that such cases of liability may not yet have reached a point of crystallisation. This, in conjunction with possible legislative actions of the EU, may have prompted the Belgian legislator to refrain from allocating any specific legislative provisions to this matter. Nevertheless, should this prove necessary, the structure of Book 6 'Tort Law' allows the addition of a new, specific liability regime for damage caused by AI systems in Chapter 7, which is dedicated to specific liability regimes (see below no 13).

b) Enhancing Accessibility

7 The second objective of the reform is aimed at enhancing the accessibility of tort law. This is most evident in the more transparent structure of the new Code. In addition, the articles in the Code are numbered by book, following the Dutch example, rather than continuous (as in the French model). To further enhance accessibility, each provision is accompanied by a heading, following the example of the German Civil Code (*Bürgerliches Gesetzbuch*, BGB), and various soft law instruments, such as the Draft Common Frame of Reference and the Principles of European Tort Law. Enhancing accessibility also requires the legislator to use more modern terminology. For instance, within the reform of tort law, the traditional term 'good housefather' (*bonus pater familias*) has been replaced by the gender-neutral expression 'prudent and reasonable person'.[11]

8 The principle of enhancing accessibility also has substantive implications. It calls for the *clarification* and *rationalisation* of complex doctrines where possible.

---

9 Explanatory Memorandum of Book 6, DocParl Chamber 2022–23, no 55–3213/001, 15.

10 Ministerial Decree 14 May 2024, Belgian Official Gazette 2 July 2021, 65,591.

11 See eg, art 6.6 § 2 on personal misconduct.

Clarification is pursued, for instance, by providing definitions of several concepts, such as that of fault (art 6.6 § 1) – with criteria to assess the general standard of care (art 6.6 § 2) –, of principals (*commettans/aanstellers*) in the context of their strict liability for auxiliaries (*préposés/aangestelden*) (art 6.14 § 1 para 2), and of custodians in the context of their strict liability for defective objects (art 6.16 para 2) and for animals (art 6.17 para 2). Today, the Code also provides definitions of causation (art 6.18 § 1), damage (art 6.24) and the purposes and modes of compensation (art 6.31), which were lacking under the former Civil Code.

Besides clarifying, the objective to enhance accessibility also commands *simplification* wherever possible. Examples in this regard are the rationalised regime in the case of a plurality of liable parties (art 6.19), which from now on gives rise to *in solidum* liability – the distinction made in the past between common faults (which used to give rise to joint and several liability) and concurrent faults (which used to give rise to *in solidum* liability) is no longer made – and recourse claims between liable parties (art 6.21). 9

c) Modernisation and Innovation

The third objective aims to modernise and innovate the law of torts, ensuring it aligns with contemporary society. The majority of the innovations introduced by the recodification are geared toward achieving this objective. Comparative law played a significant role in shaping these reforms. 10

Under the law of torts, as developed under the *Code civil* of 1804, Belgium is traditionally regarded as a legal system with a victim-friendly stance.[12] This perspective remains largely unchanged in the reform.[13] Therefore, the reform does not introduce a requirement of relativity or *Schutznorm* (such as provided for under art 6:163 Dutch Civil Code or § 823 para 2 German Civil Code). Instead, the objective of modernisation is to establish a *new equilibrium* between the pro- 11

12 This is also recognised by the legislature, see Explanatory Memorandum of Book 6 (fn 9) 5. See also *M Kruithof*, Tort Law in Belgium, International Encyclopaedia of Laws: Tort Law (2018) 34, 42 and 102.

13 Also observed in comparative analyses, see, for instance, *JS Borghetti*, Le soleil se lève au nord: ou comment la réforme belge de la responsabilité extracontractuelle fait pâlir le projet français, Recueil Dalloz (D) 2024, 643 ff; *J Knetsch*, Le Projet de réforme du droit de la responsabilité civile en France et en Belgique. Le droit français a-t-il encore quelque chose à dire? in: T Vansweevelt/ B Weyts (eds), Recente ontwikkelingen in het aansprakelijkheids- en verzekeringsrecht (2022) 271 ff; see also *B Dubuisson* (ed), La réforme du droit de la responsabilité en France et en Belgique. Regards croisés et aspects de droit comparé (2020).

tection of the victim's interests and those of the tortfeasor, and therefore between the individual and the community. For instance, while the victim-friendly nature of causality rules is retained, the reform moderates the extreme results that the *conditio sine qua non* test and the doctrine of the equivalence of conditions could produce under the previous legal framework: indeed, according to art 6.18 § 2, '(t)here is no liability … if the link between the fact giving rise to liability and the damage is so remote that it would be manifestly unreasonable to attribute the damage to the person held liable'.

In other areas, it is precisely the rights of victims that are reinforced, for example, through the introduction of a claim for disgorgement of profits for violations of personality rights (art 6.31 § 3, see below no 43), and stronger protection of harm to physical or psychological integrity, for instance, by providing for a possibility to claim additional compensation for new damage or aggravation of such injury (art 6.37).

12 Other aspects of modernisation involve adapting tort law to the *contemporary social context*. This includes, for example, regulating the liability of legal entities (arts 6.4 and 6.15 § 1) and of the State (arts 6.14 § 2 and 6.15 § 2), as well as adapting parental liability to modern family structures (art 6.12) and reformulating the liability of educational institutions (art 6.13). The reform is also correct to acknowledge the close relationship between tort law and insurance law.[14] Indeed, unlike a century ago, the defendant will now often be backed by a liability insurer. Another innovation that is consistent with the aspiration of modernisation is the introduction of remedies other than purely compensatory remedies (see no 18), such as preventive remedies (arts 6.28 and 6.40), and 'restitutionary damages' aimed at disgorgement of illegitimate profits (art 6.31 § 3).

2. Structure of Book 6 'Tort Law'

13 The new Belgian tort law is found in Book 6 'Tort Law' of the new Belgian Civil Code. It is structured as follows:

14 See eg, art 6.10 para 3: 'When the liability of the minor is covered by a contract of insurance, the court cannot decide that no damages are due nor limit the damages to an amount less than that for which the contract of insurance provides coverage'. A similar provision is enacted for the liability of persons with a mental disorder (art 6.11). Hence, where liability insurance, initially, was aimed at protecting the victim against the tortfeasor's insolvency, it now becomes a measure of the damages awarded.

Chapter 1. Introductory Chapter (arts 6.1 – 6.4)

Chapter 2. Facts Generating Liability (arts 6.5 – 6.17)

Chapter 3. Causation (arts 6.18 – 6.23)

Chapter 4. Damage (arts 6.24 – 6.29)

Chapter 5. Consequences of Liability (arts 6.30 – 6.39)

Chapter 6. Orders and Prohibitions (art 6.40)

Chapter 7. Specific Liability Regimes (arts 6.41 – 6.55)

Although the Commission preparing the reform initially proposed creating a specific regime for liability related to 'hazardous activities', it encountered significant resistance, and Chapter 7 now includes one specific liability regime only: that of product liability (see arts 6.41 – 6.55). These provisions implement the rules of European origin, which were, prior to the reform, contained in a separate, standalone legislative piece.[15] However, the new provisions do not yet encompass the new Product Liability Directive (EU) 2024/2853.[16] Consequently, a reform of these provisions is already required before the transposition deadline of this Directive, which is 9 December 2026.

The scope of application of Book 6 'Tort Law' is, however, not limited to extra-contractual claims. Indeed, when it comes to contractual liability, the legislator makes a cross-reference to the application of Book 6 in art 5.237, the latter being found in Book 5 'Obligations'. It follows that the provisions of Book 6 also apply to claims based on contractual liability. This means that the provisions on causation, damage, consequences of liability, etc on tort liability, apply to claims based on contractual liability as well. Book 6, therefore, encompasses a field of enquiry that extends beyond the confines of tort law. **14**

On the other hand, Book 6 does not provide a comprehensive framework for all cases of non-contractual liability. Indeed, the Civil Code also addresses cases of non-contractual liability that are not covered in Book 6 'Tort Law'. One may cite, for instance, the liability for nuisance caused by neighbours (art 3.101), liability for *culpa in contrahendo* (art 5.17), and third-party complicity in another's breach of contract (art 5.111). Besides, apart from the rules on product liability (see arts 6.41 – 6.55), specific liability regimes, such as those on liability of motor vehicle drivers to vulnerable road users, compensation for workplace and medical acci- **15**

15 See Act 25 February 1991, Belgian Official Gazette 22 March 1991, 5884.

16 Directive (EU) 2024/2853 of the European Parliament and of the Council of 23 October 2024 on liability for defective products and repealing Council Directive 85/374/EEC [2024] Official Journal (OJ) L 2024/2853.

dents, are not found in Book 6 of the Civil Code, but are still found in separate, stand-alone legislation.

3. General Provisions

a) Introductory Provisions

16 Turning to the provisions of Book 6 'Tort Law', the first chapter includes four introductory provisions of a general nature. Article 6.1 asserts that the provisions in this book are, in principle, of a supplementary nature. This reflects the current stance of the Belgian *Cour de cassation*. Consequently, Belgian legislation permits the discharge or limitation of liability based on tort, provided that the requisite conditions for a valid exemption clause are met. These conditions are found in art 5.89. Hence, the clauses exempting the liable party from damage caused by intentional fault, or from the fault that causes harm to the life or physical integrity of another person, are void. The same applies to faults by auxiliaries (art 5.89).

17 Only one provision of Book 6 has explicitly been designated by the legislator as not being of a supplementary nature: according to art 6.37, injured parties who have been compensated for injury resulting from harm to their physical or psychological integrity may seek additional damages for new injuries or aggravation of the injury resulting from the same harm but which have not yet been taken into account and of which they could not reasonably have been aware of at the time of the court's decision or out-of-court settlement. It is not possible to deviate from this rule: 'The renunciation of that right is without effect' (art 6.37 para 2). Apart from this, the largely non-mandatory view of tort liability is further reflected in art 6.2, which provides that the application of a provision from Book 6 does not preclude the application of other provisions, unless otherwise specified by law or contract.

18 Article 6.4 concludes the introductory provisions by establishing a principle of equal treatment between natural persons and legal persons.[17] Moreover, although this does not receive a specific provision, the new rules generally apply to public legal entities as was formerly the case, since Belgian law does not have an autonomous administrative liability system.[18]

17 Cf art VI.–1:103(b) DCFR.

18 This also follows from arts 6.14 § 2 and 6.15, which extend the rules of strict liability to public legal entities.

b) Concurrence between Contract and Tort

The legislator's willingness to overturn case law is most evident in the question of the *concurrence between contract and tort*. This question is particularly relevant in Belgian law because of its broad concept of damage, resulting in almost any contractual damage also qualifying as recoverable harm under tort. As evidenced by the comprehensive commentary in the Explanatory Memorandum, the concurrence issue is of significant complexity and sensitivity. During the reform process, the matter was the subject of extensive debate among legal scholars.[19] At one juncture, it appeared that the ultimate disposition of the reform of tort law was contingent upon the resolution of this matter. However, following the consideration of multiple draft versions and proposed alternatives,[20] the legislator ultimately reached the following conclusion: in contrast to the approach taken by the *Cour de cassation*, which has since its ruling of 7 December 1973[21] adhered to a 'prohibition of concurrence', according to which contracting parties, in principle, can only be held liable on a contractual basis, art 6.3 § 1 represents a reversal of this principle. In the absence of a stipulation to the contrary in the contract or any statutory provision to the contrary, the aggrieved party is at liberty to elect whether to base their claim on a breach of contract or on tort. Despite the absence of explicit mention in the text, it is evident from the legislative trajectory that an aggrieved party opting for tort liability must demonstrate the fulfilment of all the requisite conditions for such liability. Indeed, although already controversial in legal scholarship, in this instance, it is not possible to consider that any breach 19

19 See eg, *A Fourrez/S Larielle*, Les relations entre responsabilité contractuelle et extracontractuelle dans le projet belge, in: B Dubuisson (ed), La réforme du droit de la responsabilité en France et en Belgique. Regards croisés et aspects de droit comparé (2020) 153–172; *H Bocken*, Samenloop in het ontwerp buitencontractuele aansprakelijkheid, Tijdschrift voor Privaatrecht (TPR) 2021, 151 ff; *J Vananroye/O Roodhooft*, Toerekening aan rechtspersonen en aansprakelijkheid van uitvoeringsagenten in het ontwerp buitencontractuele aansprakelijkheid, TPR 2021, 177 ff; *J Vananroye/O Roodhooft*, Aansprakelijkheid van uitvoeringsagenten in het wetsvoorstel buitencontractuele aansprakelijkheid, in: Tendensen in het bedrijfsrecht (2023) 157; *I Samoy/S Van Eekert*, De terechte afschaffing van het samenloopverbod en de leer van de quasi-immuniteit van de hulppersoon: ander en beter, Rechtskundig Weekblad (RW) 2023–24, 437; *I Claeys/C Desmet*, Rechtstreekse aansprakelijkheid van de hulppersoon via de rechtstreekse vordering? RW 2023–24, 796; *P Thiriar*, Afschaffing van het samenloopverbod en leer van de quasi-immuniteit van de hulppersoon: gooi het kind niet met het badwater weg, De Juristenkrant (DJK) 2023, vol 480, 8; *A Keukeleire*, De uitvoeringsagent: niet zo immuun voor het nieuwe aansprakelijkheidsrecht, DJK 2023, vol 480, 9; *A Cataldo*, Le concours des responsabilités entre cocontractans, in: P Colson/F George (eds), Le nouveau livre 6 du Code civil (2024) 393–420.

20 See Amendements nos 10–15, 43, 44 and 67, DocParl Chamber 2022–23, no 55–3213.

21 Arrêts de la Cour de cassation (Arr Cass) 1974, 395 and Pasicrisie Belge (Pas) 1974, 376.

of contract automatically constitutes an extra-contractual fault.[22] However, in the event that the aggrieved contracting party elects to pursue a claim in tort because the conditions of tort are met, the party in breach may then raise defences derived from the contract itself, from provisions on specific contracts (such as on sales, lease, etc), or from the specific prescription periods applicable to the contract. This 'correction' preserves, to a certain extent, contractual equilibrium and the risk-allocation reflected in the contract. An exception to this correction is made for claims seeking compensation for physical or psychological harm or for intentional wrongdoing, where 'full' concurrence is possible without the party in breach being able to invoke these defences.

20 This solution is extended to the *auxiliaries* of the party in breach (art 6.3 § 2). In contrast to previous case law, which granted the aggrieved party, in principle, no recourse against the auxiliary of the party in breach (the so-called 'quasi-immunity' of auxiliaries), the new legislation permits such a claim, but the auxiliary may then invoke the same defences as their principal (derived from the contract between the principal and the aggrieved party), as well as any defences derived from their contract with the principal (the contract between the principal and the auxiliary).

The rationale underlying this solution can be traced back to two fundamental tenets. First, it is predicated on the expectation that the aggrieved party, as a contracting party, can anticipate that their co-contractor, the principal, will engage auxiliaries for the performance of the contract. Consequently, it is deemed reasonable for the aggrieved party to have no greater claims against these auxiliaries than against the principal. Second, this solution is founded on the idea that the auxiliary anticipates that their contract with the principal will serve as the foundation of their liability, the reason why they are allowed to invoke against the aggrieved party the defences derived from the contract between the principal and the auxiliary.

4. Facts Generating Liability

21 For liability to attach under Belgian tort law, three constituent elements are required: the person claiming compensation has to have suffered (1) damage that

22 See *B Dubuisson*, Le livre 6 du Code civil portant réforme de la responsabilité extracontractuelle. La fin d'un long héritage (1804–2024), Journal des tribunaux (JT) 2025, 1 para 5; *F Auvray/R Jafferali*, Une cure de jouvence pour le droit de la responsabilité, le Livre 6 du nouveau Code civil, Tijdschrift voor Belgisch Burgerlijk Recht/Revue Générale de Droit Civil Belge (TBBR/RGDC) 2025, 82 para 17.

was (2) caused by (3) a fact generating liability. Regarding the facts generating tort liability, the Code addresses (a) liability for personal misconduct, (b) liability for the conduct of others, and (c) liability for objects and animals.

a) Liability for Personal Misconduct

First, concerning liability for personal misconduct, the Code restates the underlying principle of the former arts 1382 and 1383, but with a new formulation: 'Any person is liable for the damage they cause to others through their fault' (art 6.5). Fault is then defined as 'a breach of a statutory rule imposing or prohibiting specific behaviour or of the general standard of care that applies in social relations' (art 6.6 § 1). Contrary to Dutch and German law,[23] Belgian law has not shifted from a two-tier to a three-tier system by incorporating the infringement of a subjective right as a third fault category.[24] 22

It is art 6.6 § 2 that clarifies the scope of the general standard of care by stating that it 'requires behaviour consistent with that of a prudent and reasonable person placed in the same circumstances'.[25] The benchmark is the conduct of a fictitious reference person; however, that reasonable person must be put into the shoes of the tortfeasor in the particular historical situation *ex ante*. It follows that, as before, Belgian tort law, like most continental legal systems, provides for an open category of 'tort': rather than a system with a variety of individual wrongs, tortious liability for personal misconduct is based on a general clause. Article 6.6 § 2 para 2 provides for a list of factors to assess the general standard of care: 23

(1) the reasonably foreseeable consequences of the behaviour;
(2) the proportionality between the risk that the damage would occur, its nature, and extent, and the efforts and measures necessary to avoid it;
(3) the state of the art in technology and scientific knowledge;
(4) the rules of the art and good professional practices; and

---

23 See art 6:162 para 2 Dutch Civil Code and § 823 German Civil Code.
24 Explanatory Memorandum of Book 6 (fn 9) 43: 'In this case, the material component of the fault is the failure to comply with the obligation to abstain from the exercise of subjective rights that are opposable to third parties. This failure can be considered a violation of a standard of conduct that imposes a defined behaviour. Therefore, the fault in this case is the violation of a norm that imposes a well-defined conduct'.
25 Cf art VI.–3:102(b) DCFR.

(5) the principles of good administration and organisation.[26]

The list of circumstances is neither exhaustive nor binding. This effort to better delineate the contours of the general standard of care, without confining it to a rigid definition, reflects a commendable intention to assist the courts and improve legal predictability.

24 Article 6.6, defining fault as a breach of a statutory rule imposing or prohibiting specific behaviour or of the general standard of care, enshrines an objective conception of fault. This marks a shift in Belgian tort law. Indeed, wrongfulness (as an *objective* element) was not sufficient to establish a 'fault' under former arts 1382 and 1383. As opposed to other legal systems, Belgian law required the wrong to be attributable or imputable to the free will of the person who committed it for them to be liable. This second, *subjective* element of a fault was culpability. Although this element is not included in the definition of fault under art 6.6, it remains relevant to some extent. Indeed, under the new framework, this element is treated differently.

First, the subjective element will resurface in cases pertaining to the exclusion of liability. There is indeed no liability when there is force majeure (art 6.7), defined as the 'impossibility of complying with the applicable rule of conduct'. Other causes for exclusion of liability for fault are provided for under art 6.8: error in fact or in law, physical or psychological constraint, state of necessity, lawful authority or order, self-defence, and the consent of the victim provided that the harm involves interests that the person may legally dispose of.[27]

Second, the reform tempers the absence of the subjective element in the definition of fault for persons lacking discernment, by providing that minors under the age of 12 cannot be held liable (art 6.11), and that the court may equitably moderate the liability of older minors and those with mental disabilities, considering, where applicable, the existence of an insurance contract (arts 6.12 and 6.13).

---

26 Interesting is a comparison with the criteria in art 4:102(1) PETL: 'The required standard of conduct is that of the reasonable person in the circumstances, and depends, in particular, on the nature and value of the protected interest involved, the dangerousness of the activity, the expertise to be expected of a person carrying it on, the foreseeability of the damage, the relationship of proximity or special reliance between those involved, as well as the availability and the costs of precautionary or alternative methods'.

27 Cf art 7:101 PETL. For an analysis, see *O Evrard/M Moulin*, Les causes d'exclusion de la responsabilité pour faute, in: P Colson/F George (eds), Le nouveau livre 6 du Code civil (2024) 345–393.

b) Liability for the Conduct of Others

With regard to liability for the conduct of others, the reform remains faithful to the cases of liability contained in the Civil Code of 1804. The list is still exhaustive (see arts 6.12 to 6.15). 25

First, art 6.12 states that parents, adoptive parents, tutors and foster parents, provided that they have authority over the person of a minor under the age of 16, are liable without fault for damage caused to third parties by the minor's fault or any other fact generating liability. For minors under the age of 16, this liability is strict. For minors aged 16 or older, this liability can be countered by proving a lack of fault on the part of those who have authority over the minor. The burden of proof is on those who are held liable. 26

Second, a new liability category is created for those legally, judicially, administratively, or contractually responsible for globally and sustainably organising and supervising others' lifestyles, such as youth institutions, retirement homes, prisons, etc.[28] Indeed, those who are tasked, based on a statutory or regulatory provision, a judicial or an administrative decision, or a contract, with organising and monitoring the lifestyle of other persons in a global and sustainable manner are liable for injury caused by these persons to third parties by their faults or other facts leading to liability while under the supervision of the former. They are, however, not liable if they prove that the injury was not caused by a fault in the supervision on their part (art 6.13 para 1). Additionally, a teacher's liability under former art 1384 para 4 is eliminated, but a new liability is imposed on educational institutions for damage caused by their pupils to third parties (art 6.13 para 2). This liability is also based on a rebuttable presumption of fault, meaning that the burden of proof is on the accused institution to prove that the damage was not caused by a fault in their supervision. 27

Third and finally, art 6.14 § 1, confirms the rule of former art 1384 para 3: principals (*commettants/aanstellers*) face liability for the damage caused to third parties by their auxiliaries (*préposés/aangestelden*) during and as a result of the performance of their duties, as a result of their fault or any other fact leading to liability. This is a form of strict liability. For auxiliaries who are not subordinate within a legal person, art 6.15 states that legal persons are liable for damage caused to third parties by their governing bodies or members thereof during and 28

---

28 Cf art VI.–3:104(b) DCFR. On this innovation, see *E Gillard*, La responsabilité des personnes chargées de la surveillance d'autrui, in: P Colson/F George (eds), Le nouveau livre 6 du Code civil (2024) 79–100.

as a result of the performance of their duties. This form of liability, applicable to both private and public legal persons, is thus treated as a form of liability for the conduct of others.[29] This is in contrast to the previous so-called 'organ theory', developed under the former Code by the courts, which equated the fault of the organ with that of the legal person itself.[30]

c) Liability for Objects and Animals

29 Liability may also exist for the damage caused by defective objects. Here, the reform abandons the strict liability for damage caused by the collapse of buildings (former art 1386). This case of liability is now covered by the general provision on liability for damage caused by defective objects, enacted in art 6.16. Inspired by the definition of product liability from European origin, an object is defective when, 'because of one of its characteristics, it does not provide the safety which a person is entitled to expect under the given circumstances' (art 6.16 para 3). Liability for damage caused by an animal is found in art 6.17: there is liability without fault for the injury caused by an animal.

30 For both objects and animals, liability rests with the custodian, defined as the person who has non-subordinate power of direction and control over the object or animal, with ownership presuming custodianship (arts 6.16 para 2 and 6.17 para 2). Both cases involve strict liability, without the possibility to counter this liability by proving a lack of fault on the part of the custodian (arts 6.16 para 1 and 6.17 para 1).

5. Causation

31 From just one word in former art 1382, the legislature now devotes six provisions to causation (arts 6.18–6.23).[31] As a starting point, the legislator enshrines the principle of *conditio sine qua non* and the principle of the equivalence of condi-

---

29 This solution was inspired by art VI.–3:201(2) DCFR. See Explanatory Memorandum of Book 6 (fn 9) 73 f.

30 On this theory, see *C von Bar*, The Common European Law of Torts, vol 1 (1998) para 12.

31 It has been observed that the Belgian reform, compared to the French reform project, presents the most significant originality in its approach to causation, see *Borghetti*, D 2024, 643, para 25.

tions (art 6.18 § 1).[32] However, this starting point is immediately tempered by two 'corrections'.

First, a correction was necessary with respect to this *conditio sine qua non* test. The correction relates to facts occurring simultaneously, which, each in themselves, would be sufficient to cause the same damage. Under such circumstances, the application of the *conditio sine qua non* test would result in the determination of no liability as, for each fact, other simultaneous facts are sufficient to establish the condition for the damage.[33] Therefore, if a fact leading to liability is not a necessary condition for the damage for the sole reason that one or more other simultaneous facts, together or separately, are a sufficient condition for the damage, it is nonetheless also considered as a cause (art 6.18 § 1 para 1). This 'logical' correction, inspired by the USA *Restatement of Torts*,[34] should prevent that the application of the *conditio sine qua non* test leads to no liability. 32

Second, a correction was needed to address the principle of the equivalence of conditions. The doctrine of equivalence asserts that all necessary conditions are equivalent and must be treated equally.[35] Consequently, no distinction is made between direct and indirect causes. However, with the objective of preventing an infinite sequence of causal facts, the legislature has introduced a correction to the principle. Indeed, under art 6.18 § 2, liability is excluded where 'the link between the fact leading to liability and the damage is so remote that it would be manifestly unreasonable to impute the damage to the person whose liability is invoked. In this assessment, particular consideration is given to the improbability of the damage in light of the normal consequences of the fact leading to liability and the circumstance that this fact did not significantly contribute to the occurrence of the damage'.[36] This correction, which is new to Belgian law, represents a departure from previous legal standards by allowing for a distinction between factual causation and legal causation. 33

There are also cases of *causal uncertainty*. These are addressed under art 6.22 ('loss of a chance') and art 6.23 ('alternative causation'). 34

32 For a comparative overiew of the different approaches on causation, see *M Infantino/E Zervogianni*, The European Ways to Causation, in: M Infantino/E Zervogianni (eds), Causation in European Tort Law (2017) 85; *E Tjong Tjin Tai*, Tort Law. A Comparative Introduction (2022) para 9.3.

33 On this question, see eg, *Van Dam* (fn 2) 330 f.

34 See § 26 'Factual cause' and § 27 'Multiple sufficient causes' in Restatement of Torts (Third) (2011). See Explanatory Memorandum of Book 6 (fn 9) 90.

35 See *Kruithof* (fn 12) para 205.

36 Cf art 6:98 Dutch Civil Code.

First, art 6.22 addresses the issue of uncertainty regarding the causal nature of fault. To remedy this, case law had developed under the former Code the doctrine of loss of a chance, which recognises a separate form of damage to address cases where the causal nature of the fault in relation to the damage is uncertain. This doctrine does not provide compensation for the damage actually suffered by the injured party (in the absence of causal certainty), but rather for the loss of a chance, which is considered as a separate form of damage (and which has a certain causal relation with the fault). With the rule laid down in art 6.22, it is no longer necessary to apply the doctrine that establishes a separate form of damage. Instead, the resolution of this issue is sought in the concept of 'proportional liability'. This approach provides compensation for the damage suffered by the injured party, albeit exclusively for the proportion of the actual damage that is commensurate with the probability that the fault caused the damage. In the spirit of the legislator, compared to the former solution on loss of a chance, 'this does not alter the ultimate outcome'.[37]

Second, art 6.23 deals with uncertainty regarding the identity of the liable party, introducing 'alternative causation'. It imposes proportional liability on each potential responsible party according to the probability that their conduct caused the damage.[38] This is an innovation for the Belgian legal tradition, fulfilling a gap in previous tort law.[39]

6. Damage

a) General Provisions

35 Article 6.24 para 1 defines damage as 'the economic and non-economic consequences of harm to a legally protected personal interest'. Hence, this provision has an open scope of protected interests. It follows that there is no such provision as, for example, under German law, that limits the scope of negligence liability to the infringement of such protected interests specifically enumerated by the Code (see eg, § 823 para 1 German Civil Code). Because of its broad concept of damage, Belgian tort law allows claims for economic losses and contains no rule that would exclude compensation for pure economic loss.[40] Indeed, under Belgian tort law, a

37 See Explanatory Memorandum of Book 6 (fn 9) 9.

38 Cf art 3:103 PETL. See, however, art VI.–4:103 DCFR (which does not impose proportional liability, but full liability of each of the actors in terms of solidary liability).

39 This is rightly identified as a break with French law: *Borghetti*, D 2024, 643, para 26.

40 This was also true under the Civil Code of 1804, see *Kruithof* (fn 12) para 58.

tortfeasor is liable even if their negligence affects nothing but the plaintiff's future income or business prospects.

However, harm is only considered as damage if the injured interest is 'personal' to the claimant. In the case of injury to a public interest, the harm is considered, in principle, not to be suffered by any individual person. As a result, tort law has not been a very efficient instrument to protect public or collective interests in Belgium. Hence, cases on environmental and climate protection gave rise to considerable tensions. Case law, which interprets the concept of 'personal interest' in a broad manner, appears to evolve rapidly, particularly in environmental cases where public authorities and, to a lesser extent, environmental associations, bring claims for the reparation of ecological damage.[41] This is why the Commission for the reform of tort law had proposed to include a special provision stating that harm to a collective interest is compensable within the cases and under the conditions determined by law. However, this provision was not adopted during the parliamentary discussions.[42] The Minister of Justice subsequently committed to the formation of a special *ad hoc* commission tasked with the development of a detailed proposal on this matter (see above no 6). 36

Other provisions on damage address the requirement of certainty of the damage (which may be future; art 6.25), the distinction between patrimonial and non-patrimonial damage (art 6.26)[43] – the latter, in the case of legal persons, only compensable provided that it is compatible with the legal person's nature. Also addressed is ricochet damage (art 6.27), ie damage suffered by a person as a result of harm previously inflicted on the interest of another person with whom the first person has a legal or sufficiently close emotional connection. Finally, the question on predispositions or the victim's pre-existing condition is addressed in art 6.29: a victim who has a predisposition to suffer the injury is entitled to full compensation for the injury even if this predisposition is one of its causes; the victim who, prior to the fact leading to liability, was in a proven pre-existing state that had already resulted in harmful consequences is only entitled to compensation for the new injury caused by this same fact or for the aggravation of the existing injury. 37

41 See eg, on this evolution under Belgian tort law: *C Devillers*, La réparation du préjudice écologique: de l'évolution à la révolution? in: B Dubuisson (ed), La réparation du dommage (2022) 217–252.

42 See Amendement no 60, DocParl Chamber 2023–24, no 55–3213/005, 8.

43 Inspired by art VI.–2:101 DCFR. See Explanatory Memorandum of Book 6 (fn 9) 137.

b) Personal Injury

38 Although Belgian tort law assumes a very broad concept of damage, it follows from the reform that not every type of damage is on an equal footing: in particular, since the reform, Belgian tort law gives broader protection to the harm to physical or psychological integrity.[44] This is reflected, for instance, in the fact that the 'full' concurrence of contractual and tortious claims is allowed for compensation for such injury (see above no 18). Another articulation of this trend is found in art 6.37: injured parties who have been compensated for injury resulting from harm to their physical or psychological integrity may seek additional damages for new injuries or aggravations of the injury resulting from the same harm but which have not yet been taken into account and of which they could not reasonably have been aware at the time of the court's decision or out-of-court settlement. It is not possible to deviate from this rule: 'The renunciation of that right is without effect' (art 6.37 para 2).

7. Consequences of Liability and Remedies

a) Compensation in Full

39 A well-established consequence of liability under Belgian tort law is the principle of *full compensation*, now enshrined in art 6.30. However, the Code distinguishes between patrimonial and non-patrimonial damage, stating that compensation of the latter 'aims to provide injured parties with fair and adequate compensation for this damage' (art 6.31 § 1). This implicitly acknowledges that for this type of harm, full compensation is somewhat of an 'aspirational ideal'. This is further reflected in art 6.36, which allows the courts to assess the damage approximately when its exact extent cannot be determined or when a precise assessment would incur excessive costs (para 2), and authorises the courts to award damages in equity when the extent of the damage cannot be ascertained in any other way (para 3).

40 Further, the Code confirms that the damage is determined as closely as possible to the time of actual compensation (art 6.32), that the elements of damage must be individually identified (art 6.36 para 1), and that the injured parties are free to dispose of the awarded damages as they wish (art 6.39). Furthermore, it provides

44 This has also been observed in comparative analyses, see *Knetsch* (fn 13) para 32; *Borghetti*, D 2024, 643, para 16.

for a choice between lump-sum, capitalisation, and annuity for compensating future injury resulting from physical or psychological harm. Indeed, to protect the victim, art 6.34 allows the court to impose an annuity, even if it is not requested, when compelling reasons related to the protection of the victim justify such an award.

A provision also addresses how to assess the compensation for damage to goods, clarifying the relationship between damages for repair and for replacement (art 6.38): 'In the case of damage to a good, the victim has the right to compensation for the expenses of its repair. If these expenses exceed the costs of replacing the good with one of the same characteristics, the compensation is limited to the amount of the latter. The victim is also entitled to compensation for any potential decrease in value of the good after its repair. In the case of destruction of the good or when its repair is not possible, the victim is entitled to compensation for the expenses necessary to replace the good with one of the same characteristics that fulfils the same functions'. 41

The Code does not allow for monetary compensation (damages) only, but for non-monetary relief (*réparation en nature/herstel in natura*) as well. To this end, the court may alter the legal situation of the parties or order measures to be taken by the tortfeasor or a third party, at the expense of the tortfeasor, and may authorise the injured party to substitute for the tortfeasor for this purpose (art 6.33 § 1). For instance, in cases of non-patrimonial harm, case law has accepted that non-monetary relief allows for the enforcement of an apology by the tortfeasor.[45] In regard to the relationship between monetary damages and non-monetary relief, the Code clarifies in art 6.33 § 2 that if non-monetary relief is requested by the injured party, it should be granted by the court, unless the requested measure turns out to be impossible or clearly unreasonable, requires the use of coercion against the tortfeasor, or is contrary to human dignity. Rather than monetary damages, the tortfeasor may offer non-monetary relief, but the injured party is entitled to refuse such an offer if there are 'valid reasons' to do so. 42

A notable innovation is the availability of a claim for disgorgement of profits. Indeed, in cases of lucrative faults, art 6.31 § 3, allows the court to grant the plaintiff an additional indemnity equal to part or all of the net profit gained by the liable party when personality rights or reputation have been intentionally violated 43

45 See Cour de cassation, Première chambre civile (Cass civ 1) 26 November 2021, ECLI:BE:CASS:2021:ARR.20211126.1F.5, JT 2022, 206, obs *P Wéry*; Revue générale des assurances et des responsabilités (RGAR) 2022, no 15858, obs *J Van de Voorde*; TBBR/RGDC 2023, 424, obs *S De Rey*. For a summary in English, see *S De Rey*, Apologies as a Private Law Remedy: Emerging on the European Continent, and Beyond? ERPL 2023, 1013–1023, followed by ten country reports on the subject.

to obtain profit. Although the new Code does not provide for punitive damages or civil fines, this new remedy does indicate that there is room for more than just compensation of damage under the new Belgian tort law.[46] This form of 'restitutionary damages' is not presented as a deviation of the principle of full compensation, nor as a private punishment. In the spirit of the legislature, it should be regarded as compensation that can be cumulated with the damages awarded to compensate for non-patrimonial damage.[47] Some authors have expressed regret that these illegitimate profits are awarded to the injured party rather than a compensation fund.[48] However, the solution adopted by the legislator is undoubtedly a condition for the effectiveness of the mechanism put in place.[49]

b) Judicial Intervention to Prevent Damage

44 Furthermore, the Code also provides for a more preventive function of tort law. This is found, for instance, in art 6.28 para 1, organising the reimbursement of costs resulting from measures taken to prevent imminent damage or the worsening of damage. These costs are borne by the tortfeasor, or the person who would have been liable if the damage had occurred. In order for the provision to apply, the measures must be urgent and reasonable, regardless of whether or not they were unsuccessful. For example, a non-profit association or public authority that has intervened to prevent pollution could find in this provision a means of obtaining reimbursement for its expenditures. Additionally, art 6.28 para 2 confers upon the court the power to order an injunction or interdiction against the liable party to prevent the aggravation of the damage that could result from the repetition or continuation of the harmful fact. This possibility is predicated on

46 Already advocated such a remedy under former Belgian tort law, see *M Kruithof*, Disgorgement of Profits in Belgian Private Law, in: E Hondius/A Janssen (eds), Disgorgement of Profits. Gain-Based Remedies throughout the World (2015) 89–120. See also *T Gladinez*, Voordeelafdracht in het privaatrecht (2020).

47 Explanatory Memorandum of Book 6 (fn 9) 148. Also under the former tort law, 'Occasionally, one can find court decisions awarding relatively high moral damages to such a victim, not so much as a reaction to the seriousness of the wrong committed but rather to tackle the profits the wrongdoer has realised by negating the exclusive right of the injured party. Even though these judgments are formally based on reasons invoking civil liability and valuing moral damages, one could also recognise in these decisions a form of disgorgement as a remedy based on the bad faith infringed of a subjective (personality) right' (*Kruithof* [fn 12] para 287).

48 *P Colson*, Les conséquences de la responsabilité, in: P Colson/F George (eds), Le nouveau livre 6 du Code civil (2024) 201.

49 See *Dubuisson*, JT 2025, 1, para 68.

the assumption that the damage in question has already occurred, and the primary objective is to forestall any exacerbation of the damage that might ensue from the repetition or continuation of the harmful event.

Another expression of this tendency is found in art 6.40, not laid down in the chapter on the consequences of liability, but in a separate chapter, devoted to injunctions or interdictions. It allows the court to intervene even before the damage occurs: 'In the case of an established or a seriously imminent breach of a statutory provision imposing specific behaviour, the court, upon request of a party demonstrating that it will suffer damage to one of its goods or harm to its physical integrity as a result, may issue an injunction or an interdiction aimed at enforcing this statutory provision'. 45

This provision considerably restricts the conditions under which such preventive measures may be ordered. Indeed, it requires, first of all, a proven violation or a serious threat of violation of a statutory rule. Moreover, the violation or serious threat of violation should relate to a statutory rule imposing specific behaviour, which excludes the application of this provision in the case of a violation or threat of violation of the general standard of care. In such a case, it is in fact the court itself which is called upon to concretise the rule of conduct with regard to what a prudent and reasonable person would have done, which was found to give it excessive powers. Therefore, the legislator has reserved the power to order injunctions and interdictions to violations or threats of violations of a statutory rule imposing specific behaviour.

In addition, the person claiming such an injunction or interdiction must demonstrate that they will suffer harm to their physical integrity or damage to property as a result of the violation. It follows that the threat of mental harm is excluded. On several occasions, the legislator has equated physical and mental harm (see above no 38), but this is not the case here. This choice, although already subject of criticism in the extant literature,[50] does appear to have been given due consideration. In the spirit of the legislator, making preventive injunctions and interdictions available for a threat to mental integrity would enable anyone to bring a case before the courts in the name of collective anguish or anxiety, the reality of which is often difficult to verify.[51]

---

50 See eg, *N Schmitz/E Vanstechelman*, La fonction préventive de la responsabilité civile dans le nouveau livre 6 du Code civil: une consécration contrastée, in: P Colson/F George (eds), Le nouveau livre 6 du Code civil (2024) para 35.

51 On this choice, see *Dubuisson*, JT 2025, 1, para 75.

B. Literature

46 The subsequent section presents an overview of the extant literature addressing the reform of Belgian tort law.

1. *H Bocken*, Het ontwerp van de Commissie tot herziening van het aansprakelijkheidsrecht. Een overzicht in context [The Commission's draft revision of tort law. An overview in context], Tijdschrift voor Privaatrecht (TPR) 2019, 11 – 30

47 This article, in Dutch, provides an overview of the reform at the stage when the provisions were drafted by the Commission for the reform of tort law, co-chaired by the author. It is followed, in the same journal that devoted a special issue to the reform in this early stage, by several contributions that focus on a particular aspect of the reform at the drafting stage.

2. *JS Borghetti*, Le soleil se lève au nord : ou comment la réforme belge de la responsabilité extracontractuelle fait pâlir le projet français [The sun rises in the north: or how the Belgian reform of tort law makes the French project pale in comparison], Recueil Dalloz (D) 2024, 643 – 649

48 This article, in French, provides an overview of the reform from a comparative perspective by comparing the key changes and innovations of the reform with French reform initiatives.

3. *P Colson/F George* (eds), Le nouveau livre 6 du Code civil [The new Book 6 of the Civil Code] (Anthemis 2024) 476 pp

49 This book, in French, provides an overview of the reform by addressing, in a first part, liability for personal misconduct (by *B Goffaux/G Maschiet*), liability for the conduct of minors (by *A Pütz*), liability of persons responsible for the supervision of others (by *E Gillard*), and liability for objects (by *M Thiry*). In a second part, the book addresses the notion of damage (by *B Fosséprez*), damage resulting from an

infringement to a collective interest (by *C Devillers*), the consequences of liability (by *P Colson*), and preventive measures (by *N Schmitz/E Vanstechelman*). In a third part, the book addresses causation (by *V De Wulf*), proportional liability (by *C Joisten*), and the grounds for exclusion of liability (by *O Evrard/M Moulin*). Finally, in a fourth part, the book addresses the concurrence of contract and tort between co-contractors (by *A Cataldo*), and the position of auxiliaries (by *F George*).

4. *C De Koninck*, Het nieuwe buitencontractuele aansprakelijkheidsrecht. Een eerste commentaar op grond van de parlementaire stukken [The reform of tort law. A first commentary based on the parliamentary documents] (Intersentia 2024) 286 pp

This book, in Dutch, is a useful working tool that restates, in the form of an article- 50
by-article commentary, the content of parliamentary documents.

5. *S De Rey,* The Reform of Belgian Tort Law: Overview, Methodology, and Why it Succeeded, European Review of Private Law (ERPL) 2025, 135 – 172

Following an explanation of the rationale behind the reform, this article, in En- 51
glish, provides an overview of the potential reasons for the reform's conclusion. These may include the presence of sufficient political determination, the methodology employed in the reform process, and the reform's objectives. This is followed by an overview of the new Belgian tort law, focusing on its key innovations and identifying the most notable changes from a comparative perspective.

6. *B Dubuisson* (ed), Le nouveau livre 6 du Code civil portant réforme du droit de la responsabilité civile extracontractuelle [The new Book 6 of the Civil Code reforming the law of torts], Commission Université-Palais vol 229 (Anthemis 2024) 270 pp

This book, in French, provides an overview of the reform by addressing the con- 52
currence of contract and tort (by *A Rigolet*), liability for personal misconduct (by *F*

Auvray), liability for the conduct of others and for objects and animals (by *T Malengreau*), causation (by *C Joisten*), and the new provisions on physical or psychological harm (by *P Colson*).

7. *B Dubuisson*, Le livre 6 du Code civil portant réforme de la responsabilité extracontractuelle. La fin d'un long héritage (1804 – 2024) [Book 6 of the Civil Code reforming tort law. The end of a long legacy (1804 – 2024)], Journal des tribunaux (JT) 2025, 1 – 31

53 This article, in French, provides a comprehensive overview of the entire reform, addressing all provisions of Book 6 'Tort Law', with numerous references to case law, legal scholarship and parliamentary documents.

8. *F Auvray/R Jafferali*, Une cure de jouvence pour le droit de la responsabilité, le Livre 6 du nouveau Code civil [A facelift for tort law: Book 6 of the new Civil Code], Tijdschrift voor Belgisch Burgerlijk Recht/Revue Générale de Droit Civil Belge (TBBR/RGDC) 2025, 82 – 128 (part 1)

54 This article, in French, provides a comprehensive overview of the reform, with numerous references to case law, legal scholarship and parliamentary documents.

9. *G Jocqué*, Het buitencontractuele aansprakelijkheidsrecht. Van oud naar nieuw [Tort law. From old to new] (die Keure 2024) 207 pp

55 This book, in Dutch, discusses the new Belgian tort law rules. All provisions of Book 6 'Tort Law' are covered. The author explains where the new provisions differ from the former Civil Code and for which provisions the case law of the Court of Cassation remains relevant.

10. *G Jocqué*, Het nieuwe Belgische buitencontractueel aansprakelijkheidsrecht [The new Belgian tort law], Weekblad voor Privaatrecht, Notariaat en Registratie (WPNR) 2024, 549–555

This article, in Dutch, provides an overview of the reform, addressing its key in- 56
novations and identifying the most notable changes.

11. *M Kruithof*, Boek 6 BW (deels) toegelicht: de aansprakelijkheid genererende feiten en de causaliteit [Book 6 of the Civil Code (partly) explained: facts generating liability and causation], in: P Lecocq/M Dambre, Rechtskroniek voor de vrede- en politierechters 2024 [Legal chronicle for Justice of Peace and Police] (die Keure 2024) 319–376

This book chapter, in Dutch, focusses on how the reform reshaped the rules on 57
facts generating liability and on causation, with numerous references to case law, legal scholarship and parliamentary documents.

12. *T Malengreau* (ed), Le droit de la responsabilité civile extracontractuelle réformé [Tort law reformed] (Larcier 2024) 377 pp

This book, in French, provides an overview of the reform by addressing liability 58
for personal misconduct (by *N Schmitz*), liability for the conduct of others and for objects and animals (by *MH de Callataÿ/R Deutsch*), causation (by *A Duriau*), plurality of liable parties (by *B De Coninck*), the notion of damage (by *P Colson*), compensation for personal injury (by *N Estienne*), injunctions and interdictions (by *T Derval/CE Lambert*), and the concurrence of contract and tort (by *F George*).

13. *I Samoy/G Jocqué*, Het nieuwe buitencontractuele aansprakelijkheidsrecht in Boek 6 BW [The new tort law in Book 6 of the Civil Code], Rechtskundig Weekblad (RW) 2024–25, 682 ff (part 1) and 722 ff (part 2)

59 This article, in Dutch and published in two parts, provides a comprehensive overview of the entire reform, addressing all provisions of Book 6 'Tort Law', with numerous references to case law, legal scholarship and parliamentary documents.

14. *V Schollaert*, Het nieuwe buitencontractueel aansprakelijkheidsrecht. Een verkennende analyse [The new tort law. An exploratory analysis], Nieuw juridisch Weekblad (NjW) 2023, 374–381

60 This article, in Dutch, provides an overview of the reform, addressing its key innovations and identifying the most notable changes at the stage when the provisions were drafted but not yet final.

15. *T Vansweevelt/B Weyts*, Handboek Buitencontractueel Aansprakelijkheidsrecht [Handbook of tort law] (Intersentia, 2nd edn 2025) 1392 pp

61 This book, in Dutch, is a handbook that deals with tort law in Belgium, covering all topics that are relevant for lawyers in legal practice or in their research and studies, seasoned with critical and personal theses. In addition to a thorough legal analysis of this area of law, this book places tort law in a broader context and situates it in relation to social security, insurance and compensation funds. Also, the relationship to criminal (procedural) law, contract law and European law is addressed.

Viktor Tokushev and Hristina Tancheva

III. Bulgaria

A. Legislation

In 2024, the Bulgarian Parliament did not adopt any new legislation relevant to tort matters and no substantial changes were made to existing regulations. 1

B. Cases

This year, the subject of analysis will be new and significant case law of the Supreme Court of Cassation. In addition, the issue of compensation in personal injury cases is discussed. 2

1. Supreme Court of Cassation (SCC) Judgment No 50051 of 12 April 2024, Case No 1822/2022, II Civil Chamber, Civil Division: Damages for Non-Enforcement of a Penalty

a) Brief Summary of the Facts

On 1 January 2018, the mother and sister of the plaintiff were deliberately killed by a person who had already been convicted of intentional crimes. 3

In a verdict dated 13 May 2009, the perpetrator of the offence was convicted of 'molestation' under conditions of dangerous recidivism and was sentenced to eight years' imprisonment under an initially 'strict' regime. The sentence was confirmed by the Supreme Court in a judgment of 22 December 2009. 4

The sentence, which entered into force on 13 May 2009, was not enforced for over eight years because the convicted person was not traced. Over the years, there were reports from the Ministry of Interior authorities that the perpetrator had not been found because of the ineffective methods used in this case; however, the Public Prosecutor's Office of the Republic of Bulgaria did not exercise its powers by instructing other search measures (undertaking checks of the National 'Population' Database, tracking bank transactions, pursuing information from the database of mobile operators, etc). If the sentence had been enforced at the time of the offence, the offender should have been serving a custodial sentence. 5

https://doi.org/10.1515/9783111389271-004

6 On that basis, the plaintiff brought an action against the Public Prosecutor's Office, claiming that its failure to exercise its powers to enforce the penalties imposed had caused him to suffer non-pecuniary damage as a result of the death of his relatives. Both the Court of First Instance and the Court of Appeal upheld the claim and awarded compensation in favour of the plaintiff.

7 The Court of Appeal held that the work of the prosecution authorities entrusted with the supervision of the execution of sentences, was nominal, ineffective, insufficient and untimely and this was the reason for the objectives of the punishment not being achieved, to wit: having a corrective effect on the convicted person, but also providing a deterrent effect by generating a disinclination for him to commit a new crime.

8 The Court found that, as a result of the inaction of officials within the Prosecutor's Office, there was a causal link between such inaction and the 'damage' in the form of the moral suffering of the plaintiff resulting from the loss of loved ones whose lives were criminally taken by a convicted individual.

9 The appeal was allowed on the following question: 'Does the failure of officials in the Public Prosecutor's Office to enforce a "deprivation of liberty" sentence which has entered into force constitute an exceptional ground for the imposition of an obligation to pay compensation for the damage caused by murder committed by the convicted person at a time when he should have been serving the "deprivation of liberty" punishment imposed on him?'

b) Judgment of the Court

10 According to the Supreme Court, the evidence in the case supported the conclusion that after the sentence entered into force, and that, for a period of eight years, typical actions were undertaken without effect, and no specific instructions were given by the Prosecutor's Office as the body supervising the execution of the sentence, to instigate investigative measures that could have led to the effective enforcement of the sentence. The result of the prosecutor's inaction was not only a failure to implement particular and general preventive measures and to have an impact on the correction and re-education of the convicted person, but also created an opportunity for the convicted person to commit a new crime.

11 The SCC held that where the action was not the sole cause of the outcome (ie the damage resulted from the cumulative effect of multiple phenomena/events), liability for tort is not excluded, but this factor is to be taken into account in determining the scope of liability. In this case, the main cause of the damage's occurrence was the specific criminal act of the convicted individual and the failure of the Prosecutor's Office to act could be regarded as a *conditio sine qua non.*

The SCC assessed the ratio between the contributions of the two unlawful acts and held that the act of the convicted offender contributed to the damage suffered by the plaintiff to 70 %, while the inaction of the public authority contributed 30 %. 12

Taking into account the circumstances established in the case, namely: the nature and intensity of the relationship established between the plaintiff and his mother and sister; the sudden nature of the loss suffered and its impact on the plaintiff's psyche; the age of the victims and of the plaintiff; and the economic situation in the country at the time of the injury, the Court found that fair compensation amounted to € 75,000 for the damage caused by the death of the plaintiff's mother, and € 50,000 for the damage caused by the death of his sister. Accordingly, the liability of the Public Prosecutor's Office was limited to a payment of the sum of € 23,000 in respect of the death of the plaintiff's mother and € 15,000 in respect of the death of his sister. 13

c) Commentary

The key points in this case are the establishment of the unlawfulness of the conduct of the State authority, manifested in inaction (failure to take adequate and timely measures to search for a person whose 'deprivation of liberty' sentence had entered into force and was subject to execution), and the existence of a causal link between this inaction and the result – the intentional killing of the plaintiff's relatives. The Court correctly held that, had the punishment been effectively imposed, the offender would still have been in prison at the time of the murders, and that the deprivation of liberty could have acted as a deterrent. This latter by reforming and re-educating the individual and warning him that, if he committed another crime, he might be imprisoned again, would act as a deterrent. 14

Interestingly, the Court held that the conduct of the prosecution authorities had created an opportunity for that individual to commit a crime and thereby cause harm to the plaintiff, but without defining this as a 'joint act' within the meaning of art 53 of the Obligations and Contracts Act (OCA). Had it been held that the tort had been occasioned by *both* the prosecution *and* the offender who had killed the plaintiff's mother and sister, the liability would have been joint. That is to say, each of them would have been liable to the injured party for the full amount of compensation. In the judgment under consideration, the SCC took a different approach by applying the concept normally reserved for determining the contribution to an injurious result as in the case of a joint act by the injured party and the tortfeasor (in which case the compensation is reduced in proportion to the contribution of the injured party), which was not the case here. 15

16 It can be said that the Court was guided more by natural justice than by legal logic, which, in this case, may well be considered justified. However, this is unlikely to form an enduring practice in such cases. Still, it cannot be denied that if the action had been brought against the actual perpetrator of the offence, he would have been liable for the full amount of the damage, but only up to 70 % of the amount of the damages.

2. Supreme Court of Cassation (SCC) Ruling No 2204 of 8 May 2024, Case No 3890/2023: Joint Act of a Minor

a) Brief Summary of the Facts

17 The victim of a road traffic incident was a two-and-a-half-month-old child at the time of the accident. The accident itself was the result of a two-car collision, and both drivers were at fault. One (the victim's father) had moved into the left-hand lane without giving a right of way to the vehicle already travelling in that lane. The other was driving at excessive speed in that left-hand lane. The victim was riding, in an unrestrained booster seat, in the back seat of the vehicle. The action was brought against the insurer of the 'civil liability' insurance carrier of the driver who hit the victim's car. A claim for compensation for the personal tort suffered was filed for € 600,000.

18 Taking into account all of the child's injuries, the Court of Appeal determined that fair compensation amounted to € 500,000. It was pointed out that the child (at the time of suit aged four years and three months) was unable to move independently, had profound mental disabilities, no prospect of improvement in the future, and had developed epilepsy for which periodic hospitalisation was required.

19 The Appellate Panel held that the drivers of the cars involved in the incident, *and* the unlawful failure to properly restrain the child had equally brought about the harmful outcome. Therefore, it fixed the amount of compensation payable for non-pecuniary damage at € 250,000. Account should also be taken here of the Court's analysis of the provisions of the Road Traffic Act concerning, on the one hand, the driver's enhanced 'duty of care' to ensure that passengers are properly restrained and, on the other, the particular safety obligations of passengers.

20 In this case, there was a cassation appeal both on the issue of the amount of compensation and on various aspects of the question of whether a minor can co-contribute to the damage suffered by them.

b) Judgment of the Court

The case was not admitted to cassation. The SCC first ruled on the question of compensation, holding that the amount of compensation for non-pecuniary damage in the amount of € 250,000 was fair and proportionate *in re* the damage suffered. It took into account the substantial impairment of the child's quality of life, to wit: the inability to walk independently; feed himself; control his pelvic organs and functions; speak; as well as his cognitive developmental regression to the degree of severe mental retardation with no optimistic prognosis for recovery. 21

On the more substantive issue, from a legal perspective, the SCC relied on Supreme Court interpretative case law from the 1960s and held that, where a minor contributed to the tortious outcome, in accordance with the circumstances of the case, the provision on contribution should apply, notwithstanding that such a person cannot have acted culpably. It is also recognised that the rules on contribution also apply where a minor, injured in an accident, has contributed to the injurious outcome through inadequate parental supervision. It is sufficient that the injurious result be causally linked (albeit through the innocent act or omission of the injured minor) for contributory causation to be established. 22

In view of these arguments, the SCC held that the judgment of the Court of Appeal was correct and should not be subject to cassation review. 23

c) Commentary

The judgment given adopts the principle of 'contribution' being objective and irrelevant to the injured party's ability to act reasonably and to foresee the possible negative consequences of their actions and omissions. According to the SCC, it is the existence of a causal link between the conduct of the victim and the tortious outcome that is relevant for the application of the institute of 'contribution', and not the 'fault' of the victim. 24

As mentioned above, this understanding is also based on the interpretative practice of the Supreme Court from the 1960s. In our view, however, this interpretation neglects the obligation, imposed on a driver by the Road Traffic Act, to take the utmost care to ensure the safety of passengers and does not take into account the difference in the psychological maturity of persons between the ages of zero and fourteen, those generally falling into the group of 'minors'. 25

In this sense, we deem it unjustified to seek contribution on the part of a baby who travelled unrestrained because, in such a case, only the parents can be guilty of culpable and unlawful conduct. Were this not so and the claim was filed by the injured minor against his parents who caused the damage, we would end up with 26 the absurd situation that their unlawful conduct would lead to a reduction in the compensation payable on the ground of their own 'contribution' (to events).

27 It should also be recalled that a number of SCC panels have rendered opposing decisions in similar cases. For example, SCC Decision No 50064[1] stated: 'The injured minor does not contribute to the occurrence of the damage under art 51, para 2 of the OCA when travelling in a vehicle driven by the tortfeasor without the proper use of a safety system, in view of the heightened duty of care imposed on the driver in such cases.'

28 On the basis of such contradictory practice created by the President of the SCC's Resolution of 9 August 2024, Interpretative Case No 2 of the Civil and Commercial Division was initiated to consider a position: 'On the link between the actions of the tortfeasor-driver of the motor vehicle and the conduct of the injured party in determining whether the injured party contributed to the occurrence of the damage under art 51, para 2 of the OCA, where the victim is a minor and was travelling in a motor vehicle driven by the tortfeasor without the use of a restraint system in breach of the Road Traffic Act.'

3. Supreme Court of Cassation (SCC) Ruling No 835 of 27 February 2024, Case No 2655/2023, I Civil Chamber, Civil Division: Damages for Subsequent Prejudice to Health

a) Brief Summary of the Facts

29 Since early childhood, the plaintiff had suffered from the disease haemophilia, for which he has been systematically treated with anti-haemophilic globulin/A. On 4 January 1995, the plaintiff received a transfusion of anti-haemophilus globulin/A, as a result of which he became infected with the HIV virus and Hepatitis C.

30 In 2005, a judgment entered into force which held that, as compensation for damage caused to the plaintiff by an object (blood product), the owner of that object, in this case the Ministry of Health, was liable, and was ordered to pay the plaintiff, jointly with the National Centre for Clinical and Transfusion Haematology, compensation under art 50 of the OCA for the damage caused to him by the contamination. This was in the amount of € 25,000. The plaintiff was initially awarded compensation precisely because of the fact that he had suffered damage by contracting HIV and Hepatitis C.

1 Decision of 7 February 2024 in Commercial Case No 1692/2022, II Commercial Chamber, Commercial Division.

Later, in 2012, another Court judgment held that a deterioration in the plaintiff's state of health, ascertained in January 2010, had been proven and he was therefore awarded compensation for the existence of an exacerbation. This was in the amount of € 50,000. The judgment found that, from 2010, the plaintiff's illness had progressed to the stage of AIDS, which is the final stage in the development of an HIV infection. At this stage, the weakened immune system of the patient leads to the development of multiple disease processes, frequent severe infections of various kinds emerge, and damage to various organs occurs. These significantly impaired the general state of health of the patient and put his life at permanent risk. 31

In 2017, there was a further deterioration in the health of the plaintiff, which was the subject of the proceedings outlined above. He therefore brought a new action against the Ministry of Health for payment of compensation for non-pecuniary damage suffered as a result of the exacerbation, in effect, the aggravation of his haemophilia, the deterioration of which had occurred as a result of his being infected with the HIV virus and Hepatitis C. 32

The Court held that, because the plaintiff suffered from haemophilia, he received monthly prophylactic treatment aimed at avoiding spontaneous, life-threatening haemorrhages, and joint problems. Although the plaintiff had been regularly undergoing prophylactic treatment for haemophilia, his condition had deteriorated and there were increasingly frequent haemorrhages caused by the use of antiretroviral medication for the treatment of his HIV infection. Thus, the treatment of the plaintiff's second illness, HIV, led to a worsening of the underlying illness, haemophilia, as the most effective treatment for HIV causes haemorrhages (sometimes life-threatening) and the Hepatitis C infection leads to a strain on the liver and further exacerbates the condition and course of the underlying haemophilia. The treatment of the HIV infection is considered to have a persistent negative impact on the manifestation of haemophilia but as stopping treatment would result in a fatal outcome for the patient, he has no such option, but perforce suffer a progressive worsening of the underlying disease. 33

The Court of Appeal awarded € 25,000 in compensation for the aggravation of the plaintiff's underlying disease, haemophilia, based on the nature of the deterioration in the plaintiff's state of health and its consequences and taking into account his physical and mental suffering. These latter, in practice, had an immediate and ongoing impact on the quality of the victim's life, and rendered him unable to work despite being of working age. 34

b) Judgment of the Court

35 The SCC did not allow the case to proceed to cassation, holding that, on the basis of the evidence gathered, the panel of judges had rightly decided that the previous judgments, as entered into force, had compensated for the damage caused by the HIV infection, but had not awarded compensation for the negative impact of that infection on the underlying disease, haemophilia, for the damage from which compensation was also sought in the new claim.

c) Commentary

36 In this most recent case there was an exacerbation, that is, a further impairment of deterioration in the injured person's state of health, which occurred some time after the original injury and was not taken into account in determining damages in the first two cases because it was not known at the time. The Court took into account that a new deterioration in the plaintiff's condition had been established, due to the medication used at the time to treat the HIV virus, which had had a negative impact on the plaintiff's underlying condition.

37 The Court rightly held that, if the victim's state of health deteriorates in comparison to the condition for which compensation was awarded, he is entitled to 'new' compensation for that deterioration if it is causally related to the original tort and not due to other factors and causes. In the more recent case, the compensation awarded did not duplicate that already granted for the original suffering, because it concerned the aggravation of a condition which the plaintiff had prior to the tort, and the exacerbation was precisely the result of the infection with HIV and Hepatitis C and treatment of those diseases. Had the plaintiff not been infected with these, he could have treated his haemophilia more effectively, and the two therapies would not have interfered and worsened his state of health.

4. Supreme Court of Cassation (SCC) Judgment No 121 of 22 February 2024, Case No 1148/2023: Damages for Failure to Perform a Routine Preventative Examination

a) Brief Summary of the Facts

38 In 2012, the plaintiff was employed by the defendant in the position of a 'mine superintendent'. According to the regulations governing the employment relation-

ship, the employer had an obligation to provide its employees with medical examinations, at its own expense. These were not performed regularly. It was established that, for the period of six and a half years in which the plaintiff worked for the defendant company, only one routine preventative medical examination was undertaken, that being in 2013.

For that reason, the plaintiff claimed that his cancer was not detected in time and this led to irreversible damage to his health, whereby he suffered non-pecuniary damage. In 2019, two years after his employment with the defendant terminated, the plaintiff was diagnosed with prostate cancer at clinical stage three of four possible stages, which is a common (not occupational), socially significant, disease. The plaintiff also maintained that the late detection of the tumour in his prostate caused irreversible damage to his health, and the pain and suffering he endured in terms of stress, fear for his life, and for the future of his family, for all of which he claimed compensation. 39

The District Court dismissed the claim, holding that the Labour Code (LC) does not provide for compensation for workers for an employer's failure to provide mandatory medical examinations. 40

b) Judgment of the Court

The Court of Cassation held that, where an employee claims payment of compensation for non-pecuniary damage caused by an employer's failure to comply with a mandatory obligation under the LC, and where such compensation is not expressly provided for in the LC, the general rules of tort liability apply. 41

The Court took into account the provision of art 289 of the LC, pursuant to which, an employer is obliged to take measures for the prevention of, and reduction in, the incidence of employment-related injuries, occupational diseases, and general sickness. Also, pursuant to art 287, paras 1 and 2 of the LC, all employees are subject to mandatory preliminary and periodic medical examinations, the periodic ones being at the employer's expense. 42

The Court found that the tumour had been detected in a Magnetic Resonance Imaging (MRI) scan performed in 2019, but considered that this investigation was not included in the mandatory annual medical examinations that the employer was required to arrange and, therefore, in the Court's view, failure to comply with such an obligation cannot constitute a reason for the late detection of the disease. Consequently, it was not established that there was a direct and proximate causal link between that unlawful omission on the part of the employer and the non-pecuniary damage at issue suffered, personally, by the plaintiff. 43

c) Commentary

44 The SCC rejected the contention that a full medical history would have been taken when the plaintiff underwent regular planned check-ups, and that these would have included ascertaining the family history, such as the plaintiff had given in this case, and that this would, in turn, have provided the basis for referral for further examination to identify a tumour marker. In the Court's view, the taking of the medical history is very much dependent on the conduct of both the examining physician and the patient and, therefore, it cannot reasonably be concluded that, had the employer complied with its obligation to perform the annual planned check-up of the plaintiff, the plaintiff would have declared specific complaints and indicated a family history when the medical history was recorded (it was established that, when examined by the personal physician earlier in 2019, the plaintiff did not indicate any issues), which in turn would have given rise to a referral of the plaintiff for further examination to establish the condition.

45 Furthermore, under Ordinance No 39 of 16 November 2004 on 'preventative examinations and regular medical reviews', persons over 18 years of age are subject to annual planned check-ups, which include the recording of the medical history and a detailed (current) status. That is to say, a planned check-up, to which all adults (and not just those in an employment relationship) are subject, could, theoretically, also have established the plaintiff's state of health in good time.

46 Therefore, firstly, it was not certain that, even if the plaintiff had regularly undergone planned check-ups organised by the employer, he would have been diagnosed with a tumour in good time. Secondly, the plaintiff had had the opportunity to benefit from planned check-ups provided by law.

5. Supreme Court of Cassation (SCC) Ruling No 5406 of 25 November 2024, Civil Case No 2783/2024, I Civil Chamber, Civil Division: Damages Following a Rock Collapse

a) Brief Summary of the Facts

47 A woman perished when rocks collapsed in the grounds of a natural landmark (a public municipal property) where an eco-trail had been created. Her children and husband claimed compensation from the municipality for non-pecuniary damage resulting from her death.

The Court held that the claim is brought on the ground of art 50 of the Obligations and Contracts Act (OCA), which provides that the owner of a chattel and the person under whose supervision the said chattel is, are liable jointly and severally for the damage caused by said chattel. The Court declared that there was a causal link between the properties (nature) and qualities (condition) of the chattel and the damage, as the latter 'originated' exactly with the chattel itself. 48

The Court awarded compensation of € 50,000 to each of the plaintiffs, taking into account, in its determination, that the loss was of a close relative – a mother and wife (aged 45 years) who was an active, effective, physical and moral support to everyone in the family, managed the household and was a devoted mother and wife. The Court took into account the fact that the loss of the mother and wife, to whom the plaintiffs were deeply attached, would remain with them throughout their lives, depriving them of both her emotional and moral comfort and support. 49

b) Judgment of the Court

The Supreme Court dismissed the appeal in cassation against the decision of the Court of Appeal, holding that the Court of Appeal had considered the specific circumstances established in the case, which were relevant in determining the fair amount of compensation. 50

c) Commentary

The Court reasonably held that the municipality was liable under no-fault liability for 'damage caused by a chattel', as owner of the natural landmark where the rockfall had occurred. It rejected the defendant's objection that force majeure was involved, holding that the incident was deemed to have occurred because of the properties (nature) and qualities (condition) of the chattel. 51

By comparison, in another case from last year, Judgment No 4851,[2] in respect of damage caused by fallen branches of trees owned by the State, and under the supervision of the Road Infrastructure Agency, the Court held that this was due to force majeure and exempted the defendants from liability. The trees were found to have fallen due to high winds, which were defined as a hurricane on the Beaufort scale. 52

2 Judgment of 25.10.2024 of the SCC in Civil Case No 5274/2023, I Civil Chamber, Civil Division.

6. Court of Cassation (SCC) Judgment No 385 of 21 June 2024, Case No 3551/2023, I Civil Division: Liability of a Manager for Damages

a) Brief Summary of the Facts

53 The plaintiff in the case was a commercial company which claimed damages for the actions of its manager. The company had a subsidiary to which three real estate properties (the main assets of the parent company) were transferred 'in kind'. The tortfeasor was the manager of both the parent company and the subsidiary. Acting on behalf of the parent company, the manager sold the entire going concern of the subsidiary to a third party for a price of € 500, even though the value of the properties in the subsidiary were worth over € 500,000 at the time. Subsequently, the manager acquired shares in the recipient company thus, in effect, selling the properties to himself at a significantly discounted price.

54 The manager had been convicted in criminal proceedings for embezzlement. The company brought an action against him for 'damages in tort' in the amount of approximately € 500,000 suffered as a result of his deeds. The Court of Appeal held that, in accordance with the factual allegations set out in the Statement of Claim and the clarifications made before the appellate instance, the legal classification of the claim fell under art 145 of the Commerce Act (which was the legal classification originally given by the Court of First Instance) and it was in accordance with this that the defence of both parties to the dispute had been conducted.

55 The Court also argued that it was not bound by the legal qualification indicated by the plaintiff, but was obliged to determine that rule of law applicable in light of those of the plaintiff's factual assertions on which he, the plaintiff, based the establishment and realisation of the right claimed by him and was the subject of the protection sought. It was submitted that, in this case, the allegations of the plaintiff company related to acts committed by the defendant as its manager which allegedly caused the damage to the company, by reducing the assets of its subsidiary. It was held that these allegations covered the factual composition of the so-called 'managerial tort' within the meaning of art 145 of the Commerce Act, which governs the special liability of a manager for compensation of any damage caused to the company due to culpable and unlawful failure to perform contractual and authorised obligations arising from this capacity. It was submitted that the fact that some of those acts may constitute a criminal offence does not derogate from that ground and does not give rise to a claim under the general provisions of art 45 of the OCA. It was on this basis that the appellate judgment was rendered.

The judgment of the Court of Appeal was admitted to cassation for the purpose of assessing its admissibility in view of the legal qualification of the claim as submitted by the Appellate Court. 56

b) Judgment of the Court

The SCC held that the judgment in question was valid but procedurally inadmissible as having been rendered on an unclaimed action. In a situation in which the former manager of the company had been convicted by a judgment which had entered into force, and it had been held that the actions taken by him in that capacity constituted a criminal offence, the company had the option of bringing an action to hold the manager liable both under art 145 of the CA and under art 45 of the OCA. The Court would have been obliged to qualify the claim on the basis of these allegations, in the Statement of Claim, concerning the facts from the establishment of which the claimant derives its claim. If the company based its claim on the fact that the former manager had been convicted by a judgment for undertaking the actions by which it claimed it had suffered damage, which had entered into force, and expressly stated in doing so that it was bringing its action under art 45 of the OCA, the Court should have considered the claim so presented. 57

In addition, the SCC pointed out that, given the existence of several remedies available to the party, the exercise of that party's right to choose between them cannot be qualified as an 'abuse of right'. It should be noted, however, that in such an exercise of choice (between a contractual claim and a tort claim), the party carries the risk that its claim will be rejected as unfounded. 58

c) Commentary

The Court's decision was correct and should be supported. It should be taken into account that it continues the trend of Decision No 128[3], which distinguished between an action under art 145 of the CA and an action under art 45 of the OCA and found that both could be brought against managers of companies, something which was denied in practice only 10–15 years ago. 59

The question of which claim a court will rule upon is not a formal one, it is based on whether the claim is for damages for breach of contract, or for tort. This also serves to overcome the highly inappropriate concept of 'managerial tort' to 60

3 Decision of 13.1.2021 in Commercial Case No 2167/2019, I Commercial Chamber.

something that is a form of contractual default. Moreover, beyond the basis of liability, this issue is also of great importance with regard to the limitation periods to be applied.

7. Supreme Court of Cassation (SCC) Judgment No 606 of 22 October 2024, Case No 1265/2023: Contribution; Joint Liability

a) Brief Summary of the Facts

61 The plaintiff's mother died during a flood in the Asparuhovo district of Varna. The plaintiff brought an action against the Municipality of Varna, the Varna Regional Administration and the Ministry of Regional Development and Public Works for compensation for non-pecuniary damage resulting from her death.

62 The Court of First Instance jointly ordered the Municipality of Varna and Ministry of Regional Development and Public Works to pay compensation in the amount of € 45,000 but dismissed the case against the Varna Regional Administration.

63 The Court of Appeal dismissed the case against the Ministry of Regional Development and Public Works and reduced the compensation awarded against the Municipality of Varna to € 31,000. In order to reach that decision, the Court of Appeal found that third parties not involved in the proceedings had contributed to the occurrence of the damage, to wit: the builders of the unlawful residential property where the plaintiff's mother had been a guest; and those responsible for clearing the culvert (drainage ditch) of construction and household waste and plants, namely the Ministry of Environment and the State Forestry Enterprise Varna. Those findings motivated the Court of Appeal to accept the defendant municipality's objection and to determine 30 % third-party contributory causation to the tortious outcome and to determine that the municipality should pay only the remaining 70 % of the amount of the fair compensation (€ 45,000).

64 In order to verify the conformity of the contested decision with the case law of the SCC, the cassation appeal was admitted on the question: '… where the damage was caused by several persons and the injured party has brought his claim for full compensation against only one of them, should the Court determine the quotas of contribution of the other, uncited, parties and reduce thereby the amount of compensation due for the damage caused?'

b) Judgment of the Court

The SCC held that the judgment under appeal was partly incorrect. According to the Court, the Court of Appeal, having found that third parties not involved in the proceedings had also contributed to the damage, erred in examining the specific contribution of each of the said contributors since, under art 53 of the OCA, they were jointly liable and the creditor might seek performance of the entire obligation from *any* of the debtors, as is accepted in settled case law. The Court should not apply *ex officio* joint liability, nor may a jointly liable debtor object, to the affected creditor, that other persons are liable for the damage. Accordingly, it also annulled the reduction of the amount and confirmed a fair compensation of € 45,000. 65

c) Commentary

The SCC's judgment was correct and in line with accepted positions in both case law and doctrine. In the case of a contribution to damage, the tortfeasors are jointly liable: this is so uncontroversial that it is rather surprising that the Appellate Court decided to impose proportional contributory negligence. The only explanation for this approach is the finding of 'contribution', but such an approach is nevertheless incorrect and has been rightly corrected by the SCC. The apportionment of liability, and recovery thereof, could be an issue for the jointly liable parties to fight out among themselves, in a separate action, after the claimant has been satisfied by the cited party. 66

8. Personal Injury

a) Supreme Court of Cassation (SCC) Judgment No 705 of 26 November 2024, Case No 609/2023

The compensation awarded for non-pecuniary damage amounts to € 365,000. The Court took into account the fact that the plaintiff suffered a road traffic accident when he was 17 years old, sustaining severe physical injuries as a result of which he needed the assistance of others to carry out activities of daily living (ADLs), not only immediately after the accident but probably for the rest of his life, as he remained immobile. He had undergone several surgeries, including the removal of one kidney. In addition, the plaintiff's mental state was severely affected and he exhibited depression, mood swings, increased irritability, a distressing sense of in- 67 ability to cope with the situation, and a painful feeling of inferiority. It was reported that, at a young age, he was deprived of significant vital functions being rendered immobile and totally dependent on the help of others, unable to take a variety of food (only liquidised solids and liquids), obliged to use diapers and a catheter. The negative prognosis for possible recovery, both in physical and psychological terms, was taken into account with experts concluding not only that there was an absolute minimum possibility of any recovery, but rather a negative development of the physical and mental state of the person.

b) Supreme Court of Cassation (SCC) Judgment No 528 of 16 August 2024, Case No 1706/2023

68 In this case, the plaintiff was seriously injured in a road traffic accident, as the result of which he suffered multiple injuries and disabilities, and his condition after the accident was described as 'severe' and life-threatening with no reactions and only cardiac activity registered. The individual was left paralysed in the lower part of the body, and it was further clarified in the case that no improvement in the motor function of the lower limbs was expected, and there was an ongoing tendency to trophic ulceration in the lower part of the body. Thus, the plaintiff was only able to use his arms and would continue to suffer numerous limitations, including the inability to move the lower part of his body, sit independently or to have offspring. In reviewing the case, the SCC also considered the mental state of the victim and his age at the time of the accident, namely 19 years old. The fact that there was contributory negligence on the part of the injured party in this case, in that he knew that the driver of the motor vehicle, of which he was a passenger, had consumed a significant amount of alcohol, was also taken into account. The SCC concluded that the fair compensation in this case was € 300,000 but, taking into account the contributory negligence of one-third, the claim was justifiable at € 200,000. In addition, the out-of-court settlement of € 50,000, paid by the insurer, was also taken into account, and the compensation further reduced by that amount. The plaintiff was finally awarded compensation of € 150,000.

c) Supreme Court of Cassation (SCC) Judgment No 201 of 3 December 2024, Case No 2263/2022

69 In this case, too, the victim was an individual injured in a road traffic accident who sustained an extremely severe mid-body injury for which there was a surgical intervention. In this case, the Court of Appeal held that fair compensation was

€ 43,500, over and above the voluntary compensation of € 21,500 paid by the insurer. This took into account the victim's age at the time of the accident (24 years old) and the fact that the incident had also had a negative impact on her future professional development. In addition, the SCC considered the fact that the injury had not led to an interruption of the victim's studies and the possibility that she might suffer some residual inconvenience, pain and limitations did not justify a finding of fair compensation in excess of € 50,000. Therefore, the SCC set aside, in part, the judgment of the Court of Second Instance and decided that fair compensation would be € 45,000, comprising € 23,500 from the compensation due, and € 21,500 from the out-of-court settlement by the insurer.

C. Literature

1. *Margarita Balabanova*, Is there contribution to damage in the failure of a minor to wear a seat belt? published at <www.lex.bg> 17 June 2024

The author begins with an analysis and attempts to clarify the prerequisite of 70
'contribution to damage' and, in particular, whether the victim's conduct must be unlawful and culpable. After comparing the requirements of the law for the tortfeasor and judgments in foreign legal systems, she formulates her conclusion. In her view, a contribution to loss or injury is objective in nature, an element of which is the victim's failure to exercise due care in their own affairs.

On that basis, the author examines the specific issue of whether there is con- 71
tribution to tort on the part of a minor who was not using safety restraints in a vehicle. In the author's view, a minor is not capable of tortious conduct and cannot be a contributory cause of damage within the meaning of art 51 para 2 of the OCA in the case of the absence of a seat belt because the duty of care for its use is not ascribed to the child but to their parents and the driver of the motor vehicle. In that sense, any claim as to the contribution to the loss or injury is unfounded in respect of a minor child and compensation should be awarded in full.

2. *Raina Nikolova*, Recognition of the right of legal entities to compensation for non-pecuniary damage is tantamount to censorship, published at <https://news.lex.bg> 10 July 2024

72 The author points out that to grant a legal entity the right to claim compensation for non-pecuniary damage is to equate its status with that of natural persons. Such an interpretation contradicts recognised constitutional rights of citizens, namely the freedom of expression and right to information.

73 She also takes the view that the possibility of legal entities to seek compensation for non-pecuniary damage would frustrate media investigations of corrupt practices and bankrupt the investigator. The author adds that the possibility of awarding compensation to legal entities for non-pecuniary damage contravenes not only the Constitution of the Republic of Bulgaria, but also the international treaties it has ratified (European Convention on Human Rights, Treaty on the Functioning of the European Union) and legislative acts of Community law, including the Charter of Fundamental Rights of the EU.

74 The author concludes that legal entities do not have the capacity to receive awards for non-pecuniary damage resulting from a tort, and that to accept the contrary is to depart from modern democratic values.

3. *Ivan Ruschev*, Opinion on Interpretative Case 1/2023 of the General Assembly of the Criminal, Civil and Commercial Division of the SCC and the Supreme Administrative Court (SAC) I and II Division, Lawyers' Review 4 (2024) 79 ff

75 The author highlights that non-pecuniary damage is caused when the injury has had a psychological impact on the victim, and this is not applicable to a legal entity.

76 Ruschev does not exclude the possibility that a legal entity, as an artificially created legal person, may suffer reputational damage in the form of damage to its good name but excludes that this damage may be perceived as being suffered by the legal entity itself.

77 Given that, under Bulgarian law, a legal entity is not liable in tort for personal wrongdoing, nor criminally liable, precisely because of its lack of mental capacity, it stands to reason that it cannot, by the same token, suffer non-pecuniary damage caused to it by another.

78 The conclusion is that a legal entity could claim compensation for non-pecuniary damage only to the extent that the law provides for a 'fiction' by virtue of

which it can suffer and sustain such damage. Such a general rule does not currently exist in the legislation in force and, if the legislator so decides, such a 'fiction' could be provided for by exception, but only in certain cases.

4. *Trayan Konov*, Do Legal Entities Possess Legitimation such as to Merit the Award of Compensation for Non-Pecuniary Damage Arising from Tort? published at <https://news.lex.bg> 1 July 2024

The author argues that there is a clear trend in our national law aimed at overcoming the traditional view that only individuals can claim compensation for non-pecuniary damage. 79

According to the author, a legal entity, although not a person, acts in law as a distinct entity, not as a community of separate persons. Behind the legal entity there are always people, which we designate as the 'personal substrate', and which includes not only the organs forming its will, but its members, employees, and the multitude of people who identify themselves as related to it and its purposes – supporters, fans, believers, customers, etc. 80

Since the legal entity is responsible for the actions of its 'personal substrate', it is clear that the missing psyche of the legal entity is replaced by the collective psyche of the people forming that 'personal substrate'. Assuming that the will, actions and mistakes of the 'personal substrate' of the legal entity are the will, actions and mistakes of the legal entity itself, we must also accept that the negative emotions of the 'personal substrate' are negative emotions of the legal entity. 81

It follows that legal entities are entitled to claim compensation for non-pecuniary damage. 82

5. *Margarita Balabanova/Daniel Georgiev*, Does the Principle of 'Fairness' in Art 52 of the OCA Constitute a Special Mandatory Rule? published at <https://news.lex.bg> 27 January 2025

The authors discuss whether art 52 of the OCA, which provides that compensation for a personal tort shall be determined in fairness by the Court, qualifies as a 'special mandatory rule' within the meaning of the Rome II Regulation. The question arises in connection with a case brought before the Bulgarian court, in which it was determined that the applicable law should be German law because the dam- 83 age (death of the plaintiffs' son as a result of an accident) occurred in the territory of the Republic of Germany. According to established case law of the German Supreme Court at the time of the tort (car accident), compensation for pain and suffering caused by the death of a loved one is granted only if these negative emotions have led to a pathological impairment of health manifesting as an illness.

84 According to the principle of fairness laid down in art 52 of the OCA, all damage suffered, irrespective of whether it has resulted in pathological damage to health, is subject to compensation. In this respect, German and Bulgarian law are based on completely different conceptions of the right to compensation. If the Bulgarian SCC had applied German law at the time the damage occurred, it should have dismissed the plaintiffs' claims because the pain and suffering from the death of their child had not resulted in pathological damage to their health.

85 It was for the Court that received the referral to determine whether a national rule is of such decisive importance as to qualify as a 'special mandatory rule' and to apply it as such.

86 It is accepted that the right to compensation is an historical, cultural phenomenon of Bulgarian legal thinking, a part of the national legal system, which is enjoyed by every Bulgarian citizen wherever and whenever they suffer damage.

87 In conclusion, the authors hold that the ruling of the SCC should be to the effect that the principle of fairness, enshrined in art 52 of the OCA, corresponds to the definition in art 16 of the Rome II Regulation and therefore does constitute a 'special mandatory rule' derogating from the application of the national law of another Member State.

Marko Baretić

IV. Croatia

A. Legislation

1. Zakon o provedbi Uredbe (EU) 2023/1114 o tržištima kriptovalute (Law on Implementation of Regulation (EU) 2023/1114 on Markets in Crypto-Assets) Narodne novine (NN) No 85/2024

This Law aims to enable the implementation of Regulation (EU) 2023/114 on crypto-assets in Croatia. 1

Article 9 of this Law provides for liability for damage caused to a holder of crypto-assets in case the information from the so-called white book on crypto-assets was not accurate, complete, unclear or was misleading. Responsible persons – who may include the issuer of the crypto-assets, the members of the relevant managerial or supervisory body, or persons assuming responsibility for accuracy and completeness of the information – must be clearly stated in the white book. If more persons are liable, their liability will be joint and several. This liability extends to the legal successors of the holder of the crypto-assets. The request for compensation for damage shall be time-barred two years from the moment the holder of the crypto-assets learned that the information from the white book was inaccurate, incomplete or misleading, and in any case, five years after the day the white book was published. This liability cannot be excluded or limited in advance. 2

Pursuant to art 10 of this Law, a responsible person can be freed from liability if they prove that they did not know or ought to have known that the information in the white book was inaccurate, incomplete or misleading; if such flaw in the information did not contribute to a decrease in market value of the crypto-assets; or if the correction of the inaccurate, incomplete or misleading information was published before the holder acquired the crypto-assets. 3

https://doi.org/10.1515/9783111389271-005

2. Zakon o upravljanju i održavanju zgrada (Law on Management and Maintenance of Buildings) NN No 152/2024

4 This Law intends to regulate in detail the management and maintenance of multi-apartment buildings and multi-storey garages. It gives a significant role to the co-owners' community, a legal person responsible for decision-making regarding management and maintenance of such buildings, and to the so-called manager, a professional chosen by the co-owners to perform the management and maintenance tasks on a daily basis.

5 Article 14 of this Law specifically regulates liability for damage caused by failure to properly manage and maintain buildings. Pursuant to this article, the co-owners' community is responsible for any damage which occurs as a result of the non-fulfilment or improper fulfilment of the works connected to the maintenance of the building. Since, the co-owners' community is a legal person, it follows that the owners themselves will not be liable in person. The co-owners' community is also liable for any damage caused by a part of the building if it is not possible to determine which particular part of the building the damage originates from. In the case of damage caused to third parties, the co-owners, the co-owners' community and the manager are jointly and severally liable. In such a case, the manager will be freed from liability if they prove they informed the owners in writing about the works necessary to avert the danger, and the co-owners ignored such information.

B. Cases

1. Presuda Županijskog suda u Slavonskom Brodu (Judgment of the County Court in Slavonski Brod) No Gž-161/2023 – 2 of 30 August 2024: No Compensation of Non-Material Damage for Deceased Pet

a) Brief Summary of the Facts

6 The victim owned two cats and hired the tortfeasor to castrate them. During the operation, one of the cats died. The victim sued the tortfeasor, claiming that the death of her cat resulted from the tortfeasor's unprofessional and negligent con-

duct, and therefore claimed compensation for non-material damage consisting in a violation of her personality right to mental health in an amount of € 995,42.

The first instance court dismissed the victim's claim as to the merits, opining 7 that the tortfeasor's alleged wrongful act was not directed towards the victim but towards her cat (hence, towards a thing owned by the victim), and that the Civil Obligations Act (COA) does not provide for the possibility to award compensation for non-material damage caused by damaging a thing owned by the victim, but only in cases of damage inflicted on the close members of the victim's family.

b) Judgment of the Court

The County Court in Slavonski Brod, acting as an appellate court, rejected the vic- 8 tim's appeal and confirmed the first instance judgment.

This court reasoned that, in order for a victim to be entitled to compensation 9 for non-material damage, the wrongful act must be directed towards the victim's person, and, in the case at hand, the wrongful act was directed towards the victim's property (the cat), and not herself. In this respect, the County Court in Slavonski Brod took the position that, in the case at hand, the claimant is an indirect victim, and that art 1101 of the COA provides for the possibility of awarding non-material damages to indirect victims only in the case of death or especially severe disability of close family members. On these grounds, and without prejudice to the victim's obvious exceptional bond with her deceased cat, the County Court in Slavonski Brod rejected the victim's appeal.

c) Commentary

This decision merits mention for two reasons; first, for the rather dubious legal 10 position of the courts deciding this case and second, for reflecting new realities which will, no doubt, have a notable impact on tort law in the years to come.

As described above, the first instance court and the County Court in Slavonski 11 Brod, acting as an appellate court, took the position that the victim was not entitled to compensation for non-material damage because she was an indirect victim. Substantiating this position, the County Court in Slavonski Brod invoked art 1101 of the COA, regulating liability for non-material damage in the case of death or especially severe disability of a close relative. According to the County Court in Slavonski Brod, in the case at hand, the wrongful act was directed towards a thing the victim owned (her cat), rather than the victim herself, which is why this court described the claimant as an indirect victim.

12 Pursuant to art 1046 of the COA, non-material damage is defined as a violation of a personality right. Pursuant to art 19 of the COA, every person is entitled to protection of their personality rights, and according to this Law, personality rights are the right to life, bodily and mental health, reputation, honour, dignity, name, privacy of personal and family life, freedom and others. Pursuant to art 1100 para 1 of the COA, in the case of a violation of a personality right, the court can, if this is justified considering the gravity of the violation and other circumstances, award just pecuniary compensation, irrespective of material damage, and even in the absence of it.

13 The described legislative framework defines a rather liberal, open-ended, victim-friendly liability regime, which generally permits every serious violation of personality rights to be remedied through pecuniary compensation, regardless of the source of violation, ie, regardless of how the personality right was violated. It is true that some further provisions limit to some extent this general liability scheme. Thus, for example, pursuant to art 1101 para 1 of the COA, in the event of death or especially severe disability of a person, the immediate family members (spouse, children and parents) are entitled to just pecuniary compensation for non-material damage, and pursuant to para 2 of the same article, such compensation may also be awarded to siblings, grandparents and grandchildren and a common law spouse, provided that there was a more permanent co-habiting union between them and the deceased or injured person.

14 Hence, according to the cited provision of art 1101 of the COA, indirect victims who suffer non-material damage as a result of the direct damage inflicted on someone else's legally protected interests (eg, another person's personality rights) are entitled to compensation for non-material damage only in limited cases, under restrictive conditions provided for in this article. The County Court in Slavonski Brod based its decision in this case precisely on this provision of the COA.

15 However, it seems that this court misinterpreted not only the provisions of art 1101 of the COA, but also the very concept of indirect victim. Pursuant to art 1101 of the COA, the term 'indirect victim' refers to a person who suffered certain loss as a result of a violation of another person's legally protected interests, such as the other person's life and limb. In this particular case, as established by the first instance court and the County Court in Slavonski Brod, the alleged wrongful act was directed towards the victim's cat. Regardless of the fact that animals enjoy special protection under the Croatian legal system, the fact is that, in legal terms, animals are still considered to be things (objects), hence property. Therefore, in this particular case, the alleged violation was directed towards the victim's property. Speaking in terms of the contemporary Croatian legal system, the victim's bereavement in the case at hand was the result of a violation of a

property right. Accordingly, the victim in the case at hand is a direct, and not an indirect victim.

Article 1101 of the COA, upon which the County Court in Slavonski Brod relied in this case, applies in situations where a person's bereavement is a result of a violation of another person's life and limb, and not in a situation where a person's bereavement is a result of a violation of that person's property. In this respect, it seems there was no room for application of this provision to the case at hand. 16

Second, even if art 1101 of the COA were to be applied in the case at hand, this case inevitably raises the question of the interpretation of the concept of 'family', enshrined in the provisions of art 1101 of the COA, and opens up the delicate, perhaps even controversial, issue as to whether a pet can be considered 'family' for the purposes of the application of this provision. 17

The Croatian legal system even today defines animals as things,[1] admittedly specially protected,[2] but still things. Hence, animals are considered property. 18

Some other national legal systems have explicitly moved away from treating animals as objects, either by expressly providing that animals are not regarded as things, as is the case in Germany[3] and Austria,[4] or even by defining animals as sentient living beings, as is the case in Portugal.[5] Of course, these changes do not imply that in these legal systems animals are considered as *subjects* of legal relationships,[6] but they certainly represent a considerable shift in the treatment of animals in modern societies. 19

These legislative changes are obviously the result of the broader phenomenon of anthropomorphization or humanisation of pets.[7] According to some surveys, up 20

---

1 See *N Gavella/T Josipović/I Gliha/V Belaj/Z Stipković*, Stvarno pravo [Property law], Narodne novine (Croatian Official Gazette, NN) 2007, 70; See also art 132 para 3 and art 144 of Zakon o vlasništvu i drugim stvarnim pravima [The Ownership and Other Rights in Rem Act], NN 91/1996, 68/1998, 137/1999, 22/2000, 73/2000, 114/2001, 79/2006, 141/2006, 146/2008, 38/2009, 153/2009, 90/2010, 143/2012, 152/2014.

2 See Zakon o zaštiti životinja (The Protection of Animals Act) NN 102/2017, 32/2019, 78/2024.

3 See § 90a of Bürgerliches Gesetzbuch (Civil Code).

4 See § 285a of Allgemeines bürgerliches Gesetzbuch (General Civil Code).

5 See *A Dias Pereira/M Martins/A Pedrosa*, Portugal, in: E Karner/BC Steininger (eds), European Tort Law 2017 (2018) 484, nos 1–11.

6 Thus, *Dias Pereira/Martins/Pedrosa* (fn 5) no 2.

7 *EMC Bouma/A Dijkstra/RS Arnt*, Owner's Anthropomorphic Perceptions of Cats' and Dogs' Abilities Are Related to the Social Role of Pets, Owners' Relationship Behaviors, and Social Support. Animals (Basel). 2023 Nov 24;13(23):3644. doi: 10.3390/ani13233644. PMID: 38066995; PMCID: PMC10705108.

to 94% of dog owners consider their pets to be part of their families.[8] The surveys also suggest that pet owners confirm the same strong emotional bond with their pets often identified with emotions people develop for their family members.[9] This is why some authors,[10] but also the courts in some countries, as is the case with the Bogota Superior Court in Columbia,[11] speak of the so-called multi-species families, consisting not only of humans, but of other 'sentient living beings' as well. Due to this emotional bond between humans and their pets, some authors suggest that, in the case of a loss of a pet, people mourn in a way that is very similar to the feelings associated with the loss of a human family member.[12] In fact, deceased pets nowadays are commonly buried and commemorated in a manner similar to humans.[13] Based on these facts, some authors advocate the idea that the owners should be compensated for their emotional harm in the case of the loss or injury of their pets,[14] and apparently this stance is supported by case law in some jurisdictions, as was the case in Florida, when the Supreme Court reached its decision in the *La Porte vs Associated Independents, Inc* case.[15] Moreover, some jurisdictions, such as Tennessee in the USA[16] or Portugal,[17] have adopted specific legislative provisions allowing pet owners to be compensated for their emotional loss caused by their pets being wrongfully killed or injured.

---

8 *S Coren*, Are Dogs Truly (and Legally) Members of the Family? Psychology Today 2023, at <https://www.psychologytoday.com/us/blog/canine-corner/202311/could-dogs-be-legally-considered-members-of-the-family>.

9 *Coren*, Psychology Today 2023 (see link fn 8).

10 See *MC Truyenque*, Multispecies Families in Latin America, Protecting Animals by Protecting Human Rights, ReVista – Harvard Review of Latin America 2023, at <https://revista.drclas.harvard.edu/familias-multiespecie-en-latinoamerica/>.

11 See *Coren*, Psychology Today 2023 (see link fn 8).

12 *L Carver*, The Conversation: When pets are family, the benefits extend into society, Queen's Gazette 2019, at <https://www.queensu.ca/gazette/stories/conversation-when-pets-are-family-benefits-extend-society>.

13 See *A Doré/J Michalon/T Líbano Monteiro*, The Place and Impact of Pet sin Failies, Enfances Familles Générations, Revue interdisciplinaire sur la famille contemporaine 32 (2019) 4, at: <http://journals.openedition.org/efg/8073>.

14 *WC Root*, "Man's Best Friend:" Property or Family Member? An Examination of the Legal Classification of Companion Animals and Its Impact on Damages Recoverable for their Wrongful Death or Injury, 47 Villanova Law Review (Vill L Rev) 423, 2002, at <https://www.animallaw.info/article/mans-best-friend-property-or-family-member-examination-legal-classification-companion>.

15 *Root*, 47 Vill L Rev 423, 2002 (see link fn 14).

16 See ibid.

17 *Dias Pereira/Martins/Pedrosa* (fn 5) no 8.

Should these current trends in other legal systems be sufficient to justify the expansion of understanding of the concept of 'family' from art 1101 of the COA to also include pets? According to the stance of the Supreme Court in Slavonski Brod, apparently not, at least for the time being. However, judging from some other cases decided before Croatian courts, including the Supreme Court of the Republic of Croatia, the answer should not be that firmly negative. 21

The case law of the Supreme Court reveals the readiness of that court to interpret the provisions of art 1101 of the COA considerably beyond their wording, both with respect to the personal and substantial scope of application. Thus, for example, the Supreme Court allowed protection from art 1101 of the COA to persons not specifically mentioned in this provision, as is the case with stepparents or those who raised the deceased or injured person without their relationship being formalised as custody or adoption, opining that 'the statutory phrase "close relative" should not be interpreted formalistically but instead a broader interpretation should be accepted in order to allow the statutory rule to be applied with the substantive meaning the lawmaker intended to give to this rule'.[18] In substantiating the term 'permanent living community' from art 1101 para 2 of the COA, the Supreme Court reasoned that in order for a 'permanent living community' to exist, it is not necessary to establish common habitation between the relatives, but instead, an exceptionally strong emotional bond is sufficient.[19] The Supreme Court explained that the characteristics of a 'permanent living community' are consistent and close emotional bonds or closeness, and a firm sense of belonging to the same community.[20] 22

Hence, according to the Supreme Court, an exceptionally strong emotional bond lies at the essence of the provision of art 1101 of the COA and the principal reason why the lawmaker allows family members to be compensated for non-material damage in the case of death or especially severe disability of their loved ones. If we acknowledge that the same emotional bond existing between family members can exist between humans and their pets, and accepting the Supreme Court's broader, teleological interpretation of this provision, there is a strong case for arguing that art 1101 of the COA should equally apply to persons suffering emotional distress due to their pets being killed or severely injured. 23

---

18 See *M Baretić*, Croatia, in: E Karner/BC Steininger (eds), European Tort Law 2014 (2015) 88, nos 48–53.

19 See *M Baretić*, Croatia, in: E Karner/BC Steininger (eds), European Tort Law 2021 (2022) 66, nos 10–20.

20 See *M Baretić*, Croatia in: E Karner/BC Steininger (eds), European Tort Law 2018 (2019) 70, nos 65–72.

24 Be that as it may, the mere fact that this case appeared before Croatian courts suggests that certain changes in this area will soon have to be made. In fact, some elements of this case imply that the claimant initiated proceedings as a 'test' for the Croatian judiciary. Thus, the County Court in Slavonski Brod noted that the claimant in her appeal stated that: 'it is time for the case law to take the stance that animals belong to those whose death deeply affects people, which should justify awarding compensation for non-pecuniary damage.' Hence, such cases will most probably appear in practice more often, highlighting the need for a change in approach to the treatment of bereavement caused by the loss or severe injury of a pet. Whether this change will come about through a shift in case law, like in Florida or through legislative intervention, as in Portugal, is of secondary importance.

2. Presuda Županijskog suda u Velikoj Gorici (Judgment of the County Court in Velika Gorica) No Gž-381/2024-1 of 23 July 2024: Liability of the State for Passing the Law; Scope of Liability; Non-Material Damage

a) Brief Summary of the Facts

25 As already reported in the 2015 Yearbook,[21] after the Constitutional Court of the Republic of Croatia proclaimed that, by adopting the Act on the Cessation of Applicability of the Public Enforcers' Act, the Republic of Croatia violated legitimate expectations of those who were previously appointed as public enforcers and that therefore, these persons are entitled to compensation for damage resulting therefrom, a number of those who were previously appointed as public enforcers initiated proceedings against the Republic of Croatia requesting compensation for both material and non-material damage sustained by adopting the Act on the Cessation of Applicability of the Public Enforcers' Act.

26 As already reported in the 2024 Yearbook,[22] in one of the cases decided by the County Court in Velika Gorica, this court partially accepted the claim of a person who was appointed as a public enforcer awarding her compensation for material and non-material damage.

21 See *Baretić* (fn 18) nos 24–28.

22 See *M Baretić*, Croatia in: E Karner/BC Steininger (eds), European Tort Law 2023 (2024) 87, nos 21–38.

In this particular case, the victim, as a person who was appointed as a public enforcer, claimed compensation in an amount of € 13,272 for non-material damage caused by an alleged violation of her personality right to mental health and her personality right to honour and dignity. 27

b) Judgment of the Court

The first instance court sustained the victim's claim, with the reasoning that the victim had legitimate expectations that she would have commenced with her service as a private enforcer, expectations which were frustrated when Parliament adopted the Act on the Cessation of Applicability of the Public Enforcers' Act. 28

The County Court in Velika Gorica, acting as an appellate court, accepted the defendant's appeal, reversed the first instance court's judgment and dismissed the victim's claim. 29

The County Court in Velika Gorica first noted that the first instance court rightly concluded that, based on the Decision of the Constitutional Court of the Republic of Croatia in case U-I-5612/2011 and others of 23 January 2013, the Republic of Croatia is generally obligated to compensate persons previously appointed as public enforcers for both the material and non-material damage they sustained when the Act on the Cessation of Applicability of the Public Enforcers' Act was adopted. 30

However, the County Court in Velika Gorica took the position that the circumstances of this particular case do not justify awarding compensation for non-material damage. 31

Thus, this court explained that, bearing in mind that the victim was not placed in a financially precarious situation with the adoption of the Act on Cessation, since she never closed her attorney office, one cannot accept the argument that the victim's mental health suffered due to the alleged existential insecurity. Furthermore, the court also rejected the argument of the alleged violation of the victim's honour and dignity, holding that it was common knowledge that the Act on Cessation was a political whim, rather than something attributable to those who were appointed as public enforcers. Accordingly, adopting the Act on Cessation could not have possibly violated the victim's honour and dignity. Finally, even though the County Court in Velika Gorica permitted the possibility that the victim felt hurt, angry and disappointed after the public enforcers' service was abolished, the intensity of this violation of her personality rights was not such as to justify awarding pecuniary compensation. 32

c) Commentary

33 Commenting in last year's Yearbook on the judgment of the County Court in Velika Gorica No Gž 2587/2021–10 of 28 February 2023, in which this court partially upheld the victim's claim for compensation of non-material damage, I noted that the court rather poorly substantiated its decision concerning the criteria based on which the quantum of compensation for non-material damage should be assessed.[23]

34 In the case at hand, the County Court in Velika Gorica was much more elaborate in this respect, shedding new light on the issue of awarding compensation for non-material damage.

35 First of all, this court expressly permitted the possibility of awarding compensation for non-material damage for those who suffered damage by the adoption of the Act on Cessation. However, this court also clearly noted that every award of compensation of non-material damage must be based on the facts of each particular case.

36 Second, on a more general note, the County Court in Velika Gorica convincingly explained why compensation for non-material damage caused by an alleged violation of the victim's honour and dignity could hardly be expected in cases like this. As this court noted, no one ever suggested that people appointed as public enforcers in general or any of those persons in particular contributed in any way to the abolition of the public enforcers' service. Hence, the professional and/or personal integrity of these persons was never called into question and therefore, they could hardly convincingly argue that their honour and dignity were violated by the abolition of the public enforcers' service.

37 Third, the County Court in Velika Gorica emphasised the importance of the gravity of the violation of personality rights for possible compensation of non-material damage. Indeed, pursuant to art 1100 para 1 of the COA, compensation for non-material damage will only be awarded if this is justified considering the gravity of the violation of the personality right and other circumstances of the case. In this particular case, the County Court in Velika Gorica confirmed that 'normal' anger, disappointment or even frustration caused by the abolition of the public enforcers' service is, in principle, not sufficient to justify awarding compensation for non-material damage. In this respect, this decision ties in nicely with the decision of the same court in case No Gž 2587/2021–10 of 28 February 2023,[24] where this court took the view that more serious violations of the right

23 *Baretić* (fn 22) no 37.

24 See ibid.

to mental health will generally have to be proven with medical documentation. Hence, only those violations of mental health which have left some more permanent consequences will, in principle, be compensable.

For these reasons, this decision will no doubt be instrumental for similar cases in the future. 38

3. Presuda Vrhovnog suda Republike Hrvatske (Judgment of the Supreme Court of the Republic of Croatia) No Rev 1024/2023 – 2 of 3 January 2024: Modification of the Claim for Compensation of Non-Material Damage after the Adoption of the New Orientation Criteria

a) Brief Summary of the Facts

The victims claimed compensation for non-material damage caused by the death of their close relative (son and grandson). The quantum of damages sought in the initial claim was determined in accordance with the Orientation Criteria and the Amounts for Determining the Value of Just Pecuniary Compensation for Non-Material Damage (the Orientation Criteria), which the Supreme Court of the Republic of Croatia adopted on 29 November 2002. 39

At the second session of the Civil Law Department of the Supreme Court (No SU-IV-47/2020 – 2) held on 5 March and 15 June 2020, the Civil Law Department of the Supreme Court adopted a legal position in which the Orientation Criteria of 2002 were amended in such a way as to increase the amounts provided for therein by 50 %.[25] 40

Based on these new Orientation Criteria of 2020, the victims modified their request for compensation as to the quantum by increasing the compensation sought by 50 %. The modification of the victims' request for compensation was made after the preliminary hearing was closed and before the closing of the main hearing. 41

25 See in more detail, *M Baretić*, Croatia, in: E Karner/BC Steininger (eds), European Tort Law 2020 (2021) 66, nos 84 – 95.

b) Judgment of the Court

42 The first instance court allowed the victims' motion for modification of the request for compensation of non-material damage, upheld the modified request awarding the first and second claimants compensation for non-material damage in an amount of HRK 352,000 (€ 46,718) and an amount of HRK 43,353 (€ 5,754) each, and awarding the third and fourth claimants compensation for non-material damage in an amount of HRK 115,000 (€ 15,263) each.

43 The second instance court partially upheld the claimants' request for compensation but only up to the amount defined in accordance with the Orientation Criteria of 2002, quashed the first instance court's decision allowing the claimants to modify their request for compensation and dismissed the claimants' request for compensation exceeding the amounts defined in the Orientation Criteria of 2002.

44 By its decision No Revd-1580/2022–2 of 30 November 2022, the Supreme Court allowed the claimants to apply for revision regarding the question:

> Can a claimant modify their request for payment by increasing the quantum of compensation in accordance with the Orientation Criteria of 2020 after the preliminary hearing is closed, provided that the preliminary hearing is closed after the second session of the Civil Law Department of the Supreme Court held on 5 May 2020 and 15 June 2020, in which this Department adopted a legal opinion by which the Orientation Criteria of 2002 are amended, applying the provision of art 190 para 2 of the Civil Procedure Act, particularly taking into consideration that the Orientation Criteria of 2020 expressly provided that they should also apply to pending proceedings?

45 Based on the Supreme Court's decision of 30 November 2022, the claimants applied for revision, the Supreme Court accepted the application, quashed the second instance court's decision, allowed the claimants' modification of the claim and upheld the first instance decision.

46 The Supreme Court recalled that, pursuant to art 190 paras 1–3 of the Civil Procedure Act (CPA), a claimant is entitled to modify their claim before the preliminary hearing is closed, and only exceptionally will a claimant be allowed to modify the claim until the closing of the main hearing if, without their fault, they were not able to modify their claim before the preliminary hearing was closed. After the claim was submitted, the claimant needs the respondent's permission to modify the claim, unless the court considers that accepting a modification would be useful for the final resolution of the dispute.

47 In this particular case, the Supreme Court held that adopting the new Orientation Criteria of 2020 represents a justified reason to allow the modification of a claim. Substantiating this position, the Supreme Court explained that before the Orientation Criteria were amended in 2020, case law regarding the quantum of

compensation for non-material damage was mainly based on the Orientation Criteria of 2002, and based on this, the claimants could have foreseen that their request for compensation exceeding the amounts provided for in the Orientation Criteria of 2002 had a slim chance of succeeding. Only after the Supreme Court adopted the new Orientation Criteria were the claimants able to justifiably modify their claims by increasing the quantum of compensation sought in accordance with these new Orientation Criteria. In this respect, the Supreme Court recalled that the Orientation Criteria of 2020 specifically provided that they should also apply to pending cases.

The Supreme Court concluded that one cannot blame claimants for abstaining from requesting the increased amount of compensation before the new Orientation Criteria of 2020 were adopted, since if they did so, based on the then prevailing case law, their request would have been dismissed. 48

Based on the foregoing, the Supreme Court took the position that the claimants' question should be answered as follows: Claimants are entitled to modify their request for compensation by increasing the amount sought in accordance with the Orientation Criteria of 2020, based on art 190 para 2 of the CPA, and taking into consideration that the Orientation Criteria 2020 also apply to pending proceedings. 49

c) Commentary

Although this judgment predominantly concerns procedural issues, it is of vital practical importance in thousands of cases involving compensation for non-material damage which are currently being dealt with before Croatian courts. 50

As already presented in the 2020 Yearbook,[26] in 2020, the Supreme Court decided to amend the Orientation Criteria in order to increase the amounts provided for therein by 50 %. The Orientation Criteria are not a source of law but a useful tool, which is intended to assist courts by giving them some guidance in determining the amount of just pecuniary compensation for non-material damage and thus, to harmonise the case law with respect to this type of damage. Although the Orientation Criteria do not represent the law, but only a soft-law instrument, Croatian courts generally strictly adhere to the Orientation Criteria as if their application were mandatory, presumably because the Supreme Court would generally quash the lower courts' decision if they deviated from the amounts defined in 51

26 *Baretić* (fn 25) nos 84–95.

the Orientation Criteria. Hence, the Orientation Criteria have an enormous practical importance in cases involving compensation for non-material damage.

52 Regardless of how dubious this is,[27] the Orientation Criteria of 2020 provided that they apply even to all pending cases, hence they have retroactive effect. Therefore, since they were adopted, the new Orientation Criteria apply to all cases pending before Croatian courts. For this reason, after the new Orientation Criteria were adopted, claimants claiming compensation for non-material damage who defined the quantum of their compensation on the basis of the old Orientation Criteria of 2002 wanted to modify they requests for payment by increasing the quantum of compensation in accordance with the new Orientation Criteria of 2020.

53 However, a procedural problem arose, consisting in some limitations to modifications of the claim, provided for in art 190 of the CPA. As already noted by the Supreme Court in this case, pursuant to art 190 para 1 of the CPA, a claimant is entitled to modify their claim before the preliminary hearing is closed, and only exceptionally, and pursuant to art 190 para 2 of the CPA, will the claimant be allowed to modify their claim until the closing of the main hearing if, without their fault, they were not able to modify their claim before the preliminary hearing was closed. Pursuant to art 190 para 3 of the CPA, after the claim is submitted, the claimant needs the respondent's permission to modify their claim, unless the court considers that accepting a modification would be useful for the final resolution of the dispute.

54 Regular courts which were deciding cases concerning compensation for non-material damage were taking opposite positions regarding the question of whether the adoption of the new Orientation Criteria of 2020 justifies a modification of a claim, pursuant to art 190 para 2 of the CPA. As is evident from the first and second instance courts' decisions in this case, some courts allowed modification of the claim due to the adoption of the new Orientation Criteria of 2020 even after the preliminary hearing was closed, others did not. Of course, such divergent positions created a significant level of legal uncertainty regarding this issue. For this reason, the Supreme Court, which is constitutionally bound to harmonise case law, decided to react by providing a general interpretation of the relevant provisions of art 190 of the CPA that should be applied by all lower courts.

55 Pursuant to art 382 of the CPA, revision is an extraordinary remedy which can be lodged only if the party is specifically allowed by the Supreme Court to do so. Pursuant to art 385a of the COA, the Supreme Court will allow revision if it considers that the question raised in revision is of importance for the unified appli-

27 See in more detail, *Baretić* (fn 25) nos 92–95.

cation of the law. Hence, revision will, in principle, only be allowed if it concerns an issue of general interest, ie an issue which will likely appear in a number of similar cases and it is, therefore, necessary to adopt a common position regarding this issue.

Allowing revision in this case, the Supreme Court obviously confirmed the importance of this issue for the unified application of the law. Thousands of cases concerning compensation for non-material damage are currently pending before Croatian courts, clearly confirming the importance of the issue raised in this case. 56

As presented above, the Supreme Court answered the question posed in this revision in the affirmative. This Court thus took a general position that a claimant is entitled to modify their request for compensation by increasing the amount sought in accordance with the Orientation Criteria of 2020, based on art 190 para 2 of the CPA. Bearing in mind the constitutional position of the Supreme Court as the only court responsible for harmonising case law, by the Court adopting this general position, this issue is finally resolved in a general fashion. 57

4. Rješenje Županijskog suda u Rijeci (Decision of the County Court in Velika Gorica) No Gž 47/2024 – 2 of 9 July 2024: Condition Precedent in Media-Related Cases for Compensation of Non-Material Damage

a) Brief Summary of the Facts

The victim, a natural person who acted as a director of a company, requested that the editor-in-chief of a newspaper issue a corrective statement in relation to an article in which the victim personally was allegedly slandered. The claim was based on art 22 of the Media Act. The document which contained the request to issue a corrective statement was signed by the victim, and it contained the seal of the company in which the victim was a director. 58

The editor-in-chief of the newspaper, to which the request for publication of a corrective statement was sent, refused to publish a corrective statement, claiming that procedural conditions provided for in art 22 of the Media Act were not fulfilled. In particular, the editor-in-chief argued that the victim did not request publication of a corrective statement in his personal capacity, but in his capacity as the director of the company. 59

After receiving a negative reply from the editor-in-chief, addressed personally to him, the victim filed a claim against the publisher, requesting compensation for 60 non-material damage caused by violation of his personality right to honour and dignity.

b) Judgment of the Court

61 The first instance court dismissed the claim for procedural reasons, arguing that the victim filed the claim in his personal capacity, whereas the request for publication of a corrective statement addressed to the defendant was sent in his capacity as the director of a company. Since, pursuant to art 22 para 2 of the Media Act, requesting publication of a corrective statement is a condition precedent for initiating court proceedings against a media publisher, and since the victim, according to the first instance court, sent this request in his capacity as the director of a company and not in his personal capacity, the first instance court concluded that, in the case at hand, the procedural conditions for filing the claim from art 22 para 2 of the Media Act were not met.

62 The County Court in Rijeka, acting as an appellate court, quashed the first instance decision and remanded the case for re-examination.

63 Substantiating its decision, the County Court in Rijeka took the position that, in the case at hand, the first instance court had misinterpreted the facts of the case and the relevant provision of the Media Act. Indeed, the County Court in Rijeka expressly established that the first instance decision represents a blatant example of excessive formalism and, as such, it violates the victim's right to access a court protected by the Constitution of the Republic of Croatia and the European Convention on Human Rights (ECHR).

64 The County Court in Rijeka established that the facts of the case clearly indicate that the victim sent and signed the request for publication of a corrective statement in his personal capacity, and that the editor-in-chief of the newspaper addressed his reply, rejecting the request, to the victim personally. Hence, according to the County Court in Rijeka, there is no doubt that the victim sent the request for publication of a corrective statement in his personal capacity, and not as the director of a company. The County Court in Rijeka continued by noting that the mere fact that the document in which the request for publication of the corrective statement was formulated contained the seal of the company in which the victim was a director could not call into question the conclusion that the victim sent this request in his personal capacity, and therefore characterised the first instance court's conclusions as excessive formalism.

In support of its decision, the County Court in Rijeka specifically invoked the judgment of the European Court of Human Rights (ECtHR), in case *B v C*,[28] according to which, excessive formalism of the domestic courts in interpreting the existence of procedural conditions for filing a claim in media-related cases represents an unjustified limitation of access to a court. 65

c) Commentary

The County Court in Rijeka should be commended for its rather sensitive approach to the issue of formalism in civil proceedings. In this respect, it seems to be of particular importance that the County Court in Rijeka based its decision on findings of the ECtHR. 66

One cannot help but observe that Croatian courts sometimes tend to apply the laws rather formalistically, without any recourse to the reasons why particular formalities are provided for in laws in the first place. The position of the first instance court in this case is a perfect example of excessive formalism. The first instance court never determined the rationale behind the provision of art 22 para 2 of the Media Act, ie why this provision requires the potential victim to request the publication of a corrective statement before they go to court. Moreover, the first instance court clearly failed to interpret the facts correctly. Solely based on the fact that the document in which the request for publication of a corrective statement was contained was marked with the seal of the company, the first instance court concluded that the request was sent on behalf of the company, while, at the same time, neglecting the fact that the substance of the document clearly suggested that the victim sent the request on his own behalf, and not on behalf of the company and the fact that the editor-in-chief's reply was addressed to the victim personally, and not the company. These circumstances undoubtedly demonstrated that the publisher was well aware of the substance of the request and who the sender was. Hence, the conditions laid down in art 22 para 2 of the Media Act were clearly fulfilled by the request sent by the victim. However, the first instance court focused exclusively on formalities rather than on the substance of the claim. 67

Bearing in mind that this rather obscure reasoning of the first instance court is unfortunately not an isolated case, it is comforting to know that the upper courts are prepared to fulfil their role of administering justice, including by reacting to cases of excessive formalism. 68

28 ECtHR *Buvac v Croatia*, 4.4.2019, no 47685/13.

69 Another point worth mentioning is the County Court's invocation of the ECtHR's case law. The willingness of domestic courts to follow case law of international courts, as demonstrated in this decision of the County Court in Rijeka, is of utmost importance for the development of domestic case law and this decision of the County Court in Rijeka proves this statement to be true. The concept of excessive formalism and inconsistency of this concept with the requirements of proper administration of justice, applied by the County Court in Rijeka in this case, is developed and promoted precisely by the ECtHR.

5. Rješenje Vrhovnog suda Republike Hrvatske (Decision of the Supreme Court of the Republic of Croatia) No Rev-668/2021 – 3: Beginning of the Limitation Period in Damage-Related Cases

a) Brief Summary of the Facts

70 The defendant rented some business premises from the claimant but refused to vacate them upon the expiry of the contract. Due to the defendant's refusal to hand back the business premises to the claimant, the claimant as a lessor failed to fulfil his obligation towards the new lessee. The new lessee filed a claim against the lessor and obtained compensation for damage due to the non-fulfilment of a contract. In these proceedings, the claimant attempts to recoup from the defendant the damages it paid to the new lessee.

b) Judgment of the Court

71 The first instance court partially accepted the claim, awarding the claimant compensation in an amount of HRK 319,631 (€ 42,422), and dismissed the claim in the remaining amount of HRK 5,500 (€ 730). Hence, the claimant was awarded what it had to pay to the new lessee, based on a judgment the new lessee had obtained in a separate proceeding initiated against the claimant.

72 The second instance court partially quashed the first instance court's decision in the part where the first instance court upheld the claimant's claim, holding that the claim was time-barred. The second instance court explained that the limitation period started to run as of the moment the claimant learned about the defendant's wrongful act, which is the moment when the defendant refused to vacate

the rented premises, and that, therefore, the claim for compensation for damage was time-barred at the moment the claimant filed the claim.

By its decision No Revd 62/2021–2 of 23 February 2021, the Supreme Court allowed the claimant to apply for revision regarding the question: 'Does the limitation period for a claim for compensation for damage start to run as of the moment the victim learned of the wrongful act and the tortfeasor or from the moment the victim learned of the damage and the tortfeasor?' 73

Based on the Supreme Court's decision of 23 February 2022, the claimant applied for revision, the Supreme Court accepted the application, quashed the second instance court's decision, and remanded the case to the second instance court for re-examination. 74

The Supreme Court reasoned that, pursuant to art 230 para 1 of the COA, a claim for compensation for damage is time-barred three years from the time the injured party became aware of the damage and the person causing the damage, and, pursuant to art 230 para 2 of the COA, in any case, such claim is time-barred five years from the moment the damage occurred. 75

Based on such a statutory framework, the Supreme Court generally concluded that the beginning of the limitation period is connected to the occurrence of damage and the moment the victim learned about the damage. The Supreme Court continued that the moment of damage occurrence and the moment of occurrence of the wrongful act do not always coincide and that, in terms of limitation, the moment of damage occurrence is decisive. According to the Supreme Court, damage occurs when the consequences of the wrongful act materialise and when the victim learns of the scope and quantum of damage. 76

In this particular case, concluded the Supreme Court, this occurred when the claimant in these proceedings actually paid the amount to the new lessee based on the court order, and not when the defendant committed a wrongful act (the moment the defendant refused to vacate the premises). 77

Addressing the question posed in revision, the Supreme Court took a general position that 'the limitation period for a claim for compensation for damage starts to run as of the moment the victim learned of damage and the tortfeasor, and not as of the moment the victim learned of the wrongful act and the tortfeasor.' 78

c) Commentary

There are good reasons why this question should never have been raised. The provision of art 230 of the COA is perfectly clear and unambiguous – this provision leaves no room for any doubts as to its meaning. According to this provision, the moment of damage occurrence and not the moment of occurrence of the 79 wrongful act is decisive for the beginning of the limitation period. Hence, the answer to the question posed by the claimant is not a matter of interpretation, but a matter of a literal reading of art 230 of the COA.

80 This statutory solution is quite logical and self-explanatory: in order to substantiate their claim for compensation, a victim must know the scope and quantum of damage and who the tortfeasor is. Hence, before the victim gains knowledge of the damage and the tortfeasor, it makes no sense for the limitation period to start to run.

81 Unfortunately, as one can conclude from the decision of the second instance court in this case, a literal reading of statutory provisions and logical thinking may cause problems to some courts. Moreover, the mere fact that the Supreme Court decided to react by accepting the revision in this case shows that a misunderstanding as to the moment when the limitation period starts to run, shown by the second instance court in this case, is not just an isolated incident, but something which clearly occurs more frequently.

82 Bearing in mind that the Supreme Court is constitutionally empowered to harmonise case law, the issue of the moment when the limitation period in damage-related cases starts to run should be finally settled with this decision.

C. Literature

1. *Hrvoje Lisičar/Marko Jurić*, Pravna regulacija sustava umjetne inteligencije s osvrtom na pitanja izvanugovorne odgovornosti za štetu [Legal regulation of Artificial Intelligence systems with reference to issues of non-contractual liability for damage], Pravo u gospodarstvu 1–2 (2024) 115–140

83 This article examines a contemporary phenomenon of Artificial Intelligence systems and focuses on issues of non-contractual liability arising from the use of these systems. The authors emphasise that on the European level, two directives are being developed, aimed at addressing the specific problems associated with liability for damage caused by Artificial Intelligence systems, notably a new directive on liability for defective products and a new Artificial Intelligence liability directive. They conclude that these two directives, should they be adopted with the same content as drafted, could considerably improve the position of victims who suffered damage from Artificial Intelligence systems; a new directive on liability

for defective products by including software in the definition of products, thus extending the scope of protection envisaged by this directive to damages caused by Artificial Intelligence and a new Artificial Intelligence liability directive by providing for special rules on evidence collection and disclosure and by providing for presumption of a causal link with respect to damage caused by Artificial Intelligence. However, the authors also warn that these two directives provide for only a minimum regulation of liability and that in this respect, domestic laws will continue to be of paramount importance in regulating this specific case of tort liability.

The article provides a comprehensive and yet intelligible description of the 84 functioning of different Artificial Intelligence systems and the perils associated with the use of these systems. The authors convincingly explain the specific problems the victims of these systems may face in the course of obtaining compensation for the damage sustained and analyse to what extent the new rules provided for in two European directives could contribute to successfully addressing these problems.

2. *Ana Lovrinov*, Odgovornost za naknadu štete zbog povrede Opće uredbe o zaštiti podataka [Liability for damage caused by violation of the General Data Protection Regulation], Informator 6856 (2024) 9–14

The author examines conditions under which liability arises under the General 85 Data Protection Regulation (GDPR). In this respect, the author focuses on art 82 of the GDPR, according to which, a controller or a processor of the victim's personal data is liable for material and non-material damage resulting from a violation of the GDPR, unless they prove that they are not in any way responsible for the event giving rise to the damage. The author also emphasises that the concept of joint and several liability of all those who contributed to the occurrence of a harmful event significantly improves the position of the victim and facilitates the compensation of the damage sustained. An added value of this article is the analysis of the recent case law of the ECJ regarding art 82 of the GDPR, in particular case C-300/21 *UI v Österreichische Post AG* (ECLI:EU:C:2023:370), case C-456/22 *VX, AT v Gemeinde Ummendorf* (ECLI:EU:C:2023:988), case C-340/21 *VB v Nacionalna agencija za prihodite* (ECLI:EU:C:2023:986), case C-667/21 *ZQ v Medizinischer Dienst der Krankenversicherung Nordrhein* (ECLI:EU:C:2023:1022) and case-687/21 *BL v MediaMarktSaturn Hagen-Iserlohn GmbH* (ECLI:EU:C:2024:72), in which this Court gave valuable guidance as to how to properly interpret art 82 of the GDPR.

Given the growing frequency of application of the GDPR and the importance of the CJEU's interpretation of the relevant provisions of the GDPR, this article provides valuable information to the general public on how to properly apply the GDPR's provisions on liability for damage.

Michael Chatzipanagiotis

V. Cyprus

A. Legislation

In 2024, there were no legislative developments in Cyprus in the field of tort law. 1

B. Cases

1. Supreme Court, 15 July 2024, *Aki Ioannou et al v Cyprus Broadcasting Corporation*, Civil Appeal no 214/2015: Defamation; Injurious Falsehood

a) Brief Summary of the Facts

Plaintiff 1 was a technology importer and one of the two shareholders of the company, TAS Ophthalmos Laser Center Ltd (plaintiff 2). In May 2005, the company introduced the 'Allegretto' laser machine. To promote it, plaintiff 1 gave an interview, which was broadcast on television, and presented the capabilities of the machine regarding the laser treatment of refractive errors of the eye, with particular reference to presbyopia. On 7 June 2005, three ophthalmologists who were involved in the correction of refractive errors by laser convened a press conference and referred to the presentation of plaintiff 1. Part of their statements were republished the same evening on the newscast of the respondent/defendant television station, Cyprus Broadcasting Corporation (RIK). 2

The plaintiffs brought an action against RIK on defamation and injurious (ie, malicious) falsehood. Plaintiff 1 claimed that the statements broadcast were false and defamatory, had been made maliciously, and caused plaintiff 2 enormous financial damage. 3

Regarding plaintiff 1, the trial court accepted that there was a defamatory statement, which, however, was true. Thus, no liability could be established for 4

Acknowledgement: The author would like to thank Myrianthi Panayiotou, Attorney-at-Law, LLM, Research Assistant at KOIOS Center of Excellence, University of Cyprus, for her kind assistance in the preparation of the case summaries of this report.

Note: In the cases cited, a European Case Law Identifier (ECLI) is provided only where available.

https://doi.org/10.1515/9783111389271-006

defamation. As to plaintiff 2, the trial court found that it had not been proven that these statements referred to plaintiff 2, which is a requirement for both defamation and malicious falsehood. In any case, the company had not suffered any damage as required by sec 7 of the Civil Wrongs Law (CWL), which provides that proof of damage is a condition for a legal entity to receive compensation for a tort. Hence, the trial court also dismissed the action of plaintiff 2.

5 Both plaintiffs appealed to the Supreme Court.[1]

b) Judgment of the Court

6 As to plaintiff 1, the Supreme Court accepted the ground of appeal that the truth of the statement had not been proven.

7 On the issue as regards the reference of the defamatory statement to plaintiff 2, the Court clarified that this matter should be examined in terms of a claim of injurious falsehood. In the case of injurious falsehood, the 'reference to the plaintiff' does not have the same meaning as in defamation. It is not necessary for the defamatory statement concerning a business activity to reveal the name of the legal entity conducting the activity. Plaintiff 2, the company that invested in importing and presenting the 'Allegretto' machine to the public in Cyprus, was associated with the statement at hand, because it would suffer loss due to the defamatory statement, although the company's name was not mentioned in the statement and possibly very few knew that it was the machine's importer. Thus, the Court accepted the relevant ground of appeal.

8 For injurious falsehood to be established, malice is an essential requirement, as provided by sec 25(1) CWL. The Supreme Court observed that although the three ophthalmologists had acted maliciously, the same could not be said of the television station (defendant). The station's failure to verify the statements of the ophthalmologists before including them in its newscast was merely negligent. Therefore, the defendant station could not be held primarily liable for injurious falsehood.

9 Moreover, the Supreme Court examined whether the defendant could be held vicariously liable for the malicious statement of the three ophthalmologists. The answer was no, because they were neither employees nor agents of the defendant. Thus, the Supreme Court dismissed the pertinent grounds of appeal.

1 Under the previous Civil Procedure Rules, which still apply to older cases, the Supreme Court functions as a Court of Appeal.

Lastly, the Supreme Court ruled on the damages to be awarded to plaintiff 1 for defamation. The Court took into account that damages had already been awarded to the plaintiff in a separate action against the three ophthalmologists and awarded reduced damages in the present case. 10

c) Commentary

Cypriot law provides for defamation and injurious (ie, malicious) falsehood in the CWL, which largely reflects the development of English law on these torts up to 1959. The relevant provisions are based mainly on the UK Defamation Act 1952 and Cypriot courts follow closely the evolution of English case law on these issues. 11

In this case, the legal bases of the claims were defamation and injurious falsehood. Under Cypriot law, the two claims can only be brought alternative to each other.[2] 12

The trial court had rejected the claims of the company (plaintiff 2). The company had failed to prove damage, which under sec 7 CWL, is a general requirement for legal entities to receive compensation for torts committed against them. The Supreme Court in this case affirmed the judgment of the trial court, since the corresponding finding of the trial court had not been appealed. 13

In this respect, there is old case law in Cyprus[3] that the general requirement for proof of damage under sec 7 CWL does not apply where the special provisions on injurious falsehood exempt the plaintiff from proving special damage. Section 25(2) CWL provides that no proof of special damage is necessary if (a) the words upon which the action is founded are calculated to cause pecuniary loss to the plaintiff and are published in writing or other permanent form, or (b) the said words are calculated to cause pecuniary loss to the plaintiff in respect of any office, profession, calling, trade, or business held or carried on by them at the time of publication. The term 'are calculated' means 'more likely than not'.[4] However, the Greek translation of the original English text of the CWL inaccurately reads 'σκοπεύουν' (are intended to). The English text and the construction thereof under English law prevail over the Greek translation by virtue of sec 2(1) CWL, entitled 'Interpretation', which provides that: 'This Law shall be interpreted in accordance with the principals of legal interpretation obtaining in England and ex- 14

2 *Kemsley Newspapers Ltd v Cyprus Wines & Spirits Co, Ltd, 'KEO'*, Civil Appeal no 4235, 5.12.1957, (V23) 1 Cyprus Law Reports (CLR) 1; *P Polyviou*, Civil Wrongs in the Law of Cyprus (2020) 993.
3 *Kemsley Newspapers Ltd* (V23) 1 CLR 1.
4 See Gatley on Libel and Slander (13th edn 2022) para 22.14; *Tesla Motors Ltd & Anor v BBC* [2013] England & Wales Court of Appeal (Civil Division) (EWCA Civ) 152, para [27].

pressions used in it shall be presumed, so far as it is consistent with their context, and except as may be otherwise provided, to be used with the meaning attaching to them in English law and shall be construed in accordance therewith'.

15 The Court also analysed the issue of the reference of the defamatory statement to the plaintiff. The trial court had accepted such reference regarding plaintiff 1 (the natural person), but not regarding plaintiff 2 (his company). The Court, citing English authorities,[5] clarified that such reference does not have the same meaning in injurious falsehood as in defamation. In defamatory statements regarding business activities, it is not necessary that the name of the legal entity carrying out the business is explicitly mentioned. Plaintiff 2 was the importer of the medical device at hand and would suffer loss due to the statement. Therefore, the Court accepted the relevant ground of appeal. This part of the judgment should be considered an *obiter*, since the Court had already rejected the company's claim on the ground that it had failed to prove that it had suffered any damage.

16 Another issue was whether the defendant TV station had acted with malice in broadcasting the defamatory statement of the ophthalmologists. The Court accepted that the defendant had acted negligently by failing to verify the statements of the three ophthalmologists, but such failure did not amount to malice. Therefore, there was no primary liability, but the issue was one of vicarious liability, as the Court found, again citing English authorities.[6] Since the ophthalmologists were neither servants nor agents of the TV station, there was no malice, and malicious falsehood had to be rejected. It is noteworthy that, again, the Court referred to plaintiff 2 (the company). However, the issue of malice also affected the pertinent claim of plaintiff 1 (its owner), so the analysis in the judgment cannot be deemed an *obiter*.

17 As to the assessment of damages, the Court took into account the damages that had been awarded to the plaintiff in an action he had brought against the three ophthalmologists, based on the same facts. Although sec 23(b) CWL provides for the award of reduced damages only in cases of licensed newspapers, the Court seems to have applied a broad interpretation of 'newspaper', as is the case under English law,[7] and to have implicitly considered the general principle of prohibiting any enrichment of the plaintiff, as deduced from sec 61–63 CWL.[8]

5 Gatley on Libel and Slander (fn 4) para 22-005.

6 Gatley on Libel and Slander (fn 4) paras 9-029, 9-032, 9-033, which refers to the Australian case *Falcke v The Herald and Weekly Times Ltd* (1925) Victorian Law Reports (VLR) 56.

7 See sec 12 of the Defamatory Act 1952 'In any action for libel or slander the defendant may give evidence in mitigation of damages that the plaintiff has recovered damages, or has brought actions for damages, for libel or slander in respect of the publication of words to the same effect

2. Court of Appeal, 27 June 2024, *Apollonio Private Hospital Public Company Ltd v C Moleskis* and *C Moleskis v Apollonio Private Hospital Public Company Ltd et al*, Civil Appeals nos 139/2018 and 168/2018: Medical Negligence; Informed Consent; Non-Delegable Duty; Punitive Damages

a) Brief Summary of the Facts

The plaintiff/appellant (in civil appeal no 168/2018), 35 years old at that time, had problems with urination, ejaculation, and pain in the lumbar region. He sought treatment from a doctor (defendant 2/respondent 2) at Apollonio Private Hospital (defendant 1/respondent 1). The doctor diagnosed the plaintiff with prostate cancer and told him that he would have to undergo surgery to remove his prostate. The doctor recommended a transurethral prostatectomy (TURP) and explained that this operation would be 100 % successful; however, the plaintiff would be unable to have any children in the future and would have 'some potential complications', which the doctor did not further specify. The patient clarified that he preferred to undergo an 'open' operation, not a prostatectomy, because in the latter operation, his prostate would be removed. The hospital also gave the plaintiff a blank informed consent document to sign, which he did. 18

The plaintiff underwent a TURP, and his prostate was fully removed. The prostate was found to be small, normal, and cancer free. After the removal and during the same operation, the doctor considered it necessary to proceed to a transurethral bladder neck incision (TUIP), because of the condition of the bladder neck (hard and fibrous). The possibility that a patient suffers from erectile dysfunction after TURP is 13 % and after TUIP 4.6 %. A few weeks after the operation, the plaintiff's urination issues reappeared. Moreover, the plaintiff had become impotent. 19

It was later discovered that the plaintiff's real problem was bladder outlet obstruction, which could have been detected before the operation upon appropriate diagnostic examinations, such as an urethrocystoscopy. The plaintiff had to undergo many additional, serious operations and treatment to overcome his urination problems. Furthermore, his pain and impotency seriously affected his mental health, which led to three suicide attempts. 20

---

as the words on which the action is founded, or has received or agreed to receive compensation in respect of any such publication'.

8 These are entitled: sec 61 'Compensation only to be recovered once', sec 62 'Compensation not to be recoverable under this Law and the Workmen's Compensation Law', sec 63 'No action to be brought on contract if compensation awarded for civil wrong'.

21 The plaintiff filed an action against the doctor and the hospital on the basis of negligence and battery. The trial court found both defendants liable for negligence.

22 The doctor had misdiagnosed the plaintiff with cancer and had not ordered appropriate diagnostic examinations. Moreover, the plaintiff's consent to the operation had been based on insufficient information: the defendant had failed to explain the nature of the operation in an intelligible manner, he had failed to inform the plaintiff of the risks of erectile dysfunction and recurrence of the urination problems, and he had not informed him of any alternative treatment. Nonetheless, the trial court found no causal link between the plaintiff's urination issues and the invalid informed consent. The stenosis of the neck of the bladder which caused these issues is a condition that cannot be cured by surgery and may recur. Furthermore, it was an indisputable fact that the plaintiff had undergone many major operations after the disputed case, which had affected his condition.

23 On these facts, the hospital had also violated its duty of care towards the plaintiff, which could not be delegated to the doctor. It was immaterial in such cases whether the doctor who treated the patient was an employee of the hospital or self-employed. The exact relationship between the hospital and the doctor did not affect the plaintiff's legal position.

24 Hence, the trial court found in favour of the plaintiff and awarded him € 70,000 in general damages, plus € 3,024 in special damages.

25 The patient and the hospital appealed, and their appeals were joined.

b) Judgment of the Court

i) Regarding the appeal of the patient

26 The patient/plaintiff appealed on the ground that although the trial court had found the conduct of the defendant to be negligent, it had not accepted a causal link between the negligent behaviour and his urination problems.

27 The Court of Appeal observed that doctors and hospitals have a duty to inform patients of the risks of an operation and of any alternative treatment, so that the patients can decide whether to undergo the operation. If the doctor and the hospital violate such duty, then they are liable to the patient, provided that the patient's health problem is due to a risk for which appropriate information should have been provided. The causation requirements in such cases are less strict than the standard but-for test. However, causation does not cover everything that follows surgery for which the risks were not explained. There is no causation regarding an event that would have existed even without the surgery. In the present

case, the plaintiff's urination issues constituted a condition unrelated to the surgery. Therefore, these issues were not a materialisation of the surgery risk about which the plaintiff should have been informed. These observations did not apply to the matters concerning erectile dysfunction, which clearly constituted a materialisation of risks from the operation, of which the appellant had not been informed.

The patient also appealed on the ground that the trial court did not consider 28 his claims regarding assault and the award of punitive damages. The trial court drew a distinction between cases where there is no consent at all and cases where consent is given without proper prior information. If the patient consents to an operation but the consent was given without the patient being provided with all relevant information, then this constitutes negligence and not battery. The Court underlined that despite the grossly negligent behaviour in the present case, there was no evidence that justified an award of punitive damages.

Hence, the Court of Appeal affirmed the decision of the trial court. Nonethe- 29 less, the Court increased the award of damages to the plaintiff from € 70,000 to € 100,000 for the issue of his impotence, accounting for the young age of the plaintiff at the time of the surgery (35 years old) and the effects on his mental health.

ii) Regarding the appeal of the hospital

The hospital appealed on the ground that the trial court had erroneously attribut- 30 ed vicarious liability for the behaviour of the doctor and had erroneously accepted that the hospital had not discharged its duty of duty of care.

The Court clarified that the trial court had not found the hospital vicariously 31 liable; it had found it personally liable for negligence on the basis of a non-delegable duty of care. Under the facts of the case, the doctor could not be considered an employee or an agent of the hospital. Nevertheless, among others, the patient had signed an agreement with the hospital for his treatment and all invoices had been issued in the name of the hospital. Thus, the hospital had a duty of care to the patient, which it could not discharge simply by having the doctor operate on and treat the patient.

Hence, the Court rejected the appeal of the hospital. 32

c) Commentary

This judgment is important because it clarifies the consequences of informed con- 33 sent in the medical context, the effect of doctors' negligence on the hospital where they work, and the requirements for awarding punitive damages.

34 Regarding informed consent and causation, Cypriot courts tend to deviate from the standard but-for test, following *Chester v Afshar.*[9] In *Chester*, the House of Lords ruled that where a surgeon had failed to warn a patient about a risk of injury inherent in an operation, and, as a result of that failure, the patient had the operation and the risk materialised, it was sufficient for the patient to prove that, if properly warned, they would not have consented to the operation which was in fact performed and which resulted in the injury. The legal principles of this judgment were applied by the Supreme Court of Cyprus in *Varianou v Vorka*[10] and in other cases. The present judgment clarifies that the 'relaxed' causation requirements in cases of consent based on insufficient information do not entail that there are no requirements at all. Hence, if an operation is performed following such consent and the patient develops medical issues after the operation, then the patient still needs to prove that these issues resulted from the operation, and that they had not been properly informed thereof.

35 Moreover, this judgment affirms the position of Cypriot courts[11] that clinics and hospitals have a personal duty of care to their patients, which cannot be delegated to the doctors who undertake the patients' treatment. The duty of care in such cases is not discharged, even if the doctors are regarded as independent contractors. Hospitals and clinics have personal, not vicarious, liability for negligent behaviour of the doctors who work in their hospitals and clinics. This position is based on English case law, especially the dicta by Lord Denning in *Cassidy v Ministry of Health,*[12] which is frequently cited by Cypriot courts. It is also noteworthy that the Court of Appeal in the present case approved the judgment of the trial court, which referred among others to the more recent case of *Woodland v Essex Country Council.*[13] The latter clarified that a non-delegable duty can arise, when: (1) the claimant is a patient or child or for some other reason is especially vulnerable or dependant on the protection of the defendant against the risk of injury; (2) there is an antecedent relationship between the claimant and the defendant, independent of the negligent act or omission itself (i) which puts the claimant in the actual custody, charge or care of the defendant, and (ii) from which it is

9 [2004] United Kingdom House of Lords (UKHL) 41. Interestingly, the present judgment cited the judgment of the Court of Appeals in *Chester v Afshar* [2002] 3 All England Law Reports (All ER) 532.

10 (2010) 1 Judgments of the Supreme Court (AAD) 1541.

11 *Katina Hadji Theodossiou v Petros Koulia & Anor* (1970) 1 CLR 310; *Aggeli v Vorka* (2007) 1 AAD 761; *Polykliniki Ygeia Ltd & Anor v T Lambrou as an administrator of the estate of the deceased P Lambrou & Anor* [2016] 1 AAD 2634.

12 [1951] 1 All ER 574, 585.

13 [2013] United Kingdom Supreme Court (UKSC) 66.

possible to impute to the defendant the assumption of a positive duty to protect the claimant from harm in the performance of those obligations and not just a duty to refrain from conduct which will foreseeably damage the claimant; (3) the claimant has no control over how the defendant chooses to perform those obligations; (4) the defendant has delegated some function which is an integral part of the positive duty which he has assumed towards the claimant and the third party is exercising the defendant's custody or care of the claimant and the element of the control that goes with it; and (5) the third party has been negligent in the performance of the very function assumed by the defendant and delegated by the defendant to him.[14]

Another issue clarified were the legal consequences of the invalid consent of the patient. Such consent can only give rise to negligence, not to battery. The Court of Appeal cited English doctrinal writings[15] and indirectly referred to *Sidaway v Bethlem Royal Hospital*, which regarded battery for such cases as an inappropriate cause of action under English law.[16] 36

Connected thereto was the issue of punitive damages. Since there could be no battery but only negligence due to invalid consent, the Court held that the trial court was correct not to examine the issue of punitive damages. This is in line with the position of Cypriot courts that punitive damages are awarded only in exceptional circumstances;[17] negligence, however gross, will not suffice.[18] 37

3. Court of Appeal, 29 April 2024, *Konnaris v Republic of Cyprus*, Civil Appeal no 201/2018: State Liability for Violation of Human Rights

a) Brief Summary of the Facts

The plaintiff, a lawyer, filed an action against the Republic of Cyprus, alleging that during the execution of an arrest warrant against him, the police officers unreasonably handcuffed him and deliberately treated him in a derogatory and humil- 38

---

14 Ibid, at [23] per Lord Sumption.

15 *J Steele*, Tort Law (3rd edn 2014) 58.

16 [1985] 1 All ER 643, at 650 (per Lord Scarman).

17 *Yiallouros v Nicolaou* (2001) AAD 558; *Attorney General v A Palma et al* (2015) 1 AAD 2489. On the issue of punitive damages under Cypriot law, see also *M Chatzipanagiotis*, Cyprus, in: E Karner/BC Steininger (eds), European Tort Law 2023 (2024) 118.

18 *M Theophilou as an administrator of the estate of the deceased P Theophilou v Attorney General*, Action no 3604/2011, 19 May 2016, ECLI:CY:EDLAR:2016:A82.

iating manner in front of his clients. In addition to the arrest warrant, a search warrant was executed in his office that lasted about four hours, during which time he was handcuffed, and his condition was visible to all his clients who came for scheduled meetings, which the police did not allow to be cancelled. Two lawyers who were working in the law firm, as well as two secretaries, were also present. The legality and validity of the warrants were not disputed.

39 The trial court found that the handcuffs were unnecessary at the relevant time and, even if the handcuffs were considered reasonable and necessary, they should have been avoided in the presence of the appellant's/plaintiff's clients, given his capacity as a lawyer. It was also proven that there was no possibility of escape since the office was located on the second floor and had only one entrance-exit door. Nevertheless, the trial court considered all the circumstances of the case, including that the arrest was lawful; that no force was used to place the handcuffs; that the incident had occurred inside the appellant's/plaintiff's law office and he had not been not seen in handcuffs in a public place. Hence, the trial court was unable to conclude that the specific treatment of the appellant/plaintiff by the police was inhuman or degrading.

40 The plaintiff appealed on the ground that there was a violation of his right not to be subject to inhuman and degrading treatment pursuant to art 3 of the European Convention on Human Rights (ECHR).

b) Judgment of the Court

41 The Court of Appeal, citing judgments of the European Court of Human Rights (ECtHR), stated that handcuffing as such does not amount to degrading treatment under art 3 ECHR. The circumstances of a particular case have to be considered, such as the place of arrest, the period for which the handcuffs were used, the intention of the police authorities to humiliate the detainee, the use or non-use of physical violence, any physical and emotional harm to the detainee.

42 The Court of Appeal affirmed the judgment of the trial court that the specific treatment of the appellant did not reach the minimum level of seriousness to be considered as inhuman or degrading. It was not proven that the police officers had intended to humiliate or degrade the appellant, and no evidence indicated that the police officers had acted with prejudice against him, or to damage his reputation. This was supported by other factors, such as the fact that the arrest was lawful, no force was used to place the handcuffs, and the appellant did not suffer any physical or emotional harm.

43 As a result, the appeal was dismissed.

c) Commentary

The violation of human rights, as these are enshrined in the Constitution and in the ECHR, can found a cause of action for the affected individuals. According to the case law of the Supreme Court of Cyprus, there is an actionable right for such violations irrespective of whether the alleged perpetrator is the State or a private individual, since the judiciary, exercising State power, must protect its citizens from such violations.[19] 44

In practice, alleged violations of human rights are often combined with specific torts, especially negligence. The result is that the requirements of the tort in question are interpreted in the light of protection of the pertinent human rights.[20] Nevertheless, if the facts of the case do not fall under an existing tort, the violations of fundamental rights may constitute a standalone cause of action.[21] 45

The rights violated may be vested in the Constitution and/or the ECHR. Although the part of the Cypriot Constitution on fundamental rights is largely based on the ECHR, claimants often refer to both, apparently because it facilitates invoking the case law of the ECtHR. 46

The remedies provided for violations of human rights are based on the principles of *restitutio in integrum* and of equitable compensation.[22] Compensation covers both pecuniary and non-pecuniary damages. The latter include hardship, distress, pain and suffering, loss of employment opportunities, etc.[23] In practice, there is no difference between awarding equitable compensation for violations of fundamental rights and general damages for torts. Punitive damages may also be awarded, albeit only in very exceptional cases, when the defendant's behaviour indicates extreme arrogance or oppression.[24] 47

---

19 *Yiallouros v Nicolaou* (2001) AAD 558.

20 Eg *Attorney General v Palma & Ors* (2015) 1 AAD 2489, ECLI:CY:AD:2015:A765, where the alleged violation of the right to life under art 2 ECHR was combined with the tort of negligence; *Pantelas v Attorney General & Anor,* Action No 1313/13, 11 November 2020, ECLI:CY:EDPAF:2020:A103, regarding battery, false imprisonment and the fundamental rights to liberty and security, bodily integrity, and inhuman or degrading treatment or punishment.

21 *Yiallouros v Nicolaou* (2001) AAD 558, which concerned a violation of the right to private life and the right to free communication.

22 Ibid.

23 Ibid.

24 *Attorney General v Palma & Ors* (2015) 1 AAD 2489, ECLI:CY:AD:2015:A765.

4. Court of Appeal, 10 July 2024, *Violetta Management Committee v Graham Blackburn*, Civil Appeal no 181/2019: Jointly Owned Buildings; Trespass to Immovable Property

a) Brief Summary of the Facts

48 The plaintiff, the managing committee of a block of flats, claimed that the behaviour of the respondent/defendant, owner of an apartment in the said block of flats, constituted trespassing on the common and/or jointly owned areas, and requested damages and an injunction.

49 Specifically, the defendant, without the plaintiff's permission and the consent of the other owners of the building, had built an external wooden staircase which started from the balcony of his apartment and ended on the roof of the building. He also placed various objects on the roof, such as chairs, sunbeds, umbrellas, etc, which he later removed. The plaintiff claimed that the actions of the defendant violated the rights of the other owners and endangered their safety, as well as public safety: the staircase had not been constructed in a durable manner, the required building permit had not been obtained, while the objects placed on the roof had not been secured and could cause injuries.

50 The trial court dismissed the action on the grounds that the plaintiff failed to prove that the roof constitutes a jointly owned property. The plaintiff appealed.

b) Judgment of the Court

51 The Court of Appeal reversed the judgment of the trial court.

52 According to sec 38 A of the Immovable Property (Tenure, Registration and Valuation) Law, the term 'unit' includes an apartment, and the term 'jointly owned property' means any part of a jointly owned construction or building which has not been registered as a unit. Additionally, under sec 38B, 'each unit of a jointly owned construction shall be owned, occupied and enjoyed separately as private property'. A certain percentage of a jointly owned area within such building may be granted for the exclusive use of a specific unit. In such a case, this percentage shall be specifically described in the registration of that unit. Concerning the rights of the units' owners, the Law provides that the owner of each unit may make alterations, additions or repairs to their unit, provided that 'they do not prejudice the rights of the owner of any other unit nor interfere with its enjoyment by its owner; or do not in any way affect the jointly owned property, its smooth operation or enjoyment; or do not in any way affect the walls support-

ing the jointly owned construction, the external walls of the jointly owned construction or any part of the frame of the jointly owned construction or do not in any way endanger the safety or do not alter the external appearance of the jointly owned construction'.

The Court of Appeal found that the roof of the building is jointly owned prop- 53
erty, since it had not been registered in the defendant's/respondent's title deed as a unit. Consequently, the roof as a jointly owned property belongs proportionately, in undivided shares, to all co-owners of the building.

In the light of the above, the appeal succeeded. The Court of Appeal concluded 54
that the construction of a wooden staircase on the external wall of the building is an action of trespassing. The Court issued an injunction prohibiting the defendant from interfering with the said areas. Furthermore, the Court issued an injunction in which it ordered the defendant to demolish the external wooden staircase within ten days of the serving of the injunction. Given that the appellant did not prove any actual damage, the Court of Appeal awarded € 50 as nominal damages, with legal interest from the date of filing of the action.

c) Commentary

This is one of the very few Cypriot cases relating to trespassing on co-owned build- 55
ings.

Legal issues related to co-owned buildings are regulated in secs 38 A-38ΛΓ of 56
the Immovable Property (Tenure, Registration and Valuation) Law. Section 38 A defines 'jointly owned property' as 'any part of a jointly owned building that has not been registered as a unit'. A 'unit' is 'a floor or section, or part of a floor, room, office, apartment or shop or any other part or space of a jointly owned building which can be suitably and conveniently occupied and used as a completely separate and independent unit for any purpose for which a building permit has been obtained'. Thus, jointly owned property consists of jointly owned areas and 'units' owned separately. The typical example are flats within a multi-storey building. Furthermore, sec 38H provides that 'the unit area consists of the covered space enclosed by the external walls of the unit and includes the covered and uncovered verandas and the covered and uncovered balconies of the unit'.

57 The present judgment follows a recent judgment of the Supreme Court, which clarified that the external walls of a co-owned building are not part of the 'unit'.[25] Hence, the person who owns or possesses a flat may not make any amendments, either provisional or temporary, to external areas without the consent of the other co-owners. Such consent is usually given by the administrative committee of the building, which is elected by the co-owners. Among others, the administrative committee is entitled to manage the jointly owned areas and sue or be sued on issues regarding such areas. The committee merely represents the co-owners and does not itself own the jointly owned areas.[26]

58 Nonetheless, in practice, individual owners often use parts of the external walls and the roof of the building for installations serving their own apartment, like water boilers and external air-conditioning units. Such installations are tolerated by the other co-owners without protest, to the extent that they are reasonable, and they do not interfere with the use and enjoyment of their own property. In the case at hand, the defendant had practically converted part of the roof area to an extension of his own property, hence the action brought by the administrative committee against him.

5. Supreme Court, 19 June 2024, *Kyriakos P Kosiaris & Ors v Andrea Leonidou* and *Andreas Leonidou v Cyprus Ski Club & Ors*, Civil Appeals nos 60/2016 and 61/2016: Negligence; Contributory Negligence

a) Brief Summary of the Facts

59 The plaintiff, 12 years old at the time of the accident, was skiing on a public path, trying to go from one skiing piste to another, on the Troodos Mountain. Defendants 2 and 3 were passengers in a car driven by defendant 1. Defendant 1 took his car off the road, due to heavy traffic, but heavy snow made it impossible to drive his car any further. Defendants 1, 2 and 3 tried to use the car's winch to free the car from the snow. They pulled the wire tow rope from the car's winch, which was located at the front of the car, and tied it to a tree. The plaintiff noticed at a distance of 3–4 metres the wire tow rope in front of him, but he did not have time to react and hit the wire tow rope with his stomach. He was taken to

25 *Isthmos Trading Ltd & Anor v Vardaris Snack Ltd*, Civil Appeal no 506/2012, 30.9.2009, ECLI:CY:AD:2019:A403.
26 Ibid.

hospital and underwent surgery. He filed an action based on negligence and breach of statutory duty against the three persons who had placed the wire tow rope on the slope (defendants 1–3), but also against the Cyprus Ski Club and the Cyprus Ski Federation (defendants 4 and 5), which managed the two ski pistes.

The trial court found only defendants 1–3 liable and awarded the respondent/ 60 plaintiff € 80,000 in general damages, and € 4,747 in special damages, plus interest and costs.

Defendants 1–3 and the plaintiff appealed. 61

b) Judgment of the Court

Defendants 1–3 argued that the trial court had wrongly concluded that they had 62 breached their duty of care towards the plaintiff. In any case, the plaintiff had been contributory negligent. The Supreme Court, affirming the trial court's decision, observed that the way the appellants had placed the wire created an extremely dangerous trap for the users of the path. The cause of the accident was their negligent act in placing the wire tow rope, which constituted a danger for the plaintiff.

Regarding contributory negligence, the Supreme Court reiterated that contrib- 63 utory negligence is not based on a duty of care owed by the plaintiff towards the defendant, but on a duty of the plaintiff to self-protect by demonstrating appropriate care. The standard of care depends on the circumstances of the particular risk at the given moment. A plaintiff is not usually required to guard against the negligence of third parties, unless such negligence is usual under the circumstances. In the present case, the Supreme Court affirmed the findings of the trial court that the plaintiff could not have foreseen that the snowy path on which he was skiing could have been blocked by the placement of a wire tow rope. There was no question that the said risk would arise in the mind of a reasonable person who was skiing on that path. Furthermore, the wire tow rope was grey, half-an-inch thick, and could only be seen from a very close distance. Thus, the plaintiff had no possibility at all to avoid skiing into it, while there had been no evidence that the speed at which the respondent was skiing had contributed to the accident.

Regarding the alleged negligence of the Cyprus Ski Club and the Cyprus Ski 64 Federation, the Supreme Court applied sec 51(2)(b) CWL on the duty of care of occupiers.[27] Since the accident occurred on a path within the forest and outside the

---

27 'A duty not to be negligent shall exist in the following cases, that it to say … (b) the occupier of

area owned, rented and controlled by the respondents, they had no duty of care towards those using the path, and no causation was proven between their acts or omissions and the plaintiff's injury.

c) Commentary

65 This judgment reiterates some important elements of contributory negligence, namely whether the plaintiff ought to have accounted for the negligence of third persons.

66 The provisions on contributory negligence can be found in sec 57 CWL, which reflects the provisions of the UK Law Reform (Contributory Negligence) Act 1945. Their interpretation by Cypriot courts is based on English judgments.

67 Contributory negligence requires foreseeability of harm to oneself.[28] The standard of care in contributory negligence is what is reasonable in the particular circumstances of each case; and, in most cases, this corresponds to the standard of care in negligence.[29] The present judgment underlines that a claimant is not contributory negligent for a failure to account for the negligence of third parties, unless experience shows that such negligence is usual under the circumstances.[30] A prudent person will guard against the possible negligence of others, when experience shows such negligence to be common.[31] The question is whether on these facts, the plaintiff took sufficient precautions to avoid the accident and whether those precautions were sufficient in the circumstances.[32]

---

any immovable property shall owe a duty to those who are ... lawfully in, or upon, or so near to such immovable property as to the usual course of things to be affected by negligence'.

28 *Odysseos v Mantovani & Sons* (1989) 1 CLR 321.

29 *Patsalides v Yapani & Anor* (1969) 1 CLR 84, 100 (per Hadjianastasiou J), citing *Jones v Livox Quarries Ltd Same v Same* [1952] 2 Queen's Bench (QB) 608, 615 (per Lord Denning).

30 *Vlassios v Antoniou* (1990) 1 AAD 815; *Charilaou v Nicolaou* (2003) 1 AAD 1460.

31 *Elpiniki Panayiotou v Georghios Kyriacou Mavros* (1970) 1 CLR 215, citing *Grant v Sun Shipping Co Ltd* [1948] 2 All ER 238, 247.

32 *Pourikkos v Fevzi* (1963) 2 CLR 24; *Karikatou v Soteriou* (1979) 1 CLR 150.

6. Personal Injury

a) Supreme Court, 18 October 2024, *P I v Aristocleous & Anor*, Civil Appeal no 14/2016: Negligence; Road Traffic Accident

The plaintiff was 17 years old when he was involved in a traffic accident in 2006. 68
He suffered a serious head injury with permanent brain damage, especially in the frontal lobes. The injury resulted in permanent mental and emotional impairments. These caused changes in the appellant's personality, namely emotional instability, depression, outbursts of anger, moral decline, impulsive behaviour, excessive irritability, and emotional disorders. In 2007, the appellant was diagnosed with clinical depression and post-traumatic stress disorder, and he has received psychological support ever since. The appellant also suffered severe and multiple injuries to various parts of his body, underwent many operations and more would follow to treat osteoarthritis of the knee. He suffers from permanent scars and injuries, including mobility restrictions. He has shown early signs of osteoarthritis and will need surgical assistance for arthroscopy of the knee or a total arthroscopy as a final treatment. He is unable to engage in various sports and manual work.

The trial court found the defendants liable for the accident and awarded the 69
amount of € 155,000 in general damages for pain, suffering and loss of amenities and the amount of € 90,000 for loss of future earnings. The plaintiff appeal, requesting a higher amount of damages.

The Supreme Court increased the amount of general damages for pain, suffer- 70
ing and loss of amenities to € 250,000. Regarding the loss of future earnings, the Supreme Court increased the amount awarded to € 150,000 to account for the plaintiff's age and residual working capacity. At the same time, the Supreme Court affirmed the decision of the trial court to award a lump sum and not apply the method of the multiplier and multiplicand (monthly loss of earnings times the number of months for which the loss would be sustained), because the plaintiff had not worked for four years since the date of the accident.

b) Supreme Court, 21 November 2024, *Aitidis & Anor v The Republic*, Civil Appeal no 33/2016: Battery; Punitive Damages

Officers of the Cyprus police force had beaten and abused the plaintiffs when they 71
arrested them and while they detained them. Plaintiff 1 suffered a laceration wound to the left eyebrow, swelling of the left cheek, swelling of the left ear, neck pain, a bruise on the left shoulder blade, swelling of the wrists, dizziness

and headaches. Plaintiff 2 suffered skin abrasions, pain, swelling and abrasions on the wrists, bruising, swelling of the left earlobe, swelling under the right eye, bruising in the eye area and injury to the capillaries of the left eye causing severe pain and temporary reduction in vision, a minor laceration wound and abrasion on the upper surface of the right lower limb.

72 The trial court found the Republic of Cyprus vicariously liable for the battery and awarded € 8,000 to plaintiff 1 and € 12,000 to plaintiff 2 in general damages and aggravated damages for their pain and suffering. However, it refused to award punitive damages against the Republic, judging that only when an employer encourages the unlawful act may punitive damages against the employer be awarded.

73 The plaintiffs appealed requesting an award of punitive damages.

74 The Supreme Court observed that punitive damages can be awarded only in exceptional cases, when the defendant's conduct is so reprehensible as to justify punishment by a civil court. Behaviour is considered reprehensible when it is accompanied by strong elements of arrogance, imprudence, or improper motive, or a tendency to humiliate the victim. It was a huge error of the trial court to rule that only in cases where employers have encouraged the behaviour of their employees can punitive damages be awarded against the employer. As a result, the Court awarded € 3,000 to each plaintiff in punitive damages.

c) District Court of Nicosia, 26 April 2024, *BAR v GG Farm and Butcher Shop To Dikomo Ltd & Anor*, Action No 5434/16: Employer's Negligence

75 At the time of the accident the plaintiff was a 22-year-old, unskilled employee at the defendant company, a butcher shop (defendant 1). Defendant 2 was the director, representative and shareholder of the company, and the plaintiff's supervisor. The plaintiff's duties included grinding meat in the mincer machine. On 3 October 2014, while manually pushing meat in the grind machine, her right hand was trapped in the moving parts of the machine, and she sustained grave injuries.

76 As a result, she had her hand amputated from the wrist and underwent plastic surgery to restore the skin on her hand. The amputation caused her deformities in various body parts and rendered her incapable of any manual work. On 4 February 2016, the Medical Board of the Social Insurance Services declared the plaintiff permanently incapable of work with a disability rate of 66 %. Furthermore, the plaintiff needed psychological support and a prosthesis for her right hand.

The plaintiff was earning a net salary of € 655 per month from the defendant company, as well as € 220 per month providing cleaning services for residential homes. 77

The court found the defendants liable for negligence. Deducting the social insurance benefits that the plaintiff was entitled to receive, the Court awarded € 600,000 in general damages, which include: (a) € 48,100 for loss of future earnings with a multiplier of 20 (ie, for 20 years); (b) the future need to have an artificial limb, for which the court awarded compensation of € 70,000; and (c) damages for pain and suffering. The court also awarded € 22,107 in special damages. 78

Nevertheless, the Court found the plaintiff 35 % contributory negligent and reduced the damages accordingly. 79

d) District Court of Nicosia, 8 August 2024, *A-M P v P M*, Action no 3664/16: Medical Negligence

The plaintiff was 30 years old and in excellent health when she sought medical assistance. After an examination in which she was diagnosed with an ovarian cyst, she underwent gynaecological surgery on 26 January 2016, performed by the defendant, an obstetrician-gynaecologist. On 31 May 2016, the plaintiff experienced vomiting and abdominal pain, and went to the Emergency Department of the Nicosia General Hospital. She was seen by the defendant, who diagnosed gastritis. On 1 June 2016, she was rushed to the Emergency Department because the symptoms persisted. Two days later, she was diagnosed with ileus (bowel) obstruction, caused by the presence of a foreign body within the pelvic area. She underwent surgery under general anaesthesia, during which a piece of gauze was removed from her small intestine. The gauze had been left in her intestine after the operation conducted by the defendant. Without the timely intervention of a surgeon, she could have lost her life from sepsis. The plaintiff faces a serious possibility of intestinal obstruction for the rest of her life. Moreover, she has a permanent scar in her abdomen, for which she will need plastic surgery. 80

The Court found the defendant doctor liable and awarded € 70,000 in general damages for pain and suffering. 81

C. Literature

1. *Polyvios Polyviou*, Culpa, Αμέλεια, Ευθύνη [Culpa, Negligence, Liability] (Chrysafinis and Polyviou 2024) 419 pp, ISBN 978-9925-7765-2-8

82 The author examines the evolution of the tort of negligence under three legal systems, namely common law, Roman law, and civil law.

83 The book is divided into 19 chapters of varying length, including an introduction and conclusions. The author starts from the concept of *culpa* under Roman law, to which he dedicates around 90 pages (chapter 2) of his book. He shows that this concept did not have the same meaning as negligence under modern law. The concept of *culpa* has evolved over time and could indicate different things in different periods and different contexts, such as wrongful behaviour, causation between one's behaviour and loss caused to another person, or fault (intent or negligence). At the same time, the author finds that modern common law is similar to Roman law, since both apply a casuistic methodology, ie, that the law is created 'bottom-up', on the basis of specific case scenarios.

84 The author dedicates three short chapters, around 30 pages in total, to the notion of negligence under civil law as a legal family (chapter 3), makes a special reference to Greek law (chapter 4), and European law as laid down mainly in the Principles of European Tort law of the European Group on Tort Law (chapter 5).

85 Subsequently, the author proceeds to an extensive analysis of the tort of negligence under common law, especially as applied in England (chapters 7–18, around 265 pages).

86 The most interesting part of the book is chapter 19, where the author presents his conclusions in the form of common elements and differences of the legal systems examined. In general, the author finds that all these legal systems have common requirements for liability, other than liability for breach of contract and liability for unjust enrichment: wrongful behaviour, loss, and a causal link between the behaviour and the loss. Moreover, in all these systems, there is no liability, in principle, for omissions and pure economic loss. However, in common law, the duty of care is the main method applied to limit or expand liability, whereas in civil law, other methods are employed, such as the use of interests and rights of the persons affected. Moreover, while Roman law and common law adopt a case-by-case (bottom-up) approach, civil law uses an overarching legal principle/provision, from which legal doctrine and courts deduct the legal consequences (top-down approach).

Overall, the book is insightful and makes very interesting reading. The book would have benefitted from a more symmetrical analysis of the legal systems examined. In any case, it is one of the very few books in Cypriot legal literature to undertake a historical-comparative analysis of a legal concept. 87

2. *Polyvios Polyviou*, Η ανάληψη ευθύνης στο αστικό δίκαιο [Assumption of responsibility in civil law] (Chrysafinis and Polyviou 2024) 329 pp, ISBN 978-9925-7765-3-5

The author explores the concept of assumption of responsibility in the common law as applied mainly in English private law, which Cypriot law closely follows, as well as the analysis and methodology that should be applied to this concept. 88

The core of the author's analysis is the *Hedley Byrne* principle, both in its basic and extended form. The elements of the *Hedley Byrne* principle were laid down by the House of Lords in its respective judgment:[33] when a person with special knowledge or skill undertakes, irrespective of contract, to apply that knowledge or skill to assist another person, who reasonably and foreseeably relies upon such knowledge or skill, then the former person has a duty of care to the latter to prevent economic loss. A series of judgments, such as *Henderson v Merrett Syndicates Ltd*,[34] *Spring v Guardian Assurance plc*[35] and *White v Jones*[36] extended this principle to cases of provision of professional services and professional conduct. 89

The book is divided into 19 chapters of varying length, including an introduction and conclusions. It starts with the taxonomy and categories of 'civil law' (ie, core private law in the sense of continental legal systems, *droit civil, Zivilrecht*), namely contracts, torts and unjust enrichment. It proceeds with an analysis of the tort of negligence, especially of the notion of the duty of care under the landmark case of *Caparo Industries v Dickman*,[37] followed by comments on the law of contracts, especially regarding the notion of 'consideration'. It then analyses the series of cases that established the '*Hedley Byrne* principle' and the 'extended *Hedley Byrne* principle': *Hedley Byrne, Spring, Henderson* and *White v Jones.* The chapters thereafter are dedicated to the assumption of responsibility in the context of 90

33 *Hedley Byrne & Co Ltd v Heller & Partners Ltd* [1964] AC 465.
34 [1995] 2 AC 145.
35 [1995] 2 AC 296.
36 [1995] 2 AC 207.
37 [1990] 2 AC 605.

public authorities, including the police. Next are chapters on omissions, US law, economic loss, assumption of personal responsibility by company representatives, the evolution of the English case law after *Hedley Byrne*, the provision of free services, and some comments on the relationship between the law of contracts and the law of torts as to assumption of responsibility.

91 The final chapter is dedicated to the conclusions of the author and provides some overarching thoughts. The author concludes that the *Hedley Byrne* judgment is important not because it is innovative, but because it returns to the roots of common law, before the division into the law of contracts and torts was established, when the concept of assumption of responsibility could impose liability on a person who it was assumed would provide services or complete an undertaking. The author observes that in modern law, 'assumption of responsibility' cannot fall under the law of contracts for lack of consideration. Hence it should be considered either as part of the law of torts or as an autonomous category of law. The *Hedley Byrne* principle marks a departure from the prevalent 'mechanism' of tort law (mainly negligence), since the duty of care is based on voluntary commitments of the defendant and not on the imposition of such a duty by law. However, this is alleviated by the extended *Hedley Byrne* principle, under which the law imposes a duty of care for the appropriate provision of professional services or professional conduct. According to the author, the 'assumption of responsibility' is dictated by social necessity and by common perceptions of justice, and this is also how this concept should be regarded in the future.

92 The book is the first monograph in Cypriot legal literature on this topic. It provides some very interesting insights and analyses the pertinent issues in depth, although not always in the most systematic way. The *Hedley Byrne* principle has also been applied by Cypriot courts.[38] However, the author does not refer to Cypriot cases, apparently because he is interested in a wider analysis of the concept, upon which Cypriot case law has had no significant impact.

38 Eg, *Premier Chemical Co Ltd v Bank of Cyprus Ltd & Anor* (1998) 1 AAD 1951.

Jiří Hrádek

VI. Czech Republic

A. Legislation

1. Act no 30/2024 Coll, Motor Third-Party Liability Insurance[1]

The new regulation transposes Directive 2009/103/EC relating to insurance against civil liability in respect of the use of motor vehicles and monitoring the obligation to insure against such liability (codified version), the so-called Motor Directive as amended by Directive (EU) 2021/2118. 1

The main purpose of the legislation remains the protection of persons injured as a result of accidents caused by the use of vehicles. However, there are also other important principles of the new regulation: 2

- amendments to the existing legislation so that it is fully in line with the changes made to the EU legislation on civil liability in respect of the use of motor vehicles;
- ensuring the free movement of vehicles normally based in the EU and of persons travelling in them;
- ensuring that persons injured by the operation of vehicles are treated in a comparable way, regardless of where in the EU the injury occurs;
- ensuring the movement of vehicles within the 'green card' system; and
- taking account of changes in the regulation of insurance and road vehicle operation that have occurred since the previous legislation was adopted.

Regarding the specific regulation, the following points should be mentioned: 3

a) Vehicle and its Operation

The new Act extends the scope of the types of vehicles subject to compulsory third-party liability insurance compared to the current one, thus covering all motor vehicles with a declared maximum design speed exceeding 25 km/h, as 4

1 Zákon č. 30/2024 Sb., o pojištění odpovědnosti z provozu vozidla, commentary is based on the explanatory memorandum to the Act.

https://doi.org/10.1515/9783111389271-007

well as vehicles with a declared maximum design speed exceeding 14 km/h if their operating weight exceeds 25 kg.

5 At the boundary of the vehicle concept is a moped, as its design allows human power to serve as an auxiliary source of locomotion despite being equipped with a standard electric motor. To maintain the existing protection of victims, a legal fiction has been introduced, classifying vehicles with purely mechanical propulsion as mopeds, except in cases where, similar to motorcycles, the supplementary engine serves only an auxiliary pedalling function.

6 The Act also contains a definition of vehicle operation. This means any use of the vehicle corresponding to its normal function as a means of transport, regardless of the characteristics of the vehicle and the terrain in which the vehicle is operated. The term operation also does not take into account whether the vehicle is stationary or in motion.

7 The operation of a motor vehicle also includes the preparation for driving and the immediate acts following the end of a journey, as well as the acts necessary for the maintenance of the vehicle. Merely starting the engine constitutes part of the operation of a motor vehicle, regardless of whether the vehicle is set in motion, located on a road or other publicly accessible place, or still in a garage, and whether the engine is started by the operator or their employee. A motor vehicle is also in use if, as a result of the driver's failure, it creates an obstacle for other road users.

b) Insurance and Territory

8 The operator of a domestic vehicle must ensure that liability insurance covers the risk of incurring an obligation to compensate for damage arising from the vehicle's operation. This obligation applies throughout the vehicle's registration period if it is subject to road vehicle registration or, if unregistered, for the period during which it is in running order.

9 The territory in which a vehicle is normally based is the territory of a State

- whose registration plate or registration mark the vehicle bears;
- in which a plate assigned to the vehicle by an insurance company was issued if a registration plate is not required for such vehicle;
- where the operator of the vehicle is resident or established, if the vehicle is not required to have a registration plate or any other distinguishing mark equivalent to a registration plate; or
- where the accident occurred if the vehicle is without a registration plate, although it should have had such a plate, or if the vehicle has a registration plate that does not correspond to the vehicle.

c) Operator

The operator of the vehicle is usually its owner, but it may also be a person other than the owner who is authorised to operate the vehicle by an agreement with the owner. In such a case, the content of that agreement, or the scope of the rights and obligations that the owner has transferred to that person by agreement, is decisive for determining the operator of the vehicle. This concept of operator is consistent with the approach stipulated under § 2927 of Act No 89/2012 Coll, the Civil Code (CC), upon which the Act is directly based. 10

11 However, the concept of operation requires a certain long-term use. Therefore, if the vehicle is rented or borrowed for a short period of time, the renter or borrower does not become the operator of the vehicle.

12 If the operator of the vehicle cannot be determined, similarly to § 2930 of the Civil Code, the owner of the vehicle is deemed to be the operator. Although this presumption is formally formulated as irrebuttable ('shall apply'), by being linked to a situation where the operator of the vehicle cannot be determined, it is in fact rebuttable, since it will not apply if someone else is determined to be the operator.

d) Scope of Insurance

13 Liability insurance covers claims arising from the operation of the vehicle while it was used as a means of transport, ie, for the carriage of persons, animals or goods. Transport means the purposeful and intentional movement on transport routes, the result of which is transport as the purposeful movement of persons, goods or animals by the means of transport. It follows from the foregoing that liability insurance cannot exclude any damage caused by the operation of a vehicle, as defined in the Act, that is caused by a vehicle used as a means of transport, irrespective of where the vehicle is operated.

14 The insured party has the right to have the insurer indemnify the injured party on their behalf to the extent and in the amount covering: (i) the loss or damage resulting from bodily injury or death; (ii) expenses reasonably incurred in connection with the care of the injured animal and the damage caused by the damage, destruction or loss of an item, as well as the damage caused by the theft of an item if the natural person has lost the ability to care for it; (iii) loss of earnings; and (iv) reasonable legal costs incurred in the exercising of their rights.

15 The limit of the insurance benefit in the event of damage to health is to be at least CZK 50,000,000 (approx € 2,000,000) for each injured party. In respect of

damage to a thing, it is to be at least CZK 50,000,000, irrespective of the number of victims.

16 Compensation for damage caused by the operation of a vehicle, to the extent that the insured party is obliged to compensate for such damage, may not be refused or reduced.

e) Motorsport Insurance

17 One of the exceptions to liability insurance allowed by this EU legislation is insurance for the organiser of a motor race or motorsport competition. In response to this exception, the Act thus regulates in its § 8 the basic conditions for this type of insurance.

18 The insurance covers injuries arising from the operation of vehicles during motorsport events, including races or competitions taking place in a defined area outside the normal operation of vehicles on closed motorsport tracks or routes.

19 This insurance must be taken out by the organiser of the motorsport event if no alternative insurance is provided.

B. Cases

1. Constitutional Court of the Czech Republic (Ústavní soud České republiky) 13 March 2024, Pl ÚS 27/23: Compliance with Constitution; Compensation for Harm to Health

a) Brief Summary of the Facts

20 The District Court in Vyškov filed an application to annul the contested provision in connection with proceedings under Case no 6 C 337/2022, in which the claimant sought payment of CZK 117,344 (approx € 4,720) from the respondent as compensation for non-pecuniary damage to his health. The District Court submits that, in these proceedings, it must apply § 2958 of the Civil Code,[2] the second sentence of which it considers to be contrary to the constitutional order.

2 Where harm to health is caused, the wrongdoer shall redress such harm by means of a monetary sum fully compensating the pain suffered and other immaterial loss; if the harm to his

The District Court submits that if the courts determine the damages in accordance with the contested provision, ie in accordance with the principles of decency, it has two options: either it will proceed according to the subjective perception of the injured party and then the compensation awarded will be random and unpredictable, or it will approach it from an objective point of view. 21

Since Decree no 440/2001 Coll of the Ministry of Health on compensation for pain and impairment of social position was repealed, the general courts now proceed 'objectively' in accordance with the Methodology for compensation for non-pecuniary damage to health (pain and impairment of social position pursuant to § 2958 of the Civil Code). 22

The District Court considers the inconsistency of the contested provision with the constitutional order on two levels: 23

- Directly in relation to the second sentence of § 2958 of the Civil Code, stating that the contested provision, being unpredictably applicable, contradicts the principle of legal certainty, predictability of judicial decision-making, and the rule of law; and
- the filling of the constitutional gap mentioned earlier by the Methodology.

In the District Court's view, the legislator was aware that the general courts cannot decide on compensation without an implementing regulation or other supporting material based on which 'quantification' of non-pecuniary damage would be seen as predictable compensation. The deliberately created 'vacuum' served to allow a group of 'interested persons' to establish the Methodology as the 'centre of application' of § 2958 of the Civil Code. The Methodology, however, is a commercial product, created without authorisation or public scrutiny, which 'deliberately bypassed the legislature'. 24

b) Judgment of the Court

The Civil Code in force is based on the concept of compensating the injured party for material and non-material damage, including mental anguish (§ 2956[3] of the 25

---

health interferes with the future prospects of the injured party, the wrongdoer shall also compensate him for the difficulties in attaining his proper social position. If the amount of compensation cannot be determined in this way, it shall be determined in accordance with the principles of equity.

3 If the wrongdoer comes under an obligation to redress harm to another's natural rights as protected by the provisions of the first part of this Code, he shall compensate the damage and

Civil Code). Thus, there has been a significant conceptual change compared to the legal regulation in force until the end of 2013, when the so-called aetiological approach was the determining factor, based on the classification of painful conditions according to the impairment of individual organs or body parts and expressing the degree of pain as physical and mental hardship. Since the entry into force of the Civil Code, the determination of the amount of compensation in relation to the reduction in social position is now assessed according to the way in which the damage to health will manifest itself in the (future) life of the person (the injured party in the particular case).

26 This new concept is not revolutionary; it has been built based on existing case law. When the previous legislation was in force, the general courts of various instances had already frequently deviated from the amount of compensation provided for in Decree no 440/2001 Coll on the basis of art 95 para 1 of the Constitution, or art 7 of that Decree, which allowed for a reasonable increase in the amount of compensation determined in 'particularly exceptional cases worthy of extraordinary consideration'. The Constitutional Court has repeatedly found such a procedure to be constitutionally compliant in cases where the amount of compensation determined under the Decree was not disproportionate to the harm suffered.

27 The purpose of § 2958 of the Civil Code is to provide the injured party with compensation (satisfaction) for all the hardship and suffering they have had to endure as a result of the personal injury. Therefore, in the case of personal injuries, a monetary amount compensates for pain, impairment of social life and other non-pecuniary damage.

28 Thus, the second sentence of § 2958 of the Civil Code is not intended to lay down a 'secondary rule' as to how compensation for personal injuries is to be awarded. A procedure which takes into account the principles of equity or fairness in the particular case, or a fair assessment which takes into account all the individual circumstances, including how the personal injury is reflected in the victim's life, is, and must be, an integral part of any compensation for personal injury. Accordingly, the requirement of fair compensation in the case of compensation for impairment of social life (permanent consequences) is not compatible with the above aetiological approach.

29 The separate emphasis on the principles of decency in the second sentence of § 2958 of the Civil Code should therefore be understood primarily as a reminder that the courts should always bear in mind the individual circumstances when de-

---

immaterial loss caused thereby; mental suffering caused by such harm shall also be redressed by the wrongdoer as compensation for immaterial loss.

termining the specific amount of compensation for non-pecuniary damage to health, even when applying objectifying criteria. § 2958 of the Civil Code should always be interpreted in the spirit of the principles of decency, even without an express normative reference in its second sentence.

It is clear from the foregoing that it is precisely and only by applying the principles of decency that a constitutionally consistent assessment of the amount of compensation respecting the fundamental rights of the injured party can be achieved in the decision on a particular case by a general court. 30

As regards the Decree, the proposed 'return to the points' regulation would inappropriately shift the focus of decision-making on the amount of compensation back to the executive, whose discretion would determine the value of the 'points' and the 'points' of the various injuries. The amount of compensation would be decided by an independent court based on a free evaluation of the evidence. The Constitutional Court sees no reason to change its earlier conclusions, in which it was critical of the mechanical assessment of the amount of compensation for personal injury (see the previously referred to judgment File no Pl ÚS 50/05), which is still maintained in the field of labour law (File no II ÚS 2925/20). 31

Indeed, the Constitutional Court's earlier comments on the prevailing interpretation of § 2958 of the Civil Code, which took into account the Methodology, were directed in the exact opposite direction to the District Court's argumentation. The Constitutional Court has previously stated that 'from the point of view of the protection of constitutionality, even a limited scoring according to the Supreme Court's Methodology may be problematic, since the decision on compensation cannot be conceptually based on certain tabulated scores, but must be based solely on the evidence and with regard to the circumstances of the particular case, which, in fact, has been given effect since 1 January 2014 by the legislator'. Therefore, the Constitutional Court also criticised the de facto departure from the declared general non-binding nature of the Methodology towards its increasingly rigid application (File no I ÚS 1010/22). In other words, the Constitutional Court emphasises the need to individualise compensation for injury before seeking to unify it. It is precisely this approach that corresponds to the relative vagueness of the statutory regulation, which provides sufficient flexibility to assess each case according to its individual circumstances within the framework of judicial discretion. 32

c) Commentary

The Constitutional Court decided in this case under art 95 of the Czech Constitution on the compliance of said provision with the Czech Constitution in the broad- 33 er sense (constitutional order). Thus, it is not a standard decision of the court, but a constitutionally defined check based on the application of a general court.

34 The Constitutional Court did not find that the contested second sentence of § 2958 of the Civil Code was contrary to the constitutional order, in particular to the principles of the rule of law in its formal dimension (the principles of predictability of law and legal certainty). The principles of decency constitute an elementary requirement for any assessment of compensation for personal injury. It is a generally formulated and broad (vague) legal concept. Its purpose is to give the courts scope to assess a case reasonably and fairly in the context of its individual circumstances, for which they are then responsible.

35 It is clear from the case law of the Constitutional Court that, given the meaning and purpose of § 2958 of the Civil Code and the nature of the Methodology, the Methodology must be understood as not binding, but only as a supporting basis for determining the amount of compensation for non-material damage for pain suffered and aggravation of social position.

36 It is not a binding regulation implementing the second sentence of § 2958 of the Civil Code and the courts cannot treat it as binding legislation. The general courts are not obliged to apply the Methodology exactly, but to ensure that their own decisions on compensation for personal injury are predictable, in accordance with the principle of full compensation and the principle of decency. It is precisely these principles that the general courts are obliged to reflect in their decisions.

2. Supreme Court of the Czech Republic (Nejvyšší soud České republiky) 27 March 2024, 30 Cdo 3909/2023: Breach of EU Law; Legislator's Liability; Basis of Regulation

a) Brief Summary of the Facts

37 Through an action against the Czech Republic, the claimant sought an apology from the respondent as satisfaction for the non-pecuniary damage caused to him (and to the citizens of the Czech Republic) by the incorrect implementation of Directive 2002/58/EC. It was the incorrect implementation that led to the widespread collection and further processing of traffic and location data on electronic communications of users of electronic communications services. In that collection, the claimant perceives an interference with his rights to privacy and to informational self-determination.

The court of first instance dismissed the action, as it concluded that the damage allegedly caused to the claimant through the supposed inconsistency between national legislation on the one hand, and EU law on the other, is merely potential damage, which is not eligible for the legal protection provided by § 81 para 1[4] and § 2956 of the Civil Code. 38

The court of second instance upheld the decision. It stated that, although the enactment of a law is an exercise of public authority, it is the result of a normative activity of the State, which cannot be regarded as an improper official procedure under the State Liability Act and therefore liability for damages cannot be inferred. Article 36 para 3 of the Charter of Fundamental Rights and Freedoms (as part of the Czech Constitution) does not establish a right to compensation for damage caused by the exercise of Parliament's legislative power. If the legislator exceeds its limits, the Constitutional Court may intervene and repeal the law or declare it unconstitutional and that did not happen in this case. 39

b) Judgment of the Court

If the Czech Republic is held liable for a breach of EU law, the victim may be entitled to compensation for both the damage suffered and non-pecuniary damage, provided other conditions are met. 40

In accordance with the fundamental principle of EU law enshrining the principle of equivalence, claims for breaches of EU law must also include the possibility of claiming compensation for non-pecuniary damage, provided the statutory conditions are met. This conclusion then applies even if the violation of EU law was committed by legislative action, even though the normative (in)action cannot be regarded as maladministration within the meaning of Act no 82/1998 Coll, the State Liability Act, and this Act does not apply to legislative action by the State in purely domestic situations. 41

A contrary interpretation would inadmissibly lead to a de facto division of liability for breaches of EU law. If the breach of EU law corresponds to an incorrect official procedure or was committed by means of an unlawful decision, the victims would be awarded compensation of both pecuniary and non-pecuniary damage, whereas in the case of a breach of EU law by legislative (in)action, only pecuniary damages would be awarded. 42

4 Personality of an individual including all his natural rights are protected. Everybody is obliged to respect the free choice of an individual to live on their own.

43 There is no rational reason for introducing any compensation exclusively for breaches of EU law. On the contrary, the Act is the best legislation that is reasonably applicable in order to determine the extent and form of the compensation awarded.

44 As regards the merely potential damage suffered, even in the case of non-pecuniary damage caused by the incorrect processing of personal data, the existence of damage suffered is one of the conditions of the right to compensation for damage. So too is the existence of a breach of a legal obligation and a causal link between that damage and the breach, the three conditions being cumulative. Therefore, it cannot be concluded that any 'breach' of an EU provision inherently gives rise to the said right to compensation for damage in favour of the data subject.

c) Commentary

45 The Court decided on several fundamental issues in connection with the liability of the State. However, the most important issue is whether the State is to be held liable for damage caused by the improper implementation of EU law into Czech laws and whether damage must be specified by the claimant.

46 The Court correctly concluded that the State Liability Act is the specific basis for the State's liability, and the State will always be held liable for a breach of law if the conditions stipulated in the case law of the CJEU are present. The general principle that legislators are not liable for damage caused by national legislation, as they exercise sovereign powers, does not apply to EU law. The Czech Republic is obliged to implement EU law in accordance with its standards, and any breach thereof establishes a liability relationship in line with EU case law.

47 Moreover, a contrary interpretation would inadmissibly lead to a de facto division of liability for breaches of EU law. If the breach of EU law corresponds to an incorrect official procedure or was committed through an unlawful decision, both being subject to the State Liability Act, the victims would be awarded both pecuniary and non-pecuniary damages, while in the case of a breach of EU law by legislative action or inaction, only pecuniary damages would be awarded.

48 As for whether a specific regulation is needed, this requirement was rejected by the Supreme Court, as the State Liability Act provides sufficient legal regulation enabling compensation for both pecuniary and non-pecuniary damage.

49 Nevertheless, the conclusion that the State might be liable for legislative activity is not new. The doctrine that the State is not liable for damage caused by legislative activity, or its absence, has already been challenged in the past. The Supreme Court held in 2012 that the State is liable for legislative errors in the case of a breach of EU law (File no 28 Cdo 2927/2010) and the Constitutional

Court due to errors in legislative activity relating to rent regulation (File no I ÚS 92/94), and in 2023, the Supreme Court decided on damage caused by COVID-19 measures (File no 30 Cdo 63/2023).

3. Supreme Court of the Czech Republic (Nejvyšší soud České republiky) 27 February 2024, 6 Tdo 1132/2023: Concept of Unborn Child and its Parents; Secondary Victims

a) Brief Summary of the Facts

A driver did not fully concentrate on driving a vehicle and collided head-on with an oncoming passenger car travelling in the opposite direction. This car was thrown off the road by the intensity of the impact, where it collided with a parked Peugeot 308, causing serious injuries to the female passenger in the vehicle. The female passenger was in the 33rd week of pregnancy. She sustained severe injuries, including head injuries, chest contusion, abdominal wall contusion with placental abruption, and skull fractures with intracranial bleeding of the foetus, which led to the subsequent death of the foetus in the womb. Despite receiving comprehensive professional care, including psychotherapy and pharmacotherapy, she developed post-traumatic stress disorder, significantly limiting her ability to lead a normal life. 50

In addition to the criminal punishment, the wrongdoer was ordered to compensate the parents who lost their unborn child for emotional harm (pain of grief) pursuant to § 2959 of the Civil Code.[5] The mother was granted CZK 720,000 (approx € 28,800) and the father CZK 360,000 (approx € 14,400). This was the decision of the court of first instance and the court of second instance upheld it. Both courts argued for an analogous application of § 2959 of the Civil Code. 51

The respondent filed an extraordinary appeal, arguing that § 2959 of the Civil Code is inapplicable in the case of both victims. In his opinion, both courts misin- 52

5 Where death or especially serious harm to health is caused, the wrongdoer shall redress any mental suffering of the spouse, parent, or child of the injured party or other person close to him by means of a monetary sum fully compensating their suffering. If the compensation amount cannot be determined in this way, it shall be determined in accordance with the principles of equity.

terpreted this provision, as well as § 25 of the Civil Code,[6] which defines a 'nasciturus'. The unborn child is a bearer of a private law status and personal rights only if born alive. At this stage of development, the foetus is granted only so-called conditional personal status in private law relations.

b) Judgment of the Court

53 The current legal regulation in the Civil Code stipulates that, in the case of homicide or particularly serious bodily injury, the wrongdoer must compensate the mental suffering of the spouse, parent, child or other close person through monetary compensation that fully addresses their suffering. If the amount of compensation cannot be precisely determined, it is to be assessed in accordance with the principle of equity.

54 Unlike the previous legislation, which unambiguously stipulated in § 444 para 3 lit d) of the (former) Civil Code that parents were entitled to lump-sum compensation of CZK 85,000 (approx € 3,400) in the event of the death of an unborn child, logically implying that they were the persons entitled to compensation (now referred to as compensation for mental suffering) in the event of foetal death, the current Civil Code, whose application is at issue, does not contain a similar provision. However, it cannot be inferred from this that the parents of an unborn child who has been killed by the culpable conduct of a wrongdoer are not entitled to such a claim. Although the Explanatory Memorandum to the Civil Code, as well as the commentaries on the issue do not take any position, one cannot ignore the trend manifested in the legislation towards strengthening the position of victims.

55 A teleological interpretation leads to the conclusion that the purpose of § 2959 of the Civil Code is to ensure the most comprehensive form of compensation for damage, in relation to all persons who may have suffered it. This is also apparent from the use of the term 'other persons close to the victim', which considerably broadens the range of persons entitled to satisfaction. The purpose and aim of the law in this case is to establish a right of a purely personal nature for persons close to the deceased. The harm to be compensated consists primarily in the psychological distress (grief, sorrow) caused by the perception of the loss of a loved one. Such rights of a personal nature are undoubtedly also affected by the parents

6 A conceived child is considered to be already born if it suits the child's interests. A child is presumed to have been born alive. However, if the child is not born alive, he is considered never to have existed.

of a child who was conceived but could not be born due to the negative impact of the harmful event, which prevented the parents from establishing family relations with their child.

In other words, the Supreme Court concludes that § 2959 of the Civil Code is 56 precisely the provision which is intended to compensate for the harm caused by the death of the foetus, and which is to be applied directly and not by analogy. If the previous legislation also referred to parents as those subjects whose child was not born as a result of its killing in the prenatal period, there is no reason why the concept of parent should not be interpreted in the same way in the current wording of § 2959 of the Civil Code.

c) Commentary

This case is really topical as the Supreme Court has, for the first time, ruled on 57 whether the parents of an unborn child who died as a result of an illegal action should be compensated as parents. If answered positively, the second fundamental question in this case is whether § 2959 should be applied directly or by analogy to people who conceived a child but never became parents in the legal sense.

The standard interpretation and application of § 2959 of the Civil Code leaves 58 no doubt that a secondary victim, who may bring their claim against the wrongdoer, is the parent of the already born and therefore independently living child. The existence of close emotional ties between these individuals (apart from extreme exceptions, which cannot be ruled out) is, as a rule, beyond doubt. However, there was no direct interpretation as to whether a child who is not born alive can establish those ties.

Based on the historical interpretation, it can be concluded that the legislator 59 did not intend to make compensation for such harm impossible, especially since nothing of the kind is apparent from the explanatory memorandum of the Civil Code. Even though § 2959 of the Civil Code is more generally defined than the past Civil Code, explicitly mentioning the parents of an unborn child as individuals entitled to compensation, it does not preclude a claim for compensation for non-pecuniary damage caused by the death of an unborn child.

The Supreme Court is convinced that there is no reason to exclude from the 60 parent-child relationships defined above those whose child was conceived but not yet born. Not only the interference with the physical integrity of a loved one, but also the termination of a child's development due to the death of a human foetus may cause comparable, if not greater, mental distress to the parents than the physical injury itself.

61 The Supreme Court maintains that the scope of § 2959 of the Civil Code is wider than the respondent believes, since it also concerns the relationships (emotional ties) formed by parents to a child conceived by them but not yet born. It can reasonably be assumed that they develop in relation to the approaching time of the expected birth of their child.

62 Although such a decision is well reasoned and the Supreme Court is entirely correct in defining the scope of application of § 2959 of the Civil Code, its direct application collides with the definition of mother and father as established by the Civil Code. A man only becomes a father when the child is born. We therefore do not define the father as a close person entitled to compensation for the death of the child.

63 If we examine the purpose of § 2959, it is clearly to atone for the trauma a person experiences upon the death of a loved one. The bottom line is that people typically regard the death of an unborn child as the death of a loved one. Jointly with the historical interpretation, which clearly shows that the legislator did not intend to change the personal scope of compensation, such a gap should be filled by analogy rather than by a direct application.

64 The Supreme Court's approach establishes a narrow and independent definition of 'nasciturus', which might be deemed complicated from the point of view of uniformity of legal terms. For the legal clarity and uniformity of legal institutes in the legal order, the approach established by analogy is more sensitive and reasoned. Therefore, both parents whose unborn child dies should be entitled to compensation for emotional harm but based on an analogous application of § 2959.

4. Supreme Court of the Czech Republic (Nejvyšší soud České republiky) 25 April 2024, 25 Cdo 3742/2023: Operation of a Vehicle; Circumstances Stemming from Operation of the Vehicle

a) Brief Summary of the Facts

65 An accident occurred when a deer suddenly ran into the path of a driver and operator of a vehicle and rebounded off the front of the vehicle onto an oncoming Škoda Octavia, causing damage. The claimant, as the insurer under the accident insurance contract for the Škoda Octavia, sought compensation in the amount of CZK 62,312 (approx € 2,490) for the insurance benefit paid to another vehicle operator for damage caused to their vehicle.

The court of first instance assessed the claimant's claim under § 2927 of the Civil Code[7] and concluded that the damage to the Škoda Octavia was caused by the special nature of traffic but was not caused by circumstances originating in the operation of another vehicle. Its driver was exempted from liability under the second sentence of § 2927 para 2 of the Civil Code, as he could not have avoided the collision with the deer even if he had made all reasonable efforts. Therefore, the claimant was not entitled to a recourse claim against the respondent pursuant to § 9 para 1 of Act no 168/1999 Coll, on Motor Third-Party Liability Insurance. 66

The court of second instance upheld the judgment. The case concerned an event that could not have been prevented or objectively averted by the operator, even if such efforts had been made. It is essentially a so-called qualified (not simple) coincidence or force majeure (*vis maior*). The unforeseeable behaviour of the animal cannot be regarded as a circumstance originating in traffic and, therefore, the exemption ground under § 2927(2) of the Civil Code is fulfilled, resulting in the operator of the other car not being liable for the damage caused by the collision between their vehicle and the deer subsequently rebounding on the Škoda Octavia. 67

b) Judgment of the Court

The car operator may be exempted from liability only in the case of circumstances that are not related to the operation of the vehicle but that nevertheless have an adverse effect on the specific characteristics of the transport or means of transport. He must also prove that he could not have prevented the damage even if he had made every effort to do so, ie, that he could not have prevented and eliminated the effect of the circumstances that caused the adverse effect on the operation of the vehicle. 68

The propelling of a forest animal, which ran into the road, onto another vehicle cannot be regarded as a circumstance that did not originate from the operation of the vehicle that struck the animal. Similarly to defects in passability or objects lying on the road, wildlife is one of the objects that can be associated 69

7 (1) A person who operates transport shall compensate damage caused by the specific character of that operation. The same duty also pertains to any other operator of a vehicle, boat or plane, unless the means of transport is operated by human power. (2) An operator cannot be exempted from the duty to compensate damage if the damage was caused by circumstances that have their origin in the operation. Otherwise he shall be exempted from liability if he proves that he could not prevent the damage, even by exercising all due care.

with the nature of traffic, since it is likely to interfere with the movement of vehicles (thus falling within the operator's 'sphere of traffic') passing through a wooded area or near fields.

70 The negative effects of the movement of game are countered by a number of measures, including chemical deterrents, fencing or underpasses or bridges for game, from which it is clear that the presence of game (or the risk of it) on roads is by no means exceptional. Therefore, the mere collision with a vehicle does not, as a rule, constitute such a strong external influence that overrides the characteristics of the moving vehicle as to make it a circumstance that does not originate from the operation of the means of transport.

c) Commentary

71 This decision is important because it defines conditions under which an operator cannot exempt themselves from liability. In 2023, the Supreme Court defined such circumstances in case File no 25 Cdo 154/2023 with respect to trams. The current decision defines game as a trigger.

72 The legal regulation of the obligation to pay damages caused in connection with the operation of transport or means of transport does not require the breach of a legal obligation as a condition for the establishment of a liability relationship if the damage is caused by the specific nature of the operation of transport or the means of transport. It is a strict liability, which is based on the occurrence of a circumstance specifically qualified by law that causes a harmful effect, regardless of the wrongdoer's fault. The responsible person (operator) cannot, therefore, exempt themselves from the obligation to compensate for the damage by proving a lack of fault. Their liability is excluded only if a so-called exemption reason is provided (§ 2927 para 2 of the Civil Code).

73 Such an exemption reason is defined in the second sentence of § 2927 para 2 of the Civil Code by requiring the operator to make all reasonable efforts to prevent the occurrence of damage during transport activities. It is irrelevant from where (or from what place) these circumstances originate, but rather how and with what result they manifest in relation to the means of transport, causing harmful effects due to the specific characteristics of traffic.

74 The concept of circumstances not originating from traffic applies only to those factors that trigger negative effects specific to traffic that would not have occurred otherwise. In the context of strict liability, this means that the negative effect of the movement of the vehicles and their operation was 'set in motion' by an external circumstance that does not lie within the sphere of the operator of the vehicle or means of transport.

5. Constitutional Court of the Czech Republic (Ústavní soud České republiky) 28 May 2024, Pl ÚS 14/24: Causation; Interruption of Causal Nexus; Theory of Adequacy; Secondary and Primary Victims

a) Brief Summary of the Facts

The claimant sought (pecuniary) compensation from the wrongdoer's third-party liability insurer for personal injury in the form of loss of earnings and reasonable medical expenses, claiming that the personal injury was caused by a traffic accident on 5 July 2016. Members of the claimant's family – her daughter-in-law and two minor grandchildren – were killed in the accident. Her son suffered serious injuries with consequent psychological damage from the loss of his family. 75

The court of first instance concluded that, in the present case, a causal link could be established between the wrongful conduct of the respondent and the claimant's injuries. The tragic death of the family members caused by the respondent was undoubtedly a substantial and decisive cause that contributed to the claimant's injury to her own health as an adverse consequence. This conclusion is reached since the injury to the secondary victim's health would not have occurred without the interference with the primary victim's absolute right; both injuries result from the same wrongful act of the respondent. 76

The court of second instance found that the claimant's personal injury was not caused directly by the traffic accident, in which the claimant was not personally involved, but only as a consequence of the accident – the death of close family members. There is therefore only a causal link between the claimant's injuries and the death of her family members. In the present case, therefore, the injury is a secondary cause and must be assessed under § 2959 of the Civil Code[8] and not under § 2910[9] or § 2956 of the Civil Code, as the court of first instance concluded. 77

8 Where death or especially serious harm to health is caused, the wrongdoer shall redress any mental suffering of the spouse, parent, or child of the injured party or other person close to him by means of a monetary sum fully compensating their suffering. If the compensation amount cannot be determined in this way, it shall be determined in accordance with the principles of equity.

9 A wrongdoer who through his fault breaches an obligation set by law and in doing so interferes with an absolute right of the injured party shall compensate the harm he causes by doing so. The duty to provide compensation also applies to a wrongdoer who interferes with another right of the injured party by breaching through his fault a duty established by law for the protection of that right.

b) Judgment of the Court

78 The Czech legal doctrine in relation to secondary victims has distinguished between psychological harm to health, ie, harm so intense that it constitutes an interference with a person's mental integrity, and emotional harm, which refers to emotional distress or emotional hardship that does not reach the intensity required to constitute an interference with a person's health. Whereas the former is referred to as 'shock damage', the latter is referred to as 'emotional damage' in cases of interference with personal and family life (§ 2959 of the Civil Code). The secondary victim may therefore suffer not only damage to their private and family life involving mental distress but also damage to their health as the primary victim of the death of a close person.

79 According to current case law, compensation for shock damage is provided in a non-systematic way under § 2959, ie, by increasing the compensation for the emotional harm caused. While in the case of compensation for emotional injury, the private and family life of the secondary victim is protected by law, in the case of shock injury consisting of post-traumatic stress disorder, it is the victim's health.

80 If there is a causal link between the harmful event and the injury caused, there is no reason why the general courts should be obliged by the case law to substitute claims for compensation for pecuniary damage arising from breach of health with increased compensation for non-pecuniary damage under § 2959 of the Civil Code.

81 In interpreting the causal link, the courts of general jurisdiction rely on the case law of the Supreme Court, according to which, a causal link cannot be inferred from a fact which is itself a consequence. However, this is merely an assertion presented as a postulate, not a legal argument based on a broader logical foundation. No further explanation of this conclusion can be found in the original reasoning of Rc 7/1979. Moreover, this decision, the purpose of which is normally to draw a general rule of conduct from a case, cannot be taken out of the context of the case. Taken to its *ad absurdum* conclusion, the application of this conclusion of the Supreme Court would lead to the exclusion of liability for indirect damage, which is characterised precisely by the fact that it is caused only as a product of the damage suffered by the primary victim.

82 With regard to adequate causation, it may be noted that if a road traffic accident results in serious bodily injury or even the death of a person close to the victim, this usually represents an enormous psychological burden for the person close to the victim as a secondary victim. Then, it is reasonably probable that the secondary victim's psychological health may have been affected as a result of the road accident and the deaths of those close to her, ie causally linked to those events. In other words, the impact on the psychological health of a person

close to the victim can be regarded as being expected and adequate in similar situations.

c) Commentary

The importance of this case is extraordinary, since the Constitutional Court has attempted to change long-standing case law regarding the interruption of the causal link, which has been deduced despite the fact that, under the theory of adequacy, there is a chain of causes and consequences. The same exact situation also occurred in this case, as the claimant suffered damage to health due to shock when she found out that her family had died in a car accident. In this case, the car accident was a substantive and decisive cause that led to damage to health. In other words, without the accident, there would be no interference in the absolute right of the claimant. **83**

The theory of adequacy uses a criterion whereby damage is regarded as the result of a wrongful activity if, in addition to being the condition of the damage, the wrongful act or event is, by its general nature or in the usual course of events and experience, a common result of such damage. Non-attributable consequences are those that the wrongdoer could not expect, because they are too extraordinary and unforeseeable (adequacy of the extent of the consequences), or which are too distant from the consequence (adequacy of causal nexus). In determining the adequacy of causation, the criterion is a hypothetical experienced (so-called optimal) observer, ie an imaginary person with all their life experience. **84**

As for the interruption of the causal link, Czech law understands this situation as one where the chain of causes does not establish a causal link between the wrongdoer's actions and the damage caused when another event, independent of the wrongdoer's actions, occurs and is decisive for the damage. The same conclusion is reached, however, in a situation where the cause of the damage is a fact that is itself a consequence for which the wrongdoer is liable for another legal reason. Meanwhile, the problem is not the denial of the causal nexus itself but the way the case law disregards the standard normative criteria of imputability and how Czech law addresses the issue of indirect damage. **85**

It seemed that this latter approach was changed by the decision of the Supreme Court File no 25 Cdo 1946/2000. The reason for this surprising conclusion was that the Court preferred a factual consideration over a chronological one in establishing the damage, focussing on the claimant's absence from the business meeting rather than the fact that the meeting took place after the accident and the claimant was not present. However, the Supreme Court did not consider either the general principle of adequacy, especially foreseeability, or the theory of protective **86** purpose of a norm. Moreover, this case was overruled many times by subsequent decisions.

87 However, the Constitutional Court seems to have expressed a clear and well-reasoned disagreement with the past case law. It refused an automatic application of the notion of interruption of the causal link and insisted on an examination of the question of the adequacy of the cause.

88 It assumes that it is not easy to establish and objectively prove an interference with an individual's mental health. As follows from the above, it will be essential to distinguish between a medically detectable interference with physical and mental integrity (apparently most often a mental illness) and a 'mere' interference with private and family life. For this reason, general courts should approach the awarding of compensation very carefully, but are obliged to examine the causal link and not to automatically refuse compensation with respect to the doctrine on the interruption of the causal link.

6. Supreme Court of the Czech Republic (Nejvyšší soud České republiky) 22 August 2024, 25 Cdo 227/2024: Liability for Operational Activity; Scope of Care Required

a) Brief Summary of the Facts

89 The claimant fell on 8 December 2017 in a supermarket when she slipped on radish leaves. She suffered a dislocated fracture of the patella of her left knee and underwent surgery on the same day as the accident. The subject matter of the proceedings was compensation for personal injury consisting of compensation for the pain caused by the accident and the operation, which an expert assessed at a total of 230 points, corresponding to compensation for pain of CZK 63,455 (approx € 2,540).

90 The court of first instance concluded that the respondent, the operator of the supermarket, must compensate the claimant for the non-pecuniary damage caused by the operational activity pursuant to § 2924 of the Civil Code,[10] without the respondent being exonerated under the second sentence of that provision.

10 A person who operates a business or other facility with the aim of making a profit shall compensate damage resulting from the operation, regardless of whether it is caused by the operational activity itself, by a thing used for it or by the effect of the activity on its surroundings. The duty shall not apply if the person proves that he made all reasonable efforts to prevent the occurrence of damage.

The court did not find the respondent's conduct to be sufficient in terms of all the care that could reasonably be required of the operator to prevent damage. A certain employee was in charge of checking the cleanliness of the shop floor and the shop manager then checked the employee's rounds. The interval between the floor checks was set by the respondent at every two hours, and the last time the respondent's employee checked the cleanliness of the shop floor prior to the accident was at 12:00 pm. Moreover, the employee in the fruit and vegetable department cleaned up any mess herself, even outside the prescribed intervals, almost immediately, if necessary, as she was present in the section almost all the time. 91

The court of second instance also concluded that the respondent had not been exonerated from its liability, as it had failed to prove that it had taken all the care that could reasonably be required to prevent the injury. 92

b) Judgment of the Court

In the case of § 2924 of the Civil Code, the liability is objective, but due to the establishment of the exemption reasons, it is not absolute. When interpreting the conditions under which the wrongdoer may successfully invoke the exemption reason, it follows from the explanatory memorandum to the Civil Code that the expression 'reasonably required' means not only the obligations agreed in the contract or laid down by law, but everything that appears to be rational in that respect with regard to the nature of the operation, ie not all conceivable measures that are feasible and which would place excessive demands on the operator. The operator will be released from liability if they prove they acted with the degree of caution corresponding to the level of knowledge in the relevant field and general experience (ie as a proper and competent operator). 93

It is clear from the proven circumstances of the case that the occasional presence of waste from the vegetables sold on the floor of the shop in the area in question cannot practically be prevented, since it is a circumstance that ultimately depends on the conduct of customers and not on the conduct of the respondent's employees. The operator of a shop can reasonably be required to take appropriate measures to minimise the risk arising therefrom. As the proceedings have shown, the respondent took such measures. In addition to the fact that the entire premises had a sufficiently high-quality non-slip floor, the respondent placed a bin in the area for the disposal of waste, and the relevant worker in the area cleaned up the waste that fell on the ground as and when required. The respondent could not reasonably be required to monitor every customer purchasing vegetables every minute to see if a few leaves had fallen. 94

c) Commentary

95 The Supreme Court interprets § 2924 as allowing the wrongdoer to exempt themselves from liability if they prove that they exercised all care that could reasonably be required.

96 The Supreme Court considers the reasoning of the lower courts on the issue to be manifestly unreasonable and unfounded. The Supreme Court observes that the measures taken to prevent damage cannot be assessed as insufficient simply because damage occurred, since, in such a case, the operator could never, in principle, discharge its obligation to compensate for damage and that obligation would become absolute. Even if the formal organisational measures taken by the respondent to ensure cleaning were not in themselves sufficient to discharge the obligation to compensate for damage within the meaning of the second sentence of § 2924 of the Civil Code, what is relevant is how the respondent (including its employees) actually managed the prevention measures, including by carrying out cleaning in excess of the timetable according to the specific situation and the need to keep the floor sufficiently clean of vegetable residues.

97 Thus, the Supreme Court was entirely correct in denying the liability of the respondent. Nevertheless, the Supreme Court clearly points out that § 2924 provides for a case of strict liability. This author does not share this view, since unlike simple operational activity, it will be subject to liability based on fault. As to the strict liability regime, this will only cover the liability of extraordinarily dangerous operations under § 2925 of the Civil Code.

98 Nevertheless, liability based on fault is based on a reversal of the burden of proof and the enhanced position of the injured party. The injured party does not need to prove the breach of the duty (both the fault and wrongfulness) since the operator has to prove that they made all reasonable efforts to prevent the occurrence of damage.

7. Supreme Court of the Czech Republic (Nejvyšší soud České republiky) 20 August 2024, 25 Cdo 3108/2023: Motocross Race; Particularly Dangerous Operation

a) Brief Summary of the Facts

99 The claimant, a spectator at a motocross qualifying practice organised by the first defendant, sustained injuries after he was hit by a bike in the spectator area by the second defendant, who failed to control his motorcycle and flew off the

marked track. The first defendant regularly organises motocross races, including qualifying practice sessions, approximately two or three times a year, always at the Merklin track.

The court of second instance confirmed the decision of the court of first instance and found the first defendant liable for compensation for pain and suffering under § 2925 of the Civil Code,[11] as the organising of motocross qualifying practice sessions constitutes a particularly dangerous operation. The racers ride very fast on the track and have no regard for traffic laws, their motorcycles are a source of increased danger during the ride, they have limited control, and they are at risk of running off the track and causing injury to the participants of the race. This risk cannot be eliminated even if the track is properly laid out and prepared or if a safe zone for spectators is properly defined. The second defendant was found liable as a vehicle operator under § 2927 of the Civil Code.[12] 100

The question at stake was whether the categorisation of liability under § 2925 of the Civil Code is correct. 101

b) Judgment of the Court

§ 2925 of the Civil Code defines a particularly dangerous operation as one for which the possibility of serious damage cannot be reasonably excluded in advance even if due care is taken. 102

11 (1) A person who operates an extraordinarily dangerous business or other extraordinarily dangerous facility shall compensate damage caused by the source of the increased danger. An operation is considered extraordinarily dangerous if the possibility of serious damage occurring cannot reasonably be excluded, even with the exercise of due care. The duty to compensate shall not apply if it is proved that the damage was caused by force majeure, by the actions of the injured party or by the unavoidable actions of a third party. Other exclusions of liability that have been agreed shall not be taken into account. (2) If it is apparent from the circumstances that the operation significantly increased the risk of damage occurring, even though other possible causes can also be identified, the court shall require the operator to provide compensation for damage to an extent that corresponds with the probability of the operation having caused that damage. (3) An operation shall be deemed extraordinarily dangerous if it is operated as a factory or if it operates or deals with explosives or similarly dangerous substances.

12 (1) A person who operates transport shall compensate damage caused by the specific character of that operation. The same duty also pertains to any other operator of a vehicle, boat or plane, unless the means of transport is operated by human power. (2) An operator cannot be exempted from the duty to compensate damage if the damage was caused by circumstances that have their origin in the operation. Otherwise he shall be exempted from liability if he proves that he could not prevent the damage, even by exercising all due care.

103 In addition to operations that are particularly dangerous absolutely, ie always and in all circumstances, an operation may also be particularly dangerous if, although usually not particularly dangerous, it is not fully controllable in the given conditions in terms of the consequences it may cause, rendering it a source of increased risk of serious damage to its surroundings. The particular conditions under which such an operation is carried out may also be the source of the increased risk of damage.

104 Cases where the operation becomes particularly dangerous due to the specific conditions under which it is carried out include the operation of motocross races. The organiser of such races organises repeated runs of specific racing motorcycles using a special track located in the open air. Motocross qualification training sessions present an increased danger, as the competitors attempt to reach the finish line in the shortest possible time (the fastest lap counts, which then determines their ranking at the start of the race), are not bound by traffic rules on the road, drive their motorcycles at the limit of their physical capabilities on a difficult and rugged course laid out in the terrain, and take jumps.

105 An injury to a spectator of a motocross qualifying practice session caused by a motorcycle that has gone off the designated track is caused by particularly dangerous traffic (§ 2925 of the Civil Code) and is the responsibility of the race organiser.

c) Commentary

106 The relevance of this case arises from the fact that it has not yet been sufficiently determined under which circumstances operational activity should be considered extraordinarily dangerous.

107 Such a qualification is crucial for any potentially liable party, since liability in this case is strict, with minimal possibility for exemption, even if due care is exercised. If an operational activity is not deemed extraordinarily dangerous, the case will fall under § 2924 of the Civil Code[13] (standard operational activity), which is qualified as a case of liability based on fault.

108 In this case, however, the Supreme Court correctly pointed to the character of the race and all risks connected thereto. It concluded that the motorcycles may become uncontrollable and, therefore, there is a risk that the drivers will fall and

13 A person who operates a business or other facility with the aim of making a profit shall compensate damage resulting from the operation, regardless of whether it is caused by the operational activity itself, by a thing used for it or by the effect of the activity on its surroundings. The duty shall not apply if the person proves that he made all reasonable efforts to prevent the occurrence of damage.

can be thrown off the designated racecourse. Even with due care exercised by the race operator, it cannot be ruled out that the motorcycle will fall outside the track laid out by the organisers into places designated for spectators (and that should therefore be safe) in accordance with the rules and standards of the Autocross Association of the Czech Republic, which is what happened in the present case.

In addition, to be deemed an operation, the time-test must be passed. It is not 109
the sporadic off-road riding of a motocross motorcycle per se that constitutes a particularly dangerous operation, but the repeated holding of motocross races or qualifying practice sessions. Organising motocross races and qualifying training for races, even if only a few times a year, can be considered a regular and recurrent activity, not a one-off use of a source of increased danger.

Thus, the driving of racing vehicles (already) in qualifying practice for a mo- 110
tocross race involves an increased risk of serious harm, particularly to the health of the competitors and spectators. Therefore, the organisation of such races constitutes a particularly dangerous operation within the meaning of § 2925 of the Civil Code. The condition is, of course, that the damage arises from the nature of the particularly dangerous operation, ie that it is caused by the special characteristics of the operation rendering it dangerous and objectively capable of causing the damage (in the present case, the dangerous riding of motorcycles that are restricted in their control).

A mention must be made of the new legislation. By Act no 30/2024 Coll, the 111
Czech legislator enacted the possibility of organisers of motocross racings to take out an insurance policy under third-party vehicle liability insurance (see above nos 17–19).

8. Supreme Court of the Czech Republic (Nejvyšší soud České republiky) 25 April 2024, 25 Cdo 1034/2023: Damage Caused by an Item

a) Brief Summary of the Facts

A tree (western aspen) growing on the respondent's property in the central green 112
belt between two roads uprooted and fell onto the adjacent asphalt road as well as the claimant's property, damaging the claimant's fence.

The fallen tree was the subject of a 'check of greenery' carried out by the re- 113
spondent in 2014, where, according to the 'tree card', it was assessed as generally healthy and its stability was assessed as grade 2 (a tree with slight defects). The last visual inspection of the tree was carried out nine days prior to the incident

and no obvious defects (crown drying, change in vitality or inclination) were found.

114 Based on the expert examination, the court found that the cause of the uprooting was the combination of the tree's unbalanced crown and external factors (wind blowing, extreme rain).

115 The courts concluded that the uprooting of the tree was not caused by force majeure, since the extreme rainfall in June 2020 had only a marginal effect on the condition of the tree. The main cause was the failure to carry out planting measures, which should have been done by a legal entity established by the municipality to manage public greenery in the city. The court of second instance further concluded that the respondent may be sued for damage.

b) Judgment of the Court

116 Pursuant to § 2937 of the Civil Code,[14] a person who should have supervised an item is obliged to compensate for the damage. The entity legally liable for damage caused by an item of which it is the owner cannot transfer its liability to another entity which it has set up to ensure maintenance and repair of the item or if it concludes a service contract with another entity.

117 The person liable for compensation is (above all) the person who, at the time of the damage event, supervised the item and who had it effectively in their possession (eg a lessee, a borrower or the person who actually took it over to carry out a certain activity).

118 It follows from the above interpretation that a person other than the owner who exercises control over an item is a person who uses (holds) the item for themselves. In other words, the person who has taken over the item from the owner for the purpose of using it for their own benefit (a tenant, a borrower, but also a thief or a person who uses it for their own benefit without having any legal reason to do so), or the person who has taken over the item, for example, for the purpose of repairing or modifying it and has the item in their possession (supervises it) for that period of time.

119 However, a person who is entrusted by the owner with the performance of some of their duties (eg professional care) is not a person who has supervision over the owner's property within the meaning of § 2937 of the Civil Code, since

---

14 1) If damage is caused by the thing itself, the damage shall be compensated by the person supervising the thing; if such a person cannot be identified, it is deemed that the owner of the thing was supervising it. A person who proves that he did not neglect to provide due supervision shall be relieved of the duty to provide compensation.

they do not hold, use or manage the property for themselves, but for the person who entrusted them with this activity. Therefore, in such a case, the person who has supervision over the item is still the owner who has entrusted another with partial care of the item. The item is still at their actual disposal, and they decide, manage and supervise it only with the assistance of another.

c) Commentary

This case is important in terms of who might be liable for an item and whether the owner can assign the duty of care over the item to a third party and under what circumstances. 120

In the present case, the respondent claims that the person who supervised the tree was the legal entity set up by the defendant for the purpose of, inter alia, looking after the greenery, and which actually carried out that care for the defendant, including the care of the tree in question. The owner's duties include ensuring that their property, including items, is sufficiently managed so as not to cause harm to another. To comply with that duty, the respondent set up a legal entity to take care of the greenery in the municipality for him. 121

However, the court came to the conclusion that a person who is thus entrusted by the owner with the performance of some of their duties (eg professional care) is not a person who has supervision over the owner's property within the meaning of § 2937 of the Civil Code, since they do not hold, use or manage the property for themselves, but for the person who entrusted them with this activity. 122

We believe that such an interpretation is incorrect as it does not take into account the purpose of the norm. The provision of § 2937, which is inspired by the regulation in the Quebec Civil Code, is intended to improve the position of the injured party by reversing the burden of proof that the item was properly supervised and managed. Moreover, the reversal of the burden of proof applies both to fault and wrongfulness since the wrongdoer has to prove that they did not neglect to provide due supervision. 123

This regulation is practical also from the point of view of the owner who in most cases does not possess the skills to carry out the proper care. Then, if the person who is entrusted with the supervision of the item is a professional, it is their conduct that most satisfies the requirement of due supervision. 124

Therefore, if the law refers to supervision, then such supervision should be exercised by any person authorised by the owner of the thing, irrespective of whether they are in possession of the thing or not. Otherwise, there would be an unreasoned dichotomy of arrangements between the person who is entrusted 125 by supervision and who has to have possession over the item, and a person with supervision in the position of a helper.[15]

126 Consequently, any restriction on persons who are potentially liable, as proposed by the court, is not consistent with the aim of the regulation and should not apply.

9. Personal Injury

a) Supreme Court of the Czech Republic, 25 April 2024, 25 Cdo 1313/2023

127 The Court's conclusion that the circumstances at stake fell within the concept of compensation for pain, since it was only of a temporary nature, is incorrect. That would be the case when the state of health improves and those conditions subside, but not where the primary injury, in connection with the complications that arose, results in the death of the victim. In such a case, the conditions must be deemed to have had a definitive negative impact on the individual's state of health.

128 The victim was discharged from hospital after four months, but because of his total dependence on the care of third parties, he was placed in an institution and died some seven months after the accident. This is undoubtedly an interference with the fundamental human right to health (§ 81 para 2 of the Civil Code[16]) for a vulnerable person who, at an elderly age, was permanently removed from his accustomed environment and spent the latter part of his life battling with an increasing number of various difficulties, which also led to a worsening of his existing illnesses and limitations. Such impairment of his life gives rise to a claim for compensation for further non-pecuniary damage under § 2958 of the Civil Code.

---

15 In the case of a non-independent helper, the injured party would be able to sue both the helper who breached the duty to supervise and the principal to whom the breach of this duty is attributed according to § 2914 of the Civil Code. In the case of an independent helper, the injured party may sue the helper who has breached the duty of supervision, the principal being liable only for *culpa in eligendo*.

16 Life and dignity of an individual, their health and the right to live in a favourable environment, their respect, honour, privacy and expressions of personal nature enjoy particular protection.

b) Supreme Court of the Czech Republic, 28 February 2024, 25 Cdo 3542/2023

Pursuant to § 2960 of the Civil Code,[17] the wrongdoer must also reimburse the person who has incurred costs related to the care of the injured party's health, their person or their household. 129

In addition to the costs of the victim's medical care that is not covered by public health insurance, the costs associated with healthcare also include the costs of personal care that is not only of a medical nature (eg personal hygiene, food preparation and feeding, washing and dressing, which the injured person is wholly or partly unable to do themselves), and expenses for the care of their household (eg shopping, cleaning, laundry and dealing with other necessary matters at the post office, public offices, etc). Compensation covers the costs of acquiring the necessary aids and of providing for activities that the injured person is unable to carry out. The reasonableness of the costs associated with the care of the injured person's health must be measured not only in economic terms but also more broadly in terms of society's efforts to integrate disabled people into social life. 130

The interpretation of § 2960 of the Civil Code adopted by the court of first instance does not correspond with the concept of household care. It does not include garden care on the grounds that the garden is not a regular part of the household. Therefore, it is necessary to consider the ordinary household, as well as the tasks associated with the normal running of a household, as they would be undertaken by the average victim. 131

C. Literature

1. Books

F Púry/P Vojtek, Nároky poškozeného v adhezním řízení [Claims of the injured party in adhesion proceedings] (CH Beck 2024) 280 pp 132

D Kubová, Odčiňování duševních útrap primárních obětí [Compensation for the mental suffering of primary victims] (CH Beck 2024) 152 pp 133

17 The wrongdoer shall also compensate all direct costs reasonably incurred in connection with the medical care provided to the injured party, and with the personal and household care provided to the injured party, to the person who has incurred such costs; upon that person's request, the wrongdoer shall pay him a reasonable advance for such costs.

2. Articles

134 *J Bártů*, Nebezpečnost zvířete jako předpoklad vzniku odpovědnosti za škodu [Dangerousness of an animal as a prerequisite for liability for damage], Právník 9/2024, 879–891

135 *F Melzer/V Zorinčáková*, Náhrada škody a bezdůvodné obohacení z jednání falešného zástupce [Compensation for damage and unjust enrichment from the actions of a false representative], Bulletin advokacie 7–8/2024, 9–15

136 *F Eichel*, Pokračující škoda a promlčení v německém právu [Continuing damage and statute of limitations in German law], Bulletin advokacie 3/2024, 27–34

137 *P Bezouška*, Odpovědnost za škodu při použití pomocníka při plnění dluhu [Liability for damage when using a helper in debt fulfillment], Bulletin advokacie 10/2024, 25–30

138 *T Veselý*, Kdo odpovídá za škodu způsobenou pádem sněhu ze střechy? [Who is liable for damage caused by snow falling from a roof?], Právní rozhledy 3/2024, 81–85

139 *F Melzer*, Předvídatelnost v deliktním právu [Foreseeability in tort law], Právní rozhledy 5/2024, 135–144

140 *P Mertelová*, Deliktní nezpůsobilost poškozeného a náhoda [Tortious incapacity of the injured party and accident], Právní rozhledy 6/2024, 187–193

141 *M Dlabolová*, Doktrína "ztráty šance" a její aplikace v českém právním řádu [The doctrine of 'loss of chance' and its application in the Czech legal system], Právní rozhledy 11/2024, 352–389

142 *P Bezouška*, Otázka protiprávnosti při zásahu do absolutního práva dle § 2910 věty první ObčZ [The question of wrongfulness in the event of interference with an absolute right pursuant to § 2910, first sentence, of the Civil Code], Právní rozhledy 19–20/2024, 613–619

Søren Bergenser and Andreas Bloch Ehlers

VII. Denmark

A. Legislation

There was no relevant legislation in the field of tort law in Denmark in 2024. 1

B. Cases

1. Højesteret (Supreme Court) 20 November 2023, UfR (Ugeskrift for Retsvæsen, Weekly Law Report) U 2024.746 H: Bech-Bruun Law Firm Liable for Damages in the Amount of DKK 400 million for the Tax Administration's Loss

a) Brief Summary of the Facts

This decision concerns the liability of lawyers. In this case, a law firm advised the German Bank, North Channel Bank, in 2014 on the bank's potential liability as a result of participating in transactions with Danish listed shares. The transactions involved the bank issuing dividend notes that could be used when submitting applications to the Danish Tax Administration for a refund of dividend tax. 2

During 2014 and 2015, North Channel Bank issued the dividend credit advice mentioned above, which was attached to applications for a refund of dividend tax. Based on the applications, the tax authorities paid out approximately DKK 1.135 billion. The refund claims subsequently turned out to be unjustified on the whole, because the claims were based on fictitious transactions, as there were no shares, dividends or cash flows. The main issue in the case was whether Bech-Bruun, based on its advice to North Channel Bank, was liable for the tax administration's loss because of the unjustified refunds of dividend tax. 3

The Supreme Court stated that when assessing whether a lawyer, when advising a client, has acted in a manner that gives rise to liability towards the tax authorities, it is decisive whether the lawyer recklessly disregarded the interests of the tax authorities. Whether this is the case depends on an overall assessment of the circumstances at the time when the lawyer gave the advice. 4

https://doi.org/10.1515/9783111389271-008

5 A key element in the assessment is whether the transactions that the lawyer advised on had a commercial purpose and whether the transactions were of an unusual nature.

b) Judgment of the Court

6 The Supreme Court thus found that Bech-Bruun had acted negligently towards the Tax Administration. Furthermore, the Supreme Court found that it had to be assumed that there was the necessary causal link between Bech-Bruun's negligent advice and the fact that the Tax Administration had suffered a loss as a result of the wrongful refund of dividend tax.

7 The Supreme Court found that Bech-Bruun must have realised that there was an obvious risk that North Channel Bank, together with others, was involved in preparing a model for an unjustified refund of dividend tax and as such recklessly disregarded the interests of the tax authorities by advising the bank as it did, including by stating in its legal opinion that the bank 'should not be subject' to civil or criminal liability for its participation. Bech-Bruun was thus liable towards the tax authorities. Under the present circumstances, the fact that Bech-Bruun had included a number of assumptions and reservations in its legal opinion could not lead to a different assessment.

8 The case concerned an amount of just over DKK 700 million plus interest, as the Tax Administration had reduced its claim totalling approximately DKK 1.135 billion with payments that the Tax Administration had received through settlements with various parties.

9 Based on considerations of adequacy, the Supreme Court found that Bech-Bruun's liability for damages, based on an overall assessment, should only include an amount of DKK 400 million and thus not the Tax Administration's full claim of just over DKK 700 million.

c) Commentary

10 The main question in the case was whether Bech-Bruun, on the basis of its advice to North Channel Bank, was liable for the loss that the tax authorities suffered as a result of unjustified reimbursement of dividend tax to the bank's customers. The Supreme Court examined whether a tax advisor acts in a manner that gives rise to liability to the tax authorities, when giving advice to a client, by – in performance of its advisory role to the bank – recklessly disregarding the interests of the Tax Administration.

The Supreme Court thus assesses to what extent Bech-Bruun – based on the knowledge available to them – had to realise that there was an obvious risk that the advice would be used as a basis for North Channel Bank to become involved in devising a manner in which to receive an unauthorised refund of dividend tax. 11

Although it has been discussed whether this case endorses a stricter assessment of liability of tax advisors, the decision is in accordance with prior cases regarding liability of tax advisors. 12

2. Østre Landsret (High Court, Eastern Division) 28 September 2023, UfR (Ugeskrift for Retsvæsen, Weekly Law Report) U 2024.172 Ø: Liability for Collision between Grandchild and Ironman Sports Participant

a) Brief Summary of the Facts

This case concerns the assessment of liability and duty of care for a child in relation to personal injury. 13

C and his granddaughter, B, born in 2012, were spectators at an Ironman competition, where A crashed his bike when he and B collided on a road. 14

A was cycling in a straight line on the road when the accident occurred. B had run across the road several times prior to the collision, at times alone. 15

The District Court had acquitted C of liability for any damages as C and a witness, L, had stated that C, shortly before the collision, was holding onto B's hands and C had not neglected any duty of care. 16

As a result, A appealed the decision to the High Court. 17

b) Judgment of the Court

The High Court found that C had breached his duty of supervision in relation to the child and thereby incurred liability for the injury suffered by A. Based on the evidence, including the nature of the event and the course of events and the fact that B, prior to the collision, had run across the road several times. The High Court found no basis for reducing or cancelling the liability for damages due to A's own fault or acceptance of risk. 18

The High Court further found that the nature of the incident was not such that A could be deemed to have accepted the risk of the collision with the child on the road by accepting the organisers' conditions and disclaimers. 19

c) Commentary

20 The main question in the case was whether C had neglected his duty of care for his grandchild by letting her run across the road at an Ironman event. Even though there were several other spectators close to the road, the High Court found that C was liable for A's injuries from the collision as B was free to run across the road several times, which C should have prevented her from doing. This case highlights that adults who bring children to sporting events are subject to a duty of care for the children they bring, and, as such, are liable for damage that the children cause.

21 Furthermore, the case shows that even though participants in public sporting events such as an Ironman competition know that there are spectators on the road, the participants cannot be held liable due to their own fault or their acceptance of risk for injuries occurring when spectators run onto the road.

3. Østre Landsret (High Court, Eastern Division) 20 February 2024, UfR (Ugeskrift for Retsvæsen, Weekly Law Report) U 2024.2317 Ø: Product Liability for Electricity Company for Supply of Electricity

a) Brief Summary of the Facts

22 The main issue in this case concerns the liability of an electricity company for property damage caused by a fire resulting from the supply of electricity with excessive voltage.

23 In 2017, a fire broke out in a heating unit in D's property, causing damage to the building and personal property. D was compensated by his insurance company, A Forsikring A/S, which sued the electricity company, El A/S, as there had been a supply failure on the same day that affected the supply of electricity to D's property, among others. The cause of the fire was considered to be an overvoltage in the local electricity supply system.

24 The question was whether El A/S was liable under the Danish Product Liability Act.

b) Judgment of the Court

The High Court found that El A/S is a grid company as defined in the Danish Electricity Supply Act, that El A/S operates a distribution grid, and that El A/S transforms voltages in the distribution grid from 50 kV down to 0.4 kV through substations, which supply consumers with electricity at a voltage of 230 V. 25

The High Court stated that sec 4(1) of the Danish Product Liability Act must be understood to mean that El A/S is to be considered a 'producer' within the meaning of the provision. The High Court found that there was a causal link between the damage and the claim raised. 26

The voltage had exceeded 230 V by approximately 33% and, as a result, the electricity supplied had to be considered defective under the Danish Product Liability Act. El A/S therefore had to compensate for the damage caused by the fire, unless El A/S was exempt from liability under sec 7 of the Danish Product Liability Act. 27

The question was whether El A/S had proved that the overvoltage was not present at the time the electricity was put into circulation. 28

It appeared from the connection provisions that El A/S made the distribution network available to and from the 'point of connection', and that the company had to maintain a satisfactory voltage quality at the point of connection. 29

The supply failure was due to a spontaneous cable fault that occurred on a cable between two cable cabinets and resulted in fuses tripping in a substation. As the cable fault and the resulting overvoltage occurred at a point prior to the cable cabinet which D's property was connected to, the High Court found that El A/S had not yet put the electricity into circulation within the meaning of sec 7(2) of the Danish Product Liability Act at that time. 30

Thus, El A/S had not proved that there were grounds for exemption from liability under sec 7 of the Danish Product Liability Act. There was no basis for reducing or cancelling the compensation. The High Court therefore upheld the insurance company's claim and found El A/S liable. 31

c) Commentary

This case states the extent of arts 5, 6(1) and 7(2) of the Product Liability Act and provides an elaboration as to when a producer is liable for damage caused by their product. Furthermore, it answers the question of whether the producer is exempt from liability as regards the question of when the defect occurs. It shows that electricity companies are liable for any damage present before the 32 electricity was introduced on the market within the meaning of sec 7(2) which in this case is when it reaches the cable cabinet.

4. Østre Landsret (High Court, Eastern Division) 15 August 2024, UfR (Ugeskrift for Retsvæsen, Weekly Law Report) U 2024.5043 Ø: Proof of Causation between a Car Collision and Physical and Mental Harm

a) Brief Summary of the Facts

33 The case concerns the legal assessment of causation versus the medical assessment of causation in a case where the claimant suffered WAD (whiplash associated disorder) after a car accident.

34 In February 2013, the claimant (27 years old) suffered physical pain and metal problems after a car accident where he collided with a taxi travelling at 60 km/hour and crashed into a tree. The car caught fire immediately after the claimant had managed to escape from the vehicle.

35 It appeared from the policeman's report conducted on-site, the pre-hospital journal (from the ambulance), phone messages the next day, as well as the record of questioning the day after that, that the claimant was suffering from pain. However, this was not reflected in the discharge papers from the emergency ward, as the claimant explained that the pain emerged when he arrived at his home after being discharged.

36 Subsequently, the claimant experienced mental issues of a multifactorial nature, inter alia: sadness, apathy, despondency, flashbacks, restlessness, dyssomnia and irritability. The claimant's general practitioner diagnosed 'moderate depression', for which the claimant was prescribed antidepressants. The dose was not reduced until June 2016 and the claimant was still suffering from said symptoms in 2018. Physically, he suffered from radiating pain in his neck, which rendered him unfit to work.

b) Judgment of the Court

37 Like the District Court (*byretten*), the Eastern High Court, in upholding the judgment, found that there was a causal link between the accident and both the mental and physical problems.

In reaching this result, the court relied, among other things, on an opinion given by the Medico-Legal Council in February 2017. 38

The Medico-Legal Council noted that the pre-hospital report only referred to 'pain in the neck' and that the claimant did not express any pain in the emergency ward. The neck pain was not mentioned specifically until the end of April 2013. Because there were no medical statements about the accident immediately following the accident, the Medico-Legal Council could not establish a causal link between the *physical pain* and the accident. 39

Despite a lack of medical statements, the Medico-Legal Council established that it was more than 50 % likely that there was a causal link between the accident and the *mental harm* suffered by the claimant. This result was deduced from the severity of the accident itself and from the fact that there were no recorded mental issues before the accident. 40

c) Commentary

Firstly, the ruling illustrates that a court can, and will, set aside the assessment of the Medico-Legal Council in favour of a legal assessment. This is clearly reflected in the court's approach: 'Af de anførte grunde og ud fra en samlet vurdering af sagens omstændigheder, herunder de lægelige vurderinger og karakteren af ulykken, finder retten det herefter ud fra en erstatningsretlig bedømmelse tilstrækkeligt sandsynliggjort …'.[1] 41

Overall, the decision highlights that the test of causation is basically a legal assessment ('en erstatningsretlig bedømmelse') where various considerations can be taken into account, including the onset of the claimant's symptoms and whether the claimant had full working capacity before the incident. Since the Medico-Legal Council stated that no medical records of any pain existed within three days after the accident, it was unable to establish a causal link. However, based on an assessment of the full facts of the case, the court concluded that the requirement of causation was fulfilled with regard to the acute neck pain. The reference to the nature of the accident ('karakteren af ulykken') underscores that the court took into account that the harm to the claimant was caused by a so-called high-energy or high-speed accident. 42

1 Which may be translated as follows: 'For the reasons stated and based on a comprehensive assessment of the circumstances of the case, including the medical evaluations and the nature of the accident, the court therefore, based on an assessment under tort law, finds it sufficiently demonstrated …'. The author's translation.

C. Literature

1. *Søren Halling-Overgaard/Thomas Bøgelund Norvold*, Revisors erstatnings- og disciplinæransvar [Auditors' liability] (DJØF Forlag, Jurist- og Økonomforbundets Forlag, 5th edn 2024)

43 This book is an updated version of the previous editions. The book thus includes the latest regulations, legal basis, judgments and rulings that are relevant for assessing accountants' liability and disciplinary liability.

44 Based on the Danish Auditing Act, the book discusses the conditions for the establishment of auditors' liability for damages when issuing endorsements and statements.

45 The book also examines auditors' liability for damages outside the scope of the Danish Auditors Act, for example in connection with tax advice, financial advice and the preparation of financial statements.

46 The Supreme Court's judgments in the *E-hus*, *Memorycard* and *Bech-Bruun* cases are reviewed, as well as the High Courts' judgments in the compensation cases against the auditors of Roskilde Bank, EBH-Bank, EIK-Bank and Løkken Sparekasse.

2. *Søren Halling-Overgaard/Birgitte Sølvkær Olesen*, Er erstatningsansvaret for skatterådgivere blevet skærpet efter U.2024.786H? [Has the liability for tax advisors increased after U.2024.786H?], Revision og regnskabsvæsen (RR) RR.7.2024.36

47 This article examines the decision of the Danish Supreme Court in November 2023 in the case that the Danish tax authorities brought against the law firm Bech-Bruun. Several scholars have raised the question of whether the Supreme Court's judgment has increased tax advisors' liability for damages. The authors examine tax advisors' liability in this case in connection with earlier cases that were brought before the Supreme Court.

48 The article focuses on the factors the authors find to have been of importance for the result reached by the Supreme Court in U.2024.746H and at the same time examines the extent to which the judgment is likely to have an impact on the tax advice (and other advice) currently provided by accountants, lawyers and other tax advisors.

3. *Niels Anker T Rostock-Jensen*, Post-M&A garantibrudstvister i erstatningsretlig belysning, særligt om tabsopgørelser og 'Multipelspørgsmålet' [Post-M&A breach of warranty disputes in tort law, especially on loss calculations and the 'Multiplier Question'], Erhvervsjuridisk Tidsskrift (ET) ET.2024.184

This article deals with loss calculations and the assessment of evidence in post-M&A cases, which is a sparsely covered topic in Danish law. As part of the treatment of the topic, several comments are made on the context of the law of damages for a post-M&A dispute, including the way in which losses are calculated. The article further addresses the interaction between the transfer agreement and the calculation of losses, the significance of the purchase price and some more general observations related to the burden of proof. 49

4. *Vibe Ulfbeck/Anne Sofie Bagger Tranberg*, Produktansvar for elektricitet i et liberaliseret marked [Product liability for electricity in a liberalised market], Erhvervsjuridisk Tidsskrift (ET) ET.2024.002

This article examines the question of who the producer is in cases regarding damage caused by electricity. 50

The article examines this question based on Danish case law and in light of a recent judgment from the European Court of Justice, which states that electricity is only fully produced when it has been transformed into a usable voltage. In addition, the article considers whether a claim can be brought against either the grid operator or the electricity trading company under the rules on intermediary liability or on a contractual basis. 51

5. *Tina Braad/Esben Korsgaard*, Byggeledelsens erstatningsansvar for forsinkelse [Construction management liability for delays], Tidsskrift for Bolig- og Byggeret (TBB) TBB2024.213

This article deals with liability of the construction management as delays in building and construction projects often result in the developer having to compensate 52 the contractors' financial losses if the causes of delay justify the contractors' claim for an extension of time. In this article, both older and newer arbitration case law is considered in order to examine the legal and evidentiary basis for the client's claim for damages against the technical consultant in situations where the developer attributes the delay of a construction project to the consultant's inadequate construction management.

Colm Peter McGrath

VIII. England and Wales

A. Legislation[1]

1. The Damages (Personal Injury) (England and Wales) Order 2024 (SI 2024/1261)

There was no major primary legislation relevant to tort law in England and Wales in 2024. 1

Yet, whilst it can hardly be said that this secondary legislation, introduced by the Lord Chancellor in December 2024 under the powers vested in her by the Damages Act 1996, would attract true headline attention, it is important and worth noting nevertheless in that it updates the personal injury discount rate. 2

That rate is the statutorily set multiplier which the courts, when calculating the lump sum damages payable to the claimant, use to adjust that sum in an effort to avoid over-compensation and take into account the benefit of being awarded damages in one go. The rate is also informally known as the so-called Ogden Discount Rate named after the Ogden Tables calculated by a government-led group of relevant actuarial experts, which, based on the relevant multipliers, are used in practice by lawyers and insurers to arrive at final sum calculations.[2] 3

Having been at 2.5% for over a decade, a controversial decision in February 2017 by the then Lord Chancellor (and future, if short-lived, Prime Minister) Liz Truss saw it set it at -0.75%. Having crept up in 2019 to -0.25%, the new rate will, from 11 January 2025 be 0.5% and, as such, sums will return to being discounted in practice rather than inflated to a degree as under the years of negative rates. This change was undertaken after an extended review by an expert panel which, given the current economic climate, identified a risk of significant over-compensation if the previous rate was to be maintained.[3] 4

Whilst the change drew little particular criticism by the sector, two potential consequences of it are worth noting. The first is that the attendant risk of large 5

---

1 My thanks to my student Camille Golowski, who provided excellent research assistance in relation to this year's report.

2 The current tables can be found here: <https://www.gov.uk/government/publications/ogden-tables-actuarial-compensation-tables-for-injury-and-death>.

3 See the materials available from the Panel, as well as a Statement of Reasons and a likely Impact Assessment here <https://www.gov.uk/guidance/personal-injury-discount-rate>.

https://doi.org/10.1515/9783111389271-009

lump sums, say in the case of catastrophically injured children in need of lifelong care, now being subject to a discount may tempt claimants towards greater uptake of the opportunity to recover damages by way of a periodical payment order. The second is that this will inevitably reduce to some extent the overall damages bill faced by the National Health Service.[4]

B. Cases

1. *Paul and another v Royal Wolverhampton NHS Trust; Polmear and another v Royal Cornwall Hospitals NHS Trust; Purchase v Ahmed*, United Kingdom Supreme Court (UKSC) 2 [2024] Weekly Law Reports (WLR) 417:[5] Negligence; Psychiatric Harm; Secondary Victims; Medical Negligence

a) Brief Summary of the Facts

6 In these three joined decisions, heard together by the Supreme Court, the Justices were faced with slight variants on a heart-rending theme. In all three cases, the negligence of the defendant's employee medical staff was responsible for the death of a patient that was witnessed by each of the respective claimants, who were family members of the deceased in each case. As a result of what they had witnessed, all the claimants had suffered from a recognised psychiatric injury and brought suit in the tort of negligence.

7 In *Paul* the deceased had been negligently misdiagnosed over a year earlier, dying of a heart attack during a shopping trip in front of his two young daughters, the claimants.

8 Likewise, in *Polmear*, over a year earlier, the deceased, a six-year-old girl, had been misdiagnosed. The underlying condition returned during a school trip and her parents, the claimants, were summoned to take her home. She deteriorated rapidly and, having tried to resuscitate her in advance of medical assistance arriving, both her parents were present when she died.

4 See the musings of the Impact Assessment, above.

5 Judgment available online at <https://www.supremecourt.uk/cases/uksc-2022–0038>. Noted by *J Morgan* [2024] 83 Cambridge Law Journal (CLJ) 214; *R Stevens* (2024) 140 Law Quarterly Review (LQR) 346; C *Purshouse* (2024) 40 Professional Negligence (PN) 139; *R Mulheron* (2025) 93 Medico-Legal Journal (MedLegJ) 5.

Finally, in *Purchase*, the claimant's twenty-year old daughter had been misdiagnosed only days earlier. The claimant returned home in the evening to find her daughter motionless on her bed but still warm. Opening her daughter's mouth to attempt resuscitation, the claimant was faced with blood and bodily fluids spilling out. Her daughter was confirmed deceased by the paramedics on arrival. The claimant had not noticed that, very shortly before she had arrived home, her daughter had phoned her mobile phone. The minutes long voicemail had captured her daughter's dying breaths. 9

As harrowing as these cases undoubtedly were for those involved, the shared doctrinal gist was simple. It was beyond a doubt that the defendants were causally responsible for a negligently inflicted recognised form of actionable damage. As such, the case hinged on the question of whether the defendants owed a duty of care in the tort of negligence *in relation to* such harm. If they did not, then no claim could be advanced. 10

The law in relation to when a duty of care is owed in relation to psychiatric harm in England and Wales is, at best, a messy sub-category where successive decisions of the apex court have resulted in the steady accretion of special rules and restrictions on recovery here. The nakedly policy-driven nature of much of the decision-making here has been the subject of much academic commentary throughout this period. Indeed, famously, as Lord Hoffmann put it himself, the 'search for principle has been called off',[6] albeit the one keystone of liability here is that to have any hope of recovery, the claimant must suffer a medically recognised psychiatric illness as a result of the defendant's negligence. 11

Where the claimant is objectively imperilled themselves, it suffices that it was reasonably foreseeable that physical harm would result, even if all that results is psychiatric harm. Such 'primary' victims thus benefit from a relatively straightforward route to recovery. Where the claimant has merely witnessed another's death or imperilment, matters are rather less generous. In the argot the law has adopted here, they are 'secondary' victims. Here, the main bar on whether a duty will be owed are the so-called *Alcock* factors[7]: the claimant must witness the event with their own unaided senses, they must have a close relationship of love and affection with the person, and they must witness the event or the immediate aftermath of it. 12

6 *Frost v Chief Constable of South Yorkshire Police* [1999] 2 Appeal Cases (AC) 455, per Lord Hoffmann at 511B.

7 Drawn from the seminal decision in *Alcock v Chief Constable of South Yorkshire Police* [1992] 1 AC 310, these impose restrictions on the relationship between the claimant and the deceased or endangered party and the means of experience and temporal relation between the claimant and the relevant event.

13 The second of those requirements often damns any potential claim. Whilst one may well love one's fellow man in principle, bystanders cannot, the logic of the English law goes, love a stranger sufficiently that they deserve protection against the effects of witnessing their negligently-caused death. Here, however, this was, sadly, not a challenge for the claimants. Nor was the need to experience first-hand and immediately. Rather, the cases hinged on the thornier matter of what exactly it was that needed to be witnessed. Was it sufficient that the claimants had ultimately only witnessed what was undoubtedly the most impactful culmination of the negligence, even if they had not seen the negligence itself? In context, did the duty owed by medical staff extend beyond their patients to encompass the risk of psychiatric harm as a result of witnessing the death of a family member?

14 At first instance, the claims in *Paul* and, subsequently, *Polmear* had been allowed to proceed. The claim in *Purchase* had been struck out. All three were taken together in the Court of Appeal. There,[8] the Court held that in cases such as these, it was necessary that the relevant event that the secondary victims had to witness could not be removed in time from the negligence.[9] In essence, a later horrific event caused by the negligence was insufficient as the basis for a claim here. Were that the case, there would not be sufficient proximity between the claimant and defendant to justify imposing a duty of care.

15 In practice, the decision hinged on the simple matter of whether the governing authority here could be avoided. This was the earlier decision of the Court of Appeal in *Taylor v A Novo (UK) Ltd.*[10] There, the claimant had witnessed her mother die from a condition caused by an accident in the workplace weeks earlier. The Court of Appeal had there denied the claim on the basis that merely witnessing the latter consequence of the defendant's negligence was insufficient to establish the necessary proximity. The difficulty of drawing a temporal line past which a duty would not be owed, and the general trend of restricting recovery in this area supplied the decisive policy reasoning here.[11]

16 Despite discussion of whether a distinction could be drawn between the medical negligence context in *Paul* and the classical cases of secondary victims recovering for psychiatric injury in which the relevant rules had been developed and where the defendant's negligence occasioned an 'accident' that was witnessed by the claimant, the court in *Paul* felt themselves bound to apply *Novo* and deny any duty here. That said, there was much open doubt about the logic and defen-

8 [2022] 2 WLR 917: [2022] Court of Appeal, Civil Division (EWCA Civ) 12.

9 Para 95.

10 [2014] Queen's Bench (QB) 150.

11 See the Court of Appeal's decision (no 9 above) paras 54–58.

sibility of such restrictions on recovery here, with the Master of the Rolls, Sir Geoffrey Vos noting quite bluntly, 'If I were starting with a clean sheet, I can quite see why secondary victims in these cases ought to be seen to be sufficiently proximate to the defendants to be allowed to recover damages for their psychiatric injury. Since, however, this court is bound by *Novo*, it is for the Supreme Court to decide whether to depart from the law as stated...'.[12]

Thus, to the Supreme Court the claimants went, where an enlarged bench of 17
seven justices heard the gathered cases, suggesting that for the first time in decades, the law here might be ripe for some active pruning and re-orientation.

b) Judgment of the Court

By a majority of six to one, the Supreme Court dismissed the appeal, confirming 18
that there was no duty of care owed in such situations. Lord Leggatt and Lady Rose JJSC provided the majority judgment, with Lord Carloway JSC providing a brief concurring opinion considering the relationship to Scots law here. Lord Burrows JSC wrote a lengthy dissent.

For the majority, the tenor of the decision was clear from two foundations. 19
First, the gravity of the starting point. A reminder that at common law (and despite statutory intervention from the nineteenth century onwards)[13] the death of one person did not found a cause of action in another person.[14] From this cheerful foundation, any such duty owed to a third party in relation to harm occasioned to another must be seen as exceptional and, as such, tightly controlled. This was particularly the case where, as in the category of cases at hand, it is not the death itself, but witnessing the death that lies at the heart of the claim.[15]

Second, the recognition that the rules here had been developed in the context, 20
as they put it, of 'accident' cases. That is, the happenstance that the law here has been made in the context of the secondary victim witnessing an accident brought about by the defendant's negligence, which has injured or at least imperilled another with whom the secondary victim has the necessary close bond of love and affection. As they framed it, the key question was whether the rules developed to account for an already exceptional category of duty in that context could be taken

12 Para 12.
13 Whilst the original dates from 1846, the presently applicable version can be found in the Fatal Accidents Act 1976.
14 Para 2.
15 Para 4.

to include cases where the death was caused not by an 'accident' but by a medical condition that the defendant had failed to diagnose or otherwise properly treat.[16]

21 From this shared starting point, the answer appeared inevitable. No such duty could be owed. The Justices were clear that it is impossible to conclude an answer without considering the principles that apply generally to the liability of medical practitioners to third parties.[17] But, as it was, the case as presented by the claimants was focused on demonstrating that no such consideration was required. This was not, they suggested, any sort of novel duty, rather it clearly fell within the framework of the rules established by previous cases in the area of psychiatric injury. In reaching the opposite conclusion, this question dominated much of the majority's reasoning.

22 Central to their conclusion was framing the central trio of authorities – none of which the claimants suggested should be revisited – as involving 'accidents', in that they involved a sudden incident, witnessed by the claimant, in which persons had been imperilled or killed.[18] Likewise, the clear impetus throughout these cases was both restrictive and attuned to avoiding distinctions which would 'offend most people's sense of justice'.[19]

23 Whilst there had, since that framework had been established, been a range of cases in the medical negligence context, these cases had adopted different approaches to that medical context and had been heard by lower courts. Given, as they framed it, the central doctrinal requirements for imposing a duty in favour of secondary victims here have been decided in the context of 'accidents', it remained an open question whether this was the case in the medical context where there was, as it were, no such 'accident'. This assumed distinction was crucial to the ultimate result.

24 The key reasoning in this part of the judgment lay in rejecting the view of the lower courts that there could be no recovery where what one had witnessed was the consequence of an earlier act of negligence. This idea that recovery was impossible where the negligence had caused two events separated in time, only the latter of which the claimant had witnessed, which was central to how the lower courts had understood *Novo*, was rejected.[20] Rather, the claim had failed as the claimant had not witnessed an 'accident'. The same could be said of each of the claimants in the combined cases in *Paul*.

16 Para 5.
17 Paras 24 f, 50.
18 Paras 26–50.
19 Para 49.
20 Para 90.

As is clear, the concept of an 'accident' was elevated to crucial importance in secondary victim cases. It was this, rather than any length of time between the negligence and the event witnessed by the claimant, that matters.[21] The majority defined this as 'an unexpected and unintended event which causes injury (or a risk of injury) to a victim by violent external means'.[22] Turning to the claimants before them, they had not witnessed any such 'external, traumatic, event which immediately causes injury or death to a primary victim'.[23] As such, no duty was owed. 25

The preference for this emphasis on 'accident' was supported by three justifications.[24] First, as it is a discrete event, this provides a relatively clear distinction between those who have experienced it and those who have not. Second, the general public would intuitively understand a line drawn between those who had witnessed a loved one being put in harm's way and those who had not. Third, whilst it is difficult to distinguish between primary and secondary victims in the context of an accident case, in the cases at hand, there was no question that the secondary victim might have concurrently been in fear for their own wellbeing. These distinctions supported reliance on 'accident' as the crucial distinction here. 26

Whilst there was little by way of reinvention evident in *Paul*, the majority did amend the existing rules in two important ways. The requirement that what the claimant witness be a 'horrific' event was discarded. There was, as the majority put it, 'no available Richter scale of horror' against which different incidents could be judged.[25] It had been a mistake for earlier cases to elevate this to the status of a formal requirement for a duty of care.[26] Likewise, it was not necessary for the claimant to suffer a sudden shock as the relevant causal mechanism. Discarding this rather nineteenth century notion of how psychiatric illness arises, the majority confirmed that all that is required is a causal connection rather than demonstrating 'the neurological or psychological mechanism by which the illness was induced'.[27] 27

Turning to the broader principled basis that the majority regarded as the necessary basis for any decision here, the same denial of a duty of care was evident.[28] Acting as a cross-check on the approach through the cases on secondary victims 28

---

21 Para 91 f.
22 Paras 24, 52.
23 Paras 90, 142.
24 Paras 107–110.
25 Para 75.
26 Para 76.
27 Para 74.
28 Para 124 ff.

and psychiatric illness, the question here was simply whether a medical practitioner could owe a duty of care to third-party family members. Whilst it was not impossible that this might be the case where, say, a patient was negligently discharged with an infectious or sexually transmissible disease,[29] or the clinician has otherwise assumed responsibility to the family member,[30] on orthodox principles it was not the case that a duty was owed to third-party family members in relation to their mental wellbeing.[31] To put it bluntly, any such duty on hospitals and doctors would 'go beyond what, in the current state of our society, is reasonably regarded as the nature and scope of their role'.[32]

29 In a lengthy and powerful dissent, Lord Burrows took a rather different view of the matter. Central to his analysis was a focus on the death of the primary victim as the relevant event, not any concept of 'accidents or external events'.[33] As he noted, it was obvious that, if the death was the relevant event, then all other existing doctrinal requirements were met. It was also clearly the case that it was witnessing the actual death that was the gist of the claimants' harm here.[34]

30 Whilst he regarded this, as had the claimants, as a plausible application of the existing doctrinal framework, if it were instead viewed as a development of that framework, he felt that it was clearly a justifiable and merely incremental step.[35] In answer to the majority's concern for a crisp delineation of responsibilities here, Lord Burrows noted that the fact there might be a lag between the defendant's negligence and the relevant injurious consequence was not usually regarded as a barrier on owing a duty. As he pithily observed, if a builder negligently builds a doorframe, it is no objection to liability that it does not collapse for a number of months after that point.[36] Most concerningly, he noted that the law as set out by the majority would effectively rule out claims for psychiatric illness suffered by secondary victims in the medical negligence context almost entirely.[37] Such a decision only risked arbitrary distinctions in the rare situations the requirement would be met in the healthcare context. Ultimately, in a world where Parliament had, by its inaction, left the courts to police the acceptable boundaries of liability

29 Para 134 f.
30 Para 131.
31 Para 136 f.
32 Para 138.
33 Para 198.
34 Para 199.
35 Para 201.
36 Para 227 f.
37 Paras 205–211, 250.

here, treating such a factual distinction as, in effect, a legal one, was unattractive and unprincipled.[38]

c) Commentary

Paul is a seminal but somewhat odd decision for the English law here. As much as it is clearly conservative (if not, indeed, regressive) in its approach to the boundaries of recovery in this area, it represents the first time in decades that the apex court has been able to squarely consider the law in relation to recovery for secondary victims. Hope that this might be the cause for reconsideration of some of the odder rules here went unrewarded, albeit there were some positive signs that can be taken from it. As one leading commentator rightly described it, it was 'a leading case that never was'.[39] 31

Primarily, *Paul* can be seen as supplying clarity here. Even if one disagrees with the underlying reasoning or its doctrinal expression, it is now undoubtedly the lynchpin of the law here, and the lens through which the law on recovery by secondary victims must now be seen. The regime as established in the decades prior has been affirmed and, if anything, placed on a firmer footing than it was before. As with previous recent cases reported in the Yearbook,[40] a particularly striking aspect of the case was the analytical spin placed on this rather intricate edifice of rules designed to limit liability for negligently inflicted harm here. Far from the restrictive and almost arbitrary rules that they have often been taken to represent by both scholarship and, famously (see Lord Hoffmann above) by the courts themselves, the majority in *Paul* performed a cunning reversal. From the starting point that there is no recovery in principle in relation to death, this framework (indeed arguably any framework to reduce the scope of liability) was in fact true to the underpinning principle. It is one thing to uphold settled legal rules, no matter how much criticism they have drawn, it is an altogether more impressive feat to inform the audience that the criticism has missed the point all along! 32

The cost here in practice is clear and, frankly, unconvincingly dealt with by the majority. In an attempt to adopt a principled approach not only have we been left with a maddingly frustrating definition of an 'accident' but the law 33

38 Para 208.

39 *Morgan*, [2024] 83 CLJ 214.

40 See eg, *McCulloch*, noted in *CP McGrath*, England and Wales, in: BC Steininger/E Karner (eds), European Tort Law (ETL) 2023 (2024) 179, no 38.

has been allowed to take on the shape of the emblematic (but far from exclusive) type of case in which these issues have traditionally arisen, to wit large-scale sudden accidents. Furthermore, an entire factual setting, the one at stake in *Paul* has, effectively, been ruled on by operation of these principles rather than through the application of any particularly decisive policy argument here.[41]

34 It may well be in line with a different broader set of principles starting from the question of what duty doctors owe to third parties, and it is not wrong to suggest that this question likewise tends to receive a restrictive response, but such reasoning clearly played second fiddle to an approach that sought to vindicate the previous authorities here in general. Indeed, some commentary has been critical not of the result, but the fact that that principled approach led straightforwardly to the given result and the Court, in effect, took the long way round to get there themselves.[42]

35 The switch to a principle-based approach to the question at hand, and the relative brevity of the treatment the central question gets using this approach raises a puzzling conundrum: If the law here really is principled, as those final pages assumes, what was the need for the preceding, more traditional approach to parsing the authorities? Come to think of it, if such principles are present, why have successive courts previously failed to identify them? Despite the rebuff that Lord Hoffmann's earlier and admirable honesty drew from the majority in *Paul*,[43] it is hard to believe that successive generations of leading English jurists had somehow overlooked such handy principles in seeking an answer to an undoubtedly thorny legal problem. As has been flagged in previous Yearbook reports, the turn towards principle in the duty of care cases continues to be one of the defining characteristics of contemporary tort law in England and Wales.[44]

36 Whilst for naught in the case itself, it is impossible not to be somewhat sympathetic to Lord Burrows' dissent here, whether on policy grounds, or at least the manner in which he approached the case. There was clearly another way to draw the undoubtedly necessary line on recovery here, and not one that would rule out almost any event grounded in the healthcare context. Cuttingly, as Lord Burrows

---

41 *Purshouse* (2024) 40 PN 139 notes, at 141, that this might well be a feature not a bug.

42 See *Stevens* (2024) 140 LQR 346. As he not unfairly suggests; '*Paul* itself involved what was, straightforwardly, a failure to prevent others to whom no duty had been voluntarily assumed from suffering injury'.

43 Described variously as a 'lament' with which they did not agree and, by Lord Burrows, as a counsel of despair at paras 58 and 204 respectively.

44 See eg, *N v Poole Borough Council* [2019] UKSC 25; [2020] AC 780; reported by *K Oliphant*, England and Wales, in: K Oliphant/BC Steininger (eds), European Tort Law (ETL) 2019 (2020) 141, no 6.

noted, even where we to wish to adopt the 'accident' model set out by the majority, there is a pressing and unanswered question about to whom the event must be external?[45] It is evidently the case that one's relative falling dead in front of you as a result of the negligence of a third party medical professional is an event convincingly analysed as being external to the claimant as much as the majority sought to suggest that it must be external to the deceased victims in *Paul.*

In an irony impossible to miss, with the broader discussion in *Paul* hinging in part on the appropriate role of the courts in developing the law around Parliament's inaction (evident in the choice *not* to implement the Law Commission's 1998 report into liability for psychiatric harm), Lord Burrows had himself been the Law Commissioner who oversaw that report. Having missed one opportunity to put the law on a firmer footing, he has now missed a second with the decision of his judicial colleagues to plough a different furrow. 37

Ultimately, if there is any positive to be taken from *Paul* (other than by the insurers of healthcare institutions), it is in the degree of pruning that took place along the way. It is clearly a positive move to abandon any requirement that the court attempt to parse the gravity of horror of a situation that has befallen a claimant and caused a psychiatric illness, likewise the mechanism by which it has been caused. Whilst the law is correct to police a necessary causal requirement here, it strays into either unanswerable moral or medical territory to have ever required them to do more. 38

2. *Tindall v Chief Constable of Thames Valley Police* [2024] UKSC 33, [2024] 3 WLR 822:[46] Negligence; Public Authority; Omission; Failure to Warn; Preventing Alternative Aid

a) Brief Summary of the Facts

In the early hours of the morning, Mr Kendall lost control of his car due to a patch of black ice on the road. Drawing on his knowledge from previous work as a road-gritter, Mr Kendall realised that the black ice posed an imminent danger to other road users and, despite his injuries, stood by the road waving in an effort to slow oncoming traffic and reduce the chances of a further accident. 39

45 Para 211.
46 Judgment available online at <https://www.supremecourt.uk/cases/uksc-2023-0059>. Noted by *J Lee* (2025) 41 PN 5; *R Geraghty* (2025) 1 Journal of Personal Injury Litigation (JPILi) C1.

40 He called the non-emergency police number. The call handler acknowledged that the road could cause problems in that state and, having dispatched officers to the scene, informed Mr Kendall that the officers had been made aware about the ice, and that the road was 'dark and fast'.[47] Whilst at the scene, they had placed a 'Police Slow' sign on one side of the carriageway informing oncoming drivers, swept the road for debris and, albeit without communicating the need for urgency, requested a road gritter. Shortly thereafter, with Mr Kendall safely dispatched to the hospital, they packed up the sign and returned to the station along with the other emergency services who had attended.

41 The claimant's husband, Mr Tindall, was killed less than half an hour later when a third party driving in the opposite direction lost control on the same patch of ice, causing a fatal head-on collision. The case was straightforward. The defendant accepted that but for the arrival of the police, Mr Kendall would have continued to try and alert other road users and the claimant and that nothing had been done by the police to encourage, direct, or require Mr Kendall to stop his efforts and leave to hospital.[48]

42 The claimant brought suit in negligence, the action hinging on whether a duty of care was owed in this situation. The primary challenge lay in how one might frame the action. If the situation was one in which the police officers had simply failed to confer a benefit by their actions, then copious recent authority suggested that no duty would be owed. If, however, by their intervention, they had in fact made matters worse, or created the relevant danger, or assumed responsibility in relation to the claimant for the harm they suffered, a duty would plausibly be owed and the case could proceed to trial.

43 Given the fact-sensitive nature of this exercise in categorisation, the claim had been allowed to proceed at first instance, but struck out on the duty point by the Court of Appeal. As Lord Justice Stuart-Smith saw it, the mere presence of the police had led Mr Kendall to silently assume they would behave in a certain way, influencing his decision to go to hospital.[49] Although they had responded 'ineffectually', this was a case in which that had simply failed to confer the benefit that greater competence might have done. Nor did the officers' control over the scene (or power to take control) suffice to justify a duty and there could be no assumption of responsibility to drivers at large in relation to a danger that the police were not responsible for.

44 The claimant appealed to the Supreme Court.

47 Para 6.
48 Para 17.
49 Para 19.

b) Judgment of the Court

In a unanimous decision, Lords Leggatt and Burrows dismissed the appeal. There was no duty of care owed in this situation and, as such, there could be no claim in negligence for the attendant harm. 45

As a starting point, the Justices emphasised that it was beyond dispute that the failure to take steps to protect drivers from the danger was a 'serious dereliction of their public duty *owed to society at large*'.[50] Indeed, the officers had been referred for criminal prosecution by an independent panel (albeit the state declined to bring charges), had been subject to disciplinary proceedings, which found two of the officers guilty of misconduct offences, and a public inquest into the deaths that had resulted from the crash had recorded a series of criticisms and recommendations for how the officers ought to have behaved.[51] Nevertheless, the Supreme Court emphasised that none of this could be taken to suggest in itself that there would be resulting liability in the tort of negligence. The duty breached had been a public one, not a private one. Whether there was such a latter duty owed was the subject of the proceedings here, and in considering this, the courts must bear in mind the persisting and fundamental distinction between 'making matters worse and failing to confer a benefit'.[52] 46

From there, the Justices rehearsed a line of cases involving public authorities, whether the police or otherwise, which have come to act as the spine around which the current law relating to the duty of care is owed. In each instance, this fundamental distinction was emphasised, with the court taking care to identify what elements of each case were decisive in the respective result.[53] Each could be explained as an application of that orthodox distinction and whilst there were clearly exceptions to the principle of no liability where the defendant has merely failed to confer a benefit on the claimant, none of these key authorities were in fact examples of any of those exceptions.[54] 47

In clearing the ground to apply it in the case before them, the Justices clarified a helpful matter that has proven challenging in some of the earlier cases: How does one actually identify whether the defendant's actions have made the situation worse? The relevant counterfactual was confirmed as asking what would have happened if the defendant had done nothing at all? It must be the case 48

---

50 Para 20, emphasis added.
51 Paras 13–15.
52 Para 20 f.
53 Paras 22–44.
54 Ibid.

that carrying out the relevant activity made the claimant worse off than if it had not been undertaken if the case is to be convincingly framed as falling on the crucial 'making things worse' side of the line.[55] The Justices emphasised that the defendant's whole activity had to be considered, rather than approaching the matter on a more granular level. Such an approach was confidently asserted as dispelling the objection that parsing the act/omission borderline can be difficult or arbitrary.[56] By way of an example, they noted that this approach explained why there would be a duty (on the basis of making things worse) where a defendant driver might be said to have merely failed to confer a benefit by not putting on his handbrake to prevent his car rolling down a hill into another. Asking whether the damage would have resulted had he not undertaken his whole activity (ie, driving at all) the answer was, said the Justices, obviously, no and hence a duty would be owed on orthodox principles.[57]

49 Turning to the case before them, the claimant contended that it was straightforwardly the case that the defendants had made matters worse in that had they not attended the scene, Mr Kendall would have continued to attempt to warn other motorists and, in leaving the scene, they had done nothing to otherwise protect against the risk the ice posed.[58] In particular, they contended that they did not need to show a specific act by the police to coerce or dissuade Mr Kendall from seeking to warn other motorists and instead go to hospital.[59]

50 In doctrinal terms, this aspect of the claimant's case hinged on an argument that the relevant academic literature had assumed for a number of years, but for which there was no direct authority in the case law. If, knowing someone else is in need of help, the defendant puts off or prevents another from providing that help, is there a duty of care? Is this a case where, all things being equal, the defendant has in fact made things worse?[60]

51 This so-called 'interference principle' had been framed in the literature as an exception to the basic principle of no liability for failing to confer a benefit.[61] Notable textbook authors had also set out its tacit acceptance in a range of relevant cases,[62] although the most recent edition of that work had, conscious of the Court

---

55 Para 44.
56 Para 45.
57 Ibid.
58 Para 46.
59 Para 48.
60 Paras 48–58.
61 Para 42, discussing *S Tofaris/S Steel*, Negligence Liability for Omissions and the Police [2016] 75 CLJ 128.
62 Para 50, discussing *N McBride/R Bagshaw*, Tort Law (6th edn 2018).

of Appeal's decision in *Tindall*, suggested their earlier confidence may now need reassessment.[63]

Happily for all concerned, the Supreme Court confirmed the existence of such a principle, indeed pointing to a steady process of relying on it post hoc to offer a more convincing explanation of some older cases in the more recent caselaw.[64] In fact, as they noted, it was not even an exception to the general principle, but rather, an example of an instance of what it means to 'make things worse'.[65] The crux, however, was that it would not be enough for the defendant's act to simply have the effect of preventing the relevant aid, it was necessary that the defendant knew or ought to have known that their conduct would have this effect.[66] 52

From here, the case was straightforward. There was, taking the evidence at its strongest, simply nothing to suggest that the officers had known that Mr Kendall had, before their arrival, been trying to warn other motorists of the hazard here. This posed, as they gently put it, a 'major factual difficulty' for the claimant's case.[67] Ultimately, and perhaps not surprisingly, in the absence of any specific information about what he had been doing, Mr Kendall was, as far as the officers had been concerned, a victim of a car accident, not a rescuer.[68] As such, it was clearly the case that there could be no duty of care owed on the basis that the defendant's activities had made the situation worse by preventing a third-party intervenor from acting.[69] A heroic attempt by the claimant to shift focus from having prevented Mr Kendall's assistance, to that of the fire brigade, was met with the clear objection that their attendance had been focused on helping Mr Kendall and his vehicle and was not in any way related to dealing with or otherwise related to the underlying ice hazard.[70] 53

Having disposed of the claimant's case on orthodox grounds, the Justices considered the alternative arguments that a duty might be owed by way of the accepted exceptions to the general principle. Thus, a duty may have been owed either on 54

63 Para 54.

64 Para 56. Notably, the Justices thought there was a strong analogy with the firefighter case of *Capital & Counties plc v Hampshire County Council* [1997] QB 1004, arguing that this suggested there was no principled way to distinguish between a case where someone prevented an object from providing aid to the claimant (with analogy to the sprinklers the defendant had negligently disabled in *Capital*) and preventing a person from doing so.

65 Para 49.

66 Para 58.

67 Para 59.

68 Para 62.

69 Paras 60–70.

70 Para 72.

the basis that they had assumed responsibility to Mr Tindall,[71] or had a special degree of control over the danger due to having taken over the scene and then left without doing anything to remove or reduce the danger,[72] or by reason of their status as police.[73]

55 The first and third of these were summarily dismissed. There was simply no evidence (how could there be in a normal situation?) that the officers had said or done anything that the later drivers like Mr Tindall were aware of. It was impossible to assert an assumption of responsibility on such facts.[74] Likewise, the idea that a duty would be owed by reason of the fact that the defendants were the police, in a situation where other actors or individuals would not, was clearly unsustainable on the basis of the last decade of authorities.[75]

56 Rather it was the so-called 'control' argument that provided the best option here. Here the court distinguished clearly between the sort of control that the defendant's officers in fact had, which was control over the scene of the accident. This was not, as it would have had to have been in order to found a duty, control over the source of the danger itself.[76] This, the ice patch, was not only spatially different to the scene of the accident, but also nothing that the officers had done could be regarded as taking control of the ice. Indeed, as the court noted, the gist of the allegation all along was precisely that: that the police had done nothing about the ice, going so far as to emphasise that they had not even inspected it. All told, this was fatal to the argument and, with that, the last chance of founding a duty of care melted away.

c) Commentary

57 *Tindall*, which arrived so late in the year that it is yet to be subject of much academic commentary in response, is nevertheless clearly emblematic of a number of trends in the tort of negligence. Its conclusion has not been controversial and, if anything, it has stilled interests that might have been piqued in the wake of the decision in the lower courts. The centrality of the act/omission distinction (or, to use the language increasingly, and usefully, adopted, making things worse/failing to confer a benefit) is inescapable. It is the gravitational nexus around which the

71 Para 75 ff.
72 Para 78 ff.
73 Para 85 ff.
74 Para 76.
75 Para 85.
76 Para 83.

modern duty of care orients itself. That the case turned, ultimately, on the fairly blunt evidence as to what the officers knew of Mr Kendall permits a reading that is fairly narrow, and given those facts. it is undoubtedly the correct result, but a number of issues stand out for further consideration.

Centrally, whilst *Tindall* did much to simply reaffirm existing principles in relation to the duty of care, confirmation that the interference principle forms part of the broader duty of care framework is welcome and will hopefully help courts identify earlier and more clearly whether there is a triable issue at hand. 58

Less convincing perhaps is the insight for future scholarship to build on, that the interference principle is not an exception but, essentially, simply a way in which the defendant, in so behaving, will in fact make things worse. The modern framework for analysing the duty of care in negligence, in which one looks to the 'established categories' before turning to principle, treats equally categories in which what has been established is that there either is *or is not* a duty. The doctrinal or systematic distinction between a case representing an established category of duty (say, the duty owed by drivers to pedestrians) and one representing an exception to an established category of no duty is yet to be fully explored, but clearly, as in *Tindall* itself, is capable of leading both counsel and the courts down the supposedly wrong analytical path. 59

Likewise, as was shown here, the increasingly settled list of exceptions to the 'omissions' category leads to claimants pleading any and all in the alternative. Here the defendant had either made things worse … or had infringed any of the duties established by the alternative rationales. Treating such 'exceptions' as, in effect, safety valves from the inevitability of finding no duty otherwise drives claimants to frame their arguments in somewhat artificial and cascadingly overlapping ways. It will shock no-one, for instance, that there was no finding of an assumption of responsibility here (or indeed the defendant's 'control' over the danger) but it is likewise hard to blame claimants for seeking to avail themselves of what are, in effect, presented as emergency analytical escape routes. 60

More positive points that can be taken from *Tindall*, even if hopeless for the claimant, include the recurring and constructive admission in passing that the modern English law of tort now likely recognises different conceptual variants of the assumption of responsibility as a means of grounding a duty of care. This clears much ground to bring greater coherence to the law generally if, in public authority cases, it remains clear just how challenging such arguments are likely to be. 61

Equally, the forceful manner in which the Court rejected the idea that the law here was still in flux. Whilst that was perhaps more evident two decades ago, the last decade has seen only an inexorable move (at least outside of the more chaotic enclaves represented by *Paul* above no 6) towards rigid, supposedly principled 62 clarity in relation to the duty of care. The scope for counsel to hope that an action will not be summarily struck out and that trial will uncover the necessary facts – distinct from the abstract assumption about the facts that pertain in the sort of strike out hearing that *Tindall* represents – is increasingly limited. If there was greater flexibility for such tactics before, as the Court put it in *Tindall*, 'That is not true now'.[77]

63 Finally, in dismissing the last of the potential exceptions that could have generated a duty, the Court speculated that one point that might have been fatal in any case, even if the police officers had somehow engaged with the ice patch, was the fact that it is not clear in English law whether this logic of 'control' generating a duty actually applies to artificial or natural hazards outside of the defendant having control qua their role as occupier. Quite fairly the Court noted that the control principle has traditionally been deployed where there is some sort of parental, quasi-parental relationship or analogously custodial relationship at play,[78] none of which can be said to be the case in relation to the emergency services and a hazard on the road.

3. *Rabot v Hassam* [2024] UKSC 11, [2024] 2 WLR 949:[79] Negligence; Road Traffic Accident; Whiplash; Non-Pecuniary Losses; Tariff Awards

a) Brief Summary of the Facts

64 In this pair of decisions, two claimants had sued in negligence to recover small sums of damages for non-pecuniary loses in relation to personal injury following respective car accidents. In the standard terminology, such damages cover pain and suffering, and loss of amenity, referred to collectively as PSLA. They had each suffered whiplash injuries to their neck and back alongside, and concurrently with, other low-level physical injuries to other parts of their body. At first instance, there was a dispute within each case, and indeed between their respective resolutions at trial as to what damages were in fact recoverable here. The issue

77 Para 68. See also the delightful reference to Dickens' Mr Micawber to describe the perhaps overly optimistic view of claimants' counsel here that if only they could get to trial something might turn up to save the day.
78 Paras 79–81.
79 Judgment available online at <https://www.supremecourt.uk/cases/uksc-2023–0025>. Noted by *B Dixon* (2024) 2 JPILi C119; *M Johnson* (2024) 121 Law Society's Gazette (LSG) 26.

arose as a consequence of legislation in 2018 to create, by later statutory regulations in 2021, a fixed tariff for the amount of such damages recoverable for whiplash.[80] What, if anything, was in fact recoverable beyond this tariff in such concurrent injury situations?

In each case, the defendant insurers disputed whether it was possible, and if so to what extent, to recover beyond the scope of the tariff amount in situations like this. The Court of Appeal had, by majority, adopted an approach broadly favourable to the claimants, holding that the court ought to calculate the whiplash injury in line with the statutory tariff, calculate the non-whiplash injury in line with the usual common law rules and then stand back from that overall sum and consider whether a deduction needed to be made to reflect the extent to which the injuries might overlap. That said, if any deduction was to be made, it would have to come from the non-tariff award as the tariff award was, naturally, fixed by statutory regulation.[81] 65

One judge in the Court of Appeal had adopted the position advocated by the defendants that the matter should be approached by starting from the tariff award and requiring that the claimant then demonstrate that the injuries are not concurrent and, if they can, build up the final sum from the tariff award.[82] On the claimant's part, their primary case was that one should simply add together the tariff sum and the non-tariff sums without any consideration of whether a deduction was required.[83] 66

Whilst the sums were relatively trivial individually, around £3,000– £4,000 in each case, the point in *Rabot* was taken to the Supreme Court as a test case given there were 'many thousands' of cases that could stand to be affected by the result.[84] 67

b) Judgment of the Court

In a unanimous decision delivered by Lord Burrows, he began by restating the basic proposition that damages in tort, including damages for PSLA are intended to compensate the claimant by putting them, as much as money can, back in the position they were in before the tort.[85] The quantum of PSLA awards is a matter 68

80 Civil Liability Act 2018 sec 3.
81 Para 9.
82 Para 7.
83 Para 8.
84 Para 4.
85 Para 10.

left to individual judges to award something that is just and fair and 'takes into account the interest of claimants, defendants and society as a whole'.[86] Consistency here is achieved through publication of informal judicial guidelines so that common ranges of recovery (depending on the seriousness of the claimant's situation) are available to consult in deciding on what to do in a given case.

69 Indeed, these guidelines have, since 2012 cited judicial dicta on the naturally challenging matter of how to assess PSLA in the context of concurrent injuries generally, consistently adopting a view that in such cases it is appropriate that the judge step back and consider whether the situation requires that the combined sum be reduced, raised or left alone, with an assumption that the third category will, in practice, be the outlier.[87] This had become, as the Court noted, the 'standard approach at common law'.[88] What effect, if any, the statutory regime introduced by the 2018 Act had was the central question here.

70 Rehearsing the statutory background, Lord Burrows noted that the 2018 Act had left open the possibility of including in the relevant regime the possibility of an uplift in exceptional circumstances (where the whiplash was, say, particularly severe) and this had been put into practice when the regulations had been introduced, allowing a maximum uplift that did not exceed 20 % of the relevant tariff amount.[89]

71 Turning to the majority judgment in the Court of Appeal, Lord Burrows noted that the court had there given consideration to the fact that the statutory regime under the 2018 Act said nothing about common law damages for non-whiplash injuries and that the relevant sums fixed under the tariff were considerably lower than the sum that would otherwise have been recovered at common law before the introduction of the tariff.[90] Central to the dissenting judgment were the arguments that the statutory language suggested it applied to cases where 'a person suffers a whiplash injury' so the tariff award would, there, cover concurrent injuries as well, and the fact that the standard 'stepping back' exercise was designed to be deployed where the goal was full compensation for each one of multiple injuries, but of course that goal had been abandoned in the case of whiplash injuries given the tariffs.[91]

72 Adopting the 'well-established' modern approach to statutory interpretation, which 'requires courts to ascertain the meaning of the words used in the light

86 Para 11.
87 Paras 14–16.
88 Para 18.
89 Paras 22 f, 24.
90 Para 32 ff.
91 Para 34.

of their context and purpose of the provisions'[92] Lord Burrows held that the wording of the statute 'plainly does not extend the tariff amount to PSLA in respect of non-whiplash injuries'.[93] There was nothing to suggest the standard common law stepping back approach was displaced or departed from, albeit must be exercised in the context of the limits imposed by the tariffs and could not be inconsistent with it. As such, the approach adopted by the majority of the Court of Appeal was endorsed.[94]

Whilst it was clear that Lord Burrows felt there were convincing positive reasons to adopt the approach advocated, he spelled out the disadvantages of the other potential results here. Staring from the view that the statute said nothing about extending beyond whiplash, he suggested the dissenting view in the Court of Appeal was apt to require a greater degree of detail and complexity from the relevant medical experts, running contrary to the overall goal of the statutory regime to simplify awards here. Asking such precision was at odds with what was inevitably a 'rough and ready' or 'avowedly impressionistic' attempt to calculate the PSLA damages in cases of concurrent injury.[95] Indeed, there was likewise a risk that it would introduce an absurdity of a claimant ignoring their whiplash injury for fear that raising it in court might lead to an overall lower award and generally such risks of absurd consequences were to be avoided when undertaking statutory interpretation.[96] 73

As to the claimant's primary position, this could be discarded given the obvious manner in which it overlooked the risk of double counting by eschewing any such deductive exercise in a case that merited it. Whilst the goal was to compensate the claimant, it was obviously important to avoid the risk of over-compensation in such concurrent injury cases.[97] Indeed, it was no argument to suggest that such fears could be set aside precisely because the tariff award was a conscious choice towards under-compensation in the first place, as to do so would be, albeit from a different direction, again to undermine the point of the statutory regime in the first place.[98] 74

As such, the Supreme Court confirmed that the correct approach in such cases is to assess the tariff amount for PSLA in relation to whiplash (taking into account where appropriate the potential for an uplift under the statute), assess the com- 75

92 Para 36.
93 Para 37.
94 Paras 39–42.
95 Para 46.
96 Para 47.
97 Para 49 f.
98 Para 50.

mon law damages for PSLA relating to any other concurrent injury, sum these and then step back and consider whether an adjustment is required, conscious that the goal is to avoid double recovery. Respecting the choice to abandon full compensation for the tariff award, any deduction should be made from the non-tariff award, but the final award cannot sink beneath what would have been awarded for PSLA at common law had it only been those injuries at stake.[99]

c) Commentary

76 *Rabot* has all the classic markings of a test case. The stakes are at once low but impactful. The ground on which the decision was fought was caught between the abstract tensions of a system's methodological approach to statutory interpretation and the normative force of the respective positions that appear plausible. Added to that, and at the heart of the case, was the inevitably knotty problem of how one resolves a specific statutory enactment with a broader common law approach that can easily, as here, overlap.

77 That challenge was all the more evident as the effect of the 2018 legislation was, as Lord Burrows frankly acknowledged, to depart from the settled rule of full compensation. How one resolves an unavoidably and, as the frequent medical evidence in such situations reveals, inevitably overlapping conflict between full compensation for some injuries and otherwise for others is a naturally difficult question. Whilst much of the solution could be found in parsing the statutory regime itself, with respect to Lord Burrows the positions that were rejected were hardly implausible and in the absence of sufficient clarity the Court is, in effect, legislating through interpretation, choosing not simply the meaning of the text, but selecting between the plausible valencies of Parliament's concern to identify *the* purpose of the legislation to begin with.

78 A clearly compelling argument in favour of the Court's solution is, as Lord Burrows noted,[100] ultimately that it represented a more minimal departure from the common law than the alternatives. Lord Burrows has previously written convincingly in his academic career on the relationship between statute and common law and it is a fine reminder that for all their clear democratic legitimacy and the respect that ought to be accorded to statutes in the hierarchy of legal sources, they are often, in the law of tort, islands of normative or structural-doctrinal certainty in a sea of more malleable and often long-standing common law rules.

99 Para 52 f.
100 Para 48.

This restated preference for a minimal rather than a maximal assumption about the effect of statutes on common law rules provides an excellent example of the continued dominance of the common law within the English law of tort.

Finally, and as in many jurisdictions, the Supreme Court is to be commended for defending the admirably intuitive approach at common law (ie outwith the ambit of the tariffs) to awarding damages for PSLA. There is, as all tort lawyers know, no right answer to the question of what ought to be recovered here and, indeed, some European systems take a far more minimal approach to their respective responses here. The Master of the Rolls' view was rejected, in part, precisely because in striving to be more 'principled' and 'scientific', it failed to account not just for the procedural reality of how these sums are arrived at, but arguably because this was a subject matter – setting the niceties of statutory interpretation aside – where such an approach simply lacked normative heft. 79

Whilst narrowly focused on the important point it raised, *Rabot* must be seen as a thorough and resounding vindication of the broader toolbox that the English common law has developed here. Whilst we have to accept that on this topic justice may on occasions need to be rough, the system must always be ready to provide a coherent response and *Rabot* reminds us that coherence can at least be found in abiding by a settled practice where settled answers are elusive. 80

4. *Davies v Bridgend County Borough Council* [2024] UKSC 15, [2025] AC 434:[101] Nuisance; Japanese Knotweed; Existing Encroachment; Factual Causation; Counterfactuals

a) Brief Summary of the Facts

Here, the defendant council had allowed Japanese Knotweed to spread onto the claimant's land around 2004. Japanese Knotweed is a perniciously disruptive plant that is incredibly difficult to remove once it invades a piece of land and can have destructive effects on the property generally. Whilst not initially tortious, it had become an actionable nuisance from around 2013 on the basis of developing knowledge around the risk the plant posed and it was not until 2018 that the defendant implemented a practical programme of measures designed to treat and manage the situation. In cases concerning natural hazards, it is necessary to prove that the defendant was at fault in not taking reasonable care on the basis of their 81

101 Judgment available online at <https://www.supremecourt.uk/cases/uksc-2023–0028>. Noted by *I Gasgoigne* (2024) 174 New Law Journal (NLJ) 12; *N Dobson* (2024) 121 LSG 31.

own personal circumstances and resources. There was no dispute between the parties that there was a suitable breach of duty during this period.

82 The claimant's action here, in the tort of private nuisance, was in part to recover damages of £4,900 for the residual diminution in the value of their land even once the treatment programme had been introduced. The evidence suggested that the rhizomes, which are the source of the infestation, can remain on land, even after successful treatment, and may, if disturbed, regrow. Likewise, the fact that soil so contaminated would likely require specialist disposal and, as such, the ability to develop the land was impaired. Finally, the claimant argued that the stigma attached to properties that had been infested with Japanese Knotweed would adversely affect the value of the property.

83 The claim was ultimately dismissed at first instance on the basis that any residual diminution had all been caused prior to the breach of duty by the earlier, non-actionable presence of the plant on the property before 2004. Applying a classic authority concerning nuisance by encroachment, where, by definition, the situation is an ongoing or 'continuing' one over time, the Court of Appeal allowed the claim and awarded the damages sought for the residual diminution.[102] The defendant appealed to the Supreme Court on the narrow matter of causation. Was their breach the factual cause of the damage complained of? On a further issue, the claimant contended that as the residual stigma would diminish over time, the burden was on the defendant to identify the lower sum that should be awarded if the treatment had started earlier in 2013, rather than 2018. There was an outstanding question as to whether this had been properly pleaded in the lower courts, but the question was taken to the Supreme Court as part of the appeal.

b) Judgment of the Court

84 Across two judgments, with Lord Stephens giving the main judgment and Lord Burrows a short concurrence, the Supreme Court allowed the appeal, the claimant could not recover the damages sought. The further issue was also rejected as improperly pleaded and lacking in any evidence.[103] It did not form a central part of the reasoning before the Supreme Court.

85 As such, the heart of the decision turned on factual causation. Lord Stephens started from the foundation clarified in the earlier case of *Williams v Network*

---

102 Para 7.
103 Para 36.

Rail[104] that the tort of private nuisance does not protect claimants against pure economic losses. It does not protect the value of property as an investment or financial asset.[105] This had been central to the decision at first instance, as if the relevant diminution was merely in the abstract, without a further associated loss of amenity in the property, this principle would appear to rule out recovery for the relevant head of damage.

Lord Stephens confirmed that the basic test of causation here was the classic 'but for' test, noting that the, 'purpose of the but for test is to eliminate irrelevant causative factors'.[106] If the diminution of value would have occurred despite the defendant's breach, then it was an irrelevant causal factor and could be discounted as such. Whilst he acknowledged that there are, of course, situations where the 'but for' test breaks down and, as such, exceptional approaches to the question of factual causation have been developed,[107] in upholding the claimant's case, the Court of Appeal had regarded it as obvious that none of these exceptions were necessary on the facts and, indeed, causation could be established on conventional grounds with reference to the earlier decision in *Delaware Mansions.*[108] 86

The crux of the decision thus rested on the strength of the analogy here. Did the claimant's case fall within the scope of that earlier decision? In *Delaware*, damages had been awarded where roots of a tree situated on an adjoining pavement had caused cracks in the claimant's apartment block before they had taken ownership of it. The Court of Appeal had awarded the claimant substantial damages in nuisance to reflect the cost of repair despite the fact that there was arguably no further damage after the date they had acquired the building. This was justified on the basis that the cost of the remedial work in the context of an ongoing or, in the language of English tort law, 'continuing' nuisance was recoverable without proof of further physical damage.[109] This was upheld in the House of Lords. 87

As Lord Stephens interpreted it in *Davies*, *Delaware* was authority for the proposition that a claimant can recover the reasonable costs of abating a continuing nuisance.[110] Crucially, damages for the diminution in value of property were, clearly, not any part of such damages for abating a continuing situation, they could be distinguished and did not fall under the cover of authority provided 88

104 [2018] EWCA Civ 1514; [2019] QB 601.
105 Para 18.
106 Para 56.
107 Para 58.
108 *Delaware Mansions Ltd v Westminster City Council* [2001] UKHL 55, [2002] 1 AC 321.
109 Para 62 f.
110 Para 66.

in *Delaware*, regardless as to whether that diminution occurred before the defendant's breach.[111]

89 Turning to the causal issue, the finding that the Japanese Knotweed had encroached onto the claimant's land before 2004 was fatal. The relevant question would be to ask, given this, would the diminution of value have occurred 'but for' the defendant's admitted breach between 2013 and 2018? The answer was to be found in the fact that at first instance there had been no finding that that breach had increased or materially contributed to the diminution of value, revealing that any diminution had occurred well before the defendant's breach. Given that, there could, obviously, be no recovery on the facts.[112]

90 In his short concurring judgment, Lord Burrows took time to set out some comments on the topic of factual causation in the context of private nuisance, noting that it was not a topic that had drawn much attention from the courts.[113]

91 Emphasising that there was no dispute that the diminution was the same before and after the start of the breach in 2013 and that the claimant had not at any stage either sought an injunction against the defendant's behaviour or, as a result, suggested that this was in fact a case of continuing nuisance, Lord Burrows noted that whilst there were, of course, classic examples of situations where the 'but for' test produces analytically unsatisfactory results, there was no reason not to apply it to the facts of this case. That was true even if one thought this was a case where the damage had been brought about by, as he put it, 'two successive sufficient events, the first being a natural event and the second being a breach of duty'.[114] The failure to prove factual causation damned the claimant's case.

c) Commentary

92 *Davies* is an entirely orthodox decision that reaffirms basic principles of recovery in tort. The outcome has not been the cause of much commentary in the broader literature, likely due to the orthodox nature of the judgment.

93 It is, of course, unquestionable in a straightforward case that if the claimant cannot demonstrate factual causation using the 'but for' test, that the claim must fail. What perhaps stands out in *Davies* is the acknowledgement in passing that there is no reason in principle why the exceptional approaches to the law of factual causation could not be drawn on in the right case as a means of demonstrat-

111 Paras 67, 69.
112 Para 70 f.
113 Para 75.
114 Paras 78, 82.

ing factual causation. It is evident that these were not created in the context of private nuisance, and whether they are well suited to that tort remains to be seen.

The main insight to be drawn is the continued challenge that the tort of pri- 94
vate nuisance faces on two fronts. On the more prosaic, Japanese Knotweed has in recent years driven a considerable amount of litigation and it is no surprise that the pernicious damage it can create and the manner of its spreading continues to bring parties before the court. Here, the party responsible for much of England's rail tracks intervened in the action given the fact that it is often a challenge for their own land management.

On the more doctrinal, despite the recent fundamental restatement of the law 95
relating to private nuisance in *Fearn v Tate*[115] it continues to be a source of litigation before the Supreme Court. There is no doubt that *Delaware* remains a good, if narrow, authority, but as *Davies* shows, if the parties and, indeed, with respect, the courts are confused as to whether it applies in a given case, and whether the nuisance is actually a continuing one or not, it can lead to some odd and expensive results. The confusion here may suggest that the historic tendency in English law to categorise abstract types of nuisance-creating interference (of which 'encroachment' was one) is now apt to mislead rather than ground greater coherence and certainty.

5. Personal Injury

a) Trends in Personal Injury Claims

Previous annual reports have noted the general decline in personal injury actions, 96
and the role of the Government's efforts to tackle the perceived problem of compensation culture through both regulation of personal injury actions and, in some limited cases, direct intervention in the quantum of damages recoverable in common cases.[116] The effect of the pandemic has also become clear since the 2020/2021 year, where there was a reduction in actions (itself already part of an overall trend of decline) from 829,252 in 2019/2020 to 564,359 in 2020/2021.[117] The same trend

115 *McGrath*, (fn 40) no 2 ff.

116 The details of the most relevant recent reforms can be found here, *A Morris/K Oliphant*, England and Wales, in: K Oliphant/BC Steininger (eds), European Tort Law (ETL) 2012 (2013) 163, (fn 40) no 1 ff.

117 Statistics on the number and type of claims pursued each year are publicly available from the Department for Work and Pensions' Compensation Recovery Unit: <https://www.gov.uk/

continued in 2023/2024 with 477,220 claims. Of this, and without surprise, road traffic accident claims continue to represent the bulk of all claims brought but were down somewhat, numbering 348,806 over the same period. Across the other categories of collected data, there was a slight rise in clinical negligence claims, from 14,443 to 15,839 and a slight climb in public cases from 53,403 to 58,933 such that it is a drop in road traffic accident claims that, as with the previous year, explains most of the year-on-year decline here.

b) Significant Decisions

97 A general development of obvious significance for personal injury in 2024 was the arrival of the new edition, the 17th, of the Judicial College's Guidelines. This slim but hugely important volume is used in courts across the country to calculate and, in so far as possible, standardise awards of non-pecuniary losses. Whilst the Guidelines are, clearly, not a single judicial decision, they are an effort to capture judicial practice in courts all across the country and so represent a cumulation of judicial decisions on quantum of awards in the area of personal injury. Colleagues interested in quantum of damages in this area are advised to consult this work as an excellent guide to practice in England & Wales.

98 Of note here are primarily two points. The first is that the Guidelines continued to retain the Retail Price Index (rather than the alternative Consumer Prices Index) as the relevant means of calculating the effect of inflation on the scope of awards as listed in the Guidelines. Secondly, in light of the current inflationary era, there is an average uplift of 22 % in many but not all categories of award covered by the Guidelines.

99 The question of relying on such extra-judicial tools in the course of calculating damages in personal injury cases was indeed at stake in one decision this year. *Price v Marston's PLC*,[118] was a straightforward personal injury case where the claimaint's husband had sadly died following an accident in the workplace. On appeal to the High Court, the decision of the first instance judge faced with calculating the claimant's loss of financial dependency to depart from using the established and commonly relied on actuarial tables,[119] as well a judicial 'rule of

government/publications/compensation-recovery-unit-performance-data/compensation-recovery-unit-performance-data>.

118 [2024] EWHC 1352 *King's Bench Division* (KB).

119 See above, no 1.

thumb' developed in previous caselaw to aid with this,[120] was sufficient to ground the claimant's successful appeal on the point. As Griffiths J noted, whilst exceptions to this dual-pronged practice are, of course, inevitable, such cases are rare, and there was nothing in this case to justify such a departure.[121]

The most significant tort decision in the field of personal injury was likely 100 *Lewis-Ranwell v G4S Health Services.*[122] There, the claimant, who had been diagnosed with schizophrenia and had spent time in psychiatric intensive care, sued a series of defendants for their negligence in providing healthcare services to him during periods of detention following arrest. Mere days after being released, he went on to murder three people whilst suffering from a delusional belief about them. His case was that the defendants had been negligent in releasing him given it should have been obvious that, if released, there was a real risk he might, as indeed he did, hurt others. He claimed damages for personal injury, loss of liberty, reputation and pecuniary losses as well as an imdemnity against the potential claims resulting from his actions during that period. During the preceding criminal trial for his actions, he had been found not guilty by reason of insanity and detained in mental health facilities. The crux of the tort action lay in the defendants' attempts to rely, not implausibly, on a defence of illegality and the question of whether this could be deployed against a claimant who the criminal law had, in the form of the insanity defence, found to lack criminal responsibility for their action. If by law the claimant does not know what they are doing is unlawful, can a defendant rely on a defence of illegality in a tort action brought against them? Having lost at first instance, the defendants appealed. A majority of the Court of Appeal dismissed their case arguing that this would not create an inconsistency with either the criminal law (having held that he was not responsible for his actions) or the civil law (as this concerned the liability of others to the claimant, not the claimant's liability to others where his insanity would evidently not allow him to avoid liability). Finally, that allowing his claim would not otherwise undermine public confidence or adversely impact healthcare providers charged with the care of patients in a similar situation. Lady Justice Andrews, dissenting, argued that there was nothing disproportionate in barring the claim and that, given closely analogous authorities, the decision to prevent such claims 'should not rest on nice distinctions between having little or no personal responsibility for the killing because of the state of the claimant's mental health at the

120 See *Harris v Empress Motors Ltd* [1984] 1 WLR 2125, namely the idea that when calculating dependency, one assumed the deceased would retain one-third of their joint net income for themselves personally with two-thirds going towards their family and household expenses.
121 140 f.
122 [2024] EWCA Civ 138 [2024] KB 745.

time.'[123] The case is currently on appeal, awaiting a hearing before the Supreme Court, and will inevitably appear in a later iteration of the Yearbook.

C. Literature

1. *Sandy Steel*, Omissions in Tort Law (Oxford University Press, 2024)

101 This is the first substantial monograph on a topic that has dogged English tort lawyers in recent decades. Authored by one of our leading tort lawyers, this is a necessary study of an area that is now of central importance to the modern law of tort, particularly the issue of when and why a duty of care is owed within the tort of negligence. Indeed, the Foreword to the book comes from the current President of the Supreme Court and an insightful address given at the book's launch by another Justice of the Supreme Court may be found in the Court's archives.[124] The author brings his background as a legal theorist and philosopher of private law to bear on the problem offering an account of the basic distinctions in the modern law (and, crucially, the exceptions to them) that is rooted in understanding the law as it stands, but strives to offer a normative account of the area alongside this.

2. *Haim Abraham,* Tort Liability in Warfare (Oxford University Press, 2024)

102 A hugely novel and sadly timely monograph from another scholar who is as much a tort lawyer as they are an engaging and insightful legal theorist of private law. Bringing these interests to bear on the knotty question of the state's responsibility to civilians for harm flowing from combat, the work covers both negligent wrongs and intentional wrongs as well as the tension between, and operation of, vicarious liability and direct liability for such wrongs. The work is impressive for its treatment of an area where it is too easy to (as practice perhaps suggests here) assume that there is something about warfare that circumscribes the role of tort. In a pair of well-reasoned opening chapters, the author builds a powerful case rooted in corrective justice for tort's relevance here and suggests that the idea of an immu-

123 Para 137.

124 See, <https://supremecourt.uk/speeches/omission-in-tort-law-by-sandy-steel>.

nity from liability in combat can, likewise, be challenged from a rule of law perspective.

3. *Kylie Burns/Jodi Gardner/Jonathan Morgan/Sandy Steel,* Torts On Three Continents: Honouring Jane Stapleton (Oxford University Press, 2024)

First amongst equals, Professor Jane Stapleton's contribution to modern tort practice and scholarship is unmatched. This worthy volume of essays celebrating her career, overseen by a collection of excellent scholars who each bear the imprint of her influence, brings together a stellar field of contributions from leading tort scholars. Fitting to Stapleton's life and scholarship, the chapters range not only broadly across the common law world, with US, Australian and UK scholars and topics all on show, they range across the broad span of ways in which one might be interested in the law of tort. Covering everything from the role of damage, the place of compensation schemes, pluralist ways of thinking about tort and, of course, inevitably, causation, this is hugely recommended for those seeking insight into, and reflection on, the common law of tort and one of our leading scholars herself. 103

4. Selected Journal Articles

General Tort Law: *E Eldridge,* Rights That (2024) 44 Oxford Journal of Legal Studies (OJLS) 808; *A Fell/I Field,* The Actual Loss Illusion [2024] 83 CLJ 301; *U Grušić,* The Law Governing United Kingdom Government Tort Liability In The 'War On Terror.' (2024) 73 International and Comparative Law Quarterly (ICLQ) 1045; *J Murphy,* Unpicking Torts: Elements, Conditions of Actionability and Standing Rules (2024) 87 Modern Law Review (MLR) 1519; *C Purshouse,* Tort theory and the interpretive sleight of hand (2024) 140 LQR 301; *P Sales,* Constitutional Values in the Common Law Of Obligations [2024] 83 CLJ 132. 104

Negligence: *I Benson/C Jones,* Professional negligence annual case review 2023 (2024) 40 PN 5; *H Evans,* The scope of duty and purpose (2024) 40 PN 47. 105

Clinical Negligence: *S Attinger/I Kerridge/C Stewart/I Karpin/S Gallagher/R Norman/W Lipworth,* Money matters: a critique of 'informed financial consent' (2024) 32 Medical Law Review (Med L Rev) 356; *E Wicks,* The role of the right to life in respect of deaths caused by negligence in the healthcare context (2024) 32 Med L 106

Rev 81; *M Leitch*, Disclosing alternative treatments: towards a Bolam-Montgomery partnership (2024) 40 PN 107.

107 **Defective Products:** *D Fairgrieve/C Busch/E Buyuksagis/ZG Garrett/G Straetmans/A Karaiskos/RD Linley/ C Markou/JM Paterson/CM Sharkey*, Product liability and online marketplaces: comparison and reform (2024) 73 ICLQ 477.

108 **Privacy:** *E Descheemaeker*, Legal Persons and The Right to Privacy [2024] 83 CLJ 465.

109 **Tort and Climate Change:** *D Palombo*, Business, Human Rights and Climate Change: The Gradual Expansion of the Duty of Care (2024) 44 OJLS 889.

110 **Directors' Liability:** *M McHugh*, Directors' liability for inducing a breach of trust or fiduciary obligation, (2024) 140 LQR 223.

111 **Legal History:** *M Lunney*, Subversion Down-Under: Innovation, Ambition and the Introduction of Survival of Causes of Action Legislation in South Australia and Victoria (2024) 45 Journal of Legal History (JLH) 88.

112 **Vicarious Liability:** *M Cappelletti*, A pluralist view of vicarious liability in tort (2024) 140 LQR 61.

Janno Lahe and Irene Kull

IX. Estonia

A. Legislation

1. Motor Insurance Act (Liikluskindlustuse seadus) of 26 March 2014, (2014) Riigi Teataja (RT) I, 11.4.2014, 1

1 Of the laws more indirectly affecting tort law, the Motor Insurance Act[1] (MIA) was amended. In particular, it is worth referring to the amendment of the definition of insured event. The previous regulation in § 8(1) of the MIA provided that:

> An insured event means the causing of damage to a third party, provided that the following conditions exist at the time: 1) the damage was caused by a vehicle that is subject to the insurance obligation arising from this Act or the legislation of the state where the vehicle is normally based; 2) the damage was caused by the realisation of the risk characteristic of the operation of the vehicle in traffic and there is a causal link between the movement or location of the vehicle and the damage caused; 3) the damage was caused on the road or in another area used for conventional vehicle traffic.

2 According to § 8(2) of the MIA, the following is not deemed an insured event: 1) damage caused in a vehicle (including aircraft and water craft), except upon driving on or off a ferry engaged in regular services; 2) damage caused in a place closed and separated for racing, training or another similar event; 3) damage caused in the territory of an aerodrome closed for traffic; 4) damage caused on the road or in another area used for conventional vehicle traffic at a time when the area was closed for public traffic, and if the vehicle with which the damage was caused is used in field or construction work or another similar purpose and the damage was caused directly in the course of the performance of work.

3 The amended § 8(1) MIA defines an insured event as an occurrence where damage is caused to a third party by the use of a vehicle covered by the insurance obligation as a means of transport.

4 The amendment of the Law was necessary because the previous definition of an insured event was too restrictive and did not correspond to the interpretation

1 Liikluskindlustuse seadus (Motor Insurance Act) of 26 March 2014, available in English at <https://www.riigiteataja.ee/en/eli/505012025004/consolide>.

https://doi.org/10.1515/9783111389271-010

given by the European Court of Justice to the term 'use of a vehicle' in Art 3 of Directive 2009/103/EC of the European Parliament and of the Council.[2]

2. Compulsory Liability Insurance of Health Care Providers Act (Tervishoiuteenuse osutaja kohustusliku vastutuskindlustuse seadus) of 13 April 2022, (2022) Riigi Teataja (RT) I, 29. 4. 2022, 1

5 On 1 November 2024, the Compulsory Liability Insurance of Health Care Providers Act[3] finally entered into force. According to this Law, all health care providers are obliged to conclude a liability insurance contract. The timing of the entry into force of the Law proved problematic, as only one insurance company started to offer this insurance service, and there was considerable resistance from health care providers to the obligation to contract. This was probably due in particular to the fact that premiums were higher than expected.

6 It is hoped that other insurance providers will join the market in the coming year, which will lead to more reasonable premiums. Mandatory liability insurance for health care providers will help to ensure better protection of the rights of both patients and providers.

B. Cases

1. Supreme Court (Riigikohus) Judgment no 2-20-3847, 10 April 2024, ECLI:EE:RK:2024:2.20.3847/48: Defamation

a) Brief Summary of the Facts

7 The plaintiff worked for a short time as an adviser in the Estonian Ministry of Economic Affairs and Communications. The employment was terminated by

2 Directive (EU) 2021/2118 of the European Parliament and of the Council of 24 November 2021 amending Directive 2009/103/EC relating to insurance against civil liability in respect of the use of motor vehicles, and the enforcement of the obligation to insure against such liability [2021] Official Journal (OJ) L 430/1.

3 Tervishoiuteenuse osutaja kohustusliku vastutuskindlustuse seadus (Compulsory Liability Insurance of Health Care Providers Act) of 13 April 2022, available in English at <https://www.riigiteataja.ee/en/eli/516092024001/consolide>.

agreement between the parties. The defendant posted on the plaintiff's Facebook page allegations which the plaintiff considered to be untrue and offensive to his honour and dignity. The allegations posted by the defendant were that: 1) the plaintiff worked against his minister; 2) the actions of the plaintiff as a public official were corrupt; 3) the plaintiff is the representative of the Russian taxi company Yandex in Estonia; 4) the plaintiff's actions were sufficient to be investigated by the Security Police Office; 5) the plaintiff used his position (acting as a consultant) in his own interests and those of the taxi company Yandex.

The plaintiff applied for compensation of at least € 5,000 for the non- 8
pecuniary damage suffered.

The county court upheld the action and ordered the defendant to pay the 9
plaintiff € 2,000. The circuit court left the county court's judgment unchanged.

b) Judgment of the Court

The Supreme Court annulled the decisions of both the county and circuit courts 10
and dismissed the claim.

With respect to the defendant's first allegations (see point 4 above), the Su- 11
preme Court held that not every publication of a valuation need be considered unlawful within the meaning of § 1046 of the Law of Obligations Ac (LOA).[4] Under § 1046 of the LOA, every minor infringement of personal rights is not unlawful, since, according to the law, the type of violation, the reason and motive for the violation and its gravity have to be taken into account. Also, not every negative value judgement published on social media must be followed by an award of damages. An allegation posted on social media that a public official is working against a minister does not damage the honour of the official while it should be considered to be not more than a trivial attack on his honour. In the view of the Supreme Court, such an assessment does not exceed the threshold of unlawfulness under § 1046(1) of the LOA and is not of a nature to degrade, humiliate or ridicule the official.

As regards pleas 2 to 5 (see point 4 above), the Supreme Court did not consider 12
the defendant to be the author of the Facebook posts, since they had been made by a third party and the defendant had merely 'liked' them.

---

4 Võlaõigusseadus (Law of Obligations Act, LOA) of 26 September 2001, available in English at <https://www.riigiteataja.ee/en/eli/ee/512122022006/consolide/current>.

c) Commentary

13 This decision is more important in shaping Estonian case law than it may seem at first glance. In Estonia, there has recently been a tendency (especially in the case of well-known people) to claim compensation even for minor breaches of honour and dignity on social media. As the courts have often upheld such claims, this has provided further incentives to go to court. In the present judgment, the Supreme Court has attempted to reverse this trend by stating that not every negative value judgement published on social media must be followed by an award of damages. In the case of invalid infringements, the victim does not always have to receive monetary compensation.

14 The assessment as to whether the plaintiff is entitled to damages has to be made on the bases of unlawfulness of the published allegation. In particular, § 1046 of the LOA is relevant as sec 1 provides that: 'The defamation of a person, inter alia by passing undue value judgement, by the unjustified use of the name or image of the person, or by breaching the inviolability of the private life or another personality right of the person is unlawful unless otherwise provided by law. Upon the establishment of unlawfulness, the type of violation, the reason and motive for the violation and the gravity of the violation relative to the aim pursued thereby shall be taken into consideration'. According to sec 2 of § 1046 of the LOA, 'The violation of a personality right is not unlawful if the violation is justified considering other legal rights protected by law and the rights of third parties or public interests. In such case, unlawfulness shall be established based on the comparative assessment of different legal rights and interests protected by law'.

15 The fact that not all cases of defamation should lead to an award of damages has also been emphasised by the Supreme Court in the following judgment.

2. Supreme Court, Judgment no 2-20-2328, 3 July 2024, ECLI: EE:RK:2024:2.20.2328/112: Defamation

a) Brief Summary of the Facts

16 Defendant 2 published an article about the plaintiff in the newspaper LõunaLeht owned by defendant 1, entitled 'Suspicious offer lured the gullible'. The article contained, inter alia, the text '170 euros for every customer brought in, immediately!' This offer was circulated on social media groups in south-east Estonia on the plaintiff's Facebook account. Immediately after LõunaLeht tried to contact the person who had shared the offer, the person deleted all posts and, in addition

to it, also the Facebook account, which had managed to gather 5,000 new 'friends' after posting the offer.

According to the plaintiff, the article gave the impression that she had made a dubious offer to lure gullible people and that she was a criminal who defrauded people. 17

The plaintiff asked the defendants jointly and severally to pay damages of € 20,000 or other compensation as the court might consider just. In addition, the plaintiff requested that the defendants be ordered to delete the article. 18

The county court dismissed the action, finding that the published article did not contain any incorrect factual allegations or false information about the plaintiff. The circuit court partially annulled the county court's decision and ordered defendant 1 to pay the plaintiff € 300 in damages. The circuit court explained that defendant 2 could not be considered as the author of the article and therefore the action against her was dismissed. 19

b) Judgment of the Court

The Civil Chamber of the Supreme Court annulled the judgment of the circuit court and upheld the judgment of the county court. The Supreme Court noted that, as was previously clarified under § 1046 of the LOA, minor infringements that a person must reasonably endure in certain circumstances, taking into account the manner, context or content of the publication, should not be considered unlawful. Every negative value judgement published in the press need not be followed by an award of damages. An allegation that a person encourages others to enter into transactions with dubious content should not be considered to be more than a trivial defamation of the person's honour. Such an assessment does not, in the view of the Chamber, exceed the threshold of unlawfulness under § 1046(1) of the LOA. 20

The Civil Chamber agreed that the allegation made by the defendant that the plaintiff deleted her Facebook account was incorrect, but the making of such an incorrect allegation does not constitute such a breach within the meaning of § 1046(1) of the LOA, which should entitle the plaintiff to claim compensation for non-pecuniary damage. 21

c) Commentary

22 This judgment sends the same signal as the judgment in case no 2-20-3847 that not every minor breach of the law is above the threshold of defamation and therefore does not give rise to a right to compensation for non-pecuniary damage.

23 It can be hoped that, as a result of these two judgments, persons who feel that their personal rights have been infringed will, before going to court, consider more carefully in the future whether the infringement committed against them was serious enough to justify legal proceedings. The authors believe that both decisions send a legitimate signal to society.

3. Supreme Court, Judgment in Criminal Case no 1-22-5835, 3 July 2024, ECLI:EE:RK:2024:1.22.5835/33: Non-Pecuniary Damages

a) Brief Summary of the Facts

24 Defendant 1 (driver of a motor vehicle) was convicted on charges of driving a motor vehicle in breach of the rules of the road, thereby causing serious injury to the victim (the plaintiff). The criminal case also involved a civil claim against the insurer of defendant 1 (defendant 2).

25 In the criminal proceedings, the plaintiff sought an order that defendant 1, as the accused, and his insurer, jointly and severally pay to him the sum of € 16,500 in non-pecuniary damages. The insurer had voluntarily paid the sum of € 13,500.

26 The county court upheld the civil claim, ordering the defendants jointly and severally to pay the injured party € 16,500 in compensation for non-pecuniary damage. As the amount was exceptionally high in comparison to other awards in similar cases in Estonia, the county court added an explanation of why it awarded such an amount. In particular, the county court found that it cannot be considered correct that the amount of compensation for non-pecuniary damage must always correspond to the compensation awarded in similar cases. In such a case, the compensation cannot increase over time. However, the circuit court took a different view and dismissed the plaintiff's civil claim, stating that the € 13,500 voluntarily paid by the defendant to the injured party corresponded to the amount of the non-pecuniary damage suffered by the injured party and was in line with damages awarded in similar circumstances in the case law.

b) Judgment of the Court

The Supreme Court annulled the decision of the circuit court and upheld the decision of the county court. In its judgment, the Supreme Court outlined the circumstances to be taken into account in deciding the amount of non-pecuniary damages. The Court further stated that previous case law must be taken into account when awarding compensation for non-pecuniary damage, but that it does not impose a rigid upper or lower limit on the compensation for non-pecuniary damage, which the court may not exceed on the basis of the circumstances of the case and its own discretion. 27

Compensation for non-pecuniary damage must go hand in hand with increases in the cost of living and general welfare, as well as with possible changes in society's values. Thus, the amounts of compensation awarded in the past for non-pecuniary damage, while a factor to be taken into account by the court, together with all other relevant considerations, does not take precedence over other considerations. 28

c) Commentary

In the present case, although it is a criminal case, in a situation where the victim brings a civil claim in the course of criminal proceedings, it must be resolved on the basis of the LOA in the same way as an ordinary civil claim. 29

In this case, the main issue was the amount of the non-pecuniary damages, namely the relevance of the previous case law to the resolution of the case. The Supreme Court held that previous case law need not be decisive in determining the amount of compensation. This position can be considered justified, as due to Estonia's small size, there is also very little comparable previous case law. In addition, each case usually has a certain peculiarity in the factual circumstances. However, it can be said that previous case law is all the more important in deciding on the amount of compensation, the more similar the circumstances of the cases are. 30

As the circuit court based its decision on previous case law from 1 June 2018 to 31 May 2020, the Supreme Court referred, inter alia, to the fact that, for example, the consumer price index increased by 36.4 % between August 2020 and November 2023 and the average gross monthly salary increased by 26.5 % between 2020 and 2023. 31

Although the Supreme Court has not indicated that the change in the amount of non-pecuniary damages should be mathematically calculated on the basis of the consumer price index and the percentage change in salaries, the approach of the 32 circuit court that the change in the consumer price index alone allows for a 'fair and just' amount of compensation for non-pecuniary damage to be determined on the basis of a mathematical operation is certainly incorrect. If the consumer price index increases over the relevant period, but salaries do not, then the overall welfare of society (over the relevant period) has been reduced.

4. Supreme Court, Court Order no 2-22-14182, 20 March 2024, ECLI:EE:RK:2024:2.22.14182/32: Causing Pecuniary Damage by Means of a Ban on Competition

a) Brief Summary of the Facts

33 The plaintiffs, the Estonian Karting Association and two natural persons, were banned from engaging in motorsports in Estonia and internationally for three years by a decision of the defendant, the Estonian Automobile Sports Association. The plaintiffs brought an action against the defendant seeking an order that the defendant refrain from preventing the plaintiffs from engaging in motor sport. The plaintiffs requested that the court declare the defendant's decision void or to order the defendant to annul it.

34 The plaintiffs' claim was dismissed by the county court and the circuit court.

b) Judgment of the Court

35 The Supreme Court annulled both the county and circuit court judgments and returned the case to the county court for review. The Supreme Court first held that the plaintiffs may have a legal interest in a declaration that the defendant's decision is void. Next, the Supreme Court stated that if the defendant's decision prevents the plaintiffs from engaging in motor sports activities, it cannot be excluded that the defendant unlawfully causes damage to the plaintiffs by such a decision. The defendant's conduct may constitute an abuse of a dominant position within the meaning of the Competition Act.[5] Insofar as the plainitffs were prohibited from participating in international motor sport, that prohibition may also infringe art 102 of the Treaty on the Functioning of the European Union (TFEU).

5 Konkurentsiseadus (Competition Act) of 5 June 2001, available in English at <https://www.riigiteataja.ee/en/eli/ee/508012025002/consolide/current>.

The provisions of the Competition Act are special rules of protection in tort within the meaning of LOA § 1045(1)(7). Article 102 of the TFEU also constitutes an equivalent standard of protection. Accordingly, the defendant's conduct may be qualified as unlawful conduct causing damage to the plaintiffs within the meaning of §§ 1043 and 1045(1)(7) of the LOA if it infringes the prohibition on abuse of a dominant position and the plaintiffs suffer damage as a result. 36

If the defendant's conduct constitutes a continuing wrongful act, the plaintiffs have the right to claim the cessation of the wrongful conduct on the basis of LOA § 1055(1). In the present case, a claim under § 1055(1) of the LOA could consist of an order that the defendant do all that is necessary to put an end to the prohibition imposed on the plaintiffs to engage in motor sport. Under § 1055(1) of the LOA, it is also possible to claim restraint from further infringement. 37

c) Commentary

There are very few so-called sports law cases in Estonia. In the present case, the plaintiffs challenged the ban imposed on them by the defendant as an umbrella organisation. The case law to date was unclear on what legal grounds this was even possible. The judgment of the Supreme Court in this case has clarified the situation. 38

However, it is questionable whether the law of tort is still the appropriate basis for resolving disputes arising from a non-competition clause. LOA § 1055(1) provides that: 'If unlawful damage is caused continually or a threat is made that unlawful damage will be caused, the victim or the person who is threatened has the right to demand that behaviour which causes damage be terminated or the making of threats with such behaviour be refrained from.' In order for this remedy to apply, the plaintiffs must be able to show that the defendant's conduct causes them lasting unlawful harm or that there is a likelihood of unlawful harm. 39

It would likely make more sense if there were a separate mechanism for appealing against decisions of the sport's governing body. Tort law, by its nature and purpose, is not the most appropriate basis for this type of dispute. 40

5. Personal Injury

There were no Supreme Court cases concerning compensation for personal injury in 2024. However, there were judgments from the lower courts awarding pecuniary and non-pecuniary damages in connection with personal injury. As a general tendency, courts have started to award a higher amount of non-pecuniary dam- 41 ages than in previous cases and this is mainly due to the guidelines of the Supreme Court in criminal case no 1-22-5835 of 22 April 2024 (see above no 24 ff). The Supreme Court held in the above-mentioned judgment that compensation for non-material damage must go hand in hand with an increase in the cost of living and an increase in the general level of well-being, as well as take account of possible changes in society's values.

42 For example, in criminal case no 1-23-4097 (11 September 2024), Tartu County Court awarded € 100,000 in compensation for non-pecuniary damage to a person who had suffered life-threatening injuries caused by a dog attack. The Tartu District Court reduced the compensation and awarded € 50,000. It should be recalled that in 2020 – 2022, the highest amount of compensation for non-material damage for bodily injury or damage to health was € 12,000.[6] Considering that the average amount of compensation for non-pecuniary damage caused by a health injury was previously € 1,752, the decision of the Tallinn District Court no 2-23-7499 of 12 March 2024 must also be considered relevant. In this case, the district court awarded compensation of € 7,800 to a person who, as a result of a traffic accident, suffered injuries, which required surgical intervention and left the victim with scars that disfigured his appearance.

43 However, the above-mentioned case law of the Supreme Court did not influenced the practice of lower courts in cases of compensation for non-material damage caused to third parties in 2024. For example, the county court dismissed a claim for an award of non-pecuniary damages to the spouse and two minor sons of a mother killed in a road accident. The county court relied on § 134(3) of the LOA, according to which, persons close to the injured person may claim compensation for non-material damage only if the payment of compensation is justified by exceptional circumstances, such as, according to the case law, the physical proximity of the close person to the victim at the time of the accident, subsequent survival from seeing the injuries or suffering, or other similar circumstances. In this case, the significantly broader interpretation of the provision given by the Criminal Chamber of the Supreme Court in judgment no 1-21-3082 of 7 October 2022 was not taken into account. According to the aforementioned judgment, whether and to what extent one of the relatives saw the body after the accident is not decisive in a situation where the circumstances of the loss of life are so tragic

6 The analysis is available (in Estonian): <https://www.riigikohus.ee/sites/default/files/analyys/Mittevaraline_kahju_2020–2022.pdf> The analysis is commented on by *J Lahe*/*I Kull* in: E Karner/BC Steininger (eds), European Tort Law (ETL) 2023 (2024) 211, no 59 f.

that learning about them in any way has an extremely traumatic effect on the relatives of the deceased.[7]

C. Literature

1. *B Koppel*, Deliktiõiguslik vastutus tegevusetuse eest [Tort liability for failure to act] Juridica 1 (2024) 12 ff

In this article, the author discusses the current legal problems related to failures to act and analyses whether and how such can be distinguished from other forms of conduct; how the structure of the overall composition of the tort could be shaped in the case of a breach of the standard of protection and of the duty to maintain safety; and what the allocation of the burden of proof should be in determining the presumptions of liability. 44

The article is an important contribution to the developments in Estonian law as the idea that unlawful conduct may result not only from active action but also from failure to act is now generally accepted in all European legal orders but not regulated in Estonian law. The author proposes an answer to the question of whether there is a need for further legal regulation of failure to act as a basis for liability. 45

2. *K Krillo/K Piho*, Mittevaralise kahju hüvitiste väljamõistmine isikuõiguse rikkumise korral. Kohtupraktika 2020 – 2022 ja arengutendentsid [Award of compensation for non-pecuniary damage in the event of infringement of personal rights. Case law 2020 – 2022 and trends in developments] Juridica 3 (2024) 222 ff

The article was based on judgments of regional and circuit courts that were handed down over a three-year period and in which the courts awarded compensation for non-pecuniary damage. The authors' aim is to investigate whether and how the amount of compensation for non-pecuniary damage awarded by the courts has changed in recent years, and whether and how it differs for different offences. 46

7 The judgment of the Criminal Chamber has been commented on by *J Lahe/I Kull*, Estonia, in: E Karner/BC Steininger (eds), European Tort Law (ETL) 2022 (2023) 187, no 4 ff.

The authors express concern that the sums awarded as non-pecuniary damages have not increased but rather decreased. Courts are mostly basing their analyses on previous case law and take into account the increase in the cost of living in only a few cases. The article concludes that compensation for non-pecuniary damage must be in line with the general level of welfare of society: the amount of compensation awarded should be somewhat higher than that indicated in the analyses of previous case law.

47 The article is particularly important as the Supreme Court has repeatedly criticised lower courts for determining the amount of compensation solely on the basis of previous case law.

3. *O-J Luik/R Kinkar*, Tehisaru ja lepinguväline vastutus: kas kindlustussüsteem asendab tulevikus deliktisüsteemi? Autonoomsete sõidukite näide [AI and non-contractual liability: will insurance replace tort in the future? The example of autonomous vehicles] Juridica 7 (2024) 496 ff

48 The authors analyse whether and how the current harmonised motor insurance system in the EU needs to be changed with regard to autonomous vehicles. In particular, they address the questions as to whether liability arising from the use of autonomous or fully autonomous vehicles should be subject to another insurance system and if the extent of liability cannot be mitigated through another insurance system, or if it is not practical, would the pan-European motor vehicle insurance system need to be changed.

49 This article is an important contribution to scholarship concerning the harmonisation of EU law on compulsory motor vechicle insurance according to Directive 2009/103/EC of 16 September 2009, amended by Directive 2021/2118 of 24 November 2021.[8]

8 Directive (EU) 2021/2118 of the European Parliament and of the Council of 24 November 2021 amending Directive 2009/103/EC relating to insurance against civil liability in respect of the use of motor vehicles, and the enforcement of the obligation to insure against such liability (Text with EEA relevance) [2021] OJ L 60/1.

Päivi Korpisaari

X. Finland

A. Legislation

1 In 2024, there were no significant legislative developments in the field of tort law in Finland.

B. Cases

1. Supreme Court (Korkein oikeus, KKO) 23 October 2024, KKO 2024:64:[1] Damages; Basis of Liability; Limited Liability Housing Company, ECLI:FI:KKO:2024:64

a) Brief Summary of the Facts

2 A company, A Ltd, rented a residential apartment from a shareholder of a limited liability housing company B for the use of its own employees, foreigners who were football players. The employees did not speak or understand Finnish.

3 Renovation work, where the sewage pipes were coated, was carried out in the limited liability housing company B. The residents were prohibited from using certain facilities while the work was being done on the sewage pipes. The employees of A Ltd who lived in the apartment had nevertheless used the facilities while the work on the sewage pipe was being carried out, causing water damage to the two apartments located below.

4 B, who had paid the repair costs incurred to remedy the water damage, claimed compensation from A Ltd for the damage in question, which amounted to € 18,417. B considered that A Ltd had failed to take such reasonable precautions as would have prevented the violation of the prohibition on using the facilities connected to the sewage system and thus the occurrence of the damage. The ten-

Acknowledgement: The author thanks research assistant Matias Koivulehto LLB, MSc in Political Science for help with this contribution.

1 Cases are available at <https://www.finlex.fi/en>.

https://doi.org/10.1515/9783111389271-011

ant was responsible for the proper use of the apartment, regardless of whether it was used by the tenant or by someone they had subletted it to.

5 According to B, A Ltd had acted negligently in failing to ensure that the foreign employees of A Ltd who were staying in the apartment understood the meaning of the notice concerning the sewage repair work and the prohibition on using facilities connected to the pipes. A Ltd denied liability, arguing that it had not acted negligently and that its actions or omissions were not causally linked to the damage.

6 The question to be resolved by the Supreme Court was whether A Ltd was liable to compensate the limited liability housing company B for the damage caused by its employees.

b) Judgment of the Court

7 The Supreme Court stated that the damage had not been caused to the landlord of A Ltd, but to the limited liability housing company B. The Tort Liability Act (412/1974, TLA) was therefore applied as a general law on extra-contractual liability for damages.

8 According to ch 2, sec 1, subsec 1 of the TLA, a party who intentionally or negligently causes damage to another is liable for damages. The decisive factor in assessing the degree of negligence is the degree of care that could be expected of the person concerned in the circumstances of a given situation. The basis for liability under the provision could be the act or omission of the party causing the damage.

9 The employees of A Ltd who were staying in the apartment rented by A Ltd had used the facilities connected to the sewage system during the prohibition period, causing water damage to the two apartments located below.

10 The housing company B had informed the residents of the building about the sewage pipe work and the related prohibitions of use several times and in many ways. A Ltd had not even claimed that it was not aware of the repair of the sewage pipes and the prohibition of use and the related instructions to residents.

11 As the employees living in the apartment rented by A Ltd were foreigners and did not speak Finnish, there was a greater than usual risk that the residents would not understand the prohibition on using the drains or its meaning and that extensive damage could be caused to the building of the limited liability housing company. Given these special circumstances, A Ltd had a particular duty to ensure that the employees staying in its apartment were aware of the sewage repair work and the associated prohibition of use and the meaning of the prohibition. By not even claiming to have contacted its employees about the repair work, A Ltd had acted negligently.

The damage could have been avoided by discussing the prohibition of the use of the facilities connected to the sewage system and the meaning of the prohibition with the employees of A Ltd who were staying in the apartment. Furthermore, it was not unforeseeable for A Ltd that failure to comply with the prohibition to use the facilities connected to the sewage system could result in water damage, the repair costs of which could be considerable. Therefore, there was a causal link between A Ltd's negligence and the damage. 12

A Ltd had also argued that the party which caused the damage was not A Ltd but an unknown employee of A Ltd, for whose actions A Ltd was not responsible. In this respect, the Supreme Court stated that in established case law concerning damages, it is common that damage may be considered to be causally linked to the acts or omissions of more than one person, even if they did not act together (see eg, KKO 2022:21, para 34). Therefore, the fact that the damage was directly caused by one of A Ltd's employees did not exclude A Ltd's liability in this case. 13

c) Commentary

The negligent act of causing damage, within the meaning of ch 2, sec 1, subsec 1 of the TLA, can be considered not only an active act but also an omission, that is, the failure to act to prevent damage (reasoning of the judgment, para 6). In an extra-contractual situation, the general rule is that no one is obligated, without a specific reason, to take actions that would reduce the risk of damage or otherwise benefit another person. In the present case, A Ltd's active obligation to expressly inform the employees living in the apartment it rented of the prohibition to use the facilities connected to the sewage system was justified by the fact that sec 25 of the Act on Residential Leases (481/1995) provides for the tenant's obligation to take care of the apartment they have rented. 14

In addition, B had informed the residents about the repairs to the sewage system and the related prohibitions of use several times and in various ways. A Ltd had not even maintained that, as a tenant, it had not been aware of the repairs to the sewage system and the prohibition of use and the related instructions. 15

The decision KKO 2024:64 provides a new example within the case law on liability for damages, clarifying the circumstances under which a person may, in an extra-contractual context, have a duty to take active steps to prevent harm to another.[2] The decision places the risk on the tenant to ensure that the persons using 16

2 *Olli Norros*, KKO 2024:64, Tiedottamisen laiminlyönnillä aiheutettu vahinko, in: KKO:n ratkaisut kommentein 2025 I.

the apartment with the tenant's permission have been properly informed of the fairly obvious and clear risk of damage.

17 By imposing liability on the tenant, the potentially difficult question of proof as to who or which of the people living in the apartment had used the facilities connected to the sewage system in violation of the instructions was also avoided.

18 The judgment also achieves a fair distribution of risk, as A Ltd would have had the opportunity to influence the realisation of the risk, while the shareholders of limited liability housing company B, who pay for the repair costs in the apartment building, have limited opportunities to influence the behaviour of the people living in each apartment.

2. Supreme Court (Korkein oikeus, KKO) 23 October 2024, KKO 2024:67: Selling a Car; Damages, ECLI:FI:KKO:2024:67

a) Brief Summary of the Facts

19 On 3 June 2020, A bought a car from B. Due to a defect in the car's engine, the car was withdrawn from service on 19 August 2020 and the contract of sale was declared avoided. B was ordered to refund the purchase price to A, less the benefit A had obtained from the use of the car, with interest.

20 In addition to the refund of the purchase price, A demanded that B be ordered to compensate him for the period of immobilisation of the car at the rate of € 2.67 per day from the date of the commencement of the action on 20 August 2020 until the date on which the purchase price was refunded to him. The question to be resolved by the Supreme Court was whether A was entitled to this compensation for the loss of use of the car for the period after it was withdrawn from service.

b) Judgment of the Court

21 Pursuant to sec 30 of the Sales of Goods Act (355/1987, SGA), a buyer is entitled, as a consequence of a defect in the goods, to declare the contract avoided as well as to claim damages. Pursuant to sec 40, subsec 1 of the Act, a buyer is entitled to damages for losses that they suffer because of a defect in the goods, unless the seller proves that there was an impediment beyond the seller's control. No such impediment was proven to have existed.

22 According to sec 67, subsec 1 of the SGA, damages for breach of contract consist of compensation for expenses, price difference, lost profit and other direct or indirect losses due to the breach. According to subsec 2 of the same section, indi-

rect loss consists of, inter alia, losses arising because the goods cannot be used as intended. According to Government Proposal 93/1986, p 123, the starting point is full compensation, meaning that the injured party is to be placed in the same financial position as if the other party had properly fulfilled the contract.

The Supreme Court referred to case KKO 2005:66 and stated that compensation for the loss of the use of property was based on the fact that the financial investment made to acquire the property became useless when the object could not be used for its intended purpose. In addition, this often resulted in direct costs, as the owner of the object has to purchase a replacement. 23

The Court of Appeal had rejected A's claim for compensation for the loss of use of the car, because the parties' payments were restored to the pre-trade situation upon avoidance of the contract. However, the Supreme Court stated that under the SGA, the buyer was entitled to claim damages in the event of avoidance of the contract. The question was one of a consequence of a breach of contract which was distinct from the avoidance of the contract and its effects, the purpose of which was to place the buyer in the financial position in which he would have been if the seller had performed the contract correctly. In such a case, compensation could, for example, be awarded for the damage resulting from the fact that the object of the sale could not be used as intended because it was defective. 24

A had to withdraw the car from service because of its defect. A suffered loss of use of the property, which was reduced by the fact that interest had to be paid on the refund of the purchase price. In the assessment, consideration could also be given to the injured party's duty to mitigate his loss. As regards the amount of the loss of use, it was generally not reasonable to require specific evidence, as the court could, in most cases, estimate the amount pursuant to ch 17, sec 2, subsec 3 of the Code of Judicial Procedure (4/1734). 25

The question was one of indirect damage, for which the buyer was only entitled to compensation if the defect or damage was due to negligence on the part of the seller or if the goods at the time of the conclusion of the contract deviated from what the seller had specifically agreed to. It was therefore necessary to assess whether the defect was due to negligence on the part of B. 26

The car had been in B's possession for only a few weeks before being sold to A. B had changed the oil during the period of ownership and the car had been inspected. In the light of the evidence presented, the defect could not be considered to have been detectable during B's ownership of the car. B had not been shown to have given any information about the characteristics or use of the vehicle in the marketing or sale of the goods which he should have known to be incorrect or misleading. 27

Therefore, no failure or other circumstance had been proved in connection with the conclusion or performance of the contract on the part of B which 28 could be attributed to negligence on his part. A's claim for compensation for the loss of use was dismissed.

c) Commentary

29 The decision KKO 2024:67 is similar to KKO 1992:86, in which compensation for the loss of use was considered. Also, in KKO 1992:86, the claim for compensation was dismissed due to the absence of negligence on the part of the seller. It is worth noting that the Supreme Court in KKO 2024:67 dealt with the general conditions for the compensability of loss of use and the assessment of the amount of damages, although it could have refrained from doing so, as the claim was dismissed due to a lack of negligence.[3]

C. Literature

1. *Anton Hartzell/Tom Vapaavuori*, Törkeä huolimattomuus liikesopimussuhteissa ja vastuunrajoitukset [Gross negligence in business contracts and limitations of liability], Liikejuridiikka 2024/2, 8 – 38

30 The threshold for gross negligence in business contracts is high and rarely met. The assessment is always an overall assessment of the concrete situation. The article discusses the different assessment criteria and assumes that the situation is assessed largely on the basis of objective facts. However, the decisive criterion is the subjective assessment of whether the contracting party has shown a clear disregard or indifference to its conduct and its consequences.

31 In the case of gross negligence, the various limitations of liability in contracts are overridden by the general principle of contract law. Gross negligence also has other consequences, such as the effect on the contracting party's liability to make a claim, the right of rescission and the possibility of obtaining insurance compensation.

3 *Olli Norros*, Auton käyttöhyödyn menetyksen korvattavuus, in: KKO:n ratkaisut kommentein I (2025).

2. *Mikael Koskinen*, Etätöissä sattuneen tapaturman korvaaminen [Compensation for an accident during remote work], Lakimies 2024/1, 79 – 98

Compensation for occupational accidents is governed by the Workers' Compensation Act, which came into force on 1 January 2016.[4] This Law specifies the circumstances in which accidents can be compensated as occupational accidents. 32

One of the unclear questions relates to the compensation of accidents that occur during remote work. This issue has not been addressed in jurisprudence. However, the Insurance Court and the Accident Appeal Board, have issued several published and unpublished decisions on this issue. 33

The research question in this article is: when should an accident that occurred while working remotely be compensated under the Workers' Compensation Act? In the absence of jurisprudential opinions, the question is examined by researching published and unpublished decisions of both the Insurance Court and the Accident Appeal Board. The preparatory work for the Workers' Compensation Act also plays an important role. 34

The result of the research is that the extent of compensation protection should be understood by the following question: What caused the accident? If the main cause of the accident has an essential causal connection with the work, compensation protection applies. In addition to the performance of the actual work tasks, various related tasks, such as travelling to obtain work equipment, may also be covered by compensation protection. However, the author concludes that the distance travelled in transporting equipment does not have to be significant for compensation protection to apply. The author also notes that the extent of statutory compensation protection depends on the employer. From the beginning of 2023, the statutory compensation protection for civil servants will be much broader than for other employees. This is because on 1 January 2023 the Act on Compensation of State Employees for Accidents caused by Remote Work came into force. 35

4 The author has modified the text from the English summary published in the original publication.

Jonas Knetsch and Zoé Jacquemin

XI. France

A. Legislation

1. Act no 2024-346 of 15 April 2024 on the Adaptation of Tort Law to Current Challenges: Enshrining the Doctrine of Private Nuisance (*troubles anormaux de voisinage*) in the Civil Code

1 The title of this Act may suggest to regular readers of our national report that the French lawmakers have finally resumed their plans for a comprehensive tort law reform.[1] Unfortunately, that has not happened and this legislation comes as a political 'window dressing' rather than being a serious attempt to 'adapt tort law to current challenges'. In fact, despite the Act's pompous and misleading title, its scope is limited to the doctrine of private nuisance, which is now enshrined in art 1253 of the Civil Code.

2 The reason for this surprising legislative step, while there is still no prospect of a comprehensive tort law reform, is to be found in the vociferous protests arising from the farming community against new country dwellers objecting to agricultural livelihood and, in particular, to noise and odour nuisances related to farming activities. The case of *Maurice*, a particularly noisy cockerel, which so annoyed a retired couple that they took its owner to court in order to obtain injunctive relief,[2] gave rise to harsh criticism of the rural community complaining that the litigiousness of urban population threatens the 'living together' (*vivre ensemble*) in the countryside. The aim of the bill, introduced by a rural representative of Central Britanny, herself a poultry farmer, was thus to set out a stricter framework for the case law-based doctrine of private nuisance.

1 For a comprehensive survey of the reform plans, see *J Knetsch/Z Jacquemin*, France, in: E Karner/BC Steininger (eds), European Tort Law (ETL) 2016 (2017) 191, nos 13–23; *J Knetsch/Z Jacquemin*, France, in: E Karner/BC Steininger (eds), ETL 2017 (2018) 187, nos 1–8; *J Knetsch/Z Jacquemin*, France, in: E Karner/BC Steininger (eds), ETL 2019 (2020) 186, nos 1–5; *J Knetsch/Z Jacquemin*, France, in: E Karner/BC Steininger (eds), ETL 2020 (2021) 178, nos 1–5; *J Knetsch*, France, in: E Karner/BC Steininger (eds), ETL 2021 (2022) 174, no 1 f.

2 The case even attracted some attention in the United Kingdom. See eg *A Chrisafis*, French court hears case of Maurice, the famous 'noisy' cockerel, The Guardian 4 July 2019 ('a retired couple say rooster's "abnormal noise" disturbs them at holiday home').

https://doi.org/10.1515/9783111389271-012

3 As in other jurisdictions, the remedy for disturbances between neighbours is based on the idea that in the enjoyment of their premises, individuals must take care not to interfere excessively with their neighbours.[3] The Court of Cassation converted this maxim to an autonomous ground of civil liability, progressively abandoning the reference to the doctrine of *faute* under art 1382 Civil Code. In accordance with a landmark decision in 1844, a claimant does not have to establish fault but only a *trouble anormal de voisinage*, that is, a serious disturbance exceeding the normal inconvenience or discomfort between neighbours.

4 The new art 1253 reaffirms the main features of the doctrine of *troubles anormaux de voisinage*, while specifying in the Civil Code the 'defence of preoccupancy' (*exception de préoccupation*). This defence excludes civil liability in cases in which the litigious activity, 'whatever its nature', pre-existed the settlement of the person complaining and continues under the same conditions as before or 'under new conditions that do not cause the abnormal disorder to worsen'. It was previously enshrined, more discreetly and more narrowly defined, in art L 112-16 Construction and Housing Code. The new text allows farmers to bar compensation claims even in the case of a modification of their business, which comes with an aggravation of a nuisance, if this modification is to ensure compliance with regulations or is not deemed 'substantial as to its nature or intensity'.[4]

5 Along with many other commentators,[5] we can only regret that both Parliament and the Government agreed to waste time on such a 'mini-reform' without an obvious need other than to satisfy the expectations of a small, but noisy electoral group. The only consolation that remains is that there is no longer any doubt as to the legal nature of the rules on private nuisance: with the 2024 Act, the doctrine has definitely dropped out of the laps of property law and is now solidly entrenched in tort law.[6]

---

3 For a recent overview in English, see *J Knetsch*, Tort Law in France (2nd edn 2025) nos 202–206.

4 This defence is only limited to farming activities, introducing a differentiation with other activities producing disturbances. For a critical assessment of this difference in treatment, see *C Latil*, Les troubles anormaux du voisinage: le régime de responsabilité fait son entrée dans le Code civil!, La Semaine Juridique. Édition Notariale 2024, no 1129.

5 See *P Delebecque*, Troubles de voisinage : pourquoi légiférer? Énergie Environnement Infrastructures 2024, repère 4; *H Bosse-Platière*, L'activité agricole: en trouble normal de voisinage, Revue de droit rural 2024, repère 6; *C Quézel-Ambrunaz*, La codification du régime des troubles excédant les inconvénients normaux du voisinage, Revue Lamy Droit civil (RLDC) 2024, no 228, 26.

6 On this aspect, see *N Rudulier*, Codification des troubles anormaux du voisinage, Revue trimestrielle de droit civil (RTD civ) 2024, 813; *N Reboul-Maupin*, Une responsabilité pour troubles anormaux de voisinage insérée dans le code civil : le droit des biens sacrifié sur l'autel de la responsabilité civile! Recueil Dalloz (D) 2024, 65.

B. Cases

1. Cour de cassation, Troisième chambre civile (Cass Civ 3) 4 April 2024, no 22-21132: No Disproportionality Defence in Extra-Contractual Liability Cases

a) Brief Summary of the Facts

A landowner residing in Réunion (a French overseas *département* in the Indian 6
Ocean) sued her neighbour to have him ordered to bring his house into compliance with the height rules and his plantations with the distance rules, set out in the local planning scheme. The reason was that she felt deprived of a large part of the panoramic view of the coastline and of the brightness of her living room. Accordingly, she not only sought injunctive relief, but also compensation for loss of enjoyment (*préjudice de jouissance*).

b) Judgment of the Court

After a long procedure, the Saint-Denis Court of Appeal granted these claims on 7
the ground of fault-based liability (art 1240 Civil Code), ordering the partial demolition of the house, the ridge height of which turned out to be 70 cm too high. The defendant brought the case before the Court of Cassation, arguing that the trial judges failed to assess whether the ordered injunctions were not disproportionate with regard to the extent of non-compliance and to the (considerable) cost of the necessary construction work.

Referring to the principle of full reparation (*réparation intégrale*), the Court of 8
Cassation upheld the decision on the grounds that 'the trial judges, when dealing with non-contractual cases, cannot assess the reparation due to the victim in the light of its disproportionate cost for the tortfeasor'.

c) Commentary[7]

The principle of full compensation (*réparation intégrale*) is one of the fundamen- 9
tal concepts of French tort law, with only few exceptions. There are countless

7 See also *JS Borghetti*, L'exigence de proportionnalité en responsabilité délictuelle, La Semaine

cases in which the Court of Cassation reminds that 'the proper function of civil liability is to re-establish as exactly as possible the balance disturbed by the harm and to replace victims in the situation in which they would have been if the harm had not occurred'.[8] This principle is one of the legal grounds underlying the present case, explicitly referred to by the Third Civil Chamber, and it means that 'the victim shall be compensated without loss or profit'.

10 Given the importance of the idea of full reparation, it may be surprising that the Court of Cassation had to deal with a 'disproportionality defence' in the present case. It may be even more surprising to the foreign reader that, in 2023, the same Third Civil Chamber decided, in a contractual case, that a trial judge, to which a claim for demolition of a building was presented under contractual liability rules, 'must investigate, if so requested, whether there is a manifest disproportion between the cost to the debtor ... and its interest for the creditor in the light of the harmful consequences of the non-conformities'.[9] The contrast between both judgments, one admitting the disproportionality defence, the other rejecting it vigorously, could not be more striking.

11 One could argue that, in contractual matters, the current Civil Code provisions facilitate the admission of such a defence. Since the 2016 Law of Obligations reform, art 1221 provides that: 'a creditor of an obligation may ... seek performance in kind unless performance is impossible or if there is a manifest disproportion'.[10] This new rule led the Court of Cassation to extend the 'disproportionality bar' to contractual damages, most probably because the distinction between the specific enforcement (*exécution forcée*) of an obligation and contractual damages is not that clear. While this solution seems to be covered by the legislator's intention, the Third Civil Chamber is reluctant to introduce the same defence in extra-contractual matters, probably for two reasons. First, such a step could be regarded as exceeding the powers of the courts, the tort law reform being still outstanding. Second, the situation between contractual parties is a specific one, as the duty to

juridique. Édition générale (JCP G) 2024, no 653; *M Cormier*, Mise en conformité d'une construction: inachèvement du chantier de l'exclusion de la proportionnalité, D 2024, 1311; *P Jourdain*, Rejet du contrôle de proportionnalité d'une demande de réparation en nature en matière de responsabilité extracontractuelle, RTD civ 2024, 661; *S Pellet*, Exclusion de tout contrôle de proportionnalité en matière de responsabilité extracontractuelle: triomphe de la licéité ou de l'esprit de vindicte? Revue des contrats (Rev contrats) 2024, no 3, 17.

8 See eg, Cour de Cassation, Chambre commerciale (Cass Com) 10 January 2012, no 10-26837. The formula is borrowed from *R Savatier*, Traité de la responsabilité civile en droit français (2nd edn 1951) vol 2, no 601.

9 Civ 3, 6 July 2023, no 22-10884.

10 On this provision, see in English *S Rowan*, The New French Law of Contract (2022) 203 f.

act in good faith (*bonne foi*), laid out in art 1104 Civil Code, is not applicable to parties who are not committed to a contractual relationship.[11]

2. Cour de cassation, Assemblée plénière (Cass Ass plén) 28 June 2024, no 22-84760: Judicial Rewriting of the Parental Liability of Art 1242(4) Civil Code

a) Brief Summary of the Facts

A 14-year-old boy had been found guilty of setting fire to different plots of woodland on 17 occasions. The owners of the burned land claimed compensation from both parents of the child, although the parents were divorced and the child lived permanently with his mother alone. The claimants argued that, contrary to what was indicated in the custody order, the boy had been living regularly with his father, both before and after the offences. 12

Having found the child guilty of the destruction of the claimants' property, the juvenile court also recognised the civil liability of both parents under art 1242(4) Civil Code. The father appealed against this judgment. The Aix-en-Provence Court of Appeal ruled in his favour on the grounds that *cohabitation* was one of the prerequisites for parental liability and that the custody order clearly stated that the child's residence was with his mother only. 13

The outcome of the case was of the upmost importance for the mother, as the coverage limit of her insurance policy was of € 1 million only, leaving her to compensate the victims for the remainder. She therefore decided to bring the case before the Court of Cassation, so as not to bear the share of the compensation not covered by her insurance alone. 14

b) Judgment of the Court

Sitting in full bench (*Assemblée plénière*), the Court of Cassation decided to abandon its previous interpretation of art 1242(4) Civil Code. According to the case, 15

11 This was the argument raised by the *rapporteur* in the present case. See *P Brun*, Éviction du contrôle de proportionnalité en cas de demande de démolition sur le fondement de la responsabilité extracontractuelle, JCP G 2024, no 652. For a critical assessment of this reasoning, see *S Pellet*, Exclusion de tout contrôle de proportionnalité en matière de responsabilité extracontractuelle: triomphe de la licéité ou de l'esprit de vindicte? Rev contrats 2024, no 3, 17, 18–20.

'from now on, the notion of *cohabitation* is to be interpreted as the consequence of the joint exercise of parental authority'. This means that '(the) *cohabitation* (of parents) with a minor child over whom they jointly exercise parental authority only ceases when administrative or judicial decisions entrust the minor to a third party'. In other words, both parents must bear the civil liability for the loss caused by their son, although a custody order indicates that he was living with one of his parents only.

c) Commentary[12]

16 Under French law, parental liability is laid out in art 1242(4) Civil Code according to which, 'the father and mother … are jointly and severally liable for the damage caused by their minor children *who live with them*'. This requirement of *cohabitation* has been of particular importance as long as this liability regime was based upon a presumption of the parents' fault, as originally conceived in the Civil Code. According to this rationale, the courts had to determine whether the defendant(s) had properly supervised their child, which is only possible when there is physical proximity between them.

17 Over the years, due to the 'objectivation' of parental liability, that is the change from a presumption of fault (*présomption de faute*) to strict liability,[13] the *cohabitation* test has progressively become less and less consistent. During the 2000s and the 2010s, it was deemed sufficient that the child 'usually lived' with their parents, a standard that was very widely interpreted by French courts. In a symbolic case, the Court of Cassation held that parents could be liable for the actions of their 13-year-old daughter, even though she had resided with her grandparents from the age of one.[14] While for many authors the *cohabitation* requirement became a purely 'virtual' one, the Court of Cassation applied a stricter test. However, in cases in which the parents lived separately, it decided that only the

12 See also *AM Leroyer*, Quel est le vrai fondement de la responsabilité des père et mère? RTD civ 2024, 628; *L Perdrix*, La cohabitation de l'enfant avec ses parents : une condition de la responsabilité parentale entre effacement et mutation, D 2024, 1751; *L Vitale*, La condition de cohabitation de l'enfant avec ses père et mère est désormais consubstantielle à l'autorité parentale, JCP G 2024, no 992; *JS Borghetti*, La Cour de cassation poursuit sa réécriture du Code civil en matière de responsabilité des parents du fait de leurs enfants, Gazette du Palais (Gaz Pal) 2024, no 27, 20.
13 For a presentation of this transformation in English, see *Knetsch* (fn 3) nos 145–149.
14 Cour de Cassation, Chambre criminelle (Cass Crim) 8 February 2005, no 03-87447. In light of this case, it goes without saying that trips to relatives, holiday camps and even stays at boarding schools did not terminate 'cohabitation' between children and their parents.

parent with whom the child resided would be subject to art 1242(4) Civil Code, while the other parent (in most cases, the father) could escape civil liability.[15] Those inconsistencies led to criticism and voices had been raised to fundamentally revise the liability regime, for example by introducing parental authority as the sole criterion for the establishment of liability.[16]

In the present case, the Court of Cassation responds to this criticism without, however, formally abandoning the *cohabitation* requirement. According to the judgment, *cohabitation* is now inferred from parental authority, the judges upholding somewhat artificially the distinction between both prerequisites. It is very likely that the Court did not feel at ease with the idea of a radical overhaul of this liability regime, which is the prerogative of Parliament.[17] This case is thus a further illustration of the effects of legislative inertia in the field of tort law: the courts must deal with statutory provisions which date back more than two centuries, while hesitating about the limitations of their own prescriptive power. However, the French parliament has decided, for once, to enshrine this case-law development in the Civil Code. A last-minute amendment to a 2025 Act on juvenile delinquency modified the wording of art 1242(4) Civil Code, deleting the requirement of *cohabitation*.[18] 18

3. Cour de cassation, Chambre commerciale (Cass Com) 3 July 2024, no 21-14947: Liability of Contracting Parties towards Third Parties; Extension of Contractual Provisions to Extra-Contractual Liability

a) Brief Summary of the Facts

The defendant, a transport company, was appointed by the French branch of a corporate group specialised in packaging solutions to handle and unload machines belonging to its Italian parent company. After one of the machines was 19

15 Cass Civ 2, 21 December 2006, no 05-17540. For a critical assessment of this case, see eg, *L Bloch*, Résidence alternée de l'enfant: responsabilités solidaires des parents? Responsabilité civile et assurance (Resp civ assur) 2013, alerte 35.

16 For a comparative overview of the different options available, see *M Martín-Casals* (ed), Children in Tort Law, vol 1 Children as Tortfeasors (2006).

17 This was also the opinion delivered by the Prosecutor-General, according to whom, the 'de-activation' of the cohabitation test is a task for lawmakers, not the courts.

18 Art 3 of Act 2025-568 of 23 June 2025. This legislative change, which entered into force on 25 June 2025, will be commented on in our next annual report.

damaged, the parent company reported the loss to its insurer and was awarded direct compensation for it. The insurance company, subrogated to the rights of the machine owner, sued the transport company which was responsible for damaging the machine on the basis of contractual liability and in tort.

20 The Paris Court of Appeal held that the transport company had breached its contractual duties towards the French branch of the corporate group. However, considering that the insurance company was exercising the rights of the parent company, which was not party to the contract, the liability of the transport company could only be extra-contractual in nature. The Court of Appeal also decided that the limitation clause provided for in the contract could not be invoked vis-à-vis the claimant, since the parent company was a third party.

21 The transport company brought the case before the Court of Cassation, arguing that the limitation clause should be considered when a third party invokes a breach of contract to obtain compensation under tort law.

b) Judgment of the Court

22 Quashing the Court of Appeal judgment, the Court of Cassation decided that 'in order not to frustrate the expectations of the debtor, who has themself committed in consideration of the general scheme of contract (*économie générale du contrat*), and not to confer on the third party which invokes the contract a more advantageous position than that which the creditor themself can claim, the third party to a contract, which invokes, on the basis of tort liability, a contractual breach which caused a loss may be subject to the conditions and limits of liability which apply in the relationship between the contracting parties'.

c) Commentary[19]

23 The liability of contracting parties towards *third* parties is one of the major sources of complexity when it comes to the interplay between contractual and extra-

19 See also *D Bakouche/YM Serinet*, Responsabilité du débiteur à l'égard des tiers: où va la chambre commerciale? JCP G 2024, no 1074; *D Houtcieff*, Opposabilité des clauses limitatives de responsabilité aux tiers: le nœud gordien, D 2024, 1607; *C François*, Revirement partiel de la jurisprudence Myr'Ho: enfin un rééquilibrage en faveur du débiteur! Revue Lamy Droit des affaires (RLDA) 2024, no 207, 26; *A Gouëzel*, Opposabilité des clauses limitatives à l'action en responsabilité délictuelle du tiers: quelle place pour l'opportunité dans l'élaboration de la jurisprudence? D 2024, 1577. For a detailed assessment in German, see also *J Knetsch*, Haftung der

contractual liability under French law.[20] Since the *Bootshop/Myr'Ho* case of 2006,[21] if the non-performance of a contractual obligation (*inexécution contractuelle*) causes a loss to a third party, such non-performance may be invoked by the defendant as the legal grounds for a compensation claim in tort without further proof of fault under art 1240 Civil Code. This solution has always given rise to criticism as it allows a third party to invoke a contractual failing without proof of the violation of a general duty towards them and without being subject to stipulations, such as exemption or limitation clauses, which affect the right to damages between contracting parties.

The present case (also known as the *Clamageran* case) is a direct response to 24 this criticism addressed in legal scholarship and, at first sight, it appears to be a major turning point in an area where the law of contract and tort law are often in conflict. It must be noted, however, that the judgment was given by the Commercial Chamber and not by the Court of Cassation sitting in full bench, which reduces the authority of this case. The diverging views among the chambers of the Court, which made necessary the intervention of the full bench in the *Bootshop/Myr'Ho* case, make it uncertain that this solution will be endorsed by the Civil Chambers. Given this context, it is likely that the Commercial Chamber wanted to run a test to determine whether a change of the *Bootshop/Myr'Ho* solution may generate acceptance among other formations of the Court.

As innovative as it is, the *Clamageran* case raises quite a few questions. First 25 of all, it creates a sort of hybrid liability regime which cuts across the dividing lines between contractual and extra-contractual liability. While there is a growing trend in international and European law to dismantle this distinction, it is still a strong and characteristic feature of the French law of obligations – and be it only for the sake of the *non-cumul* principle[22]. Asserting that a contracting party may invoke limitation clauses vis-à-vis third parties even though the claim for damages is based on extra-contractual liability seems a rather unconventional solution in

---

Vertragsparteien gegenüber Dritten in Frankreich: Ist der gordische Knoten endlich gelöst? Zeitschrift für Europäisches Privatrecht (ZEuP) 2025, no 4 (forthcoming).

20 On this, see in English *P Stoffel-Munck*, Liability of Contracting Parties Towards Third Parties, in: JS Borghetti/S Whittaker (eds), French Civil Liability in Comparative Perspective (2019) 55; *JS Borghetti*, Breach of Contract and Liability to Third Parties in French Law: How to Break the Deadlock? ZEuP 2010, 279, 290–292. See also *Knetsch* (fn 3) no 64.

21 Cass Ass plén, 6 October 2006, no 05-13255. For a commentary, see *O Moréteau*, France, in: H Koziol/BC Steininger (eds), European Tort Law (ETL) 2006 (2008) 196, nos 32–41.

22 According to this principle, a contracting party is not entitled to damages from the other contracting party in tort as long as the loss was caused by the non-performance of a contractual obligation. For more details, see *Knetsch* (fn 3) nos 59–61.

this regard. In particular, the recognition of such a hybrid regime[23] gives rise to doubts as to where exactly the action should be 'located' in terms of rules on limitation of actions, conflicts of jurisdiction and insurance guarantees, as all of them are distinct for contractual and extra-contractual cases.

26 Second, it is not quite clear what is meant by 'the conditions and limits of liability', which the defendant may rely upon vis-à-vis third parties invoking the non-performance of a contract as the basis of their tort claim. Are only exemption clauses, limitation of liability clauses or penalty clauses subject to this new extra-contractual enforceability or would it not be consistent to extend the solution also to contractual limitation periods, to jurisdiction and arbitration clauses? Regarding contractual liability caps, courts will also have to decide whether they must be divided between contracting parties and third parties or, on the contrary, have to be duplicated in order to not frustrate the expectations of the contractual partner.

27 Last but not least, it is highly uncertain to what extent this solution will affect the case law on so-called 'contractual groups' (*groupes de contrats*). In two landmark decisions from 1986 and 1991, the Court of Cassation decided that a client at the end of a contractual chain can sue for damages in contract even though the defendant is not the contracting party but a more distant entity in the chain, provided that the individual contracts are 'homogeneous' and imply a transfer of ownership (*chaînes de contrats translatifs de propriété*).[24] The *Clamageran* case largely deprives the case law on contractual groups of its interest, as an action in tort will come with the same 'conditions and limits of liability' as an action on the grounds of contractual liability.[25]

23 *J Knetsch*, L'hybridation du régime de responsabilité pour manquement contractuel ayant causé un dommage au tiers: ouverture ou aveu d'échec? Rev contrats 2024, no 4, 15 ('responsabilité délictuelle à coloration contractuelle').

24 Cass Ass plén, 7 February 1986, no 83-14631; 12 July 1991, no 90-13602 (for an English translation, see <https://law.utexas.edu/transnational/foreign-law-translations/french/case.php?id=1294> and <https://law.utexas.edu/transnational/foreign-law-translations/french/case.php?id=1289>). For a critical assessment of this solution, see *Borghetti*, ZEuP 2010, 279, 284. See also *S Whittaker*, Privity of Contract and the Law of Tort: The French Experience (1995) 15 Oxford Journal of Legal Studies (OJLS) 327, 354–357.

25 On this, see in particular *M Latina*, Responsabilité d'un contractant vis-à-vis d'un tiers: nouveau rebondissement…, Rev contrats 2024, no 4, 12.

4. Cour de cassation, Deuxième chambre civile (Cass Civ 2) 5 September 2024, no 21-23442: Application of Liability for the Action of Things to a Toxic Cloud; Civil Immunity of the Employer

a) Brief Summary of the Facts

Two employees of a surveillance company suffered an accident requiring immediate medical attention, due to the inhalation of a toxic substance, while carrying out a patrol on one of the construction sites of Airbus A380 airplanes. According to the compensation scheme for workplace accidents (*régime des accidents du travail*), they were awarded partial compensation by their statutory health insurance fund, before filing a claim for additional compensation against the company of the Airbus group, which owned the premises on which the accident had taken place. 28

The Toulouse Court of Appeal granted additional compensation to both employees on the grounds of strict liability for things under art 1242(1) Civil Code. The Airbus company brought the case before the Court of Cassation, arguing that the toxic substance had not been formally identified and that, consequently, it could not be held liable as its guardian (*gardien*). 29

b) Judgment of the Court

The Court of Cassation upheld the Court of Appeal judgment, deciding that, despite the lack of identification of the toxic substance, the Airbus company could be held liable. For the Second Civil Chamber, the 'toxic cloud which emanated from the company and while under its guardianship, was the cause of the symptoms suffered by the victims'. 30

c) Commentary[26]

One of the specific features of French tort law is the existence of a strict liability regime for things, which the Court of Cassation created at the end of the 19th cen- 31

26 See also *P Jourdain*, Un nuage toxique est une chose susceptible de garde au sens de l'article 1242, alinéa 1er, du code civil! RTD civ 2024, 895; *X Aumeran*, Accident du travail et responsabilité civile: des règles imbriquées, La Semaine juridique. Édition sociale 2024, no 1337; *C Latil*, De la

tury, on the basis of former art 1384(1) Civil Code (now art 1242(1)), although this provision was only conceived as a formal introduction rather than a genuine ground of liability.[27] However, since the enactment of a specific regime for traffic accidents, cases in which this regime is applied have become so rare that it is important to draw attention to this judgment, especially since it illustrates the flexibility with which the Court of Cassation interprets the requirements of this liability regime.[28]

32 The liability regime based upon art 1242(1) Civil Code covers all kinds of 'things' (*choses*), whether intrinsically defective or not, whether moving or inert, whether dangerous or not, whether liquid, gaseous or in solid form and whether movable or immovable. The present case, in which a toxic cloud was observed, is thus in line with the existing case law.[29]

33 The central issue, however, was whether the trial judges could consider that an unidentified toxic substance was under the guardianship of the owner of the premises. In the famous *Franck* case from 1941, the *Chambres réunies* held that a guardian was the person who possesses the 'use, direction and control' (*usage, direction et contrôle*) of the thing.[30] Soon after this case, trial courts began to apply this formula on condition that the owner would be presumed to be the guardian of a thing unless this presumption could be rebutted by showing that the guardianship had been transferred. In the present case, it was this presumption which made it possible to hold liable the Airbus company, which was considered the *gardien* of all substances located on its premises, regardless of their identification.

34 The third specific requirement of the liability regime for things is the 'active role' of the thing, meaning that the *chose* has to be 'the instrument of the harm caused'.[31] In practice, the defendant has to establish the causal link between the thing and the damage.[32] The trial judges held that the claimants had presented

garde d'un nuage toxique, Resp civ assur 2024, comm 234; *E Jeansen*, L'accident de travail survenu au cours de l'exécution d'un contrat de prestation de service, Bulletin Joly Travail 2025, no 1, 40.

27 See the extensive study by *E Tomlinson*, Tort Liability in France for the Act of Things: A Study of Judicial Lawmaking, 48 Louisiana Law Review 1299, 1322–1357 (1988).

28 For an up-to-date presentation, see *Knetsch* (fn 3) nos 167–175.

29 Further illustrations of incorporeal things qualified as *choses* in the sense of art 1242(1) Civil Code are dust, steam, odours, among others.

30 Cass Ch réunies, 2 December 1941, S 1941, 1, 217, note *H Mazeaud.*

31 See eg, Cass Civ 2, 25 October 2001, no 99-21616.

32 See *J Bell/S Boyron/S Whittaker*, Principles of French Law (2nd edn 2008) 386 ('the courts have taken a broad but nuanced approach to the causal relation between the thing and the injured person's harm, using causation to reflect a normative sense of the proper attribution of responsibility for the claimant's harm').

the first symptoms during their rounds of the premises and that at the same time, an employee of the Airbus company had noticed a white cloud. This led the Court of Cassation to acknowledge the findings of the Court of Appeal as to the existence of a causal link between the exposure to the toxic cloud and the symptoms suffered by the claimants.

5. Cour de cassation, Première chambre civile (Cass Civ 1) 16 October 2024, no 22-23433: Liability of Health Professionals; Presumption of Fault in the Case of Insufficient Medical Documentation

a) Brief Summary of the Facts

A hip arthroscopy had led to the rupture of a metal pin, which could not be recovered, in the patient's body, leading to the replacement of the damaged joint with a prosthesis. According to the report of a medical expert, the accident could be the consequence of either the patient's anatomy or the doctor's method of carrying out the arthroscopy. The uncertainty as to its origin was due to an incomplete operative report, as it was not known whether the doctor followed the recommendations of the French Society for Arthroscopy on the performance of the medical act. Despite the unknown reason for the accident, the patient sued the doctor for damages. 35

The Aix-en-Provence Court of Appeal rejected the claim, holding that in the absence of proof of clinical negligence, the doctor could not be held liable. The patient brought the case before the Court of Cassation, arguing that the incomplete operative report made it impossible for him to establish this proof. 36

b) Judgment of the Court

The Court of Cassation quashed the Court of Appeal judgment on the basis of art L 1142-1 Public Health Code and art 1353 Civil Code. According to the First Civil Chamber, 'in the case of lack of information on the health care provided to the patient or in the case of insufficient information thereon, making it impossible for the patient to ascertain whether the medical act was performed appropriately, it is up to the health professional to prove this appropriateness'. 37

c) Commentary[33]

38 Under French law, the liability of doctors and other healthcare professionals is laid out in the 2002 Patients' Rights and Quality of the Health System Act (*Loi relative aux droits des malades et à la qualité du système de santé*).[34] At the time of the enactment of this Act, Parliament deemed it necessary to reaffirm the principle of fault-based liability, to which doctors and other healthcare professional attach the greatest importance. According to art L 1142-1(1) Public Health Code, 'medical practitioners … and all establishments, services and organisations in which medical acts of prevention, diagnosis and care are given, shall only be liable for fault'. While this text refers to statutory exceptions, such as strict liability for defective medical products or hospital-acquired infections *(infections nosocomiales)*, doubts have been raised about the possibility for courts to recognise medical liability on the basis of a presumed fault.

39 Although in some, rather isolated cases, the Court of Cassation had inferred a medical fault from a lacking or incomplete medical record,[35] the present case was the first one in which such a presumption was established in general terms to the benefit of patients. This is consistent with the rationale of the 2002 Act, which enshrined in legislation a right of access to one's medical data (art L 1111-7 Public Health Code). The acknowledgement of a (rebuttable) presumption of fault is thus a way to improve the effectiveness of this facet of patients' right to information.

40 A number of uncertainties remain, however, in particular as to the extent of the presumption. While the Court recalls that 'the proof of fault and causation be-

---

33 See also *S Hocquet-Berg*, Faute déduite de l'absence d'éléments permettant d'établir le respect d'une recommandation médicale, Resp civ assur 2024, comm 271; *R Mesa*, La présomption de faute technique du médecin attachée au défaut d'information du patient sur la prise en charge, RLDC 2025, no 232, 15.

34 On this Act, see in English *S Taylor*, Clinical Negligence Reform: Lessons from France? 52 International & Comparative Law Quarterly (ICLQ) 737; *D Thouvenin*, French Medical Malpractice Compensation Since the Act of March 4, 2002: Liability Rules Combined with Indemnification Rules and Correlated with Several Kinds of Proceedings, 4 Drexel Law Review 165; *S Taylor*, Providing redress for medical accidents in France: conflicting aims, effective solutions? (2011) 2 Journal of European Tort law (JETL) 57; *F G'sell-Macrez*, Medical Malpractice and Compensation in France: Part I: the French Rules of Medical Liability since the Patients' Rights Law of March 4, 2002, 86 Chicago-Kent Law Review 1093 (2011). See also the comprehensive presentation given by *S Taylor*, Medical Accident Liability and Redress in English and French Law (2015) 53–60, 93–115.

35 Cass Civ 1, 9 April 2014, no 13-14964; 8 February 2017, no 16-11527; 26 September 2018, no 17-20143.

tween the fault and the harm has to be established by the claimant' according to the general rules of proof, it is not clear why the Court limits the presumption to the sole fault in the following paragraph. Furthermore, trial courts will need to determine to what degree the incompleteness of medical records triggers the presumption of fault. It will be interesting to monitor the future case law developments in medical law, especially as the link between insufficient information and presumption of a tortious act is present in other fields of tort law.[36]

6. Cour de cassation, Chambre commerciale (Cass Com) 6 November 2024, no 23-10772: Limits of the Personal Liability of a Partner in a Company towards Third Parties

a) Brief Summary of the Facts

The case, which received considerable media coverage in France, concerned a former coach of the national rugby team, who became a partner of a real estate company. A claim was brought by private individuals who had invested in a tourist residence project in a well-known ski resort in the *Massif Central* region. The project was, however, structurally underfunded and the company quickly became bankrupt. Due to the fact that the sued partner had used his reputation to the benefit of the real estate project, the investors filed a claim in order to hold him personally liable for the economic loss caused. 41

The Grenoble Court of Appeal followed the claimants' argument and declared the partner personally liable on the grounds that he was aware of the financial problems of the company and that 'he acted with wrongfulness thoughtlessness (*légèreté fautive*) in accepting to communicate on and advertise this real estate project'. 42

b) Judgment of the Court

The Commercial Chamber quashed the Court of Appeal judgment, considering that the trial judges did not provide sufficient evidence to prove sufficiently serious misconduct. For the Court of Cassation, partners of companies can only be 43

36 For example, art 10 § 2 of the new Product Liability Directive provides for a presumption of the product's defectiveness if 'the defendant fails to disclose relevant evidence' even though they were required to do so according to art 9.

held personally liable 'if they have committed a particularly serious intentional fault, incompatible with the normal exercise of the prerogatives attached to their status'.

c) Commentary[37]

44 Relatively little attention has been paid, in comparative tort law, to the civil liability of directors and partners. Legal literature in the English language on the current state of French law is relatively scarce[38] and even in France, one can notice a certain lack of interest among tort law scholars in this area of civil liability, despite its practical significance.[39]

45 Directors (*dirigeants sociaux*) can be held personally liable vis-à-vis third parties for corporate fault. Even though statutory law provides for their personal liability in the case of an infringement of mandatory rules or mismanagement,[40] they are subject to a specific protection regime that is even more protective than that applicable to employees and other *préposés.*[41] According to the *Sati* case of 2003, their personal liability can, indeed, only be recognised when their fault can be 'detached' from their functions (*faute détachable*). This is particularly the case when 'a director intentionally committed a serious fault incompatible with the normal exercise of his corporate duties'.[42]

46 This immunity was extended to actions by third parties against partners in the *Macris* case of 2014. In this case, the Commercial Chamber already held that partners are personally liable vis-à-vis third parties only 'if they have committed a particularly serious intentional fault, incompatible with the normal exercise

37 See also *JB Barbièri*, L'introuvable (mais indispensable) faute séparable de l'associé, JCP G 2025, no 43; *T Duchesne*, Faute détachable de l'associé… ou l'art d'aller à contresens, D 2025, 135; *E Miglietta*, La faute détachable de l'associé, protection absolue contre l'engagement de sa responsabilité par les tiers, Bulletin Joly Sociétés 2025, no 2, 19.

38 See however *C Mauro*, France, in: H Anderson (ed), Directors' Personal Liability for Corporate Fault: A Comparative Analysis (2008) 139; *A Pietrancosta/PH Dubois/R Garçon*, Corporate Boards in France, in: P Davies et al (eds), Corporate Boards in Law and Practice: A Comparative Analysis in Europe (2013) 175, 209–232; *J Buhart/N Lafont*, France, in: A Loss (ed), Directors' Liability. A Worldwide Review (3rd edn 2016) 189.

39 Most often, scholars and practitioners specialising in company law (droit des sociétés) address this issue in their publications.

40 See eg art L 225-251 Commercial Code (Code de commerce) concerning public companies (sociétés anonymes).

41 On the civil immunity granted to employees and agents (préposés), see *Knetsch* (fn 3) no 101.

42 Cass Com, 20 May 2003, no 99–17092. On this case, see *Mauro* (fn 38) 147.

of the prerogatives attached to their status'.[43] A closer look at the case law shows, however, that this solution only applied to cases in which partners committed a fault in exercising their voting prerogatives. Outside these cases, the Court of Cassation and, more specifically, its Social Chamber, held that partners can also be liable personally for a simple 'fault and blameworthy thoughtlessness' (*faute et légèreté blâmable*).[44]

The present case seems to abandon this subtle distinction between the circumstances in which a partner committed a fault, imposing a single standard for the personal liability of partners and extending the immunity to all tortious acts, whatever their context and regardless of whether the partner is a natural or legal person. What makes this new general approach all the more surprising is that it comes at a time when national and EU legislation is strengthening corporate due diligence duties which apply to parent companies which, by definition, qualify as partners. Seen from this perspective, this general immunity, as established in the present case, comes completely at the wrong time.[45] 47

7. Personal Injury

a) Cour de cassation, Première chambre civile (Cass Civ 1) 11 July 2024, no 23-10068 and 18 December 2024, no 24-14750: Redefining the Outlines of 'Prejudice of Anxiety' (*préjudice d'anxiété*)

One of the most original features of the recent case law on compensation for personal injury is the acknowledgement of a 'loss for fear of future harm' (*préjudice d'anxiété*) in various situations ranging from exposure to asbestos to the fear of imminent death in the context of traffic accidents, terror attacks or ordinary crimes.[46] In two recent cases, the Court of Cassation provided clarification on the limits of those types of loss. 48

In the case from 18 December 2024, related to a possible contamination of drinking water on the island of Mayotte (an overseas *département* in the Indian Ocean), the Court of Cassation provided a general definition of *préjudice d'anxiété*. From now on, claimants have to establish 'anxiety resulting from exposure to a high risk of developing a serious pathology', which is a far more restrictive formu- 49

43 Cass Com, 18 February 2014, no 12-29752.

44 See eg, Cour de Cassation, Chambre sociale (Cass Soc) 8 July 2014, no 13-15573.

45 In this sense, see also *Duchesne*, D 2025, 135.

46 See in English *E Lemaire*, The Fear of Future Illness: An Analytical Comparison of English and French Law (2016) 7 JETL 27.

lation than that from 2023, when the Court of Cassation suggested that the sole 'exposure to a risk of loss' would be sufficient.[47] This redefinition of *préjudice d'anxiété* is a welcome step to sharpen the edges of a sprawling head of loss, which is increasingly being invoked by personal injury lawyers.

50 In the case from 11 July 2024, the Court of Cassation reassessed the fear of imminent death, known as *préjudice d'angoisse de mort imminente*. In a landmark case from 2022, already commented on in a previous report,[48] the Court had acknowledged the autonomy of this head of loss, but only in cases in which the victim ultimately died. The present case offered the First Civil Chamber the opportunity to assert the autonomy even when the victim survives. However, unlike in the case of death, the judgment holds that no specific amount is to be awarded to the surviving victim, but only a sum in addition to the damages for pain and suffering (*souffrances endurées*).

b) Cour de cassation, Deuxième chambre civile (Cass Civ 2) 10 October 2024, nos 23-12612 and 23-13932: Award of Damages for Loss of Income in the Case of (Partial or Total) Inability to Carry Out an Occupational Activity

51 The assessment of loss of income is always a complex and technical exercise, as the judge or an insurer must adopt a prospective view on the future income situation of claimants, especially when they have not resumed a professional activity. A particularly thorny issue arises when victims cannot return to their former work position, but still have limited work capacity. While some trial judges tend, in this context, to award the claimant compensation of the total loss of income, the Court of Cassation rejects this solution in this case, recalling that this is only possible if, 'after consolidation, the claimant is permanently unable to carry out any professional activity providing them with earnings'.

52 In other words, compensation for total loss of income implies that claimants are unfit to return to *any* professional activity and not only to return to their previous job. This solution has raised criticism among personal injury lawyers and some tort law scholars, who argue that this restrictive approach is not consistent with the absence of a duty for claimants to mitigate their losses under French law.[49] Furthermore, the Court of Cassation does not provide any clarity on how to precisely assess the partial loss of income in cases of partial work capacity.

47 Cass Civ 1, 18 October 2023, no 22-11492.
48 Cour de cassation, Chambre mixte (Cass Ch mixte) 25 March 2022, no 20-15624. See *Z Jacquemin/J Knetsch*, France, in: E Karner/BC Steininger (eds), ETL 2022 (2023) 215, nos 6–14.
49 On this aspect, see in English *Knetsch* (fn 3) no 316 f.

C. Literature

1. Doctoral Theses and Monographs

H Méral, La perte de chance en droit privé: essai critique [Loss of a chance under private law: a critical essay] (Paris, Panthéon-Assas 2024) coll Thèses, préface *JS Borghetti* 53

2. Textbooks

C Biguenet-Morel, Responsabilité civile du notaire [Civil liability of public notaries] (Francis Lefebvre 2024) coll Thèmexpress 54

C Radé, Droit de l'indemnisation des victimes de dommages corporels: principaux régimes d'indemnisation [The compensation of personal injury victims: a presentation of the main compensation regimes] (Paris, LexisNexis 2024) coll Droit & Professionnels 55

3. Symposium Proceedings and Collective Works

Perspectives: droit de la responsabilité civile [Perspectives on tort law] Revue de droit d'Assas 2024, no 27, 112–150 56

P Abadie/G Leray (eds), Le juge et le devoir de vigilance [The judge and the duty of due diligence] RLDA 2024, no 200 supplément, 3–71 57

B Dubuisson/P Jourdain (eds), Les responsabilités et les garanties du vendeur en droit belge et en droit français : approche de droit comparé [Liabilities and guarantees of the vendor under French and Belgian law] (Brussels, Larcier 2024) coll du GRERCA 58

A Guégan (ed), Le dommage corporel face au temps [Personal injury in the light of time] Proceedings of 3 March 2023 Conference at the Paris 1 Panthéon-Sorbonne University, Resp civ assur 2024, dossier 1–10 59

J Lete (ed), La crise sanitaire: la responsabilité et l'assurance [Public health crisis: liability and insurance] Proceedings of 21–22 April 2023 Conference at the Santiago de Compostela University (Brussels, Larcier 2024) coll du GRERCA 60

A Maitrot de la Motte & C Tréhin (eds), La responsabilité des conseils fiscaux [The liability of tax advisors] Revue de droit fiscal 2024, no 49, 12–39 61

62 *S Maljean-Dubois/F Ippolito* (eds), La réparation des dommages climatiques. Enjeux juridiques et perspectives [The compensation of climate-related harm. Legal issues and perspectives] Revue juridique de l'environnement 2024, 531–632

63 *B Parance/J Rochfeld* (eds), Les grandes notions de la responsabilité civile à l'aune des mutations environnementales [Major tort law concepts in the light of environmental changes] (Paris, Dalloz 2024) coll Thèmes & Commentaires

64 *O Robin-Sabard* (ed), Les divergences de jurisprudence entre les juridictions du fond et la Cour de cassation en droit de la responsabilité civile [Divergences in tort-related case law between trial judges and the Court of Cassation] Resp civ assur 2024, dossier 11–23

65 *A Tardif* (ed), Présomptions et responsabilités [Liability rules and presumptions] (Paris, Mare & Martin 2024)

4. Articles

66 *A Akam Akam*, La distinction des responsabilités contractuelle et délictuelle à l'épreuve du droit des transports [The distinction between contractual and extra-contractual liability in the light of transportation law] Écrits sans esprit de système. Mélanges Philippe Delebecque (Paris, Dalloz 2024) 19–33

67 *M Bacache*, Devoir de vigilance et responsabilité civile [Duty of due diligence and tort law] Écrits sans esprit de système. Mélanges Philippe Delebecque (Paris, Dalloz 2024) 115–131

68 *P Bonfils*, Le dommage réparable devant les juridictions pénales [Reparable loss before criminal courts] Écrits sans esprit de système. Mélanges Philippe Delebecque (Paris, Dalloz 2024) 233–243

69 *T Bonneau/L-M Pillebout*, Le devoir de vigilance des entreprises en matière de durabilité [The duty for corporate sustainability due diligence] Revue des sociétés 2024, 223–237

70 *JS Borghetti*, Consacrer un régime de responsabilité en matière d'intelligence artificielle dans le code civil? [Do we have to enshrine a liability regime for AI in the Civil Code?] Le renouvellement du droit civil sous l'influence du numérique (Paris, Dalloz 2024) 149–159

71 *M Celaya/C Grimaldi*, Les incohérences de l'évaluation du préjudice en cas de rupture brutale d'une relation établie [Inconsistencies in the assessment of reparable loss in the event of unexpected termination of established business relations] JCP G 2024, no 1104

72 *A Danis-Fatôme*, Repenser la responsabilité civile [Rethinking tort law] JCP G 2024, special issue '1804–2024 : quel Code civil à l'heure de l'Anthropocène?' 53–59

F Debove/R Chouvel, Soigner quoi qu'il en coûte! À propos de la responsabilité des directeurs d'hôpital dans un contexte médical dégradé [Providing healthcare whatever the cost! On the liability of hospital directors in a deteriorating medical context] Mélanges en l'honneur de Louis Vogel. La vie du droit (Paris, LexisNexis/Dalloz/LGDJ 2024) 779 – 790 73

A Dumery, La digitalisation du droit de la responsabilité civile à la rencontre de la logique indemnitaire [The digitilisation of tort law and the compensatory rationale] Dalloz IP/IT 2024, 19 – 22 74

M Dupré/B Moron-Puech/C Cousin, La réparation des victimes de violences sexuelles par la Commission reconnaissance et réparation. Regards civilistes sur une entreprise de réparation hors norme [The compensation awarded by the Commission for recognition and compensation of victims of sexual abuse in the Catholic Church. A private law view on an outstanding redress process] D 2024, 430 – 437 75

L Friant, Nutri-score, Yuka et autres 'applis' alimentaires : quelles implications du point de vue du droit de la responsabilité? [Nutri-score, Yuka and other food apps: what are the tort law implications?] Cahiers Droit, Sciences & Technologies 2024, 117 – 127 76

J Heinich, Les clauses de force majeure [Force majeure clauses] Rev contrats 2024, no 3, 114 – 118 77

J Knetsch, Consacrer une indemnisation forfaitaire en cas de manquement au droit des données à caractère personnel? [Do we have to create lump sum-based compensation in GDPR infringement cases?] Le renouvellement du droit civil sous l'influence du numérique (Paris, Dalloz 2024) 173 – 191 78

L Leveneur, Les clauses limitatives, exonératoires ou de non-garantie à l'épreuve de l'obligation essentielle : splendeurs et misères de la force obligatoire [Exclusion, limitation and disclaimer clauses vs the essential obligation: the splendour and misery of binding force] Rev contrats 2024, no 4, 92 – 97 79

P Maimone, Loi n° 85 – 677 du 5 juillet 1985 et catastrophes climatiques: des 'liaisons dangereuses'? [The 1985 Badinter Act and weather-related disasters: 'dangerous liaisons'?] Resp civ assur 2024, étude 9 80

R Mesa, L'appréhension du dommage, distincte de celle du préjudice, par le droit de la responsabilité civile délictuelle [The distinction between 'dommage' and 'préjudice' in extra-contractual civil liability] RLDC 2024, no 229, 44 – 50 81

J Mouly, La perte de chance de conserver son emploi. À propos de la responsabilité civile des tiers au contrat de travail [The loss of a chance to keep one's job: on the civil liability of third parties to an employment contract] Droit social 2024, 335 – 341 82

83 *P Oudot*, La créance en réparation du dommage corporel [The right to compensation in personal injury cases] Mélanges en l'honneur de Natalie Fricero. Procédure civile sans frontières (Paris, LGDJ/Dalloz 2024) 487–499

84 *B Parance*, De nouveaux devoirs pour les entreprises à l'heure de l'Anthropocène? [New corporate duties in the anthropocene era?] JCP G 2024, special issue '1804–2024 : quel Code civil à l'heure de l'Anthropocène?' 65–70

85 *Y Picod*, Concurrence déloyale et responsabilité civile : un couple infidèle [Unfair competition and tort law: an unfaithful couple] Mélanges en l'honneur de Louis Vogel. La vie du droit (Paris, LexisNexis/Dalloz/LGDJ 2024) 611–622

86 *S Porchy-Simon*, Quel encadrement de l'usage des outils d'intelligence artificielle pour l'évaluation des préjudices? [What framework for the use of AI tools to assess losses?] Le renouvellement du droit civil sous l'influence du numérique (Paris, Dalloz 2024) 161–172

87 *S Prétot*, Abus sexuels dans l'Église [Sexual abuse in the church] RTD civ 2024, 553–576

88 *P Stoffel-Munck*, Les clauses limitatives de responsabilité: état de la question [Limitation clauses: a status report] Rev contrats 2024, no 3, 119–128

89 *P Stoffel-Munck*, La responsabilité du contractant défaillant envers les tiers: quelles perspectives en l'absence de réforme? [The liability of defaulting contracting parties towards third parties: what prospects without a tort law reform?] Écrits sans esprit de système. Mélanges Philippe Delebecque (Paris, Dalloz 2024) 961–994

90 *L Vitale*, Clair-obscur en matière de parasitisme économique [Light and shade in trademark infringement cases] Resp civ assur 2024, étude 11

91 *L Vitale/S François*, Réflexions sur le principe d'assimilation des fautes contractuelle et extracontractuelle à la lumière de la jurisprudence récente de la Cour de cassation [Thoughts on the assimilation of contractual and extra-contractual faults in the light of recent Court of Cassation case law] Resp civ assur 2024, étude 10

Jens Kleinschmidt and Lukas Glöckner

XII. Germany

A. Legislation

1. Introduction of a 'Guideline Decision Procedure' (*Leitentscheidungsverfahren*)

'However satisfactory they may appear on paper, legal rights are of little value unless it is practicable to enforce them.'[1] For this reason, our report has time and again widened its scope beyond substantive law and taken into consideration legislative (and judicial) developments concerning the *enforcement* of (delictual) claims.[2] Probably the most important legislative development in the context of this year's report is the introduction of a novel instrument before the German Federal Court of Justice (*Bundesgerichtshof*, BGH): the 'Leitentscheidungsverfahren' (Guideline Decision Procedure). The 'Act introducing a guideline decision procedure before the Federal Court of Justice' (*Gesetz zur Einführung eines Leitentscheidungsverfahrens beim Bundesgerichtshof*) entered into force on 31 October 2024.[3] 1

The Act is a reaction to recent mass claims, ie actions brought in considerable numbers before courts all over Germany and based on essentially similar sets of facts, sometimes going back to one particular event.[4] Prominent examples from tort law are actions brought against car manufacturers in the wake of the diesel 2

Note: The authors wish to thank Mike Faust for assistance in collecting material for this report.

1 *S Whittaker*, Consumer protection, in: M Bridge (ed), Benjamin's Sale of Goods (10th edn 2017) no 14-246.
2 See eg, *J Kleinschmidt*, Germany, in: E Karner/BC Steininger (eds), European Tort Law (ETL) 2018 (2019) 221, nos 1 ff and 40 ff.
3 Federal Law Gazette (Bundesgesetzblatt, BGBl) 2024 I, no 328.
4 On the background of the new provisions, see Printed Documents of the German Parliament (Bundestagsdrucksache, BT-Drucks) 20/8762, 10; *B Rentsch*, Kollektive Rechtserkenntnis oder Revision 'light'? Zeitschrift für Rechtspolitik (ZRP) 2023, 135, 135 f; *J Rapp*, Zwischen Wunsch und Wirklichkeit – Das geplante "Leitentscheidungsverfahren beim BGH", ZRP 2024, 34 ff; *G Vollkommer*, Das Leitentscheidungsverfahren beim BGH, Neue Juristische Wochenschrift (NJW) 2024, 3257 ff. For a balanced perspective on mass claims that considers both their effects on the court system and their function to serve individual justice of the claimants and contribute to private enforcement, *T Riehm*, Massenverfahren und kein Ende? JuristenZeitung (JZ) 2024, 945, 946.

https://doi.org/10.1515/9783111389271-013

scandal[5] or those following the so-called Facebook data leak (see below no 55 ff).[6] Often, not only the sets of facts are similar but also the legal issues involved are essentially the same. Due to a lack of functioning and attractive means of collective redress in German civil procedure,[7] these legal issues must be dealt with and answered in individual proceedings[8] by judges in many different courts who may unsurprisingly arrive at divergent conclusions and whose conclusions will necessarily disappoint one of the parties. Arguably, an appeal decision by the Federal Court of Justice would be able to provide guidance for the lower courts and reduce uncertainty for potential claimants and defendants. Whether it may also reduce the number of new proceedings initiated or incite a settlement of pending proceedings and thus relieve first instance courts from being clogged by essentially similar actions prepared (or defended) by law firms using powerful IT tools, is subject to debate.[9] In any event, experience has shown over the past years that parties attempted to avoid an unfavourable appeal decision that could have influ-

5 See, *J Kleinschmidt*, Germany, in: E Karner/BC Steininger (eds), European Tort Law (ETL) 2022 (2023) 233, no 61 ff; *W Wurmnest/J Kleinschmidt/S Gasche*, Germany, in: E Karner/BC Steininger (eds), European Tort Law (ETL) 2021 (2022) 194, no 50 ff; *J Kleinschmidt*, Germany, in: E Karner/BC Steininger (eds), European Tort Law (ETL) 2020 (2021) 206, no 34 ff.

6 Examples from other areas of the law mentioned in this context include rights of withdrawal from bank or insurance contracts, claims brought by Wirecard investors, or restitution of wagers in online gambling or sports betting. Air passenger rights might also present a mass phenomenon that keeps courts busy but are different in that each claim is based on its individual fact pattern, see *Riehm*, JZ 2024, 945, 946 (distinguishing 'parallel' and 'serial' mass claims).

7 *Riehm*, JZ 2024, 945, 947; *Rapp*, ZRP 2024, 34; see also the criticism by, eg, *G Albers*, Kampf ums Recht? Massenverfahren und Rechtsverwirklichung im Lichte der neusten Gesetzgebung, JZ 2024, 261, 264 ff; *C Meller-Hannich*, Kollektiver Rechtsschutz im Privatrecht und die Umsetzung der Verbandsklagenrichtlinie, Versicherungsrecht (VersR) 2023, 1321 ff. On the criticism levelled against the 'Musterfeststellungsklage' (and its failure to arrive at a decision against Volkswagen), see *Kleinschmidt* (fn 2) no 1 ff. On the implementation of representative actions *W Wurmnest/N Riemann*, Germany, in: E Karner/BC Steininger (eds), European Tort Law (ETL) 2023 (2024) 263, no 1 ff.

8 Tens of thousands of proceedings have been initiated by individual claimants against Volkswagen.

9 It can be observed that the decisions which established in principle the liability of Volkswagen under § 826 BGB did not have the effect of reducing significantly the number of claims, *Vollkommer*, NJW 2024, 3257, 3259; see also the numbers reported for 2022 by *Rapp*, ZRP 2024, 34; the Annual Report of the Civil Senates of the Federal Court of Justice for 2024 reports over 650 new cases and more than 1,700 pending cases before the Senate that was created specifically for dealing with delictual claims emerging from the diesel scandal.

enced many other proceedings.[10] Appeals were withdrawn or cases were settled by the parties, thus depriving the Federal Court of Justice of the opportunity to render a decision (a procedural tactic often called the 'escape from appeal' – 'Flucht aus der Revision'). At times, the Federal Court of Justice tried to stand up to this tactic by making public, after the appeal had been withdrawn, procedural orders that had initially been addressed to the parties only and summarised the preliminary views of the Senate on the legal issues involved.[11]

The new § 552b of the German Code of Civil Procedure (*Zivilprozessordnung*, 3
ZPO) entitles the Federal Court of Justice to issue, after expiry of certain delays, an order that designates a pending appeal procedure (*Revisionsverfahren*) to be a 'guideline decision procedure' (*Leitentscheidungsverfahren*) where the appeal raises legal issues the decision of which is relevant for a number of other proceedings. The order states the facts and the legal issues the decision of which is relevant for a number of other proceedings (and which the Federal Court of Justice thereby reserves to answer[12]). The question whether a pending procedure is designated as a *Leitentscheidungsverfahren* and, if so, which one remains at the discretion of the Federal Court of Justice.[13] Although this is not expressed in the provision, the legislator expected the (anonymised) order to be published (for example, by a press release or on the court's homepage) so that lower courts, interested parties and the general public become aware of an imminent statement on the legal issues.[14] The existence of the order enables, in principle, any court before which

10 Concerning claims against Volkswagen, where the first judgment by the BGH dates from May 2020, ie almost five years after discovery of the allegations, see *Rapp*, ZRP 2024, 34. On the decision by the BGH, see *Kleinschmidt*, ETL 2022 (fn 5) no 34 ff.

11 BGH 8 January 2019 – VIII ZR 225/17, NJW 2019, 1133; BGH 22 March 2024 – I ZR 88/23, NJW 2024, 1950; for details, see *B Laukemann*, Die Veröffentlichung richterlicher Hinweisbeschlüsse, Zeitschrift für Zivilprozess (ZZP) 134 (2021) 67 ff; *W Voß*, Publikation von Hinweisbeschlüssen und vorläufigen Rechtseinschätzungen der Gerichte – praeter legem oder contra legem? JZ 2020, 286 ff.

12 *Vollkommer*, NJW 2024, 3257, 3258.

13 *C Feskorn*, Das neue Leitentscheidungsverfahren beim BGH, Monatsschrift für deutsches Recht (MDR) 2024, 1413, 1414 f; *P Rädler*, Die neuen Leitentscheidungsverfahren – Justizentlastung und Rechtsfortbildung? NJW 2025, 473.

14 BT-Drucks 20/8762, 15. The duty to publish the order may be derived from constitutional law, see eg, *M Heese*, Veröffentlichung gerichtlicher Entscheidungen im Zeitalter der Digitalisierung, in: Festschrift für Herbert Roth (2021) 283 ff; *J Kleinschmidt*, La portée des arrêts de revision en droit allemand, in: C Chainais/J-F van Drooghenbroeck/A Saletti/B Hess (eds), Quel avenir pour les juridictions suprêmes? (2021) 393, 397 ff; *Voß*, JZ 2020, 286, 289 f. According to § 329 ZPO, the parties must be notified of the order.

a case depends on legal issues which are subject to a pending *Leitentscheidungsverfahren* to stay the proceedings until the resolution of the latter.[15]

4 Upon this order, two alternative scenarios may be envisioned. In the first scenario, the appeal procedure moves forward and is not terminated by the parties. This scenario raises no peculiarities. The appeal proceedings will eventually lead to a 'regular' motivated appeal judgment on the substance of the case that is no different from a judgment as it would have been entered without the designation as *Leitentscheidungsverfahren.*[16] In the second scenario, however, where the appeal is still terminated without a judgment as to the substance, the new § 565 ZPO kicks in: the Federal Court of Justice renders a 'guideline decision' by issuing an order without an oral hearing which declares the appeal to be terminated and answers the legal issues stated in the designation order. Despite the public interest in a 'guideline decision', no representative of the public is involved.[17] The order must be motivated, with the motivation being restricted to the considerations necessary for answering the legal issues. The 'guideline decision' has to be published.[18] Consequently, the designation as *Leitentscheidungsverfahren* enables the Federal Court of Justice to express its position on the legal issues irrespective of the parties' procedural behaviour.[19]

5 The 'guideline decision' has no effect whatsoever on the parties to the appeal since the appeal procedure has already been terminated at the time it is issued[20] (for that reason, it can strictly speaking not be called a 'decision' as it does not close a procedure[21]). As with 'regular' judgments by the Federal Court of Justice, the 'guideline decision' can have no formal binding effect on the many other proceedings for which it is relevant, either.[22] However, and again as with 'regular' judgments,[23] it may exert a persuasive authority. In the words of the legislator,

15 § 148 (4) ZPO. This possibility is thought to relieve the burden weighing on lower courts, *Vollkommer*, NJW 2024, 3257, 3259.

16 BT-Drucks 20/8762, 14.

17 *Riehm*, JZ 2024, 945, 948; *Vollkommer*, NJW 2024, 3257, 3258, pointing out that it might apparently be possible for interested parties to submit opinions; against a participation of third parties, *Rädler*, NJW 2025, 473, 474.

18 Again, this is not expressly provided for but is thought to follow from the Constitution, BT-Drucks 20/8762, 15.

19 BT-Drucks 20/8762, 15.

20 BT-Drucks 20/8762, 15; *Rädler*, NJW 2025, 473, 476.

21 *Vollkommer*, NJW 2024, 3257, 3260.

22 BT-Drucks 20/8762, 15; *Rapp*, ZRP 2024, 34, 35; *Vollkommer*, NJW 2024, 3257, 3258.

23 See eg, Bundesverfassungsgericht (Federal Constitutional Court, BVerfG) 15 January 2009 – 2 BvR 2044/07, NJW 2009, 1469, 1475; *O Klein*, Zur Frage der Bindung höchster Gerichte an ihre Rechtsprechung, JZ 2018, 64, 65; *F Maultzsch*, Streitentscheidung und Normbildung durch den

it is to provide 'guidance and orientation' to lower courts and to the general public as to how an appeal judgment would have looked like.[24]

First reactions to this new instrument appeared to be mainly reserved. While 6 at least the possibility to stay proceedings and the guidance flowing from the 'guideline decision' are considered by some a welcome relief,[25] even critics concede that the new provisions may indeed counter the 'escape from appeal' (see below no 8). The new provisions do, however, not really speed up or facilitate the resolution of controversial legal issues,[26] nor are they expected to contribute effectively to a reduction of the enormous number of similar actions.[27] Furthermore, a *Leitentscheidung* will still be based on the underlying set of facts; guidance in related but different scenarios (as they exist, for instance, in the diesel complex) is limited and does not relieve lower courts of verifying whether the *Leitentscheidung* covers the case before it.[28]

The instrument must not be confused with a request for a preliminary ruling 7 which is known not only in EU law (art 267 Treaty on the Functioning of the European Union [TFEU]) but also in various national laws, such as Italy (*rinvio pregiudiziale*, art 363*bis Codice di procedura civile*) or France (*saisine pour avis*, art 1031-1 ff *Code de procédure civile*).[29] Generally speaking, such instruments en-

---

Zivilprozess (2010) 30 ff; *A von Ungern-Sternberg*, Normative Wirkungen von Präjudizien nach der Rechtsprechung des Bundesverfassungsgerichts, Archiv des öffentlichen Rechts (AöR) 138 (2013) 1, 45 ff.

24 BT-Drucks 20/8762, 15.

25 *S Ernst*, Zur Bestimmung eines Leitentscheidungsverfahrens durch Revisionsgericht, hier: zum Facebook-Scraping, Zeitschrift für Wirtschaftsrecht (ZIP) 2025, 250, 251 (new regulation is a 'blessing' – 'Glücksfall'); *Rapp*, ZRP 2024, 34, 35; *Vollkommer*, NJW 2024, 3257, 3260.

26 *Feskorn*, MDR 2024, 1413, 1417; *Rapp*, ZRP 2024, 34, 35 ff; *Rentsch*, ZRP 2023, 135, 137; *Vollkommer*, NJW 2024, 3257, 3259; in contrast, the advantages of a case having already passed two instances are emphasised by *Albers*, JZ 2024, 261, 269.

27 *Albers*, JZ 2024, 261, 268; *Riehm*, JZ 2024, 945, 947 ff (suggesting the development of effective mechanisms for collective redress and a strengthening of court infrastructure); *Vollkommer*, NJW 2024, 3257, 3259 f. In particular, lower courts will still have to adjudicate all pending individual actions, unless the 'guideline decision' incites the parties to settle, *Riehm*, JZ 2024, 945, 951. But see *Ernst*, ZIP 2025, 250, 251 (mass claims can be resolved in a considerably more effective manner).

28 *Rädler*, NJW 2025, 473, 476; *MP Lerch/C Valdini*, Herausforderungen an den Zivilprozess bei Massenverfahren, NJW 2023, 420, 422; adding that this set of facts may be incomplete for lack of an oral hearing and active participation by the parties, *Riehm*, JZ 2024, 945, 950.

29 On this approach, and generally in favour of it, *M Heese/E Schumann*, Ein Vorabentscheidungsverfahren beim BGH, NJW 2021, 3023 ff; *J Rapp*, Die ‚saisine pour avis' zum BGH – ein Zukunftsmodell für den Zivilprozess? JZ 2020, 294 ff; *J Rapp*, Revision, Kassation, Final Appeal (2024) 446 ff; critical *B Gsell*, Kollektive Schadensereignisse erfordern kollektive Klageinstrumente, ZRP 2021, 166 ff; *Riehm*, JZ 2024, 945, 951 ff.

able a lower court to single out a legal issue which is relevant for a greater number of cases and refer it to the Supreme Court (*Corte di cassazione*, *Cour de cassation*) for an opinion. The opinion is not binding in other proceedings but may nevertheless provide valuable guidance. Arguably, such a preliminary ruling may allow lower courts to obtain the desired guidance more swiftly than under the technique employed by the German legislator because it is not necessary to wait for a number of cases to have gone up through all previous instances to the Supreme Court.[30] Yet, the German legislator did not follow this alternative approach.[31]

8 Ironically, it seems most likely that the order designating an appeal to be a *Leitentscheidungsverfahren* will turn out to be the most powerful tool to prevent parties from resorting to an 'escape from appeal'.[32] Once the order is issued, parties will be certain that an answer to legal issues which affect them in other cases as well will be published. In such a scenario, they will prefer to remain an active party (including the possibility to present their position in an oral hearing) to the procedure that will eventually lead to this answer one way or the other.[33] This expectation proved right upon the very first order for a *Leitentscheidungsverfahren.* On the very same day on which the new instrument entered into force, the Federal Court of Justice issued an order based on § 552b ZPO in a pending appeal.[34] The appeal concerned a claim for damages for immaterial harm under Art 82 General Data Protection Regulation (GDPR) following the so-called Facebook data leak, an incident which had led to innumerable proceedings before first instance courts all over Germany. After the order, the appeal was not withdrawn nor did the parties reach a settlement; rather, the appeal procedure moved forward, and the Federal Court of Justice was able to enter a 'regular' appeal judgment (see below no 55 ff).

---

30 *Rapp*, ZRP 2024, 34, 35 f and 37; *Vollkommer*, NJW 2024, 3257, 3260.

31 *Feskorn*, MDR 2024, 1413 reports that reservations had been voiced by the Federal Court of Justice.

32 *Rädler*, NJW 2025, 473, 474; *Rapp*, ZRP 2024, 34, 35; *Riehm*, JZ 2024, 945, 950; *Vollkommer*, NJW 2024, 3257, 3260. *Rentsch*, ZRP 2023, 135, 138 regards the instrument therefore as a 'missed opportunity'.

33 *Rapp*, ZRP 2024, 34, 35.

34 BGH 31 October 2024 – VI ZR 10/24, NJW 2024, 3595.

2. Transposition of Directive (EU) 2021/2118 relating to Compulsory Motor Vehicle Insurance

A statute transposing Directive (EU) 2021/2118 of the European Parliament and the Council of 24 November 2021 amending Directive 2009/103/EC relating to insurance against civil liability in respect of the use of motor vehicles, and the enforcement of the obligation to insure against such liability[35] entered into force on 17 April 2024.[36] The statute modified or amended the Act on compulsory insurance (*Pflichtversicherungsgesetz*, PflVG).[37] At the same time, it replaced the Act on liability insurance for foreign motor vehicles and motor vehicle trailers (*Gesetz über die Haftpflichtversicherung für ausländische Kraftfahrzeuge und Kraftfahrzeuganhänger*). 9

3. (Unsuccessful) Draft Establishing the Heritability of Compensation Claims for Infringements of Personality Rights

It may seem quite unusual to include a legislative initiative in this report that did 10 not advance beyond the status of a ministry draft – and will not advance any further due to the premature end of the term of parliament after the breakdown of the German government coalition. However, the backstory of the proposed legislation warrants a brief note. The draft (*Referentenentwurf*) published by the Ministry of Justice in May 2024 proposed the amendment of § 1922 (1) of the German Civil Code (*Bürgerliches Gesetzbuch*, BGB) which is the introductory provision to the German law of succession and enshrines the principle that, upon the death of a person, that person's assets devolve as a whole to the heir(s). A new second sentence was to clarify that these assets include a claim for monetary compensation for an infringement of personality rights: 'The succession also includes a

35 Official Journal (OJ) 2021 L 430/1.

36 Gesetz zur Umsetzung der Richtlinie (EU) 2021/2118 im Hinblick auf die Kraftfahrzeug-Haftpflichtversicherung und die Kontrolle der entsprechenden Versicherungspflicht und zur Änderung anderer versicherungsrechtlicher Vorschriften vom 11. April 2024, BGBl 2024 I, no 119.

37 For details, see *C Burmann/JL Kemperdiek*, Die Umsetzung der RL (EU) 2021/2118 in nationales Recht – das neue PflVG, Deutsches Autorecht (DAR) 2024, 61 ff; *JL Kemperdiek*, Das neue Pflichtversicherungsgesetz vom 16.4.2024 – Update, DAR 2024, 323 ff.

claim of the deceased for monetary compensation because of an infringement of personality rights.'[38]

11 The proposal is remarkable for two reasons. First, the amendment would have constituted the first express legislative mention of a claim for monetary compensation for infringement of personality rights in the BGB. As is well known, the claim is a creation by the judiciary and, for lack of mention in the Civil Code, the general right of personality has been based on the Constitution (art 1 (1), 2 (1) Basic Law, *Grundgesetz*, GG).[39] The legislator did not seize the opportunity to enshrine (and possibly elaborate) the claim in the Civil Code on the occasion of the reform of the provisions on damages in 2002. Although the new § 253 (2) introduced by the reform considerably expanded the availability of compensation for immaterial harm (damages for pain and suffering, *Schmerzensgeld*) to contract law and to strict liability, the provision did not add the general right of personality to the list of rights and interests the violation of which may lead to compensation for immaterial harm; rather, the legislator followed the distinction established by the courts between damages for pain and suffering on the one hand and compensation for an infringement of the general right of personality on the other and therefore declared that the provision would not be a suitable place for a codification of the latter type of claims. The question whether such infringements ought to be regulated more generally was expressly left open;[40] and it may indeed be subject to

38 Proposed § 1922 (1) 2 BGB: 'Die Erbschaft umfasst auch einen Anspruch des Erblassers auf Entschädigung in Geld wegen einer Persönlichkeitsrechtsverletzung.', Referentenentwurf des Bundesministeriums der Justiz vom 15.5.2024 'Entwurf eines Gesetzes zur Änderung des Bürgerlichen Gesetzbuchs – Einsichtnahme in die Patientenakte und Vererblichkeit bei Persönlichkeitsrechtsverletzung', accessible at <https://www.bmj.de/SharedDocs/Gesetzgebungsverfahren/DE/2024_Einsichtnahme_Patientenakte.html> (last accessed 26 March 2025); for a critical analysis, see *H Grziwotz*, Persönlichkeitsrechtsverletzung – Schutzlücken bei der Vererblichkeit? ZRP 2024, 173 f.

39 The development is recounted with further references by *G Wagner*, Deliktsrecht (14th edn 2021) ch 7 nos 1 ff, 47 ff; and, in English, by *BS Markesinis/J Bell/A Janssen*, Markesinis's German Law of Torts (5th edn 2019) 43 ff.

40 BT-Drucks 14/7752, 24 f; *D Olzen* in: J von Staudinger Kommentar zum Bürgerlichen Gesetzbuch (2024) Einleitung zum Schuldrecht §§ 241–243 no 234; *L Jaeger/J Luckey*, Das Zweite Schadensersatzrechtsänderungsgesetz – Ein Überblick über das neue Recht, MDR 2002, 1168, 1169; *C Karczewski*, Der Referentenentwurf eines Zweiten Gesetzes zur Änderung schadensersatzrechtlicher Vorschriften, VersR 2001, 1070, 1072; *G Wagner*, Das Zweite Schadensrechtsänderungsgesetz, NJW 2002, 2049, 2056 f. The Bundesrat had requested the adoption of a special provision on personality right infringements to no avail, BT-Drucks 14/7752, 49. An earlier attempt of 1959 at extensive codification of the protection of personality rights in private law (BT-Drucks III/1237) failed due to opposition from the press, see *H-J Ahrens/A Spickhoff*, Deliktsrecht (2022) § 45 no 47.

debate whether a codification is even possible.[41] Up to this day, the courts regard the claim for monetary compensation for infringement of personality rights as different from damages claims for pain and suffering because of a violation of the protected interests enumerated in § 253 (2) BGB (for a recent example, see below no 27 ff). Arguably, the proposed amendment would not have affected this special status.[42] However, it would have affirmed that the legislator approves of the award of monetary compensation for infringements of personality rights.

Secondly, and more importantly, the amendment would have served to over- 12
turn a line of cases that had denied the heritability of such claims for monetary compensation. A recent and famous example of this case law can be found in the litigation initiated by former German Chancellor Helmut Kohl against two authors and the publisher of a biography for infringement of his personality rights. Here, the *Bundesgerichtshof* confirmed, after the original claimant had died and his widow had taken over the dispute, that claims for monetary compensation for violation of personality rights cannot be inherited unless a final judgment had been obtained.[43] This position was upheld by the Federal Constitutional Court (*Bundesverfassungsgericht*, BVerfG).[44] However, it met with exceptionally strong and convincing criticism in legal scholarship, not least for turning the enforcement of a justified claim into an unworthy 'race against time'.[45] The ministry draft intended to heed to this criticism, which was shared by the Ministers of Justice of the *Bundesländer*, and to eliminate the anomaly compared to other personal, yet inheritable claims such as the damages claim for pain and suffering or the claim for monetary compensation for secondary victims (*Hinterbliebenengeld*, § 844 (3) BGB).[46]

---

41 *J Hager* in: J von Staudinger, Kommentar zum Bürgerlichen Gesetzbuch (2017) § 823 no C2; deploring the missed opportunity *Ahrens/Spickhoff* (fn 40) § 11 no 64.

42 However, at the price of adding a special rule to a fundamental provision of succession law, *Grziwotz*, ZRP 2024, 173, 174.

43 BGH 29 November 2021 – VI ZR 258/18, NJW 2022, 868; *Wurmnest/Kleinschmidt/Gasche* (fn 5) no 60.

44 BVerfG 24 October 2022–1 BvR 110/22, NJW 2023, 757; *Kleinschmidt*, ETL 2022 (fn 5) no 2 f.

45 See, in particular, *B Gsell*, NJW 2022, 871; *H Schack*, JZ 2022, 747; *C Schubert/J Ipsen*, Geldentschädigung wegen der Verletzung des allgemeinen Persönlichkeitsrechts – vom Anspruch sui generis zum Schadensersatzanspruch, JZ 2022, 737; *A Spickhoff*, Leitsätze mit Kommentierung (LMK) 2014, 359158; *R Rixecker* in: Münchener Kommentar zum BGB (MünchKomm BGB) vol 1 (10th edn 2025) Anh § 12 no 63 ff; for details on the discussion, see *Wurmnest/Kleinschmidt/Gasche* (fn 5) no 60; *W Wurmnest/M Gömann*, Germany, in: E Karner/BC Steininger (eds), European Tort Law (ETL) 2017 (2018) 207, no 41 ff.

46 Referentenentwurf (fn 38) 12 f.

13 For the time being, it is uncertain whether the next government will take up this welcome initiative.

B. Cases

1. BGH 16 January 2024, VI ZR 253/22:[47] Garage Risk

a) Brief Summary of the Facts

14 The subject matter of the case is repair costs in connection with a road traffic accident in which the claimant's vehicle was damaged by the party insured by the defendant insurance company. The full liability of the insured party was undisputed between the parties. On the day of the accident, the claimant obtained an expert opinion which estimated the repair costs to be € 4,415; subsequently, she commissioned a car repair shop to carry out the repair work on her vehicle. The garage invoiced € 4,683 to the claimant after completion of the work, which the claimant has not paid to date. Relying on its own expert report, the defendant considered these costs to be excessive and only reimbursed the claimant for a part of them. The claimant requests the balance of € 1,054 from the defendant in court. Following a court expert opinion, the Local Court (*Amtsgericht*, AG) Kitzingen also found that the garage's invoice was too high; it awarded the claimant only a further € 389 and otherwise dismissed the claim. The Regional Court (*Landgericht*, LG) Würzburg dismissed the appeal. With the appeal before the BGH, the claimant continues to pursue compensation for the remaining repair costs of € 665, which she still owes to the garage.

b) Judgment of the Court

15 The BGH sets the judgment of the Regional Court aside and remands it to the court for a new hearing. The claimant has a direct claim against the insurer of the party who was solely responsible for the accident pursuant to § 7 (1) Road Traffic Act (*Straßenverkehrsgesetz*, StVG) in conjunction with § 115 (1) sent 1 no 1 Insurance Contract Act (*Versicherungsvertragsgesetz*, VVG). According to § 249 (2) BGB, the injured party can demand the amount of money necessary for the repair of her

47 ECLI:DE:BGH:2024:160124UVIZR253.22.0; Entscheidungen des Bundesgerichtshofs in Zivilsachen (BGHZ) 239, 208 = NJW 2024, 2031.

car (as the restoration in kind owed by the injurer), and she can freely choose the type and form of repair. However, the amount recoverable is limited to what a reasonable, economically minded person in the position of the victim would deem expedient and necessary from an economic point of view (cost efficiency principle, *Wirtschaftlichkeitsgebot*). Where the victim may reasonably influence the amount of costs for repair, she is required to choose the most cost-effective, having regard, however, to the special situation of the victim and her subjective possibilities of knowledge and influence. Furthermore, costs recoverable pursuant to § 249 (2) 1 BGB must fully indemnify the victim but must not allow her to make a profit by placing her in a financially better position than she would be in but for the damaging event (*Bereicherungsverbot*).

In a seminal judgment of 29 October 1974,[48] the BGH had deduced from these **16** principles that the so-called 'garage risk' (*Werkstattrisiko*) must be borne by the injurer: having regard to the necessary subjective assessment of damages, the victim, who had her damaged car repaired in a garage, may request from the injurer full reimbursement of the invoiced repair costs as necessary costs under § 249 (2) 1 BGB even if they are unreasonable (eg by excessive rates for work or parts or by improper or uneconomical work), provided she was not at fault in selecting or monitoring the garage. If, however, the invoiced costs are excessive, the victim must assign, against reimbursement by the injurer, any potential claims she has against the garage to the injurer to prevent her from making an unjust profit. Absent the victim's fault in selecting or monitoring the garage, the question whether invoiced costs were excessive is exclusively a matter between the garage and the injurer, since this issue would also be on the injurer had he commissioned the garage himself. After entrusting her car to a carefully selected garage, the victim is rather limited in her possibilities of influencing the repair work effected. Rather casually, the BGH adds that this reasoning also applies if the garage also invoiced works which it had not carried out, provided that this is not recognisable to the injured party.

Contrary to the opinion of the Regional Court – that could rely on widespread **17** support in legal scholarship – the BGH now expressly extends these principles on the garage risk to cases in which the victim has not yet (fully) settled the garage invoice. The underlying rationale of the principles does not depend on whether the invoice has been settled. However, the BGH recognises that an unmodified application of the principles may conflict with the *Bereicherungsverbot* if the victim receives full reimbursement of the costs invoiced and then only pays the garage a reduced amount (eg, what would have been reasonable). This would also put the

48 BGH 29 October 1974 – VI ZR 42/73, BGHZ 63, 182.

injurer in a worse position compared to the situation in which he himself would have commissioned the repair because then he would be able to reduce the amount paid to the garage himself.

18 To avoid this consequence, the BGH modifies the 'garage risk' principles for cases in which the victim has not yet (fully) paid the garage to the effect that the victim may only request payment from the injurer to the garage and not to herself. The victim remains the creditor of the claim, but payment must go to, and may only be received by, the garage. At the same time, the victim must, as always, assign her potential claims against the garage to the injurer, who may then argue with the garage about the reasonableness of the invoice. A court may inform the claimant about the need to request payment to the garage. If the victim nevertheless continues to request payment to herself, she must bear the garage risk and the full burden of demonstrating and proving that the invoiced repair costs had in fact been necessary according to § 249 (2) 1 BGB.

19 If the victim requests payment to the garage, any dispute over the reasonableness of the invoice will not be part of the proceedings between victim and injurer. However, the victim must still show that the works appearing on the invoice were in fact due to the accident, and she must not have been at fault in selecting or monitoring the garage. The mere fact that the final invoice exceeds the expert's estimation, which the victim had commissioned before the repair by about 6 %, does not indicate fault on her part.[49]

c) Commentary[50]

20 The decision is noteworthy, and has received the deserved attention in legal writing, for its meticulous application of basic principles of the law of damages and

---

49 In the parallel case BGH 16 January 2024 – VI ZR 266/22, DAR 2024, 256, even 27% was not considered as indicating fault.

50 See the case notes by *T Almeroth*, Neues zum Werkstattrisiko, Neue Zeitschrift für Verkehrsrecht (NZV) 2024, 153; *F Böhm/M Nugel*, Schadensersatz und Werkstattrisiko bei unbezahlten Rechnungen nach der aktuellen Rechtsprechung des BGH, Zeitschrift für Schadensrecht (ZfS) 2024, 543; *HW van Bühren*, ZIP 2024, 619; *H Grams*, Fachdienst Versicherungsrecht (FD-VersR) 2024, 806448; *H-P Freymann*, Das Werkstattrisiko: Grundlagen und aktuelle Entwicklungen, Recht und Schaden (r+s) 2024, 341; *J Hager*, Juristische Arbeitsblätter (JA) 2024, 775; *E Hettwer*, Werkstattrisiko – "Die fünf Entscheidungen des BGH", juris die Monatszeitschrift (jM) 2024, 249; *D Looschelders/T Hoffmann*, Die Rechtsprechung des BGH zum Werkstattrisiko, Juristische Rundschau (JR) 2025, 1; *G Mäsch*, Juristische Schulung (JuS) 2024, 698; *J Pamer*, Die Reparaturkostenrechnung beim Kfz-Haftpflichtschadenfall und das Werkstattrisiko, DAR 2024, 242; *F Scheu*, juris PraxisReport Versicherungsrecht (jurisPR-VersR) 7/2024 Anm 1; *A Staudinger/*

for its high relevance in practice. In fact, the judgment discussed here is one of a series of five judgments regarding garage risk handed down by the BGH on the same day.[51] The facts of the cases are essentially similar: all deal with repair costs following a road traffic accident. With these judgments, the BGH concretises its case law on garage risk and creates legal clarity.

The BGH was able to build on its established case law, which had assigned the garage risk to the injurer where the garage invoice had been settled.[52] Contrary to the opinion of some courts and parts of the legal scholarship, the BGH now unequivocally and clearly holds that these principles also apply if the injured party has not yet settled the garage's invoice in full.[53] This is convincing because the interest of the parties involved generally do not depend on whether the victim has already paid the garage in full. If the garage risk were to remain on the victim until she has fully paid the invoiced amount, this would place a victim, who is in a financially weak situation and unable to pay the garage immediately, in a significantly worse position than a wealthy victim because she would be required to demonstrate the reasonableness of the invoice to request indemnification. 21

At the same time, the solution adopted by the BGH in order to avoid that the victim who has not yet fully paid may derive a profit is equally convincing in view of the *Bereicherungsverbot* prevailing in the law of damages. However, where the victim has not yet paid, one may ask which potential claims she has against the garage to assign to the injurer so that the latter may argue with the garage about the reasonableness of the costs incurred. As long as there is no overpaid amount, it might seem that there can be no potential claim in unjustified enrichment, as it would be in the case of an invoice settled before compensation is 22

K Runge, Werkstattrisiken und Nebenwirkungen, NJW 2024, 1996; *M Zwickel*, Risikotragung für fehlerhafte oder überhöhte Rechnungen im Haftungsrecht des Straßenverkehrs, MDR 2024, 809.

51 BGH 16 January 2024 – VI ZR 38/22, DAR 2024, 253; BGH 16 January 2024 – VI ZR 239/22, r+s 2024, 332; BGH 16 January 2024 – VI ZR 266/22, DAR 2024, 256; BGH 16 January 2024 – VI ZR 51/23, r+s 2024, 335; see the case notes for all five judgments by *Almeroth*, NZV 2024, 153; *Freymann*, r+s 2024, 341; *Hettwer*, jM 2024, 249; *Looschelders/Hoffmann*, JR 2025, 1; *Pamer*, DAR 2024, 242; *Staudinger/Runge*, NJW 2024, 1996; *Zwickel*, MDR 2024, 809.

52 Cf *I Ebert* in: Erman BGB-Kommentar (17th edn 2023) § 249 no 5; *H Rüßmann* in: juris PraxisKommentar BGB (10th edn 2023) § 249 no 95 ff.

53 Cf LG Essen 27 July 2020-13 S 97/19, Beck online Rechtsprechung (BeckRS) 2020, 39303 para 35 ff; *F de Biasi*, Der Fahrzeugschaden in Zeiten von Corona, NZV 2021, 113, 114; *S Exter*, Der Regress des Kraftfahrthaftpflicht-Versicherers bei der die Reparatur ausführenden Werkstatt als Kehrseite des Werkstatt- und Prognoserisikos, VersR 2022, 729, 730; *N Hoppe*, Indizwirkung der nicht beglichenen Reparaturrechnung? Straßenverkehrsrecht (SVR) 2021, 168, 169 f; *JL Kemperdiek*, Der Schädiger im Spannungsfeld zwischen Werkstattrisiko, Indizwirkung und eigenen Regressansprüchen, r+s 2021, 372, 374.

claimed, and a contractual or delictual claim for damages fails for lack of damage suffered by the victim.[54] The puzzle is solved by the BGH with the need to request payment to the garage: once the injurer pays the garage, the garage may be unjustly enriched and damage corresponding to a contractual or delictual claim may have occurred.[55]

23 In practice, it is quite common that a victim assigns her claim for damages, which she has against the injurer, to the garage and then the garage itself asserts the claim. The question as to who is to bear the garage risk in this situation was the subject of two other decisions in the series of judgments. The BGH holds that, unlike the victim, the garage as assignee of the victim's claims cannot rely on the garage risk and must therefore demonstrate the necessity of all invoice positions.[56] The BGH justifies this result by pointing out that the principles of garage risk should only benefit the victim and not the garage. Otherwise, the garage would have an undesirable incentive to charge excessive costs.[57] Moreover, as long as the claim for damages is in the hands of the victim, the injurer is protected because they can request the assignment of the victim's claims against the garage in return for a reimbursement in full. When the claim for damages is assigned to the garage, this protection would no longer be available, were the injurer still be required to pay in full. The doctrinal justification for this unquestionably convincing result is, however, not easy.[58]

24 Finally, in another of the five judgments, the BGH deals with the issue whether the victim is negligent in selecting the garage and must therefore bear the risk of an unreasonable invoice if she has not obtained an expert report before bringing her car to the garage.[59] The Court holds that the *Wirtschaftlichkeitsgebot* (see above no 15) does not require the victim to consult an expert before commissioning the repair at a specialised garage (*Fachwerkstatt*). Rather, she may expect the garage to proceed in an economical manner and to carry out only work that is objectively necessary. The standard for holding the victim at fault in selecting and monitoring the garage is therefore high.[60] As the injurer would also have

54 *van Bühren*, ZIP 2024, 619, 620 who therefore prefers to place the garage risk on the victim.
55 *Mäsch*, JuS 2024, 698, 699; *Freymann*, r+s 2024, 341, 348; but see *Böhm/Nugel*, ZfS 2024, 543, 545 who criticise that this solution places an additional burden on insurers and who argue that the insurer should be entitled to set-off a repayment claim against the garage.
56 BGH 16 January 2024 – VI ZR 38/22, DAR 2024, 253; BGH 16 January 2024 – VI ZR 239/22, r+s 2024, 332.
57 *Mäsch*, JuS 2024, 698, 699.
58 See the discussion and the criticism levelled against the BGH by, eg, *Mäsch*, JuS 2024, 698, 699 (resorting to good faith under § 242 BGB); *Hager*, JA 2024, 775, 777.
59 BGH 16 January 2024 – VI ZR 51/22, r+s 2024, 335.
60 *Staudinger/Runge*, NJW 2024, 1998, 1998.

to reimburse reasonable costs for obtaining an expert report, not requiring the victim to resort to an expert in every case may also benefit the injurer. Unfortunately, it remains unanswered when a garage will be considered a 'Fachwerkstatt', and a future clarification by the BGH is desirable.[61]

Overall, the series of cases strengthens the procedural situation of the injured 25
party.[62] As long as the victim is diligent in selecting and monitoring the garage, she does not have to pay the repair costs in advance, nor does she have to consult an independent expert before commissioning the garage.

In a judgment that was handed down two months later, the BGH refers (in 26
part verbatim) to its recent decisions and extends the principles of garage risk to potentially excessive costs charged by a motor vehicle expert commissioned to evaluate the damage to the victim's car after a traffic accident.[63] The BGH justifies this extension, neatly labelled 'expert risk', by the fact that even in the case of experts, the injured party has a limited influence on the third-party sphere and, as a layman, can hardly assess the reasonableness of the invoiced costs.[64] The injurer had refused to reimburse € 20 charged by the expert as a 'supplement for corona protection measures'. As the claim for damages had been assigned to the expert, the 'expert risk' was on him (see above no 23) and he had to demonstrate the reasonableness of this supplement. The BGH did not object in principle to the possibility of charging a supplement and remanded the case.

2. BGH 12 March 2024, VI ZR 1370/20:[65] Compensation for Immaterial Harm in the Event of Secret Video Monitoring of a Flat Entrance by the Property Owner

a) Brief Summary of the Facts

The claimant, a state-owned housing company, demanded the eviction and sur- 27
render of two rented flats from four tenants due to unauthorised subletting. Despite repeated warnings to the defendants, the claimant continually received in-

---

61 *Almeroth*, NZV 2024, 153, 158; *Staudinger/Runge*, NJW 2024, 1996, 1999.
62 Cf *Mäsch*, JuS 2024, 698, 700; *Scheu*, jurisPR-Vers 7/2024 Anm 1; *Almeroth*, NZV 2024, 153, 157 f; for an alternative approach to achieve the same objective, see *Zwickel*, MDR 2024, 809, 815.
63 BGH 12 March 2024 – VI ZR 280/22, NJW 2024, 2035.
64 Cf *Staudinger/Runge*, NJW 2024, 1996, 1998, who also want to apply the principles of garage risk, developed for liability insurance of an injurer, to fully comprehensive vehicle insurance of the injured.
65 ECLI:DE:BGH:2024:120324UVIZR1370.20.0; BGHZ 240, 45 = NJW 2024, 2836.

formation from third parties to the effect that the defendants sublet the two flats on a regular basis. In order to be able to prove the subletting, the claimant hired a private detective agency. For four weeks, the private agency monitored the entrance area of the flats with a hidden camera and recorded who entered and left the flats. The camera was installed in the staircase in such a way that the entrance area inside the flats was also monitored when the door was open. The monitoring revealed that the flats rented by the defendants had in fact been sublet to third persons, and the claimant terminated the tenancy. Before the AG Berlin-Mitte, the claimant requested that the defendants vacate the flats. One of the defendants counter-claimed a total of € 10,000 in compensation because of unlawful video monitoring.[66] The Local Court granted the claim and dismissed the counter-claim. The LG Berlin dismissed both claim and counter-claim. It held that the secret video monitoring violated fundamental rights and could therefore not provide evidence for unauthorised subletting that had otherwise been contested by the defendants. With the appeal, both parties continue to pursue their claims.

b) Judgment of the Court

28 The BGH confirms the judgment of the LG and thus dismisses both the action for eviction and the defendant's counter-claim for compensation.

29 The clear focus of the judgment is certainly on the claim for eviction which is also denied by the BGH. However, the reasoning concerning this aspect will be summarised only very briefly. As the secret video recordings were considered inadmissible evidence and the claimant could not otherwise prove the alleged unauthorised subletting, the claimant was not entitled to terminate the rent agreement. Gathering evidence by secret video recordings violated applicable data protection laws. The fact that evidence was gathered in an unlawful manner does not necessarily prevent its admissibility in court. Rather, the rights infringed upon have to be balanced in the individual case against the private and public interests in an effective administration of civil justice, having regard to the GDPR, which also applies to the processing of data before the court but leaves room for national civil procedure. In the present case, admitting the recordings as evidence would violate the defendants' right to inviolability of the home (art 13 (1) GG) and their right to informational self-determination, which is an accepted part of the

66 The defendant counter-claimed € 5,000 in her own right and another € 5,000 as assignee of claims from two other defendants.

general right of personality (art 2 (1), 1 (1) GG); both violations outweigh the claimant's interest in enforcing his claim.

The defendant's appeal as to her counter-claim is also unsuccessful. She is not entitled to monetary compensation for a violation of her general right of personality under § 823 (1) BGB in conjunction with art 1 (1), 2 (1) GG. With reference to its established legal practice, the BGH clarifies that monetary compensation in the event of a violation of the general right of personality is only awarded in exceptional circumstances. Monetary compensation is only to be recognised if there is a serious infringement of the general right of personality and the impairment cannot be satisfied in any other way than by money. According to the BGH, these criteria are necessary to ensure a sufficient protection of personality rights. Whether a serious infringement exists depends on the circumstances of the individual case. In particular, the significance and scope of the infringement, the cause and motive of the infringer and the degree of fault are important. In applying these criteria, the BGH concludes that the infringement of the defendant's rights was not sufficiently serious to warrant monetary compensation as had been requested in the counter-claim. Although there was a significant infringement of the general right of personality with regard to the defendant's private sphere and her right to informational self-determination, the core of her personality and of her private life were not affected. Furthermore, the claimant had only acted negligently, as it was convinced of the lawfulness of the hidden monitoring, and the claimant was driven by the fact that the defendants had given sufficient cause for monitoring in the past due to their unauthorised subletting. Finally, it must be taken into consideration that the defendants had already received some kind of satisfaction for the violation of their personal rights in that the video recordings were not admitted as evidence in civil proceedings. 30

Moreover, the BGH emphasises that an alleged significant injury to health asserted by the counter-claiming defendant must be ignored for the overall assessment of whether the infringement of the general right of personality was sufficiently serious. An injury to health, as a legally protected absolute right, is relevant for claiming damages for pain and suffering pursuant to § 253 (2) BGB. However, the latter claim must be strictly distinguished from the claim for monetary compensation for infringements of the general right of personality in issue. According to the BGH, the claim for monetary compensation for violation of the general right of personality is a 'special legal institution' that is derived from the protection afforded to fundamental rights by the Constitution. It merely serves to provide satisfaction in cases where no other form of satisfaction is possible. However, it does not serve to protect other absolute rights, such as health. In the opinion of the BGH, the difference in essence between the two forms of compensation can also be seen in the fact that a claim for damages for pain and suf- 31 fering under § 253 (2) BGB can be inherited, whereas this is not the case with a claim for monetary compensation based on the infringement of personality rights. If conduct does not only infringe personality rights but also leads to an injury to health, the latter injury cannot be used to justify the seriousness of the infringement of personality rights but must be made the subject of a claim for damages for pain and suffering.

c) Commentary[67]

32 To be sure, the dispute between the housing company and its tenants is a contract law case. However, its main issue as to whether secret video recordings can provide evidence in trial can easily arise in tort law cases as well, as can be seen from the seminal decision of the BGH on the admissibility of dash cam recordings as evidence in traffic accident litigation.[68] Two questions must be distinguished: Was the evidence gathered unlawfully? Is the unlawfully gathered evidence nonetheless admissible in civil proceedings? The present judgment draws on this established line of reasoning and refers it to the multi-level system established by the GDPR and to the Regulation's requirements for data processing by public authorities. Although the focus of the judgment is clearly on this issue, and the case has received great attention in legal writing for this very aspect,[69] it is included in this report rather because of the Court's succinct statements on compensation for immaterial harm.

33 In an almost apodictical manner, the BGH reiterates its clear distinction between monetary compensation for infringements of the general right of personality, on the one hand, and damages for pain and suffering because of injury to health, on the other. The Court sees a difference in essence ('Wesensverschiedenheit') between the two. Infringements of personality rights may only be compensated in money if they are sufficiently serious and the impairment cannot be sat-

67 See the case notes by *O Elzer*, MDR 2024, 1094; *A Eufinger*, Zeitschrift für Datenschutzrecht (ZD) 2024, 636; *M Fuhlrott*, Gesellschafts- und Wirtschaftsrecht (GWR) 2024, 253; *J Hager*, JA 2024, 949; *A Luedtke*, Gewerblicher Rechtsschutz und Urheberrecht in der Praxis (GRUR-Prax) 2024, 544; *P Schlüter*, JZ 2024, 888; *A Siegmund*, Mietrecht kompakt (MK) 2025, 24; *M Wünschelbaum*, Recht Digital (RDi) 2024, 506.

68 BGH 15 May 2018 – VI ZR 233/17, BGHZ 218, 348; see the discussion of the case in *Kleinschmidt* (fn 2) no 40 ff with further refs.

69 *Schlüter*, JZ 2024, 888; *Elzer*, MDR 2024, 1094; *Eufinger*, ZD 2024, 636; *Fuhlrott*, GWR 2024, 253; *Luedtke*, GRUR-Prax 2024, 544; *Siegmund*, MK 2025, 24; *Wünschelbaum*, RDi 2024, 506.

isfied in any other way.[70] This requires a balancing of interests in each individual case according to established criteria. Injury to health as a legally protected right is not among these criteria.[71] The main purpose of the monetary compensation is, therefore, satisfaction of the claimant (and deterrence of the tortfeasor), while damages for pain and suffering have a double purpose of compensation and satisfaction.[72] An important corollary of this difference in purpose, in the eyes of the BGH, lies in the fact that a claim for damages may be inherited while a claim for compensation for an infringement of personality rights is not inheritable.[73]

The character of the latter claim as a 'special legal institution' must be ex- 34 plained historically. As is well known,[74] the claim is a creation by the courts that was very controversial at the time because the drafters of the BGB wished to afford only very limited protection to personality rights and these rights were, unlike health, not among the legally protected interests enumerated in the BGB as warranting damages for pain and suffering. In order to justify its creation, the BGH, with the blessing of the Constitutional Court, gave the claim a basis in constitutional law; ever since, it has received this special status that is somehow different from other claims under the general law of delict. In this respect, the distinction emphasised in the present judgment reflects the established case law.

However, the special status of monetary compensation for infringements of 35 personality rights has recently been called into question.[75] In particular, the non-heritability of these claims is heavily criticised as no longer corresponding to the spirit of the times and as producing unjust results.[76] As reported above (see above no 10 ff), a legislative initiative attempted (without success) to reverse this particularly unfortunate corollary of the distinction. It is possibly because of this criticism that the BGH emphasises its insistence on its position concerning the lack of heritability although this aspect was not even relevant in the present case.

---

70 For details, see MünchKomm BGB/*Rixecker* (fn 45) Anh § 12 no 336 ff.

71 On the relationship between the general right of personality and the protection of bodily integrity and health as specific emanations, see *G Wagner* in: Münchener Kommentar zum Bürgerlichen Gesetzbuch (MünchKomm BGB), vol 7 (9th edn 2024) § 823 nos 220, 466.

72 *A Slizyk*, Handbuch Schmerzensgeld (21st edn 2025) no 165 ff; *Schubert/Ipsen*, JZ 2022, 737, 738 f, both with further refs.

73 BGH 29 November 2021 – VI ZR 258/18, NJW 2022, 868; confirmed by BVerfG 24 October 2022 – 1 BvR 110/22, NJW 2023, 757; see the discussion above no 12; *Slizyk* (fn 72) no 466 f.

74 See above fn 39.

75 See *Schubert/Ipsen*, JZ 2022, 737 ff with further refs summarising the discussion; MünchKomm/*Rixecker* (fn 45) Anh § 12 no 334 f; *Grziwotz*, ZRP 2024, 173, 174; but see also, emphasising differences between the two types of redress, *Wagner* (fn 39) ch 7 no 51 f; *Ahrens/Spickhoff* (fn 40) § 45 no 48 f.

76 See above no 12.

36 Without any real discussion, the case seems to draw another surprising consequence from the distinction between the two types of claims. While it is convincing that injury to health may not affect the monetary compensation for infringements of personality rights, the BGH did not consider whether an (alternative) claim for damages for pain and suffering existed because of this allegation (nor did it remand the case for this purpose).[77] From a procedural perspective, one would be led to believe that the issue in dispute (to be considered by the court) is defined by the incident on which the action is based and the request formulated in the (counter-)claim. It seems that pleading an infringement of personality rights is so different from pleading an injury to health that the two cannot even be considered as the same issue in dispute. That would hardly be convincing.[78] As the BGH shows its firm attachment to the traditional reasoning, it would indeed be the task of the legislator to eliminate the special status and to enshrine the claims arising from the infringement of the general right of personality in the law of damages of the BGB.[79]

37 It should be noted that the video recordings took place before 25 May 2018, hence at a time when the GDPR was not yet applicable. For violations of the obligations created by the GDPR, the strict requirements for monetary compensation in the event of a violation of the general right of personality are no longer relevant: art 82 GDPR contains an independent basis of claim that does not require a degree of seriousness (see below no 61). The provision also applies to minor infringements and does not require the non-material damage to be significant. The immaterial harm suffered by the counter-claiming defendant in the present case could potentially be compensated under this provision.[80] This situation once again underlines the need for a more coherent coordination of the respective claims.[81]

77 *Hager*, JA 2024, 949, 952.
78 Ibid.
79 See above no 11.
80 *Fuhlrott*, GWR 2024, 253.
81 *Schubert/Ipsen*, JZ 2022, 737, 740 f.

3. BGH 11 June 2024, VI ZR 381/23:[82] Animal Keeper's Liability for a Dog under Human Direction

a) Brief Summary of the Facts

The claimant, a statutory health insurer, is asserting claims in court against the defendant as an animal keeper for medical treatment costs reimbursed to the insured person in the amount of € 11,640 and for a declaration of the obligation to pay further damages.[83] The claim is based on the defendant's liability as an animal keeper for the damage suffered by the insured person as a result of an encounter between her and the defendant's dog. 38

On 2 July 2020 at around 6 pm, the defendant's daughter went for a walk with the defendant's dog on a country path. There she met the insured and later injured woman, who was also walking her dog. Both dogs charged towards a mouse hole in a field overgrown with tall grass. The defendant's dog was on a drag line which it was pulling behind. The insured stepped onto the field to get her dog away from the hole. In doing so, she stepped, unnoticed because of the tall grass, into a 'snare' that the defendant dog's drag line had formed. The defendant's daughter also wanted to separate the defendant's dog from the mouse hole, so she called it to her by command. Immediately, the dog followed this command and ran back to the defendant's daughter. This caused the drag line to tighten around the insured person's leg and to knock her over. The fall caused a fracture to the insured's right leg that had to be treated in hospital. The treatment costs were covered by the insurer and are now mainly part of the claim. 39

b) Judgment of the Court

The LG Bonn as first instance and the Higher Regional Court (*Oberlandesgericht*, OLG) Köln as court of appeal both dismissed the action.[84] Unanimously, both courts denied the materialisation of a risk specific to the animal (*spezifische oder typische Tiergefahr*) of the defendant's dog in the damaging event and therefore rejected the animal keeper's liability under § 833 sent 1 BGB as the only conceivable basis of claim. The BGH reverses the decision by the previous court. It 40

82 ECLI:DE:BGH:2024:110624UVIZR381.23.0; BGHZ 240, 377 = NJW 2024, 3293.

83 In the meantime, the defendant has died, so that the action in the further proceedings is directed against the heirs, who are represented by a curator of the estate.

84 LG Bonn 28 July 2021 – 17 O 457/20, ECLI:DE:LGBN:2021:0728:17O457.20.00; OLG Köln 3 March 2022 – 18 U 131/21, ECLI:DE:OLGK:2022:0303:18U131.21.00.

clearly affirms the defendant's liability as an animal keeper under § 833 sent 1 BGB and remands the case.

41 The BGH recalls in detail the requirements for the strict liability under § 833 sent 1 BGB. According to this provision, the keeper of a 'luxury' animal, ie an animal which is not 'intended to serve the profession, the business activities, or the support'[85] of its keeper, is liable if a person is killed or injured or a thing is damaged by the animal. The decisive factor for liability is essentially the materialisation of the specific or typical risk of the animal in the damaging event. A specific risk materialises where an unpredictable and autonomous behaviour, in line with its animal nature, has become causal for the violation of a legally protected interest. The specific danger of the animal lies in the fact that the keeper exposes others to a living being whose characteristics and behaviour they cannot fully control. When keeping an animal, it is often impossible to influence the occurrence of dangerous situations through proper control. In this vein, the animal keeper's strict liability is the flip side of recognising the permitted risk of keeping an animal and exposing others to the only insufficiently controllable danger of the animal.

42 However, the materialisation of an animal risk is traditionally rejected in two cases: on the one hand, if no energy of the animal itself contributes to the event, and, on the other hand, if the animal solely follows the direction and will of a human. The case turns on the scope of this second exception which the lower courts had used to refuse the defendant's liability. The BGH confirms that, where an animal merely follows the direction and will of a human, the injury is caused not by the animal but by the human so that no claim can lie in § 833 sent 1 BGB. To illustrate, the BGH cites an old judgment by the Imperial Court (*Reichsgericht*, RG) in which the liability of a coachman as an animal keeper had been denied when a horse had been harnessed to a coach and obeyed the will of the coachman; in such a case, the horse is merely a tool in the hands of the coachman and it is consequently he who inflicted the damage by careless driving. While typical cases of autonomous animal behaviour include animals lashing out, charging, kicking, biting, barking, jumping up, shying or bolting, cases where the animal is just a mechanical tool or does not behave autonomously due to the will or direction of a human are outside the scope of § 833 sent 1 BGB. In contrast, an animal does not only follow the will and direction of a human where a riding horse reacts to the horseman's – possibly erroneous – command in a different way than intended. In such a case, the horse's reaction is a consequence of the

85 *Markesinis/Bell/Janssen* (fn 39) 212.

unpredictable nature of an animal, and the general supervision of the horseman cannot exclude autonomous and arbitrary behaviour.

The BGH takes account of numerous authors in legal writing who object to an exclusion of cases in which an animal acted under the direction or will of a human because the animal still contributed to the damage through its own strength. According to these authors, the human direction does not efface the risk arising from the specific energy of the animal. The damage is still caused by the animal's ability to move autonomously. Human direction may even increase the risk. 43

The BGH does not fully embrace this position but seems to accept the criticism in principle: if the keeper of a living being to which he exposes others is often unable to fully control this living being precisely because of its nature as a living being, then direction by a human cannot necessarily exclude all risks arising from the animal's nature. At least in cases such as the present one, where the human direction is just the impetus for the animal's behaviour, but the behaviour itself is outside human control for lack of physical access, there is no reason to deny the materialisation of the specific animal risk resulting from the autonomous movement of the animal, its energy and strength. Hence, the key criterion is the lack of physical access of the human to the animal. This line of reasoning can be referred back to the underlying purpose of strict animal liability. 44

Moreover, the BGH quite generally invokes the protection of victims. From the victim's perspective, it makes no difference whether a dog breaks free, runs away from home, follows the human's command directly or reluctantly or not at all. The victim's need for protection exists in all cases, irrespective of the presence of a human. 45

Applying these considerations to the case at hand, the BGH holds that the specific risk of the defendant's dog materialised in the damaging event. The command of the defendant's daughter was just the impetus for the dog's behaviour and the daughter did not have physical access to the dog. This is shown by the fact that the dog autonomously decided at what speed, with what strength and with what use of energy it ran back to the defendant's daughter. The dog could not recognise the fact that the drag line presented a danger to others, and it was unable to stop upon noticing that the drag line was resisting. 46

Finally, the BGH mentions that indirect causation is sufficient for an animal keeper's liability, so the fact that the injured woman was damaged by the drag line and not by direct contact with the dog is therefore enough. 47

c) Commentary[86]

48 In principle, delictual liability under German private law is based on fault. It may only be strict where expressly provided for by statute. The strict liability of the keeper of a 'luxury' animal is the only case of strict liability to be found within the BGB. Other cases are enshrined in special statutes outside the BGB but may not be extended by way of analogy. Their underlying rationale is, as recalled by the BGH in the present judgment, the creation of a permitted risk to which the person who keeps this risk under control exposes others. As a consequence, strict liability can only exist where the specific risk materialised. Otherwise, the keeper of this risk can only be held liable for fault.[87] The specific risk of an animal lies in its unpredictable and autonomous behaviour as a living being.

49 In the present judgment, the BGH declares that it continues its previous case law; upon closer inspection, however, it extends the scope of liability as is apparent from the fact that the lower courts had denied liability based on the established case law. According to this case law, the materialisation of a specific animal risk is denied in cases where the animal was subject to the directions and the will of a human.[88] In these cases, the courts saw the origin of the harm in the human's and not in the animal's behaviour. More recently, the BGH introduced a distinction and excluded cases from this reasoning in which the animal disobeyed the human direction, thus displaying its unpredictable behaviour.[89] The BGH mentions the example of the riding horse that does not react as intended in this regard. Consequently, the animal keeper's liability depended on the obeyance of

---

86 See the case notes by *N-J Biller-Bomhardt/T Rieth*, r+s 2025, 78; *C Eberl-Borges*, LMK 2024, 826444; *M Ehmer*, NJW 2024, 3295; *G Mäsch*, JuS 2025, 363; *FT Schrader*, JA 2025, 73; *A Staudinger/LA Sprick*, juris PraxisReport Internationales Wirtschaftsrecht (jurisPR-IWR) 6/2024 Anm 3.

87 Similar considerations have given rise to numerous cases in the past years, in which it was discussed whether the operation of a motor vehicle had been the cause of harm, see *Wurmnest/Riemann* (fn 7) no 29 ff on the keeper's liability for explosion of a removed vehicle battery, with reference to earlier cases; BGH 27 February 2024 – VI ZR 80/23, VersR 2024, 1170; BGH 18 July 2023 – VI ZR 16/23, VersR 2024, 321 (damage caused by emission of oil from a vehicle used for harvesting grapes); BGH 12 December 2023 – VI ZR 76/23, NJW 2024, 1037 (scope of liability upon vehicle fire); OLG Schleswig 31 July 2024 – 7 U 48/24, MDR 2024, 1515 (collision of vehicles parked on a car transport train).

88 Cf RG 6 February 1902 – VI 383/01, Entscheidungen des Reichsgerichts in Zivilsachen (RGZ) 50, 180; RG 26 February 1903 – VI 352/02, RGZ 54, 73; BGH 25 September 1952 – III ZR 334/51, VersR 1952, 403.

89 Cf BGH 12 July 1966 – VI ZR 11/65, VersR 1966, 1073; BGH 6 July 1999 – VI ZR 170/98, NJW 1999, 3119; BGH 20 December 2005 – VI ZR 225/04, Neue Juristische Wochenschrift Rechtsprechungs-Report (NJW-RR) 2006, 813; LG Koblenz 14 October 2022 – 9 O 140/21, Neue Juristische Online Zeitschrift (NJOZ) 2023, 81.

the animal. As in the case at hand the defendant's dog reacted just as intended upon the command given by the defendant's daughter, liability would have been excluded. Furthermore, as the daughter had not been negligent, the injured person would not have received compensation.[90]

50 One commentator points out that the BGH could have solved the case based on this previous case law by tying the materialisation of the dog's risk not to the return of the dog upon the human command but to the earlier spontaneous decision of the dog to run to the mouse hole that was clearly a consequence of the dog's unpredictable behaviour and that still continued in the need for the daughter to call back the dog.[91] However, the BGH did not follow this path but instead used the case to heed, at least in principle, to critical voices in legal scholarship and limit the exception even further.

51 The distinction according to whether an animal obeyed the human's command is subject to extensive criticism in legal scholarship, with some authors rejecting the exclusion of a typical animal risk in cases of human direction in general.[92] Excluding the keeper's liability for animals under human direction is criticised for a whole series of arguments.[93] First, these scholars invoke the legislator's intention to establish a comprehensive liability of the animal keeper.[94] Secondly, they compare the animal keeper's liability with the liability of a vehicle keeper under § 7 (1) StVG, which is also strict, and find an implausible discrepancy: while the keeper of a vehicle is liable if a person uses their car as a weapon, the keeper of an animal is not liable if a person sets the (obedient) animal on another person.[95] Finally, critics refer to the purpose of establishing strict liability, which is to compensate for the risks arising from a living being. These risks are

---

90 But see *Mäsch*, JuS 2025, 363, 364 who sees the daughter at fault because she had let go of the drag line. This is however not evident from the facts stated in the judgment.

91 *Ehmer*, NJW 2024, 3295.

92 See eg, *Eberl-Borges*, LMK 2024, 826444; *C Eberl-Borges* in: J von Staudinger, Kommentar zum Bürgerlichen Gesetzbuch (2022) § 833 no 57; *A Spickhoff* in: beck-online.Grosskommentar BGB (BeckOGK BGB) (1 August 2024) § 833 no 77; *C Förster* in: Beck'scher Online-Kommentar BGB (73rd edn 1.2.2025) § 833 no 11; MünchKomm/*Wagner* (fn 71) § 833 no 22; *R Wilhelmi* in: Erman, BGB-Kommentar (17th edn 2023) § 833 no 4.

93 See the overview in, eg, *Eberl-Borges*, LMK 2024, 826444; BeckOGK BGB/*Spickhoff* (fn 92) § 833 no 77; MünchKomm/*Wagner* (fn 71) § 833 no 21 ff; even more extensive *K Moritz* in: juris PraxisKommentar BGB (10th edn 2023) § 833 no 29, who considers the requirement that a typical risk of the animal's nature materialised as entirely dispensable.

94 Staudinger/*Eberl-Borges* (fn 92) § 833 no 57; but see for a different understanding of the legislator's intention, *Ehmer*, NJW 2024, 3295.

95 Staudinger/*Eberl-Borges* (fn 92) § 833 no 57; BeckOK BGB/*Förster* (fn 92) § 833 no 11; BeckOGK BGB/*Spickhoff* (fn 92) § 833 no 77; MünchKomm/*Wagner* (fn 71) § 833 no 22.

also present when an animal is under the direction of a human; the fact that animals follow human commands is an inherent part of their dangerousness.[96] It would run counter to the purpose of the provision to exclude liability for a well-trained and obedient animal which is deliberately used for putting others at risk.[97] Only where a person could have brought about the same injury with the help of an inanimate object did the animal's risk not play a role.[98]

52 Obviously, the BGH sympathises with this opinion although the court does not fully embrace it – possibly not to break abruptly with its previous case law. However, it replaces the criterion of obeyance with that of physical access to the animal: where this physical access is lacking, the independent behaviour of a living being is still at work.[99] In other words, the human command is just the impetus of the animal's own behaviour.[100]

53 The judgment is to be commended. The criterion of obeyance led to random and unjust results, leaving victims harmed by the autonomous movement of an animal without compensation. Although victim protection may be a difficult argument in itself, in the present case it is relevant, as the BGH rightly emphasises.[101] Even an obedient dog runs (and does not stop) by its own volition; from the victim's perspective, it does not make any difference whether the victim is run over by a dog that set itself into motion because of a human command or by a dog that had broken free from its leash. In both situations, it is the independent and autonomous movement and strength of a living being (and not so much its unpredictability)[102] that gives rise to the damage. It could even be claimed that the possibility of influencing the behaviour of an animal increases the dangerousness of the animal.[103] Physical access seems to be the criterion used by the BGH to describe situations in which the animal's movement was not autonomous or independent. It remains to be seen in future cases whether this is a suitable criterion that fully captures the underlying idea. In any event, strict limits ought to be placed on the requirement of physical access.[104] It should only be possible to

96 Staudinger/*Eberl-Borges* (fn 92) § 833 no 57; MünchKomm/*Wagner* (fn 71) § 833 no 22.
97 *Ahrens/Spickhoff* (fn 40) § 35 no 13.
98 MünchKomm/*Wagner* (fn 71) § 833 no 22.
99 It is not clear from the judgment whether the BGH would still exclude cases in which the animal obeyed the human command if the human (such as a coachman) did have physical access, see *Biller-Bomhardt/Rieth*, r+s 2025, 78, 79 who still consider the criterion relevant in cases where the person has physical access.
100 Emphasising this aspect, *Eberl-Borges*, LMK 2024, 826444.
101 *Eberl-Borges*, LMK 2024, 826444.
102 Cf *Ehmer*, NJW 2024, 3295.
103 Staudinger/*Eberl-Borges* (fn 92) § 833 no 57.
104 Cf *Biller-Bomhardt/Rieth*, r+s 2025, 78, 79.

speak of physical access if the human has complete control over the animal in the situation, so that the latter cannot move independently. Use of a long drag line, as in the present case, may give access to the animal but it does not grant full control. In practice, this will never be the case with large animals due to their superior strength over humans, meaning that animal keeper's liability will always arise.[105] This may put the keeper of a large animal at a disadvantage compared to the keeper of a small animal, but this difference is justified by the fact that the potential danger of a horse, for example, is significantly greater than that of a hamster.

On the continuum from fault-based liability to strict liability, the present judgment expands the scope of strict liability in cases of animal accidents. However, it does not turn the risk-based liability for animals into a liability for the mere existence of the animal or the mere fact of keeping it.[106] Rather, it fleshes out more clearly the underlying rationale of holding the keeper strictly liable. Time will tell whether the BGH will extend its more victim-friendly approach to other cases in which it has so far denied the materialisation of a specific risk of the animal.[107] 54

4. BGH 18 November 2024, VI ZR 10/24:[108] Compensation for Immaterial Harm after Facebook Data Leak ('Scraping')

a) Brief Summary of the Facts

The claimant, a private Facebook user, is taking legal action against the operator of Facebook for violating the General Data Protection Regulation. The claimant asserts various claims. In particular, he requests compensation for the loss of control over his own data in the amount of a least € 1,000 based on the following event:[109] 55

The claimant registered on Facebook with the details of name, gender and user ID, which were required for registration and publicly visible to everyone. In addition, he publicly indicated his place of work on his profile. By changing 56

105 Cf Biller-Bomhardt/Rieth, r+s 2025, 78, 79.
106 Ibid; but see the criticism by *Ehmer*, NJW 2024, 3295.
107 *Eberl-Borges*, LMK 2024, 826444; cf recently OLG Dresden 12 September 2024 – 5 U 633/24, BeckRS 2024, 28992 (no contributory liability of an animal keeper whose dog was merely present at the scene of the accident without exerting any energy of its own).
108 ECLI:DE:BGH:2024:181124UVIZR10.24.0; NJW 2025, 298.
109 Other claims asserted by the claimant include a declaration that the defendant is liable to compensate future material and immaterial loss, as well as requests for information and omission. This report will not deal with these claims.

the default settings, the claimant made his mobile phone number visible to himself only. Although this would have been possible, the search function of user profiles via telephone number was, however, not changed by the claimant to a limited circle of persons, so that the default setting was retained. Therefore, any Facebook user could find the claimant's profile by entering his mobile phone number. From January 2018 to September 2019, unknown persons collected Facebook profile data via the search function using random sequences of digits as telephone numbers, a technique known as 'scraping'. In April 2021, a list of around 533 million Facebook user profile data collected worldwide through scraping was published on the internet. The claimant was also listed there, along with his telephone number, name, gender and working place. He asserts that, because of this listing, he has suffered a tangible loss of control over his data, leading to a massive increase in scam attempts.

b) Judgment of the Court

57 While the LG Köln as first instance court had awarded the claimant immaterial damages in the amount of € 250, the OLG Köln as Court of Appeal dismissed the action entirely, including the claim for damages.[110] This does not convince the BGH, which remands the case for a new hearing. The judgment meticulously deals with all claims advanced by the claimant; yet it clearly focuses on the claim for compensation for immaterial harm.

58 According to the BGH, a claim based on art 82 (1) GDPR may not be ruled out.[111] Article 82 (1) GDPR reads: 'Any person who has suffered material or non-material damage as a result of an infringement of this Regulation shall have the right to receive compensation from the controller or processor for the damage suffered.' Although the claimant complained of several data protection violations by the defendant, the BGH clarifies that only one unitary claim of compensation exists. It is impossible to split the claim according to the respective data protection violation because the claim for compensation is based on a single event, the scraping incident. Concerning the requirements of a claim for compensation, the BGH refers to decisions of the Court of Justice of the European Union (CJEU), according to which the claimant has to establish three cumulative conditions: an infringe-

110 OLG Köln 7 December 2023 – 15 U 67/23, ECLI:DE:OLGK:2023:1207.15U67.23.00.

111 International jurisdiction of German courts over the Ireland-based defendant therefore follows from the claimant's habitual residence in Germany, art 82 (6) GDPR together with art 79 (2) GDPR.

ment of the GDPR, material or immaterial damage suffered by the claimant and a causal link between that damage and that infringement.[112] In contrast, the claimant does not have to show that the person held liable was at fault but that person may exonerate himself by proving that 'it is not in any way responsible for the event giving rise to the damage' (art 82 (3) GDPR).

With regard to the first condition, the BGH assumes an infringement of the 59
GDPR for the purposes of the appeal. Whether obligations under the GDPR had in fact been infringed will have to be examined by the Court of Appeal to which the case is remanded. However, the BGH elaborates that it clearly regards a default setting of the search function via the mobile telephone number to everyone at the time of the scraping incident as an infringement of the principle of data minimisation which is concretised by an obligation to implement data protection-friendly default settings.[113] The question whether the processing was nevertheless lawful because of consent given by the claimant[114] will be a matter for the Court of Appeal.

With regard to the second condition, ie the requirement of harm suffered, the 60
BGH disagrees with the reasoning of the OLG Köln. The OLG Köln had rejected the argument that a loss of control over one's own data may constitute immaterial harm. Rather, it regarded the loss of control in itself as a kind of intermediate stage that can lead to immaterial harm. Fears, worries and discomfort as well as an increase in spam had not been sufficiently established by the claimant, in particular because the allegations were pleaded not concretely enough and by using boilerplate text.

Again relying on CJEU case law,[115] the BGH emphasises that the concept of im- 61
material damage must be given an autonomous definition under EU law. While a mere infringement of the GDPR without the occurrence of damage cannot confer a right to compensation, the third sentence of Recital (146) of the Regulation sets out the EU legislator's intention to adopt a wide interpretation of damage. In particular, art 82 (1) GDPR does not require that any immaterial damage suffered has reached a certain degree of seriousness and precludes a national rule that establishes a minimum threshold. Nevertheless, despite the lack of any threshold, the provision still puts the claimant under an obligation to prove that they actually suffered (material or immaterial) damage.

---

112 CJEU 25.1.2024, C-687/21, *MediaMarktSaturn*, ECLI:EU:C:2024:72, para 58 with further refs.

113 Art 5 (1) (c) and art 25 (2) GDPR.

114 Art 6 (1) (a) GDPR.

115 Among others, CJEU 4.5.2023, C-300/21, *Österreichische Post*, ECLI:EU:C:2023:370; CJEU 20.6.2024, C-590/22, *PS GbR*, ECLI:EU:C:2024:536.

62 Furthermore, the BGH refers to Recital (85) and recent judgments of the CJEU, according to which even the loss of control over personal data, even for a short period of time, constitutes immaterial harm and does not depend on additional tangible negative consequences (such as an actual misuse of the data).[116] Where the data subject can prove such loss of control, this in itself constitutes immaterial damage without the additional need to show fears or worries stemming from this loss of control. Such fears or worries would only be able to increase the damage.

63 Applying this standard, the BGH regards the claimant's submissions as sufficient to establish immaterial damage. The standard adopted by the *Oberlandesgericht* had been set too high. The BGH is aware of the fact that the scraping incident has led to numerous actions with obviously (partly) 'standardised' submissions lacking concreteness for the individual case. However, it also concedes that the incident has affected millions of users so that submissions in individual cases must necessarily be similar at least at the outset. Nevertheless, the claimant could sufficiently substantiate his loss of control by stating that he has never disclosed his mobile telephone number to the general public but only in a conscious and targeted manner. Even if one considers telephone numbers to be less sensitive data, this could only affect the amount of damages but not the occurrence of damage itself; there is still a considerable difference between the risk associated with the voluntary sharing of a telephone number with consciously selected persons and the loss of control caused by the scraping and the ensuing permanent availability of the number on the internet. The BGH adds that, in the present case, further consequences such as discomfort and worries about a potential misuse of the data have been shown in an equally sufficient manner by asserting an increased mistrust towards emails or calls from unknown senders or callers as well as an increased number of scam emails or calls.

64 While the conditions of the claim are a matter of EU law, the amount of damages is determined by national law, having regard to the principles of equivalence and effectiveness. In Germany, the provision of § 287 ZPO can be applied, which leaves the assessment of damages to the free estimation of the trial judge. Nevertheless, the BGH outlines the criteria and considerations which the judges to whom the case is remanded will have to take into account. Damages under art 82 (1) GDPR have a compensatory and not a punitive function.[117] Therefore, neither the gravity of the violations, nor their frequency, nor the degree of fault on the part of the defendant play a role in the assessment of damages. Rather,

116 Among others, CJEU 4.10.2024, C-200/23, *Agentsia po vpisvaniyata*, ECLI:EU:C:2024:827, para 145; CJEU 20.6.2024, C-590/22, *PS GbR*, ECLI:EU:C:2024:536, para 33; CJEU C-687/21, *MediaMarktSaturn*, para 66.

117 Among others, CJEU C-590/22, *PS GbR*, para 42; CJEU C-687/21, *MediaMarktSaturn*, para 47.

the focus must be, if only loss of control over personal data is at stake, on the sensitivity of the personal data and on their typical use, furthermore on the type and duration of the loss of control, and on the possibility to regain control over or change the personal data. In the particular case, this could include the hypothetical burden of changing one's mobile telephone number. All these factors taken together, the BGH considers a 'single-figure amount' as it had been suggested by another Court of Appeal[118] to be incompatible with the principle of effectiveness. In contrast, an amount in the region of € 100 should represent reasonable compensation in the present case. Psychological impairment which goes beyond the loss of control suffered by everyone may justify a higher amount but would require additional findings by the trial court.

Finally, the BGH states that the legal situation regarding the loss of control over personal data as damage has been sufficiently clarified by the recent case law of the CJEU in order to be considered *acte éclairé*. A preliminary reference to the CJEU is deemed unnecessary. 65

c) Commentary[119]

Nowadays, social media are used across generations and technical progress means that more and more personal data are being collected. This development increases the importance of protecting one's own data from misuse by third parties and of retaining control over one's own data. The scraping incident shows that this is not always successful. Millions of Facebook users were affected by the incident that gave rise to the present decision: by means of 'scraping', unknown persons had collected and subsequently published personal data which users had not made 66

---

118 OLG Celle 4 April – 5 U 31/23, Gewerblicher Rechtsschutz und Urheberrecht-Rechtsprechung (GRUR-RS) 2024, 6435 para 102.

119 See the case notes by *S Dienst/L Stegemann*, GRUR-Prax 2025, 153; *S Ernst*, ZIP 2025, 366; *A Golland*, Verbraucher und Recht (VuR) 2025, 71; *J Heine*, RDi 2025, 161; *J Hofmann*, juris PraxisReport IT-Recht (jurisPR-ITR) 1/2025 Anm. 3; *J Horn*, ZD 2025, 165; *S Kremer/P Laue*, Zeitschrift für Europäisches Daten- und Informationsrecht (EuDIR) 2025, 37; *R Mantz*, Schadensersatz für Datenlecks, Gewerblicher Rechtsschutz und Urheberrecht (GRUR) 2024, 1878; *B Paal*, NJW 2025, 261; *J Pohle/P Adelberg*, Der Betrieb (DB) 2025, 239; *M Rössel*, IT-Rechtsberater (ITRB) 2025, 8; *A Schürgers/JE Hirschberger*, Immaterieller Schadensersatz nach Art. 82 DS-GVO – Fokus auf die Darlegungs- und Beweislast, Neue Zeitschrift für Arbeitsrecht (NZA) 2025, 216; *HC Schwenker*, juris PraxisReport BGH-Zivilrecht (jurisPR-BGHZivilR) 8/2025 Anm. 2; *J Spittka/Y Zirnstein*, DSGVO-Massenklagen: 'Leitentscheidung' für die Praxis?, Computer und Recht (CR) 2025, 24; *J Voigt/L Mugler*, InfrastrukturRecht (IR) 2025, 104; *O Zöll/R Soeder*, juris PraxisReport Compliance & Investigations (jurisPR-Compl) 1/2025 Anm. 4.

available to the public. The incident has led to tens of thousands of essentially similar actions against Meta as the operator of Facebook, all of them based on art 82 GDPR, keeping German courts busy. It transpires from the judgment that the underlying actions are often prepared in a comparable manner, many of them by the same law firms, and are essentially based on similar allegations. The question whether the incident warranted compensation and, if so, in what amount touched on uncharted territory. Unsurprisingly, first instance courts arrived at diverging results.[120] Courts of Appeal, however, seemed reluctant to grant compensation: loss of control over personal data cannot constitute immaterial harm.[121] Eventually, appeals against these judgments in favour of Meta reached the Federal Court of Justice.

67 Quite remarkably, the Federal Court of Justice, in view of the interest in a uniform resolution of the claims stemming from this alleged 'mass tort', seized the opportunity to designate one of the appeals pending before it as a 'guideline decision procedure' on the very same day this new instrument entered into force on 31 October 2024 (see above no 1 ff).[122] This underlines the significance accorded to the legal issues involved; and it may express a certain fear that an appeal might be withdrawn before a judgment, as had happened before.[123] The order refers to 25 other pending appeals and to several thousand cases pending before lower courts.[124] The case thus represents the first *Leitentscheidungsverfahren* in Germany. Less than three weeks after this order, the present judgment was handed down. After the designation as *Leitentscheidungsverfahren*, the parties probably had lost any interest in terminating the appeal procedure without a court decision as to the substance (see above no 8), so that the judgment did not have to take the peculiar form of a 'guideline decision' under the new provisions but came in the form of a 'regular' appeal judgment.

68 The present judgment reverses the reluctant approach prevalent among Courts of Appeal. The BGH declares the mere loss of control over one's own

120 See the numerous references in *Wurmnest/Riemann* (fn 7) no 46.

121 Eg, OLG Hamm 15 August 2023 – 7 U 19/23, GRUR 2023, 1791 (cf *Wurmnest/Riemann* [fn 7] no 36 ff); OLG Köln 7 December 2023 – 15 U 67/23, GRUR-RS 2023, 37347; OLG Dresden 23 January 2024 – 4 U 1313/23, GRUR-RS 2024, 2992; OLG Celle 4 April 2024 – 5 U 31/23, GRUR-RS 2024, 6435; OLG München 24 April 2024 – 34 U 2306/23 e, GRUR-RS 2024, 8563; OLG Saarbrücken 3 May 2024 – 5 U 72/23, GRUR-RS 2024, 10977.

122 BGH 31 October 2024 – VI ZR 10/24, NJW 2024, 3595.

123 Appeals for which an oral hearing had been scheduled for 8 October 2024 were withdrawn shortly before the appeal. The oral hearing for the present case was scheduled for 11 November 2024, together with a second case for which the appeal had likewise been withdrawn shortly before, see Press Release no 206/2024.

124 BGH NJW 2024, 3595, 3596.

data, even if only for a short time, to be a compensable immaterial damage if shown by the claimant. The claimant does not have to establish an actual misuse of the data nor any further negative effects. This seems quite understandable in view of the difficulty of proving mental impairment in the event of data loss.[125]

The BGH bases its position on a number of recent judgments of the CJEU. Hav- 69
ing regard to the language of these judgments,[126] the decision of the BGH is no surprise.[127] It should be mentioned that the interpretation of the case law is disputed among legal scholars; pointing to the distinction between infringement and damage, some authors argue that the mere loss of control does not constitute the immaterial harm but may lead to immaterial harm such as the fear of misuse.[128] This, however, does not seem to be the position of the BGH.

From a purely German perspective, the granting of damages for immaterial 70
harm appears a little strange at first sight due to the restrictive approach of the BGB,[129] but with its reference to an autonomous understanding of the concept of damage within the GDPR, the BGH convincingly does not take into consideration such a national understanding in applying EU law.[130] The GDPR does not

---

125 *Rössel*, ITRB 2025, 8, 10.

126 See eg, CJEU C-200/23, *Agentsia po vpisvaniyata*, para 145 ('the EU legislature intended to include in the concept of "damage" that may be suffered by data subjects, inter alia, the mere "loss of control" over their own personal data, as a result of an infringement of that regulation, even if there had been no actual misuse of the data in question'); CJEU C-590/22, *PS GbR*, para 33 ('The loss of control over personal data, even for a short period of time, may constitute "non-material damage", within the meaning of Article 82(1) of the GDPR, giving rise to a right to compensation, provided that the data subject can show that he or she has actually suffered such damage, however slight, bearing in mind that the mere infringement of the provisions of that regulation is not sufficient to confer a right to compensation on that basis'); CJEU 11.4.2024, C-741/21, *GP/juris*, ECLI:EU:C:2024:288, para 42; CJEU 14.12.2023, C-340/21, *Natsionalna agentsia za prihodite*, ECLI:EU:C:2023:986, para 82 ('It is apparent ... that the EU legislature intended to include ..., in particular, the mere "loss of control" over their own data, as a result of an infringement of that regulation, even if there had been no misuse of the data in question to the detriment of those data subjects.').

127 *Golland*, VuR 2025, 71; *Hofmann*, jurisPR-ITR 1/2025 Anm 3; *Horn*, ZD 2025, 165.

128 *Paal*, NJW 2025, 361, 263 f referring to CJEU 14.12.2023, C-456/22, *Gemeinde Ummendorf*, ECLI:EU:C:2023:988 para 22 and CJEU C-687/21, *MediaMarktSaturn*, para 66 ('the loss of control of the personal data for a short period of time may cause the data subject "non-material damage"'); *Spittka/Zirnstein*, CR 2025, 24, 27 f; *O Brand/L Jaeger*, VersR Report: Ausgewählte Rechtsprechung zum Haftungs- und Schadensrecht 2023–2024, VersR 2024, 1588, 1596; *Kremer/Laue*, EuDIR 2025, 37, 37; *Pohle/Adelberg*, DB 2025, 239, 240 ff; *Schürgers/Hirschberger*, NZA 2025, 216, 221; more sceptical also *Mantz*, GRUR 2024, 1878, 1879; *Heine*, RDi 2025, 161, 163.

129 Cf § 253 BGB.

130 Cf *S Nabulsi*, "Dauerbrenner" beim EuGH: Der Ersatz immaterieller Schäden nach Art. 82 DS-GVO, Zeitschrift für Europäisches Privatrecht (ZEuP) 2024, 912, 927; *Golland*, VuR 2025, 71, 71 f.

know a minimum threshold; it does not require a degree of seriousness. Therefore, the judgment is also an example of the successful interaction between EU law and national law.

71 In contrast, the reasoning of the BGH on the amount of damages is enlightening and new. The BGH now provides the courts with the criteria they can use to assess the amount of damages. In particular, the sensitivity of the data affected and the existence of further psychological consequences play a crucial role. In this context, the BGH also mentions a concrete guideline value of € 100. It can be expected that courts will use this amount as orientation and guidance when dealing with the still enormous number of pending cases.[131] In decisions handed down since the present judgment, various Courts of Appeal moved into the BGH lane.[132]

72 As happy as the claimant may be about the standard for establishing damage adopted by the BGH, the envisaged amount of damages will probably disappoint him. Remember that the claimant had claimed compensation of at least € 1,000. If the court to which the case is remanded awards him damages in the amount of € 100, he will have lost 90 % of the case (with the corresponding cost consequences). From a lawyer's perspective, the judgment with its low value in dispute leads to the economic unprofitability of clients complaining of loss of control over their own data.[133] As a result, the number of individual claims in this field is expected to decrease considerably.[134] One way out of this unprofitability situation could be for the injured parties to assign their claims.[135] Whether damages claims under the GDPR can be assigned at all has not yet been decided by the Supreme

131 *Ernst*, ZIP 2025, 366, 367.

132 See eg, OLG Dresden 10 December 2024 – 4 U 808/24, GRUR-RS 2024, 35688 (award of € 100 for mere loss of control instead of the € 3,000 requested by the claimant); OLG Celle 9 January 2025 – 5 U 173/23, GRUR-RS 2025, 192; OLG Koblenz 11 February 2025 – 3 U 145/24, GRUR-RS 2025, 2048; OLG Koblenz 11 March 2025 – 3 U 950/24, GRUR-RS 2025, 4337; OLG Düsseldorf 13 March 2025 – 16 U 135/23, GRUR-RS 2025, 4634; OLG Düsseldorf 14 March 2025 – 16 U 94/24, GRUR-RS 2025, 4597; OLG Celle 20 March 2025 – 5 U 129/24, GRUR-RS 2025, 5402; but see OLG Hamm 18 December 2024 – 11 U 168/23, GRUR-RS 2024, 41292 (no loss of control proven).

133 Cf *Golland*, VuR 2025, 71, 73; *Paal*, NJW 2025, 261, 265; *Spittka/Zirnstein*, CR 2025, 24, 29; more optimistic, *Mantz*, GRUR 2024, 1878, 1880 f.

134 *Spittka/Zirnstein*, CR 2025, 24, 29; *Zöll/Soeder*, jurisPR-Compl 1/2025 Anm 4; but see *Kremer/Laue*, EuDIR 2025, 37, 38 and *Poehle/Adelberg*, DB 2025, 239, 243 who anticipate an increased risk of mass proceedings due to standardised lawsuits filed by specialised law firms.

135 Cf the discussion in *Golland*, VuR 2025, 71, 73; *Spittka/Zirnstein*, CR 2025, 24, 29 f.

Court.[136] It therefore remains to be seen whether an assignment will be a common way of enforcing such claims in the future.

Another way could be collective redress: shortly after the present judgment, on 9 December 2024, the *Verbraucherzentrale Bundesverband* filed a model declaratory action against Meta before the OLG Hamburg.[137] As soon as the application is entered in the register of model declaratory actions administered by the Federal Office of Justice (*Bundesamt für Justiz*), persons affected by the scraping incident are entitled to register their claims. In particular, this will suspend the prescription period for a potential claim ensuing from the publication of the data collected in the scraping incident which would otherwise have expired by the end of December 2024.[138] However, the model declaratory action is a two-step procedure:[139] even if the court finds in favour of the claimant consumer association, the model declaratory action does not end with a judgment granting relief to the individuals. Rather, the court will issue a declaratory ruling on a number of specific factual and legal issues that are relevant for the existence or non-existence of the consumers' individual claims and have previously been defined as the objectives ('Feststellungsziele') of the model action. Only in a second step will a court be concerned with individual claims; each registered individual has to pursue their claim individually by bringing an action in court, unless the claims can be settled.[140] In such an individual action, the claimant will be able to rely on the factual and legal findings contained in the declaratory ruling. However, apart from that, each individual action follows the ordinary civil procedure, and in particular it is not free of charge. 73

Therefore, the saga continues. The present judgment provides an important point of reference for the courts and clarifies important questions in relation to compensation for immaterial harm under art 82 (1) GDPR.[141] Nevertheless, not 74

136 Recently, in favour of an assignment of the claims, OLG Hamm 24 July 2024 – 11 U 69/23, GRUR-RS 2024, 24099.

137 Docket no 11 VKl 1/24; for further information, see <https://www.sammelklagen.de/verfahren/facebook> (last accessed 2 April 2025).

138 *Ernst*, ZIP 2025, 366, 367.

139 See the discussion in *Kleinschmidt* (fn 2) no 1 ff with further refs.

140 When introducing the novel model declaratory action, the German legislator hoped that a declaratory ruling finding against the defendant would encourage them to settle individual claims swiftly, BT-Drucks 19/2507, 16. However, a recalcitrant defendant may be able to take each individual action through more than one instance, *A Stadler*, Musterfeststellungsklagen im deutschen Verbraucherrecht? VuR 2018, 83, 86 f.

141 In the BGH judgment, it was out of dispute that the case was within the temporal scope of application of the GDPR. OLG Stuttgart 4 December 2024 – 4 U 97/24, GRUR-RS 2024, 34271 rejected a

all questions have been solved. First of all, although the BGH quite clearly indicated its position on the issue whether obligations under the GDPR had in fact been infringed, it could not rule on the question but remanded it.[142] The issue has therefore also been made an important element of the model declaratory action. Furthermore, it has rightly been pointed out that the CJEU case law is silent as to what exactly is required from the claimant to demonstrate loss of control.[143] Bearing in mind that the mere infringement of obligations under the GDPR is not sufficient to constitute damage, claimants will have to show they did in fact have control over the data affected before the scraping incident.[144] In the present case, it was sufficient that the claimant had not shared his telephone number on the internet but only in a conscious and targeted manner. This could mean that claimants who had published their telephone number previously did not suffer immaterial harm.[145] Moreover, it is unclear whether the amount of € 100 must be regarded as a kind of minimum compensation.[146] The judgment is often read that way[147] but the BGH has only indicated an amount 'in the region of € 100'. Finally, the guideline value for the amount of damages with regard to the loss of control is not useful if more sensitive data than the mobile telephone number are affected. One could think of an email address, date of birth, home address, or relationship status. These are examples mentioned in the model declaratory action; for each item, the *Verbraucherzentrale Bundesverband* deems an increase by € 100 (€ 200 in the case of relationship status) appropriate.[148] Nor does the guideline amount help courts that have to assess actual further negative consequences if demonstrated by the claimant.[149] Of course, all these issues may also require an answer in the many individual actions that are still pending.

---

claim because the claimant could not prove that his data had been affected by the scraping incident after 25 May 2018.

142 The indications given by the BGH on this issue are therefore not binding on the lower court, see *Paal*, NJW 2025, 261, 262 f who expresses doubts as to the position of the BGH.

143 *Nabulsi*, ZEuP 2024, 912, 921 f.

144 *Paal*, NJW 2025, 261, 263; *Golland*, VuR 2025, 71, 71 f; *Mantz*, GRUR 2024, 1878, 1879.

145 *Hofmann*, jurisPR-ITR 1/2025 Anm 3; OLG Hamm 18 December 2024 – 11 U 168/23, GRUR-RS 2024, 41292; but see OLG Celle 20 March 2025 – 5 U 129/24, GRUR-RS 2025, 5402 para 18 (the claimant does not have to show that they did not previously disclose the affected data).

146 Lower amounts are possible according to *Dienst/Stegemann*, GRUR-Prax 2025, 153, 153; *Golland*, VuR 2025, 71, 72; *Horn*, ZD 2025, 165, 166; *Paal*, NJW 2025, 261, 265; *Spittka/Zirnstein*, CR 2025, 24, 29.

147 See eg, *Ernst*, ZIP 2025, 366, 367; *Rössel*, ITRB 2025, 8, 9.

148 In application of the BGH judgment, the OLG Dresden 21 January 2025 – 4 U 738/24, GRUR-RS 2025, 3222 awarded € 100 for loss of control over an email address.

149 *Golland*, VuR 2025, 71, 73; *Mantz*, GRUR 2024, 1878, 1880.

Consequently, one may doubt to what extent this long-awaited judgment and the guidance contained therein may provide actual relief to lower courts that still have to struggle with similar actions in tremendous numbers. 75

5. OLG Koblenz 10 July 2024, 5 U 1375/23:[150] No Liability of Producer for Alleged Injury to Health upon Covid Vaccination

a) Brief Summary of the Facts

The claimant is claiming compensation for pain and suffering in the amount of at least € 100,000 from the producer of the coronavirus vaccine Comirnaty as well as compensation for future damage due to an alleged vaccination injury. The claimant was vaccinated against the coronavirus with the Comirnaty vaccine (produced by the defendant BioNTech/Pfizer) for the first time on 30 or 31 August 2021 and for the second time on 30 September 2021. The vaccine received conditional authorisation from the European Commission on 21 December 2020 and standard authorisation on 10 October 2022. 76

The claimant alleges that she suffered from severe headache and dizziness already after the first vaccination and that these symptoms worsened considerably after the second vaccination, so that she could hardly stand and often had to be propped up. Aside from that, she also alleges permanent fatigue and pain, a gait disorder and other symptoms that continue to this day. The claimant asserts that her impairment is a consequence of the coronavirus vaccination. She claims that there is no scientific basis for the effectiveness of the vaccine and that the vaccine was reported to have significant side effects. The risk of the vaccination was claimed to be significantly higher than the benefits. According to the claimant, the relevant benefit-risk analysis had to be carried out in the individual case and, because of the adverse effects, would be negative in her case. In addition, she submits that the labelling of the vaccine did not correspond to the state of medical science. The claimant asserts that she would have refused a corona vaccination with the particular vaccine if she had been properly informed about the side effects. Consequently, she claims that the defendant is liable pursuant to § 84 (1) Medicinal Products Act (*Arzneimittelgesetz*, AMG), § 823 (1) BGB and § 826 BGB. The defendant disputes the claimant's arguments. The LG Mainz 77

150 ECLI:DE:OLGKOBL:2024:0710.5U1375.23.00; Pharma Recht (PharmR) 2024, 535.

dismissed the claim in its totality. The claimant is continuing to pursue her claim on appeal before the OLG Koblenz.

b) Judgment of the Court

78 The OLG Koblenz dismisses the claimant's appeal with an exceptionally detailed reasoning of which only some essential aspects can be outlined here. The court examines every possible basis for the claim in depth and comes to the conclusion that the defendant is not liable.

79 At the beginning, the court considers a claim based on the strict liability established by § 84 (1) AMG. According to this provision,[151] the pharmaceutical entrepreneur who placed a medicinal product on the market is liable for the damage caused if, as a result of the administration of a medicinal product intended for human use, which was distributed to the consumer and which is subject to compulsory marketing authorisation or is exempted by ordinance from the need for a marketing authorisation, a person dies or the body or health of a person is not insignificantly injured. While it is undisputed that the vaccine is such a medicinal product, that it was placed on the market by the defendant and that it was distributed to a consumer, the further requirements of a claim are not met. Especially, § 84 (1) sent 2 AMG sets out two alternative conditions for liability which at the same time limit the strict liability of the pharmaceutical entrepreneur.

80 § 84 (1) sent 2 no 1 AMG requires that the medicinal product, when used as intended, has harmful effects that go beyond what is tolerable according to the knowledge of medicinal science. In other words, liability depends on a negative benefit-risk analysis. This criterion is closely related to § 5 (2) AMG that prohibits the marketing or use of 'questionable' unsafe medicinal products. As all medicinal products may have undesired side effects, § 84 (1) sent 2 no 1 AMG requires that the risks of the vaccine have to be balanced against its benefits. Two points deserve particular attention in this context, and the court carefully discusses both. First, contrary to the claimant's argumentation, the OLG emphasises that this analysis does not depend on harmful effects in the individual case, but on the entire targeted patient group in general. When balancing the factors, the better the therapeutic benefit and the more serious the disease without vaccination, the more likely it is that serious harmful side effects are acceptable. It is impossible

151 Translation based on the translation published by the Federal Ministry of Justice: <https://www.gesetze-im-internet.de/englisch_amg/englisch_amg.html#p1748> (last accessed 9 April 2025).

to exclude risks for the individual entirely, and therefore these risks must be accepted the greater the beneficial use for the entire group of potential users.

Secondly, the OLG addresses the question of the point in time relevant for determining the knowledge on which the assessment of benefits and risks must rest. The details of this question are disputed among courts and legal scholarship. In accordance with the predominant opinion, the OLG states that, as a starting point, the knowledge existing at the time of the last oral hearing is relevant but it adds that, contrary to the predominant opinion, this knowledge must be projected back to the point in time when the vaccine was administered. This solution corresponds best with the nature of § 84 (1) AMG as a strict liability. 81

Applying this standard, the OLG arrives at a positive result of the benefit-risk analysis. First, the court refers to the authorisation granted by the European Commission, the legality of which must be presumed. Both the conditional and the standard authorisation affirmed a positive benefit-risk assessment. According to the OLG, these determinations are binding for the civil courts. As the vaccine is still authorised by the EU, this binding effect still exists. An individual would be able to refute the presumption by demonstrating that the producer was aware of circumstances that were not taken into account in the authorisation procedure and could lead to a different result in the authorisation decision or that side effects arise after authorisation, the earlier knowledge of which would have led to a refusal of authorisation. However, the claimant did not provide any evidence in this regard. Secondly, even if one were to deny such binding effect, there would still be a positive benefit-risk assessment. In doing so, the court relies on the evaluations of various expert committees, namely the European Committee for Medicinal Products for Human Use, the European Pharmacovigilance Risk Assessment Committee and the national Paul-Ehrlich-Institute. All committees confirm that the benefits of the vaccine clearly outweigh the risks. These scientific commissions have the highest level of expertise and must be regarded as equivalent to expert evidence, so that a single expert could not come to a different conclusion and, therefore, the court is not required to take further expert evidence on the matter. Consequently, the prerequisites of § 84 (1) sent 2 no 1 AMG are not fulfilled. The risk that has materialised in the individual patient must be considered a 'social sacrifice' for the community of users of the vaccine that is accepted by liability law. 82

However, the producer could still be liable if the requirements of § 84 (1) sent 2 no 2 AMG were met. According to this provision, the damage must have occurred as a result of labelling, expert information or instructions for use that do not correspond to the knowledge of medical science. The OLG explains in detail that the claimant was unable to provide any evidence to the effect that the product information did not correspond to the state of scientific knowledge. 83

84 As the requirements of both alternative provisions are not met, the court would not have to address the difficult question of a causal link between the vaccination of the claimant and the alleged impairment. Nevertheless, it expressly denies causation. The claimant cannot benefit from the presumption of causation laid down in § 84 (2) AMG, as this would require that a specific suitability of the medicinal product to cause the injury be demonstrated. The claimant did not provide evidence of her state of health before the vaccination. In addition, her complaints were too unspecific and were not supported by medical records. Even the doctor did not link the diagnosed gait disorder to the vaccination. Finally, the OLG explains that for § 84 (1) sent 2 no 2 AMG – in contrast to no 1 – a double causality would be required. The violation of a legally protected interest must be based on the use of the medicinal product and at the same time have occurred due to the inadequate medicinal product information. This would only be the case if the injury to health would not have arisen if proper information had been provided. The OLG considers the claimant's statement that she would have refrained from being vaccinated if she had been informed about the persistent dizziness to be implausible. The product information of the vaccination contained side effects that could lead to death and these side effects did not prevent the claimant from being vaccinated. Thus, double causality was also absent.

85 The OLG also denied further potential bases of a claim for damages. A claim under the Product Liability Act (*Produkthaftungsgesetz*, ProdHaftG) fails because the Product Liability Act cannot apply within the scope of the special liability rule of the AMG, § 15 ProdHaftG. A claim under § 823 (1) BGB fails for the lack of proof of causality. A claim under § 823 (2) BGB in conjunction with § 5 AMG would require a negative benefit-risk assessment, which the court had denied.

c) Commentary[152]

86 The covid-19 pandemic confronted the world with a major challenge. A global effort in politics, science and society finally succeeded in defeating the virus. However, the legal implications of public and private measures against the coronavirus continue to lead to court disputes on various issues, including questions of tort law.[153] Mainly, the coronavirus vaccinations that were successfully developed in

152 See the case note by *C Wever*, Medizinrecht (MedR) 2024, 931.

153 Cf eg, the case reported above no 26 as well as a recent decision on the compensability of costs for disinfection against the coronavirus incurred by a garage, BGH 23 April 2024 – VI ZR 348/21, NJW 2024, 2324 (costs of € 158 disproportionate); with case note by *M Stürner*, Juristische Ausbildung (Jura) 2024, 1139.

a very short time made a huge contribution to the fight against the disease. Up to 30 June 2024, 64.9 million people in Germany had been vaccinated with these vaccines, making up a large proportion of the German population.[154] However, these vaccines cannot only have positive effects, but in rare individual cases can also cause negative health impacts as undesired side effects.[155] Under certain conditions, persons injured by vaccinations may be entitled to compensation benefits in public law according to social security legislation.[156] By April 2025, competent authorities have acknowledged such claims in at least 573 cases.[157] Whether it is also possible to hold the producer of the vaccine liable for damages in private law is the subject of the judgment.

This decision by the OLG Koblenz deals with the Comirnaty vaccine from pro- 87
ducer BioNTech/Pfizer and answers key questions on the liability of vaccine producers. In particular, the comments on the German Medicinal Products Act, which was considered specialised knowledge before the coronavirus pandemic, are valuable for the entire legal community. The judgment helps to shed light on a statute which establishes a specific strict liability.[158] The OLG emphasises that benefits and risks of the vaccines must not be balanced with regard to the individual patient but to the entire community of users, accepting that absolute security does not exist and that individual users may indeed suffer from unwanted side effects.[159] With its decision on the relevant time of knowledge for the benefit-risk assessment, the OLG brings further dynamics into the debate.[160] Furthermore, it

---

154 Statistics of the Robert Koch Institute <https://www.rki.de/DE/Themen/Infektionskrankheiten/Impfen/Impfungen-A-Z/COVID-19/Impfquoten/Impfquoten-Tab.html?nn=16906862> (last accessed 9 April 2025).

155 See the statistics summarised in *W Voit*, Die Haftung für Gesundheitsschäden durch Impfstoffe in und nach dem Ende der pandemischen Lage, PharmR 2022, 597.

156 See §§ 24, 141 Social Security Code Book XIV – Social compensation (Sozialgesetzbuch Buch XIV – Soziale Entschädigung, SGB XIV), see *R Martis/M Winkhart-Martis*, Schadensersatzansprüche bei Impfschäden (COVID 19), MDR 2025, 422, 429 f. Suggesting an extended liability of the State, *A Dutta*, Haftung für etwaige Impfschäden, NJW 2022, 649, 654 f.

157 See *KB Becker*, Mehr als 500 anerkannte Corona-Impfschäden, Frankfurter Allgemeine Zeitung 22 April 2025, 4.

158 On the character of § 84 (1) AMG as a strict liability, *Ahrens/Spickhoff* (fn 40) § 40 no 2 f with further refs. At the same time, the liability rule contributes to private enforcement of medicinal safety, *KF Gärditz*, JZ 2024, 1039, 1040.

159 *Gärditz*, JZ 2024, 1039, 1043 points out that (societal) benefits of a vaccination outside the immediate pharmaceutical benefits must not be taken into consideration when balancing risks and benefits.

160 The Court states that lower courts which had already dealt with the issue had chosen slightly different approaches, see LG Hof 3 January 2023 – 15 O 22/21, r+s 2023, 275, 277; LG Hannover 4 December 2023 – 2 O 76/23, BeckRS 2023, 38485 para 27; LG Arnsberg 21 December 2023 – 1 O 39/

is interesting that the OLG refers to the authorisation of the vaccine to decide whether a positive benefit-risk assessment exists and feels bound by this administrative decision. The court also refers to the statements made by the expert committees during the authorisation procedure. This method is unconventional for court proceedings, as the court independently examines whether the requirements for a claim are met. Nevertheless, the approach chosen is to be endorsed. The authorisation procedure by the EU is purely science-based and is influenced by recommendations from a large group of experts. As the OLG itself states, these experts have the highest expertise on the subject and are best placed to assess the benefits and risks of the medicinal product. It would be unrealistic for the court to place its own findings on the basis of a single expert over the expertise of these expert committees. This would lead to random results and massively reduce trust in science. The approach of the Higher Regional Court creates a certain interlocking of science-based administrative proceedings and civil procedural law, which is to be welcomed from the point of view of procedural economy.[161] The reasoning was followed by other Higher Regional Courts.[162]

88 Unusually for an appeal judgment, the OLG addresses each of the claimant's arguments in exhaustive detail and barely refers to the lower court's decision. At the same time, the OLG doubles down on each individual step of its decision by providing additional reasons. This shows how emotional and sensitive the topic of vaccinations is. Underlying many liability disputes over coronavirus vaccinations, and in the present case as well, one seems to sense a more general disagreement amongst claimants with the measures taken against the pandemic.[163] By explaining in detail the scientific composition of the expert committees, referring to the expertise of the deciding Senate of the OLG as a specialised Senate for medical liability and the knowledge gained from other proceedings, the Higher Regional Court counters any mistrust of vaccinations or even potential conspiracy theories.

89 In the meantime, claims for damages against producers of coronavirus vaccines have been dismissed not only by first instance courts but also by other High-

23, BeckRS 2023, 38483 para 29; LG Rottweil 8 January 2024 – 2 O 153/23, BeckRS 2024, 1988 para 26; LG Detmold 13 February 2024 – 2 O 85/23, Rechtsdepesche für das Gesundheitswesen (RDG) 2024, 210, 212; LG Frankfurt 14 February 2024 – 2 – 12 O 264/22, PharmR 2024, 213, 218; see also *Ahrens/Spickhoff* (fn 40) § 40 no 15.

161 Cf *Gärditz*, JZ 2024, 1039, 1041 ff; see also *Martis/Winkhart-Martis*, MDR 2025, 422, 423 f.

162 OLG Oldenburg 18 December 2024 – 5 U 53/24, BeckRS 2024, 36092; OLG München 12 December 2024 – 14 U 3100/24 e, BeckRS 2024, 36083.

163 This impression is shared by *Gärditz*, JZ 2024, 1039, 1040.

er Regional Courts for which the present judgment provided valuable guidance.[164] In other proceedings, claims against the vaccinating doctors equally failed.[165]

6. Personal Injury

The year 2024 again provided the courts with the opportunity to flesh out the claim for monetary compensation afforded to secondary victims by § 844 (3) BGB (bereavement damages).[166] The provision was introduced in 2017.[167] The provision awards reasonable pecuniary compensation to surviving persons in a close personal relationship to the victim of a wrongful death for their pain and suffering; such personal relationship is presumed for the surviving spouse, parent or child of the deceased. Of particular interest is the development of the amount recoverable under this provision. The provision itself is, of course, silent. Interestingly, the legislative materials indicate an amount of € 10,000 based on the perception of the drafters that this amount was the average award in nervous shock cases.[168] In 2022, the BGH had provided important guidance on the assessment of compensation:[169] despite the figure mentioned in the legislative materials, each case has to be assessed individually; however, it is bound to fall short of the amount to which one would be entitled if the emotional distress suffered by an individual had the quality of an injury to health.[170] The following decisions, all of which were handed down in 2024, may give an impression of the developing case law. 90

164 See for BioNTech/Pfizer OLG München 5 November 2024 – 14 U 2313/24 e, BeckRS 2024, 31623; OLG München 12 December 2024 – 14 U 3100/24 e, BeckRS 2024, 36083; OLG Oldenburg 18 December 2024 – 5 U 53/24, BeckRS 2024, 36092; for AstraZeneca OLG Koblenz 18 September 2024 – 5 U 1139/23, BeckRS 2024, 27414 with case note *Gärditz*, JZ 2024, 1039; but see (hardly convincing) *E Staebe*, Arzneimittelhaftung für Corona-Impfstoffe, Deutsches Verwaltungsblatt (DVBl) 2025, 138, who proposes to share liability under § 84 (1) AMG equally between pharmaceutical entrepreneur and injured person.

165 OLG Hamm 19 June 2024 – 3 U 119/23, BeckRS 2024, 16818; OLG Stuttgart 25 June 2024 – 1 U 34/23, BeckRS 2024, 14555; *Dutta*, NJW 2022, 649, 651 f. Discussing a potential liability of employers whose medical service offered vaccinations to employees, *R Stöbe/D Stach*, Die Haftung des Arbeitgebers für Impfschäden, NJW 2024, 2430.

166 A parallel provision exists in § 10 (3) StVG for the strict liability of the keeper of a motor vehicle and in other statutes on strict liability.

167 *Wurmnest/Gömann* (fn 45) no 1 ff.

168 BT-Drucks 18/11397, 11.

169 BGH 6 December 2022 – VI ZR 73/21, NJW 2023, 1438; see *Kleinschmidt*, ETL 2022 (fn 5) no 40 ff; see also BGH 23 May 2023 – VI ZR 161/22, NJW 2023, 2878.

170 On this latter point, see also BGH 6 December 2022 – VI ZR 168/21, NJW 2023, 983.

91 The OLG München[171] approved of an award of € 12,000 to the daughter of a 77-year-old woman who had been killed in a road traffic accident and who had lived only a few kilometres away and visited for lunch every Sunday as well as several times per week by bicycle. During the covid lockdowns, the daughter had taken Mondays off to spend with her mother. The mother's death had caused the daughter severe emotional distress. The court emphasised that the victim's advanced age did not present a reason to reduce the amount, in particular because the victim kept herself fit by cycling every day and there were no indications for an impending death. Moreover, the court expressly refers to the seminal decision of the BGH according to which the amount of € 10,000 is not an upper limit but merely a guideline and awards in individual cases may be higher or lower.[172] Interestingly, the court invokes the general increase of prices since 2017 to justify an amount that is higher than the guideline of € 10,000.

92 The OLG Brandenburg[173] arrived at an amount of € 5,000 for the son of a cyclist run over by a bus and at an amount of € 2,500 for the son's partner who had lived with the son for seven years and developed a parent-child-like relationship with the deceased. The son asserted regular personal contact with his mother, an increased need to look after the father and difficulties in explaining the loss to their child. On the other hand, the court considered that the claimant was independent and had a family and a household of his own. The court considered in particular a significant contributory negligence on the part of the deceased as one factor justifying a reduced amount. Concerning the son's partner, the court expressed considerable doubts as to the required close personal relationship, since she was not among the persons for whom the law presumes such a relationship. Neither is she a daughter-in-law. However, the court leaves open whether it regards her as entitled to claim monetary compensation because the awarded amount had been out of dispute.

93 The LG Berlin II[174] awarded € 10,000 in an unusual constellation: the defendant's brother had embezzled a gun belonging to the defendant from a locked weapons cabinet in the defendant's apartment to which he had a spare key and in which he knew where to find the key to the cabinet. He carried the gun with him to Spain where he used it to kill the claimant's wife because he wanted to

171 OLG München 19 March 2024 – 24 U 541/24 e, NJW-RR 2024, 768.

172 BGH 6 December 2022 – VI ZR 73/21, NJW 2023, 1438; see *Kleinschmidt*, ETL 2022 (fn 5) no 40 ff.

173 OLG Brandenburg 15 May 2024 – 12 U 173/23, NJW-RR 2024, 1278.

174 LG Berlin II 25 June 2024 – 67 O 89/24, MDR 2024, 1110. German law applied because the deceased (not the claimant, CJEU 10.12.2015, C-350/14, *Lazar/Allianz SpA*, ECLI:EU:C:2015:802) and the defendant had their common habitual residence in Germany, art 4 (2) Rome II Regulation.

steal the claimant's camper van. The court basically referred to the guideline amount.

In a decision on legal aid, the OLG Frankfurt[175] also took the guideline amount as its starting point. As the court could not find any arguments in the claimant's submissions that would justify a higher amount, it regarded an amount of € 10,000 as appropriate. The defendant stepfather had killed the claimant's mother. 94

Unlike the OLG Brandenburg (see above no 92), the OLG Celle[176] found a doctrinal explanation for reducing the amount in a case of contributory negligence. According to § 846 BGB, the provision on contributory negligence (§ 254 BGB) applies to the claim of a third party if fault on the part of the injured person contributed to causing the damage suffered by the third party.[177] In application of this provision, the OLG Celle awards € 3,333, corresponding to one-third of the guideline value, because it assumed a contributory negligence of the injured person of two-thirds. The court regarded the guideline value as appropriate for the death of a grown-up only child of the claimant. 95

It should be added that the relationship between nervous shock (as an injury to health suffered by the claimant) and monetary compensation for secondary victims has given rise to an ongoing discussion in legal scholarship.[178] Furthermore, the CJEU established high requirements for qualifying a provision such as § 844 (3) 96

---

175 OLG Frankfurt 21 November 2024 – 3 U 103/24, MDR 2025, 385.

176 OLG Celle 18 December 2024 – 14 U 119/24, DAR 2025, 152.

177 On the application of this provision to claims for bereavement damages, see MünchKomm/*Wagner* (fn 71) § 844 no 110.

178 *JP Bergmann*, Das Hinterbliebenengeld im Wandel – ein aktueller Überblick, DAR 2025, 8; *N Biller-Bomhardt/M Steinbock*, Hinterbliebenengeld und Schockschaden, NJW 2025, 113; *M Dregelies*, Schockschäden – alle Fragen geklärt? VersR 2024, 1515; *C Huber*, Das "neue" Hinterbliebenengeld und sein Verhältnis zum Schockschaden, SVR 2025, 4 (including a very helpful detailed analysis of recent case law and scholarship); *C Jansen*, Das Hinterbliebenengeld als kleines Schmerzensgeld? JZ 2024, 64. – The issue was also the subject of a working group at the 63rd Deutscher Verkehrsgerichtstag, see the report by *M Pfliefke*, Der 63. Deutsche Verkehrsgerichtstag vom 29.–31. Januar 2025 in Goslar, DAR 2025, 133, 135 f. The report summarises an interesting statistic on 340 insurance cases dealt with by one large motor vehicle liability insurer between 2017 and October 2024: while monetary compensation under § 844 (3) BGB amounted to € 7,678 up to € 10,070 on average, without regard to contributory negligence and a total of 462 payments, damages for pain and suffering because of nervous shock totalled between € 1,000 and € 30,000 with an average of € 8,779 without regard to contributory negligence and a total of only 14 claims. Moreover, it reports that several proposals for reform were unsuccessful: entitlement of the unborn child, presumption of a close personal relationship for siblings and increase of the guideline value according to inflation.

BGB as an overriding mandatory provision within the meaning of art 16 Rome II Regulation.[179]

97 In the context of nervous shock, a decision by the OLG Köln[180] follows the recent judgment by the BGH[181] to regard § 1664 (1) BGB as a provision that not only establishes the standard of care a parent owes to their child but also a basis for liability claims of the child against its parent. A father had to witness his three-and-a-half-year-old son being severely injured in a road traffic accident and sustained psychological impairment. As the father had neglected his duties in letting his son play with his balance bike near a street unsupervised, he was also held liable to his son so that the motor vehicle's liability insurer could take redress against him, as a jointly and severally liable debtor, for three-quarters of the payments made to the son and of the medical costs reimbursed to the son's health insurer. The fact that the liability of the motor vehicle's keeper was strict while the father's liability was fault-based could not exclude the claim. Because of the considerable contributory negligence, the father's claim for damages for pain and suffering was reduced to an amount of € 750 (one-quarter of € 3,000 that would otherwise have been justified).

98 Finally, an interesting decision by the OLG Brandenburg[182] elaborates on the scope of duties of care owed by the owner and landlord of a residential complex adjacent to a pond and the extent to which he may rely on third parties' being aware of dangers and behaving accordingly. Some of the houses were built on concrete stilts in this pond and called 'fishing houses'. The part of the pond that was accessible to the public was surrounded by a fence that, however, ended at the fishing houses so that it was possible to access the water freely below these houses. There were no fences or other enclosures that separated the properties from each other or from the street so that all properties were freely accessible. The rent agreements expressly prohibited access to the area underneath the fishing houses and to the pond outside designated paths. The defendant had requested the removal of a small fence installed under the house of one of the tenants. When a two-year-old child left his parents' neighbouring house unnoticed and climbed under the fishing house, he was severely injured by falling into the pond. The defendant was held liable for violating a duty of care owed to the claimant. However,

179 CJEU 5.9.2024, C-86/23, *HUK-COBURG-Allgemeine Versicherung AG II*, ECLI:EU:C:2024:689. For details, see the report on the European Union.

180 OLG Köln 5 March 2024 – 9 U 66/23, BeckRS 2024, 4504.

181 BGH 19 January 2021 – VI ZR 210/18, VersR 2021, 452; see *Wurmnest/Kleinschmidt/Gasche* (fn 5) no 26 ff.

182 OLG Brandenburg 30 January 2024 – 3 U 30/22, NJW 2024, 2327.

the amount of damages was reduced by 70 % because of the contributory negligence of the claimant's parents in failing to supervise the claimant.

C. Literature

Animals: *H Christokat*, Einblick, Überblick, Durchblick: Die Tierhalterhaftung gem. § 833 BGB, JA 2024, 358; *N Schmidt*, Haftung und Haftpflichtversicherung von Hundehaltern, VersR 2024, 271; see also the case reported above no 38 ff. 99

Artificial Intelligence and Autonomous Systems: *C Danda*, Auswirkungen der KI-Verordnung und der KI-Haftungs-Richtlinie auf die Haftung beim KI-Einsatz in der Finanzbranche, LTZ 2024, 9; *D Essers*, Haftungsfragen automatisierter Systeme (Duncker & Humblot, Berlin 2024); *KF Furch*, Stimmlokalisierung von Games, MMR 2024, 728; *M Gebauer/S Huber* (eds), Künstliche Intelligenz – Zurechnung, Vertrag, Verantwortung (Mohr Siebeck, Tübingen 2024); *V Kraetzig*, Deliktsschutz gegen KI-Abbilder, CR 2024, 207 and 276; *D Linardatos*, Hochrisiko-KI-Systeme und Verantwortungsverschiebung in der Wertschöpfungskette, ZIP 2024, 2497; *A-K Mayrhofer*, Die Haftung des Verwenders von KI-Systemen auf der 'ersten Stufe', EuZW 2024, 882; *D Messner-Kreuzbauer/J Pehm*, Taming AI Through Presumptions: A Softer Approach to Tort Law Harmonisation? ZEuP 2024, 161; *M Martini/C Wendehorst* (eds), KI-VO: Verordnung über Künstliche Intelligenz (CH Beck, München 2024); *L Rolfes/M Engeler*, Unterlassungsansprüche bei der Erzeugung von ehrverletzenden Falschinformationen durch LLMs, ZD 2024, 496; *R Theis*, Auswirkungen der KI-Verordnung und der KI-Haftungs-Richtlinie auf die Haftung beim KI-Einsatz in der Finanzbranche, BKR 2024, 414; *M Thöne*, Deliktische Haftung im Internet der Dinge, RDi 2024, 318; *C Wendehorst*, Künstliche Intelligenz und Produkthaftung, EuZW 2024, 876. 100

Automated Driving: *H Steege/D Winkler*, Rechtsfragen zu Testfeldern zur Erforschung automatisierter und vernetzter Mobilität, NZV 2024, 353; *M Stöber/A Möller/D Willmer*, Das Gesetz zum autonomen Fahren und seine Auswirkungen auf die zivilrechtliche Haftung im Straßenverkehr, NZV 2024, 353. 101

Capital Markets: *J Bauerschmidt*, Keine Amtshaftung der BaFin im Zusammenhang mit dem Fall 'Wirecard', BKR 2024, 701; *G Bayat*, Die Prospekthaftung im Abhilfeverfahren, BKR 2024, 219; *M Cornils/E Gurlit*, Staatshaftung für fehlerhafte Finanzmarktaufsicht, ZBB 2024, 157; *H Fleischer*, 50 Jahre Herstatt-Zusammenbruch: Ein Bankskandal und seine regulatorische Aufarbeitung, WM 2024, 1929; *H-C Grigoleit*, Haftung des Wirtschaftsprüfers aus § 826 BGB gegenüber Dritten, ZIP 2024, 1293; *TH Lorenz*, Kapitalmarktrechtliche Abschlussprüferhaftung (Duncker & Humblot, Berlin 2024). 102

103 **Civil Procedure:** *G Albers*, Kampf ums Recht? Massenverfahren und Rechtsverwirklichung im Lichte der neusten Gesetzgebung, JZ 2024, 261; *T Almeroth*, Rechtsanwaltskosten im Zusammenhang mit der Unfallschadensbearbeitung, NJW 2024, 2891; *T Höfling/M Killisch*, Schätzung der Anspruchshöhe anhand von statistischen Methoden – ein Vorschlag zur Anwendung des Monetary Unit Sampling, IWRZ 2024, 266; see also the references cited above no 1 ff.

104 **Climate Change and Environment:** *S Deuring*, Klimaschutz und Demonstrationsschäden, AcP 224 (2024) 663; *M Habersack*, 'Klimaschützende Unterlassungsklagen' gegen Pkw-Hersteller vor dem BGH, ZIP 2024, 1513; *R Harnos*, Keine Korrektur klimapolitischer Kompromisse durch die deliktsrechtliche Hintertür, AG 2024, R92; *J Neuner*, Die ökologisch orientierte Auslegung und Fortbildung des Privatrechts, ZfPW 2024, 127; *S Nitsch*, Microplastics Litigation: eine rechtsvergleichende Orientierung, ZEuP 2024, 316; *R Podszun/T Rohner*, Nachhaltigkeit und Recht (CH Beck, München 2024); *J Sauerwald*, Haftung für den Klimawandel im Zivilrecht (Duncker & Humblot, Berlin 2024); *J-E Schirmer*, Klimahaftung: Überforderung der Gerichte? ZfPW 2024, 159; *M-P Weller/T Hößl/C Seemann*, Klimaneutralität im Privatrecht, ZEuP 2024, 575.

105 **Collective Redress:** *A Bruns*, Dogmatische Grundfragen der Verbandsklage auf Abhilfeleistung in Geld, ZZP 137 (2024) 3; *W Büscher*, Die Umsetzung der Verbandsklagenrichtlinie, WRP 2024, 1; *B Gsell*, Die Umsetzung der Verbandsklagenrichtlinie, GRUR 2024, 979; *TB Lühmann*, Die Entwicklung des kollektiven Rechtsschutzes im Jahre 2023, WM 2024, 1199; *R Schaub*, Die Umsetzung der Verbandsklagenrichtlinie, GRUR 2024, 655; *V Schreier*, Das Verbraucherrechtedurchsetzungsgesetz (VDuG) und seine Auswirkungen auf die Versicherungswirtschaft, VersR 2024, 144; see also no 103.

106 **Company Law:** *H Fleischer*, Geschäftsleiterhaftung in der Personengesellschaft, NZG 2024, 1639; *J Koch*, Ad-Hoc-Pflicht: Knowledge statt Knowledge Governance, AG 2024, 97; *F Mahdi*, Rechtmäßiges Alternativverhalten im Organhaftungsrecht (Duncker & Humblot, Berlin 2024); *M Schockenhoff/A Duttig*, Die Haftung der Stiftungsorgane – Voraussetzungen und Durchsetzung, ZIP 2024, 2433.

107 **Competition Law:** *M Bach*, Die Anwendbarkeit von kartellrechtsspezifischen Hemmungstatbeständen auf Ansprüche nach § 852 S. 1 BGB, NZKart 2024, 382; *R Dewenter/R Gasper*, Kartellverfahren auf der Überholspur? Ein Ansatz zur Beschleunigung der Kartellschadensersatzverfahren, NZKart 2024, 671; *C Krüger*, Mit Voll(ab)gas zum kartelldeliktsrechtlichen Mindestschaden? NZKart 2024, 152; *H Schläfke/M Leck*, Kartellschadensersatzverfahren, GRUR-Prax 2024, 526; *A Weitbrecht*, Kartellschadensersatz 2023, NZKart 2024, 170.

108 **Data and Internet:** *S Apel/C Huber*, Das neue Datenrecht der EU, JuS 2024, 514; *C Gomille*, Informationshaftung von Influencern, JZ 2024, 286; *C Heinze*, Schutzgesetzhaftung und Schadenszurechnung bei Online-Glücksspielen, ZfWG 2024, 308;

T Hoeren, Unternehmenshaftung nach der DSGVO – ein Spagat zwischen Datenschutzrecht und Kartellrecht, in: Daten, Information, Recht. Festschrift für Andreas Wiebe zum 65. Geburtstag (facultas/Nomos, Wien/Baden-Baden 2024) 269; *G Horstmeier*, Schadensersatz für 'ungute Gefühle'? Der Art. 82 DSGVO im Arbeitsrecht, BB 2024, 2740; *H Ludyga*, Beseitigungs- und Unterlassungsanspruch gegen soziale Netzwerke wegen antisemitischer Inhalte, NJW 2024, 703; *M-R McGuire/H Schulte-Nölke*, Ansprüche des Nutzers gegen den Dateninhaber nach dem Data Act, ZdiW 2024, 73; *T Nägele*, Die Haftung von Internet Service Providern für rechtswidrige Inhalte nach dem Digital Services Act, NJW 2024, 1137; *BP Paal*, Schufa-Scoring und Schadensersatz bei Übermittlung von Positivdaten, NJW 2024, 1689; *S Thönissen*, DS-GVO-Schadensersatz durch kollektiven Rechtsschutz? ZD 2024, 253; see also no 112.

Diesel: *T Almeroth*, Neuer zum Diesel-Thermofenster, NZV 2024, 111; *J Drechsler*, Deliktsrecht als Vehikel des Unionsprivatrechts, EuZW 2024, 357; *MB Fontana*, Freiheitsschutz durch Schadensersatz: Der unerwünschte Vertrag in der Diesel-Rechtsprechung des BGH, ZIP 2024, 1940; *L Hübner*, Bestimmung des anwendbaren Rechts für Ansprüche gegen Hersteller im sog. Dieselskandal, IPRax 2024, 173; *O Klein*, Die 'Dieselverfahren' vor dem BGH, NZV 2024, 105; *A Sievers*, Sentenzen und Tendenzen: Aktuelle Rechtsprechung zum Dieselskandal – Teil X, DAR 2024, 496. 109

General: *O Brand/L Jaeger*, VersR Report: Ausgewählte Rechtsprechung zum Haftungs- und Schadensrecht 2023–2024, VersR 2024, 1588; *M Ellerbeck*, Die Haftungseinheit – das oftmals unbekannte Wesen, VersR 2024, 974; *F Faust/H-B Schäfer* (eds), Deutsches Deliktsrecht aus ökonomischer Perspektive (Mohr Siebeck, Tübingen 2024); *HG Ganter*, Der Einwand rechtmäßigen Alternativverhaltens im Haftungsrecht, WM 2024, 281; *B Kannowski*, Das Märchen vom räumlich-gegenständlichen Bereich der Ehe, JZ 2024, 19; *FJ Säcker/R Rixecker/H Oetker/B Limperg* (eds), Münchener Kommentar zum Bürgerlichen Gesetzbuch, vol 7: §§ 705–853 BGB (9th edn, CH Beck, München 2024); *P Schlüter*, Obligatorische Gefahrentlastung zwischem funktionalem Deliktsrecht und 'formalem' Sachenrecht, ZfPW 2024, 44. 110

Insurance: *J Rapp*, Krisenbewältigung durch Privatrecht? ZfPW 2024, 465. 111

Karlsruher Forum 2024: In 2024, the traditional annual conference on liability and insurance law focused on 'Legal issues of digital platforms' (Rechtsfragen digitaler Plattformen). While the first presentation approached the topic from the perspective of liability law (*M Schmidt-Kessel*, Verantwortung digitaler Plattformen, VersR 2024, 1241), the second placed its emphasis on analysing insurance aspects (*C Armbrüster*, Rechtsfragen der Nutzung digitaler Plattformen im Versicherungssektor, VersR 2024, 1262). Both presentations evoked a rich discussion (reported by *G Lüders/P Schultess*, VersR 2024, 1277). 112

113 **Liability for Others:** *F Bernau*, Die Aufsichtshaftung über Minderjährige im Straßenverkehr, DAR 2024, 121.

114 **Medical Liability:** *D Hart*, Zur Entwicklung des Medizinhaftungsrechts, MedR 2024, 299; *A Spickhoff*, Die Entwicklung des Arztrechts 2023/2024, NJW 2024, 1704; *A Spickhoff*, Die Reform der Arzthaftung im europäischen Umfeld, MedR 2024, 559; *R Waltermann*, Haftungsrechtlicher Rahmen des Einsatzes von Ersteinschätzungsverfahren in der Notaufnahme des Krankenhauses, NZS 2024, 441.

115 **Personal Injury:** *T Almeroth*, Abfindung von Personenschäden nach Verkehrsunfällen und anderen Schadensereignissen, NJW 2024, 1457; *R Balke*, Das Hinterbliebenengeld, SVR 2024, 451; *R Balke*, Haushaltsführungsschaden, SVR 2024, 3; *M Dregelies*, Schockschäden – alle Fragen geklärt? VersR 2024, 1515; *SM Gafus*, Crowd-Crush (Nomos, Baden-Baden 2024); *C Huber*, Der Haushaltsführungsschaden in Deutschland: tatsächlich voller Ausgleich der erlittenen Einbuße? NZV 2024, 7; *C Jansen*, Das Hinterbliebenengeld als kleines Schmerzensgeld, JZ 2024, 64; *D Messner-Kreuzbauer*, Das deutsche Haushaltsschadenssystem auf dem Prüfstand des Rechtsvergleichs, NZV 2024, 393; *C Syrbe*, Verweis auf Tabellenwerke genügt nicht zur Darlegung eines Haushaltsführungsschadens, NZV 2024, 548; cf also the cases reported above no 90 ff.

116 **Personality Rights:** *MF Lörrach*, Die zivil- und datenschutzrechtlichen Folgen eines Cold Calls, VuR 2024, 373; *C Gomille*, Das postmortale Persönlichkeitsrecht des Künstlers, ZUM 2024, 413; *H Grziwotz*, Persönlichkeitsrechtsverletzung – Schutzlücken bei der Vererblichkeit? ZRP 2024, 173; *HP Schwintowski*, Schadensersatz wegen Persönlichkeitsrechtsverletzung – Die Herausgabe von Nutzerdaten, VuR 2024, 218; see also above nos 10 ff and 27 ff.

117 **Prescription:** *C Thomale*, Die Anatomie des Verjährungseinwands, AcP 224 (2024) 215.

118 **Product Liability and Product Safety:** *M Becker/A Bell/H Meyer*, Die neue EU-Produkthaftungs-RL und ihre Folgen für das deutsche Produkthaftungsrecht, NJW 2024, 3745; *L Feuerhake/S Schäfer*, Rechtsprechungsreport Lebensmittelrecht 2023, WRP 2024, 438; *A Kapoor/T Klindt*, Aktuelle Entwicklungen im Produkthaftungs- und Produktsicherheitsrecht, NJW 2024, 1551; *T Voigt*, (Medizin-)Produkthaftung zwischen traditionellem und extensivem Produktfehlerbegriff, MedR 2024, 331; *F Graf von Westphalen*, Neue beweistechnische und beweisrechtliche Herausforderungen des EU-Rechts, IWRZ 2024, 9.

119 **Road, Railway and Ship Traffic:** *KU Bahnsen*, Gefährdungshaftung des Reeders für Drittschäden? NZV 2024, 48; *M Burmann/J Jahnke*, Das Fahrrad im Recht und Unrecht, NZV 2024, 464; *I Drewes*, Der verkehrsrechtliche Betriebsbegriff im Wandel, NJW 2024, 2497; *W Halm/M Fitz*, Versicherungsverkehrsrecht 2023/2024, DAR 2024, 301; *R Heß/M Burmann*, Die aktuellen Entwicklungen im Straßenverkehrsrecht, NJW 2024, 1078 and 3053; *F-R Herber*, Aktuelle Rechtsprechung

zur Straßenverkehrssicherungspflicht, NZV 2024, 522; *P Jaklin*, Gefährdungshaftung und Anscheinsbeweis bei Verkehrsunfällen in Europa, DAR 2024, 549; *A Kaufmann/J Kurczinski*, Abgestellte E-Scooter – Ein Haftungsproblem, NZV 2024, 207; *H Lang/T Mergner*, Amokfahrten mit Kfz, VersR 2024, 1177; *D Looschelders*, Berücksichtigung von Vorschäden bei Abwicklung von Verkehrsunfällen, VersR 2024, 329; *C Oehler*, Die Rechtsprechung des BGH zum Haftpflichtrecht im Straßenverkehr, DAR 2024, 421; *MF Peters*, Haftungsrechtliche Problem- und Fragestellungen bei der Nutzung von Autowaschanlagen, JA 2024, 808; *K Ramming*, Haftung aus dem Zusammenstoß von Schiffen, RdTW 2024, 291; *M Wessel*, Rechtsprechung der Oberlandesgerichte zum Haftpflichtrecht im Straßenverkehr, DAR 2024, 181; *F Wilting*, Ausgewählte Rechtsprechung zum Verkehrsträger Schiene aus den Jahren 2021 bis 2023, RdTW 2024, 82; *W Wurmnest*, Auf dem Weg zu einer Verschärfung der Haftung von Schiffseignern? LogR 2024, 37; *W Wurmnest*, Die Haftung des Reeders für Drittschäden – de lege lata und de lege ferenda, TranspR 2024, 41; *M Zwickel*, Risikotragung für fehlerhafte oder überhöhte Rechnungen im Haftungsrecht des Straßenverkehrs, MDR 2024, 809; see also the case reported above no 14.

Sports: *M Castendiek/P Czaka*, Schutzpflichten der Fußballspiel-Veranstal- 120
terin, SpuRt 2024, 267; *S Reif/S Strauß*, 'Fanproteste' in Fußballstadien, NJW 2024, 1069.

State Liability: *R Dickmann*, Die Ministerhaftung und der Fall Andreas 121
Scheuer, NJOZ 2024, 481; *P Itzel*, Neuere Entwicklungen im Amts-, Staatshaftungs- und Entschädigungsrecht, MDR 2024, 207; *A Janssen*, Kirchenrechtlicher Schadensersatzanspruch und zivilrechtlicher Regress, VersR 2024, 457; *S Knickrehm*, Soziales Entschädigungsrecht und sexualisierte Gewalt, VersR 2024, 265; *M Ogorek*, Zur Amtshaftung der Kirchen in Fällen sexuellen Missbrauchs, JZ 2024, 271; *S Schmidt*, Der Amthaftungsanspruch unter straßen- und verkehrsrechtlicher Berücksichtigung, DVP 2024, 7; *T Vießmann*, Entschädigung für das coronabedingte Herunterfahren selbstständiger Erwerbstätigkeit, NJW 2024, 188.

Supply Chain (Corporate Due Diligence): *S Deuring*, Geschädigtenschutz im 122
Lieferkettenszenario de lege lata und de lege ferenda, RIW 2024, 633; *L Hübner/M Lieberknecht*, Mehr Pflichten für weniger Unternehmer? – Kerninhalte der EU-Lieferketten-RL und ihre Umsetzung im deutschen Recht, NJW 2024, 1841; *S Kalss*, Wie sollen die Verhaltenspflichten nach der Lieferkettensorgfalts-Richtlinie (CSDDD) erfüllt werden – ein rechtspolitischer Zuruf! ZfPW 2024, 181; *EM Kieninger*, Zivilrechtliche Haftung für Sorgfaltspflichtverletzungen nach Lieferkettengesetz und Sustainability-Richtlinie, ZIP 2024, 1037; *T Kindt*, Menschenrechtsschutz für Unternehmen? ZVglRWiss 123 (2024) 443; *PC Leyens/JM Goetsch*, Das neue Lieferkettenrecht, Jura 2024, 221; *M Nietsch*, Die zivilrechtliche Haftung nach der EU-Lieferketten-RL – ein Gamechanger? NJW 2024,

2865; *B Steinbrück/S Traub*, Die EU-Lieferketten-Richtlinie (CSDDD) Verbesserter Schutz für Menschenrechte und Umwelt in Liefer- und Wertschöpfungsketten, MDR 2024, 1141; *PS Stöbener de Mora/P Noll*, Anpassungsbedarf beim LkSG, NZG 2024, 1391; *G Wagner*, Lieferkettenhaftung zwischen Spezialgesetz und Kodifikation, in: Gedächtnisschrift für Peter Mankowski (2024) 837.

Zafeirios Tsolakidis

XIII. Greece

A. Legislation

1. Law 5086/2024:[1] National Authority for Cyber Security and Other Provisions

Article 26 of Law (L) 5086/2024 amends art 11 para 1 of L 4508/2017, which establishes the regulatory framework for the licensing and supervision of space activities. Article 11 regulates the international liability of a person conducting space activities for damage caused by space objects. Paragraph 1 of art 11 provides for an obligation of this person to conclude an insurance contract. 1

After its amendment, art 11 para 1 reads as follows: 2

> In order to provide coverage for liability for damages, the operator shall take out an insurance policy covering this liability up to an amount of sixty million (60,000,000) euros, which may be adjusted according to the size, weight, technical characteristics/specifications, value or other operational parameters of the space object by decision of the Minister of Digital Governance, following a reasoned request from the operator, prior to the submission of the supporting documents referred to in para 2 of art 5. If the space activity is carried out in the public interest, the Minister of Digital Government may, by decision, set a lower amount or exempt the operator from the insurance obligation, considering the size, weight, technical properties/specifications, value or other operational parameters of the space object, as well as the risks associated with the space activity of this object. Space activities are carried out in the public interest, in particular, if they serve national defence and security, science, research or education. Insurance is not required if the Greek State itself is the operator.

2. Law 5143/2024:[2] Regulations on Land Border Stations, the Enhancement of Local Authorities and Other Provisions

Article 47 of L 5143/2024 amended art 9 para 2 of L 4830/2021,[3] which regulates the liability of the owner of a companion animal ie domestic animals regarded as 3

1 Published in the Official Gazette (FEK) A' 23/14.02.2024.
2 Published in the Official Gazette (FEK) A' 161/11.10.2024.

https://doi.org/10.1515/9783111389271-014

pets. The amendment stipulates that municipalities are not held liable for damage resulting from traffic accidents caused by stray animals.

4 Following its amendment, art 9 para 2 now reads as follows:

> The owner or fosterer of a companion animal is liable for any harm or damage caused by the animal, in accordance with art 924 of the Greek Civil Code (Presidential Decree 456/1984, A' 164). For stray animals that are not accommodated in a foster home, the liability shall be held by the person whose details have been registered in the National Register of Companion Animals for the particular animal (municipality or animal welfare association or non-profit animal welfare organisation or private person with a shelter), provided that they have not complied with their obligations under this Law and, in particular, that they have not sterilised those animals, unless civil compensation for the damage or injury caused is paid by another entity, such as an insurance company. For stray animals that have not been tagged, liability shall be borne by the municipality within the boundaries of which the damage or injury was caused. In any event, municipalities shall not be liable for any damage or injury resulting from a traffic accident caused by a stray animal, whether or not tagged.

B. Cases

1. Areios Pagos (Greek Supreme Court, AP) 24 February 2024, no 433: Liability for Assistants

a) Brief Summary of the Facts

5 The plaintiff was hired by the first defendant company as a lorry driver. On the day following the commencement of his employment, a few minutes before the end of working hours, the plaintiff was in the yard of the company with four other drivers, employees of the defendant. The second defendant, also a driver, who had earlier had an altercation with another employee, took a gun from his car, which was parked nearby, approached the place where the drivers, including the plaintiff, were standing and fired at them twice with the barrel of the gun pointing toward the ground, apparently to intimidate the driver with whom he had been arguing. However, a bullet, which had previously ricocheted off the ground, hit the plaintiff in the right arm, causing him grievous bodily injury.

---

3 See *Z Tsolakidis*, Greece, in: E Karner/BC Steininger (eds), European Tort Law 2021 (2022) 234, no 9.

b) Judgment of the Court

According to the provision of art 922 of the Greek Civil Code (GrCC), the master or the person who appoints another person to perform a task is liable towards a third party for the damage unlawfully caused to the latter by that person in the execution of their tasks. For this provision to be applicable, the following conditions have to be met: 6

(a) A relationship of 'dependence' between the principal (the master or the person who has assigned to another the task of performing a service) and the auxiliary person (the servant or the person assigned). This relationship exists when, in the framework of a juridical or other connection, permanent or occasional, between these two persons, the principal appoints the auxiliary person to provide a service, with or without remuneration, and the latter is subject to the control or at least to the general instructions of the principal. Binding specific instructions are not necessarily required, but general instructions are sufficient in a context of loose dependence, which allows for general supervision of the master. 7

(b) An unlawful and faulty action of the auxiliary person, ie, a tort that fulfils the requirements of art 914 GrCC. 8

(c) Such action of the auxiliary person has to have taken place in the performance of the service entrusted to them, or on the occasion of, or in connection with, their service, or even in abuse of their service. The latter ('abuse of service') occurs when the unlawful act took place within the limits of the auxiliary's duties but in contravention of the orders and the instructions of the principal or in excess of the limits of their duties, provided that between the unlawful act and the service entrusted there exists an internal causal connection, in the sense that the tort would not have been committed without the assignment of duties to the auxiliary person or that this assignment constituted the necessary means for the commission of the tort. 9

The aforementioned violent incident against the plaintiff took place in the course of his employment and caused him grievous bodily injury. The plaintiff's injury, caused by the assault of another employee, occurred in the workplace, the supervision and security of which was the sole responsibility of the first defendant company. However, no claim can be established against the first defendant company on the basis of vicarious liability for the unlawful action of the second defendant, to whom it had entrusted some tasks, since the tort committed by the latter, despite temporal and geographical proximity, *lacks an internal causal link* with the performance of the defendant's duties in the present case. Conversely, the action in question pertains to the employee's personal motivations, rather than his professional obligations, as the possession and utilisation of weapons by employees for the resolution of disputes falls outside the scope of their authority. 10

The assertions made by the plaintiff that the first defendant had failed to select its employees appropriately, had not ensured the presence of security and supervisory staff, and had not provided a sheltered waiting area for them were not found to be causally related to the incident, since it was not proven that the company knew or could have known of the existence of the weapon in the possession of the second defendant at the time of his hiring. In any case, the company's obligations do not include, among the security measures which it must take to protect its employees, daily physical control of them. The plaintiff's claim against the first defendant must therefore be dismissed as unfounded.

c) Commentary

11 The main problem in the application of art 922 GrCC is the determination of the relationship that must exist between the assignment of specific tasks to an auxiliary person and the commission of an unlawful act on their part, ie, when it will be considered that the assignee acted 'in the course of their service' and not merely 'on the occasion of their service'.

12 It is a firm position of Greek scholars and case law that the criterion for limiting the liability of the principal cannot be whether the auxiliary person complied with the provided instructions and orders. Therefore, the Greek Supreme Court has consistently held, as in the current case, that the principal is liable even when the auxiliary has acted 'in abuse of their service'[4] and in violation of the instructions received, provided that there exists an 'internal causal connection' between the unlawful act and the performance of the duties entrusted to them. According to Greek jurisprudence, such a connection exists if these duties were the 'necessary means' of the unlawful act or, in other words, if the unlawful act could not have been committed if these duties had not been assigned.[5] However, if the mere fact that the relationship between the principal and the auxiliary made the person or property of the injured third party accessible to the auxiliary is regarded sufficient, almost every assignment of duties would be considered adequate: the assignment would be regarded as a *conditio sine qua non* for the unlawful act, which, in Greek tort law theory, is not considered sufficient to establish a causal link.[6] Furthermore, neither the geographical nor the temporal proximity of the unlawful act to the duties of the assignee can be considered a sufficient cri-

4 Indicatively AP 2058/2022; AP 1230/2021; AP 93/2019.
5 Indicatively AP 203/2023; AP 221/2022; AP 93/2019; AP 974/2018; AP 1329/2017; AP 899/2014.
6 *Z Tsolakidis*, Contractual and Delictual Liability for Assistants (in Greek) (2008) 400 f.

terion for establishing a causal connection between them, since the unlawful act may be entirely incidental to the duties assigned and not functionally linked to them.

The prevailing view among Greek scholars is that the decisive factor lies in 13 whether the unlawful acts of auxiliaries are associated with the 'typical risks' of the activity entrusted to them.[7] According to this approach, which has also been adopted by recent court decisions,[8] if the unlawful act or omission falls within the typical risks of the activity in question, it is deemed to be related to it, so that the principal may be held liable. Typical risks are defined as risks 'arising from the actions of the auxiliary that are common or usual for the activity in question'.[9]

Typical risks may, in particular, be considered as risks of damage to the legal 14 interests of third parties, which arise or are aggravated by the nature and character of the activity assigned to the auxiliary, as well as by the special opportunities which it offered to the person to whom it was entrusted.[10] Decisive factors include the special possibilities afforded to the auxiliary by the type of activity entrusted to them, the actions required for its performance, the means at their disposal for those actions, as well as the circumstances surrounding both the entrustment and the performance. Objective criteria are used primarily to determine the 'typical' or 'atypical' nature of a risk in relation to a particular activity. This judgment is based on the perception of an average observer, rather than that of the principal or the injured party.

In the case under consideration, the Court held that, while the intentional 15 shooting and injury of the plaintiff had temporal and geographical proximity to the performance of his duties, it did not have an *'internal causal connection'* with them. This is because the act originated from a personal motive and was unrelated to his professional responsibilities. The Supreme Court does not refer to *typical risks*, but it is clear that, even under this criterion, the employer company could not be held liable. The injury of a colleague with a weapon following an ar-

7 *M Stathopoulos*, Law of Obligations, General Part (5th edn 2018) (in Greek) § 7 no 70; *A Georgiades*, Law of Obligations, Special Part, Handbook (2nd edn 2024) (in Greek) § 48 no 41; *P Kornilakis*, Law of Obligations, Special Part (3rd edn 2023) (in Greek) § 221 no 15; *G Georgiades* in: A Georgiades (ed), Short Commentary of the Greek Civil Code I (2nd edn 2023) (in Greek) art 922 no 45; *Tsolakidis* (fn 6) 409 ff.

8 AP 586/2013; AP 882/2008; Athens Court of Appeal 29/2019; Piraeus Court of Appeal 6/2017; Piraeus Court of Appeal 207/2015; Larissa Court of Appeal 99/2014; Thessaloniki Court of Appeal 2126/2012.

9 *A Georgiades* (fn 7) § 48 no 41; *Kornilakis* (fn 7) § 221 no 15; *G Georgiades* (fn 7) art 922 no 45.

10 See in detail, *Tsolakidis* (fn 6) 411 ff.

gument does not constitute a risk related to driving vehicles, nor is the likelihood of its occurrence increased by undertaking the activity assigned. On the contrary, it is an act entirely incidental to the duties the perpetrator had assumed. The answer would probably be different if the tort was committed by a security officer or a policeperson, since the use of a weapon would be considered a 'typical risk', connected with the activities entrusted to the tortfeasor.

2. Areios Pagos (Greek Supreme Court) 26 March 2024, no 450: Unlawful Omission

a) Brief Summary of the Facts

16 The plaintiff was walking through a supermarket owned by a public limited company. After completing his purchases, he proceeded along a corridor leading to the checkout area when he slipped on a liquid substance (soft drink) that had been spilled earlier in the day. The store manager had been notified of the spill and had issued instructions for the aisle to be cleaned. However, at the time the plaintiff passed the spot where the soft drink had been spilled, no employee informed or warned him of the aisle's slipperiness, nor was there any evidence that a verbal warning had been issued. As a result, he continued walking unsuspectingly until he slipped and fell to the ground, sustaining a fracture. He was hospitalised for four days and was granted medical leave for six months. The victim filed a lawsuit: (a) against the company that owned the supermarket, (b) against the company's CEO, (c) against the store manager, and (d) against the store's health and safety officer.

b) Judgment of the Court

17 According to the provision of arts 914, 297, 298, and 330 GrCC, the prerequisites for the obligation to compensate are: an unlawful act or omission; fault; damage; a causal link between the injurious conduct (legal basis of liability) and the result (damage).

18 The unlawful conduct, as a condition of the tort, may consist not only of a positive act, but also of an omission, provided that, in the latter case, the tortfeasor was obliged to act by law, by contract or by good faith. A person who creates dangerous situations is obliged, in good faith, to take all the necessary protective measures appropriate to the circumstances, in accordance with the principles of science and common experience, to prevent harm to third parties. This obligation

exists even if it is not explicitly provided for by a specific legal provision, since the violation of such a provision would already constitute unlawful conduct.

In the case of a public limited company, its directors are not personally liable 19 for the company's debts. However, they may incur personal liability for tortious acts under art 914 GrCC. The rule of directors' non-liability is set aside and does not apply when their faulty conduct constitutes a tort under general principles (art 914 GrCC), thereby giving rise to their personal liability.

The plaintiff's injury is primarily attributable to the fault of the third defen- 20 dant (the store manager), an auxiliary of the company, whose legal representative was the second defendant (the CEO of the company). In particular, the third defendant failed to exercise the required diligence and care (art 330 sec b GrCC) that she could, given the objective circumstances and her capabilities, and should have demonstrated, due to the pre-existing dangerous situation, within the scope of her professional activities and the duties assigned to her by the employer company. Such diligence and care would have enabled her to foresee the injurious outcome. Specifically, the third defendant was obligated to take all appropriate measures to prevent harm to the physical integrity of the supermarket's customers, either by directly securing the aisle herself, or by having an appointed person remain at the location to notify customers, or by placing special warning signs at a sufficient distance before the hazardous area, or at least by blocking the access to the aisle until the warning signs were placed. However, she failed to comply with the aforementioned obligations, and did not maintain constant vigilance, even though, as she claims, she had already noticed the spilled soft drink and had instructed the cleaning of the area in question. It was not proven that she had given instructions to supervise the area until the proper warning signs were placed, and as a result neither she nor the store's employees alerted the plaintiff, who, thus, walked unsuspectingly down the aisle, lost his balance, and fell, sustaining a fracture.

The fourth defendant is also at fault, as, despite holding the position of the 21 store's health and safety officer, it was not proven that he implemented adequate measures to inform the company's employees about the necessary actions to be taken in similar instances of liquid spillage on the store's floors and aisles. Nor was there any evidence that he had issued the necessary instructions to ensure that, in cases of floor slipperiness from any cause, employees would promptly and thoroughly clean the area, or that he had informed them about methods for restricting customer access to parts of the store that posed risks due to similar incidents.

The third and fourth defendants are deemed jointly liable for the aforemen- 22 tioned accident, as they violated art 13 para 1 of Presidential Decree 17/96 (Measures for improving the safety and health of workers during work), which requires employees to comply with health and safety regulations and ensure the safety and health of others affected by their actions or omissions, as well as art 20, art 32 para 1, art 36 para 6, and art 44 para 16 of the A1b/8577/83 Health Regulation, which mandate that those responsible for maintaining cleanliness on the store's premises, in any capacity, must ensure, through appropriate instructions, that the floor areas remain clean.

23 Furthermore, the second defendant, as the legal representative of the company at the time of the accident and responsible for the store's operation, is also considered jointly liable for the resulting harm. In addition to the responsibility arising from the provisions of art 7 paras 1–3 of Presidential Decree 17/1996 (which stipulates that the employer is obliged to ensure the safety and health of employees and take measures to protect the health and safety of third parties), the second defendant failed to take the necessary action as the person who appointed the third and fourth defendants (as well as the rest of the company's staff) by neglecting to provide appropriate instructions regarding the immediate placement of signs and other warnings, and by failing to continuously supervise them to ensure that, in the event of any liquid spillage on the floor that rendered it slippery, the area would be immediately blocked off and the floor would be cleaned thoroughly to prevent related risks.

24 Therefore, all the aforementioned individuals, through their concurrent negligence, were liable for the plaintiff's injury because, despite having a legal obligation, they failed to prevent the harmful incident. Their omissions, as described above, rendered their conduct unlawful by contravening imperative legal provisions and violating the obligation under art 914 GrCC, which requires taking necessary positive actions to prevent potential risks and ensuing damage when a hazardous situation has been created, thus causing harm through fault.

c) Commentary

25 According to art 914 GrCC, a prerequisite for liability in tort is 'unlawful' conduct. Unlawful conduct refers to behaviour that is contrary to a rule of law that prohibits or imposes certain behaviour.[11] The rule infringed must establish an absolute right or protect private legal interests.[12] For over 50 years, Greek jurisprudence has held that unlawfulness does not require the violation of a specific rule but is *sufficiently established when conduct violates the general duty of*

11 AP 90/2023; AP 1145/2022; AP 914/2021; AP 751/2019.
12 *A Georgiades* (fn 7) § 46 no 13; *Kornilakis* (fn 7) § 214 no 2 ff.

care, providence, and protection of the rights of others, derived from the principles of good faith and public usage.[13] According to the theory of the 'dual function of negligence', negligence exists when a person infringes the obligation generally required of every member of society to exercise the care that a reasonable person is capable of, regardless of whether a specific legal duty is violated.[14]

For an omission to be considered unlawful, the person must be obligated to perform the specific act either by law, by contract or by good faith. In the latter case, the principle of good faith, alongside the obligation to protect the legal interests of third parties, may require specific actions to prevent any potential harm to them. A typical example of such an obligation to take protective measures arises when prior conduct by the tortfeasor has created a hazardous situation from which damage may result: in such cases, a duty to take measures to prevent the harm is established, under the principle of good faith.[15] **26**

In the case in question, the Greek Supreme Court held that duties of care and providence were established for all the defendants. The court attributed negligent conduct to all of them, considering that their actions violated the general duty of care and protection of the rights of third parties with whom each individual comes into contact. The Court even deemed their failure to take preventive measures to avert the risk as unlawful, despite the fact that they had not caused the hazardous situation through their own actions. Their obligation was obviously considered to derive from their position within the company, which also resulted in a duty to prevent any harm to customers. **27**

Two particularities are noteworthy in the aforementioned case: firstly, different duties of care were established for each of the individuals involved (the CEO, the store manager and the health and safety officer). It was determined that, depending on their position and scope of responsibility, each individual had a different duty of diligence to prevent damage similar to that caused. Since all the individuals were defendants, the Court did not have the opportunity to examine the issue of the causal link, namely whether each of them contributed equally to the final result. This issue will arise in the event of recourse between them, in accordance with art 927 GrCC ('A person who has paid compensation for the whole of the prejudice pursuant to the preceding section shall have a right of recourse against the others'). **28**

---

13 See the recent case law of the Greek Supreme Court: AP 258/3023; AP 1083/2022; AP 957/2022; AP 266/2021; AP 1007/2019; AP 1359/2018; AP 1284/2017; AP 1801/2014.

14 AP 1054/2022; AP 1121/2021; AP 1510/2014; AP 974/2014; AP 1361/2013; AP 1796/2012. For the analysis of this theory, see *Stathopoulos* (fn 7) § 6 no 75 ff.

15 AP 410/2022; AP 293/2022; AP 54/2019; AP 2075/2013; AP 114/2012; AP 1485/2010.

29 It is also noteworthy that the Court, in justifying its decision, refers not only to the general duty of care and the obligation to take protective measures to prevent imminent risk, but also to the violation of legal provisions (administrative rules regarding health and safety in the workplace). It explicitly states that the defendants' conduct was contrary *both to the general duty of care and to the specific prohibitive provisions.* It seems that the Court merely sought to strengthen its reasoning and did not intend to depart from the prevailing principle that the creation of a hazardous situation imposes an obligation to take protective measures, grounded in the principle of good faith and the overall spirit of the law.

3. Council of State (Symvoulio tis Epikrateias) 21 May 2024, no 704: State Liability

a) Brief Summary of the Facts

30 The plaintiffs, in their lawsuit against the Greek State, claimed that the State should compensate them for damage corresponding to the rents they lost as owners of properties leased under commercial lease agreements during the period from March 2020 to March 2021. This loss resulted from the compulsory reduction of rent for businesses affected by the COVID-19 pandemic, pursuant to special laws mandating such reductions as compensation for the loss of profits incurred by lessee businesses during the lockdown.

31 The plaintiffs assert that the provisions of these laws are invalid, as they contravene art 2 para 1, art 4 paras 1 and 5, art 5 para 1, arts 17 and 25 of the Hellenic Constitution, as well as art 1 of the First Additional Protocol to the European Convention on Human Rights (ECHR).

b) Judgment of the Court

32 Article 105 of the Introductory Law to the Civil Code stipulates: 'The State is liable for compensation for unlawful acts or omissions committed by its public servants in the exercise of the public authority entrusted to them, except when the act or omission violates a provision enacted in the interest of the general public…'. Under this provision, for the State to incur liability for compensation due to an act or omission by its public servants in the exercise of the public authority entrusted to them, it is required, inter alia, that the act or omission be unlawful. Since the legislator, either through a statute or a regulatory administrative act issued pursuant to statutory authorisation, generally defines the conditions of un-

lawfulness, it follows that *no liability for compensation can arise against the State* under art 105 of the Introductory Law to the Civil Code *as a result of legislation* enacted by the State through its constitutionally authorised bodies or their omission to legislate, unless such legislation or omission conflicts with legal norms of superior formal validity.

In this latter case, a necessary condition for establishing the State's civil liability is the existence of a causal link between the resulting damage and the legislation or omission to legislate that is contrary to legal norms of superior formal validity. Specifically, in the case of such legislation, the State's liability to compensate the injured party arises, in an exceptional manner, only if the harmful consequences *directly result from the contested provision*, prior to and independently of any implementation, whether through an administrative act or through a bilateral legal transaction (contract). 33

When the harmful consequences emanate primarily from the application of the aforementioned legal rule, that is, from the administrative act implementing it in an individual case, liability towards the injured party does not derive from the legal rule itself but rather from this latter act. The same applies when the regulation in question presupposes the existence of a contract in order to be applicable in a specific case. In particular, when the legal rule pertains to a contractual term and, therefore, can only be applied within the framework of a contractual relationship, the harmful consequences do not arise directly from the enactment of the contested provision but from its application during the performance of the contract. Consequently, in this case, the exceptional civil liability of the State arising from an act of a legislative body or the regulatory administration cannot be established, as the aforementioned condition is not satisfied (namely, that the damage must be caused directly by the legislative or regulatory provision) and, as a result, the required causal link between the aforementioned legislation and the resulting damage does not exist. Consequently, a claim for compensation cannot be established. 34

Councillor X dissented, arguing that when the legislator intervenes authoritatively in a contract for reasons of public interest through a law or a regulatory act that establishes a new contractual framework, adopting general and abstract measures that impact on the terms of individual contractual relationships, the harmful consequences arise directly from this regulatory provision. This is because the provision, not being the result of negotiation between the contracting parties, does not become a contractual term. 35

Article 1 of Law 4683/2020 (A' 83) provides: 36

> The lessee of a commercial lease for the establishment of a business, for which special and exceptional measures have been implemented regarding the suspension or temporary pro-

hibition of operations for preventive or restrictive reasons related to the COVID-19 pandemic, shall be exempt from the obligation to pay 40 % of the total rent for the months of March and April 2020, notwithstanding the provisions applicable to leases … .

37 This exemption was extended through corresponding provisions (Laws 4690/2020, 4722/2020, 4753/2020) until December 2020. For the period from January to March 2021, full exemption was granted.

38 In the present action, the plaintiffs seek a declaration that the defendant, the Greek State, is obligated to pay each of the plaintiff companies, as owners of properties leased to third parties under commercial lease agreements, the rent amounts they lost due to the implementation of the compulsory rent reduction measure – by 40 % (from March to December 2020) and 100 % (from January to March 2021) – pursuant to the aforementioned provisions. The plaintiffs claim that these provisions are invalid as they contravene art 2 para 1, art 4 paras 1 and 5, art 5 para 1, arts 17 and 25 of the Greek Constitution, as well as art 1 of the First Additional Protocol to the ECHR. Specifically, it is argued that these provisions impose a restriction on economic freedom, particularly on the freedom of contract, as the rent reduction measure constitutes a direct interference in an established contractual relationship, without being justified by reasons of compelling public interest and without considering factors such as the economic situation of both parties to the lease agreement, especially in light of the pandemic. It is further argued that no alternative, milder measures were sought, such as State subsidies for rent to support the affected businesses. In view of these factors, the duration of the contested measure, as well as the partial compensation provided to lessors-legal entities such as the plaintiffs (since compensatory measures were foreseen for the support of lessors, but mainly for individual persons, not legal entities), it is argued that the measure in question was ineffective, unnecessary, and disproportionate in relation to the intended objective. At the same time, it is argued that this measure also contradicts art 1 of the First Protocol to the ECHR, as it disrupts the fair balance that, according to this article, must exist between the pursued objective of the public interest and the right to property.

39 Under the specific protective legislative provisions mentioned in the previous paragraph, a measure was imposed for certain months in favour of lessees of commercial leases, as the weaker party, granting partial (40 % of the total monthly rent) and full (100 %) exemption from the obligation to pay the agreed rent to lessors. These provisions constituted an intervention in contracts for commercial leases established between private parties and introduced a detrimental modification for the lessor in order to address the adverse effects of the COVID-19 pandemic on professional or business activities. However, their mere enactment is not, by itself, sufficient to cause the damage (both property and non-property/moral dam-

age) claimed by the plaintiff companies – lessors – in their lawsuit against the Greek State. This is because the harmful consequences for the lessors of commercial properties did not arise directly and immediately from the provision of the contested measure (partial or full exemption) under the aforementioned laws, but rather from the altered execution of the relevant contracts by the lessees, who adjusted their contractual behaviour based on the provisions of the above legislative regulations (see Council of State 2423/2023), and as a result, did not pay part or all of the owed rents. Consequently, the claim against the Hellenic State for the restoration of the damage (both property and non-property/moral damage) allegedly suffered by the plaintiff companies as a result of legislation in violation of provisions of superior formal validity cannot be grounded on art 105 of the Introductory Law to the Civil Code. Therefore, the lawsuit should be dismissed as legally unfounded.

In the dissenting opinion of Councillor X, however, the lawsuit based on art 105 of the Introductory Law to the Civil Code is founded, because the contested provisions constitute an intervention by the legislator in already existing contractual relationships, which results in a restriction on the freedom of contract for reasons of public interest. Specifically, through these provisions, the legislator, within the framework of social and economic policy aimed at protecting lessees during the pandemic, granted the lessees of the plaintiff companies the contractual right to pay a reduced rent – instead of the initially agreed amount – or even no rent at all, through the direct payment of part of the rent by the State. If the lessees did not waive this right, a modification occurred in their lease relationship regarding the amount of the rent owed, without this being subject to free negotiation between the contracting parties. Consequently, the damage caused to the plaintiffs directly arose from the provisions of the laws. 40

c) Commentary

The decision adopts in its reasoning the prevailing position of the Council of State regarding the liability of the State arising from acts of legislative authority. According to this position, since the legislator defines which conduct is lawful and which is unlawful, the State cannot, in principle, incur liability for compensation arising from the enactment or non-enactment of a law. An exception is recognised when legislation (or failure to enact a law) is contrary to rules of superior formal validity (such as those of the Constitution, international law, or EU law). In this case, however, liability arises only if the damage was caused directly by the provision of the law and not by its implementation through an administrative act. If 41 the damage results from the issuance of an administrative act in application of the law, liability is not based on the law but on the administrative act.[16]

42 The decision in question extends this reasoning, distinguishing between 'direct' and 'indirect' causes of damage, and applies it not only to administrative acts but also to contracts. The Court holds that, when a rule (which is contrary to a provision of superior formal validity) pertains to a contract, 'the harmful consequences do not arise directly from the enactment of the contested provision but from its application during the execution of the contract'. This reasoning, however, is not convincing. The case is not the same as the application of the law through the issuance of administrative acts (for example, when a law contrary to the Constitution stipulates a reduction in an individual's pension, and the infringement actually arises from the decision of the social security organisation that reduces the pension). In the case of a contract, if a legislative provision intervenes in the contractual relationship and imposes heteronomous terms, these terms will govern the contract not by the will of the parties, but by virtue of the legislative provision. Therefore, the individual's damage does not arise from the contract itself, but from the legislative provision that altered or abolished its terms. In any case, the dispute arising from the contract remains a private dispute, and, therefore, the injured party could not seek compensation from the State, grounded on the contract, as the State is not a contracting party.

43 In the case in question, the Council of State did not assess whether the legislative provision mandating the reduction of rents owed by businesses that ceased operations due to the COVID-19 pandemic complied with the Constitution, as it determined, in a prior stage, that the lessors' collection of reduced rent resulted from the execution of the contracts by the lessees. However, the opinion of the dissenting Councillor seems to be more accurate, as it asserts that the damage resulted from the legislator's intervention in the pending contract and the alteration of its terms, and, consequently, arose directly and immediately from the relevant legislative provisions, which should have been examined for their compatibility with the Constitution and the ECHR.

16 Council of State 2113/2021; 479/2018; 4741/2014; 450/2013; 2773/2010; 3093/2009.

4. One-Member Court of Appeal of Athens, 12 June 2024, no 2403: Long-Term Partners as 'Family of the Victim'

a) Brief Summary of the Facts

Due to the exclusive fault of the defendant, a traffic accident occurred, resulting in 44
the fatal injury of X, who had been the long-term partner of the first plaintiff.

b) Judgment of the Court

Article 8 ECHR, which has supra-legislative force, pursuant to art 28 para 1 of the 45
Greek Constitution, states: 'Everyone has the right to respect for his private and family life, his home and his correspondence'.

From the interpretation of the notions of 'family life' and 'family', as formu- 46
lated in the case law of the European Court of Human Rights (ECtHR), the defining criteria for determining the above-mentioned key concepts, essential for the application of the provision in question, are derived. According to the ECtHR, whether 'family' or 'family life' exists is essentially a question of fact, depending upon the actual existence of close personal ties. In particular, the ECtHR has repeatedly held that art 8 ECHR does not distinguish between 'legal' and 'de facto' families, stating that the notion of 'family life' protected under this provision is not limited to marriage-based relationships, but extends to other de facto relationships of cohabitation, which also create family ties. The existence of a 'family' or 'family relationships' is examined by the Court on a case-by-case basis, as a question of fact, considering various factors, such as cohabitation and mutual support (emotional or material) between the parties, the duration and stability of the relationship and any expression of commitment by them, such as when they choose to have children and assume shared responsibility for their upbringing, as well as long-term and consistent caregiving relationships. Therefore, according to the ECtHR, the notion of 'family' also includes any situation in which two individuals cohabit without having entered into a legal marriage or a civil partnership, provided that their cohabitation results from love, devotion, and a serious and stable intention for companionship and a shared life. Thus, within this framework and under the aforementioned conditions, the ECtHR encompasses extra-marital cohabitation (where the parties are living together outside marriage) within the protective scope of art 8 ECHR. In any event, the ECtHR has held that marriages or cohabitations, even if not recognised by the legal order of the Member State, constitute a 'family' if they meet the criteria for the existence of genuine and factual family ties, as outlined above.

47 According to art 932 GrCC, in the case of tort, independently from the damages for pecuniary damage, the court may award a reasonable, according to its judgment, monetary compensation for moral harm. This applies especially to a person who has suffered an offence to their health, honour or chastity or who has been deprived of their liberty. In the case of death of a person, this monetary compensation may be awarded to the family of the victim for pain and suffering.

48 From the provision in question, it follows that the Court has discretion to award monetary compensation and to determine a reasonable amount by considering various factors, such as the degree of fault of the tortfeasor, the nature of the offence, the importance of the harm sustained, the economic and social status of both the tortfeasor and the victim, and the specific personal characteristics of the victim (eg, age, gender, and, especially in cases of death, the family relationships), based on the principles of common experience and logic.

49 The legislator deliberately does not define the meaning of the term 'family of the victim' in art 932 GrCC, obviously because it did not want to delimit the boundaries of an institution, which, because of its nature, is subject to the influence of social differentiations over the course of time. However, according to the true meaning of the provision, as derived from the purpose of its enactment, the 'family of the victim' includes the closest and most intimate relatives of the deceased, who have suffered emotional distress as a result of their loss, and whose relief from such emotional pain the provision seeks to address, regardless of whether they lived together or separately.

50 According to the prevailing opinion in jurisprudence, the application of art 932 sent c GrCC in the case of a person living in a free union with the deceased is not permitted, neither by the wording nor by the purpose of the article. Therefore, the possibility of granting monetary compensation for emotional distress caused to the surviving partner by the death of their partner is not provided for by law. An opposing view would be *contra legem* and would also subvert the constitutionally established institution of marriage.

51 Neither can art 932 sent c GrCC apply by analogy, since there is no legal gap regarding the regulation of cohabitation and individuals in a free union, as the legislator chose not to regulate this union. Free unions are placed among the 'de facto family relationships', ie, from the legal point of view, informal or irregular situations that are at the margin of the legal reality. Furthermore, as can be inferred from the provisions of arts 1444 sent b, 1456, 1457, 1471, 1479, 1350 ff and 1386 ff GrCC, in conjunction with art 21 para 1 of the Greek Constitution, this is a conscious choice of the legislator, which, although aware of the term 'free union', did not wish to regulate the issues and legal matters arising from this form of union. Free unions without children are not recognised in the Greek legal system, as their formation does not produce legal consequences and, therefore, cannot be

included in the notion of 'family', nor are they protected. In fact, those who choose to form a free union do not wish to be subject to legal regulations or obligations, making it contradictory for them to be granted legal protection. Taking all this into account, the necessary similarity for the analogous application of the provision of art 932 sent 3 GrCC does not exist between the unregulated case and the regulated one (AP 775/2011; AP 1141/2007; AP 1735/2006; AP 434/2005).

The aforementioned prevailing view refers to free unions without children. 52
Regarding free unions from which children have been born, the following points should be noted: the provisions of art 21 of the Greek Constitution, which establish marriage and family as constitutionally protected institutions, urge the legislator to adopt positive measures for the protection of marriage and the family, as well as motherhood, childhood, and large families. This protection does not always have a specific content; rather, its specific forms and extent are to be determined by the legislator and, under its authorisation, by the administration in the exercise of its regulatory functions, within the boundaries defined by other constitutional provisions and principles. The legislator is not prevented by the above constitutional provision from amending the regulations concerning the ways of establishing a family or from recognising, within the framework of the also constitutionally enshrined principles of freedom of personal development, equality, and protection of private life, alternative forms of cohabitation and the creation of family ties through them. This is because the constitutional protection of the 'family' does not pertain solely to families established through marriage, since, in any case, the institution of the family, as it is acknowledged, 'by its nature, necessarily suffers the effects of social variations over time', being subject to evolution and redefinition.

In light of the above, taking into account not only modern social perceptions, 53
which recognise free unions as an alternative, more relaxed form of common life within the context of tolerance and respect for free choices, but also the significant amendments and reforms that family law has undergone in recent years, it is clear that the national legislator, following the example of almost all European legal systems, is moving away from the narrow, traditional view that a 'family' is formed solely through marriage.

Following all of the above, regarding individuals who have neither married 54
nor entered into a civil partnership, but live in a free union from which they have had children, it should be accepted that such individuals also fall within the concept of 'family' and are included in the protective scope of art 932 sent c GrCC and art 8 ECHR. This view takes into account not only the aforementioned definition of the notion of 'family', as clearly outlined in the decisions of the ECtHR, interpreting art 8 of the supra-legislative ECHR, according to which, the notion of protected 'family life' extends to de facto cohabitation relationships

that also create family ties, provided that the decisive criterion of close personal ties between the individuals is met, and their cohabitation results from love, devotion, and a serious and stable intention of companionship and partnership, but also the evident tendency of the national legislator to no longer accept marriage as the exclusive form of 'family' creation. Therefore, in the case of a traffic accident, the person who lives in a free union, from which children have been born, along with the victim of the accident, is legally entitled, and has the right, to pursue monetary compensation for emotional distress, in accordance with the provisions of art 932 sent c GrCC.

55 In the case in question, the first appellant complained about the rejection, as unlawful, of her claim for the award of monetary compensation, based on the emotional distress she experienced due to the loss of her partner of 14 years, with whom she shared a strong emotional bond based on a loving and mutually understanding relationship, trust and partnership and with whom she came to Greece from their home country (Moldova) and lived in their shared home, intertwining their lives and solidifying the substantial notion of 'family', despite not having children together. Nevertheless, according to the aforementioned reasoning, the cohabitation of two individuals in a free union from which no children have been born does not legally establish the creation of 'family ties' or the existence of a 'family' within the meaning of the provisions of art 932 sent c GrCC. Therefore, the claim of the first appellant for the award of monetary compensation for emotional distress due to the loss of her partner, who passed away in the accident, is rejected as unlawful.

c) Commentary

56 Article 932 sent c GrCC provides that, in the case of the death of a person, monetary compensation for emotional distress is granted to the 'family' of the victim. The provision does not specify who falls within its scope of application. Greek jurisprudence has held that the determining factor is whether the individuals were closely connected to the victim through bonds of kinship, love and affection.

57 In the case of individuals living in a free union without having entered into a civil partnership, the Greek Supreme Court has consistently ruled that they are not considered a 'family' within the meaning of art 932 GrCC and are not entitled to monetary compensation.[17] The Court's primary argument was that the legisla-

17 AP 51/2018; AP 775/2011; AP 1541/2009; AP 1735/2006; AP 434/2005. Only certain decisions of the Greek courts have ruled otherwise (Athens Court of Appeal 6862/2007 EllDik (Greek Justice, Greek

tor, despite being aware of the institution of free union and having regulated other aspects of family law over time, did not grant rights to individuals cohabiting in a free union.

The jurisprudence of the Greek Supreme Court partially shifted in 2022.[18] The Court acknowledged that free unions should fall within the notion of 'family', provided that children have been born from such unions and there is evidence of a serious and stable intention for cohabitation between the partners. The Supreme Court's primary argument relied on the case law of the ECtHR, according to which, de facto cohabitation relationships, not based on marriage or civil partnerships, also fall under the protection of 'family life' (art 8 ECHR). Additionally, it referred to specific legislative provisions through which the Greek legislator recognises legal consequences of free unions. Consequently, the Court stated that: 'it is evident that the national legislator, aligning with the approach of nearly all European legal systems, is gradually moving away from the narrow, traditional assumption that "family" is formed solely through religious or civil marriage, as defined by the provisions of the Greek Civil Code' (AP 1159/2022). 58

The Greek Supreme Court, in both cases, accepted that 'the notion of family' includes cases where two individuals cohabit, without having entered into a legal marriage or civil partnership, provided that the decisive criterion, the actual existence of close personal ties between them, is met and their cohabitation is the result of love, devotion, and a serious and stable intention for companionship and togetherness. However, it is unclear why the Court imposed the additional requirement that children must be born from the cohabitation, as it is evident that close ties can exist even in cohabitations where no children have been born, and the ECtHR does not link the recognition of family life to the presence of children. 59

In both cases ruled by the Greek Supreme Court, the individuals living in free union *had had children*, and therefore, the request for monetary compensation for emotional distress was accepted. In contrast, in the case under consideration, which was adjudicated by the Athens Court of Appeal, the individuals in the cohabiting relationship did not have children. The Court of Appeal fully endorsed the reasoning of the Supreme Court, also adopting the limitation that it had accepted, namely that a precondition for the qualification of cohabitation as a 'fam- 60

law journal) 2008, 822; Athens Court of Appeal 727/2001 EllDik 2001, 1358; Thessaloniki Court of Appeal (single-member) 2/2020 EllDik 2020, 826; Athens Court of Appeal (single-member) 1815/2019 NoV (Nomiko Vima, Greek law journal) 2019, 1644. Greek scholars, also, were in favour of the inclusion of individuals cohabiting in a free union within the notion of 'family' and of the awarding of monetary compensation. Indicatively, *Stathopoulos* (fn 7) § 15 no 105; *Kornilakis* (fn 7) § 236 no 16.

18 AP 1159/2022; AP 1194/2023 followed in the same direction.

ily' is the presence of children. Consequently, it rejected the relevant request. However, it can be argued that the condition of having children (in order for cohabitants to be recognised as a 'family') is not a necessary indication of the 'seriousness' of the cohabitation nor is it an essential requirement for the existence of close ties. It remains to be seen (if a Cassation is filed) whether the Supreme Court will take the next step, by recognising the existence of a family even in the absence of children, or whether it will adhere to its (recent) case law.

5. Three-Member Court of Appeal of Athens, 12 July 2024, no 3095: Risk Liability

a) Brief Summary of the Facts

61 The plaintiff was the owner of an estate with olive trees, covering an area of 50,000 square metres, within which a commercial olive mill was operating, with a surface area of approximately 400 square metres. On 20 August 2012, a fire broke out, and within a short period of time, it spread to the area where the plaintiff's estate was located. The plaintiff filed a lawsuit against the Public Power Corporation SA (PPC, or DEI in Greek), which, at that time, owned the electric power distribution network, claiming that the fire was caused by an explosion at a PPC substation.

b) Judgment of the Court

62 The rapid modern scientific and technological development has inevitably created a number of sources of increased risk that pose an unpredictable threat to people and their property. Such sources of increased risk of damage include terrestrial, waterborne, and airborne means of public transportation, electricity generation facilities and distribution networks, facilities for nuclear power, natural gas, and other flammable and explosive chemical substances, automated mass production, etc.

63 Damage caused by such a source of increased risk places the injured party in a difficult position to recover their loss, as the principle of subjective liability (fault-based liability), governing the rules of non-contractual liability, excludes compensation from the owner or the person having control of such a source of risk when the damage cannot be attributed to the fault of any specific individual. As a result, 'accidental' damage is ultimately borne by the injured party. It is difficult for the injured party to prove the fault of the person who caused the dam-

age, while the latter, as the holder of the relevant expertise, can more easily demonstrate that there was no fault on their part. Therefore, the victim of a modern source of increased risk is left without compensation, which constitutes an unacceptable outcome and highlights the inability of the principle of subjective liability to regulate, in a socially just manner, the modern issues of extra-contractual liability.

A different legal approach to liability for damage caused by such sources of 64 increased risk is therefore required, commonly referred to as 'risk liability'. This is the recognition of an obligation to compensate regardless of fault when the damage is associated with sources from which an 'increased risk' emanates – a risk that, on the one hand, cannot be controlled through the standard level of diligence required in transactions and, on the other hand, threatens individuals who, due to the structure and organisation of modern societies, are compelled to be exposed to it. Consequently, the 'principle of risk' implies that the owner or controller of such a source of increased risk is obligated to compensate for any damage caused by these particular risks, regardless of whether the damage is attributable to their fault or not. Risk liability, which is typically extra-contractual and may concur with tortious or contractual liability, does not require an act, unlawful conduct, or fault on the part of the liable party. It may arise from natural events, technical operations, or even human behaviour that does not constitute an act. It requires, however, an appropriate causal link between the source of the risk and the damage. The person liable for compensation is the owner or controller of the source of particular risks. This obligation is morally justified both by the legal recognition of the operation of such sources within the Greek legal order and by the typically significant economic benefits derived from them.

The sole adherence to the doctrine of subjective liability results in the inabil- 65 ity of the legal order to compensate for a significant proportion of the damage suffered by the modern citizen, and, therefore, a reorientation of the regulation of extra-contractual liability is required, within the framework of the modern welfare state, directed towards the full compensation of the injured party, provided that the cause of their damage originates from such a source of risk. Only in this way can the constitutional rights of individuals be fully safeguarded and fulfilled, including the right to the free development of their personality, the participation in social and economic life, the protection of life and health, and the protection of property (art 5 para 1 f and art 17 para 1 of the Greek Constitution). These constitutional rights, in the light of the general principle of the rule of law, aim, particularly following the explicit establishment of the principle of the horizontal effect of individual and social rights (art 25 para 1 of the Greek Constitution), to secure and protect the relevant legal interests, not only against sovereign State interventions but also against violations by private entities within the context of interpersonal relationships. In this sense, extra-contractual liability (and thus risk liability, as part of it) constitutes a secondary protective function for the aforementioned legal individual rights and, for this reason, is promoted as an essential element of the constitutional order. Otherwise, the protection of these rights sought by the Constitution would remain incomplete.

66 The legislator, implementing these constitutional provisions, did not establish a general rule for risk liability, but instead regulated (in addition to art 924 para 1 and art 925 GrCC) risk liability on a case-by-case basis. These statutes are the following: (a) Law 3950/1911 on liability for damage caused by motor vehicles accidents; (b) Law 1815/1988 on liability of the operator of an aircraft for damage during air transport; (c) Law 1758/1988 on liability of damage in the field of nuclear energy, as amended by Law 1897/1990; (d) Law 1650/1986 on liability for damage caused by the pollution or the degradation of the environment, as amended by Law 1892/1990; (e) Law 563/1977 on liability for damage caused by objects launched into space; (f) Law 314/1976 on liability for pollution caused by oil; and (g) Law 2251/1994 on liability of the producer for defective products.

67 In cases not regulated by law, such as liability for damage caused by electricity generation facilities and distribution networks, the obligation of the owner or the controller of the source of 'increased' risk is directly grounded in the aforementioned constitutional provisions, which impose on private individuals the duty to respect and protect the relevant legal rights. In any case, the aforementioned legislative 'imperfection', consisting in the absence of relevant regulation, which is deemed necessary based on the intrinsic teleology of the law and, above all, on the legal principle of equal treatment of similar situations, can be addressed through the application by analogy of the provisions governing the already regulated cases. This is because the legislator, by regulating only certain cases in this manner, did not intend (given the universality of the aforementioned constitutional provisions) to regulate only those exceptional cases and exclude others from similar provisions, but rather, due to the case-by-case regulation that was adopted, articulated the scope of the law more narrowly than was ultimately intended. Otherwise, the result would be the paradoxical phenomenon where the owner of a source of 'increased' risk (eg, an electricity generation facility and distribution network) would incur tortious liability, ie, 'lighter' liability since fault must be proven, while the owner of an animal would bear 'heavier' liability under the provisions of risk liability, which is objective and independent of any fault.

c) Commentary

A general principle of civil liability in the Greek legal system is that liability for compensation presupposes the fault of the wrongdoer.[19] A fundamental expression of this principle in the field of tort law is art 914 GrCC.[20] By exception, the law obliges, in specific cases, the individual who caused damage to repair it, even if they are not at fault (strict liability). Among these cases is risk liability. The justification for risk liability lies in the notion that the individual who controls a particular source of risk, which cannot be adequately controlled and can cause particularly large and/or frequent damage, should also restore the damage caused by the operation of that source, as they derive benefits from it.[21] 68

Risk liability has not been established by the legislator as a general basis of liability. While tortious liability is regulated by a general provision (art 914 GrCC), the legislator has chosen to regulate *specific cases of risk liability* on a case-by-case basis. Many sources of risk still remain unregulated. In Greek legal theory, following an international debate dating back to the 1940s,[22] the introduction of a general clause on risk liability has been proposed *de lege ferenda*.[23] 69

Decision 1904/2022 of the Greek Supreme Court ruled that even in unregulated cases, when 'the damage is associated with a source of increased risk', an obligation to compensate should be recognised for the owner of that source. This judgment *contradicts the clear legislative choice to limit risk liability only to the cases explicitly provided by law* and to refrain from establishing a general clause that would encompass all activities creating a specific source of risk. The Court of Appeals' decision in question adopts almost verbatim the reasoning of the Supreme Court. 70

The reasoning of the Court is supported by two main arguments. First, it follows the path of analogy. Specifically, it states that '...the establishment of risk liability...can also be possible through the application by analogy of the provisions already in force for the aforementioned regulated cases, since the legislator, by regulating only certain cases...expressed itself more narrowly than intended'. However, no intention of the legislator to regulate all cases of risk liability in a general manner can be inferred, as the debate on this issue has been ongoing for decades, and the legislator continues, even recently, to regulate only specific sources of risk. Therefore, no legislative intent emerges to extend the scope of 71

19 *Stathopoulos* (fn 7) § 6 no 120.
20 *A Georgiades* (fn 7) § 45 no 3.
21 *Stathopoulos* (fn 7) § 15 no 91; *A Georgiades* (fn 7) § 51 no 2; *Kornilakis* (fn 7) § 239 no 1 ff.
22 *J Esser*, Grundlagen und Entwicklung der Gefährdungshaftung (1941).
23 *Kornilakis* (fn 7) § 240 no 14; *Stathopoulos* (fn 7) § 15 no 93.

risk liability to other cases beyond those explicitly provided for by the legislator, and thus, an application by analogy is not possible.

72 The second argument presented by the Court of Appeal (and the Supreme Court) relies on constitutional provisions. According to this reasoning, an application by analogy is not merely permitted, but is mandated by the Constitution. In particular, the Constitution imposes the protection of certain legal interests. Since this protection has a horizontal effect, ie, it applies not only against the State but also against private individuals, a comprehensive safeguarding of these interests is required through a claim for compensation. However, this argument also does not appear convincing. The Constitution may safeguard specific goods (such as health or property) and impose on the legislator the obligation to protect them. However, it is up to the legislator to balance this protection with other constitutionally protected rights, such as individual freedom of action. The legislator does not protect all goods, nor does it consider every infringement unlawful; instead, it grants specific rights. In cases of risk liability, the legislator considers that the infringement is both highly likely and significant, given the specific risk involved, and thus imposes liability without requiring either fault, or even unlawful conduct by the holder of the source of risk.[24] At the same time, however, this liability is subject to special regulation (quantitative limits, short prescription periods, exemption due to force majeure, etc). This balancing act is the task of the legislator and it cannot be argued that it was directly entrusted to the judge by constitutional provisions.[25]

6. Personal Injury

a) Notable Decisions

73 In **Decision no 42/2024** of the **Single-Member Court of Appeal of Piraeus** it was held that *res judicata* established by a judicial decision which awards monetary compensation for moral harm does not preclude a subsequent claim for additional monetary compensation, through a new lawsuit, when the health of the injured party deteriorates further, provided that this deterioration is causally linked to the tortious act. This is only possible, however, under the condition that the consequences of the tort in question *occurred later and could not have been foreseen*

---

24 *Kornilakis* (fn 7) § 240 no 1; *Stathopoulos* (fn 7) § 15 no 91.

25 See also, *M Stavrakakis*, Commentary on AP 1904/2022, XrID (Chronicles of Private Law, Greek law journal) 2023, 434.

by the Court that initially adjudicated and awarded the compensation. If, on the other hand, the consequences of the tort had been raised in the initial claim and examined in the course of its adjudication, they are covered by the *res judicata* effect of the decision issued in the first trial, rendering the subsequent claim inadmissible. The critical point for asserting the consequences of the tort and for determining the foreseeability, or lack thereof, of the injured party's future health deterioration is the time of the oral hearing before the trial court that adjudicated the initial claim, as only the arguments advanced up to that point can be considered in determination of the initial monetary compensation.

If, on the other hand, additional monetary compensation is sought to alleviate 74
the mental harm the injured party will endure due to a future medical or surgical procedure necessitated by the deterioration of their health, the court examines whether, based on the facts presented, the occurrence of such a procedure is certain or merely probable according to the ordinary course of events, and whether it is dependent on other unforeseeable factors that may arise in the future, whose potential realisation cannot be predicted with certainty under the principles of common experience. In the latter case, the claim is rejected as 'premature' and compensation can only be awarded once it arises. The final decision rejecting the claim as prematurely filed does not create *res judicata* regarding the existence of the right.

In **Decision no 425/2024** of the **Single-Member Athens Court of Appeal** it 75
was held that a person who suffered damage to their body or health and, as a result, has become incapable of working, has the right to claim, from the party legally liable for compensation, everything they would have earned in the future with a probability, according to the usual course of events, had they not become incapable of working due to the injury to their body or health. The facts that determine the expectation of certain profits, based on the probability according to the usual course of events, as well as the special circumstances and the preparatory measures taken, must be clearly presented in the lawsuit. Therefore, it is not considered sufficient for the plaintiff to merely repeat the general provisions of the law on loss of profits, nor to simply state the total amount of profit claimed as lost. Instead, a specialised and detailed case-by-case analysis is required, emphasising the specific facts, circumstances, and measures that make the profit 'probable' with respect to the individual claims. However, it is not necessary to specify in the lawsuit the identity of the employer for whom the injured party would have worked in the future, nor whether this employer would indeed have the capacity to employ them. Similarly, it is not necessary for the elements that contribute to the amount of the expected profit to be specified, by referencing specific transactions or counter-parties. On the other hand, it is not sufficient to establish a claim for compensation by merely invoking the injured party's subjec-

tive intention to exercise a profession in the future, nor by referring to occasional involvement in a specific activity, but specific factual circumstances have to be cited to make the future practice of the relevant profession probable.

76 In **Decision no 1492/2024** of the **Single-Member Athens Court of Appeal** it was held that the type and extent of the compensation owed due to a tort (art 914 GrCC) are determined by the provisions of arts 297 and 298 GrCC, as well as by the provision of art 929 GrCC, which states that, in the case of injury to a person's body or health, the compensation includes, among other things, medical expenses. The term 'medical expenses' includes costs necessary for the restoration of the injured party's health, such as, by way of example, expenses for the purchase of medicines, doctors' fees, hospital or clinic stays, physical therapy (especially in cases of fractures and dislocations), rental of a car or taxi to transport the injured party to the hospital or for visits to medical examinations and follow-up, hiring of a private nurse either at home or in the hospital, provision of specialised food if required for the specific case, general expenses for the accompanying person (who may be a close relative) when travelling to another city, provided that the presence of the accompanying person is deemed necessary, as well as the potential costs for services provided by the injured party's relatives in the event of their inability to self-care. If the amount of the expenses is due to over-precaution on the part of the injured party, it would be subject to reduction (art 300 GrCC – reduction due to contributory negligence). Specifically, the injured party is free to choose a therapeutic institution (public or private hospital), attending physician, and treatment method. In other words, the victim of a tort is not obliged, in order to avoid imposing a burden on the liable party, to limit themselves to accepting the services offered by their insurance fund, regarding the therapeutic institution, the available treatment methods and doctors, as the obligation of the injured party to mitigate the damage cannot be considered superior to the right and the interest of protecting their health.

b) Compensation of Non-Pecuniary Damage

77 A worker died as a result of a work-related accident while performing tasks on a bridge of the National Highway. The Court of Appeal ruled that the husband of the victim's sister was not entitled to monetary compensation for pain and suffering, as he did not fall under the category of 'family' of the deceased, being a relative by marriage beyond the first degree. The **Greek Supreme Court (AP 5/2024)** upheld the decision of the Court of Appeal. The Court of Appeal awarded the following monetary compensation for pain and suffering to the victim's family: (a) € 70,000 to the father and € 70,000 to the mother of the deceased,

(b) € 40,000 to each of the three siblings of the deceased, (c) € 80,000 to the widow of the deceased, (d) € 4,000 to the father-in-law and € 4,000 to the mother-in-law of the deceased. The Greek Supreme Court upheld the decision of the Court of Appeal.

A woman died from heart disease due to complications during childbirth. It 78
was determined that her death was caused by the negligence of the cardiologist who treated her. The Court of Appeal awarded monetary compensation for pain and suffering as follows: (a) € 70,000 to the father and € 70,000 to the mother of the deceased, (b) € 40,000 to the deceased's sister, (c) € 70,000 to the deceased's husband, (d) € 85,000 to the deceased's minor child. The **Greek Supreme Court (AP 309/2024)** ruled that the Court of Appeal did not violate the principle of proportionality, nor did it exceed the extreme limits of its discretion, as the amounts awarded, based on common experience, judicial practice, and public conscience, did not exceed, and in fact were clearly within, the usual amounts awarded in similar cases. It also confirmed that the minor child is entitled to monetary compensation, as the child will experience emotional pain when they reach an age at which they are affected by the outside world and may feel orphaned, particularly during the pre-school and school age.

During childbirth, a newborn suffered brain damage due to perinatal asphyx- 79
ia, resulting in permanent spastic quadriplegia. It was determined that the gynaecologist was at fault for failing to use the cardiotocograph for continuous monitoring of the foetus's heart rate and for not promptly performing a caesarean section when foetal heart rate abnormalities were detected. The Court of Appeal awarded € 400,000 as monetary compensation for moral harm to the newborn, stating that 'the minor child suffered significant moral harm, consisting of the physical and psychological pain endured due to the permanent condition from which the child suffers, a condition that deprived them for life of the opportunity to develop their personality and to live a normal childhood and adult life'. The **Greek Supreme Court (AP 823/2024)** ruled that the Court of Appeal did not violate the principle of proportionality and did not exceed the extreme limits of its discretion. Given that this amount, based on common experience, judicial practice, and the sense of justice, is not higher (and is in fact clearly within) the usual amounts awarded in similar cases of monetary compensation for moral damage due to lifelong disability, it is not considered excessive.

In a traffic accident, a 17-year-old riding as a passenger on a motorcycle was 80
killed. The **Eastern Crete Court of Appeal (Decision no 25/2024)** recognised contributory negligence on the part of the deceased in the causation of the damage, amounting to 20 %. It awarded the following monetary compensation for pain and suffering: (a) € 42,000 to each of the deceased's parents, (b) € 24,000 to each of the deceased's siblings, (c) € 10,000 to each of the deceased's grandparents.

81 In a traffic accident, a 61-year-old woman was killed due to the exclusive fault of the other driver who caused the accident. The **Crete Court of Appeal (Decision no 46/2024)** awarded the following monetary compensation for pain and suffering: (a) € 50,000 to each of the deceased's children, (b) € 10,000 to each of the spouses of her children, (c) € 20,000 to each of her grandchildren, (d) € 20,000 to each of her sisters.

82 In a traffic accident, a pedestrian was injured while walking on a zebra crossing in the middle of the roadway, due to the exclusive fault of the driver. As a result of the injury, the pedestrian underwent two operations, enduring significant discomfort, anxiety, and fear about their outcome. During recovery, the pedestrian experienced severe pain and had to take sedatives and strong painkillers to manage it. The court of first instance awarded € 6,000 as monetary compensation for moral harm. The **Dodecanese Court of Appeal (Decision no 55/2024)** ruled that the compensation should be increased to € 15,000, as the court of first instance violated the principle of proportionality and exceeded the extreme limits of its discretion. The amount awarded (€ 6,000), based on common experience, judicial practice, and the sense of justice, was deemed significantly lower than the amounts typically awarded in similar cases.

C. Literature

1. *Dimitrios Koutsoukis*, The Claim for Compensation for Damage from Horizontal Collusion of Undertakings (Cartel) under Law 4529/2018 (Nomiki Vivliothiki, Athens 2024)

83 The study deals with the issue of claims by persons affected by horizontal collusion of undertakings, in violation of the rules of free competition. The specific solutions provided by Law 4529/2018, which incorporated Directive 2014/104/EU ('on certain rules governing lawsuits for damages under national law for infringements of competition law provisions'), are examined. This study examines, in particular, the differences from the general provisions of compensation law, which arise in many crucial issues, especially in active and passive standing, the concept of unlawfulness and damage, and the causal link. Special attention is also given to the specific rules facilitating access to evidence, the statute of limitations, and the restitution of the benefit obtained by the infringer to the detriment of the harmed party.

2. *Konstantinos Leon*, Compensation for the Deterioration of the Victim's Health (Sakkoulas, Athens-Thessaloniki 2024)

The book addresses issues related to compensation for future and progressive damage. In particular, it examines whether damage arising in the future due to the deterioration of an already existing injury can be compensated. The key issue is whether the damage resulting from the worsening of bodily harm or health impairment should be classified as new or as part of a continuous injury that merely progresses over time. The author also analyses the issue of contributory negligence by other parties, particularly in cases of medical malpractice, as well as the concurrence of multiple potential causes, which creates uncertainty regarding the actual cause of the deterioration. A chapter is devoted to moral damage, with a focus on cases of post-traumatic stress, as well as the moral damage suffered by third parties connected to the victim who experience the adverse progression of their health. 84

3. *Euripides Rizos*, Violation of Good Morals and Tortious Liability (Sakkoulas, Athens-Thessaloniki 2024)

This monograph analyses the interpretive issues arising from the application of art 919 GrCC ('Whoever intentionally causes damage to another in a manner contrary to good morals (*bonos mores*) is obliged to compensate them'). The concept of good morals in art 919 GrCC is examined primarily in terms of its function within this provision, as well as its role within the broader system of tort liability. For this reason, the study explores the relationship between art 919 GrCC and related provisions, particularly art 914 GrCC. The monograph advocates for an interpretation of good morals based on legal value judgements rather than social morality and formulates a set of generalisable legal criteria for defining good morals, which can be applied beyond the cases that currently fall within the established typology of its application. Beyond the issue of violation of good morals, the author also examines the other conditions set out in art 919 GrCC, as well as issues arising from its application and consequences. 85

Attila Menyhárd

XIV. Hungary

A. Legislation

In 2024, there were no significant legislative developments in the field of tort law in Hungary. 1

B. Cases

1. Supreme Court, BH 2024 no 38, Kúria Pfv.III.20.239/2023/5, 2024 January: Liability for Accident at a Sports Event

a) Brief Summary of the Facts

The plaintiff's late spouse, the victim of the accident, attended a motorcycle race, as a spectator, with his child. Together with several others, he stood on the outer perimeter of the track, in the 'empty staging area' as indicated on the track sign, outside the border of the track, in an area open for spectators. During the race, one of the racers lost control of his bike, left the track and hit the victim, who suffered a skull fracture and died shortly afterwards. 2

The plaintiff based her claim on the rules of liability for extra-hazardous activities of the Civil Code, according to which, the person liable to pay damages is the person who qualifies as the operator of the activity (§ 6:535 of the Hungarian Civil Code). These rules of the Hungarian Civil Code provide that a person carrying out extra-hazardous activities shall compensate for the resulting damage. It is exempted from liability if it can prove that the damage was caused by an event which was unavoidable and fell outside the scope of the extra-hazardous activity. The operator is the person in whose interest the extra-hazardous activity is carried out. Such person is considered the person carrying out the extra-hazardous activity. 3

The plaintiff claimed *solatium doloris*, functionally equivalent to non-pecuniary damages, as compensation for losing her husband. In support of her claim for damages, the plaintiff argued that the loss of her spouse had interfered with her right to live in a complete family and her right to mental health. The defendant sport clubs pleaded that they should not be qualified as operators of an extra-hazardous activity and, thus, they are not liable. 4

https://doi.org/10.1515/9783111389271-015

b) Judgment of the Court

5 The Court ordered the defendants to pay *solatium doloris* of HUF 8,000,000 (approx € 20,000). The starting point for the court was that the operator is not necessarily the actual user, but the person for whose benefit the hazardous activity was operated. It held that the defendants, one of them a sports club organising the race and the other, which announced and promoted the racing season, are both to be held as operators of the race. The Court found no contributory negligence on the part of the victim. In the case at hand, the motor racing itself was considered as an extra-hazardous activity, resulting in no-fault liability. The Court concluded that such activity requires the implementation of extra preventive measures, and the fact that damage occurred means that the protection was inadequate, with the consequence that strict liability was established.

c) Commentary

6 The central issue in the case was who should be deemed as the operator of the extra-hazardous activity. While assessing the issue, the lower courts as well as the Supreme Court qualified the motorcycle race – and not simply the motorcycle as a vehicle – as an extra-hazardous activity. The Court decided that the two clubs, that is, the organiser of the actual race as well as the other which announced and promoted the racing season, are to be qualified as operators of the race as a hazardous activity. According to § 6:535 of the Hungarian Civil Code, a person carrying out hazardous activities is to be held liable for the resulting damage. The operator is exempted from liability only if it can prove that the damage was caused by an unavertable event falling outside the scope of the hazardous activity. § 6:536 provides that the person in whose interest the hazardous operations are carried out is considered the person carrying out the hazardous activity (operator). If the hazardous activity is linked to several operators, they are considered as the persons causing damage together and are held jointly and severally liable.

7 According to the reasoning of the Court, that the defendants were required to implement extra preventive measures and failed to do so was irrelevant to the question of the establishment of liability.

2. Supreme Court, BG 2024 no 39, Kúria Pfv.III.20.223/2023/5, 2024 January: Annuity to Compensate the Lost Income of the Victim's Relative

a) Brief Summary of the Facts

Plaintiff 1 was the driver of a motorcycle and he was involved in a traffic accident 8 caused by another driver, insured by the defendant insurance company. The plaintiff's severe spinal cord injury resulted in partial paralysis of the upper limbs and total paralysis of the lower limbs. He lost his ability to live independently. Plaintiff 2, the spouse of the victim, gave up her job in order to take care of the victim. Plaintiff 2 claimed compensation for lost income. The defendant insurance company pleaded that plaintiff 1 had already been compensated for the costs of taking care of him and that it was solely the decision of plaintiff 2 to stop working.

b) Judgment of the Court

In the judgment of the Court, the defendant was ordered to pay an annuity, equal 9 to €1,100 per month, in order to compensate plaintiff 2 for the income she lost as a result of giving up her job due to her husband's accident. The Court agreed with the plaintiffs that the care and maintenance allowance provided to the primary victim was not sufficient to compensate the loss of income of plaintiff 2. The Court considered that, since plaintiff 1 was in receipt of a care allowance for 14 hours per day, plaintiff 2 could claim compensation for the remaining period for her loss of income. A claim for compensation for expenses may therefore be justified not only by the victim but also by his dependant. If the relative carrying out these activities suffers a loss of income, this may give rise to a separate claim for compensation.

The Supreme Court established that according to consistent case law, the tort- 10 feasor is also obliged to compensate the additional expenses incurred if the assistance was provided free of charge by a relative of the victim. In such cases, it is actually the victims who suffer loss, as they are in need of care, domestic help and assistance, regardless of whether these tasks are performed by relatives, who are in fact acting on behalf of the person who caused the damage and at their expense, but in the interests of the victim. In view of this, not only the victim but also the relative assisting them may claim compensation for the costs incurred. As a further consequence of the same situation, the relative performing the activities in question may suffer a loss of income, which may give rise to a separate claim for compensation. In this case, the obligation of the victim to mitigate the damage is of particular importance, and it must be examined whether the relative fulfilled this obligation when they terminated their employment or other income-generating activity in order to assist the direct victim. However, since the two types of compensation claims are intended to compensate different types of damage, the annuity to compensate the costs of tasks performed for the victim cannot be taken into account when determining the loss of income. The Supreme Court also upheld its position, which was also applicable in this case, that the disputed claims are additional claims based on other grounds, which must be assessed on a different legal basis, and that they are not covered and offset by any allowances received under other headings. These claims have different factual and legal bases, and the fact that the annuities and benefits were granted on different grounds does not preclude activities of a different nature and for different purposes being carried out at the same time.

c) Commentary

11 According to § 6:528 of the Civil Code, a person whose capacity to work has been reduced by damage may request an annuity to supplement their income if, following the harmful event, it does not reach the income they earned for the period preceding the harmful event for a reason for which they are not at fault. In this case, the Court found it justified to compensate the costs of taking care of the victim beyond such annuity. The question was, however, how such costs are to be calculated if caring is provided by a relative who gave up her job in order to do this for the victim. By compensating such costs, the general approach would be that the amount of the costs should be assessed and awarded. The Court, however, followed a different approach and assessed such costs as the income lost by the relative. The starting point for this approach was that the duty of the victim to mitigate loss was fulfilled by the relative as she gave up her job. The approach of the Supreme Court does not seem to be correct in the sense that the duty to mitigate loss should not result in spending more on mitigating the loss than the costs that are actually needed, because this may lead to overcompensation.

3. Supreme Court, BH 2024 no 84 Case 2, Kúria Pfv.I.20.191/2023/7, 2024 February: Establishing Compensable Loss

a) Brief Summary of the Facts

The defendant caused damage to the structures, fixtures and fittings of the building owned by the plaintiff, while possessing it. The plaintiff claimed the repair costs as specified in the claim. The defendant pleaded that the plaintiff sold the building in the meantime and ownership of the building was transferred to the buyer accordingly. Thus, the plaintiff is no longer in a position to repair the building. Further, because the price at which the plaintiff sold the building was not reduced due to expected repair works, the plaintiff suffered no compensable loss. 12

b) Judgment of the Court

The court of first instance decided for the plaintiff and awarded damages. The court of second instance reversed this judgment and rejected the claim entirely. According to the arguments of the court of second instance, the wrongful conduct and the occurrence of damage may be separated in time, but compensation is due when the damage occurs. However, due to the reparative function of compensation, it is still possible that facts which occur later may have an impact on compensation. If, for example, the victim fails to comply with their obligation to mitigate the damage after the damage has occurred and does not act as would be expected under the given circumstances of the case in order to reduce the loss, the resulting damage should not be compensated. However, within the scope of the rules concerning unjust enrichment, any benefit resulting from the damage must be deducted from the compensation. That is, any financial benefits arising from the damage caused to the victim, even if they arise later, must be deducted from the damages. Thus, compensation is due immediately upon the occurrence of the damage, but it is still possible that subsequent events may affect the compensation, because its purpose is reparation, ie the restoration of the interest of the victim that has (still) been impaired. The right to claim costs is relevant in determining liability for damage if the tortfeasor's conduct causes the victim a loss, the elimination or reduction of which requires the payment of certain costs, based on the decision of the victim: in such cases, the court has to decide on the justification of the costs claimed. However, if the financial interest ceases to exist in the 13 meantime, there is no financial disadvantage that would need to be repaired, and therefore the payment of costs in this connection can no longer be justified.

14 The court of second instance established its decision on the fact that the plaintiff had not actually carried out the repairs and could no longer do so due to the sale of the building and did not refer to the fact that the purchase price paid to him had been reduced due to the dilapidated condition of the farm building. According to the buyer's witness statements cited by the court of second instance, the farm was in a satisfactory condition for them, and they were interested in the location of the farm rather than the buildings on it, which they considered to be dilapidated and neglected, but they did not find any signs of damaging behaviour. The court of second instance concluded that there is no financial disadvantage that needs to be eliminated or reduced, and therefore the costs claimed by the plaintiff as compensation are not justified, taking into account the criteria of reasonableness and expediency.

15 The Supreme Court upheld the judgment of the court of second instance on the same grounds.

c) Commentary

16 The approaches of the court of first instance and the approach of the higher courts were different. The starting point of the court of first instance was that the loss occurred when the building was damaged and once this loss occurred, a claim emerged to compensate it. That is, as the right to have the loss compensated emerged, such a right, and the claim enforcing it, is not extinguished by the fact that the ownership of the damaged object has been transferred. The building was a part of the plaintiff's assets and did not cease to be so. The higher courts, however, concluded that the fact that such claim emerged does not mean that it cannot be rejected as a result of facts that no longer support such a claim. If the plaintiff was able to prove that the price of the farm sold was reduced by the decrease in the value of the building, the higher courts also would have assessed the case differently.

4. Supreme Court, BH 2024 no 131, Kúria Pfv.III.20.881/2023/6, 2024 March: Victim's Contributory Negligence in Context of Liability for Extra-Hazardous Activity

a) Brief Summary of the Facts

A person without a driving licence was driving a car that belonged to someone else. The car was designed for five people, but there were six passengers. The rear row of seats was equipped with three three-point seat belts, but none of the passengers in the rear seats were wearing seat belts. All of them had consumed alcohol before starting the journey. The driver was travelling at a speed of 140–145 kilometres per hour in a rural area, instead of the permitted 90 kilometres per hour, on a section of road with a left-hand bend. Noticing the bend, he corrected with an extreme steering movement, as a result of which he lost control of the vehicle. He first drove onto the right-hand shoulder, then returned to the left-hand side, collided with a road sign, and the front right of the vehicle crashed into the wall of a ditch next to the road. The vehicle then spun around several times around its vertical axis, in the course of which, the rear right side of the vehicle hit the ditch wall, causing the passengers in the rear seats to be thrown out of the vehicle. The plaintiffs were the passengers who suffered serious personal injury and their close relatives. The defendant was the insurer of the car's owner. The plaintiffs claimed damages as compensation for their losses which resulted from the accident. The defendant pleaded that the plaintiffs contributed to their personal injury negligently as, at the time of the accident, and with their consent and knowledge, an intoxicated person without a driving licence was driving the vehicle, and the plaintiffs accepted the increased risk of damage by this conduct and assumed the risk of serious damage by their conduct. The defendant also referred to the fact that the plaintiffs entered the vehicle in an irregular manner, with four of them sitting in the back, and that they did not wear seat belts. In its interpretation, only that damage must be compensated which would have occurred even if the plaintiffs had not acted negligently. 17

b) Judgment of the Court

The court of first instance, in its interim judgment, established the defendant's liability and reduced liability only vis-à-vis one of the plaintiffs. The court assessed whether wearing a seatbelt could have prevented such serious personal injury. As 18 to plaintiff 2, the opinion of the expert appointed by the court that the proper use of the seat belt would have prevented injuries requiring medical treatment and no permanent disability would have been expected for the passengers travelling in the left and middle seats, was considered relevant. For this reason, it considered that a causal link between the more serious injuries sustained by plaintiff 2 and the failure to fasten the seat belt could be clearly established, and, assessing the hazardous nature of the activity to the detriment of the defendant, it determined the extent of the defendant's liability at 40 % of the damage suffered by plaintiff 2. In determining the extent of contributory negligence, no significance was attached to the fact that the first and second plaintiffs had consumed alcohol prior to the accident. Furthermore, in determining the extent of contributory negligence, the court did not attach any significance to the fact that the plaintiffs had consumed alcohol before the accident and that there were four people sitting in the back seat, as these factors could not be causally linked to the injuries suffered. Liability for contributory negligence should be determined on a percentage basis and is not limited to loss that would have occurred even with the contributory negligence of the victim.

19 The court of second instance upheld the judgment. It confirmed that, according to § 6:537(1) of the Civil Code, when determining the proportion of contributory negligence, the primary consideration is the fault of the victim, which may be taken into account as a mitigating factor in relation to liability for the consequences of the damage. It emphasised that the contributory conduct, the causal link between the damage and that conduct, and the fault of the victim had to be proven by the operator or, in the present case, by the defendant liable for the damage caused by the operator. The court of second instance agreed with the defendant's argument on appeal that, in the case of compensation for damage caused by an extra-hazardous activity, the proportion of the damage to be shared should be determined in proportion to the degree of contributory negligence. It also pointed out that, in the causal chain leading to the damage, only the contributory conduct of the victim that can be linked to the damage should be assessed. The court of second instance also emphasised that, according to the expert opinion, the direct cause of the accident was the driver's absolute and relative speeding and the extreme steering manoeuvre he made as a result of the dangerous situation that arose. It pointed out that there was no evidence from the case file from which it could be concluded that the driver's lack of a driving licence or his alcohol consumption were causally linked to the accident and thus to the damage suffered by the first and second plaintiffs.

20 The court of second instance confirmed that the court of first instance had decided on the percentage distribution of damages in accordance with consistent and established case law and saw no legal basis for reviewing this decision. In

its view, the contributory negligence ratio determined by the court of first instance was also considered appropriate, taking into account the driver's culpable conduct in exceeding the speed limit. In the case of plaintiff 1, the court of appeal agreed with the court of first instance that the failure to fasten the seat belt constituted contributory negligence on the part of the victim, giving rise to a share of the damage. It also agreed with the court of first instance that, since according to the expert opinion, the injuries resulting in permanent disability could have occurred with a 50 % probability even if the seat belt had been worn, and since the extra-hazardous nature of the activity had to be assessed to the detriment of the defendant, the conduct of the first plaintiff did not, in essence, justify a division of damages. Therefore, it attached significance to the fact that plaintiff 1 would most likely have suffered the same damage even if he had fastened his seat belt.

The Supreme Court upheld the judgments of the lower courts. 21

c) Commentary

According to § 6:537 (1) of the Civil Code, providing the rules on contributory negligence in the context of the specific form of liability for extra-hazardous activities, an operator is not required to compensate any loss which arises as a result of the fault of the victim. While apportioning liability for damages, the hazardous nature of the activity is to be taken into account to the detriment of the operator. 22

The judgments suggest that within the scope of liability for extra-hazardous activities, while applying § 6:537(1), which sets out the rules on contributory negligence on the part of the victim, there is no need to consider the fault of the operator or, in its place, the actual wrongdoer. However, this does not mean that in cases where the operator or the actual wrongdoer caused the damage resulting from an extra-hazardous activity through culpable conduct, this should not be taken into account when determining the proportion of damage to be shared. Such conduct justifies the application of a more stringent apportionment of damage to the operator. 23

That is, the risk of the driver's fault had been shifted to the operator vis-à-vis the victims of the accident. 24

5. Supreme Court, BH 2024 no 184, Kúria Pfv.I.20.807/2023/5, 2024 April: Civil Law Liability for Legislation

a) Brief Summary of the Facts

25 On 20 May 2016, the Parliament amended the regulations on reducing smoking among minors and on the retail sale of tobacco products. With this legislation, the legislator prohibited the retail sale of electronic cigarettes, refill bottles and electronic devices that imitate smoking in shops other than national tobacco shops. At the same time, it prohibited the distance selling of electronic cigarettes and refill bottles. As a result, the plaintiff's online sales activities became impossible and it was forced to close its shops.

26 In its decision 3/2020 (I. 3.) AB, the Constitutional Court found that the Parliament had committed a fundamental violation of the Fundamental Law by failing to provide adequate compensation for those affected by the restriction of the right to engage in business by limiting the retail sale of electronic cigarettes and related products to tobacco shops subject to a licence. It called on the Parliament to fulfil its legislative obligation by 30 June 2020. The plaintiff claimed damages as compensation for the loss caused by the legislation according to § 6:519 of the Hungarian Civil Code providing the general rule of fault-based liability. According to the claim, the defendant Hungarian State failed to implement the decision of the Constitutional Court properly, because the defendant still does not allow the plaintiff to continue its activities by establishing new concession sites. As a result, the plaintiff is unable to sell electronic cigarettes in retail outlets, which results in loss. According to the plaintiff, the specific legislation providing for compensation did not remove the unlawfulness of the wrongful conduct of the legislator. The unconstitutionality could only have been remedied by the adoption of legislation which, on the one hand, ensures the continuation of the activity and, on the other hand, provides for compensation for the loss caused. This would only be capable of remedying the unlawfulness for the future; in the meantime, the defendant is obliged to pay full compensation. The specific legislation on compensation does not affect the right to full compensation under the Civil Code in any way.

b) Judgment of the Court

27 According to the court of first instance, as a rule, the disadvantages arising from legislation must be borne by everyone, including the plaintiff. The Constitutional Court qualified the restriction leading to the impossibility of the plaintiff's business activity as constitutional but found that compensation for the disadvantages

is needed and called on the Parliament to enact rules in this regard. In its claim, the plaintiff sought compensation for lost profits due to the impossibility of carrying out its activities, which is not related to the unconstitutionality established in the Constitutional Court's decision. The damage claimed arises from the loss of profit which is causally connected with the introduction of the restriction, even though the Constitutional Court did not find the introduction of the restriction to be contrary to the Fundamental Law. In the absence of this, no related claim for damages can be enforced. The Constitutional Court found that the legislature had failed to provide for adequate compensation, and therefore the plaintiff could only claim such compensation. The amount of such compensation may be determined by law or, in the absence of legislation, by the court. In the case at hand, the legislature fulfilled its obligation under the Constitutional Court's decision, thereby remedying the unconstitutionality. The Court therefore had to examine whether it had jurisdiction to review the compensation to determine whether it was adequate. The legislature determined the amount of compensation in legislation. The purpose of the legislation is to comply with the legislative obligation laid down in the Constitutional Court's decision and to provide for full compensation. Although the Court examines in every case whether a piece of legislation is contrary to the Fundamental Law, it does not have the power to disregard the application of the legislation if it finds that it is contrary to the Fundamental Law. It only has the power to refer the matter to the Constitutional Court. In the present case, the court of first instance did not raise any concerns regarding the constitutionality of the legislation ordering compensation. According to the Constitutional Court's decision, the plaintiff is only entitled to compensation, the amount of which is determined by law. The court has no power to disregard the law and cannot award a different amount of compensation. Therefore, the court rejected the claim.

The court of second instance upheld the judgment and the judgment of the 28
lower courts was confirmed by the Supreme Court as well.

c) Commentary

Liability of the legislator for improper law-making is a controversial issue in Hun- 29
garian legal theory and practice. While lower courts are tending to establish such State liability on the basis of the general doctrine that causing loss creates a private law relationship between the State and the citizen in tort, the Supreme Court follows the principle that law-making, including omissions of it, is governed by public law. That is, improper legislation is a failure to comply with obligations stemming from public law and the consequences are also to be governed by public

law. The doctrine that damages for improper legislation should be awarded if the Constitutional Court established law-making or omissions that are incompatible with the Fundamental Law of Hungary is a compromise followed by the Supreme Court.

30 The specific element of this case was that the State provided compensation via specific legislation, in line with the judgment of the Constitutional Court. The questions were whether this excludes establishing liability for improper legislation in private law and whether the compensation provided by the legislator could be overruled by the court. The answer of the courts was affirmative as to the first question, while negative as to the second one. Thus, if the Constitutional Court finds that non-compliance with the Fundamental Law can be eliminated by providing compensation, the legislator eliminates unconstitutionality and the ground for liability by providing such compensation. Whether the compensation is fair should be decided by the Constitutional Court again, because ordinary courts cannot do so due to lack of competence.

6. Supreme Court, BH 2024 no 207, Kúria Pfv.III.20.282/2024/5, 2024 May: Liability for Accidents

a) Brief Summary of the Facts

31 Plaintiff 1, a relative of plaintiffs 2–6, was involved in a traffic accident while riding a motorcycle. As a result of serious fractures, both of his lower limbs were amputated. His overall health impairment is 80 %. He is unable to care for himself without assistance.

b) Judgment of the Court

32 The court of first instance decided for the plaintiff and awarded damages. With regard to the additional costs for medical aids, based on witness testimony and expert medical evidence, the court of first instance established that the use of an active prosthesis would enable plaintiff 1 to move around safely and his movements would become more dynamic and smoother. At the same time, it took into account that it had already awarded damages to plaintiff 1 and ordered the defendants to compensate him for other damage on other grounds. In the court's view, this other damage and the claim for annuity due to the active prosthesis overlapped, and therefore dismissed the claim for the latter. It also pointed out that plaintiff 1 is free to dispose of the amount of compensation and may therefore

use the amounts awarded on other grounds to purchase the active prosthesis at his discretion.

The court of second instance confirmed the grounds of the judgment of the court of first instance but increased the sums awarded. With regard to the additional costs for medical aids, the court of first instance found that the use of the type of bilateral active prosthesis specified in the claim was justified for plaintiff 1 and that the submitted price quotations also supported the amount claimed. In contrast, in view of the arguments put forward in the appeal and the counter-appeal, it took the view that the action was premature before the optimal body weight for wearing the active prosthesis had been reached and that the conditions for awarding the costs on a lump sum basis were not met. It explained that the expert finding that the insertion of an active prosthesis on both sides could result in an exponential improvement in the first plaintiff's living conditions did not in itself mean that certain costs covered by the allowance would not arise at all in the future. It also pointed out that, from an expert point of view, there was no reason that would objectively preclude the use of an active prosthesis by plaintiff 1, and therefore he could claim the cost of purchasing the active prosthesis regardless of when he would reach his desired body weight. 33

c) Commentary

The most important implication of the judgment sems to be that the essential criterion for compensation is that it serves to compensate damage that will arise regularly in the future, at precisely calculable intervals, and whose amount can be determined in advance. Where applicable, factors of uncertainty such as technological developments or changes in the victim's needs due to their condition mean that the cost for medical aids does not constitute damage that would justify a claim for compensation, even if it is already foreseeable that replacement will be necessary after a certain period of time. 34

7. Supreme Court, BH 2024 no 265, Kúria Pfv.I.21.045/2023/8, 2024 May: Transfer of Land on the Basis of Forged Contract

a) Brief Summary of the Facts

35 The plaintiff purchased the property in question from the owner listed in the land register, paid the purchase price, registered his ownership, cleared the property of any encumbrances and began to develop it. After this, in cancellation proceedings brought by the actual owner of the property, the court found that it was not the actual owner who had sold the property but an unknown person who had forged the document and had signed the contract of sale, whereby the first purchaser acquired the property and then sold it to the plaintiff's seller. Thus, no contract was concluded between the owner and the first buyer, and the contract concluded by the plaintiff was invalid. On the basis of the final judgment, the real estate authority deleted the plaintiff's ownership and re-registered the ownership of the original owner. The plaintiff brought an action for damages against the real estate authorities involved in the case.

b) Judgment of the Court

36 In its judgment, the court of first instance found that the conduct and omissions complained of by the plaintiff had been committed by the defendants in the exercise of public authority. On the basis of an examination of the merits of the claim, it concluded that defendant 2 was not liable for damages. With regard to defendant 1, it proceeded from the fact that the plaintiff had referred to two acts of defendant 1: firstly, that it had registered the ownership despite a formal defect in the contract between the owner and the first purchaser, and secondly, that when it became aware of the suspicion of a criminal offence in connection with the contract, it did not withdraw the registration decision. With regard to the latter, the court found that referring to such omission was not correct. However, it held that defendant 1 had acted unlawfully in registering the ownership of the first purchaser.

37 On the basis of the available evidence, it could be established that the document on which the registration was based contained only the post office box address of the countersigning lawyer and not the registered office of the law firm, and, therefore, it did not meet the formal requirements for registration. The court pointed out that the examination of the requirements is not a legal activity

based on assessment, therefore, in the present case, there can be no question of the incorrect application of the law. Defendant 1 is liable for the damage caused by registering the change of ownership contrary to the provisions of the law by failing to indicate the registered office of the countersigning lawyer.

In examining the causal link, the court of first instance explained that, accord- 38
ing to the *conditio sine qua non* theory, any antecedent event of the damage shall be deemed as the cause of the damage without which it would not have occurred. However, if causality is defined in this way, a number of circumstances that are only remotely related to the damage could also be considered causes. Therefore, judicial practice examines which of the conditions identified are relevant from a civil law perspective. According to the theory of adequate causality, only those conditions are considered causes which have an adequate link to the damage. In the view of the court, if defendant 1 had not unlawfully registered the ownership of the first purchaser, the latter would not have been able to transfer the property to the intermediate acquirer from whom the claimant purchased it, and the plaintiff would not have paid the purchase price for the property he hoped to acquire. Therefore, the claim for damages in respect of the purchase price is causally linked to the unlawful registration by the first defendant. It is clear that the initial link in the chain of causation is the forged contract of sale, but if the first defendant had fulfilled its obligation under the law, the registration would not have taken place and the claimant would not have suffered any damage. The court of first instance found that, in the absence of unlawful registration, the plaintiff would not have acquired ownership and the original owner of the property would not have had to bring an action for cancellation, and thus the claimant would not have incurred any costs in connection with the proceedings. Therefore, the claim for damages to compensate the costs of the cancellation proceedings is also causally linked to the unlawful registration by defendant 1.

The court of second instance reversed the judgment and dismissed the claim 39
against defendant 1 as well. The court of second instance agreed with the lower court that the omission of defendant 1 was unlawful and negligent. However, in the opinion of the court of second instance, the plaintiff's damage can be attributed to two relevant reasons: on the one hand, the deletion of the original owner was the result of a criminal offence, based on a forged sales contract, and on the other hand, the plaintiff was not the direct contractual partner of the original owner and the plaintiff's seller is still unwilling to repay the purchase price. The registration based on the false document actually caused damage to the original owner of the property, who transferred his damage to the plaintiff through the cancellation proceedings. It was the plaintiff who ultimately suffered damage because the seller did not repay the purchase price, even though he was obliged to do so. Therefore, overall, the plaintiff's damage was caused by the fact that he pur-

chased a property of which he was ultimately unable to obtain ownership and for which he was unable to recover the purchase price. According to the arguments of the court of second instance, these two circumstances are not linked to the omission of defendant 1. If any of the events had occurred differently, ie if defendant 1 had noticed the formal deficiency in the document, the original owner would have appealed, the lawyer would have taken more decisive action, and it is highly likely that the first defendant would have been able to prevent the damage. If the formal defect in the document had been noticed, if the original owner had appealed, or if the lawyer had taken more decisive action, it is highly likely that the damage could have been prevented and the chain of events leading to the damage could have been broken, but these events, either individually or together, did not cause the loss.

40 The court of second instance concluded that there was no causal link between the omission of defendant 1 and the loss suffered by the plaintiff. Therefore, the liability of defendant 1 for damages could not be established. The Supreme Court upheld the final judgment.

c) Commentary

41 In the case at hand, the courts disagreed on how to establish the causal link between the omission of the authority and the loss of the plaintiff. The difference was that while the court of first instance held the omission of the authority as a causal link, the higher courts did not. The courts agreed that, according to the but-for test, natural causation can be established but the higher courts did not establish legal causation. Although it has not been articulated in the arguments, it seems that the higher courts did not assume that the duty of the authority to control the compliance of the documents with legal requirements for the transfer of land has as its purpose the protection of the interests of third parties, especially subsequent buyers. For this reason, they rejected establishing a causal link between the omission of the authority and the plaintiff's loss.

8. Supreme Court, BH 2024 no 267, Kúria Pfv.III.20.424/2024/4, 2024 August: Liability for Traffic Accident

a) Brief Summary of the Facts

On 30 June 2016, plaintiff 1 was involved in a traffic accident on a motorway in Germany as a passenger in a vehicle, in which he suffered life-threatening injuries and damage to his health. The accident was preceded by a vehicle slowing down and stopping in the right-hand lane of the motorway due to the traffic situation ahead. The driver of a semi-trailer combination (ie an articulated truck) travelling behind in the same lane noticed this too late and was forced to brake suddenly. As a result, the articulated truck lost stability and swung to the left and collided with the vehicle in front. The vehicle carrying plaintiff 1 as a passenger was travelling directly behind the articulated truck that lost stability due to the emergency braking. In order to avert the danger, the driver of the vehicle where the plaintiff was a passenger steered to the left without any error on his part and then applied the brakes forcefully, but due to the shortened braking distance caused by the collision of the vehicles in front of him, he was unable to avoid an accident and his vehicle collided with the semi-trailer that had swung out to the left. The operator of the vehicle transporting plaintiff 1 had a compulsory motor vehicle liability insurance relationship with the defendant. Plaintiffs 1 and 2 were the children of plaintiff 1. In their claim, the plaintiffs requested that the defendant be ordered to pay damages to plaintiff 1 and compensation for pain and suffering to all three plaintiffs. In their plea, which also included a statute of limitations defence, the defendant requested that the claim be dismissed. 42

b) Judgment of the Court

The court of first instance, in its interim judgment, established the liability of the defendant. The judgment was upheld by the court of second instance and also by the Supreme Court. 43

c) Commentary

According to § 6:535 of the Hungarian Civil Code, which provides for the rules on liability for extra-hazardous activities, a person carrying out a hazardous activity 44 is liable to compensate for the resulting damage. They are exempted from liability if they prove that the damage was caused by an unavertable event outside the scope of the hazardous activity. The case was covered by this form of liability. In the context of this rule, the unavoidable cause required for exoneration, falling outside the scope of activities involving an increased risk, means that two conditions must be met simultaneously: firstly, the cause of the damage must not fall within the scope of the hazardous operation, ie it must be external, and secondly, it must be unavoidable. Consequently, if either condition is not met, it is not necessary to examine the other condition. When examining external causes outside the scope of the dangerous operation, the traffic situation leading to the accident must also be assessed.

C. Literature

1. *Ákos Szalai*, A deliktuális felelősség joggazdaságtana [Law and economics of tort law] (Budapest, Orac – ELTE ÁJK 2024) 369 pp

45 This book is the first monograph in Hungarian on the economic analysis of tort law. The incentive-based approach applied in this book provides answers to the question of what social and economic impact court decisions have. Without this understanding, it is difficult to imagine responsible court decisions. In this formula, as the author emphasises, the victim is also a real actor, since the injuring party and the victim always cause the damage together, and liability for damage concerns allocating the risk of damage among the various actors. This approach is also important because one of the characteristic trends of recent decades in relation to liability for damage has been an almost compulsive search for someone to blame: the general idea is that if something bad happens, someone must always be held responsible; if no one can be found, then it must be someone who had a duty to prevent the damage but failed to do so. In other words, the phenomenon described by the author as hindsight bias seems to be gaining ground. Against this backdrop, individual responsibility for one's own actions, which is a prerequisite for autonomy in a free society, is being pushed into the background. Freedom comes with responsibility, while responsibility can only be linked to free action. The principle of prevention, which the author also supports and considers a primary requirement in the functions of the law of damages, also suggests this link, because defence can only be expected in the case of free action. If the person actually or potentially affected, whether the victim or the party liable for compen-

sation, is unable to change their behaviour, there is no point in sending them a preventive message

2. *Balázs Tőkey*, Szerződésen kívüli kötelmek: károkozás és az egyéb kötelemkeletkeztető tények [Non-contractual obligations: damage and other facts creating obligations] (Budapest, Orac 2024) 281 pp

This textbook discusses tortious liability and other facts giving rise to obligations 46
outside of contracts. In addition, as a summary of the specific aspects of the law of obligations, it provides a detailed analysis of the issues of damage and risk allocation, primarily with a view to helping students prepare for their final exams. The book also covers case law to the extent necessary for educational purposes.

3. *Marianna Dzsula/Bálint Kovács/Mónika Major/Tibor Molnár/Péter Szabó*, A határon átnyúló kartellkár iránti perek gyakorlati kérdései [Issues of cross-border antitrust claims in court practice] (Budapest, Orac 2024) 248 pp

The breakthrough in the development of EU competition policy came with Regu- 47
lation (EC) No 1/2003 and Directive 2014/104/EU, which supplemented public law rules with private law instruments and made it easier to bring actions for damages for breaches of competition law. In addition to regulation, increasing attention is being paid in practice to private enforcement, where victims can claim compensation directly from cartel members. Effective enforcement of such claims, the amounts of damages awarded, together with the fines imposed in competition proceedings, are more effective in deterring undertakings from engaging in anticompetitive conduct. The current wave of competition law damages litigation began in 2018, following the European Commission's decision in the so-called truck cartel case. These 'follow-on' actions against truck manufacturers are pending in almost all Member States, implicitly triggering a 'competition' between national courts to see which forum system can provide the fastest and most effective legal protection for the injured parties. This could have serious implications for the future: since, under EU jurisdiction rules, the injured parties can choose between several Member States in which to bring their claims, they will do so where they have the best chance of success. Hungarian courts will also have to prove themselves in this 'European championship'. This volume compiles the pro-

cedural and substantive legal issues that have arisen so far in the truck cartel cases before Hungarian courts, as well as providing an insight into the results of the relevant court practice in four other European countries. The authors are judges who have dealt with such cases.

4. *András Pethő*, A kár és a sérelemdíj meghatározása az egészségügyi szolgáltató felelőssége körében [Defining harm and solatium doloris in medical malpractice cases] (Budapest, Wolters Kluwer Hungary Kft 2024) 212 pp

48 The aim of the book is to define the conceptual and substantive elements of damage as a consequence of causing harm and of compensation for pain and suffering among the conjunctive elements of civil liability, with particular emphasis on the tortious branch of civil liability. The author specifically aims to define damage and compensation for injury arising within the scope of healthcare providers' liability. The book primarily aims to provide feedback on types of cases that repeatedly arise in practice from the perspective of healthcare services, but at the same time, it provides examples that can be used for comparison to show what further claims may be possible in practice.

49 In line with the doctoral research on which it is based, the book reaches the level of theoretical abstraction by processing and evaluating the legal practice applied in litigation. Accordingly, it was written with the intention that its findings can be used in practice, not only in cases involving the civil liability of healthcare providers, but also in cases involving compensation and damages in general.

Eoin Quill

XV. Ireland

A. Legislation

1. Motor Insurance Insolvency Compensation Act 2024 (No 32 of 2024)

This Act implements the 2021 amendment to the Motor Insurance Directives[1] and 1
the Motor Insurers' Bureau of Ireland (MIBI) is nominated as the authorised compensation body for the purposes of the Directive.[2] The MIBI has carried out the function of providing compensation in respect of unidentified or uninsured drivers for many years and is now tasked with covering cases involving the insolvency of insurance undertakings.[3]

2. Patient Safety (Notifiable Incidents and Open Disclosure) Act 2023 (Commencement) Order 2024 (Statutory Instrument [SI] No 482 of 2024)

Article 2 of this SI commences the 2023 Act from 26 September 2024, except for a 2
single provision governing incident reviews by the Chief Inspector of Social Ser-

1 Directive (EU) 2021/2118 of the European Parliament and of the Council of 24 November amending Directive 2009/103/EC relating to insurance against civil liability in respect of the use of motor vehicles, and the enforcement of the obligation to insure against such liability [2021] Official Journal (OJ) L 430/1.

2 The Act came into force on 17 October 2024 by virtue of the Motor Insurance Insolvency Compensation Act 2024 (Commencement) Order 2024 (SI No 537 of 2024), art 2. Irish legislation can be accessed on the website of the Attorney General's Office (AG), <http://www.irishstatutebook.ie/home.html> and on the British and Irish Legal Information Institute website (BAILII), <http://www.bailii.org/>.

3 As required by arts 10a and 25a of Directive 2009/103/EC of the European Parliament and of the Council of 16 September 2009, relating to insurance against civil liability in respect of the use of motor vehicles, and the enforcement of the obligation to insure against such liability [2009] OJ L 263/11, as inserted by Directive 2021/2118 (fn 1).

https://doi.org/10.1515/9783111389271-016

vices.[4] Some technical details in respect of incidents just before or after birth were also added in a later SI.[5] The legislation introduces a mandatory notification procedure for certain adverse medical incidents; disclosures may not be used as evidence in tort proceedings but they may make persons aware of the potential for tort action.

3. Representative Actions for the Protection of the Collective Interests of Consumers Act 2023 (Commencement) Order 2024 (SI No 181 of 2024)

3 Article 2 of this SI commences the 2023 Act from 30 April 2024, making Ireland belatedly compliant with EU Collective Redress Directive.[6] The 2023 Act is briefly noted in last year's report.[7] The Act has been supplemented by two statutory instruments on procedural aspects of claims under the legislation.[8] It remains to be seen if the legislation will have any significant impact, though in principle it is useful to have this redress mechanism for cases where individual actions are unlikely due to the small amounts of individual losses.

4. The Court Proceedings (Delays) Act 2024 (No 12 of 2024)

4 This legislation is a belated response to the judgment of the European Court of Human Rights in *McFarlane v Ireland* and provides for compensation for court delays.[9] Section 11 establishes a statutory right to have proceedings conclude within a reasonable time and the Act provides a compensation mechanism if the right is breached. Part 4 establishes an administrative assessment procedure and, for applicants that do not accept the assessment, there is provision for an authorisation

4 The 2023 Act is noted by *R Byrne/W Binchy*, Annual Review of Irish Law 2023 (2024) 453 ff and briefly by *E Quill*, Ireland, in: E Karner/BC Steininger (eds), European Tort Law (ETL) 2023 (2024) 333, no 9.

5 Patient Safety (Notifiable Incidents and Open Disclosure) Regulations 2024 (SI No 501/2024).

6 Directive (EU) 2020/1828 [2020] OJ L 409/1.

7 *Quill* (fn 4) no 10.

8 Representative Actions for the Protection of the Collective Interests of Consumers Act 2023 (Prescribed Forms) Regulations 2024 (SI No 182 of 2024) and Representative Actions for the Protection of the Collective Interests of Consumers Act 2023 (Section 29) (Maximum Fee) Regulations 2024 (SI No 183 of 2024).

9 [2010] ECHR 1272, noted by *R Byrne/W Binchy*, Annual Review of Irish Law 2010 (2011) 642 ff.

to proceed to the Circuit Court (IECC). Part 5 governs proceedings in the IECC and includes provision for the award of compensation, based on the compensation levels of the European Court of Human Rights. Section 27 provides for an appeal to the High Court (IEHC) on a point of law. Section 8 provides that assessors are not liable in respect of the performance of their functions unless they do so in bad faith. Section 33 provides that judges or courts may not be held liable for a breach of the right in sec 11. The Act has not yet commenced at time of writing.

B. Cases

1. *Urban and Rural Recycling Limited & RSA Insurance v Zurich Insurance PLC*, Irish Supreme Court (IESC) 10 October 2024, [2024] IESC 43: Scope of Mandatory Motor Insurance[10]

a) Brief Summary of the Facts

An employee of URRL was injured by a recycling bin that he was loading on to a 5
truck, using an automated lifting device; the bin fell from the lifting device and struck the employee on the head. He took a tort action against his employer in respect of the personal injuries suffered.[11] Zurich provided motor insurance cover to URRL, while RSA provided the company with employers' liability cover. Neither insurance company accepted that the incident was covered by their policy. The central question was whether the incident was covered by the mandatory motor insurance provisions;[12] if so, Zurich would have to indemnify URRL, if not, then RSA would have to indemnify the employer.[13] The litigation was conducted between the two insurance companies, even though it was initiated by the employer seeking declaratory relief.[14] The IEHC found that the incident was covered

10 Most of the Irish cases cited can be found on BAILII (fn 2) and the Courts Service of Ireland's judgments database, <https://beta.courts.ie/judgments>.

11 The claim was settled for € 4.75 million, see [2024] IESC 43, [6].

12 Section 56 of the Road Traffic Act 1961 and art 12(1) of Directive 2009/103/EC (the Sixth Motor Insurance Directive) [2009] OJ L 263/11.

13 Strictly speaking, indemnity is not mandated in this case, since liability was never actually established but both insurers seem to have conducted the litigation on the assumption that the loser would indemnify the employer.

14 The claim was dealt with under the Special Case procedure in Order 34 of the Rules of the Superior Courts.

by the mandatory insurance provisions.[15] The Irish Court of Appeal (IECA) overturned the IEHC.[16] The IESC granted leave to appeal.[17]

b) Judgment of the Court

6 The IESC allowed the appeal and concluded that, if the employee's injury was the result of negligence by the employer, then it was covered by the mandatory insurance provision in the domestic legislation.[18] In doing so, the court determined three issues. First, the operation of the automated lifting device constituted use of the vehicle under the provision. Secondly, where the victim is a user of the vehicle, they are not excluded from the mandatory insurance cover. Thirdly, the owner of the vehicle can be a user of the vehicle through the agency of another.

7 The court did not have to resort to the interpretation of the Sixth Motor Insurance Directive to resolve the case and so, did not need to refer the case to the Court of Justice of the European Union. The court did expressly draw the legislature's attention to the fact that the domestic legislation may not properly implement aspects of EU law and that legislative amendments may be needed to ensure compliance with Ireland's obligations; otherwise, the State may be exposed to liability under the *Francovich* principle.[19]

c) Commentary

8 It is slightly surprising that the core issue – whether a user of a vehicle injured when operating machinery attached to the vehicle is covered by the statutory mandatory motor insurance provisions – had not been determined before. At first sight, the case looks more like one of product liability or employers' liability, rather than a motor accident case but, on closer inspection, it is difficult to fault the reasoning of the IESC on the key issues. The IESC noted that use of the vehicle

15 *Urban And Rural Recycling Ltd and Anor v Zurich Insurance Plc* [2021] IEHC 661 (Reynolds J); this judgment is not available on BAILII at the time of writing but is available on the Courts Service of Ireland's judgments database.
16 *Urban and Rural Recycling Ltd and Anor v Zurich Insurance Plc* [2023] IECA 11.
17 *Urban and Rural Recycling Limited and Anor v Zurich Insurance plc* [2023] IESCDET 63.
18 Section 56 of the Road Traffic Act 1961.
19 CJEU joined cases C–6/90 and C-9/90, *Andrea Francovich and Danila Bonifaci and others v Italian Republic*, ECLI:EU:C:1991:428 – [1991] ECR I-5357, [1993] 2 Common Market Law Reports (CMLR) 66.

had to be connected to its function as a means of transport and had regard to EU and English cases in determining that, since the contents of the bin were being loaded to be transported, this requirement was met in respect of the operation of the lift.[20] On the second issue, the IESC noted that the Irish legislation did not confine the insurance obligation to 'third party risks', unlike the equivalent English provision.[21] Thus, the fact that the claimant was a user of the vehicle at the time of injury could not be a basis for excluding his claim from the mandatory insurance obligation. There could be more than one user of the vehicle and injury of one by the other is included in the required insurance cover.[22] On the third issue, the IESC noted that use 'includes not merely driving but any act of control, management or operation'.[23] The court accepted that an owner of a vehicle could act through the agency of another to use the vehicle,[24] distinct from any issue of vicarious liability.[25] On the present facts, it could be the case that the employer was a user through the agency of the plaintiff, but any negligence by them in the management or maintenance of the vehicle would be distinct form the plaintiff's operation of the vehicle.

It is somewhat disconcerting to find that the court has doubts about Ireland's 9 compliance with the Motor Insurance Directives in other possible scenarios. The IESC specifically noted that there could be problems with the Irish legislation

20 Cases included CJEU 28.11.2017, C-514/16, *Rodrigues de Andrade v Proença Salvador*, ECLIEU: C:2017:908; CJEU 11.12.2019, C-431/18, *Bueno Ruiz and Zurich Insurance v Sánchez*, ECLIEU: C:2019:1082; CJEU 29.4.2021, C-383/19, *Ostrowski v Ubezpieczeniowy Fundusz Gwarancyjny*, ECLI:EU: C:2021:337; *Brown v Roberts* [1965] 1 Law Reports, Queen's Bench division (QB) 1 and *R&S Pilling v UK Insurance Ltd* [2019] United Kingdom Supreme Court (UKSC) 16, [2020] Law Reports, Appeal Cases (AC) 1025.

21 *Cooper v Motor Insurers' Bureau* [1985] 1 QB 575 found that a driver's injuries were not covered because of the wording of the English statutory provision. The IESC noted that the employee in the Irish case was no longer acting as a driver but was a user. The IESC noted *obiter* that even drivers would be included in the mandatory cover in Ireland where the injury to the driver was caused by another user.

22 Citing *Ö Gürses*, The Law of Compulsory Motor Vehicle Insurance (2020) at para 5.63–5.82.

23 [72] relying on *John T Ellis v Hinds* [1947] 1 Law Reports, King's Bench (KB) 475; *Briggs v Gibson's Bakery Ltd* [1948] Northern Ireland Reports (NI) 165 and *Turnbull v MNT Transport (2006) Ltd* [2010] Scottish Court of Session, Outer House (CSOH) 163, [2011] Scottish Law Times (SLT) 650.

24 Citing *RM Merkin/M Hemsworth*, The Law of Motor Insurance (2nd edn 2015) at para 5–69: *K McCormac/P Brown/N Watson/P Veits/J Woodhouse* (eds), Wilkinson's Road Traffic Offences (29th edn 2019) at para 10–49: synopsising the position in the English cases.

25 Citing *Gürses* (fn 22) at 5.63 on the distinction.

specifying that use must occur in a public place to be covered by the compulsory insurance provision and that it must be negligent.[26]

2. *Angela Kerins v Dáil Éireann, Ireland and the Attorney General*, IESC 18 June 2024, [2024] IESC 24: Misfeasance in Public Office; Parliamentary Immunity

a) Brief Summary of the Facts

10 The appellant, Ms K, was the Chief Executive of a not-for-profit health and social care organisation. Due to media disquiet about a number of issues, she was invited to appear before Parliament's Public Accounts Committee (PAC). She agreed and was questioned in an often-hostile manner for seven hours with only one short break and the questions went far beyond the issues identified in the request. Ms K was traumatised by this and was hospitalised shortly afterwards and attempted suicide on release from hospital. She was then asked to appear again before PAC, but declined; other members of the organisation agreed to appear instead. Despite being informed of her illness, PAC invited the other representatives of the organisation to criticise Ms K and sought to compel her appearance before the Committee and applied to the Committee on Procedures and Privileges (CPP) to do so. The CPP ruled that the investigation was *ultra vires* and it was discontinued. Ms K brought a judicial review action and included a claim for damages in respect of misfeasance in public office and breach of constitutional rights. In the module of the litigation concerned with declaratory relief, the IESC ruled that the individual members of PAC had immunity from suit in respect of all relief sought but left open the question of whether Dáil Éireann (the lower house of the Irish Parliament) could be liable in damages.[27] The present case concerned that question of liability. While the present case involves the appeal of a discovery application in the claim against the State defendants, the IESC ad-

26 Negligence has been interpreted to include deliberate misuse of a vehicle – *Mongan v Mongan* [2020] IEHC 262, [2020] 3 Irish Reports (IR) 678 – but there is a lack of authority on whether other tortious forms of liability, such as strict liability, are included in the compulsory insurance obligation under sec 56.

27 *Kerins v McGuinness* [2019] IESC 11, [2020] 1 IR 1 (*Kerins (No 1)* and *Kerins v McGuinness (No 2)* [2019] IESC 42, [2019] 2 Irish Law Reports Monthly (ILRM) 361), noted by *E Feldman*, Constitutional Law, in: R Byrne/W Binchy (eds), Annual Review of Irish Law 2019 (2020) 207 ff. A declaration of unlawfulness was granted against the Dáil in the latter decision.

dressed the substantive question as to whether the constitutional parliamentary privilege provided the defendants with immunity in respect of the damages claims.[28]

b) Judgment of the Court

The IESC concluded that privilege applied: as the defendants were immune from liability for damages, no discovery could be ordered in respect of the proceedings. Articles 15.10, 15.12 and 15.13 of the Irish Constitution[29] protect freedom of parliamentary debate and exclude judicial jurisdiction over members in respect of utterances in parliament (including parliamentary committees). The earlier litigation indicated that this could not be circumvented by collateral means by making the institution rather than the individual members accountable. However, institutional accountability for actions, as distinct from utterances, was possible. The core question here was whether the damage claimed by the appellant was caused by, or sufficiently closely connected to, utterances as distinct from actions. The IESC concluded that the PAC could have exceeded its authority in proceedings politely conducted and caused no harm; thus, in the present case, the harm flowed from the manner of questioning and not merely the unlawfulness of the scope of enquiry and so was sufficiently connected to protected utterances. 11

c) Commentary

As with the previous case (*Urban and Rural Recycling Limited*), it is unusual that this issue has not previously been determined in Irish law, given the long history of judicial consideration of the separation of powers. It helps to have clarity on the parameters of constitutional immunity in respect of the State, as well as the individual parliamentary representatives, in parliamentary committees. It is unfortunate for the appellant that she should be without redress for significant harm, both to reputation and to her health, that may have resulted from what were plainly unwarranted behaviours by members of PAC. It serves as a reminder that the ordinary principles of corrective justice through tort claims have to give way to the collective interest in the unfettered functioning of parliamentary 12

---

28 As did Owens J in the IEHC, *Kerins v Dáil Éireann & Ors* [2022] IEHC 489, refusing discovery as the proceedings were precluded due to the scope of the immunity.
29 Bunreacht na hÉireann (1937).

democracy and the vindication of individual rights in these circumstances is confined within the process of parliament's own oversight mechanisms.

3. *A v The International Protection Appeals Tribunal*, IECA 29 May 2024, [2024] IECA 133: *Francovich* Claim; Breach of Constitutional Rights

a) Brief Summary of the Facts

13 The second and third applicants applied for international protection in Ireland in December 2016. They later obtained permits to work while their applications were pending. The applications were unsuccessful and in February 2020 they lost their permission to work. Their child, the first applicant, was born in Ireland in April 2021 and in July 2021 his mother applied for international protection on his behalf; in November 2021 the parents reapplied for permits to work, based on vicarious exercise of their child's right of access to the labour market as an international protection applicant or, alternatively, a derived right to work based on the child's rights to reside in the State and to enjoy an adequate standard of living. This was rejected through the various levels of the administrative process. The applicants brought judicial review proceedings before the IEHC, claiming that Irish law did not properly implement the relevant EU Directive[30] and included a claim for damages under the *Francovich* principle and for breach of constitutional rights.[31] The IEHC rejected the application;[32] the child did not have a right of access to employment, due to his age, so the parents did not have a right to work on his behalf. The obligation to ensure living standards for the applicant child rested on the State, not the parents, so an entitlement to work could not be derived from

30 Directive 2013/33/EU of the European Parliament and of the Council of 26 June 2013 laying down standards for the reception of applicants for international protection [2013] OJ L 180/96.

31 CJEU C–6/90 and C-9/90, *Francovich*. For the principles governing a claim for breach of constitutional rights, see *BME McMahon/W Binchy*, The Law of Torts (4th edn 2013) [1.45] ff; *E Quill*, Torts in Ireland (4th edn 2014) 356 ff; *G Hogan/DG Morgan/P Daly*, Administrative Law in Ireland (5th edn 2019) ch 20, sec A; *W Binchy*, *Meskell*, The Constitution and Tort Law (2011) 33 Dublin University Law Journal (DULJ) 339; *G Hogan*, The Farthest – December 1972 (2019) 62 Irish Jurist (Ir Jur) 1.

32 *A (A Minor) v International Protection Appeals Tribunal (Labour Market Access)* [2023] IEHC 141 (Simons J). During the course of the proceedings, the parents were granted permission to reside and work in Ireland and the child was granted international protection. The damages claim remained a live issue.

this. On the constitutional right to seek employment, the restrictions on child labour were found to be proportionate and clearly within the legislative area of discretion.[33] A leapfrog appeal to the IESC was refused and the appeal went to the IECA.[34]

b) Judgment of the Court

The IECA held that the *Francovich* claim fails, as there was no vicarious or derived right of the parents to work and, consequently, there was no breach of EU law. The court accepted that a child has a right of access to the labour market under EU law but that its exercise may be restricted in practice (eg on grounds of age); that right is individual and personal and cannot be exercised vicariously and does not give rise to any derived right on the part of parents to work to provide for the child's needs. On the constitutional claim, the court found the exclusion of the parents from seeking work for the limited period involved on the facts was not a breach of their rights and they had no vicarious or derived entitlement based on their child's constitutional rights. 14

c) Commentary

The case raises another layer of complexity in the fraught area of rights of applicants for international protection. The decision ultimately rejects the development of the proposed additional layer. It is probably a correct interpretation of the law as the legislation at EU and domestic level currently stands – though predicting how the CJEU will interpret the EU provisions is difficult. As no rights were found to have been breached, the court did not have to engage with the other elements of either a *Francovich* claim or a breach of constitutional rights claim. The court did note, *obiter*, that the calculation of damages could be particularly problematic in a case such as this; if the parents' entitlement was vicarious or derivative, calculation would have to focus on the loss to the child, not on the total loss. 15

---

33 The restrictions are contained in the Protection of Young Persons (Employment) Act 1996; these provisions are also incorporated in the Statutory Instrument (SI) implementing Directive 2013/33/EU – The European Communities (Reception Conditions) Regulations 2018 (SI 230/2018), as amended.

34 *LA (A Minor Suing by his Mother and Next Friend AA) AA & NA v The International Protection Appeals Tribunal & Ors* [2023] IESCDET 81.

16 Another aspect of the international protection regime – the impact of delay – came before the IESC in a case that also involved a *Francovich* claim; this case has been referred to the CJEU, so we will have to await the outcome of that reference.[35]

4. *Hosford v Minister for Employment Affairs and Social Protection*, IECA 4 December 2024, [2024] IECA 294: Whistleblower; Victimisation Claim; Choice of Process

a) Brief Summary of the Facts

17 The claimant took proceedings before the Workplace Relations Commission (WRC) for victimization and wrongful dismissal, alleged to be breaches of sec 13(1) of the Protected Disclosures Act 2014.[36] The claim was held to be time-barred. He then instituted tort proceedings in the IEHC; the Minister applied to have that claim dismissed on the basis that the 2014 Act required claimants to elect between the WRC process and the courts. The IEHC refused to dismiss, as the WRC had not adjudicated on the substantive claim but had dismissed it on procedural grounds.[37] The Minister appealed.

b) Judgment of the Court

18 The IECA overturned the IEHC and dismissed the claim. Section 13(2) of the 2014 Act excludes a tort action where the plaintiff has taken a claim before the WRC on the same complaints against the same defendant.[38] The fact that the claim was

35 *LK v The International Protection Appeals Tribunal* [2024] IESC 42.

36 The 2014 Act is noted by *D Ryan*, Employment Law, in: R Byrne/W Binchy (eds), Annual Review of Irish Law 2014 (2015) 328 ff and *E Feldman*, Whistleblower Protection, in: R Byrne/W Binchy (eds), Annual Review of Irish Law 2014 (2015) 708 ff; also noted briefly by *E Quill*, Ireland, in: E Karner/BC Steininger (eds), European Tort Law (ETL) 2014 (2015) 263, no 2.

37 *Hosford v Minister for Employment Affairs and Social Protection* [2024] IEHC 154 (Mulcahy J). The claim considered in this report was one of four instituted by the plaintiff; the other three were dismissed by Mulcahy J and are the subject of a leapfrog appeal to the IESC, see [2024] IECA 294, [10].

38 The language of the 2014 Act is to 'make or present' a claim, while the Unfair Dismissals Acts 1977–2007 refer to 'initiating' a claim; the IECA ruled that there is no material difference in the three terms.

ruled out on procedural rather than substantive grounds makes no difference to the application of subsec 2. The meaning of the provision is clear and unambiguous and does not require any complex or convoluted interpretation to distinguish categories of cases decided on different grounds; the mere initiation of one process precludes the use of the other for the dispute raised.[39] The commencement of the process is the trigger for the exclusion of the alternate process, not the determination of the dispute under the chosen process. As a result, the present case was entirely suitable for striking out on the defendant's motion to dismiss.[40]

c) Commentary

It is useful to have clarification of the scope of the right of election between processes in sec 13(2). For claimants, it reinforces the importance of being alert to time limits, which are quite stringent in respect of WRC claims.[41] While such claims may have some advantages over litigation, they are not without some disadvantages and the time limit is clearly one of the latter. The claim is one of a series of complaints being litigated by the claimant against the Minister; an issue mentioned in the claimant's arguments to the IECA, but not forming part of the present appeal, is the constitutionality of sec 13(2). We may yet see this dispute arise before the courts in another guise. 19

5. *Enoch Burke v Mediahaus Ireland Ltd*, IEHC 13 June 2024, [2024] IEHC 348: Defamation; Defamatory Effect

a) Brief Summary of the Facts

The plaintiff has been involved in a long running dispute with his employers and has been imprisoned for contempt of court a number of times, due to persistent breaches of injunctions. During one such period of imprisonment, the defendants published an article in print and online alleging that the plaintiff had been moved 20

39 This is based on the principles of statutory interpretation, as set out in *Heather Hill v An Bord Pleanala* [2022] IESC 43, [2022] 2 ILRM 313.

40 The jurisdiction to dismiss is contained in Order 19 Rule 28 of the Rules of the Superior Courts; the current version of the rule is in the Rules of the Superior Courts (Order 19) 2023 (SI 456 of 2023).

41 6 months, with a possibility of being extended to 12. The time limit for the tort claim is 6 years for a financial loss claim.

from the general prison population to a different part of the prison for his own safety because he was annoying other prisoners by being outspoken on his religious beliefs. Following complaints from the plaintiff's family, the online version of the article was withdrawn and a clarification and apology were published in print and online, noting that he had never been in the general prison population and that a change of cell occurred for operational reasons and not for the reasons asserted in the article. The plaintiff instituted defamation proceedings in the IEHC and neither party sought a jury trial, so the case was heard and determined by a judge alone.

b) Judgment of the Court

21 Mulcahy J rejected the claim, finding that the factual inaccuracies in the story had no defamatory effect. The meanings of the various statements complained of were held to be that the plaintiff expressed his religious beliefs in a manner that tended to annoy others to the extent that some might turn violent against him, that he was oblivious to the impact his behaviour had on others and that he had an extremely poor relationship with some of his fellow prisoners. Mulcahy J then addressed whether such meanings could injure a person's reputation.[42] He held that a false allegation of the repeated expression of religious views could not injure reputation, given the constitutional rights to freedom of expression and religion.[43] He also found that continuing the expression of such views in situations where they may get an unfavourable reception could not be defamatory and may even be creditable, as being true to one's beliefs; the fact that it may be ill-advised to continue to do so was not considered defamatory either. On the final point, Mulcahy J noted that a person imprisoned for contempt might have more difficulty adapting to prison life than some other prisoners and so a false statement about failure to adjust well would not detract from his reputation among reasonable persons.

22 Mulchy J added *obiter* that, even if the false allegations had in principle been capable of any defamatory meanings, they did not injure the plaintiff's actual reputation. He further added that had there been any injury to reputation, the defen-

42 Section 2 of the Defamation Act 2009 defines defamatory effect as 'a statement that tends to injure a person's reputation in the eyes of reasonable members of society'.
43 Mulcahy J did acknowledge that attributing beliefs a person did not hold could be defamatory, but that did not arise in the present context.

dants would not have been able to avail of the defence of fair and reasonable publication, as the story was not one of sufficient public interest and its publication was not furthering any discussion of public benefit.[44]

c) Commentary

The rulings on the meaning of the publication and whether they are capable of defamatory effect are based on well-established principles, though an appeal court might draw different inferences as to meaning and effect from the primary facts established.[45] The interesting aspects of the judgment are the *dicta* on evidence of poor reputation and the fair and reasonable publication defence. On the first of those issues, sec 31(6) of the Defamation Act 2009 provides the court with a discretion to admit evidence on 'any matter that would have a bearing upon the reputation of the plaintiff, provided that it relates to matters connected with the defamatory statement'. Mulcahy J makes it clear that sec 31(6) represents a significant departure from the common law principles on reputational evidence.[46] Up to now, it has not been clear whether the discretion to admit evidence would be exercised in a similar fashion to the old rules, since there were no cases on the issue, but this ruling makes it clear that a greater degree of latitude is now afforded to defendants on this issue and this is a welcome development. On the facts of the case, Mulcahy J found that the plaintiff's reputation could not be harmed by anything in the impugned publication, due to what was widely known about the plaintiff in relation to his public expression of his religious views, his dispute with his employer and his imprisonment for contempt of court in proceedings related to that dispute. In this instance, the information on the plaintiff's reputation was used to show that there was no defamatory effect at all, although sec 31(6) specifies that the reputational evidence may be admitted 'for the purposes of mitigating damages'; conscious of this difference, Mulcahy J noted that if it was to be considered only in the context of damages, then he 23

44 The defence is contained in sec 26 of the Defamation Act 2009; see *N Cox/E McCullough*, Defamation Law and Practice (2nd edn 2022) ch 9; *McMahon/Binchy* (fn 31) [34.300] ff; *Quill* (fn 31) 340 ff.

45 The plaintiff subsequently asserted that several errors were made in the judgment, but these claims were addressed and rejected during the costs ruling – *Burke v Mediahuis Ireland Ltd* [2024] IEHC 424, [29] ff. On meaning and defamatory effect, see *Cox/McCullough* (fn 44) ch 3; *McMahon/Binchy* (fn 31) [34.50] ff; *Quill* (fn 31) 317 ff.

46 Relying on the analysis in *Cox/McCullough* (fn 44) [13–266 ff]. See also *McMahon/Binchy* (fn 31) [34.355]; *Quill* (fn 31) 328 ff.

would assess the damages as zero. The judge may be correct to say that in exceptional cases, a reputation may be so tarnished on an issue that a false and derogatory statement could have no adverse effect capable of being regarded as defamatory, but the law has not previously gone this far.

24 The treatment of the fair and reasonable publication defence is of some concern. The defence, derived from the expansion of qualified privilege in other jurisdictions,[47] was intended to provide expanded free speech protection to curb the high pro-plaintiff slant of traditional defamation law. After 15 years in force, it has had little impact and hardly any judicial consideration of its parameters. The interpretation of the defence here and in another IEHC decision, *Desmond v Irish Times*,[48] suggests that it will be a difficult defence to establish. On the facts, the defence might have failed on the narrow ground that the publishers did not afford the plaintiff, or his family, an opportunity in advance to give any comment or counter-narrative; this might have undermined the fairness aspect of the article. However, the judge's view that the story lacked public interest and that the discussion was not for the public benefit suggests that a wide range of stories will fall at these hurdles. Given that incarceration for contempt is a contentious issue and the plaintiff's story is a very prominent one, touching on a variety of important matters, some detail on the conditions of incarceration could well be regarded as meeting both requirements. It is also worth mentioning that an attempt to develop a broad version of the qualified privilege defence as generally available to the media was unsuccessful.[49] It is not surprising that the judiciary is not keen to develop a public interest version of qualified privilege alongside the fair and reasonable publication defence; a preference for focusing protection of public interest speech within the defence expressly designed for that purpose is understandable.

25 Apart from this case, the plaintiff's dispute with his employers was also back in the IEHC and a brief clarification on the civil contempt case reported last year is necessary. My earlier report suggested the fine for contempt was payable to the employer, but the IEHC has now clarified that the fine for civil contempt is payable to the State, though the employer, as the plaintiff in the civil action, has an entitlement to bring the enforcement proceedings.[50]

47 Particularly the approach developed in *Reynolds v Times Newspapers* [1999] United Kingdom House of Lords (UKHL) 45, [2001] 2 AC 127.

48 [2024] IEHC 134.

49 *Bird v Iconic Newspapers Limited* [2024] IECA 62.

50 *The Board of Management of Wilson's Hospital School v Enoch Burke (No 1)* [2024] IEHC 746; the fine was increased to € 1,400 daily. The earlier decision was *The Board of Management of Wilson's Hospital School v Burke* [2023] IEHC 144, noted by *Quill* (fn 4) no 22 ff. A garnishee order

6. Personal Injury

a) General Statistics

The Personal Injuries Resolution Board (PIRB) Annual Report 2023 showed a 10 % rise in claims compared to 2022, but this is still 35 % lower than 2019.[51] The total compensation awarded was significantly higher than in 2022, but still considerably lower than 2019.[52] The average award was € 18,537, representing a 23 % reduction from 2020 (the last full year assessed under the Book of Quantum, now replaced by the Personal Injury Guidelines).[53] The highest award made in 2023 was € 691,000, a slight increase on the previous year.[54] The distribution of claims showed a drop in the proportion of motor claims.[55] The acceptance rate for awards was 48 %, a slight increase.[56] A more detailed breakdown of PIRB awards is available in their two Personal Injuries Award Value Reports for 2023.[57] Preliminary figures for 2024 indicate a slight decline in the number of claims and a slight 26

to enforce the fine was made in *The Board of Management of Wilson's Hospital School v Burke (No 3)* [2025] IEHC 104.

51 Available at <https://www.injuries.ie/eng/about-injuries-resolution-board/reports/annual-report-2023.html>, accessed 19 May 2025. There were 20,263 claims in 2023, compared to 18,453 in 2022. There is a comparison of statistics from 2019 to 2023 in the report; some tables include figures back to 2016.

52 In 2023 there were 9,144 awards totalling € 170 million, up from € 141 million in 2022, but € 105 million lower than 2019.

53 The 2023 average for special damages was € 3,111, similar to the average of € 3,001 in 2022, but up 53 % on the 2020 average of € 2,027. The average for general damages was down 29 %, from € 21,850 in 2020 to € 15,426 in 2023. The Guidelines are discussed in *E Quill*, Ireland, in: E Karner/BC Steininger (eds), European Tort Law (ETL) 2021 (2022) 283, no 35 ff.

54 The highest award in 2022 was € 655,678. Serious injuries, leading to awards of over € 100,000, represented 1.2 % of all awards in 2023, compared to 0.9 % in 2022.

55 Motor claims down from 65 % in 2022 to 57 %; public liability claims 24 % (up 4 % on 2022); employer's liability claims 18 % (up 3 % on 2022); a new category – Garda (police) Compensation claims comprised 1 % of the 2023 claims.

56 The overall acceptance rate for 2022 was 44 %; the 48 % figure I reported last year was for November 2022, representing the high point of recovery since the introduction of the Personal Injury Guidelines in April 2021; *Quill* (fn 4) no 26.

57 The Personal Injuries Award Value Report Jan – June 2023, available at <https://www.injuries.ie/eng/about-injuries-resolution-board/reports/personal-injuries-award-value-report-jan-june-2023.html> and Personal Injuries Award Values 1 July 2023 – 31 December 2023, available at <https://www.injuries.ie/eng/personal-injuries-award-values-report-h2-2023.pdf>, both accessed 19 May 2025.

increase in the value of awards.[58] Under its research function, the PIRB produced a Report on Accidents involving Cyclists and E-Scooter Users at the end of 2024: amongst the wealth of detail in the report, it indicates that injured bicycle riders tend to be older and injured e-scooter users tend to be younger. There were 329 awards involving cyclists and 32 involving e-scooters, generating awards totalling € 9.84 million.[59] The PIRB has extended its mediation function to public liability and motor claims, having started with occupational injuries cases in 2023.[60]

27 The Courts Service Annual Report 2023 showed a slight increase in the number of incoming personal injury cases, with most of the increase occurring at IEHC level.[61] The IEHC awarded a total of € 256,515,241 in compensation in 336 cases – just over € 3 million more that in 2022. The IECC awarded € 16,700,875 in 871 cases – almost € 1.7 million more than in 2022. The District Court (IEDC) awarded € 2,158,170 in 403 cases – approximately € 0.64 million less than in 2022. The number of medical negligence cases was similar to 2022, but the total value of awards fell substantially, though they still represent a very substantial amount of the total compensation awarded by the courts.[62] The State Claims Agency (SCA) paid out € 376.8 million in compensation, incurring € 161.2 million in costs: this is an increase of 3 % on 2022.[63]

58 See Personal Injuries Award Values 1 January – 30 June 2024, available at <https://www.injuries.ie/eng/about-injuries-resolution-board/reports/personal-injuries-award-values-report-jan-june-2024.pdf> and the Personal Injuries Award Values Report No 8 H2 2024, available at <https://www.injuries.ie/eng/about-injuries-resolution-board/reports/personal-injuries-award-values-report-no-8-h2–2024.html>, both accessed 19 May 2025.

59 Available at <https://www.injuries.ie/eng/about-injuries-resolution-board/reports/report-on-accidents-involving-cyclists-and-e-scooters-users.pdf>, accessed 19 May 2025. Reports on public liability claims and motor claims were published in 2025 and will be noted in next year's ETL report; these can be viewed on the PIRB website.

60 The service was commenced on 8 May 2024 for public liability claims by the Personal Injuries Resolution Board Act 2022 (Commencement) Order 2024 (SI No 187/2024) and on 12 December 2024 for motor claims by the Personal Injuries Resolution Board Act 2022 (Commencement) (No 2) Order 2024 (SI No 681/2024).

61 Available at <https://www.courts.ie/acc/alfresco/2b552955-e0f9–41a2–80e7-c526d24651e2/Courts%20Service%20Annual%20Report%202023.pdf/pdf/1>, accessed 20 May 2025. There were 13,434 cases, compared to 12,459 in 2022. The breakdown of the 2023 cases by court is 4,538 IEHC (up from 3,766); 7,495 IECC (up from 7,151); 1,401 IEDC (down from 1,542).

62 € 167,162,945 awarded in 106 cases, compared to € 178,711,076 in 107 cases in 2022. The highest award was € 20.5 million, up from € 19 million in 2022.

63 National Treasury Management Agency Annual Report 2023 (2024); the extracts on the State Claims Agency are available at <https://stateclaims.ie/uploads/banner/State-Claims-Agency-Extracts-2023.pdf>, accessed 20 May 2025. The SCA handles claims against the State; activities are divided between 'clinical' and 'general'. There is overlap between the SCA figures and the Court Service Report figures. The SCA is reported to have paid out considerably less in 2024, see Irish

The National Claims Information Database indicates that motor insurance premiums rose by 2 % and claims as a percentage of premiums rose from 62 % in 2022 to 67 % in 2023.[64] Claims cost per policy is now similar to pre-COVID levels, with an increase in the number and value of damages claims, though there is a decrease in the number and value of injury claims. Direct settlement between insurance companies and claimants is still the most prevalent and quickest means of resolution.[65] The Personal Injury Guidelines are having a significant impact in reducing claims costs.[66] In respect of non-motor claims, there was an increase in the number and value of claims in 2023.[67] Insurance premiums rose by 4 %.[68] As with motor claims, claim costs were significantly reduced by the introduction of the Personal Injury Guidelines.[69] Contrary to motor claims, litigation is more widely used in employer's liability and public liability claims.[70] 28

Legal News, State Claims Agency paid out € 287 million in 2024 (5 March 2025); the report indicates the figure was obtained in answer to a parliamentary question.

64 *Central Bank of Ireland*, Private Motor Insurance Report 6: National Claims Information Database (2024), available at <https://www.centralbank.ie/docs/default-source/statistics/data-and-analysis/national-claims-information-database/private-motor-insurance-report-6-ncid.pdf?sfvrsn=1608671a_5>, accessed 20 May 2025. The 5th report had actually reported claims as 61 % of premiums.

65 45 % of cases, with an average resolution time of 1.9 years; PIRB settlements account for 17 % of cases and average 2.7 years; 37 % of cases resolved through the litigation process, averaging 5.1 years to resolve. For the purposes of these reports, 'cost' includes compensation levels and associated costs.

66 The cost of claims settled directly, without going to PIRB, was 38 % lower than under the Book of Quantum. The cost reduction for claims via the PIRB was 22 %. Claims settled immediately after the PIRB assessment were 39 % lower. There was insufficient data on the effect of the Guidelines in litigated cases, as 73 % of these cases in the latter half of 2023 were still governed by the Book of Quantum.

67 *Central Bank of Ireland*, Employers' Liability, Public Liability and Commercial Property Insurance Report 4: National Claims Information Database (2025), available at <https://www.centralbank.ie/docs/default-source/statistics/data-and-analysis/national-claims-information-database/ncid-annual-employers-liability-and-public-liability-insurance-report-4.pdf?sfvrsn=4b786a1a_10>, accessed 20 May 2025.

68 This figure relates to package policies (ie combining the different categories covered), not standalone policies; 86 % of all policies were package ones.

69 For employer's liability claims, the reduction was 31 % for claims settled prior to the PIRB process, 13 % for claims resolved via PIRB and 36 % for claims settled directly after the PIRB process. For public liability claims, the reductions were 29 % for pre-PIRB settlements, 22 % for claims resolved via PIRB and 35 % for claims settled directly after PIRB. There were not enough cases litigated under the Guidelines to gauge the impact on this category of case.

70 Only 10 % were resolved by direct settlement pre-PIRB; 14 % settled via PIRB; 5 % settled directly after PIRB; 68 % settled via litigation, before a court award and 3 % resolved via litigation, with a court award.

b) Constitutionality of Personal Injury Guidelines

29 In *Delaney v The Personal Injuries Assessment Board* a majority of the IESC upheld the constitutionality of the Judicial Council's Personal Injury Guidelines.[71] The principal reason for upholding the Guidelines was the fact that they had been subsequently endorsed by parliament in the Family Leave and Miscellaneous Provisions Act 2021; the original basis for the Guidelines in the Judicial Council Act 2019 was found by a majority to be unconstitutional, either as an impermissible delegation of the legislative function or an impermissible constraint on the judicial function. The detail of the decision will likely be of greater interest to constitutional lawyers rather than tort lawyers. From the perspective of tort law, we can be assured that the Guidelines will continue to be used in practice. The Judicial Council approved a draft second edition of the Guidelines in January 2025, recommending a 16.7% increase in damages levels to reflect inflation since the first Guidelines were introduced; the new edition will now need approval from the legislature to take effect.[72] The revised process governing the introduction of amended Guidelines is set out in Part 6 of the Courts, Civil Law, Criminal Law and Superannuation (Miscellaneous Provisions) Act 2024.[73]

c) Cases

30 There were several cases in the IEHC and IECA addressing the issue of damages in cases of multiple injuries, two of which are worth a brief mention.[74] In *Coughlan v CGR Construction Ltd*,[75] the plaintiff was injured when his stationary vehicle was struck in the rear by a truck; he suffered soft tissue injury to his right shoulder,

71 [2024] IESC 10, [2024] 1 ILRM 189.

72 The Harmonised Index of Consumer Prices (HICP) was used as the basis for the proposed increase. The new draft guidelines are available at <https://judicialcouncil.ie/assets/uploads/documents/Personal%20Injuries%20Guidelines%20-%20Draft%20Amendments%20as%20modified%20by%20the%20Board.pdf>, accessed 5 March 2025. The Government rejected the proposed increase, see <http://www.rte.ie/news/2025/0709/1522647-personal-injury-awards/>, accessed 9 July 2025.

73 The amendments came into force immediately upon enactment of the legislation, see sec 1 of the Act.

74 The appropriate process for assessment was discussed in a number of cases noted in last year's report, *Quill* (fn 4) no 30 ff. It principally comprises determining the damages for the dominant injury and adding an uplift for the other injuries (as opposed to assessing each injury independently and adding up the totals).

75 [2024] IECA 78.

neck, left wrist and chest; he also complained of headaches. The IEHC awarded him € 90,000 in general damages for non-pecuniary loss and € 6,758 for special damages; the shoulder injury was held to be the dominant one (involving significant rotator cuff damage) and most of the special damage related to the cost of a future operation to address the continuing shoulder injury.[76] Noonan J for the IECA reduced the amount for the dominant injury, based on two considerations. The first was an analysis of the Guidelines: the IEHC judge had classed the injury as being in the lowest of three sub-categories of serious shoulder injury but awarded damages at the highest point in the scale. Secondly, the comparison to other recent cases indicated that more significant injuries were getting significantly lower amounts than the IEHC awarded here.[77] Noonan J substituted an award of € 40,000 for the IEHC award of € 75,000 for the dominant injury; the revised amount represents the lower end of the serious category of shoulder injury and the upper end of the moderate category. The IECA found that the calculation of the uplift was based on some flawed reasoning, given that the medical evidence on the question of headaches was weak and the IEHC had allowed a significant amount in respect of this item. However, the € 15,000 uplift was not disproportionately high and so was allowed to stand. As the medical evidence on the need for an operation was weak, this item of special damage was disallowed by the IECA.[78]

In *Collins v Parm*,[79] the plaintiff was a passenger in a car driven by the defen- 31
dant: due to the defendant's negligence, the car crashed causing a range of injuries to the plaintiff. The trial judge assessed general damages at € 95,000, and applied a 15% deduction for contributory negligence because of the failure to wear a seat belt.[80] On appeal, Noonan J for the Court, noted that the parties in their arguments did not properly address the Personal Injuries Guidelines or the cases on their interpretation and, as a result, the trial judge did not have regard to the Guidelines or cases, bar some passing indications of some awareness of both.[81] In light of this, it is not surprising that the IECA found a failure to follow

76 *Coughlan v CGR Construction Ltd* [2023] IEHC 639 (Stewart J).
77 Noonan J used these cases as a 'reality check' considering the principle discussed in *Zaganczyk v Pettit* [2023] IECA 223, noted by *Quill* (fn 4) no 30.
78 Noonan J had regard to *O' Daly v Bus Éireann (Irish Bus)* [2023] IECA 232, noted by *Quill* (fn 4) no 33, in addressing the evaluation of evidence.
79 [2024] IECA 150.
80 Unreported, 25 October 2023, *ex tempore*; the judgment is not available on BAILII or the Courts Service of Ireland's judgments database at the time of writing. There was also an assessment of just over € 4,000 in special damages.
81 The judge divided the damages into a dominant injury and an uplift, showing some awareness of the Guidelines and methodology and made passing reference to one of the key decisions on

the statutory obligation to engage with the Guidelines.[82] After a careful evaluation of the plaintiff's injuries in light of the detailed factors in the relevant parts of the Guidelines and assessments in suitable comparator cases, the IECA reduced the assessment of general damages to € 55,000 and applied the contributory negligence deduction (which had not been appealed). The interesting aspects of the decision are the *dicta* of Noonan J. He acknowledges *obiter* that, while multiple injuries cases generally involve deductions to avoid overcompensation due to overlapping effects of injuries, the sum of multiple injuries may be greater than the total of the individual parts in exceptional cases.[83] He also noted that the precise method of calculation does not matter as long as the overall assessment provides a holistic view of the effects of injuries, including overlaps or exacerbations.[84] He further acknowledges there may be cases without a dominant or most severe injury, where multiple equally serious injuries arise and notes that judges should be careful not to undercompensate by discounting all of the injuries as non-dominant.[85]

32 In *Germaine v Day*,[86] the IEHC had to determine whether the plaintiff could recover damages for a psychiatric injury alleged to result from the defendant's negligent failure to diagnose her husband's terminal cancer. The defendant admitted a negligent failure to diagnose but denied liability on a number of grounds. It was clear that, even at the time of misdiagnosis, the husband's cancer was too advanced for him to be saved. The crux of the claim was that the plaintiff witnessed his rapid deterioration and death without being duly prepared. Egan J rejected the claim, as it failed to satisfy three of the required conditions set out in the leading IESC authority.[87] First, the plaintiff did not witness a sudden shocking event.[88] Sec-

multiple injuries – *Meehan v Shawcove* [2022] IECA 208, noted by *E Quill*, Ireland, in: E Karner/ BC Steininger (eds), European Tort Law (ETL) 2022 (2023) 307, no 34.

82 Under sec 99 of the Judicial Council Act, 2019 (amending sec 22 of the Civil Liability and Courts Act, 2004) as substituted by sec 30(a) of the Family Leave and Miscellaneous Provisions Act 2021.

83 Endorsing a *dictum* to that effect of Coffey J in *Keogh v Byrne* [2024] IEHC 19, [13].

84 Again, endorsing the view of Coffey J in *Keogh v Byrne* [2024] IEHC 19, [12]; he also referred to the principles in *Zaganczyk v Pettit* (fn 77) used in *Coughlan v CGR Construction Ltd*, above no 30.

85 The possibility of there being no dominant injury in a multiple injury scenario was also acknowledged by Noonan J in *Coughlan v CGR Construction Ltd*, above no 30, where he simply noted that the issue would have to be addressed in a suitable case; see also Coffey J in *Keogh v Byrne* (fn 84).

86 [2024] IEHC 420.

87 *Kelly v Hennessy* [1995] IESC 8, [1995] 3 IR 253; see *McMahon/ Binchy* (fn 31) ch 17; *Quill* (fn 31) 57 ff; *P Casey/P Brady/C Craven/A Dillon*, Psychiatry and the Law (2nd edn 2010) ch 9; *G Kelly*, Post Traumatic Stress Disorder, Mental Injury and the Law (2nd edn 2008); *B O'Hanlon*, PTSD and the Law [2020] 4(2) The Irish Judicial Studies Journal 79.

ondly, the plaintiff lacked proof of causation; even if she had been notified of her husband's condition in a timely manner, there was no evidence that the outcome for her mental health would have been any better. While these were given as the primary reasons for the decision, Egan J offered a third reason for rejecting the claim – even if the plaintiff could establish the necessary proximity and foreseeability for the purposes of a duty of care, it would not be just and reasonable to impose such a vague duty of uncertain scope on the defendant. The judgment offers an extensive discussion of the duty of care in respect of psychiatric injury and acknowledges the scope for differing interpretations of the foreseeability and proximity criteria. This opens the possibility for further developments in this area.[89] The case also demonstrates the limits of the existing criteria: depending on one's perspective, one could find grounds for criticism of the constraints generated by them and might question whether they are necessary.

Scanlan v Michael McDonnell t/a The Woodlands Caravan and Camping Park 33
provides yet another example of the courts treating an occupiers' liability claim as resulting from the plaintiff's own failure to take care.[90] The plaintiff tripped over an electrical cable providing power to the caravan she was staying in; Coffey J found that some element of trip hazard was an inevitable facet of providing electricity to the caravans and the plaintiff could easily have avoided the risk if she paid more attention to what she was doing. In those circumstances, he found no breach of duty on the defendant's part.

---

88 The possibility of a flexible approach to continuing events for the purposes of the sudden shock requirement was effectively foreclosed by the decision in *Harford v Electricity Supply Board* [2021] IECA 112, [2022] 2 IR 541, noted by *Quill* (fn 53) no 18 ff.

89 The discussion of foreseeability suggests the possibility of a wider interpretation than that applied in *Morrissey v HSE* [2019] IEHC 268 (Cross J) and *Mitchell v HSE* [2023] IEHC 394 (O'Connor J), noted by *Byrne/Binchy* (fn 4) 582 ff; *Quill* (fn 4) no 36. Egan J also noted that the approach to duty of care in Ireland need not be as constrained as that in *Paul v Royal Wolverhampton NHS Trust* [2024] UKSC 1, [2025] AC 459, noted by *CP McGrath*, England and Wales, in this volume, 167, no 6 ff.

90 [2024] IEHC 324, citing *Lavin v Dublin Airport Authority plc* [2016] IECA 268, noted by *R Byrne/W Binchy*, Annual Review of Irish Law 2016 (2017) 618 ff, and *White v Doherty* [2019] IECA 295, noted by *R Byrne/W Binchy* (eds), Annual Review of Irish Law 2019 (2020) 689 f; *E Quill*, Ireland, in: E Karner/BC Steininger (eds), European Tort Law (ETL) 2019 (2020) 289, no 34.

C. Literature

1. Articles

34 *J McGrath*, Ten Years Since the Protected Disclosures Act 2014: A Critical Review of the Enhancements to Whistleblowing Laws in Ireland (2024) 72 The Irish Jurist (Ir Jur) 25; *P Gavin*, Newcomer Injunctions: Equitable Innovation or Constitutional Challenge? (2024) 72 Ir Jur 50; *RÁ Costello*, The Test in *Kelly v Hennessy* and Article 82(1) of the General Data Protection Regulation (2024) 8(2) Irish Judicial Studies Journal 22; *M MacGrath/L Powell*, *Res Ipsa Loquitur* – A Rule, a Principle, a Maxim, a Doctrine, a Myth or a Convenient Label? (2024) 8(2) Irish Judicial Studies Journal 67; *E Gormley*, A Slapp in the Face for Legal Intimidation? Daphne's Law, The Defamation Bill, and the Future of Irish Legislation to Tackle Strategic Lawsuits against Public Participation (2024) 23 Hibernian Law Journal (Hibernian LJ) 57; *D Gilligan*, Constitutional Torts as Private Wrongs: *McGee v Governor of Portlaoise Prison* (2024) 6 ISCR 181; *H Biehler*, Dismissal of Proceedings on Grounds of Delay: Recent Developments (2024) 42 Irish Law Times (ILT) 6; *KA Richard*, Informed Consent in Nigeria: Addressing Cultural Challenges to the Norm of Individual Autonomy (2024) 42 ILT 91; *C Cass*, Vulnerability and the Irish Personal Injury Plaintiff (2024) 42 ILT 112; *M Donnelly*, Representative Actions: A New Frontier for Consumer Redress? (2024) 31 Commercial Law Practitioner (CLP) 55; *C Pepa*, A New Era for Whistleblower Rights? An Examination of the Amendments Introduced by the Protected Disclosures (Amendment) Act 2022 (2024) 21 Irish Employment Law Journal, (IELJ) 51; *KJ Sutton*, Navigating the Threshold: Exploring Disparities Between the Age of Responsibility in Criminal Offences and the Age of Consent to Medical Treatment (2024) 27 Irish Journal of Family Law (IJFL) 47; *M Peart*, Win/Win (2024) 118(2) Law Society Gazette (Gaz) 20 (Mediation, Personal Injuries); *J Verbruggen*, Could We, Should We Do More? (2024) 118(4) Gaz 20 (Catastrophic Injury, Rehabilitation, Costs); *K Walsh*, Serve and Protect (2024) 118(8) Gaz 34 (Civil Restraint Orders, Stalking & Harassment); *Á Bhreathnach*, Waiting on Redress (2024) 118(9) Gaz 22 (Historic Child Sex Abuse); *K Ahern*, Untangling the Threads (2024) 118(9) Gaz 42 (Causation); *O Kelleher*, Possibilities for a Right to Clean Air after Case C-61/21 *JP v Ministre de la Transition Écologique and Premier Ministre* (2023) 25 Irish Journal of European Law (IJEL) 133.

Elena Bargelli and Giulia Puleio

XVI. Italy

A. Legislation

1. Ministerial Decree (Decreto ministeriale, DM) 15 December 2023, no 232, entered into force on 16 March 2024: Medical Liability; Compulsory Insurance; Implementation of Medical Liability Law

This piece of secondary legislation does not directly impact on medical or hospitals' liability, being rather aimed to implement the compulsory insurance introduced by Law 8 March 2017 no 24 (Medical Lability Law – Gelli-Bianco Law). In essence, the decree establishes the minimum requirements for insurance coverage for public and private health and social care facilities and for healthcare professionals. It further regulates the minimum requirements of guarantees and the general conditions of operation of similar measures, including the direct assumption of risk and the rules for the transfer of risk in the event of a contractual takeover by an insurance company. It states that hospitals have to provide for a specific fund to cover the risks identified at the end of the financial year and another one including the total amount necessary to meet the requests for compensation presented during the financial year or during previous years. 1

2. Interministerial Decree (Decreto interministeriale) 25 November 2024, entering into force on 5 March 2025: Personal Injuries – *danno biologico* Tables

This important piece of secondary legislation aims to enforce the provision of the Insurance Code (Legislative Decree 7 September 2005 no 209) regarding the criteria for the calculation of damages for personal injuries (*danno biologico*). In particular, art 138 of the Insurance Code delegated to decrees of the President of the Republic the task of issuing tables for compensation for personal injuries for permanent invalidity between 10 % and 100 %. While the table for injuries up to 10 % 2

Note: Elena Bargelli authored nos 1-44, 75-77. Giulia Puleio authored nos 45-74.

https://doi.org/10.1515/9783111389271-017

was issued, the legislator did not implement the criteria for the calculation of damages corresponding to injuries up to 100 %. After twenty years of inactivity, on 24 November 2024, the Council of Ministries finally approved the table containing the amounts of damages corresponding to each point of invalidity, which varies according to the age of the victim and the severity of the injury. After a long legislative process,[1] the aforementioned Interministerial Decree upholds the 'Milan Tables', which have been elaborated by the Tribunal of Milan and used by courts of the whole national territory over the last twenty years for calculating *danno biologico* in the absence of a legislative provision.

3 The Interministerial Decree has been approved by Decree from the President of the Republic 13 January 2025, no 12 and will enter into force on 5 March 2025. After this date, the compensation for *danno biologico* following road traffic accidents and in cases of medical liability will be harmonised in the whole of Italy.

B. Cases

1. Corte di Cassazione (Italian Supreme Court, Cass) 24 January 2024, no 2375: Damage Caused by Thalidomide taken during Pregnancy; Prescription of the Action; *dies a quo*

a) Brief Summary of the Facts

4 The actor was born with phocomelia (a rare condition that affects babies at birth, causing the upper or lower limbs of the child to be underdeveloped or missing) because his mother, during pregnancy, took Thalidomide. He sued the Health Ministry for the consequential damage suffered as a consequence of his personal injuries. The defendant objected that the plaintiff's right to damages was prescribed, but the Tribunal rejected it by reasoning that the *dies a quo* starts to run on the date of submission of the claim. As a consequence, it upheld the claim and awarded € 319,573. Instead, the Court of Appeal reasoned differently and rejected the claim. It argued, in particular, that the Ministry withdrew the medicine from the market three years after the birth of the plaintiff as a consequence of its per-

1 See the advisory opinion of the Council of State 13 February 2024, <https://portali.giustizia-amministrativa.it/portale/pages/istituzionale/visualizza?nodeRef=&schema=consul&nrg=202400194&nomeFile=202400164_26.html&subDir=Provvedimenti>.

nicious effects. Against this background, it held it likely that paediatricians or other medical doctors informed the plaintiff or his relatives about the cause of his illness.

The plaintiff appealed to the Supreme Court, arguing that, according to well- 5
established doctrine, prescription starts from the time when the injured party has knowledge or perceives that the harm suffered is due to the wrongful conduct of a third party.

b) Judgment of the Court

The Supreme Court upheld the appeal. 6

The Court started by reminding that, according to well-established doctrine, 7
the limitation period of the right to compensation for damage runs not from the day on which the damage is caused or manifests itself, but from the time when the illness is perceived, or may be perceived, as unlawful damage by the injured party. To this end, the ordinary standard of diligence is required, which is assessed on the basis of the level of the scientific knowledge of the harmful effects of the product, to be appreciated according to the actual circumstances of the case. In particular, whether or not the medical doctor or the hospital duly informed the patient is a circumstance that plays a decisive role in assessing the latter's diligence. This doctrine, which was developed by the Supreme Court regarding damages for infected blood transfusion, was extended to Thalidomide cases.[2]

The Court concluded that the *exordium praescriptionis* coincides with the ap- 8
plication for the payment of the indemnity provided for by art 1 of Law no 229 of 29 October 2005, unless the defendant proves otherwise.

Against this background, the Supreme Court held that the judgment under ap- 9
peal was erroneous because it did not correctly apply the aforementioned doctrine by holding that the plaintiff had prior knowledge of the causal consequences of taking the medicine.

In considering it unlikely that the plaintiff's family members had not been in- 10
formed by paediatricians or general practitioners about the possible cause of the illness, it dated such knowledge to the year in which the diagnosis of phocomelia was given. In doing so, however, the Court based its reasoning on mere conjecture that was based 'on uncertain facts', thus violating the prohibition of *praesumptiones de praesumpto.*

2 Cass, ord 3 June 2020, no 1051.

11 The Court rejected the appeal and referred the case to another court of appeal for its further examination in the light of the following statement: 'The limitation period applicable to the claim for compensation for damage suffered in the prenatal phase as a result of consumption of medicine with teratogenic effects runs, as a general rule, from the submission of the administrative application for the payment of the compensation provided for by art 1 of Law no 229 of 29 October 2005, unless the defendant proves the previous knowledge of the causal link between the taking of the drug and the suffered pathology'.

c) Commentary

12 This judgment deserves to be mentioned because it deals with mass damages caused by the use of the drug Thalidomide, whose harmful effects were discovered years after its introduction. Compensation in the form of a public subsidy is provided for by Law no 229 of 29 October 2005.

13 The judgment does not address the issues related to the amount of such subsidy,[3] being rather focused on the claim for damages, and, more specifically, with the starting time of its prescription. According to art 2935 CC, the limitation period starts from the time at which the right can be exercised. While this starting point was originally understood as the time when the harmful event occurred, its interpretation has profoundly changed over the years. The turning point of this development is represented by the 2008 decision of the Plenary Session of the Italian Supreme Court concerning damages due to infected blood transfusions, which identified the starting date of the limitation period with the objective perception of the illness as a consequence of the transfusion.[4] From then on, prescription is held to run from the time at which a disease is perceived or could be perceived by the injured party as an unlawful consequence of a tort. An injured party's due diligence as well as the accessibility of scientific knowledge and the dissemination of the information are elements to be taken into account by courts in establishing the starting time.

14 Against this background, the present judgment does not elaborate an innovative interpretation of prescription rules, being rather aimed to apply the aforementioned doctrine to Thalidomide cases. In doing so, it confirms both the line

3 See eg, Cass 7 November 2018, no 28460.

4 Corte di cassazione, Sezione Unite (Cass SU) 11 January 2008, no 581 at www.dejure.it. Its line of thought has been subsequently confirmed and further elaborated by several judgments (see eg, Cass 28 June 2019, no 1742; Cass 19 June 2023, no 16468).

of thought affirmed by the Supreme Court in 2020[5] and the general change in the interpretation of art 2935 CC. Indeed, the 2020 decision was cited by the plaintiff and recalled by the present judgment.

2. Cass 26 June 2024, no 17634: Medical Malpractice; Administrative and tort Law Liability of Medical Doctors; Concurrence of Actions

a) Brief Summary of the Facts

The defendants are three medical doctors and two nurses who were condemned according to arts 113 and 589 of the Italian Criminal Code, for having culpably caused the death of a patient as a result of an incorrect dose of anti-blastic therapy. Criminal liability had been definitively ascertained with the passing of *res judicata* of the judgment of the Court of Appeal of Palermo. The criminal court further held that one doctor had to pay damages in the amount of € 875,497 and each of the others € 318,363. 15

As a further consequence, the hospital (*Azienda Ospedaliera Universitaria Policlinico Paolo Giaccone of Palermo*) was held jointly and severally liable to pay damages for the total amount of € 1,989,766. 16

The public prosecutor filed an administrative action against the defendants for the pecuniary loss caused to the public hospital as a consequence of their medical malpractice. The administrative court (*Corte dei Conti*) condemned the medical doctors to reimburse the amount which the hospital had paid in compensation. Its decision was confirmed by the Court of Appeal, which also reaffirmed the jurisdictional competence of the administrative court. 17

The doctors appealed to the Supreme Court by contesting the jurisdiction of the administrative court. In particular, they argued that the action for damages proposed by the hospital in front of a civil court would render the administrative one filed by the Public Prosecutor unnecessary, as both actions are based on the same medical malpractice and are aimed to compensate the financial loss suffered by the hospital for compensating the damage of the injured patient. 18

5 Cass 3 June 2020, no 10515.

b) Judgment of the Court

19 The Court dismissed the appeal.

20 The Court held that if a hospital has to pay damages to patients as a result of the medical malpractice of its employees, such damages constitute an indirect financial loss to be compensated by its employees. This subsequently allows the Public Prosecutor to claim for the medical doctors' administrative responsibility for damages to public funds, while, at the same time, the hospital is also allowed to claim civil damages.

21 The Court confirmed that the administrative action for financial loss caused to public funds by the hospital's employees and for the economic damage suffered by the hospital are independent and autonomous and serve different goals.

22 In particular, the administrative liability serves public and general interests, as it concerns the proper functioning of the public administration and the correct use of public resources. Conversely, according to the Supreme Court, the hospital claims for damages for the sole purpose of obtaining full compensation for the loss it suffered. Given the diversity of the two actions, the Court confirmed that the plaintiffs are liable under both administrative and tort law.

23 A further defence raised by the plaintiff concerned the applicability of art 9 of Law no 24 of 2017 (Medical Liability Law) to the present case. Article 9.6 entitles the Public Prosecutor to file an action for administrative responsibility if the damage was inflicted with intent or gross negligence. Since the medical malpractice occurred before the Medical Liability Law entered into force, the appellants argued that the competence of the administrative court stated by the cited provision did not exist in the present case.

24 However, the Supreme Court rejected even this second defence by holding that the competence of the administrative court existed even before Law no 24/2017 entered into force.

c) Commentary

25 The decision deserves to be cited as it focuses on the relationship between civil and administrative liability of medical staff employed by public healthcare institutions after their medical malpractice has been ascertained and damages have been paid to the injured party.

26 The general admissibility of a concurrence of civil and administrative actions was confirmed by a decision of the plenary session of the Court of Cassation in

2022, which underlined the diversity of functions pursued by the two actions,[6] even if outside the field of medical malpractice. Previously, the autonomy and independence of the two actions was affirmed by the plenary session of the Supreme Court in 2020 and 2019.[7]

In the field of medical liability, art 9.1 of the Medical Liability Law grants public healthcare institutions the right to seek recourse against their staff (only) if these inflicted any damage with intent or gross negligence. Under the same circumstances, art 9.6 further allows the Public Prosecutor to file an action for administrative responsibility against the healthcare employees who have been held liable if their employer is a public body. On this point, the court clarifies that the Medical Liability Law did not introduce a new kind of action, rather confirming a pre-existing one. 27

The present judgment reaffirms a well-established trend in Italian jurisprudence in recent years and applies it to the field of medical liability. 28

3. Cass 30 July 2024, no 21261: Concurrent Causes; Material and Legal Causality

a) Brief Summary of the Facts

The plaintiff suffered an acute myocardial infarction, as a result of which he fell to the ground, hitting his head. He was taken to hospital and treated for a heart attack with anticoagulant and antiplatelet therapy. As a result of the treatment, he remained significantly and permanently disabled. 29

The plaintiff brought an action for damages against the hospital and claimed that, in addition to the permanent effects of the heart attack, he had suffered bodily injuries due to the incorrect administration of the antiplatelet medication, as the medical staff had not carried out a CAT scan to check for the presence of a head injury. 30

He argued that, while anticoagulant therapy was appropriate to counter the effects of the heart attack, before also administering antiplatelet therapy, the hospital, given that the patient also had an abrasion on his head as a result of the fall, should have checked that he did not have a head injury. 31

6 Cass SU 15 February 2022, no 4871.
7 Cass SU 7 May 2020, no 8634; Cass SU 19 February 2019, no 4883.

32 The claim for damages was accepted in the first instance by the Court of Busto Arsizio, which ordered the hospital to compensate the plaintiff for the damage in the amount of € 69,397.

33 The plaintiff appealed and sought an increase in the amount of compensation. The Court of Appeal upheld the appeal and ordered the hospital to pay € 214,842.

34 The hospital appealed to the Supreme Court and contested the amount of damages awarded to the plaintiff.

b) Judgment of the Court

35 The Supreme Court followed the appellant's arguments and upheld the appeal.

36 The appellant argued that the Court of Appeal had not correctly calculated the damages due to the patient. In particular, the Court of Appeal determined the total percentage of permanent invalidity suffered by the plaintiff according to the Milan Tables of *danno biologico* (50 %), and reduced such amount by calculating the rate of invalidity due to the myocardial infarction, which was duly treated by the medical doctors. The Court awarded damages corresponding to the remaining invalidity of 20 %, which was caused by the incorrect treatment with anticoagulant medication. According to the appellant, however, this reasoning would fail to take into account that the harmful consequences of the heart attack should not be taken into account in calculating damages, as they did not impact on the damage due to medical malpractice. These two types of damage were coexistent, not concurrent.

37 The Supreme Court held that the Court of Appeal wrongfully calculated the 'extra rate' of permanent invalidity suffered by the plaintiff as a consequence of the medical malpractice by applying the doctrine affirmed by Cass no 6341 of 2014. According to this doctrine, damages are determined by calculating the personal injuries as a whole and, subsequently, by deducting the percentage of invalidity that the patient would have suffered even if the unlawful event had not occurred. However, according to the Supreme Court, this doctrine takes into account only cases in which a personal invalidity is aggravated by medical malpractice which, therefore, leads to a worsening of the patient's condition. This would happen if a wrongful surgical intervention worsened the consequences of the invalidity that the patient would have suffered even if the operation had been duly performed.

38 In the present case, as the Court stressed, the Court of Appeal did not clarify whether the invalidity consequent on the heart attack – which was duly addressed by the medical doctors – was independent from that related to the administration of the wrong medication or rather aggravated its harmful consequences.

As a consequence of the aforementioned reasoning, the Supreme Court quashed the Court of Appeal's decision and referred the case to the Court of Appeal of Milan. 39

c) Commentary

The aforementioned decision is interesting for focusing on additional damage due to two different concurring causes: a heart attack which was duly treated by the medical doctors and the anticoagulant and antiplatelet therapy wrongfully provided to the patient notwithstanding the presence of a head injury. 40

The Court noted a subtle distinction between two kinds of situations: on the one hand, unlawful conduct that aggravated the harmful consequences that would have occurred even if the medical intervention had been duly performed; on the other hand, unlawful conduct that caused damage and which coexisted with a physical impairment due to a health issue that was diligently treated. 41

The idea behind both situations is that, as a general rule, tortfeasors are responsible for all damage materially linked to their misconduct, even if natural events concur with the unlawful conduct (eg skull rule or principle of the equivalence of concurrent causes).[8] However, such a strict rule is 'softened' by reducing the total amount of the damage not attributable to tortfeasors' misconduct according to legal causality. This concept actually works as a limit to liability, and applies by reducing the amount of damages to be awarded (art 1223 CC: damage to be compensated must be the direct and immediate consequences of the unlawful conduct). This reasoning applies whenever the harmful conduct concurs with a pre-existing illness and aggravates its consequences.[9] 42

However, according to a recent line of cases (Cass 11 November 2019, no 28986, which is cited by Cass 15 January 2020, no 514), the aforementioned doctrine should not apply whenever the concurrent 'natural' causes do not aggravate the consequences of the tortfeasor's misconduct, but produce consequences which remain unchanged. According to this line of thought, in the latter situation, the harmful natural events would not concur with the unlawful misconduct, but merely coexist with it, as they do not worsen its consequences. In this situation, damages are not calculated by reducing the total amount of compensation, but are limited to those directly related to the tortfeasor's misconduct. 43

---

8 See eg, Cass 8 November 2023, no 31058, <www.federalismi.it>; Cass 19 September 2023 no 26851 in Foro italiano, 2024, I, 880.

9 This doctrine has been reported by *E Bargelli*, Italy, in: E Karner/BC Steininger (eds), European Tort Law 2020 (2021) 326, no 23 ff.

44 The commented decision is a manifestation of this new trend, whose ultimate result is to 'soften' the tortfeasor's liability if natural causes of injury occur together with their misconduct.

4. Cass 1 February 2024: Right to the Protection of Minor's Image

a) Brief Summary of the Facts

45 During the arrest of a Mafia fugitive, the crew of a national television channel also filmed a minor who happened to be present at the scene. The video of the arrest was subsequently broadcast during a news programme and later distributed several times to television and digital platforms. The parents, who had custody of the minor, filed a lawsuit seeking both an injunction against the further unlawful distribution of the video and compensation for the pecuniary and non-pecuniary damage suffered as a result of the unauthorised publication of the minor's image.

46 The Court of Rome, following a procedural amendment to the special procedure for disputes under art 152 of Legislative Decree no 196/2003 – concerning matters of privacy, which are not subject to appeal – dismissed the case, ruling out any unlawful conduct. According to the court, even if the parental consent for the publication of the image of the minor was lacking (according to art 96 of Law no 633/1941), art 97, para 1 of the same Law was applicable in this case. The images were linked to a legitimate public interest in information, falling under the right to report news, as they were intended to document the 'live' arrest of a Mafia fugitive by the police on a public street. Furthermore, the minor was captured in the footage by chance, as his presence in the public street at the time of the fugitive's arrest was purely coincidental.

47 The plaintiffs appealed to the Court of Cassation, arguing that the reasoning of the lower court was flawed. According to the appellants, the lower court's decision was contradictory. On the one hand, it acknowledged that the purpose of the journalistic report was to depict a 'sick' social context in which members of the community, instead of distancing themselves from the arrested person, watched the arrest and even approached him to greet him. On the other hand, it asserted the accidental nature of the filming of the minor.

48 The appellants argued that these two statements were contradictory. If the journalist's real intention had been to portray a 'sick' social context in which homage was paid to an arrested Mafia fugitive, such an objective would necessarily have implied a deliberate focus on the identity of the persons involved and their recognisability. This, according to the appellants, rendered the publication

of the minor's image unlawful, on the one hand, because it was detrimental to the honour, reputation and dignity of the person portrayed (pursuant to art 97(2) of Law no 633/1941), and, on the other hand, because it unduly highlighted the identity and recognisability of a minor who was unlawfully associated with a convicted Mafia fugitive.

b) Judgment of the Court

The Court of Cassation declared the appeal inadmissible. According to the Court, 49
the lower court had established the existence of one of the specific cases in which the publication of a person's image is authorised by law, irrespective of their consent, because it is linked to an event – such as the arrest of a fugitive in the social context in which they had gone into hiding – characterised by a public interest in information and which took place in a public place.

Furthermore, there were no objective circumstances that would have made 50
the publication of the minor's image unlawful. The minor was filmed incidentally during a television news report, in the midst of an undifferentiated crowd, without any intention of making the minor identifiable or recognisable to those who viewed the footage.

The appellants' argument that the publication of the image harmed the mi- 51
nor's honour, reputation and dignity and was intended to draw attention to her identity and recognisability did not point to an *error in iudicando*. Rather, it was an attempt to force the Court of Cassation to make a new assessment of the merits of the case, contrary to the reasoned judgment already given by the lower court, in accordance with the legal principles applicable to the case.

c) Commentary

Beyond the negative outcome of the appeal, the decision is noteworthy because it 52
provides an opportunity to establish a set of principles regarding the right to one's image and news reporting.

The right to one's image falls within the category of personality rights which 53
are enshrined in the Italian Constitution (art 2). For this reason, the Italian legal system grants individuals the *jus excludendi*, ie, the right to prevent the use and dissemination of their image, as laid down in art 10 of the Civil Code and art 96, para 1 of Law no 633/1941. Consequently, the dissemination of images generally requires the consent of the person portrayed. In order to be valid and legitimate, this consent must be given by an adult with full legal capacity. Therefore, in

accordance with the general rules on legal capacity, minors cannot independently authorise the use of their image unless such use is a natural consequence of a pre-existing legal relationship established by the minor themselves. Apart from this scenario, it is the legal representative of the minor or otherwise incapacitated person who must consent to the dissemination of the image, within the limits established by the applicable laws, provided that it benefits the individual and does not cause them harm.

54 In this regard, the Court of Cassation emphasised that the growing social recognition of a person's right to appear in public when they have an interest in doing so has led to the legal protection (art 1322, para 2 Civil Code) of a person's financial interest in the commercial exploitation of their image in return for payment. This recognition has had a twofold effect. On the one hand, it has led to the proliferation of atypical sponsorship contracts. On the other hand, it has recognised the right to compensation for financial loss resulting from the unauthorised commercial use of one's image, in line with the American concept of the 'right of publicity'. The ruling defines this right as the right of individuals (primarily, but not exclusively, public figures) to control the commercial exploitation of their identity or image.

55 The Court of Cassation has held that the right to one's image has both a negative and a positive dimension. From a negative perspective, it protects the individual's interest in preventing the public dissemination or display of their image, thereby imposing a corresponding duty on others (*erga omnes*) to refrain from such acts. From a positive perspective, it protects the individual's interest in appearing in public when they choose to do so, and imposes a corresponding duty on others (*erga omnes*) to tolerate such appearances.

56 Furthermore, the judgment clarified that the prohibition on displaying or publishing a person's image may be either absolute or relative, depending on the circumstances. The prohibition is not absolute if the dissemination does not harm the honour, dignity or reputation of the person portrayed. In such cases, dissemination is exceptionally permitted with the consent of the person (art 96 of Law no 633/1941) or in the presence of specific legal exceptions (public notoriety of the person; public office held; judicial or police requirements; scientific, educational or cultural purposes; connection with events of public interest or taking place in public, art 97, para 1 of Law no 633/1941). On the other hand, the prohibition is absolute if the dissemination damages the honour, dignity or reputation of the person. In such cases, the need to protect the privacy of the individual outweighs the public interest in knowing the image of the person, and no exceptions to the prohibition apply (art 97, para 2 of Law no 633/1941).

57 With regard to the relative nature of the prohibition under art 97 of Law no 633/1941, the Court emphasised the exceptional nature of this provision,

which must be interpreted restrictively. Furthermore, with regard to the information provided by television reports, the Court reiterated that the existence of conditions legitimising the exercise of the right to report does not automatically justify the publication or dissemination of the images of the persons concerned. The legality of such dissemination depends not only on compliance with art 10 of the Civil Code and arts 96 and 97 of Law no 633/1941, but also on compliance with art 137 of Legislative Decree no 196/2003 and art 8 of the Journalists' Code of Ethics, as well as on a concrete assessment of whether there is a specific and independent public interest in revealing the identity of the parties involved, ensuring that such disclosure is essential for the completeness and accuracy of the information provided.

The judgment under review linked the right to one's image to the protection 58 of privacy, stressing that in balancing the right to one's image against the right to report news, greater weight should be given to the protection of private life, particularly in the case of minors.

5. Cass 18 April 2024, no 25872: Compensation to Crime Victims

a) Brief Summary of the Facts

In the aftermath of a brutal criminal case, the question of compensation for the 59 victim's relatives arose. As it was not possible to obtain compensation from the offender, the victim's relatives invoked the application of Council Directive 2004/80/EC of 29 April 2004. This Directive required the Member States to set up, by 10 July 2005, a general compensation scheme aimed at providing adequate and fair compensation to the victims of all violent and intentional crimes in cases where they are unable to obtain full compensation for the damage suffered from the direct perpetrators. Contrary to the first instance court, the Court of Appeal, in upholding the appeal, condemned the Italian State, represented by the Presidency of the Council of Ministers, to compensate the families of victims of intentional violent crimes for failing to transpose the European Union Directive in time.

b) Judgment of the Court

The Court of Cassation referred the matter to the Court of Justice under art 267 60 Treaty on the Functioning of the European Union (TFEU). The preliminary question referred for interpretation by the Court of Justice was as follows: should the compensation provided for by Directive 2004/80/EC be interpreted restrictively, so as to refer only to the person directly injured, namely the holder of the interest protected by the criminal provision, to the exclusion of those whom the appellant refers to as 'collateral victims'?

61 In the case before the Court, the collateral victims were represented by the parents, siblings, grandparents, aunts and uncles of the victim of the violent crime.

62 The Court emphasised that different interpretations of European legislation are possible. According to para 2 and 2-bis of art 11 of Law no 122 of 2016, compensation is granted to the surviving spouse – or cohabiting partner – and children, and only in their absence to the parents; if the parents are also absent, compensation is granted to the siblings, but only if they lived with the deceased and were financially dependent on them at the time of the crime. If the conditions for access to compensation are not met, no compensation can be claimed for the delay in adopting such legislation.

63 However, art 2 of Directive 2012/29/EU adopts a much broader definition of 'crime victim' (in the case of homicide), which also includes a 'member of the family of a person whose death was directly caused by a criminal offence', provided that they 'have suffered damage as a result of that person's death'.

64 It is therefore necessary to ask whether the choice of the Italian legislator is contrary to EU law by granting unconditionally the compensation – established for the victims of the intentional violent crime of voluntary homicide – only to the spouse (or cohabitant) and children of the deceased, while recognising it for the parents of the deceased only in the absence of primary beneficiaries, and for siblings only in the absence of both primary and secondary beneficiaries. Indeed, the concept of 'crime victim' seems to be interpreted much more broadly in both EU and national law. It is now well established in case law that the right to compensation for the loss of a family relationship has a broad scope, as it is a direct consequence of the harm inflicted on the close relative. This harm is thus considered to be a 'multi-offensive' act that affects different but equally direct victims. For this reason, the term 'secondary victim' is inappropriate, except for purely descriptive purposes.

c) Commentary

65 Delays in implementing Directive 2004/80/EC in Italy have resulted in a number of court cases because of difficulties in interpreting art 12 of said Directive. In fact, two conflicting approaches had emerged in Italian case law. Some judgments

have held that compensation was only required for victims of cross-border violent crime, arguing that Member States were not obliged to establish a similar compensation scheme for purely domestic situations. Other judgments, however, have maintained that the State's obligation to establish a compensation scheme should also extend to purely domestic situations.

The Court of Justice resolved this question of preliminary interpretation in its judgment *Presidenza del Consiglio dei Ministri v BV.*[10] Specifically, the Court ruled that art 12(2) of Directive 2004/80/EC imposes a general obligation on Member States to establish a compensation scheme for victims of violent intentional crime committed on their territory. The EU legislator opted for the application of national compensation schemes to cross-border victims in Chapter 2 of the Directive, rather than for each Member State to set up a separate compensation scheme for cross-border victims. The absence of national compensation schemes makes it impossible to establish compensation schemes for cross-border victims and thus gives rise to State liability. 66

Similarly, the question of interpretation raised by the Court of Cassation in judgment no 25872/2024 is whether the Court of Justice will support a broad or a restrictive interpretation of the compensation scheme set out in the Directive. 67

6. Personal Injury

In 2024, the main issues in personal injury cases were still related to methods of defining and quantifying damage. 68

Firstly, issues of definition and quantification were addressed by the Court of Cassation, Order no 10787/2024, which dealt with the distinction between biological and moral damage. Following arthroscopic surgery, a woman suffered an injury to the femoral nerve and the right patellar tendon. Furthermore, due to a difficult post-operative course, the woman developed an adjustment disorder with chronic depressive mood, which was medically diagnosed during the trial. The Court of Appeal of Bologna included this disorder among the factors justifying the personalisation of the damage. In particular, the Court of Appeal recognised the appellant's right to compensation for non-pecuniary damage, part of which was awarded as compensation for biological damage, based on the percentage of disability established by the second expert opinion appointed by the court at first instance. Another part of the compensation was awarded as personalisation, 69

10 Court of Justice of the European Union (CJEU) 16.7.2020, C-129/19, *Presidenza del Consiglio dei Ministri v BV*, ECLI:EU:C:2020:566.

quantified at 25% of the biological damage, recognised in the light of the psychopathological condition resulting from the surgical intervention. When asked to rule on the matter, the Court of Cassation, in line with a trend of interpretation that has been developing for several years, clarified that when the subjective suffering caused by a life event constitutes a medically ascertainable condition that amounts to an actual impairment of the psychological integrity of the individual, it does not fall under moral damage, but rather constitutes biological damage. In the present case, the lower courts also recognised the causal link between the plaintiff's post-operative condition and the emergence of an 'adjustment disorder with chronic depressive mood'. According to the Court of Cassation, this situation went beyond the realm of subjective suffering and constituted a pathological psychological condition sufficient to fall within the category of biological damage rather than moral damage. The lower court had wrongly considered the appellant's depressive psychopathological state as a basis for personalising the non-pecuniary damage. Since this was a medically ascertainable and established psychopathological condition, the lower court should have taken into account the psychological damage alleged and proven by the appellant when determining the total compensation for biological damage. In other words, the Court of Cassation found that the same wrongful act had caused multiple violations of the appellant's psychophysical integrity, namely the injury to the femoral nerve and the right patellar tendon, as well as the depressive psychopathological state, with biological damage being a unified concept. Order no 10787 of 2024 fitted seamlessly into the jurisprudential evolution of recent years, although some concerns remain. While the distinction between biological and moral damage appears to be entirely consistent from the perspective of legal classification, the assessment entrusted to the lower courts in concrete cases may prove problematic. This is particularly true when the violation of the right to health results in psychological damage, which by definition not only affects the dynamic and relational dimension of the individual but also causes inner suffering.

70 Cassation Order no 26185/2024 dealt with the question of the qualification and quantification of moral damage in a case of loss of family relations. The lower courts had ruled on the liability of a Port Authority for the exposure of one of its workers to asbestos, which caused his illness and death. The appealed judgment of the Court of Appeal had denied compensation for the moral damage suffered by the deceased's siblings as a result of the loss of the family relationship on the grounds that there was no evidence to support the alleged suffering. This decision was overturned by Order no 26185/2024 of the Court of Cassation, which referred to a well-established approach to the equitable compensation of damage caused by the loss of a family relationship. Specifically, in the case of close relatives belonging to the nuclear family (spouses, parents, children, brothers and sis-

ters), the loss of genuine bonds of mutual affection and solidarity with the deceased can be presumed by virtue of their belonging to the same 'minimal family unit', within which such bonds are still considered the norm in today's society, according to the usual course of events (*id quod plerumque accidit*), unless the defendant proves otherwise, even presumptively (Cass no 9010/2022). The Order also upheld the Port Authority's appeal to the Court of Cassation, which had challenged the erroneous application of the tabular criteria for calculating damages to the victim's relatives in relation to the victim's widow. In determining the compensation for the widow's loss of family relations, the lower court had failed to take into account – in order to reduce the amount – the short duration of the widow's survival, as she died just over ten months after her husband's death. The appeal was considered valid because compensation for the loss of a family relationship must be calculated using a points-based system, which includes not only the adoption of the point-based criteria, but also the extraction of the average value of a point from precedents, along with flexibility and a list of relevant factual circumstances, such as the age of the victim and the age of the survivor. The decision provided a further opportunity to reflect on the reasons justifying compensation for the loss of a family relationship, emphasising that the real damage lies in the suffering, not in the relationship itself: it is the moral pain, not the changed life, that must be compensated.

The Court of Cassation, Civil Section III, in its Order of 28 March 2024, no 8371, 71
addressed a problem relating to the quantification of damage resulting from the violation of the right to health. As a result of a car accident, the victim suffered very serious injuries and claimed pecuniary damages for 'future medical expenses'. The referring judge awarded the pecuniary damages 'for future medical expenses' without distinguishing between past and future pecuniary damage arising from medical expenses. The appellant complained that the contested judgment had wrongly applied, even to medical expenses already incurred, a calculation system based on a 'foreseeable expenditure for home care', using the 'daily wage of domestic workers' according to the 'wage tables of the National Collective Agreement for Domestic Workers (CCNL Colf e Badanti) applicable *ratione temporis*'. However, the appellant argued that this amount improperly included assistance expenses that the plaintiff should have documented as actually incurred, since the aforementioned 'expenditure forecast' could only apply to future expenses. The Court of Cassation upheld these appeals, albeit with certain clarifications. Firstly, it is important to recognise that this is a case of permanent damage, which the judge has to assess and which has two components. The pecuniary damage resulting from the need to pay a person to provide personal assistance to a disabled person is permanent damage that occurs 'de die in diem'. Since the judge intervenes to liquidate this damage at a point in time after it has occurred

and the associated economic burden has been incurred, they have to quantify both the damage that has already occurred and the damage that will occur. Clearly, these two operations cannot be governed by the same criteria. This question arises in all cases of future permanent damage that will require periodic expenditure for the duration of the victim's life. In such cases, the damage cannot simply be liquidated by multiplying the current expenditure by the estimated number of years of the victim's life but can be addressed in different ways. One approach is to quantify the future permanent damage in the form of an annuity. Another is to multiply the annual loss by the number of years it is expected to be borne and to discount the result using an expectation coefficient. Finally, the third method is capitalisation, which involves multiplying the annual loss by a capitalisation coefficient for life annuities. The Court of Cassation, no 8371/2024 reiterated the position already expressed: the pecuniary damage for the cost of lifelong assistance, which includes the need to pay someone to provide personal assistance to a disabled person, constitutes permanent damage that occurs 'de die in diem'. In order to assess this damage, it is necessary to distinguish between past damage, ie damage that has already occurred and for which the injured party must prove that they have incurred such expenses, and future damage, ie damage that has not yet occurred at the time of the decision but which can reasonably be expected to occur during the remainder of the injured party's life.

72 The Court of Cassation, no 4289/2024 also dealt with the question of quantifying the pecuniary damage resulting from a violation of the right to health. Following an accident, the injured party became disabled and lost all capacity to work. The Court of Appeal had quantified the pecuniary damage resulting from the loss of working capacity as a loss of opportunity rather than as pecuniary damage for the loss of a specific working capacity. This was because, at the time of the accident, the injured party, who normally worked as a labourer, was unemployed. However, the Court of Cassation ruled that since the unemployment was due to contingent reasons not attributable to the injured party, the future pecuniary damage should be quantified as loss of specific working capacity. More precisely, the damage had to be calculated by multiplying the lost income by an appropriate capitalisation coefficient. The Court of Cassation specified that this should be based on the following criteria: the average remuneration over the entire working life of the occupational category concerned, derived from legally relevant parameters or equitably estimated, and capitalisation coefficients established by regulatory provisions for the capitalisation of social security or welfare pensions.

73 As this brief review has shown, the quantification of damage remains the most difficult aspect of personal injury liability litigation. In this regard, it is important to recall that in cases of non-pecuniary damages, judicial tables of compensation are used to ensure uniformity in awards. These tables are drawn up

by the main Italian courts of merit. Among them, the most important are the so-called Milan Tables, for which an updated version was published in 2024. In addition, the National Uniform Tables have been published, as described in the first part of the report.

The order of the Court of Cassation, no 14245/2024 does not concern the quantification of non-patrimonial damage, but its qualification. Tizio was diagnosed with incurable lung cancer and began treatment with chemotherapy and morphine. Dr Mevio, who was contacted by Tizio's family at the suggestion of Dr Caio, persuaded Tizio to abandon traditional treatment and take only one drug, which would guarantee his recovery. After Tizio's death, his wife and children filed a lawsuit against Dr Mevio, seeking compensation for the pecuniary and non-pecuniary damage suffered. In particular, the plaintiffs complain that the defendant took advantage of their vulnerability by creating false hopes of recovery for their loved one in order to profit from them. The patient's family also brought criminal charges against Dr Mevio, who was convicted under art 444 of the Code of Criminal Procedure for criminal conspiracy, the unauthorised practice of pharmaceutical biochemistry, the sale of unlicensed medicines and fraud. In the first and second judgments, the defendants were sentenced to pay patrimonial damages equal to the cost of the alternative medication sold by the doctor and to compensate the non-patrimonial damage. The Court of Cassation dismissed the doctor's appeal and upheld the judgment of the Court of Appeal: the damage suffered by the family members was both *iure proprio*, for the suffering they had endured as a result of having hoped for their loved one's recovery, and *iure hereditatis*, for the violation of the deceased's right to self-determination. 74

C. Literature

1. *C Scognamiglio* (ed), Responsabilità civile (Tort law) series Enciclopedia del diritto Tematici VII (Giuffré 2024)

The volume belongs to one of the most well-known and frequently consulted encyclopaedias. It covers all tort liability matters and highlights the most recent developments in the field by selecting and collecting 53 entries in alphabetical order written by different authors. Anti-competitive behaviour, environmental damage and climate change litigation, Artificial Intelligence, digital platforms, punitive damages, violation of privacy, and product liability are a few examples of subjects included in the volume. Classical topics such as causality, fault, third parties' un- 75 lawful interferences in contractual liability, and non-pecuniary damages are also embraced in the volume.

2. *A Bertolini*, Intelligenza artificiale e responsabilità civile (Artificial Intelligence and tort law) (Il Mulino 2024)

76 If an Artificial Intelligence system malfunctions, who will pay for the damage? This question inevitably arises when discussing technology and the need to regulate it. After all, civil liability defines the scope of action for those who create, develop, use and benefit from innovation. The answer is complex – just as AI itself is complex – and requires a careful framing of the issue within the legal system, as well as reflection on the functions of liability rules. Starting from the definition, the author shows that it is impossible to adopt a uniform approach that regulates an autonomous vehicle, a social robot, an exoskeleton or a large language model in the same way. The possibility of considering AI as a 'moral agent' that can be held liable is ruled out, and a critical analysis of the current legal framework is undertaken, starting with the European product liability regime, which appears inadequate both to encourage ex ante investment in safety and to ensure ex post compensation for victims. From this perspective, the author reconstructs the emerging regulatory landscape at European level and identifies future challenges and inconsistencies that risk undermining the new frontier of EU law. Finally, the study outlines possible alternatives and interpretative solutions that focus on functionality while maintaining coherence with the systematic structure of liability law.

3. *R Calvo*, La responsabilità civile. Principi ordinatori e regole applicative (Tort law. Guiding principles and applicable rules) (Zanichelli 2024)

77 This volume provides a comprehensive and up-to-date overview of Italian tort law. The most recent case law developments are taken into account. It provides guidance on any question in the field for both students and practitioners.

Agris Bitāns

XVII. Latvia

A. Legislation

1. Amendments to the State Administration Structure Law (Grozījumi Valsts pārvaldes iekārtas likumā) Latvijas Vēstnesis no 230, 26 November 2024

On 14 November 2024, the Latvian Parliament adopted amendments to the State Administration Structure Law, which has been in force with amendments since 1 January 2003. These amendments became effective from 10 December 2024. 1

The main goal of these amendments was to clarify and simplify the rules for cooperation between institutions. These amendments also include improvements in tort law. 2

The Law replaced the term 'personal harm' with the words 'non-pecuniary loss' ('non-material harm') in this Law, because, since the 2018 amendments to the Law on Compensation for Damage Caused by State Administrative Institutions[1] and later amendments to the Administrative Procedure Law, the term 'personal harm' is no longer used in administrative law. 3

Now arts 44 and 53 clearly determine the obligation to compensate pecuniary loss and non-pecuniary loss caused to third parties as a result of performing specific delegated administration tasks or improper performance of the task by the authorising person from the State or public entity budgets. 4

2. Amendments to the Pharmaceutical Law (Grozījumi Farmācijas likumā) Latvijas Vēstnesis no 128 A, 4 July 2024

On 20 June 2024, the Latvian Parliament adopted amendments to the Pharmaceutical Law, which has been in force with amendments since 8 May 1997. These amendments became effective from 18 July 2024. 5

The main goal of these amendments was to facilitate the monitoring of medicines and medical devices intended for human use. The amendments also im- 6

1 See the brief description and my comments in *A Bitāns*, Latvia, in: E Karner/BC Steininger (eds), European Tort Law (ETL) 2018 (2019) 344, nos 21–26.

https://doi.org/10.1515/9783111389271-018

proved the regulation regarding gene therapy medicinal products, including tissue engineering products and somatic cell therapy medicinal products – advanced therapy medicinal products (ATMP) – which, as an exception, are not subject to registration, manufacturing and medical use authorisation in accordance with EU legislation (these medicinal products are referred to as 'hospital exemption of ATMP') in the Pharmaceutical Law.

7 Accordingly, the new art 32 determines the right of the patient to receive compensation for injury to their health or life caused by the use of exceptional advanced therapy medicinal products in medical treatment, in accordance with the regulatory enactments on these medicinal products (part 1).[2]

8 A medical institution that uses the hospital exemption of ATMP in its medical treatment is obliged to insure against its own civil liability, ie to cover the treating physician and medical personnel for any damage caused to the health or life of a patient involved in the use of the hospital exemption of ATMP. In order to implement such liability, the Cabinet of Ministers is to determine the procedure for civil liability insurance, the minimum liability limit of the insurance contract and the mandatory risks insured by a medical institution that has the right to use the ATMP exemption. The Cabinet of Ministers will issue the relevant regulations by 1 July 2025.

3. Amendments to the Compulsory Civil Liability Insurance of Owners of Motor Vehicles Law (Sauszemes transportlīdzekļu īpašnieku civiltiesiskās atbildības obligātās apdrošināšanas likumā) Latvijas Vēstnesis no 230, 26 November 2024

9 On 14 November 2024, the Latvian Parliament adopted amendments to the Compulsory Civil Liability Insurance of Owners of Motor Vehicles Law (OCTA Law),[2] which has been in force with amendments since 1 May 2004. The majority of these amendments became effective from 10 December 2024, but some of them have been postponed.

10 The purpose of the adoption of the amendments to the Law is to transpose the requirements of Directive (EU) 2021/2118 of the European Parliament and of the Council of 24 November 2021 amending Directive 2009/103/EC relating to insurance against civil liability in respect of the use of motor vehicles, and the enforce-

---

2 See the brief description and my comments in *A Bitāns*, Latvia, in: H Koziol/BC Steininger (eds), European Tort Law (ETL) 2004 (2005) 395, nos 1–7.

ment of the obligation to insure against such liability (Directive).[3] The drafters of the amendments indicated four main areas, namely, (1) compensation for victims of accidents in the event of the insolvency of the relevant insurer; (2) minimum amounts of compulsory insurance cover; (3) checks on motor vehicle insurance carried out by Member States; and (4) the use of reports on the claim's history of policyholders by a new insurance company. In addition to the four areas mentioned, amendments were drafted in relation to dispatched vehicles (ie vehicles that have been assigned a task or route by a dispatcher to fulfill the assignment, such as a delivery or service call), accidents involving trailers towed by a vehicle, independent motor vehicle insurance price comparison tools and information centres and information for victims. In addition, the Law provides for a number of amendments to the OCTA Law not directly related to the transposition of the Directive.

In subpara a) para 12 part 1 art 1 of the OCTA Law, the definition of a motor 11 vehicle which is subject to the compulsory insurance obligation was clarified. The OCTA Law now applies to a road motor vehicle, including a trailer (semi-trailer), which is registered with the Road Traffic Safety Directorate or the State Technical Supervision Agency, or with a local government or is registered in a foreign country. Also, now in additional to trams from 1 July 2025, an electric scooter that is registered with the Road Traffic Safety Directorate will also be considered as such a means of transport under the OCTA law.

Amendments were made to art 15 of the OCTA Law regarding the amounts of 12 insurance indemnification, but contrary to art 9 of the Directive, which provides for minimum amounts, art 15 of the OCTA Law, in turn, provides the limits of an insurer's liability, ie a maximum liability. Accordingly, in Latvia there is a limit on the payment of insurance indemnification to injured parties as a result of an accident involving a motor vehicle: 1) for indemnification of personal loss, up to € 6,450,000, regardless of the number of injured persons; and 2) for indemnification of property loss, up to € 1,300,000, regardless of the number of third persons.

Article 28 has been amended as result of the judgment of the European Court 13 of Justice (ECJ) in case C-707/19.[4]

The most heated discussions in society and an unprecedented action in Par- 14 liament followed the amendment that determined the obligation to have compulsory civil liability insurance for vehicles that do not actually participate in traffic due to the fact that the amendments to the Law provide that the insurance event also includes an accident related to the use of the vehicle for the transport func-

3 [2021] Official Journal of the European Union (OJ) L 430/1.
4 ECJ 20.5.2021, C-707/19, *K.S. v A.B*, ECLI:EU:C:2021:405.

tion, regardless of the place of use of the vehicle and whether the vehicle was in motion. The fact that all vehicles that are registered, including those that participate in traffic seasonally, will have to be insured caused public outrage. At the *Saeima* session, both coalition and opposition members supported the amendments to the Law, but later, several opposition members, responding to criticism, admitted on social media that they did not really understand or know what they had voted for and even apologised to drivers.

15 Accordingly, the Parliament adopted urgent new amendments on 5 December 2024 which postponed the requirement to purchase compulsory insurance policy for all vehicles until 1 November 2025, and also ordered the Cabinet of Ministers to provide an assessment of the scope of the European Union Directive by 30 April as regards whether it has been transposed appropriately and does not provide for any derogations, while the ministries and institutions involved will prepare a solution so that OCTA policies do not have to be purchased for vehicles that are not in motion or are used seasonally.

4. Amendments to the Law on the Rights of Patients (Grozījumi Pacientu tiesību likumā) Latvijas Vēstnesis no 124, 28 June 2024

16 On 13 June 2024, the Latvian Parliament adopted amendments to the Law on the Rights of Patients, which has been in force with amendments since 1 March 2010.[5] These amendments, with the exception of the amendment to art 3 with part 7, became effective from 12 July 2024. Part 7 art 3 of the Law enters into force on 1 July 2025, since time is needed to develop a guideline plan for the protection of patients' rights.

17 The main goal of these amendments was to clarify existing norms and supplement them with new rights and obligations in order to improve the compliance with, and monitoring of, the rights of patients, including minor patients, to establish new obligations for both the heads of medical institutions and medical practitioners, to clarify the rights of patients' legal or authorised representatives, and to provide for the possibility of the patient's chosen person (support person) to participate in the patient's treatment choice, etc.

18 The new wording of part 1 art 1 of the Law specifies the term 'attending physician', stipulates at what point and under what circumstances a medical practition-

5 See the brief description and my comments in *A Bitāns*, Latvia, in: E Karner/BC Steininger (eds), European Tort Law (ETL) 2009 (2010) 360, nos 3–8.

er is considered an attending physician and is responsible for the patient's treatment. This change is important because treatment in most cases consists of several treatment measures, with the involvement of doctors of different specialties (sometimes treatment also continues in another medical institution), so one doctor cannot be held responsible for all treatment measures and the actions of another doctor. Therefore, also the term 'healthcare service provider' is introduced in this Law in part 6 of art 1 and this has been defined as a medical institution, medical practitioner or medical support person who is directly or indirectly involved in the patient's healthcare process.

Now, the Law determines, as a general obligation, for a medical institution not only to provide treatment to the patient, but also to systematically promote respect for patients' rights, to ensure the protection and implementation of patients' rights in every healthcare situation. An inpatient medical institution and a multi-profile outpatient institution is obliged to develop a patient's rights implementation plan and ensure its implementation (part 7 art 3). 19

With the amendments to the Law, the right to information under the existing art 4 was divided into: (1) the right to information about healthcare services and their providers; and (2) the right to information about the patient's health. Accordingly, art 4 now regulates the patient's right to information about healthcare services and their providers and art 4^1 regulates the patient's right to information about their health. 20

Article 4^1 provides a broader catalogue of rights to the patient regarding information about their health. For example, the medical institution and the treating physician are obliged to promptly provide the patient with information about an unexpected outcome of treatment, explaining the reasons and further action. In this situation, the patient must be provided with information about the legal remedies available in the relevant situation (part 5). The patient has the right to indicate information about the person whom the patient authorises or has authorised to make decisions related to the treatment on their behalf, as well as a person who is not entitled to receive information about the patient or to make decisions related to their treatment on their behalf (part 7). 21

The Law expands the cases when, during a surgical or other invasive intervention, the treating physician has a right to perform unplanned treatment without the patient's informed consent. This may occur in cases where there is significant harm to the patient's health or life or a risk of such harm, or if the failure to perform the treatment could result in incomparably greater harm to their health (part 9 art 7). 22

The new wording of art 13 aims to strengthen and ensure the better observance of the rights of a minor patient (up to 14 years of age), that arise from the Convention on the Rights of the Child. Despite the fact that decisions on the 23 treatment of a minor patient are made by their legal representative, the medical practitioner must also listen to the opinion of the minor patient and ensure the participation of this patient in the treatment, and such participation will ensure the achievement of more successful treatment results. Therefore, the Law introduces the concept of 'the best interests of the child' in relation to a minor, which is universal, a broader legal term, which is applicable as a generalisation, which helps to reveal and use it in explanations of decisions made in medical treatment, where there are few or no legal norms or when the regulation is unclear. This concept as universal is recognised in the entire legal system of the health sector in accordance with para 3 part 2^1 art 6 of the Law on the Protection of Children's Rights.

24 Article 15, which deals with obligations of patients, has been added with several additional obligations, which could possibly be important from a tort law perspective. The patient now has an obligation to provide a translator if they cannot speak Latvian and speaks in a language that the medical practitioner does not understand, except in cases where this is not possible for objective reasons (part 2^1). And also, when the patient or the person representing the patient exercises their rights, they have an obligation to respect not only the rights of other patients, but now also treat medical practitioners and other employees of the medical institution with respect (part 6).

B. Cases

1. Decision of Assignments Hearing of the Senate of the Republic of Latvia, Department of Civil Cases, 5 June 2024, no SKC-242/2024 (C30523222) ECLI:LV:AT:2024:0605. C30523222.8.L: Compensation for Violation of Fundamental Rights[6]

a) Brief Summary of the Facts

25 Person A brought a claim against the Republic of Latvia in the person of the *Saeima* (Parliament) and the Ministry of Justice for compensation of non-pecuniary loss under art 92 of the Constitution of the Republic of Latvia and art 1635 of the Civil Law. He requested that the Republic of Latvia award compensation for

6 See on the Latvian Supreme Court website: <https://www.at.gov.lv/downloadlawfile/10111>.

non-pecuniary (moral) loss in favour of A by obliging the Riga Regional Court to publicly apologise in writing, and to recover from the defendant the costs of the lawsuit.

The claim is based on the fact, that when the claimant was in custody, he was 26
not provided with the opportunity to participate in the local government elections organised in the country. Namely, the Local Government Council Election Law (parts 4 and 8 art 32) at that time did not provide the possibility for a detained person to vote in the territory of the municipality outside the place of detention.

The judge of the Riga Regional Court, based on para 1 art 4 of the Law on the 27
Procedures for Holding under Arrest, did not allow the claimant to be escorted to the appropriate polling station.

By the judgment of the Constitutional Court of 30 March 2022 in case No 2021- 28
23-01 'On the compliance of art 32, Parts Four and Eight of the Law on Municipal Council Elections with art 101 of the Constitution of the Republic of Latvia', which was initiated following A's constitutional complaint, parts 4 and 8 art 32 of the Law on Municipal Council Elections were declared to be inconsistent with art 101 of the Constitution of the Republic of Latvia and to be invalid in relation to A from the moment of the infringement of his fundamental rights, namely from the date when the local elections were held.

A's civil claim was dismissed by the Riga City Court as the court of first ins- 29
tance with a judgment of 13 February 2023, and the Riga Regional Court, as the court of appeal, with a judgment of 26 October 2023 also dismissed the claim. A filed a cassation complaint against the judgment of the Riga Regional Court of 26 October 2023.

b) Judgment of the Court

The Senate recognised that there is a basis for refusing to initiate cassation pro- 30
ceedings, as indicated in clause 2 part 2 art 464^1 of the Civil Procedure Law, because the arguments of the cassation complaint do not create grounds to believe that the result of the case contained in the appealed judgment is incorrect and that the case under consideration is of significant importance in ensuring uniform judicial practice or the further development of the law.

At the same time, the Senate considered that it is necessary to additionally 31
indicate several conclusions. The Senate disagreed with the finding contained in the judgment of the court of appeal that the violation of fundamental rights caused to A by the Latvian State by not providing him with active voting rights in the local government elections in the regulatory framework was already compensated, namely that, with the favourable judgment of the Constitutional Court

of 30 March 2022 in case No 2021-23-01, the claimant received adequate compensation (satisfaction) for the violation of his fundamental rights. A was not deprived of the right to demand that the State compensate him for the damage caused, which has manifested itself as a specific violation of his fundamental rights.

32 The liability of the State for pecuniary or non-pecuniary loss caused to a private person is regulated by the provisions of several laws. For example, the Law on Compensation for Losses Caused by State Administrative Institutions and the Law on Compensation for Damage Caused in Criminal Proceedings and Administrative Violations. In both indicated instances, disputes are resolved in accordance with the procedure for administrative proceedings, also applying the types of compensation and procedural instruments provided for in these Laws.

33 The Senate indicated that claim regarding compensation for the violation, which was allegedly caused to the claimant by the decision of the judge of the Criminal Court of the Riga Regional Court, refusing to transport A to the appropriate polling station, is not subject to review under the civil procedure. Under part 1 art 18 of the Law on Compensation for Damage Caused in Criminal Proceedings and Administrative Violations, a private person can submit a written application for compensation for damage caused in criminal proceedings to the decision-making authority in accordance with the competence referred to in part 1 art 17 of this Law. Accordingly, under art 23, decisions taken by the decision-making authority in a case of compensation for damage may be appealed to a court in accordance with the Administrative Procedure Law, namely, to an administrative court. Consequently, the Senate recognised as justified the conclusion of the court of appeal that the legality of the judge's actions when deciding on criminal procedural issues cannot be assessed under the civil procedure.

34 In turn, with regard to the damage that the claimant, in his opinion, suffered by the regulation of the Municipal Council Election Law, which prevented his participation in the municipal elections, the Senate agreed with the Riga Regional Court's finding that the Civil Law does not provide for such a legal remedy as the claimant requested, namely an apology. The claimant chose to defend his violated rights in civil proceedings by filing a claim in a court of general jurisdiction for compensation for non-pecuniary loss and the liability of the Latvian State for the violation of the aforementioned fundamental rights was based on two legal norms – the third sentence of art 92 of the Constitution of the Republic of Latvia, which provides the right to adequate compensation in the event of an unjustified violation of fundamental rights and on art 1635 of the Civil Law, which provides a general right to claim satisfaction from the infringer for the harm (including immaterial harm) caused by a wrongful act of the infringer. However, in the specific case, the claimant unjustifiedly directly referred to art 92 of the Constitution of the Republic of Latvia to justify the legal remedy he chose. Article 92 of the Constitu-

tion of the Republic of Latvia is directly applicable in cases where the legislator has not provided for a special procedure by which a person may request appropriate compensation for the violation of their fundamental rights. The legislator has specified compensation for non-pecuniary loss in other laws, in this case, in art 1635 of the Civil Law. The second part of this article provides for monetary compensation for non-pecuniary loss (moral harm). The claimant had the right to request such legal remedy which is provided under art 1635 of the Civil Law. The second part of this article provides for the possibility to seek compensation in money for non-pecuniary loss, which the claimant did not request. Therefore, the Senate concluded that in such circumstances, there is no reason to believe that the result of the adjudication of the case could be different from the result contained in the appealed judgment, namely that the claim be dismissed.

In addition, the panel of senators considered it necessary to indicate that 35 part 3 art 1635 of the Civil Law, as a prerequisite for establishing non-pecuniary loss and, accordingly, determining compensation, provides for the victim's obligation to prove non-pecuniary loss (moral harm). In accordance with the second sentence of part 2 art 1635 of the Civil Law, the amount of compensation for non-pecuniary loss is to be determined by the court at its discretion, considering the severity and consequences of the moral harm.

When assessing the evidence submitted by the claimant, neither the first in- 36 stance nor the appellate court found that the specific violation of fundamental rights would have caused any consequences for the claimant, rightly referring to the finding expressed in case law that not every emotional experience or mental suffering (including despair, a feeling of powerlessness and anger) subjectively perceived by a person creates a basis for compensation for non-pecuniary loss.

c) Commentary

Taking into account particular requests which are mentioned in the claim state- 37 ment, including for an apology, submitted by the claimant, the final outcome provided by the Senate seems reasonable. Indeed, the Civil Law does not provide for such a legal remedy as an apology, contrary to the Law on the Press and Other Mass Media (art 21). The outcome would likely have been different if the claimant had chosen such a legal remedy as an acknowledgement of an infringement of his rights, which is very rarely used.

However, some conclusions raise some comments and questions. The first re- 38 lates to the proof to be furnished to evidence the existence of moral damage (non-pecuniary loss). The Senate still continues to interpret part 3 art 1635 narrowly. It is unclear how the claimant should prove that non-pecuniary loss has been caused. In general, non-pecuniary loss is based on a presumption that a particular wrongful act could create unpleasant feelings or emotional consequences for a reasonably sensitive person. Second, despite the fact that the Senate rightly mentioned the finding expressed in case law that not every emotional experience or mental suffering of a claimant creates a basis for compensation for non-pecuniary loss, but concluded that the specific violation of fundamental rights would have caused any consequences for the claimant seems very formalistic.

2. Judgment of the Senate of the Republic of Latvia, Department of Administrative Cases, 20 December 2024, no SKA-256/2024 (A420234319) ECLI:LV:AT:2024:1220. A420234319.31.S: Non-Pecuniary Loss for Unlawful Data Processing Through Dissemination of Video[7]

a) Brief Summary of the Facts

39 The Consumer Rights Protection Centre (the Centre) organised a social campaign, within the framework of which it published a video clip *Pārbaudi–Pērc–LietoTo sociālais eksperiments* (Test-Buy-UseIt Social Experiment) informing the public about the risks that consumers may face when purchasing a used car. Consumers were urged to check the identity and reputation of sellers, as well as to be careful, as dishonest traders may use unfair methods, trying to imitate popular experts.

40 The main character in the video imitated the applicant by another person. The applicant is well known in Latvia since he has produced broadcasts for TV and now for social media regarding road safety and cars for almost 30 years. The character in the video dressed in a manner similar to the applicant, imitated the applicant's voice and his typical expressions and phrases. Also, one fragment from a real broadcasting video had also been included in the video. The main character depicted fraudulent activities to entice buyers to purchase substandard or unsafe cars. The applicant objected to this and requested the Centre cease the dissemination of the video and publicly apologise for the damage to his reputation and compensate for the non-pecuniary loss he suffered. The Centre rejected the request.

41 The applicant took the matter to court and requested that the Centre's actions be recognised as unlawful, that it be obliged to apologise and pay € 2,000 as compensation for non-pecuniary loss.

7 See on the Latvian Supreme Court website: <https://www.at.gov.lv/downloadlawfile/10792>.

The Regional Administrative Court found that the Centre had allowed unlawful data processing and imposed an obligation to stop the use of the applicant's personal data, including the removal of the video from social media. In this part, the judgment entered into force. The Regional Administrative Court ordered a public apology as compensation for unlawful data processing. The applicant considered such compensation to be disproportionate to the damage caused and appealed the judgment in the relevant part. 42

In preparing the case for consideration, the Senate decided to refer questions to the Court of Justice of the European Union (CJEU) for a preliminary ruling. The CJEU in its judgment in the case 'Consumer Rights Protection Centre'[8] ruled that: 43

> (1) Article 82(1) of Regulation (EU) 2016/679 of the European Parliament and of the Council of 27 April 2016 on the protection of natural persons with regard to the processing of personal data and on the free movement of such data, and repealing Directive 95/46/EC (General Data Protection Regulation), read in the light of Article 8(1) of the Charter of Fundamental Rights of the European Union must be interpreted as meaning that an infringement of the provisions of that regulation is not sufficient, in itself, to constitute 'damage' within the meaning of Article 82(1).
>
> (2) Article 82(1) of Regulation 2016/679 must be interpreted as meaning that the making of an apology may constitute sufficient compensation for non-material damage on the basis of that provision, inter alia where it is impossible to restore the situation that existed prior to the occurrence of that damage, provided that that form of redress is such as to compensate in full the damage suffered by the data subject.
>
> (3) Article 82(1) of Regulation 2016/679 must be interpreted as precluding the taking into account of the attitude and motivation of the controller in order to determine compensation to the data subject that is lower than the damage they actually suffered.

b) Judgment of the Court

The Senate examined whether the regional court had correctly considered the matter when deciding on compensation for non-pecuniary damage. The Senate recognised that the appealed judgment of the Regional Administrative Court in the part on compensation is based on incorrect legal considerations and quashed it in the relevant part and remitted the case for a new examination. 44

The Senate concluded that the Regional Administrative Court's considerations regarding the basis for compensation for damage were incorrect. Both the rules for the processing of personal data and the compensation awards for unlawful 45

---

8 CJEU 4.10.2024, C-507/23, *Patērētāju tiesību aizsardzības centrs*, ECLI:EU:C:2024:854.

data processing are provided for by the General Data Protection Regulation.[9] The CJEU in case C-507/23 has explained that a person seeking compensation for non-pecuniary loss must prove not only the infringement of the provisions of this Regulation, but also that they actually suffered damage as a result of the infringement.

46 The applicant pointed to the damage to his reputation, honour and dignity. With regard to the existence of damage, which the Regional Administrative Court did not take into account, there are several important factors that must be considered. In the opinion of the Senate, in circumstances where the General Data Protection Regulation allows a person to object to the processing of their data in various incomparably less significant cases, it is difficult to understand the position of the Regional Administrative Court when it states that publication for the long term of a video clip contrary to the person's clear objections, and moreover, the deliberate use of the person's long-established public image in the relevant clip is perceived as a minor data processing infringement.

47 It should also be considered that the applicant is a publicly recognisable person who has developed his image over a long period of time and, therefore, in this case, the impact on the applicant's public image and, accordingly, on his honour and dignity may be more significant than in a case when a person is not publicly known.

48 The Senate does not find any legal basis to believe that the applicant has a legal obligation or a mission to allow others to use his long-term developed image and reputation for such purposes and in a manner that he does not want and has not agreed to. Such use must be distinguished from journalistic interests and the public's right to obtain information about a person.

49 The Senate also did not agree that the content of the video should be assessed only from the perspective of a 'sufficiently observant' person. Here it would be appropriate to take into account that honour and reputation in society are also formed by the opinions of those people who do not delve into a several-minute long story at all but rather watch it superficially or do not perceive the message of the video as deeply as was intended.

50 The Senate also drew attention to the fact that, when determining the compensation, the Regional Administrative Court considered only the substantiation (justification) indicated by the institution for the processing of data. Such considerations have been found inadmissible by the CJEU in response to the questions

9 Regulation (EU) 2016/679 of the European Parliament and of the Council of 27 April 2016 on the protection of natural persons with regard to the processing of personal data and on the free movement of such data, and repealing Directive 95/46/EC (General Data Protection Regulation) (Text with EEA relevance) [2016] OJ L 119/1.

posed by the Senate. In determining the amount of compensation for damage, only the severity of the damage caused should be considered and the amount of compensation should serve only as compensation for the damage suffered.

c) Commentary

The Senate correctly indicated that a personal data breach under the General Data Protection Regulation (the Regulation) may, if not addressed in an appropriate and timely manner, result in physical, material or non-material damage to a natural person. 51

Since in this case the applicant indicated possible harm to his reputation, honour and dignity, if such harm is established, there is a basis to apply the right to compensation for harm provided for in art 82(1) of the Regulation. 52

Also, the Senate correctly indicated that that the arguments put forward by the Regional Administrative Court for its conclusions on the absence of harm were not substantiated. 53

The argument that it could not be established that the applicant's image used in a specific manner in the Centre's video clip was aimed at offending his honour and dignity, as well as his reputation, was not substantiated, that the purpose of the 'joke' video was to promote an increase in the level of consumer knowledge so that they would be able to make an economic decision based on truthful information about the purchase of a used car. Also, it is not a mitigating factor that the video was created within the framework of the performance of the functions of a State administrative institution and was aimed at achieving a lawful and necessary goal. 54

The argument that the video did not use the applicant's sensitive personal data or such personal data that were not already generally available does not justify the absence of harm. In a situation where the Regulation allows a person to object to the processing of their data in various incomparably more minor cases, it is difficult to understand the position of the Regional Administrative Court that the publication of an extensive and prolonged video clip contrary to the person's clear wishes, and moreover, the deliberate use of the person's long-established public image in the relevant clip, is perceived as a minor data processing violation. 55

The processing of data, against the will of a person, by making them public in a manner and context unacceptable to the person, first of all affects the person's private autonomy to object to the use of their image for purposes other than those of the person themself, and this affects the person's integrity and self-respect. It should also be taken into account that the applicant is a publicly recognisable per- 56 son who has developed their image over an extended period of time: therefore, in this case, the impact on the applicant's image and, accordingly, on his honour and dignity, may be more significant than in a case where the person is not publicly known. Public recognition does not give grounds for others to use one's image for purposes and in a manner that the person does not want and does not agree with.

57 It was rightly pointed out that the Regional Administrative Court incorrectly referred to journalistic interests and the public's right to obtain information about a person.

58 The Senate rightly disagreed with such a superficial assessment of the applicant's possible violation, that the content of the video should be assessed only from the perspective of a 'sufficiently observant' person, because honour and reputation in society are also formed by the opinions of those people who do not delve into the story of the several-minute video at all, but watch it superficially or do not perceive the message of the video as deeply as it was intended. Although the Regional Administrative Court emphasised that the video does not claim that the applicant is a fraudster, the video does not particularly emphasise the opposite, and, superficially, the image of the applicant is connected to the fraudulent act depicted in the video. Accordingly, the viewer may remain unaware of the applicant's true connection or lack of such connection with fraudsters and may form general negative associations. It should also be taken into account that the applicant is recognisable precisely in the field about which the story is made, therefore the negative impact is most likely in the field that is important to him. From the perspective of public perception, one must also agree with the applicant's statement that the court did not assess the circumstances that confirm the further spread of the story and the possibility of it being perceived negatively by the public at large, including on social media. The headline alone can convey the idea of the applicant's connection with fraud, especially to people who do not even open the article itself.

59 The Senate also found that, despite the fact that the Regional Administrative Court's judgment had entered into force, which declared the publication of the video story unlawful and imposed an obligation to stop using and distributing the applicant's personal data in the story, the Centre had not removed the video from its accounts on *YouTube.com* and *Facebook.com*. In this regard, the Senate adopted an additional decision on the fact of non-compliance with the judgment.

60 The Senate also rightly rejected the assessment of the Regional Administrative Court that this case was legally complex. The fact that the Centre tried to put forward several arguments to justify its actions does not indicate legal complexity in relation to whether a violation of the Regulation was committed. The applicant's objections to the script and the use of his image were grounds for the Centre to

carefully consider the validity of its actions in accordance with the requirements of the Regulation. After a clear objection from a person, it is already an institution's duty to properly justify that it may nevertheless act at its own discretion against the person's will.

An apology may be considered as an independent or additional form of compensation for non-material loss, in accordance with art 82(1) of the Regulation, provided that such compensation complies with the principles of equivalence and effectiveness, in particular in that it must allow for full compensation for the non-material damage specifically caused by the infringement of the Regulation, which must be verified by the court, taking into account the circumstances of each case. Accordingly, when determining the amount of compensation for damage, there is a basis for applying the Law on Compensation for Losses Caused by State Administration Institutions.[10] **61**

The Senate rightly pointed out that art 82(1) of the Regulation precludes the attitude and motivation of the data controller from being taken into account in order to potentially award the data subject compensation that is less than the specific damage suffered. In determining the amount of compensation for damage, only the severity of the damage caused should be taken into account, and the amount of compensation should serve only as compensation for the damage. **62**

It remains an open question whether, indeed, in all cases 'the exclusively compensatory function' provided in art 82(1) of the Regulation precludes the taking into account of the severity and possibly intentional nature of the infringement of the Regulation committed by the controller in order to compensate for the damage caused. The intentional nature could be a decisive element when a court determines appropriate compensation for an infringement, but this is a question of future interpretation of the CJEU. **63**

10 See the brief description and my comments in *A Bitāns*, Latvia, in: H Koziol/BC Steininger (eds), European Tort Law (ETL) 2005 (2006) 380, nos 1–20.

3. Judgment of the Senate of the Republic of Latvia, Department of Administrative Cases, 27 December 2024, no SKA-297/2024 (A420340016) ECLI:LV:AT:2024:1227. A420340016.19.S: Standard of Proof of Lost Profits in Public Procurement Cases[11]

a) Brief Summary of the Facts

64 In 2013, the applicant SIA 'Skonto Būve' participated in the procurement 'Development, construction and author supervision of the 1st stage technical project of the Academic Centre of the University of Latvia in Tornakalns, Riga' organised by the University of Latvia as a contracting authority. The University of Latvia recognised another applicant, not the applicant in this case, as the winner in this public procurement.

65 Following the applicant's complaints about the actions of the University of Latvia, the Administrative District Court, by its judgment of 22 January 2015 in case No A420451113, found that the contracting authority had violated the procurement procedure. The court's judgment was subsequently left unchanged by a judgment of the Senate 22 February 2016 in case No SKA 138/2016.

66 The applicant submitted a claim for compensation for losses caused by the violation of the procurement procedure – lost profit – in the amount of € 1,655,441 against the contracting authority and then to the Administrative District Court.

67 The Administrative District Court dismissed the application by its judgment of 28 July 2023. The court found that in the event of a legal procedure, the applicant would have been recognised as the winner in the procurement and the applicant would have had the opportunity to perform the procurement contract and make a profit. However, when assessing the loss calculation submitted by the applicant, the court found that the applicant had not submitted reliable evidence that would confirm to a level of reliability that the costs related to the performance of the contract indicated in the profit calculation correspond to the average market prices at the time of the construction work and that all expected expenses were included in the costs. Thus, the court concluded that the applicant had not properly proven the amount of the loss – the loss of profit – caused by the unlawful administrative act.

68 The applicant filed a cassation complaint with the following arguments. The court had not correctly assessed the losses in accordance with parts 3 and 4 art 12 of the Law on Compensation for Damage Caused by State Administrative In-

11 See on the Latvian Supreme Court website: <https://www.at.gov.lv/downloadlawfile/10823>.

stitutions. The court also did not evaluate the expert report conducted by SIA 'LBS Konsultants' on the construction cost calculations in connection with other evidence in the case – the loss assessment conducted by the accounting and consulting services company 'Grant Thornton', as well as the certificate on the applicant's average profit indicators from its turnover in 2013–2015. The applicant objected that the court had not informed it about the inadmissibility and inapplicability of the evidence submitted by it. The court made the institute of compensation for damage illusory, because, recognising that the applicant would have made a profit, it did not determine the obligation to compensate the loss.

b) Judgment of the Court

The Senate decided to quash the judgment of the court of appeal and return the case for a new trial. 69

As regards the standard of proof of lost profits, the Senate provided the following conclusions. 70

In cases of lost profits, it would be unjustified for the court not to award any compensation where there is no doubt, in principle, that the individual has suffered loss simply because it is not possible to determine its exact amount or the maximum amount claimed by the individual. Such an approach would make it practically impossible to exercise the right to compensation guaranteed by European Union law. 71

Since lost profits are always hypothetical and therefore their amount cannot be proven precisely down to the last cent, the amount that can be reasonably expected to be proven shall be deemed to be proven. The burden of proof on the victim to prove the loss must not be so strict as to make it difficult to prove to such an extent that it would adversely affect the possibility of obtaining compensation in the event of an infringement. 72

The determination of the amount of lost profits is to be primarily based on economic calculations, taking into account the costs calculated in the estimate of the private individual and whether, at the time when the contract was enforceable, they could have been reliably estimated in the relevant amount, namely, whether there were no significant circumstances that could have affected the costs, which in turn would have increased or decreased the profits. In a situation where it is not possible to determine the exact amount of losses, the court must consider whether the relevant costs indicated by the party concerned are sufficiently reliable in general. 73

c) Commentary

74 The Senate correctly emphasised that in cases of compensation for lost profits, it would not be justified for the court not to award any compensation if there is no doubt in principle that a private individual has suffered losses simply because it is impossible to determine its exact amount or the maximum amount claimed by the individual. Such an approach would make it practically impossible to exercise the right to compensation guaranteed not only by European Union law, but also by national law.

75 Since the court had set an excessively strict standard of proof of lost profits in the appealed judgment, and moreover, the court's conclusions regarding the amount of lost profits were not based on a comprehensive, complete and objectively verified analysis of the evidence, the Senate rightly quashed the judgment of the court of appeal.

4. Personal Injury

a) Judgment of the Senate of the Republic of Latvia, Department of Civil Cases, 21 March 2024, no SKC-3/2024 (C30532919) ECLI:LV:AT: 2024:0321.C30532919.10.S: Insurance Indemnity as Compensation for Non-Pecuniary Loss Caused to a Victim of a Road Traffic Accident[12]

76 The claimant suffered a road traffic accident. In a criminal case, the court found the person who caused the accident guilty of committing a criminal offence and established the right of the claimant to compensation for non-pecuniary loss. Compensation was recovered from the guilty person and from the motor vehicle owners' civil liability insurer in the amount specified in the Cabinet of Ministers regulations in force at that time. The insurer paid the relevant amount of money.

77 Several years later, the victim filed a claim against the insurer for compensation for non-pecuniary loss in a larger amount, believing that the amount of compensation for damage determined for him was unfairly low.

78 The court of appeal satisfied the claim and awarded compensation for non-pecuniary loss from the insurer, which exceeds the amount specified in the regulations. The court referred to the Constitutional Court judgment, by which the rel-

12 See on the Latvian Supreme Court website: <https://www.at.gov.lv/downloadlawfile/9899>.

evant provisions of the above-mentioned Cabinet of Ministers regulations were declared invalid, and they were not applied in the specific case either.

The Senate decided to quash the judgment of the court of appeal and return 79
the case for a new trial. The Senate noted that the court of appeal did not take into account the fact that the Constitutional Court declared these provisions invalid with retroactive effect only in relation to the submitter of a constitutional complaint in the specific case and that, in this case, the road traffic accident had occurred before the adoption of the aforementioned Constitutional Court judgment. Therefore, the court had unreasonably applied the consequences of the Constitutional Court judgment to the claimant, because the claimant was not included in the list of persons specified in the judgment.

At the same time, the Senate drew attention to the fact that the Constitutional 80
Court judgment does not affect the court's obligation to observe the principle of the primacy of European Union law. The Senate found it possible to interpret the Latvian legal framework in a manner consistent with European Union law. The fact that the claimant in the criminal case received compensation in the amount specified in the regulations in force at the time did not prevent him from bringing a claim against the civil liability insurer of the person who caused the road traffic accident and proving that greater damage had been caused.

Such a decision of the Senate was possible because, in the Senate's view, the 81
regulations were adopted to facilitate the protection of the injured party by ensuring the possibility of receiving immediate compensation if the relevant circumstances were established. The regulations create an obligation for the insurer to pay compensation in accordance with the formulas contained in the regulations, namely, damage (harm) in such (minimum) amount was presumed.

Since the court had already partly compensated the suffered non-pecuniary 82
loss in the criminal proceedings, the Senate emphasised that the victim does not have the right to receive double compensation for the same damage under both civil and criminal law. The principle of *res judicata* must also be respected, in other words, the right to rely on the fact that issues that have already been assessed by a court decision that has entered into force will not be reviewed.

b) Judgment of the Senate of the Republic of Latvia, Department of Administrative Cases, X 2024, no SKA-[C]/2024 X ECLI:LV:AT:2024:X: Compensation Insurance Indemnity as Compensation for Late Diagnosis of Oncological Disease[13]

83 By decision No X of 2021 of the Ministry of Health, the applicant was refused compensation from the Medical Risk Fund for the harm caused to the life and health of his father. The applicant believes that the harm to his father's health and life was caused since a malignant tumour was discovered too late.

84 The Senate quashed the 2022 judgment of the Administrative Regional Court, by which the applicant's application for compensation was rejected, and sent the case for re-examination to the Administrative Regional Court. The Senate provided several conclusions from the present case.

85 In order to correctly assess whether the patient has been harmed as a result of a doctor's actions/omission, it is initially necessary to identify the harm itself as accurately as possible in order to further correctly assess the causal relationship between the harm and the action or inaction of the medical professional, as well as the severity of the harm and the circumstances affecting it. Paragraph 8 of annex 2 to the Cabinet of Ministers' Regulation No 1268 of 5 November 2013 'Regulations on the Operation of the Medical Risk Fund'[14] defines harm as arising when a patient has not been diagnosed with an oncological disease in a timely manner and/or its treatment has not been provided. Within the meaning of the norm, harm to a patient's life or health is caused simply by the fact that the diagnosis of an oncological disease was made late and/or treatment of the disease was initiated late.

86 It follows from the legal framework that the diagnosis of a malignant tumour occurs within the framework of primary and secondary diagnostics, where the first stage is performed by a family doctor, and the second by a specialist doctor as a provider of secondary healthcare services. Within the framework of secondary diagnostics, a specialist sees the patient within ten working days after the patient has been registered for a consultation by the family doctor. As part of this process of diagnosis, examinations may also be performed, with the calculation that within one month from the start of secondary diagnostics, a decision as to the patient's treatment measures would be made by the specialist doctor.

---

13 As the decision itself was anonymised, certain information is not available and is referred to here as 'X'. See on the Latvian Supreme Court website: <https://www.at.gov.lv/downloadlawfile/10758>.

14 See the brief description and my comments in *A Bitāns*, Latvia, in: E Karner/BC Steininger (eds), European Tort Law (ETL) 2013 (2014) 361, nos 11–23.

A patient has a general obligation arising from legal norms to take care of their health, as well as to provide the treating doctor with the information necessary to provide medical treatment, but within the limits of their capabilities and knowledge. At the same time, it should be taken into account that medical treatment services can only be provided by medical institutions and persons who have special knowledge in this field, and it is not reasonable to require the patient to be familiar with all the nuances of medical treatment, even if they relate to their own specific illness. Therefore, special care is expected from medical professionals and institutions in informing patients. 87

Legal norms also provide for the obligation of a specialist doctor to inform a family doctor about the secondary health service provided to the patient, also if further examinations are necessary. The legal regulation implies the obligation of both the family doctor and the specialist doctor to evaluate the secondary care services necessary for a patient's health condition, to explain their urgency and the possibilities of receiving them, in cooperation with the patient. Thus, if the legal norms do not provide that it is the specialist doctor who registers the patient for a tumour diagnostic examination, then the doctor is obliged to explain to the patient how to receive the necessary examination in order to ensure a timely decision on the treatment tactics. Otherwise, the goal of timely diagnosis of an oncological disease and timely initiation of its treatment may not be achieved. 88

The Senate also by *obiter dictum* drew attention to the goals and methods of treating oncological diseases: (1) to cure the disease (including complete or partial remission, survival as the equivalent of cure); (2) to control the disease (dynamic treatment of the disease with variable success in order to prevent or delay relapse or recurrence of the disease); (3) to prolong lifespan or palliative therapy (the goal is not radical treatment of the disease, but rather reduction of tumour mass or limitation of further progression, in order to alleviate the patient's condition and reduce the burden of the disease). 89

c) Judgment of the Senate of the Republic of Latvia, Department of Administrative Cases, 10 December 2024, no SKA-794/2024 (A420290622) ECLI:LV:AT:2024:1210.A420290622.12.S: Appropriate Compensation for Harm Caused to the Patient's Health; Informed Consent[15]

Shortly after birth, the applicant (A) was diagnosed with tetralogy of Fallot, a congenital heart disease and declared disabled. On 12 August 2020, in connection with 90

15 See on the Latvian Supreme Court website: <https://www.at.gov.lv/downloadlawfile/10777>.

the aforementioned diagnosis, the applicant underwent a planned operation at the Children's Clinical University Hospital. The patient's health condition after the operation was assessed as serious.

91 Considering that the applicant suffered harm to his health during the treatment, his representative applied to the Health Inspectorate on 5 February 2021 for compensation for damage from the Medical Risk Fund. By the decision of the Ministry of Health of 12 December 2022 No 01-23.3/4756, € 73,991 as the total compensation for damage was awarded to the applicant from the Medical Risk Fund. The applicant applied to the court for a positive administrative act, believing that compensation should be awarded in the amount of € 142,290.

92 By the judgment of the Administrative Regional Court of 28 June 2024, the application was partially satisfied and the Health Inspectorate was instructed to issue a new, positive administrative act within two months of the judgment coming into force, by which compensation would be paid from the Medical Risk Fund for the damage caused to the applicant's health, taking into account the circumstances established in the judgment and the conclusions drawn.

93 The Senate quashed the judgment of the Administrative Regional Court and sent the case for re-examination to the Administrative Regional Court. The Senate provided several conclusions from the present case.

94 When an institution and the court deciding on compensation for personal injury from the Medical Risk Fund determine the harm (which is causally related to the violation of rights) and the appropriate compensation, it not required to make considerations of utility in issuing such a decision.

95 The Administrative Regional Court has not indicated a specific legal norm that would indicate considerations of utility, such a conclusion is also not otherwise justified. If a person applies to the Health Inspectorate, requesting compensation for damage caused to health, then the task of the institution – and, when reviewing its decision, also the court – is to clarify a number of factual circumstances: (1) whether the damage itself is identifiable and what it is; (2) whether there is a causal connection between the damage and the action or omission of the medical practitioner in the medical treatment process; (3) whether the damage occurred due to the unprofessional conduct of the medical practitioner; (4) whether there are any circumstances referred to in sec 12 of the Medical Treatment Risk Fund Regulations that exclude the person's right to compensation and that have not been established in the previous stages of the examination.

96 Also further, when determining the extent of the damage, it is first necessary to clarify the factual circumstances that affect it, for example, the patient's condition before treatment, adherence to medical treatment (sec 9 of the Medical Treatment Risk Fund Regulations). In turn, when expressing the amount of damage as a percentage (subsec 10.2 of the Medical Risk Fund Regulations in conjunction with

annex 2), both the institution and the court must determine the amount of damage that directly reflects the harm caused due to unprofessional conduct in the medical treatment process.

As regards informed consent for medical treatment, the Senate indicated that 97 in order for 'informed consent' to be considered as provided by a patient or their legal representative, the healthcare professional must also explain the risks of the treatment to the patient or their legal representative. This means that information must also be provided about possible negative consequences of the treatment, the occurrence of which is not inevitable, but only probable. Furthermore, the law does not distinguish between risks with a higher or lower probability of occurrence.

d) Decision of the Senate of the Republic of Latvia, Department of Administrative Cases, 13 December 2024, no SKA-874/2024 (A420302122) ECLI:LV:AT:2024:1213.A420302122.9.L: Extension of the Treatment Period under Evaluation[16]

The applicant (A) submitted an application to the Administrative District Court for 98 the imposition of an obligation on the Health Inspectorate to issue an administrative act on determining the severity of the harm caused to the life and health of the applicant's mother (B) in the amount of 100 % and seeking compensation from the Medical Risk Fund.

After receiving the opinion of the additional expert examination ordered by 99 the court, the applicant submitted supplements to the application, indicating that the examination revealed the fact that the applicant's mother had Parkinson's disease, which, moreover, developed before 2019, but was not diagnosed and treated accordingly. The applicant believed that this revealed new possible violations in the health care of the applicant's mother, which the Health Inspectorate had not assessed.

The judge of the Administrative District Court refused to accept the supple- 100 ments to the application. The judge concluded that the applicant, in the application for compensation submitted to the Health Inspectorate, did not request an assessment of the fact that the applicant's mother was not diagnosed with Parkinson's disease before 2019. Thus, accordingly, the applicant, with the additions to the application, did not comply with the procedure for the previous out-of-court examination of the case. In addition, it can be established that the ap-

16 See on the Latvian Supreme Court website: <https://www.at.gov.lv/downloadlawfile/10791>.

plicant did not comply with the three-year period (from the date of the harm) specified in part 5 art 16 of the Law on the Rights of Patients for submitting a compensation claim to the Health Inspectorate for the treatment period before 2019.

101 The Senate quashed the decision of the Administrative District Court and sent the case for re-examination to the Administrative District Court. The Senate provided several conclusions from the present case regarding an 'extension of treatment period'.

102 Cases regarding compensation from the Medical Risk Fund are closely related to the implementation of human rights guaranteed by the Constitution of the Republic of Latvia. Therefore, if the delay in the deadline specified in part 5 art 16 of the Law on the Rights of Patients for submitting a compensation claim is not related to the person's own actions, the person may not be denied the right to appropriate compensation.

103 In order to observe and effectively ensure the rights provided for in part 1 art 16 of the Law on the Rights of Patients, in cases where new information is revealed that indicates the need to extend the period of treatment to be assessed and the determination of which required in-depth professional knowledge in medicine, non-compliance with the out-of-court examination procedure is not an obstacle to accepting the application supplements. The court has the right and obligation to itself, when extending the period of treatment to be assessed, to find an effective solution in essence for assessing the possible violation in its true extent, if necessary, also requiring the institution's active cooperation in assessing the actual circumstances in accordance with the newly obtained information.

C. Literature

1. Case Law Summary

Summary of the Case Law of the European Court of Human Rights on Art 5 of the European Convention for the Protection of Human Rights and Fundamental Freedoms regarding the application of the measure of detention (Riga, 2024)[17]

The summary contains the findings of the ECtHR's case law in relation to the right to freedom, including physical freedom of a person from restraint, guaranteed in art 5 of the European Convention on Human Rights (ECHR). Any deprivation of freedom must fall within one of the justified cases of deprivation of freedom defined in subpara (a) to (f) part 1 art 5 of the ECHR. 104

Furthermore, part 1 art 51 requires that any deprivation of freedom be consistent with the aim of protecting the person from arbitrariness. It is a fundamental principle that no arbitrary deprivation of freedom can be compatible with part 1 art 5. The summary emphasises that, in this respect, it is essential that the concept of 'arbitrary' in part 1 art 5 is interpreted more broadly than non-compliance with national law. This means that a deprivation of freedom may be lawful under national law but still be arbitrary and thus incompatible with the ECHR. 105

The aim of this summary is to provide an insight into the case law of the ECtHR on art 5 of the ECHR in relation to the application of the measure of security – detention. The findings and examples of the case law of the ECtHR are systematised according to the possible articles of the Criminal Procedure Law of the Republic of Latvia, which provide both the grounds for the application of detention provided for in the Criminal Procedure Law, and the circumstances to be assessed in certain procedural aspects related to the application of detention. However, the summary does not refer to examples of Latvian court practice. 106

17 See on the Latvian Supreme Court website: <https://www.at.gov.lv/files/ uploads/files/6_Judikatura/Tiesu_prakses_apkopojumi/2024/ECT_judikaturas_atzinas_apcietinajums_2024.docx>.

2. Legal Articles

107 **Compensation for Personal Injury:** *K Silionovs/R Ivanovs*, Miesas bojājumu kompensācijas apmērs (I) [Amount of compensation for bodily injury (I)] Jurista Vārds, 1.10.2024, No 40 (1358) 28–33; *K Silionovs/R Ivanovs*, Miesas bojājumu kompensācijas apmērs (II) [Amount of compensation for bodily injury (II)] Jurista Vārds, 10.12.2024, No 50 (1368) 38–35

108 **Damages:** *V Soņeca*, Zaudējumu atlīdzināšana saistībā ar zaudēto iespēju [Compensation for lost chance] Jurista Vārds, 5.11.2024, No 45 (1363) 2; *K Balodis*, Valdošā uzņēmuma pienākums atlīdzināt atkarīgās sabiedrības zaudējumus koncernu tiesībās [The duty of a controlling enterprise to compensate for losses of the dependent company in groups of companies law], Legislation and Its Outcome in Latvia: Lessons from the Past, Current Trends, Problems and Solutions. Legal Science Proceedings of the 82nd International Scientific Conference of the University of Latvia (Rīga, LU Akadēmiskais apgāds 2024) 36–42; *V Reinfelds*, Zaudējuma atlīdzināšana par nepamatotu mantas arestu [Compensation for unjustified property seizure], Legislation and Its Outcome in Latvia: Lessons from the Past, Current Trends, Problems and Solutions. Legal Science Proceedings of the 82nd International Scientific Conference of the University of Latvia (Rīga, LU Akadēmiskais apgāds 2024) 168–174

109 **Liability for Malpractice:** *A Slokenberga*, Veselības aprūpes riska augstā cena [The high price of healthcare risk] Jurista Vārds, 15.10.2024, No 42 (1360) 33–37; *J Dzērve-Pavloviča*, Ārstniecības radīta kaitējuma atlīdzināšanas problemātika [Issues of compensation for harm caused by medical treatment] Jurista Vārds, 27.8.2024, No 35 (1353) 13–19

110 **Damages for Violation of Competition Law:** *A Gūtmane*, Pierādījumu nodrošināšanas un kaitējuma prezumpcijas mijiedarbība zaudējumu prasībās hibrīdlietās [The interaction of securing evidence and the presumption of harm in damages claims in hybrid cases] Jurista Vārds, 10.9.2024, No 37 (1355) 30–34

111 **Insurance:** *J Alfejeva* Kompensācijas principa būtība apdrošināšanas līgumtiesībās [The essence of the compensation principle in insurance contract law] Jurista Vārds, 5.3.2024., No 10 (1328) 11–14

112 **Quasi-Delict:** *A Bitāns*, Kvazideliktu regulējuma Latvijā pagātnes mācības un mūsdienu tendences [Past lessons and current trends of quasi-delict regulation in Latvia], Legislation and Its Outcome in Latvia: Lessons from the Past, Current Trends, Problems and Solutions. Legal Science Proceedings of the 82nd International Scientific Conference of the University of Latvia (Rīga, LU Akadēmiskais apgāds 2024) 89–95

113 **Civil Liability for Violation of Human Rights and Environmental Abuses in Value Chains:** *A Artamonova*, Uzņēmumu civiltiesiskā atbildība par cilvēk-

tiesību un vides aizskārumiem vērtību ķēdēs [A company's civil liability for violation of human rights and environmental abuses in value chains] Jurista Vārds, 26.11.2024, No 48 (1366) 47–56

Loreta Šaltinytė

XVIII. Lithuania

A. Legislation

1. Amendment of the Law on the Rights of Patients and Compensation of Damage to Patients' Health, 25 June 2024, No XIV-2797[1]

This is an amendment of the Law which introduced the model of no-fault liability in Lithuania in 2020. This amendment further modifies the Law on the Rights of Patients and Compensation of Damage to Patients' Health (the Law), which was already modified in 2022[2] and 2023.[3] It focuses on art 13, which provides for the right to compensation for non-pecuniary damage. 1

Before this amendment, art 13 provided that the right to compensation of material and non-material damage under the law was ensured to a patient and a person who received maintenance from the deceased patient or had the right to it on the day of the patient's death. This list included minor children (including adopted children), a spouse, incapacitated parents (including adoptive parents), or other actual incapacitated dependents, as well as a patient's child who was born after their death. This right was also granted to the deceased patient's parents (including foster parents) and adult children (including foster children) if they had a particularly proximate and affectionate relationship with the patient. The other persons who were proximate to the injured patient and wished to claim compensation for non-material damage could not do so under the special extrajudicial procedure established by the Law, which provides for a no-fault liability regime. Instead, they were required to seek compensation through a court procedure and to fulfil the general conditions for the establishment of civil liability. 2

1 Lietuvos Respublikos pacientų teisių ir žalos sveikatai atlyginimo įstatymo Nr. I-1562 13 ir 26 straipsnių pakeitimo įstatymas (TAR 05–07–2024, No 12617).

2 Discussed by *L Šaltinytė*, Lithuania, in: E Karner/BC Steininger (eds), European Tort Law (ETL) 2022 (2023) 383, nos 1–4.

3 Discussed by *S Drukteinienė/I Maculevičienė*, Lithuania, in: E Karner/BC Steininger (eds), European Tort Law (ETL) 2023 (2024) 407, nos 1–5.

https://doi.org/10.1515/9783111389271-019

3 After the amendment, the right to compensation for non-material damage has been extended to other individuals who had a particularly close and intimate relationship with the patient.

4 The amendment follows a ruling by the Constitutional Court of the Republic of Lithuania (the Constitutional Court) of 24 January 2024,[4] in which the Court had been asked to review the compatibility of the now amended art 13 with the Constitution. The question focused on whether the distinction between the individuals who were eligible to compensation of their non-pecuniary damage under a simplified procedure and those who were required to meet the general civil liability conditions to be able to claim compensation did not contradict the principle of equal treatment. The Constitutional Court found that it did. The Court emphasised that it was unconstitutional to allow only certain groups to claim compensation for non-material damage in extra-judicial proceedings. The ruling of the Court led to legislative amendments to ensure equal access to compensation under this Law to all individuals who suffer non-pecuniary damage.

B. Cases

1. *UAB 'Vlantana' v Daimler AG (Mercedes-Benz)*, Court of Appeal (CoA) 15 December 2023, no e2 A-653–934/2023: Compensation of Cartel Damage

a) Brief Summary of the Facts

5 The claimant (UAB 'Vlantana') brought an action seeking compensation of damage against Daimler AG (Mercedes- Benz) because of the anticompetitive practices which this company engaged in. The action was brought in view of the finding of the European Commission of 19 July 2016 that a number of truck manufacturers, including Daimler, had infringed art 101 of the Treaty on the Functioning of the European Union (TFEU) and art 53 of the Agreement on the European Economic Area by agreeing, first, on the setting of prices and the increase of gross prices

4 Ruling of the Constitutional Court of the Republic of Lithuania on persons entitled to compensation for non-pecuniary damage in accordance with the procedure established by the Law on the Rights of Patients and Compensation for Damage to Health, 24 January 2024, No KT10-N1/2024, case No 9/2023–16/2023. The texts of most rulings of the Constitutional Court are available in English at <http://www.lrkt.lt>.

of medium and heavy trucks, and second, on the timing and the passing on of costs for the introduction of emission technologies required by EURO 3 to EURO 6 standards. This cartel operated from 17 January 1997 to 18 January 2011.[5]

The claimant had purchased trucks from an authorised dealer of Mercedes-Benz (the defendant) in Lithuania.[6] It had regularly bought the defendant's trucks from 23 October 2004. It argued that because of the cartel agreement in which Daimler participated, it had overpaid and thus suffered damage. It also argued that it should have been compensated for the damage it suffered even after the cartel ceased to exist, because its negative effects continued and the prices for the trucks were not reduced. 6

In a judgment of 8 June 2023, the Vilnius district court upheld the action in part and ordered the defendant to pay compensation of € 1,689,762 as well as 6% of this amount as procedural interest (ie interest on the amount claimed in court). 7

The court agreed that the prerequisite of damage resulting from a cartel agreement could be presumed in view of the decision of the European Commission and considered that it was the duty of the claimant to prove that the other prerequisites for the establishment of liability were met. 8

The court rejected the defendant's argument that the Commission's decision was irrelevant to the case at hand because it only concerned gross prices, which did not affect the actual prices paid by the buyers. As the defendant failed to establish that the price applicable to VIP clients was different to the cartel price, the court rejected its argument that, in view of actual price discounts, the claimant had not suffered any damage. 9

It also rejected the argument that, as an unregistered business in Lithuania, it could not inflict damage on the Lithuanian market. The court was not persuaded that the decision to raise prices concerned only the German market and did not affect the pricing in Lithuania, as the European Commission concluded that the colluded pricing applied in the entire European Economic Area. 10

The court assessed the damage in view of the conclusions of its appointed expert. It accepted that the claimant had suffered damage in the form of higher truck sale prices. However, it reduced the damage calculated by the expert, because, first, it should have been calculated in view of the claimant's lease payment rather than the full truck price, and second, that it was not correct to take into consideration the markup of the seller, the third party, who did not take part 11

5 Commission decision of 27.9.2017 relating to a proceeding under art 101 of the Treaty on the Functioning of the European Union and art 53 of the EEA Agreement (AT.39824 – Trucks).

6 The data about the specifics of the transaction was omitted from the judgment as sensitive.

in the cartel. Consequently, the court concluded that the claimant suffered damage in the amount of € 1,644,762.

12 The claimant also sought compensation of a higher amount paid as lease interest which it had to pay because of the higher purchase price of the trucks. The court reduced the amount that was calculated by the expert who assessed it by the method of approximation.

13 The defendant appealed, challenging the findings in respect of unlawful conduct and causation as well as damage. It argued that: (1) the court failed to take into consideration that the defendant could not affect the end contract price because the trucks were purchased from the third party which was not a member of the cartel; (2) the court erred by finding that damage resulting from breaches of competition law could be presumed; (3) it erred by relying on the expert conclusion rather than on the expert reports presented by the defendant; (4) the court failed to take into consideration that a part of the award of damages was calculated for a period after 18 January 2011, when the cartel had officially ended; (5) further, the court failed to take into consideration that the trucks had been sold at a significantly discounted price; and (6) the court failed to take into consideration that the claimant had passed on the charges to third parties, and the court should have established this fact on the basis of the *contra spoliatorem* rule.

b) Judgment of the Court

14 The Court of Appeal rejected the appeal.

15 Relying on the *Cogeco*[7] and *Skanska*[8] decisions, the CoA accepted the defendant's argument on the point that any infringement of competition law does not automatically entail damage and that it was necessary to establish causation. The CoA then applied the doctrine of causation as developed by the Supreme Court of Lithuania (LSC), reiterating that causation may be either direct, when damage is inflicted directly by the conduct of the tortfeasor, or indirect, when the conduct (omission) of the tortfeasor contributes to the occurrence or aggravation of the damage.[9] It found that the mere circumstance that the defendant did not set the final price of the trucks did not mean that the trucks at issue were sold for the same price which would have applied had the defendant not participated

7 Court of Justice of the European Union (CJEU) 28.3.2019, C-637/17, *Cogeco Communications Inc v Sport TV Portugal SA and Others*, ECLI:EU:C:2019:263, para 40.

8 CJEU 14.3.2019, C-724/17, *Vantaan kaupunki v Skanska Industrial Solutions Oy et al*, ECLI:EU:C:2019:204, para 26.

9 LSC 3 March 2014, no 3K-7–144/2014.

in a cartel. Therefore, although the defendant was correct in stating that the final price was subject to individual negotiations with the buyer, the process of setting the price confirmed the connection between the gross and net price of the trucks.

The CoA further relied on the findings of the European Commission in its decision that, occasionally, the participants to the cartel also discussed net prices for some countries.[10] In view of this, the CoA found that the truck cartel did indeed affect the Lithuanian market and that the intervention of the direct seller of the trucks did not interrupt the chain of causation. 16

The CoA agreed that, at the time the damage was inflicted, competition law did not provide for a presumption of damage resulting from breaches of competition law. The legislative rule which implemented the EU directive on compensation of damage and which provided for this presumption only entered into effect on 1 February 2017.[11] The CoA thus concluded that it was necessary to apply art 46(1) of the Competition Law that was in force until 1 May 2012 and its art 43(1) (in force after 1 May 2012), which provided that damage was to be compensated under the rules that were in force at that time. Accordingly, the Court concluded that damage inflicted by breaches of competition law was to be compensated based on general rules governing tortious liability. 17

The CoA reasoned that although this principle was not explicitly provided for in the competition law of Lithuania, a similar conclusion could be made in view of the principle of *res ipsa loquitur*, which means that certain conduct as such may entail damage. Accordingly, the CoA considered that it was appropriate to apply a factual presumption of damage in view of clarifications of the CJEU to the effect that certain collusive behaviour, such as that leading to horizontal price-fixing by cartels, may be considered so likely to have negative effects, in particular on the price, quantity or quality of the goods and services, that it may be considered redundant to prove that they have actual effects on the market, and that it leads to the detriment of consumers.[12] 18

The CoA further cited the European Commission's guidelines on the point that 93 % of all cartels involve overcharges. In view of this, the CoA applied the presumption that the claimant had suffered damage. It did not establish any circumstances which would have denied this presumption. In particular, the fact that the Commission did not investigate the impact of the conduct of producers on the 19

---

10 European Commission Decision No AT.39824, para 51.

11 The Law on amendment of the Competition Law [Konkurencijos įstatymo Nr. VIII-1099 pakeitimo įstatymas] 18 January 2017, No 2017–01075.

12 CJEU 11.9.2014, C-67/13 P, *Groupement des cartes bancaires (CB) v European Commission*, ECLI:EU:C:2014:2204, para 51; 19.3.2015, CJEU 19.3.2015, C-286/13 P, *Dole Food Company Inc. and Dole Fresh Fruit Europe v European Commission*, ECLI:EU:C:2015:184, para 115.

market and did not calculate a possible overcharge in the market did not mean that damage was not proved. As the Commission established the cartel by purpose, not by effect, the CoA assumed that the cartel was harmful by its nature. The CoA further relied on the expert opinion and on evidence collected by the Commission in its investigation to the effect that the gross prices of the trucks were raised by all cartel participants in November 2010 and January 2011.

20 The CoA also affirmed the findings of the court of first instance in respect of awarded damages for the vehicles which were acquired after the official closing date of the cartel ('lingering effect of the cartel'). The CoA reiterated the rule formulated by the CJEU that the duration of an infringement may be assessed by reference to the period during which the undertakings concerned engaged in prohibited conduct, which can include the whole period in which the unlawful prices were applied.[13] The CoA thus assessed whether the cartel had a lingering effect on the truck prices at issue.

21 The CoA rejected the defendant's challenge on this point. The publicly available text of the decision only specifies that although a certain number of trucks had been delivered to the claimant at a time when the cartel was no longer effective, those trucks had been purchased during the period of operation of the cartel. The CoA still affirmed the conclusion of the court of first instance that the cartel agreement had a lingering economic effect until a date that was concealed from the public.

22 Finally, the CoA agreed with the defendant that if it were established that the overcharge had been passed on to its clients, this would be a legitimate ground to reduce the compensation, as the opposite decision would lead to the unjust enrichment of the claimant. However, under the facts, the CoA concluded that the defendant failed to prove that the overcharge had indeed been passed on to the defendant's clients. The CoA equally did not think that the defendant had met the duty to provide the necessary data justifying the application of the *contra spoliatorem* presumption, therefore the appeal was rejected.

---

13 Para 115, citing CJEU 30.5.2013, C-70/12 P, *Quinn Barlo Ltd and Others v European Commission*, ECLI:EU:C:2013:351, para 40; CJEU 14.1.2021, C-450/19, *Kilpailu- ja kuluttajavirasto*, ECLI:EU:C:2021:10, para 30.

c) Commentary

The truck cartel case is one of the most relevant recent EU cartel decisions which in some EU Member States, particularly Spain, has already led to settled case law.[14] The commented decision was handed down by the Court of Appeal in December 2023; however, it became accessible to the public only in 2024, hence it is reported this year. This is the first known successful decision of a court of higher instance concerning compensation of damage inflicted by competition law breaches. These torts have not yet been assessed by the LSC. Also, as the damage at issue was inflicted before the adoption and national implementation of the competition damages directive,[15] the case is invaluable as an example of judicial interpretation of the general Lithuanian delictual framework in the context of competition law. 23

The most important legal consequence of this decision concerns the presumption of damage in cartel damages cases. The CoA concluded that although this presumption was not applicable under Lithuanian law at the relevant time when Daimler participated in the trucks cartel, the CoA reached the same conclusion in view of the principle of *res ipsa loquitur*, or a factual presumption that such damage occurs, because horizontal price-fixing cartels always entail negative effects on the market, which lead to negative consequences for consumers. 24

This decision is an important reminder that possible victims of cartels in Lithuania have not yet explored the legal possibilities to be compensated for their damage, and this claimant-friendly decision will likely encourage an increase in the number of claims in this category of torts. 25

Regrettably, the other information which might be relevant for subsequent practice was either not discussed in the judgment or the discussion was 'concealed' due to the fact that it contained sensitive data. For example, although the publicly available decision discloses the total amount of damages that were awarded to the claimant, excluding procedural interest, information is lacking as regards the percentage of the paid price that was considered to constitute cartel damage or other information about the methodology of calculating the damages. 26

Also, there are indications in the decision that the case involved a problematic issue when assessing damage after the termination of cartel, (lingering effect of 27

---

14 *F Marcos*, The Truck Cartel's "Lingering Effects", <https://competitionlawblog.kluwercompetitionlaw.com/2024/10/03/the-truck-cartels-lingering-effects/>.

15 Directive 2014/104/EU of the European Parliament and of the Council of 26 November 2014 on certain rules governing actions for damages under national law for infringements of the competition law provisions of the Member States and of the European Union, Official Journal of the European Union (OJ) L 349/1.

the cartel).[16] The CoA concluded that the contract for the purchase of the relevant trucks had been concluded when the cartel was still functional. Consequently, the fact that some trucks had been delivered by the defendant already after the expiry of the cartel does not appear to be legally significant. Thus, it is not certain whether this decision could serve as a relevant example of case law in respect of compensation of damage for the lingering effects of cartels.

2. *UAB 'Sostinės investicijos' v the Republic of Lithuania*, represented by the Ministry of Justice, Supreme Administrative Court of Lithuania (SACL) 20 March 2024, no eA-708 – 624/2024: Solidary Liability in Tort of the Centre of Registers for Pecuniary Damage Inflicted by Criminal Conduct

a) Brief Summary of the Facts

28 In this case, a private company filed a claim for compensation of pecuniary damage against the Centre of Registers. The company became a victim of a crime when two individuals falsified a company document certifying that a certain individual became its sole shareholder and appointed himself as a company director. Based on this document, the Centre of Registers changed the official company data. After this change, the alleged new company director gained access to the company's bank account and withdrew over € 23,820. The company argued that the Centre of Registers acted negligently and should be found liable *in solidum* for the company's damage.

29 The Vilnius district administrative court agreed that the Centre of Registers had a duty to verify the authenticity of documents prior to entering data into a public register, but it decided that the Centre of Register's liability was several, finding it liable for 20 % of the damage, or € 9,528. The court attributed 80 % of the damage to two individuals who committed the crime.

16 See *Marcos* (fn 14).

b) Judgment of the Court

The SACL amended the decision, finding that the Centre of Registers was liable *in solidum* with the individuals who falsified the document and appropriated the company's assets. 30

The SACL's conclusion is based on an LSC decision from 2018[17] in which the LSC clarified that solidary liability in damages applies to all actors whose conduct contributed to the victim's damage even if that conduct was not its immediate cause. The SACL reiterated the reasoning of the LSC and found that the victim's damage was caused by the conduct of both the individual tortfeasors and the Centre of Registers, because the victim would not have suffered any damage had the Centre of Registers met its duty of care in ascertaining the veracity of the document before entering the data in the public register. 31

c) Commentary

Establishing solidary liability under similar circumstances has for a long time been challenging for victims who brought claims either before courts of general competence or before the administrative courts. Although art 6.279 (4) CC explicitly provides for solidary liability[18] and this rule has been in force since the entry into force of the Civil Code in 2001, the courts have generally apportioned liability between the tortfeasors, especially when the case involves the liability of a public institution. The courts of general competence have finally begun to fully apply the rule on solidary liability, but the case law of administrative courts has not been consistent on this issue. The commented decision is the first clear decision confirming that the rule has also been fully acknowledged by administrative courts. 32

---

17 LSC 30 October 2018, no e3K-7–143–684/2018.

18 Article 6.279(4) CC provides: 4. Where damage may have resulted from different actions performed by several persons and they are liable to compensation, even though it is determined that the damage actually resulted from actions of only one of those persons, the obligation to compensate the damage shall rest upon all these persons jointly unless the other persons prove that the damage could not have resulted from the event (actions) for which they are liable.

3. *PM v UAB 'Colagena', Kauno klinikos and RM*, LSC 6 February 2024, no e3K-3-39-313/2024: Clinical Liability; Compensation for Loss of Earning Capacity

a) Brief Summary of the Facts

33 The claim concerned compensation of the damage suffered by a patient, which had been inflicted while undergoing surgery which cost € 206 at a private clinic. The decision omits to mention any information about the nature of the surgery, the facts about the breach of medical duties and the specific damage to the patient's health.

34 The claimant's surgery had first been scheduled with a doctor RM at a public hospital (*Kauno klinikos*), where RM worked. This operation had to be rescheduled because of the claimant's health condition. The doctor then advised him to have the surgery at a different, 'Colagena', private clinic, where he also worked, because of allegedly long waiting times at the public clinic.

35 The Commission for Compensation of Medical Damage to Patients later determined that the patient suffered damage during the operation because of the doctor's error, and the complications were noticed by the clinics far too late. It also transpired that the private clinic did not have a licence to carry out operations such as the one at issue on the premises where it took place, even though neither the Commission nor the courts thought that this was causally linked with the patient's damage. The Commission awarded the claimant € 6,225 in pecuniary and € 10,000 in non-pecuniary damages.

36 The patient then filed a claim for compensation of damage against both the public and private clinics, and the doctor. He argued that the first clinic should have been held liable for his damage *in solidum* with the clinic which carried out the surgery. He reasoned that the option to carry out the surgery at a private clinic was made by the doctor, who had been employed by both clinics. Also, the public clinic failed to separately inform the patient about the possibility to reschedule the surgery on its premises.

37 Sitting as a court of first instance, the Vilnius Regional Court upheld the claim in part: it ordered the defendant private clinic to pay the claimant € 57,413 in respect of pecuniary damage and € 30,000 in respect of non-pecuniary damage as well as procedural interest. It dismissed the direct claim against the doctor and the public clinic, considering that even if the doctor's conduct might suggest some issues in relation with ethical considerations, there was no ground to consider that the doctor's conduct led to any legal consequences for the clinic.

The court also agreed to award compensation of future expenses. Because of the damage at issue, the claimant had to have a certain medical device installed, with a warranty period of two years. In view of this and the general male life expectancy, the court considered that the claimant would have to purchase this device at least 18 times, and, therefore, it agreed to award compensation of € 49,320 on this ground. An additional amount of € 5,751 was awarded as compensation for lost income for the period between 23 October and 24 November 2017. 38

The court, however, rejected the claim for compensation of future lost income (€ 250,000), pointing out that the claimant had not taken all the necessary and possible measures to ensure the maintenance of his working capacity. The court also relied on the fact that the claimant's working capacity had not been formally assessed, and it was not persuaded that the claimant intended to be engaged in the same activities for the remaining 27 years until his retirement age. Finally, the court was not persuaded by the claimant's expert opinion on the assessment of loss of earnings. 39

On appeal, the compensation of non-pecuniary damage was reduced to € 15,000, pecuniary damage to € 10,833, and the remaining part of the claim was dismissed. 40

The CoA pointed out that there was no objective evidence on the alleged severity of the damage suffered by the claimant, as he could still engage in professional activities, he could drive, his working capacity had been preserved, even if somewhat reduced, especially as he had neither purchased nor wore the recommended medical device. For these reasons, the CoA found that adequate compensation of his non-pecuniary damage would be € 15,000. The CoA also reduced the award of compensation of likely future expenses to € 2,740. The CoA agreed with the court of first instance that the claim for the alleged lost earnings (€ 250,000) should be rejected. 41

The claimant filed a cassation appeal to the LSC challenging all findings of the CoA and arguing that the award of € 15,000 was inadequate, especially compared with the legal expenses of the defendant clinic (€ 24,000). He also raised an objection to the fact that the court did not invoke an exception from the general procedural rule that the losing party must bear the litigation costs and challenged the decision not to award compensation for lost income. 42

b) Judgment of the Court

The LSC affirmed the decision of the CoA. It reiterated that although civil liability generally serves a compensatory function and is applied when actual damage has already been suffered and relevant expenses have been incurred, under certain 43 circumstances, damage might be manifest, although assessing it might take time, and the interest of the injured party requires that it be paid out sooner. Under these circumstances, pursuant to art 6.249(3) CC, the court may assess the future damage depending on a realistic probability of its occurrence and award a specific sum of money, periodic payments or oblige the tortfeasor to compensate it.

44 In the case at hand, the dispute focused on the need to compensate the acquisition of a medical device which the claimant was recommended to use but had not yet acquired. The court of first instance awarded € 49,320 for this purpose, considering that the claimant would have to regularly acquire a new device in view of its two-year warranty period. The CoA reduced this amount to € 2,790. The LSC affirmed considering that the warranty period of a device does not as such demonstrate that it can only be used for that duration and does not give any indication as to how many of them the claimant may need in the future.

45 In respect of the lost future earnings, the LCS reiterated that although the case law primarily focuses on the loss or reduction of actual income because of personal injury, it also assesses the loss or impairment of a person's ability to earn that income in the future, even if the individual was not earning any income before they suffered personal injury. The LSC specified that this interpretation is in line with art 10:202 of the Principles of European Tort Law (PETL) on personal injury and death, according to which, damage to health includes the impairment of earning capacity, regardless of whether the earning capacity is already exploited or will be exploited in the future.

46 The LCS emphasised that establishing the loss of earnings in view of the claimant's impaired earning capacity is a more challenging exercise, as pre-injury earnings is only one of multiple criteria that need to be considered. It is also necessary to determine how much the victim would have been able to earn had it not been for the injury.[19]

47 As loss of capacity to work results in some degree of impairment of the ability to work and earn an adequate income equal to the pre-injury level, the percentage of that person's loss of working capacity that corresponds to the extent of the damage suffered should be considered, as affirmed by the LSC in its earlier case law.[20]

48 Also, a victim's loss of earning capacity reduces their possibilities to engage in economic activity and generate income. As a result, it is necessary to consider the percentage of loss of earning capacity, which reflects the scope of damage caused by the personal injury. As was previously affirmed by the LSC, the loss suffered by

19 LSC no e3K-3–164–1075/2019, para 62.
20 LSC 20 April 2023, no e3K-3–123–1075/2023, para 63 f.

an injured worker because of personal injury is a partial loss of earning capacity. Therefore, the assessment of compensation of pecuniary damage should take into consideration the degree of loss of earning capacity, which means a monetary expression of a percentage of the loss of earning capacity during a given period.[21]

The LSC also reiterated that the burden of establishing the loss of earning capacity is on the claimant, who needs to persuade the court that it is reasonably expected that the claimant would have earned this amount but for the damage that he suffered.[22] 49

In the case at hand, the gist of the dispute was whether it was necessary to present a certificate on lost earning capacity from a medical commission for the purpose of claiming compensation of lost earnings for self-employed individuals. The LSC found that the courts of lower instance had not violated the rules of evidence in the case at hand. It confirmed that a victim of personal injury may claim compensation of any lost income, regardless of whether it was earned via employment or other legal relationships. Although loss of earning capacity is one of the relevant criteria, the reason that the victim suffers damage is not that their working capacity is reduced or lost, but because of the diminution or, loss, of the prospect that the victim will earn that income in the future.[23] 50

The LSC concluded that determination of the loss of earning capacity may be important for assessing the lost income of self-employed individuals. Such an individual should prove that the reduction of their future earnings is caused specifically by their reduced working capacity, and that they would have earned it had they not suffered personal injury. The LSC further noted that the certificate of working capacity, which is issued by the Disability and Working Capacity Assessment Office under the Ministry of Social Security and Labour, may serve as an official document with a probative value, which would allow the person's reduced capacity to work to be substantiated. Nevertheless, the LSC emphasised that the courts may accept as evidence any relevant factual data which corroborates the party's statements. 51

In the case at hand, although the courts had emphasised that the claimant had failed to provide the certificate of his lost working capacity, this could have been assessed in view of other objective evidence, which had not been provided by the claimant. 52

21 LSC 23 May 2019, no e3K-3-164-1075/2019, para 66.
22 Ibid.
23 LSC 20 November 2015, no 3K-3-604-219/2015.

c) Commentary

53 The case involves several separate legal issues which deserve discussion. First, many medical personnel who are employed by public clinics also work in private clinics. Having received some treatment at a public clinic, quite a number of patients turn for further services of the same doctor to private clinics.

54 This LSC decision is the first known decision in which the claimant attempted to argue that a public clinic should also be held liable for medical negligence of the private clinic because of the latter's alleged organisational failures. On this occasion, the argument did not succeed, but the legal analysis of the issue was not extensive, and this line of reasoning might be explored in further detail in the future.

55 Secondly, the significant differences between the estimate of damages by the court of first instance and the CoA in the case at hand reflects a lack of predictability as regards the assessment of damages. In this case, the LSC sided with the more conservative estimate of damages by the CoA, which appears to be reasonable in view of the moderate nature of the personal injury that the claimant suffered.

56 Lastly, the LSC decision in this case is noteworthy for its detailed discussion of legal criteria that apply for the assessment of damages resulting from loss of earning capacity. Notably, in this discussion, the LSC explicitly referred to art 10:202 PETL, which demonstrates the importance of these Principles in deciding legal issues that have been underdeveloped in Lithuanian tort law.

4. *AL v Lithuania*, represented by the Ministry of Justice, LSC 14 August 2024, no e3K-3-158-1075/2024: Public Liability for Judicial Refusal to Apply Interim Measures of Protection

a) Brief Summary of the Facts

57 In this case, a creditor claimed damages from the State because the courts had refused to apply interim measures of protection against the debtor and the debtor subsequently sold property and concealed the money gained.

58 The claimant, the creditor, was an 84-year-old man who had lent € 28,962 to a woman in 2014. In 2019, he filed a claim for the annulment of the contract and recovery of funds gained without justification. The claimant also asked to apply an interim measure of protection – ie to seize the only asset held by the defendant, her apartment. In 2020, the defendant sold that apartment for € 47,000

and concealed the money. The interim measures of protection were then imposed, but the defendant did not have any other assets that could be seized and her only income was a € 365 pension.

59 The court of first instance agreed with the claimant that the State should be liable for his pecuniary damage, but rejected the claim for non-pecuniary damages.

60 The court of appeal instance entirely rejected the claim and emphasised that under art 6.272 (2) CC, the State may incur liability for judicial conduct only if the court has committed manifest and grave errors of interpretation and application of law. In the case at hand, such errors were not identified. On the contrary, the panel established that the request to apply interim measures of protection had been rejected because the claimant had failed to present adequate arguments justifying their imposition: first, the precarious financial condition of the defendant as such does not indicate a threat of enforcement of the future judicial decision; second, the loan contract was open-ended, the claimant requested repayment of the debt less than 30 days before he initiated judicial proceedings on this issue; third, the creditor submitted a document from 2014 certifying that the debtor had difficulties paying her utilities fees, but this document was not recent and, in addition, this fact did not stop the creditor himself from lending her € 30,000.

61 In the cassation appeal, the claimant argued that the court of appeal instance failed to take into consideration that the judicial refusal to apply temporary protective measures in the case at hand was negligent.

b) Judgment of the Court

62 The LSC affirmed the decision of the court of appeal instance. It reiterated that in order to establish a manifest and serious judicial error of interpretation and application of the law, it is necessary to take into account such circumstances as the ordinary meaning of the applicable legal provision, its precision, clarity of the evidence, the complexity of the circumstances of the case, whether, in the light of the clear circumstances of the case and of the applicable provision of the law, it was necessary for the court to apply it. The fault of the court can be established only if it commits manifest errors of interpretation and application of the law which a qualified judge should not have made (art 6.248 CC). Also, judicial fault can only be established if the court had clearly violated the law, and if another judge in the same situation would have arrived at a different decision.

63 The LSC reiterated the approach of the CoA that temporary protective measures can be imposed only under exceptional circumstances, when the court is presented with convincing arguments and evidence about the dishonesty of the

defendant, the conduct by which they seek to avoid the execution of a judicial decision against them, and the court might accept as relevant both the party's conduct prior and during the judicial procedure.

64 Although the LSC agreed that the prevention of similar situations was one of the aims of temporary protective measures, it emphasised that this aim does not prevail over the interest to ensure its exceptional nature. A contrary interpretation would mean that these measures should be imposed in every claim.

65 Because of this, the sole fact that the debtor had sold her immovable property does not as such mean that the court had committed a gross and manifest error when it refused to impose temporary protective measures.

c) Commentary

66 This LSC decision was included in the report because of two reasons. First, it is a rare example of claims for State liability for judicial decisions. Second, this is the first LSC decision in which the LSC has coherently discussed the legal prerequisites that need to be met in order to find the State liable for its refusal to impose temporary protective measures.

5. *AB v Lithuania*, represented by the National Health Insurance Fund, LSC 24 September 2024, no e3K-3-162-1120/2024: Clinical Liability for Loss of a Chance

a) Brief Summary of the Facts

67 The claimant, who was 29, suffered severe pain in his neck and his hand and his feet felt numb. The doctor in the emergency room gave him painkillers and recommended he begin massage therapy. After two hours in the emergency room, the claimant was sent home. Later that day, the claimant experienced pain again, but this time he stopped feeling his body from the waist down. He was taken to the same hospital again, and he was finally examined by a neurologist who diagnosed, correctly, that the patient had had a spinal cord stroke.

68 Pursuant to the medical protocol, the patient needed to have surgery as soon as possible. However, it was Sunday, the hospital was operating under the Covid-19 regime, and it did not have the necessary equipment. An MRT test was carried out only seven hours later, on Monday, and surgery was performed two hours later.

In addition, the doctors failed take into consideration the patient's individual medical condition – vascular myelopathy – and, after the surgery, prematurely gave him blood thinning medication, which led to a repeated rupture of his blood vessels and further damage to his spinal cord. 69

As a result, the patient became paralysed from his waist down and permanently lost his full working capacity. 70

He claimed pecuniary damages in the amount of € 1,341,128 (€ 1,315,245 in lost income and € 25,884 in medical expenses) as well as € 200,000 in non-pecuniary damages. His calculations of lost income were based on the salary he was earning prior to the relevant event, minus social security payments. 71

The Commission for the determination of damage inflicted on patients' health rejected his claim, having concluded that the damage at issue could not have been avoided. The Commission considered that the patient became disabled because of a sudden aggravation of his own illness. Although the clinic failed to timely diagnose the illness that was developing aggressively and led to the damage to his spinal cord, in the Commission's view, this consequence could not have been avoided even with the best medical practices. Under the Law on the Rights of Patients and Compensation of Damage, such damage was not compensable. 72

The court of first instance took a different view. It decided to award the claimant € 25,530 in pecuniary and € 100,000 in non-pecuniary damages. The court found that the failure to meet the applicable professional standard of due care was causally linked with the claimant's damage and that it could have been prevented. 73

The court, however, rejected the claim for lost income. It is also important to note that the claimant had explicitly refused to request the court to appoint an expert in order to assess, inter alia, whether his working capacity would have been preserved but for medical negligence. The court thus considered that the claimant failed to establish that his full working capacity could have been preserved had the clinic met its duty of professional medical care. 74

This decision was affirmed on appeal. The panel found that although there was no objective data confirming that the patient's damage could have been completely avoided with the timely intervention of a neurologist as well as a timely MRT test, these services had not been provided because of negligence, thus there was no reason to refuse compensation of damage. However, the panel considered that the patient's damage could have been avoided to a certain extent, even though it was hardly likely that the harmful consequences could have been averted with adequate treatment and that his capacity to work would have been preserved. Accordingly, the court concluded that the claimant failed to establish that his lost earnings were 'real'. This part of the claim was thus rejected. 75

76 The claimant filed a cassation claim, pointing out that it was the court's duty to assess lost earnings *ex officio* if it considered that the claimant had failed to establish to what extent specifically his working capacity was affected by medical negligence and what share of his lost income was real. The claimant argued that to ensure an effective remedy, the court should have itself assessed the amount of damage. For this, it should have invoked the principle of 'practically impossible to prove', or it could *ex officio* have appointed an expert to present an opinion on this point.

b) Judgment of the Court

77 In this context, the LSC observed, for the first time in its practice, that the legal ground to award compensation to the claimant was the doctrine of loss of a chance.

78 Under the facts, because of medical malpractice, the patient had lost the chance to have the negative consequences of his own illness reduced. His interest is protected by law and the failure to take the necessary steps to ensure it leads to a right to compensation, even if the probability of success is less than 51 %. Under these circumstances, damage is calculated based on the value of the lost chance.

79 The LSC concluded that, in such cases, the courts have to assess the extent to which the probability of the patient's damage would have been smaller if the patient had been provided with due medical care, and only award compensation for that share of the damage which corresponds to the probability that the damage was caused by the defendant.

80 In the case at hand, the burden of proving the likelihood that his capacity to work would have been preserved had the clinic met its professional duty of care lay on the claimant. Thus, the LSC concluded that the courts had met their duty to assess damage; however, it clarified that the courts failed to award compensation for lost income under the facts of the case because the claimant had failed to establish that his working capacity could have been preserved with timely and adequate treatment of his condition. Consequently, the courts had no legal ground to consider the question of compensation of lost income.

c) Commentary

This new approach of the LSC is very different from its earlier established practice which this author discussed in a 2017 publication on assessing causation under Lithuanian law.[24] 81

Previously, the LSC would first assess whether a clinic had acted in accordance with its professional standard of due care. If this standard was not met, it would then consider whether the patient suffered actual damage. However, *de facto* it would not look for evidence that the damage was caused by medical malpractice.[25] 82

Now, the LSC emphasises that the claimant must prove causation, and damage must be assessed depending on the likelihood that the damage was the result of medical negligence. 83

The LSC has further clarified that the responsibility to assess damage shifts to the court only if the claimant cannot establish damage with sufficient certainty, but not when the claimant does not even present evidence in this respect. 84

Thus, in this decision, the LSC has introduced a significantly stricter approach to causation in medical negligence cases, which makes the judicial process more difficult for claimants. In other words, this decision makes causation a significant notion to focus on again in Lithuania. 85

Recognising that the loss of a chance doctrine is a part of Lithuanian tort law, the LSC has shifted the perspective. The decision suggests that a failure of clinics to meet their duty of due diligence would generally lead to the defendant's liability; however, damages would only be awarded to the extent of the likelihood that the claimant can establish that their working capacity would have been preserved had the hospital met its duty of care. 86

---

24 *L Šaltinytė* in: E Zervoggiani/M Infantino (eds), Causation in European Tort Law, The Common Core of Private Law (2017).

25 Ibid.

6. *UAB 'Kulpės slėnis' v Andrius Bespalovas*, LSC 17 December 2024, no e3K-7-127-823/2024: Professional Negligence Liability of a Bailiff

a) Brief Summary of the Facts

87 The case concerned a bailiff's liability for negligent enforcement. The bailiff had unsuccessfully been pursuing a judicial award of € 136,208 from two private individuals since 2011. It had failed to recover a single euro during the entire enforcement period.

88 The creditor, who instituted legal proceedings against the bailiff, argued that the reason for such failure was the bailiff's negligence. Specifically, the claimant, inter alia, pointed out that his request to seize one account of the debtor had been ignored by the bailiff.

89 Both the court of first instance and the court of appeal instance agreed that such a failure was wrongful. However, both rejected the claim, having concluded that the claimant failed to establish damage as a precondition of liability. They also agreed that during the period when the account had not been seized, the debtor had an income of € 25,457, and this money was not subjected to enforcement measures. The courts considered that this money could not be viewed as damage because the claimant failed to establish that it would have been used for the recovery of its claims, as the claimant was not the only creditor at issue. In addition, the courts considered that the claimant did not really suffer damage but could only have complained about the late recovery of a debt, because the recovery process was still pending. However, the claimant had not argued that it had suffered damage of this nature, and this was identified as a reason to reject the claim.

b) Judgment of the Court

90 The LSC, sitting in an extended composition, agreed to consider the cassation appeal in respect of the issue of damage and the court's duty to assess the extent of the damage if the claimant cannot determine it accurately.

91 The LSC reiterated that if a claimant establishes wrongful conduct of the defendant, a claim for compensation of damage cannot be rejected solely on the ground that their assessment of damage is not accurate or that the claimant fails to provide adequate evidence in support of the extent of its damage.

The LSC further emphasised that this provision should not be interpreted as shifting the burden of proof to the court – the court's duty to establish damage only arises if the victim cannot accurately assess its damage because of objective reasons. 92

On the other hand, the LSC emphasised that even though the burden of proof lies on the parties to the dispute, the judicial process is guided by the court, which has a duty to guide the parties and to seek to ensure a prompt resolution of the dispute. For this purpose, the court may not deny a claim merely because it does not think that the evidence presented by a party is not sufficiently clear to it. The court has an explanatory duty. In the case at hand, the courts established that the bailiff failed to seize the account of one of the debtors. It was also established that there was € 25,457 in this account, and this money was not subject to enforcement measures. Although the courts accepted that the bailiff's failure to seize this account was wrongful, they rejected the claim on this issue because the claimant allegedly failed to establish damage and its extent. 93

The LSC emphasised the contradictory reasons on which the courts justified this conclusion. On the one hand, they specified that the amount of money which had not been recovered could have constituted the claimant's damage, however, they considered that the claimant had failed to establish that that amount would have (and could have) been used for recovery of the debt that was owed to the claimant. On the other hand, the courts stated that the damage only concerns late payment, which was not the focus of the claim. 94

In respect of this argument, the LSC emphasised that the claimant's possibility to change the method of calculating damage was not restricted – it also could provide evidence in respect of an alternative calculation of damage, and such conduct does not constitute an amendment of the nature of the claim. Accordingly, the LSC found that if the court considered that the claimant has chosen the wrong method of calculating damages, they should have clarified to the claimant its burden of proof in this respect. Consequently, the courts could not have rejected the claim on this ground. 95

The LSC further concluded that the courts erred in stating that the nature of the damage suffered by the claimant at hand is exceptionally linked with late payment. If the bailiff acted wrongfully, damages could encompass the amount which could have been recovered had the bailiff carried out its duties in accordance with the law. 96

Furthermore, the mere circumstance that the creditor's right had not expired does not as such deny the fact that damage has occurred. The damage at issue consists of the value of the lost opportunity, which is calculated as the difference between the actual value of the creditor's claim and the creditor's share of the recoverable assets. 97

98 Accordingly, the LSC formulated a new rule in respect of assessing damage for professional negligence of a bailiff: where the bailiff's unlawful acts (omissions) result in the loss of the possibility to recover certain assets of the debtor, the damage caused to the claimant can be calculated as the value of the lost opportunity (the difference between the amount not recovered for the benefit of the claimant as a result of the bailiff's unlawful act [omission], and the real value of the claimant's claim over the debtor's assets for the corresponding amount of the bailee's right to the debtor's assets).

99 Finally, the LSC emphasised that the courts had erred in the case at hand by shifting the burden of proof to the claimant. The LSC clarified that after the claimant had successfully established that the debtor's account had not been seized by the bailiff, the burden of proof to establish that this amount could not have been used for the recovery due to the claimant lay with the defendant. In particular, the LSC stated that had the bailiff seized the money, it would have been under a duty to carry out enforcement from this money, unless the debtor presented evidence that this money was not subject to recovery.

100 In light of this, the LSC returned the case for reconsideration to the court of appeal instance.

c) Commentary

101 The significance and complexity of the case is demonstrated by the fact that it was decided by the LSC sitting in an extended composition.

102 The case constitutes an important and rather rare example of LSC jurisprudence in respect of the notion of damage and its assessment in tort liability cases for professional negligence of a bailiff. The clarification of the notion of damage is welcome as reflecting a strengthened protection of the interests of creditors during enforcement proceedings.

7. *DVJ v Lithuania*, represented by General Prosecutor and Vilnius district police commissariat, LSC 28 November 2024, no e3K-3-228-823/2024: Compensation of Litigation Expenses in Non-Pecuniary Damage Claims

a) Brief Summary of the Facts

The claim concerned compensation of pecuniary and non-pecuniary damage inflicted by the unlawful initiation of a pre-pretrial investigation and criminal prosecution proceedings. The court of first instance rejected the claim. On appeal, the claim was upheld in part and the court awarded € 500 in non-pecuniary damages. In light of 'the loser pays' principle, the court awarded the claimant compensation of € 1,000 of the € 3,180 litigation expenses which the claimant had incurred. 103

As a result, the actual effect of the decision was that the claimant found herself in a situation where her litigation costs significantly exceeded the amount of the compensation awarded to her by the court, and this means, in essence, that after the proceedings, the applicant was placed in a more disadvantaged position than she was in before she initiated the proceedings. 104

b) Judgment of the Court

The LSC agreed to consider whether such a result could be justified under the facts of this case. 105

The LSC first reiterated that the general rule governing the allocation of litigation costs is art 93 of the Code of Civil Procedure (CPC), which provides for the principle of the 'loser pays' and means that litigation costs are allocated in view of the outcome of the proceedings. However, if the application of this rule does not result in a fair apportionment of litigation expenses, as an exception, the court may rely on art 93(4) of the CPC, which allows taking into consideration the procedural conduct of the parties as well as the reasons for incurring the litigation costs. 106

The LSC then discussed the finding of the European Court of Human Rights (ECtHR) that the 'loser pays' principle as well as the requirement to cover litigation expenses in proportion to the procedural result may constitute a restriction of the right to a fair trial. Such a restriction may be held to be incompatible with the European Convention on Human Rights (ECHR) if it does not have a legitimate 107 aim and is not proportional to that aim.[26] Referring to the practice of the ECtHR, the LSC restated that unreasonable litigation expenses may be primarily problematic if the claim was successful at least in part, because they may constitute a large part of the compensation awarded by the court. In the absence of any solid justification for such a result, such a situation makes litigation pointless and renders that party's right to a court merely theoretical and illusory.[27]

108 The LSC further reminded that a strict application of the 'loser pays' principle in cases of compensation of non-pecuniary damage may lead to a disproportionate restriction of the right to a fair trial.[28]

109 In light of this, the LSC clarified that even if the CPC does not provide for exceptions from the 'loser pays' principle, when it comes to compensation of non-pecuniary damage, the courts must apply the criteria of justice, reasonableness and fairness in accordance with art 3(7) CPC and the exception under art 93(4) CPC.[29]

110 Although art 6(1) of the ECHR does not completely preclude situations when litigation expenses exceed the compensation awarded by a court, it is necessary that such a result has a legitimate aim and is proportionate to this aim. The LSC thus instructed the court to consider the claimant's conduct (eg whether the claimant raised manifestly unfounded claims for compensation of non-pecuniary damage; in this context it may be relevant whether jurisprudence on the issue was developed and accessible, the guidelines on reimbursable amounts, etc), the nature of the case, its importance for the applicant (whether the dispute concerned a civil claim between private parties, whether it concerned State liability for damage inflicted by its institutions or the duty of a private person to compensate damage to health, whether the defendant's litigation costs were affected by an excessive claim for compensation, the final result of apportionment of litigation costs and its effect on the final compensation, etc).[30]

111 In the case at hand, the LSC agreed that the decision on reimbursement of litigation costs did not comply with the ECHR standard, because the court of appeal instance did not take into consideration that the claimant lost financially having initiated litigation, even though the court agreed with her claim in part. Also, the court failed to consider whether such a result was appropriate under the facts.

---

26 ECtHR *Klauz v Croatia*, 18.7.2013, no 28963/10.

27 ECtHR *Čolić v Croatia*, 18.11.2021, no 49083/18, para 46.

28 ECtHR *Klauz v Croatia*, 18.7.2013, no 28963/10, para 97; also see LSC 4 January 2023, no e3K-7–75–916/2023, para 31.

29 LSC 31 May 2021, no e3K-3–117–969/2021, para 51; LSC 13 July 2021, no e3K-3–225–943/2021, para 35.

30 LSC 4 January 2023, no e3K-7–75–916/2023, para 31.

The LSC pointed out that, under the facts, the case concerned the compensation of damage inflicted by pre-trial officers by unlawful detention. The CoA did not establish that the claimant's legal expenses were excessive or manifestly unnecessary to ensure the effective protection of her interests before the courts, or that these expenses could have been lower had the claimant sought a lower amount of compensation for her damage. In light of this, the result cannot be considered as compliant with the principles of justice, reasonableness and fairness, as her right to initiate litigation becomes meaningless, whereas the judicial protection of her rights becomes ineffective. 112

The panel concluded that the amount of requested compensation of non-pecuniary damage did not affect the extent of legal remedies that she had invoked. Consequently, the LSC found that, under the facts, there was adequate legal ground to derogate from the 'the loser pays' principle and to order the defendant to reimburse all litigation expenses incurred by the claimant. 113

c) Commentary

The first decisions where the LSC suggested that the courts are under a duty to take into consideration additional criteria when applying the rules of apportioning litigation expenses in cases regarding the compensation of non-pecuniary damage can be traced to 2021.[31] For example, the LSC had found that if an individual claims a higher amount of non- pecuniary damages than is actually awarded by the court, this does not mean that he only has a right to compensation of his legal costs proportionate to the share of the amount that was awarded by the court.[32] 114

In 2023, the LSC, sitting in an extended composition, formulated the rule that the courts must separately discuss whether the apportionment of litigation expenses is just and fair when the claimant becomes financially worse off because of it even if he (partially) succeeds in his claim. In the case at hand, the claimant proved that her pre-trial detention was unlawful and was awarded € 500 compensation on this ground. However, because the court only ordered reimbursement of € 1,000 of her lawyer's fees, financially she had 'lost' € 1,680. 115

On the one hand, such a situation demonstrates that the costs of legal expenses may discourage parties from bringing claims while, on the other, it suggests 116

31 LSC 13 July 2021, no e3K-3 – 225 – 943/2021, para 37; LSC 10 March 2021, no e3K-3 – 47 – 916/2021, para 21; LSC 17 November 2021, no e3K-3 – 275/823/2021, para 13.

32 Ibid.

that the awards of compensation are far too low, rendering the right to a trial elusive.

117 In 2024, there were several cases where the issue of inadequacy of compensation was raised, however, the LSC has refused to pursue this line of argument.

118 Instead, it has formulated a more flexible rule, which requires the courts to fully appreciate the result of the litigation for the claimant if they succeed on the merits of their claim. Although under these circumstances the procedural rules become much 'friendlier', arguably the 'loser pays' principle calls for further development even in those situations when the claimant fails, because this rule may be used to discourage parties from initiating judicial proceedings. For example, in 2024, the LSC considered a case of unlawful dismissal against the Faculty of Law of Vilnius University, in which the CoA decided that the claimant, a dismissed lecturer who had worked for the same university for 17 years under temporary employment contracts, had failed to establish that her dismissal was unlawful. The claimant was ordered to pay over € 10,000 as a reimbursement of the legal representation expenses of the Faculty of Law.[33] The chilling nature of this award is evident in view of the fact that the claimant's monthly salary was € 1,100. Under the facts, the LSC amended the decision to the effect that the employer had a duty to compensate her € 2,000 in non-pecuniary damages for failure to communicate with her before deciding not to conclude a contract with her for the next academic year. However, the court still ordered the claimant to pay € 2,000 as compensation for her employer's legal expenses because she failed to establish that she had been unlawfully dismissed.

8. Personal Injury

119 Arguably the most important personal injury legal development in 2024 was the confirmation by the LSC that Lithuanian law provides for the possibility to apply the doctrine of the loss of a chance to medical negligence cases. The case *AB v Lithuania* has been discussed separately (see no 67 above). Another topic that has also been discussed as a separate case study is compensation of loss of earning capacity for self-employed victims (see *PM v UAB 'Colagena' et al* no 33 above).

120 Two other noticeable topics as regards the compensation of personal injury are: a) reimbursement of litigation costs in personal injury cases; as well as b) compensation of non-pecuniary damage to the secondary victims of tort. In

33 See LSC 10 June 2024, no e3K-154 – 684/2024.

2024, the former issue arose at least twice. First, the Constitutional Court found that the legislative restriction of the list of individuals who can claim extra-judicial compensation in cases of medical negligence was unconstitutional, which led to the amendment of the law on the compensation of patients' damage. This development has been also separately discussed as a legislative development.

Secondly, the topic of secondary victims' right to claim non-pecuniary damages was also discussed by the LSC considering a criminal case.[34] The case concerned a traffic incident during which a truck failed to stop because of technical issues, as a result of which the truck hit a man. The victim was pushed into a wall, his pelvis was broken and his urinary system was damaged. The court of first instance awarded the victim € 27,000 in non-pecuniary damages. A further € 5,000 was awarded to his wife and € 2,000 each to his son and daughter. On appeal, the decision to award compensation of non-pecuniary damage to the wife and children was overturned. The court argued that compensation of non-pecuniary damage to the relatives of a surviving primary victim can only be awarded if the primary victim is a minor child, and the secondary victims are their parents. The LSC disagreed, considering that this was incorrect as it had already been accepted by the LSC that the children and spouse of a primary victim as well as other individuals, listed in art 6.284 CC, who maintain proximate relationships with them, may also suffer significant non-pecuniary damage, which is compensable. The LSC, however, emphasised that these secondary victims may claim damages in criminal cases only under exceptional circumstances. Mere negative emotional experiences are insufficient for this purpose – it is necessary to establish that the health injury that was inflicted on the primary victim also had a negative effect on the life of the secondary victim. Under the facts, the LSC noted that as the primary victim lost 60 % of his working capacity, he could no longer engage in housekeeping activities, including grass mowing, logging, etc, which now had to be performed by his wife. Also, because of the injury, the couple's intimate relationships have suffered. Accordingly, the LSC awarded € 5,000 in non-pecuniary damages to the victim's wife, but not to his children. 121

In 2024, out of more than 100 cases considered by the SACL concerning State liability, a significant portion (around 50) involved complaints from inmates regarding inadequate detention conditions. One such case deserves mention because of its specific factual circumstances. An inmate, who was serving a life imprisonment sentence, claimed compensation for non-pecuniary damage because he was refused permission to attend his father's funeral.[35] The reason for this re- 122

34 LSC 29 November 2024, no 2K-248 – 1214/2024.

35 SACL 10 July 2024, no TA-19 – 968/2024.

fusal was art 67(1) of the Code of Execution of Sentences, which specified that short-term departures from prison were allowed only for those inmates who were serving fixed term imprisonment sentences. The SACL decided to refer the case for consideration to the Constitutional Court, which found the provision unconstitutional.[36] In view of this finding, the SACL agreed that the refusal to allow the inmate to attend his father's funeral was unlawful and awarded him € 1,000 in non-pecuniary damages.

123 There were no noticeable changes in respect of the amounts of compensation awards in personal injury cases in 2024, although victims repeatedly appealed against judicial decisions complaining about low awards.

124 In one such case, the victim of an intentional crime as a result of which she suffered from a broken hip complained about an award of € 3,000. She assessed her damages at € 8,000 in view of the intentional and malicious nature of the conduct of the tortfeasor who used the victim's own crutch and hit her already injured legs to inflict further pain and suffering. The victim had to spend two weeks in hospital for the treatment of her injuries. The LSC disagreed, emphasising that the awards in cases of intentional crimes which lead to similar personal injuries do not exceed € 4,000.[37]

125 In an apparently similar case, when the victim suffered personal injury inflicted by her partner, the award was a little higher. In this case, a man hit his partner while the couple were on holiday at a health resort. He kicked her body at multiple places, including on the head, and broke her ankle. The courts awarded the victim € 4,786 in pecuniary and € 5,000 in non-pecuniary damages.[38]

126 Similarly, a victim who was attacked on the street and was hit multiple times was awarded € 5,000, although one could assume that his injuries were more severe, as the public health bureau was awarded over € 13,000 as compensation of his treatment expenses, compared with € 130 that it had been awarded in each of the previous two cases.

127 The LSC reviewed quite a few cases involving personal injury inflicted by proximate family members, including by parents on their children. In one such shocking case, two parents were ordered to pay damages to their minor children whom their father systemically physically abused from 2017 until 2022 with a belt, a broom, pulling them by their hair and wiping urine from the floor with the hair

36 Ruling of the Constitutional Court of the Republic of Lithuania on the right of sentenced persons serving a life sentence to short-term trips for important reasons from the place of serving the sentence, 4 June 2024, no KT47-N7/2024, case no 19/2023.

37 LSC 28 November 2024, no 2K-254–1214/2024.

38 LSC 14 February 2024, no 2K-29–594/2024.

of one of the daughters.[39] The court of first instance awarded one of these children € 3,000, another € 1,500, the third one € 1, 000. On appeal, the award to the first child was reduced to € 1,500.

In another case, the LSC awarded € 8,000 to a minor victim from her stepfather who had sexually abused her and attempted to rape her via anal intercourse for four years since she was seven years old.[40] 128

In yet another shocking case, a husband was convicted for exploiting his minor spouse for prostitution.[41] The LSC considered that, from the perspective of criminal law, the victim was a child and underaged, even though she had full capacity because she got married when she turned sixteen. She was awarded € 1,500 in non-pecuniary damages, but this award was raised to € 4,000 on appeal. 129

The last case concerns a criminal case for manslaughter by two hospital workers who negligently carried a patient who was tied to a stretcher. The victim fell on asphalt, hit his head and died from a brain injury.[42] 130

The court of first instance awarded the wife of the primary victim € 18,000 and the son € 12,000 in non-pecuniary damages. The court instructed the damages to be covered by the insurer of the health clinic for which the two employees of the clinic worked. However, the total amount of awarded damages exceeded the insurance coverage of the clinics, and this issue was referred to the LSC. The case was returned for reconsideration to the court of first instance. 131

C. Literature

1. *I Izarova/Y Hartman/S Nate*, Mechanisms for the Compensation of War Damage: Toward a Fair Solution for Ukraine, International Comparative Jurisprudence 2024 No 10 (1) 29–49

The article discusses the issue of compensation of damage resulting from Russia's invasion of Ukraine. Following the invasion, numerous countries took action to freeze Russian assets. The article discusses the practice of Canada, the US, the UK, Belgium, Estonia and Switzerland in respect of confiscation of Russian assets. 132

39 LSC 26 November 2024, no 2K-250–628/2024.
40 LSC 20 March 2024, no 2K-46–648/2024.
41 LSC 22 February 2024, no 2K-64–654/2024.
42 LSC 30 January 2024, no 2K-12–511/2024.

It also discusses investment arbitration cases as a means to receive compensation for private businesses for their lost properties in Crimea.

133 The article emphasises the need to establish compensation mechanisms which could be funded by the frozen assets of the Russian Federation. It discusses legal and practical hurdles precluding the confiscation of Russian assets and argues that it is insufficient to merely freeze them. It advocates for the establishment of national legislation to facilitate the confiscation process.

134 The article concludes by asserting that the international community must coordinate efforts to confiscate Russian assets for Ukraine's reconstruction, stressing the need for a comprehensive international mechanism to ensure complete compensation for all damage inflicted by Russia on Ukraine and Ukrainians since 2014.

2. *A Mažrimaitė*, Medical Liability: No-Fault Liability System in Lithuania, Medicine and Law 2024, 209–214

135 The article discusses the no-fault medical liability system of Lithuania, which became effective on 1 January 2020. It examines the historical context, legal framework and the first judicial decisions in respect of the application of this model. The author concludes that while still in its early stages, the model aims to simplify the compensation process and foster a safer healthcare environment and represents a significant shift towards more patient-friendly, efficient handling of medical liability claims.

3. *R Paukštė*, Lithuania: (In)Effective Private Antitrust Enforcement in Lithuania? European Competition and Regulatory Law Review 2024, 111–117

136 The author, a Mykolas Romeris university lecturer and a former associate partner and co-head of the EU, Competition and Regulatory specialisation group at TGS Baltic, discusses Lithuania as a jurisdiction where damages actions for breaches of competition law are rare and rarely successful. Although a relevantly sufficient national legal framework on competition law has existed in Lithuania for decades, the number of successful cases has been very low and it has also not increased since the implementation of the Damages Directive 2014/104/EU in 2017. In this publication, the author discusses the legislative landscape governing this issue in Lithuania and provides an overview of all publicly available national cases re-

garding damages claims for infringements of arts 101 and 102 TFEU. She also offers an explanation of the reasons for the reluctance of claimants to bring claims on this ground for consideration of the courts.

4. *D Rimkutė*, Shaping Civil Liability in the Digital Age: AILD and the Revisited PLD, Teisė 2024, No 130, 129 – 143

Written by a Vilnius University doctoral student, the article explores the European Commission's proposals for the Artificial Intelligence Liability Directive (AILD) and the revised Product Liability Directive (PLD). 137

The article criticises the AILD for not providing for strict liability, which could limit the rights of those harmed by AI incidents. It also questions the restriction of evidence disclosure to high-risk AI, as lower-risk systems can also be dangerous. Concerns are raised about the AILD's exclusion clause, which might allow circumvention of the Directive. The revised PLD expands liability beyond manufacturers to include economic operators and broadens the definition of a product to encompass digital files and software. While this is a positive step, it might change the Directive's core nature, necessitating careful consideration to ensure consumer protection. 138

The article advocates for the inclusion of strict liability in the AILD, extending evidence disclosure to low-risk AI systems, and aligning presumption mechanisms between the Directives. These enhancements aim to better protect individuals affected by AI-related harm and ensure the Directives achieve their intended goals. 139

5. *T Stundys*, Bendrovės kaip *de facto* vadovo civilinė atsakomybė Lietuvos teisėje [The civil liability of the *de facto* manager of a company under Lithuanian law], Jurisprudencija 2024, No 31(1) 143 – 159

The article considers the concept of the 'de facto manager' and its implications for civil liability in Lithuanian law. The author begins by addressing the fiduciary duties of company management as codified in Lithuania's Civil Code, emphasising the obligation of management members to compensate for damage arising from improper performance of their responsibilities. He emphasises how this principle aligns with broader legal traditions in both continental and common law systems, focusing on the requirement that managers act solely in the interests of the company. 140

141 The article critically examines the 'de facto manager' concept, which encompasses individuals or entities who, while not formally appointed as managers, effectively control a company and make decisions on its behalf. Through a comparative analysis, the author explores how jurisdictions like France, Germany, and the UK have expanded this concept to include parent companies and other entities exerting substantial control. However, Lithuanian law is more restrictive, confining the 'de facto manager' designation to natural persons, thereby excluding legal entities such as parent companies. Calling for reform, the author advocates for Lithuanian courts to adopt a broader interpretation of the 'de facto manager' concept and to align national practice with international standards, thus ensuring accountability of those effectively managing companies.

6. *L Šaltinytė*, Nesutartinės atsakomybės už dirbtinį intelektą reglamentavimo ES aspektai [Challenges of developing regulation of non-contractual liability for Artificial Intelligence in the EU], Lietuvos Teisė 2024: Esminiai pokyčiai [Lithuanian Law 2024: Fundamental changes] 323 – 332

142 In this article, the developing framework of the EU legal regulation on liability for AI-related damage is discussed. The focus is on the changes to the legal regulation of non-contractual liability that have been introduced by the new Product Liability Directive, and the relationship between this Directive and the proposed directive on non-contractual liability for AI, which has now been withdrawn by the Commission. Having discussed the reasons why the existing tort liability system is inadequate for the assessment of non-contractual liability for AI, the article analyses the new legal regulation, its impact on the legal system of the EU Member States, including Lithuania, and assesses the prospects for its further development. It concludes that the new Product Liability Directive has made it easier for consumers to initiate claims for damage caused by defective products. Nevertheless, this does not replace the need for a separate legal act governing liability for AI. It would be preferable if the framework were adopted as a regulation, however, the political will for this step seems to be currently lacking.

Giannino Caruana Demajo and Lawrence Quintano

XIX. Malta

A. Legislation

No legislation of direct relevance to tort law was enacted during 2024. 1

B. Cases

1. *Noel Borg v David Norbert Schembri and another*, Court of Appeal, 1 February 2023, no 724/2012: Liability of Public Authorities; Foreseeability

a) Brief Summary of the Facts

The plaintiff and the first defendant are both prison inmates. During a violent quarrel with the plaintiff in the infirmary within the prison precincts, the first defendant grievously injured him with a razor blade. The plaintiff sued both his assailant, the first defendant, and the prison director, the second defendant, for damages. 2

The first defendant did not file a reply. The prison director disclaimed liability. He had done all that was possible to avoid the incident, which was entirely unforeseeable. Arguments between inmates which turn violent were not unusual. After a previous incident between the two inmates, they were placed in different divisions to avoid contact. However, the incident occurred in the infirmary, which is accessible to all inmates, although under escort. The incident lasted only a few seconds, which was not sufficient time for the guards to intervene. Moreover, the weapon used by the first defendant had been put together by him using legitimately permitted components: a shaving razor, a plastic knife and masking tape. 3

b) Judgment of the Court

There was no question as regards the liability of the first defendant. As regards the second defendant, the first instance court observed that the liability of public authorities is, in the absence of specific provisions of law, governed by the same 4

https://doi.org/10.1515/9783111389271-020

principles of liability in tort applicable to private persons, including liability for omissions where there is a duty to act.

5 In this particular case, considering that the plaintiff is a prison inmate and therefore to some extent a vulnerable person in a potentially violent environment, the prison authorities were under a positive duty – arising also under art 2 of the European Convention on Human Rights – to protect him. Although the prison authorities are not automatically liable for every harm caused by violent episodes between inmates, in the present case they ought to have been more vigilant because the incident was foreseeable, particularly since the plaintiff had informed them about the previous violent incident between him and his assailant. Moreover, the assailant had committed crimes of violence – he was a convicted murderer – and the risk was therefore higher.

6 The plaintiff stated that the director had ordered that there was to be no contact between the two inmates. Observing that the evidence tendered by the prison authorities on the point was inconsistent, the first instance court believed the plaintiff, and concluded that the fact that this order had been disregarded when both inmates were allowed in the infirmary at the same time was evidence of lack of supervision and lax enforcement of orders on the part of the authorities. It was certainly logistically possible to avoid having both inmates in the infirmary at the same time, and there was no reasonable justification for not doing so.

7 Therefore, the second defendant's culpable omission was in failing to ensure that both inmates were kept separate at all times. However, it found no culpable omission in the fact that the assailant had been allowed to keep the components from which he fashioned a weapon, since these were not prohibited items.

8 For these reasons, the first instance court found both defendants liable and condemned them jointly to pay € 62,387 by way of damages for loss of earnings.

9 The prison director appealed. The grounds of appeal concerned the finding of liability, and, in particular, joint liability with the assailant, and the assessment of damages.

10 As regards liability, the Court of Appeal agreed with the reasoning and conclusions of the first instance court. As regards joint liability, however, the first instance court had wrongly applied the provisions of art 1049 of the Civil Code[1] because the second defendant had not acted with malice. It therefore reduced his

1 1049. (1) Where two or more persons have maliciously caused any damage, their liability to make good the damage shall be a joint and several liability.
(2) Where some of them have acted with malice, and others without malice, the former shall be jointly and severally liable, and each of the latter shall only be liable for such part of the damage as he may have caused.

share of liability to 40 %, leaving unchanged the first defendant's liability for the full amount.

On the matter of quantum of damages, the court dismissed the appellant's argument that the disability benefit which the plaintiff was receiving as a result of his injury ought to be deducted from the award. It followed the accepted practice that the victim's post-injury residual income is not to be taken into account. 11

c) Commentary

The fundamental principle underlying this case is that of foreseeability coupled with the reasonable possibility of avoiding the incident. The prison environment, the previous episode between victim and assailant, the assailant's history of violent crime were red flags which were properly understood by the authorities when they transferred the plaintiff to a different division; this precaution was however frustrated when they failed to adopt the easily implemented expedient of timing the inmates' visit to the infirmary so as to avoid their coming in contact with each other. 12

As in the *Etienne Ellul* case reported below,[2] the award of damages for loss of future earnings without taking into account the plaintiff's residual income after the incident goes to show that, notwithstanding the 'official' position that non-patrimonial damages are not awarded except in exceptional cases specifically provided for by law,[3] the multiplier method adopted by the courts does in fact award non-patrimonial damages. 13

2. *Etienne Ellul v Director General, Health Services Department and others*, Court of Appeal, 6 February 2024, no 31/2016: Medical Malpractice

a) Brief Summary of the Facts

The plaintiff was admitted to a public hospital to undergo surgery for the removal of a swelling on his neck and he signed a standard consent form. The surgery was 14

2 See no 14.

3 Damage caused by a wilful criminal offence against the person or affecting the dignity of persons subject to imprisonment of at least three years.

performed on 16 March 2013 by the third defendant, a general surgeon belonging to the firm headed by the second defendant.

15 Although this particular surgical procedure is normally performed under local anaesthetic, the procedure on the plaintiff was performed under general anaesthesia. The surgeon (the third defendant) reported that he encountered difficulties 'because the lump was a bit deeper … in the neck region'. He further reported that the lump was an intermuscular neck lipoma. Although, prior to the surgery, an ultrasound scan was performed, in the surgical safety checklist the comment 'not applicable' was entered under 'is essential imaging displayed?'.

16 During the surgery, the third defendant removed a lump measuring 55 × 30 × 8 mm. The lump was delivered to the histopathology department on 18 March 2013 and the report dated 2 April 2013 states that 'large nerves are present within the fat, accompanied by thick blood veins'. The case file reports that 'no follow-up is needed'.

17 After discharge the plaintiff noted that there was still a lump in his neck, and he also felt pain in his face, shoulder and arm. On the advice of the second defendant, an ultrasound scan was again performed and the plaintiff was referred to the pain clinic for therapy. Since the pain did not subside, a CT scan was performed and the second defendant reported that a new tumour had developed in the same spot. An electromyography test was performed and the result showed that nerve fibres had probably been damaged during the surgery.

18 The plaintiff was referred to the neurophysiological department and a report dated 5 April 2014 states that the 'trapezius muscle shows de-innervation/re-innervation changes with no evidence of active ongoing denervation. This is consistent with an incomplete lesion of the left spinal accessory nerve, with signs of regeneration'.

19 The plaintiff declared that it was only at this point that he was informed that a nerve had been damaged during surgery. Since he was still in pain, he again sought the advice of the second defendant who insisted that the surgery had been properly performed. He also informed the plaintiff that, although the lipoma had grown again, he did not advise a second operation since it was risky and that not removing the lipoma should not cause any complications.

20 On 25 August 2014, the plaintiff was again admitted to hospital complaining of severe pain. Tests revealed that the lipoma now measured 84 × 57 × 33 mm. A departmental case conference was held on 26 August 2014 and it was noted that 'large nerves are present which might have now given rise to a traumatic neuroma'.

21 The plaintiff sought the advice of a different surgeon, an ENT specialist, who advised that the lipoma could be surgically removed but that the damage to the nerve was not reversible.

The second surgical procedure was performed on 16 February 2016 by the ENT surgeon, who reported his finding that irreversible damage to the nerve had been caused during the first operation. He also reported that, in his view, the first procedure had not been correctly performed and the post-operation treatment had not been adequate. 22

The lump did not reappear after the second procedure. 23

Since he was now suffering from a permanent disability which affected his capacity for work, the plaintiff sued the hospital administration (the first defendant), the surgeon who had performed the first procedure (the third defendant) and the department head (the second defendant) for damages. 24

b) Judgment of the Court

The medical expert appointed by the first instance court reported that the ultrasound scan performed before the first surgical procedure showed that the site of the lipoma presented certain difficulties to such an extent that, contrary to normal practice, it was decided to perform the procedure under general anaesthesia. Also, under normal practice, MRI scans are not performed prior to similar procedures; however, under the particular circumstances of the case, only an MRI scan could have established that nerve fibres were running through the lipoma. 25

The ENT surgeon who had performed the second procedure reported that the lipoma he had removed typically develops over a number of years. It had grown between the two procedures probably because it had not been completely removed during the first procedure. He also stated that the damaged nerve was superficial and easily identified; it should therefore have been identified during the first procedure to avoid damaging it. 26

This contrasted with the evidence tendered by the defendants, who stated that the nerve fibres were running through the lump, which could therefore not be removed without damaging the nerve. 27

The first instance court, whilst acknowledging that every surgical procedure carries unavoidable risks and that the surgeon is responsible for the correctness of the means used and not for the result, observed that the ultrasound scan performed prior to the first procedure had shown that the case presented particular difficulties, so much so that the surgeon had decided to perform the procedure under general anaesthesia. Under the circumstances, therefore, prudence required that an MRI scan be performed, since only this could have provided a complete picture. It also observed that the evidence showed that the first procedure had also failed to completely remove the lipoma. 28

29 The court concluded that the defendants had failed to exercise proper diligence in the exercise of their profession and were therefore responsible for the harm caused to the patient.

30 The defendants appealed. In their first ground of appeal, they argued that the first instance court had not made a proper assessment of the evidence. The plaintiff had failed to submit evidence that standard accepted practice in cases of this nature required an MRI scan; indeed, standard practice did not call for an MRI scan, which exposes the patient to unnecessary radioactive rays, and, in any case, an MRI scan would not necessarily have revealed the position of the nerve. Moreover, there is always a risk of damage to the nerves, even in a preliminary exploratory procedure; in the present case, damage to the nerve was inevitable since the fibres ran through the lump which had to be removed. The plaintiff was aware of the situation and of the risks involved, and still signed the consent form.

31 The Court of Appeal observed that the trial court has a degree of discretion in the interpretation of evidence and, even if facts are amenable to a different interpretation, an appellate court will not necessarily overrule the conclusions of the trial court if these are not unreasonable. In the present case, the first instance court had relied on a reasonable and legitimate interpretation of the evidence.

32 It further observed that the burden of evidence depends on whether the relationship between the parties is one based on contract or on tort. In the latter case, it is incumbent on the plaintiff to prove negligence on the part of the defendant; on the other hand, if the relationship is contractual, it is enough for the plaintiff to prove (i) the existence of the relationship, (ii) the harm and (iii) the causal link between the surgery and the harm. Once the plaintiff satisfies this burden, it is then up to the medical professional to prove that they acted in accordance with the best accepted practice and that there was no negligence on their part. It is now firmly established, since the judgment delivered by the Court of Appeal on 31 October 2009 in *Rose Gauci v Donald Felice*, that the relationship is contractual in nature.

33 Accordingly, under the circumstances, the burden was on the defendants to show that they had exercised the standard of care and skill expected of them.

34 Furthermore, the defendants failed to show that the patient had given his informed consent. Merely having the patient sign a standard form drafted in general terms is evidence that the patient agrees to submit to the procedure, but it is not evidence that he was aware of the risk inherent in his specific case. There is no evidence to show that he was aware of the danger that the nerve may be damaged and even less that the damage was inevitable.

35 The question whether standard practice requires an MRI scan is irrelevant in the present case. The evidence showed that it was evident at the outset that the

case presented particular difficulties, so much so that the procedure was performed under general anaesthesia, and therefore normal practice was not necessarily indicated under the circumstances.

The Court of Appeal also observed that it was not conclusively established that the damage was inevitable under the circumstances; indeed, the court-appointed expert had testified that the nerve was superficial and relatively easily identified and separated. In any case, even if the damage were indeed inevitable, this called for a prudent assessment of whether it was preferable to remove only part of the lipoma avoiding the nerve, or to remove it completely including the nerve. Since it was established that the lipoma was only a cause of discomfort and not a danger to the patient's overall health, it would have been preferable to choose the course of action which avoided damage to the nerve, which carried more serious consequences. 36

The defendants also alleged that the plaintiff had failed to establish the causal link between the surgery and the harm. The neurophysiological report stated that the findings are 'consistent with an incomplete lesion of the left spinal accessory nerve, with signs of regeneration', which implies that the harm is not permanent. Moreover, the patient's symptoms can be due to other causes. 37

The Court of Appeal summarily dismissed this argument: the medical expert's report conclusively stated that the harm and resultant disability are permanent. The expert also reported that the symptoms are neuropathological in nature and therefore attributable to the damaged nerve. 38

On the matter of assessment of damages for loss of future earnings, the Court of Appeal observed that the relevant factors are the multiplier, depending on the age of the victim, his degree of disability and his pre-accident earnings; his actual earnings after the accident are not a factor. 39

The final ground of appeal concerned the responsibility of the second defendant who, although heading the surgical firm, had not actually taken part in the procedure. Dismissing this argument, the court observed that due to the contractual nature of the relationship between the surgical firm and the patient, the head of the firm answers for the acts and omissions of his subordinates. 40

The appeal was therefore dismissed. 41

c) Commentary

Although the first instance court did find for the plaintiff, its reasoning follows that of older judgments which has since been discarded. Indeed, it quotes the old case of *Victor Savona and others v Peter Asphar* (Court of Appeal, 2 April 1951), which states that a surgeon is only expected to follow 'accepted standard 42 practice' and is not liable for mistakes in the exercise of his profession unless the mistake is the result of 'gross negligence'. As regards the liability of the hospital administration and of the department head, the first instance court followed *Emmanuel Sammut and another v Chief Government Medical Officer and another* (First Hall, Civil Court, 12 December 2002) in relying on the tort law principle of *culpa in eligendo* in terms of art 1037 of the Civil Code,[4] thereby rejecting more recent judgments which consider the relationship between the hospital and the surgeon, on the one hand, and the patient on the other as being contractual in nature and not based on tort.

43 The Court of Appeal, while confirming the judgment, corrected this deviation from established jurisprudence. It reaffirmed the contractual nature of the relationship even when the procedure is carried out in a public hospital where the patient does not directly engage the surgeon.

44 Another point of interest is the statement by the Court of Appeal that the victim's post-accident residual earnings are not a factor to be taken into account in assessing his loss of future income. This reinforces the view that the multiplier method of assessment of *lucrum cessans* includes an element of non-pecuniary damages since the compensation is awarded in full even if the victim suffers no actual reduction of income.

45 Perhaps the most important contribution of the Court of Appeal judgment to the law on medical malpractice is to be found in its comments on what is required for a proper informed consent. Getting the patient to sign a standard form is not sufficient, nor are generic statements such as 'explained procedures and risk' enough; the patient must be given a proper explanation of what the procedure involves and what the risks are for their consent to be valid. However, in our view, in practice, the situation is more nuanced and depends to some extent on the patient's psychological condition. Although the patient is indeed entitled to full information, in some cases, particularly if the patient is psychologically fragile or sensitive, the information may do more harm than good and may result in a loss of morale, which impedes the healing process or indeed worsens the patient's condition. The decision is not necessarily the surgeon's alone, but it may perhaps not be practical to assess the patient's psychological condition in each case prior to surgery. The situation is not so open-and-shut as the court makes it out to be, and may lead to 'defensive' disclosure, which may be harmful in some cases.

4 1037. Where a person for any work or service whatsoever employs another person who is incompetent, or whom he has not reasonable grounds to consider competent, he shall be liable for any damage which such other person may, through incompetence in the performance of such work or service, cause to others.

Finally, it is remarkable that the defendants – all medical professionals – were allowed to get away with, in effect, attempting to mislead the court by stating that an MRI scan was disproportionate and contra-indicated in this case because it would expose the patient to unnecessary radioactive rays. It is well known that MRI scans do not emit ionising radiation. 46

3. *Vladyslava Kravchenko and another v Kevin Micallef and others*, Court of Appeal, 26 February 2024, no 966/2009: Responsibility of Event Organisers and of Public Authorities; Responsibility for Sub-Contractors; Responsibility of Company Directors

a) Brief Summary of the Facts

The first two defendants were responsible for organising an open-air show and had contracted the fifth defendant, a company, to install scaffolding to support lighting for the event. The fourth defendant was a director of the company. The event was sponsored by the local council, the third defendant, which had applied for and obtained the necessary police permits for the event. 47

During the event, strong winds caused the scaffolding supporting the lights to collapse, resulting in injuries to several attendees, including the first plaintiff, an 18-year-old paying spectator, who sustained severe injuries and subsequently became paraplegic. She sued all five defendants for damages. The second plaintiff, her mother, joined the suit as a co-plaintiff, claiming that she incurred expenses and lost income while caring for her daughter after her injury. 48

A court-appointed expert established that the first plaintiff suffered a 75 % permanent disability. 49

b) Judgment of the Court

The first instance court noted that severe weather warnings were in force before and during the event. Under these circumstances, the company responsible for the scaffolding should have taken necessary precautions to ensure the stability of the structure, taking into account the weather conditions and the fact that the structure was top heavy. The lack of these precautions resulted in the collapse of the structure due to force 5 winds. The defence of force majeure was therefore dismissed because the primary cause of the collapse was the scaffolding's instability. 50

51 The organisers should have cancelled the event due to the adverse weather conditions. Furthermore, as they had engaged the company (the fifth defendant) which lacked properly qualified personnel to install the scaffolding, they were liable for *culpa in eligendo* under art 1037 of the Civil Code.[5]

52 The local council had applied for and obtained the police permits for the event. These permits included a condition stipulating that the 'licensee must ensure that the area in the immediate vicinity of the venue does not constitute any sort of danger to patrons attending the event'. As the council failed to ensure this condition was met, it shared responsibility for the accident. Moreover, the council had taken out insurance for the event, which confirms its responsibility.

53 The court found the organisers (the first two defendants), the company (the fifth defendant), and the local council (the third defendant) jointly responsible for the incident. In view of the distinct legal personality of the company, the claim against its director (the fourth defendant) was dismissed.

54 The court awarded the first plaintiff € 25,038 for expenses incurred and a further € 438,428 for loss of future earnings. This amount was calculated based on her annual earnings of € 17,173, a 75 % disability, and an 8 % deduction from the lump sum payment over 37 years (the multiplier), together with interest from the date of filing of the claim. However, the court dismissed the claim of the second plaintiff (the mother) due to lack of evidence of expenses and losses incurred.

55 The local council, the organisers, and the company filed appeals, while the plaintiffs submitted a cross-appeal.

56 The local council raised several procedural pleas, all of which were dismissed. On the merits, the council contended that the company director should not have been absolved of responsibility, given his personal involvement and direct supervision over the erection of the structure. Additionally, the council argued that the first instance court had erred in attributing liability to it based solely on the acquisition of a police permit and insurance coverage. The final ground of appeal pertained to the commencement date for the accrual of interest.

57 The Court of Appeal first addressed the local council's primary substantive ground of appeal, which contended that the company director should not have been relieved of responsibility. This argument was also presented by both the organisers and the plaintiffs in their appeals.

58 The court examined the question of whether a company director could be held liable in tort for acts or omissions committed by the company. It determined that a company's distinct legal personality does not automatically shield its directors from tort liability. In this case, the director played an active role in the com-

5 See fn 4 above.

pany's management. He had been personally involved in the project, making decisions on technical details directing the works. The scaffolding was a physical structure erected by a physical person who, due to his lack of appropriate qualifications and failure to assess all risk factors and take necessary precautions, was to be held accountable for his actions and omissions.

Consequently, this ground of appeal was upheld. 59

The Court of Appeal then examined the local council's claim that it had been 60 wrongly held liable. The court concurred that the council's procurement of insurance was not a sufficient basis for liability, as obtaining insurance coverage was a prerequisite for securing a police licence for the event. However, as the licensee, the council had assumed the responsibility to oversee the event to ensure the safety of attendees. In this duty the council failed, as it did not seek certification from qualified individuals to ensure that the structure met technical requirements.

The local council's final ground of appeal, which was also a ground of the or- 61 ganisers' appeal, concerned the commencement date for the accrual of interest. The Court of Appeal agreed that, in accordance with established practice, interest should accrue from the date the sum due is determined in the judgment, rather than from the initiation of the action. Consequently, this ground of appeal was upheld.

Next, the court considered the organisers' remaining grounds of appeal. They 62 contended that the fault lay solely with the company contracted to install the scaffolding, and that there was no basis for attributing fault to them under art 1037 of the Civil Code. They also argued that the accident was attributable to force majeure and that the damages had been improperly assessed.

The court determined that the relationship between the organisers and the 63 first plaintiff, as a paying attendee, was contractual in nature. As such, the organisers were under a contractual obligation to take all necessary measures to avoid exposing the plaintiff to preventable harm and could not delegate this responsibility to others. Consequently, this ground of appeal was dismissed.

Regarding the defence of force majeure, the court noted that this defence can- 64 not be upheld when the harmful event results from the act or omission of the responsible party. In the present case, it was sufficiently demonstrated that the company engaged by the organisers had negligently failed to ensure the stability of the structure, which was the primary cause of the accident.

The final ground of the organisers' appeal pertained to the assessment of 65 damages, specifically the use of a 37-year multiplier and the minimal 8 % reduction of the award in light of the lump sum benefit. The organisers argued that the multiplier should not be based solely on maximum working life expectancy but should also consider the 'chances and changes of life'.

66 The Court of Appeal held that, given that the plaintiff was only 17 years old at the time of the injury, a 37-year multiplier was justified. Regarding the lump sum benefit, the court noted that, since interest was to be awarded from the date of the initial judgment and the case was being finally resolved more than ten years after its commencement, the plaintiff did not receive a benefit from the lump sum payment that warranted a greater reduction. Therefore, the court found no reason to exceed the 8% reduction decided by the first court, particularly since the plaintiff had in no way contributed to the delay.

67 Lastly, the court addressed the appeal of the company (the fifth defendant), which claimed that the structure was technically capable of withstanding the forecasted force 5 winds. The company argued that it was therefore evident that the wind was stronger than what the forecast had led them to believe, making the event unforeseeable. Moreover, the structure had been erected on other occasions without an accident occurring.

68 The court held that the weather forecast should have alerted the company to the necessity of additional precautions. The court-appointed expert noted that the structure was top-heavy and therefore unstable, which could have been mitigated by adding weights at a lower level and securing it with cables. The company's failure to take these precautions, despite the foreseeable risk of strong gusts of wind toppling the structure, led to the dismissal of its appeal.

69 Subsequently, the court addressed the plaintiffs' cross-appeal. The issue of the company director's responsibility had already been resolved.[6] The remaining grounds concerned the dismissal of the second plaintiff's (the mother's) claim for expenses and loss of earnings, as well as the first court's failure to award non-patrimonial damages and damages for future expenses which will be required for the care of the first plaintiff.

70 The second plaintiff's appeal was rejected because she did not provide evidence of lost earnings or receipts for the claimed expenses. The first instance court rightly dismissed the claim due to the lack of concrete evidence, which could have easily been presented during the trial. While the court has the authority to assess and award damages *arbitrio boni viri*, it can only do so when the plaintiff is unable to produce the necessary evidence, not when the evidence is available but not presented, as in this case. Since this evidence could have been introduced at the initial trial, the Court of Appeal refused to allow the plaintiff to submit it at the appeal stage.

71 Regarding the first plaintiff's future expenses, the Court of Appeal noted that she will certainly face additional medical costs. As her mother ages and can no

6 See no 58 above.

longer care for her as she does now, the plaintiff will likely need to hire a caregiver in the future. In such situations, the court can use its discretion to estimate future expenses, as it is clearly impossible to provide receipts at this time. Consequently, the court awarded an additional € 50,000 for future expenses.

The court then addressed the issue of non-patrimonial (moral) damages. It observed that, as amended in 2018 (with the amendments reported in the 2018 Yearbook[7]), art 1045 of the Civil Code stipulates that damage to be made good shall also include any moral harm but only in the case of damage arising from a criminal offence, other than an involuntary offence, and only in the case of crimes affecting the dignity of persons. Since the accident occurred before the 2018 amendments took effect, and the harm was not due to a voluntary offence, non-patrimonial damages cannot be awarded in this case. 72

c) Commentary

The local council's argument that the company director should not have been absolved of responsibility is compelling. The Court of Appeal's acknowledgement that a company's distinct legal personality does not shield its directors from tort liability reinforces the accountability of individuals in positions of authority, especially when directly involved in decision-making and supervision. This decision underscores the importance of personal responsibility in corporate governance. 73

The court's finding that taking out insurance coverage is not tantamount to preventively assuming liability for the harm covered by the insurance clarifies that insurance is a protective measure rather than an admission of fault, and serves to counter the moral hazard associated with insurers' 'deep pockets'. However, merely fulfilling statutory requirements (like obtaining insurance) does not equate to meeting substantive obligations (like ensuring safety). This finding reaffirms the importance of proactive oversight by local authorities, especially in public safety matters. 74

The court's decision to uphold that interest should accrue from the date the sum due is determined in the judgment aligns with established practice. This serves to mitigate prolonged legal battles by ensuring that interest penalties provide a financial disincentive against unnecessary delays. However, it may also un- 75

7 *G Caruana Demajo/L Quintano/DE Zammit*, Malta, in: E Karner/BC Steininger (eds), European Tort Law (ETL) 2018 (2019) 401, nos 1–6.

fairly punish creditors and reward defendants who retain the use of the money which is rightfully owed to the creditor.

76 The court dismissed the organisers' claim that they bore no fault under art 1037 of the Civil Code, underlining the notion that contractual relationships entail inherent responsibilities which cannot be delegated. The rejection of the force majeure defence further highlights the inadequacy of the organisers' risk management practices. By failing to ensure the stability of the structure, the organisers could not evade liability by attributing the accident to unforeseeable forces.

77 The court's rationale for using a 37-year multiplier is justifiable, given the plaintiff's young age and life expectancy. The minimal reduction of the lump sum benefit reflects a balanced approach, considering the prolonged legal proceedings and the plaintiff's lack of contributory delay. However, the reference to potential contributory delay undermines the rationale behind the lump sum deduction. This deduction is not based on fault for the delay but on the fact that the creditor is receiving anticipated future earnings in advance. If the plaintiff does not fully benefit from this advance due to delays in determining the sum due, the justification for the full reduction diminishes.

78 The dismissal of the company's appeal underscores the critical importance of adhering to safety standards and proactively mitigating foreseeable risks. The court-appointed expert's assessment that the structure was top-heavy and unstable, and the company's failure to take necessary precautions, further emphasises the need for stringent safety protocols.

79 The court's dismissal of the second plaintiff's claim for lack of concrete evidence underscores the importance of providing substantiated claims during trials. The refusal to allow new evidence at the appeal stage – provided this was readily available at the trial stage – reinforces the principle of procedural diligence.

80 However, there appears to be a notable discrepancy in the court's reasoning regarding the disallowance of the mother's claim for loss of earnings while caring for her injured daughter, contrasted with the acknowledgement that the daughter will need to hire a caregiver in the future. On one hand, the court dismisses the mother's claim due to the lack of concrete evidence, while, on the other, it recognises the inevitability of future caregiving expenses as the mother ages. This inconsistency highlights a potential oversight in the court's assessment of the practical realities of caregiving. The decision to award future expenses but deny compensation for the mother's current sacrifices could be seen as contradictory, as both scenarios involve necessary and foreseeable costs incurred due to the plaintiff's condition.

81 The Court of Appeal's award for future expenses acknowledges the practical reality that certain future costs cannot be precisely documented in advance. However, the court's refusal to award non-patrimonial damages, based on the 2018

amendments to the Civil Code, aligns with the view we expressed in the 2018 Yearbook that these amendments have effectively halted a potential case law-driven development in allowing compensation for moral harm in cases other than the limited instances expressly mentioned in the amendments.

In brief, the court's decisions collectively emphasise the importance of personal and corporate responsibility, diligent oversight by authorities, and adherence to procedural and substantive legal principles. This case serves as a robust reminder of the multifaceted nature of liability and the meticulous scrutiny required in legal proceedings to ensure that justice is served while upholding the rule of law. 82

4. *Carmelo Ellul and others v AX Hotel Operations Ltd and others*, Court of Appeal, 21 May 2024, no 1044/2015: Personal Injury due to Malfunctioning Equipment; Proper Defendant; Contract and Tort

a) Brief Summary of the Facts

The plaintiffs were guests at a hotel operated by the first two defendants. When they entered a lift to descend from the seventh floor to the ground floor, the lift descended at an excessive speed and came to an abrupt stop when the emergency brakes were activated. Consequently, the plaintiffs sustained personal injuries and required assistance from hotel employees to exit the lift. 83

During the inspection of the lift to identify the cause of the malfunction, it was found that certain cross-bars supporting the lift structure were twisted. However, it could not be determined whether this twisting resulted from the accident, contributed to it, or was caused by the hotel employees when rescuing the plaintiffs from the cabin. 84

Additionally, although the lift met European standards as certified by the health and safety authority, and had undergone regular inspections and servicing prior to the accident, it was noted that the lift was not of the latest design and lacked a compensation chain, which can help in ensuring the safe and stable operation of the lift. 85

The plaintiffs sued both defendants for damages. The defendants denied liability and requested that the company which had supplied and installed the lifts, and which was responsible for regular lift maintenance, be joined in the lawsuit as a co-defendant. Despite the plaintiffs' objection, citing the absence of a 86 legal relationship with the company, the company was subsequently added as the third defendant.

b) Judgment of the Court

87 The first instance court concluded that the hotel operators (the first two defendants) had failed in their duty to ensure that all hotel equipment was functioning correctly and safely for the hotel guests. The court also noted that the lifts were completely replaced a year after the accident, and the new lifts equipped with compensation chains, indicating that the replacement was due when the accident occurred.

88 Regarding the third defendant, the court observed that this defendant had inspected and certified the lift in question three weeks prior to the accident. The failure of the lift three weeks later showed that the inspection had not been carried out diligently, particularly in failing to identify the need for a compensation chain. Furthermore, the court held that the absence of a contractual relationship between the plaintiffs and this defendant does not absolve it from liability.

89 Accordingly, the court found all three defendants jointly liable.

90 The third defendant appealed, and the other two defendants along with the plaintiffs filed cross-appeals. The third defendant, referring to the plaintiffs' initial objection to its inclusion in the suit due to the absence of a legal relationship, argued that it was not a proper defendant and the claim against it should be dismissed. The third defendant contended that the plaintiffs' cause of action was based on the contractual relationship between the plaintiffs and the hotel operators, which could not serve as a basis for a judgment against it.

91 In response, the plaintiffs stated that in light of the first instance judgment, they were altering their initial stance. The Court of Appeal noted that, although the plaintiffs were now abandoning their initial objection and considering the third defendant a proper party to the suit, their original position was correct. The court interpreted the plaintiffs' claims as presented in the initial filing as being based on the contractual relationship between the hotel operator and the hotel guest. Since the third defendant was not a party to this relationship, the action could not succeed against it.

92 The third defendant's appeal was therefore allowed.

93 The court then addressed the cross-appeal filed by the other defendants. The hotel operators maintained that, since they had engaged the third defendant to regularly inspect, service, and certify the lift, they had not failed in any duty towards the plaintiffs and that the fault rested solely with the third defendant.

94 In light of its conclusion on the main appeal, the Court of Appeal declared that the hotel operators' attempt to transfer blame to the third defendant could not succeed. Given the contractual relationship with hotel guests, the defendants could not delegate their duty to ensure guests' safety to third parties. Consequently, the appeal was dismissed, without prejudice to the defendants' right of recourse against the third defendant, if applicable. However, this could only be pursued in a separate lawsuit based on the appropriate cause of action, and not within the present case.

95 The remainder of the hotel operators' cross-appeal, as well as the plaintiffs' cross-appeal, pertained to the quantum of damages. The defendants disputed the degree of permanent disability and the multiplier applied by the first instance court. The court summarily rejected the cross-appeal, noting that the defendants had not provided any reasons for their disagreement with the findings and conclusions of the first instance court.

96 The plaintiffs' cross-appeal addressed the assessment of loss of future earnings. They argued that the multiplicand should have been based on their gross income, rather than the income net of taxes and social security contributions used by the first instance court. Additionally, considering the number of years until final judgment, the plaintiffs contended that the court should not have applied the 20 % deduction for the lump sum payment, or at least not in its entirety. One plaintiff also claimed that her current earnings, as a university graduate and gainfully employed individual with a higher income, should have been considered, rather than her earnings while she was a student.

97 The Court of Appeal agreed with the plaintiffs that, since the final judgment was rendered ten years after the commencement of the action, no reduction for the lump sum payment should be made. It also concurred that the multiplicand should be based on gross earnings, adjusting the first instance court's figures accordingly. Additionally, the court agreed that the plaintiff's current income, rather than her income while she was a student, should have been taken into account.

c) Commentary

98 The first instance court placed clear responsibility on the hotel operators for ensuring the functionality and safety of their equipment. The court's decision to attribute liability to the hotel operators underscores the importance of maintaining high safety standards and the regular, diligent upkeep of all facilities. This underlines the fact that engaging third-party service providers does not absolve primary duty-holders of their overarching obligations to guests. The court noted the subsequent replacement of the lifts with models equipped with compensation chains,

indicating that the original lifts were outdated. This observation aligns the court's decision with the imperative to ensure that older equipment is updated in a timely manner to prevent accidents.

99 Although the Court of Appeal did not dispute the first court's conclusion regarding the third defendant's lack of diligence in inspecting and certifying the lift, particularly its failure to identify the absence of a compensation chain as a critical oversight, it upheld the third defendant's argument about its improper inclusion in the lawsuit due to the absence of a legal relationship.

100 This conclusion can be legitimately questioned. Despite the plaintiffs' objection to joining the third defendant in the suit – a strategic decision that was itself questionable – the initial pleadings were not strictly confined to contract as a cause of action. Therefore, there was no substantial hurdle in finding against the third defendant based on these initial filings.

101 Indeed, the cause of action against the various defendants would differ: contractual for the hotel operators and tortious for the third defendant. Article 161 (3) of the Code of Civil Procedure[8] specifically permits two or more plaintiffs to file a joint action even if their causes of action differ. By analogy, it should be permissible to file an action against multiple defendants even if the causes of action against each are different. Furthermore, the degree of diligence in performing contractual obligations, as regulated by art 1132 (1) of the Civil Code,[9] is identical to that in tort. Indeed, art 1132 specifically refers back to art 1032,[10] which governs tort matters.

102 The absence of a direct contractual relationship should not therefore have absolved the third defendant from liability. This would indicate that duties related to safety and maintenance can extend beyond direct contractual obligations, reinforcing the idea that all parties involved in safety-related services share a collective responsibility toward end-users.

103 Incidentally, the case highlights an unusual development where the plaintiffs altered their initial stance following the first instance judgment. Although the

8 161. (3) Two or more plaintiffs may bring their actions by one sworn application or by one not sworn application as the case may be, if the actions are connected in respect of the subject matter thereof or if the decision of one of the actions might affect the decision of the other action or actions and the evidence in support of one action is, generally, the same to be produced in the other action or actions. The cause and subject matter of the actions shall be clearly and specifically stated in respect of each plaintiff.

9 1132. (1) Saving any other provision of this Code relating to deposits, the degree of diligence to be exercised in the performance of an obligation, whether the object thereof is the benefit of only one of the parties, or of both, is, in all cases, that of a bonus paterfamilias as provided in art 1032.

10 1032. (1) A person shall be deemed to be in fault if, in his own acts, he does not use the prudence, diligence, and attention of a bonus paterfamilias.

Court of Appeal ultimately rejected this altered position, it did not do so on the grounds that a change in stance is not permissible. This underscores the fluid nature of legal arguments and the court's willingness to be receptive to logical and factual shifts in position.

The Court of Appeal's agreement with the plaintiffs on the assessment of future earnings and the reduction for the lump sum payment denotes a fair and detailed reassessment process. This signals the court's commitment to ensuring equitable compensation based on current and future income potentials, rather than outdated or incomplete financial data. 104

In its broader implications, the judgment underscores the importance of maintaining modern equipment and diligent inspection protocols. It highlights that, while engaging third-party services is common, the ultimate duty of care and accountability remains with the primary operators. 105

5. *AB and another v The Director General Health Services and another,* Court of Appeal, 10 June 2024, no 205/2009: Liability of Public Hospital

a) Brief Summary of the Facts

The two plaintiffs are a married couple. The wife, then 48 years old, was admitted to the hospital on the advice of her family physician, who diagnosed her with dehydration. This was not her first hospitalisation, as she had various underlying medical conditions. She remained hospitalised for 15 days, during which a drip was attached to her forearm. She reported the development of a haematoma around the area where the drip needle was inserted. 106

Sometime after her discharge from the hospital, the wife collapsed as her legs could no longer support her weight. At that moment, she noticed a yellowish discharge from her forearm. She was readmitted to the hospital, where she was diagnosed with Methicillin-Resistant Staphylococcus Aureus (MRSA) in her spine. She underwent surgery the same day to remove an abscess, but the infection had already spread, resulting in a permanent disability. Asserting that the infection was due to the hospital's unsatisfactory sanitary conditions, the plaintiffs filed a lawsuit against the hospital authorities for damages. 107

b) Judgment of the Court

108 After resolving a procedural dispute regarding which authority was responsible for the hospital, leading to the Chief Government Medical Officer being added as the second defendant, the first instance court noted that the relationship between the parties was contractual. It described this relationship as a 'hospitalisation contract', applicable even though the hospital is a public institution. Consequently, the hospital had a duty to provide proper medical care in a sanitary environment, while the plaintiffs bore the burden of proving that the infection was contracted during the wife's hospitalisation and that the hospital had failed to discharge its contractual obligations towards her.

109 The medical expert appointed by the first instance court noted that, due to the patient's pre-existing condition that weakened her immune system and potentially affected the bacterium's incubation period, it was difficult to conclusively determine whether she contracted the infection in the hospital or the community. The expert also observed that an observation of the patient's symptoms and a thorough examination of the haematoma at the site of the drip needle should have led the defendant to diagnose the infection at an earlier stage. Had surgery been performed at that time, the consequences would have been less severe.

110 In light of the expert's report, as well as the existence of other instances of MRSA at the hospital during that period, the court concluded that the plaintiffs had successfully demonstrated that the hospital had failed to implement the necessary measures to prevent the spread of the bacterium, leading to the probable contraction of the infection by the wife while in the hospital. The hospital, on the other hand, was unable to show that adequate precautions were in place to protect the patient, thereby failing in its contractual duty towards her.

111 Proceeding to assess the damages, the court noted that the wife was suffering from a permanent disability of 60 %. Since the plaintiff was unemployed at the time, the court, following usual practice, used the national minimum wage as the multiplicand and five years as the multiplier (the plaintiff was 48 years old at the time). Consequently, the court awarded € 69,561 as compensation for lost earnings (*lucrum cessans*) and an additional € 390 for expenses incurred (*damnum emergens*).

112 The Court of Appeal identified two primary issues: (i) whether the plaintiff contracted the infection in the hospital or the community; and (ii) if it was the case that the infection was contracted in the community, whether a more effective treatment could have been administered. This identification was based on the first instance court's correct observation that the relationship between the parties was contractual in nature.

If the plaintiffs can establish a causal link between the hospital stay and the infection, the burden then shifts to the hospital to demonstrate that it took all necessary precautions to prevent or treat the infection and that the harm occurred through no fault of its own despite these precautions. 113

On the first issue of whether the plaintiff already carried the infection when she was hospitalised, the court observed that the evidence was inconclusive. Given the rapid onset of symptoms, it was probable that the infection was not contracted during the current hospital stay, but rather during a previous admission, or, less probably, in the community, considering the higher prevalence of such infections in hospitals compared to the community. 114

Furthermore, the court noted that the plaintiff exhibited symptoms of the infection which were initially misdiagnosed. Under the circumstances, it would have been prudent to administer proper tests, leading to an earlier diagnosis and treatment before it was too late. 115

Therefore, even if, as asserted by the defendant, the hospital had taken all necessary precautions to avoid the spread of MRSA, it remains a fact that the hospital failed in what it could have done. This failure was perhaps not in preventing the microbe from infecting the plaintiff, but in ensuring that the diagnosis was made sooner when indications appeared that it would be prudent to make it immediately. 116

The appeal was therefore dismissed. 117

c) Commentary

Unlike the *Kravchenko* case discussed above,[11] the first instance court did not award additional compensation by way of *damnum emergens* for future medical expenses, considering that the plaintiff was paraplegic. This was not corrected on appeal because the plaintiffs did not appeal. Unfortunately, the wife passed away while the appeal was pending. 118

Although the Court of Appeal confirmed the first instance judgment, there is a subtle but important difference in the reasoning. The first instance court stated: 119

> It is for the plaintiffs to show that there was a contractual obligation on the Chief Medical Officer and also that the Chief Medical Officer had failed to discharge this obligation.
>
> … The plaintiffs have to show that the plaintiff contracted the infection while in hospital and that this was due to the failure of those responsible for the running of the hospital to take the measures necessary to avoid this.

11 See no 47 above.

120 The Court of Appeal, on the other hand, clearly stated that, if it were shown that the plaintiff contracted the infection while in hospital, then the burden shifts immediately to the defendant to prove that this occurred without fault on their part and despite the precautions in place.

121 Although this point was not heavily emphasised, since it was demonstrated that the hospital had, in any case, failed to diagnose and treat the infection in a timely manner, it underscores the more victim-friendly approach in recent medical malpractice cases, contrasting sharply with earlier cases that required proof of gross negligence. This shift aligns with broader trends in many jurisdictions, aiming to provide better protection for patients and holding medical institutions to higher standards. While this approach signals the critical importance of thorough and proactive patient care to medical institutions to avoid legal repercussions, it may also encourage a 'defensive' approach, leading to unnecessary tests to cover all possible contingencies.

6. *AB v CD and others*, Court of Appeal, 15 July 2024, no 985/2010: Responsibility of Parents of Suicidal Subjects

a) Brief Summary of the Facts

122 The first defendant, a 17-year-old with mental health issues, had exhibited suicidal tendencies on at least one occasion. She was admitted to psychiatric care at a hospital, where she was diagnosed with borderline impulsive personality disorder. The attending psychiatrist recommended her early discharge as prolonged hospitalisation would further worsen her condition. Consequently, she was granted a one-week leave from the hospital after eleven days.

123 Following an improvement in her condition, her leave was extended, and she was eventually discharged after six weeks, with instructions to revisit the outpatient department after two weeks for a condition review. Notable progress was observed, and her parents were advised to allow her unsupervised outings as part of her recovery. Following this advice, her parents permitted her to go out alone, provided she returned home by 10 pm.

124 One day, the first defendant, accompanied by her boyfriend, went for a walk near the Valletta Bastions. They quarrelled, and her boyfriend departed, leaving her alone. Shortly afterward, she jumped from a significant height and landed on the plaintiff, who was seated below. As a result, the plaintiff sustained severe injuries, resulting in a complete loss of mobility and total dependence on others. The first defendant survived with relatively minor injuries.

The plaintiff sued the first defendant, her parents and the public authority responsible for the upkeep of the bastions. 125

b) Judgment of the Court

The court of first instance dismissed the action against the public authority but held the first defendant and her parents liable for the damage suffered by the plaintiff, apportioning fault as follows: 60 % to the first defendant and 40 % to the parents. The damages were assessed at € 190,000 with interest accruing from the date of judgment. 126

Regarding the public authority's responsibility, the court observed that the bastions' inner side was of sufficient height and width to prevent accidental falls, requiring a deliberate and substantial effort to traverse. It is impractical to entirely restrict access to the bastions; hence, the authority cannot be deemed at fault. 127

The first defendant entered a plea under art 1035 of the Civil Code: 128

> 1035. Persons with a mental disorder or other condition, which renders them incapable of managing their own affairs, ... shall not be bound to make good the damage caused by them; saving, where competent, any action of the party injured against such persons as may be liable for such damage ....

She contended that the incident occurred during a moment when she was not in full control of her actions. She asserted that her decision to jump was made spontaneously and was unforeseeable. The court rejected this plea, noting that the defendant's actions were intentional. She consciously decided to climb the ledge, walk along its width, and jump; the entire sequence of events required deliberate decisions and did not occur instantaneously. 129

As regards the parents, the court reasoned that the first defendant was still a minor when the event occurred, and therefore her parents were liable for any harm caused by her in terms of art 1034 of the Civil Code: 130

> 1034. Any person having the charge of a minor, or of a person with a mental disorder or other condition, which renders him incapable of managing his own affairs, shall be liable for any damage caused by such minor or such person, if he fails to exercise the care of a bonus paterfamilias in order to prevent the act.

Citing previous cases that interpret art 1034 as establishing a presumption of fault, the court ruled that the burden was on the parents to demonstrate that they exercised proper diligence in caring for their daughter, especially given their aware- 131 ness of her condition. By permitting their daughter to go out unsupervised, they failed in this duty and therefore bear part of the responsibility.

132 Only the parents appealed, challenging both the determination of liability and the quantum of damages assessed by the court of first instance.

133 With respect to liability, the Court of Appeal noted that, unlike the original art 1384 of the Code Napoleon – which served as its model and created a rebuttable presumption of fault – art 1034 does not establish such a presumption. Thus, the burden of proof remained on the plaintiff to demonstrate that the parents failed to exercise proper care, rather than on the parents to prove their diligence. Presumptions can only be established by an explicit legal provision and cannot be inferred by analogy.

134 The evidence indicated that the parents had neither caused nor contributed to their daughter's mental condition. On the contrary, they had promptly sought professional assistance. While their daughter was on leave from the hospital and until her discharge, they kept her under supervision at home. They only permitted her to go out unsupervised when it was advised that this would benefit her recovery. Even then, they ensured she returned home by no later than 10 pm, often driving her back themselves. Under the circumstances, exercising proper care did not necessitate constant supervision, and the unfortunate event was unforeseeable. The plaintiff failed to establish any lack of duty on the parents' part.

135 Consequently, the parents' appeal was upheld, rendering it unnecessary to address the appeal concerning the quantum of damages.

c) Commentary

136 This case highlights the challenges involved in determining liability in situations involving mental health issues and the responsibilities of guardians.

137 The court of first instance dismissed the action against the public authority, essentially ruling that the bastions' physical structure was sufficient to prevent accidental falls, making it impossible to hold the authority at fault. This ruling underscores the inherent difficulty in assigning liability to public entities when the structures in question meet safety standards and require deliberate actions to circumvent. This judgment might elicit debate on whether public authorities should take further preventative measures or if the expectations from them are sufficiently met given practical constraints.

138 The first court's decision to hold the first defendant and her parents liable, apportioning 60 % to the first defendant and 40 % to the parents, demonstrates an intricate balance of responsibility and the legal principles surrounding the duty of care. The court rejected the first defendant's plea that her actions were

spontaneous and uncontrollable due to her mental health condition, concluding instead that her actions were deliberate. This decision may be scrutinized, especially given the complex understanding of mental health disorders and the associated behavioural unpredictability. The court did not clearly define the criteria for determining when individuals with mental health conditions are still accountable for their actions under art 1035, nor did it specify the severity of mental conditions that would exempt from liability.

As for the parents, the first court invoked art 1034 of the Civil Code, which places a duty of care on individuals responsible for minors or persons with mental disorders. The court reasoned that the parents' failure to supervise their daughter adequately contributed to the harm caused. Here, a pivotal legal question arises: What constitutes 'proper diligence' in cases where mental health conditions impact behaviour unpredictably? The parents sought professional help, supervised their daughter, and followed medical advice, raising a potential argument that they acted within the bounds of reasonable care, as indeed highlighted by the Court of Appeal. 139

The Court of Appeal's commentary on the interpretation of art 1034 is significant and is indeed the most notable aspect of this judgment. Unlike the original art 1384 of the Code Napoleon, art 1034 does not establish a rebuttable presumption of fault. In adopting this interpretation, which shifts the onus back to the plaintiff, the court departed from previous jurisprudence, which, with some exceptions, held that art 1034 does establish a rebuttable presumption. 140

The evidence in defence of the parents showed their proactive stance in seeking professional help and adhering to medical advice. Given these actions, the Court of Appeal concluded that constant supervision was not warranted under the circumstances and that the incident was unforeseeable. This ruling sets a potential precedent for interpreting parental liability in similar cases. 141

This case intricately weaves together mental health issues, legal duties, and the interpretation of statutory provisions. It serves as a critical reference for discussions on the scope of responsibility for guardians and the liabilities of public authorities. The appellate court's ruling, in particular, highlights the importance of clear statutory language in establishing presumptions of fault and delineates the complex dynamics of proving proper care in the context of mental health. 142

One unfortunate outcome of this judgment is that the plaintiff will only be able to recover 60 % of the damages, since no cross-appeal was entered by them on the first instance court's decision that the first defendant is only liable for that amount. 143

7. *Joseph Zammit v Dragonara Casino Ltd*, Court of Appeal, 16 July 2024, no 1037/2007: Liability of Casinos towards Compulsive Gamblers

a) Brief Summary of the Facts

144 The plaintiff alleged that he had frequented the defendant casino for many years due to a compulsive pathological gambling problem. He claimed that the defendant failed to follow regulations by not preventing him from staking additional money and by sending him promotional materials. Furthermore, the defendant facilitated easy access to his bank deposits through electronic machines. The plaintiff participated in various games, including slot machines, leading to substantial financial losses. From a young age, the plaintiff was exposed to an environment where games of chance were prevalent. As a working nurse, he used his entire salary for gambling, continuing this trend while working abroad. The plaintiff began visiting the Dragonara Casino in 2003 and initiated legal action in 2007.

145 The defendant asserted that it had always complied with gaming regulations and denied responsibility for the plaintiff's financial losses. It also raised the defence of contributory negligence on the part of the plaintiff.

b) Judgment of the Court

146 The first instance court noted that the casino is under the oversight of the gaming authority, which has employees stationed at the defendant company to monitor activities. The defendant had also provided training for its employees on how to handle individuals with gambling addictions.

147 The court considered the licence holder's responsibility to bar a compulsive gambler, which can only be done if the individual clearly shows signs of the disorder. It held that the licence holder can only do this after hearing the person concerned and only after that person had clearly shown that he was suffering from the disorder. It was only after he had already filed the lawsuit that the plaintiff had requested a twelve-month ban from gambling, whereupon the company had issued an order prohibiting the plaintiff from participating in any games.

148 A court-appointed medical expert confirmed the plaintiff's pathological condition as that of a compulsive gambler. Evidence revealed that the plaintiff concealed his condition from others. He had requested the promotional materials and the money he staked was not significantly high. Additionally, his attendance at the casino had decreased over time.

Taking all this into account, the court decided that the defendant could not be held responsible for the losses suffered by the plaintiff. 149

The plaintiff appealed, arguing that the defendant had not complied with art 26(3) of the Gaming Act[12] then in force. The Court of Appeal acknowledged that the law imposed certain obligations on the defendant. However, it added that not preventing the plaintiff from playing did not automatically make the defendant liable for the plaintiff's losses, as the article in question does not impose strict liability. The plaintiff needed to prove an illicit failure by the defendant that was directly linked to the damage suffered and provide evidence of the extent of the damage. The Court of Appeal found that the plaintiff failed to prove the initial element since there was no evidence that his condition was apparent. 150

The defendant maintained records of all visitors and was aware of the plaintiff's decreasing attendance after 2003. Typically, those with compulsive gambling tendencies increase their visits over time. The plaintiff also failed to provide evidence of the amount of money he gambled during his visits and was considered a 'small player' by casino employees, who did not even recognise him. 151

The plaintiff only provided bank statements from 2005 to 2007 and did not submit any documents showing his losses at the casino in 2003 and 2004. Without records for those years, the defendant could not have known about the plaintiff's psychological condition. Additionally, the plaintiff admitted to visiting other casinos, and there was no evidence of significant cash withdrawals while gambling at the defendant's casino. Friends of the plaintiff also did not inform the casino of his gambling issues. Even after filing the lawsuit, the plaintiff continued visiting casinos. 152

Holding that the plaintiff failed to prove that the defendant did not fulfil its obligations under art 26(3) of the Gaming Act, the Court of Appeal dismissed the appeal and upheld the first instance court's judgment 153

c) Commentary

The judgments highlight the complexities in cases involving compulsive gambling. The courts scrutinized both the casino's adherence to regulatory duties and the plaintiff's behaviour and evidence. The rulings stress the importance of clear, demonstrable proof of a defendant's negligence and its direct link to claimed dam- 154

12 26. (3) Without prejudice to the other provisions of this Act, admission to a casino shall be at the discretion of the licensee who shall ensure that persons who may have a problem of pathological gambling are not given access to the gaming area.

ages under the Gaming Act for a successful claim. Ultimately, the plaintiff's failure to provide consistent evidence undermined his case, leaving the defendant unaccountable for his financial losses.

155 Nevertheless, operating a casino involves certain duties, including a duty of care towards individuals who may need assistance despite their intentions to seek fortune. It is essential for legislators to find a balance between business profits and the well-being of those who are vulnerable to gambling addiction.

8. *Michael Vella on behalf of his minor son v Marjan Lee Pantalleresco and another*, Court of Appeal, 15 October 2024, no 353/2020: Liability for Animals

a) Brief Summary of the Facts

156 On 20 August 2018, an American Pitbull bit and injured the plaintiff, who was still a minor. Although the dog was registered in the name of the first defendant, the second defendant, his mother, was at the time in charge of it, although she could not control it because it ignored all commands. The dog was without a muzzle and not on a leash.

157 The plaintiff sued both defendants.

158 The second defendant – the mother – did not file a reply. The first defendant pleaded that he was not the proper defendant and should therefore be non-suited. He was not present at the time of the accident and it was not he who had allowed the dog outside without a leash and muzzle. Subordinately, he contested the damages claimed by plaintiff.

b) Judgment of the Court

159 On the liability of the second defendant, the first instance court observed that this was not the first time that she had allowed the dog outside without a leash and muzzle. It then referred to art 1040 of the Civil Code[13] and reg 3 of the Control

13 1040. The owner of an animal, or any person using an animal during such time as such person is using it, shall be liable for any damage caused by it, whether the animal was under his charge or had strayed or escaped.

of Dogs Regulations (Subsidiary Regulations 312.01)[14], which makes it quite clear that a dog must always be kept on a leash, even more so in the present case because Pitbulls are notoriously dangerous animals. Her failure to observe this regulation makes the second defendant liable for the harm caused.

Turning to the first defendant, the dog's owner, the first instance court made it quite clear that the owner of an animal is responsible for any damage that the animal may cause to others irrespective of whether the animal was under the control of the owner or whether it had run away. This is a matter of strict liability and the owner can only avoid responsibility if there was some form of force majeure or if the animal had been provoked by the person who suffered the harm. The fact that the first defendant had repeatedly warned his mother to keep the dog on a leash when allowing it outside but she ignored all his warnings did not exonerate him from liability. **160**

The first instance court therefore held both defendants jointly liable. **161**

In determining the quantum of damages, the court took into account that the plaintiff was merely 14 years old at the time of the incident, and could commence employment at the age of 16. He was employed as a petrol station attendant, with the retirement age presumed to be 65. The court observed that no evidence had been presented concerning the *damnum emergens* (the actual loss suffered). Concerning the permanent disability, the court considered two expert reports: the expert on reconstructive surgery assessed the disability at 9 % and the psychiatric expert assessed 12 %. The court averaged the findings of both reports, concluding an 18 % disability. Given that the case had been ongoing for only three and a half years, the Court adjudged that a deduction of 18 % to account for a lump sum payment was appropriate. Additionally, € 10,000 was added to account for potential inflation, in total € 104,021, which the defendants were to pay *in solidum* with interest to run from the day of the judgment. **162**

The first defendant appealed, mostly on procedural grounds. The Court of Appeal however dismissed the appeal, which it considered as vexatious, and confirmed the first instance judgment, stressing that liability in this case is objective and does not depend on fault or on foreseeability; it can only be excluded if the defendant proves the harm was due to *vis major* or to the fault of the injured party. **163**

---

14 3. (1) No person who has any dog under his control shall allow such dog to stray and, where the dog is taken out in any street, the dog shall be kept on leash:

…

(2) If a person knows or suspects that the dog under his control is temperamental or dangerous or can cause harm to any person, he shall also keep the dog muzzled at all times in any public place.

c) Commentary

164 Both the first instance court and the Court of Appeal adhered to the traditional interpretation of sec 1040 of the Civil Code. The language of this section unequivocally establishes strict liability for animal owners or caretakers. They can only escape liability if they prove force majeure or that a third party provoked the animal. This provision does not concern negligence. The legislator adopted a different stance when dealing with liability for animals, and no arguments can impose an alternative interpretation of this specific provision.

165 The courts also correctly assessed damages in this case. The plaintiff was 14 years old at the time of the damage, thus not yet eligible for legal employment. Similar situations arise when young children, pensioners, or elderly individuals suffer harm. In such cases, the courts have found solutions. In this instance, the courts endeavoured to be reasonable in assessing the years considered and made minimal adjustments for inflation. Additionally, the courts followed jurisprudence regarding the deduction for a lump sum payment. Instead of applying a 20 % deduction, which is traditionally the maximum, the courts determined that 18 % was more reasonable, given that the case took three and a half years to reach a final judgment.

166 The only unanswered question concerns the finding of joint liability. Presumably both defendants may be considered to have acted with gross negligence: the second defendant in allowing the dog outside without a leash and muzzle, and the first defendant in entrusting the dog with the second defendant knowing that she had repeatedly ignored his instructions not to allow the dog outside without a leash and muzzle. Gross negligence is equivalent to malice for the purposes of art 1049 of the Civil Code.[15]

9. *Andrew Cilia and others v Angelo Spiteri and others*, Court of Appeal, 2 December 2024, no 1143/2019: Abuse of Judicial Procedure

a) Brief Summary of the Facts

167 Several years earlier, the defendants had initiated judicial proceedings against the plaintiffs ('the first case'), claiming they were owed a sum of € 638,642. Despite the plaintiffs disputing the claim, the defendants secured a precautionary garnishee

15 See fn 1 above.

order against the plaintiffs. This was to ensure the payment of the sum should the judgment be in the defendants' favour. In response, to counter the effects of the garnishee, the plaintiffs provided a bank guarantee, incurring substantial expenses – in total € 35,040 – to maintain its validity during the ongoing litigation against them.

Ultimately, the judgment in the first case was delivered against the defendants, dismissing their claim. Both the appeal and application for a rehearing of the appeal were also dismissed. Consequently, the plaintiffs filed a lawsuit against the defendants to recover the costs and losses incurred due to the garnishee order, which had proven baseless following the dismissal of the defendants' original action. 168

The defendants argued that their actions in obtaining the garnishee order were a legitimate exercise of their right to secure the payment of their claim. 169

b) Judgment of the Court

The first instance court noted that the defendants had exercised their right under art 829 of the Code of Civil Procedure: 170

> 829. It shall be lawful for any person, without the necessity of any previous judgment, to secure his rights by one or more of the following precautionary acts, which shall be issued and carried into effect on the responsibility of the person suing out the act, provided he shall have complied with the conditions prescribed by this Code.

The court stated that the exercise of this right would remain legitimate even if the claim eventually failed, as long as the precautionary act was not issued with vexatious intent or to exercise undue pressure, and provided there was a reasonable possibility of success at the time it was issued and during the time while it was kept in force. 171

However, the court observed that the defendants should have reassessed their position after the initial judgment dismissed their claim. Instead, they not only appealed but also sought a rehearing of the appeal – an extraordinary remedy granted under exceptional circumstances – even though the appeal judgment clearly indicated that their claim was baseless. In fact, the ruling on the rehearing application described it as frivolous. 172

The only reason the defendants persisted with the garnishee order was out of stubbornness. Hence, their continued insistence was not deemed a legitimate exercise of their rights under art 829. 173

The first court therefore found for the plaintiffs. 174

175 In assessing damages, the court observed that, from the date of the first instance judgment against them, the defendants had acted in bad faith for the purposes of art 1047 of the Civil Code:

> 1047. (1) The damage which consists in depriving a person of the use of his own money, shall be made good by the payment of interest at the rate of eight per cent a year.
>
> (2) If, however, the party causing the damage has acted maliciously, the court may, according to circumstances, grant also to the injured party compensation for any other damage sustained by him, including every loss of earnings, if it is shown that the party causing the damage, by depriving the party injured of the use of his own money, had particularly the intention of causing him such other damage, or if such damage is the immediate and direct consequence of the injured party having been so deprived of the use of his own money.
>
> (3) The sum to be awarded in respect of such loss of earnings shall be assessed by the court having regard to the circumstances of the case.

176 The court therefore awarded damages of € 3,000 per annum for every year since the first instance judgment in the first case. Additionally, the defendants were ordered to pay € 35,040, covering the costs incurred by the plaintiffs for maintaining the bank guarantee, along with interest on that sum from the date of the initial judgment.

177 The defendants appealed the judgment, contending that they neither acted in bad faith nor were required to reassess their position following the first judgment, arguing that the judgment was not final. They further asserted that the plaintiffs had not suffered any actual loss or damage. The dismissal of their rehearing application as frivolous at most indicated that they could be deemed to have acted incorrectly only after the appeal judgment.

178 The Court of Appeal observed that the question of whether the defendants acted in bad faith, and from when, was largely irrelevant. The critical issue was whether the garnishee order had caused the plaintiffs to incur a loss. Given the existence of such a loss, the logical conclusion was that the burden should not fall on the plaintiffs, who rightly contested the baseless claim against them and were in no way at fault, but on the defendants, who had secured the garnishee order based on an unfounded claim. Article 829 of the Code of Civil Procedure explicitly states that precautionary acts are 'issued and carried into effect on the responsibility of the person pursuing the act'. This responsibility is objective, with the only pertinent factor being the outcome of the case on its merits, rather than the good or bad faith of the individual pursuing the act, which is relevant only when assessing the quantum of damages.

179 Despite having made this point, the Court of Appeal nevertheless agreed with the first instance court that the defendants had indeed acted in bad faith. It was evident from the outset that their claim against the plaintiffs was groundless, as

even the first judgment described their arguments as no more than 'a feeble effort' to sway the case in their favour.

On the matter of damages, the Court of Appeal considered that the first instance court had identified: (i) judicial costs and bank fees to replace the garnishee order with a bank guarantee; (ii) interest at 8 % on those costs and fees; and (iii) loss of earnings, as the defendants were deemed to have acted maliciously. 180

The first two heads were objectively determined. Indeed, the first court should have awarded interest also on the monies which the plaintiffs could not use because they were tied down with the garnishee and subsequently with the bank guarantee, not solely on the cost of the bank guarantee. 181

The third head of damages – the loss of earnings – assessed at € 3,000 per annum, though necessarily speculative, was conservative. Furthermore, the loss of earnings was assessed from the date of the first judgment rather than from the outset, as it should have been. 182

Therefore, the damages awarded by the first instance court were, if anything, insufficient, and there was no reason to reduce them further on appeal. Consequently, the appeal was dismissed. 183

c) Commentary

This judgment presents a rigorous analysis of a protracted legal battle where both judicious prudence and procedural rights of the parties were scrupulously examined, and underscores the critical importance of discretion, the implications of procedural actions, and the balance between legitimate legal measures and the obligations of fairness and responsibility in litigation. 184

One of the Court of Appeal's key points – indeed, the most significant in our view – is that responsibility of the individual pursuing the precautionary act is objective, depending solely on the outcome of the claim and not on negligence. Although this was in effect mentioned *obiter*, since the court found the defendants to have acted in bad faith anyway, it remains noteworthy because it overturns prior jurisprudence that stipulated bad faith as a basis for liability. This new approach is undoubtedly more just; it provides no solace for the injured party to simply know he was correct in contesting the claim, yet still has to shoulder the costs. Essentially, *chi rompe paga* ('he who breaks, pays'). 185

10. Personal Injury

186 In 2024, although there were no significant new trends or departures from established practices in personal injury cases, a number of cases touched on various aspects and there was a notable affirmation and clarification of principles that enhance consistency and predictability, particularly in assessing damages for loss of earnings and incurred or anticipated expenses.

a) Responsibility for Industrial Accidents

187 In the case of *Roberta Cassar and another v Polidano Brothers Ltd* (no 203/2011), decided on 25 April 2024, the Court of Appeal affirmed that employers do not bear strict liability for workplace accidents. However, while the plaintiff must prove fault, the employer is required to demonstrate that it implemented a safe system of work. This includes conducting proper risk evaluations, taking measures to mitigate unavoidable risks, and providing supervision and instruction on appropriate work practices.

188 In *Joseph Cordina v Wasteser v Malta Ltd and another* (Court of Appeal, 17 October 2024, no 81/2017), the Court of Appeal reiterated these principles, emphasising that employers are not absolved of liability when they dispatch employees to work in areas under the control of third parties. Instead, they share responsibility with such third parties for the failure to ensure a safe system of work.

b) Future Expenses

189 In the case of *Jonathan Abela on behalf of another v Maria Spiteri and another* (no 41/2017), decided by the Court of Appeal on 14 March 2024, compensation was awarded for expenses that, although not yet incurred, were deemed necessary. The plaintiff had suffered extensive injuries requiring life-long care and medication, and the court assessed and awarded a sum to cover these future expenses. Likewise, compensation awarded for expenses still to be incurred was approved by the Court of Appeal in *Sharon Coleiro v Ahmed Fatmalla and another* (Court of Appeal, 21 November 2024, no 54/2009).

190 The same principle was applied in the case of *George Cuschieri v Anthony Cuschieri* (no 59/2018), decided by the Court of Appeal on 9 April 2014. In this instance, the plaintiff sustained an injury necessitating the implantation of a dental bridge, which he could not afford at the time. Nevertheless, the court awarded the cost of the bridge, stating that the plaintiff's health damage was incurred regard-

less of whether he proceeded with the implant or not. This case holds even more weight as the plaintiff passed away (due to reasons unrelated to the accident) before the final judgment was rendered, and consequently, the awarded sum will not be utilised for the bridge.

Likewise in *Lee Tanti v Clayton Bugeja and another* (Court of Appeal, 21 May 2024, no 763/2017), the plaintiff experienced hearing loss due to his injury and required a hearing aid costing € 4,000. However, because he could not afford the hearing aid, he only provided an invoice rather than a receipt for this amount. The first instance court dismissed his claim for this item on the grounds that there was no evidence to suggest that he would use the awarded amount to purchase the hearing aid. The Court of Appeal reversed this part of the judgment, again asserting that once it is established that the need for the expense arose from the injury, the plaintiff should be compensated regardless of whether the expense has already been incurred or will be incurred in the future. Possibly inconsistently, the court held the disability is no less permanent if it can be corrected, as in this case, by a hearing aid. **191**

However, the court emphasised that it is always the plaintiff's responsibility to demonstrate that the incurred or anticipated expenses resulted from the accident. Therefore, the court concurred with the first instance court in dismissing an additional claim for € 3,550 to cover the cost of a course of studies. The plaintiff contended that he undertook the course to learn a new trade because his injury prevented him from continuing his previous part-time employment. The court held that, while the plaintiff would be compensated for loss of earnings, he should not receive additional compensation for the cost of the course, which would only serve to enhance his earning capacity. **192**

c) Assessing Loss of Income – the Multiplicand

Regarding the loss of future earnings, the Court of Appeal confirmed that, when applying the multiplier method to assess future earnings, the victim's gross pre-accident earnings, adjusted for inflation, should be considered. In the aforementioned *Lee Tanti* case, the Court of Appeal overturned the first instance judgment, which had calculated the loss of earnings based on the victim's net income after tax and social security contributions. Furthermore, the Court of Appeal affirmed that, when making inflation adjustments, the duration of the multiplier period should be taken into account. In the *Lee Tanti* case, the court increased the basic income by 20 % instead of 10 % as determined by the first instance court, due to the considerable 38-year multiplier period. **193**

194 In the case of *Dax Fernandes v Thomas Barr* (Court of Appeal, 27 February 2024, no 495/2015), the plaintiff argued that the basic income (the multiplicand) should be calculated based on the date closest to the judgment rather than the date of the accident. The Court of Appeal dismissed this argument, not on principle, but because the evidence presented by the plaintiff to prove his income was unreliable. It is interesting to consider what the outcome might have been had the evidence been satisfactory. Calculating the income closest to the date of judgment as the multiplicand minimises the uncertainty concerning the inflation rate but may result in over-compensation for the preceding years. A more equitable solution might be to take the latest figures as an average and adjust the compensation accordingly, depending on the number of years since the accident and the remaining years of the multiplier.

195 However, in the *Jonathan Abela* case, the Court of Appeal implicitly rejected this argument when it adopted the average between the last two full years before the accident, before adjusting for inflation.

d) Assessing Loss of Income – Tax Evasion

196 In the *Roberta Cassar* case, the first instance court used the victim's actual income as the multiplicand, instead of the income declared to the fiscal authorities for tax purposes. In line with previous cases, the Court of Appeal overturned this part of the judgment, stating that it could not ignore instances of tax evasion.

197 A somewhat unusual case concerning fiscal evasion is that of *Radoslav Yurokov v GasanMamo Insurance Limited* (no 1107/2019) decided by the Court of Appeal on 7 October 2024. In this case, the defendant, the plaintiff's employer, for some reason – probably to reduce social security payments – underdeclared the plaintiff's income in its accounts. However, there was no evidence that the plaintiff likewise underdeclared his income for tax purposes; on the contrary, he produced bank statements showing that his full income was deposited in his account. The Court of Appeal held that if there was some form of evasion, this was on the part of the defendant, not of the plaintiff, who should not therefore be prejudiced thereby.

e) Assessing Loss of Income – Varied Disability Factors

198 In cases where the victim suffers multiple injuries resulting in various disabilities, the final percentage of disability is determined by using a weighted average rather than the arithmetic total of the individual disabilities so as to create a

balanced consideration of multiple disabilities. In the *Lee Tanti* case and also in *Paul Saliba and another v Michael Portelli and another* (Court of Appeal, 26 November 2024, no 48/2017), the Court of Appeal approved and adopted a mathematical formula to assess total disability as follows:

$$\frac{f = a^2 + b^2 + c^2}{\mathrm{a + b + c}}$$

where *a*, *b* and *c* represent the percentages of distinct disabilities, and *f* is the final percentage.

In *Jonathan Abela* the first instance court adopted a different formula: 199

$$\frac{f = (100 - M) \times m}{100}$$

where *M* is the higher disability percentage and *m* is the lower percentage.

The Court of Appeal somewhat inconsistently accepted different formulae in 200 the two aforementioned judgments, despite the fact that they yield different results. The formula used in the *Lee Tanti* case enhances predictability and consistency in awarding compensation; however, it can be criticised for producing a final figure lower than that for the highest single disability. This creates an anomalous situation where the victim would have received higher compensation if he had only suffered from the most severe disability. The formula in the *Jonathan Abela* case avoids this issue. Nevertheless, consistency is compromised if a uniform formula is not adopted in all cases.

f) Assessing Loss of Income – the Multiplier

A notable trend observed in recent years is that courts have become less hesitant 201 to adopt a multiplier that more closely aligns with the difference between the victim's age at the time of the accident and the expected retirement age. Although the multiplier adopted is rarely equivalent to this difference due to the 'chances and changes of life' – a practice reaffirmed in most judgments, eg the *Dax Fernandes* case mentioned above – the gap is progressively narrowing.

In the *Lee Tanti* case, where the victim was 21 years old and the retirement 202 age is 65, a difference of 44 years, the first instance court adopted a multiplier of 38 years. The defendants' appeal, which argued that the multiplier should be 30 years based on a table consistently followed in earlier judgments, was dismissed by the Court of Appeal. The court emphasised that the table serves only as a guide and is not binding.

203 In *John Tanti v Luke Anthony Saliba* (Court of Appeal, 14 March 2024, no 161/2021), the first instance court applied a full multiplier of 16 years for the 49-year-old victim, which the Court of Appeal upheld. In the *Roberta Cassar* case, involving a 32-year-old victim, the first instance court used a multiplier of 28 years, assuming the victim would retire at 60 due to the physically demanding nature of his work as a quarry worker. The Court of Appeal rejected the defendant's appeal and upheld this part of the judgment, noting that although the official retirement age for quarry workers is 65, the victim's right to change to less strenuous employment must be considered. In the *Emanuel Farrugia* case, the multiplier was 40 years for a 21-year-old victim. In *André Borg on behalf of another v Gzira Local Council* (Court of Appeal, 18 June 2024, no 615/2017), the multiplier was 27 years for a 33-year-old victim.

204 In the *Joseph Cordina* case, the first instance court applied a full 25-year multiplier, mistakenly assuming the victim was 40 years old, although he was actually only 35. The Court of Appeal noted that the multiplier was appropriate given the victim's correct age.

205 In *John Baldacchino v Malta Transport Authority* (Court of Appeal, 22 October 2024, no 885/2015) a multiplier of five years was adopted for a 59-year-old victim. In *Christine Hannah Burns on behalf of another v Paul Ebejer and others* (Court of Appeal, 7 November 2024, no 723/2009), the first instance court applied a full multiplier of 16 years for a 48-year-old victim; this was however reduced to 14 years on appeal.

206 In *Reuben Fenech and others v Francis Montebello and others* (Court of Appeal, 20 June 2024, no 181/2010) where the victim was a two-year-old child, the first instance court applied a multiplier of 37 years, which was increased to 40 years by the Court of Appeal.

207 In *Emanuel Farrugia and another v Mario Magri* (Court of Appeal, 20 June 2024, no 1018/2009), an action filed by the parents of the victim who died as a result of overdosing on illegal drugs supplied by the defendant, the first instance court applied a multiplier of 40 years for a 21-year-old victim. In this case, the Court of Appeal appeared to go against the more victim-friendly trend mentioned earlier when it reduced the multiplier to 30 years. However, the court clarified that this decision was due to the special circumstances of the victim's history of drug abuse, which resulted in a lower working life expectancy than normal.

208 In *Ivan Azzopardi and another v Alfred Sciberras and others* (Court of Appeal, 30 July 2024, no 615/2021), the court of first instance applied a 12-year multiplier for a 57-year-old victim, reasoning that the victim, being self-employed, would likely work beyond the standard retirement age of 65. However, the Court of Appeal reduced the multiplier to six years, asserting that there was no justification to dif-

ferentiate between self-employed persons and employees, as both have the option to work beyond the retirement age.

The court did however differentiate between housewives and other victims, 209
noting that household chores do not cease upon reaching retirement age. In the case of *Paul Saliba*, involving a 54-year-old unemployed housewife, the Court of Appeal applied a 16-year multiplier and the national minimum wage as the multiplicand.

Determining the appropriate multiplier becomes increasingly challenging 210
when the victim is a pensioner or has already surpassed or is very close to retirement age. In the case of *George Cuschieri*, the plaintiff was 63 years old and retired at the time of the accident. He initiated legal proceedings almost nine years after the incident, at the age of 72, and passed away before the final judgment was rendered. The first instance court, adhering to the established practice for victims over 60 years of age, applied a five-year multiplier, which was subsequently affirmed by the Court of Appeal. In the *Radoslav Yurokov* case, the plaintiff was 60 years old but still in employment. The Court of Appeal approved the eight-year multiplier adopted by the first instance court.

A novel approach was adopted by the first instance court in *Joanne Darmanin* 211
and another v Manuel Camenzuli (Court of Appeal, 3 September 2024, no 297/2019). The victim was 84 years old and suffered a 20 % disability. The court discarded the multiplier method, which it considered inappropriate for someone of the victim's age. Instead, an 'equitable' compensation of € 5,000 was awarded. The Court of Appeal approved the award.

g) Interest on the Sum Awarded

One principle which seems consolidated is that interest on the damages awarded 212
starts to run only from the date of the first instance judgment (*Lee Tanti*; *Emanuel Cordina v Paul Vella*, Court of Appeal, 15 February 2024, no 750/2016; *Jonathan Abela*).

h) Lump-Sum Deduction

In the *Roberta Cassar* case, the first instance court deducted 4 % from the sum as- 213
sessed for loss of earnings to account for the benefit of receiving future earnings as a lump sum although judgment was delivered ten years after the accident.

In the *Jonathan Abela* case, the first instance court deducted 20 %, even 214
though the judgment was delivered four years after the accident. The Court of Ap-

peal reaffirmed that this 20 % reduction should be decreased by 2 % for each year until the judgment is delivered since compensation for those years will be paid in arrears rather than in advance. However, the starting point should be the date of filing the action rather than the date of the accident. Conversely, the end point is the final judgment. This was also affirmed in the *Roberta Cassar* case.

i) Deduction for Personal Consumption in Case of Fatalities

215 In the *Roberta Cassar* case, where the victim died as a result of the accident, the plaintiffs were his widow and daughter. The Court of Appeal followed earlier rulings, determining that the plaintiffs in such cases are considered dependents of the deceased rather than heirs. Consequently, their loss is not the full amount of the lost earnings, as the victim's personal consumption must be accounted for. Therefore, the Court of Appeal reduced the amount awarded by the first instance court by 25 %. In *Emanuel Farrugia*, where the plaintiffs were the parents of the deceased, and the degree of dependency was deemed to be less, the first instance court deducted one-third of the amount for personal consumption. The Court of Appeal however reduced the deduction to 25 %.

C. Literature

1. *Ivan Mifsud*, 'The Duty of Care' in Maltese Court Judgments: Adding Value or just a Cliché (Malta University Press 2024)

216 In this insightful book, the author differentiates between 'a duty to care' and 'the duty of care'. He posits that 'a duty to care' represents the foundational obligation of the modern state to look after those within its jurisdiction. Conversely, 'the duty of care' is the standard individuals must adhere to in order to avoid liability, as reflected in Maltese court jurisprudence since 2001. The courts have applied this concept across civil, criminal, commercial, and constitutional cases.

217 Initially, the author examines how the duty of care is conceptualised in various countries, including Germany, France, and England and Wales. He then delves into the Maltese context, referencing arts 1029 to 1051 A of the Civil Code, with emphasis on arts 1030 to 1033. The concept of the *bonus paterfamilias* – interpreted today as 'a mature, responsible person raising his family to the best

of his abilities' – plays a key role. Commentaries on the Maltese Civil Code draw from continental doctrine and jurists to elucidate the laws on tort and quasi-tort.

In contrast, although the criminal law provisions of the Maltese Criminal Code are influenced by the Italian Code of 1889, the courts often rely on Anglo-Saxon literature to define criminal negligence as 'a reckless disregard for the safety of others'. In company law, art 136 A(3) of the Companies Act is particularly significant. Findings of negligence are determined by Maltese civil law principles, which do not encompass a duty of care. However, in environmental legislation, the duty of care is explicitly mentioned in reg 12 of the Waste Regulations (Legal Notice 184 of 2011), a transposition of Directive 2008/98/EC. 218

The author further analyses how the duty of care is interpreted in Maltese civil, criminal, commercial, and constitutional judgments. He also considers decisions from the Small Claims Tribunal, providing an extensive list of judgments where Maltese courts have relied on English doctrine, despite Malta's laws being based on Continental principles. Additionally, the author highlights that certain special laws, such as those related to employment, health, and safety, are influenced by English law. 219

2. *Christopher Aquilina,* Artificial Intelligence: Establishing the Causal Link in Tort: The Implications of Article 4 of the Proposal of the Artificial Intelligence Liability Directive on the Maltese Legal System (Dissertation, University of Malta 2024)

Artificial Intelligence (AI) represents a category of Information Communication Technologies (ICTs) that inherently possess the capacity to replicate human behavioural traits dynamically and autonomously through independent learning, reasoning, thinking, and data-driven decision-making. While AI systems offer numerous benefits, these same characteristics are central to academic debates, particularly when their outputs result in harm, challenging the fundamental principle that all harm should be compensated. 220

In many civil law jurisdictions, non-contractual fault-based liability provisions are grounded in centuries-old principles that have largely remained unchanged since their inception. However, technological advancements have necessitated the introduction of new laws to maintain equilibrium. The ICTs that have previously challenged our legal systems are relatively unsophisticated compared to AI-enabled goods and services (AI systems). 221

222 A significant question arises: how does one recover damages from an autonomous entity that causes harm? In 2022, the European Commission proposed the Artificial Intelligence Liability Directive (AILD) to bridge these domains by promoting the adoption of AI systems while safeguarding non-contractual fault-based liability rights when harm occurs. Following a detailed examination of AI and Maltese non-contractual liability provisions, this dissertation analyses the potential impact of the AILD on the Maltese legal system. The findings indicate that the AILD will have a substantial impact and, in some instances, present outright incompatibilities.

3. *Andrew Joseph Mifsud*, Moral Damages: The Maltese Judicial Experience (Dissertation, University of Malta 2024)

223 The concept of moral damages has significantly evolved since its exclusion from Malta's Civil Code. For an extended period, this omission required the Maltese courts to interpret and clarify the term through their judgments. This landscape shifted dramatically with the legislative amendments introduced in 2018 via Act XIII and Act XXXII of that year. These amendments marked the first instance of the legislator explicitly recognising compensation for moral damage, representing a progressive milestone. However, the formulation of these amendments unfortunately also regressed in certain aspects.

224 This work aims to evaluate whether the initial regression has been rectified and to ascertain if our legal framework on moral damages is realigning towards *restitutio in integrum*. Through an analysis of numerous judgments, this study illustrates the approach of the Maltese courts in addressing moral damages. Despite the highly regressive legislation, the Maltese courts have adeptly navigated these challenges, devising innovative methods to award compensation for emotional pain and suffering.

4. *Gabriella Vella*, Determining Liability and Compensating Damage Suffered by Passengers in the Use of Public and Private Transport (Dissertation, University of Malta 2024)

225 Establishing liability is a multifaceted endeavour. To obtain compensation for personal injury, it is imperative first to identify a liable party. This dissertation delves into the principles of liability and compensation within the realms of both public and private transportation, with a particular emphasis on three European legal

systems: Maltese law, English law, and French law. The author investigates the duty of care owed by transportation operators, the responsibilities of drivers towards passengers, and the rights of individuals to seek compensation for injuries sustained during transit.

Furthermore, this study scrutinizes relevant case law to discern how courts have interpreted liability and calculated damages in judgments involving road traffic accidents. Through an in-depth analysis of these issues, the author aims to identify convergences and divergences among the legal systems under review, providing valuable insights into best practices for potential legislative reform. 226

Additionally, the dissertation examines transportation laws with the intent to elucidate the duty of care expected from drivers within various legal jurisdictions. From a tort law perspective, it explores the concepts of liability and damages, contrasting them with the contract law approach. This comparison reveals the fundamental standards of conduct mandated by law and addresses the issue of responsibility by constructing a framework for remedial action. 227

Ultimately, assigning responsibility presents a significant challenge. An examination of various international cases reveals that courts meticulously consider the complexities involved before attributing liability. 228

5. *Hannah Vella,* Causation in Toxic Torts (Dissertation, University of Malta 2024)

Causation is a fundamental requirement in tort actions across all jurisdictions. However, due to the lack of consensus on the concept of 'causation', various theories have emerged through jurisprudence. Traditional causation theories were designed to address conventional injuries and were not tailored to the complexities of toxic torts. This is primarily because toxic torts are a relatively recent development, arising from society's industrialisation. As such, these torts were not prevalent when traditional causation theories were formulated. 229

This discussion aims to provide an overview of the prevalent causation theories in toxic tort litigation, with a particular focus on English and American case law. These jurisdictions have significantly advanced the area of causation in toxic tort litigation. 230

Emanuel GD van Dongen and Anne LM Keirse

XX. The Netherlands

A. Legislation

1. Besluit van 13 december 2024, houdende wijziging van het Besluit van 6 april 2011, houdende vaststelling van de bedragen waartoe de aansprakelijkheid van de vervoerder bij vervoer door de lucht is beperkt ter uitvoering van de artikelen 1359, 1399 en 1400 van Boek 8 van het Burgerlijk Wetboek (Stb 2024, 417) [Decree of 13 December 2024, amending the Decree of 6 April 2011, laying down the Amounts to which Air Transport Carriers' Liability is limited in the Implementation of Articles 1359, 1399 and 1400 of Book 8 of the Dutch Civil Code]

The Montreal Convention for the Unification of Certain Rules for International Carriage by Air[1] provides for carriers' liability in the event of damage to persons, baggage or cargo during international carriage by air. It also regulates the extent of that liability and the periodic review of liability amounts. This Decree implements the revision of the International Civil Aviation Organisation, which took place in June 2024 and which entered into force on 28 December 2024. For the Netherlands, the basis for the limitation of liability is implemented in arts 8:1359, 8:1399 and 8:1400 of the Dutch Civil Code (*Burgerlijk Wetboek*, DCC). A general administrative order (Decree of 6 April 2011) determines to which amounts the carrier's liability is limited in the case of transport by air. The extent of liability is expressed in units of account (*rekeneenheden*), special drawing rights as defined by the International Monetary Fund. One unit of account is currently approximately € 1.22. This Decree ensures that the liability amounts laid down in 1

Note: Dr Emanuel GD van Dongen and Prof Dr Anne LM Keirse are, respectively, Associate Professor and (part-time) Professor at the Molengraaff Institute, Utrecht University, and researchers at the Utrecht Centre for Accountability and Liability Law. Anne Keirse is also a judge at the Court of Appeal, Amsterdam, and Emanuel van Dongen a deputy judge at the Court of Appeal, Arnhem-Leeuwarden.

1 Tractatenblad van het Kroninkrijk der Nederlanden (Trb) 2000, 32.

https://doi.org/10.1515/9783111389271-021

the Decree are adjusted in line with the revision of these amounts by the International Civil Aviation Organisation.

2. Regeling van de Staatssecretaris van Binnenlandse Zaken en Koninkrijksrelaties van 2 september 2024, nr WJZ/ 53021307, tot wijziging van de Regeling Tijdelijke wet Groningen in verband met het toevoegen van een vergoeding voor overlast bij vertraging in de versterking en enkele andere wijzigingen (Regeling Tijdelijke wet Groningen, Scr 2024, 27983) [Regulation of the State Secretary of the Interior and Kingdom Relations of 2 September 2024, no WJZ/ 53021307, amending the Groningen Temporary Act Regulation in Connection with the Addition of Compensation for Disturbances in the Event of Delays in Reinforcement and Some Other Amendments]

2 The Groningen Temporary Act Regulation contains the elaboration of certain provisions of the Groningen Temporary Act and the Groningen Temporary Act Decree. In response to a measure from the Dutch government following the report of the Parliamentary Inquiry Committee on natural gas extraction in Groningen, the Regulation was amended in order to extend the existing regulation of 'disturbance' compensation, to include compensation for the long waiting time which elapsed before the restoration of the affected homes. At the same time, some other changes have been made to the provisions in the Regulation on reinforcement. These include the extension of the compensation scheme to allow assistance by a financial adviser for tenants and some updates.

B. Cases

1. Hoge Raad (Supreme Court, HR) 15 December 2023, ECLI: NL:HR:2023:1750: Duty of Care during Excavation Work (*Liander/Krinkels*)

a) Brief Summary of the Facts

Krinkels is a contractor working in the ground (*grondroerder*) that installed shoring on a canal for which it was necessary to carry out work underground, the work being subject to a guideline on prudent soil excavation: the Directive on Prudent Soil Excavation from the Initiation Phase to the Use Phase (CROW 500). This guideline, drafted by the excavation sector itself, is an elaboration of the Information Exchange on Overground and Underground Networks and Networks Act (*Wet informatiewisseling bovengrondse en ondergrondse netten en netwerken*, Wet WIBON) by private parties and stipulates the standards of care when carrying out excavation work. 3

Prior to the start of its operations, the contractor issued an excavation notification. In response, the local network operator, Liander, informed the contractor that the excavation site contained a gas pipeline and a cable. The contractor did not find the cable, and carried out the work manually (using a spray lance). A few weeks later, a failure of the local electricity grid occurred. The local network operator then cut the cable on both sides of the canal and installed a bypass. In these proceedings, the local network operator claims that the contractor is liable for this damage, stating the contractor acted in breach of the due care owed under the circumstances. According to the local network operator, the contractor did not comply with CROW 500. The court of first instance and the Court of Appeal rejected the claim. 4

b) Judgment of the Court

In cassation, the local network operator argued that the contractor acted negligently. The *Hoge Raad* followed its earlier judgment in 2018[2] and argued that in order to define the required duty of care of a groundskeeper, one should in principle follow the CROW 500. As the Court of Appeal rightly held, the scope and func- 5

2 HR 25 May 2018, ECLI:NL:HR:2018:772.

tion of the CROW 500 make a uniform interpretation desirable and, as a result, great importance is attached to the wording of CROW 500. According to the local network operator, the contractor breached CROW 500 by digging without having located all cables and pipes present beforehand (ie in the 'design phase'). According to the *Hoge Raad*, this is insufficient to constitute negligence. In fact, the CROW 500 states that excavation work is allowed in places where not all cables and pipes have been mapped, provided certain precautionary measures are taken. One such measure is to carry out the work considering the unmapped area a 'risk area', which was the method the contractor opted for. Thus, the mere fact that the contractor did not find the location of the cables and pipelines does not make his actions negligent.

6 The local network operator also argued that, since the contractor worked in a so-called 'risk area', the mere fact that damage occurred is sufficient to establish liability. The local network operator based this argument on the provision in the CROW 500 that the soil excavator, when working in a high-risk area, is obliged to 'ensure that the excavation is carried out safely without damaging the cables and pipelines present'. According to the *Hoge Raad*, however, no provision in the CROW 500 states that damage caused by work in a high-risk area automatically leads to liability. In an *obiter dictum*, the *Hoge Raad* noted that if damage occurs during excavation work in a high-risk area to a cable or pipeline previously located or whose theoretical location was in the search area, and it is established that the damage resulted from the excavator's work, it is presumed that the excavator did not work sufficiently safely and acted negligently. This presumption can be invoked by the party who suffered damage due to excavation work in a high-risk area.

c) Commentary

7 Pursuant to the *Wet WIBON*, as *grondroerder* ie working in the ground, a contractor must investigate the exact location of cables and pipelines at an excavation site prior to excavation work. The contractor may not simply assume the accuracy of information received after an excavation notification has been issued but will have to locate cables and pipes based on this information before starting their activities. In 2017, a form of private regulation, the CROW 500, was introduced.

8 In 2018, the *Hoge Raad* created some clarity by ruling that liability for excavation damage to cables and pipelines involves a weighing-up process in which, among other things, the objectionability of precautions to be taken by the excavator and the network operator must be considered against the possible consequences of damage to cables or pipelines. According to the *Hoge Raad*, the

CROW 500 guideline is of great importance in this assessment, because it reflects the views of the professional sector as to careful action. A court may only deviate from that guideline if it explicitly states why it does so.[3] The circumstances of the case remain decisive.

In the present judgment, the *Hoge Raad* explicitly ruled that the CROW 500 does not imply a strict liability for excavators. The duty of localisation under the CROW 500 is a best-efforts obligation rather than a result obligation. Thus, even in the case of damage to unlocated cables in a high-risk area, negligence on the part of the actor must be proven. Such proof was lacking in this case, since the excavator had taken additional measures to prevent damage, not digging with a machine but with a spray lance. In order to accommodate the excavation practice in similar cases, the *Hoge Raad* formulated a presumption of proof in favour of the network operator in the aforementioned case. 9

2. HR 12 January 2024, ECLI:NL:HR:2024:17: Standard of Care towards Third Parties (*Immersion Pit*)

a) Brief Summary of the Facts

When constructing a new building, contractor Multi-Bouwsystemen B.V. was commissioned by a plot owner to install an immersion pit. Although measures were taken to prevent subsidence, the adjacent property was damaged (broken shop window and severe cracking). Damage was caused to the neighbours – in the building of one of the neighbours, a wine business was based, and the upper floor was inhabited. Although the Construction All Risk-insurer (CAR) had indicated – after an obstacle in the ground was hit, tearing away part of the basement wall – that all parties involved, including the neighbours, should be consulted, under penalty of termination of coverage, this was disregarded: the plot owner instructed the contractor to continue the work without consultation. The residents of the neighbouring property sought a declaratory judgment that the contractor acted unlawfully, aiming to recover their damage, based on an unlawful act. Both the court of first instance and Court of Appeal denied the claims, as it was not established that the contractor had acted negligently, either in preparation or in execution of the work. 10

---

3 HR 25 May 2018, ECLI:NL:HR:2018:772.

b) Judgment of the Court

11 The users of the adjacent property appealed in cassation. Two relevant complaints were brought: firstly, that an unlawful act occurred through the infringement of a right (damage to the building) and secondly, that the duty of care was violated. According to art 6:162(2) DCC, a wrongful act consists of a violation of a right, an act or omission breaching a duty imposed by law or a rule of unwritten law pertaining to proper social conduct (except in the presence of a ground of justification). With regard to the first ground of appeal, the *Hoge Raad* ruled that a violation of a right as referred to in art 6:162 para 2 DCC does not occur on the basis of the mere fact that an act can foreseeably cause injury or property damage, because this category must be interpreted restrictively. Such an act is only unlawful if the conduct directly constitutes a violation of a norm of written or unwritten law which serves to prevent personal or property damage. The *Hoge Raad* refers to legislative history.[4]

12 With regard to the second complaint, the *Hoge Raad* ruled that if the contractor had acted carefully and properly when installing the immersion pit, he still may have acted unlawfully in other ways. The construction work at hand involved a significant risk of damage to the neighbouring property, even if measures were taken to prevent damage and the work was carried out carefully. When this risk subsequently materialised, it cannot simply be accepted in all cases that the owners of the neighbouring property should bear the resulting damage. In this case, it is relevant that the work was carried out in the interest of (the principal of) Multi and did not bring any benefit for the owners of the neighbouring property, that their damage is not simply (part of) what must be tolerated by a third party in public life when someone else carries out construction work, and that it was rather up to Multi to arrange insurance coverage against liability for damage to third parties. The work carried out by Multi, resulting in damage to the neighbouring property, may thus constitute an unlawful act and lead to an obligation to compensate the resulting damage. The *Hoge Raad* referred to its decision of 3 April 1987:[5] in this case a fence had been erected to screen off a building site. This made the shop less visible. This act in itself was not unlawful, but because no compensation for this invisibility was offered (eg compensation of part of the shop's turnover), a lawful action became an unlawful action after all.

4 Parliamentary History Book 6 BW 1981, at 614 (Explanatory notes by *EM Meijers*).
5 HR 3 April 1987, ECLI:NL:HR:1987:AG5569 (*Van Gastel/Van den Heuvel*).

c) Commentary

The judgment on the first cassation plea repeats the view already held in the Meijers Explanatory Memorandum and thus follows the prevailing doctrine: a violation of a right in the sense of art 6:162 DCC only occurs if the act, regardless of its consequences, infringes a subjective right.[6] In the literature, regret has been voiced that the *Hoge Raad* did not take the opportunity to clarify the relationship between the unlawfulness categories of infringement of a right and of breach of duty of care.[7] Even more so because the category of an infringement of a right is an important one, not only for the injured party in question because of its evidentiary benefits (an infringement is in principle unlawful, unless there is a justification ground) but also in general because of the increasing importance of fundamental rights in private law.[8] 13

The judgment on the second cassation plea is interpreted by some as a tightening of the standard of care in high-risk construction activities (to 'substantial risk', as a number of circumstances are mentioned by the *Hoge Raad* that may lead to a high degree of required care in order to bring the duty of care in construction activities more in line with the risk profile of the activities in question).[9] Although these circumstances resemble those mentioned to justify strict liability,[10] no strict liability was accepted in this case. The *Hoge Raad* ruled that the plea succeeds insofar as it objects to the fact that the Court of Appeal recognised that Multi could be liable for the damage suffered, even in the event of careful preparation and execution of the work. In addition, it would also be difficult to reconcile strict liability with the ruling of the *Hoge Raad* on the first cassation plea.[11] 14

Much has been written about this case in the literature, critical comments have been voiced and various explanations have been given on this judgment: that, although not a violation of a right, the subjective right nevertheless, to a large extent, forms the basis for a judgment of unlawfulness, that the judgment would be a form of compensation for lawful action and that it should be con- 15

6 See also *CH Sieburgh*, Toerekening van een onrechtmatige daad (2000).
7 *CE Drion*, Wanneer is een rechtsinbreuk onrechtmatig? Nederlands Juristenblad (NJB) 2024/308.
8 *KJO Jansen*, Het enigma van de Afzinkkelder: subjectieve rechten als bron van aansprakelijkheid, Nederlands Tijdschrift voor Burgerlijk Recht (NTBR) 2024/6.
9 Cf Note *FJ Berkelder*, Het afzinkkelder-arrest: zorgvuldigheidsnorm onrechtmatige daad bij risicovolle bouwwerkzaamheden aangescherpt, Jurisprudentie in Nederland (JIN) 2024/30.
10 Cf *A Verheij*, Onrechtmatige daad (2023) para 1.7.
11 Note *Berkelder*, JIN 2024/30.

sidered a matter of unlawful nuisance, resulting from construction work.[12] All in all, it is our opinion that this ruling brings no fundamental changes, firstly because a violation of a norm is still a requisite for liability.[13] This also stems from the reference by the *Hoge Raad* to a ruling from 1987:[14] the company did not have to abstain from its activities, but if damage is caused to someone, it might be unlawful to not compensate the loss.

3. HR 12 January 2024, ECLI:NL:HR:2024:18/ECLI:NL:HR:2024:19: Limitation Period of Interest Rate Swap Claims (*Claimants/Deutsche Bank*)

a) Brief Summary of the Facts

16 The directors of Bomo III B.V. (hereafter: claimant) entered into interest rate swaps (ie an agreement between different parties to exchange one stream of interest payments for another over a specified time period) with the Deutsche Bank in 2005 and 2008. Two interest rate swaps entered into in 2005 were terminated in January 2008, but a new interest rate swap was entered into in June 2008. In 2012, the duration of this interest rate swap was extended to 2022. In 2010, the claimant took over a € 26.3 million debt from its directors to the bank and in 2011 also assumed all rights and obligations under the 2008 interest rate swap. The credit relationship ended in 2016. At that moment, the 2008 interest rate swap had a negative value of € 7.38 million. The claimant paid this amount to the bank. In court, the claimant sought (i) annulment of the 2008 interest rate swap for entering into the contract under influence of an error (*dwaling*); (ii) a declaratory judgment that the bank had imputably failed in its obligations and/or acted unlawfully; and (iii) to order the bank to pay over € 18 million in damages or restitution of the amount unduly paid. Both the court of first instance and the Court of Appeal rejected these claims.

---

12 *EF Verheul*, Het Afzinkkelder-arrest in burenrechtelijk perspectief, NTBR 2024/16, issue 6, 119 ff.

13 Cf *JN Potharst*, Risicoaansprakelijkheid of 'aanmerkelijk risico' aansprakelijkheid? NTBR 2024/11.

14 HR 3 April 1987, ECLI:NL:HR:1987:AG5569.

b) Judgment of the Court

In cassation, among other things, the claimant challenged the judgment that the claim for damages against the bank was time-barred. The *Hoge Raad* ruled that art 3:310 (1) DCC requires actual awareness of the damage and of the liable party. The limitation period only starts to run at the moment the injured party is actually in a position to bring a claim for compensation, meaning that the injured party obtained sufficient certainty, not necessarily absolute certainty, that damage was caused by a breach of contract or wrongful act of the liable party. The answer to the question as to at what point in time the injured party obtained sufficient certainty that damage was caused by breach or wrongful act depends on the relevant circumstances of the case.[15] 17

According to the *Hoge Raad*, this means that the court must assess whether the injured party had actual knowledge of the facts and circumstances relating to (i) the damage – ie, that loss is suffered due to the breach or wrongful act of a third party; and (ii) the liable person. In assessing whether the injured party had actual knowledge of the liable person's breach or wrongful conduct, the judge should consider whether the injured party had the knowledge and understanding required to assess the soundness of the conduct. This does not necessarily mean that the client should have a clear notion of the precise content of the bank's duty of care, but the client must understand that the other party failed to fulfil its obligations, for example by deceiving, misleading or withholding relevant information. Complaints were brought against the Court of Appeal's judgment that, with regard to various breaches of duty of care alleged by the claimant, he already had acquired knowledge and insight enabling him to assess the soundness of the bank's actions earlier than five years before he filed his claim. The *Hoge Raad* endorsed the premise that the circumstance that reassurance notices are made may imply that the injured party did not (yet) have the knowledge and insight to be able to assess the soundness of the actions. However, conversely, the absence of reassurance notices cannot independently contribute to the opinion that the injured party was actually aware of the damage and the liable party. To be able to file a claim – and thus for the subjective limitation period to start running – the plaintiff must understand well enough that the counterparty has failed or acted wrongfully. 18

15 See, amongst others, HR 21 April 2023, ECLI:NL:HR:2023:653; HR 9 October 2020, ECLI:NL:HR:2020:1603; HR 31 March 2017, ECLI:NL:HR:2017:551.

4. HR 12 January 2024, ECLI:NL:HR:2024:19: Commencement of Limitation Period

a) Brief Summary of the Facts

19 The relationship between the claimants and the bank began in 2006 – originally between the claimants and ABN AMRO, later taken over by the Deutsche Bank – and ended in 2014 with a settlement agreement, including a settlement clause to the effect that the parties declared they no longer have any claims against each other under the interest rate derivative contract. The banking credit relationship between the parties ended in 2017. The claimants (growers, breeders and sellers of lilies) suffered losses. In proceedings initiated in 2018, the claimants primarily sought to have the settlement clause set aside, among other things on the basis of incorrect advice by the bank (advising them without making them aware of the risks of interest rate swaps) in 2006, which they only found out about during a conversation with a lawyer in 2016, in the wake of which they also sought to sue the Deutsche Bank for damages on other legal grounds. Central to their argument were contentions on grounds of their ignorance as to what they exactly agreed to in the 2014 agreement. The court of first instance and the Court of Appeal concluded that the annulment claim could not succeed since it was time-barred in view of the short limitation period. With regard to the interest rate swap, the Court of Appeal also ruled that the 'settlement clause' from 2014 precludes a claim in cassation, since the parties thereby waived all possible claims in connection with that interest rate swap. The Court of Appeal also held that the absence of reassurance notices in itself may contribute to a conclusion that the injured party was aware of the damage and the liable party.

b) Judgment of the Court

20 The *Hoge Raad* ruled that it is not sufficient that the injured party actually knows about the damage suffered for the short limitation period of art 3:310(1) DCC to start. The injured party must also have sufficient certainty that the damage was caused by a breach or wrongful act of the liable party. The answer to the question as to at what point in time the injured party obtained sufficient certainty, not nec-

essarily absolute certainty, that damage was caused by a breach or wrongful act depends on the relevant circumstances of the case.[16]

In assessing whether the injured party had actual knowledge of the facts and circumstances relating to (i) the damage and (ii) the liable party, the judge should consider whether the injured party had the necessary knowledge and insight to assess the soundness of the other party's actions. The circumstance that the latter sent reassuring messages may imply that the injured party did not (yet) have that knowledge and insight. However, the reverse – ie the absence of reassuring communications – cannot independently contribute to the opinion that the injured party actually knew about the damage and the liable party.[17] 21

In the assessment of the question of the exact meaning of the settlement clause and whether or not, according to standards of reasonableness and fairness, it was acceptable for the Deutsche Bank to rely on it (cf art 6:248(2) DCC), it may also be important to consider the insight the claimants had at the time they signed the agreement with this provision about claims they could have against the Deutsche Bank in connection with the interest rate derivative contract and what Deutsche Bank could expect in that respect, in terms of knowledge on the part of the claimants. According to the *Hoge Raad*, from the Court of Appeal's reasoning, it is not clear that the court included these elements in its assessment, and therefore the relevant cassation complaint is well-founded. 22

c) Commentary

The short limitation period of art 3:310(1) DCC starts to run from the moment the injured party has become aware of both the damage – ie, disadvantage suffered as a result of a third party's faulty or wrongful act – and the liable/responsible party. In settled case law, the *Hoge Raad* specified that the time limit of art 3:310(1) DCC starts to run the moment (or rather, the day after) the injured party is 'actually in a position to bring a legal action for the compensation of its loss'.[18] 23

The mere presumption of being in that position is not sufficient. In legal practice, the question as to when an injured party is actually in such a position gives rise to debate. In particular, the question whether a lack of knowledge and insight to assess the performance delivered may play a role in proceedings has been sub- 24

16 See HR 21 April 2023, Jurisprudentie Onderneming & Recht (JOR) 2023/229; HR 9 October 2020, JOR 2020/302.

17 Cf HR 9 October 2020, ECLI:NL:HR:2020:1603.

18 See eg, HR 31 October 2003, ECLI:NL:HR:2003:AL8168, Nederlandse Jurisprudentie (NJ) 2006/112 with note *Du Perron*.

ject of discussion. Legal error does not prevent the commencement of the limitation period, but this main rule was set by a *Hoge Raad* decision in 2020,[19] in which the concept of 'awareness' is interpreted subjectively. This means that a lack of knowledge and insight on the part of the injured party to assess the soundness of the performance delivered may prevent the commencement of the limitation period. In other words, this concerns the situation in which an injured party, in relation to the party held liable, was entitled to rely on the latter's expertise and in that context had no reason (yet) to doubt the soundness of its actions.

25 The present judgments (2024:18 and 2024:19) concern and confirm the line followed in the 2020 judgment, and holds that the nuance/exception is not limited to cases in which the injured party turns to legal counsel, but may also apply beyond.[20]

5. HR 16 February 2024, ECLI:NL:HR:2024:249: Loss of a Chance (Professional Misconduct of a Lawyer)

a) Brief Summary of the Facts

26 A self-employed entrepreneur – owner of a clothing workshop (*confectie-atelier*) – took out compulsory insurance against work disability under the Self-Employed Persons Disability Insurance Act (*Wet Arbeidsongeschiktheidsverzekering zelfstandigen*, WAZ). After reporting disability due to back and leg complaints, the insurer did not accept that there was 25% incapacity for work or more. The entrepreneur then turned to a lawyer, who committed professional misconduct by allowing the expiry period of one year, set out in the policy terms of the insurance, to pass without filing a claim. As a result, his client had no possibility whatsoever to enjoy insurance benefits. He held the lawyer liable for the damage suffered and for future damage.

27 The court of first instance (in proceedings on the merits, *bodemprocedure*) decided that, in order to determine whether, and if so, to what extent, damage has been suffered as a result of professional misconduct, the court should weigh up the probability of what the situation would have been without professional misconduct (hypothetical situation) and compare it with the situation after the professional misconduct (ie, the actual situation). The question arose as to whether

19 HR 9 October 2020, ECLI:NL:HR:2020:1603.

20 See *T Wouda/K Wunderik*, Aanvangsmoment korte verjaringstermijn: Hoge Raad bevestigt subjectieve toets, blog at dirkzwager.nl d.d. 11 November 2024.

or not the client would have received benefits had the misconduct not taken place. The court of first instance declared the lawyer liable towards his client as a result of this professional misconduct (it is assumed that benefits would have been gained). In this declaratory judgment, the lawyer was ordered to pay damages, to be assessed further by the court (referring the case to damages assessment proceedings [*schadestaatprocedure*], art 612 Code of Civil Procedure [*Wetboek van Burgerlijke Rechtsvordering*, Rv]). In the damages assessment procedure, the damages were initially set at € 136,000, but upon appeal, the Court of Appeal rejected the claim on the grounds of lack of a causal relationship and ruled that the payment by the insurer would have been refused even if a claim had been lodged in time.

b) Judgment of the Court

In cassation, it was argued that the court of first instance had already made a binding finding of loss of a chance of at least a certain magnitude and had only left it to the court in the damages assessment procedure to determine the amount of compensation in more detail. The argument was that, since professional misconduct and a causal link had already been established in proceedings on the merits, a finding of liability cannot be dismissed in damages assessment proceedings. However, the *Hoge Raad* ruled that it is still possible to decide to dismiss a claim in the damages assessment procedure because the professional misconduct in question did not actually lead to damage, since, if it is sufficiently plausible that, as a result of professional misconduct, a chance of success has been lost (a *conditio sine qua non* connection), the requirement for referral to the damages assessment procedure has been met, and all that remains is to determine the damages on the basis of an evaluation of probability. This, however, does not yet mean that the chance of success has a value. That remains to be determined. In the case at hand, the Court of Appeal had ruled that the plaintiff did not suffer any damage due to his lawyer's misconduct because the plaintiff would not have gained any insurance benefits even if the request to the insurer had been lodged in time. The claim of the plaintiff was therefore dismissed. The *Hoge Raad* confirmed this decision. 28

c) Commentary

29 For a referral to the damages assessment procedure, the grounds for liability must be pre-established.[21] Furthermore, the possibility that damage has been or will be suffered must be plausible, as recently reiterated by the *Hoge Raad.*[22] If a lawyer fails to lodge an appeal in time, in order to answer the question of whether and to what extent the client suffered detriment as a result, in principle it must be assessed how the appeal should have been decided upon, or at least the amount to be awarded must be assessed on the basis of the probability of the client's success in the hypothetical case of a timely lodged appeal.[23]

30 Causality is assessed in two stages. In the first phase, liability is established, requiring a *conditio sine qua non* connection between the violation of a norm, *in casu* the professional misconduct, and an altered situation related to the damage.[24] In the second phase, the scope of liability, losses are attributed according to reasonableness (art 6:98 DCC). If the central question is the extent of the damage (estimate of damage), the doctrine of loss of a chance arises. However, if an injured party lost a chance, it is still possible that the damages assessment procedure concludes a zero value, according to the *Hoge Raad.* This can be detrimental to the disappointed client, namely when (in the court's view in the damages assessment procedure) there was no real chance of a better result, ie, of setting aside the judgment left uncontested, or of success in the proceedings not commenced (within the limitation period). In this case, the *Hoge Raad* ruled that the court had only taken a decision on causation in the question as to the establishment of liability (in fact whether the client was deprived of a chance *in abstracto*), not also (already) as to the scope of liability (and whether he was deprived of a chance *in concreto*).[25]

---

21 *E Tjong Tjin Tai,* De schadestaatprocedure, 2024/4.1.

22 HR 8 March 2024, ECLI:NL:HR:2024:328 (*Solidiam vorderingen/erfgenamen*).

23 HR 24 October 1997, ECLI:NL:HR:1997:AM1905 (*Baijnings/mr H*).

24 See HR 21 December 2012, ECLI:NL:HR:2012:BX7491 (*Deloitte/Hassink*).

25 See *M Hengeveld,* De verhouding tussen hoofdzaak- en schadestaat bij causaliteitsvraagstukken, Jurisprudentie Burgerlijk Procesrecht (JBPr) 2024/33.

6. HR 12 April 2024, ECLI:NL:HR:2024:568: Estimating the Extent of Damage and Undeclared Work (*Achmea cs/defendant*)

a) Brief Summary of the Facts

A contractor suffered (ankle) injuries as a result of an accident while carrying out work for a school, falling from a ladder, provided by the school. The school admitted liability for the accident. During the claim settlement process, it emerged that the contractor had received a considerable sum of income from undeclared work, ie income for which he had paid no income tax. The school's insurer (*Achmea cs*) took the position that this income should not be taken into account when estimating the loss of earning capacity. The court of first instance (in partial dispute proceedings, cf art 1019w ff Rv) and the Court of Appeal ruled against the insurer: income from undeclared work – if proven – is to be taken into consideration when estimating the loss of earning capacity. 31

b) Judgment of the Court

The school's insurer appealed in cassation. According to settled case law of the *Hoge Raad*, the existence and extent of damage due to reduced working capacity, as a result of an event giving rise to liability, must be determined by making a comparison between the income of the injured party in the actual situation after that event and the income that the injured party would have acquired in the hypothetical situation without that event. In principle, the obligation to furnish facts (*stelplicht*) and the burden of proof (*bewijslast*) of the existence and extent of the damage rests on the injured party. However, no strict requirements may be imposed on the injured party when comparing the actual and hypothetical situations. When comparing the actual situation with the hypothetical situation, reasonable estimates must be made of how the injured party's income will develop or how it would have developed in the absence of the damage event. These estimates have to rely on reasonable expectations of future developments in the injured party's working capacity after that event or without that event. In that respect, the probabilities must be weighed up, in the assessment of which the court has a considerable degree of freedom.[26] 32

---

26 Cf HR 15 May 1998, ECLI:NL:HR:1998:ZC2654; HR 14 January 2000, ECLI:NL:HR:2000:AA4277; HR 17 February 2017, ECLI:NL:HR:2017:273; HR 22 April, ECLI:NL:HR:2022:590.

33 Furthermore, the *Hoge Raad* ruled that when estimating the extent of damages due to a diminished work capacity, insofar as it concerns work performance that is lawful as such, income from undeclared work of the injured party in the period before the damage event can be taken into account.[27] The *Hoge Raad* responded to the question of how to estimate income from undeclared work. If the injured party before the damage event received income from undeclared work which is lawful as such, it is necessary to assess (i) whether, and if so, to what extent, the injured party would have performed this work in the hypothetical situation that the accident did not occur, or if he would have performed other work instead, and (ii) what net income, after withholding or remitting due tax and other contributions, the injured party would have gained from such work.

c) Commentary

34 Already in 2000, the *Hoge Raad* (implicitly) ruled that undeclared income from work to be regarded as lawful as such is eligible for compensation, not from illegal activities, to be regarded as non-legal damage,[28] for which there is no obligation to pay compensation (usually based on the so-called principle of relativity cf art 6:163 DCC – eg for activities of drug dealers). However, a court of first instance in 2020 clearly ruled against compensation for lawful undeclared ('black') forms of income.[29] Opinions are also divided in legal doctrine.[30] In the present judgment, the *Hoge Raad* ruled on the question of whether loss of undeclared income is eligible for compensation when estimating loss of working capacity. In terms of content, it follows the approach it took in the past. Nevertheless, this ruling led to many reactions in the Dutch legal world.

35 In this (abstract) assessment of damages, income from undeclared work has to be included, because the situation after a norm violation and the situation if there had been no norm violation (hypothetical situation, estimated or assumed[31]) must be compared. In this comparison, the working capacity has to be taken into account, and it has to be determined whether that has deteriorated. In this calculation, the working capacity at the time of the breach (or just before) is indicative

27 HR 24 November 2000, ECLI:NL:HR:AA8453.

28 A (later) exception, in which was ruled otherwise, was ECLI:NL:RBNHO:2020:284.

29 Rechtbank (Rb) Noord-Holland, ECLI:NL:RBNHO:2020:284.

30 *Salva Schaderecht*, Schadevergoeding voor gemiste zwarte inkomsten? De Hoge Raad oordeelt, d.d. 17 April 2024

31 Cf Conclusion *AG Lindenbergh*, 22 December 2023, ECLI:NL:PHR:2023:1203, para 4.10.

for the hypothetical situation without a breach. In that respect, income from undeclared work is important, being an indication of working capacity. Therefore, it should be allowed to include it. The *Hoge Raad* however uses the word *can*, which seems to be understood as *must* (with a limited scope to disregard it).[32] Otherwise, if income from undeclared work is not included, the work capacity level will be estimated much lower than it actually is.

The calculation should not be based on undeclared work gross income, but 36
from what the net income would have amounted to. Then the income the victim would have earned if there had been no violation of standards, for undeclared work or comparable declared work, after tax, is calculated. Although the above is to be assessed and determined on a case-by-case basis, as a rule, the estimate of loss of earning/working capacity will come down to the undeclared 'grossed-up' income, although there may be special circumstances, eg if there is concrete evidence that the injured party's undeclared income, irrespective of the incident, would have increased or decreased at some point in time.[33]

7. HR 5 July 2024, ECLI:NL:HR:2024:1022: Capacity as Driver of a Vehicle in the case of Intervention by an Occupant (*Stichting Koskea/Nationale Nederlanden*)

a) Brief Summary of the Facts

While a group of footballers were travelling as in a passenger van, one of the pas- 37
sengers, previously their coach, sitting in the back seat, pulled the emergency brake. The van went into an uncontrolled cross-slip, hitting a concrete pillar. One of the passengers died. The driver – who, incidentally, was under the influence of alcohol and, possibly, drugs – suffered severe brain damage and became permanently and fully unfit to work. The driver claimed a declaratory judgment that the SVI insurer (*Schade Verzekering Inzittenden*) of the van, insured under the Motor Insurance Liability Act (*Wet Aansprakelijkheidsverzekering Motorrijtuigen*, WAM) is liable for his damage. According to art 4(1) WAM,[34] the insurer does not

32 Note *R Zwanenberg*, Zwarte inkomsten van de benadeelde van voor de aansprakelijkheidsvestigende gebeurtenis kunnen worden meegenomen bij de begroting van schade wegens verlies aan arbeidsvermogen, JIN 2024/128, 9.

33 JIN 2024/128, 10, referring to *Bloembergen*, note in NJ 2001/195.

34 This provision elaborates on the exception of art 12(1) Directive 2009/103/EC [2009] Official Journal (OJ) 263/11.

have to provide coverage for damage of a driver of a motor vehicle that caused an accident. For this reason, the central issue was whether the victim, as the driver, 'lost' his capacity as a driver when a passenger suddenly pulled the emergency brake, causing the collision.

38 Although the court of first instance, in partial dispute proceedings (*deelgeschilprocedure*), answered that question in the affirmative, the Court of Appeal ruled otherwise. According to the Court of Appeal, the person behind the wheel remained a driver after he occupied the driver's seat behind the wheel, set the van in motion and determined its speed and direction. He did not cease to be a driver merely because another person also performed a driving act by pulling the handbrake.

b) Judgment of the Court

39 The Koskea Foundation, trustee (*bewindvoerder*) of the injured party, appealed this ruling to the *Hoge Raad*. Among others, it complained that the Court of Appeal had misapplied the law, and that the injured party was no longer a driver after a passenger pulled the emergency brake. The *Hoge Raad* considered that the concept of 'driver' in the WAM should be interpreted in accordance with the European rules on compulsory motor vehicle insurance, in respect of which, the Court of Justice of the EU has highlighted the importance of passengers' protection in several of its judgments. According to the *Hoge Raad*, in this case, the question is whether the exception in art 12(1) Directive 2009/103, as codified in Dutch law, also applies in the event a passenger interferes with the steering of a motor vehicle, resulting in an accident. Nor is it clear how and when a driver 'loses' their capacity as a driver. The question is thus whether art 12(1) of Directive 2009/103 should be interpreted as meaning that the WAM insurance should cover liability for the (initial) driver's loss when a passenger interferes with the steering of the motor vehicle, resulting in an accident. A second question is whether other circumstances may be relevant to the question of whether a driver can 'lose' their capacity as a driver in order to be able to claim coverage under the WAM as a passenger. According to the *Hoge Raad*, the answer to those questions cannot be deduced from EU law beyond reasonable doubt. Thus, the *Hoge Raad* decided to file a preliminary question as to the question of the capacity as a driver to the European Court of Justice.

c) Commentary

In this case, the question is whether compulsory motor vehicle insurance, also based on European Union directives, should also cover damage caused by the (initial) driver of a car when a passenger interferes with the steering of a motor vehicle, resulting in an accident. According to the Advocate General, it is clear that the person behind the wheel ceases to be a 'driver' if they can no longer exercise 'control' of the car due to the actions of a passenger. The Advocate General refers to how this WAM issue is decided in Belgium in civil case law. The Belgian Act of 21 November 1989 on compulsory motor vehicle liability insurance (*Belgische Wet van 21 november 1989 betreffende de verplichte aansprakelijkheidsverzekering inzake motorrijtuigen*) is strongly influenced by the Benelux roots that also gave birth to the Dutch WAM and therefore, according to the Advocate General, constitutes interesting comparative information. Under Belgian law, a driver is considered a driver as long as they have control over the car. If the driver loses control at any time, due to the actions of a passenger, they are no longer considered a driver.[35] Yet, according to the *Hoge Raad*, it is not clear when exactly a driver ceases to be a driver. The Dutch criminal courts had less difficulty with this question in related criminal proceedings. Both the court of first instance and the Court of Appeal ruled in the criminal case that, by his action, the former coach behaved legally towards the driver of the bus. 40

8. HR 27 September 2024, ECLI:NL:HR:2024:1311: Limitation Period for Claims Subsequent to Collective Action (*Groeivermogen NV/defendant*)

a) Brief Summary of the Facts

In 1997 and 1998, the defendant in cassation had entered into two securities leasing agreements with Groeivermogen, the claimant in cassation. In 2005, the Consumer and Money Association (*Vereniging Consument & Geldzaken*, VCG) brought a collective action against Groeivermogen under art 3:305a (former) DCC. The Court of Appeal ruled in 2019 that Groeivermogen had acted unlawfully in respect of certain securities lease products by breaching its special duty of care. In 2020, the defendant in cassation claimed payment from Groeivermogen, inter alia, of all sums paid to Groeivermogen according to the securities lease agreements. Groeivermo- 41

35 Conclusion *GRB van Peursem*, 15 December 2023, ECLI:NL:PHR:2023:1166, at 4.21.

gen invoked prescription in those proceedings. The court of first instance (cantonal judge: *kantonrechter*)) upheld the prescription plea. The Court of Appeal, however, dismissed it by interlocutory judgment, ruling that a new limitation period of five years, equal to the original limitation period, started to run after the *res judicata* of the class action judgment.

b) Judgment of the Court

42 The limitation period for individual claims related to collective actions is interrupted, inter alia, by the submission of a claim, in this case the submission of the collective action by VCG, until the judgment in the collective action has become *res judicata* (art 3:316(1) DCC). In cassation, arguments were based on art 3:316(2) DCC, which states that when a filed legal claim is rejected by the court, the prescription period will only have been interrupted if, within six months after the legal proceedings have ended due to a final and binding decision or because of another reason for its ending, a new legal claim is filed, which is ultimately upheld by the court.

43 The view that the (partial) granting of VCG's claim in the collective action cannot be regarded as rejecting or granting the claim referred to in art 3:316 (2) DCC vis-à-vis the individual interested parties on whose behalf VCG acted in the collective action is incorrect, since these individual claims were not decided upon in the collective action. That would entail that the judgment in a collective action vis-à-vis individual interested parties by definition cannot be considered as rejecting or granting the claim within the meaning of art 3:316(2) DCC, and that these individual parties, who take no part in the collective action and may not even be aware of such proceedings, must always bring a new claim by themselves within six months after the judgment in the collective action becomes final in order to prevent their claim from being time-barred. This is inconsistent with the effective and efficient legal protection of individual interested parties intended by the provision of art 3:305a DCC.

44 The *Hoge Raad* first of all ruled that, pursuant to art 3:319 (1) and (2) DCC, the interruption of the limitation period of a legal action causes a new limitation period to commence equal to the original period, but not exceeding five years. An exception only occurs if there is an awarding enforceable judgment (*voor tenuitvoerlegging vatbare toewijzende uitspraak*), in which case, pursuant to art 3:324 DCC, a limitation period (of 20 years) for the enforcement starts to run. However, a declaratory judgment is not enforceable. In those cases, there will usually be no need for a new limitation period. The situation is different in a case such as the present one, in which the interruption of an individual claim ended because the

judgment became final. The *Hoge Raad* ruled that it must be assumed that in such case, in accordance with the main rule of art 3:319(1) DCC, a new limitation period begins to run for the claims of individual interested parties after the collective action, equal to the original limitation period, but not longer than five years.

c) Commentary

VCG's collective action was based on art 3:305a DCC, as this provision applied until the entry into force on 1 January 2020 of the Act on Settlement of Mass Damages in Collective Action (*Wet afwikkeling massaschade in collectieve actie*, WAMCA). Until then, art 3:305a(3) DCC stipulated that the aim of a collective action could not be monetary compensation. 45

According to the general rules on the interruption of the limitation period of a legal action in arts 3:316–3:318 DCC, the limitation period may be interrupted by the submission of a claim or another act of legal action (*rechtsvervolging*; art 3:316 DCC), by written summons or notice (art 3:317 DCC) or by acknowledgement (art 3:318 DCC). These grounds for interruption may co-exist, ie if one interruption ground is not or no longer valid, this does not prevent the prescription period from being interrupted on another ground. This case concerns interruption on the basis of art 3:316 DCC. 46

In settled case law, the bringing of a claim in a collective action also interrupts the limitation period of the individual claims of those whose interests are promoted by the collective action.[36] In this judgment, the *Hoge Raad* clarifies which limitation period applies if such an individual claim is brought after the collective action has ended, ie, a period of five years (art 3:319(1) DCC), provided that the claim in question was not already time-barred at the moment the interruption of the collective action took place. 47

9. HR 4 October 2024, ECLI:NL:HR:2024:1384: Mitigation of Damages (*Chairman/BZV*)

a) Brief Summary of the Facts

This Curaçao case concerns the (internal) liability of two directors towards the *Stichting Buro Ziektekostenvoorzieningen* (BZV) of which they were directors for 48

36 HR 28 March 2014, ECLI:NL:HR:2014:766.

two years. BZV filed several charges against the directors for suspected financial irregularities. In these proceedings, BZV sought a declaratory judgment that the chairman and secretary had culpably failed in the proper performance of their management duties under art 2:14 of the Civil Code Curaçao, and claimed damages. The court (*Gerecht*) and the common court (*Gemeenschappelijk Hof*) partly upheld that claim. The common court reduced the amount of compensation to be paid by the directors.

b) Judgment of the Court

49 In cassation, BVZ complains, inter alia, about this reduction. According to art 6:109 DCC, if the full award of damages in the given circumstances, including the nature of the liability, the legal relationship between the parties and their mutual capacity to pay, would lead to manifestly unacceptable consequences, the court may reduce the amount of an obligation to pay damages. According to the *Hoge Raad*, this provision should be regarded as a special application of the rule on the restrictive effect of reasonableness and fairness (arts 6:2 and 6:248 DCC).[37] The standard laid down in art 6:109 DCC, which requires caution and objectification of insight, compels the court to use its power to reduce the amount of a legal obligation to pay damages with restraint. Article 6:109 (1) DCC leaves the judgment on mitigation entirely to the court, whereby it will have to consider all the circumstances of the case. For the circumstances mentioned in the provision that may be of particular importance, namely the nature of the liability, the legal relationship between parties and their financial resources, and for other circumstances, namely those not mentioned in the legal provision, it is a matter of weighing the interests on the side of both parties.[38]

50 The *Hoge Raad* ruled that the starting point in the application of art 6:109 (1) DCC is that the court, when deciding on the merits of a case, has the freedom to moderate the statutory obligation to pay damages if it is of the opinion that awarding full damages would lead to manifestly unacceptable consequences in the given circumstances. However, this is subject to the basic principle of due process that every judicial decision must at least be motivated in a way in which sufficient insight into the underlying reasoning is provided. Moderation is not limited to (or particularly intended for) cases of strict liability. It can even be applied in the case of a high degree of fault. As a general rule, moderation of the amount of

37 HR 2 March 2001, ECLI:NL:HR:2001:AB0382; HR 14 January 2005, ECLI:NL:HR:2005:AR0220.
38 Parliamentary History Book 6 BW, 449 f.

an obligation to pay damages will be considered after having determined the full extent of the damage. If appropriate, the court may, for example for reasons of procedural economy, take a different approach. If a court does so, it does not have to priorly, ie before applying mitigation, determine the full extent of the damage.

c) Commentary

This judgment confirms that mitigation of damages pursuant to art 6:109 DCC (the 51
wording of which is identical to that of the Curaçao version of art 6:109 Curaçao Civil Code which applied in this case, as well) is a rare exception. It constitutes a special application of the rule on reasonableness and fairness. Only if, according to the standards of reasonableness and fairness, it is unacceptable to award full damages, may there be room for the court to reduce an amount of damages to be paid. The fact that both the Court of Appeal and the *Hoge Raad* provided such extensive reasons for their judgments was necessary according to the *Hoge Raad*, because, in order to come to a mitigation judgment, it must be extensively motivated. The standard to be applied in mitigation requires restraint on the part of the court, precisely because the standard requires caution and the case to be looked at objectively, abstracting from its own insights. The judgment rests with the court of facts, but it must consider all the circumstances of the case and must weigh all the interests of both parties (not just of one party), and substantiate its decision very well (on objective grounds). The Court of Appeal did so, moderation was related to a very unusual situation, related to the Schotte government in Curaçao. The *Hoge Raad* also ruled that even when full damage is not (yet) determined, this does not mean that it is not acceptable to mitigate the damages.

10. HR 15 November 2024, ECLI:NL:HR:2024:1661: Consequences for Violating the Equality Principle (*Didam 2*)

a) Brief Summary of the Facts

The Municipality of Montferland owns the site of the former town hall in the centre of Didam. A car park next to this site serves a Coop supermarket. Didam Have 52
c.s. operate an Albert Heijn supermarket elsewhere in Didam. The municipality had drawn up a master plan for the redevelopment of the centre of Didam, includ-

ing the town hall and the Coop supermarket sites. Groenstaete, representative of the interests of the Coop supermarket, participated in a sounding board group, set up for the development of the master plan while Didam Have, which had also wanted to buy the town hall site in order to move their supermarket to the centre of Didam, were not given such an opportunity.

53 Initially in the summary proceedings (*kort geding*) and later in the proceedings on the merits, Didam Have demanded it still be given the opportunity to acquire the plot. In the summary proceedings, the *Hoge Raad* ruled that governmental bodies, when disposing of their land, must give an equal opportunity to acquire it to everyone interested.[39] In the case on the merits, the Court of Appeal ruled that the municipality acted unlawfully toward Didam Have by entering into the purchase agreement and ordered the municipality to compensate Didam Have for the damage suffered, to be specified in detail in a damages assessment proceeding.

b) Judgment of the Court

54 The *Hoge Raad* ruled that these 'Didam Rules' also apply to actions of a public body that took place prior to the *Didam* judgment in 2021,[40] because the Didam Rules are based on general principles of proper administration (applying art 3:14 DCC), to which public bodies were subject already before 2021. Moreover, the *Hoge Raad* ruled that the Didam Rules do not purport to render void or voidable the validity of legal acts that conflict with these rules. Thus, an agreement, even if concluded in violation of the Didam Rules, is not void or voidable on that ground (cf art 3:40 (2) DCC). The agreement remains intact from the point of view of legal certainty. A government body that proceeds to the sale of real estate in violation of the Didam Rules, in principle, acts unlawfully toward (potential) prospective buyers who have been unjustly denied an equal opportunity in that sale. On that ground, that public body may be liable to pay damages. Also, as long as no agreement has been concluded obliging the public body to deliver the immovable property (the plot), or as long as the real estate has not been transferred to a new owner, under certain circumstances there may be cause to prohibit the public body from proceeding with the sale or transfer on the basis of an action brought by the party on that ground.

---

39 HR 26 November 2021, ECLI:NL:HR:2021:1778.
40 HR 26 November 2021, ECLI:NL:HR:2021:1778.

c) Commentary

If a governmental body enters into agreement with a party without giving other parties sufficient scope to compete, thus violating the principle of equality, it may be acting unlawfully. In *Didam 1*, the *Hoge Raad* indicated that the principle of equality implies that room for competition must be provided if a government body wants to enter into an agreement. Governments must in fact adhere to the general principles of proper administration, including the principle of equality. If a public body wants to enter into an agreement with one party and does not consider the possibility of other parties, and then enters into an agreement without considering other potential parties, it does not treat everyone equally, putting one party ahead of another and this is not allowed. This means that a public body has to provide 'competition space' (*mededingingsruimte*) to potential parties, unless it is clear that there is only one suitable party. In the case of more interested parties, a public body must use objective criteria to determine which party wins (the tender). The *Didam* rulings were the subject of lively debate. For governments, it is difficult to comply with competition law requirements. 55

The current ruling, *Didam 2*, deals with the question of what consequences result in the case of non-compliance with the Didam Rules. The *Hoge Raad*, in line with the conclusion of the Advocate General, ruled that agreements concluded in violation of the Didam Rules are not void or voidable, because the Didam Rules do not have that scope (art 3:40 (2) DCC). Legal acts remain valid, but may be unlawful toward other parties who are not treated equally, which may lead to liability for damages. Should a purchase contract be concluded but not transferred, it is possible that, under certain circumstances, a prohibition is imposed. The *Hoge Raad* ruled that the Didam Rules have a broad scope, and that they also apply to cases prior to *Didam 1*, since the principle of equality always applies, being one of the general principles of proper administration. 56

11. Personal Injury

The possibility to compensate immaterial damage was first created in case law, and subsequently codified in the Civil Code 1992. Immaterial damage only qualifies for compensation if the law provides a right to such damages (art 6:95 DCC). A right to immaterial damages arises if the liable person intended to inflict such harm. Under certain conditions, if the harm consists of injury to the memory of a deceased person; and if the person suffering the immaterial loss sustained physical injury, their honour or reputation is injured or their person has been otherwise negatively affected ('op andere wijze in zijn persoon is aangetast'; 57

art 6:106 DCC). In addition, there are other statutory provisions that may form a basis for entitlement to damages, including arts 6:107 and 6:108 DCC.

58 The compensation is estimated, to be determined in fairness (art 6:106 DCC) on the basis of all the circumstances of the case and taking into account amounts of compensation previously awarded by courts in similar cases.[41] For a long time, the ANWB Compensation Guide for immaterial damage (*Smartengeldgids*), including examples, was used for this purpose.[42] The Guide provides little information and therefore it is difficult to find similar cases. It is also worth mentioning that judges do not always give reasons for how they calculated the compensation amount. For many years there has been a debate about the budgeting of damages and a demand for more insight, consistency and efficiency. The need for this has been reinforced by the increase in the number of cases in which criminal courts assess immaterial damages.[43]

59 With the goal of obtaining more guidance in the determination of immaterial damages, the Erasmus School of Law conducted research, commissioned by the Judicial Council (*Raad voor de rechtspraak*) and funded by the Dutch Ministry of Justice and Security. The so-called 'Rotterdam scale' is a scientific study in which injuries are categorised into a scale in order to simplify and harmonise the calculation of immaterial damages, as an aid when determining the extent of damages in concrete cases, by civil or criminal courts and also for out-of-court settlements. The researchers drew inspiration from the English Guidelines for the Assessment of General Damages in Personal Injury Cases and the Irish Personal Injury Guidelines, which also build heavily on the English model.

60 The Rotterdam Scale is a product of research into a more insightful representation of the amount of immaterial damages in the event of injuries and other personal injuries. A first draft was recently published (September 2024), by the end of 2024 the input from the consultation round will be incorporated, and the final version will appear mid-2025. The scale describes which compensation amounts are suitable for various types of cases. The basic structure is that an injury category, type of standard violation or offence is described, together with a range that indicates the extent of the compensation amounts. To use this model, customisation is required, since various factors determine the final amount. Examples of relevant factors for the determination of the extent of the compensation are: age, nature,

41 HR 17 November 2001, ECLI:NL:HR:2000:AA8358.

42 *M Donkerlo*, Smartengeld. Uitspraken van de Nederlandse rechter over de vergoeding van immateriële schade (2024).

43 Consultatie Rotterdamse Schaal smartengeldbedragen gestart, NJB 11 September 2024; De Rotterdamse Schaal. Ordening van smartengeldbedragen bij letsel en andere persoonsaantastingen, consultatieversie september 2024, at 6.

severity and duration of the injury and the resulting symptoms, the scope of impact on the quality of life and leisure activities, and the prognosis.

The scale is also already referred to and applied by courts.[44] In two cases, courts ruled differently. The court of first instance in Rotterdam, contrary to what was argued on behalf of the injured party, found no reason to use the Rotterdam Scale. The court stated that this Scale is still in the consultation phase and not yet used by the judiciary.[45] The court of first instance in Gelderland noted that the Rotterdam Scale is still in the consultation phase. According to the court, this is sufficient justification not to apply the principles contained in that Scale.[46] 61

C. Literature

1. *T Hartlief/WH van Boom/ALM Keirse/SD Lindenbergh*, Verbintenissen uit de wet en schadevergoeding [Obligations arising from the law and damages] (Wolters Kluwer, 10th edn 2024)

This publication provides insights into the law of obligations, extra-contractual liability law and the law of damages. This tenth edition is fully updated and includes the consequences of the Law on Compensation for Disproportionate Damage (*Wet op de Nadeelscompensatie*), which came into force on 1 January 2024, as well as current developments resulting from European regulations relating to product liability and Artificial Intelligence. 62

44 Rb Rotterdam, 11 December 2024, ECLI:NL:RBROT:2024:12404; Rb Oost-Brabant, 13 January 2025, ECLI:NL:RBOBR:2025:128; Rb Oost-Brabant, 13 January 2025, ECLI:NL:RBOBR:2025:130; Rb Oost-Brabant, 13 January 2025, ECLI:NL:RBOBR:2025:131; Rb Rotterdam, 13 November 2024, ECLI:NL:RBROT:2024:11541; Rb Noord-Holland, 6 December 2024, ECLI:NL:RBNHO:2024:12636; Rb Zeeland-West-Brabant, 14 October 2024, ECLI:NL:RBZWB:2024:6942; Hof Den Haag, 4 February 2025, ECLI:NL:GHDHA:2025:141.

45 Rb Rotterdam, 31 December 2024, ECLI:NL:RBROT:2024:13307.

46 Rb Gelderland, 5 November 2024, ECLI:NL:RBGEL:2024:7666.

2. *AU Janssen/TF Walree*, Winstafdracht in het privaatrecht [Surrender of profits in private law] (Wolters Kluwer 2024)

63 In this work, new insights, perspectives and thoughts are provided on the claim for the surrender of profits (art 6:104 DCC). The topic is important, since interest groups increasingly invoke this legal provision to initiate collective proceedings. The contributors to this book address various aspects of the surrender of profits, such as its place in the private law system, its function(s), the historical context, the existing legal and factual obstacles to a surrender of profits and its assessment in various cases.

3. *CNJ Kortmann*, Égalité et justice [Equality and justice] (Wolters Kluwer 2024)

64 In this inaugural address, Kortmann discusses how to prevent a simplification of the assessment of damages leading to individual injustice and relational injustice. Those who suffer damage as a result of an unlawful government action can go to court if they fail to settle the matter amicably. Based on all the information provided by the parties, the court will determine the amount of damages. The downside of this emphasis on accuracy is that court proceedings are often lengthy, costly and place a heavy burden of proof on the injured party. For large groups of victims (mass damage), the court process may even become overburdened and, for this reason, the national government sometimes works out separate compensation schemes for mass damage, such as that for the damages following the earthquake in Groningen. Such a compensation scheme must be designed in such a way that it leads to an efficient settlement of damages without its outcomes being perceived as unfair.

4. *SD Lindenbergh*, Smartengeld [Compensation for pain and suffering] (Wolters Kluwer, 2nd edn 2024)

65 This is the second edition of a dissertation on the legal rules on compensation for pain and suffering, published in 1998, now fully updated by the author with the developments which have taken place for more than 25 years. It contains an elaboration on the legal rules on compensation for pain and suffering in the Dutch Civil Code and beyond. Not only does it discuss current legislation in detail, it also relates it to European law (EU and ECtHR). The most important case law and literature of the past 25 years are also included in this second edition.

5. *CH Sieburgh*, Mr. C. Asser's handleiding tot de beoefening van het Nederlands burgerlijk recht, 6-I: De verbintenis in het algemeen, eerste gedeelte [Mr C. Asser's Manual for the practice of Dutch civil law, 6-I: The obligation in general, first part] (Wolters Kluwer, 17th edn 2024)

This new edition of the well-known Asser series provides a systematic, well-considered and thorough commentary on the first part of the 'law of obligations in general'. This includes the concept of obligations, the different types and the sources of obligations, the plurality of creditors and debtors, fulfilment and non-fulfilment of obligations. The doctrines are treated in outline and references are made to other doctrines in private law. Developments in legislation and case law are included. Legislation, case law and doctrines have been updated since the last edition. Attention is also paid to fundamental rights, European law and comparative law. 66

6. *DFH Stein*, Hoofdelijke aansprakelijkheid [Joint and several liability] (Wolters Kluwer 2024)

This dissertation describes the contents and a personal evaluation of joint and several liability when several debtors owe the same performance or are obliged to compensate the same damage. The relevant legal rules for joint and several liability can be found throughout European Union law, Dutch substantive civil law, and Dutch civil procedural and insolvency law, which are discussed by the author, also including relevant procedural and insolvency law rules. He also indicates the influence of rules of liability in European Union law. This dissertation also examines how civil procedural law and insolvency law facilitate the exercise of rights arising from joint and several liability. In these analyses, the author does not limit himself to a discussion of the applicable legal rules, but also analyses whether these rules are based on common legal principles and what space parties have to fulfil their legal relationship themselves. 67

7. *MKG Tjepkema*, Schappelijk schadevergoedingsrecht [Fair law of damages] (Wolters Kluwer 2024)

The settlement of damages by the national government is an important current issue, eg settlement of the Groningen earthquake damage, settlement of disaster 68 damage in South Limburg and personal losses incurred by victims of the Dutch childcare benefits scandal. Citizens expect a human dimension and generosity from the government, which sets up new regulations, which in turn give rise to new procedures. At the same time, public support for overly generous regulations seems limited. In his inaugural lecture, Tjepkema uses recent damage cases from an administrative law perspective in order to explore challenges faced by administrators, legislators and courts.

8. *RP Wijne*, Aansprakelijkheid voor zorggerelateerde schade: de geneeskundige behandeling en de aansprakelijkheid bij schade van de patiënt [Liability for care-related damage: medical treatment and liability for harm incurred by patients] (Boom Juridisch, 4th edn 2024)

69 One of the needs of patients after an accident is to obtain compensation for care-related damage. Usually, civil liability law is applied in order to receive such compensation, and that is the theme of this book. Based on national and European legislation, national and European case law and literature, civil liability law and the procedure to recover care-related damage are described. Recent case law on the handling of medical information and medical opinions are included. This also applies to the proposed legislation relating to Artificial Intelligence and product liability.

Knut Martin Tande

XXI. Norway

A. Legislation

1. Proposal of Changes in Standardised Compensation Regarding Occupational Injuries and Income Loss for Children

The Norwegian Government has reviewed standardised compensation regarding occupational injuries and income loss for children. A legislative consultation process launched in May 2024 based on this review proposed comprehensive reforms to align compensation frameworks for occupational injuries and child income loss with modern economic principles, addressing systemic undervaluation caused by outdated capitalisation rates.[1] The proposal suggested replacing the 1990-era 6% rate for occupational injuries and the 2018 4% rate for child compensation with standardised rates of 2.5% in general and 1.5% for guardianship-managed funds. 1

These adjustments aimed to uphold the principle of full compensation while harmonising calculations across tort categories and mirrored the 2022 reform, which reduced the general capitalisation rate from 4% to 2.5% for standard cases, and to 1.5% for cases where compensation must be placed in bank deposits under guardianship laws. However, the 2022 reforms did not extend to the specialised compensation frameworks for children and occupational injury victims. 2

Despite completing consultations, the implementation stalled. In May 2025, the Supreme Court upheld existing rates in their verdict in *HR-2025–978-A*, emphasising that existing frameworks remain binding until the formal legislative amendments are enacted. 3

1 <https://www.regjeringen.no/no/aktuelt/utredning-av-nye-regler-for-erstatning-til-barn-og-etter-yrkesskade-pa-horing/id3037548/>.

https://doi.org/10.1515/9783111389271-022

B. Cases

1. Norges Høyesterett (Norwegian Supreme Court, HR) 29 January 2024, HR-2024-431-A: Non-Pecuniary Compensation following a Severe Traffic Accident

a) Brief Summary of the Facts

4 On 29 January 2022, a 21-year-old man (A) was driving a newly acquired high-performance Audi RS 6 Avant with over 500 horsepower, and collided with another car, causing serious injury to this car's driver.

5 In a tunnel, where the speed limit was 90 km/h, A filmed the car's speedometer showing 220 km/h with the intention of sending the video to a friend. Inside the tunnel, the road expanded from two to three lanes. The defendant passed several cars on the right side, despite knowing this was prohibited. The collision happened when the victim's car was changing lanes from the middle to the right lane. The victim, B, was in the car with his spouse.

6 According to the State Road Administration's accident and analysis group, the defendant's car was travelling at 207 km/h immediately before the collision, while the other car was moving at 99 km/h.

7 The District Court convicted A of negligently causing significant bodily harm under sec 280 of the Norwegian Penal Code (*straffeloven*), along with violations of the Road Traffic Act related to speeding. The court concluded that while the defendant had caused serious injury, he had not acted intentionally regarding the harmful consequences. The District Court sentenced him to sixty days imprisonment and ordered him to pay B non-pecuniary compensation of NOK (Norwegian kroner) 175,000.

8 Following appeals by both the prosecution and the injured party, the Court of Appeal reconsidered the case. The Court of Appeal maintained the District Court's finding that the defendant had acted negligently rather than intentionally, though this decision was not unanimous as one lay judge dissented, believing the defendant had acted with intent. The Court of Appeal significantly increased both the prison sentence and the compensation amount, sentencing the defendant to two years and six months imprisonment and ordering him to pay NOK 500,000 in non-pecuniary compensation to the injured party.

9 The defendant subsequently appealed to the Supreme Court regarding both the sentencing and the compensation amount.

b) Judgment of the Court

The Supreme Court addressed the defendant's degree of culpability in a case involving reckless driving causing significant bodily harm. While one lay judge in the Court of Appeal believed the defendant acted with intent (*dolus eventualis*), the majority found he acted with conscious negligence, as he was aware of the risks but did not accept a collision as part of his actions. 10

The Supreme Court emphasised that conscious negligence, where an offender knows they are taking a significant risk, approaches the boundary of intent. The Court found the defendant's actions constituted gross negligence, warranting strong reproach. The Court considered it particularly aggravating that the defendant had no reason to expose others to danger except to satisfy his own desire for speed and excitement, possibly to impress a friend. This made the offence particularly reckless under sec 77(d) of the Penal Code. 11

The extremely serious injuries suffered by the victim exceeded what is typically required for being recognised as significant bodily harm under sec 11 of the Penal Code, further elevating the culpability. The Court rejected the defendant's confession as a mitigating factor, finding it lacked significance in terms of the question of pecuniary compensation. 12

In determining the appropriate sentence, the Court reviewed historical precedents for traffic offences causing bodily harm. The Court referenced cases from 1991 and 2009 involving similar reckless driving resulting in serious injuries or death, noting that the penalty level had gradually increased after legislative changes in 1988. The Court found no basis for further increasing penalties beyond established levels, as there was no evidence that such offences constitute a greater societal problem today. 13

Based on this analysis, the Supreme Court concluded that the appropriate sentence was one year and eight months imprisonment, which stood in reasonable proportion to previous judgments establishing that grossly negligent and aggravated driving with fatal consequences warranted sentences exceeding two years and six months. 14

After determining the sentence, the Court addressed the question of non-pecuniary compensation (*oppreisning*). According to sec 3–5, para 1 of the Norwegian Compensatory Damages Act (*skadeserstatningloven*, skl), a person who has intentionally or through gross negligence caused personal injury may be ordered to pay the injured party a lump sum as the court finds reasonable as compensation for the pain and suffering caused and for other non-pecuniary damage. It was undisputed that the conditions for awarding B non-pecuniary compensation were met. The question was the amount to be awarded. 15

16 The Court noted that, according to established case law, the compensation should reflect the objective gravity of the act, the culpability of the tortfeasor, and the extent and effects of the injury for the injured party, referring to Retstidende (Rt)-2011–769 para 28 and HR-2021-1332-A para 17. The focus in justifying the award of compensation has gradually shifted from retribution and prevention to the injured party's need for compensation, according to Rt-2006–61 para 17 and HR-2020–1345-A para 28 with further references. This has led to a certain general increase in compensation levels, according to Rt-2012–1773, the Supreme Court stated.

17 Unlike some other offences where compensation is standardised in the form of fixed levels that are only deviated from in special cases, such standardisation has not been considered possible for the negligent causation of significant bodily harm. The injuries, and thus the need for compensation, the Court stated, vary too much, referring to Rt-2012–1773.

18 In determining the compensation amount in this case, the Supreme Court took Rt-2012–1773 as a starting point. In that case, the perpetrator had, unprovoked and with homicidal intent, shot at people who were in a public place. The purpose was to settle scores in a drug environment. The two injured parties in the case were life-threateningly injured. Both had to undergo lengthy hospital stays. They suffered paralysis, were dependent on wheelchairs, and required care. One also lost the sight in one eye and had problems speaking. Both suffered pain and psychological problems. The compensation to the injured parties was set at NOK 400,000 and NOK 500,000 respectively. Adjusted in accordance with the development of the National Insurance basic amount, this corresponds to approx NOK 570,000 and NOK 715,000 today.

19 The Court noted that the sentence for the defendant in Rt-2012–1773 – imprisonment for 15 years – was significantly more severe than in the present case. This did not prevent the judgment from being considered a guide for the compensation level, but in the specific assessment, the present case involved a less serious act.

20 The Supreme Court also considered HR-2024-219-A, where the injured party received NOK 375,000 in compensation after being inflicted with two stab wounds in the upper part of the back. It was coincidental that the injuries were not life-threatening. After the incident, the victim suffered from post-traumatic stress disorder and had not returned to work. The injury had major consequences for her daily functions, and she would probably be completely or partially disabled for the foreseeable future.

21 Based on this analysis, the Supreme Court concluded that the harmful act in the present case was less serious than in Rt-2012–1773 and HR-2024–219-A, and that the degree of culpability was lower. At the same time, in determining the compensation, significant weight had to be placed on the life-destroying and ir-

reparable injuries that A had inflicted on B through his grossly negligent and aggravated driving. The individual injury to B was clearly closer to Rt-2012–1773 than HR-2024–219-A. The Court concluded that the compensation in this case could appropriately be set at NOK 450,000.

One judge dissented regarding the compensation amount, arguing that it 22 should be set at NOK 250,000 instead of NOK 450,000. The dissenting judge agreed with the majority that the compensation should be based on the objective gravity of the act, the tortfeasor's culpability, and the effects on the injured party. However, the judge believed that the compensation should be more in line with the sentence in the case and that there were no legislative signals indicating that compensation should be raised to a higher level than previously.

The dissenting judge argued that many convicts are in practice unable to pay 23 the compensation. The compensation is then paid by the Office for Compensation for Victims of Violence, which then claims the amount back from the convict. The reason why convicts often have problems settling their debts is complex. Many have mental illnesses and substance abuse problems. Many are young and have neither income, assets, nor housing when they are released.

The dissenting judge noted that the legislature had not, to their knowledge, 24 expressed that compensation levels should be increased. Recently, it was decided that convicts could be exempt from paying any penalty interest that accrued during their term of imprisonment. The justification included statements from the majority in the Parliament's Justice Committee about the challenges high claims pose for individuals after they complete their sentences.

Based on this background, the dissenting judge argued for moderation in de- 25 termining the amount. It is a fundamental consideration in Norwegian criminal law that the convict should be able to rehabilitate themselves. Starting life after serving a sentence with a high debt, which increases in line with the penalty interest rate of 12.5 %, can make rehabilitation almost impossible and, in the worst case, lead to continued criminality.

c) Commentary

This Supreme Court decision provides important guidance on sentencing and 26 compensation in cases of reckless driving causing severe bodily harm.

The Court emphasises that reckless driving, characterised by excessive speed, 27 repeated overtaking in prohibited ways, and filming the speedometer while driving, represents a particularly dangerous form of traffic violation that warrants severe punishment.

28 The Court's approach to determining non-pecuniary compensation is instructive. The majority's decision to award NOK 450,000, while less than what might be awarded for intentional acts causing similar harm, reflects the gravity of the injuries sustained by the victim. The majority clearly prioritised the victim's need for compensation given the life-altering nature of his injuries.

29 The dissenting opinion on compensation raises important societal questions about the purpose and effect of awarding high compensation. The opinion highlights the practical challenges many convicts face in paying such amounts and the potential negative impact on rehabilitation. This perspective adds a valuable dimension to the ongoing debate about how to balance the need to compensate victims with the goal of rehabilitating offenders.

30 Overall, this judgment represents a balanced approach to a serious traffic offence, emphasising both the need for significant punishment to reflect the gravity of the offence and the importance of compensating the victim for life-altering injuries. The decision provides guidance for future cases involving reckless driving causing severe bodily harm and contributes to the development of Norwegian jurisprudence in this area.

31 The Court's decision to reduce the sentence from the Court of Appeal's two years and six months to one year and eight months, while still maintaining a substantial non-pecuniary compensation award, can be argued to reflect a balanced understanding of the different purposes of criminal punishment and civil compensation.

2. HR 16 April 2024, HR-2024-708-A: Non-Pecuniary Compensation after Attempted Murder

a) Brief Summary of the Facts

32 This case involves a victim (B) who was stabbed in the side of his body during an attempted murder. The perpetrator (A) was found guilty of attempted murder by the Court of Appeal and sentenced to six years and nine months in prison. The Court of Appeal also awarded B compensation for loss of amenities (*ménerstatning*) of NOK 877,548 and non-pecuniary compensation (*oppreisningserstatning*) of NOK 210,000.

33 The victim suffered severe injuries from the stabbing. He had to have one kidney removed, and experienced extensive blood loss that nearly cost him his life. Both the wound from the knife and the surgical scar left scar tissue that increases the risk of intestinal obstruction. The victim had visible scars and continues to experience pain in his abdomen and back, making it difficult to sit still for extended

periods. He also experiences rib pain when lying down. Additionally, the victim has developed post-traumatic stress disorder (PTSD) and hypochondriacal disorder (health anxiety), which have prevented him from working since the incident. His medical disability has been assessed to be 35%.

B appealed to the Supreme Court regarding the non-pecuniary compensation, 34
specifically challenging the legal interpretation. Initially, B claimed NOK 250,000 in non-pecuniary compensation but later increased the claim to an amount at the court's discretion.

b) Judgment of the Court

The Supreme Court began by establishing the legal framework for non-pecuniary 35
compensation and compensation for permanent injury (*ménerstatning*). These are regulated by secs 3-5 and 3-2 of the Norwegian Damages Act, respectively.

The Court noted that sec 3-5 allows for non-pecuniary compensation to be 36
awarded regardless of whether compensation for permanent injury is granted under sec 3-2. This wording suggests that the two forms of compensation can be awarded independently of each other.

The Court then examined the legislative history of these provisions. When the 37
rules on non-pecuniary compensation were moved from the Norwegian Penal Code to the Norwegian Compensatory Damages Act in 1973, the preparatory works stated that such compensation could be granted without regard to whether the injured party is entitled to compensation for permanent injury, and non-pecuniary compensation can be granted even if the injured party has received full compensation for permanent injury.

The Court discussed the historical development of non-pecuniary compensa- 38
tion, noting that its primary purpose has shifted over time. While it originally had a more punitive function, since the late 1990s, the focus has been on compensating the victim for the harm suffered.

Compensation for permanent injury, on the other hand, is meant to compen- 39
sate for medical disability that can have a significant impact on the injured party's situation, such as reduced ability to engage in leisure activities.

The Court emphasised that while both forms of compensation cover non- 40
pecuniary losses related to lost quality of life, there are clear differences between them. Compensation for permanent injury is tied to medical disability; the injury must be significant and permanent. Non-pecuniary compensation has no such requirements and is more flexible in its application.

41 The Court then analysed previous Supreme Court decisions on this issue. In Rt-2005–289, the Court had held that non-pecuniary compensation and compensation for permanent injury should be treated independently of each other.

42 However, in Rt-2014–392, the Court suggested that some coordination between the two forms of compensation might be appropriate, reducing the non-pecuniary compensation, based on the principle that the same loss should not be compensated twice.

43 In the present case, the Supreme Court criticised the 2014 decision, noting that it did not address the 2005 decision or the practice that has developed in the intervening years. The Court also questioned whether the principle of avoiding double compensation, which is primarily relevant to economic losses, is as applicable to non-pecuniary losses that are inherently difficult to quantify.

44 The Court highlighted several practical issues that would arise if the two forms of compensation were to be coordinated in the sense that the non-pecuniary compensation was reduced because of the compensation for permanent injury.

45 Non-pecuniary compensation is often decided in connection with the criminal case, while compensation for permanent injury may be determined later. This makes coordination difficult.

46 The calculation of compensation for permanent injury is regulated by law and regulations, including rules for coordination with other benefits. It would be challenging to incorporate a discretionary reduction based on non-pecuniary compensation.

47 The total compensation should be the same regardless of whether the claims are decided in the same case or separate cases. An unwritten rule on coordination would make this difficult to achieve.

48 Based on these considerations, the Supreme Court concluded that neither the wording of the law, the purpose of the provisions, the preparatory works, nor practical considerations support coordinating non-pecuniary compensation and compensation for permanent injury. While there may be some overlap between the two forms of compensation, they fundamentally aim to compensate different types of non-pecuniary harm. Therefore, they should be treated independently of each other, in line with the 2005 decision.

49 The Court then turned to the consideration of non-pecuniary compensation in the present case. It noted that the amount should reflect the objective severity of the act, the degree of culpability of the perpetrator, and the extent and effects of the injury on the victim.

50 The Court referenced recent Supreme Court verdicts that had increased the standardised amounts for non-pecuniary compensation in similar cases. A verdict

in HR-2024–219-A had awarded compensation of NOK 375,000 to a victim of attempted homicide.

Considering the severe injuries suffered by the victim in this case, including the loss of a kidney, ongoing pain, post-traumatic stress disorder, and health anxiety, as well as the recent adjustments to standardised compensation amounts, the Court agreed with the parties that NOK 325,000 was an appropriate amount of non-pecuniary compensation. 51

c) Commentary

This Supreme Court decision is interesting in several respects. The Court has provided a clear and comprehensive analysis of the relationship between non-pecuniary compensation and compensation for permanent injury. By deciding that these two forms of compensation should be treated independently, the Court resolved an ambiguity in Norwegian tort law that had persisted since the conflicting decisions in 2005 and 2014. 52

The Court's detailed examination of the legislative history and purpose of the relevant provisions demonstrates a commitment to understanding and respecting the intentions of the legislature. This approach provides valuable guidance for future cases involving a statutory interpretation in tort law. 53

The Court's discussion of the practical difficulties that would arise from coordinating these two forms of compensation illustrates an awareness of the real-world implications of legal decisions. This pragmatic approach is likely to be welcomed. 54

The decision strikes a balance between ensuring adequate compensation for victims of serious crimes and maintaining a coherent and manageable system of tort law. By allowing both forms of compensation to be awarded independently, the Court ensures that victims can be fully compensated for different aspects of their suffering and loss. 55

While the Court did not set a new standardised amount for attempted murder cases, its approval of the NOK 325,000 figure provides useful guidance for future cases. This amount, considered in relation to the recently adjusted amounts for homicide cases, helps to establish appropriate guidelines regarding compensation for victims of violent crimes. 56

The Court's reference to recent decisions on compensation levels demonstrates its commitment to maintaining consistency and relevance in its jurisprudence. 57

3. HR 31 May 2024, HR-2024-990-A: Bank's Liability for Damages to a Business Customer Tricked by Fraudsters

a) Brief Summary of the Facts

58 In autumn 2019, the CEO of the company Edison Norge AS was tricked by external fraudsters into transferring about NOK 130 million from the company's account at Danske Bank to accounts in Hong Kong. The fraud began when the CEO (A) received an email from a fraudster posing as the CEO of the parent company, Edison International, regarding a purported acquisition in China.

59 The fraudster instructed A to maintain complete discretion and communicate through a 'lawyer' (also a fraudster) who provided account information for transfers to Hong Kong. A total of 13 payments were made between 24 September and 8 October 2019, all authorised by the CEO who had sole signature authority for Edison Norge.

60 Danske Bank had an automated system for detecting suspicious transactions (a 'fraud engine'), but for unknown reasons, it was not activated for Edison Norge's payments. The fraud was discovered on 10 October 2019, with most of the money lost. Edison International subsequently filed a lawsuit against Danske Bank, claiming damages for the lost funds.

b) Judgment of the Court

61 The Supreme Court first established that the three basic conditions for awarding damages are a basis of liability, economic loss, and causal connection between these. In this case, Edison had undoubtedly suffered a loss of up to 130 million kroner.

62 The Court then examined Edison's principal claim that the payment transactions were unauthorised and thus triggered liability under sec 35, para 1 of the Financial Agreements Act 1999 (para 44). The Court concluded that all 13 payments to the accounts in Hong Kong were authorised by Edison Norge. The CEO, A, had the authority to give instructions as regards the 13 payments. This was not affected by the fact that the company may have used double approval for some previous payments. It was not proven that the parties had an agreement that required double approval when A requested payments outside of online banking.

63 Having ruled out liability for unauthorised payments, the Court then considered whether Danske Bank could be liable based on negligence even though the payments were authorised.

The Court noted that the negligence rule is the fundamental rule of damages both in and outside of contract. The question was whether Danske Bank or employees in the bank should have acted differently, ie, whether the bank had a duty to monitor transactions and act if there was something that could indicate fraud, even though it was clear that the payment had been performed on instructions from the CEO of Edison Norge. 64

The Court observed that this case involved pure economic loss. At the same time, the alleged harmful act was an omission not connected to a risk created by the bank. If one takes as a starting point the negligence assessment outside of contract, liability for damages can only be relevant if there is a breach of an established duty to act. 65

The Court emphasised that the agreement on payment services and its purpose is central to the negligence assessment, regardless of the approach taken. 66

Beyond the claim related to double authorisation, which the Court had already dismissed, Edison had not claimed that Danske Bank had otherwise violated the written contractual provisions. 67

The Court noted that neither the framework agreement nor the account agreement between Edison and the bank stated that Danske Bank had a duty to control the customer's payment decisions to prevent internal or external fraud. A partial conclusion was therefore that the bank had not breached any explicitly contracted obligation. 68

The Court then examined whether different kinds of regulation imposed requirements on banks for protection against fraud in the case of authorised payments: 69

The Court found that the Financial Agreements Act 1999 (*Finansavtaleloven*) sec 40 presupposes that a bank carries out transactions initiated by the customer, but the law does not contain provisions on the obligation to monitor transactions. On the contrary, sec 43, first paragraph, states that a bank is not liable if the customer entered an incorrect account number. A bank is also not liable even if the customer has written the correct name of the recipient, but the wrong account number, cf sec 43, second paragraph. Certain modifications follow from sec 43a, but this provision only covers online payment services. The Financial Agreements Act 1999 contains no obligation to monitor and control payment transactions aimed at detecting fraud related to a customer's payment decisions. On the contrary, the regulation in the law showed a starting point that a customer is responsible for their own mistakes (para 65). 70

The Court found support for this in the preparatory works of the law (Ot prp no 94 (2008–2009)), which was the Norwegian preparatory works for the implementation of Directive 2007/64/EC in Norwegian law. On pages 157 f in the proposition, the Department of Justice states that the Directive provides that a customer 71 has to cover the loss for their own mistakes. Furthermore, the Department states that one cannot have solutions in national law that imply that losses which, according to a full harmonisation Directive should lie with the customer, are regularly shifted to the banks in such a way that it undermines the solution in the Directive.

72 The Court also examined the Regulation on Systems for Payment Services of 15 February 2019, No 152, but found no basis for a duty for banks to develop general systems or routines to prevent or reduce the risk of financial dishonest behaviour in a business or fraud initiated by an actor outside the business (paras 67–69).

73 The Court noted that the European Banking Authority (EBA) in its report, EBA/REP/2022/14 on page 81, identifies social manipulation as an area 'where further improvements … are needed.' Based on this, the Court found it clear that the EBA, neither in 2019 nor 2022, could have meant that banks had a duty to develop systems and procedures to prevent or reduce the risk of economic misconduct.

74 The Court also referred to the European Commission's proposal for a new regulation on payment services from June 2023, COM (2023) 367, cf COD 2023/0210. In the preamble to sec 79, consumer fraud by 'social engineering' is described as an increasing problem. Increasingly sophisticated fraud methods blur the distinction between authorised and unauthorised transactions, making the regulation in Directive 2015/2366/EU no longer sufficient. However, the proposed new liability rule in art 59 no 1 is limited to consumers and cases where the fraudsters pretend to be bank employees. The legislative proposal would therefore not have applied in this case.

75 The Court noted that the proposal somewhat resembles the current regulation in the Financial Agreements Act sec 3-49, para 3. This provision determines that a bank, under certain conditions, is responsible for the customer's loss if someone claims to represent the bank. But that was not the situation in this case, the Court noted.

76 The Court added that if legal requirements for systems or routines against fraud in authorised transactions could be derived from Directive 2015/2366/EU, one would likely have seen indications of this in legislation or practice from EU countries. Such indications have not been demonstrated.

77 In summary, the Court could not see that regulations in force at the time of the damage had established requirements for banks regarding systematic measures against the risk of fraud in the case of authorised payments.

78 The Court considered whether breaches of money laundering rules could form a basis for liability. The Court explained that if a rule of conduct in an area of life is to be relevant in the negligence assessment, it must primarily aim to protect the interest that the damage has affected. The purpose of the

money laundering rules follows from the Anti-Money Laundering Act sec 1, first paragraph, namely to prevent and detect money laundering and terrorist financing. The measures in the Law are intended to protect the financial and economic system and society, according to sec 1, second paragraph. The purpose of the Law is not to prevent or detect other criminal acts, such as fraud or other economic crime.

The Court noted that the Anti-Money Laundering Act sec 27, first paragraph, 79
states that a suspicious transaction cannot be carried out before the National Authority for Investigation and Prosecution of Economic and Environmental Crime (*Økokrim*) is notified. The bank has a duty not to disclose investigations, the transmission of information to *Økokrim*, or investigation under the Anti-Money Laundering Act to the customer, according to sec 28, first paragraph.

The Court concluded that a bank customer who has been subjected to fraud 80
cannot base a claim for damages solely on violations of money laundering rules. The Court did not rule out that gross violations of money laundering rules could be relevant in a negligence assessment in combination with other violations of law or norms, but that was not the case here.

The Court noted that when there is no industry standard, possible violations 81
of Danske Bank's internal procedures for control of authorised payment transactions cannot provide a basis for liability for damages. This must at least be clear when these internal procedures are not made known to the customers, as was the case here. When Edison Norge, from November 2015 onwards, was erroneously exempted from the bank's fraud engine, this did not in itself represent grounds for liability.

c) Commentary

This Supreme Court decision clarifies the scope of a bank's liability in cases of au- 82
thorised payments that turn out to be fraudulent. The Court emphasises that when a payment is authorised by someone with the proper authority within the company, the bank is generally not liable for executing that payment, even if it later turns out to be part of a fraud scheme.

The Court's analysis of liability based on negligence is noteworthy. The Court 83
establishes that for pure economic loss resulting from an omission, liability can only arise if there is a breach of an established duty to act. This clarifies the high threshold for liability in such cases.

The Court's analysis of various regulations provides valuable guidance on the 84
extent of a bank's duty to prevent fraud. The Court found no legal obligation for banks to have systems or procedures in place to prevent or reduce the risk of fi-

nancial misconduct or external fraud in cases of authorised payments. This finding is significant as it establishes that such obligations, if desired, must be created through explicit legislation.

85 The decision of the Supreme Court underscores the importance of clear contractual agreements between banks and their business customers. The Court found no contractual basis for requiring the bank to perform additional checks on authorised payments. This suggests that businesses seeking such protection should explicitly include it in their agreements with banks.

86 The discussion of industry practice and internal procedures by the Supreme Court is significant. It suggests that banks have some discretion in how they implement fraud prevention measures if they meet the relevant legal requirements. The Court's finding that a bank's internal procedures do not create liability when they are not made known to customers provides important guidance for banks in managing their risk.

4. HR 26 June 2024, HR-2024-1169-A: Mother's Claim for Non-Pecuniary Compensation After her Daughter was Taken into Care by Child Welfare Services

a) Brief Summary of the facts

87 In May 2013, a mother (A) gave birth to her daughter (B) two months prematurely. She already had a son from a previous relationship who was in his father's care. During the first month after birth, mother and daughter stayed together in the hospital. Upon discharge, the child welfare services issued an emergency care order.

88 On 21 June 2013, the County Social Welfare Board upheld the emergency care order, citing serious concerns about the mother's care abilities and the child's special needs due to premature birth. On 17 September 2013, the Board issued a regular care order, placing the child in foster care and setting visitation rights to 12 times per year (monthly) for the first year, with a reduction plan if reunification did not occur (six visits the second year, four the third year).

89 In September 2014, when the daughter was about 16 months old, the mother requested the return of her child. On 22 January 2015, the Board rejected this request and reduced visitation to three times per year, one hour each time. In March 2016, the mother again requested the return of her child or increased visitation. The Board rejected both requests on 2 August 2016.

In September 2018, the municipality applied for adoption of the child by the foster parents. On 2 June 2019, the Board rejected the adoption request but maintained the limited visitation schedule, though extending each visit to two hours. The mother had another daughter in 2018, for whom child welfare services found no need for intervention after initial investigation. 90

On 10 March 2022, the mother filed a lawsuit against the municipality claiming compensation for violation of her right to family life. The District Court ruled in favour of the municipality. The Court of Appeal found that the municipality had violated the mother's rights under art 8 of the European Convention on Human Rights (ECHR) and ordered compensation of NOK 100,000. 91

b) Judgment of the Court

The Supreme Court started by considering whether the mother's right to family life was violated. 92

The Supreme Court established that the right to family life is protected both by art 8 of the ECHR (incorporated into Norwegian law through the Human Rights Act) and sec 102 of the Norwegian Constitution, noting that these provisions are interpreted similarly as established in HR-2022-718-A para 85. 93

Based on its plenary decisions from 2020 (HR-2020-661-S, HR-2020-662-S, and HR-2020-663-S), the Supreme Court stated several key principles regarding interventions in family life: they must address a pressing social need, be proportionate, and respect the strong presumption for preserving family bonds. The Court emphasised that care orders should be exceptional and temporary, authorities must actively work toward reunification, and contact must be sufficient to maintain family bonds with reunification in mind. 94

While acknowledging legitimate reasons for child welfare services to investigate, the Supreme Court criticised the preparation and justification of both the emergency and regular care orders. The Court found that the Board's decision failed to demonstrate the 'very exceptional circumstances' required to justify removing a child from their parent, referencing HR-2020-662-S para 56 and the European Court of Human Rights case *Hernehult v Norway*[2] to establish this high threshold. 95

The Supreme Court was particularly critical of the automatic reduction plan for contact, finding it incompatible with the obligation to work toward reunifica- 96

2 ECtHR *Hernehult v Norway*, 10.3.2020, no 14652/16, para 62.

tion. Citing the *Strand Lobben* case[3], the Court emphasised that the duty to work toward family reunification increases 'with progressively increasing force as from the commencement of the period of care.' The Court found that the municipality's decision to progressively reduce contact to just a few visits per year effectively abandoned the reunification goal without the special and strong reasons required by law.

97 The Court noted that by 2018, when the mother had demonstrated improved parenting abilities with her second child, the damage to her relationship with her first daughter was already done due to the severe restriction of contact in 2014–2015. The Court gave limited weight to the mother's periods of poor cooperation, noting that significant communication issues arose only after the municipality had effectively abandoned the reunification goal.

98 After concluding that there was a violation of art 8 ECHR and sec 102 of the Constitution, the Court considered the legal basis for awarding non-pecuniary damages.

99 The Court found that art 13 ECHR, which requires an effective remedy for Convention violations, can necessitate compensation for non-pecuniary damage when other remedies are insufficient. The Court referenced the ECtHR case *T.P. and K.M. v the United Kingdom*[4] to establish when compensation is necessary for violations of art 8 ECHR.

100 In this case, compensation was awarded because the mother had been deprived of the opportunity to develop natural family bonds with her daughter due to the premature abandonment of the reunification goal. The Court explained that it cannot be determined for certain whether the child would have been returned to the mother if the authorities had fulfilled their duties, but the limited contact did cause harm by unnecessarily weakening the family bonds. The family was deprived of the opportunity to develop bonds, which caused the mother great despair, sorrow, and a sense of injustice, the Court argued.

101 The Court noted that while art 13 ECHR requires effective remedies, it grants Member States discretion regarding implementation. Therefore, national courts must determine whether compensation is justified, who is liable, and the appropriate amount.

102 The Supreme Court then considered if the municipality could be held liable.

103 The Court examined the division of responsibilities under the Norwegian Child Welfare Act (*barnevernloven*), noting that municipalities are responsible for preparing cases for the County Board, implementing decisions, and continuing

3 ECtHR *Strand Lobben and Others v Norway*, 30.11.2017, no 37283/13, para 208.
4 ECtHR *T.P. and K.M. v the United Kingdom*, 10.5.2001, no 28945/95.

follow-up work. Municipalities also have a duty to facilitate reunification and regularly assess whether a care order can be lifted. This duty existed before it was explicitly added to the Norwegian Child Welfare Act in 2018, as it was already implicit in the law and follows from human rights obligations.

The Court rejected the municipality's argument that it should be judged by the 104
less stringent standards that existed at the time of the alleged violation. The Court found that the ECtHR's *Strand Lobben* judgment[5] and the Supreme Court's plenary decisions from 2020 did not represent such a significant shift in the legal situation that they could only apply prospectively. The *Strand Lobben* judgment was based on existing ECtHR case law, and the Supreme Court in HR-2020-661-S para 170 had established that there was no conflict between this case law and the provisions of the 1992 Child Welfare Act.

The Court found that the municipality had failed in its case preparation and 105
had prematurely abandoned the reunification goal without proper grounds. The Court noted that while it was the County Board that had made the formal decisions on care orders and limited visitation, the municipality had a separate duty to provide the Board with a good decision-making basis and to facilitate reunification.

The Supreme Court rejected the municipality's argument that it was bound by 106
the County Board's decisions and therefore could not allow more contact: both County Board decisions explicitly stated that the contact that they established was a minimum and that additional visits could be granted if the parties wish and the child welfare service finds it justifiable, and in the child's best interests. The Court also noted that if the municipality felt bound by the Board's decisions, it had a duty to bring the case back to the Board with a recommendation for increased contact.

The Court dismissed the municipality's claim that the mother's lack of coop- 107
eration made their work difficult, noting that the major communication challenges arose after the municipality had effectively abandoned the reunification goal.

The Court set the compensation at NOK 200,000. 108

While acknowledging that national courts have discretion in determining ap- 109
propriate compensation, the Court noted that the amount must effectively compensate for the harm and cannot be unreasonably low compared to that which the European Court of Human Rights awards in similar cases. The Court refer-

5 ECtHR *Strand Lobben and Others v Norway*, 30.11.2017, no 37283/13.

enced the ECtHR cases *Apicella v Italy*[6] and *McFarlane v Ireland*[7] to establish these principles.

110 The Supreme Court considered the nature of the violation and its consequences for the mother, finding the Court of Appeal's award of NOK 100,000 insufficient. The Court acknowledged that the amount of NOK 200,000 was somewhat lower than that which the European Court of Human Rights has awarded in similar cases (such as € 25,000 in the *Strand Lobben* case), but deemed this acceptable given the Norwegian legal tradition, which generally takes a cautious approach to compensation and awards moderate amounts.

c) Commentary

111 This landmark decision in Norwegian tort law significantly develops Norwegian law regarding State and municipal liability for human rights violations in child welfare cases. The Supreme Court has established that art 13 ECHR can serve as a basis for awarding compensation for non-pecuniary harm when other remedies are insufficient. This represents an important development in Norwegian law, creating a pathway for individuals to receive compensation for human rights violations from the Norwegian courts without having to pursue their case in the European Court of Human Rights.

112 The judgment clarifies that municipalities can be directly liable for human rights violations within their area of responsibility. This is significant as it establishes that claimants do not always have to sue the State for such violations but can hold the responsible public entity directly accountable. This approach promotes local accountability and potentially more efficient remedies. The Supreme Court made it clear that while the State is ultimately responsible for Convention compliance, municipalities have independent obligations to respect human rights in carrying out their duties under Norwegian law.

113 The judgment reinforces and elaborates on the high threshold for removing children from their parents established in the 2020 Supreme Court plenary decisions. The Court emphasises that care orders must truly be exceptional measures, authorities have an ongoing and increasing obligation to work toward reunification, and contact must be sufficient to maintain and develop family bonds. The Court also stresses that procedural safeguards, including thorough investigation and proper reasoning, are essential.

6 ECtHR *Apicella v Italy* [GC], 29.3.2006, no 64890/01.
7 ECtHR *McFarlane v Ireland*, 10.9.2010, no 31333/06.

The Supreme Court's approach to the assessment of damages acknowledges the discretion afforded to national courts under art 13 ECHR but also establishes that compensation must effectively repair the harm caused and cannot be unreasonably low compared to ECtHR awards in similar cases. The doubling of the compensation amount from NOK 100,000 to NOK 200,000 signals the seriousness with which such violations should be treated, though the Court maintained a characteristically Norwegian moderation in the actual amount compared to ECtHR practice. 114

5. HR 29 November 2024, HR-2024-2188-A: Settlement Date as the Dividing Line between Individually Calculated and Standardised Compensation

a) Brief Summary of the Facts

The plaintiff (A) worked as a helicopter pilot from 1996 to 2016. Through his work, he developed tinnitus and hypersensitivity to sound, which has prevented him from working since November 2016. He filed a claim for occupational injury compensation against Tryg Forsikring (*Tryg*) under the Occupational Injury Insurance Act (*yrkesskadeforsikringsloven*). 115

In April 2019, Tryg informed A that for procedural economic reasons and to establish a cut-off point between past and future income loss, they chose to pay 100 % standardised compensation, totalling NOK 1,947,231 after adjustment for the National Insurance basic amount (G) in May 2019. However, Tryg did not acknowledge liability. 116

A believed he was entitled to higher compensation, and the parties negotiated without reaching an agreement. The case was brought before the Financial Complaints Board (*Finansklagenemnda*), which ruled in favour of A, finding that his health problems were covered by the Occupational Injury Insurance Act and that the settlement date was when the decision was made that the basic compensation was to be paid in April 2019. 117

Tryg did not accept the Board's statement, and in October 2021, A filed a lawsuit with the District Court. During the case preparation, it was clarified that the case would only concern the amount of disability compensation (*ménerstatning*) and the determination of the settlement date. 118

The Oslo District Court ruled in favour of A, ordering Tryg to pay NOK 7,130,355 plus interest. The court determined that the disability compensation should be based on a disability degree of 10 % and that the settlement date was the date of the court's decision. 119

120 Tryg appealed to the Court of Appeal. After the question of disability compensation was settled, the case only concerned the settlement date. The Court of Appeal upheld the District Court's decision that the settlement date should be the date of the court's decision.

b) Judgment of the Court

121 The Supreme Court began by establishing the legal framework for the case. Under the Occupational Injury Insurance Act, employees are entitled to compensation for injury and illness caused by work processes. Full compensation should be provided, including for lost income and loss of future income.

122 According to sec 13, first paragraph of the Act, the assessment rules in Chapter 3 of the Damages Act apply unless otherwise specified in, or pursuant to, this Act. Section 13, second paragraph gives the King authority to issue rules on the assessment of compensation, which have been provided in Regulation No 1027 of 21 December 1990, on standardised compensation under the Occupational Injury Insurance Act.

123 According to sec 2-3, first paragraph of the Regulation, compensation for lost income up to the 'settlement date' is determined individually, while compensation for loss of future income is determined according to standardised formulas in Chapter 3 of the Regulation. Since standardisation leads to under-compensation for high-income earners, the choice of settlement date is important. For A, the difference between the payment date and the court decision date amounts to several million kroner.

124 The Court noted that since sec 13, first paragraph of the Occupational Injury Insurance Act states that the assessment rules in the Damages Act Chapter 3 apply unless otherwise specified, the starting point must be the settlement date as established in general tort law.

125 The Supreme Court referred to several previous Supreme Court decisions that have consistently established that the settlement date in general tort law is either the date of agreement between the parties or, in the case of litigation, the date of the court's decision (paras 29–33). The Court referred to Rt-1997-1044, Rt-2006-684, Rt-2009-425, and HR-2022-1132-A to support this position.

126 None of these decisions directly addressed whether a unilateral partial payment of compensation could establish a settlement date, the Court admitted, but noted that case law clearly indicates that the settlement date is the date of agreement or court decision, with no indication of other alternatives.

127 There were also other sources supporting this interpretation, the Supreme Court stated. In the Norwegian Official Report NOU 2011:16 on Standardised Per-

sonal Injury Compensation, it was proposed to define the settlement date as the time when the parties reach an agreement, or a decision becomes legally binding. This proposal was intended as a codification of existing law, specifying that the tortfeasor cannot unilaterally determine the settlement date by paying a part of the compensation.

The Court noted that a special rule was introduced in the Norwegian Damages Act sec 3-2a regarding the compensation of future income loss for children, where the settlement date can be 'the time of payment' when compensation is substantially paid before the parties reach an agreement or a legally binding decision is made. However, the preparatory works emphasise that this is a special rule not intended to affect cases outside child compensation, including the distinction between past and future losses. 128

Also, the Supreme Court argued, legal literature consistently holds that the settlement date in general tort law is the time of the agreement or judgment that concludes the compensation settlement, with no support for the position that a unilateral payment of compensation for future income loss can establish a settlement date. 129

The Court rejected Tryg's argument that the legal principles on monetary claims should lead to the conclusion that such a payment can constitute a settlement date. The Court noted that while a debtor has the right to make a payment that discharges their obligation, this right does not determine the extent of the payment obligation. A partial payment does not give the debtor the right to unilaterally define the extent of the compensation. 130

After establishing that the general tort law settlement date is the time when the parties agree on the settlement or, in the case of disagreement and court proceedings, the date of the court decision, the Court examined whether sec 2-3 of the Regulation stipulates something different that would allow the time of payment of compensation for future income loss to be considered a settlement date. 131

The Supreme Court noted that the reference made in sec 13, first paragraph of the Norwegian Occupational Injury Insurance Act to the Norwegian Damages Act Chapter 3 was added by the Justice Committee to emphasise the importance of assessment principles in general tort law, including that the individual employee should receive full compensation for their specific, individual loss. The regulatory authority in sec 13, second paragraph was also amended during parliamentary proceedings to ensure that there was no unlimited authority to standardise compensation payments. The Court found that this has some significance for the interpretation of the settlement date in sec 2-3 of the Regulation, particularly for deviations from the general tort law cut-off point to the detriment of the injured party. 132

The Court observed that sec 2-3 of the Regulation provides no definition of what is meant by the 'settlement date' and unlike the Norwegian Damages Act 133 sec 3-2a on compensation for future income loss for children, there is no explicit special rule for occupational injuries that deviates from the principle that the settlement date is the time of agreement or court decision.

134 A normal linguistic understanding of the wording 'settlement date' points to the time of completion of the entire compensation settlement, which occurs when agreement is reached between the parties or when a dispute is resolved by the courts. If, on the other hand, a partial payment has been made unilaterally and the parties disagree, there is no final clarification of how the compensation settlement should be made. It is then linguistically less natural to view the payment as the 'settlement date' and the wording provides little support for such an interpretation (para 45 f).

135 The Supreme Court found that neither the regulation's wording, preparatory works, nor case law suggests that sec 2-3 of the Regulation establishes a different settlement date than that which follows from the assessment rules in general tort law. The general tort law rules, on the contrary, are established as a part of the legal system, and substantial justification would be needed to deviate from them.

136 The Court acknowledged Tryg's argument that policy considerations should be given significant weight in interpreting sec 2-3 of the Regulation. Tryg argued that if a unilateral payment cannot establish a settlement date, high-income claimants would have an incentive to delay the compensation settlement and bring the case to court to get as late a settlement date as possible, which would drive litigation and have adverse societal effects.

137 While the Court agreed this was a relevant consideration, it found it had limited impact. During the preparation of the Law, the Department of Justice was aware that long processing times could benefit some injured parties but placed less weight on this when considering whether compensation should be standardised. The Department considered it more important that most injured parties prefer a quick settlement, which removes uncertainty and provides compensation when the need is greatest, ie immediately after the time of injury.

138 The Court noted that other policy considerations point in the direction that a unilateral partial payment cannot be considered to establish a settlement date. For high-income earners, there may be some tension between standardised compensation and the law's premise of full compensation – a starting point that the Justice Committee of the Parliament emphasised when adopting the Occupational Injury Insurance Act. If insurance companies could unilaterally 'lock' the settlement date for this group of injured parties, it would further deviate from the premise of full compensation.

139 Furthermore, it would create an imbalance between the parties if companies could unilaterally influence the settlement by paying part of the compensation for income loss without assuming liability for the other part in the form of past loss.

This can be unfortunate when the two parts of the compensation for income loss are interdependent.

Considering the legal sources, the Court concluded that policy considerations clearly cannot lead to the 'settlement date' in sec 2-3 of the Regulation including a unilateral payment of compensation for future income loss. There are no indications in the preparatory works that the legislature wanted to deviate from general tort law rules in this way. 140

Based on this interpretation, the Court concluded that the settlement date in this case is the date of the Supreme Court's decision. 141

c) Commentary

This Supreme Court decision provides an important clarification of the concept of 'settlement date' in occupational injury compensation cases. The Court has definitively established that insurance companies cannot unilaterally set the settlement date by making a partial payment, even when they claim this is done to establish a cut-off point between past and future income loss. 142

The decision reinforces the principle that the settlement date is either when the parties reach an agreement or, in the case of litigation, the date of the court's decision. This interpretation aligns with general tort law principles and respects the legislative intent behind the Occupational Injury Insurance Act, which emphasises the right to full compensation for individual losses. 143

The Supreme Court verdict has significant practical implications, particularly for high-income earners who may be 'underpaid' by standardised compensation formulas. By establishing that the settlement date cannot be unilaterally determined by insurance companies, the Court ensures that the period for which individualised compensation is calculated extends until the case is fully resolved, either by agreement or court decision. This approach better fulfils the law's purpose of providing full compensation for occupational injuries. 144

The Court demonstrates a careful and thorough approach to statutory interpretation. The Court not only examined the text of the relevant provisions but also considered legislative history, case law, legal literature, and policy considerations. This analysis provides guidance for future cases involving the interpretation of compensation regulations. 145

The decision also addresses the balance of power between insurance companies and claimants. By rejecting the insurer's ability to unilaterally establish a settlement date, the Court prevents companies from strategically preventing individualised compensation calculations to minimise their liability. This ensures a fairer negotiating position for injured workers seeking compensation. 146

147 While the Supreme Court acknowledged the insurance industry's concern that this interpretation might incentivise litigation by high-income claimants, it found this consideration outweighed by the fundamental principle of full compensation and the need for balance between the parties.

148 The ruling also highlights the relationship between standardised and individualised compensation assessments. While standardisation serves important purposes such as efficiency and predictability, the Court's decision ensures it does not unduly compromise the principle of full compensation, especially for those who would be most disadvantaged by standardised formulas.

6. HR 12 December 2024, HR-2024-2273-A: Question of Deduction of Insurance Payments from the Compensation Amount

a) Brief Summary of the Facts

149 This case concerns the determination of compensation for the loss of a provider and specifically addresses whether insurance payments should be deducted from the compensation amount under the discretionary deduction rule in sec 3-1, third paragraph, second sentence of the Damages Act.

150 On 5 April 2022, B was stabbed and killed by her then-partner, A. She left behind two children, D and E, who were approximately five and almost three years old, respectively, at the time of their mother's death. The children had different fathers (para 3).

151 In the District Court, A was sentenced to 15 years in prison for intentional homicide. The court also ruled on civil claims, including claims from the two surviving children for compensation for the loss of a provider. These claims were upheld, and the District Court awarded compensation for loss of a provider in the amount of NOK 830,579 to D and NOK 901,994 to E. Each child was also awarded NOK 400,000 in non-pecuniary compensation.

152 B was covered by group life insurance policies through her employer. The District Court did not deduct the insurance benefits paid to the children from the compensation, stating that it did not find it reasonable that the insurance benefits should benefit A in the form of a reduction in his liability to compensate the children's loss of their provider.

153 A appealed the criminal conviction, including the civil claims. The Court of Appeal also sentenced A to 15 years in prison for intentional homicide. The Court of Appeal awarded each child NOK 425,000 in non-pecuniary compensation

but reduced the compensation for loss of provider to NOK 570,000 for D and NOK 590,000 for E due to new calculations based on changes to the rules regarding children's pensions. Unlike the District Court, the Court of Appeal made a discretionary deduction of NOK 150,000 from the compensation to each child because they had received insurance payments of approximately NOK 1.6 million each.

D and E, through their guardians, appealed to the Supreme Court regarding 154 the Court of Appeal's handling of the case and its application of law related to the deduction issue in the compensation for loss of a provider (para 9).

For the Supreme Court proceedings, a new adjusted calculation of the com- 155 pensation for loss of a provider before any deductions was presented. It was agreed that the loss amounted to NOK 613,906 for D and NOK 742,576 for E. After the Court of Appeal's judgment, the children had also received a payment under an additional group life insurance policy that B had through her membership in the Education Association (*Utdanningsforbundet*). In total, each child had received insurance benefits amounting to 17.5 times the National Insurance basic amount (G), which, with the G-rate that applied at the time of the homicide, amounted to slightly less than NOK 1.9 million.

b) Judgment of the Court

The Supreme Court began by establishing the legal framework for compensation 156 for loss of a provider. Section 3-4 of the Norwegian Damages Act provides rules for compensating surviving dependents whom the deceased wholly or partly supported at the time of death. The purpose of the compensation is to enable the survivors to maintain their accustomed standard of living, insofar as this was a result of the deceased's support.

Section 3-4, second paragraph refers to the general deduction rule in sec 3-1, 157 third paragraph, which in the first sentence states that when determining compensation, deductions shall be made for sick pay and similar benefits, social security benefits, benefits from pension schemes in employment or occupation, and for insurance benefits to the extent that the premiums have been paid. Furthermore, the second sentence states that insurance benefits not covered by the previous sentence, other significant financial support that the injured party has received or will receive based on the injury, and other circumstances may be considered.

The discretionary deduction rule appears in the second sentence. The wording 158 indicates a concrete assessment, both as to whether an insurance benefit should lead to a reduction in compensation, and how large a deduction should be made.

The law does not provide further guidance on what factors should be taken into account in this assessment.

159 The Court noted that the legislative rationale for the rule is that the tortfeasor should not automatically benefit from insurance that the injured party may have taken out. The discretionary nature of the deduction means that the basic principle of tort law – that the injured party should have their full economic loss covered, but no more – does not fully apply to insurance benefits. The law's starting point is that the injured party should have their economic loss covered through compensation and may also receive insurance payments in addition.

160 The Supreme Court referred to its recent decision in HR-2023–268-A, which addressed the deduction rule in a case involving a wrongful death due to medical negligence. After reviewing the relevant statements in the legislative history, the Court in that case summarised that it would normally not be appropriate to deduct more ordinary life insurance benefits. A deduction would only be relevant for more significant insurance benefits, and courts should show generosity in their assessment.

161 Based on this and other sources, the Court in HR-2023–268-A provided the following guideline: no deduction should be made for life insurance payments in the case of compensation for loss of a provider if the payments are 15 G or less for adults and 5 G or less for children. For insurance payments above these levels, considerable caution should be exercised in making deductions. Only payments that are substantially above these levels should trigger a more detailed assessment.

162 In the present case, the payments to each child exceed the level indicated for children in HR-2023–268-A. However, the main reason for this is that B's children were the only beneficiaries under the insurance policies, resulting in the entire coverage going to them. The guidelines from the 2023 decision were not formulated with this situation in mind.

163 The Court noted that on the one hand, these were ordinary life insurance benefits that B had through her regular employment in the care sector and her union membership. On the other hand, the insurance payments to each child, totalling 17.5 G, were relatively substantial.

164 The Court addressed the argument that the nature of the criminal act and the degree of culpability should be considered. While acknowledging that, as a general starting point, these factors can only be given limited weight in the assessment of whether deductions should be made for insurance payments, the Court noted that such circumstances should primarily be reflected in the compensation for non-pecuniary damage, which the Court of Appeal had done in this case.

165 At the same time, the Court highlighted the connection mentioned in the preparatory works between the discretionary reduction rule in the Compensatory

Damages Act sec 5-2 and the possibility of reducing the tortfeasor's liability. The preparatory works state that in cases where a reduction of liability is not relevant, there is a high threshold before an insurance benefit can lead to reduced compensation for the injured party.

Based on this, the Court concluded that in cases where a reduction of compensation is not relevant according to sec 5-2, as in the case at hand, there is reason to show additional caution when considering whether deductions should be made for insurance payments. This must also apply where a reduction according to sec 5-2 is not relevant due to the harmful act and the culpability shown by the tortfeasor, the Court noted. 166

The Court found this approach to be consistent with the legislative rationale behind the discretionary deduction rule – that the tortfeasor should not automatically benefit from insurance that the injured party may have taken out. The provision is a more flexible rule that, to a greater extent, allows for consideration of concrete fairness. 167

Based on its review, the Court summarised the following principles: 168

When assessing whether paid life insurance benefits should be deducted from the survivors' compensation for loss of provider, the extent of the insurance coverage for the individual injured party is important, but deduction is only relevant where the payments substantially exceed what can be characterised as an ordinary level. Generosity should be shown to the injured party in the assessment. 169

If a reduction of the tortfeasor's liability according to sec 5-2 of the Compensation Damages Act is not made due to the harmful act and the tortfeasor's culpability, there is a high threshold before it can be considered reasonable to deduct life insurance payments. 170

In its concrete assessment, the Court noted that B was covered by group life insurance through her employment in the care sector and had additional basic insurance through her union membership. These are, in principle, 'ordinary' life insurance benefits. The level of the total insurance coverage of 35 G was high, but the Court considered that this did not warrant a deduction in the compensation for loss of a provider. Moreover, the Court emphasised that the assessment should be made separately for each child entitled to compensation. 171

The insurance sum paid to each child of 17.5 G was relatively high and would – economically – provide a real benefit to them. The consideration of preventing overcompensation could, from this perspective, suggest a discretionary deduction in the compensation to each of them. However, the children were the only beneficiaries under the insurance policies, and this was the reason for the high amount of compensation for each child. A similar payment to an adult survivor would clearly not have led to a deduction based on the guidelines given in HR-2023–268-A. 172

173 Despite some hesitation, the Court eventually concluded – based on the caution that the preparatory works indicate in the application of the discretionary deduction rule and the presumption that there should be a high threshold for a reduction of liability – that a deduction in this case would not be reasonable.

c) Commentary

174 This Supreme Court decision provides important clarification on the application of the discretionary deduction rule in the Damages Act, particularly in cases involving life insurance payments to children who have lost a parent due to a criminal act.

175 The Court maintains and reinforces the principles established in HR-2023-268-A regarding when insurance benefits should be deducted from compensation. It confirms that 'ordinary' life insurance benefits generally should not lead to deductions, and that considerable caution should be exercised when considering deductions for payments above the established thresholds.

176 The decision introduces an important nuance by emphasising that when a reduction of the tortfeasor's liability is not relevant due to the nature of the act and the degree of culpability, the threshold for making deductions becomes even higher. This creates greater protection for victims of serious crimes, ensuring that they receive both the compensation they are entitled to and the insurance benefits that the deceased had arranged for their benefit.

177 The Supreme Court's analysis of the specific situation – where the children received higher insurance payments because they were the only beneficiaries – is particularly noteworthy. The Court recognises that the size of the payments alone should not determine whether deductions are made, but rather the context and nature of the insurance coverage must be considered. This approach ensures a more equitable outcome that considers the specific circumstances of each case.

178 The decision also reflects a balanced consideration of different principles and interests in tort law. On the one hand, there is the principle that the injured party should not receive more than full compensation for their economic loss. On the other hand, there is the principle that the tortfeasor should not benefit from insurance arrangements made by the victim. The Court's approach gives greater weight to the latter principle, especially in cases involving serious criminal acts.

7. Personal Injury

All the cases review above, except HR-2024–990-A, can be seen as important cases regarding personal injury. 179

C. Literature

1. *Bjarte Thorson*, Oppreisning for menneskerettigheter – et foreløpig punktum [Clarifications from the Supreme Court for human rights violations] Tidsskrift for erstatningsrett (TfE) 1 (Volume 21, 2025) 1–4

Bjarte Thorson's editorial analyses two landmark Norwegian Supreme Court rulings from June 2024 that establish new principles for compensation claims arising from violations of the European Convention on Human Rights (ECHR). The cases, HR-2024–1169-A (concerning child welfare interventions under ECHR art 8) and HR-2024–1170-A (regarding degrading treatment during prison strip searches under ECHR art 3), clarify the legal basis for State liability and compensation standards in human rights cases. Thorson assesses these decisions within the broader evolution of Norwegian tort law and ECtHR jurisprudence, while discussing their implications for future litigation and legislative reforms. 180

Thorson identifies that the Norwegian Supreme Court, in its 26 June 2024 rulings, established an independent legal basis for the establishment of liability to pay compensation on public authorities for violations of ECHR rights. According to his analysis, this legal framework contains three cumulative requirements: an ECHR right must have been violated, the violation must have caused damage to the victim, and awarding compensation must be necessary to provide sufficient protection of the violated ECHR right. 181

Thorson notes that this development was not so surprising given that the Supreme Court had presupposed such authority existed in Rt 2001–428, though he observes that while the Court now stated this authority was 'established' in Rt 2008–588, this was done rather presumptively. He suggests that the disagreement on this very issue was likely what led to these cases coming to trial in the first place. 182

According to Thorson's analysis, the Supreme Court established that liability to pay compensation can be imposed on municipalities through a concrete assessment. He explains that this evaluation resembles the approach outlined in the 183

Damages Act's preparatory works regarding whether public employer liability should be attributed to municipalities or the State.

184 Thorson identifies the assessment factors as including who generally has responsibility for the administrative area and who is concretely responsible for the damage occurring. He provides the example of situations where municipal administrative errors can be traced back to deficiencies in State (non-delegated) legislation.

185 His analysis anticipates that these evaluations are not always simple, and that questions about liability for various public law bodies may arise. He identifies the potential for systemic failures involving multiple public actors at different levels, often involving rule development, practice management, and individual decisions. In such cases, Thorson suggests joint liability may be relevant.

186 Thorson presents the Supreme Court's guidance on the calculation of compensation as being based on discretionary amounts within established traditions. He details the specific awards: NOK 200,000 in the child welfare case, and NOK 50,000, NOK 90,000, and NOK 100,000 respectively to the three victims in the strip search case.

187 According to his analysis, the Supreme Court in the strip search case considered the connection between pre-trial detention credits, rates for compensation for wrongful detention, and the compensation awarded. He notes that the Court looked to compensation levels awarded by the European Court of Human Rights in similar cases under ECHR art 41.

188 Thorson explains the Court's recognition that the ECtHR makes significant cost-of-living adjustments, resulting in completely different compensation levels for different countries. He presents the Court's acceptance that national levels may be somewhat lower than that which the ECtHR awards under ECHR art 41 without violating ECHR art 13, referencing the ECtHR's decision in *Ananyev and others v Russia*[8].

189 Thorson identifies a significant change in judicial approach, noting that the Supreme Court has not previously, in such a pure form as now, examined whether public authorities in their handling of a child welfare case showed sufficient respect for the involved parties' family life under ECHR art 8.

190 The author distinguishes this from the Supreme Court's previous practice of commenting on how this right must be safeguarded in the application of child welfare regulations as part of ongoing child welfare cases, characterising the direct assessment of individual rights violations as something quite different.

8 ECtHR *Ananyev and others v Russia*, 10.1.2012, nos 42525/07 and 60800/08, para 230.

While the ECtHR has repeatedly found violations of ECHR art 8 in such cases in recent years, the differences between child welfare cases and cases on ECHR violations have received little attention in Norway, Thorson states. He notes that ECHR violation findings have instead been discussed through assumptions about different child-rearing cultures or traditions of especially careful language used in Norwegian court verdicts compared to other countries. 191

According to Thorson's analysis, the Supreme Court's approach may illustrate that courts might be more inclined to find ECHR violations when the question of violation is directly addressed, when courts must actually interpret the ECHR and subsume facts regarding the specific person claiming violation under ECHR rules, rather than just using the ECHR as an interpretive element or argument in applying other rules. 192

In the future, the Supreme Court will possibly proceed less cautiously than the ECtHR, Thorson argues. Thorson notes that in child welfare cases, the ECtHR has placed significant weight on how national authorities during the child welfare case have considered what they believed to be in the child's best interests, something not readily found in the Supreme Court's judgment. 193

Thorson states that this type of more direct examination of individual complaints about rights violations will contribute to the ECtHR being able to take a more subsidiary role in cases where subsequent complaints are filed there, potentially resulting in fewer complaints against Norway to the ECtHR and even fewer substantive assessments and violation findings in cases where complaints are made. 194

Thorson presents the question of whether the now more clearly established right to demand compensation for violations of rights derived from ECHR art 8 may become a remedy that complainants must exhaust before the ECtHR can proceed to a substantive analysis under ECHR art 35. 195

He provides a comparative context, noting that the ECtHR frequently dismisses complaints against Sweden if compensation has not been sought nationally, referencing the ECtHR's decision in *Eriksson v Sweden*[9], while complaints against Norway have been assessed more concretely. 196

Thorson describes the Swedish system: if someone believes their rights have been violated, they can, besides filing a compensation claim in the courts, present the claim to the Chancellor of Justice free of charge. He notes that Norway has no corresponding institution. 197

9 ECtHR *Eriksson v Sweden*, 12.4.2012, no 60437/08, paras 50–52.

198 Thorson notes that specifically in the child welfare field, the ECtHR has indicated that it has detected a systemic element to the violations in Norway, referencing *Abdi Ibrahim v Norway*[10].

199 Under such special circumstances, he presents the possibility that the State could consider establishing a collective, extra-judicial solution for families who have experienced violations related to the premature use of the most intrusive coercive measures. He specifically identifies denial of contact or severe contact restrictions and forced adoptions as measures that have led to violations in the ECtHR.

200 Thorson emphasises that discussions of human rights in the child welfare sector should be conducted as ordinary and grounded legal discussion and not only be explained by differences in cultures between different countries. He advocates that such discussions should address not only family members' right to respect for their family life under ECHR art 8, but also the child's right not to be separated from their parents without their consent under art 9 of the Convention on the Rights of the Child. The Supreme Court's decision can potentially demystify some of these issues, Thorson argues, and contribute to the discussion.

10 ECtHR *Abdi Ibrahim v Norway* [GC], 10.12.2021, no 15379/16, para 184.

Ewa Bagińska and Paulina Wyszyńska-Ślufińska

XXII. Poland

A. Legislation

There was no new legislation referring to, or affecting, tort law in 2024. 1

B. Cases

1. Sąd Najwyższy (Supreme Court, SN) 12 April 2024, II CSKP 1873/22, (OSNC-ZD[1] 2024 no 4 item 42): Medical Malpractice; Loss of a Chance of Giving Birth to Children; Right to Procreate is a Personal Interest?

a) Brief Summary of the Facts

A healthy 28-year-old woman (plaintiff A), who experienced a healthy pregnancy, 2 suffered from the failure to make a timely decision to terminate the birth by caesarean section. The child was born healthy; however, soon after the surgery, the plaintiff developed uterine rupture, hematoma and atony, and consequently unstoppable bleeding, which generated the need for life-saving surgery, ie removal of the uterus. The latter was properly performed by the hospital chief of the clinic and the plaintiff recovered physically.

Plaintiff A and her husband (plaintiff B) sued for: 1) compensation for non- 3 pecuniary loss in the amount of PLN 500,000 (approx € 119,000) for A, claiming that in addition to A's health and physical integrity, the defendant's action also caused a violation of her other personal rights; 2) the award of PLN 100,000 (approx € 23,800) to plaintiff B for the violation of his personal interests; 3) a certain sum for the cost of A's psychological treatment; 4) the declaration of the defendant's liability for the future consequences of the event. As to the ground for non-pecuniary loss, the plaintiffs invoked: 'the right to have children', or 'the right to procreate' – in the sense of the entitlement to decide on the model and shape of one's family, uninhibited by third parties and in accordance with

1 Orzecznictwo Sądu Najwyższego Izba Cywilna, Zbiór Dodatkowy (Decisions of the Supreme Court, Civil Chamber, Supplement, OSNC-ZD).

https://doi.org/10.1515/9783111389271-023

one's own will and convictions, hence such a right is a personal interest (right) as such, or an element of the right to family planning or the right to privacy (protection of private, family and personal life).

4 The Regional Court dismissed the lawsuit on the facts (it found no fault of the defendant). The Court of Appeals, in partial acceptance of A's appeal, supplemented the evidence with a new expert opinion, and reached the opposite result on the facts. It established that the defendant bears liability for the consequences of its failure to terminate the plaintiff's labour by caesarean section in time. The decision to terminate the labour in its second stage was significantly prolonged (by approx 90 minutes), which led to severe complications. A's claim for non-pecuniary and pecuniary damage was grounded in art 430 of the Civil Code (*kodeks cywilny*, KC),[2] as a healthcare institution is liable for damage caused by the fault of doctors providing medical services to patients. The Court of Appeals awarded A the amount of PLN 100,000 (approx € 23,800) as compensation for non-pecuniary loss, the cost of psychological treatment and dismissed B's appeal and the demand to establish the defendant's liability for any future damage. Further, the Court of Appeals determined that the removal of the plaintiff's uterus was not an event leading to a violation of the plaintiff's personal rights. A and B filed a cassation.

b) Judgment of the Court

5 The Supreme Court agreed with plaintiff A that the Court of Appeals, having correctly cited the premises which determine the amount of compensation for non-pecuniary loss in connection with bodily injury (in the light of art 445 § 1 KC), incorrectly assessed the amount of compensation. The extent of the harm suffered depends on the degree of suffering (its intensity, duration, irreversibility of consequences and other similar circumstances). The non-quantifiable nature of these circumstances means that the court has a degree of discretion when determining the extent of the harm and the amount of compensation. The Supreme Court referred to its judgment of 22 March 2022 (II CSKP 124/22), and confirmed that the subjective nature of the harm and the rule of the individualisation of compensation do not render useless the reference to sums awarded in similar cases, although such reference is particularly useful when controlling whether, against the background of other cases, the compensation sought or awarded is not grossly

2 Ustawa z dnia 23 kwietnia 1964 r., Kodeks cywilny, Dziennik Ustaw (Journal of Laws, Dz U) 2024, item 1061.

modest or excessive. The sense of justice validates the striving for uniformity in judicial decisions in this regard – while respecting the distinctiveness of the facts and individual circumstances of each case. Although medical events with consequences such as those at hand have not often been assessed by the courts, plaintiff A rightly argued that the harm of patients who found themselves in a similar situation to her because of the removal of an organ as a consequence of medical malpractice was compensated with higher amounts.[3] For these reasons, the Supreme Court awarded plaintiff A additional PLN 50,000 (approx € 12,000).

As regards further compensation for A and the compensation for B, the Supreme Court raised several arguments to justify its opinion that this was not a case of violation of personal interests. The Court reiterated the definition of personal interests and fundamental tenets of their protection. A subjective right established for the purpose of securing the protection of a personal interest entails the possibility to demand from others that they do not infringe that value attached to the person either by action or by omission. 'A right to…' does not constitute an object of protection, but rather an instrument which serves to protect a value, which is a personal interest (right). By binding itself to the European Convention on Human Rights (ECHR), the State has declared that its organs will act in a manner that respects the rights and freedoms recognised as human rights in the Convention, but also that these organs will make law that enforces respect for human rights in horizontal relations, and thus between the participants in the community in which the law is to be made. The rights protected under art 8 of the ECHR and art 47 of the Polish Constitution (ie the right to legal protection of private life, family life, honour and good name and to decide on one's personal life) are not identical to the personal rights protected under civil law, although their realisation is a form of enjoyment of intangible values connected with a human being and constituting their personal interest and a form of safeguarding their protection. 6

The Court then acknowledged that the plaintiffs did not allege that the State and its organs had directly violated their right to respect for private and family life, which consists of the 'right to have children', the 'right to procreate'. They were deprived of the possibility to realise the plaintiffs' freedom in this sphere by the defendant hospital and not by the State. The Court then observed that a 7

3 The courts quotes the following judgments of the Supreme Court: 28 February 2023, II CSKP 677/22 (damages for non-pecuniary loss were reduced on appeal from PLN 200,000 to PLN 100,000, confirmed on cassation by the Court of Appeals in Poznań judgment of 7 April 2020, I ACa 310/19); 10 March 2006, IV CSK 80/05 (reported by *E Bagińska* in: H Koziol/BC Steininger (eds), European Tort Law (ETL) 2007 [2008] 451, nos 13–17), as well as the judgment of the Court of Appeals in Warsaw of 8 October 2010, VI ACa 660/10.

'right to have children' ('right to procreate') is not a personal interests per se, but a form of enjoyment of a personal interest such as health, physical integrity, autonomy. Whether one has or does not have biological children is determined by one's health and physical integrity, and by life choices, which are often, but not always, motivated by beliefs (such motivation is referred to by the plaintiffs). Until a person finds themselves in a situation requiring a decision to have or not to have children, any declarations made on this subject are not personal interests, but a certain manifestation of views, plans, a vision of the world, which are subject to constant change. However, as health is undoubtedly a personal interest, the removal of an organ necessary for a woman to give birth to a child deprives her of this possibility. The harm a woman suffers in such a case is compensated in the Polish legal system based on art 445 § 1 KC and such compensation was awarded to the plaintiff. The factors considered in determining its amount included the fact that she had been deprived of the possibility to give birth to another child. Hence, the same harm cannot be compensated twice, ie under art 448 KC as well.

8 As concerns B's claim, he did not suffer bodily injury or a health disorder as a result of the medical event concerning his wife. At most, the effects of the event must have altered his plans for his family life with A. However, the Court stated, 'such plans – created before the marriage and verified by various events, including tortious acts committed by third parties to the detriment of one of the spouses – cannot possibly be qualified as personal interests and create entitlement to compensation in connection with events that modify them'. The Supreme Court confirmed the view of the Court of Appeals that such interest could not be considered the plaintiff's personal interest under art 23 KC.

c) Commentary

9 First, the Supreme Court rarely uses the possibility of raising the amount of compensation for non-pecuniary loss and it was correct and just to do so for the young woman who will never be able to give birth to another child. Also, it rightly emphasised that justice requires a certain level of uniformity of awards, subject to a concrete and individual assessment of the facts. The trend for standardisation is hence developing slowly also in the highest judiciary body.

10 It is worth noting that cases involving depriving a woman of the ability to have biological children due to medical malpractice (removal of the uterus or other organs, misdiagnosis of cancer, etc), some of which were cited in the motives, have been, and are being, reported in Poland. According to established jurisprudence, damage can be defined as the erroneous removal of a uterus thus causing a patient's infertility; such damage is compensated with damages for

non-pecuniary loss stemming from a personal injury (art 444 in conjunction with art 445 KC). In this respect, the decision follows the established practice.

Because a claim for a loss of a chance is not (yet) expressly recognised in Polish law, in personal injury cases, the courts award damages for lost chances within the framework of compensation for non-pecuniary loss. A primary example can be found in a case similar in facts to the commented one. A patient lost her capacity to work and to have children as a result of medical malpractice during labour (she suffered injury to her pubes); that damage was described by the Supreme Court as 'a loss of a chance to give birth to a child' (SN, 1 September 1978, CR 510/77, OSNC 11/1978, item 210). Unfortunately, in the 2024 case, the Supreme Court did not see a perfect occasion to develop the concept of a loss of a chance, albeit it properly assessed the damages for the harm. 11

One of the problems (a dogmatic one) lies in the fact that art 448 refers to all personal interests, and art 445 (*lex specialis* in relation to the former provision) applies specifically to personal injuries, deprivation of property and sexual misconduct. Although not everyone agrees with this traditional interpretation, it is still a dominant one. Thus, A would have obtained double recovery if her award was increased based on art 448 KC. This notwithstanding the concept of a loss of a chance would possibly provide some solution to B's claim (the husband). 12

B's claim and part of A's claim were rejected for the reasons which are equally surprising as are questionable. In the judgment, the Court in fact plainly rejected the long-established view that a right to procreate (freedom to procreate) is to be recognised as a personal interest. 13

It is worth recalling to the Yearbooks' readers that the Polish Supreme Court has repeatedly held that a right to plan a family is protected as a personal interest by the Civil Code (art 23 KC), and as a personal liberty by the Constitution. Protection of privacy and dignity were mainly invoked in cases concerning wrongful birth and so-called reproductive torts, reported over the years in this series. Accordingly, if abortion was wrongfully denied to a raped woman and she was compelled to give birth to a child, her right to plan a family was violated, which provided a ground to seek compensation on the basis of art 448 KC.[4] A woman's right to privacy and her right to prenatal tests are violated when she has been forced to give birth to a disabled child, when the pregnancy could have been legally terminated.[5] A violation of these rights constitutes moral harm, which entitles the 14

4 SN 21 November 2003, V CK 16/03, OSNC 6/2004, item 104; SN 22 February 2006, III CZP 8/06, Orzecznictwo Sądu Najwyższego (OSN) 7–8/2006, item 123.

5 SN 13 October 2005, IV CK 161/05, OSP 6/2006, item 71; SN 6 May 2010 II CSK 580/09, Orzecznictwo Sądu Polskich (OSP) 2/20011, item 13 cmt *M Nesterowicz*.

woman to compensation pursuant to art 448 KC.[6] The view is shared by the Courts of Appeals. In a judgment of 12 May 2015, I ACa 204/15, the Court of Appeals in Kraków acknowledged that a right to plan a family, and a right to legal abortion stemming therefrom, is a personal right protected by the Civil Code. In view of the above established case law, we cannot see a rationale behind the differentiation: the right to plan a family is protected as a personal interest (right) in the context of entitlements to abortion or prenatal test and cannot be protected as such in situations where, due to a tort, a healthy and fertile woman is deprived of the possibility to plan and give birth to another healthy child. Arguments raised by the Supreme Court are utterly unconvincing, and moreover, not only fail to attempt to scrutinise the doctrinal views and the dominant line of earlier court practice, but also fail to indicate *differentia specifica* between abortion cases and 'regular' malpractice cases.

15 The lost chance of having more biological children is certainly an ultimate loss for the female plaintiff, but it is not necessarily so as concerns her husband, who theoretically might have children with another woman (as could be read between the lines). However, such an approach is wrong, as in tort cases we assess the facts in the whole context and the facts say that a husband, who has already formed a family with his wife and the first child, will not have a chance to naturally expand this family. An alternative chain of events cannot be considered and is not at stake here.

16 The final comment pertains to the above problem of the entitlement of the child's father, which was noted by the Supreme Court in 2019, although this Court seems to have overlooked that decision. In the judgment of 27 November 2019,[7] the Supreme Court extended the protection of art 4 of the Patients' Rights Act to a father's right to information about a foetus' congenital disorder. While the Court of Appeals dismissed the father's claim arguing that the father of the child was not a patient within the meaning of the Patients' Rights Act, and therefore had no legal standing, the Supreme Court held that each parent had the same rights to information about the condition of their children and a broad understanding of 'patient' should be adopted. As the plaintiff was present both during the prenatal tests and at the childbirth, when he learned of the physical defect of the child, he suffered psychological harm similar to that of his wife and mother of their child.

---

6 SN 12 June 2008, III CSK 16/08, Orzecznictwo Sądu Najwyższego Izba Cywilna (OSNC) 3/2009, item 48, reported by *E Bagińska* in: H Koziol/BC Steininger (eds), European Tort Law 2009 (2010) 475, nos 51–56. See *E Bagińska*, The development of liability for 'reproductive torts' in Polish law, in: H Koziol/U Magnus (eds), Essays in Honour of Jaap Spier (2016) 8–18.

7 II CSK 491/18, OSNC-ZD 2020/3, item 54, reported by *E Bagińska/P Wyszyńska-Ślufińska* in: E Karner/BC Steininger (eds), European Tort Law (ETL) 2020 (2021) 487, nos 14–20.

There was no question that the right to information is a personal right. However, the recognition that the child's father is a patient in light of the Patients' Rights Act has raised serious doubts, as the medical services were provided exclusively to the mother and the child. Moreover, the Supreme Court approved the concept of awarding compensation to the father on the basis of the Civil Code rules concerning the violation of personal rights (arts 24 and 448 KC). As we commented in 2020, the statutory definition of a patient is too narrow to be extended to the father of an unborn child,[8] and the correct basis for the father's claims is the infringement of his personal rights.

2. Sąd Apelacyjny w Szczecinie (Court of Appeals in Szczecin) 10 July 2024, I ACa 1400/22 (LEX no 3781048): Violation of General Data Protection Regulation and Compensation for Moral Harm (Non-Pecuniary Damage)

a) Brief Summary of the Facts

In the autumn of 2020, the plaintiff (a lawyer running his own business) received 17 several calls, during which he was offered the chance to purchase a payment terminal. Because he had explicitly refused to receive such offers, he reacted angrily and lost his focus on work and family matters. During one conversation, the plaintiff found out that his phone number had been obtained from the defendant Z. The plaintiff immediately demanded that Z stop processing his personal data. Z informed him that he had obtained the data from X, based on a licence agreement between Z and X, and that the data were transferred to companies that made the phone calls. The plaintiff indicated that he had not consented to the processing of his personal data (the phone number) to these companies, and therefore Z's action was unlawful.

The plaintiff alleged a violation of the General Data Protection Regulation[9] 18 (GDPR) and a violation of his personal interests, particularly his right to privacy. The plaintiff sued Z and X demanding: 1) a statement of apology in the form and content indicated in the petition; and 2) the payment of PLN 10,000 (approx

8 See comment to the reported judgment by *N Karczewska-Kamińska*, OSP 12/2020, 10.

9 Regulation (EU) 2016/679 of the European Parliament and of the Council of 27 April 2016 on the protection of natural persons with regard to the processing of personal data and on the free movement of such data, and repealing Directive 95/46/EC (General Data Protection Regulation), Official Journal (OJ) L 119/1.

€ 2,380) for the indicated social cause. The district court dismissed the claim and the plaintiff appealed.

b) Judgment of the Court

19 The appellate court broadly shared the arguments presented by the district court. The district court pointed out that the plaintiff identified the provisions of the Civil Code on the protection of personal interests (arts 23 and 24 KC) and the provisions of the GDPR as the bases for his claims. Hence, the plaintiff had to identify the protected personal interest and to prove that it had been unlawfully violated. Any assessment of unlawfulness involved the determination of whether the processing of his personal data was done in accordance with the GDPR. The grounds for processing of personal data as set forth in art 6 GDPR include the legitimate interest of the controller. Such an interest may exist, inter alia, if there is a 'substantial and appropriate type of connection between the data subject and the controller, for example, if the data subject is a client of the controller or acts on behalf of the controller.' Furthermore, the court drew attention to the information duty under art 14 GDPR, which applies when personal data is not obtained from the data subject. The court referred to Recital 60 of the Preamble to the GDPR, which states that the principles of fair and transparent processing require that the data subject be informed of the processing of their data, as well as the purposes of that processing.

20 The court then analysed arts 79 and 82 GDPR, which are the grounds for the right to an effective judicial remedy. In the light of Polish regulations, the remedy includes compensation for both pecuniary (*damnum emergens* and *lucrum cessans*) and non-pecuniary damage. The court referred to the interpretation of the Court of Justice of the European Union (CJEU), stressing that the concept of harm should be understood broadly, thereby reflecting the objectives of the GDPR, and be defined in accordance with the principles of autonomous interpretation of EU law, in the spirit of *effect utile*, and in accordance with the CJEU case law.

21 Applying the above rules to the facts of the case, the court held that both defendants were controllers of the plaintiff's personal data. The decisive criterion is the exercise of actual control over data processing. Since defendant Z obtained the plaintiff's data from X and subsequently shared them with other companies, it may be considered to have had actual control over the data and thus become a controller. The court stated that although the mere listing of phone numbers does not indicate an individual, the phone number allows direct contact with a person, and therefore it is personal data. According to the court, the defendants

failed to comply with their information obligation under art 13 GDPR. The sending of a text message with a link to an information clause cannot be considered as the fulfilment of the obligation. The plaintiff did not read the text message, which, however, should be considered as prudent behaviour in times when such messages may contain computer viruses.

The court held that the plaintiff's right to privacy had been violated. Nevertheless, the key question remains whether he suffered non-material damage in the form of moral harm as a result of the defendants' conduct. The court referred to the definition of moral harm understood as an element of the sphere of human experiences (pain and suffering). According to art 448 KC, compensation for moral harm can be awarded if personal interests have been violated and according to the case law, the size of the award is determined by the nature of the violated personal interest, the intensity and duration of the violation, and the degree of fault of the tortfeasor. 22

The court also referred to the Supreme Court judgment of 18 October 2011 (III CZP 25/11), in which it was held that in the case of a violation of a personal interest, a court may or may not award compensation, but it is obliged to give reasons for refusing compensation despite the fulfilment of the prerequisites for liability. Such reasons may include the insignificance of the moral harm, the voluntary efforts of the tortfeasor to compensate the victim and the insignificant causal involvement of the tortfeasor in the occurrence of the harm. 23

The first instance court pointed out that in the case at hand, while the plaintiff's reaction to the phone calls was subjective, there is no evidence that the said calls significantly affected his daily functioning. The plaintiff, as an entrepreneur, should expect to receive calls from potential customers, and unexpected calls should not 'throw him off balance'. The assessment of the violation of a personal interest should be made according to objective criteria. It is necessary to consider not only the subjective feelings of the person seeking legal protection, but also societal reactions to the violation. The jurisprudence of the European Court of Human Rights (ECtHR) indicates in the context of art 8 ECHR that the interference with privacy must have a minimum level of annoyance. This assessment is relative and depends on all the circumstances of the case, including the intensity and duration of the interference, the physical and psychological effects and the factual context as a whole. In the case at hand, the defendants undoubtedly violated the GDPR, however, their violation cannot be considered as a violation of the plaintiff's personal interest. The offers received were not intrusive in nature. The plaintiff received only two calls, while further calls were not made at his express request. For these reasons, in the court's opinion, there was no violation of the plaintiff's personal interests. The court found that the harm suffered by the plaintiff was very minor. Moreover, the defendant stopped contacting the plaintiff 24 immediately after his request to cease contact. For these reasons, the court dismissed the plaintiff's claim, but did not order him to pay legal costs.

25 The Court of Appeals confirmed that the defendants were the controllers of the plaintiff's data and that they processed the plaintiff's data unlawfully due to a failure to comply with the obligation to provide information and the lack of a legal basis for processing the data, as indicated in art 6 GDPR. The Court of Appeals also addressed the scope of protection measures in the event of a violation of the GDPR. The court found that the civil law claims arising from a violation of personal data protection law are provided for by art 82 GDPR, which constitutes an independent basis for claims for damages.

26 Further the court pointed out that art 79 GDPR, unlike art 82 GDPR, is a competence norm, which refers to the provisions of the Civil Code on the protection of personal interests. According to art 92 of the Polish Personal Data Protection Act,[10] the provisions of the Civil Code are applied to claims for the violation of the provisions on personal data protection referred to in arts 79 and 82 GDPR. Polish law provides for the remedies in arts 24 and 448 KC. Both pecuniary and non-pecuniary damages claims can be pursued, but due to the above cited reference, they can be sought in connection with the allegation of a violation of personal rights (arts 23, 24 and 448 KC).

27 Thus, in the opinion of the Court of Appeals, the asserted claims had to be considered through the prism of the violation of personal interests. Focusing on the concept of the right to privacy, the court stressed that this is a constitutionally protected right and pointed out that in the context of the plaintiff's situation, privacy was to be understood as the ability to freely decide whether and to what extent information about one's person should be shared with others. The court adhered to the view of the Supreme Court (judgment of 13 December 2018, I CSK 690/17), according to which, personal data is not the same as a personal interest, although certain types of data may comprise elements of identity and privacy. The court pointed out that the protection of personal data works alongside the protection of personal interest. In the case under review, it should have been taken into account that the plaintiff is a legal advisor who runs a business, and both calls concerned an offer to a businessperson; the call was preceded by a request for permission to present an offer and ceased on the plaintiff's request. Since the plaintiff has a phone number for both private and professional purposes (after contacting the plaintiff's law firm, the secretariat was able to forward the plaintiff's number to clients), the plaintiff should expect to receive such calls.

10 Ustawa z dnia 10 maja 2018 r. o ochronie danych osobowych (consolidated text, Dz U 2019, item 1781).

For these reasons, while there was a violation of the GDPR provisions, the plaintiff's privacy was not violated. From an objective viewpoint, the inconvenience of the calls received was minor. Not every inconvenience or annoyance constitutes a violation of personal interest.

The GDPR construct of objection, which the plaintiff used, proved effective, as 28
the defendant company made no further calls to the plaintiff and deleted his data from the database.

As to the plaintiff's claims, the claim for apology has its basis in art 24 KC. The 29
court noted that the defendant company apologised three times to the plaintiff for the situation. The second claim, ie payment to a designated social cause, has its basis in art 448 § 1 KC. In the court's opinion, the plaintiff failed to prove both the violation of his personal interest and harm resulting from the violation. The court added that a mere violation of GDPR does not justify a claim for damages. The court stressed that in light of the case law of the CJEU, a person who claims a violation of the GDPR must demonstrate the consequences of the violation in the form of non-pecuniary damage, other than the GDPR violation itself.[11] Also the Civil Code regulations applicable under arts 79 and 82 GDPR require that damage must have occurred.

In light of the above, the claims were ultimately dismissed. 30

c) Commentary

It seems that the case at hand follows other judgments of Polish common courts 31
on the compensation of moral harm caused by a violation of the GDPR.[12] However, it is the first time that a court has paid special attention to the boundaries between an infringement of personal interests and a violation of the GDPR and provided a broader explanation on this topic.

It is interesting to note that the court expressly indicated that the claim for the 32
compensation of moral harm requires the establishment of a violation of personal interests in accordance with domestic law (here: arts 24 and 448 KC), although, at the same time, art 82 GDPR provides, in the court's opinion, a sole basis for the compensation of pecuniary and non-pecuniary damage. This clearly stands in contradiction. Thus, it is still unclear what situations (and/or claims) can be covered solely by art 82 GDPR, as the court unfortunately did not offer any examples. It

11 CJEU, 14.12.2023, C-456/22, *Gemeinde Ummendorf*, ECLI:EU:C:2023:988.

12 Reported by *E Bagińska/P Wyszyńska-Ślufińska*, Poland, in: E Karner/BC Steininger (eds), European Tort Law 2023 (2024) 513, no 17 ff.

might be that the unique problem of the case lay in the fact that the plaintiff demanded legal protection not only on the basis of the GDPR, but also of the Civil Code, namely the statement of apology and the payment of a sum of money for a special social cause, which are not expressly mentioned in art 82 GDPR, but appear in domestic law (arts 24 and 448 KC).

33 In Polish legal doctrine, two views can be distinguished as to the proper basis of compensation claims in cases of violations of the GDPR. According to the first, art 82 GDPR constitutes a sole (and sufficient) basis of a victim's claim. According to the second, the violation of the GDPR must result in the violation of a personal interest.[13] Although Polish legal writers are divided on this matter, it seems that the view provided by the Court of Appeals might prevail.

3. SN – Izba Pracy i Ubezpieczeń Społecznych (Chamber of Labour and Social Insurance) 22 May 2024, III PSKP 17/23 (OSNP[14] 2024 no 10 item 98): Liability of a Petrol Station Operator for an Employee's Injury Caused by a Robbery Attack

a) Brief Summary of the Facts

34 The plaintiff was employed at a petrol station. He was familiar with the safety manual and received training provided by the station manager, including, on the risks of robbery. On 18 January 2012, an armed man entered the petrol station and, having threatened the plaintiff with a cleaver, ordered him to open the cash register. The plaintiff followed all commands throughout the robbery, according to the prior instructions he had received from his employer. The investigation into the robbery was discontinued due to the failure to detect the perpetrator. The plaintiff continued to work at the petrol station for seven more months, but after the incident he developed PTSD (post-traumatic stress disorder) and depressive-anxiety symptoms. The incident suffered by the plaintiff was classified as a work accident, for which he was awarded a lump sum compensation payment. In this lawsuit, the claimant sought PLN 30,000 (approx € 7,143) as compensation for the moral harm he suffered (under the provisions of the Civil Code). The court

13 *A Pązik*, Szkoda wynikająca z naruszenia przepisów RODO. Wybrane problemy, Zeszyty Naukowe Uniwersytetu Jagiellońskiego 3 (2020) 127, 141 ff.

14 Orzecznictwo Sądu Najwyższego Izba Pracy i Zabezpieczeń Społecznych (Decisions of the Supreme Court, Labour and Social Insurance Chamber).

of first instance rejected the argument that the employer operated an enterprise set in motion by natural forces and was strictly liable for damage based on art 435 KC.[15] Neither was the employer liable for fault (art 415 KC). The plaintiff's claims were dismissed in two instances. The plaintiff filed a cassation.

b) Judgment of the Court

First, the Supreme Court pointed out that the bases of liability under art 435 KC (strict liability of the owner of an enterprise set into operation by natural forces) and art 415 KC (the general clause of liability) are mutually exclusive. As to the first provision, the absence of fault on the part of the employer is irrelevant and does not absolve the operator from liability. As to art 415 KC, liability will not arise if no fault can be proven. 35

In order to establish liability under art 435 KC, it does not suffice to show that the enterprise uses elementary forces (energy), but it must be shown that the operation of the enterprise is based on the use of machinery and equipment that use such energy. The court referred to earlier case law which indicated the following criteria for the determination of the scope of application of art 435 KC: 1) the degree of danger caused by the equipment used; 2) the degree of complication in the processing of elementary energy at work; and, 3) the general level of technology. The rationale for strict liability is the increased danger linked to the use of natural forces, which in turn causes an increased risk of harm. The natural forces must be essential to the operation of the entire enterprise, in other words, without their use, the enterprise would not achieve the purpose for which it was created. Therefore, a court must determine whether the use of these forces was a *conditio sine qua non* for the existence and operation of the enterprise in question. The definition provided in art 435 KC makes it impossible to denote a closed catalogue of enterprises, but based on the case law, it is possible to build a non-exhaustive list, which includes, inter alia, 'a mine (mining plant), an industrial plant emitting poisonous substances, a gas plant, a power plant, a railroad transport enterprise, a state machinery centre, a transportation enterprise using mechanical means of transport, a tramway enterprise, a mill, an agricultural cooperative, an enterprise 36

15 Art 435 § 1: A person conducting on his own account an enterprise or business set into operation by natural forces (steam, gas, electricity, liquid fuel, etc) is liable for any damage to persons or property caused through the operation of the enterprise or business, unless the damage was caused by force majeure or exclusively by the fault of the injured party or of a third person for whom he is not liable. § 2 The above provision shall apply correspondingly to enterprises or businesses producing or using explosives.

using aircrafts for agrotechnical treatments, a shipping enterprise, a construction enterprise, a container terminal, a farm'.

37 Applying these considerations to petrol stations, the Supreme Court regarded that such stations do not process energy in the form of fuel, but store it, and given that safety and caution are observed, the storage does not cause a particularly high level of danger. What is more, the petrol pumps require the use of electricity, but the use of hand-powered pumps is not excluded. According to the court, petrol stations derive their main profits from the sale of goods and catering services, not from the sale of fuel. For these reasons, the defendant is not liable under art 435 KC. As a side note, the Court pointed out that were the given petrol station to be considered an enterprise set into operation by natural force, strict liability would be excluded by the exclusive fault of a third party.

38 Referring to fault liability (art 415 KC), the Court underlined that the employer has a general duty to ensure safe and healthy working conditions, based on labour law.[16] A breach of this duty can be classified as a tort. In order for the employer to be held liable, it is necessary to show the negligent breach of that duty, and an adequate causal link with the damage. The Court stressed that the higher the risk of injury to the employee, the higher the employer's standard for addressing this risk. However, the Court referred to the Supreme Court's judgment of 13 September 2016 (III PK 146/15), which held that the employer's duty to ensure safety cannot go so far as to burden the employer with the duty to provide all possible protective measures. To attribute unlawfulness to the employer's conduct, it is necessary to show that the employer failed to implement effective mechanisms to protect the employee, aimed at minimising the danger. In the Court's opinion, in the case at hand, the measures adopted by the employer (inter alia, training materials, training programme) were sufficient and there were no grounds for the defendant's liability.

c) Commentary

39 Our first point is that the workers' compensation scheme is not exclusive, and the 'regular' civil liability of an employer for labour accidents is governed by the general principles of tort law (fault, strict liability or equity) and its scope is determined by arts 361–363 KC (pecuniary damage, causation) and arts 444–449 KC (compensation for personal injury). Risk is the most important principle and

16 The Labour Code (Ustawa z dnia 26 czerwca 1974 r., Kodeks pracy, Dz U 2023, item 1465).

source of an employer's liability, often coming into play under the regime of art 435 KC.

As in most other European jurisdictions, in Poland, strict liability attaches to dangerous activities or objects creating a risk of damage. There are many strict liability rules within and outside of the Civil Code. The rule which can be considered as general, or at least more general than others, is art 435 KC, discussed in the commented case. The Civil Code requires a case-by-case examination of whether a given enterprise 'fits' the definition of art 435 KC. If the answer is in the affirmative, the entrepreneur is liable for any damage caused through the operation of the enterprise, unless the damage was caused by force majeure or exclusively by the fault of the injured party or of a third person for whom they are not liable. In a situation where, despite the danger of the activity in question, the court does not classify the given enterprise as one which is set into operation by natural forces, the injured party may still use the general clause of fault liability: however, this is usually a 'dead-end' option evidence-wise. 40

As observed by the Court, in determining the scope of application of art 435 KC, it is necessary to consider the degree of danger from the equipment used, the degree of complication in the use of elementary energy, and the general level of technology. It is therefore necessary to estimate whether the activity set into operation by means of natural forces is of a supportive or fundamental character.[17] Generally, Polish courts interpret art 435 KC broadly by an extensive interpretation of all the elements of the tort. 41

Nevertheless, the risk which attaches to a person operating an enterprise run with the use of natural forces is not unlimited. An event that is completely independent from the person who is strictly liable cannot influence the extent of their duty to compensate.[18] 42

4. SN 11 June 2024, II CSKP 2357/22:[19] Bathing in Illegal and Unguarded Water Basin; Lack of Causation

a) Brief Summary of the Facts

In 2015, the plaintiff and his colleagues went to a water reservoir that had been formed in the excavated area used by a mine, the property of the State Treasury 43

17 SN 18 December 2018 (IV CSK 483/17, OSNC-ZD 2019, no 4, item 60).

18 See *M Nesterowicz/E Bagińska*, Contributory Negligence under Polish Law, in: U Magnus/M Martín-Casals (eds), Unification of Tort Law: Contributory Negligence (2004) 155.

19 <www.sn.pl>.

and under the management of the State Forestry Administration. The plaintiff had known the basin for several years. It is considered as an ecological utility, and not for recreational purposes. There were no signs saying 'no trespassing' and 'no swimming'. The Municipal Office published information in the Legal Information Bulletin that it is prohibited from swimming in all reservoirs in the municipality, while the municipality's head official stated that there was no lifeguard-provided bathing area in the municipality.

44 After the plaintiff and his friends had fired up a barbecue, they entered the water and performed jumping jacks. The plaintiff was standing at the edge of the water basin, when his friend, while jumping, pushed him and, as a consequence, the plaintiff fell into the one-metre-deep water. As a result of the fall, he suffered serious personal injuries, has become an invalid and is confined to a wheelchair.

45 The plaintiff sued the State Treasury and the municipality claiming compensation in the amount of PLN 1,500,000 (approx € 357,143) for his pain and suffering, as well as an award of a monthly pension of PLN 21,450 (approx € 5,107). The courts of first and second instances dismissed the plaintiff's claim, due to a lack of unlawfulness of the defendants' conduct and the lack of a causal link between the defendants' omissions and the plaintiff's injury. The plaintiff filed a cassation, requesting that the judgment of the second instance court be reversed and the case be remanded for reconsideration.

b) Judgment of the Court

46 Firstly, the Supreme Court stated that Directive 2006/7/EC[20] was not applicable in the present case. Then, the Court pointed out that surface waters are divided into flowing and standing waters, and the reservoir in question was subject to the provisions of water law (the 2001 Water Law Act).[21] While the reservoir did not constitute a bathing area within the meaning of the EU Directive or a bathing site within the meaning of Polish water law, it could be classified as a so-called 'place customarily used for bathing' or a place occasionally used for bathing, which are defined in the Act of 18 August 2011 on the safety of persons visiting (present at) water areas.[22] Among other things, this Act defines the safety condi-

20 Directive 2006/7/EC of the European Parliament and the Council of 15 February 2006 concerning the management of bathing water quality and repealing Directive 76/160/EEC, OJ L 64/37.

21 Ustawa z dnia 18 lipca 2001 r. Prawo wodne (Dz U 2001, no 115, item 1229).

22 Ustawa z dnia 18 sierpnia 2011 r. o bezpieczeństwie osób przebywających na obszarach wodnych (Dz U 2011 no 208, item 1240).

tions for people swimming, bathing or practising sports or recreational activities in water areas.

The Court noted that the duty to ensure safety rests with the head of the municipality and is one of the municipality's own tasks (art 4 of the Law of 18 August 2011). This duty requires, among other things, that a risk analysis be performed, including the identification of places where there is a threat to the safety of people using the water area for swimming, bathing, sports or recreation; marking and securing areas, facilities and equipment intended for swimming, bathing, sports or recreation in water areas; carrying out preventive and educational activities regarding safety in water areas. The Court stated that the area where the reservoir in question was located is classified as a public inland surface water, an ecological utility and a State forest, so everyone had a right of access to it and it could not be fenced in such a way as to prevent physical access to it. 47

The plaintiff with his friends violated the prohibition on camping in the forest (art 30 of the Forest Law of 28 September 1991[23]); however, as the area had been used by many as an informal bathing area for an extended period of time, both the owner of the area and the authorities responsible for ensuring safety should have marked the area with a ban on bathing. The fact that the municipality had disclosed information that there were no legal bathing areas in its territory was deemed insufficient by the Court. Similarly, it concluded that the State Treasury should have posted a sign prohibiting camping and bathing. Such an omission of the municipality and the State Treasury must be considered unlawful. On the other hand, however, both the plaintiff and his friends failed to exercise due diligence (art 355 § 1 KC) by using the bathing area, whereas any reasonable person would have realised that the site was neither a guarded bathing area nor formally organised by the competent authorities, and that it had no professional infrastructure. 48

On the issue of causation, the Court pointed out that if the accident had occurred in connection with the typical use of the reservoir, ie while bathing, then the plaintiff's conduct could have been considered as his contribution to the damage. However, in the Court's opinion, there was no adequate causal link between the unlawful conduct of the defendants in failing to place signs prohibiting bathing and the plaintiff's injury. Causation is an objective category and should be determined by the facts of a particular case. It was stressed that the cause of the injury was the act of the plaintiff's friend, not the lack of prohibitions on swimming and camping. The Supreme Court agreed with the appellate court's reasoning that even if the bathing area had been guarded, due to the conduct of 49

23 Ustawa z dnia 28 września 1991 r. o lasach (Dz U 1991, no 101, item 444).

the plaintiff's friend, the plaintiff's injury would have occurred anyway. It is impossible to show that the erection of a sign prohibiting swimming would have prevented the conduct of the injured party's friend. For these reasons, due to the lack of an adequate causal link, the Court dismissed the injured party's claims.

c) Commentary

50 In this rather ordinary tort case, the plaintiff's claims failed on the question of causation, more specifically they failed to pass the *conditio sine qua non* test. The Court, on the other hand, failed to address the discussion of public liability, in particular whether the alleged omission should be classified as an *acte de iure imperii* (no-fault liability) or *acte de dominii* (fault liability).

51 Overall, the reasoning of the Court appears to be in line with previous case law. Regarding omissions of public authorities, the courts have held that any non-compliance with regulations on safety of public places leads to a finding of fault resulting in the establishment of tort liability of the State or a local authority. According to that case law, any person who is obliged to remove sources of danger (eg holes in a road, a building threatening to collapse, etc) should exercise due diligence in taking preventive measures. Due diligence requires that authorities react if the danger is known or should have been known. To illustrate, the Supreme Court (judgment of 4 March 1965 (III CR 9/65 OSN 1966, item 17) awarded damages to a plaintiff who, when bathing in the sea, injured his leg on a broken iron barrel lying in the shallow water close to the beach. The defendant municipality claimed that the plaintiff had been swimming at an unguarded beach, which was not an arranged bathing area. A warning sign had been put up on that beach stating, 'Unguarded beach. Visitors bathe at their own risk.' However, the officials of the municipality were aware of the barrel's existence as there had already been cases of people being injured while bathing there. In two instances, the claims were dismissed as the courts regarded the plaintiff to have acted at their own risk. The Supreme Court held that the municipality should not have limited itself to placing a warning notice close to the beach of a frequented sea resort but since it kept the beach tidy and removed dangerous objects from the beach, it should have done so also regarding coastal waters. Although the warning did not state that bathing was forbidden, it could have been read as meaning that there would be no rescuer there, so the swimmer ran the risk of drowning. If the municipality had put up a notice prohibiting bathing, this would also have been inefficient.

52 As in the 1960s, also today, municipalities are under a statutory duty to make beach and coastal waters that are open to the public safe and to prevent harm to swimmers. On the other hand, a general duty of care, a duty to the public, should

not be construed too broadly. We should return to the point made by the Court that the water basin in the commented case was known to be used by the public. Had the access to it been prevented or limited, if only through the warning against shallow waters, the unlawfulness of the conduct of local officials might not have been established. A related point is the doctrine of assumption of risk, which is not regulated in Polish law. Such a defence sometimes overlaps and sometimes runs parallels to the defence of contributory conduct, or to consent of a victim. Legal scholars generally follow the approach, according to which, a victim assumes the risk of damage in a situation when they expose themselves to a hazard known to them voluntarily, consciously and for no important reason. According to various theories, the victim is assumed to have accepted the possible occurrence of a hazardous situation which may, but does not have to, involve adverse consequences. After all, it is not improbable to foresee that when people use water areas for recreation, unintentional accidents can happen.

5. Personal Injury

Several judgments published in 2024 illustrate the problems related to the assessment of damages for non-pecuniary harm in personal injury cases. The level of compensation in cases of severe personal injuries is generally on the rise. 53

In a judgment of the Court of Appeals in Lublin of 31 July 2024 (I ACa 465/23), the court considered the amount of compensation for moral harm for the parents and adult siblings of X, who died because of a car accident. The tortfeasor had been convicted in criminal proceedings. The parents and siblings sued the motor vehicle liability insurer. Three months after the accident, X died at the age of 25 due to the injuries he sustained. He was a student at a catholic church seminary and was described by his parents as their most talented child. The siblings had a very good relationship with the deceased. Both the tragic accident and the victim's struggle for life were a traumatic experience for the plaintiffs, whose emotional health was negatively affected. The court of first instance awarded each of the deceased's parents PLN 200,000 (approx € 47,619), and each sibling PLN 100,000 (approx € 23,809). The awarded amounts were reduced by 30 % due to X's contribution to the damage. In the court's opinion, although the relationship with the deceased's siblings was very close, it did not equate with the emotional bond with his parents. The verdict was appealed by both parties. The Court of Appeals pointed out in the context of siblings that the sister's harm was much greater than her brother's, because due to her illness (schizophrenia), she received special support from her deceased brother, who was particularly close to her, also because of his ecclesiastical functions. In addition, she could count on X to take 54 care of her after the death of her parents. These circumstances, in the court's opinion, resulted in the need to increase the compensation for the deceased's sister to PLN 150,000 (approx € 35,714). However, the court did not accept the argument that the harm of the parents is equal to the harm of the siblings. Such a conclusion is contrary to life experience, since the degree of pain and suffering caused by the sudden death of a child affects the parents the most, which justifies awarding them higher amounts of compensation for moral harm.

55 In another judgment of the Court of Appeals in Lublin of 13 August 2024 (ref no I ACa 1117/23),[24] the court considered the issue of the contribution to the injury of a mentally disabled minor under art 362 KC (contribution to damage). In the case at hand, the minor plaintiff, while getting off a bus, suddenly crossed the road from behind the stationary bus, ignoring basic traffic rules. In the opinion of the court, the plaintiff's medical condition and his partial impairment are not factors to account for the reduction of damages, as the minor's legal guardians allowed him to function normally in public, and the victim did indeed function without the care of third parties. The court stressed that since the injured party's parents agreed that their child should use public transportation independently, they considered the minor to know and apply the rules related to traffic. The court considered the plaintiff's conduct to be a typical reckless act of a teenager, which can happen regardless of their level of mental maturity. The court also emphasised that the plaintiff did not prove that his mental impairment affected his conduct. It was held that in such circumstances, the plaintiff should have been considered to have contributed 50 % to the injury. Referring to this judgment, it should be considered that the mere fact that the parents allowed the child to use public transportation should not *ipso facto* lead to the conclusion that this is tantamount to a finding that the plaintiff understood the consequences of his actions.

24 The judgment was issued with the participation of persons appointed to the position of judge with the participation of the National Council of the Judiciary formed under the Act of 8.12.2017 amending the Act on the National Council of the Judiciary and certain other acts (OJ 2018, item 3).

C. Literature

1. *K Szczepanowska-Kozłowska K* (ed), Odpowiedzialność deliktowa. Księga pozjazdowa Zjazd Katedr Prawa Cywilnego [Liability in tort. The Collection of papers from the Conference of Civil Law Chairs] (CH Beck, Warszawa 2024)

This book is the collection of papers presented at the Biannual Conference of Civil Law Chairs, which took place in 2023 in Warsaw. It contains 20 scholarly articles devoted to the main subject of the congress, namely tort law. All texts are in Polish. They have been arranged in five sections. The first part, entitled 'Personal injury', includes three chapters on: the definition of non-pecuniary loss (*A Pyrzyńska*); reforms of compensation for non-pecuniary loss in the new Civil Code (*E Bagińska*); and personal injury and related harm in international trade: qualification issues (*Ł Dyrda, E Figura-Góralczyk*). The second part combines articles devoted to the topic 'Damage in intellectual property law': the relevance of the occurrence of damage to the determination of the remuneration for the infringement of copyrights (*Ł Maryniak*); the function of liability for damage for infringement of intellectual property rights (*K Gliściński*); and the relationship between a claim for damages and a disgorgement claim in cases of violations of intellectual property rights (*Ł Żelechowski*). The third section, entitled 'Developments in strict liability and the concept of unlawfulness', contains five texts on: concepts of fault and unlawfulness and strict liability in selected legal systems (*S Castillo-Wyszogrodzka*); the question of the need for a systemic change to the rules of tort liability detaching the liability issue from the attribution of fault in the light of the achievements of neuroscience (*M Olczyk*); the basis for tort liability of a legal person for its own act (art 416 KC) (*B Gnela*); tort liability for damage caused by AI on the example of autonomous vehicles (*W Kocot*); and functions of strict liability in tort (*M Wilejczyk*). Part IV, entitled 'Between tort and contract', comprises works on the *cumul* rule, in particular, the importance of contractual modifications and exclusions of tort liability (three chapters by *M Gutowski, B Kaczorowska, P Konik)*; tort liability arising from the conclusion of an invalid legal transaction (*M Bławat*); and setting standards of conduct and the law of torts (*W Borysiak*). The book closes with four papers presenting the results of research conducted by doctoral students, concerning strict liability of independent contractors, the limits of contractual liability, liability for damage caused by an infringement of business secrets, and strict liability of quasi-producers. 56

2. *A Kappes*, Naprawienie szkody wyrządzonej wspólnikom mniejszościowym. Majątkowa ochrona mniejszości w spółkach kapitałowych [Reparation of damage caused to minority shareholders. Pecuniary protection of minorities in limited liability companies] (CH Beck, Warszawa 2024)

57 The book examines the admissibility and the prerequisites of liability for damage suffered by minority shareholders because of the conduct of the majority shareholders in limited liability companies. The protection of minority shareholders is a hot subject in the field of commercial law and the problem of liability towards such shareholders has been quite controversial in Polish legal writings and case law. The book covers the subjective scope of liability, interests of shareholders, interests of groups of companies, the duty of loyalty of shareholders, the legal nature of liability (the entitlement of shareholders to seek recovery for lost value of shares) and its elements, as well as selected means of redress (*action pro socio*) and preventive actions.

58 The author interprets the changes to the Commercial Companies Code, adopted in 2022,[25] including the rules on the business judgement rule and the regulation of group companies. As there are no specific mechanisms in that Code designed to protect the pecuniary interests of minor shareholders, through a compensatory claim, the main value of the analysis pertains to the scope of applicability of the provisions of the Civil Code to the reparation of damage suffered by minority shareholders. The damage primarily consists of a decrease in the value of the shares. Accordingly, many factual situations (including practical examples taken from the legal practice of the author) containing an element of disadvantage for the shareholders deprived of influence over the operation of the company's business are examined. The author argues that not only direct damage, but also indirect damage is subject to compensation if it remains in an adequate causal relationship with the unlawful conduct of the tortfeasor. A detailed analysis of the rules, doctrinal views and court practice, as well as proposals for legislative changes are provided in the book. Comparatively, only German law is referred to, which is justified, as explained by the author, by the systemic proximity of Polish and German company law and the relative similarity of Polish and German contract law.

25 Ustawa o zmianie ustawy – Kodeks spółek handlowych oraz niektórych innych ustaw of 9 February 2022, Dz U 2022, item 807.

3. Selected Articles

E Bagińska, Zadośćuczynienie za naruszenie praw i wolności człowieka w dobie kryzysu praworządności (uwagi de lege lata i de lege ferenda) [Damages for violations of human rights in times of the rule-of-law crisis: Observations about the law as it is and as it should be], Państwo i Prawo 3 (2024) 158–170 59

M Deptalski/P Dziewałtowski-Gintowt, Tortious Liability Regime for Medical Devices Using Artificial Intelligence. Analysis of Current Solutions, Transformacje Prawa Prywatnego 2 (2024) 37–64 60

P Kaniewski/K Kowacz, Odpowiedzialność cywilna za szkody spowodowane funkjconowaniem sztucznej inteligencji – uwagi de lege lata i de lege ferenda [Civil liability for damage caused by the operation of artificial intelligence], Palestra 11 (2024) 6–33 61

WJ Kocot, Podmiotowość sztucznej inteligencji w nowym kodeksie cywilnym [The subjectivity of artificial intelligence in a New Civil Code], Pańswto i Prawo 5 (2024) 108–134 62

P Drapała, Odpowiedzialność Skarbu Państwa za szkody spowodowane ograniczeniami praw i wolności w czasie epidemii Covid-19 (polemika z M. Pyziak-Szafnicką i R. Strugałą) [The State Treasury's liability for losses caused by restrictions on rights and freedoms during the Covid-19 epidemic (Polemic with *M.* Pyziak-Szafnicka and R. Strugała)], Państwo i Prawo 1 (2024) 159–171 63

A Paleczna, The concept of rationalising damage and the scope of insurer's liability, Wiadomości Ubezpieczeniowe 1 (2024) 33–46 64

P Wyszyńska-Ślufińska, Compensation for moral harm caused to a legal entity – does the new Polish Supreme Court Resolution of 2023 provide a remedy for the Polish legal system? Some critical remarks in a comparative perspective, Wiadomości Ubezpieczeniowe 1 (2024) 47–59 65

Rui Cascão, Inês Oliveira Martins and André Pereira

XXIII. Portugal

A. Legislation

1. Law no 10/2024, 19 January (Legal Regime on the Professional Services of Attorneys and Solicitors)

This Law approved a new legal regime on the professional services of attorneys and solicitors in Portugal. It revokes previous legislation on the scope of professional services and combatting the illegal practice of law (Law no 49/2004, 24 August). 1

Article 4 of Law no 10/2024 provides for the scope of the legal services that are legally reserved to registered attorneys and solicitors. According to art 4 (2), only attorneys or solicitors can provide legal representation (*mandato forense*) of clients before the courts of law, tribunals, arbitration boards, or justices of the peace. Furthermore, pursuant to art 4 (3), attorneys have the exclusive prerogative of assisting defendants in criminal procedures and ensuring the constitutional right of citizens to be accompanied by an attorney before any authority enshrined in art 20 (2) of the Constitution. 2

Article 4 (4) of Law no 10/2024 provides that attorneys and solicitors *also* have the capacity to provide legal advice, to draft contracts and juridical acts, and to engage in debt recovery negotiation. Pursuant to art 4 (5), legal advice is, as a rule of thumb, legally reserved to these legal professionals when the act, on behalf and on account of a third party, lies within the scope of their professional activity. 3

The most significant innovation of Law no 10/2024 is that it allows for persons and entities other than attorneys and solicitors to lawfully provide certain legal services (eg provision of legal advice, the drafting of contracts and juridical acts, the negotiation of debt recovery). In previous legislation, the sole exception to the exclusive capacity of attorneys and solicitors to provide legal services was the prerogative recognised to law professors of providing legal advice in writing to third parties (art 1 (3) Law no 49/2004). While the latter has been retained in art 7 (2) of Law no 10/2024, several other persons and entities are now legally entitled by this statute to provide the said legal services, albeit with some limitations: notaries; enforcement agents; holders of a law degree retained by (or providing ser- 4

https://doi.org/10.1515/9783111389271-024

vices to) a company or entity, within the scope of their duties;[1] companies acting within the scope of their corporate purpose (insofar as a holder of a law degree is retained); and companies whose exclusive corporate purpose is debt collection negotiation. Strangely enough, other service providers whose activity intersects with legal advice (eg, Data Protection Officers, tax advisers, realtors) are omitted, which could lead to legal uncertainty and increased litigation.

5 Providing legal services in violation of the provisions of Law no 10/2024 can trigger criminal liability and/or administrative sanctions for illegal practice in the area of law if legal services that are legally reserved to registered attorneys and solicitors are arrogated, as provided by arts 11–14 of Law no 10/2024.

6 Article 15 of Law no 10/2024 is of particular significance to tort and insurance law, as it provides for a presumption of fault if the conditions set forth by art 4 (legal services reserved to attorneys and solicitors), art 7 (provision of legal advice by other entities), art 8 (drafting of contracts), and art 9 (negotiations regarding debt recovery). It also provides that the Portuguese Bar Association, as well as the Order of Solicitors and Enforcement Agents have legal standing to bring a liability claim for the protection of the public interest in these cases.

7 It is not immediately evident whether art 15 of Law no 10/2024 applies to contractual or non-contractual liability (or both). In contractual liability, the general law of obligations already provides for a presumption of fault (art 799 CC). Therefore, including such a provision would be redundant.[2]

8 As regards non-contractual liability, at a first glance, the provision of art 15 also looks unnecessary, considering that the dominant opinion in literature and case law leans towards an overlap (*cumul*) between contractual and non-contractual liability.[3] Supposing that a client incurred damage caused by substandard care by a legal services provider (other than an attorney or a solicitor) in breach of the provisions of arts 4 and 7–9, at a first glance there would be no advantage in this provision, as the presumption of fault of art 799 CC would apply in any case.

9 Nevertheless, this provision can be advantageous in cases where the contract between the client is deemed null and void on grounds of illegality, pursuant to art 280 CC. In this case, the presumption of fault burdening an unauthorised

1 Pursuant to art 7 (6) of Law no 10/2024, for this purpose, law degree holders and companies are obliged to take out compulsory third party professional liability insurance.

2 *A Barroso Rodrigues*, Sobre a responsabilidade civil profissional do advogado e das sociedades de advogados, Revista da Ordem dos Advogados I/II (2022) 77.

3 *AG Dias* Pereira, Direitos dos Pacientes e Responsabilidade Médica (2012) 653; *A Vaz Serra*, Responsabilidade civil contratual e responsabilidade extracontratual, Boletim do Ministério da Justiça 85 (1959) 115–139.

legal services provider will make it easier for an aggrieved client to be compensated for damage incurred by virtue of a substandard legal service. The presumption also has a deterrent effect on unauthorised legal service providers.[4]

Furthermore, the nature and purpose of the standing to sue granted by art 15 (2) of Law no 10/2024 to the Bar Association, as well as the Order of Solicitors and Enforcement Agents is unclear. It does not appear to mean an extension of the aggrieved party's standing to sue or a right to claim to indirect damages (*par ricochet*), but rather an autonomous standing which is institutional in nature (as these two institutions are responsible for the self-regulation of the legal professions) aiming at protecting the public interest, consumers, and deterring the illegal practice of law. This is consistent with the provision of art 15 (3) in consigning the compensation awards to a fund aiming at implementing measures to promote awareness, preventative action, and deterrence of the illegal practice of law.[5] **10**

The provision of art 15 is not innovative and is identical to art 11 of the forerunner Law no 49/2004. In the context of the previous law, the borderline between legal and illegal practice was rather clear: legal services provided on behalf and on account of third parties were legal if they were provided by an attorney or a solicitor (or a law professor in the case of written legal advice), whereas legal services provided by any other entity (with few exceptions) were deemed illegal. As Law no 10/2024 created more exceptions and expanded the catalogue of entities permitted to provide legal services, the complexity of the legal framework of this activity increased. It was a missed opportunity to improve the clarity and conciseness of this provision. There will be grey areas between legal and illegal practice, which will lead to legal uncertainty and increased litigation. **11**

4 *Barroso Rodrigues*, Revista da Ordem dos Advogados I/II (2022) 75.
5 *Barroso Rodrigues*, Revista da Ordem dos Advogados I/II (2022) 77.

B. Cases

1. Supreme Administrative Court, 6 June 2024 *(Pedro Machete)*, ECLI:PT:STA:2021:061.19.9BEPRT.A4: Delay in an Administrative Decision; Non-Contractual Liability of Public Entities; Delay in the Administration of Justice

a) Brief Summary of the Facts

12 This case relates to legal proceedings between the plaintiff and the Portuguese Bar Association and the Portuguese State due to an excessive delay in disciplinary procedures against the plaintiff (an attorney) initiated by the Bar.

13 The plaintiff initiated an administrative action on 11 January 2019, with the Porto Administrative and Tax Court against the Portuguese State and the Portuguese Bar Association, seeking € 16,000 in compensation for non-pecuniary and pecuniary damage due to the excessive length of disciplinary procedures against him, which lasted approximately nine years and seven months. The plaintiff argued that the Bar breached its obligation to issue a decision within a reasonable time and that the State shared liability because of its failure to adequately supervise the Bar's regulatory and disciplinary activity.

14 The State contested the claims, arguing that it was not liable, the action against it was manifestly unfounded, and the right to bring the action had expired. It also asserted that all legal formalities were observed during the disciplinary proceedings. On the other hand, the Bar contended that the disciplinary process followed the regular procedure and that the delay was due to waiting for essential certificates from the courts to substantiate the facts related to the alleged disciplinary offences. The Bar also maintained that it was not responsible for the delay and that the plaintiff's rights to a defence were always duly safeguarded.

15 In first instance, the Porto Administrative and Tax Court partially upheld the plaintiff's claims, acquitting the State and ordering the Bar Association to pay the plaintiff € 2,500 in non-pecuniary damages due to the excessive delay in the disciplinary procedures.

16 Both the plaintiff and the Bar appealed the decision to the Northern Central Administrative Court, which upheld the initial ruling and denied both appeals. Not content with the ruling, both the plaintiff and the Bar appealed the decision to the Supreme Administrative Court, which admitted the appeal on 12 October 2021. In his appeal, the plaintiff argued that the Northern Central Administrative Court's decision was illegal, breached the principles of equality and non-discrim-

ination, and failed to provide adequate compensation, pursuant to the European Convention on Human Rights (ECHR) standards, only awarding token compensation.

The State and the Bar requested the dismissal of the appeal and that the original decision be upheld, as the necessary legal criteria for the establishment of liability were not met. The Bar argued that the case law on this matter was unclear, citing a recent decision by the Southern Central Administrative Court, which established a difference between procedural and judicial delays, and questioned the applicability of the ECHR to administrative disciplinary procedures.[6] 17

Both the plaintiff and the State responded to the Bar's motion, with the plaintiff underscoring the applicability of European Court of Human Rights (ECtHR) standards to disciplinary procedures and arguing for the recognition of the delays as violations of the reasonable length guarantees in light of art 6 (1) ECHR. 18

b) Judgment of the Court

The Supreme Administrative Court partially overruled the appealed decisions and awarded the plaintiff € 7,875 in non-pecuniary damages, in line with ECtHR standards for the calculation of damages awards, holding the Portuguese Bar Association liable. It accepted the acquittal of the Portuguese State, considering that it is the exclusive responsibility of the Bar Association, as the association of legal professionals, to regulate and exercise discipline over its members, and this entity enjoys full autonomy in relation to such attribution, namely vis-à-vis the State. 19

The Court also considered that the professional status of an attorney and their experience or competence, the effectiveness of their defence or the fact that the proceedings have been terminated due to limitation periods should not be considered as relevant or appropriate factors for the purposes of a fair assessment of the non-pecuniary damage caused by an excessive delay in deciding disciplinary proceedings brought by the respective professional association. 20

The Court held that the right to a timely administrative decision, especially in disciplinary procedures, benefits from a multilevel protection both at the national level and the international level, requiring interpretative adjustments of different regimes to optimise the intended protection. The Court held that, due to the principle of subsidiarity, the ECHR is not directly and immediately applicable in cases of excessive duration of disciplinary proceedings: the punishment of violations of 21

6 Southern Central Administrative Court, 18/03/2021 (*Ana Celeste Carvalho*) Proc No 865/16.4BELSB.

rights subject to simultaneous protection at the constitutional and ECHR levels is primarily the responsibility of the competent national authorities at the domestic law level. Nevertheless, it is the sovereign State in the international legal order that is responsible for violations of ECHR rights committed within its jurisdiction by public authorities (international responsibility of the State).

22 The exercise of the legal profession is considered a civil right under art 6(1) ECHR, making disciplinary proceedings against attorneys subject to this provision. The practice of the profession of attorney is a 'civil right' for the purposes of this article: as such, disciplinary proceedings brought against attorneys in relation to the exercise of their profession – in the context of which sanctions may be applied that call into question, temporarily or permanently, the exercise of such right – give rise to a dispute on civil rights to which the aforementioned rule of the Convention in its civil aspect applies.

23 Furthermore, the Court held that the excessive procedural delays could indicate an abnormal functioning of the administrative entity, relevant for liability allocation purposes, pursuant to the Regime of Extra-Contractual Civil Liability of the State and Public Entities (in particular, art 7).[7]

c) Commentary

24 This case is a good example of the functioning of the multilevel protection of human rights, on how the domestic jurisdiction engages with the ECHR/ECtHR system, and the impact of this system on how tort law is applied. Excessive length of administrative and judicial procedures is a significant systemic problem in the Portuguese judiciary and public administration. This is widely perceived by the stakeholders in these sectors, as well as the public, as a problem that is highly detrimental to the quality of justice, administrative efficiency, economic competitiveness, as well as a risk to the rule of law and democratic institutions.

25 Portugal has been repeatedly held liable by the ECtHR for breach of art 6 (1) (right to a fair trial), art 13 (right to an effective remedy), as well as art 2 (right to life, procedural limb) due to the excessive length of procedures.[8]

26 However, the multilevel protection of human rights has been successful, and the case law of the ECtHR has been influential and helpful for the courts and the

---

7 Law 67/2007 of 31 December on the Non-Contractual Liability of the State and Public Law Entities.

8 ECtHR *Valada Matos das Neves v Portugal*, 29.10.2015 [Section I] no 73798/13; ECtHR *Flores Cardoso v Portugal*, 29.5.2012 [Section II] no 2489/09; ECtHR *Lopes de Sousa Fernandes v Portugal* [GC] 19.12.2017, no 56080/13.

legislator in addressing this systemic problem. Compliance with ECtHR case law has had a significant impact in the length of court procedures, notably by adopting the standards defined by said case law, particularly as regards the calculation of damages and the reasonable time concept, as this case illustrates.[9]

However, a significant legislative reform of procedural laws is urgently required. It ought to include innovative rules on case management, criteria regarding reasonable time periods for proceedings, and rules allowing the acceleration of proceedings. In addition, issues related to the lack of human resources in the courts must be addressed. 27

2. Supreme Court of Justice, 23 May 2024 (*Nuno Ataíde das Neves*) ECLI:PT:STJ:2024:3489.17.5.T8STR.E1.A.D0: Compulsory Motor Liability Insurance; Insurer's Right of Recourse.

a) Brief Summary of the Facts

In the early morning, while driving on a two-way road, A, who was travelling with B, swerved his car into the opposite lane and collided with a farm tractor coming from the opposite direction. The crash resulted in B's death and caused severe damage to the tractor. A underwent toxicological exams, which revealed the presence of cannabis-related chemicals in his blood, specifically 4.3 ng/ml of THC-COOH and 0.8 ng/ml of THC. A's motor insurer settled claims with both B's mother (her sole heir) and the tractor's owner. The insurer then sought reimbursement of these amounts from A, on the basis of art 27(c) of the Compulsory Motor Liability Insurance Act (CMLIA),[10] which grants insurers a right of recourse against a driver who causes an accident while exceeding the legal blood alcohol limit, or testing positive for narcotics, other drugs, or toxic substances. 28

A contested this claim, citing the provisions of the Road Traffic Act (RTA)[11] that prohibit driving under the influence of psychoactive substances. Under the RTA, a driver is considered to be under the influence of such substances only if 29

9 *R Pedro*, The Portuguese Legal Framework of State Liability for Delayed Justice: The Relevance of ECtHR Case-Law, International Journal for Court Administration 15(2) (2024) 6, doi: 10.36745/ijca.486; *MB Urbano*, Duração Excessiva do Processo, in: P Pinto de Albuquerque (ed), Comentário da Convenção Europeia dos Direitos Humanos e dos Protocolos Adicionais, vol II (2019) 965.

10 Decree-Law no 291/2007 of 21 August.

11 Decree-Law no 114/94 of 3 May.

a medical or expert report, following an examination conducted in accordance with applicable laws and regulations, establishes this (art 81(1) and (5) of the RTA, supplemented by the Regulation on the monitoring of driving under the influence of alcohol or psychotropic substances and by the Decree on medical exams for the detection of alcohol or psychotropic substance influence[12]). The defendant argued that since the chemical levels detected in his blood were below the thresholds mentioned in one of these regulations, there was no proof that he had been driving 'under the influence'. Consequently, the insurer had no right of recourse.

30 The first instance court ruled in favour of the plaintiff. The defendant appealed and won on appeal. The plaintiff then appealed to the Supreme Court, which overturned the appellate ruling.

31 The Supreme Court held that the thresholds cited by the defendant apply to urine tests used for screening purposes, and not to blood tests like the one he had undergone. The Court further ruled that the law does not establish a minimum threshold for psychoactive substance levels to be considered relevant, nor does it require proof that the substance actually impaired the driver's faculties. The mere fact that a driver who caused an accident tests positive for psychoactive substances is sufficient to trigger the insurer's right of recourse.

32 The defendant considered that this ruling contradicted previous case law issued by the Supreme Court, and appealed to the plenum of the civil law sections of the Supreme Court, under the special right to appeal based on conflicting jurisprudence. This right applies when a Supreme Court ruling contradicts previous decisions by the same court on identical factual and legal issues (arts 688 to 695 of the Civil Procedure Code, on the recourse for the uniformisation of case law).

33 The defendant referred to the decision issued by the Supreme Court on 25 March 2021, case 313/17.2T8AVR.P1.S1. In that case, which also involved a driver who caused an accident and tested positive for cannabinoids, the Court ruled that the mere detection of the substance was insufficient. For the insurer to invoke art 27(c) of the CMLIA, it had to prove through the exams mentioned in art 81(5) RTA and complementary regulations that the substance had indeed impaired the driver's ability to operate the vehicle.

12 Respectively, Law no 19/2007 of 17 May and Decree no 902-B/2007 of 13 April.

b) Judgment of the Court

The Court acknowledged that the decisions cited contained contradictory interpretations of art 27(c) of the CMLIA as regards similar facts. Guidance was needed as to whether the insurer's right of recourse under art 27(c) of CMLIA was satisfied merely by proof of the presence of psychoactive substances in the driver's blood at the time of the accident, or whether it required proof of actual influence, to be established exclusively through the medical and expert examinations set out in art 81(5) RTA and complementary regulations. The Court should thus issue a ruling on this question and then decide the case accordingly. 34

The Court began by analysing art 27 of the CMLIA, which exhaustively lists the circumstances in which an insurer has the right to recover amounts paid to a victim. Under art 27(c), the insurer has a right of recourse against a driver who causes an accident either while driving with a blood alcohol level above the legally permitted limit or testing positive for narcotics, other drugs, or toxic substances. The Court identified the purpose of art 27(c) as that of shielding insurer from risks beyond those normally associated with motor vehicle use. Given the exhaustive nature of art 27, the Court emphasised that the right of recourse must be strictly confined to cases where the damage was caused by those specific circumstances. 35

The Court then examined the law governing the consumption of alcohol, as compared to the use of other psychoactive substances in the context of driving, as well as scientific data underpinning these regulations. Regarding alcohol, the RTA defines 'driving under the influence' as having a blood alcohol concentration of 0.5 g/l or higher (art 81(2) RTA). This is supported by the available scientific data, which indicates that the human faculties involved in driving are materially impaired at that threshold. 36

By contrast, no statutory threshold exists for levels of other psychoactive substances above which a driver is presumed to be under their influence. The threshold initially cited by the defendant applies only to preliminary urine screening tests, which require confirmation through further examinations. Under art 81(5) RTA and its supplementary regulations, the influence of psychoactive substances can only be established by: either a blood test accompanied by a medical statement confirming that the substance detected could affect driving ability; or, when it is not possible to collect sufficient blood from the driver, through a medical examination assessing physical and mental parameters to determine impairment.[13] 37

13 Art 12(2)-(3), and art 13 of the Regulation on the monitoring of driving under the influence of

38 The Court then proceeded to review the current state of medical knowledge in this field, as well as legislative approaches in other jurisdictions. Unlike alcohol, there is no universally accepted threshold for the bloodstream levels of psychoactive substances that reliably indicate impairment. Cannabis-related chemicals, in particular, can remain in the bloodstream well beyond their period of active influence, and their effects on driving vary significantly among individuals, depending on factors such as habitual use. Moreover, unlike alcohol, cannabis compounds can be passively inhaled, potentially leading to positive test results without actual consumption. With all these caveats, there seems to be scientific support to take a THC blood level of 2 ng/mL as a reasonable indicator of impairment on average. This threshold has been adopted in UK law, but Portuguese legislators have not incorporated it into domestic law.

39 Against this background, the Court rejected the interpretation that art 27(c) grants insurers a right of recourse whenever a driver merely tests positive for psychoactive substances. Especially in view of the long afterlife of these substances in the bloodstream, a positive test alone does not conclusively prove actual influence at the time of the accident. Under current legal provisions, such influence must be ascertained by medical or expert reports. The Court further reasoned that a 'zero tolerance' approach – where any trace of a substance would trigger recourse – would introduce moral considerations not supported by law. It would further unjustifiably relieve insurers of part of the insured risk, thereby unbalancing the contract in their favour.

40 The Court thus ruled that. in order to avail themselves of the right of recourse set out in art 27(c) based on the presence of psychotropic substances, insurers must prove that the driver was under the influence of those substances at the time of the accident. This must be established through medical or expert reports, as required by the RTA and its supplementary regulations.

41 Turning back to the case at hand, the Court found that no such medical or expert examination had been conducted on the defendant. Consequently, the insurer had failed to provide the necessary proof to exercise its right of recourse, leading to the rejection of its claim.

42 The court was split on its voting. Of the 29 judges voting on the decision, 10 dissented, most of them sharing the same position.

43 According to this dissenting view, the majority ruling contradicted the wording and legislative history of art 27(c). The previous version of CMLIA explicitly required the driver to be under the influence of alcohol or another substance,

alcohol or psychotropic substances and arts 23 and 25 of the Decree on medical exams for the detection of alcohol or psychotropic substance influence.

and case law had interpreted this to mean that insurers had to prove not only such state of influence, but also that such state had been the cause, or at least one of the concurring causes, of the accident. However, the revised text of art 27(c) CMLIA omits the phrase 'under the influence.' According to the dissenters, this omission signified a legislative intent to abandon the previous requirement, and a rejection of earlier case law.

Furthermore, the dissenting judges argued that art 27(c) should not be interpreted in conjunction with art 81 RTA (which does require the influence of substances upon driving), since the latter governs road traffic rules and imposes administrative and criminal sanctions, but it does not regulate the scope of compulsory insurance coverage. Thus, art 27(c) should be applied literally, meaning that the insurer only needs to prove that the driver caused the accident and tested positive for psychoactive substances other than alcohol. The driver bears the burden of proving that such substances did not influence their driving. 44

c) Commentary

The majority opinion is well-founded and deserves approval. By contrast, the dissenting view supported by the largest opposition relies primarily on formal arguments – the wording of art 27(c) CMLIA and the supposed intentions of its drafters – which appear rather weak. 45

This dissenting position refers to case law developed under the predecessor of art 27(c), which required proof that the driver was under the influence of alcohol or other substances at the time of the accident. Under that framework, insurers had to establish both impairment and a causal link between the impairment and the accident. In the absence of any evidentiary leniency, this could pose a significant burden on the insurer's right of recourse. 46

Given this context, it is plausible that the lawmakers of the current CMLIA deliberately omitted the phrase 'under the influence' from art 27(c) to avoid an interpretation that would once again require proof of causation. In the case of alcohol, this omission is inconsequential because driving with a blood alcohol level above the legal threshold already constitutes driving under the influence under art 81(2) RTA. It is, in itself, an unlawful act. Furthermore, as noted earlier, this definition is supported by scientific evidence, which confirms that driving faculties are materially impaired above this threshold. 47

However, it is quite another matter to assume that lawmakers intended the same principle to apply to all psychoactive substances and that drivers should automatically lose coverage merely for testing positive. As established, the mere presence of a psychoactive substance in the bloodstream does not conclusively 48 indicate impairment – nor does it necessarily prove that the driver even consumed the substance knowingly. Testing positive is not equivalent to a legal violation. Therefore, such an interpretation would systematically deny coverage in cases where there is no evidence that the driver acted unlawfully or was cognitively impaired. Although drivers would, in theory, be allowed to prove they were not under the influence, the burden of proof would shift to them – placing them at risk of being unable to establish their innocence.

49 It is the duty of public authorities to ensure that a driver suspected of substance use is taken to a public health care facility, where either a definitive blood test or an alternative observational examination can be conducted. However, if the authorities fail to fulfil this duty – as appears to have happened in this case – and the driver is unaware of the importance of such tests for protecting their rights, they may be left defenceless. Moreover, logistical issues – such as the lack of properly staffed facilities in remote locations or procedural errors that render the tests invalid – could wrongfully expose the driver to recourse claims from the insurer.

50 There is no clear evidence that lawmakers intended such a rigid and punitive approach, which appears incompatible with the constitutional principle of proportionality. In fact, no legislative documents exist that would allow for a reliable reconstruction of the drafters' intent. When laws are issued by the government, as was the case with CMLIA, they are not accompanied by an official explanatory report, nor are there any publicly available records of legislative discussions. Under these conditions, historical interpretation becomes speculative, and conclusions drawn from it may have little connection to the actual legislative intent.[14]

51 Indeed, the reasoning of the majority is persuasive. From the perspective of the insured party, the insurer's right of recourse functions as an exclusion of coverage. Such exclusions must not be triggered by circumstances that are, in themselves, immaterial to the level of risk or the quality of coverage. Contrary to the primary dissenting argument, art 27(c) CMLIA must be interpreted in conjunction with the provisions of the RTA, which define the legal standard of unlawfulness concerning alcohol and drug use in connection with driving. Drivers should be able to trust that they retain their insurance cover when they comply with the law. A driver with a blood alcohol level below the legal threshold is act-

---

14 The interpretation of the law according to the intention of historical legislators (interpretation according to the genesis of the law) must be based upon proper sources – namely, on the documents involved in the political and drafting process leading up to the enactment of the law, and only exceptionally in other statements made by those involved in the process (*F Reimer*, Juristische Methodenlehre [2nd edn 2020] 172 f; *R Wank*, Juristische Methodenlehre [2020] 293; *B Rüthers/C Fischer/A Birk*, Rechtstheorie und Juristische Methodenlehre [11th edn 2020] 489).

ing within the bounds of the law, despite having consumed alcohol. The same principle applies to a driver who tests positive for a psychoactive substance, since, under the RTA, only further testing can determine whether the driver's faculties were impaired.

An interpretation of the CMLIA that denies coverage to drivers who have not 52 violated the law would be inconsistent and unduly favourable to insurers. If a general contractual clause were to exclude coverage solely on the basis of a positive drug test, such a clause would rightly be deemed contrary to the reasonable expectations of the insured party and would be null and void under the Act on Standard Contract Terms for unfairly shifting the balance of the contract in favour of insurers.

3. Supreme Court of Justice, 17 April 2024 (*Júlio Gomes*) ECLI: PT:STJ:2024:179.19.8T8GRD.C1.S1.A.B1: Work Accident; Safety Measures; *conditio sine qua non*

a) Brief Summary of the Facts

The plaintiff works for the one of the defendants, a construction company. While 53 installing a heavy PVC tube, which he held in place using a belt attached to his hand, the plaintiff fell into the seven-metre-deep pit where the tube was being placed. Since the belt was secured to his hand, he remained suspended by it, and the weight of his body caused the belt to tighten around his hand, compressing it.

The employer acknowledged its duty to compensate the damage under the 54 general rules of the Act on Compensation for Work Accidents and Occupational Diseases (ACWA).[15] These general rules establish a regime of strict liability, granting workers a limited amount of compensation. However, the employer rejected the plaintiff's claim that it had failed to comply with workplace safety regulations and was therefore subject to liability under the fault-based provisions of the ACWA (art 18), which entitle workers and their families to full compensation for the damage incurred.

The plaintiff then brought an action against his employer and its insurer, seek- 55 ing full compensation on the basis of breach of workplace safety rules. The decision does not provide information as to what happened in the lower courts before the case initially reached the Supreme Court, which ultimately ruled in favour of

15 Law no 28/2009 of 4 September 2009.

the plaintiff. The Court held that the employer had indeed violated workplace safety regulations by failing to secure access to the pit or ensure the plaintiff's safety while working at its edge. Moreover, although it could not be proved whether such breach was a *conditio sine qua non* of the damage, causation could still be established, as the type of accident suffered by the plaintiff was a foreseeable consequence of failing to comply with such safety regulations.

56 The defendant employer argued that this ruling contradicted previous case law issued by the Supreme Court, and appealed to the plenum of the civil law sections of the Supreme Court, under the appeal for the uniformisation of case law (arts 688–695 Civil Procedure Code). The plaintiff cited the Supreme Court's decision of 8 May 2012, in case 908/08.5TTBRG.P1.S1, which, in similar circumstances involving a breach of excavation site safety regulations, had denied causation on the grounds that it had not been established that the breach of these rules was a *conditio sin qua non* of the accident.

b) Judgment of the Court

57 The Court agreed that the decisions were indeed contradictory, and thus a uniformising ruling was necessary to clarify whether, in order to establish liability for breach of a safety duty, it was necessary to prove that such breach was a *conditio sine qua non* of the damage.

58 The Court began by ascribing a preventive function to the special regime on liability for fault of the ACWA, which encompasses cases of breaches of safety duties. This conclusion stemmed from the fact that, unlike the general rule on strict liability of the ACWA, the special rule on liability for fault grants the plaintiff full compensation, besides making only the employer, and not its insurer, liable for the damage exceeding the compensation ceiling set out for strict liability (arts 18(1) and 79(3) of the ACWA). The Court then highlighted that, although breaching a safety duty typically increases the risk of harm to workers, it is not necessarily a *conditio sine qua non* for every accident that follows. Workplace accidents involve multiple risk factors, making it particularly difficult to conclude with certainty that the accident would not have occurred if the safety rule had not been breached. The Court illustrated this difficulty with an example: an accident involving explosives might have been caused by insufficient worker training or simply by human error. This uncertainty in proving that a breach of duty was a *conditio sine qua non* of the damage could compromise the preventive function of the special liability for fault regime.

59 Although the Act could, in the Court's view, provide arguments to construe liability for workplace accidents as more pro-victim than the general rules on lia-

bility (notably in that under art 11(1) ACWA, the predisposition of the victim to disease, unless deliberately concealed by the victim, does not exclude the right to full compensation), the Court held that the issue could be resolved through general liability principles. The *conditio sine qua non* criterion is used to establish causation in a naturalistic sense, and has traditionally been applied together with the doctrine of adequate causation, which, in its broad negative sense, holds that causation exists unless the damage could only have resulted from the conduct under exceptional circumstances.

However, according to the Court, the present doctrinal approaches to causation have shifted away from requiring naturalistic causation, which is often difficult for the plaintiff to prove, and have embraced purely normative theories of causation, such as the scope of protection theory, or theories based upon the distinction between spheres of risk or upon the creation or aggravation of unlawful risks. Under any of these normative approaches, the plaintiff does not even need to establish causation in a naturalistic sense, and thus does not need to establish that the breach was a *conditio sine qua non* of the harm. Even if one were to apply the traditional doctrine of adequate causation, it would be sufficient that the plaintiff establishes the breach of duty and the damage; the burden would then shift to the defendant to prove that the damage was caused by an exceptional circumstance. 60

Based on these premises, the Court concluded that the plaintiff did not bear the burden of proving that the absence of measures to prevent him from falling had been a *conditio sine qua non* of the accident, and dismissed the defendant's appeal. Finally, it set as uniform case law that, for the purposes of art 18(1) ACWA, to establish that a breach of safety duty caused a workplace accident and its resulting harm, it is necessary to determine whether, under the specific circumstances of the case, the breach increased the probability of an accident with the particular characteristics of the one that occurred, while it was not necessary to establish that the accident would not have occurred but for the breach. 61

c) Commentary

This case exposes the harsh realities of workplace conditions, marked by a total disregard for worker safety. It is particularly striking that the method used to perform the task – involving the attachment of a heavy object to the worker, standing above a pit – needlessly created a serious risk of accident with potentially grave consequences for the worker's health. One can thus fully understand the Court's concern with the effectiveness of liability rules for workplace accidents and the 62 need to deter unsafe practices. However, the rule it established, and the reasoning underpinning it, are highly controversial.

63 The Court appears to have replaced the traditional *but-for* causation test in cases involving a breach of safety duties with a test requiring only that the breach increased the risk of the accident. It seemingly precludes the tortfeasor from proving that the accident would have occurred even if the appropriate safety measures had been taken.

64 The Court does refer to the heightened importance of prevention in the context of workplace liability, and could have grounded its decision in arguments tailored to that specific context. The relevant ACWA provision, which guarantees full compensation even when the victim has a pre-existing condition, could arguably be interpreted as extending compensation beyond the general causation rules (art 11).[16] However, it should be noted that the fact that the ACWA provides full compensation when an accident is due to the employer's fault does not necessarily imply a deterrent purpose of the provisions of the ACWA. On the contrary, it adheres to the principle of compensating actual harm, without providing any additional entitlements. The Civil Code follows the same general principle of full compensation, which – unsurprisingly – is not in itself indicative of a preventive rationale. Rather, the limitation of compensation through a statutory ceiling constitutes an exception, justified by the exceptional nature of strict liability regimes. Furthermore, the fact that mandatory insurance for strict liability does not extend to fault-based liability has no bearing on the interpretation of fault liability. The latter is not accompanied by mandatory insurance, but that does not imply that it extends beyond compensating actual damage – it simply means such damage is typically borne by the tortfeasor.

65 Yet the Court's reasoning is grounded in the general rules on liability. Now, the dismissal of factual causation seems difficult to reconcile with Civil Code provisions that require the infringement of a right as a condition for compensation (art 483), or that limit the duty to compensate the damage caused (art 563). These provisions demand a substantial – not merely speculative – assessment of causation.[17] The Court's approach also appears inconsistent with the case law of the Civil Law Sections of the Supreme Court, which recently reaffirmed

16 This point does not seem settled in Portuguese scholarship, though. See *JC Brandão Proença*, A conduta do lesado como pressuposto e critério de imputação do dano extracontratual (2007) 196 f; *P Mota Pinto*, Interesse contratual negativo e interesse contratual positivo, I (2008) 696; for a different perspective, *ML Pereira*, Direito da responsabilidade civil, A obrigação de indemnizar (2021) 564.

17 *Pereira* (fn 16) 273–275.

the necessity of establishing a *conditio sine qua non* and even set a high evidentiary threshold for doing so.[18]

Moreover, theories that reject the *but-for* test are far from universally accepted, and it would be inaccurate to claim that legal doctrine is trending toward abandoning factual causation. On the contrary, traditional approaches that combine *conditio sine qua non* with normative causation assessments have gained renewed support in recent scholarship.[19] The theories the Court refers to – such as the 'scope of the norm' theory, the 'sphere of risk' theory, and the theory of 'creation or aggravation of unlawful risks' – form a heterogeneous set, and within each, the doctrinal approaches are nuanced.[20] For instance, the 'scope of the norm' theory is generally not applied in isolation. Rather, it typically serves to qualify or correct outcomes reached under the doctrines of *conditio sine qua non* and adequate causation; other approaches are often combined with the 'creation or aggravation of unlawful risks' theory.[21] 66

It remains to be seen whether the decision will remain confined to the specific context of workplace accidents or whether it will influence broader rulings on liability in general.[22] 67

18 See Supreme Court of Justice, 3 November 2022, Proc no 1479/16.4T8LRA.C2.S1-A, reviewed by *de Oliveira Martins/Pereira*, Portugal, in: E Karner/BC Steininger (eds), European Tort Law 2022 (2023) 501, nos 13–42.

19 See traditionally *J Matos Antunes Varela*, Das obrigações em geral, I (10th edn 2000) 881 ff; *J Sinde Monteiro*, Rudimentos de responsabilidade civil, Revista da Faculdade de Direito da Universidade do Porto (RFDUP) 2005, 379 ff; *A Menezes Cordeiro*, Tratado de Direito civil português, II, Direito das obrigações, III, Gestão de negócios, enriquecimento sem causa, responsabilidade civil (2010) 549 f; more recently *Pinto* (fn 16) 673 ff; *R Soares Pereira*, O nexo de causalidade na responsabilidade delitual (2017) 1259 f; *Pereira* (fn 16) 273–275.

20 On the theory of the spheres of risk, *AM Castanheira Neves de Miranda Barbosa*, Do nexo de causalidade ao nexo de imputação, II (2013) 1063 ff; on theories relying on the creation or aggravation of unlawful risks, *R Mascarenhas Ataíde*, Direito da responsabilidade civil (2023) 292 ff and, for environmental liability, *A Perestrelo de Oliveira*, Causalidade e imputação na responsabilidade civil ambiental (2007) 75.

21 For the first approach, see eg, *Monteiro*, RFDUP 2005, 379, 383; for the latter, *Ataíde* (fn 20) 292 ff.

22 Moreover, in view of the fact that the Judge Rapporteur is a very respected private law scholar who has written many insightful texts on civil liability.

4. Supreme Court of Justice, 27 November 2024 (*Rui Machado e Moura*) ECLI:PT:STJ:2024:28.24.5T8CTB.S1.DE: Accident Insurance; Multiple Insurance; Cumulation

a) Brief Summary of the Facts

68 A worked as a firefighter for the Association of Voluntary Firefighters of the municipality of Z. In 2020, while A and several other firefighters were driving on a mountain road in response to an emergency, the truck they were in – driven by another firefighter – went off the road, overturned, and caught fire. A, who was inside the vehicle, died as a result of the accident.

69 Under Decree-Law no 241/2007 of 21 June, which governs Portuguese firefighters, municipalities are required to take out personal accident insurance upon the lives and to the benefit of firefighters in their service. Accordingly, the municipality had taken out a personal accident insurance contract with insurer X to the benefit of A.

70 A's parents filed a claim with insurer X for the payment of the sums specified in the personal accident insurance contract in the event of death, and were paid such amounts. Additionally, A's parents brought a claim against insurer Y, which provided motor liability insurance cover in regard of the vehicle involved in the accident. The action was partially successful, and A's parents received from insurer Y a part of the amounts they had claimed.

71 Insurer X, the personal accidents insurer, then brought an action against insurer Y, the motor liability insurer, seeking reimbursement of the amounts paid to the insured's parents. Insurer X argued that both insurance policies were indemnity contracts, rather than fixed sums insurance. Specifically, the personal accidents insurance should be considered indemnity insurance, as its wording referred to the payment of compensation, subsidies or expenses arising from personal accidents. It did not function as a long-term savings contract. Since both contracts covered the same risk – the risk of accidents – the rules on multiple insurance applied, meaning that the total costs of the insurance indemnity should be divided between the insurers (arts 180(2) and 133 of the Insurance Contract Act, ICA[23]). Consequently, insurer Y should reimburse insurer X for the part of the compensation it had paid.

72 The first instance court rejected the claim. The plaintiff then appealed directly to the Supreme Court, under the special right of appeal *per saltum* set out in art 678 of the Civil Procedure Code (which requires in particular that the parties

---

23 Decree-Law no 72/2008 of 16 April.

raise only questions of law in their allegations and the value of the cause exceeds the jurisdictional threshold of the Appellate Courts).

b) Judgment of the Court

The Court began by emphasising that the two insurance contracts in question covered different risks: the policy with insurer X covered the risk of a firefighter suffering an accident in the line of duty, whereas the policy with insurer Y covered risks of liability connected with the vehicle involved in the accident. As a result, the rules on multiple insurance did not apply and it was not necessary to delve into them. Moreover, under the ICA, payments received under fixed sums insurance can be cumulated with payments received from both fixed sums and indemnity insurance (art 180(2) ICA). Since the personal accidents insurance contract gave the beneficiary the right to a fixed amount (€ 150,000) in the event of the insured person's death, the Court concluded that it was a fixed sums insurance. 73

Additionally, insurer X did not have a right of subrogation against the liable third party (the firefighter driving the truck) or the insurer covering his liability (insurer Y). Under art 181(1), the payment of insurance benefits does not subrogate the insurer to the rights of the insured person or the beneficiary against a third party responsible for the loss, unless otherwise agreed with regard to indemnity payments made by the insurer. For those purposes, art 181(2) establishes that indemnity payments are necessary payments incurred by the insurer to compensate for the damage suffered (a) and that, in case of doubt, the indemnity nature of the insurer's payment depends on an explicit and clear contractual provision to that effect (b). 74

The Court cited previous case law which had refused the application of these provisions to life insurance taken out as fixed sums insurance, highlighting its function as a savings and investment contract, expressing its approval. Closely following the reasoning of that case law, the Court held that under art 181, there is no right of subrogation in the case of fixed sums insurance, unless the parties agree otherwise. Since no such agreement existed in this case, insurer X had no right to claim reimbursement from insurer Y. The payment of the insured sums was made in fulfilment of its contractual duties rather than in the fulfilment of duties of a third party and thus insurer X had no right to recover from that party. 75

c) Commentary

76 The case is quite straightforward. The decision is nonetheless important because it confirms a body of case law that establishes fundamentally correct principles regarding personal insurance.

77 Insurance contracts may be classified as either indemnity insurance or fixed sums insurance, depending on whether the insurance payout corresponds to the damage caused by the insured event or whether the payout is determined by predefined criteria set out in the contract, independent of the damage incurred. Traditionally, only personal insurance can be taken out as fixed sums insurance.[24] The distinction is relevant since there are a number of limitations that apply exclusively to indemnity insurance, such as the limitation of insurance payments to the damage caused (art 128 ICA), the prohibition of receiving cumulative payments from different insurers in regard of the same risk (art 133 ICA) and the attribution of a right of subrogation against a liable third party (art 136 ICA). These provisions apply, albeit with some adaptations, to personal insurance when structured as indemnity insurance (arts 180(2) and 181(2) ICA). They do not apply – contrary to the Court's decision – to fixed sums insurance; nor can the parties opt to apply them in that context. The parties may only agree to exclude cumulative payments from multiple insurers for the same risk (see arts 180(2) and 181(1) ICA).

78 Although in some cases the qualification of a contract as indemnity or fixed sums insurance is straightforward (eg, unit-linked life insurance is unequivocally an insurance of fixed sums, while health care expenses insurance is unequivocally indemnity insurance), in other cases there may be doubts. This is particularly true for accidents insurance, where payouts vary based on the occurrence of death or disability, and even according to different degrees of disability. Nonetheless, even in these cases, the contract functions as a mechanism to ensure access to an amount of savings, upon the occurrence of an event that results in the loss of saving capacity. Insured parties do not expect that the compensation or savings amounts they receive or have access to in the case of an accident may be jeopardised by their personal accidents insurance. In fact, many insured individuals would be unwilling to pay premiums – or require their employer to do so – if this were the case.

79 Personal insurance contracts should thus be presumed to be fixed sums insurance, unless they clearly state otherwise.[25] This principle is now explicitly set out

24 Parametric insurance has, however, recently brought fixed sums insurance to the realm of non-personal insurance.

25 For this conclusion and the foregoing reasoning, see *MI Oliveira Martins*, Contrato de seguro e conduta dos sujeitos ligados ao risco (2018) 289–294.

in art 181(2-b) ICA, quoted above, which was introduced in 2015 to protect insured parties from the unexpected application of indemnity insurance rules on subrogation.

The present decision should therefore be welcomed, as it reinforces these concerns and underscores the importance of construing personal insurance as *prima facie* fixed sums insurance. Nonetheless, for the sake of clarity, two remarks should be added. 80

First, as is evident from the wording of art 181, subrogation is not permitted in fixed sums insurance. Only indemnity personal insurance contracts may include rights of subrogation. Once the Court classified the personal accidents contract as a fixed sums insurance, subrogation was out of the question. The fact that the Court suggests otherwise appears to result from relying on the pre-2015 version of art 181 – which may have been an error induced by the case law quoted by the decision. 81

Second, the Court emphasises that there was no subrogation in this case because the insurer paid the insured sums in fulfilment of its contractual duties, rather than in the fulfilment of duties of a third party. This reasoning seems to imply that subrogation would only arise in cases where the insurer discharged a third party's duty. 82

Such a conclusion would be incorrect, as an insurer's duty to pay upon the occurrence of an insured event arises directly from the insurance contract – it is an obligation of the insurer itself.[26] By making this statement, the Court may have intended to clarify that the general provisions of the Civil Code on subrogation (arts 589 to 594) – which indeed govern cases where a party fulfils a debtor's obligation to a creditor and is therefore subrogated into the creditor's rights – do not apply to the case. It seems, however, to have been more confusing than illuminating. 83

---

26 *JM Vieira Gomes*, Da sub-rogação legal do segurador à luz da nova lei do contrato de seguro (Decreto-Lei n.º 72/2008, de 16 de Abril), in: P Otero/F Araújo/J Taborda da Gama (eds), Estudos em memória do Prof. Doutor J. L. Saldanha Sanchez, II (2011) 449–484, 450.

5. Supreme Court of Justice, 10 April 2024 *(Jorge Arcanjo)* ECLI:PT:STJ:2024:404.14.1T8BJA.E1.S1.EB: Biological Damage; Pecuniary Loss; Non-Pecuniary Loss; Indirect Damage; Supremacy of EU Law; Interpretation of Directive 2009/103/EC; Preliminary Reference to CJEU; Acte Clair Doctrine

a) Brief Summary of the Facts

84 In this case, the bereaved parents of a deceased daughter, who died almost instantly from injuries sustained in a car accident, sought compensation from the insurance company Lusitânia S.A. for both pecuniary and non-pecuniary loss. The Supreme Court of Justice deliberated on several issues, including the extent and calculation of damages and the applicability of national and EU law.

85 The plaintiffs' daughter died on 17 August 2013, in a traffic accident involving two vehicles. She was a passenger in one of the vehicles involved in the collision. They requested compensation for patrimonial and non-patrimonial loss amounting to € 253,481; € 20,000 for the pain and suffering of their daughter between the accident and death; € 85,000 for the loss of the right to life; € 5,131 for funeral expenses; € 3,450 for medical expenses; € 45,000 for each of the plaintiffs for non-pecuniary loss incurred as a consequence of their daughter's death, and € 25,000 for each of the plaintiffs for biological damage and loss of earning capacity.

86 While the insurance company admitted exclusive responsibility for the accident, it contested the extent of the damages claimed by the plaintiffs, rejecting the claims for pain and suffering of the daughter between the accident and death, as well as any compensation for the plaintiffs' biological damage and loss of earning capacity. The insurance company made an offer of € 125,000 for a reasonable settlement agreement, which was rejected by the plaintiffs.

b) Judgment of the Court

87 At first instance, the court awarded the plaintiffs € 185,131; € 120,000 for the loss of their daughter's right to life; € 30,000 to each of the plaintiffs for non-pecuniary loss suffered because of their bereavement; and € 5,131 for funeral expenses. The court did not consider proven that between the moment of the accident and her death, the plaintiffs' daughter was aware of her impending death or suf-

fered physical suffering and pain from being violently crushed because of the impact of the collision.

The court of first instance had rejected the plaintiffs' claim in this respect, rejecting the application to the case of the doctrine contained in the Case Law Uniformisation Decision of the Supreme Court of Justice No 6/2014 on whether or not indirect, 'reflex' non-pecuniary loss of a third party, in the event of the loss of life of the injured party in a traffic accident can be compensated, arguing that the case judged in that decision is significantly different from the situation discussed in these proceedings, as regards the material damage suffered by each of the plaintiffs by the alleged loss of earning capacity caused by the death of their daughter.[27] 88

The court held that the emotional effects felt by the plaintiffs because of the death of their daughter are included in the compensation for moral damage already awarded. As for the alleged pecuniary injury suffered by the plaintiffs, it was stated that the rules that attribute the possibility of awarding compensation to a person other than the injured party (arts 495 and 496 CC) are of an exceptional nature. The court affirmed that said rules do not permit awarding the compensation sought by the plaintiffs. The court considered that it can be affirmed, without the need for thorough evidence, that such an event irremediably changes the lives of those who experience such great suffering. However, from the point of view of the established law, the court held that the compensation sought by the plaintiffs can only be awarded to the (direct) victim of an accident. 89

Both plaintiffs and defendants appealed this decision to the Appellate Court of Évora, which dismissed the appeal and confirmed the first instance decision, holding that art 495 CC should be interpreted strictly. Article 495 CC only provides for the compensation of pure economic loss as regards the expenses incurred to aid the injured person, and to cover funeral expenses and income loss of those who were entitled to a maintenance allowance.[28] 90

The plaintiffs appealed to the Supreme Court of Justice, claiming, besides the awards already made for non-pecuniary loss, € 25,000 each as compensation for pecuniary loss due to biological damage and loss of earning capacity caused by their extreme suffering because of the loss of their only daughter. This is one of the key issues that was analysed in this decision. 91

---

27 Supreme Court of Justice, Acórdão de Uniformização de Jurisprudência no 6/2014, of 22 May (*João Bernardo*), ECLI:PT:STJ:2014:6430.07.0TBBRG.S1.1C held that: 'Art 483 (1) and 496 (1) CC must be interpreted as covering particularly serious non-pecuniary loss suffered by the spouse of a surviving victim who is affected in a particularly serious way'.

28 *M Santos Silva*, The Draft Common Frame of Reference as a Toolbox for Domestic Courts: A Solution to the Pure Economic Loss Problem from a Comparative Perspective (2017) 150–160.

92 The Supreme Court of Justice partially ruled, unanimously, in favour of the plaintiffs, overruling the previous decisions, increasing the compensation award concerning non-pecuniary damages to € 50,000 to each of the plaintiffs, due to the lasting psychological and emotional distress suffered because of the bereavement. The Court considered that the evolving concept of 'moral damage' (avoiding the concept of 'biological damage', as sought by the plaintiffs) encompassed broader impacts on an individual's psychosomatic structure and 'life project' and underscored the importance of full compensation for non-pecuniary damage. Furthermore, the Court also decided on the costs to be paid by each party (90 % by the defendant, 10 % by the plaintiffs).

93 The Court held that the Civil Code does not explicitly contain any provision specifying the circle of persons entitled to compensation for damage resulting from an accident in the field of tort liability. In principle, the right to compensation belongs only to the person or persons holding the legally protected right or interest: the injured parties. While indirect damage should also be considered for compensation, it does not seem, in terms of positive law, that in the event of a person's death, the law grants any third party a *prima facie* right to compensation, under art 483 (1) CC.

94 The Court also reaffirmed that art 495 CC is an exceptional provision: only in the cases provided therein does the law award compensation for indirect patrimonial damage caused to third parties. As such, reflex damage, indirectly caused to third parties outside the provision, does not give rise to compensation.

95 The appeal to the Supreme Court of Justice also raised the question of whether Directive 2009/103[29] provides for compensation of indirect damage suffered by third parties due to the death of an individual unless specified by national law. Considering that the CJEU has consistently upheld the interpretation that it does not, leaving it to the Member States to legislate on the substantive legal regime applicable to motor vehicle liability,[30] the Supreme Court of Justice declined to

29 Directive 2009/103/EC of the European Parliament and of the Council of 16 September 2009 relating to insurance against civil liability in respect of the use of motor vehicles, and the enforcement of the obligation to insure against such liability (Text with EEA relevance) [2009] Official Journal of the European Union (OJ) L 263/11.

30 CJEU 15.12.2022, C-577/21, *HUK-COBURG-Allgemeine Versicherung*, ECLI:EU:C:2022:992; CJEU 10.6.2021, C-923/19, *Van Ameyde España SA v GES*, ECLI:EU:C:2021:475. The obligation of coverage by insurance for damage caused to third parties by motor vehicles is defined and guaranteed by EU secondary law, while the extent of compensation for this damage under the civil liability of the insured is regulated, essentially, by the national law of the Member States.

make a Preliminary Reference to the CJEU pursuant to art 267 of the Treaty on the Functioning of the European Union (TFEU) under the *Acte Clair* doctrine.[31]

c) Commentary

This decision by the Supreme Court of Justice highlights the difficulties related to the calculation of damages awards by the courts, especially when non-pecuniary damage and pure economic loss are concerned. 96

In this case, the Court accepted the strict interpretation of art 495 rendered by the Appellate Court as regards the compensation to third parties in the case of death or personal injury (pure economic loss), restricting the scope of application to the expenses incurred to aid the injured person, to cover funeral expenses and income loss of those who were entitled to a maintenance allowance, considering that this provision is of an exceptional nature. 97

The Court also analysed the implications of the extreme distress and post-traumatic stress disorder suffered by the plaintiffs due to their bereavement under the lens of the concept of 'biological damage', a hybrid concept that relates to the psycho-somatic and functional decrease of the injured person, with a recognisable impact on the personal and professional life of the aggrieved. Biological damage is compensated independently, according to an equitable assessment by the court, irrespective of whether classified as pecuniary damage or non-pecuniary damage.[32] While the Court did not recognise those implications as biological damage or pure economic loss, it increased the compensation awards to the plaintiffs for the non-pecuniary damage they suffered, achieving an identical compensation level as that sought by the plaintiffs. 98

Biological damage is a relatively new concept.[33] It first appeared in art 3 (b) Ordinance no 377/2008 of 26 May as a category of personal injury, where it is defined as damage emerging from an offence to physical or mental health, which can result, or not, in a loss of earning capacity.[34] The adaptation of case law to 99

31 ECJ 6.10.1982, C-283/81, *Srl CILFIT and Lanificio di Gavardo SpA v Ministry of Health*, ECLI:EU:C:1982:335.

32 Supreme Court of Justice, 27 November 2024 (*Maria de Deus Correia*) ECLI:PT:STJ:2024:9774.21.4T8PRT.P1.S1.6D.

33 *MI Oliveira Martins/J Pinto Monteiro/A Dias Pereira*, Portugal, in: E Karner/BC Steininger (eds), European Tort Law 2018 (2019) 501, no 75.

34 Portaria no 377/2008 de 26 de Maio. This ordinance regulates the criteria and reference values for reasonable settlement agreements, complementing Decree-Law 83/2006 of 3 May and Decree-

this concept, which is imported from Italian law, has been gradual.[35] The courts, in some cases, have not recognised the autonomy of biological damage and have not deviated from the traditional dicothomy between pecuniary and non-pecuniary damage,[36] in others have considered it to exclusively cover either non-pecuniary damage[37] or pecuniary damage.[38] More recent case law tends to consider biological damage as encompassing both non-pecunary loss and future pecuniary loss.[39]

100 Biological damage has a significant potential to address damage that straddles the razor-thin borderline between pecuniary and non-pecuniary damage: loss of self-esteem, life relationship damage, aesthetic damage, psychic damage, sexual damage, and labour capacity damage, loss of family or affective skills, loss of procreative capacity, loss of ability to engage in sports or recreational activities, loss of enjoyment of youth, loss of the possibility to pursue certain studies, loss of life expectancy, etc. However, a clarification of the legal framework, in particular as regards the autonomy of this category vis-à-vis pecuniary and non-pecuniary damage would be desirable to prevent legal uncertainty and differences in adjudication.[40] There is a growing trend in the adoption of this doctrine: in 2024, there were 31 cases decided by the Supreme Court of Justice where biological damage was one of the legal matters to decide.[41]

Law no 291/2007 of 21 August, which implemented Directive no 2005/14/CE of the European Parliament and the Council.

35 *MG Trigo*, Adopção do Conceito de Dano Biológico pelo Direito Português, Revista da Ordem dos Advogados 72 I (2012) 163.

36 Supreme Court of Justice, 24 September 2009 (*Maria dos Prazeres Pizarro Beleza*) ECLI:PT:STJ:2009:09B0037.6C.

37 Supreme Court of Justice, 20 January 2010 (*Isabel Pais Martins*), ECLI:PT:STJ:2010:203.99.9TBVRL.P1.S1.BC.

38 Supreme Court of Justice, 27 October 2009 (*Sebastião Póvoas*), ECLI:PT:STJ:2009:560.09.0YFLSB.2 A.

39 Supreme Court of Justice, 27 November 2024 (fn 32).

40 *Trigo*, Revista da Ordem dos Advogados 72 I (2012) 177.

41 Up from an average of 21.6 (2019–2023). Until 2016, the number of cases was in the one digit range: Supreme Court of Justice case law database <juris.stj.pt>.

C. Literature

1. *Man Teng Iong*, Responsabilidade Civil na Medicina Tradicional Chinesa: Análise na Perspetiva do Ordenamento Jurídico Português [Medical liability in Traditional Chinese Medicine: Analysis from the perspective of the Portuguese legal system] (Almedina 2024)

This monography by Man Teng Iong, Professor at the University of Macau, China, analyses the issues as regards medical liability related to Traditional Chinese Medicine (hereinafter abbreviated as 'TCM') from the perspective of the Portuguese legal system. This is a highly topical issue, as there is a growing interest from patients and health care stakeholders in complementary and alternative forms of medical treatment (hereinafter abbreviated as 'CAM'), such as TCM, in Portugal and Europe. The TCM market was valued at over € 350 billion worldwide, with the European share of the market approaching 15 %.[42] 101

The analysis carried out departs from the unique vantage point allowed by the similarity between the legal systems of the author's native Macau and the Portuguese legal system and the cultural and economic importance of TCM in Macau.[43] This allows the author to draw a parallel and establish a concise framework for medical liability related to TCM and non-conventional therapeutic techniques in Portuguese law. 102

The author adroitly depicts the state of the art of Portuguese medical liability law and its topical questions (nature of liability, allocation of liability, loss of a 103

42 *G Litscher*, The Global Economics of Acupuncture and Traditional Chinese Medicine – A Strategic and Financial Perspective, MDPI Sci, 7:4 (2025), doi:10.3390/sci7010004.

43 Macau is currently a Special Administrative Region of the People's Republic of China. Its specific constitutional status (identical to the one enjoyed by neighbouring Hong Kong) grants it a wide autonomy and limited personality in international law. It was administered by Portugal until the handover to China in 1999 and was significantly influenced by Portuguese law and administrative practice: *P Cardinal*, The Role and Influence of Portuguese Law in the Macau SAR of People's Republic of China: Issues and Perspectives in: P Duarte/A Tavares/R Albuquerque (eds), The Role and Influence of Portuguese Law in the Macau SAR of People's Republic of China: Issues and Perspectives (2023) 73; *R Cascão*, Shifts in Medical Liability in the Macau SAR, The Chinese Journal of Comparative Law, vol 1 (2025), doi:10.1093/cjcl/cxaf001.

chance, informed consent) and takes a position on some of the debated or unsettled dogmatic problems.[44]

104 The author advances to analyse the specific liability questions that can be raised in relation to TCM treatment in the Portuguese legal system: defining the *leges artis* of TCM, integrative medicine, informed consent in TCM, living wills and advanced directives in TCM, as well as diagnosis and therapeutic errors in TCM.

105 Man Teng Iong's conclusions provide a concise and thorough framework that will be very useful to judges, lawyers and stakeholders in the health care sector in the adjudication of TCM/CAM liability cases in the future and in the adoption of public policies in this area.

2. *Anabela Gonçalves/Bruna de Sousa/Diana Coutinho*, Direito Médico: Responsabilidade Civil Médica, Reprodução Humana Assistida [Medical law: Medical liability, assisted human reproduction] (Gestlegal 2024)

106 This book consists of two parts: the first on medical liability, the second on assisted human reproduction. This review will focus on the first part of the book.

107 The authors thoroughly describe the state of the art of Portuguese literature and case law on medical liability, judiciously analysing the most important issues and debated topics in this field: grounds for liability, strict liability, State liability for health care provided in public facilities, the issues raised by contractual liability, and the convoluted debate around Demogue's infamous distinction between obligations of means and obligations of result (and what that distinction actually means – if anything at all – in Portuguese law).

108 After examining the general aspects of medical liability in Portugal, the authors delve into a thorough analysis of three specific challenging issues in contemporary medical liability: the theory of loss of a chance (*perte de chance*) and its

44 For instance, regarding the disputed issue of whether contractual and non-contractual overlap (*cumul*), the dominant stream of opinion considers that both sources of liability overlap (see fn 3). In pp 86–91, the author explains in detail the several different streams of opinion in Portuguese literature and case law, making a compelling case to demonstrate that the most adequate interpretation is that contractual and non-contractual liability do not, as such, overlap (*non-cumul*). A comparative analysis of this topic can be found in *R De Graaf*, Concurrent Claims in Contract and Tort: A Comparative Perspective, European Review of Private Law 25(4) (2017) 701–726, doi:10.54648/erpl2017046.

admissibility in Portuguese tort law, liability related to aesthetic surgery, and liability for lack of, or insufficient, informed consent.

This book is an innovative and welcome addition to Portuguese literature on medical liability and a very useful *vade mecum* for lawyers, judges, and scholars dealing with medical and tort law. 109

3. *Jorge Sinde Monteiro*, Acidentes de Viação – Adaptação do Código Civil à Legislação e Jurisprudência da União Europeia [Road accidents – Adaptation of the Civil Code to European Union legislation and case law] (Almedina 2024)

This book represents the conclusion of several studies by the author on the link between compulsory civil liability insurance, as defined by European harmonisation directives, and its application by the Court of Justice. Some decisions by the Court of Justice of the EU regarding preliminary questions brought by Portuguese courts have raised the question of whether there has not been a reduction in the protection, particularly of non-motorised road traffic participants. Subsequent decisions have shown that this is not the case. The need to interpret the provisions of the Portuguese Civil Code in a way that respects not only the legislation but also consolidated European case law has been confirmed. 110

The book debates whether driving a vehicle could be considered a dangerous activity, a theory that was denied by Decision 1/80 of 1980. Secondly it provides a more humanistic interpretation of art 504 concerning the fault of the victim, especially when they are a minor. The book analyses in detail the adaptation of the Portuguese Civil Code to the case law of the European Union, notably the ECJ cases *Ferreira Santos*[45], *Ambrósio Lavrador*[46] and *Marques de Almeida*[47]. Prof Sinde Monteiro, in the course of his 50-year academic career, has always supported legislation that protects the victims of the risky activity of road traffic. Monteiro has had a great influence on the evolution of Portuguese case law and legislation in this extremely important area of tort law. 111

45 CJEU 17.3.2011, C-484/09, *Manuel Carvalho Ferreira Santos v Companhia Europeia de Seguros SA*, ECLI:EU:C:2011:158.

46 CJEU 9.6.2011, C-409/09, *Ambrósio Lavrador and Olival Ferreira Bonifácio*, ECLI:EU:C:2011:371.

47 CJEU 23.12.2012, C-300/10, *Vítor Hugo Marques de Almeida v Companhia de Seguros Fidelidade-Mundial SA*, ECLI:EU:C:2012:656.

Lucian Bojin and Sergiu Căileanu

XXIV. Romania

A. Legislation

1. Law no 320/2024 approving the Emergency Ordinance of the Government no 170/2020 concerning the Actions for Damages for Infringements of the Competition Law Provisions

This is a Law enacted in order to implement the provisions of Directive 2014/104/ 1
EU of the European Parliament and of the Council of 26 November 2014 on certain rules governing actions for damages under national law for infringements of the competition law provisions of the Member States and of the European Union.[1] The domestic legal instrument was approved with quite a delay, due to a series of circumstances, as explained hereinafter. The first instrument of implementation was Emergency Ordinance no 39/2017, but the law of approval was struck down as unconstitutional by the Constitutional Court in 2020. A new Emergency Ordinance was promptly adopted in order not to leave the field unregulated. The law of approval was issued only in 2024.

The Law, essentially, reproduces the content of the Directive, which concerns 2
the rules and procedures to be followed for compensation of damage caused by infringements of competition law. It refers to infringements of both domestic law (Law no 21/1996 on competition) and EU law (arts 101 and 102 of the Treaty on the Functioning of the European Union). Most of the provisions are related to aspects of civil procedure, but there are also specific rules on substantive law. One of the interesting rules, derogatory from the default legal regime, is that concerning the limitation period which, according to the Directive, should be at least five years. This period was also recognised in the Romanian implementing law (art 10). By comparison, the general length of the limitation period in Romanian law is three years (art 2517 of the Civil Code). Another rule which differs from the default legal regime of the limitation period is that concerning its com-

1 Directive 2014/104/EU of the European Parliament and of the Council of 26 November 2014 on certain rules governing actions for damages under national law for infringements of the competition law provisions of the Member States and of the European Union [2014] Official Journal (OJ) L 349/1.

https://doi.org/10.1515/9783111389271-025

mencement. According to the Directive (and to the Romanian implementing law) the limitation period will not start to run before the infringement of competition law has ceased. According to the general Romanian legal regime of limitation periods for tort liability, their commencement is related to knowledge of the existence of damage, rather than being related to the cessation of the wrongful act.

B. Cases

1. Constitutional Court of Romania, Decision no 324 of 9 July 2024:[2] Damage by Ricochet; Injury to Physical Integrity or Health of the Immediate Victim; Non-Pecuniary Loss

a) Brief Summary of the Facts

3 The judgment discussed here was issued in a procedure of plea of unconstitutionality in front of the Constitutional Court of Romania. According to art 146 (d) of the Romanian Constitution, the Constitutional Court is competent to decide on pleas of unconstitutionality of laws, which are raised in front of ordinary courts or arbitral tribunals by the parties to the dispute. This judgment decided upon the constitutionality of art 1391 (1) of the Civil Code, based on a plea raised before the Bucharest Court of Appeal. Article 1391 is the rule in the Romanian Civil Code referring to non-pecuniary loss and is included in the section of the Civil Code devoted to reparation of damage (Book VI On Obligations, Title II. The Sources of the Obligations, Chapter IV. Civil Liability, sec 6. Reparation of Damage in Tort Law). Its para (1) reads as follows: 'In cases of the violation of physical integrity or health, compensation may also be granted for diminished opportunities for a family life or social life'. The main practical problem raised in relation to this provision was that it was interpreted (including by the High Court of Cassation and Justice) as prohibiting the compensation of ricochet damage suffered by indirect victims.

2 Published in Monitorul Oficial no 1000 of 7 October 2024, online at <https://www.ccr.ro/wp-content/uploads/2024/10/Decizie_342_2024.pdf>.

b) Judgment of the Court

The Constitutional Court declared the unconstitutionality of the provision in art 1391 (1) of the Civil Code 'to the extent it limits the possibility of indirect victims to obtain compensation for diminished opportunities for a family or social life as a result of the harm to physical integrity or health of the immediate victim'. 4

The Constitutional Court started by acknowledging that previously, and as late as 2022,[3] it rejected other pleas of unconstitutionality raised in relation to the same provision. However, the Court announced that it follows the 'living law doctrine', as the only jurisdictional authority that may provide an 'evolutive interpretation' of the Constitution, therefore it does not exclude overturning its previous judgments. In this case, ultimately, it did precisely that. 5

The Constitutional Court recalled that art 1391 (1) was authoritatively interpreted by the High Court of Cassation and Justice in a preliminary ruling procedure[4] in the latter's Decision no 12/2016 on the interpretation of the provisions of art 1391 para (1) of the Civil Code.[5] According to the High Court's mandatory interpretation, only the immediate victim of a wrongful act who has suffered damage is entitled to compensation for the limitations of family and social life. Such compensation is available for the relatives or other persons close to the direct victim, ie, for the victims by ricochet, only in the case of the victim's death (as expressly stipulated in art 1391 para (2) of the Civil Code) and not if the victim remains alive, while suffering injuries, regardless of how serious they are. The High Court's interpretation was based on comparing the wording of the provisions of paras (1) and (2) of art 1391. The first paragraph, concerning compensation for non-pecuniary loss due to harm to physical integrity or health, contains no specific provisions on the persons entitled to compensation. In contrast, the second paragraph, concerning compensation for non-pecuniary loss due to the death of the victim, contains a list of persons entitled to compensation. The High Court concluded that this difference of wording means that, in the case of non-pecuniary loss due to harm to physical integrity or health, only the immediate (direct) victim is entitled to compensation. 6

The Constitutional Court then presented the various approaches to the issue of non-pecuniary loss and damage by ricochet adopted over the history of modern 7

---

3 Decision no 229 of 28 April 2022, published in Monitorul Oficial no 762 of 29 July 2022.

4 The 'preliminary ruling procedure' is a procedure in Romanian civil procedure law, the purpose of which is to provide interpretations of ambiguous legal provisions, interpretations that become mandatory for all courts.

5 *C Alunaru/L Bojin*, Romania, in: E Karner/BC Steininger (eds), European Tort Law (ETL) 2018 (2019) 533, nos 35–39.

Romanian law, starting with the Old Civil Code of 1864. It also conducted a comparative analysis of the approaches in various legal systems, concluding that some of them are more restrictive while others are more liberal with regard to awarding moral damages by ricochet, but the principle is recognised by almost all of them.

8 The Constitutional Court started its own legal reasoning by acknowledging that Romanian private law establishes the principle of full reparation of damage. This principle is not absolute, but its limitations should be expressly provided by law.

9 Then, the Court noted that the wording of art 1391 (1) is, indeed, imprecise and, for that reason, open to two possible interpretations: the narrow one, given already by the High Court of Cassation and Justice in its Decision 12/2016 and which would limit the moral damages for affecting the social and family life to the immediate victim of the wrongfulness; and a broader one, which would allow, on a case by case basis, awarding compensation for non-pecuniary loss also to indirect victims.

10 The Constitutional Court was of the opinion that the interpretation provided by the High Court was unnecessarily restrictive. The Constitutional Court offered some hypothetical examples in which the indirect victims did indeed suffer harm related to their social and family life and concluded that there is no imperative reason for which such harm should not be compensated. The Constitutional Court reminded that the right to psychological integrity of the person is protected by art 22 of the Romanian Constitution, while art 26 of the same instrument protects the right to private and family life. Both rights require from the public authorities not only negative duties, but also positive duties.

11 According to the Constitutional Court, art 1391 (1) of the Civil Code, as was interpreted by the High Court of Cassation and Justice, introduces a discriminatory treatment of immediate victims and indirect victims of wrongful acts which do not cause death, because the right to compensation for injuries to family life is recognised only to the former, and not to the latter. Such different treatment is not provided or authorised by the Constitution, nor is it justified by an 'objective criterion'. Consequently, the Constitutional Court declared art 1391 (1) of the Civil Code to be unconstitutional 'to the extent it limits the possibility of indirect victims to obtain compensation for diminished opportunities for a family or social life as a result of the harm to physical integrity or health of the immediate victim'.

c) Commentary

The topic of 'damage by ricochet' was among the most discussed in the Romanian tort law literature and case law over the last decade. This is proven also by our reports from previous years, where we referred various times to cases concerning damage by ricochet.[6] These many discussions were, at least in part, due to the practical (and moral) difficulties when dealing with cases in which the indirect victims had clear moral grounds for claiming compensation, but no plain legal text to obtain it in court. The restrictive interpretation provided by the High Court of Cassation and Justice in 2016 only fed the debates, as its restrictive interpretation generated some criticism. From this perspective, the Constitutional Court's intervention on the topic with a more 'protection of rights-oriented' approach is more than laudable. 12

One point that deserves to be emphasised from the outset is the determination with which the Constitutional Court showed its readiness to overturn its previous judgments on this topic. The explicit reliance on the 'living law doctrine', as the Court named it, is something that we see rather rarely in the case law of the constitutional jurisdiction. The Court mentioned a handful of previous judgments in which it relied on this doctrine, that it itself formulated in a case from 2011.[7] According to this doctrine, 'the law is alive', including constitutional law, therefore one of the tasks of the Constitutional Court is to 'establish new (constitutional) requirements for law-making bodies or to adapt the existing constitutional requirements' (para 13 of the Decision commented). The doctrine seems to be a Romanian version of the 'living instrument doctrine' of the European Court of Human Rights (ECtHR). 13

Another interesting and rather novel argument in the reasoning of the Constitutional Court is that related to the idea that between the two possible interpretations of the rule in art 1391 (1) of the Civil Code, the High Court should have chosen the broader one and not the narrower one (para 39 of the Decision). Without naming it so, the argument greatly resembles the principle of *effet utile* applied in European Union law to provide the broadest effect possible to EU law. The Constitutional Court states that when interpreting rules that protect constitutional rights, the criterion of the greatest protection to the right should be a fully-fledged rule of interpretation, although there is no such specific explicit rule in Romanian law. 14

6 *L Bojin/S Căileanu*, Romania, in: E Karner/BC Steininger (eds), European Tort Law (ETL) 2022 (2023) 523, nos 23–47; *C Alunaru/L Bojin/S Căileanu*, Romania, in: E Karner/BC Steininger (eds), European Tort Law (ETL) 2021 (2022) 520, no 27.

7 Decision no 766 of 15 June 2011, published in Monitorul Oficial no 549 of 3 August 2011.

15 Another beneficial effect of the intervention of the Constitutional Court in a field of tort law, considered as one of the fields of classical private law, is underlining the firm link between the classical rights in private law (the so-called 'subjective rights' in the French-inspired Romanian legal theory) and the constitutional human rights. Ordinary Romanian courts faced some practical difficulties when dealing with issues where tort law intersects with human rights.[8] Ordinary Romanian courts have never been at ease with balancing opposing rights or the proportionality test and, thus, tended to apply the rules of tort law according to the classic doctrines in Romanian private law and to avoid, as much as possible, approaches to the same issues from the standpoint of human rights. It might be that the commented judgment will contribute to overcome this (probably inertial) approach of the ordinary courts.

16 Yet another good impulse that might be given by the judgment of the Constitutional Court to the ordinary courts concerns the methods of interpretation used by the latter. Among the main methods of interpretation recognised by Romanian doctrine (textual, teleological, systematic), the ordinary courts traditionally preferred the textual interpretation, deemed as more predictable and more deferential to the legislature. Such an approach is certainly not without its own merits when referring to ordinary courts. But the High Court of Cassation and Justice, in particular when rendering preliminary rulings, is not an ordinary court. Its function in the procedure of preliminary ruling is much closer to that of the Constitutional Court than to ordinary courts. In the preliminary ruling procedure, the High Court has a function of interpretive authority with regard to laws, which is similar to the one held by the Constitutional Court with regard to the Constitution. Both the judgments of the Constitutional Court and the preliminary rulings of the High Court are mandatory for the entire judiciary. It is, therefore, adequate for the High Court, when deciding in a preliminary ruling procedure, to act more boldly, especially when the issues at stake also touch upon questions relevant for constitutional and human rights law.

17 Finally, a more technical remark. The decisive argument for the Constitutional Court to declare the unconstitutionality of art 1391 (1) of the Civil Code was based on the unjustifiable difference between legal treatment in two relatively similar situations. In other words, a type of discrimination. The Constitutional Court noted that the relatives of the immediate victims were entitled to compensation of non-pecuniary loss in the case of the death of the immediate victims, while the same relatives had no entitlement if the immediate victim survived. The High Court, in its Decision 12/2016, noted this discrepancy, but did not treat it

8 See also below nos 18–27.

as discrimination. It simply remarked that this seemed to have been the 'will of the lawmakers'. Differences in treatment, discrepancy or discrimination might seem close concepts, but only the last offers the instruments for a thorough legal scrutiny. When the Constitutional Court noted the difference in legal treatment, it almost automatically triggered the discussion on the need to objectively justify the difference of treatment. And this proved to be the decisive argument for the judgment, although the Court did not make economy of other arguments, closer to the classical discussions in private law.

2. High Court of Cassation and Justice, Civil Section I, Decision no 380 of 13 February 2024: Tort Liability for Violation of Fundamental Rights; Balancing of Rights[9]

a) Brief Summary of the Facts

In 2020, claimant A filed a lawsuit against defendant B, requesting Bucharest Tri- 18
bunal order B to pay compensation of RON 220,000 (approx € 44,000) for damage caused as a result of an infringement of the claimant's right to dignity and reputation. The case concerned a relatively well-known situation of a public park in Bucharest, which was built on land that was confiscated after 1948 and returned in the mid-2000s to the heir of the original owner, claimant A. After having the property returned, disputes between A and the municipality of Sector 3 in Bucharest arose concerning the status of the land, the future of the park, etc. Some of the city's council officials took public positions (on TV, on social media and in public meetings) calling for keeping the park and adopting zoning regulations to this effect. The claimant filed a series of lawsuits, based on tort liability, against these officials. The case discussed here is one of the several claims brought by A.

The claimant alleged that the contentious stances taken by B, whom she ac- 19
cused of lying, affected her reputation. She also argued that such stances do not represent a lawful exercise of the freedom of expression.

Bucharest Tribunal, by its Civil Sentence no 654 of 23 April 2021 denied the 20
request of A. A's appeal was also denied by the Bucharest Court of Appeal, in its Decision no 106 A of 27 January 2023. Claimant A submitted a request for review of the judgment of the Court of Appeal in front of the High Court of Cassation and Justice.

9 Online at: <https://www.scj.ro/1093/Detalii-jurisprudenta?customQuery%5B0%5D.Key=id&customQuery%5B0%5D.Value=214997#highlight=##>.

b) Judgment of the Court

21 The High Court upheld the judgments of the lower courts and denied the request for review. On the merits of the case, the High Court reviewed the legal arguments for which A's claim was rejected and declared them lawful.

22 The High Court reminded that in similar cases, when the claimant relies on the right to dignity and reputation and the defendant relies on the freedom of expression, a balance must be struck between the two opposing rights. The High Court also relied on the consolidated case law of the ECtHR concerning the limits of the lawful exercise of the freedom of expression. The High Court concluded that B's statements were within the admissible limits of the freedom of expression because they were made on a topic of public interest and because B's purposes were legitimate – maintaining and increasing green areas within the territory of the Bucharest municipality. The High Court confirmed the assessment of the Court of Appeal, namely that it was not B's intention to damage A's reputation and dignity.

23 The High Court also responded to specific criticism A raised in the request for review: that the Court of Appeal did not discuss and assess the issue of the damage she suffered. The High Court explained that this was indeed not necessary because the Court of Appeal, by finding that B was lawfully exercising their freedom of speech, basically found that there was no wrongful act. The High Court added that, for tort liability to be triggered, all the four legal requirements provided in art 1389 of the Civil Code must be cumulatively met. These four requirements are a wrongful act, fault, damage and a causal link between the wrongful act and the damage. Consequently, since the Court of Appeal found that there was no wrongful act, assessing the other three requirements would have been pointless.

c) Commentary

24 The commented judgment seems to evidence that the 'saga' of Romanian courts struggling to find a compatible formula between legal reasoning in terms of tort liability and legal reasoning in human rights cases[10] has finally come to an end.

---

10 *C Alunaru/L Bojin/B Șerb*, Romania, in: E Karner/BC Steininger (eds), European Tort Law (ETL) 2020 (2021) 535, nos 39–42; *C Alunaru/L Bojin/S Căileanu*, Romania, in: E Karner/BC Steininger (eds), European Tort Law (ETL) 2019 (2020) 513, no 17, *C Alunaru/L Bojin*, Romania, in: E Karner/BC Steininger (eds), European Tort Law (ETL) 2014 (2015) 502, no 46.

The argumentative problem to be solved by the ordinary Romanian courts was how to link the subsumption formula of the tort liability (wrongful act + fault + damage + causal link) with the balancing exercise required by cases involving fundamental rights and freedoms.[11] The subsumption mindset implies a successive independent assessment of the four requirements for tort liability. The balancing approach is more holistic and less analytical. While the balancing of the opposing rights looks closer to the stage of assessment of the wrongfulness in the subsumption approach, it is true that some of the elements normally related to damage might come into play in the balancing process.[12] Because of this, Romanian courts have hesitated between simply applying the subsumption formula supplemented with some references to the case law of the ECtHR and omitting references to balancing,[13] making an implied balancing and referring to it under a different name (a circumstance affecting the analysis of the wrongful act, such as 'provoking' retaliatory statements)[14] or dealing with the balancing in the stage of assessing the damage or the causal link between the wrongful act and damage.[15] 25

In this case, the High Court was clear and explicit about the stage at which the balancing should be made: at the stage of assessing the existence of the wrongful act. As such, Romanian case law in the field of tort liability for violation of fundamental rights acknowledges that fundamental rights are not simple rules, but principles, in the meaning used by Dworkin.[16] Assessing the violation of a principle is different from assessing a breach of a rule, but the outcome of the legal analysis is the same: both violation of a principle and breach of a rule constitute a wrongful act. 26

There is no doubt that the crystallisation of this doctrine in the case law of the High Court will serve as a basis of orientation for future judgments of the lower courts and thus, we expect more coherence in the legal reasonings in disputes related to liability for violations of fundamental rights. 27

---

11 *R Alexy*, On Balancing and Subsumption. A Structural Comparison, Ratio Juris, vol 16 no 4 (2003) 433–449.

12 *Alunaru/Bojin/Șerb*, ETL 2020 (fn 10) no 39.

13 *Alunaru/Bojin*, ETL 2014 (fn 10) nos 45–47.

14 *Alunaru/Bojin/Căileanu*, ETL 2019 (fn 10) no 17.

15 *Alunaru/Bojin/Șerb*, ETL 2020 (fn 10) nos 39–42.

16 *R Dworkin*, Taking Rights Seriously (1978).

3. High Court of Cassation and Justice, Civil Section I, Decision no 93 of 18 January 2024: Relation between Tort Liability and Contractual Liability; Contributory Fault[17]

a) Brief Summary of the Facts

28 The claimant, bank A SA, filed a lawsuit against the defendants B and C in front of Bihor Tribunal, requesting that the defendants pay compensation for damage amounting to RON 10,105,118 (approx € 2,000,000), based on the tort liability of the defendants. In 2009, the bank concluded a loan agreement with company D, the shareholders of which were B and C, and whose administrator was B. The conclusion of the agreement was conditioned upon the debtor presenting a sale-purchase agreement concluded with Oradea municipality for 100 apartments in the real estate project developed by company D. Moreover, the drawdowns from the loan facility were to be made based on periodical works statements confirming the advancement of the building works. After company D withdrew an amount of approx RON 12,000,000, it was discovered that the agreement presented to the bank was forged and that the periodical works statements (based on which the drawdowns were made) did not correspond to the real advancement of the works. An insolvency procedure was opened against company D, during which the bank recovered a part of the amounts withdrawn by company D. The non-recovered difference was requested in the present case. In the meantime, criminal proceedings brought against B and C ended in the acquittal of the two. Consequently, the bank filed a tort law-based claim against the defendants, seeking compensation of the damage represented by the non-recovered amount of the loan.

29 The Bihor Tribunal, in its Civil Sentence no 122 of 16 June 2022, denied the request as inadmissible. The Tribunal considered that the damage relied upon was contractual, therefore only a claim based on contractual liability would be admissible.

30 On appeal, the Oradea Court of Appeal, in its Decision no 516 of 12 April 2023, reversed the judgment of the first instance court and admitted in part the request, granting the bank A SA half of the amount sought. The Court of Appeal based its decision on the fact that the claimant, through the negligence of its own employees, contributed to the damage.

17 Online at: <https://www.scj.ro/1093/Detalii-jurisprudenta?customQuery%5B0%5D.Key=id&customQuery%5B0%5D.Value=219809#highlight=##>.

b) Judgment of the Court

The High Court of Cassation and Justice upheld the judgment of the Court of Appeal. In his request for review, defendant B argued that the request based on tort liability was inadmissible (as the Bihor Tribunal had decided in first instance) because contractual liability, which takes precedence with respect to tort liability, was applicable in this case. B argued that the alleged damage resulted from the (non-)performance of the contractual obligations. Thus, the type of claim available to the bank was a request for compensation of damage based on contractual liability. The High Court rejected the argument. It accepted that the source of the damage was contractual, ie the loan agreement that was not repaid by company D. However, the High Court emphasised that defendants B and C were not parties to the loan agreement (which was concluded between the bank A SA and company D). Therefore, the legal relationship between the bank and the defendants was not contractual. Because of this, the bank was entitled to file a lawsuit based on tort liability, which is the default regime of civil liability. 31

The High Court also noted that the Court of Appeal had correctly assessed that the requirements for the establishment of tort liability were met in the case. The wrongful act was represented by B and C misleading the bank representatives by presenting them works statements that did not reflect the real status of the works and by presenting a forged sale-purchase agreement for the apartments to be built. The fault of the defendants was evident, as they acted with direct intent. The damage was represented by the non-recovered amounts withdrawn by company D based on the loan agreement. The causal link between the wrongful act and the damage results from the way that the wrongful acts were committed. 32

c) Commentary

As the facts of the case date back to 2009, the substantive applicable law in the case was the old Romanian Civil Code, in force between 1864 and 2011. However, there are no major differences between the old and the new Civil Code as to the rules and principles of civil liability applicable to the case. 33

The Court's decision brings to attention once again the classic topic of the possibility of the concurrence of contractual liability and tort liability. The old Civil Code did not have an explicit rule to that effect but, traditionally, Romanian case law and legal literature affirmed the mutual exclusion of the two legal mech- 34 anisms. When contractual liability is applicable, tort liability will be excluded, the former being derogatory to the latter.[18] The new Civil Code has a specific provision in this sense, art 1350 (3).[19]

35 Thus, the claimant does not have an option between the two legal bases. Also, a claimant cannot combine features of each in order to obtain a more favourable legal situation. The only exception to this principle accepted by the Romanian legal system is the case of a criminal offence which would also constitute a breach of a contractual obligation. In such a case, tort liability will be applied by criminal courts. In the case discussed, the criminal procedure ended, however, without the criminal court deciding on the civil action.

36 In the present case, the defendants tried to have the claim brought against them rejected by relying on the source of the damage. The legal argument of the defendants was developed around the source of the damage as determining the type of liability. The first instance court accepted this argument. Indeed, the damage resulted from the non-performance of the loan agreement, namely from the non-reimbursement of the loan. However, the claim was not brought against the contracting party (company D), but against its former shareholders. Moreover, the basis of the claim was not the non-reimbursement of the loan. On the contrary, the claimant argued that, absent the misleading statements of the shareholders, it would not have concluded the agreement or, at least, would not have authorised the withdrawals. These aspects were better clarified by the Court of Appeal and then by the High Court. The higher courts correctly identified that the defendants were not in a contractual relationship with the claimant, so there was no place for a claim based on contractual liability.

37 However, the intersection of elements of contractual liability and tort liability is not always simple. In the case discussed, it is without a doubt that the source of the damage was the agreement. Is this enough to change the nature of civil liability? Apparently not, because the distinction between the two types of liability is based on the type of wrongful act that triggered the liability. It is true that damage is an element of liability, but liability itself is triggered by the wrongful act. The intersection between contractual and tort elements could be exploited, instead, in the area of the causal link. One of the defendants argued that the existence of a causal link between the wrongful act and the damage was not met in the case, because the damage was the outcome of the non-performance of the agreement. The High Court dismissed this argument rather elliptically. However, the

18 *C Stătescu/C Bîrsan*, Drept civil. Teoria generală a obligaţiilor. Ediţia a IX-a, revizuită şi adăugită (2008) 139 – 141.
19 *P Vasilescu*, Drept civil. Obligații (2012) 531.

analysis of the facts reveals that the tort committed by the defendants did cause the damage. In the absence of that tort, there would have been no opportunity for concluding the loan agreement and no opportunity to make the drawdowns. Thus, ultimately, the cause of the damage was, indeed, the tort, and not the non-performance of the agreement.

4. Personal Injury

One of the decisions issued by the High Court of Cassation and Justice in the preliminary ruling procedure in 2024 dealt with an interesting issue of *locus standi* in tort liability-based claims. The purpose of **Decision no 49 of 7 October 2024**[20] was to interpret art 198 (1) of the Criminal Code and art 1370 of the Civil Code. Article 198 (1) of the Criminal Code refers to the offence of a scuffle, meaning a spontaneous fight, involving several people. The specific element of a scuffle is that it cannot be determined who started the fight. The criminal responsibility for scuffles lies on each of the participants, irrespective of their role. The question addressed to the High Court was whether a participant in a scuffle, convicted for the offence, may nevertheless file a claim for tort liability against another participant in the scuffle, equally convicted. Article 1370 of the Civil Code (entitled 'Uncertain identity of the author of a wrongful act') provides that: '(i)]f damage has been caused by the simultaneous or successive actions of several persons and there is no possibility to ascertain that it was caused, or, as the case may be, that it could not have been caused, by the act of any single one of those persons, all those persons will be held jointly liable towards the victim'. The High Court decided that if a person involved in a scuffle suffered an injury to their physical integrity, the damage cannot remain uncompensated, therefore such a person should have the *locus standi* to request compensation for damage from the other participants. Besides the above-mentioned art 1370 of the Civil Code, also art 1371 (1) should apply. This rule refers to the contributory fault of the victim and reads as follows: 'If a victim has intentionally or negligently concurred in either wholly or partially causing or aggravating damage or culpably failing to avoid it, although they could have done so, those who are held responsible will only be liable for such part of the damage that they themselves have caused'. The preliminary ruling is mandatory for all ordinary courts, according to art 521 of the Civil Procedure Code. 38

20 Published in Monitorul Oficial no 1102 of 5 November 2024.

39 In its **Decision no 145 of 23 January 2024**, the High Court of Cassation and Justice discussed the amounts awarded as moral damages to the family of a victim of a traffic accident. The High Court confirmed that an amount of € 75,000 for the spouse and for each of the minor children was a fair amount, considering, in particular, that the minors were only two and five years old and they have been deprived of the possibility to effectively know their father. The Court also noted that the minors' psychological suffering will continue and take different forms as they grow up and they will fully understand the significance of the situation.

40 The liability for damage caused by animals was discussed by the High Court in **Decision no 708 of 18 March 2024.** The case regarded compensation for damage resulting from physical injuries caused by a bear. The Court discussed the relation between the general rule in art 1375 of the Civil Code and the special rules in Law no 707/2006 of Hunting and Protection of Wildlife Stock. The latter Law establishes which authorities are liable to pay compensation dependent on the type of animal that caused the damage. However, it also contains some specific rules on the amount of moral damages to be awarded. The problem in the case was that the law provided that the Government should have issued a methodology for awarding the damages, which had not yet been enacted. The High Court decided that the rules concerning the liability for damage caused by wild animals are directly applicable even in the absence of the methodology. It ordered that the case be returned for retrial and requested the court of appeal to directly apply the rules provided by the law and not to wait until the methodology was enacted by the Government.

C. Literature

1. *Florin I Mangu*, Capacitatea delictuală – componentă a capacității juridice [The tort capacity – component of legal capacity], Revista română de drept privat 1/2024, 79–123

41 The article discussed here is a good example of a classic approach in the Romanian private law towards the so-called 'fundamentals' of private law, an approach that was less popular in the last decades, but which has an honourable tradition in Romanian private law doctrine. There were two tendencies in the last decades of reflection in Romanian private law. The more theoretical one was concerned with the 'novelties', ie, the new social phenomena regulated by private law (data protection, Artificial Intelligence, etc), and the 'challenges' they pose to the established framework of concepts in private law. The second orientation was con-

cerned with the technicalities of day-to-day legal practice. There was less interest in what used to be called 'fundamental reflection' in law and which resulted in a direct questioning of the bases of the fundamental legal rules and principles, such as tort liability. This approach was, historically, the more respected one in the legal literature, as it was deemed to be the 'more intellectual' one. The great names in Romanian legal literature all practised this type of thinking.

This type of approach has some interesting characteristics that were rarely 42 (and almost never critically) analysed. The approach combines elements of legal philosophy and legal theory. The legal philosophy element of the approach consists in the underlying questions, formulated as 'whys?'. Why do we have the idea of legal responsibility? Why do we have these specific rules on responsibility and liability and so on. These are philosophical questions that would call for ethical reflections. However, lawyers, although accepting the extra-legal (meta-legal) implications of such questions, intentionally tried to formulate answers from within the legal system, by relying on the existing positive rules and refraining from going too deep into philosophy, sociology or economics. This approach created the body of legal literature which is still the 'canon' in Romanian private law.

If only for trying to keep alive this tradition, the article is already laudable. 43 Starting from the very general concept of legal capacity in tort law, the author attempts to 'dig' at the roots of the way the legal environment conceives civil responsibility.

The starting point of the reflection is, indeed, the idea of 'tort capacity' as a 44 sub-category of legal capacity. Legal capacity is generally conceived as the aptitude of natural and legal persons of having rights and duties, ie, of being parties to 'legal relationships'.[21] Defined in this way, legal capacity looks just like another name for 'legal personality', the mechanism through which the subjects of the legal order enter this legal order. Thus, from a functional approach, the role of legal capacity is to be a 'door', a connecting mechanism, between the social system and the legal system. But the author is not satisfied with this minimalistic function of legal capacity. The aim of the article may be described as trying to give some substantive content to the seemingly 'dry' functional approach towards legal capacity. The main idea of the article is that 'tort capacity' expresses an implicit legal requirement to trigger tort liability, that of the freedom of will of the legal subject. The author argues that the requirement of fault in triggering tort liability includes not only the reference to the discernment of the individual (which is expressly provided by the Civil Code in arts 1349 (1), 1366 and 1367), but necessarily

21 *FI Mangu*, Capacitatea delictuală – componentă a capacității juridice, Revista română de drept privat 1/2024, 80.

also to the freedom of will. The actions that trigger liability are conscious choices of the subject, and conscious choice presupposes both discernment and free will. The latter is not expressly provided by any rule of the Civil Code in the field of tort liability. Therefore, the author argues that the usefulness of the category of 'tort capacity' rests in its ability to tacitly describe the subject of tort law as both free and responsible (with discernment).

45 The first part of the article is a dense restatement of the fundamental concepts in the field of legal responsibility: the importance of rules and sanctions in social life, the importance of an effective legal order, and the basic requirements for an effective legal order. Within this theoretical framework, the author underlies the importance of having generally recognised standards of assessing conduct from a legal perspective, but also the need to have instruments to be able to make accurate individual assessments based on these general standards. In this context, the two functions of legal consequences of responsibility are discussed: the reparatory function and the preventive function. Another insightful remark is that when analysing the reasons for the action of a wrongdoer, the courts actually scrutinise not only the conduct, but also the personality of the wrongdoer. Also in this part, in order to complete his demonstration, the author relies on extra-legal sources, as he cites several studies in psychology and social psychology. This is a good example of integrating an interdisciplinary approach into an essentially legal positivist enterprise.

46 The second part of the article is devoted to the exegesis of the articles of the Civil Code related to tort liability from the standpoint of the ethical foundations of liability. The author notes that, while discernment is dealt with explicitly in various sections of the Code, freedom of will is not explicitly mentioned, not even in the articles related to fault. Based on this, the author develops his main idea, according to which, freedom of will, as a necessary requirement for fault, although not explicitly mentioned, is always presumed. Thus, his main argument is the idea that 'tort capacity' expresses the necessary link between discernment, freedom of will and fault. In this way, 'tort capacity' does not only have the functional role of linking the social system and the legal system, but also has a substantive function, that of expressing the relevance of free will in the mechanism of tort liability.

47 Some of the claims of the author to support his argument can be questioned. The author provides examples of some causes precluding liability (such as force majeure or legitimate defence) as illustrating his point. While it is clear that in such cases, indeed, liability is not triggered because of the lack of free will (and, as such, absence of fault), it is instead disputable whether one could say that the legal subject did not have 'tort capacity' in these cases. This illustrates

well the difficulties of attempting to transform a functional concept into a substantive one.

However, the positive elements of this legal reflection is not affected by these issues. The text remains a solid groundwork for an honest discussion in the Romanian legal environment on the foundations and policies of tort liability. 48

2. *Lucian Bercea*, Acționarul ca victimă prin ricoșeu: despre prejudiciul prin reflectare în materie societară [The shareholder as a ricochet victim: on reflective loss in corporate matters], Revista română de drept privat 4/2024, 330–345

The author is one of the leading exponents of the economic analysis of law in Romania. His writings deal, usually, with matters of corporate law but, many times, as the reflection deepens, they go beyond the conventional limits of the so-called 'branches of law'. This article is a good example of bringing to light the deep connections between corporate law and liability, between corporate personhood and reparation of damage. When compared with the article discussed supra, the present approach illustrates a different trend in Romanian legal literature, that of following one of the contemporary courses of legal reflection in the world (law and economics, law and society, critical legal studies, etc) but integrating the results of the research in the Romanian general legal 'language', so that even non-academics might understand the relevance of the topic. 49

The article deals with a problem that is very relevant for practice and raises important theoretical questions. Sometimes, a wrongful act (be it in the field of competition law, intellectual or industrial property, environmental law, etc) may cause both a 'corporate loss' (a loss for the company) and an 'individual loss' (a decrease in value of the shares). In such a situation, do the shareholders have a distinct entitlement to recover their loss or it is only the company that may act to see its damage compensated? 50

The conceptual mapping of the problem starts with the idea of corporate legal personality with its consequence of the patrimonial separation between company and shareholders. The separation does not equate, though, with disconnection. The value of the shares reflects, up to a certain extent, the value of the business. Thus, a corporate loss might be followed by a decrease in value of the shares, so a loss for the shareholders. But this is not the same as saying that it is the same loss that is simply visible in two places. The author explains that shares do not 'represent' (from a legal point of view) the economic value of the company. From a legal 51 perspective, the shares are incorporeal goods, titles issued by the company, and they have an autonomous economic value themselves. They do not replace the funds that have been invested in them. Both the funds invested and the shares obtained are two different goods, both circulating in the economic flow of resources. The author refers to this consequence as 'multiplication' of the economic value of the investment (as opposed to 'representation' of the latter by the shares).[22]

52 The loss suffered by shareholders based on a loss incurred by the company is called a 'reflective loss'. The analysis of the 'reflective loss' and its comparison with 'ricochet damage' is contained in the part of the article relevant for the issue of tort liability. The author explains from the outset that 'reflective loss' is not 'ricochet damage'. The latter represents a loss suffered by the indirect victim of wrongfulness, but stemming from the same cause as the loss suffered by the immediate victim. Both losses are necessary consequences of the wrongful act. The immediate damage does not precede the mediate damage from a temporal perspective, it simply explains the mediate damage.

53 On the other hand, the author argues, the 'reflective loss' is not, properly speaking, a consequential loss, that is, in principle, not subject to compensation. A consequential loss is one where there is a second cause, besides the wrongful act, that intervenes in the causal link of the damage and in the absence of which there would be no damage. The author explains that in the case of 'reflective loss' of the shareholder, the 'corporate loss' and the 'individual loss' are both direct consequences of the wrongful act and, most of the time, simultaneous. Thus, the eventual exclusion of a legal mechanism for the recovery of the 'reflective loss' cannot be explained by mere reference to the principle of non-recovery of the consequential loss.

54 Due to a scarcity of discussions on this topic in the Romanian literature, the author refers to the legal regime of the mechanisms to compensate 'reflective loss' in the United States and the United Kingdom. He shows that the principle is that the 'individual loss' is not recoverable. There are several explanations for this: the inherent business risk assumed by shareholders, the priority of action in favour of the company for losses of a company's assets (based on the principle of entity shielding), the need to avoid a 'double recovery' (from the company and from the shareholder). However, some exceptions are also accepted, the main one being the case of derivative actions, where shareholders are entitled to act 'on behalf' of the company against the wrongdoers that generated the loss. The author notes that this exception is, actually, a quasi-exception because the shareholders

22 *L Bercea*, Acționarul ca victimă prin ricoșeu: despre prejudiciul prin reflectare în materie societară, Revista română de drept privat 4/2024, 334.

promoting the derivative action do not seek compensation of the 'individual loss', but of the 'corporate loss'. However, there might be situations (that are regulated in some national legal systems) in which shareholders do, sometimes, have the right to direct action to compensate the 'individual loss', but only if the action to recover the 'corporate loss' ceased to be available.[23]

The author's conclusion is that the legal regime of the (non-)recovery of the 55
'reflective loss' is a policy choice in the various legal systems. In the words of the author, this is not a 'perfect solution, nor a definitive one'. Based on this conclusion, the author also assesses the possible transplant of this principle into the Romanian legal system.

23 *Bercea*, Revista română de drept privat 4/2024, 344.

Martin Hogg

XXV. Scotland

A. Legislation

There was no new legislation in the field of delict in 2024. 1

B. Cases

1. *Galbraith Trawlers Ltd v Advocate General for Scotland*, Court of Session (Inner House) 10 January 2024, [2024] CSIH 1, 2024 Session Cases (SC) 255, 2024 Scots Law Times (SLT) 43, 2024 Scottish Civil Law Reports (SCLR) 162: Measure of Damages for Unlawful Detention of Fishing Vessels

a) Brief Summary of the Facts

The pursuers, Galbraith Trawlers Ltd, owned a fleet of prawn fishing vessels. The 2
Home Office investigated them as part of an operation to counter illegal working within the UK fishing industry. They suspected the pursuers of facilitating breaches of immigration law by employing Filipino workers on their vessels. In August 2015, during a routine port visit, Border Force officers came across four Filipino workers working aboard one of the pursuers' vessels. The workers were detained under the Immigration Act 1971. Three of the pursuers' fishing vessels were also later detained by an acting chief immigration officer.

The pursuers raised an action challenging the legality of the detention of the 3
vessels on the basis that, as the detaining officer was only acting as a chief immigration officer, he was not a 'senior officer' within the definition of the 1971 Act and therefore lacked the authority to authorise the detention of the vessels. They sought damages for the unlawful and wrongful detention of their vessels from the Advocate General for Scotland (representing the Home Office).

At first instance, the sheriff found in favour of the pursuers, holding the de- 4
tention of the vessels to have been unlawful and the Advocate General liable for the pecuniary losses caused to the pursuers. The sheriff rejected an argument advanced by the Advocate General that only nominal damages of £ 1 should be payable, an argument which had been advanced by reference to English cases on

https://doi.org/10.1515/9783111389271-026

false imprisonment in which detainees had not suffered any patrimonial losses. The Sheriff noted that those authorities had not been applied in Scotland: the Scottish decisions had held compensatory damages would normally be payable in all but highly exceptional cases. In any case, patrimonial losses had been suffered by the pursuers in this case as a result of deprivation of their use of the vessels.

b) Judgment of the Court

5 On an appeal by the Advocate General to the Inner House of the Court of Session, the court rejected the appeal, holding: (1) when a wrong has been committed, the court will order the wrongdoer to compensate the person affected by assessing what, in monetary terms, would put that person back into the same position as they would have been in had the wrong not occurred. In a detention situation, if the detention would have occurred anyway in the absence of the wrong, only nominal damages would be payable; (2) the question in this case was what would, as a matter of fact, have happened if the vessels had not been wrongfully detained. On the facts, the vessels would *not* have been detained lawfully; and (3) the sheriff had therefore been entitled to conclude, as he did, that that the wrongful detention had had a 'severely detrimental effect on the (pursuers') financial situation'.

6 The appeal court added its opinion that care must be taken when applying the term 'nominal damages' to cover circumstances of unlawful detention which might only cause inconvenience. In two cases from the later nineteenth and early twentieth centuries, so-called nominal damages awards of £ 10 would equate to amounts in excess of £ 1,000 when adjusted for inflation. Such a quantum of nominal damages ought to serve 'as a modest deterrent of unlawful detentions'.

c) Commentary

7 This appeal is of interest in relation to damages awards in delict for at least two reasons. First, there is an extensive review by the court of the question of the correct counterfactual to be applied when considering what would have occurred in the absence of an unlawful detention. In looking at that matter, the court considered a number of prior English judgments, including *R (Lumba) v Secretary*

of State for the Home Department,[1] *R (Kambadzi) v Secretary of State for the Home Department*,[2] *Parker v Chief Constable of Essex*,[3] as well as the decisions of the High Court of Australia in *Lewis v Australian Capital Territory*[4] and the Irish Supreme Court in *GE v Commissioner of An Garda Síochána*.[5] The outlier in this line of judgments is *Parker*, a claim of damages for false imprisonment, in that the Court of Appeal in *Parker* had assessed the proper counterfactual as being 'what would have happened had it been appreciated what the law required' rather than what would have happened in the absence of the unlawfulness.[6]

By contrast, in *Lewis* it was said by Edelman J that: 8

> The 'but for' or counterfactual approach 'directs us to change one thing at a time and see if the outcome changes'. The change is the removal of the wrongful act. If the loss would lawfully have occurred but for the wrongful act then the wrongful act was not necessary for the loss. The counterfactual approach thus involves a hypothetical question where no other fact or circumstance is changed other than those which constituted the wrongful act.[7]

Edelman J specifically criticised the approach taken in *Parker*, commenting that: 9 'The correct counterfactual approach, which removes only the wrongful act, does not require the court to ask what would have happened if it had been appreciated what the law required'.[8] The Inner House in *Galbraith* was of the same view: 'the court disagrees with the reasoning in *Parker* in favour of that in Australia and Ireland … The correct counterfactual is simply what would, on the balance of probabilities, have happened; not what might or could have happened'.[9]

Of interest secondly is the court's analysis of the law concerning nominal 10 damages claims for unlawful detention of claimants. Certain authorities had been relied upon by the Advocate General to support an argument that nominal damages of only £ 1 should be payable to the pursuers, on the basis that, although procedural failings rendered the detention of the vessels unlawful, they did not of themselves merit an award of substantial damages. The appeal bench upheld the

---

1 [2011] United Kingdom Supreme Court (UKSC) 12, [2012] 1 Appeal Cases (AC) 245, [2011] 2 Weekly Law Reports (WLR) 671.
2 [2011] UKSC 23, [2011] 1 WLR 1299.
3 [2018] England & Wales Court of Appeal, Civil Division (EWCA Civ) 2788, [2019] 1 WLR 2238, [2019] 3 All England Reports (All ER) 399.
4 [2020] Hight Court of Australia (HCA) 26; (2020) 271 Commonwealth Law Reports (CLR) 192.
5 [2022] Supreme Court of Ireland (IESC) 51.
6 *Parker*, per Sir Brian Leveson, at para 104.
7 *Lewis*, per Edelman J, at para 178.
8 *Lewis*, per Edelman J, at para 182.
9 Para 42.

sheriff's view that there was no rule or principle in cases of unlawful detention that only nominal damages could be awarded, clearly signalling the approach of Scots law on that point.

11 The court's *obiter* comments on the quantum of nominal damages are also noteworthy. The appeal bench was clearly alive to the danger that the terminology of damages being 'nominal' can be misleading, especially given the differing approach taken in some other jurisdictions. In US common law, for instance, nominal damages typically amount to only $ 1, though in some US states a marginally higher sum might be awarded (for instance, in one fairly recent Ohio case concerning conversion, nominal damages of $ 100 were awarded by the court[10]). By contrast, 'nominal' damages in Scots law are not necessarily a trivial sum. The court cited *United Horse Shoe and Nail Co Ltd v Stewart & Co*,[11] in which the First Division of the Court of Session had awarded a sum of £ 50 (equivalent to about £ 8,000 in today's money), *Aarons & Co Ltd v Fraser*,[12] in which they awarded damages of £ 10 (equivalent to £ 1,000 today), and *Webster & Co v Cramond Iron Co*,[13] also an award of £ 10 (equivalent to £ 1,500 today). The point made by the court in describing the appropriate quantum of nominal damages – that it should be such sum as would serve as a 'modest deterrent' against the unlawful act – explains why one would not expect nominal damages in Scots law to be trivial: trivial sums do not act as a deterrence.

2. *X v Brown and Lord Advocate*, Court of Session (Inner House) 12 April 2024, [2024] CSIH 6, 2024 SC 309: Whether the Crown was Vicariously Liable for Alleged Assaults Committed by a Judge

a) Brief Summary of the Facts

12 The first instance decision in this case was reported in the 2023 Yearbook.[14] By way of a reminder of the facts, the pursuer, who was a legal practitioner, had sought damages of £ 120,000 based upon an alleged series of sexual assaults

10 *Fisher v Barker* (2005) 159 Ohio Appellate Reports (Ohio App 3d) 745.

11 (1885) 15 Rettie, House of Lords ([R] [HL]) 45.

12 1934 SC 137,

13 (1875) 2 Rettie (R) 752.

14 Reported in *M Hogg*, Scotland, in: E Karner/BC Steininger (eds), European Tort Law (ETL) 2023 (2024) 575, nos 8–17.

and harassment in 2018 said to have been committed by the first defender, Brown, who was a judge (a sheriff), for which the second defender (representing the Crown) had been argued to be vicariously liable. The four separate incidences of assault were claimed to be individual delictual acts at common law and, taken together, to also constitute a chain of harassment under the Protection from Harassment Act 1997.

At first instance, the court held that § 2(1) of the Crown Proceedings Act 1947 plainly applied vicarious liability for delictual acts of Crown servants, which class included judicial office-holders. That section provides that the Crown could be subject to vicarious liability, but only in the same way as applied to other liable parties. That being so, the test of the relationship being akin to that between an employer and employee still required to be met. The key features of Crown and government involvement in the position and payment of sheriffs met this part of the test, and the independence of the judiciary did not negate that relationship. The court ordered a proof before answer (a trial of the facts before a debate on the law) in order to assess whether, as a matter of fact, the judge had abused the special position in which the Crown had placed him. Both parties appealed against aspects of the first instance decision.[15] 13

b) Judgment of the Court

In the Inner House of the Court of Session, the court held: (1) the first instance court had treated the claim as being against the Scottish Government in respect of the Crown's vicarious liability for the first defender. As there had been no appeal against that part of the court's decision, it was therefore an essential part of the pursuer's case that sheriffs were akin to employees of the Scottish Government; (2) in a case of vicarious liability, a two-stage test had to be met: at stage one, the question was whether the relationship between a defender and the wrongdoer was one of employment or akin to employment; at stage two, the question was whether the wrongful conduct was so closely connected with acts that the wrongdoer was authorised to do that it could fairly and properly be regarded as done by the wrongdoer while acting in the course of the wrongdoer's employment or quasi-employment; (3) as to stage one, the issue was whether judicial office-holders, not being employees of the Scottish Government, were nonetheless akin to employees. As to that question, because of the absence of control by the 14

15 Not all aspects of the judgment are considered in this report. For instance, an issue of time bar relating to two of the claims against the defenders is not discussed.

Crown over them, judicial office-holders were not to be regarded as Crown servants for the purposes of the 1947 Act (they were rather 'officers' of the Crown). Even if judicial office-holders were Crown servants (which the appeal bench did not believe), that would not be a weighty factor in favour of them being akin to employees; (4) while the Scottish Government was the funder of sheriffs' remuneration, allowances, and pension benefits, it had no control over the performance by sheriffs of their judicial functions, nor did it exercise control over the judiciary as an institution. The absence of any effective control by the Scottish Government was deliberate and based on sound constitutional principles: the operation of the rule of law, central to which are judicial independence and the separation of powers. Treating judicial office-holders as akin to employees of the Scottish Government, and thus (where stage two of the vicarious liability test was met) rendering the Government vicariously liable for them, would be inimical to judicial independence, notwithstanding the common law and statutory guarantees that judicial independence be maintained; (5) the lack of control by the Scottish Government and the importance of maintaining judicial independence (both actual and perceived) were cogent factors which weighed heavily against judicial office-holders being akin to employees, factors which were not outweighed by any countervailing arguments; (6) therefore, as judicial office-holders were not akin to employees, the case of vicarious liability against the Crown failed.

c) Commentary

15 This judgment is of note in that it entirely up-ends the approach of the judgment at first instance. It analyses in detail the legal responsibility in delict of the Lord Advocate (a law officer of the Crown), as a representative of the Scottish Government, for the misconduct of judges. The key question for the appeal court was whether a judge can be considered in a position akin to employment, the appeal court answering this question very emphatically in the negative. Its view, that judges are *not* akin to employees, is explained by reference to established principles of constitutional law (supported by citation of caselaw, statute, and academic writing) and further justified by citation of the same approach taken in some other legal systems (mention is made of Ireland and Singapore).

16 Given the court's finding, the pursuer was unable to meet stage one of the modern vicarious liability test. That test has been recently reviewed, in light of all the recent caselaw, by Lord Burrows JSC in *Trustees of the Barry Congregation*

of Jehovah's Witnesses v BXB[16], whom the appeal bench in this case cites at length. Application of the 'akin to employment' test is particularly challenging in relation to judges, given their complex constitutional position in relation to the Crown. A holistic assessment of their position requires consideration of their remuneration and other emoluments, the processes for their appointment and removal from office, their independence of action (which statute says the Government must maintain), and the role of Scotland's senior judge (the Lord President) in relation to them, among others. The analysis of these matters is entirely at odds with that taken by the judge at first instance.

In exonerating the Crown from vicarious liability for the misconduct of judges, the judgment leaves those who find themselves the victims of judicial misconduct without an obvious remedy for any losses they may suffer, other than suing the wrongdoer personally; seeking an official investigation into alleged judicial misconduct does not alleviate the losses of any victim of such misconduct.[17] It is doubtful whether the availability of these others avenues of redress will in all cases fully satisfy the victims of judicial misconduct.[18] 17

3. *Centenary 6 Ltd v TLT LLP*, Court of Session (Inner House) 4 June 2024, [2024] CSIH 13: Assessment of a Loss of a Chance Claim against a Law Firm

a) Brief Summary of the Facts

This case concerned the negligence of the defenders (TLT), a firm of solicitors, in 18 failing properly to advise their client, the pursuer (Centenary 6), in relation to the requirements for lodging a security in proceedings brought by the pursuer against the joint liquidators of a third party, Centenary Holdings III Limited, of which the pursuer was the sole shareholder.

The defenders' failure had resulted in the court refusing an insolvency claim 19 by the pursuer for payment of £ 22.3 million. The defenders admitted their negli-

16 [2023] UKSC 15, [2024] AC 567, [2023] 2 WLR 953.

17 Neither the procedures in the Judiciary and Courts (Scotland) Act 2008, asp 6, concerning investigations into judicial conduct (sec 28) or the removal from office of a judge (secs 35–39, 41), nor those of the Courts Reform (Scotland) Act 2014 (secs 21–25), provide for any remedies for persons who may be adversely affected by judicial misconduct. The first defender in *X v Brown* was removed from his shrieval office with effect from 7 June 2024.

18 For an expression of this doubt, see *L Cowan*, Vicarious Liability of Judicial Officers, 2024 (28) Edinburgh Law Review (Edin LR) 417, 421 f.

gence but denied that the pursuer had sustained any loss as a result, arguing that the pursuer had a nil or negligible chance of achieving any success in the insolvency proceedings. One of the reasons was that any challenge which might have been made by the pursuer to a compromise agreement reached by the joint liquidators of the third party had, so the defenders argued, prescribed (under sec 6 of the Prescription and Limitation (Scotland) Act 1973) by the time of the insolvency proceedings.

20 The pursuer argued that it had been deprived of a reasonable chance of challenging the compromise agreement under the insolvency proceedings and that the right to challenge this agreement had not prescribed. Had such a challenge been successful, the pursuer claimed that, following the deduction of various costs, it would have recovered approximately £ 14.9 million.

21 At first instance, the defenders having admitted their negligence, the judge held that the pursuer had been deprived of a real and substantial chance of recovery because of this negligence. He assessed the level of the lost chance as being 65 %. Applying this percentage to the sum which would have been secured in successful insolvency proceedings (the £ 14.9 million), he quantified the recoverable lost chance damages as £ 9.1 million.

22 The defenders appealed, arguing that: (1) for the purposes of the law of prescription, the 'creditor' in any claim for damages against the liquidators had been the pursuer and not the third party. Because the pursuer had been entitled to raise a claim more than five years before the insolvency proceedings, the claim had prescribed under § 6 of the 1973 Act; and (2) the commercial judge had erred in holding that the value of the chance lost by the pursuer was 65 %. Where the quantum of a lost chance was dependent upon a number of discrete contingencies, if any of those individual contingencies was properly quantified as zero (or as negligible), taking a mathematical approach to the overall assessment of the lost chance, it should also be assessed at zero.

b) Judgment of the Court

23 The court refused the defenders' appeal, holding that: (1) the creditor, for the purposes of applying § 6 of the 1973 Act to the joint liquidators' obligation, was the person to whom that obligation was owed. The relevant obligation was the obligation to make reparation for loss caused by the joint liquidators' breach of duty. That obligation was owed to the company whose assets they were alleged to have misapplied, ie, to the third party, and not to its shareholder (the pursuer). That obligation had not prescribed at the time of the insolvency proceedings; (2) where a lost chance includes more than one hurdle for a claimant to surmount,

the English courts had, in certain cases, regarded it as appropriate to adopt a mathematical (or, as some might prefer to call it, an arithmetical) approach, multiplying the percentage prospects of each uncertain outcome to produce an overall loss of a chance percentage. The commercial judge had rejected using such a mathematical approach, on the ground that the overall chance was not composed of independent contingencies but rather facets of the same contingency. The court was not persuaded that the commercial judge had erred in doing so. Although there might be circumstances in which it would be appropriate to adopt a mathematical approach to the loss of a chance, it was less obviously attractive in the context of litigation risks. The commercial judge had given reasons for selecting a broad-brush figure of 65 % and there was no reason to disturb that assessment.

c) Commentary

This judgment of the Inner House raises a number of issues of law, the two of 24 most interest for present purposes being the proper assessment of a lost chance claim and the ascertainment of the proper party to be considered as the 'creditor' for the purposes of determining whether a damages claim has prescribed.

A major point of argument between the parties was the proper assessment of 25 the value of a lost chance. The pursuer argued for a holistic, broad-brush assessment (that adopted by the commercial judge), the defenders for a mathematical/arithmetical assessment. The defenders could point to English caselaw demonstrating the use of such an arithmetical approach, such as *Joyce v Bowman Law Ltd*,[19] a case concerning the admitted negligence of a firm of licensed conveyancers. The judge in that action had identified four separate contingencies affecting the overall chance which had been lost, assessing them as, respectively, 85 %, 100 %, 40 %, and 85 %. He had multiplied those together to reach an overall figure of a lost chance of 29 %. The defenders argued that such an exercise, properly applied to the present case, would have produced an overall lost chance of 0 %, on the basis that they asserted that some of the separate contingencies had a 0 % chance of success. Had the appeal court agreed, the pursuer's case would have failed. However, the bench noted that not all English cases took such a formalistic, arithmetical approach,[20] and they specifically noted that the assessment of litigation risks is not usually approached by legal practitioners in this way:

19 [2010] High Court of England and Wales (EWHC) 251 Chancery Division (Ch).
20 See, for instance, *Hanif v Middleweeks* [2000] Lloyd's Reporter, Professional Negligence (Lloyds Rep PN) 920.

> It is not, for example, the approach that would be adopted by experienced counsel when advising a client on prospects of success or on the level at which a settlement offer ought to be made or accepted ... the uncertainties in the present case would in practical terms have been regarded by the parties ... as facets of one question.[21]

Practitioners faced in the future with actions of a lost chance of success in litigation will doubtless take note of these observations.

26 As to the second issue, the prescription point, matters were complicated by the fact that it was not the present action itself which was the subject of a prescription argument; rather, it was obligations owed to the third party by the joint liquidators of the company. If those obligations had not prescribed, then the pursuer would be entitled to participate in the insolvency proceedings, this forfeited entitlement being the subject of the lost chance claim against the defenders. If those obligations had already prescribed at the point in time when proceedings were raised, then any chance which the pursuer had lost was worthless. In considering prescription arguments in relation to the liquidators' obligations, the language of § 6 of the 1973 Act was brought sharply into focus: the section speaks of the obligations encompassed by it in terms of the 'creditor' under the obligation, the creditor being the party to whom performance under an obligation is owed. As the court explained, the party to whom the obligations of the joint liquidators was owed was the third party, and not the party who owned its shares (the pursuer). So, the question of whether the pursuer's lost chance was a valuable one depended upon whether obligations owed to a third party had or had not prescribed. As has been explained, the court thought they had not.

27 A further point worthy of note in relation to prescription is the court's observation on its determination of this issue that:

> If it be the case that English law would produce a different result (a matter on which we express no view) then that would be the consequence of differences between the respective laws of prescription and limitation, which would not occasion surprise or concern.[22]

28 The reason why the court was prompted to make this observation is that the defenders, when advancing their argument that it was the pursuer which should be considered the 'creditor' for the purposes of determining whether any action for damages against the joint liquidators of the third party had prescribed, had argued that:

21 Para 70.

22 See para 32.

> Such an interpretation accorded with the definitions of claimant and plaintiff used in English and Northern Irish limitation legislation. It would be surprising if different results were reached in different parts of the UK in respect of a UK-wide statutory insolvency regime.[23]

The court was clearly not persuaded by the argument that, in order to achieve consistency in the law of insolvency proceedings, the same approach to interpreting 'claimant'/'plaintiff' in English/Northern Irish limitation provisions and 'creditor' in Scottish prescription provisions should be adopted. The meaning of a creditor (one to whom an obligation is owed) is very clearly not the same as a claimant (one who raises legal proceedings), and the Inner House was right not to ignore that difference in meaning when determining the proper approach in this action. 29

4. *Crozier v Scottish Power UK Ltd*, Court of Session (Inner House) 4 June 2024, [2024] CSIH 14, 2024 SC 373: Whether Family of Deceased Man could Claim Damages in Respect of his Death from Mesothelioma

a) Brief Summary of the Facts

Robert Crozier died of mesothelioma in October 2018. He had been employed by the defenders between 1969 and 1992. In 2014, he had successfully settled a damages claim against the defenders, having developed pleural plaques and contracted asbestosis as a result of being exposed to asbestos in the course of his employment. A portion of the settlement in his favour related to the risk of his developing mesothelioma later in life. 30

Following Mr Crozier's death, the pursuers, who were members of his immediate family, raised an action against the defenders. They sought damages under § 4(3) of the Damages (Scotland) Act 2011 for the anxiety and distress which they suffered in contemplation of Mr Crozier's death, their loss and grief upon his death, and the loss of his society and guidance. 31

The defenders contended that the action was incompetent because, in terms of § 4(2) of the 2011 Act, the pursuers' right to claim damages upon Mr Crozier's death was precluded by the previous settlement in his favour. The pursuers accepted that § 4(2) provided that, as a generality, no claim for damages for a wrongful death can be brought by the relatives of a deceased person if the deceased has 32

23 See para 26.

settled his own claim for damages flowing from the same wrong. They however relied upon § 5(1), which provides for an exception to that rule where the deceased has died of mesothelioma. They contended that this exception applied even if he was not suffering from mesothelioma at the time of settlement.

33 At first instance, the judge held that, when Mr Crozier settled his claim with the defenders in 2014, he had discharged the defenders from all liability arising from their negligent exposure of him to asbestos, including mesothelioma. However, the pursuers' subsequent claims satisfied the conditions of § 5 of the 2011 Act. They were therefore entitled to seek damages in respect of Mr Crozier's death. The defenders appealed against this decision.

b) Judgment of the Court

34 The Inner House refused the defenders' appeal, holding that the words of the applicable statutory provisions were clear and unambiguous. The context was ensuring that the relatives of persons who had died from mesothelioma were compensated, albeit to a limited extent, for the loss of the deceased, even if he had earlier settled his own claim for *solatium* and loss of earnings. The way in which the applicable provisions did this was simply to disapply a bar on damages claims which had been settled or otherwise disposed of where 'the personal injury in consequence of which the deceased died is mesothelioma'. There was no other relevant condition; there was no ambiguity; and no absurdity was created by allowing immediate relatives to claim some damages for the loss of a relative who had previously claimed *solatium* and loss of earnings.

c) Commentary

35 This case concerned the proper interpretation of the provisions of the Damages (Scotland) Act 2011 concerning the entitlement of relatives of a deceased person to claim damages in cases where the cause of death was mesothelioma. Relatives of deceased persons to whom damages awards are owed are themselves entitled to claims under the Act for loss of society (that is, loss of love, care, company, and guidance) and loss of support (that is, loss of material provision and assistance which the deceased provided), but the claim is normally excluded if the deceased previously settled his own claim. However, that exclusion is itself excluded (under § 5) where 'the personal injury in consequence of which the deceased died is mesothelioma'.

Section 5 was enacted to deal with the problem that, previously, if a mesothelioma sufferer successfully claimed damages for their condition during their life, their relatives would lose their non-patrimonial claims. That bar was removed by § 5. But what of a case (the present action being one) where the deceased's lifetime claim was only for pleural plaques (a marker of a raised chance of contracting mesothelioma) but not for mesothelioma itself – could relatives still raise a post-mortem claim in such a case? That was a question of the proper interpretation of § 5 of the 2011 Act.[24] **36**

In interpreting the exclusion of the exclusion provided for in § 5, the court applied the 'standard canons of interpretation',[25] referencing the intention of Parliament in using the language it did, starting from the position that 'language should bear its ordinary meaning in the general context of the statute',[26] and taking into account that the words were clear and unambiguous. The defenders' contention that, in order for the relatives to succeed in their additional claims, the deceased would have had to have been suffering from mesothelioma when he himself recovered damages, was flatly rejected by the court, none of the arguments to that effect being accepted. **37**

The decision of the Inner House is supported by the clear wording of § 5 of the 2011 Act. That section specifies as one of the requirements for a claim by relatives which is additional to a claim made by the deceased during his lifetime that 'the personal injury in consequence of which A died is mesothelioma'. The section might have required, but does not, that the deceased was suffering from mesothelioma when he raised his claim. Given this, the court's decision in this action seems appropriate. **38**

24 These issues are discussed in *S di Rollo*, Veale (aka Crozier) v Scottish Power UK Ltd (Case Comment), 2024 SLT 197–200.
25 Para 26.
26 Para 27.

5. *Finlayson and others v Alban Wine Ltd and Johnstone*, Court of Session (Inner House) 9 October 2024, [2024] CSIH 32: Whether a Court was Entitled to Dismiss a Personal Injury Case

a) Brief Summary of the Facts

39 A woman died in a wine bar when a non-load bearing wooden structure, intended to be used as a drinks tray, collapsed when she and another person (the second defender) sat on it, causing the deceased to fall onto concrete steps and suffer a fatal injury. The deceased's partner, her mother, and her brother sought damages from the operators of the wine bar, Alban Wine Ltd (the first defender), and also from the second defender. The action against the first defender was subsequently settled.

40 The judge at first instance dismissed the action against the second defender, on the basis that he owed the deceased no duty of care: in the event of a danger that was not obvious, there would require to be an averment of special knowledge of the danger on the part of the second defender (which was absent), or of circumstances which could amount to an assurance to the deceased that the shelf was safe, which the deceased could rely upon. In reaching this view, the judge applied the tripartite test for establishing a duty of care laid down in *Caparo Industries plc v Dickman.*[27] That test stipulated three elements for establishing a duty of care: foreseeability of the injury; a sufficiently proximate (close) relationship between the parties; and that imposition of a duty would be fair, just, and reasonable. Only the first element (foreseeability) was present on the facts of the instant case.

41 The pursuers appealed the decision of the court at first instance, arguing that it was inappropriate to apply the tripartite test in *Caparo* to the facts of the instant case. The *Caparo* test had been developed to assess whether the imposition of a duty of care in novel circumstances was appropriate. This was not such a case: this was a standard personal injury case where death had resulted, one which could be accommodated within existing principles. It was a case of foreseeable physical damage caused by a positive act.

---

27 [1990] 2 AC 605.

b) Judgment of the Court

42 The Inner House allowed the pursuers' appeal and ordered a proof (a trial of the facts), holding that, while the case might be factually unusual, it was not complex in terms of legal analysis. It was a relatively straightforward claim for damages for personal injury based on an alleged positive, but negligent act, which created a foreseeable risk of injury to the deceased. There might be formidable obstacles in the appellants' path in terms of proving the claim, but that was not the test for the decision of the court at first instance nor was it for the appeal bench. The focus in the legal debates before the court at first instance on *Caparo* had led the first instance judge into error. More appropriate guidance was provided in the judgment of the Supreme Court in *Robinson v Chief Constable of West Yorkshire Police*,[28] in which the court had explained that it is normally only in a novel type of case, where established principles do not provide an answer to the question of liability, that the courts need to go beyond those principles in order to decide whether a duty of care should be recognised. The present claim had been advanced on entirely traditional grounds which were, or should be, well understood. In these circumstances, the tripartite test in *Caparo* had no place.

c) Commentary

43 In this judgment, the Inner House overruled a surprising first instance judgment, one which appears to have been reached because of a focus by counsel on misleading and inappropriate authorities during the debate before the judge. One would normally expect a judge to identify when there has been such a misleading focus on the wrong authorities, but this did not happen in the present case. The result was the court being led to reach a conclusion which was not consistent with the historical development of liability for negligent breach of a duty of care. That development began (pre-eminently in *Donoghue v Stevenson*[29]) with simple cases of liability for death or personal injury resting upon the criterion of the reasonable foreseeability of loss caused to the pursuer. As the law began to expand into novel categories, the courts appreciated the need to develop a more complex test, with the result that the tripartite test in *Caparo* was formulated. Crucially, however, that did not mean an adoption of that tripartite test for already well established cases, cases of liability for death and personal injury being

---

28 [2018] UKSC 4, [2018] AC 736, [2018] 2 WLR 595.
29 1932 SC (HL) 1, 1932 SLT 317, [1932] AC 562.

the most well established such cases. In those cases, foreseeability of loss to the defender remains the touchstone of liability.

44 It is unfortunate in this instance that this historical development of the law was forgotten (or at least overlooked) by the judge at first instance, but the decision of the Inner House offers a welcome correction of the first instance error. Ultimately, the pursuers may not succeed in proving negligence in this action (because it might, for instance, be argued that the defender could not reasonably have foreseen any harm being caused to the deceased, or because, if in fact there was an obvious danger, the deceased may be deemed to have accepted the risk of injury), but that will now depend upon the application of the correct test for liability.

6. *Thomson v Iceland Foods Ltd*, Sheriff Appeal Court (Civil) 18 December 2024, [2024] SAC (Civil) 50: Whether it was Appropriate to Apply the Maxim *res ipsa loquitor*

a) Brief Summary of the Facts

45 The pursuer was shopping at the defenders' store when, after paying for her shopping at the checkout, she walked towards the store exit. She tripped on a mat that was raised above floor level and injured herself. She raised an action for damages against the defenders, claiming that they were in breach of both their common law duties as well as their duty under § 2(1) of the Occupiers' Liability (Scotland) Act 1960. The pursuer argued that the maxim *res ipsa loquitor* applied to the case, this being a presumption of fact requiring a defender to demonstrate that an accident occurred without fault on its part. In the absence of such demonstration, a court will presume negligence on the part of the defender.

46 At first instance, the sheriff held the maxim to be applicable on the facts of the present case. As the defenders had not offered an explanation to displace the inference of negligence, the sheriff found for the pursuer and granted decree in her favour for the sum of £ 9,500. The defenders appealed the decision at first instance, challenging the appropriateness of applying *res ipsa loquitor* to the facts of the case.

b) Judgment of the Court

The Sheriff Appeal Court refused the appeal and upheld the judgment at first instance. They held: (1) for *res ipsa loquitor* to be applicable, (i) the thing which caused damage must have been under the defender's management; and (ii) the accident must have been of a type that does not ordinarily occur if proper care is taken; (2) the defenders accepted that the mat was under their management, thus meeting the first requirement; as to the second requirement: the mat would not ordinarily have a raised edge if proper care were taken; a raised edge of the mat close to the store entrance would give rise to the risk of injury to customers, depending on the circumstances; a defect in the mat caused the accident. Accordingly, the sheriff had been entitled to reach the conclusion on the evidence that the accident was of a type that did not ordinarily occur if proper care were taken; (3) cases of tripping on local authority pavements were not comparable with tripping on a mat in a supermarket store, and they therefore did not assist in determining the proper outcome in this case. 47

c) Commentary

The decision in this case puts occupiers of premises on notice so far as the safety of doormats and loose carpets is concerned. Occupiers need to ensure that such items are firmly affixed to the floor (making them immovable) or else are of such weight and design that, if disturbed by a visitor to the premises, they will without human intervention revert to an entirely flat, safe state after being disturbed. Such care ought to ensure an absence of the risk of injury; therefore, if injury does occur, the application of the maxim *res ipsa loquitor* will mean that it can be presumed that proper care was not taken. 48

The defenders attempted to counter liability by citing cases of pedestrians tripping on public pavements. One such case is *McClafferty v British Telecommunications plc*,[30] in which no issue of *res ipsa loquitor* was raised and in which a protruding manhole cover (raised approximately ¾ of an inch above pavement level) was not held to create a reasonably foreseeable risk of injury. The court was not persuaded by the relevance of such cases, though in its judgment it does not say why, other than to state somewhat opaquely that the 'circumstances ... were fundamentally different'. If that view is correct, then the fundamental difference may be that an outdoor, public space is more difficult to manage and monitor than an 49

30 1987 SLT 327, 1987 SCLR 473.

enclosed, indoor, private space and thus not an appropriate circumstance to which to apply the maxim *res ipsa loquitor.*

7. Personal Injury

50 So-called 'group proceedings' are gaining prominence in Scotland, these being (within a delictual context) proceedings where multiple parties seek to sue the same defender in relation to injuries arising from the same wrongful act or omission. Such cases are now dealt with under Part 4 of the Civil Litigation (Expenses and Group Proceedings) (Scotland) Act 2018,[31] though before the coming into force of that statute, court practice directions governed such cases. *McLuskey v Scott Wilson Ltd,*[32] a personal injuries claim begun before 2018, gave rise to the question of whether the action could proceed, given that the 'lead case' dealing with the same wrongful act had already been disposed of (through a finding of no breach of duty). Allowing this case to proceed raised the possibility of infringing the rule of *res judicata* (which seeks to prevent duplicate litigation). In this case, the court held that, because further facts had been pled by the pursuer as well as an alleged further breach of duty, the court was willing to allow the action to proceed on those limited additional elements.

51 Cases concerning road traffic accidents are commonplace, but one worthy of note from 2024 is *Marshall v Berkshire Hathaway International Insurance Co Ltd.*[33] At first instance, the sheriff made an award of *solatium* to the victim of a road traffic accident without having heard from any expert medical witness as to the nature of the injuries. This omission was the subject of appeal to the Sheriff Appeal Court, which refused the appeal. It held that, given the nature of the injuries sustained, it had not been necessary to hear expert medical evidence: the sheriff made a discerning judgment on the evidence which he accepted, drew inferences of causation based on common experience, and reached a judgment which was supported by the evidence and inferences. Such a course was open to a court in cases relating to uncomplicated injury amenable to assessment on the basis of common experience.

31 For examples of 2024 cases brought by reference to this statute, see *Bridgehouse v Bayerische Motoren Werke AG* [2024] CSOH 16, *Campbell v James Finlay (Kenya) Ltd* [2024] CSIH 29, *Mackay v Nissan Motor Co Ltd* [2024] CSOH 68, and *Milligan v Jaguar Land Rover Automotive plc* [2024] CSOH 96.

32 [2024] CSOH 4, 2024 SLT 853, 2024 SCLR 183.

33 [2024] SAC (Civ) 13, 2024 SCLR 306.

The question of whether damages claims are time barred is another common issue for the courts and arose in a number of cases. In addition to *Centenary 6 Ltd v TLT LLP* (discussed earlier[34]), one may also note *Tilbury Douglas Construction Ltd v Ove Arup & Partners Scotland Ltd*,[35] which held that breaches of duty alleged by a contractor in its action of damages against a subcontractor were not separate and distinct causes of action against which time started to run for the purposes of prescription; and *Drouet v Milligan*,[36] a case of a damages claim by relatives of a deceased family member (E) in which the court held that, when calculating when time began to run for the purposes of the applicable limitation period, the pursuers required to be aware of E's injuries and that the injuries were attributable to an act or omission; it did not follow that the pursuers required positively to be aware, as a matter of fact, that E's injuries were relevant injuries as a matter of law. 52

A final case worthy of note is *NM v Henderson*,[37] in which the pursuer sought to establish that an ambulance service had breached a duty of care owed to her in respect of assaults carried out against her over a period of months by an ambulance technician who had attended her during an emergency call out. The breach of this alleged duty was said to have been constituted by the ambulance service's failure to properly investigate whether the first defender had acted inappropriately with another woman in an ambulance two years before his contact with the pursuer, whose complaint to the police had been investigated but not progressed. The judge held there to be no sufficient proximate relationship between the parties and further that he was not persuaded that, in this novel situation, it would be fair, just, and reasonable to impose a duty of care on the ambulance service. 53

C. Literature

1. *F McManus*, Delict Essentials (Edinburgh University Press, 5th edn 2024)

This is the fifth edition of a popular introductory work on the law of delict, aimed primarily at the student market. 54

34 At nos 18–29.
35 [2024] CSIH 15. On 29 January 2025, the UKSC granted permission to appeal this decision.
36 [2024] CSOH 32, 2024 SLT 401.
37 [2024] CSOH 84, 2025 SLT 35.

2. *J MacLeod*, Why are the wrongs wrong? Scots lawyers' liability to justifying liability in delict, Edinburgh Law Review, vol 28(1) 2024, 1–41

55 The author considers the theoretical understandings underpinning the Scots law of delict, in part responding to prior musings on that issue by J Brown in articles in the Scots Law Times[38] (in which Brown argued that Scots law had taken a wrong turn in *Donoghue v Stevenson*[39]). The author argues that Lord Atkin's test in *Donoghue* does not appear all that radical. It was an attempt to formulate a test which explained when people can be expected to anticipate, and thus take steps to avoid, harm and, therefore, when causing it is rendered culpable. It did so in terms which presuppose the wrongfulness of knowingly causing harm. As such, it can be read as a development of the conduct-harm principle – the principle that liability is justified because conduct is culpable, but the culpability arises from the fact that it creates a risk of harm to someone else. Neither can Lord Atkin be said to depart very far from the manner in which the conduct-harm principle developed in Scotland.

56 The author continues that, however, the conduct-harm principle cannot provide a taxonomical definition and normative justification to the law of delict, because: (i) the nominate delicts tend to retain their own specific matrices; (ii) the idea of a duty of care arising has been used extensively as a threshold device, to restrict liability, even in cases where the harm is foreseeable. If it were not so restricted, a law of negligence driven simply by the conduct-harm principle would be radically over-inclusive; and (iii) the conduct-harm principle ties duties of compensation to culpable conduct, making it difficult to account for strict liability. A rights-based model seems to provide a more promising rationale, since (in relation to ownership of property) the claim-right to compensation for damage can be understood as distinct from the claim-right that others do not damage property.

57 The author concludes that, if a rights-based model is to be taken seriously, the discussion of what counts as wrongful should be removed from the law of delict and located in the law of property, the law of persons, and perhaps the law of eco-

38 *J Brown*, The mouse and the snail: reappraising the significance of *Donoghue v Stevenson:* Part 1 – a case worth celebrating? 2022 SLT (News) 229; The mouse and the snail: reappraising the significance of *Donoghue v Stevenson:* Part 2 – the 'intellectual superstructure' of Scots delict, 2022 SLT 235.

39 1932 SC (HL) 1, 1932 SLT 317, [1932] AC 562.

nomic interests. On such a rights-based model, wrongfulness is merely the relief of the rights accorded in these other spheres.

3. *E Reid*, Making law for Scotland: the Defamation and Malicious Publications (Scotland) Act 2021, Edinburgh Law Review, vol 28(1) 2024, 42–60

The author reviews the changes to Scots defamation law effected by the passage of the Defamation and Malicious Publications (Scotland) Act 2021 (which were discussed in the 2021 Yearbook[40]). 58

The author argues that, while the Act was a major achievement – producing a codifying statute for a complex area of the law in a relatively short time-frame, thereby modernising and simplifying the law – nonetheless the Act also demonstrated some of the difficulties of legislating for the law of delict, especially in the Scottish context. If, on certain issues, the link with the influential jurisprudence of the English courts is to be broken, careful consideration is needed as to formulations capable of taking the law forward independently. Furthermore, close parallels in the common laws of both jurisdictions do not remove the need for caution in new statutory constructions devised to deal with policy issues specific to England. 59

4. *J MacLeod*, Double duty: *McCulloch v Forth Valley Health Board*, Edinburgh Law Review, vol 28(1) 2024, 130–133

This short article considers the 2023 decision of the UK Supreme Court in *McCulloch v Forth Valley Health Board*,[41] which drew a distinction between a doctor's duty to disclose risks of treatment to a patient, where (following *Montgomery v Lanarkshire Health Board*[42]) a 'reasonable patient' test applies, and the disclosure to the patient of possible alternative treatments, where the traditional *Hunter v Hanley*[43] test of a responsible body of medical opinion continues to apply. The author argues that the decision is to be welcomed as it clarifies, on a plausible basis, 60

40 Reported in *M Hogg*, Scotland, in: E Karner/ BC Steininger (eds), European Tort Law (ETL) 2021 (2022) 539, nos 1–3.

41 [2023] UKSC 26, 2023 SLT 725.

42 [2015] UKSC 11, 2015 SC (UKSC) 63, [2015] AC 1430.

43 1955 SC 200.

the relationship between patient autonomy, on the one hand, and health and welfare, on the other, and thus the relationship between the *Hunter v Hanley* and the *Montgomery* tests. He further argues that it emphasises the twin responsibilities that doctors have to pursue health and to respect autonomy and helps us to understand the way that the duties to further these distinct interests interact.

5. *J Brown*, *Damnum* is where one starts from? Questions to be asked for determining liability for negligence in Scots law, Juridical Review 2024(3) 119–141

61 The author argues that Scots law does not possess either a 'law of tort' or a 'tort of negligence'. Instead, drawing on its institutional connection to civil law, Scotland possesses a law of delict which forms a part of a broader law of obligations. This has, or ought to have, consequences for any analysis of liability for civil wrongdoing in Scotland. Rather than predicating liability on a pigeonholed system of nominate wrongs, Scots law recognises general principles which may justify a remedy for wrongdoing, provided that a pursuer juridically demonstrates that the defender can legitimately be blamed for a wrong. The most commonly litigated type of wrong in Scotland is *damnum injuria datum* (loss caused by wrongful conduct), with *culpa* (fault – encompassing intentional, reckless, and negligent conduct) serving as the trigger for blame where *damnum injuria datum* is established between sufficiently proximate pursuers/defenders. Despite the prevalence of actions predicated on alleged negligence, however, *damnum injuria datum* is not the sole species of generalised wrongdoing known to the law of Scotland, and concepts other than *culpa* are required in order to explain liability under other headings within Scots law of delict.

62 The author consequently considers the general principles of delict which can be observed within Scots law and – noting that the concept of duty is of less conceptual use and significance within the law than has hitherto been thought – suggests a framework for determining liability for purported negligence in Scotland which is not predicated on the demonstration of a directional, or particular, duty of care.

6. *C Anderson*, Encroachment and public interest, Juridical Review 2024(3) 142–158

In this article, the author considers aspects of the law of encroachment, which is a wrongful intrusion onto land owned or lawfully possessed by another. The author notes that, when the owner of land seeks the removal of an encroachment, the courts will often exercise a discretion to allow the encroachment to remain. He argues that little attention has been given to the relevance of public interest considerations in the courts' decision-making in this area, for example where the encroachment is of benefit to the public. 63

He concludes that, however we understand 'public interest' (it is not easy to define precisely how it should be understood), there is very little evidence that it plays any role in judicial decision-making in encroachment disputes. That is as it should be: the court in a private law dispute is not the ideal forum for weighing up competing public interest considerations. The appropriate forum is the legislature or bodies exercising the delegated authority of the legislature. 64

Anton Dulak

XXVI. Slovakia

A. Legislation

There was no new legislation in tort law in 2024. 1

B. Cases

1. Judgment of the Supreme Court of the Slovak Republic of 26 August 2024, Case No 7CDo/103/2023, published in Collection 69/2024: Victim Status

a) Brief Summary of the Facts

The plaintiff (the husband of the deceased) sought compensation for non-pecuniary damage under the provisions on the protection of personality (art 13(2) and (3) of the Civil Code). Based on the evidence, the Court finds that the defendant failed to provide timely and effective treatment to cure and improve the condition of the plaintiff's wife, considering the current state of medical science. In doing so, it relied on the conclusions of the expert evidence and on the examination of an expert from an expert organisation, which showed that the delay in carrying out the necessary medical treatment in relation to the life-threatening haemorrhage had exhausted the plaintiff's defence mechanisms and reserves, which had led directly to the failure of vital organs. From the point of view of intensive care, the defendant's treatment of the deceased was inadequate. During treatment, there were several procedures which were not carried out correctly and in time. 2

The Court of Appeal ordered the defendant to pay the plaintiff the sum of € 50,000 and to pay the costs of the proceedings. The Court of Appeal upheld the judgment of the court of first instance. The defendant appealed against the Court of Appeal's decision. The Supreme Court held that the appeal was partly admissible. 3

https://doi.org/10.1515/9783111389271-027

b) Judgment of the Court

4 In determining the amount of compensation for non-pecuniary damage under art 13(2) and (3) of the Civil Code, it is not reasonable to limit this compensation to the highest compensation allowed under the Victims of Crime Act (Act No 215/2006 Coll on compensation of persons injured by violent crimes, or Act No 274/2017 Coll on victims of crimes).

c) Commentary

5 The Court considered the plaintiff's person and his previous life, noting that the circumstances of his previous life were markedly specific. As a child, the plaintiff had already survived a tragic event, namely the death of his mother. He grew up with his father and sister, losing his father as an adult, who took his own life; it was the plaintiff who found his deceased father. The Court found that the plaintiff's acquaintance with his deceased wife, their life together, their marriage and the joy of the expected arrival of offspring were joyous events for the plaintiff after a long time, which ended with the unexpected death of his wife, another tragedy in his life.

6 According to the Court, in view of the gravity of the harm suffered (the plaintiff had lost all hope of a happy family life after a series of tragedies in his private life), it was reasonable to assume that the amount of non-pecuniary damages awarded must be higher than in other cases of improperly provided medical care.

7 In deciding on the amount of non-pecuniary damages, the Court assessed that the plaintiff's wife's death occurred at a young age (31 years), an age which represents the most productive period of any human being. The relationship between the spouses was orderly, harmonious, and full of understanding

8 In assessing the amount of non-pecuniary damages, the Court also assessed the circumstances on the defendant's side, that the defendant is a medical institution, whereby an entity with its status is expected to observe and perform all necessary acts and procedures in fulfilling its primary duty of prevention of harm.

9 The Court of Appeal upheld the correctness of the decision by holding that it satisfied the attribute of proportionality, which is a decisive criterion for achieving the purpose of compensation. The criterion of the proportionality of the monetary compensation awarded corresponds in direct proportion to the application of the so-called victim status, which has been clarified by the European Court of Human Rights (ECtHR) in its case law, when it stated that, insofar as the compensation is compensatory in nature, the amount of the compensation need not be the same as that which the court would have awarded in comparable cases before

the courts. However, the compensation must not be manifestly disproportionate to the circumstances of the case and, in assessing that proportionality, account must also be taken of the standard of living in the country in question and whether the amount awarded is out of line with the legal tradition in the country concerned.

The Court of Appeal acknowledged that the requirement of non-abuse of this 10
remedy for unjust enrichment was also invoked.

Against the background of specific ECtHR decisions, the Court of Appeal held 11
that compensation for non-pecuniary damage in similar cases must be reasonably proportionate to the damage to reputation suffered. In determining the amount of compensation for the violation of personality rights, account must be taken of the amount of compensation awarded for personal injuries or awarded to victims of violent acts. Compensation for the violation of other personality rights should not, without compelling and sufficient reasons, exceed the maximum amount of compensation awarded for physical injuries or acts of violence.

In her appeal, the defendant complained that the courts, when deciding on 12
the amount of non-pecuniary damages, considered circumstances on the plaintiff's side which were not temporally related to the defendant's conduct, where the defendant had no influence on the occurrence and extent of the consequences. According to the defendant, the courts also erred in considering the defendant's financial circumstances, in particular the fact that the defendant was insured for the case in question.

In her appeal, the defendant argued that there had been a departure from 13
established decision-making practice and that the determination of the amount of compensation for non-pecuniary damage should have been based by analogy on the compensation of victims of crimes, referring to the appeal decisions 4Cdo/171/2005, 6Cdo/37/2021, 6MCdo/15/2012, 3Cdo/19/2018 and the decision of the Constitutional Court of the Slovak Republic (No III. ÚS 288/2017) as well as the decision of the ECtHR in *I and K.U. v Finland.*[1]

The Court of Appeal concluded that the *de lege lata* obligation to assess the 14
amount of non-pecuniary damages awarded under the statutory provision on compensation for victims of crime does not follow from the substantive provision (art 13 CC), nor does it follow from the settled practice of the Court of Appeal. Regarding the defendant's objection concerning the range of circumstances examined by the lower courts when determining the amount of compensation for non-pecuniary damage, the Court of Appeal stated that the court is given the possibility to proceed individually, to assess and evaluate the circumstances of the

1 *K.U. v Finland,* 2.12.2008, no 2872/02.

particular case and, where appropriate, to establish other criteria for assessing each case.

2. Resolution of the Supreme Court of the Slovak Republic of 31 January 2024, Case No 4Cdo/34/2023: Raising of a Statute of Limitations Contrary to Good Morals in Medical Cases

a) Brief Summary of the Facts

15 On 17 December 2012, the plaintiff filed a claim for compensation of personal injuries caused by the defendant (a medical facility). According to the plaintiff, the defendant's employee failed to provide *lege artis* medical care in the context of post-natal care on 4 November 2004, thereby causing her serious personal injury (fistula formation – pathological connection of body cavities, necessitating the performance of a colostomy). This required subsequent reconstructive operations and hospitalisation (on a total of ten occasions). As a result of the incident, the plaintiff developed anxiety-depressive disorders, which led to a general change in her personality. In addition to compensation for personal injuries, the plaintiff claimed compensation for injury to her personality, for which she did not seek monetary compensation, but an apology.

16 The district court (by its supplementary judgment) upheld the action and ordered the defendant to pay compensation for pain and suffering in the amount of € 9,716 and compensation for impairment of social life in the amount of € 135,948. The court did not uphold the claim for an apology for the interference with the protection of personality.

17 The Court of Appeal upheld the judgment of the district court insofar as it ruled on the compensation for personal injuries, set aside the judgment relating to the claim for interference with personality and referred the case back for a new trial.

18 The plaintiff appealed that decision. The Supreme Court held that the appeal was well-founded.

b) Judgment of the Court

19 The raising of a statute of limitations objection by the defendant (a health care institution) which has seriously interfered with the personal rights of a patient

by a medical procedure *non lege artis* may exceptionally be contrary to good morals (sec 3(1) of the Civil Code) even if the patient has demonstrably not been able to claim compensation for non-pecuniary damage in due time in court as a result of the medical procedure thus carried out, either psychologically or physically.

c) Commentary

The interference with personality rights occurred on 4 November 2004 and the lawsuit was filed on 17 December 2012. According to the expert reports, the victim's health condition had stabilised by 20 November 2011 or 8 February 2012 (as regards sexual and mental disorders). According to the court, the action in respect of the claim for compensation for pain and suffering and for social harassment was brought in time. 20

As regards the claim for non-pecuniary damages under the provisions on the protection of personality, this claim was time-barred. According to the court, the injured party could have exercised her right on 5 November 2004. The limitation period began to run from that date and expired on 5 November 2007. 21

The injured party defended itself on the ground that the plea of limitation was contrary to good morals. The district court did not recognise the grounds for such an objection. The court argued that such a defence was raised only rarely because it violated the principle of legal certainty. According to the court, the victim's psychological suffering could not in any substantial way have influenced her rational thought and judgement to the extent that she was unable to seek legal assistance in a timely manner. The Court of Appeal agreed with that conclusion. 22

In her appeal, the plaintiff defended herself by arguing that interference with personal rights is primarily an interference with the psyche and that it is therefore necessary to distinguish between the point at which the unjustified interference causing injury to health occurred and the point at which the right to privacy and family life was interfered with. The plaintiff argued that throughout the development of the psychological disorder, she suffered from health problems which did not allow her to deal with the question of compensation for the injury to health and the interference with her personality. 23

The Court of Appeal considered the victim's objection that the courts should not have considered the statute of limitations objection due to its conflict with good morals in the light of previous case law (Cases No 5Cdo/265/2009, 7 Cdo/226/2016). However, the Court of Appeal stressed that medical institutions under the jurisdiction of the Ministry of Health are held to a higher standard than any other entity. Such a health facility is a subject of public interest, especially when it comes to proceedings for compensation for the damage (or other harm) 24 that it caused by its actions. The defendant, a State-funded institution, as a *sui generis* entity, while respecting the values on which it is founded, must, according to the Court, also act as a 'model' for its citizens, even if that should be to the detriment of its eventual success in litigation.

25 A plea of limitation by the defendant State organisation may exceptionally be assessed as contrary to good morals within the meaning of art 3(1) of the Civil Code even if the direct intention of the representative of the State in raising that objection is not to harm the plaintiff. However, according to the Court, there are exceptional and special circumstances which, on the part of the injured party (the person affected by the unjustified interference with their personality rights), created a serious obstacle to the timely assertion of their claim; therefore, a finding that the claim was time-barred would be unduly harsh for the injured party. In doing so, the Court considered the expert's opinion, which acknowledged that 'the severity of the subjective experience of the mental disorders as they progressed may have been an obstacle to the relevant contact that was necessary to pursue a claim for damages'.

26 According to the Court of Appeal, the lower courts should have taken more careful account of the plaintiff's extremely adverse medical condition, which prevented her from being able to exercise her rights in court in a timely manner. This seriously adverse medical condition was solely the result of the improperly provided medical care.

3. Judgment of the Supreme Court of the Slovak Republic of 22 February 2024, Case No 4Cdo/197/2022, published in Collection 69/2024: Release of Liability for Damage Caused by the Operation of Motor Vehicles

a) Brief Summary of the Facts

27 The plaintiff was struck by the defendant's vehicle while crossing a road outside of a pedestrian crossing and was injured. The trial court dismissed the action on the ground that the defendant was not in breach of the law. The Court of Appeal upheld the judgment of the trial court. The Supreme Court of the Slovak Republic dismissed the defendant's appeal.

b) Judgment of the Court

If damage is caused exclusively by the actions of the injured party, the liability of the operator is completely excluded, not because of the exemption of their liability on the basis of the so-called liberalisation ground under the second sentence of sec 428 of the Civil Code (unavoidable damage), but because of the lack of a causal link between the circumstance for which the operator is objectively liable and the occurrence of damage on the part of the injured party. 28

c) Commentary

From the point of view of the conditions of occurrence, the legal regulation of liability for damage caused in connection with the operation of a means of transport does not presuppose a breach of a legal obligation. The decisive factor is whether the damage was caused by the specific nature of the operation of the vehicle, collectively referred to as means of transport. A collision between a vehicle and a pedestrian, in which the speed, weight and kinetic energy of the vehicle are such as to cause damage to health, is a manifestation of that special nature of the operation of the means of transport. This is strict liability, where the person liable (the operator) is not held liable only if the liberalisation grounds are met (art 428 of the Civil Code). 29

According to § 441 of the Civil Code, if the damage was also caused by the fault of the injured party, they have to bear the damage proportionately; if the damage was caused solely by their fault, they have to bear the entire damage. The victim's contributory fault (in terminological terms, rather more precisely, the victim's co-causation of the damage) means that the victim's act (or omission) was either the main and immediate cause of their damage or was one of the causes. The final consideration of the extent to which the injured party themself contributed to the cause of the damage, and thus to what extent they bear the damage themself, always depends on the circumstances of the case after a comparison of all the causes of the damage on the part of both the tortfeasor and the injured party. 30

The issue of the assessment of the liability of the operator for the damage suffered was disputed between the parties. According to the experts, the plaintiff, by entering the carriageway at a time when the traffic situation did not permit it, had created a sudden obstacle for the defendant; the victim had also crossed the carriageway at a point outside the pedestrian crossing in the evening in reduced visibility, wearing dark clothing without reflective elements. According to experts, the driver's (partially delayed) reaction to the plaintiff's entry into the roadway was not causally related to the accident. Nor was there any other fact which 31 would have rendered the defendant driver of the vehicle liable for the damage (driving under the influence of addictive substances, speeding, lights not switched on, etc).

32 On appeal, the plaintiff sought to show that the decisions of both courts in the case represented a departure from previous case law. He cited the opinion in Cpj 10/83 and Pls 2/83 and the conclusion that the operator cannot be released from liability (§ 428, first sent) if the damage was caused by circumstances inherent to the nature of the vehicle. According to the plaintiff, the courts should have addressed whether the driver made all efforts to prevent the damage that could be objectively required. According to the plaintiff, the courts did not address whether the driver should have foreseen the pedestrian's movement on the roadway given the circumstances. Instead, the courts merely adopted the expert's determination of the technical cause of the accident.

33 According to the Court of Appeal, if damage is caused solely by the actions of the injured party, the liability of the operator is completely excluded due to the lack of a causal link between the circumstance for which the operator is objectively liable and the occurrence of the damage on the part of the injured party. In such a case, the second sentence of sec 428 does not apply, ie, it is not necessary to examine whether the defendant has proved that the damage could not have been prevented even if all reasonable efforts had been made. According to the Court of Appeal, it would be unreasonable and disproportionate not only from a preventive and educational point of view, but also from a reparation point of view, to impose liability on the operator for the damage even if the injured party had caused it themself. The Court referred to a decision of the Constitutional Court (in its judgment of 7 September 2023, III.ÚS 184/2023). The Supreme Court of the Czech Republic also ruled in a similar manner (Case No 25Cdo/38072014) and such a conclusion is supported by the expert community.[2]

2 See *M Števček/A Dulak/J Bajánková/M Fečík/F Sedlačko/M Tomašovič et al*, Občiansky zákonník I (2nd edn 2019) 1613 f.

4. Personal Injury: Judgment of the Regional (Appeal) Court in Prešov of 10 December 2024, Case No 5Co/29/2024: Causality in Medical Cases; Loss of a Chance

a) Brief Summary of the Facts

The plaintiff's mother was admitted to the surgical department of the defendant's clinic for chronic pain. The defendant began providing medical care on 17 July 2014. Despite this, the patient's clinical condition worsened, and she died on 6 August 2014. The plaintiff's daughter claimed non-pecuniary damages under sec 13 of the Civil Code. The district court upheld the claim. The Court of Appeal examined the judgment of the court of first instance and held that there was no merit in the appeal. 34

b) Judgment of the Court

The requirement of unequivocal proof of causation, without the possibility of admitting some reasonable degree of uncertainty, specifically in disputes that originate in the physician (health care facility) and patient (client) relationship, is inappropriate in the standard type of evidentiary syllogism. It upsets the fair balance between the parties concerned by failing to take account of the objective limits inherent in the subsequent knowledge of past phenomena, of causation, and by failing to balance proportionately the mutually asymmetrical position of those parties, in which, for the reasons already stated, the medical establishment has the 'upper hand'. It places disproportionate demands on the plaintiff (the injured party) as the weaker party in their relationship, thereby making it effectively impossible for them to obtain satisfaction in proceedings. The consequence is a violation of one aspect of the right to a fair trial, which is the equality of the parties. The equality of the parties, thus defined, includes not only the exercise of their rights but also the issue of the burden of proof. In constitutional terms, then, the right to a fair trial includes the principle of equality of arms, which, in civil proceedings, also includes equality of the burdens of proof which are imposed on the parties to the dispute, and which must not be disproportionate, otherwise the proceedings cannot be regarded as fair. 35

In medical disputes, it is sufficient to show a loss of a chance or loss of expectation in the sense that the medical facility's admittedly non-compliant procedure resulted in a loss of a chance that, but for the improper medical intervention, the 36 patient's health would have suffered less or there would have been no consequences.

c) Commentary

37 According to one expert report, the failure to administer antibiotic treatment to the patient and to perform emergency surgery was an improper practice in the provision of medical care. According to the other expert report (submitted by the defendant): 'It is not possible to say with certainty, or even to give any specific mathematical percentage, that even if the therapeutically correct course of action had been followed in this case, it would have been possible to influence the circumstance of the later death'.

38 The defendant did not dispute that the 100 % rate of proof of causation should be waived. According to the defendant, the limit of a reasonable departure from a showing of causation is a showing of causation of at least 70 %.[3]

39 According to the Court of Appeal, the fact that both the substantive and procedural legislation in question does not normatively define the concept, the essence, as well as the decisive degree of proof of the existence of a causal link between the cause and its effect, the search for answers to these questions is primarily a task of the application of the law manifested in the decision-making activity of the public authorities. Determining causation not only from that point of view thus constitutes a rather demanding task in the process of proof, which, from the point of view of the basic procedural structure on which the system of litigation is built, places a burden on the plaintiff.

40 Due to the nature of the problems involved in the sensory cognition of past phenomena, it is usually never possible to confirm to 100 % the existence or course of a particular factual event that has already taken place, and therefore there will almost always be a degree of uncertainty present during proof. It follows, then, *a contrario*, that a court cannot, as a matter of principle, require as a measure of proof absolute certainty, which would leave no room for even theoretical doubt as to a different course of events; if such a requirement is imposed, it also places the party who bears the burden of proof in an objectively insurmountable evidentiary difficulty. Causality between the phenomena under examination of a particular factual event constitutes an element of it which is in principle neither sensually nor immediately and objectively observable, and therefore its presence can, as a rule, only be assumed based on a certain quantitative degree

---

3 See the judgment of the Constitutional Court of the Slovak Republic, Case No II. ÚS 716/2016.

of probability, and that usually based on previous experience based on the established course of the decisive events.

In factually and legally complex disputes, the fair ordering of procedural relations requires that account be taken of the fact that it is often not within the means of the party asserting a particular fact to also prove it. One such area is medical-legal disputes. These are characterised by their factual complexity, in particular, by the concurrence of several causes capable of producing a given effect or by the significant time period between cause and effect, which makes the evidentiary situation considerably more difficult. This is also because the current state of knowledge does not allow for a reliable explanation of the alleged causal link where the imperfection of health care procedures or the very nature of biological processes must be taken into account.[4] 41

Another characteristic of these relationships, which often plays a decisive role during legal proceedings, is that there is a significant information asymmetry between the level of knowledge of the health care institution and the patient, to the detriment of the patient. The health care establishment's professional knowledge and capacity to perceive events connected with the provision of health care services better or to find out more about their course, and its capacity to prevent or subsequently provide evidence of them, are circumstances which place the health care establishment in a more advantageous procedural position in the event of a dispute in relation to the patient, who, as a rule, does not have such capacity. 42

It is precisely the objective limits associated with proving causation that has led to unfair results in many cases, because the inadequate burden of proof of the causal link between the harmful event and the damage caused to the patient is also usually the cause of the patient's failure to succeed in litigation in the case of an all-or-nothing approach to litigation. Such a solution appears to be unfair, particularly in cases where a high degree of probability supports the truth of the plaintiff's factual allegations. 43

In medical-legal disputes, in many cases, for the reasons already stated, the actual cause of the harmful consequence cannot be clearly established but can only be established with a certain degree of probability. In such cases, other elements on which the liability law system is built must also be considered. These must be considered in the context of objective causal uncertainty and mutual inequality so that the result is consistent with the principles of the construction of liability for damages. In principle, it is a matter of balancing two opposing in- 44

4 *A Doležal/T Doležal*, Kauzalita v civilním právu se zaměřením na medicínskoprávní spory (2016) 180.

terests, namely the injured party's right to compensation and, on the other hand, the interest in ensuring that the obligation to compensate for damage is imposed only on those who caused the damage or could have prevented it by their actions. It is necessary to apportion the uncertainty in relation to causation fairly. The requirement of a fair balance between the factual inequalities of the parties to the dispute is in principle satisfied if the doubt is resolved in favour of the injured party.

45 Similarly, the ECtHR judgment in *Metalco Bt v Hungary*[5] concluded that the imposition of an impossible burden of proof on one party to a civil dispute is a violation of the principle of equality of arms. The right to equality of arms thus requires that the burden of proof placed on one party should not be disproportionate, which is based on the general requirement of achieving a fair balance between the parties to the dispute. It then referred to the ruling of the Constitutional Court of the Slovak Republic in Case No III. US 409/2021 of 14 December 2021 and the finding of the Constitutional Court of the Czech Republic, Case No I. US 1919/08 of 12 August 2008.

C. Literature

46 The author found no significant literature in the area of tort law in 2024.

5 ECtHR 1.2.2011, no 34976/05.

Barbara Novak

XXVII. Slovenia

A. Legislation

1. Zakon o postopku sodnega varstva nekdanjih imetnikov kvalificiranih obveznosti bank (ZPSVIKOB-1)[1] (Procedure for Judicial Protection of Former Holders of Qualifying Liabilities of Banks Act, ZPSVIKOB-1)

The Procedure for Judicial Protection of Former Holders of Qualifying Liabilities of Banks (hereinafter: ZPSVIKOB-1) regulates the legal basis for compensation for damage, the jurisdiction of the courts and the special rules for the procedure by which effective judicial protection is provided to former shareholders or creditors of a bank whose shares in the bank or liabilities of the bank have been partially or fully terminated, or to other persons whose rights are affected by a decision of the Bank of Slovenia by which an extraordinary measure is imposed to terminate the bank's qualified liabilities (hereinafter: former holders). The ZPSVIKOB-1 also regulates access to documents and data that the Bank of Slovenia took into account or should have taken into account when imposing an extraordinary measure to terminate the bank's qualified liabilities (hereinafter: extraordinary measure), as well as the publication of decisions of the Bank of Slovenia by which extraordinary measures were imposed and the manner of providing documents and data relating to the extraordinary measure (art 1 ZPSVIKOB-1).[2] 1

The former holder may claim compensation for the effects of a decision of the Bank of Slovenia only in accordance with the special procedure laid down in ZPSVIKOB-1 (para 1 art 3ZPSVIKOB-1). ZPSVIKOB-1 does not apply if it has been established by a final court decision that a criminal offence was committed in connection with the decision of the Bank of Slovenia and the former holder claims that damage was caused to them by this criminal offence. ZPSVIKOB-1 also does not apply to a claim by which a former holder asserts a breach of the duty of explanation of a commercial bank, nor to other claims that do not invoke compen- 2

1 Uradni list Republike Slovenije (Official Journal, RS) No 44/2024. The Act entered into force (15 June 2024) 15 days after publication (31 May 2024) in the Official Journal.

2 On these questions, see also *G Dugar*, Slovenia, in: E Karner/BC Steininger (eds), European Tort Law (ETL) 2019 (2020) 581, no 1.

https://doi.org/10.1515/9783111389271-028

sation protection under the above-mentioned rule from para 1 art 3 ZPSVIKOB-1. A person who is a former shareholder or creditor of a bank, whose shares in the bank or liabilities of the bank have been partially or fully terminated on the basis of a decision of the Bank of Slovenia, is not considered a former holder if this person asserted a claim against the commercial bank due to a breach of the duty of explanation, and the nullity of the contractual relationship on the sale of financial instruments that represented qualified liabilities of the bank was established by final court decision (para 4 art 3 ZPSVIKOB-1). The former holder is entitled to compensation for damage if, due to the effect of the extraordinary measure, they suffered damage in an amount greater than the damage that they would have suffered if the extraordinary measure had not been imposed. In proceedings under ZPSVIKOB-1, the provisions on the limitation of claims from the law governing obligations (art 4 ZPSVIKOB-1) do not apply. Unless ZPSVIKOB-1 provides otherwise, the law governing civil procedure, namely the rules of procedure in commercial disputes, applies to proceedings conducted in accordance with ZPSVIKOB-1. If a collective compensation action is filed in accordance with ZPSVIKOB-1, because the claims originate from the same decision of the Bank of Slovenia, the law governing collective action proceedings applies *mutatis mutandis* to proceedings conducted in accordance with ZPSVIKOB-1, unless ZPSVIKOB-1 provides otherwise. The Maribor District Court has exclusive jurisdiction to decide on proceedings conducted on the basis of ZPSVIKOB-1.

3 The plaintiff may, by filing a lawsuit claiming compensation protection under ZPSVIKOB-1, request that the court only establish the existence of an obligation to compensate for the damage, and may reserve the right to raise a claim for the amount and file it no later than one month from the service of the final decision on the grounds. The lawsuit is filed against the Bank of Slovenia. The burden of proof in the procedure for deciding on the existence and amount of damage lies with the Bank of Slovenia (art 34 ZPSVIKOB-1). The plaintiff may also, by filing a lawsuit, request that the court establish that they are the former holder. They may also request the acquisition of data and documents specified in art 22 ZPSVIKOB-1 (art 27 ZPSVIKOB-1).

4 With the finality of judgments addressed to the Bank of Slovenia as the defendant, the payment obligations under such judgments are transferred to the Republic of Slovenia (art 42 ZPSVIKOB-1). The compensation is subject to interest from the date of issuance of the Bank of Slovenia's decision until payment. The compensation is subject to interest at the interest rate used by the European Central Bank for main refinancing operations at the time of the interest. If the Republic of Slovenia fails to pay the compensation to the plaintiff within the time limit for performance, the compensation is subject to interest from the first day

following the expiry of this time limit, at the interest rate for default interest (art 41 ZPSVIKOB-1).

The court conducting the proceedings in which actions with claims due to the effects of a decision of the Bank of Slovenia, which on entry into force of ZPSVIKOB-1 are being conducted against the Bank of Slovenia or the Republic of Slovenia (hereinafter: referred to as the original court), and which is not the competent court in accordance with ZPSVIKOB-1, must, within two months of the entry into force of ZPSVIKOB-1, *ex officio* by decision declare itself not competent to decide on these claims. After the said decision becomes final, the original court transfers the case to the competent court in accordance with ZPSVIKOB-1. If the action contains several claims and the original court, in accordance with ZPSVIKOB-1, has declared itself not competent to decide only on some of the claims, the original court sends a copy of the action to the competent court, and it continues to decide on the claims for which it has jurisdiction. In the event that compensation is awarded to the plaintiff on the basis of ZPSVIKOB-1, they are also entitled to reimbursement of all costs related to the lawsuit filed before the entry into force of ZPSVIKOB-1 (art 48 ZPSVIKOB-1). 5

2. Zakon o spremembah in dopolnitvah Zakona o obveznih zavarovanjih v prometu (ZOZP-E)[3] (Amending Act to the Compulsory Traffic Insurance Act, ZOZP-E)

The Amending Act to the Compulsory Motor Vehicle Insurance Act (hereinafter: ZOZP-E) transposes Directive 2009/103/EC of the European Parliament and of the Council of 16 September 2009 relating to insurance against civil liability in respect of the use of motor vehicles, and enforcement of the obligation to insure against such liability ([2009] Official Journal (OJ) L 263/11, hereinafter: Directive 2009/103/EC), last amended by Directive 2021/2118/EU of the European Parliament and of the Council of 24 November 2021 amending Directive 2009/103/EC relating to insurance against civil liability in respect of the use of motor vehicles, and enforcement of the obligation to insure against such liability ([2021] OJ L 430/1). In accordance with it, the ZOZP-E ensures the payment of compensation from the assets of the compensation fund even in the event that bankruptcy proceedings have been initiated against an insurance company that provides aviation liability insurance, boat owners' liability insurance and public transport passenger insurance and 6

3 Uradni list RS No 45/2024. The Act entered into force (19 June 2024) 15 days after publication (4 June 2024) in the Official Journal.

is obliged to pay compensation. Only that part of the compensation that was not paid from the bankruptcy estate of the insurance company is paid from the assets of the compensation fund (art 13 ZOZP-E).

7 In order to ensure the payment of compensation in the event of the insolvency of an insurance company, a special office is to be established within the Slovene Insurance Association (hereinafter: the Association) to carry out the business of motor third party liability insurance (art a42.a ZOZP-E). Insurance companies that have obtained a licence to carry out motor third party liability insurance business in the Republic of Slovenia and are registered in the Republic of Slovenia pay contributions to it. The Office for the Payment of Compensation in the Event of the Insolvency of an Insurance Company Carrying Out Motor Third Party Liability Insurance Business must immediately notify equivalent authorities in other Member States of the publication of a decision to initiate bankruptcy proceedings or a decision to initiate winding-up proceedings, as defined in the law governing insurance, against an insurance company carrying out motor third party liability insurance business, which has obtained a licence to carry out motor third party liability insurance business in the Republic of Slovenia (art c42.a ZOZP-E). An injured party files a claim for compensation for damage due to destruction or damage to property or damage due to death, bodily injury and impaired health caused by the insured vehicle directly with the Association. The procedure for handling the claim differs depending on whether the injured party with residence or registered office in the Republic of Slovenia files a claim in the event of an accident that occurred in the Republic of Slovenia (art č42.a ZOZP-E) or in another Member State of the European Union (art d42.a ZOZP-E).

3. Zakon o skupnih temeljih sistema plač v javnem sektorju (ZSTSPJS)[4] (Common Bases of the Public Sector Salary System Act, ZSTSPJS)

8 The Common Bases of the Public Sector Salary System Act (hereinafter: ZSTSPJS) regulates the common bases of the salary system for officials and civil servants in the public sector, the specifics of determining the salaries of officials and civil servants within an individual salary pillar, and the conclusion of collective agreements regulating salaries in the public sector. An employment contract, decision

4 Uradni list RS (Official Journal) No 95/2024. The Act entered into force (23 November 2024) 15 days after publication (8 November 2024) in the Official Journal, but is only to be applied from 1 January 2025.

or resolution may not determine a salary for a public servant or official at a different level than that determined by law, regulations and other acts issued on their basis, and collective agreements (para 2 art 4 ZSTSPJS). A person who exercises the rights and duties of an employer is liable for damage caused by the unlawful determination and payment of salaries. Their liability is assessed according to the general rules of civil law and labour law (pt 14 art 6 in connection with para 2 art 4 ZSTSPJS). Procedures for establishing the liability for damages of a person who was responsible for the exercise of the employer's rights and duties at the time of the occurrence of the illegality or irregularity may be initiated in State bodies and local communities by the head, and in other public law entities by the founder. If the person responsible for the exercise of the employer's rights and duties is an official in office, the procedure is initiated by the person to whom the official in office is responsible. If the person responsible for the exercise of the employer's rights and duties is a public servant, the procedure is initiated by the body competent for their appointment or election or, in the case of local communities, by the representative body. The above rules also apply to officials and public servants whose salary was paid in violation of the rules of ZSTSPJS and who are no longer employed by employers in the public sector at the time of the establishment of the illegality (art 6 pt 15 of ZSTSPJS).

B. Cases

1. Judgment of the Supreme Court II Ips 61/2023, 7 February 2024: Loss of Insurance Rights due to the Technical Inadequacy of a Vehicle

a) Brief Summary of the Facts

The defendant, who was not a professional tractor driver, hired a trailer to harvest 9
corn. When he hitched up the trailer, he checked that the rear lights were working. After harvesting the corn, he returned with the tractor and trailer on a regional road in the evening and drove at a speed of 25–30 km/h. The speed limit on this road 90 km/h. While driving on the road, the rear lights on the tractor trailer failed, and the vehicle did not have the prescribed triangular marking for slow-moving vehicles. However, a working headlight was on in the rear tractor cabin. A motorcyclist, who was driving at a speed of 70–75 km/h, thought that the vehicle was in the opposite lane because of the working headlight, so he switched his headlights to low beam and did not see the tractor in his lane in time. When driv-

ing with low beam headlights, the motorcyclist could only assess the tractor's position more accurately at a distance of about 30m. When a third vehicle came towards him, the motorcyclist realised that the defendant's vehicle was in his lane. Despite being blinded by the working headlight and having a shorter field of vision due to the low beam, the motorcyclist did not adjust his speed, so he was unable to stop in time and the front of the motorcycle collided with the rear right part of the tractor trailer, resulting in the motorcyclist sustaining serious bodily injuries.

10 The defendant had motor vehicle liability insurance with an insurance company at the time of the damage event. On the basis of this insurance, the insurance company paid the motorcyclist compensation in the amount of €33,182. The insurance company (plaintiff) then demanded reimbursement from the defendant of part of the compensation paid, in the amount of €14,342, because it claimed that the defendant's tractor was not technically flawless and therefore, in accordance with its general insurance conditions, he lost rights under the insurance. The first instance court ruled in an interim judgment that the claim was justified on the merits to 60%. The defendant was accused of not having working rear lights and a reflective marking (triangle) for slow-moving vehicles on the tractor trailer, but of having a working headlight on to illuminate the surroundings, which prevented the motorcycle driver from properly and correctly assessing which lane the tractor was in. According to the first instance court, the motorcyclist also contributed to the accident by not adjusting his speed to the visibility when switching from high to low beam. The first instance court assessed that the defendant contributed to the accident to a greater extent, namely 60%, and the motorcycle driver to a lesser extent, 40%. The second instance court confirmed the interim judgment of the first instance court.

b) Judgment of the Court

11 The Supreme Court allowed revision of the decision of the second instance court on two issues, of which it is worth highlighting in particular the question of whether the courts of first and second instance correctly applied the legal standard of care in assessing the defendant's conduct in the specific case. The Supreme Court found that the parties to the dispute had agreed in the insurance contract, of which the plaintiff's general terms and conditions were an integral part, that the defendant would not lose his rights under the insurance if he proved that he was not at fault for a technical defect of his vehicle. They did not define fault in more detail, but since the intentional causing of a traffic accident is an independent reason for the loss of insurance rights under general terms and con-

ditions, the Supreme Court ruled that they had negligence in mind here. The mildest degree of negligence is presumed, namely ordinary negligence (*culpa levis*). Since the defendant was not a professional tractor driver, he was subject to the standard of ordinary (non-professional) care. The Supreme Court did not agree with the opinion of the first and second instance courts that, in order to meet the required care of a tractor driver, the defendant should have checked the operation of the lights on the tractor trailer not only when it was coupled to the tractor, but also before he drove onto the regional road again. It pointed out that when assessing his due care as a non-professional tractor driver, it was necessary to proceed from the circumstances of the specific off-road driving or work in the field. When the defendant coupled the hired trailer to the tractor, he made sure that the lights on it were working and then drove it to the assembly point in the field. No special features or additional details about driving in the field, the course of work and the handling of the trailer during this time were established. In the opinion of the Supreme Court, most reasonable people who do not drive tractors professionally would not have thought that in such a short time after a preliminary inspection of the operation of the rear lights, the rear lights might no longer be working. The standard of care applied by the first and second instance courts in assessing the defendant's guilt for the failure of the rear lights of the tractor trailer was too strict and unsustainable in the circumstances of the specific case. The Supreme Court therefore granted the appeal and amended the judgment of the second instance court by granting the appeal and amending the interim judgment of the first instance court by dismissing the claim.

c) Commentary

In addition to the Code of Obligations,[5] which contains general provisions on in- 12
surance contracts, the Compulsory Transport Insurance Act is important for transport insurance (hereinafter: ZOZP).[6] ZOZP regulates the insurance of passengers in public transport against the consequences of an accident (except for passengers in air transport), the insurance of a vehicle owner against liability for damage caused to third parties (motor vehicle liability insurance), the insurance of a boat owner against liability for damage caused to third parties, and the insurance of an aircraft owner against liability for damage caused to third parties, passengers, luggage and cargo (para 1 art 1 ZOZP). In cases specified by law or insur-

5 Uradni list RS Nos 97/2007, 64/2016, 20/2018.
6 Uradni list RS Nos 93/07, 40/12, 33/16, 41/17, 45/24.

ance conditions, an insurance company that settled the damage to the injured party or paid compensation has the right to claim reimbursement of the amounts paid, together with interest and costs, from the person responsible (designated a recourse claim, para 2 art 7 ZOZP). In motor vehicle liability insurance, an insurance company has a recourse claim only in specific legal cases (para 2 art 7 ZOZP), one of which is if the vehicle was not technically flawless (pt 7 para 3 art 7 ZOZP).

13 The case under consideration is relevant for the development of the standard of care that a driver must demonstrate in ensuring the technical condition of a vehicle in order to maintain insurance rights. In addition to the standard of care that a driver must demonstrate in checking the technical condition of a vehicle, the Supreme Court has, in its previous practice, also considered the technical condition of a vehicle from the perspective of causation. The Supreme Court has repeatedly emphasised that the technical condition of a vehicle is a broad concept that covers a wide range of defects, from those that clearly prevent safe driving to those that have no effect on driving safety.[7] The loss of insurance rights cannot depend on a circumstance that is not in any causal connection with the occurrence of the insured event. The driver cannot be required to eliminate all, even minimal, technical defects of a vehicle that have no impact on driving safety, since such a measure would be completely disproportionate from the point of view of the insurance relationship. The causal connection between the fact that the vehicle is not technically flawless and the occurrence of damage may therefore be challenged.[8]

2. Judgment of the Supreme Court II Ips 34/2024, 2 October 2024: State Liability for Damages due to the Conduct of an Administrative Body

a) Brief Summary of the Facts

14 The competent tax authority, on the basis of the then applicable art 68.a of the Tax Procedure Act (hereinafter: ZDavP-2), conducted a tax audit of the claimant for the period from 1 January 2007 to 31 December 2013 and established an unexplained increase in assets in the amount of € 4,660,681. On the basis of para 4 art 68.a of ZDavP-2, the tax authority assessed tax at a rate of 70 % of this established tax

7 Judgment of the Supreme Court II Ips 61/2023, 7 February 2024; judgment of the Supreme Court II Ips 9/2018, 5 April 2018.

8 Judgment of the Supreme Court II Ips 9/2018, 5 April 2018.

base, which amounted to € 3,262,477. The Ministry of Finance partially granted his appeal, reduced the tax base to € 4,155,465 and assessed the tax at € 2,908,826. The claimant filed an action with the administrative court against the second instance decision of the Ministry of Finance. This, at his initiative, suspended the proceedings and filed a request with the Constitutional Court of the Republic of Slovenia (hereinafter: Constitutional Court RS) to review the constitutionality of the provisions of ZDavP-2. The Constitutional Court RS, by decision no U-I-113/17 of 11 July 2017, granted the request and repealed para 4 art 68.a of ZDavP-2, insofar as it provided for the taxation of undeclared income at a tax rate exceeding the previously applicable tax rate. It also repealed para 3 art 68.a of ZDavP-2, insofar as it allowed undeclared income originating from periods before 1 January 2009 to be taxed. Following the decision of the Constitutional Court RS, the first instance tax authority assessed the plaintiff's tax to be € 185,712 with associated interest and returned € 3,795,030 to him on 22 July 2021.

The plaintiff subsequently, on the basis of art 26 of the Constitution of the Re- 15
public of Slovenia (hereinafter: Constitution RS),[9] by lawsuit claimed compensation from the State for damage allegedly caused to him by the unlawful conduct of the tax authorities. He claimed that he was forced to sell the asset management business of two mutual funds in order to pay incorrectly assessed taxes, and that he had thereby suffered material damage. The first instance court rejected his claim. It stated that for the State to be liable for damages under art 26 of the Constitution RS, it is not sufficient that the competent administrative authorities applied substantive law incorrectly or that procedural rules were violated, but that there must have been qualified illegality, which the plaintiff failed to prove. The second instance court upheld the judgment of the first instance court. Among other things, it also agreed with the assessment of the first instance court that the fact that the plaintiff had repeatedly warned the competent tax authorities about the unconstitutionality of the law did not affect the existence of qualified illegality.

b) Judgment of the Court

The Supreme Court allowed revision of the decision of the second instance court 16
on the question of whether the interpretation of the legal provisions on the liability of public servants for damage, according to which qualified illegality is a condition for the State's liability for damage caused by an official of an administrative

9 Uradni list RS Nos 33/91-I, 42/97, 66/00, 24/03, 47/04, 68/04, 69/04, 68/06, 47/13, 47/13, 75/16, 92/21.

body (hereinafter: official) in connection with the performance of the activities of the administrative body, is in accordance with art 26 of the Constitution RS. The Supreme Court emphasised in its introduction that the plaintiff asserted the State's liability for damages due to the issuance of an incorrect individual administrative act and not due to legislative illegality, therefore the assessment was limited to the question of the existence of illegality in the conduct of the competent tax authorities when issuing a specific tax decision. The institution *exceptio illegalis* can only be used by a judge in specific decision-making when they consider that a general regulatory act (and not a law) is unconstitutional or illegal, and the administrative body does not have this jurisdiction. However, the Constitutional Court RS in its decision no U-I-39/10 of 11 March 2010 warned that administrative authorities must also protect the constitutional order and human rights and fundamental freedoms in their procedures, because this obligation is not and cannot be reserved only to the courts. It stressed that administrative authorities are bound by the law in accordance with the principle of legality and cannot refuse to apply it in the event of doubt about its compliance with the Constitution RS, nor are they entitled to submit requests to the Constitutional Court RS during the procedure for an assessment of compliance of the law with the Constitution RS, since this possibility is given only to the courts (art 156 of the Constitution RS). However, it follows from administrative bodies being bound to the Constitution RS and the duty to respect the constitutional rights of individuals and legal entities that if, when deciding on the rights, obligations or legal benefits of parties, administrative bodies must apply a law that, in their opinion, is unconstitutional, they must draw the attention of the superior body to this, which should examine such a position and, in the event of doubt about the constitutionality of the law, propose appropriate action to the highest bodies of the executive branch of government.

17 In the specific case, the Supreme Court found that the unconstitutionality of art 68.a of ZDavP-2 had already been pointed out by the legislative-legal service of the National Assembly during the legislative procedure. The then leadership of the Ministry of Finance participated in the legislative procedure on behalf of the government. Despite the fact that the legislative-legal service of the National Assembly had pointed out the unconstitutionality of the regulation during the legislative procedure, this leadership did not change the draft amendment to the law. The public servants who decided on the plaintiff's tax case at first and second instance within the Ministry of Finance, given the described previous conduct of their superiors and the principle of hierarchy, cannot be criticised for not having re-submitted the issue of unconstitutionality to the management of the Ministry, but left the consideration of this issue to the court, which has the legal authority to independently initiate proceedings to assess the constitutionality of a law. The Supreme Court therefore concluded that the tax authority's conduct was not un-

reasonable and did not constitute a gross violation of the fundamental principles of administrative action, and dismissed the appeal.

c) Commentary

According to art 26 of the Constitution RS, everyone has the right to compensation for damage caused to them by the unlawful conduct of a person or body performing such a service or activity in connection with the performance of a service or some other activity of a State body, local community body or holder of public authority. It follows from this provision that the basis for liability is (1) unlawful conduct of a State body (local community body or holder of public authority); (2) conduct at work or in connection with work, ie, the exercise of authority; and (3) the consequence of which is the occurrence of damage.[10] Article 26 of the Constitution RS does not regulate key issues of State liability for damages, such as issues of legally recognised damage, causality and limitation. Since the aforementioned issues are not regulated in the legislation as a special institution of the institution of public law compensation, the rules of the law of obligations from the Code of Obligations apply.[11] However, when assessing individual assumptions of liability for damages, it is necessary to take into account the specific features that arise from the authoritative nature of the actions of its bodies, officials and employees.[12] 18

Court practice has repeatedly dealt with the liability of the State for damages due to the conduct of its bodies or persons in the performance of their duties or other activities. In the case in question, it is worth highlighting court practice in the area of the liability of the State for damages due to the conduct of a judge, since the Supreme Court also refers to the foundations of this liability when assessing the conduct of administrative bodies in issuing individual administrative acts.[13] The Supreme Court laid the foundations of the State's liability for the con- 19

---

10 *D Možina*, Odškodninska odgovornost države [Liability of the state for damage], Pravni letopis 2013, 143.

11 *Možina*, Pravni letopis 2013, 143, 144.

12 Judgment of the Supreme Court II Ips 34/2024, 2 October 2024.

13 Judgment of the Supreme Court III Ips 5/2014, 25 March 2014; judgment of the Supreme Court II Ips 201/2011, 24 April 2014; judgment of the Higher Court in Ljubljana II Cp 483/2014, 7 May 2014; judgment of the Supreme Court II Ips 879/2008, 29 March 2012; judgment of the Supreme Court II Ips 112/2021, 21 April 2022; judgment of the Supreme Court II Ips 34/2024, 2 October 2024. See also *B Novak/G Dugar*, Slovenia, in: E Karner/BC Steininger (eds), European Tort Law (ETL) 2014 (2015) 566, no 6.

duct of a judge in its legal opinion of 14 December 1995, according to which, a judge acts unlawfully only in the case of a so-called qualified degree of error.[14] The Supreme Court has taken the position in several decisions that the State is liable for damages when a judge unreasonably deviates from clear provisions of substantive law and established court practice in their decision-making or when they have grossly violated the provisions of procedural law.[15] According to the aforementioned practice, a decision in an administrative procedure is unlawful when the competent authority or holder of public authority exceeds the scope of its lawful activities to such an extent that this cannot be justified or explained based on the principles of the administrative or legal system.[16] The case under consideration is relevant for the further development of court practice regarding the definition of a presumption of unlawfulness of the conduct of an administrative body, since the Supreme Court adopted an important position regarding the assessment of this presumption in the event that a party in the proceedings points out the unconstitutionality of a provision, and the administrative body nevertheless applies the disputed provision.

3. Judgment of the Supreme Court II Ips 71/2023, 25 January 2024: State Liability for Damages due to Prison Living Conditions

a) Brief Summary of the Facts

20 The plaintiff claimed compensation in the amount of € 27,850 from the State for non-pecuniary damage due to inadequate living conditions during detention and imprisonment in Ljubljana Prison (hereinafter: ZPKZ Ljubljana). The following circumstances of the plaintiff's incarceration were established. The plaintiff spent 556 days in ZPKZ Ljubljana in 2016, 2017 and 2018, of which 213 days were in the summer. For 207 days, he had from 3.790–3.905 m^2, for 235 days from 5.053–5.277 m^2, for 92 days 6.860 m^2 and for 22 days over 7 m^2 of personal space. During detention, he had the opportunity to be outside his room daily for 6 hours and 50 minutes, and during his sentence for 11 hours and 20 minutes. Dur-

14 Legal opinion II/95, at 5.

15 Judgment of the Supreme Court II Ips 36/2018, 18 April 2019; judgment of the Supreme Court II Ips 200/2010, 9 January 2014; judgment of the Supreme Court II Ips 34/2024, 2 October 2024. See also *Novak/Dugar* (fn 13) no 5 f.

16 Judgment of the Supreme Court II Ips 34/2024, 2 October 2024.

ing this time, he could be in the hallway or in another room, and he also had the opportunity to walk outside the building. In the summer, there were unpleasant odours in the toilets. Temperatures on the second floor of ZPKZ Ljubljana did not rise above 30°C, but during heatwaves they approached this limit. The temperature of 28°C, which is prescribed as the maximum air temperature in working areas, was exceeded 12 times. In the summer of 2017, the plaintiff was in a room on the top floor, which was covered with sheet metal. During the summer, the plaintiff lived with one to three fellow inmates and did not have a portable fan in the room. As a diabetic, he had difficulty enduring the heat, and he often felt dizzy. He went for walks half of the time or did not go at all, although he was mobile. He refused to eat properly, take medication for the treatment of diabetes, or have check-ups with a diabetologist. He did not complain about the heat and unpleasant smells, and did not file any complaints during his time in prison.

The first instance court ordered the defendant to pay € 2,000 in damages with 21
statutory default interest, and dismissed the remaining part of the claim. It considered that the conditions in the plaintiff's room were unbearable and inhumane during the heatwaves in the summer months of 2016, 2017 and 2018 due to the temperatures and lack of ventilation in the bathrooms. It dismissed the plaintiff's other allegations of inhumane treatment as unfounded. The Court of Appeal granted the defendant's appeal and amended the contested judgment, rejecting the plaintiff's claim in its entirety on the grounds that high temperatures and unpleasant smells did not mean that the defendant's conduct was unlawful. In addition, the defendant had allowed the plaintiff to move outside the room and to ventilate the room with fresh air.

b) Judgment of the Court

The Supreme Court allowed revision on the question of whether unlawfulness, as 22
an element of liability for damages, is given when the State allows conditions in a prison facility to become inadequate (unbearable) for living in during the summer months, due to the heat in the premises, and do not meet the minimum standards for serving a prison sentence, even if the convicts do not complain about the situation. The central dilemma in the context of this question was how an assessment of the unlawfulness of the defendant's conduct is affected by the fact that the plaintiff did not complain about the heat. The Supreme Court, comparing the specific case with other cases,[17] considered that the claimant had more per-

17 Judgment of the Supreme Court II Ips 84/2020, 20 January 2021; judgment of the Supreme

sonal space and could spend significantly more time outside the room. Although the claimant's room was hot, the temperatures were comparable or even lower than in the cases of *Mandić and Jović v Slovenia*[18] and *Štrucl and others v Slovenia.*[19] He did live on the top floor of the building for a while, but only for one of the three summers. He could relieve the heat by taking longer walks, moving to other rooms, visiting the canteen or taking a cold shower. Due to the heat, he could have asked to be moved to another room on a lower floor, which he did not do. He also did not always take advantage of the opportunity to move freely, he went for walks half of the time or did not go at all. The plaintiff had adequate medical care, but he refused to eat properly, take medication for the treatment of diabetes and have check-ups with a diabetologist, which, according to the findings of the first instance court, undoubtedly had an impact on the deterioration of his diabetes. Based on the above findings, the Supreme Court considered that the defendant, taking into account all the options the plaintiff was offered during his imprisonment and the fact that the plaintiff did not complain about the prison conditions (the heat and the smells in the toilets), did not act unlawfully and rejected the revision.

c) Commentary

23 In its court practice, the Supreme Court has already defined certain legal bases for assessing claims for compensation for damage due to the violation of personal rights during deprivation of liberty. According to court practice, the conduct of the State is unlawful when it involves an intervention that no longer meets the minimum standards of civilization, violates human dignity or, in extreme cases, constitutes inhumane or degrading treatment.[20] Whether the State's conduct constitutes such an unacceptable situation depends on an assessment of all the circumstances of the case. For example, if a detainee has between 3 and 4 m^2 of personal space at their disposal, other conditions are also examined, in particular the

Court II Ips 88/2017, 30 November 2017; judgment of the Supreme Court II Ips 45/2017, 30 November 2017; European Court of Human Rights (EctHR) *Mandić and Jović v Slovenia*, 20.11. 2011, nos 5774/10, 5985/10; ECtHR *Štrucl and others v Slovenia*, 20.10.2011, nos 5903/10, 6003/10, 6544/10.

18 ECtHR *Mandić and Jović v Slovenia*, 20.11.2011, nos 5774/10, 5985/10.

19 ECtHR *Štrucl and others v Slovenia*, 20.10.2011, nos 5903/10, 6003/10, 6544/10.

20 Judgment of the Supreme Court II Ips 84/2020, 20 January 2021; judgment of the Supreme Court II Ips 88/2017, 30 November 2017; judgment of the Supreme Court II Ips 45/2017, 30 November 2017; judgment of the Supreme Court II Ips 84/2020, 20 January 2021.

possibility of movement outside the room, access to outdoor recreation, natural light, the possibility of ventilation, the appropriateness of the room temperature and hygiene standards. If the personal space is restricted for a short period of time and deviates only slightly from the minimum standards, the alleged violation will not normally be shown.[21]

The case under consideration is important from the perspective of the further development of court practice regarding the State's liability for damages for living conditions in prisons. It is worth highlighting that the Supreme Court, when assessing the presumption of unlawfulness, also gave special weight to the fact that the plaintiff did not complain about the conditions. In doing so, it emphasised the foreseeability of the damaging consequences as one of the central criteria for unlawful conduct.[22] The potential injured party's activity in informing the administration of the prison about the inappropriateness of the conditions or living conditions during the deprivation of liberty (eg, that there were unpleasant smells, that he felt too hot, that he had health problems) is a legally significant circumstance in assessing the unlawful conduct of the prison. If this is done, the administration of the prison can more easily foresee that its conduct may cause a harmful consequence.[23] 24

4. Judgment of the Supreme Court II Ips 70/2023, 13 February 2024: Determination of the Amount of Full Compensation

a) Brief Summary of the Facts

The plaintiff claimed payment of € 36,839 with statutory default interest from 1 December 2017 until payment and payment of a monthly annuity from 3 April 2022 in the amount of € 696 to be paid by the first day of each month. In the claim, she stated that on 12 May 2016, she was injured as a passenger in a passenger vehicle involved in a traffic accident. The person who caused the traffic accident, who was fully responsible for the traffic accident, was covered with liability insurance with 25

21 Judgment of the Supreme Court II Ips 71/2023, 25 January 2024, and the court practice cited there.

22 On Slovene court practice regarding the foreseeability of the occurrence of consequential damage, see also *B Novak/G Dugar* in: B Winiger/E Karner/K Oliphant (eds), Digest of European Tort Law, Volume 3: Essential Cases on Misconduct (2018) 474, 475.

23 Judgment of the Supreme Court II Ips 71/2023, 25 January 2024.

the defendant at the time of the damage event. The defendant paid the plaintiff € 41,000 in compensation; the only disputed issue related to the compensation claimed for inability to work during treatment, or more specifically, whether the plaintiff was entitled to the gross or net amount of lost income. The first instance court concluded that the plaintiff had claimed pecuniary damage due to loss of income, which is reflected in the difference between the salary she would have received and the salary she received due to being on sick leave while receiving medical treatment. The first instance court took the position that it may not decide on public law burdens on income (ie mandatory contributions that an employer must deduct and transfer to the State, including health and pension insurance contributions), but may only award the plaintiff the full (gross) amount of compensation for loss of income. The second instance court agreed with the first instance court and pointed out that the plaintiff's earnings are the gross salary. The plaintiff, not her employer, is the person liable for paying contributions, which is why the plaintiff is entitled to enforce them.

b) Judgment of the Court

26 The Supreme Court allowed revision on two issues, namely, (1) whether the plaintiff was entitled to receive social contributions from the compensation representing loss of personal income from employment from the insurance company with which the compulsory motor vehicle liability insurance was concluded; and (2) whether the fact that it is taxable compensation must be evident from the operative part of the judgment. The Supreme Court emphasised that earnings lost due to inability to work during treatment after a traffic accident constitute lost earnings. Lost earnings are a head of damages for material harm resulting from a bodily injury, the consequences of which are reflected in the fact that the injured party is no longer able to generate the same income with the same gainful employment as before the accident (art 174 of the Code of Obligations). A claim for the recovery of lost earnings is thus a claim for financial compensation for the gainful employment that the injured party performed before the damage event. The requested pecuniary amount is intended to restore the injured party to the financial situation that would have existed without the damage event. This amount is the gross salary, ie, the amount from which the person liable to pay taxes, ie, the recipient of the salary, must pay social insurance contributions. In the gross earnings system, the financial loss suffered by a specific injured party is defined by the difference between the gross salary before the damage event and the gross earnings (compensation) after the damage event. Payments of taxes and contributions are a matter for other (tax administrative) procedures

and not for civil proceedings in which compensation is decided. Based on the above, the Supreme Court therefore answered the first question in the affirmative and the second in the negative, and dismissed the appeal.

c) Commentary

A court awards an injured party compensation in the amount necessary to restore their financial situation to the level it was before the damage event (ie full compensation; art 169 of the Code of Obligations).[24] An injured party has the right to compensation for ordinary property damage and also for lost profits (para 1 art 168 of the Code of Obligations). When assessing lost profits, account is taken of the profit that could reasonably have been expected in the normal course of events or in special circumstances, but which could not have been achieved due to the act or omission of the person causing the damage (para 3 art 168 of the Code of Obligations). 27

The Code of Obligations, in its provision on compensation for damage in the event of bodily injury or impaired health, refers to lost earnings (art 168 of the Code of Obligations). Anyone who causes bodily injury to another or impairs their health must reimburse the latter for the costs of treatment and other necessary costs related thereto, as well as earnings lost due to their inability to work during treatment (para 1 art 174 of the Code of Obligations). If the injured party loses earnings due to complete or partial inability to work or their needs permanently increase or the possibilities for their further development and advancement are destroyed or reduced, the liable party must pay them a certain monetary annuity as compensation for this damage (para 2 art 174 of the Code of Obligations). Given that the injured party's position must be the same as it would have been if the damage event had not occurred, in the case under consideration, it is possible to agree with the position of the Supreme Court that the injured party is entitled to reimbursement of her gross salary. The gross salary is the amount from which the salary recipient must pay social contributions. This is not changed by the fact that these amounts are transferred in the name and on behalf of the salary recipient by the employer as the payer of the salary directly to the person specified by law. The payment of these deductions is therefore a pay- 28

24 *B Novak*, Osnove neposlovne odškodninske obveznosti [Bases of non-commercial tortious liability], in: M Juhart/D Možina/B Novak/A Polajnar-Pavčnik/V Žnidaršič Skubic (eds), Uvod v civilno pravo [Introduction to civil law] (2011) 237.

ment by the recipient of the salary to the State.[25] It is therefore a matter of equating the injured party's gross salary position with their gross salary position before the damage event.[26]

5. European Court of Human Rights (ECtHR) *Dolenc v Slovenia*, 22.5.2024, no 20256/20: Award of Pecuniary Damages for Failure to Ensure the Right to a Fair Trial

a) Brief Summary of the Facts

29 The case concerns recognition by the Slovene courts of judgments issued by the Tel Aviv District Court (hereinafter: the Israeli district court's judgments) in civil proceedings against the applicant. In the proceedings in Israel, the applicant was found liable for damage caused to EM as a result of surgery performed by him. The applicant was ordered to pay EM a significant amount in compensation. In a judgment delivered on 20 October 2022 (hereinafter: the principal judgment), the European Court of Human Rights (hereinafter: ECtHR) held that there had been a violation of para 1 art 6 of the European Convention on Human Rights (ECHR) because the Slovene courts had failed duly to satisfy themselves, before recognising the Israeli district court's judgments, that the trial in Israel had been fair (see *Dolenc v Slovenia*, 20.10.2022, no 20256/20, §§ 55–76).[27] Since the parties did not reach an agreement, the applicant submitted his claims for pecuniary damages and the respondent Government submitted their observations in this regard.

30 Following the recognition of the Israeli district court's judgments by the Slovene courts, several sets of enforcement proceedings were instituted against various assets of the applicant. As a consequence, sums were consistently taken from his bank account in Slovenia and from his retirement pension and paid to EM. On 23 November 2022, following the ECtHR's principal judgment, the applicant applied to the Ljubljana District Court to have the recognition proceedings reopened. The respondent State intervened in the proceedings (in support of the applicant), arguing that proceedings before the ECtHR were pending and that the resolution of the case depended to a large extent on the possibility of discontinuing the en-

25 Judgment of the Supreme Court II Ips 13/2023, 6 September 2023.

26 Judgment of the Supreme Court II Ips 70/2023, 13 February 2024.

27 For a presentation of the principal judgment, see *G Dugar*, Slovenia, in: E Karner/BC Steininger (eds), European Tort Law (ETL) 2023 (2024) 607, no 28.

forcement proceedings against the applicant. EM objected to the reopening. The Ljubljana District Court considered that art 394 of the Civil Procedure Act, setting out the grounds for reopening civil proceedings, might be unconstitutional because it did not allow proceedings to be reopened on the basis of the ECtHR's finding of a violation of the ECHR. On 7 April 2023, the Ljubljana District Court decided to suspend the proceedings concerning the application to reopen and requested that the constitutionality of art 394 of the Civil Procedure Act be reviewed by the Constitutional Court. This decision was upheld by the Supreme Court on 17 August 2023. On 8 June 2023, the applicant lodged a request to suspend the enforcement proceedings against his assets – his bank account, his retirement pension and his movable property – until the Constitutional Court's decision. On 26 July 2023, the Ljubljana District Court dismissed that request, finding that there was no indication that the Constitutional Court had started to examine the request for constitutional review. The applicant subsequently appealed. On 5 December 2023, the Ljubljana Higher Court, referring to the ECtHR's principal judgment, upheld the applicant's appeal and decided to suspend the enforcement proceedings until the Constitutional Court decided on the request for review of constitutionality of art 394 of the Civil Procedure Act. Until 30 November 2023, that is prior to the suspension of the enforcement proceedings, the applicant had paid EM € 329,306 by way of enforcement of the latter's claim with attachment of the applicant's bank account and pension.

A separate set of enforcement proceedings against the applicant concerned 31
his immovable property. It would appear that this part of the proceedings was, at least partially, suspended because the applicant's wife had objected to the enforcement and brought a claim for a share of the immovable property. On 28 February 2023, the applicant lodged a request to suspend this set of enforcement proceedings, referring to his application to reopen the recognition proceedings and the Court's principal judgment. EM, on the other hand, requested that the applicant's claims against the State based on the Court's principal judgment be attached to the enforcement. On 6 July 2023, the Ljubljana Local Court issued a decision. It held that EM's claim amounted to € 11,610,395, which would remain largely unpaid even if the immovable property in question were sold. It allowed EM's request to attach the applicant's claims in respect of non-pecuniary damage and costs and expenses awarded to the applicant by the ECtHR in the principal judgment. At the same time, it suspended that set of enforcement proceedings until the decision on reopening was given. It noted that the applicant had lodged an extraordinary remedy and took into account the ECtHR's principal judgment in the case and the Ljubljana District Court's decision to initiate proceedings before the Constitutional Court. It also noted that the applicant would not have the aforementioned sums awarded by the ECtHR at his disposal, but that they would not be

transferred to EM unless the applicant's application to reopen the recognition proceedings was turned down. EM's appeal was dismissed by the Ljubljana Higher Court on 5 December 2023. In the meantime, on 16 February 2023, the Government's representatives met with EM's representative to discuss possible solutions regarding the execution of the ECtHR's judgment. The Government's report on the meeting indicates that there was no basis for reaching an agreement because of the significant differences in the participants' position on the matter.

b) Judgment of the Court

32 The ECtHR found that the applicant had sustained pecuniary damage as a result of the recognition of the Israeli district court's judgments by the Slovene courts in proceedings that did not comply with § 1 art 6 of the ECHR, as found in the principal judgment. It reiterated that a judgment in which it finds a breach imposes on the respondent State a legal obligation to put an end to the breach and make reparation for its consequences in such a way as to restore, as far as possible, the situation existing before the breach. The Contracting States that are parties to a case are, in principle, free to choose the means whereby they will comply with a judgment in which the ECtHR has found a breach. The ECtHR observed that enforcement regarding the applicant's immovable property and the sums awarded to him in respect of non-pecuniary damage and costs and expenses pursuant to the principal judgment was for the moment suspended. Since 5 December 2023, he had therefore not incurred losses on that account. According to the latest information received by the ECtHR, € 329,306 was taken from the applicant's bank account and pension and paid to EM up to 30 November 2023.

33 The ECtHR observed that the respondent State supported the applicant in his attempt to reopen the recognition proceedings in their capacity as an intervening party in the proceedings. While the enforcement of EM's claim seemed to be now suspended, the ECtHR understood that the Government were possibly faced with a practical difficulty in that compensation paid by the Government could be withheld from the applicant at least until the decision on his application to reopen the recognition proceedings was given. The ECtHR was not in a position to determine what the best solution would be in the domestic legal system to ensure that the applicant received the sums awarded to him by the ECtHR and to discontinue the ongoing enforcement based on the domestic decisions found to be in breach of para 1 art 6 of the ECHR, especially given that the issue regarding the possibility of reopening the recognition proceedings was currently pending before the Constitutional Court. Since there was no indication of when the proceedings before the Constitutional Court would be completed and what the impact on the appli-

cant would be in the event of their favourable outcome, the ECtHR did not find it justified either to delay the judgment regarding the just satisfaction under art 41 of the ECHR, as suggested by the Government. It noted in this connection that the respondent State remained under a legal obligation to put an end to the breach and make reparation for its consequences.

In view of the above considerations, the ECtHR considered it reasonable to 34 award the applicant the sum corresponding to compensation for the pecuniary loss he sustained up to 30 November 2023, namely € 329,306. It further considered that interest should be added to the above award in order to compensate for the loss of value of the award over time. The interest should reflect national economic conditions, such as levels of inflation and rates of interest. In the circumstances of the present case, having regard also to inflation during the relevant period, the ECtHR, ruling on an equitable basis, awarded the applicant € 390,000 in respect of pecuniary damage, plus any tax that may have been chargeable on that amount. The ECtHR further considered that the respondent State should ensure that the applicant's property, including the sums awarded pursuant to the principal judgment, as well as the present judgment, were not subject to enforcement of the claim arising from the Israeli district court's judgments. The Government should also compensate the applicant for any sums taken from his bank account or pension by way of such enforcement after 30 November 2023. While the respondent State was free to choose the means of complying with this obligation, it was important that the redress, namely the payment of just satisfaction and the cessation of any further loss resulting from the violation found in the principal judgment, was provided to the applicant without delay.

c) Commentary

In 2024, the ECtHR issued two decisions against Slovenia, both of which, again this 35 year,[28] (*Dolenc v Slovenia* and *Škoberne v Slovenia*, no 19920/20, 15 February 2024[29])

---

28 Violation of para 1 art 6 of the ECHR has been among the most frequent Slovene violations of the ECHR for years. Previous reports have already drawn attention to this issue: *B Novak*, Slovenia, in: E Karner/BC Steininger (eds), European Tort Law (ETL) 2020 (2021) 588, no 29; and *B Novak/G Dugar*, Slovenia, in: E Karner/BC Steininger (eds), European Tort Law (ETL) 2016 (2017) 550, no 34; *B Novak*, Slovenia, in: E Karner/BC Steininger (eds), European Tort Law (ETL) 2018 (2019) 599, no 35; *G Dugar*, Slovenia, in: E Karner/BC Steininger (eds), European Tort Law (ETL) 2023 (2024) 607, no 28.

29 In the case of *Škoberne v Slovenia*, the ECtHR also found a violation of para 3 art 6 of the ECHR and art 8 of the ECHR due to the prolonged systematic surveillance of the applicant's telecom-

were cases involving a breach of para 1 art 6 of the ECHR. The *Dolenc* case shows not only how important it is that there is no breach of the ECHR in national proceedings, but also how important it is for the State to provide in advance rules under which it is possible to effectively and quickly ensure that the breach of the ECHR no longer occurs and to remedy the consequences of that breach. According to the court practice of the ECtHR, the State must ensure that the breach no longer occurs and make reparation for its consequences in such a way as to restore as far as possible the previously existing situation. The State must therefore create mechanisms so that the applicant can actually obtain the compensation recognised by the ECtHR (see secs 19 and 20 of the judgment). The applicant in the *Dolenc* case had not yet accessed the amounts awarded in the principal judgment. Due to the threat that enforcement based on the decision, the issuance of which violated para 1 art 6 of the ECHR, would continue, there was even a threat that the injured party would seek compensation awarded in both judgments before the ECtHR.[30] This would mean the annulment of the ECtHR judgments and a new violation of the ECHR. Apparently, the ECtHR was also aware of the risk of new violations of the ECHR, since it concluded its findings by announcing that this conclusion was without prejudice to any obligation on the part of the applicant arising from any future reopened or fresh ECHR compliant proceedings regarding the recognition of the Israeli district court's judgments or his liability for the damage sustained by EM because of the surgery performed by him in May 1992.

6. Personal Injury

36 In 2024, the courts followed the same basic principles in calculating pecuniary compensation for non-pecuniary damage as in 2023.[31] The basic principles for calculating pecuniary compensation for non-pecuniary damage are individualisation of the level of compensation and objective conditionality of the level of compensation.

37 In relation to the principle of objective conditionality of the amount of pecuniary compensation, it is worth highlighting a case of severe neglect and cruel treatment of a child by one of their parents, which left numerous consequences

munications, due to the rejection of the applicant's motion after hearing two co-defendants as witnesses.

30 The applicant, a renowned Slovene neurosurgeon, died on 16 January 2025.

31 *G Dugar*, ETL 2023 (fn 28), no 34.

on the child's physical and mental condition and psychosocial development.[32] The plaintiff's mother (the defendant) was found guilty in criminal proceedings of committing the criminal offence of neglect of a minor and cruel treatment because, in the period from 19 October 2015 to 11 April 2017, she seriously violated her parental duties towards the minor plaintiff, who was then 11 years old. Her actions caused serious consequences for the plaintiff's physical and mental well-being, namely in the form of physical pain, fear and a decrease in life activities. She left him alone several times in the afternoons and at night, without supervision or protection, and did not provide him with clothing and food, since he had not eaten a hot meal for several months. He lived in a disordered environment, because the apartment did not have electricity, heating or hot water due to non-payment of these utilities. The defendant also did not ensure that the plaintiff attended primary school regularly. The plaintiff therefore had poorer understanding of learning material and had poor follow-up with lessons, which prevented him from having a successful education and healthy psychosocial development. He was very afraid that this situation would continue, because the defendant, when he indicated distress, roughly rejected him. Regarding the consequences of the defendant's actions, a clinical psychology expert found that the plaintiff, due to the defendant's actions and omissions, had not reached the expected level of emotional, social and personal maturity given his age. The severe distress to which he was exposed, and the simultaneous overwhelming feelings of fear, rejection, his own worthlessness, sadness and despair, greatly hindered his personal development during that period and for some time after that. The fears described, which will certainly continue to arise in the future, have developed into post-traumatic stress disorder. He sleeps with the computer on, since he is very afraid of the dark. It is assumed that this has caused irreparable damage to the plaintiff's mental health. The deficits are profound, especially in his self-image, which will only be somewhat improved after long-term psychotherapeutic treatment, and he currently suffers from extremely low self-esteem, feelings of self-deprecation and severe feelings of his own vulnerability. There are also serious deficits in the area of psychosocial contacts, since he has major difficulties integrating into the social environment, and for some time he also suffered from a fear of women. He has difficulty establishing contact with peers, is insecure when making new contacts, and is filled with a painful anticipation that he will be rejected, ridiculed and humiliated again. He is hindered in basic life functions, such as sleeping and eating, and lacks a sense of security, which is a basic condition for integrating into one's social environment, as well as emotional problems, especially in terms

32 Judgment of the Supreme Court II Ips 22/2024, 4 September 2024.

of anxiety, which is also manifested through symptoms of pain. The plaintiff suffered very severe physical pain in the form of headaches and nausea, which he could not relieve himself, and the defendant did not offer him any help – he still suffers from them in a moderate to mild form. Due to the described conduct of the defendant, the plaintiff requested compensation from her in the total amount of € 291,500, namely € 55,000 for physical pain, € 200,000 for mental pain due to reduced life activities and € 36,500 for fear.

38 The first instance court granted the plaintiff's claim in the amount of € 90,000 with statutory default interest from 28 September 2008 onwards, and dismissed the higher claim. The second instance court partially granted the plaintiff's appeal and awarded him the full amount claimed for physical pain (€ 55,000 instead of € 45,000), € 50,000 for mental pain due to reduced life activities instead of the originally awarded € 25,000, but did not amend the assessment of compensation in the amount of € 20,000 for fear suffered. As regards the increase in compensation for mental pain due to reduced life activities, it emphasised that the specific case should be compared with the compensation awarded in cases of catastrophic damage.[33] The first and second instance courts based their decision on arts 179 and 182 of the Code of Obligations. In accordance with the provision of art 179 of the Code of Obligations, a court awards compensation for non-pecuniary damage for physical pain suffered, for mental pain suffered due to reduced life activity, disfigurement, defamation of good name and honour or impairment of freedom or personal rights or the death of a loved one and for fear if the circumstances of the case, in particular the degree of pain and fear of the injured party and their duration, justify this. In accordance with the provision of art 182 of the Code of Obligations, fair compensation is also awarded at the request of an injured party for future non-pecuniary damage if it is established that in the ordinary course of events, the damage will continue in the future.[34]

39 The Supreme Court allowed revision on the question of whether the first and second instance courts had erroneously applied substantive law (arts 179 and 182 of the Code of Obligations) because they had not fully awarded the plaintiff compensation for fear and mental anguish due to the reduction of life activities. According to the Supreme Court, the plaintiff suffered damage approaching catastrophic damage, especially in the area of basic human needs, as well as in the area of mental development and the ability to establish psychosocial contacts. The Supreme Court noted that there was no recorded case law in relation to

33 See decisions of the Supreme Court II Ips 587/2008, 20 November 2008; II Ips 668/2005, 17 January 2008; II Ips 32/2002, 11 December 2002.

34 Judgment of the Supreme Court II Ips 22/2024, 4 September 2024.

this type of case, which concerns consequences on a child's physical and mental condition and psychosocial development due to neglect and cruel treatment by a parent. The case under consideration therefore required an approach that corresponds to the specific circumstances and nature of the damage when assessing uniform compensation and placing it in the catalogue of cases of compensation in court practice. In doing so, the Supreme Court referred to the principle of objective conditionality of the amount of monetary compensation. Judgments of the Supreme Court referred to by the second instance court,[35] although, in the opinion of the Supreme Court, they are not directly comparable to the case under consideration, can provide guidance in determining the upper limit of compensation in the case under consideration. In these cases, compensation was determined for injuries from traffic accidents with predominantly catastrophic physical consequences (severe contusions and permanent brain damage) and mostly significantly more severe types and degrees of reduced life activities, both physical and mental. In these cases, compensation was awarded in the amount of 358, 238 and 155 average net salaries. In finding the lower limit of compensation, the Supreme Court compared the case under consideration with compensation awarded primarily in cases of sexual abuse, in which there were similar harmful consequences. In Supreme Court judgments II Ips 8/96 of 28 May 1997, II Ips 295/2012 of 26 November 2014 and II Ips 64/2014 of 26 November 2015, a single compensation award of 80 average monthly net salaries was awarded, and in case II Ips 366/2011 of 19 December 2013, 77 average monthly net salaries. The Supreme Court, having demonstrated the placement of the specific compensation in the corpus of court practice, concluded that an increase in the total amount of compensation awarded before the second instance court in the amount of € 130,000 (100 average monthly net salaries) was not justified.[36] The Supreme Court therefore rejected revision as unfounded.

In relation to the principle of individualising the amount of monetary compensation, it is worth highlighting the example of the assessment of monetary 40 compensation for non-pecuniary damage due to unjustified detention.[37] A plaintiff was arrested on 23 July 2011 on the basis of an international Interpol warrant while attempting to cross the State border at the Jelšane border crossing. On the same day, the Koper District Court ordered his detention. By decision of the Koper District Court of 24 February 2012 in connection with the decision of the Koper Higher Court of 27 March 2012, the plaintiff's extradition to Belarus was

35 Decisions of the Supreme Court II Ips 587/2008, 20 November 2008; II Ips 668/2005, 17 January 2008; II Ips 32/2002, 11 December 2002.

36 Judgment of the Supreme Court II Ips 22/2024, 4 September 2024.

37 Judgment of the Supreme Court II Ips 83/2023, 5 June 2024.

permitted. By decision Up 402/12–16 of 5 July 2012, the Constitutional Court of the Republic of Slovenia annulled the above-mentioned decisions and remitted the case to the Koper District Court for a new decision. The latter again issued a decision on the plaintiff's extradition to Belarus, which the Koper Higher Court annulled in its decision of 21 August 2012, rejecting the petition for the plaintiff's extradition and ordering his immediate release. From his arrest to his release, the plaintiff spent 396 days in detention. The plaintiff was not sentenced for any offence, and neither was any conviction issued in Belarus.

41 The first instance court awarded the plaintiff € 35,800 in damages, with statutory default interest from 20 August 2015 onwards, and dismissed the claim in excess of this amount (the difference to the requested amount of € 166,000 with statutory default interest from 20 August 2015). Of the awarded amount of damages of € 35,800, € 10,800 represented compensation for loss of income, and € 25,000, or 19 average monthly net salaries, represented compensation for non-pecuniary damage due to the deprivation of freedom and the related physical and mental pain. When assessing the compensation for non-pecuniary damage, the court took into account the following circumstances: that the plaintiff was 51 years old at the time of his arrest and had never been detained or imprisoned before the damage event; that the police officer pointed a gun at him during his arrest, which caused him intense fear, all in the presence of his family, and that upon arrest he was worried about what would happen to his family, since his wife did not have a driving licence; that he did not know the exact reason for his detention for one month, and only after three weeks did he manage to establish contact with his family; that he was worried because the courts rejected his appeals; that he was worried about the possibility of extradition to Belarus, where the death penalty is still in force and respect for human rights is at a low level; that he spent 396 days in prison; that as a foreigner, he was restricted in his communication with fellow prisoners and the prison administration and was unable to practise his religion during this time; that he was separated from his wife and two minor children, one of whom was seriously ill; that he lost his job for a certain period of time as a result of his detention; that during his detention he lost weight, experienced health problems and suffered mental pain related to the onset of an adjustment disorder, which lasted approximately one month after his imprisonment and was manifested in a lack of compensatory mechanisms for coping with stress during his imprisonment and also for approximately two years after the end of his imprisonment, when it manifested itself as a depressive reaction in the subtype of adjustment disorder, the consequences of which the plaintiff still feels today; that medical care in detention was adequate; that he was present when the guards beat a fellow prisoner and the cell was under increased surveillance for about six months when he shared a cell with him; that

the deterioration of the plaintiff's dental health was only to a minor extent a consequence of the detention. The second instance court reduced the monetary compensation for non-pecuniary damage to € 19,800. It explained that the State was obliged to execute an arrest warrant against the plaintiff under the United Nations Convention against Organized Crime, which meant that the plaintiff was arrested on reasonable grounds. It therefore did not take into account the circumstances of the arrest and the fear of extradition to Belarus when determining the amount of monetary compensation for non-pecuniary damage.[38]

The Supreme Court allowed revision regarding the assessment of the amount 42
of monetary compensation for non-pecuniary damage. The Supreme Court emphasised that when assessing the amount of compensation, the time spent in detention must be taken into account as a starting point, which is the basis for the amount of compensation in relation to other cases in court practice. The plaintiff's case belonged in the range of detentions lasting several months in terms of the length of the deprivation of liberty. The daily amounts of compensation awarded in this range vary between 0.03 and 0.083 of the average net salary. This means that the compensation awarded to the plaintiff by the second instance court was at the very bottom of this range. Converted to a daily amount, it amounted to 0.038 of an average salary per day. The length of detention in the specific case, in the opinion of the Supreme Court, therefore, is an argument in favour of increasing the fair monetary compensation. When determining the amount of monetary compensation, in addition to the objective conditionality of the amount of monetary compensation, all individual circumstances of the specific case must be taken into account. In the opinion of the Supreme Court, the second instance court's assessment of the monetary compensation for non-pecuniary damage in the amount of 15 average net monthly salaries was too low. Taking into account the violation of dignity during the deprivation of liberty, the duration of the detention and all the inconveniences related to the deprivation of liberty, the fear of extradition to Belarus, and the inconveniences and consequences caused to the plaintiff by the detention, whereby the plaintiff's reputation was not tarnished and his life activities were not permanently reduced, the plaintiff was entitled to fair monetary compensation for non-pecuniary damage in the amount of € 36,230, which represented 25 average monthly net salaries (0.06 of an average salary per day of detention). The Supreme Court believed that the amount awarded in the plaintiff's case is in line with court practice, both in terms of daily amounts, the total duration of detention, and his individual charac-

38 Judgment of the Supreme Court II Ips 83/2023, 5 June 2024.

teristics, which reflect an intense fear of lawlessness and an authoritarian regime and, finally, the violation of his dignity.[39]

C. Literature

1. *D Možina* (ed), *A Cvahte/M Dolenc/A Fakin/M Juhart*, Komentar Obligacijskega zakonika (OZ) – splošni del [Commentary on the Code of Obligations (OZ) – general part] vol 1 (Uradni list Republike Slovenije, Ljubljana, 1st edn 2024)

43 The Commentary on the Code of Obligations is a set of three books that will include a systematic commentary on 434 articles of the general part of the Code of Obligations. It also comprehensively presents the content of non-contractual tort relations. The Commentary aims to be practically oriented and to present legal rules to the reader in an understandable and structured way, to draw their attention to fundamental dilemmas in their application, and to offer them guidelines for resolving legal dilemmas.

44 Currently, only the first book has been published, which includes a commentary on arts 1 to 130. In addition to introductory explanations to the Code, it also discusses the fundamental principles of the law of obligations and the rules on the creation of obligations.[40] From the perspective of non-contractual tort relations, it is worth noting the commentary on the fundamental principle of care (art 5 of the Civil Code) and the fundamental principle of the prohibition of causing damage (art 10 of the Civil Code). The commentary on the aforementioned provisions also contains information on court practice, the literature and basic information on the historical and comparative legal context of individual provisions.

39 Judgment of the Supreme Court II Ips 83/2023, 5 June 2024.

40 <https://www.uradni-list.si/knjigarna/komentar-obligacijskega-zakonika-oz-splosni-del>, 10.12.2024.

2. *N Belopavlovič/B Kresal/K Kresal Šoltes/D Šenčur Peček* (eds), Zakon o delovnih razmerjih s komentarjem (ZDR-1) [Employment Relations Act with commentary (ZDR-1)], 3rd updated and suppl edn (Lexpera, GV Založba, Ljubljana 2024)

Ten years after the entry into force of the Employment Relations Act (ZDR-1), a third, updated and supplemented edition of the commentary to the Employment Relations Act has been published. The new edition was necessary because the field of employment law has undergone significant developments and radical changes at the Slovene, European and global levels during this time.[41] The work is also important from the perspective of tort law, since it contains a detailed analysis of the articles on an employer's liability for damages in the event of a violation of the prohibition of discrimination or harassment at the workplace (art 8 of ZDR-1); on the prohibition of harmful conduct that harms, or could materially or morally harm, the employer's business interests (art 37 of ZDR-1); on an employee's liability for damages (art 177 of ZDR-1); on the exemption of an employee from paying compensation or reducing their compensation payment (art 178 of ZDR-1); on an employer's liability for damages (art 179 of ZDR-1); and on lump sum compensation when determining that the amount of actual damage would cause disproportionate costs (art 180 of ZDR-1). 45

3. *A Fatur*, Konflikt interesov pri odobritvi kolektivne odškodninske tožbe, ki jo financira odvetniška družba [Conflict of interests in the certification of a collective action for damage financed by a law firm], Podjetje in delo 2 (2024) 328 – 346

The author discusses the risk of a conflict of interests in the financing of a collective action for damages by a lawyer. He introduces the institution of a collective action, which is comprehensively regulated by the Collective Actions Act. To protect the rights of injured parties and protect against unfair litigation, this Act introduces a number of new institutions into the legal system, by which it deviates from the general rules of civil procedure. For example, the institutions of approval 46

41 <https://gvzalozba.si/zakon-o-delovnih-razmerjih-zdr-1-s-komentarjem-3-posodobljena-in-dopolnjena-izdaja/>, 10.12.2024.

of a collective action for damages and financing of a collective action by a third party or co-financing by the lawyer in a certain percentage up to the court-awarded amount. The author concludes that in the case of a lawyer financing a collective action, the risk of conflict between the lawyer and the plaintiff is extremely high. He points out that a plaintiff can only successfully protect the interests of the group if they have sufficient knowledge and human and financial resources to constantly supervise their lawyer during the procedure and critically examine their proposals. Otherwise, the members of the group may suffer harm, since it may happen that the lawyer only considers their own payment and the financial justification of the procedure from the perspective of the work they have invested.

Albert Ruda

XXVIII. Spain

A. Legislation

1. Railway Accidents

In 2024, there were several statutory reforms in Spain related to tort liability to a greater or lesser extent. The first is the new Act on the Creation of the Independent Administrative Authority for the Technical Investigation of Railway, Maritime and Civil Aviation Accidents and Incidents.[1] The new statute creates a single multimodal body that assumes the technical investigation powers for railway, maritime and civil aviation accidents, until now attributed to three separate commissions attached to the Spanish Ministry of Transport and Sustainable Mobility. The Law aims to give the aforementioned authority greater autonomy by reinforcing its financial independence (art 1) and establishing a new mechanism for appointing its members (art 32). 1

Other new features include provisions for the participation of those affected in accident investigations, or documents that are confidential. The new regulation is based on the principles of transparency, stakeholder participation and a 'just culture' (*cultura justa*, art 7.4). The latter is understood to mean 'a culture in which operators and other front-line personnel are not punished for actions, omissions or decisions taken by them that are commensurate with their experience and training, but in which gross negligence, wilful violations and destructive acts are not tolerated' (Preamble, III). The Act makes it very clear that the purpose of the technical investigation is to establish the causes of an accident or incident and to formulate, where appropriate, relevant safety recommendations, with the ultimate aim of improving safety and preventing accidents (art 3.1). The technical investigation carried out does not seek to determine responsibility or apportion blame (art 3.2). However, there is nothing preventing the results of the investigation from being used in a possible trial on tort liability. 2

The Act defines the concept of 'railway accidents' as 'sudden, unwanted or unintentional events, or a chain of such events, with harmful consequences, such as 3

1 Act (Ley) 2/2024, of 1 August, *de creación de la Autoridad Administrativa Independiente para la Investigación Técnica de Accidentes e Incidentes ferroviarios, marítimos y de aviación civil* (Boletín Oficial del Estado [BOE] 186, 2.8.2024).

https://doi.org/10.1515/9783111389271-029

collisions, derailments, level crossing accidents, injury to persons caused by rolling stock in motion, fires and others' (art 4.2). An incident that is not an 'accident' in this sense, but which may affect the safety of railway operations, is considered a 'railway incident' (art 4.3). The authority will only investigate serious railway accidents, ie 'the collision or derailment of trains that cause at least one fatality or five or more serious injuries or extensive damage, which the authority can immediately estimate at a total of at least € 2 million, affecting rolling stock, the infrastructure or the environment, and any other accident with the same consequences that has an obvious effect on railway safety regulations and safety management' (art 4.2). Other accidents and incidents will only be investigated if they could have caused serious accidents (art 4.1 para II). There are similar rules in relation to the other types of accident mentioned above (arts 5 and 6). The regulation uses the concept of 'major damage' (*grandes daños*), ie damage that may amount to at least € 2 million and have the other consequences described in the provision – such as eg affecting the railway infrastructure (art 4.3). In relation to aviation accidents, there is an allusion, without defining it, to so-called 'relevant damage' (*daños relevantes*, art 6.1 para 2).

4 The parties involved in accidents and incidents investigated by the authority are obliged, among other things, to safeguard all information obtained before, during and after the accident or incident, not to alter it (which logically follows from the previous obligation, and was unnecessary to stipulate), as well as to diligently collect and preserve all evidence for the purposes of safety investigations (art 10.4). In general, the destruction of evidence can be considered as conduct in bad faith in legal proceedings (art 11.1 of the Law on the Judiciary)[2] and may even amount to a crime (art 464 of the Criminal Code).[3] Apart from that, the new Act establishes the right of victims and their families to access information about the accident before it is made public (art 15). If there is a judicial investigation into the same accident, the judge may request information from the authority, and both investigations will have to be coordinated, in accordance with the principle of mutual cooperation (art 20). The Public Prosecutor's Office has to ensure the proper coordination between the judicial investigation and the technical investigation (art 26.2). Despite this, it can be assumed that the investigations may lead to different conclusions. In any case, if, as a result of the investigation, the authority makes safety recommendations, these 'do not constitute a presumption of fault or liability for an accident or incident' (art 12.2).

2 Organic Act (Ley Orgánica, hereinafter LO) 6/1985, of 1 July, *del Poder Judicial* (BOE 157, 2.7.1985).

3 LO 10/1995, of 23 November, *del Código Penal* (BOE 281, 24.11.1995).

2. Forest Rangers

Another of the statutory novelties of 2024 refers to the figure of the forest ranger.[4] 5
Pursuant to the new Act, they are responsible for the policing, custody and surveillance of legal assets of a forestry and environmental nature (art 1.2.a). Moreover, they should adopt precautionary measures – including confiscation – that are proportionate and necessary, in cases where this is provided for in current legislation, to prevent the continuation of the damage caused by any allegedly infringing activity (art 5.1.d). Although as a general rule courts assess evidence freely (pursuant to the Civil Procedure Act,[5] arts 319, 326, 376, and 384), the new Act provides that: 'The reports and complaints made by forestry and environmental officers in the exercise of their duties have evidentiary value ... and are presumed to be true, subject to ratification in the event that they are denied by the persons concerned, without prejudice to the evidence that they may provide in defence of their respective rights or interests' (art 5.2). In this way, the same value is given to the reports of forest rangers as that of a police report (cf art 319 LEC).

3. Amnesty

In 2024, the political and legal debate was largely characterised by the proposal to 6
grant amnesty to those who incurred responsibilities within the framework of the Catalan independence process. The amnesty was finally passed in June,[6] and although in general terms (art 3) it extinguishes criminal (art 4) and administrative (art 5) accountability, it leaves in place tort liability 'that may correspond to damage suffered by individuals, which will not be substantiated in a criminal court' (art 8.2). Therefore, the Act only excludes liability under public law rules, but allows private individuals who are victims of damage (eg the owners of vehicles set on fire during public disturbances) to make a claim for compensation (should they find the author). Although in general terms victims under Spanish law can choose to seek compensation in criminal or civil proceedings, the new Act excludes the former option. This exclusion seems consistent with the exclusion of criminal liability mentioned above. However, it should be borne in mind that criminal liability for certain offences has been deliberately left outside the scope of amnesty.

4 Act 4/2024, of 8 November, *básica de agentes forestales y medioambientales* (BOE 271, 9.11.2024).

5 Act 1/2000, of 7 January, *de Enjuiciamiento Civil* (BOE 7, 8.1.2000) (hereinafter LEC).

6 LO 1/2024, of 10 June, *de amnistía para la normalización institucional, política y social en Cataluña* (BOE 141, 11.6.2024).

One example is terrorism (art 2.c), but also 'intentional acts against persons that have resulted in death, abortion or injury to the foetus, the loss or uselessness of an organ or limb, the loss or uselessness of a sense, impotence, sterility or a serious deformity' (art 2.a). In these exceptional cases, it seems reasonable to understand that compensation may indeed be requested in criminal proceedings, in accordance with the general rules.[7]

4. Valencia Cold-Drop

7 In October 2024, the atmospheric phenomenon known as an isolated high-level depression (DANA) or 'cold-drop' occurred in a large part of Spain. This exceptional meteorological disturbance particularly affected the region of Valencia, where torrential rains and catastrophic floods caused hundreds of deaths and destroyed numerous properties and public infrastructures, among other damage. In response to such a tragedy, the Spanish government passed various emergency laws.[8] Among other things, these laws establish extraordinary aid aimed at mitigating personal injury and material damage to homes and belongings and to industrial, commercial and service establishments; aid to individuals or legal entities that have made personal contributions and donations of goods, as well as aid to local corporations for emergency expenses. In relation to insurance coverage for extraordinary risks managed by the Insurance Compensation Consortium (*Consorcio de Compensación de Seguros*),[9] the deductible for material damage

7 As regards the right of defence, see the new LO 5/2024, of 11 November, *del Derecho de Defensa* (BOE 275, 14.11.2024).

8 Royal Decree-Act (Real Decreto-Ley, hereinafter RD-Ley) 6/2024, of 5 November, *por el que se adoptan medidas urgentes de respuesta ante los daños causados por la Depresión Aislada en Niveles Altos (DANA) en diferentes municipios entre el 28 de octubre y el 4 de noviembre de 2024* (BOE 268, 6.11.2024; correction of errors BOE 280, 20.11.2024); RD-Ley 7/2024, of 11 November, *por el que se adoptan medidas urgentes para el impulso del Plan de respuesta inmediata, reconstrucción y relanzamiento frente a los daños causados por la Depresión Aislada en Niveles Altos (DANA) en diferentes municipios entre el 28 de octubre y el 4 de noviembre de 2024* (BOE 273, 12.11.2024), and RD-Ley 8/2024, of 28 November, *por el que se adoptan medidas urgentes complementarias en el marco del Plan de respuesta inmediata, reconstrucción y relanzamiento frente a los daños causados por la Depresión Aislada en Niveles Altos (DANA) en diferentes municipios entre el 28 de octubre y el 4 de noviembre de 2024* (BOE 288, 29.11.2024; correction of errors BOE 304, 18.12.2024).

9 The Consortium is a public agency that functions as an insurer of last resort and provides coverage for extraordinary risks, among other functions. For its statutory regime, see Royal Statutory Decree (Real Decreto Legislativo, RDleg) 7/2004, of 29 October, *por el que se aprueba el texto refundido del Estatuto Legal del Consorcio de Compensación de Seguros* (BOE 267, 5.11.2004).

caused in industrial, commercial and service establishments directly caused by the weather events mentioned above, when the insured are small and medium-sized enterprises (SMEs), is eliminated.[10] For these purposes and in order to facilitate the processing of compensation, those enterprises with a net annual turnover not exceeding € 6,000,000 will be considered SMEs, in line with reference amounts provided for by commercial law.

With regard to personal injury, specifically in the case of compensation for death, and in order to facilitate the speediest processing of the compensation claim, the Consortium is expressly authorised to directly request death certificates and certificates from the register of insurance contracts covering death relating to persons[11] who have died as a direct consequence of the events in question.[12] Given the scale of the damage and the number of people affected, the question of what they can claim from insurers or the *Consorcio* has received some attention.[13] Generally speaking, a claim against the *Consorcio* can only be made by someone who has an insurance contract in force. All other persons can only apply for public assistance, if at all. The actions of the regional public administration, which apparently failed to warn the population of the risk, have also been called into question; its possible liability – both criminal and in tort – is still being discussed.[14] 8

10 Otherwise, the deductible generally foreseen for cases where the Consortium is obliged to cover extraordinary risks would apply, pursuant to Royal Decree (Real Decreto, RD) 1060/2015, of 20 November, *de ordenación, supervisión y solvencia de las entidades aseguradoras y reaseguradoras* (BOE 288, 2.12.2015). As a rule, the deductible is 7 % of damage caused, pursuant to Order (Orden) of the Ministry of Economy and Competitiveness ECC/2845/2015, of 23 December, *por la que se regula la franquicia a aplicar por el Consorcio de Compensación de Seguros en materia de seguro de riesgos extraordinarios* (BOE 312, 30.12.2015).

11 Such register is provided for by Act 20/2005, of 14 November, *sobre la creación del Registro de Contratos de Seguros de cobertura de fallecimiento* (BOE 273, 15.11.2005) and RD 398/2007, of 23 March, *por el que se desarrolla la Ley 20/2005, de 14 de noviembre, sobre la creación del Registro de Contratos de Seguros de cobertura de fallecimiento* (BOE 94, 19.4.2007).

12 Additional public aid to the victims of the DANA was provided by RD-Ley 9/2024, of 23 December, *por el que se adoptan medidas urgentes en materia económica, tributaria, de transporte, y de Seguridad Social, y se prorrogan determinadas medidas para hacer frente a situaciones de vulnerabilidad social* (BOE 309, 24.12.2024). This regulation also aims at correcting some shortcomings of the previous statutory regime on the restitution or compensation to political parties of assets seized during the Spanish Civil War, namely Act 43/1998, of 15 December, *de Restitución o Compensación a los Partidos Políticos de Bienes y Derechos Incautados en aplicación de la normativa sobre responsabilidades políticas del período 1936–1939* (BOE 300, 16.12.1998).

13 Among others, see *M López Valverde*, Breve aproximación a la reclamación de daños causados por la DANA, Sepin 4 November 2024 <https://blog.sepin.es/reclamacion-danos-causados-dana>.

14 See *A Benítez Ostos*, ¿Concurre en responsabilidad patrimonial la Administración ante los daños producidos por la DANA? Confilegal 22 November 2024 <https://confilegal.com/20241122-opinion-concurre-en-responsabilidad-patrimonial-la-administracion-ante-los-danos-producidos-

5. Development Workers

9 In 2024, the Spanish government approved the regulatory framework applicable to so-called development workers or 'cooperating persons' (*personas cooperantes*),[15] ie those professionals who work in a developing country, both in the field of development and humanitarian aid, in the service of an organisation that promotes international cooperation. This is the development of a 2023 statute.[16] In particular, the new regulation includes a provision on 'Compensation for death or physical or mental harm to cooperating persons' (art 17). In order to understand the new provisions, it should be borne in mind that, in Spanish law, there is a specific legal regime on compensation for harm caused to participants in international peace and security operations, and that this regime is applicable to Spanish development workers who have been individually and specifically accredited by the Ministry of Foreign Affairs, European Union and Cooperation to carry out their professional activity within the scope of the operations to which they are legally entitled.[17]

10 The new regulation provides that the Spanish Agency for International Development Cooperation (*Agencia Española de Cooperación Internacional para el Desarrollo*, AECID) will establish the necessary electronic means for the organisations which promote cooperation to securely communicate the data of the persons covered by this case (art 17.1). For this purpose, all development workers shall be considered accredited if (a) they meet the requirements established in the regulatory definition of 'cooperating persons' (art 2.1) and (b) the promoting organisation has complied with its obligation to communicate the list of development workers to the AECID (in accordance with art 9.a). Likewise, operations specifically approved by the government in the field of cooperation are understood to be those of 'organisation, promotion, development or execution of cooperation actions for sustainable development or humanitarian actions carried out by promoting entities' (pursuant to art 2.2), in the countries or territories provided

por-la-dana/> and *D Fierro Rodríguez*, DANA e imputación objetiva de homicidios, lesiones y daños imprudentes por omisión, Revista Jurídica Colex 38 (2024) 34–39, also available at Iberley 16 January 2025 <www.iberley.es/revista/tribuna-dana-e-imputacion-objetiva-homicidios-lesiones-y-danos-imprudentes-omision-1281>.

15 RD 708/2024, of 23 July, *por el que se aprueba el Estatuto de las personas cooperantes* (BOE 178, 24.7.2024).

16 Act 1/2023, of 20 February, *de Cooperación para el Desarrollo Sostenible y la Solidaridad Global* (BOE 44, 21.2.2023).

17 Pursuant to Additional Disposition 1.d) of the RD-Ley 8/2004, of 5 November, *sobre indemnizaciones a los participantes en operaciones internacionales de paz y seguridad* (BOE 271, 10.11.2004).

for in the regulation (art 2.3), regardless of the public or private financing of these actions (art 17.2 para 2).

In essence, the new regulation means that development workers will be entitled to the compensation provided for in the special legislation, according to a table that provides, eg, that compensation for death will be € 140,000, and for severe disability, € 390,000.[18] However, compensation for non-disabling permanent injuries will be determined in accordance with the so-called personal injury compensation system or *baremo*, which governs compensation for motor vehicle accidents.[19] Leaving aside the latter case, it is debatable whether the victims of such damage should be subject to a regime different from that provided for in the *baremo*, as the latter has, in practice, become the general criterion applicable to personal injuries, even in cases that are not traffic accidents.[20] However, the 'compensation in damages' (*indemnizaciones*) to which development workers are entitled are paid not by the tortfeasor – should there be any – but by the state, although such payment does not imply any assumption of responsibility by the same.[21] 11

6. Consumer Arbitration

In 2024, the Spanish government passed a new regulation on consumer arbitration.[22] The consumer arbitration system allows consumer complaints to be settled out of court. However, disputes in which there is prima facie evidence of a criminal offence – 'including liability for damages directly arising therefrom' – cannot 12

18 Pursuant to art 1 para 2 RD-Ley 8/2004.

19 The *baremo* is laid down in RDleg 8/2004, of 29 October, *por el que se aprueba el texto refundido de la Ley sobre responsabilidad civil y seguro en la circulación de vehículos a motor* (BOE 267, 5.11.2004). The compensation amounts are updated every year: see Resolution (Resolución) of 18 January 2024, de la Dirección General de Seguros y Fondos de Pensiones, *por la que se publican las cuantías de las indemnizaciones actualizadas del sistema para valoración de los daños y perjuicios causados a las personas en accidentes de circulación* (BOE 26, 30.1.2024). In legal scholarship, see *M López Valverde*, Valoración de daños personales 2024: Baremo e informe pericial (2024) and *I Hurtado Díaz-Guerra*, La divergente actualización de las indemnizaciones por responsabilidad patrimonial sanitaria: cuando el dinero no siempre vale lo mismo, Revista Aranzadi Doctrinal (RAD) (2024) <https://diariolaley.laleynext.es>.

20 The *baremo* considers, eg, the circumstances of the victim, unlike this regulation.

21 Pursuant to art 1 para 1 of the RDleg 8/2004. Such 'compensation in damages' is compatible with 'pensions, aid, compensation or indemnities which have been or may be recognised in the future under the provisions contained in the applicable legislation in each case' (art 6.1 RDleg 8/2004).

22 RD 713/2024, of 23 July, *por el que se aprueba el Reglamento que regula el Sistema Arbitral de Consumo* (BOE 178, 24.7.2024).

be subject to arbitration.[23] This excludes many consumers who are victims of damage whose authorship is very difficult to establish, for example in the frequent case of tampering with electrical installations.[24]

B. Cases

1. Sentencia del Tribunal Constitucional (Constitutional Court Decision, STC) 39/2024, 11 March 2024, ECLI:ES:TC:2024:39:[25] Tort and Crime

a) Brief Summary of the Facts

13 The applicant had been criminally convicted of continuous offences of forgery of official documents and fraud. In accordance with criminal law, the execution of the judgment – and, therefore, imprisonment – was suspended on condition that he did not commit another crime for three years and that he paid the € 14,442 damages award in 24 monthly instalments. Of that total, the culprit paid € 1,200 only. He argued that he was bankrupt and that it was therefore not a wilful default – but to no avail. As a result, the Criminal Court No 4 of Santander revoked the suspension of the judgment and sent him to prison. The Provincial Court of Cantabria upheld that decision.

b) Judgment of the Court

14 The Constitutional Court granted protection (*amparo*) to the applicant on the grounds that the judicial decisions did not adequately analyse the economic capacity of the convicted person when the suspension was revoked, failing to comply

---

23 Art 2.2 of the RD 231/2008, of 15 February, *por el que se regula el Sistema Arbitral de Consumo* (BOE 48, 25.2.2008).

24 On the protection of postal users in the event of shipping loss or damage now, see RD 437/2024, of 30 April, *por el que se aprueba el Reglamento de los servicios postales, en desarrollo de lo establecido por la Ley 43/2010, de 30 de diciembre, del servicio postal universal, de los derechos de los usuarios y del mercado postal* (BOE 121, 18.5.2024) (art 10.4).

25 The full text of the Constitutional Court case law from the Spanish Constitutional Court can be found under <https://hj.tribunalconstitucional.es/es>.

with the requirements of the reinforced reasoning required in these cases. For this reason, the Court declared that the contested orders were null and void and reinstated the appellant's right to effective judicial protection (art 24.1 of the Spanish Constitution [CE])[26] in relation to his personal liberty (art 17.1 CE).

c) Commentary

In 2024, there were several interesting rulings from the Spanish Constitutional Court in relation to tort. In the case under comment, the issue revolved on the relationship between liability in tort and crime.[27] In the vast majority of cases, failure to pay damages means that the convicted person's suspended sentence is revoked, on the grounds that they have seriously failed to comply with the duties imposed on it by the judgment (pursuant to art 86.1 of the Spanish Criminal Code [*Código Penal*, CP]).[28] In this particular case, the judgment is based on an earlier decision by the same court,[29] which had already pointed out that the revocation of the suspension cannot be automatic, but that it is necessary to ascertain what the person's assets are, in order to assess his true financial situation. Since the applicant had been declared insolvent by a civil court, the criminal court had sufficient elements to carry out such an assessment. The doctrine of the judgment under discussion seems open to criticism, because the Criminal Code (art 86) only considers whether the non-compliance of the convicted person is 'serious or repeated', without asking what caused the default. Although it may give the impression that the punishment for non-payment may be severe, it should not be forgotten that the debtor was convicted of an intentional crime. In sum, the Constitutional Court's doctrine may be inadvertently discouraging the enforcement of tort liability in criminal cases. 15

26 Constitución Española (BOE 311, 29.12.1978). Official English translation available at <https://www.boe.es/buscar/pdf/1978/BOE-A-1978-40001-consolidado.pdf>; for the original Spanish text, see: <https://www.boe.es/buscar/act.php?id=BOE-A-1978-31229>.

27 In legal scholarship, see generally *E Sandoval Pérez*, Reparación integral del daño a la víctima del delito, Enfoques jurídicos 9 (2024) 9–25.

28 LO 10/1995, of 23 November, *del Código Penal* (BOE 281, 24.11.1995).

29 STC 132/2002, 22 October 2022, ECLI:ES:TC:2022:132. See also STC 184/2023, 11 December 2023, ECLI:ES:TC:2023:184. Two later, similar cases, are STC 78/2024, 20 May 2024, ECLI:ES:TC:2024:78 and STC 122/2024, 21 October 2024, ECLI:ES:TC:2024:122.

2. STC 61/2024, 9 April 2024, ECLI:ES:TC:2024:61: Liability for Torture

a) Brief Summary of the Facts

16 In 2008, Morocco requested Spain extradite Alí Arrass for alleged terrorism offences. The latter informed the Spanish authorities that he would be subjected to torture in Morocco, and the UN Human Rights Committee requested that the extradition be suspended. Despite this, the extradition took place in 2010. In 2014, the Committee concluded that Spain had violated the International Covenant on Civil and Political Rights[30] (art 7) by failing to properly assess the applicant's risk of torture. Based on this opinion, in 2015, Arrass requested compensation from the Spanish Ministry of Justice for damage suffered. The claim was rejected by administrative silence and subsequently confirmed by the National Court (*Audiencia Nacional*, AN)[31] in 2018. Arrass then lodged an application with the Constitutional Court on the basis of an alleged violation of his fundamental right to physical and moral integrity, with prohibition of torture, inhuman or degrading punishment and treatment (art 15 CE) and to effective judicial protection with prohibition of arbitrariness (art 24.1 CE).

b) Judgment of the Court

17 The *Audiencia Nacional* rejected the applicant's claim because it was based on an alleged malfunctioning of the administration of justice, but such malfunctioning had not been established; the mere fact – it was added – that an international committee is of the opinion that the applicant's rights were violated does not make the Spanish judicial decisions 'wrong'. However, the fact remains that the applicant did not have the opportunity to appeal the decision of the *Audiencia Nacional*, rejecting his request for the suspension of the delivery to Morocco, because such delivery took place the very next day after the decision was adopted. The applicant was thus deprived of his right to access to justice; moreover, because he was wrongly informed about the judicial procedure to be followed. His fundamen-

30 United Nations (UN), International Covenant on Civil and Political Rights 1967 <https://treaties.un.org/doc/treaties/1976/03/19760323%2006-17%20am/ch_iv_04.pdf>.

31 The Audiencia Nacional is a special court based in Madrid. It decides on appeals against acts of the public administration, including liability claims (pursuant to LO 6/1985, of 1 July, *del Poder Judicial* [BOE 157, 2.7.1985], hereinafter LOPJ, art 66.a) and Act 29/1998, of 13 July, *reguladora de la Jurisdicción Contencioso-administrativa* [BOE 167, 14.7.1998] art 11.1.a)).

tal rights were therefore violated. In order to redress that, the proceedings should be reinstated to the time prior to the delivery of the 2018 court decision so the *Audiencia Nacional* may examine the claim and determine whether or not there is a right to compensation as a result of a hypothetical infringement of a fundamental right.

c) Commentary

The decision exposes the Spanish state's failure to follow the opinions of the UN Committee referred to above, as a result of which the extradited person suffered torture in Morocco. From a tort law perspective, it states that the failure to give enough time to appeal the judicial decision that ultimately led to the extradition was a fundamental rights violation. Furthermore, the latter stems from incorrect information being provided by the Spanish authorities regarding the judicial avenue to be pursued by the applicant. Spanish law is certainly complex in this respect, as it provides for a specific way to claim liability for a miscarriage of justice (*error judicial*, art 292 LOPJ) – other than the existing one for holding public authorities liable.[32] However, an erroneous piece of information was included in the follow-up report that Spain sent to the aforementioned Committee, although not directly to the person concerned. However, this does not preclude a finding of a violation of rights. 18

32 See Act 40/2015, of 1 October, *de Régimen Jurídico del Sector Público* (BOE 236, 2.10.2015) art 32.6. The judicial error procedure is subsidiary, so that the victim must first pursue other avenues of redress. see Decision of the Spanish Supreme Court (Sentencia del Tribunal Supremo, STS) STS 81/2024, 23 January 2024 (Repertorio Oficial de Jurisprudencia [ROJ] 361/2024, ECLI:ES:TS:2024:361); STS 202/2024, 19 February 2024 (ROJ 817/2024, ECLI:ES:TS:2024:817) and STS 269/2024, 27 February 2024 (ROJ 1030/2024, ECLI:ES:TS:2024:1030). In any case, a disagreement with the judicial interpretation is not enough: there must be a genuine error and the wrong judicial decision must be appealed, not a subsequent one that enforces it: STS 227/2024, 20 February 2024 (ROJ 818/2024, ECLI:ES:TS:2024:818); similarly, STS 1099/2024, 11 September 2024 (ROJ 4383/2024, ECLI:ES:TS:2024:4383). The error may consist in ignoring documents provided by a party, without justification – as happened in STS 647/2024, 13 May 2024 (ROJ 2521/2024, ECLI:ES:TS:2024:2521) – or considering an action which was time-barred to be imprescriptible – as in STS 1197/2024, 27 September 2024 (ROJ 4716/2024, ECLI:ES:TS:2024:4716). On the selection of judges in Spain, now see *S Iglesias/R Bustos Gisbert*, What Does it Take to Become a Judge in Spain? An Informal First Step into a Formal World, German Law Journal (2023) 24(8) 1341–1356. On the liability of public authorities in general, see *JJ Montero Pascual*, Derecho Administrativo III: Contratos, medios y responsabilidad (2024) and *N Díaz Abad*, Responsabilidad patrimonial del Estado por daños causados por el Poder Judicial: *Zoubilidis c. Grecia*, Actualidad administrativa 9 (2024) <https://diariolaley.laleynext.es>.

3. STC 116/2024, 23 September 2024, ECLI:ES:TC:2024:116: Delisting of a Defective Drug

a) Brief Summary of the Facts

19 In 1983, Agreal (veralipride), a neuroleptic drug manufactured by Sanofi-Aventis, began to be marketed in Spain and was administered to healthy women suffering from menopausal hot flushes. Among other symptoms, users suffered from fatigue, depression, anxiety, memory loss, tremors, arrhythmias, headaches and 'not wanting to get out of bed'. It was withdrawn from the market in 2005.[33] A victims' association[34] sued the manufacturer – in vain, since the courts concluded that the claims were time-barred or causation had not been established.[35] For safety reasons, the drug should not have been taken for more than three months, but such information was not included in the package leaflet and many women used it for several years. A claim against the Spanish Ministry of Health for alleged omission or inactivity was also filed, again to no avail.[36] The victims then applied to the Constitutional Court for protection.

b) Judgment of the Court

20 The inadmissibility of the appeals before the lower courts has been sufficiently reasoned by them. Once the Administration had decided to withdraw the drug at stake from the market, on the grounds that the risks exceeded the benefits, no further administrative action could be expected or demanded in this respect, and therefore the Administration cannot be accused of 'inactivity'.

33 See *Agencia Española de Medicamentos y Productos Sanitarios*, Comunicación sobre riesgos de medicamentos para profesionales sanitarios 2005/15, 7 September 2005 <https://www.aemps.gob.es/informa/notasInformativas/medicamentosUsoHumano/seguridad/2005/NI_2005–15_agreal.htm>.

34 Under the name of 'Asociación Agreal Mujeres Luchadoras de España' (Agreal Association Women Fighters of Spain).

35 However, see a case where some victims succeeded in *A Ruda*, Spain, in: E Karner/BC Steininger (eds), European Tort Law (ETL) 2011 (2012) 632, no 51. On the case in general also see *A Piga Rivero/T Alfonso Galán/F Holgado*, El caso Agreal (Veraliprida): Responsabilidad por daños por medicamentos (2011).

36 See Sentencia de la Audiencia Nacional (Decision of the National Court, SAN) 2581/2020, 14 September 2020, ECLI:ES:AN:2020:2581.

c) Commentary

The judgment puts an end to the judicial ordeal of the victims. This is a very serious case, given the high number of victims – estimated at 10,000. They suffer serious health complications, which bring them to describe themselves as the 'living dead'.[37] However, such effects are the result of the prolonged use of the drug, of the risk of which they had not been informed because this aspect was omitted from the leaflet. The decision under comment can be seen as an example of the tendency that seems to exist in Spain to blame the public administration for any adversities or disasters. But this route is often doomed to failure and thus, in practice, it may be preferable to sue the producer.[38] The question seems to be rather why the key information was not included in the package leaflet but was kept confidential for years. The manufacturer reported the risk to the European Medicines Agency in 2007 and the victims did not have access to such a report until 2011.[39] In this regard, the decision emphasises what the Administration should have done *after* delisting the drug and the answer is simple: nothing. However, it seems legitimate to ask why the obligation to include the technical data sheet of the medicine (*ficha técnica*) was not legally established until 2007, even though it was already customary in practice. The information included in such document may be essential in a tort law procedure[40] but the producer did not provide it until 2002.[41] 21

37 La Vanguardia, Afectadas por el fármaco Agreal, 'muertas en vida', 28.1.2019 <https://www.lavanguardia.com/vida/20190128/4656110251/afectadas-por-el-farmaco-agreal-muertas-en-vida.html>.

38 See *MÁ Parra Lucán*, Responsabilidad por la falta de información de los efectos indeseables de los medicamentos, DS: Derecho y salud 24(2) (2014) 9–28 <https://www.ajs.es/sites/default/files/2020-05/vol24n2_01_Estudio.pdf>, at 15. Cf *Í Navarro Mendizabal*, Algunas cuestiones acerca de la responsabilidad civil en el caso de los medicamentos en España, Revista de Derecho: Publicación de la Facultad de Derecho de la Universidad Católica de Uruguay 9 (2014) 161–184 <https://repositorio.comillas.edu/rest/bitstreams/74544/>, at 184.

39 See *D Grasso/A Villareal*, El dossier confidencial que tumbó al Agreal, la pesadilla de las menopáusicas españolas, El Confidencial 2.3.2018, <https://www.elconfidencial.com/tecnologia/ciencia/2018-03-02/documento-confidencial-tumbo-agreal-sanofi_1529209/>.

40 See *JC Villalba Cuéllar/AC Pérez Forero*, La responsabilidad civil por medicamentos defectuosos, una aproximación de Derecho comparado, Revista Facultad de Derecho y Ciencias Políticas 50(133) (2020) 501–536 <https://dialnet.unirioja.es/descarga/articulo/7574952.pdf>, at 528.

41 Also see *JE Vázquez López*, Responsabilidad sanitaria y patrimonial en relación a los efectos secundarios de un medicamento: breve apunte sobre el llamado 'caso Agreal'. Reseña de algunas sentencias de interés. La necesidad de nexo causal, y la importancia de la prueba pericial, Cuadernos de medicina forense 19(3–4) (2013) 127–130 <https://scielo.isciii.es/pdf/cmf/v19n3-4/11prueba_pericial.pdf>.

4. STC 135/2024, 4 November 2024, ECLI:ES:TC:2024:135: Undue Judicial Delay

a) Brief Summary of the Facts

22 The applicant filed a lawsuit in May 2002, but the court did not schedule the hearing until October 2025, due to court overload and structural limitations. She claimed that this delay violated her fundamental right to a trial without undue delay (enshrined in art 24.2 CE).

b) Judgment of the Court

23 While acknowledging that the causes of the delay were structural and not directly attributable to the judicial body, such shortcomings do not absolve the state of its obligation to ensure the efficient administration of justice without undue delay. However, to solve this problem, it is not possible to bring forward the hearing at stake, which could be detrimental to other people in similar circumstances. Therefore, the applicant can claim liability for malfunctioning of the administration of justice (under art 121 CE).

c) Commentary

24 The judgment is a reflection of the collapse of the Spanish courts, with almost 4 million cases pending and an average length of first instance proceedings of 9.2 months,[42] much higher than the EU average.[43] Moreover, the situation seems to be getting worse in recent times. And while it is true that, at the time of writing, a statutory reform to improve the efficiency of justice has been passed,[44] it has already been criticised as insufficient.[45] In the meanwhile, it seems unlikely

42 See *Fundación Aranzadi La Ley*, Observatorio de la actividad de la justicia (2024) <https://www.aranzadilaley.es/dossier/xviii-informe-observatorio-de-la-justicia.html>.

43 See *European Commission*, The 2024 Justice Scoreboard (2024) <https://commission.europa.eu/document/download/84aa3726-82d7-4401-98c1-fee04a7d2dd6_en?filename=2024%20EU%20Justice%20Scoreboard.pdf>, at 11.

44 LO 1/2025, of 2 March, *de medidas en materia de eficiencia del Servicio Público de Justicia* (BOE 3, 3.1.2025).

45 Among others, see *Ilustre Colegio Nacional de Letrados de la Administración de Justicia*, Ni transparencia, ni medios; imprevisión y falta de coordinación en la reforma de la ley de efi-

that the situation will improve. For that, it would be necessary to tackle the roots of the problem. Whereas everyone agrees there is a lack of resources, for which judges can certainly not be blamed,[46] there may be some room for improvement as regards the efficiency of the judges themselves[47] and also the quality of the legislative technique.[48] The use of AI to draft decisions is already being used in Catalonia as part of a pilot scheme.[49] Until these matters are properly addressed, the number of claims such as the one that gave rise to the decision under comment will probably increase. A delay in justice has traditionally been considered a denial of justice, which is clearly harmful to those affected.[50] However, it is also an indeterminate legal concept whose content will depend on the circumstances of each case, so not every infringement of procedural time limits may constitute undue procedural delay.[51]

ciencia, auguramos una situación muy difícil para la justicia española en 2025, 8.1.2025 <https://letradosdejusticia.es/ni-transparencia-ni-medios-imprevision-y-falta-de-coordinacion-en-la-reforma-de-la-ley-de-eficiencia-auguramos-una-situacion-muy-dificil-para-la-justicia-espanola-en-2025/>.

46 On judges' liability, see *E Arias-Salgado Robsy*, La responsabilidad personal del juez (2013) <https://rajylgr.es/wp-content/uploads/2017/11/elena-arias-discurso-ingreso-02.pdf>, at 18.

47 See *Agenda Pública*, Los problemas de la justicia en España no se deben solo a una falta de medios, 22.2.2025 <https://agendapublica.es/noticia/19661/problemas-justicia-espana-no-se-deben-solo-falta-medios>.

48 As pointed out by the Spanish Ombudsman: see *Defensor del Pueblo*, Retrasos en la Administración de Justicia (2019) <https://www.defensordelpueblo.es/wp-content/uploads/2019/07/Separata_retrasos_justicia.pdf>, at 46.

49 See RTVE, Cataluña prueba las sentencias judiciales escritas con inteligencia artificial, 21.3.2025 <https://www.rtve.es/noticias/20250321/cataluna-sentencias-judiciales-inteligencia-artificial/16502032.shtml>.

50 See *J Tornos Mas*, La responsabilidad patrimonial del Estado por el funcionamiento de la administración de justicia, Revista Española de Derecho Constitucional 13 (1985) 71–122 <https://dialnet.unirioja.es/descarga/articulo/241813.pdf>, at 96.

51 See *B Anglès Juanpere*, La responsabilidad de jueces y magistrados, CEFLegal. Revista práctica de Derecho 134 (2012) 107–142, <https://revistas.cef.udima.es/index.php/ceflegal/article/download/11915/11661/20965>, at 123. Also see *PÁ Orellana Gómez*, Dilaciones indebidas o deficitaria administración de justicia, Hay Derecho 5.9.2019 <https://www.hayderecho.com/2019/09/05/dilaciones-indebidas-o-deficitaria-administracion-de-justicia/>.

5. STC 142/2024, 20 November 2024, ECLI:ES:TC:2024:142: Environmental Damage

a) Brief Summary of the Facts

25 In 2022, the Spanish Parliament passed a law granting legal personality to the Mar Menor lagoon and its basin.[52] As a legal person, the Mar Menor has the right to exist and evolve naturally, to be protected, conserved and restored (art 2.2). A political party appealed against this statute before the Constitutional Court on the basis that vague and diffuse concepts were used, that they fail to specify which specific behaviour infringes those rights, that the rights themselves are generic in content and that this may lead to an arbitrary statutory interpretation.

b) Judgment of the Court

26 Such attribution of legal personality falls within the state's powers over the environment (art 149.1.23 CE). The Constitution (art 45) provides a broad framework for the legislature to adopt environmental protection measures, including innovative approaches such as the recognition of legal personality for natural elements. The new Act does not violate the dignity of the person or the right to effective judicial protection – contrary to what the applicants claimed – since attributing legal personality to an ecosystem does not equate the same with a human person but rather constitutes a legal tool for its protection. That there may be an arbitrary interpretation of the law is a mere hypothesis on which the Court should not rule. The provisions that the appellants do not like will have to be interpreted in accordance with the remainder of the legal system.

c) Commentary

27 The decision under comment lends its support to the 'ecocentric' approach that the aforementioned Act has adopted in a novel way.[53] The Court expressly states

52 Act 19/2022, of 30 September, *para el reconocimiento de personalidad jurídica a la laguna del Mar Menor y su cuenca* (BOE 237, 3.10.2022), on which see *A Ruda*, Spain, in: E Karner/BC Steininger (eds), European Tort Law (ETL) 2022 (2013) 613, no 17 ff.

53 On liability for environmental restoration costs, see STS 1540/2024, 18 November 2024 (ROJ 5776/2024, ECLI:ES:TS:2024:5776), according to which the prescription period to recover them begins to run when the public authority that decontaminated the soil certifies that it is decon-

that it is not its role to comment on the political correctness of the law but only to analyse whether it is compatible, and in this sense the Spanish Constitution is sufficiently flexible. It is also wise not to speculate about hypothetical arbitrary interpretations, as by definition they have not yet taken place. As Isaac Newton famously said: hypothesis *non fingo.*[54] However, the Court's general argument does not hold any water. The granting of legal personality to a natural resource is an exceptional solution in Spanish law – and EU law in general. It is therefore surprising that the Court should say that such recognition must be read within the framework of Spanish law as a whole.[55]

---

taminated and sets the cost of the clean-up. On climate change litigation, see *A Peñalver i Cabré* (ed), Litigación climática. El papel de la ciudadanía y los jueces (2024) and *A Ruda*, Sostenibilidad en la litigación climática. En particular, el problema de la causalidad, in: A Ruda/A Lladó (eds), Sostenibilidad en el Derecho. Los objetivos del desarrollo sostenible (ODS) en la docencia, la investigación y el mundo profesional (2024) 288–333 <https://www.colexopenaccess.com/libros/sostenibilidad-derecho-7591>. On environmental liability in movies, see *E Richard/C Mendoza*, Una Acción Civil (1998): la ley detrás del daño corporal, los defectos congénitos y la leucemia, Revista de medicina y cine 20(1) (2024) 45–60. On the Prestige oil spill, see *M Alba Fernández*, Nuevo hito en el caso Prestige: Nota sobre la sentencia de la High Court of Justice (Commercial Court) de 6 de octubre de 2023 en el litigio entre el London steam-ship owners' mutual insurance association limited y el Reino de España, Cuadernos de derecho transnacional (CDT) 16(1) (2024) 656–670.

54 Philosophiæ Naturalis Principia Mathematica (2nd edn 1713).

55 The decision includes several dissenting opinions which adhere to the anthropocentric approach. In legal scholarship, see critically *F Luque Regueiro*, El insólito reconocimiento de personalidad jurídica a un entorno natural. Nueva confrontación en el seno del Tribunal Constitucional, Revista jurídica de la Comunidad de Madrid (2025) 1–44 <https://www.comunidad.madrid/sites/default/files/el_insolito_reconocimiento_de_personalidad_juridica_a_un_entorno_natural_fernando_luque.pdf>, at 24. Also see *D Aviñó Belenguer*, La loi 19/2022 espagnole, au-delà de la personnification de la Mar Menor (région de Murcie, Espagne). Une ouverture vers une action populaire et une responsabilité civile environnementale? Actualidad jurídica Iberoamericana 20 (2024) 1370–1391 <https://revista-aji.com/wp-content/uploads/2024/02/AJI20_Art_44.pdf>; *RI Bachmann Fuentes/V Navarro Caro*, Consideraciones en torno a la constitucionalidad de la Ley 19/2022 para el reconocimiento de personalidad jurídica del Mar Menor y su Cuenca, Revista de Derecho Urbanístico y Medio Ambiente 372 (2024) 117–163; *X Bioy*, La personalidad jurídica atribuida a la naturaleza, a propósito del 'Mar Menor', in: D Marrero Guanche/A Martín Meneses/A González Navarro (eds), Derecho, justicia y sostenibilidad ambiental (2024) 71–92; *P García Guijarro*, El alcance del reconocimiento de personalidad jurídica al mar menor ante la jurisprudencia medioambiental del tribunal constitucional, in: R Martínez Dalmau/A Pedro Bueno (eds), Derechos de la naturaleza desde el Mediterráneo: El dialogo Sur-Sur (2024) 377–388; *G Pais*, El TC reconoce la personalidad jurídica del Mar Menor, Diario La Ley (2025) 10670 <https://diariolaley.laleynext.es>; *B Soro Mateo/SM Álvarez Carreño*, Derechos de la naturaleza y Constitución, a propósito del caso de la laguna del Mar Menor, Revista d'estudis autonòmics i federals 39 (2024) 61–122 <https://raco.cat/index.php/REAF/issue/view/32336/1101>, and *N Yugueros Prieto*, La visión ecocéntrica en el reconocimiento de personalidad jurídica a la laguna del Mar Menor y su cuenca:

6. Sentencia del Tribunal Supremo (Supreme Court Decision, STS) Administrative Chamber, 1113/2024, 24 June 2024, ROJ 3342/2024, ECLI:ES:TS:2024:3342: Thalidomide

a) Brief Summary of the Facts

28 A group of citizens appealed a Royal Decree from 2023 on aid to Thalidomide victims,[56] on the grounds that it imposed requirements not provided for by legislation. The regional public authorities of Andalucía had already granted the claimants the official status of persons affected by that drug, in accordance with the previously existing statutory regime,[57] but the Royal Decree created a new barrier to them by requiring them to be entered in an administrative register on rare diseases and to undergo a new validation process.

b) Judgment of the Court

29 The additional requirement provided for in the regulation has no statutory support and is therefore void. The Spanish state can grant and manage aid to victims, but it cannot ignore the recognition as such already carried out validly by a regional administration.

c) Commentary

30 This judgment is a milestone in the long judicial ordeal of Thalidomide victims,[58] deciding the issue correctly, since the principle of hierarchy of norms prevents a

breves reflexiones jurídico-procesales, in: P Arrabal Platero/JC Catalán/A Sánchez Rubio (eds), Más allá de la Justicia: nuevos horizontes del derecho procesal (2024) 647–660. More generally, see *M Ortiz García*, De la protección a la restauración de la naturaleza, Revista Aragonesa de Administración Pública (2024) Extra 62, 31–80 <https://dialnet.unirioja.es/descarga/articulo/9887265.pdf>.

56 RD 574/2023, of 4 July, *por el que se regula el procedimiento de concesión de ayudas a las personas afectadas por la talidomida en España durante el período 1950–1985* (BOE 159, 5.7.2023). On which see *A Ruda*, Spain, in: E Karner/BC Steininger (eds), European Tort Law (ETL) 2023 (2024) 633, no 40.

57 Act 6/2018, of 3 July, *de Presupuestos Generales del Estado para el año 2018* (BOE 161, 4.7.2018).

58 See *Ruda* (fn 56) no 35 ff. Now also see *I Arana de la Fuente/E Blanco Martínez*, Responsabilidad civil por daños causados por la talidomida: cómputo del plazo de prescripción. Sentencia

lower norm – a regulation – from adding requirements not foreseen by a higher one. According to one victims' association, the requirement to be registered in the rare disease registry practically left out most victims, so this has been an important judicial victory for them.[59] It is regrettable that the Spanish government should add insult to the injury suffered by victims who have been demanding a solution for more than 20 years. Fortunately, there are still judges in Berlin.[60]

7. STS 18/2024, 9 January 2024, ROJ 34/2024, ECLI:ES:TS:2024/34: Reputational Damage

a) Brief Summary of the Facts

The claimant left his job as a manager at Banco Santander and started another job 31
at Banco Pastor, which was later absorbed by Banco Popular. Following this takeover, the claimant was dismissed on the basis of data on the applicant's reputational risk. Such data had been in an internal file of Banco Santander for 12 years – and therefore related to his first period with that bank – but had been transferred to Banco Popular without the claimant's consent. Later, Banco Santander absorbed Banco Popular.

b) Judgment of the Court

Banco Santander retained and disclosed inaccurate and harmful personal da- 32
ta without consent, with a negative impact on the claimant's reputation. Admittedly, the claimant had signed an agreement waiving his right to take legal action

---

del Tribunal Supremo de 21 de julio de 2023, Anuario de Derecho Civil (ADC) 77(2) (2024) 929 – 972 and *S Ramos González*, Talidomida II y los esfuerzos de AVITE por posponer el inicio del plazo de prescripción de la acción con base en el conocimiento tardío de las patentes de la Talidomida y otros documentos inscritos en registros públicos (arts 1968.2 y 1969 CC), Cuadernos Civitas de Jurisprudencia Civil (CCJC) 124 (2024) 279 – 296.

59 See *AVITE*, El Tribunal Supremo anula varios artículos del RD de las ayudas de la Talidomida, 28.6.2024 <https://www.avite.org/el-tribunal-supremo-anula-varios-articulos-del-rd-de-las-ayudas-de-la-talidomida/>.

60 See *JR Chaves García*, Coto a los reglamentos que se extralimitan del marco legal: caso Talidomida, 26.6.2024 <https://delajusticia.com/2024/06/26/coto-a-los-reglamentos-que-se-extralimitan-del-marco-legal-caso-talidomida/> and *Eugenio Moure Abogados*, Anulación de Real Decreto de la Talidomida, 26.6.2024, <www.emoure-abogados.com/entrada/1/6382/anulacion-de-real-decreto-de-la-talidomida.html>.

in connection with his dismissal, but this waiver relates only to the dismissal as such and not to the unauthorised transfer of data. The claimant is entitled to compensation of € 50,000 and to have his data cancelled.

c) Commentary

33 In a bizarre course of events, the claimant sues the company for which he had been working for giving data to a company that ends up being taken over by the former one. Apart from this anecdotal detail, the judgment does not specify the concept for which compensation is awarded. Although the award seems – and certainly is – a very large one, the claimant had requested more (€ 600,000).

34 The present case departs from the typical defamation case, in which harm results from a denigrating statement published somewhere.[61] As usual, there were many such cases before the Spanish Supreme Court in 2024. There is no harm when the statement at stake refers to facts from the private life of a public person, which he has not denied and which he himself has exposed in the media.[62] However, the fact that a person is 'public' does not mean that intimate facts, eg about their sex life, which they have not previously disclosed, can be divulged.[63] Conversely, the fact that the affected person is not a public one does not turn an accusation of being corrupt into a defamatory statement, provided that journalists have inquired diligently.[64] The dissemination of truthful facts of public relevance

61 In legal scholarship, see *JR de Verda y Beamonte*, Honor y prestigio profesional: legitimidad del informe leído en un Consejo de Departamento en el que se denunciaba la falta de profesionalidad del docente universitario, cuya promoción se votaba. Comentario a la Sentencia del Tribunal Supremo (Civil) 1572/2023, de 13 de noviembre, ADC 77(3) (2024) 1397–1416; *S Recuenco Pérez*, Litigios sobre difamación por internet. Comentarios a la SAP Madrid 10 febrero 2023: Competencia y Ley aplicable ¿vale el silencio más que mil palabras? CDT 16(1) (2024) 900–915 and *JA Díez Ballesteros*, Responsabilidad civil por daños morales por la publicación en Facebook de comentarios ofensivos sobre un árbitro de un partido de balonmano infantil: STS 12/12/2023, Revista de responsabilidad civil, circulación y seguro (RRCCS) 2 (2024) 32–35.

62 STS 25/2024, 11 January 2024 (ROJ 239/2024, ECLI:ES:TS:2024:239). Similarly, STS 86/2024, 23 January 2024 (ROJ 291/2024, ECLI:ES:TS:2024:291); STS 488/2024, 11 April 2024 (ROJ 1956/2024, ECLI:ES:TS:2024:1956); STS 873/2024, 18 June 2024 (ROJ 3525/2024, ECLI:ES:TS:2024:3525) and STS 983/2024, 12 July 2024 (ROJ 4148/2024, ECLI:ES:TS:2024:4148). So, for instance, there is no defamation in the case of a journalistic report on the sexual life and financial management of a priest: STS 1422/2024, 29 October 2024 (ROJ 5377/2024, ECLI:ES:TS:2024:5377).

63 STS 87/2024, 23 January 2024 (ROJ 231/2024, ECLI:ES:TS:2024:231).

64 STS 294/2024, 4 March 2024 (ROJ 1336/2024, ECLI:ES:TS:2024:1336). Similarly, on the doctrine of neutral reporting, STS 487/2024, 11 April 2024 (ROJ 2015/2024, ECLI:ES:TS:2024:2015) and STS 549/2024, 24 April 2024 (ROJ 2145/2024, ECLI:ES:TS:2024:2145). Journalists have a duty to cross-check

– eg by posting a video on Facebook – prevails over the right to honour in contexts of general interest such as an election campaign[65] or the behaviour of private companies which affects the general interest.[66] Critical opinions about professional practices (eg a lawyer advertising low-cost divorces with a van) do not violate the right to honour if they are expressed on a factual basis, without personal disqualifications.[67] For the same reason, falsely accusing someone of absenteeism or other irregularities at work is defamatory.[68] A national sports coach is more exposed to criticism, so accusations in an internal complaint do not violate his honour.[69] There is also no infringement of professional reputation if a report on medical proceedings is based on solid evidence (expert or judicial), even if the trial on medical malpractice is pending.[70] Similarly, there is no defamation if a mayor publicly criticises a worker who was sanctioned for misbehaviour at work, because it is a matter of public interest, based on facts and generally known in town.[71] But the right to honour of a school headmaster is violated if the defendant relies on anonymous statements and old publications on the Internet as if they were current and coming from the school itself.[72] Accusing a com-

---

information more rigorously when the reporting is not neutral but assumes the accusation as their own: STS 852/2024, 11 June 2024 (ROJ 3107/2024, ECLI:ES:TS:2024:3107). Misattribution by journalists of a statement by a judge is not defamatory if the claimant acted similarly or in accordance with the context (a Whatsapp group): STS 511/2024, 16 April 2024 (ROJ 1967/2024, ECLI:ES:TS:2024:1967). A biased and sensationalist news story falsely attributing the commission of a fatal hit-and-run to two allegedly drunk police officers is defamatory: STS 1499/2024, 11 November 2024 (ROJ 5516/2024, ECLI:ES:TS:2024:5516).

65 STS 82/2024, 23 January 2024 (ROJ 200/2024, ECLI:ES:TS:2024:200).

66 STS 510/2024, 16 April 2024 (ROJ 1952/2024, ECLI:ES:TS:2024:1952). Even a private interest may be sufficient in that regard, eg that of the condominium owners to know that one of the tenants has been evicted: STS 1186/2024, 24 September 2024 (ROJ 4708/2024, ECLI:ES:TS:2024:4708), or is going to be: STS 1515/2024, 12 November 2024 (ROJ 5513/2024, ECLI:ES:TS:2024:5513).

67 STS 115/2024, 31 January 2024 (ROJ 332/22024, ECLI:ES:TS:2024:332). There is also more latitude as to criticism in the context of unions' activities and professional activities in general. See STS 1227/2024, 30 September 2024 (ROJ 4718/2024, ECLI:ES:TS:2024:4718). Similarly, there is no defamation in accusing a political party (Podemos) of being 'anti-democratic' – or having received funds from Venezuela, which it actually did – within the framework of political debate: see STS 1228/2024, 1 October 2024 (ROJ 4711/2024, ECLI:ES:TS:2024:4711).

68 STS 397/2024, 19 March 2024 (ROJ 1545/2024, ECLI:ES:TS:2024:1545).

69 STS 416/2024, 20 March 2024 (ROJ 1606/2024, ECLI:ES:TS:2024:1606).

70 The trial confirmed there had been medical malpractice: STS 118/2024, 1 February 2024 (ROJ 459/2024, ECLI:ES:TS:2024:459). On the other hand, defamation occurs when a reckless and biased claim against a lawyer is disseminated extensively: STS 528/2024, 22 April 2024 (ROJ 2100/2024, ECLI:ES:TS:2024:2100).

71 STS 164/2024, 7 February 2024 (ROJ 544/2024, ECLI:ES:TS:2024:544).

72 STS 153/2024, 6 February 2024 (ROJ 478/2024, ECLI:ES:TS:2024:478).

pany of being a government racket (*chiringuito*) or of acting 'cowardly' is not defamatory, because even if they are exaggerated or provocative statements, they are based on public data from the company register.[73] In a similar vein, it is not defamatory to accuse a youtuber of being 'violent towards women' for his criticism of feminism.[74] Nor is it defamatory to accuse a coaching association of professional intrusiveness and lack of credibility if the criticism is of general interest (public health) and based on reports by the College of Psychologists.[75] Calling a person a 'politician' in the context of criticism of her performance in the public administration is not defamatory.[76] But it is so to claim that someone has been arrested by the police for a case of alleged corruption when he had only been investigated;[77] or to give information the appearance of journalistic reporting when in fact it is based on assumptions and unverified opinions.[78] When the alleged defamation is carried out by a lawyer exercising the right of defence, the courts are more flexible if the facts affect the general interest (eg they refer to a municipal official).[79] The mere closure of a Facebook page for non-compliance with terms of use is not defamation of the user company at stake and the honour of legal persons is less intensively protected.[80] The publication of a news item

73 STS 165/2024, 7 February 2024 (ROJ 497/2024, ECLI:ES:TS:2024:497).

74 STS 753/2024, 28 May 2024 (ROJ 2886/2024, ECLI:ES:TS:2024:2886).

75 STS 253/2004, 26 February 2024 (ROJ 976/2024, ECLI:ES:TS:2024:976). Nor is there defamation for the criticism of the College of Psychiatrists in the framework of the so-called anti-psychiatry discourse: STS 960/2024, 9 July 2024 (ROJ 4150/2024, ECLI:ES:TS:2024:4150).

76 STS 399/2024, 19 March 2024 (ROJ 1543/2024, ECLI:ES:TS:2024:1543).

77 STS 286/2024, 27 February 2024 (ROJ 978/2024, ECLI:ES:TS:2024:978). There is no defamation if it simply refers to the fact that a person has been criminally reported: STS 962/2024, 9 July 2024 (ROJ 4072/2024, ECLI:ES:TS:2024:4072) and STS 1187/2024, 24 September 2024 (ROJ 4656/2024, ECLI:ES:TS:2024:4656). Nor does the mere dismissal of criminal proceedings mean that the complaint was defamatory, unless there is an abuse of rights: STS 984/2024, 12 July 2024 (ROJ 4074/2024, ECLI:ES:TS:2024:4074). Even in a case where a policeman publicly stated that he was convinced of the guilt of an accused (contrary to the presumption of innocence), it is concluded that there is no defamation: STS 1328/2024, 15 October 2024 (ROJ 4987/2024, ECLI:ES:TS:2024:4987).

78 STS 436/2024, 2 April 2024 (ROJ 1766/2024, ECLI:ES:TS:2024:1766).

79 STS 369/2024, 12 March 2024 (ROJ 1329/2024, ECLI:ES:TS:2024:1329). But the right of defence does not cover the excesses incurred when accusing others of possibly criminal conduct without sufficient basis: STS 507/2024, 15 April 2024 (ROJ 1937/2024, ECLI:ES:TS:2024:1937).

80 STS 408/2024, 20 March 2024 (ROJ 1579/2024, ECLI:ES:TS:2024:1579). Similarly, STS 874/2024, 18 June 2024 (ROJ 3526/2024, ECLI:ES:TS:2024:3526) and STS 1196/2024, 26 September 2024 (ROJ 4658/2024, ECLI:ES:TS:2024:4658). Also see STS 1071/2024, 26 July 2024 (ROJ 4155/2024, ECLI:ES:TS:2024:4155), where the claimant failed to establish that the defendant society was the same which defamed the first under a different name. However, see STS 1067/2024, 23 July 2024 (ROJ 4123/2024, ECLI:ES:TS:2024:4123), according to which, legal persons are protected against prolonged smear campaigns.

about a murder committed by the claimant 34 years ago violates his right to be forgotten and the right to honour when there is no current interest in those events.[81] There is also no liability for satire if it is based on a real and verified context,[82] but there is when the applicant's words have been misrepresented.[83]

In other cases, it is alleged that the right to one's own image has been violated 35
along with the right to honour. The publication of details about the possible parentage of a minor does not infringe those rights if such details have already been disclosed previously and the image was published in a distorted form.[84] There is also no liability for the publication of the defendant's wife's photos on the Facebook wall during the marriage, even if they divorce afterwards;[85] or by the publication of an image of a person taken in a restaurant while offering criminal services to another.[86] However, there is liability if a prisoner is portrayed as the alleged murderer of his cellmate, mistaking him for someone else.[87] As regards privacy, there is no violation if security cameras are installed in a condominium but they film communal areas only,[88] or if it is revealed that a member of the royal family is in fact a republican.[89] But the privacy of minors who are re-

81 STS 484/2024, 10 April 2024 (ROJ 1805/2024, ECLI:ES:TS:2024:1805). By contrast, information remains relevant when it relates to criminal acts involving public officials: STS 562/2024, 24 April 2024 (ROJ 2119/2024, ECLI:ES:TS:2024:2119).

82 STS 959/2024, 8 July 2024 (ROJ 4061/2024, ECLI:ES:TS:2024:4061). There is also no liability if satire is absurd, grotesque and exaggerated: STS 1426/2024, 29 October 2024 (ROJ 5352/2024, ECLI:ES:TS:2024:5352).

83 STS 1229/2024, 1 October 2024 (ROJ 4730/2024, ECLI:ES:TS:2024:4730).

84 STS 293/2024, 4 March 2024 (ROJ 1434/2024, ECLI:ES:TS:2024:1434). Even if the image of the child is published without pixelation, there is no liability if the child is not recognisable: STS 551/2024, 24 April 2024 (ROJ 2127/2024, ECLI:ES:TS:2024:2127) and STS 1068/2024, 24 July 2024 (ROJ 4225/2024, ECLI:ES:TS:2024:4225). There is also no liability for merely revealing that the claimant's children are Real Madrid fans: STS 550/2024, 24 April 2024 (ROJ 2188/2024, ECLI:ES:TS:2024:2188). On the liability for having hidden from the husband that a child was not his, now see STS 238/2024, 23 February 2024 (ROJ 1098/2024, ECLI:ES:TS:2024:1098): the claim fails for want of fault. In legal scholarship, see *B Verdera Izquierdo*, Responsabilidad civil en el ámbito de las relaciones familiares, Revista Boliviana de Derecho 37 (2024) 14–43 and *AI Berrocal Lanzarot*, De nuevo sobre la responsabilidad civil en el ámbito de derecho de familia, en especial, la ocultación o falta de atribución de la paternidad no biológica del hijo, Revista Crítica de Derecho Inmobiliario 805 (2024) 2909–3007.

85 STS 907/2024, 24 June 2024 (ROJ 3537/2024, ECLI:ES:TS:2024:3537).

86 STS 1194/2024, 24 September 2024 (ROJ 4662/2024, ECLI:ES:TS:2024:4662). Similarly, STS 909/2024, 24 June 2024 (ROJ 3499/2024, ECLI:ES:TS:2024:3499).

87 STS 1596/2024, 28 November 2024 (ROJ 5978/2024, ECLI:ES:TS:2024:5978).

88 STS 1399/2024, 23 October 2024 (ROJ 5075/2024, ECLI:ES:TS:2024:5075).

89 STS 567/2024, 25 April 2024 (ROJ 2059/2024, ECLI:ES:TS:2024:2059).

ferred to by name and age is violated, even if their father is a public figure and the image is pixelated.[90]

8. STS 398/2024, 19 March 2024, ROJ STS 1497/2024, ECLI:ES:TS:20024:1495: Data Security Breach

a) Brief Summary of the Facts

36 An employee of a credit reporting company unauthorisedly accessed the creditworthiness data of her brother and niece, using the company's credentials, for personal reasons. The Spanish Data Protection Agency fined the employee € 1,500. The victims sought compensation for non-pecuniary loss derived from wrongful interference with their rights to privacy, honour and data protection.

b) Judgment of the Court

37 Although the infringement of data protection law is clear, there is no harm to privacy, because the data was not disclosed to third parties, it was data that was already in other registers, and the claimants did not prove any harm. According to the doctrine of the Court of Justice of the European Union (CJEU), not every legal infringement gives right to compensation, but damage and the causal link must be established.

c) Commentary

38 The judgment argues that the data at stake were public but fails to clarify in which registers they were recorded. It does indeed say that one of these registers was the Land Register, which, in theory, is public, but it should be made clear that only persons with a legitimate interest actually have access to it and simple curiosity, snooping or gossip is not sufficient.[91] The defendant had to use secret credentials to access the information, which allowed her to request the data at stake. Should she have filed

90 STS 1152/2024, 23 September 2024 (ROJ 4696/2024, ECLI:ES:TS:2024:4696).

91 See Decree (*Decreto*) of 8 February 1946, *por el que se aprueba la nueva redacción oficial de la Ley Hipotecaria* (BOE 58, 27.2.1946) art 221. On this, see critically *J Alfaro Águila-Real*, Un registro es público hasta que lo gobierna la DGRN, 24.12.2016 <https://derechomercantilespana.blogspot.com/2016/12/un-registro-es-publico-hasta-que-lo.html>.

an application to access that data through the ordinary channel, she would most certainly have been denied it.[92]

39 The case deviates from the most typical case in Spanish courts with regard to data protection, which is that of the improper inclusion of a debtor's data in a solvency file. Inclusion is usually carried out without the debtor having been summoned,[93] or for a debt that is disputed.[94] Damage to honour occurs when the debtor is treated as a defaulter when she is not. Therefore, inclusion in the file cannot be used as a means of pressure on the debtor to pay.[95] However, case law states that the order for the debtor to pay is a merely 'functional' requirement. Therefore, if the debtor was already listed in other similar registers, it is considered that there is no defamation on the mere ground that the order was lacking.[96]

---

92 On data protection related liability, see *PA de Miguel Asensio*, Derecho a indemnización en materia de datos personales: aspectos internacionales, CDT 16(2) (2024) 487–500; *A Ruda/N Wilson Aponte*, Responsabilidad civil y datos genómicos. Reflexiones en la intersección entre el Derecho y la genómica, Papeles el tiempo de los derechos 17 (2024) 1–8 <https://redtiempodelosderechos.com/wp-content/uploads/2024/11/wp-17–24.pdf>; *MJ Santos Morón*, Reflexiones en torno a la jurisprudencia del TJUE sobre la acción indemnizatoria del art 82 RGPD (asuntos C-300/21; C-340/21; C-456/22; C-667/21; C-687/21; C-741/21), CDT 16(2) 2024) 1405–1423, and *M Orozco González*, A vueltas con los claroscuros en torno al régimen de responsabilidad civil por daños en los supuestos de perjuicios ocasionados por incumplimientos del RGPD. A propósito de las STJUE de 11 de abril y 20 de junio de 2024, La Ley privacidad 21 (2024) <https://diariolaley.laleynext.es>.

93 It is not necessary to prove receipt of the request in a reliable manner, but an ordinary mailing is sufficient if it has been properly handled, in which case it is deemed received. See STS 324/2024, 11 March 2024 (ROJ STS 1324/2024, ECLI:ES:TS:2024:1324); STS 343/2024, 11 March 2024 (ROJ 1322/2024, ECLI:ES:TS:2024:1322); STS 599/2024, 6 May 2024 (ROJ STS 2146/2024, ECLI:ES:TS:2024:2146); STS 600/2024, 6 May 2024 (ROJ 2185/2024, ECLI:ES:TS:2024:2185); STS 601/2024, 6 May 2024 (ROJ 2147/2024, ECLI:ES:TS:2024:2147); STS 648/2024, 13 May 2024 (ROJ 2491/2024, ECLI:ES:TS:2024:2491) and STS 1613/2024, 2 December 2024 (ROJ 5982/2024, ECLI:ES:TS:2024:5982). The debtor is also not entitled to compensation if he does not collect the notification for reasons attributable to him (STS 602/2024, 6 May 2024 [ROJ 2148/2024, ECLI:ES:TS:2024:2148]) or is perfectly aware of his status as a debtor, does not pay a single instalment, and remains passive for months after inclusion (STS 650/2024, 13 May 2024 [ROJ 2482/2024, ECLI:ES:TS:2024/2482]); similarly, STS 280/2024, 27 February 2024 (ROJ 954/2024, ECLI:ES:TS:2024:954).

94 However, it is not sufficient for the debtor to create doubt as to whether he really owes by means of judicial opposition to the debt: STS 651/2024, 13 May 2024 (ROJ 2484/2024, ECLI:ES:TS:2024/2484) and STS 1615/2024, 2 December 2024 (ROJ 5989/2024, ECLI:ES:TS:2024:5989), or by sending an email where he disputes the debt and pays only a part of the same: STS 649/2024, 13 May 2024 (ROJ 2483/2024, ECLI:ES:TS:2024:2483).

95 STS 281/2024, 27 February 2024 (ROJ STS 977/2024, ECLI:ES:TS:2024:977).

96 STS 34/2024, 11 January 2024 (ROJ STS 64/2024, ECLI:ES:TS:2024:64); STS 53/2024, 16 January 2024 (ROJ 140/2024, ECLI:ES:TS:2024:140) and STS 1558/2024, 19 November 2024 (ROJ 5744/2024, ECLI:ES:TS:2024:5744). Similarly, see STS 991/2024, 12 July 2024 (ROJ 4084/2024, ECLI:ES:TS:2024:4084) and STS 1373/2024, 21 October 2024 (ROJ 5187/2024, ECLI:ES:TS:2024:5187). The order is deemed to have been

In a similar vein, inclusion in the solvency files as such does not violate the claimant's honour if the debt exists and the person concerned does not act to prove otherwise.[97] The damage compensation awarded generally depends on the length of time the inclusion has lasted and on the damage resulting from the inclusion. Inclusion for only two months, without additional harm, entitles a party to an award of only € 500.[98] If inclusion in the file has aggravated the profile of the debtor as a 'defaulter', compensation is also granted, even if it is a low amount.[99] The victim is also entitled to compensation if the inclusion of her data takes place not in a solvency file but in the Central Credit Register of the Bank of Spain (*Central de Información de Riesgos del Banco de España*, CIRBE).[100]

9. STS 370/2024, 14 March 2024, ROJ 1287/2024, ECLI:ES: TS:2024:1287: Truck Cartel

a) Brief Summary of the Facts

40 A haulage company sued a truck manufacturer for overcharging for the purchase of trucks as a result of the so-called 'truck cartel', declared by the European Commission's decision of 19 July 2016. The claimant sought € 96,702 in damages.

b) Judgment of the Court

41 The defendant is liable for damage, estimated by the Court of Appeal at 8 % of the purchase price (€ 25,855) plus interest from the date of purchase. Damage can be

given even if payment of a partially different claim has been requested: STS 1559/2024, 19 November 2024 (ROJ 5741/2024, ECLI:ES:TS:2024:5741).

97 STS 117/2024, 1 February 2024 (ROJ: STS 456/2024, ECLI:ES:TS:2024/456).

98 STS 753/2024, 2 December 2024 (ROJ 5990/2024, ECLI:ES:TS:2024:5990).

99 € 1,000 in the case of STS 598/2024, 6 May 2024 (ROJ 2144/2024, ECLI:ES:TS:2024:2144). In another case, this amount was considered merely symbolic in view of the time of inclusion in the file (more than a year), the number of searches of the file (60 in total) and the defendant's refusal to delete the data, so that the compensation amounted to € 5,000: STS 597/2024, 6 May 2024 (ROJ 2173/2024, ECLI:ES:TS:2024:2173). By contrast, STS 1560/2024, 19 November 2024 (ROJ 5884/2024, ECLI:ES:TS:2024:5884) awarded € 10,000 to the claimant because the true debtor had already been sentenced for an offence of impersonation when the former was included in the file.

100 STS 47/2024, 16 January 2024 (ROJ 150/2024, ECLI:ES:TS:2024:150). Cf STS 143/2024, 6 February 2024 (ROJ 471/2024, ECLI:ES:TS:2024:471), where it is concluded that damage resulting from inclusion in the CIRBE register is not causally related to the negligence of a bank.

established by means of a judicial presumption (art 386 LEC), although the presumption established by the Competition Act[101] (art 76.3) was not applicable (for temporal reasons). The judicial presumption is based on the duration of the cartel (14 years), its scope (90 % of the market) and object (price fixing and gross price increase). The defendant's report is not sufficient to overturn the presumption of harm. However, in practice, the courts set the price increase at 5 % of the sales price and in this particular case, the Court of Appeal had set it at a higher level for no apparent reason, so it was reduced to 5 %.

c) Commentary

In 2024, there were a high number of cases (around 70) relating to compensation for 42
the damage caused by the truck cartel, after a ruling in 2023 had paved the way for them.[102] In these cases, it is obviously difficult to prove the overcharge with precision. Therefore, case law estimates damage on the basis of the reports provided by the claimants, even if the exact damage is never proven.[103] The percentage is usually set at 5 % and it follows from the decision under comment that this should be the general rule unless there are specific circumstances that justify a deviation from it.[104] Case law usually rejects the higher percentage requested by the claim, points out that the compensation cannot be symbolic and emphasises that the applicant's evidence need not be perfect either.[105] This distinguishes this case law from other

---

101 Act 15/2007, of 3 July, *de Defensa de la Competencia* (BOE 159, 4.7.2007). According to it, 'Statutory violations qualified as cartels shall be presumed to cause damage, unless there is evidence to the contrary.' (art 6.3).

102 See *Ruda* (fn 56) no 42 ff.

103 This is along the lines of ECJ case law. See *BA Koch/T Thiede*, European Union, in: E Karner/BC Steininger (eds), ETL 2023 (2024) 721, no 56.

104 Also see STS 1497/2024, 11 November 2024 (ROJ 5495/2024, ECLI:ES:TS:2024:5495) and previously STS 927/2023, 12 June 2023 (ROJ 2475/2023, ECLI:ES:TS:2023:2475).

105 STS 373/2024, 14 March 2024 (ROJ 1289/2024, ECLI:ES:TS:2024:1289); STS 377/2024, 14 March 2024 (ROJ 1292/2024, ECLI:ES:TS:2024:1292); STS 374/2024, 14 March 2024 (ROJ 1288/2024, ECLI:ES:TS:2024:1288); STS 376/2024, 14 March 2024 (ROJ 1291/2024, ECLI:ES:TS:2024:1291); STS 372/2024, 14 March 2024 (ROJ 1285/2024, ECLI:ES:TS:2024:1285); STS 1044/2024, 22 July 2024 (ROJ 4001/2024, ECLI:ES:TS:2024:4001); STS 1040/2024, 22 July 2024 (ROJ 4003/2024, ECLI:ES:TS:2024:4003); STS 1042/2024, 22 July 2024 (ROJ 4005/2024, ECLI:ES:TS:2024:4005); STS 1257/2024, 7 October 2024 (ROJ 4816/2024, ECLI:ES:TS:2024:4816); STS 1259/2024, 7 October 2024 (ROJ 4818/2024, ECLI:ES:TS:2024:4818); STS 1262/2024, 7 October 2024 (ROJ 4830/2024, ECLI:ES:TS:2024:4830); STS 1259/2024, 7 October 2024 (ROJ 4818/2024, ECLI:ES:TS:2024:4818); STS 1261/2024, 7 October 2024 (ROJ 4836/2024, ECLI:ES:TS:2024:4836); STS 1336/2024, 16 October 2024 (ROJ 5064/2024, ECLI:ES:TS:2024:5064); STS 1337/2024, 16 October 2024 (ROJ 5057/2024, ECLI:ES:TS:2024:5057); STS 1334/2024, 16 October 2024 (ROJ 5056/2024, ECLI:ES:TS:2024:5056); STS

cases where the lack of proof of harm resulting from anti-competitive conduct leads to no damages being awarded.[106] It has been recognised that the defendant must have the opportunity to challenge the claimant's evidence.[107] Case law has held that concrete mixer trucks also fall within the scope of the EC decision.[108] The lessee in a leasing contract is considered an acquirer for the purpose of claiming damages for overpricing resulting from collusive practices, even if he has not exercised the purchase option.[109] The statutory interest on the overcharge must be calculated from the date of acquisition of the trucks, not from the payment of each leasing instalment[110] or the claim's date.[111] Interest has to be paid as part of damage compensation, not because

1338/2024, 16 October 2024 (ROJ 5054/2024, ECLI:ES:TS:2024:5054); STS 1335/2024, 16 October 2024 (ROJ 5058/2024, ECLI:ES:TS:2024:5058); STS 1331/2024, 16 October 2024 (ROJ 5050/2024, ECLI:ES:TS:2024:5050); STS 1332/2024, 16 October 2024 (ROJ 5062/2024, ECLI:ES:TS:2024:5062); STS 1376/2024, 21 October 2024 (ROJ 5182/2024, ECLI:ES:TS:2024:5182); STS 1380/2024, 23 October 2024 (ROJ 5079/2024, ECLI:ES:TS:2024:5079); STS 1424/2024, 29 October 2024 (ROJ 5304/2024, ECLI:ES:TS:2024:5304); STS 1425/2024, 29 October 2024 (ROJ 5546/2024, ECLI:ES:TS:2024:5546); STS 1423/2024, 29 October 2024 (ROJ 5301/2024, ECLI:ES:TS:2024:5301); STS 1448/2024, 4 November 2024 (ROJ 5308/2024, ECLI:ES:TS:2024:5308); STS 1446/2024, 4 November 2024 (ROJ 5311/2024, ECLI:ES:TS:2024:5311); STS 1447/2024, 4 November 2024 (ROJ 5307/2024, ECLI:ES:TS:2024:5307); STS 1494/2024, 11 November 2024 (ROJ 5606/2024, ECLI:ES:TS:2024:5606); STS 1493/2024, 11 November 2024 (ROJ 5556/2024, ECLI:ES:TS:2024:5556); STS 1609/2024, 2 December 2024 (ROJ 5892/2024, ECLI:ES:TS:2024:5892); STS 1612/2024, 2 December 2024 (ROJ 5889/2024, ECLI:ES:TS:2024:5889); STS 1608/2024, 2 December 2024 (ROJ 5893/2024, ECLI:ES:TS:2024:5893); STS 1611/2024, 2 December 2024 (ROJ 5890/2024, ECLI:ES:TS:2024:5890); STS 1654/2024, 10 December 2024 (ROJ 5996/2024, ECLI:ES:TS:2024:5996); STS 1651/2024, 10 December 2024 (ROJ 5992/2024, ECLI:ES:TS:2024:5992); STS 1688/2024, 16 December 2024 (ROJ 6163/2024, ECLI:ES:TS:2024:6163); STS 1691/2024, 16 December 2024 (ROJ 6168/2024, ECLI:ES:TS:2024:6168); STS 1692/2024, 16 December 2024 (ROJ 6169/2024, ECLI:ES:TS:2024:6169); STS 1690/2024, 16 December 2024 (ROJ 6167/2024, ECLI:ES:TS:2024:6167), and STS 1693/2024, 16 December 2024 (ROJ 6170/2024, ECLI:ES:TS:2024:6170).

106 As was the case in STS 1469/2024, 6 November 2024 (ROJ 5266/2024, ECLI:ES:TS:2024:5266) and STS 1474/2024, 7 November 2024 (ROJ 5569/2024, ECLI:ES:TS:2024:5569) (not truck cartel cases, though). On antitrust and liability, see *E Pastor Martínez*, La compensación del daño antitrust (2024).

107 STS 1652/2024, 10 December 2024 (ROJ 5994/2024, ECLI:ES:TS:2024:5994).

108 STS 373/2024, 14 March 2024 (ROJ 1286/2024, ECLI:ES:TS:2024:1286).

109 STS 381/2024, 14 March 2024 (ROJ 1290/2024, ECLI:ES:TS:2024:1290).

110 STS 1043/2024, 22 July 2024 (ROJ 4000/2024, ECLI:ES:TS:2024:4000); STS 1375/2024, 21 October 2024 (ROJ 5068/2024, ECLI:ES:TS:2024:5068) and STS 1496/2024, 11 November 2024 (ROJ 5498/2024, ECLI:ES:TS:2024:5498).

111 STS 1445/2024, 4 November 2024 (ROJ 5313/2024, ECLI:ES:TS:2024:5313); STS 1495/2024, 11 November 2024 (ROJ 5573/2024, ECLI:ES:TS:2024:5573) and STS 1610/2024, 2 December 2024 (ROJ 5891/2024, ECLI:ES:TS:2024:5891). Cf STS 1066/2024, 23 July 2024 (ROJ 4152/2024, ECLI:ES:TS:2024:4152), related to a claim against a bank, where it was concluded that interest starts accruing from the date when the claim was filed.

the debtor is in default.[112] The court rejects the idea that the distributors absorbed the overcharge ('tidal effect': if the gross price goes up, so does the net price).[113] As for the prescription period, it starts to run from the publication of the summary of the above-mentioned EC decision.[114]

10. STS 384/2024, 18 March 2024, ROJ STS 1538/2024, ECLI:ES:TS:2024:1538: Prospectus Liability

a) Brief Summary of the Facts

Banco Popular Español was subjected to a bank resolution by the supervisory authorities and sold to Banco Santander in June 2017 due to its serious financial situation. A shareholder of Banco Popular brought an action against Banco Santander, on the grounds of nullity due to error of consent in the contracts for the acquisition of shares and pre-emptive subscription rights of Banco Popular. 43

b) Judgment of the Court

Banco Popular was subject to a bank resolution process due to its serious financial situation. According to Directive 2014/59/EU,[115] as construed by the CJEU,[116] those 44

---

112 STS 1041/2024, 22 July 2024 (ROJ 4004/2024, ECLI:ES:TS:2024:4004); STS 1260/2024, 7 October 2024 (ROJ 4822/2024, ECLI:ES:TS:2024:4822); STS 1258/2024, 7 October 2024 (ROJ 4819/2024, ECLI:ES:TS:2024:4819); STS 1333/2024, 16 October 2024 (ROJ 5059/2024, ECLI:ES:TS:2024:5059) and STS 1330/2024, 16 October 2024 (ROJ 5052/2024, ECLI:ES:TS:2024:5052).

113 STS 1045/2024, 22 July 2024 (ROJ 4002/2024, ECLI:ES:TS:2024:4002).

114 STS 1377/2024, 21 October 2024 (ROJ 5070/2024, ECLI:ES:TS:2024:5070); STS 1607/2024, 2 December 2024 (ROJ 5979/2024, ECLI:ES:TS:2024:5979); STS 1655/2024, 10 December 2024 (ROJ 5997/2024, ECLI:ES:TS:2024:5997) and STS 1689/2024, 16 December 2024 (ROJ 6165/2024, ECLI:ES:TS:2024:6165). On prescription in general now, see *A Domínguez Luelmo/F Toribios Fuentes,* La prescripción extintiva en el Derecho de obligaciones: aspectos sustantivos y procesales (2024). Also see *F Toribios Fuentes*, Interrupción de la prescripción por reclamación extrajudicial. Diferencia de efectos dependiendo de que se reclame contra el asegurado o exclusivamente contra la compañía aseguradora. Comentario a la STS 1219/2023, de 11 de septiembre, CCJC 124 (2024) 309–332.

115 Directive 2014/59/EU of the European Parliament and of the Council of 15 May 2014 establishing a framework for the recovery and resolution of credit institutions and investment firms and amending Council Directive 82/891/EEC, and Directives 2001/24/EC, 2002/47/EC, 2004/25/EC, 2005/56/EC, 2007/36/EC, 2011/35/EU, 2012/30/EU and 2013/36/EU, and Regulations (EU) No 1093/2010 and (EU) No 648/2012, of the European Parliament and of the Council Text with EEA relevance [2014] Official Journal (OJ) L 173/190.

116 CJEU 5.5.2022, C-410/20, *Banco Santander, SA v J.A.C. and M.C.P.R,* ECLI:EU:C:2022:351.

who acquired shares in the framework of an Initial Public Offering (IPO), issued before the resolution process, cannot bring prospectus liability actions or actions for nullity of the share subscription contract.

c) Commentary

45 In 2024, there was a veritable avalanche of rulings on potential liability arising from the Banco Popular fiasco. All cases (about 180 of them) follow the same pattern, in which claims are doomed to failure. According to case law, the aim of the European regulation is to protect financial stability, preventing resolution decisions from being reversed by civil claims with restitutionary effect – as a prospectus liability claim would allegedly be. Any loss suffered by the investor cannot be qualified as an effect of the consent's error, but of a legitimate resolution decision.[117] The termination of Banco Popular entails the extinction of the subject matter of the contract and thus the impossibility of making any restitution.[118] In any event, the lower court cannot

117 Similarly, STS 411/2024, 20 March 2024 (ROJ 1530/2024, ECLI:ES:TS:2024:1530); STS 383/2024, 18 March 2024 (ROJ 1536/2024, ECLI:ES:TS:2024:1536); STS 410/2024, 20 March 2024 (ROJ 1533/2024, ECLI:ES:TS:2024:1533); STS 440/2024, 2 April 2024 (ROJ 1683/2024, ECLI:ES:TS:2024:1683); STS 437/2024, 2 April 2024 (ROJ 1729/2024, ECLI:ES:TS:2024:1729); STS 460/2024, 8 April 2024 (ROJ 1832/2024, ECLI:ES:TS:2024:1832); STS 465/2024, 8 April 2024 (ROJ 1828/2024, ECLI:ES:TS:2024:1828); STS 466/2024, 8 April 2024 (ROJ 1827/2024, ECLI:ES:TS:2024:1827); STS 459/2024, 8 April 2024 (ROJ 1907/2024, ECLI:ES:TS:2024:1907); STS 499/2024, 15 April 2024 (ROJ 1946/2024, ECLI:ES:TS:2024:1946); STS 501/2024, 15 April 2024 (ROJ 1905/2024, ECLI:ES:TS:2024:1905); STS 520/2024, 22 April 2024 (ROJ 2048/2024, ECLI:ES:TS:2024:2048); STS 519/2024, 22 April 2024 (ROJ 2047/2024, ECLI:ES:TS:2024:2047); STS 559/2024, 24 April 2024 (ROJ 2125/2024, ECLI:ES:TS:2024:2125); STS 552/2024, 24 April 2024 (ROJ 2051/2024, ECLI:ES:TS:2024:2051); STS 558/2024, 24 April 2024 (ROJ 2052/2024, ECLI:ES:TS:2024:2052); STS 569/2024, 29 April 2024 (ROJ 2169/2024, ECLI:ES:TS:2024:2169); STS 568/2024, 29 April 2024 (ROJ 2168/2024, ECLI:ES:TS:2024:2168); STS 589/2024, 6 May 2024 (ROJ 2165/2024, ECLI:ES:TS:2024:2165); STS 590/2024, 6 May 2024 (ROJ 2166/2024, ECLI:ES:TS:2024:2166); STS 605/2024, 7 May 2024 (ROJ 2178/2024, ECLI:ES:TS:2024:2178); STS 1366/2024, 21 October 2024 (ROJ 5181/2024, ECLI:ES:TS:2024:5181); STS 1363/2024, 21 October 2024 (ROJ 5178/2024, ECLI:ES:TS:2024:5178); STS 1368/2024, 21 October 2024 (ROJ 5184/2024, ECLI:ES:TS:2024:5184); STS 1362/2024, 21 October 2024 (ROJ 5177/2024, ECLI:ES:TS:2024:5177); STS 1370/2024, 21 October 2024 (ROJ 5186/2024, ECLI:ES:TS:2024:5186); STS 1511/2024, 12 November 2024 (ROJ 5531/2024, ECLI:ES:TS:2024:5531); STS 1508/2024, 12 November 2024 (ROJ 5529/2024, ECLI:ES:TS:2024:5529); STS 1551/2024, 19 November 2024 (ROJ 5743/2024, ECLI:ES:TS:2024:5743); STS 1547/2024, 19 November 2024 (ROJ 5748/2024, ECLI:ES:TS:2024:5748); STS 1550/2024, 19 November 2024 (ROJ 5827/2024, ECLI:ES:TS:2024:5827), etc.

118 STS 425/2024, 1 April 2024 (ROJ 1668/2024, ECLI:ES:TS:2024:1668). In a different case, which does not involve Banco Popular but Bankia, the investor plaintiff did obtain the requested compensation, despite being a qualified investor, because he did not have access to other relevant information: STS 929/2024, 1 July 2024 (ROJ 4102/2024, ECLI:ES:TS:2024:4102).

award damages in tort where the claim is based on contractual liability.[119] Finally, if the claim is not based on the prospectus (thus in tort) but on contract breach, the prescription period is not three years (art 6.3 Securities Market Act)[120] but the general period of five years (art 1964.2 CC).[121]

11. Personal Injury

In 2024, the Supreme Court reiterated its doctrine on loss of opportunity (*pérdida de una oportunidad*) in medical liability. In one case,[122] the court held an insurer liable arising from medical negligence in the diagnosis of acute transverse myelitis; although it was not proven that timely treatment would have eliminated the sequelae, the victim lost the real opportunity to reduce them and was thus awarded € 297,000 plus interest. In contrast, one woman claimed that she was not diagnosed in time with ductal breast carcinoma, which would have allowed her to undergo more aggressive treatment, but the court concluded that there was no causal link between the delay in diagnosis and the alleged consequences, so the claim against the insurer was dismissed.[123] In a case of negligent obstetric care, where doctors ignored signs of foetal distress and failed to perform an emergency caesarean section, with serious consequences for the newborn, the court concluded that the parents are also entitled to compensation, totalling € 1,500,000 plus interest.[124] In another case, however, it was concluded that there was no obstetric negligence simply because a vacuum cup was used during the baby's delivery – the claimants failed to establish the causal link and fault, and the burden of proof could not be eased because there was no evidentiary 46

119 STS 424/2024, 1 April 2024 (ROJ 1806/2024, ECLI:ES:TS:2024:1806).
120 Act 6/2023, of 17 March, *de los Mercados de Valores y de los Servicios de Inversión* (BOE 66, 18.3.2023).
121 STS 936/2024, 1 July 2024 (ROJ 4108/2024, ECLI:ES:TS:2024:4108). For another case of contract-based liability for bad advice by the bank, see STS 625/2024, 9 May 2024 (ROJ 2184/2024, ECLI:ES:TS:2024:2184). On the contract-tort divide now, see *P del Olmo García*, Responsabilidad contractual y extracontractual. La situación doctrinal en España, ADC 77(4) (2024) 1629–1676.
122 STS 204/2024, 19 February 2024 (ROJ 822/2024, ECLI:ES:TS:2024:822), commented upon by *MA Calzadilla Medina*, El quantum de un daño incierto: la oportunidad perdida en el ámbito de la responsabilidad civil médico-sanitaria. Comentario de la STS (Sala de lo Civil, Sección 1.ª) 204/2024, de 19 febrero (JUR 2024, 62960), Revista Aranzadi de derecho patrimonial (RDPat) 64 (2024) <https://www.aranzadilaley.es/>. Also see *MJ Santos Morón*, A vueltas con la pérdida de oportunidad en la responsabilidad sanitaria, Indret: Revista para el Análisis del Derecho 2 (2024) 1–44 <www.indret.com>.
123 STS 334/2024, 6 March 2024 (ROJ 1466/2024, ECLI:ES:TS:2024:1466).
124 STS 774/2024, 3 June 2024 (ROJ 3046/2024, ECLI:ES:TS:2024:3046). The girl was awarded € 1,000,000, the mother € 346,000 and the father € 154,000.

impossibility.[125] Case law has also reiterated its doctrine that an insurer is not allowed to delay the payment of compensation by arguing against the claim, but has to pay as soon as it becomes aware of the claim. Otherwise, it has to pay penalty interest[126] (pursuant to the Insurance Contract Act[127] art 20). As regards informed consent, it is considered irrelevant that one of the documents lacked the patient's signature if the patient was informed of the surgical technique to be performed, and the oedema he suffered could not be causally attributed to medical malpractice.[128]

47 In a case where a customer broke the glass door of a bar, causing damage to a bystander's eye, the Supreme Court excluded (a) the application of the strict liability rule for things that 'fall or are thrown' from a property (art 1910 Spanish Civil Code [CC]),[129] because damage was not caused by the owner but a third party, and (b) the application of the general fault liability clause (art 1902 CC), because the event was neither foreseeable nor avoidable and the safety regulations had been complied with.[130]

48 In a case of damage caused by a defective hip prosthesis, the Supreme Court concluded that the ten-year prescription period (pursuant to the Consumer Protection Act,[131] art 144) starts to run from the time the distributor (and not the manufacturer) put the product into circulation, and that the product liability statutory regime does

---

125 STS 870/2024, 18 June 2024 (ROJ 3547/2024, ECLI:ES:TS:2024:3547).

126 STS 853/2024, 11 June 2024 (ROJ 3299/2024, ECLI:ES:TS:2024:3299).

127 Act 50/1980, of 8 October, *de Contrato de Seguro* (BOE 250, 17.10.1980) (hereinafter, LCS).

128 STS 908/2024, 24 June 2024 (ROJ 3544/2024, ECLI:ES:TS:2024:3544). In legal scholarship, see *E Moure*, Sobre Derecho sanitario: Conversaciones, tribunas y estudios (2024); *J Domingo Monforte*, Responsabilidad civil médica. Medicina estética. Discordancia entre el consentimiento verbalmente ofrecido y el firmado. Valor probatorio de las grabaciones médico-paciente, El notario del siglo XXI 114 (2024) 50–53, and *J Vicente Mediavilla*, Errores de diagnóstico prenatal y responsabilidad (2024). On professional liability in general, *MC Crespo Mora*, Responsabilidad civil por negligencia profesional (2024). On liability for vaccines, see *E Pérez López*, La responsabilidad patrimonial de las Administraciones Públicas por los daños derivados de la vacunación (2024).

129 RD of 24 July 1889, *por el que se publica el Código Civil* (Official Gazette [Gaceta de Madrid] 206, 25.7.1889).

130 STS 116/2024, 31 January 2024 (ROJ 364/2024, ECLI:ES:TS:2024:364). Concerning a different case, also see *P Martínez Espín*, Lesiones sufridas por el titular de un bar como consecuencia de la explosión de una botella de cerveza. Comentario a la STS 1516/2023, de 2 de noviembre (RJ 2023, 5731), CCJC 125 (2024) 121–142.

131 RDleg 1/2007, of 16 November, *por el que se aprueba el texto refundido de la Ley General para la Defensa de los Consumidores y Usuarios y otras leyes complementarias* (BOE 287, 30.11.2007) (hereinafter TRLGDCU).

not exclude the possibility of suing under general tort liability law for fault under art 1902 CC.[132]

As regards motor vehicle liability, the Supreme Court recalled that compulsory insurance covers damage caused to third parties only, and that allowing compensation for damage caused to the policyholder (the driver, who was the victim's wife) would imply an inappropriate extension of third-party insurance, unduly assimilating it to first-party insurance.[133] Regarding penalty interest in the case where the insurer fails to issue a motivated compensation offer (*oferta motivada*) to the victim (art 120 LCS), the court recalled well established case law that, for that offer to be effective, it must be accompanied by the payment or effective consignment.[134] 49

C. Literature

1. *Araceli Donado/Francisco J Jiménez Muñoz* (eds), La responsabilidad civil de la IA [AI liability] (Dykinson, 2024)

A collective work that explores the implications of the use of AI from the perspective of tort law.[135] 50

132 STS 161/2024, 7 February 2024 (ROJ 470/2024, ECLI:ES:TS:2024:470), on which see *MJ Reyes López*, Algunas cuestiones sobre Derecho de consumo al hilo de la STS 161/2024, de 7 febrero, RDPat 64 (2024) <https://www.aranzadilaley.es/>. On product liability, see *A Hernández Manzanares*, La responsabilidad civil por producto defectuoso tras la Sentencia de Pleno de la Sala Civil del Tribunal Supremo 1516–2023, de 2 de noviembre, Diario La Ley 10440 (2024) <https://diariolaley.laleynext.es> and *J Maseda Rodríguez*, Responsabilidad del fabricante por sus productos, contrato de seguro y acción directa: panorámica breve de la práctica española de Derecho internacional privado, Revista Jurídica Digital UANDES 8(1) (2024) 44–77.

133 STS 444/2024, 2 April 2024 (ROJ 1730/2024, ECLI:ES:TS:2024:1730). In legal scholarship, see *PJ Vela Torres*, Cobertura del seguro de responsabilidad civil obligatorio del automóvil, Diario La Ley 10546 (2024) <https://diariolaley.laleynext.es> and *V Magro Servet*, No cobertura del seguro obligatorio por daño moral del conductor asegurado culpable del siniestro por muerte de su pareja (Análisis de la STS 444/2024, de 2 de abril de 2024), Tráfico y seguridad vial 297 (2024) <https://diariolaley.laleynext.es>.

134 STS 1321/2024, 15 October 2024 (ROJ 5173/2024, ECLI:ES:TS:2024:5173). Regarding penalty interest, also see STS 161/2024, 18 January 2024 (ROJ 161/2024, ECLI:ES:TS:2024:161), involving damage because of the collapse of a tunnel.

135 Also see *N Álvarez Lata* (ed), Derecho de contratos, responsabilidad extracontractual e inteligencia artificial (2024); *C Celeste Danesi*, Derechos del consumidor en la encrucijada de la inteligencia artificial: la necesaria reforma de la Directiva de productos defectuosos (2024); *TG García Micó*, Robótica quirúrgica y derecho de daños (2024); *M Martínez Muñoz*, Responsabilidad civil de los daños causados por drones y su aseguramiento, RRCCS 4 (2024) 6–30; *I Herbosa Martínez*, Encaje de los

2. *Juan Carlos Velasco Perdigones*, Autonomía progresiva y responsabilidad civil del menor [The minor's autonomy and tort] (Dykinson, 2024)

51 The author decries that minors who cause damage to others usually go scot-free even though they are autonomous in practice – so it is usually the parents or guardians who ultimately bear the liability.[136]

sistemas de IA en la definición de producto en la legislación de productos defectuosos. Análisis de la legislación vigente con la vista puesta en la Propuesta de Directiva del Parlamento europeo y del Consejo de 28 de septiembre de 2022 (COM/2022/495), Indret 3 (2024) 1–47 <www.indret.com>; *R Lafuente Sánchez*, Inteligencia artificial y vehiculos autónomos: Responsabilidad civil extracontractual internacional (2024); *JA Moreno Martínez/PJ Femenía López* (eds), Inteligencia artificial y derecho de daños: cuestiones actuales (2024); *F Ramón Fernández*, Régimen jurídico de los drones: inteligencia artificial, responsabilidad, usos y conflictos (2024), and *A Rubí Puig*, Una lectura del reglamento de inteligencia artificial desde el derecho privado, Indret 4 (2024) 1–8 <www.indret.com>. On cybercrime, see *L Matarredona Chornet/C Peñalosa Torné*, Ciberdelincuencia. La responsabilidad civil bancaria, Diario La Ley 10431 (2024) <https://diariolaley.laleynext.es>. On tort law and compensation in general, *MJ Herrador Guardia* (ed), Daño y resarcimiento (2024) and *J López y García de la Serrana*, XXIII Congreso Nacional de la Asociación Española de Abogados Especializados en Responsabilidad Civil y Seguro (2024). On the Belgian reform, see *F Oyarzún Vargas*, Acerca del proyecto de reforma de la responsabilidad civil recientemente aprobado en Bélgica, ADC 77(2) (2024) 771–820.

136 By the same author, see La responsabilidad civil de la persona con discapacidad y de las instituciones de apoyo, RAD 2 (2024) <https://www.aranzadilaley.es/>. See also *S Algaba Ros*, La responsabilidad civil de los centros docentes de enseñanza no superior por los daños causados por sus alumnos menores de edad, Indret 4 (2024) 1–50 <www.indret.com> *AM Pérez Vallejo*, Discapacidad y responsabilidad por daños extracontractuales (2024).

Sandra Friberg

XXIX. Sweden

A. Legislation

There were no changes in Swedish tort law in 2024. 1

B. Cases

1. Supreme Court (Högsta domstolen) 25 January 2024, Nytt Juridiskt Arkiv (NJA) 2024, 52: Interpretation of Insurance Terms and Conditions; Sudden and Unforeseen Damage?

a) Brief Summary of the Facts

After closing time on the afternoon of 25 March 2018, the roof of the Mio furniture store in Boden collapsed. The collapse completely destroyed the store and the property in the building. Möbellind owns the property in which the store was located. 2

Möbellind is covered by a company insurance policy that covers certain risks listed in clause 5b, including those related to snow load. The insurance also states under the all-risk section (clause 5k) that compensation is paid for sudden and unforeseen physical damage caused by a damage event other than those specified in clause 5b. 3

Möbellind claims that the insurance company should pay insurance compensation according to the terms of clause 5k (the all-risk section), while the insurance company disputes this and argues that the damage event was snow load, which is not covered by the all-risk section. The District Court and the Court of Appeal came to opposite conclusions in their rulings. 4

b) Judgment of the Court

The Supreme Court acknowledges that the parties agree that clause 5b in the insurance policy is not applicable in the present situation. The condition states: 'The insurance applies to physical damage to the building, to this fixed property and to 5

https://doi.org/10.1515/9783111389271-030

property in the building due to ... snow load on the roof arising directly in connection with extreme precipitation or other extreme weather conditions, provided that it has not been possible to eliminate the snow pressure due to the weather conditions and that previous snow load on the roof has not affected the damage. Damage due to storm, hail or snow load means that the property has been damaged by ... the weight of snow.'

6 The Supreme Court notes that the insurance clause 5b covers certain specifically specified risks, while the all-risk section covers all unspecified risks that are not excluded. After a comparison with other provisions in the insurance terms and conditions, the Supreme Court concludes that the relevant condition (clause 5k) in the all-risk section cannot be understood as covering only damage events that are not at all covered by clause 5b's conditions regarding natural disaster. Instead, the damage event must be covered by clause 5b in order for compensation to be excluded from the all-risk section. The all-risk section can therefore include damage events linked both to snow loads on roofs and to defective building construction.

7 The investigation into the case revealed that the frame structure of the store building had not been reinforced during various renovations. The defective building structure was therefore considered to be the main cause of the collapse.

8 The damage that occurred when the roof collapsed was almost immediate. The damage was therefore sudden within the meaning of the insurance terms.

9 Neither the previous nor the current representatives of Möbellind were aware of the defective building structure and the lack of load-bearing capacity was not possible to detect with the naked eye. During an inspection of the building in 2016, nothing was found to indicate that the building structure was defective. Against this background, and given that the amount of snow that had fallen at the time and the snow load on the roof were not abnormal for the time of year, the damage was not foreseeable for Möbellind. The damage was therefore unforeseen within the meaning of the insurance terms, according to the Supreme Court, and thus covered by the all-risk element of the insurance.

c) Commentary

10 The current case largely confirms already settled questions of principle that the Supreme Court has ruled on. Among other things, the Court recalls that when in-

terpreting insurance terms and conditions, an overall assessment must be made,[1] that the policyholder has the burden of proof for circumstances that fall within the scope of the insurance contract, while the insurer bears the burden of proof for circumstances that relate to exceptional conditions in the insurance,[2] and that in an insurance context where there have been interacting causes of damage, it is sufficient for an insured event that one of the causes can be identified as the 'main cause' (in this case, it was considered that the defective roof construction was the main cause of the collapsed roof; the amount of snow in itself could not have caused the collapse).

The case might not provide any great novelties, but does provide guidance to 11 insurance companies to clarify the limits of the all-risk section in their terms and conditions if they want to exclude certain natural damage that is otherwise compensable as long as it is sudden and unforeseen.

2. Supreme Court (Högsta domstolen) 4 April 2024, Nytt Juridiskt Arkiv (NJA) 2024, 229: Is Minor Assault Serious Enough to Warrant Liability?

a) Brief Summary of the Facts

A 15-year-old boy (A) hit a boy of the same age (B) in the head with an open hand. 12 The incident occurred in the schoolyard after the end of the school day and after A had physically attacked B earlier in the day by, among other things, pushing him. The blow was inflicted in front of several other pupils in the schoolyard outside the school, which they all attended.

The district court convicted A of minor assault and ordered him to pay non- 13 pecuniary damages to B of SEK 8,000.

A appealed to the Court of Appeal, which decided not to grant leave to appeal. 14 The Supreme Court decided to examine the question of whether the minor assault for which A was convicted is to be considered such a serious violation that entails liability for damages under ch 2, sec 3 of the Tort Liability Act. The question of leave to appeal in the Court of Appeal in the damages section was declared suspended pending this examination.

1 See also NJA 2018, 834 and NJA 2023, 630 – the latter case commented on by *S Friberg*, Sweden, in: E Karner/BC Steininger (eds), European Tort Law (ETL) 2023 (2024) 667, no 32 ff.

2 With reference to NJA 2021, 983.

b) Judgment of the Court

15 The Supreme Court began by outlining the general conditions for damages for infringement under ch 2, sec 3 of the Tort Liability Act to be awarded.

16 The Supreme Court sets out to describe the general requirements. It must be a criminal attack on certain specifically designated protected interests: the person, freedom, peace or honour; and it must be a serious attack. The latter means that damages proceedings concerning 'trifles' should not be encouraged, that individuals in everyday interactions must be able to tolerate certain irritations and that society's resources should be used where they are most needed.

17 The Supreme Court continues by explaining the latest legislative amendment concerning compensation for injury (2022). The overall purpose was to significantly increase the level of compensation, which means enhanced protection of bodily integrity, according to the Supreme Court. As before, however, a comprehensive assessment must be made of whether the injury can be characterised as serious under ch 2, sec 3 of the Tort Liability Act.

18 A was convicted of minor assault and the Supreme Court finds that such a crime may give rise to a right to non-pecuniary damages, but that some additional element of infringement or violation of integrity is required for the minor crime to be considered a serious injury.

19 According to the Supreme Court, the investigation revealed that A was in a superior position in relation to B, that he was well aware of this and took advantage of it to insult B several times a day. The Supreme Court further emphasises that the blow was inflicted in front of several other pupils in the schoolyard outside the school they all attended. According to the Supreme Court, it is thus clear that B was in a vulnerable situation, which meant that he was particularly humiliated by the blow.

20 The situation thus included such additional elements of violation of integrity that the attack, when assessed as a whole, was considered to constitute such a serious violation that the boy was entitled to non-pecuniary damages under the Tort Liability Act, ch 2, sec 3.

c) Commentary

21 This ruling is one of the first after the latest amendment to the Tort Liability Act 2022, which was motivated, among other things, by the need to increase the compensation levels for assault. To achieve this, without specifying specific compensation levels in the text of the law and continuing to leave the detailed considerations regarding the determination of compensation to the courts, more

circumstances were introduced in ch 5 sec 6 of the Tort Liability Act (the rule on the determination of compensation in the event of assault) that must be considered in the application of the law.

Of particular interest in the case at hand is the fact that the compensation should contribute to the victim being given redress for the assault. Previously, it also had to be considered whether the assault involved particularly shameful or degrading elements. 22

It is clear that the majority of the Supreme Court attaches importance to circumstances that preceded the actual assault earlier in the day – that the defendant had physically attacked the boy by, among others, pushing him – and that the defendant was in a superior position and that the assault took place in front of his schoolmates, which meant, according to the Supreme Court, that the attacked boy was in a particularly vulnerable situation and was thus particularly humiliated by the assault. Under such circumstances, an otherwise, relatively minor, violation is considered serious enough to give rise to a right to damages. 23

The Supreme Court, however, did not agree, with two of the five judges considering that the violation was not serious enough. They did not attach importance to what had happened between the boys earlier in the day, but focused their assessment on the time of the act. They emphasised that although the blow was inflicted in front of some schoolmates, it did not attract any public attention and did not cause any comments to the victimized boy for more than a week or so. They further emphasised that it was a rapid, transient sequence of events and that there was no specific intention in the defendant's actions. It can be said that the minority of the court attaches less importance to the context than the majority did. 24

It can be noted that the same type of circumstance surrounding an act can sometimes be considered as aggravating and sometimes mitigating. On the one hand, the fact that a sequence of events is short-lived can be said to be mitigating when the violation was not prolonged in time, but, on the other hand, can be aggravating if it is described as a sudden blow for which the victim is unprepared. This is one of the inherent difficulties with compensation for non-pecuniary damage, namely, the determination of the extent to which the context should be allowed to shape the court's assessment and how the same circumstance can be given weight both for and against a finding of liability damages. 25

However, this ruling confirms the premise that minor assaults typically do not give rise to liability for damages unless there are aggravating circumstances surrounding the act – and it is then, according to the majority in the ruling, possible to consider a larger context than the moment of the act – which means that the violation can be considered serious enough for the threshold for liability for non-pecuniary damages for the perpetrator to be crossed. 26

3. Supreme Court (Högsta domstolen) 8 May 2024, Nytt Juridiskt Arkiv (NJA) 2024, 277: Patient Compensation and the Issue of Proof Requirements in Cases of Treatment Injury

a) Brief Summary of the Facts

27 A woman sought care from a healthcare provider for a complaint with her left foot. The foot was first treated with a cortisone injection and the woman subsequently underwent surgery. Two weeks after the surgery, the woman was diagnosed with Complex Regional Pain Syndrome (CRPS), a chronic pain condition. The parties agree that the woman suffered from CRPS as a result of the surgery but disagree as to the extent to which her current complaints are a result of CRPS.

28 The healthcare provider had patient insurance with Zurich and the woman requested compensation from the company. After the Patient Injury Board had issued a statement and determined that she was not entitled to compensation, Zurich rejected the claim for compensation.

29 The woman brought an action in the District Court and demanded that Zurich be ordered to pay patient injury compensation. Zurich contested the action and stated, among other things, that the operation was medically justified and that the injury could not have been avoided. Both the District Court and the Court of Appeal rejected her action as the courts found that the reduced standard of proof contained in the Patient Injury Act (1996:799) – preponderance of probability – applies in cases examining whether there is a causal connection between the treatment and the personal injury, but not to cases as to whether the injury could have been avoided by another procedure.

b) Judgment of the Court

30 After giving a general description of patient injury compensation and the relevant legal framework in the Patient Injury Act (sec 6, para 1, point 1), the Court states that compensation presupposes, first, that *the treatment is the direct cause* of the injury, and second, that *the injury could have been avoided* either by performing the selected procedure differently or by choosing a different procedure (procedure refers to both treatment method and treatment technique). The question of whether the injury could have been avoided includes the question of whether the treatment was medically justified and whether an accepted method was used.

In the case of treatment of injuries, the patient has the burden of proof concerning both the claim that the treatment caused the personal injury, and that the injury could have been avoided. However, sec 6, first paragraph, of the Patient Injuries Act clearly states that a lower standard of proof is to be applied in terms of causation. It is sufficient that there is a preponderant probability that the personal injury was caused by, for example, the treatment. 31

The Supreme Court then states that, on the other hand, it is not possible to clearly read from the text of the judgment which standard of proof is to be applied to the latter part of the provision, ie, that the injury could have been avoided. The preparatory work does not provide a clear answer to the question either. A clearly stated starting point, however, was that any boundary-drawing problems that the law could give rise to should not affect the patient in the form of lost rights to compensation. 32

The Supreme Court then makes a comparison with the previous voluntary patient insurance (the predecessor to the Patient Injury Act) and states that the same situation prevailed when the insurance was terminated as in the current Patient Injury Act with regard to the burden of proof and evidentiary requirements. 33

The Supreme Court then moves on to compare the corresponding legislation in the Nordic countries and states that there too the burden of proof lies with the patient, with a relaxed requirement for the proof of causation. The texts of the Danish, Finnish and Icelandic Patient Injury Acts state that a relaxed evidentiary requirement also applies in cases where the question of whether the injury could have been avoided arises. 34

Furthermore, the Patient Injury Board explained in a statement that the Board applies the lowered evidentiary requirement also in cases when the injury could have been avoided. 35

After this comparative review, the Supreme Court finds that the reasons for the lower standard of proof regarding causation are related to the fact that a causal relationship cannot always be investigated in all its aspects, even with the best medical expertise. Corresponding difficulties exist when a patient has to prove that the harm following the treatment could have been avoided, as such an examination usually concerns complicated medical conditions where the patient has to rely to a large extent on assessments by doctors with specialist expertise, who may have different opinions. According to the Supreme Court, this in itself speaks in favour of a lower standard of proof. 36

The Court further stated that such a lower standard of proof can be reconciled with the wording of the law and the general wording of the section. The Court also stated that such a position is consistent with the Patient Compensation Board's practice and is in line with both what was valid under the previous voluntary insurance system and with the legislation of other Nordic countries. 37

38 The Supreme Court's conclusion is therefore that the standard of proof is that there must be a preponderance of probability that the woman's injury could have been avoided by performing the chosen procedure differently or by choosing another available procedure that, according to a retrospective assessment from a medical point of view, would have satisfied the need for care in a less risky manner.

39 In view of this, leave to appeal should be granted in the remainder of the case (ie if the woman is entitled to compensation), the Court of Appeal's judgment should be set aside and the case should be returned to it for further proceedings.

c) Commentary

40 It has been argued in legal research that the division between two different stages in the causality assessment does not serve any direct function. If – which was undisputed in this case – there is a connection between the treatment and the personal injury that occurred, then the injury could have been avoided, ie, the treatment entailed risks that are not attributable to the underlying disease. If, on the contrary, no other measure could have prevented the injury, then it is not the treatment but the underlying disease that is the cause of the injury.[3]

41 In short: there was medical malpractice on the part of the doctor that caused a harmful effect, and according to sec 6 of the Patient Injury Act, compensation of a patient's injury is to be awarded if there is a preponderant probability that the injury was caused by the treatment in a situation where the injury could have been avoided by a procedure that met the need for care in a less risky way. The doctor's insurance company claimed that the operation had been medically justified and that the injury could therefore not have been avoided.

42 However, given that it was already noted at the initial stage of the liability issue that there are complicated problems as regards the causal link in medical matters, higher evidentiary requirements should not, according to the Supreme Court, be imposed in a subsequent examination of whether the damage could have been avoided with a different procedure, and it is easy to concur in this assessment. Whether or not this ruling from the Supreme Court will lead to damages for the woman remains to be seen, since the case has now been sent back to be tried by the lower courts.

3 See *H Andersson*, Orsaksdilemman i patientskaderätten, InfoTorg 27 May 2024, <www.infotorg.se>.

4. Supreme Court (Högsta domstolen) 13 June 2024, Nytt Juridiskt Arkiv (NJA) 2024, 369: Compensation from the Tortfeasor when a Third Party has Received Payment due to the Damage

a) Brief Summary of the Facts

A woman A entered into an agreement to sell her property and the associated residential building. Before the buyers took possession, A hired a company, Pressateljén, to clean the property prior to the new owners moving in. After the cleaning was completed, the buyers took possession of the property and then discovered water damage. 43

The buyers claimed compensation from A for the water damage and eventually the parties reached a settlement which meant that A paid SEK 70,000 to the buyers. 44

A then claimed compensation from Pressateljén in the corresponding amount. She claimed that the company had caused the water damage when performing the cleaning service and that the amount of the damage she suffered corresponded to the amount that she had paid to the buyers. Pressateljén opposed the claim. As for the amount of compensation, the company objected that there was no investigation showing that the damage amounted to the amount claimed. Pressateljén further considered that the damages should in any case be adjusted to zero SEK, considering that the company, due to certain deficiencies in the doorstep and bathroom floor, had not been able to foresee or prevent the damage. 45

Both the district court and the court of appeal concluded that Pressateljén was liable for the water damage but arrived at different conclusions when it came to determining the extent of the damage. The Supreme Court granted leave to appeal on the basis that Pressateljén was liable for the damage. The question in the case was under what conditions an injured party is entitled to compensation from the person who caused the damage for a payment that has been made to a third party in accordance with a settlement due to the damage. 46

b) Judgment of the Court

The Supreme Court begins the reasons for its judgment with a comprehensive account of the liability of traders for damages under the Consumer Services Act, compensation for property damage under the Torts Act, including the issue of adequate causality, payment to third parties, the duty to limit damage, special issues 47 regarding damage to property that is the subject of transfer, and evidentiary issues.

48 In its assessment of the specific case, the Supreme Court finds that the buyers were entitled to a price reduction for the water damage that occurred. It cannot therefore be considered an incalculable consequence of the damage that A compensated the buyers for it. Nor was the settlement between the parties conditioned on any circumstances other than the water damage.

49 Initially, the buyers demanded compensation from A in a significantly higher amount (based on quotes for removal of the water damage and other measures). The Supreme Court therefore finds that the buyers were entitled to a price reduction of at least the amount that A undertook to pay in the settlement. The cost was therefore also compatible with A's obligation to limit the damage.

50 A's payment to the buyers is therefore in its entirety a compensable cost that is covered by Pressateljén's liability for damages.

c) Commentary

51 This is, in my opinion, an unnecessarily extensive judgment to clarify the not particularly complicated issue of the liability of the person who caused the damage and the right to recourse. In the lower courts, the differences actually consisted mainly in how the claim should be valued. The District Court considered that Pressateljén was indeed liable for damage, but that it was not possible to determine the extent of the damage based on the evidence presented. Since there had been no difficulties in presenting evidence, the court could not reasonably estimate the damage, and the claim was therefore dismissed.

52 The Court of Appeal also found that there was liability for damage and, unlike the District Court, considered that it was possible to reasonably determine the extent of the damage at the amount claimed.

53 The Supreme Court's examination concerned the conditions under which an injured party is entitled to compensation from the tortfeasor for a payment that has been made in connection with the damage pursuant to a settlement with a third party. These conditions are: (1) that there was, in principle, an obligation for the injured party to compensate the third party and that the obligation to compensate was conditioned by the specific damage in question (otherwise, the adequacy requirement is lacking); (2) the injured party must prove their damage using the standard of proof that normally applies to civil cases; and (3) in situations where the damages consists of compensation paid after a settlement, the injured party does not have to prove that they would have been obliged to pay a certain amount if a settlement had not been reached.

The case must be understood from the context that in a situation such as the one in question, there is no clear rule on recourse claims. But at the same time, it is clear, according to the rules in the Consumer Services Act, that a consumer is entitled to compensation for damage that the trader causes to the consumer's property and that this includes the financial consequences that the physical damage has caused to the injured party. This makes it evident that Pressateljén is liable for damage that they caused to the consumer. 54

Also, the injured party has an obligation in general to limit their damage, which means that costs that could have been avoided are in principle not compensated. In the present ruling, the Supreme Court develops more concrete criteria for how this duty to limit damage should be understood in a context where the parties have settled on an amount for damages. What is particularly emphasised is that the terms of the settlement must be reasonable so that the person liable is not obliged to pay an excessive amount if the injured party has voluntarily assumed too great a liability to pay. The injured party should thus not be able to cause the person who caused the damage too great a financial loss through a voluntary agreement. It can be understood from the case that if the injured party agrees to an unfavourable settlement, the entire cost cannot be transferred to the person who caused the damage. 55

5. Supreme Court (Högsta domstolen) 14 June 2024, Nytt Juridiskt Arkiv (NJA) 2024, 424: Foster Care Placement

a) Brief Summary of the Facts

From 1972 to 1974, the claimant (TR) was placed in foster care, and during this time, she was allegedly subjected to sexual abuse. In her claim, TR refers to the municipality's failure to fulfil its supervisory responsibilities under the Child Welfare Law of 1960, thereby violating her rights under art 3 of the European Convention on Human Rights (ECHR) concerning inhuman treatment and art 8 concerning respect for family life. She refers to State liability for fault or negligence in the current ch 3, sec 2, of the Tort Liability Act, to the provisions on Convention damages in ch 3, sec 4, and to the case law and general principles regarding liability for violations of the ECHR. In the latter respect, she refers to the case law on the right to damages based directly on the ECHR which, without any explicit legal basis, has been developed by the Supreme Court in a number of judgments since 2005. 56

After the municipality objected that TR's claim for damages was time-barred, the district court decided to adjudicate that question by an intermediate judg- 57 ment. The district court found that the claim is time-barred. The Court of Appeal arrived at the same conclusion.

b) Judgment of the Court

58 The Supreme Court firstly provided general information about limitations of actions and how the application of the Limitation Act relates to the ECHR.

59 The right to access a court (art 6 para 1) is not absolute. Limitation of actions may be acceptable and within the State's margin of appreciation if it pursues a legitimate aim and there is proportionality between the aim and the measure. The Supreme Court also stresses that there is a wide margin of appreciation as regards the starting point and length of the limitation period.

60 Limitations of actions may also violate the right to an effective remedy under art 13 ECHR and the Supreme Court notes that the European Court of Human Rights (ECtHR) has taken into account the extent to which the individual has had a real opportunity to assert their claim in time.

61 The Supreme Court then turns to the question of limitations of actions and damages for fault or negligence on the part of the municipality. Since the limitation period normally commences when the harmful action or omission occurs, and the claimant referred to the municipality's negligence during her foster care placement between 1972 until 1974, the claim is time-barred under the Limitation Act. The Supreme Court finds that such an application of the law is clearly compatible with the requirements of the ECHR.

62 The right of individuals to receive compensation from the State for immaterial damage in the event of a violation of the ECHR came into effect on 1 April 2018 and applies only to violations occurring after that date.

63 However, the right to damages in the event of a violation of the ECHR developed in the Supreme Court's case law from 2005 and onwards, and is a right which thus exists without any explicit legal basis and which applies irrespective of the temporal limitation under the statutory right to Convention damages. This right to compensation is instead based on Sweden's obligation, under art 13, to provide an effective remedy for violations of the ECHR.

64 The Supreme Court reiterates that since precedents are established over time, it is natural that new case law may have implications, not only for the future, but also for the past, regardless of whether the legal situation at that time was perceived differently or appeared unclear. The fact that the ECHR became Swedish law in 1995, 20 years after the foster care placement, does not affect the assessment of whether a claim, based on the right to damages that later developed in case law, is time-barred.

Since it was not possible to claim compensation directly on the basis of the ECHR at the time when the alleged violations occurred (i.e, in principle at the end of the foster care placement in 1974), the Supreme Court finds that the starting point for the limitation period in this case cannot be the time when the harmful act or omissions occurred. Such an application would be questionable from an ECHR perspective. 65

Instead, the Supreme Court refers to a ruling from the ECtHR where it is stated that, since early December 2009, there is a generally applicable principle in Swedish law that permits damages to be awarded for violations of the ECHR. The Supreme Court therefore finds that the date, 3 December 2009 – set by the ECtHR in its ruling with reference to a ruling from the Swedish Supreme Court – must be decisive in assessing whether Swedish law provides an effective remedy under art 13 ECHR. 66

According to the Supreme Court, it would therefore be consistent to also make that date the starting point for the limitation period for claims based on an earlier violation of the ECHR. The Supreme Court also finds this to be most consistent with the notion that a statutory limitation provision in such cases should be applied in a way that gives the individual a legally effective opportunity to recover their claim. 67

The claim in this case was thus time-barred ten years after 3 December 2009, and since there has been no interruption of the limitation period and the action was not brought until December 2021, the claim can no longer be enforced. 68

c) Commentary

In this judgment, the Supreme Court had to refer to a previous ruling – NJA 2018, 103 – regarding the issue of prescription of claims for damages and what point in time should be the starting point for when the prescription period begins to run. 69

The 2018 case concerned an incorrect deregistration of citizenship in 1989. In another preceding decision concerning an incorrect deregistration of citizenship,[4] the Supreme Court determined that the affected person was entitled to damages for a violation of the fundamental freedoms and rights that citizenship constitutes according to the Swedish Constitution, the Instrument of Government. There was no legal basis for the right to damages, but the claim was based directly on the rights provision. This means that there were no sanctions connected to infringe- 70

4 NJA 2014, 323.

ments of the right to citizenship, and thus no legal basis existed to award damages. When compared with the right to damages that had been introduced in the Tort Liability Act for violations of the ECHR, the Supreme Court considered that such a fundamental right as citizenship should reasonably enjoy the same protection against violations. Thus, in the 2018 case, the basic conditions for liability were already established, but the question was whether the claim was time-barred.

71 The parties agreed that the limitation period should be calculated successively (day by day) during the time that the infringement of rights was ongoing, ie, until the incorrect registration was revoked. However, if limitation occurs in this manner, it means that the claim relating to the years between 1989 (when the incorrect registration took place) and 2004 (ten years before the 2014 judgment established that there was a possibility of claiming damages from the State) is time-barred.

72 The Supreme Court discusses slightly different possible times for when the limitation period should begin to run, on the basis that it would not be reasonable to start from the date of the incorrect registration, which in itself could be said to be the day when the damage occurred. Instead, it is considered that the limitation period should start to run when there has been a realistic possibility for the injured party to assert their claim. When it comes to claims against the State and which are based on a right that is as central and fundamental to the individual as citizenship, the reasons behind the institution of prescription do not apply with any particular force, according to the Supreme Court.

73 However, there is no given time for when there was a real possibility to assert a claim for damages. The Supreme Court rejects the view that one should start from the date of the 2014 ruling, when the injured party at least became aware at that time that the possibility of compensation existed. The Court considers that it would be 'in principle inappropriate to link the beginning of the limitation period in this way to the development of the law in court practice.' The Supreme Court instead finds that one should start from the time when the incorrect information was corrected, since the injured party then has a real possibility to present a claim for compensation. In the 2018 case, the claim for damages was therefore not time-barred in any way.

74 Just as in the 2018 case, the Supreme Court considers that it would be unreasonable to base the date on the time when the violation of rights took place, since at that time there was no possibility of claiming damages directly under the ECHR. Instead, as already stated above, it chooses to take the date (early December 2009) that the European Court of Human Rights has ruled was the starting point for establishing a generally applicable principle in Swedish law that damages can be awarded in the event of a violation of the Convention. Since it is the European Court of Human Rights that has so clearly identified a specific date when an individual has the opportunity to assert their right, the Supreme Court considers that

there are no fundamental concerns about linking the limitation period to developments in case law, contrary to what was considered in the 2018 case. How can this be?

It is not clear from the Supreme Court's reasons for its judgment why there are no fundamental concerns, but they may be related to the fact that it is not the Supreme Court's own development of case law that is decisive. It is certainly not predictable for anyone which cases the European Court of Justice will choose to take up for decision, or at what point in time this will be done, but the decisions are nevertheless issued by an authority that is separate from Sweden's own Supreme Court, which can itself control its own legal development and thus, at least to some extent, indirectly determine when the legal development that becomes decisive both for the future and sometimes retroactively takes place. This is just a hypothesis, an attempt to find reasons for two apparently contradictory conclusions. Because it certainly seems a little illogical when in one case you have strong principled objections to the very approach to how the limitation period should be assessed, with which in another case you see no objections. 75

Another issue that is likely to recur in the Supreme Court's decisions and perhaps in the legal literature is the question of the compatibility of the statute of limitations with arts 6 and 13 of the ECHR. The European Court of Human Rights has emphasised that national statutes of limitations may not be applied in an 'excessively formalistic' manner so as to infringe the right to an effective remedy. However, statutes of limitations may certainly be acceptable if they pursue a legitimate aim and there is proportionality between the aim and the measure. The interest of foreseeability and the possibility of an acceptable legal procedure, eg, concerning the preservation of evidence, may be such legitimate aims. 76

The question is, however, if certain circumstances do not deserve to be highlighted in particular when assessing the question of proportionality and legitimate purpose. In a case such as the present one, it is the State that, through compulsory care, was responsible for the well-being of children placed in foster care. It is also the State that had the opportunity to carry out checks on the placement and document all deviations and any abuse to which children have been subjected, especially when there have been circumstances that should have made the authorities aware of the abuse. Those who were subjected to neglect and abuse during foster care placements were children without the opportunity to exercise their rights until much later in life. 77

It can therefore be questioned whether the reasons behind the prescription rules should apply in a case such as the present one, when it is the State's shortcomings that created difficulties for the individual to bring a claim in time. There may be reasons to look further into whether the outcome of the case is compatible with the minimum requirements set out in art 13 of the ECHR regarding citizens' 78 right to an effective remedy and what is actually meant by their having had a 'real possibility' of making a claim for damages.

6. Supreme Court (Högsta domstolen) 18 June 2024, Nytt Juridiskt Arkiv (NJA) 2024, 445: The Structure

a) Brief Summary of the Facts

79 From 2004–2008, MB and RC jointly owned the company IMS Europe AB, which mainly operated activities focused on mail handling.

80 BB, who was an employee and partner of Grant Thornton, was appointed auditor of IMS in the spring of 2005. Grant Thornton assisted MB and RC in preparing their private income tax returns for the tax years 2007 and 2008 and also in selling IMS to Swiss Post International Sweden AB in January 2008.

81 In December 2013, the Swedish Tax Agency rejected a scheme in IMS, referred to by the parties as 'the structure',[5] and decided that MB and RC should be taxed on the basis that the funds paid to them through the structure should be considered as salary. This meant that MB and RC were charged tax, fees, interest and tax surcharges.

82 MB and RC claim that an agreement was formed with Grant Thornton, at least by implied action, and that Grant Thornton, through BB, provided negligent advice. Grant Thornton is therefore liable to MB and RC for the financial damage they suffered through the Swedish Tax Agency's decision to impose tax, fees, interest and tax surcharges on them.

83 Grant Thornton, for its part, claims that no agreement on tax advice was ever concluded between the parties. If this were the case, the general terms and conditions of the Swedish Association of Certified Public Accountants (FAR) should apply, which means that Grant Thornton cannot be held liable as oral advice must be confirmed in writing. MB and RC also did not complain in time.

84 Grant Thornton further states that the advice in any case was not negligent, and taking all the circumstances into account, MB and RC, through their own conduct, were complicit in the damage to such an extent that the damages should be adjusted to zero.

5 'The structure' was a scheme to avoid taxation. It consisted of IMS entering into a licensing agreement with an English company for a mail handling system. IMS paid licensing fees in accordance with the agreement. These fees were then transferred in various ways to MB and RC, who through this scheme received disguised wages.

b) Judgment of the Court

The Supreme Court notes that the investigation in the case showed that MB and RC assumed that Grant Thornton, through BB, was their personal tax advisor and that Grant Thornton must have realised this without informing MB and RC that the company was of a different opinion. This means that a tax advisory engagement relationship arose between the parties. However, the general terms and conditions (FAR) did not constitute contractual content as these were not mentioned by the parties in any relevant respect. 85

Regarding liability for damages, the Supreme Court finds that MB and RC do not appear to have initially acted in such a way that BB could have been suspected of being prepared to take any particular risks. However, as, for example, when they themselves were provided with significant amounts that were not taxed and when funds were transferred out of their company without being taxed, MB and RC must have understood that there were significant risks with 'the structure'. In addition, MB and RC implemented all the measures that were required of them in order for the structure to be implemented. 86

In an overall assessment, the Supreme Court therefore finds that the circumstances are such that even if the advice had major shortcomings, it is not, considering MB's and RC's own risk-taking and risk awareness, a ground for awarding damages. 87

c) Commentary

The case is a clear example of how a fault assessment is made in a contractual relationship regarding advice, in particular the issue of the importance of the client's risk-taking and risk awareness and how this impacts the fault assessment. The Supreme Court states, with references to its own previous rulings regarding advice liability,[6] that 'the client's awareness of the risks resulted in the advisor not being deemed to have committed any negligence giving rise to damages'. 88

It is not only the risk that is considered within the framework of the assessment of fault, but also the position of the parties is important. In a situation such as the current one, the advisor's presentation of their given assessments, which must be based on a professional investigation of the factual and legal situation, is weighed against the client's knowledge and attitude on the subject matter. If the client has demonstrated both risk awareness and willingness to take risks, 89

6 See eg, NJA 2018, 414 and NJA 2019, 877.

this may be weighed against proven risks in the advice. In this case, it became clear that the injured parties' own risk-taking meant that the advisor's own risk-taking was not grounds for liability, ie, not even culpable (an alternative outcome could have been that the advisor was indeed considered to have acted culpably, but that the damages were adjusted to zero taking into account the client's complicity).

90 Particularly when it comes to the question of 'method liability' rather than liability concerning an intended contractual result, the parties' conduct throughout the contract period is of importance for the assessment of whether the advisor (in this case: tax advisor) acted without showing the due care required by the assignment. In that assessment, the client's own conduct, including insight into and willingness to take risks, must also be factored in.

7. Supreme Court (Högsta domstolen) 23 December 2024, Nytt Juridiskt Arkiv (NJA) 2024, 911: No Strict Liability outside of Electricity Legislation

a) Brief Summary of the Facts

91 A fire broke out in a tunnel in central Stockholm. The fire originated in a high-voltage cable belonging to company X. The fire damaged, among other things, cables belonging to another company, Y, that were also in the tunnel.

92 The fire was caused by overheating in a conductor joint on the high-voltage cable. The power was automatically turned off after 70 milliseconds, but the fire could not be avoided.

93 Company Y requested that company X pay just over SEK 9.8 million in compensation for the damage caused to the company in the fire. The District Court decided to examine in an interlocutory judgment whether company X is liable for compensation on any grounds. The question was answered in the negative and the Court of Appeal upheld the District Court's judgment.

b) Judgment of the Court

94 The Supreme Court examined whether company X could be held liable on any of the following four legal grounds: (1) strict liability under electricity legislation;[7]

7 The Electricity Act (SFS 1997:857), now regulated in the Electrical Safety Act (SFS 2016:732).

(2) strict liability under general legal principles; (3) liability for the negligence of an independent contractor; or (4) liability for its own negligence through omission.

(1) Strict liability under the Electricity Act: according to ch 10 sec 1 para 1, the owner of a high-voltage installation is liable for property damage caused by the impact of electricity from the installation, even if this does not follow from general compensation provisions. The second paragraph of the section states certain exceptions from this strict liability, including if the damage was caused by the impact of electricity from the installation 95

Section 8 contains a special statute of limitations rule, according to which, a claim brought on the basis of liability provided for in sec 1, first paragraph, is time-barred if an action for compensation is not brought within two years of the date on which the damage occurred. 96

In the case, it was undisputed that company X's liability under ch 10, sec 1 of the Electricity Act is time-barred and that this liability does not apply to the damaged copper cables, since these fall under the exception in the second paragraph of the section. 97

(2) Strict liability under general legal principles? According to the Supreme Court, it is a given that the provisions on strict liability with a short limitation period in the electricity legislation do not prevent liability for damages from being asserted on the basis of negligence and that liability is associated with a limitation period of ten years. But can there also be strict liability on a general tort law basis for the disputed event? Company Y referred to the fact that the case concerns dangerous activities and that this, according to general principles, justifies the strict liability of company X. 98

The Supreme Court recalls that no general principle of strict liability for dangerous activities has been established in case law, and that strict liability on a general tort law basis for the damage caused in the case would have to be justified by the inherent danger of electrical power. At the same time, it is precisely this danger that underlies the strict liability in the electricity legislation, and there is therefore no scope for establishing a more far-reaching strict liability through the application of the law. The electricity legislation must be understood as an exhaustive regulation with regard to strict liability in the area in question. 99

(3) Liability for negligence of independent contractors? Company Y in the alternative claimed that company X is liable due to company Z's negligence. According to company Y, the fire was caused by defective welding work that company Z carried out in 2007 in connection with the high-voltage cable. Although company Z assumed an independent position in relation to company X, company Y claims that it was a task with obligations that cannot be transferred to an independent 100

contractor and that company X is therefore liable for damages for the negligently performed work.

101 The Supreme Court recalls that in the case of non-contractual damages, there is no general statutory liability for an independent contractor. The Supreme Court did not consider that there were circumstances in the case at hand that justified a departure from this principle of tort law. The rules on damages in the Electricity Act mean that the owner of a high-voltage installation, within the framework of the strict liability prescribed therein, may be obliged to compensate damage caused by an independent contractor, and that there is no basis for extending this liability determined by the legislator.

102 The Supreme Court added that the examination of the case did not provide any support for the claim that company Z had acted negligently.

103 (4) Liability for one's own negligence through omission? Company Y also claimed that company X had been negligent by failing to take the necessary safety measures. However, the Supreme Court held that the company failed to prove such negligence.

104 The conclusion was therefore that the Court of Appeal's judgment should be upheld, ie, that company X is not obliged to compensate company Y for the damage they suffered as a result of the fire.

c) Commentary

105 In this case, the Supreme Court decides the question of whether there is scope for strict liability outside the statutory area regulated in the Electrical Safety Act, which is answered in the negative. The conclusion is not particularly surprising since the damage that occurred falls within the very area of damage that justifies strict liability in the law. Here we can see how the legislator balances strict liability for the operator, with a relatively short limitation period and a clearly and distinctly delimited area for the scope of liability.

106 Regarding the second central issue in the case concerning liability for independently engaged contractors, the Supreme Court's assessment is in line with previous rulings in similar cases.[8] A contractor acting on behalf of a party has, as a starting point, independent responsibility for their actions. This is motivated by the fact that the contractor works independently and performs their own management tasks, including control of any employees and how the assignment is car-

8 One of the first cases where the Supreme Court established that there is no general statutory liability of the same nature as the principal liability of an independent contractor is NJA 1947, 23.

ried out. Since the person that engages the contractor does not have the opportunity to exercise insight and control, it is an unreasonable starting point that they should still be liable for any damage which is caused.

In special cases, however, vicarious liability may be extended to include independent contractors when it is considered objective and justified in terms of legal policy.[9] For example, if it has been stated in law that a certain legal entity is responsible for a certain task that is typically of great importance to third parties, there may be reasons to extend the vicarious liability to independent contractors. 107

In the present case, however, the Supreme Court held that there were no such special circumstances. It was noted in particular that the rules on damages in the Electricity Act mean that the owner of a high-voltage installation, within the framework that follows from the strict liability prescribed therein, may be obliged to pay compensation, even for damage caused by an independent contractor. Since the legislator has already taken a position on extended principals' liability, it can be understood that liability should not be extended beyond that. 108

It is interesting to note that the Supreme Court sometimes emphasises in its rulings that when there is clear legislation in an area, there is no reason for the application of the law to go beyond what has been legally stipulated, while in other cases, the Supreme Court has considered itself prevented from contributing to the development of the law when the legislator has *not* instituted specific regulation in a certain area. There is reason to return to this issue at some other time. 109

8. Personal Injury

Supreme Court (Högsta domstolen) 8 May 2024, Nytt Juridiskt Arkiv (NJA) 2024, 277: Patient Compensation and the Issue of Proof Requirements in Cases of Treatment Injury

In this case, the Supreme Court rules that a reduced standard of proof should be applied to the question of whether a treatment injury could have been avoided. 110

9 See NJA 2019, 94.

C. Literature

1. *Harald Ullman/Bertil Bengtsson*, Företagsförsäkring [Business insurance] (Jure 2024) 198 pp

111 The book is designed as a commentary on the Insurance Contracts Act's provisions on business insurance and on the most common basic terms and conditions for business insurance. It describes the additional coverage to business insurance that is commonly taken out, as well as current case law and standards for claims settlement. The book provides an overview of legislation, insurance coverage and claims settlement and also contains in-depth comments on the most central provisions in the terms and conditions for business insurance as well as on a couple of current industry agreements.

112 This is a welcome addition by two well-regarded authors with exceptional knowledge of (among other things) the field of insurance law. The book will be useful both in teaching and as a handbook in practical legal application.

2. *Bertil Bengtsson*, Grundlagsskydd för egendom och näringsverksamhet [Constitutional protection for property and business activities] (Norstedts Juridik 2024) 102 pp

113 The book deals with the latest developments in the area of constitutional protection for property and business activities. Much has happened in recent years and, among other things, property protection has been strengthened and clarified through various legislative amendments; the right to conduct business now receives protection in the Constitution; the ECHR has become Swedish law and has led to important changes in terms of public liability for damages; the idea of proportionality, with its balancing of public and individual interests, has gained increasing importance; the possibility of legal review has been expanded; and legislation has been enacted on the right to damages also in the event of a violation of the fundamental rights laid down in the Instrument of Government (eg, the right to citizenship and to demonstrate, the protection of free speech and the protection against corporal punishment and torture). One result of this development has been a changed attitude towards constitutional rules, which can now also be invoked in individual cases and matters. The book provides an overview of the legal situation that has emerged in this way and discusses the new problems that have arisen.

The author, Bertil Bengtsson, is – indeed – Sweden's 'grand old man' in tort and insurance law, and has been a special investigator regarding, among other things, the issue of constitutional damages. This book provides a brief and precise, yet comprehensive description of the most central changes in the current area. 114

3. *Joakim Nergelius*, Skadestånd vid rättighetskränkning – Skadeståndslagen 3 kap 4 § i ett konstitutionellt perspektiv [Damages in the event of a violation of rights – Damages Act ch 3 sec 4 in a constitutional perspective] (Norstedts Juridik 2024) 161 pp

The latest amendment to ch 3, sec 4 of the Tort Act means that violations by the State and municipalities of individuals' rights under the ECHR and ch 2 of the Instrument of Government now establish liability for damages for 'the general public'. The amendment followed a development in practice lasting more than a decade, whereby courts in general and the Supreme Court in particular have gradually shown an increasing understanding of individuals' need for compensation in situations where the State has violated their rights. 115

The author argues that this legal development was initially met with scepticism within tort law, but has gradually gained wider acceptance in doctrine as well. This book analyses legal developments in the area in the 2000s, primarily from a constitutional perspective, where the amendments are placed in connection with other constitutional changes such as the increased importance of European law and the strengthened position of the courts. Bearing this perspective in mind, the book provides a contribution to still unclear legal issues within tort law, such as liability for compensation for private objects, the role of the Constitutional Court as the State's agent and compensation for violations of constitutional rules other than those that have now been protected. 116

4. *Måns Jacobsson*, Skadestånd vid sjötransport av olja och andra farliga ämnen – internationell och svensk reglering [Damages in the maritime transport of oil and other hazardous substances – international and Swedish regulation] (Jure 2024) 342 pp

This book deals with the international compensation systems for damage caused by discharges of oil from oil tankers, of bunker oil from other ships and of chem- 117 icals and other hazardous substances from all types of ships. The basis for these compensation systems is the 1992 Liability and Fund Conventions, the 2001 Bunker Convention and the 2010 HNS Convention[10]. The book also contains a detailed account of the Swedish legislation that incorporates these Conventions. Particular focus is on the practice that has developed through the tens of thousands of claims for compensation that have been processed by the international oil damage funds.

118 Furthermore, the compensation system that will be set up by the HNS Convention when it enters into force is discussed in detail. In light of the international legal developments that have taken place in environmental law in recent years, the treatment of claims for compensation for environmental damage is also discussed in detail.

119 For those who have an interest in environmental damage, and damage caused by oil and other hazardous chemicals in particular (and is able to read Swedish!), this book provides a valuable contribution from a practical perspective. The author has been, among other things, a judge of the Court of Appeal and a ministerial advisor. For 22 years, he was a director and CEO of the International Oil Pollution Compensation Funds (IOPC Funds) in London and before that for many years Sweden's representative on the IMO's legal committee.

5. *Marcus Radetzki*, Enligt vilka principer bestäms ersättning enligt 15 § epizootilagen? Särskilt om ersättning för annat än döda djur [According to what principles is compensation determined under sec 15 of the Epizootic Diseases Act? Especially regarding compensation for other than dead animals], Juridisk tidskrift 2023/24, vol 3, 574–598

120 In this article, Radetzki concludes that the right to and the extent of the compensation that the State may have to pay under sec 15 of the Epizootic Diseases Act shall be determined in accordance with general principles of tort law. This includes: the principle of full compensation and the compensable items (costs, loss of income and loss of income); the third-party damage principle (the author argues that the principle should be applied with some caution, so that, in case of doubt, it should lead to a decision that is beneficial to the affected party); the difference principle; the adequacy principle (it is unusual for the principle to cause

10 The 2010 Hazardous and Noxious Substances Convention.

difficulties in applying the law); the protective purpose doctrine (the doctrine rarely causes difficulties in assessment); the duty to limit damage.

The article has a – clearly expressed – purpose to provide guidance in practical application, which is also fulfilled through a thorough review of the possible challenges that result from decisions made in accordance with the Epizootic Diseases Act. 121

6. *Maxim Del Río Diaz*, Skadeståndsrättsligt underlåtenhetsansvar i förändring [Tort liability in change], Juridisk tidskrift 2024/25, vol 2, 323–339

In the article, the author asks whether certain special conditions need to exist for negligence to be able to trigger liability for damages, and if so, what these conditions are. The author examines three specific problems that he believes distinguish liability for negligence from liability for active action: the difficulty of distinguishing negligence from active action, the fact that the causal link partially fails to fulfill the function of establishing a specific connection to the tortfeasor, and the fact that this deficiency in establishing a causal link is compensated for by a normative assessment of the tortfeasor's connection to the risk factor, which is expressed through the existence of a duty. 122

This article can be seen as a contribution to the debate concerning a case from the Supreme Court (NJA 2013, 145) and whether the case established a new model for examining liability for negligence and what the model entails. The author argues that the distinction between active action and negligence has become more significant and liability for negligence is a more important practical issue. However, it is difficult to agree with the assessment that the liability model can have a wider scope of application than the narrow scope of application that NJA 2013, 145 may refer to. However, the discussion is likely to continue. 123

Peter Loser

XXX. Switzerland

A. Legislation

1. Revision of Civil Procedure Act (Schweizerische Zivilprozessordnung, SR 272) – Collective Legal Protection for Liability Proceedings Probably Not to Come

1 A bill to strengthen collective redress has been under discussion in the Swiss Parliament since 2021. The preliminary committee of the Parliament has had a difficult time with the draft and has dealt with it at a total of five meetings over the past two years. The draft has been reported on in previous reports.[1]

2 On 17 March 2025, the first chamber of Parliament concerned (the Grand Chamber) decided not to take a position on the draft law and not to deal with the details of the bill at all.[2] The majority of the Grand Chamber feared that Switzerland would give up an important competitive advantage with the introduction of such an instrument and that the introduction of collective remedies could lead to an Americanisation of the Swiss legal system with incalculable risks.

3 Parliament referred to a recent study by the European Centre for International Political Economy, which examined the development of the legal basis for collective legal protection in Europe, the effective development of collective litigation and the economic impact therof.[3] While there were hardly any collective actions

---

1 See *P Loser*, Switzerland, in: E Karner/BC Steininger (eds), European Tort Law (ETL) 2021 (2022) 636, no 10 ff; and *P Loser*, Switzerland, in: E Karner/BC Steininger (eds), European Tort Law (ETL) 2023 (2024) 689, no 3 ff.

2 The Federal Assembly – The Swiss Parliament, business no 21.082, at <https://www.parlament.ch/de/ratsbetrieb/suche-curia-vista/geschaeft?AffairId=20210082>. Cf the reporting in Neue Zürcher Zeitung (NZZ) 2025, 17 March 2025: National Council fears lawsuit excesses like in the USA – and scuttles Swiss class action system with a run-up <https://www.nzz.ch/schweiz/nationalrat-befuerchtet-klage-exzesse-wie-in-den-usa-und-versenkt-schweizer-sammelklagen-system-mit-anlauf-ld.1875760>.

3 *European Centre for International Political Economy (ECIPE)*, The Impact of Increased Mass Litigation in Europe, Occasional Paper – No 03/2025, at <https://ecipe.org/wp-content/uploads/2025/02/ECI_OccasionalPaper_03–2025_LY07.pdf>.

https://doi.org/10.1515/9783111389271-031

in the EU until 2010, the number increased in the following years and literally skyrocketed in certain countries after 2020. The EU Directive on representative actions,[4] which creates a minimum standard for collective redress, is a key driver here. In the Netherlands in particular, lawsuits have increased many times over in individual years. The study anticipates costs of up to € 84 billion for companies operating in the EU in the long term. There are fears in Parliament that a significant proportion of these sums will not benefit consumers, but lawyers and litigation financiers.

4 The judgment against Switzerland by the European Court of Human Rights (ECtHR), *Verein KlimaSeniorinnen Schweiz and Others v Switzerland* presumably also had a negative impact.[5] Conservative politicians fear that class actions could be co-financed by large NGOs in the future – just like the plaintiffs (the 'climate senior citizens' *'KlimaSeniorinnen'*) financed by Greenpeace.

5 The bill will now be discussed in the Small Chamber of the Parliament. However, the likelihood of the Grand Chamber's decision being reversed there is small. There is therefore a high risk that the legislative project to introduce Collective Legal Protection in Switzerland will fail.

B. Cases

1. Swiss Federal Supreme Court (Schweizerisches Bundesgericht) 21 February 2024, Federal Supreme Court Decision (Bundesgerichtsentscheid, BGE) 6B_987/2023: No Reimbursement of Costs for Preventive Measures to Avert Damage[6]

a) Brief Summary of the Facts

6 The company A&B built a glass staircase in the home of Mr and Mrs C, which, in the opinion of experts, did not comply with the rules of engineering. As the staircase had significant defects and was dangerous, it had to be completely dismantled and replaced.

4 Directive (EU) 2020/1828 of the European Parliament and of the Council of 25 November 2020 on representative actions for the protection of the collective interests of consumers and repealing Directive 2009/22/EC [2020] Official Journal (OJ) L 409/1.

5 Cf no 137 below.

6 At <http://www.bger.ch/jurisdiction-recht>.

It was disputed in court whether the company A&B owed the owners of the house the costs of repair and restoration. 7

Contractual claims were not the subject of the proceedings, presumably because they were time-barred. 8

The question was therefore whether the company A&B had to reimburse the repair and restoration costs of the staircase on a non-contractual basis – based on tort law. The court of second instance ruled in favour of the company. 9

b) Judgment of the Court

The company A&B claimed that this judgment violated the general tortious liability provisions of art 41 of the Code of Obligations. 10

The Federal Supreme Court agrees and denies a non-contractual liability claim with the following considerations: 11

(i) According to the case law of the Federal Supreme Court, an act is unlawful if it violates an absolute right of the injured party (so-called 'wrongfulness of the result or the harmful outcome of an action' '*Erfolgsunrecht*') or damages their assets (pure economic damage). 12

(ii) In the latter case of pure economic damage, the violation of a behavioural norm (a protective rule) must still be proven, which is intended to protect the injured party in the rights impaired by the incriminated act (so-called 'wrongfulness of the action itself' '*Verhaltensunrecht*'). Such protective norms can be found throughout the Swiss legal system (in private law, administrative law or criminal law). They can be written or unwritten, under federal or cantonal law. In the case of purely economic damage, this can only lead to compensation due to the unlawfulness derived from the behaviour if the damaging act violates a norm whose purpose is to protect the injured party in the rights violated by the act. 13

(iii) The Federal Supreme Court then examined whether the criminal provision of art 229 of the Swiss Criminal Code (SCC) constitutes such a protective rule, but denied this: 'Article 229 SCC penalises the conduct of persons who intentionally or negligently violate the rules of technology by directing or carrying out a construction or demolition, thereby knowingly endangering the life or physical integrity of persons.' This provision, therefore, protects the specific endangerment of life and limb, but not the endangerment of assets or property. 14

(iv) Consequently, the harmful act is unlawful if the danger caused by the violation of the rules of architecture materialises and leads to an injury to life or physical integrity because it violates an absolute right. However, non-compliance with the rules of architecture within the meaning of art 229 SCC cannot justify compensation for purely economic damage, in particular the costs of repair. 15

This is because the sole purpose of art 229 SCC is to protect the physical integrity of other persons.

c) Commentary

16 In its practice, the Swiss Federal Supreme Court is very reluctant to award damages for *preventive measures to avert damage*.

17 In a leading case from 1991, for example, it rejected non-contractual claims for damages by a landowner who had taken structural measures at his own expense to protect against falling stones from a neighbouring property.[7] The preventive measures were taken because the person responsible for the falling stones had not carried out such protective measures despite being requested to do so. The threatened property owner wanted to pass on the costs of the preventive measures to the person responsible for the threat due to unlawful damage in accordance with the general tort law rule of art 41 of the Swiss Code of Obligations. The threatened landowner saw the unlawful behaviour in the fact that the unstable embankment posed a danger to life and limb and to his property, according to experts. However, the Federal Supreme Court stated: 'However, these absolutely protected legal interests are only violated when the slope actually slides. The damage caused to property and people must then be compensated. However, the plaintiffs prevented the occurrence of this damaging event by carrying out the remediation. Contrary to their opinion, art 41 CO does not provide a sufficient basis for passing on the costs of such preventive damage defence to a third party.' It was then analysed whether a special norm that was intended to protect purely financial interests and therefore justified compensation for purely financial losses had been violated. However, such a protective purpose was rejected for the criminal offence of violating the rules of construction mentioned (above no 14 f).

18 The reason for the cautious practice is thus that the Federal Supreme Court traditionally equates the *concept of unlawfulness* in the area of absolute legal interests (life, limb, property) with the violation of life, limb, property (cf above no 12).

19 This approach is increasingly being criticised.[8] Preferably the unlawfulness should not be seen in the result or the harmful outcome of an action, but in

---

7 Swiss Federal Supreme Court, 9 July 1991, BGE 117 II 259, 269 f consideration 3, at <http://www.bger.ch/jurisdiction-recht>.

8 Cf in particular – with reference to the leading case of 1991 – *P Gauch*, Grundbegriffe des ausservertraglichen Haftungsrechts, recht 1996, 232 f; and *M Anderegg*, Schadenabwehr: Zwischen

the behaviour that leads to the harm (the action itself). However, there are two remarks:

(i) This approach does not mean that the distinction between absolute legal interests and pure financial losses is abandoned for the purposes of unlawfulness. According to the case law of the Federal Supreme Court and the prevailing doctrine to date, unlawfulness in tort liability should result from the legal system *determined by the legislator* and not from the creation of law *by judges*. In the area of pure pecuniary loss, a statutory norm for the protection of pecuniary interests is therefore required. The protection of absolute legal interests also results from the legal regulation. This concept of unlawfulness is therefore also a requirement of the separation of powers and the principle of democracy and is convincing in principle. 20

(ii) It seems useful to clarify the traditional concept of unlawfulness when absolute legal interests (like life, limb and property) are affected. This is because, correctly considered, *unlawfulness also lies in behaviour* in these cases. A distinction could be made as follows:[9] (1) If the dangerous behaviour leads directly to an injury, eg a collision on a ski slope, there is a duty to avoid this injury or to avoid the *success* of the risky behaviour (*Erfolgsvermeidungspflicht*). (2) If the behaviour only indirectly leads to injuries, eg when machines with inadequate safety devices are placed on the market, or if a failure to provide safety devices after creating dangerous situations is relevant, there is a duty to avoid *danger* (*Gefahrvermeidungspflicht*). 21

In the particular case, as with the placing of a machinery on the market, the unlawfulness would lie in the fact that a construction with a potential risk was placed 'on the market'. In the precise concept as mentioned above, it would not only be the infringement of the absolute legal interests (ie property) that would be unlawful, but already their endangerment. This would then also make it possible in principle to reimburse preventive costs in the event of a risk to absolute legal interests (ie property), because these costs do not – as the Federal Supreme Court has previously stated – merely represent pure economic damage. 22

Of course, the compensability of preventive measures to avert damage must be limited so as not to establish unlimited liability. This could be based either on the intensity of the risk or on the foreseeability and closeness of the consequences (within the meaning of art 3:201 of the Principles of European Tort Law, PETL). Overall, damage defence measures must be proportionate. 23

Schadenprävention und Schadenminderung, Zeitschrift Haftpflicht und Versicherung (HAVE) 2015, 117.

9 For a detailed explanation, cf *K Larenz/C W Canaris*, Lehrbuch des Schuldrechts, Zweiter Band Besonderer Teil 2. Halbband (13th edn 1994) § 76 III 1.

24 In addition, it would easily be possible for statutory provisions to permit a more generous replacement if corresponding special provisions exist in the legal system (eg in the Criminal Code), ie if corresponding decisions by the legislator exist.

25 And, of course, claims for compensation can go further if the parties are in a *contractual relationship*. However, it is not the task of tort law to protect expectations in the behaviour of other people with whom one is, so to speak, merely in contact by coincidence. The primacy of contract law applies to the protection of expectations in the behaviour of other people. And if contractual claims are ruled out, eg because they are time-barred, tort law does not necessarily have to fill the gap.

26 As a result, this approach would come close to the concept that the Principles of European Tort Law provide for this issue: 'Expenses incurred to prevent threatened damage amount to recoverable damage in so far as reasonably incurred' (art 2:104 PETL). The basic concept of Swiss unlawfulness would not have to be thrown overboard. However, the Swiss Federal Supreme Court's narrow understanding of the recoverability of costs for preventive measures to avert damage requires correction.

2. Swiss Federal Supreme Court, 25 September 2024, BGE 2C_1016/2022: Forum Shopping for Asylum Procedures – No Unlawfulness for Lost Social Benefits[10]

a) Brief Summary of the Facts

27 Syrian spouses A and E and their three sons (born in 2012, 2010, 2008) were on an overnight train from Milan to Paris on the night of 3 to 4 July 2014. They were travelling in a group with other family members and people from Syria. The French border police carried out an identity check on the train in the early hours of 4 July 2014 and refused to allow them to continue their journey. The group was handed over to the Swiss border police at around 10:45 for repatriation to Italy. The police took the group by minibus to Brig, a town on the border with Italy, where they arrived at around 14:20. The onward journey to Domodossola in Italy was not immediately possible. The group was therefore accommodated in the control rooms of the Border Guard post at Brig railway station from around 14:50. The Border

10 At <http://www.bger.ch/jurisdiction-recht>. Cf *C Frey*, Alternative or cumulative causation of total causes, ius.focus 2024, No 201.

Guard decided to transfer them to Domodossola in an extra carriage of the regional train departing at 16:44 according to the timetable.

Mother A was about 27 weeks pregnant at the time. She had been suffering from increasing pain since her arrival in Brig. During her stay with the border police, she lay on a wooden couch in one of the control rooms. Her husband E contacted the border police several times to request medical assistance for her, including the head of operations of the border police, who organised the further repatriation and was responsible for it. The border police refrained from calling in medical assistance. 28

After the train arrived in Italy, the group made their way to the extra carriage at around 16:35. Due to her physical condition, mother A was carried to the train and into the carriage by her relatives. The train left Brig station at 16:50. The Swiss border police informed the Italian police by telephone that a pregnant woman with health problems was on the next train to Italy. After arriving in Italy at 17:12, the Italian police called for medical assistance. At 17:46, the ambulance arrived at the station and took A to an Italian hospital. There, at 18:30, the unborn baby girl was pronounced dead. 29

Spouses A and E and their children subsequently lived in Italy for two years as asylum seekers. In 2016, mother A and her three children travelled to Germany, where they were granted a temporary right of residence in November 2017 and a permanent right of residence in November 2018. Husband E continued to live in Italy and obtained a residence permit there on 1 October 2019. On 16 March 2021, husband E also moved to Germany to join his wife A and their children. 30

The border police officer responsible was convicted of assault in 2018. He was acquitted of the charges of attempted murder and interrupting the pregnancy. According to the medical report, it was not possible to determine whether the child was still alive in the womb when the family arrived in Brig at around 14:20. Furthermore, according to the expert opinion, there was no immediate danger to the life of mother A. 31

The family members demand compensation and satisfaction from the Swiss State for the following reasons: 32

(1) Compensation of around CHF 120,000 for lost social benefits for asylum seekers in Germany, as the social benefits for asylum seekers in Italy were lower. The family claimed that had the border police behaved correctly, the mother would have been treated in a hospital in Switzerland and the whole family could have travelled on from there directly to Germany. Due to the lack of hospitalisation, they were deported back to Italy and had to stay there for a few years before they could apply for residency in Germany. 33

(2) Compensation in the amount of CHF 30,000 for the separation of the family. They argue that the whole family had to apply for asylum in Italy so that the 34

mother could be treated in hospital there. They were forced to live in Italy as asylum seekers for two and a half years. Only then, in October 2018, did the mother and her children receive residence permits for Germany. The husband was only able to apply for asylum in Germany in March 2021, meaning that the family was only reunited in Germany around seven years after the event of 4 July 2014. In essence, they take the view that the behaviour or omission of the border police caused the family members to be separated and that this constitutes an unlawful violation of personality rights, which gives rise to a claim for payment of a sum of money for non-pecuniary disadvantages.

35 (3) Compensation to the two spouses and the three sons totalling CHF 885,000 for the failure to provide medical assistance to the mother and the associated emotional distress. Following the partial acquittal of the border police officer, the amount of compensation demanded was reduced to a total of CHF 159,000. In particular, according to the expert opinion, it became clear that no causation between the actions of the border police officer and the death of the unborn girl could be proven.

b) Judgment of the Court

36 (1) The claim for damages was rejected in particular due to a lack of unlawfulness.

37 The border police were not accused of active behaviour that caused bodily harm. Rather, the accusation consisted of an omission that causally led to the asylum procedure in Italy instead of in Germany.

38 In this case, the unlawfulness does not lie per se in the violation of physical integrity (cf above no 12). Rather, the accusation of omission presupposes a duty of behaviour that obliges the person to act to protect their physical integrity. Although such a duty of behaviour exists, it does not have the purpose of protecting against financial loss due to lost social benefits in a country of asylum.

39 Compensation for purely financial losses without reference to physical damage could result from a breach of other duties of conduct. However, these duties of behaviour must have the purpose of protecting against such financial losses (cf above no 13). Although the police had violated national regulations, the purpose of these regulations was to protect life and not property. Furthermore, no protection of property or protection against lost social benefits in the area of asylum can be derived from the European regulations on asylum. Rather, the provisions of the Dublin system are based on the premise that the national asylum regulations of all Member States are equivalent.

40 (2) The claim for compensation for the separation of family life was rejected because – taking into account evaluative aspects of adequacy – no sufficient hy-

pothetical causation had been established between the conduct of the border police and the separation of the family members' residence between 2016 and 2021. Further conditions for the claim could therefore be left open.

(3) The mother received compensation of CHF 12,000 for her mental and physical suffering and her non-pecuniary disadvantages. Although her husband was not permanently medically or psychologically impaired, he was temporarily affected. Due to his long hours of fear for his wife and the unborn child, his personality was sufficiently severely violated to justify the award of compensation in the amount of CHF 1,000. 41

c) Commentary

This case shows that the Swiss concept of unlawfulness (above nos 12 and 13) is 42 perfectly suitable for reasonably limiting claims for damages. Apart from interferences with physical integrity or property rights, compensation for damage requires the violation of a provision of the legal system, which is also intended to protect against such financial losses. This means that the values of the democratically legitimised legislator come into play in the allocation of damages. However, the judge assumes an important supplementary function in the interpretation and further development of the law.

The case also makes it clear that in the area of asylum – this is not a legal 43 point of view – there is sometimes an astonishing attitude of entitlement that goes far beyond the original motives for seeking asylum, for example on the occasion of persecution during the Second World War.

3. Swiss Federal Supreme Court, 3 June 2024, BGE 4 A_411/2023: Alternative Causation in Traffic Accidents[11]

a) Brief Summary of the Facts

On 7 March 2019 at 14:43, A was involved through no fault of his own in a side 44 collision with a vehicle driven by D (driver). His damaged vehicle was towed away. He was travelling in the passenger seat of the tow truck, which was not fitted with a seatbelt. A was then involved in a second accident that occurred at

11 At <http://www.bger.ch/jurisdiction-recht>. Cf *Frey*, ius.focus 2024, No 201.

around 16:45. From 8 March 2019, A was initially on sick leave to varying degrees between 50 % and 100 % and from 27 May 2019 was on sick leave to 100 % throughout.

45 A demanded compensation from the driver D, who caused the first accident, from the owner of this vehicle, C, and from his motor vehicle owner's liability insurance B Ltd for damages in the provisional amount of CHF 32,097 and compensation of at least CHF 5,000.

46 According to the expert opinion, the diagnosis of tinnitus with the subsequent symptoms of sleep disturbance and depressive disorder was accident-related. The experts described the specific attribution of these complaints to one of the two accidents on 7 March 2019 as not reliably possible. This leaves the serious possibility that the symptoms deemed to be accident-related are exclusively attributable to the second accident on 7 March 2019.

47 Both lower courts therefore denied liability due to uncertain causation.

b) Judgment of the Court

48 The Federal Supreme Court examined whether there was a sufficiently proven causal link between the first accident and the complaints of A. In doing so, it distinguished between alternative causation and cumulative or concurrent causation of total causes.

49 The literature speaks of *alternative causation* of (total) causes when several causes can be considered as (total) causes of damage, but only one of the causes can be causal in the specific case. For example, two cars run over a pedestrian one after the other on a road; the time of death is unclear. According to the literature, there is a competition of possible causes in such a scenario.

50 *Cumulative or concurring causation* of total causes is assumed if several total causes contribute to the damage, whereby each of the causes alone would have been sufficient to bring about the (entire) damage. For example, two factories pollute a body of water independently of each other and cause a fish kill.

51 While in the case of cumulative (or concurring) causation, the tortfeasor cannot exonerate himself by arguing that another person would have caused the same damage without their intervention and the doctrine affirms the liability of all parties responsible, liability in the case of alternative causation is the subject of controversial debate. Some scholars reject liability in principle. However, this view has been criticised and the solutions proposed are (generally or in certain cases) joint and several liability, different variants of proportionate liability (according to causation or probability of causation) or a reversal of the burden of proof.

The lower court considered it possible that the first accident, if there had not been a second accident, would not have caused any of the complaints identified by the expert opinion, so that these would have been triggered solely by the second accident and would have occurred in the same way without the first accident. On the other hand, the lower court did not rule out contributory causation from the outset – this is therefore a classic causation problem, a potential total or partial cause that may not have had any influence on the damage in the specific case. With this evidence, the proof of natural causation has not been provided and liability must be rejected. 52

c) Commentary

The rejection of liability in the case of *alternative causation* is harsh for the injured party. Conversely, liability would be harsh for the effectively non-causal party. The Swiss legislator (in contrast to other national legislators, eg in Germany) has decided in these cases of lack of evidence that, apart from special cases, the victim cannot pass on the damage to other persons. The legislator therefore considered it more appropriate for the victim to remain liable for the damage than for a person to be unjustly held liable. This is because shifting the damage is the exception. 53

In the present case, the special constellation of *cumulative (or concurring) causation* was not present. It was not proven that either the first accident or the second accident would have caused the harm on their own with certainty. Rather, it was possible that the first accident was partially or not at all causal for the harm. 54

In the present case, there was the particularity that the second accident would not have occurred without the first accident. From this perspective, the first accident was certainly a cause of the harm. However, the accident victim A did not assert this argument until too late in the proceedings, so that the Federal Court did not have to address it. 55

Nevertheless, the Court had indicated that the mere causation of the first accident does not also imply responsibility for the second accident and therefore for the harm as a whole. From a legal point of view, the causal link must be limited in terms of value. The person who caused the first accident is not always responsible for all the consequences of the subsequent event. However, as mentioned above, this question did not have to be decided in the present case. 56

Another peculiarity could arise in the case of liability for road accidents if both potential perpetrators have the same liability insurer. This is because, in the area of road accidents, the injured party has a direct right of claim against 57 the insurer. From this perspective, it could be argued that the same person is ultimately liable for both events via the insurance claims and therefore liability certainly does not fall on the wrong person. In this case, it was not clear from the facts of the case whether it was the same insurance company and the courts did not deal with this question.

4. Swiss Federal Supreme Court, 15 May 2024, BGE 4 A_401/2023: Proof of the Predominant Probability of Causation in Medical Malpractice Cases[12]

a) Brief Summary of the Facts

58 B was admitted to the emergency room of a Geneva hospital after midday on 14 May 2011 because she felt unwell and was vomiting. Due to a lack of space, she was kept in the waiting room for several hours and periodically attended to by nursing staff. At 7.30 pm, she was examined for the first time by a doctor who suspected a hyperventilation attack with anxiety disorder. At 1.35 am. she was transferred to the nursing area, where the nursing staff noticed that B could no longer speak. B was immediately examined and booked in for a CT scan of the brain. A neurologist examined her at 4 am. The CT scan was performed at 5 am and revealed a possible recent cerebellar infarction due to an occlusion of the central blood vessel supplying the brain stem. This finding was confirmed in an MRI scan at 8 am and on the same day a blood clot was removed from the affected blood vessel using a catheter. After various stays in intensive care, neurology and rehabilitation, the patient was able to return home six months after the event. However, she suffered considerable consequential damage.

59 B filed a lawsuit against the hospital because she was of the opinion that the treatment in May 2011 violated the rules of medical practice, in particular due to the long waiting times.

60 The court of first instance commissioned an expert opinion, which found no breach of duty and concluded with regard to causation that it was impossible to say to what extent the incident could have been avoided through earlier action. The next instance, however, found in favour of liability and awarded B approx CHF 300,000 for pecuniary damage and CHF 30,000 for non-pecuniary damage.

12 At <http://www.bger.ch/jurisdiction-recht>. Cf *K Friedli*, Hypothetische Kausalität in der Medizinalhaftpflicht, ius.focus 2024, No 175.

The hospital lodged an appeal against this judgment with the Federal Supreme Court. 61

b) Judgment of the Court

The lower court had assumed that the hospital had caused the patient's injuries with predominant probability. The Federal Supreme Court judged this to be an obviously incorrect and therefore arbitrary application of the standard of proof of preponderance of probability. 62

According to the Federal Supreme Court, overwhelming probability means that, from an objective point of view, there are important reasons in favour of the accuracy of an allegation, that other possibilities exist, but that these do not appear to have played a decisive role or are not reasonably possible. 63

The Federal Supreme Court clarified that the case law had not defined any percentages, but that, according to doctrine, a probability of 51 % was not sufficient, but that a significantly higher degree of probability must apply: a degree of 75 % was cited. 64

In the present case, the expert had testified that only 41 % of patients who were subject to modern treatment methods had a favourable prognosis; and that only between 20 % and 44 % of patients treated with the chosen operation had a good outcome. In the case of an injury to the central blood vessel, it was not possible – unlike in the case of a classic stroke – to establish a clear correlation between the time until surgery and the prognosis for recovery, according to the expert. For this reason, the Federal Supreme Court dismissed the claim as there was no evidence of a causal link between the delayed treatment and the consequential damage caused by the stroke. 65

c) Commentary

In the present case – as in other cases – the Federal Supreme Court did not specify any exact figures as to when causation is more likely than not. 66

However, it had pointed out that, according to doctrine, the overwhelming probability is more likely to be a 75 % conviction than 51 %. 67

The Federal Supreme Court did not have to decide whether this was the case, because the probability was obviously below 50 %. Such a low probability is not sufficient when it comes to the degree of predominant probability. 68

5. Swiss Federal Supreme Court, 11 September 2024, BGE 6B_338/2024: Contributory Negligence of an Inattentive Pedestrian in a Collision with a Tram[13]

a) Brief Summary of the Facts

69 On 17 March 2018, there was a collision between a tram and a pedestrian. The pedestrian was walking in a group, crossing the road and approaching the tracks. He had been focussing exclusively on his wife – and possibly the traffic coming from the north – for a longer period of time and a longer distance and completely ignored the oncoming traffic.

70 The tram driver saw the pedestrian and observed him for 18 seconds or a distance of 200 metres. The tram driver recognised that the pedestrian was not paying attention to his side of the road and was clearly distracted. Despite the reliable evidence of the pedestrian's behaviour, the tram driver did not reduce his speed for some time and did not emit an acoustic warning signal.

71 The pedestrian also asserts liability claims against the tram driver as part of the criminal proceedings. The pedestrian claimed that the tram driver should be held wholly liable for his injuries due to the collision with the tram.

b) Judgment of the Court

72 The liability of the tram driver is governed by the rules of general fault-based liability.

73 With regard to the proportion of liability, however, the primary breach of duty was committed by the pedestrian. He had disregarded the tram's legal and generally recognised right of way. He had been aware of the situation at the scene of the accident and had been inattentive for some time, although he had first had to cross two lanes of the road and then bypass a barrier in front of the tracks.

74 The tram driver's breach of duty, on the other hand, derived from the complainant's inattention in the first place. Accordingly, the contributory negligence of the pedestrian in the collision and its consequences should be rated greater than the tram driver's breach of duty. However, the operational risk of the tram and its effect on the damage event should also be weighted heavily.

---

13 At <http://www.bger.ch/jurisdiction-recht>.

Based on the fact that, according to case law, the operating risk leads to a liability share of 50 % and the fault shares of the two parties involved (for the other 50 %) are two-thirds for the pedestrian and one-third for the tram driver, this results in a liability share of 2/3 for the tram driver. 75

c) Commentary

This liability case is unusual because it does not concern the liability of the tram company, but the tram driver personally. The reason for this was that liability was assessed as part of the criminal proceedings against the tram driver. Therefore, it was not strict liability under the Railways Act that applied, but general fault-based liability. 76

Nevertheless, the court attributed part of the operating risk of the tram to the tram driver and therefore reduced the consequences of the pedestrian's own fault. 77

The tram company was of course also liable for this accident. However, this liability and the effects of the pedestrian's own fault did not have to be examined in the present proceedings.[14] 78

6. Swiss Federal Supreme Court, 3 October 2024, BGE 6B_17/2024: No Reliance on Technology when Reversing in the Close Proximity of Children[15]

a) Brief Summary of the Facts

A, a pensioner born in 1940, drove to the home of B on 17 April 2021 at around 12 noon. Mother B and her two children, including three-year-old D, were outside the house. 79

A was at the entrance to the garage and wanted to reverse. He looked in his rear-view mirror and on the screen of his reversing camera, but saw no one. When he started reversing, no acoustic signal was triggered. Nevertheless, his car hit young D, causing him to fall over. 80

Three-year-old D subsequently suffered from anxiety and mental disorders. 81

14 See for such cases and a general legal assessment *P Loser*, Switzerland, in: E Karner/BC Steininger (eds), European Tort Law (ETL) 2022 (2023) 673, no 55 ff.
15 At <http://www.bger.ch/jurisdiction-recht>.

82 The lower court convicted A of simple assault and sentenced him to pay compensation to D for non-pecuniary loss in the amount of CHF 800.

83 A asks the Federal Court to waive the penalty and his liability.

b) Judgment of the Court

84 The lower court found that A had looked in his rear-view mirror and on the screen of his camera while reversing and had not seen anything. No acoustic alarm had sounded.

85 However, in view of the risk associated with his manoeuvre and the circumstances of the case, A should have been all the more cautious. At the time of his manoeuvre, he knew that the mother and her two children were on their way home, so he expected them to arrive. He was therefore aware that a child – three years old at the time of the offence – was behind his vehicle and was taking the same route as him to get to his house. He also knew that the child, whom he himself had described as 'restless', was not holding his mother's hand and was walking at some distance from her. He also knew that the child was possibly in the middle of the access road, as he had overtaken the child at that exact spot a few seconds earlier and had to wait until the child moved to the side so that he could pass.

86 In these circumstances, A could not rely on the fact that no acoustic signal sounded and could content himself with checking his rear-view mirror and the display of his reversing camera. He had to check the blind spots before starting his manoeuvre and he himself had stated that he could not see the child due to his height, as the tailgate of the car was higher than him. Given the high probability that the child could escape the view of the reversing camera or the rear-view mirror, A should have taken extra precautions.

87 In addition, A had performed his manoeuvre near a bend that partially obscured his view of the footpath. These circumstances required special care on the part of A: ie (1) he should have waited until the family had overtaken him before he started reversing, (2) or asked his wife to get out of the vehicle to check that the carriageway was clear. The measures taken by A before his manoeuvre were not sufficient in the circumstances to meet his duty of care.

88 The criminal judgment and A's liability were therefore confirmed.

7. Swiss Federal Supreme Court, 31 October 2024, BGE 9C_46/2024: No Claim for Non-Pecuniary Damage based on Stress and Annoyance Resulting from Legal Proceedings against an Insurance Company[16]

a) Brief Summary of the Facts

Health insurer X had refused to allow the two insured persons A and B to terminate their insurance contracts and switch to another insurer. It is true that A and B had previously failed to pay substantial premium invoices. Nevertheless, as was established in another court case, insurance company X was not entitled to refuse cancellation on the basis of the statutory right of cancellation. 89

In this context, several court proceedings were held to calculate the loss suffered by the two insured persons. 90

A and B demanded compensation from insurance company X for the stress, anger and despair caused by these legal proceedings. 91

b) Judgment of the Court

Firstly, the Federal Supreme Court stated that the legal consequence of the impossibility of changing insurer due to the previous insurer is not that the change of insurer is recognised with retroactive effect. Rather, the previous insurer is obliged to pay compensation in accordance with the general principles of liability law. The damage consists primarily of the difference between the insurance premiums paid and the more favourable insurance premiums which could have been paid. 92

The lower court had denied the claim for compensation for non-pecuniary damage within the meaning of art 49 Swiss Code of Obligations. The Federal Supreme Court confirmed this view. 93

The award of compensation for non-material damage on the basis of art 49 para 1 Swiss Code of Obligations presupposes that the impairment has a certain objective severity and was perceived by the victim as moral suffering that is strong enough to make it seem legitimate for a person to turn to a court for compensation in these circumstances. 94

16 At <http://www.bger.ch/jurisdiction-recht>.

95 In order for a claim for compensation for non-pecuniary damage to be recognised, the impairment suffered must therefore be exceptional in the eyes of third parties and not only be perceived as such by the person concerned.

96 The fact of being prosecuted for non-payment of compulsory health insurance premiums cannot objectively constitute a serious injury to the complainants' personality. Under these circumstances, there is no reason to further investigate the intensity of the pain they feel.

c) Commentary

97 The Swiss healthcare system does not recognise a single health insurance fund, but allows a large number of health insurance companies. However, in a departure from the principles of the free market, insured persons have the right to change health insurer every year without a health check. This leads to many (unwanted) advertising calls from insurance brokers and a regular run on health insurance companies with the most favourable insurance premiums.

98 In this case, a health insurance company had wrongly attempted to prevent a cancellation due to premium arrears.

99 It is to be welcomed that no compensation is granted for the inconvenience associated with such legal disputes.

8. Swiss Federal Supreme Court, 5 December 2024, BGE 4 A_312/2024: Privileging of the Victim's Claims for Non-Pecuniary Damage at the Expense of the Insurance Company in the Distribution of Damages ('Privilege of Distribution')[17]

a) Brief Summary of the Facts

100 A was employed by company B. On 8 October 2010, he suffered severe crushing trauma to his left hand, which was drawn into a stamping machine and caught by a feed roller. He has permanent damage to his hand.

101 The treatment costs were paid by company B's insurance company. The insurance company also paid A compensation of CHF 31,500 for the impaired integrity

17 At <http://www.bger.ch/jurisdiction-recht>. Cf *T Bichsel*, Quotenvorrecht gilt uneingeschränkt auch bei Genugtuung, Aufgabe des reduzierten Quotenvorrechts, HAVE 2025, 113 ff.

(so-called 'integrity compensation' in accordance with the Accident Insurance Act).

A demands an additional payment of CHF 9,500 from company B for his non-pecuniary damage. He bases his claim on a contractual basis (due to breach of the employer's duty to protect) and on a non-contractual basis (due to inadequate safety of the machinery). 102

b) Judgment of the Court

The court of second instance ruled that A was at fault for the accident and that he has to bear a 25 % share of the liability. 103

The court of second instance then determined the amount of compensation in two phases: 104

(1) In a first phase, the court determined a base amount based on the objective immaterial disadvantage that arises as a result of a specific health impairment. The court set this basic amount at CHF 31,500, corresponding to the integrity compensation paid by the insurance company. This amount is derived from a table in which the authorities have determined sums for a variety of physical impairments. The purpose of such integrity compensation from the insurance company is mainly to compensate for non-pecuniary disadvantages. 105

(2) In a second phase, the court took into account the particularities of the individual case. It increased the basic amount by a total of 30 % (10 % each with regard to (i) the change in character that occurred after the extreme stress, on the one hand; and (ii) the post-traumatic stress disorder, on the other, and finally (iii) the unsuccessful reintegration including the impairment of economic advancement) to CHF 41,000. As part of the second phase, the court then took into account the self-inflicted fault rate of 25 % and thus calculated a total compensation of CHF 30,750 (CHF 41,000 – CHF 10,250 [25 %]). 106

As the amount of compensation calculated in this way was lower than the integrity compensation already paid out by the insurance company, the claim for compensation was rejected. 107

A appealed against this decision. He claimed that the court of second instance had not taken into account the statutory privilege of priority in the distribution of the damage ('privilege of distribution'). 108

The 'privilege of distribution' in liability law essentially has the following content: if the injured party's insurance company pays an amount for the damage incurred, the liability claims are transferred to the insurance company by law. The insurance company can then take recourse against the liable party. This is where the injured party's 'privilege of distribution' comes into play. The 'privilege of dis- 109 tribution' means that the insurance company may not have a recourse claim to the detriment of the injured party. If the insurance company only compensates part of the damage, the injured party can claim the uncovered part from the liable party, and the insurance company is only entitled to a right of recourse within the scope of the remaining liability claim.

110 This 'privilege of distribution' is a generally recognised principle in liability law. It has also been regulated by law since 2003 for damages covered by accident insurance.[18]

111 The Federal Supreme Court first had to examine whether this 'privilege of distribution' applies not only to economic damage, but also to compensation for non-pecuniary disadvantages. On the one hand, this question has long been disputed in the doctrine. And on the other hand, the wording of the relevant law from 2003 was not clear. The Federal Supreme Court has recognised that the statutory regulation also applies in principle to compensation for non-pecuniary disadvantages.

112 For the specific scope of the 'privilege of distribution', the Federal Supreme Court then had to deal with a precedent from 1997.[19] In this decision, the Federal Supreme Court had reached a compromise in view of the conflict of opinion in the doctrine. It had taken into account the fact that it is hardly possible to determine exact sums for the compensation of non-pecuniary disadvantages. The 'privilege of distribution' could therefore only be applied analogously and the proportion of the reduction in liability claims taken into account in the recourse of the insurance company. As a result, the Federal Supreme Court had only partially applied the 'privilege of distribution' at the time.

113 In the present case, the Federal Supreme Court has now corrected the previous precedent from 1997. The 'privilege of distribution' should now apply in full to compensation for non-pecuniary disadvantages.

114 The calculation of A's claims was therefore as follows:

115 (i) An unreduced compensation amount for non-pecuniary disadvantages in the amount of CHF 41,000 was to be assumed, as determined by the court of second instance (above nos 103 to 106).

---

18 Article 73 of the Federal Act on the General Part of Social Insurance Law (ATSG) of 6 October 2000, SR 830.1 <at https://www.fedlex.admin.ch/de>, in force since 2003: '1) The claims of the insured person and their survivors shall only be transferred to the insurance institution to the extent that the latter's benefits, together with the compensation owed by the third party for the same period, exceed the corresponding loss. ... 3) The claims that are not transferred to the insurance carrier shall remain with the insured person and his/her survivors. ...'.

19 Swiss Federal Supreme Court, 6 May 1997, BGE 123 III 306, at <http://www.bger.ch/jurisdiction-recht>.

(ii) A had received compensation of CHF 31,500 from the insurance company. This meant that the sum of CHF 9,500 was not yet covered. 116

(iii) A can demand this CHF 9,500 from the liable company B. 117

(iv) However, company B is only liable for the sum of CHF 30,750 (CHF 41,000 minus CHF 10,250 [25 %]) due to A's own fault (quota of 25 %). 118

(v) The insurance company therefore only has a right of recourse against company B in the amount of CHF 21,250. As mentioned above, company B only has to pay the sum of CHF 30,750. 119

As a result of the interposition of the insurance company, A receives higher compensation for his economic disadvantages than if he had only had claims against the liable employer. 120

c) Commentary

Commentary 1: Privilege of priority in the distribution of the damage

The 'privilege of distribution' has long been recognised as a general principle by the courts and doctrine in Switzerland, even if it is not regulated by law as in other countries.[20] There is only a special regulation in road traffic legislation[21] and the aforementioned 2003 regulation for social insurance. An attempt to create a statutory regulation for private insurance companies also failed as part of the work completed in 2020 to revise the Insurance Contract Act of 1908.[22] The revision was limited to urgently needed changes.[23] There was no political will for a total revision of the Insurance Contract Act. 121

The 'privilege of distribution' is intended to protect the injured party from uncovered damages, but not to enrich them. 122

The 'privilege of distribution' becomes particularly important in practice in cases where the claim for damages of the injured party is smaller than the actual 123

20 For example, in Germany (§ 86 of the Gesetz über den Versicherungsvertrag of 23 November 2007; Bundesgesetzblatt [BGBl] I at 2631) or Austria (§ 67 of the Versicherungsvertragsgesetz of 2 December 1958, BGBl No 2/1959).

21 Article 88 of the Road Traffic Act of 19 December 1958, SR 741.01, at <https://www.fedlex.admin.ch/de>: 'If an injured party is not fully covered by insurance benefits, insurers may only assert their rights of recourse against the liable party or his liability insurer insofar as this does not disadvantage the injured party.'

22 Federal Act on Insurance Contracts (Insurance Contract Act, ICA) of 2 April 1908, SR 221.229.1, at <https://www.fedlex.admin.ch/de>.

23 See *P Loser*, Switzerland, in: E Karner/BC Steininger (eds), European Tort Law (ETL) 2020 (2021) 663, no 9.

loss due to a reason for reduction (eg as a result of the injured party's own fault) and the insurance benefit does not fully cover the actual loss suffered. The following example illustrates this:[24] The loss amounts to CHF 100,000. The insurance benefit amounts to CHF 80,000, the claim for damages against the third party amounts to CHF 50,000 with a liability ratio of 50 %. The injured insured person can claim CHF 80,000 from the insurance company, while it must claim CHF 20,000 in advance from the person who caused the damage. As a result, the insurance company is only entitled to a claim of CHF 30,000, although it is obliged to pay benefits totalling CHF 80,000. In such cases, the insurance company should not be able to take recourse against the injuring party to the detriment of the insured person; rather, the injured insured person may enforce his liability claim themself until the entire loss to be compensated together with the insurance benefit is covered. In a nutshell, the prerogative of quota means: damage minus insurance benefit equals direct claim of the injured person.

124 The reason for this privilege is that insurance companies have contractually promised to cover the damage or have been obliged to do so by law and collect premiums in advance for this obligation.[25]

Commentary 2: Special features of compensation for non-pecuniary disadvantages

125 The application of the 'privilege of distribution' to compensation for non-pecuniary disadvantages was rejected by the previous doctrine due to the special features of this type of compensation.

126 This is because the quota prerogative can only be applied if two calculation variables can be determined: the full damage, on the one hand, and the reduced amount of compensation, on the other. This is not the case with compensation for non-pecuniary disadvantages. The financial impact of a reduction cannot be determined numerically. Rather, the amount to be paid to the victim must be determined *ex aequo et bono* by the judge on a case-by-case basis, taking into account all relevant factors. It was also argued that a reduction in compensation due to the victim's own fault corresponds to the less severe psychological damage suffered by the victim.[26]

---

24 See Message of the Swiss Federal Council on the total revision of the Insurance Contract Act of 7 September 2011, Schweizerisches Bundesblatt (BBl) 2011, 7705, 7781, at <https://www.fedlex.admin.ch/de>.

25 BGE 4 A_312/2024 of 5 December 2024, Consideration 2.7.1.

26 Cf BGE 4 A_312/2024 of 5 December 2024, Consideration 2.2.

Commentary 3: Harmonisation of compensation for non-pecuniary and for pecuniary disadvantages

This view (cf Commentary 2) is now outdated. There has now been a certain degree of harmonisation in the determination of compensation for non-pecuniary disadvantages and economic losses. 127

It is still true that the determination of the amount of compensation for non-pecuniary disadvantages is a decision based on equity and the assessment must therefore not be based on schematic standards. The amount awarded must not be determined according to fixed rates, but must be adapted to the individual case. In this sense, for example, art 10:301 sec 2 of the Principles of European Tort Law states: 'In general, in the assessment of such damages, all circumstances of the case, including the gravity, duration and consequences of the grievance, have to be taken into account.' 128

However, this does not preclude the valuation of the non-material impairment from being carried out in two phases:[27] (1) in an objective calculation phase with a base amount as a point of reference and (2) a subsequent phase in which the particularities of the individual case (basis of liability, [self-]fault, individual life situation of the injured party) are taken into account. 129

In the present case, the court of second instance determined the compensation for the non-pecuniary disadvantages in this way (above nos 103 to 106). In doing so, it followed the case law established by the Federal Supreme Court in a 2006 leading case.[28] 130

Compensation for non-pecuniary and economic disadvantages are still separate remedies. However, they are increasingly being harmonised.[29] 131

27 Cf BGE 4 A_312/2024 of 5 December 2024, Consideration 2.7.2.

28 Swiss Federal Supreme Court, 19 January 2006, BGE 132 III 117, at <http://www.bger.ch/jurisdiction-recht>.

29 See already *A Keller*, Haftpflichtrecht im Privatrecht, vol II (2nd edn 1998) 122 f; and *H Landolt*, Gibt es der Genugtuung genug? HAVE 2021, 185, 186 f.

9. European Court of Human Rights (ECtHR) *Jann-Zwicker and Jann v Switzerland*, 13 February 2024, no 4976/20: Time-Barring of Asbestos Victim's Case Violated the European Convention on Human Rights[30]

132 The ECtHR has condemned Switzerland for the second time in connection with asbestos claims and criticised the fact that the long latency period for asbestos claims is not sufficiently taken into account in the statute of limitations provisions. The judgment was already presented in the last report.[31]

133 The background for the complaint is that the Swiss limitation rules are governed by the *system of double time limits.* A first short and so called 'relative' period (of three years) runs de facto from the time the injured party becomes aware of the damage. The second longer and so called 'absolute' period (of 10 years or 20 years in the case of physical injury) runs from the time of the damaging act respectively of the violation of legal interests. Whether the injured party is already aware of the damage at this time is not relevant. In the revision of the statute of limitations rules of 2018, the Swiss legislator deliberately adhered to this system, in the knowledge of the earlier judgment of the ECtHR *Howald Moor v Switzerland* of 2014,[32] which criticised the shortcomings of this system in the case of long latency damage.

134 As far as can be seen, *no legislative measures* are planned in Switzerland to change this system as a result of Switzerland's new condemnation. In its report to the Committee of Ministers of the Council of Europe of 14 March 2025, the Swiss government also proposed no new measures.[33]

---

30 At <https://hudoc.echr.coe.int/eng>. Cf European Court of Human Rights Press Release no ECHR 034 (2024). Cf *C Widmer Lüchinger*, Verjährung und Asbest: Die Schweiz wird erneut durch den Europäischen Gerichtshof für Menschenrechte verurteilt, Jusletter 8 April 2024; *C Müller*, Bis repetita placent: Der Europäische Gerichtshof für Menschenrechte verurteilt die Schweiz erneut wegen der absoluten Verjährung der Ansprüche von Asbestopfern, Jusletter 8 April 2024; *M Zilla*, Tribune – En cause, la prescription absolue et son *dies a quo*, La Semaine Judiciaire (SJ) 2024, 763 ff; *P Pichonnaz*, Le point sur la partie générale du droit des obligations | Entwicklungen im Obligationenrecht, Allgemeiner Teil, Schweizerische Juristen-Zeitung (SJZ) 2025, 402, 408 ff.

31 *Loser* (fn 1) ETL 2023, no 130 ff; *C Widmer Lüchinger*, Comparative Remarks, in: E Karner/BC Steininger (eds), ETL 2023 (2024) 779, no 39.

32 ECtHR *Case of Howald Moor and Others v Switzerland*, 11.3.2014, nos 52067/10 and 41072/11 (at <https://hudoc.echr.coe.int/eng>). Cf Swiss Report in the Yearbook 2013: *P Loser*, Switzerland, in: E Karner/BC Steininger (eds), ETL 2013 (2014) 673, no 21 ff.

33 Action Report DH-DD(2025)308 of 14 March 2025, Communication from Switzerland concerning the case of Jann-Zwicker and Jann v Switzerland (at: <https://hudoc.exec.coe.int/?i=004–66214>).

Various *approaches are discussed in the doctrine* as to how the problem of long latency damage could be solved. (1) One main approach is to generally allow the second deadline to run only from the time the injured party becomes aware of their injury or damage.[34] However, this view is not compatible with the legislative intention.[35] (2) Another main approach proposes that although the limitation period begins to run from the damaging act, it is suspended during the period of uncertainty about the damage.[36] The Federal Supreme Court explicitly rejected this approach in its decision of the case *Jann-Zwicker* because this would result in the introduction of a concept in which the second period begins from the time of knowledge of the damage – a concept that the legislator had deliberately rejected[37]. The question of whether the missing knowledge of the injury is an *objective* uncertainty – as demanded by the law for suspending the prescription – or a *subjective* uncertainty is disputed. It remains to be seen whether a clear opinion will develop in this regard or whether the Federal Supreme Court will change its practice.[38] 135

Partly – by the Swiss Federal Supreme Court and by some authors – the question was also raised as to *whether the ECtHR is exceeding its competences* when criticising the statute of limitations provisions. The ECtHR justified its judgment against Switzerland on the basis of insufficient access to justice in accordance with art 6 ECHR. In particular, the Swiss Federal Supreme Court pointed out (1) that the statute of limitations is not a procedural rule, but a substantive issue of liability law, and (2) the ECtHR is not competent for substantive regulations on liability law.[39] 136

34 Cf *Pichonnaz*, SJZ 2025, 402, 411.

35 Cf *V Roberto*, Haftpflichtrecht (4th edn) 2024, no 19.09d.

36 Cf *Widmer* (fn 30) Jusletter 8 April 2024 no 35; *I Wildhaber/S Dede*, Berner Kommentar, Die Verjährung (2021) OR art 134 no 47 ff.

37 BGE 146 (2019) III 25 of 6 November 2019, consideration 3.1, on Prescription of Liability for Asbestos-Related Disease: cf *P Loser*, Switzerland, in: E Karner/BC Steininger (eds), European Tort Law 2019 (2020) 659, no 61 ff. See also the critics of *R D Däppen*, Basler Kommentar, Obligationenrecht I (7th edn 2020) OR art 135 no 10d.

38 Following the ECtHR judgment of 2024, the Swiss Federal Supreme Court overturned the previous national judgments in the *Jann-Zwicker* case and referred them back to the lower court for a new judgment (BGE 4F_22/2024 of 19 February 2025). This is because the national courts had not yet examined whether the plaintiffs had complied with the first (short) period of limitation. In this decision of 19 February 2025, however, the Federal Supreme Court did not decide how the problem of the second period should be resolved.

39 BGE 146 (2019) III 25 of 6 November 2019, consideration 8.1. See for criticism also *Roberto* (fn 35) no 19.09i.

137 An unease with the ECtHR's overly broad interpretation of the ECHR became increasingly apparent last year following the ECtHR judgment *Verein KlimaSeniorinnen Schweiz and Others v Switzerland* of 9 April 2024. The critical opinion of Parliament and the government was already mentioned in last year's report.[40] The Swiss Government (Swiss Federal Council) summarised the criticism of the Swiss Parliament – that had also negatively influenced the Government's project to introduce Collective Legal Protection in Swiss Law (cf above no 4) – in the Action Plan of 8 October 2024 to the Committee of Ministers of the Council of Europe as follows:[41]

- The Council of States and the National Council each adopted an identical statement on the ruling. They consider, among other things, that the judgment goes beyond the limits of dynamic interpretation, that the ECtHR thereby accepts that its legitimacy is called into question and that a weakening of the Court's legitimacy could lead to a weakening of the effective protection of human rights in Europe. Both Councils call on the ECtHR, in the future, to respect the principle of subsidiarity enshrined in the Convention, to pay renewed and careful attention to the text of the Convention and the historical circumstances in which it was drafted, to give the importance of the State sovereignty and the principle of consensus in international law that these two concepts still have today, and to respect the democratic processes of the ECHR Member States.
- The Swiss Government has also considered this judgment. It recognises Switzerland's position as a member of the Council of Europe and in the system of the European Convention on Human Rights. The Convention and membership of the Council of Europe, one of whose fundamental values is the protection of human rights, democracy and the rule of law, are of great importance to Switzerland. Like the National Council and the Council of States, however, it is critical of the broad interpretation of the Convention with regard to climate protection. In the view of the Swiss government, case law must not lead to an extension of the scope of the Convention.

---

40 *Loser* (fn 1) ETL 2023, no 146. Cf also the discussion in legal science in the series of articles by *B Giovanni, AT Müller, H Seiler* and *N Zimmermann* in the Journal Schweizerisches Zentralblatt für Staats- und Verfassungsrecht (ZBl) 2024, 461 ff; for criticism against the the criticism of the Swiss Parliament, see *C Heri*, Drei Missverständnisse bezüglich des KlimaSeniorinnen-Urteils, Zeitschrift für juristische Weiterbildung und Praxis (recht) 2024, 184 ff.

41 Action Report DH-DD(2024)1123 of 8 October 2024, Communication from Switzerland concerning the case of *KlimaSeniorinnen Schweiz and Others v Switzerland* (at: <https://hudoc.exec.coe.int/eng?i=DH-DD(2024)1123F>, free translation).

- The doctrine of the living instrument does not allow the guarantees of the Convention to be interpreted in a way that undermines the basic principles, such as the principle of subsidiarity. In accordance with this principle, the definition and choice of measures to be taken in this area fall within the competence of national governments and parliaments and, in the case of Switzerland, which has a system of direct democracy, of the people. The triad 'human rights, democracy and the rule of law' as well as the separation of powers and the principle of subsidiarity are of great importance and must be respected. In this connection, it should be noted that a number of these arguments were also put forward by the governments involved in the case (see judgment, § 366 ff).

In the context of the statute of limitations, which is of interest here, it is of course 138
not a question of the same legal problems. However, the question of the limits of the dynamic interpretation of the Convention also arises, particularly with regard to the extent to which the regulation of the limitation period is a substantive issue of private law or of procedural law and whether it falls under the rules of the Convention.

Bernhard A Koch and Thomas Thiede

XXXI. European Union

A. Legislation

1. Product Liability

The by far most important development in the field of tort law at the level of EU law in 2024 was the formal adoption of a new Product Liability Directive (PLD) on 23 October 2024,[1] replacing its 1985 predecessor.[2] It has to be transposed into the laws of the Member States by 9 December 2026. The promulgation of the new directive on 18 November 2024 marks a surprisingly swift conclusion of the legislative process, which had been officially launched with the publication of the underlying draft[3] on 28 September 2022. 1

A previous report in this series already presented the key novelties of this draft, which has now been finalised without major modifications to its substance.[4] The 2024 Annual Conference on European Tort Law included a special session on this new directive, the presentations have already been published.[5] Here are therefore merely some key points highlighting the most significant changes to the previous product liability regime: 2

1 Directive (EU) 2024/2853 of the European Parliament and of the Council of 23 October 2024 on liability for defective products and repealing Council Directive 85/374/EEC, [2024] Official Journal of the European Union (OJ) L 2024/2853.

2 Council Directive 85/374/EEC of 25 July 1985 on the approximation of the laws, regulations and administrative provisions of the Member States concerning liability for defective products [1985] OJ L 210/29, as amended by Directive 1999/34/EC of the European Parliament and of the Council of 10 May 1999 [1999] OJ L 141/20 (in the following oPLD).

3 Proposal for a Directive of the European Parliament and of the Council on liability for defective products, COM(2022) 495 final.

4 *BA Koch/T Thiede*, European Union, in: E Karner/BC Steininger (eds), European Tort Law (ETL) 2022 (2023) 695, no 1 ff. The original draft PLD had no separate rule on damage, which was at the time merely included in the definitions. The newly inserted art 6 PLD therefore shifts the numbering of the original draft (on which the cited report was based) by one for the following articles.

5 *BA Koch*, Product Liability on the Way to the Digital Age (2024) 15 Journal of European Tort Law (JETL) 109; *Z Jacquemin*, Product Liability Directive: Disclosure of Evidence, the Burden of Proof and Presumptions (2024) 15 JETL 126; *S Li/M Faure*, The Revised Product Liability Directive: A Law and Economics Analysis (2024) 15 JETL 140; *G Wagner*, Next Generation EU Product Liability – For Digital and Other Products (2024) 15 JETL 172.

https://doi.org/10.1515/9783111389271-032

- Expansion of the scope
  The most obvious change brought about by the new PLD (and in fact the main reason to initiate the legislative procedure leading to it) is the widening of the notion of a 'product' covered by it. While software – being intangible – was arguably not meant to be a product within the meaning of the 1985 Directive, art 4 no 1 PLD now expressly includes it. The term is not explained in the black-letter text of the PLD, but its preamble lists examples 'such as operating systems, firmware, computer programs, applications or AI systems' (recital 13). Consequently, software can also be a component of another product in the future, which means its developers can be held liable directly as contributors to the final product. More importantly, the notion of 'component' was expanded even further by also including a 'related service', which is defined by art 4 no 3 PLD as 'a digital service that is integrated into, or inter-connected with, a product in such a way that its absence would prevent the product from performing one or more of its functions'. Recital 17 PLD lists examples such as 'the continuous supply of traffic data in a navigation system, ... or a voice-assistant service that allows one or more products to be controlled by using voice commands'.
- Adjustments of what is compensable under the regime
  Apart from (finally) striking the infamous € 500 threshold of art 9 lit b oPLD, the new PLD narrows the exclusion of damage to property used professionally. Such losses are now also recoverable unless the item was used '*exclusively* for professional purposes' (art 6 para 1 lit b no iii PLD, emphasis added), therefore extending protection to dual-use property. The 'destruction or corruption of data' is listed as a separate item of compensable harm (art 6 para 1 lit c PLD). Pure economic loss continues to be excluded from the Directive's scope, as is primary immaterial harm, thereby reducing the relevance of the new PLD for standalone AI applications such as recruitment or profiling software.
- Clarifications regarding defectiveness
  While not changing the substance of the notion of defectiveness, art 7 para 2 PLD now lists factors to be considered when examining whether a product fails to provide the safety that can be expected of it.
- Updates to the list of liable persons
  As under the old regime, the new PLD maintains the cascade system of liable persons, channelling liability primarily onto the producer of the final product. Article 8 PLD simply adds novel players in the chain of (particularly online) distribution that were not yet known in 1985, such as authorised representatives, fulfilment service providers, or online platforms.

- Facilitation of proving causation and defectiveness[6]
  Article 9 PLD introduces obligations for both parties to disclose crucial evidence within their exclusive control to the respective other side if the latter needs such evidence in order to support their position. Member States must ensure that this is limited to only 'necessary and proportionate' disclosure, and that the interests concerned (including the interests of third parties) are protected.
  Article 10 PLD foresees certain instances of shifting the burden of proving causation, defectiveness, or both, eg when the claimant thereby 'faces excessive difficulties, in particular due to technical or scientific complexity' (art 10 para 4 lit a PLD), while otherwise maintaining the previous general rule that this is, in general, still for the claimants to prove (art 10 para 1 PLD).
- Adjustments to the list of defences
  While the defences of art 7 oPLD were essentially copied and pasted into art 11 PLD, a new art 11 para 2 PLD accommodates for the new situation that the producer no longer loses control over the product when putting it into circulation, but retains influence on its safety features by providing updates and upgrades thereafter.
  While the ten-year extinction period of art 11 oPLD was essentially preserved (though now acknowledging in the wording of art 17 PLD that it may also be interpreted as a mere long-stop prescription period), art 17 para 2 PLD honours the *Howald Moor* ruling of the ECtHR[7] inasmuch as the period is extended to 25 years if the 'injured person has not been able to initiate proceedings within 10 years ... due to the latency of a personal injury'.

B. Cases on Infringements of the General Data Protection Regulation (GDPR)

As in previous years, the Court of Justice of the European Union (CJEU) has continued to refine and develop its interpretation of art 82 GDPR,[8] while also providing further clarity on significant aspects of art 88 GDPR and related provisions. 3

---

6 On this point in particular, see eg, *Jacquemin* (2024) 15 JETL 126.

7 ECtHR *Howald Moor and Others v Switzerland*, 11.3.2014, nos 52067/10 and 41072/11. For more details on this ruling, see *P Loser*, Switzerland, in: E Karner/BC Steininger(eds), ETL 2013 (2014) 673, no 21 ff.

8 Regulation (EU) 2016/679 of the European Parliament and of the Council of 27 April 2016 on the protection of natural persons with regard to the processing of personal data and on the free movement of such data, and repealing Directive 95/46/EC [2016] OJ L 119/1.

Each judgment addressed below certainly arises from distinct factual circumstances; nonetheless, they collectively highlight some common themes and consistent principles.

1. CJEU 25 January 2024 – C-687/21, *BL v MediaMarktSaturn Hagen-Iserlohn GmbH*, ECLI:EU:C:2024:72

a) Brief Summary of the Facts

4 The claimant (BL) purchased an electrical household appliance from the defendant, MediaMarktSaturn Hagen-Iserlohn GmbH (Saturn). In the course of this transaction on Saturn's retail premises, the claimant provided various personal data, including his name, residential address, details of his employment, income, and banking information, to an employee of the defendant. These personal data were subsequently printed on contractual documents intended exclusively for the claimant.

5 Due to an error by Saturn's employees, these documents, along with the appliance itself, were mistakenly handed over to another customer. The error was quickly detected, and within approximately 30 minutes, Saturn retrieved the appliance and the documents and returned them to BL.

6 Although Saturn offered compensation by delivering the appliance free of charge to BL's residence, BL considered this insufficient and filed a lawsuit seeking additional compensation under art 82 GDPR. BL argued that the unintended disclosure created a risk of future misuse of his personal data, causing non-material damage in the form of distress. Saturn countered that no actual harm occurred, as there was no evidence the third party had viewed or misused the data.

7 The referring court therefore sought clarification from the CJEU as to whether art 82 GDPR is valid regarding non-material damage, whether compensation requires actual proven harm, if accidental disclosure by employees automatically violates the GDPR or constitutes unlawful further processing, if mere discomfort or fear suffices as non-material damage, how the preventability of disclosure affects the seriousness of the infringement, and if compensation under the GDPR has a punitive or purely compensatory function.

b) Judgment of the Court

8 Regarding the necessity of proving non-material damage, the CJEU upheld that the mere infringement of GDPR provisions does not automatically confer a right to

compensation. Instead, claimants must demonstrate actual material or non-material harm resulting specifically from the infringement (para 58), although this harm need not reach a minimum threshold of severity (para 59).

Turning to the accidental disclosure of personal data, the Court held that such a disclosure alone, resulting from an employee's error, is not sufficient by itself to establish a violation of arts 24 and 32 GDPR. Controllers must instead be given an opportunity to demonstrate that they had adopted appropriate technical and organisational measures suitable to the identified risks (paras 38–40, 45). 9

Consequently, accidental disclosure of personal data to an unauthorised third party does not automatically constitute unlawful further processing; rather, an individual assessment of the appropriateness of the controller's measures must take place, placing the burden of proof squarely on the data controller (paras 42–44). 10

Finally, addressing the nature and assessment of non-material damage, the Court clarified that mere discomfort or fear of potential future misuse of personal data does not constitute compensable non-material damage under art 82 GDPR if the unauthorised third party demonstrably did not become aware of the disclosed data (paras 63–69). Moreover, the Court emphasised that compensation under art 82 GDPR fulfils a purely compensatory rather than punitive function, thus excluding considerations regarding the preventability or severity of the infringement from affecting the calculation of the compensation (paras 47–50, 52–55). 11

c) Commentary

This decision adds welcome clarity to the conditions required for claims under art 82 GDPR, especially regarding accidental disclosures of personal data. Notably, the Court confirms that controllers are not automatically liable for every unintended data breach caused by employee mistakes. Instead, it reinforces the principle of accountability (arts 5(2) and 24 GDPR) by placing the burden of proof on controllers to demonstrate that adequate protective measures were indeed implemented (paras 42–44). While this prevents automatic liability and disproportionate burdens on controllers, it also ensures that data protection obligations cannot be taken lightly, compelling companies to proactively establish and document their data security protocols. 12

Moreover, the judgment significantly constrains overly speculative claims for compensation for non-material damage. By expressly rejecting claims based solely on subjective fears or hypothetical future misuse of personal data, the Court emphasises the requirement for demonstrable, actual harm (paras 63–69). This represents a necessary balance between protecting individuals from genuine harm and preventing a flood of claims based on minimal or merely theoretical discom- 13 fort. Thus, while the ruling supports data subjects' rights in genuine cases of harm, it also provides businesses with reasonable predictability regarding their potential exposure.

14 Finally, the explicit rejection of a punitive element in GDPR compensation aligns well with traditional tort law principles in the Member States. Compensation under art 82 GDPR remains purely compensatory, ensuring victims are fully indemnified without permitting disproportionate penalties that exceed actual harm suffered. This demarcation helps maintain consistency across EU law and prevents the GDPR from unintentionally becoming an instrument of punitive damages – a notion largely foreign to the European legal tradition.

2. CJEU 11 April 2024 – C-741/21, *GP v juris GmbH,* ECLI:EU: C:2024:288

a) Brief Summary of the Facts

15 The claimant, GP, a self-employed lawyer, was previously a customer of juris GmbH ('juris'), a company providing legal database services. Upon discovering that juris was using his personal data for direct marketing purposes, GP explicitly revoked all previously given marketing consents on 6 November 2018, clearly objecting to any further use of his data for marketing purposes except to continue receiving newsletters.

16 Despite these explicit objections, GP received two personalised marketing leaflets from juris in 2019. After again reminding juris of his objections by email on 18 April 2019 and demanding compensation for unauthorised processing, GP received yet another marketing leaflet in May 2019. This prompted him to formally reiterate his objections once more, this time via bailiff.

17 Each of these leaflets contained a unique 'trial personal code' linking directly to an online order form that included GP's personal data, as verified by a notary. GP subsequently initiated legal proceedings before the *Landgericht Saarbrücken*, seeking compensation under art 82 GDPR. He claimed compensation for both material damage (the costs incurred for the services of the bailiff and notary) and non-material damage, specifically asserting loss of control over his personal data.

18 juris GmbH, in its defence, argued that the continued marketing communications resulted solely from internal employee errors, despite having adequate measures in place to prevent such occurrences. juris further contested GP's claim by asserting that mere infringement of GDPR provisions, without proven consequential damage, cannot constitute compensable harm under art 82 GDPR.

The *Landgericht Saarbrücken* therefore referred several questions to the CJEU, asking inter alia, whether any infringement of GDPR automatically constitutes compensable non-material damage under art 82 GDPR irrespective of seriousness, whether controllers can escape liability by attributing breaches solely to employee error, whether the criteria for administrative fines under art 83 GDPR should influence the calculation of compensation, and whether multiple infringements require separate assessments or can be compensated as a single infringement. 19

b) Judgment of the Court

The CJEU held that the mere infringement of GDPR provisions granting rights to the data subject is not sufficient, in itself, to constitute compensable non-material damage under art 82 GDPR (paras 32–34, 40). Rather, claimants must demonstrate actual harm, though notably, the Court reiterated that there is no required minimum threshold of seriousness for such damage. It specifically highlighted that a loss of control over personal data – even temporary – may constitute compensable damage if actually proven by the claimant (para 42). 20

On the controller's exemption from liability due to employee misconduct, the CJEU firmly stated that the controller cannot avoid liability under art 82(3) GDPR by merely attributing the breach to human error or negligence of its employees acting under its authority (para 49 f). To benefit from this exemption, the controller must explicitly demonstrate a complete absence of any causal connection between its own data protection obligations and the damage caused – an evidentiary requirement explicitly intended to preserve the effectiveness of compensation rights provided by the GDPR (paras 51–54). 21

Finally, on the assessment of compensation, the Court clearly distinguished between the criteria for administrative fines under art 83 GDPR and compensation claims under art 82 GDPR, expanding that these criteria are not interchangeable due to fundamentally different purposes – administrative fines being punitive and deterrent, while compensation is exclusively compensatory (paras 59–62). Consequently, even if several infringements occurred against the same data subject, the compensation must solely reflect the actual harm suffered, without separate calculation for each infringement or cumulative assessment influenced by the number of violations (paras 63–65). 22

c) Commentary

23 The ruling significantly strengthens the accountability principle underlying the GDPR. The Court's clear statement that a controller cannot avoid liability merely by claiming human error of its employees underlines the importance of proactive and effective internal compliance measures. The judgment thus encourages controllers to implement stringent safeguards, regular training, and proper oversight, as they must ultimately prove a complete lack of causal connection to avoid liability under art 82(3) GDPR.

24 In addition, the Court draws a decisive boundary between compensatory damages and punitive administrative fines. By rejecting any analogy between the criteria for administrative fines (art 83 GDPR) and compensation assessment, it preserves the compensatory principle underlying art 82 GDPR, ensuring claimants receive precisely what is necessary to redress actual harm.

25 Finally, the ruling further clarifies that, even in situations involving multiple infringements, compensation must reflect real damage rather than aggregating penalties, thus reinforcing consistency and predictability in GDPR-related compensation claims.

3. CJEU 20 June 2024 – C-590/22, *AT, BT v PS GbR and Others*, ECLI:EU:C:2024:536

a) Brief Summary of the Facts

26 The claimants, AT and BT, clients of the tax consultancy firm PS, had informed PS of their new address, which was duly recorded in PS's internal data processing system. In July 2020, AT and BT asked PS to prepare their 2019 tax return, which PS subsequently mailed. However, due to an internal error, the envelope containing sensitive personal data – including their names, birth dates, tax identification numbers, bank details, religious affiliation, disability status, professions, workplaces, and details about various personal expenses – was mistakenly sent to their former address.

27 The new occupants at the former address inadvertently opened the letter before realising the mistake. Although these third parties claimed not to have read the contents extensively, they passed the envelope to relatives living nearby for collection by AT and BT. Upon receipt, AT and BT discovered only a copy of the tax return in the envelope and assumed that the original, containing all their detailed personal information, was lost or at risk of unauthorised disclosure. Notably, the referring court was unable to establish conclusively what documents

were originally enclosed or precisely how much personal data the third parties had accessed.

AT and BT subsequently initiated legal proceedings before the *Amtsgericht Wesel*, seeking compensation under art 82(1) GDPR for non-material damage. They argued that, due to the unauthorised disclosure, their sensitive personal data had come into the hands of third parties, warranting compensation. Given uncertainties around the extent of third-party access to their personal information and doubts regarding how to assess the compensation, the *Amtsgericht Wesel* referred to the CJEU whether the mere infringement of GDPR provisions alone suffices for non-material damage claims under art 82(1) GDPR or if additional adverse effects must be proven, if a certain magnitude of harm is required, if fear alone of potential unauthorised data disclosure is compensable, if criteria for administrative fines under art 83 GDPR or deterrent considerations should affect compensation assessments, and if simultaneous breaches of national data protection rules should impact compensation awarded under the GDPR. 28

b) Judgment of the Court

The CJEU first reaffirmed (again) that a mere infringement of GDPR provisions is insufficient, by itself, to confer a right to compensation under art 82(1) GDPR; the claimant must always demonstrate actual material or non-material harm caused by the infringement (paras 23–25). The Court explicitly clarified that there is no minimum threshold for the seriousness of the harm required for non-material damage claims, thus protecting claimants who suffer even slight harm from unlawful processing of their personal data (paras 26–28). 29

Addressing the specific question of compensable fear, the Court ruled that the fear or distress resulting from concern that personal data may have been disclosed to unauthorised third parties – despite uncertainty as to whether such disclosure actually occurred – can indeed constitute compensable non-material damage, provided that the claimant credibly demonstrates this fear and its tangible negative consequences (paras 32–36). However, mere hypothetical concerns or unsubstantiated fears remain insufficient for compensation. 30

Lastly, the Court clearly rejected applying by analogy the criteria used for administrative fines under art 83 GDPR to assess compensation under art 82 GDPR, emphasising fundamental differences in their objectives – administrative fines being punitive and deterrent, while damages are strictly compensatory (paras 38 f, 43 f). Hence, compensation under art 82 GDPR does not have a punitive or deterrent function and must strictly match the extent of actual harm suffered. Additionally, the Court clarified that simultaneous infringements of national data pro- 31 tection provisions not adopted specifically under the GDPR framework cannot increase compensation under art 82(1), though Member States remain free to offer greater protection under their own laws if they choose (paras 45–50).

c) Commentary

32 This judgment reaffirms critical guidance regarding the interpretation of non-material damage under art 82 GDPR, clearly delimiting the scope of compensation rights while ensuring appropriate protection for data subjects. By firmly restating the requirement of actual damage and rejecting claims based purely on infringements without demonstrated harm, the Court maintains a crucial balance: ensuring effective redress for genuine injuries without opening the door to an overwhelming number of trivial or unsubstantiated claims. Notably, the explicit acceptance of well-founded fear as compensable damage – even where unauthorised disclosure is uncertain – significantly extends data subjects' protection against breaches involving sensitive or personal information.

33 At the same time, the Court decisively closes the door on any blending of punitive and compensatory mechanisms. It clarifies, as in previous judgments such as *juris* (no 15 above), that the criteria used for administrative fines under art 83 GDPR cannot influence compensation amounts under art 82 GDPR, since these two measures serve distinct purposes.

34 Furthermore, the judgment elegantly navigates the intersection between EU and national data protection rules. By determining that simultaneous violations of national laws not explicitly implementing GDPR provisions cannot independently amplify compensation under art 82 GDPR, the Court reinforces the autonomy and uniformity of the European framework. Nonetheless, it prudently leaves open the possibility for national courts to award higher damages under purely domestic law, preserving Member States' ability to offer enhanced protection if they wish. This carefully nuanced position effectively safeguards both uniform EU data protection standards and Member States' legislative autonomy.

4. CJEU 4 October 2024 – C-200/23, *VX, Agentsia po vpisvaniyata v OL,* ECLI:EU:C:2024:827

a) Brief Summary of the Facts

35 OL, a member of a Bulgarian limited liability company registered in January 2021, requested the Bulgarian Registration Agency to erase personal data contained in

the company's constitutive instrument, which had been published online in the commercial register. This constitutive instrument included personal data beyond what was legally required, notably OL's identification number, address, and signature.

Initially, the Registration Agency did not respond, prompting OL to initiate legal proceedings before the *Administrativen sad Dobrich*. Although the Agency subsequently erased some of OL's personal data, it retained OL's name and handwritten signature, stating that complete erasure required OL to submit an authenticated redacted copy of the instrument. 36

The Administrative Court ruled in OL's favour, awarding compensation for non-material damage, finding that OL had suffered psychological distress due to unauthorised data disclosure and loss of control. The Registration Agency appealed this judgment to the *Varhoven administrativen sad* (Supreme Administrative Court of Bulgaria). 37

In this context, the *Varhoven administrativen sad* asked the CJEU whether the disclosure of non-compulsory personal data in a company's constitutive instrument published in a commercial register without explicit consent complies with Directive 2017/1132[9] and the GDPR, whether a presumed consent under national law is valid, how the right to erasure applies to such publicly disclosed documents, if a handwritten signature qualifies as personal data under the GDPR, whether temporary loss of control over personal data constitutes compensable non-material damage, and whether an advisory opinion of a national supervisory authority can exempt a controller from liability. 38

b) Judgment of the Court

The CJEU first clarified that Directive 2017/1132 does not impose an obligation on Member States to allow publication in a commercial register of personal data not required by law (paras 50–60). Consequently, a national authority responsible for maintaining such a register cannot rely on that Directive as justification for publishing non-compulsory personal data without consent or another valid legal ground under the GDPR. 39

Regarding consent, the Court emphasised that presumed consent, such as that established by Bulgarian law, does not satisfy the conditions set forth in the GDPR. Explicit consent, freely given and clearly informed, remains necessary for any pro- 40

9 Directive (EU) 2017/1132 of the European Parliament and of the Council of 14 June 2017 relating to certain aspects of company law [2017] OJ L 169/46.

cessing not justified by another lawful ground under art 6 GDPR (paras 99–101). The Court further held that a handwritten signature clearly constitutes personal data within the meaning of art 4(1) GDPR, as it directly identifies an individual (paras 128–136).

41 Concerning liability, the Court ruled that temporary loss of control over personal data, due to unauthorised disclosure in a publicly accessible register, can constitute compensable non-material damage under art 82(1) GDPR. Importantly, claimants must demonstrate actual harm, though this harm may be minimal and does not require additional tangible adverse consequences (paras 137–156).

42 Finally, the Court determined that an advisory opinion issued by a national supervisory authority under art 58(3)(b) GDPR cannot exempt a controller from liability. Controllers must explicitly demonstrate the absence of any causal link between their actions and the damage suffered to benefit from liability exemption under art 82(3) GDPR (paras 157–176).

c) Commentary

43 This judgment marks another significant step by the CJEU in refining the intersection between company law disclosure requirements and data protection under the GDPR. By firmly rejecting presumed consent as incompatible with GDPR principles, the Court reaffirms the strict conditions necessary for valid consent: it must always be explicit, informed, and freely given. This sets clear limits for national legislators and public authorities, ensuring that commercial transparency cannot override fundamental data protection rights by means of legal presumptions.

44 Moreover, the judgment reinforces the expansive interpretation of 'personal data', explicitly confirming that even handwritten signatures constitute identifiable personal information under art 4(1) GDPR. By doing so, the Court strengthens individual rights, obliging controllers – particularly public registers – to exercise heightened diligence and implement safeguards to prevent unauthorised or unnecessary disclosure of personal data, even in routine administrative contexts.

45 Most notably, the Court's analysis of liability under art 82 GDPR maintains its consistent protection of data subjects, emphasising that a temporary loss of control over personal data made publicly accessible is itself compensable damage, provided actual harm is demonstrable.

5. CJEU 4 October 2024 – C-507/23, *A v Patērētāju tiesību aizsardzības centrs,* ECLI:EU:C:2024:854

a) Brief Summary of the Facts

The claimant, a journalist well-known in Latvia for his expertise in the automotive sector, initiated legal proceedings against the defendant Consumer Rights Protection Centre (*Patērētāju tiesību aizsardzības centrs*, PTAC). The claimant alleged that the defendant unlawfully processed his personal data without consent during an awareness campaign intended to inform consumers about the risks associated with purchasing second-hand vehicles. Specifically, PTAC produced and widely disseminated a video online, which featured a character clearly imitating the claimant, despite his explicit objection to both the production and publication of this video. 46

After the claimant's repeated demands for the removal of the video and for compensation due to reputational harm were rejected by the defendant, he pursued judicial remedies. Before the Latvian courts, the claimant sought an official declaration that PTAC's processing of his personal data had violated the GDPR, as well as compensation for non-material damage consisting of both a public apology and monetary damages amounting to € 2,000. 47

The instance court partially granted the claimant's request, ordering PTAC to cease distribution of the video, to issue a public apology, and to pay € 100 as compensation for non-material harm. Upon appeal, the Regional Administrative Court upheld the decision that PTAC had indeed infringed the GDPR but dismissed the claimant's monetary compensation claim entirely. The appellate court reasoned that the infringement lacked sufficient seriousness, as PTAC's motivation was to perform a public-interest task rather than harm the claimant's reputation, honour, or dignity. Additionally, the court acknowledged that PTAC's infringement arose from misinterpreting statutory provisions of complex nature. 48

The claimant subsequently appealed to the Latvian Supreme Court and argued that the appellate court had erred by refusing financial compensation and had wrongly assessed the seriousness of the GDPR infringement and its impact. Moreover, he contended that an apology alone did not constitute fair and adequate compensation under art 82(1) GDPR. 49

Faced with these issues, the Latvian Supreme Court stayed the proceedings and referred to the CJEU whether the infringement of GDPR provisions alone constitutes compensable damage within the meaning of art 82(1); whether an apology could constitute sufficient compensation for non-material damage under the GDPR, particularly where restoration to the original state is impossible; and whether factors such as the defendant's public-interest motive, absence of intent 50 to cause harm, or complexity of the relevant legislation could justify setting compensation below the actual damage sustained by the claimant.

b) Judgment of the Court

51 The Court expanded that art 82(1) GDPR does not preclude forms of compensation other than monetary payment, explicitly holding that an apology can constitute sufficient compensation for non-material damage under the GDPR, particularly in circumstances where restoration to the original state is impossible. It highlighted that the GDPR does not itself prescribe the form of compensation, instead leaving such determination to Member States' procedural autonomy, provided national courts comply with the principles of equivalence and effectiveness under EU law. The national courts must therefore assess individually whether an apology genuinely provides full and effective redress for the damage actually suffered (paras 30–37 and operative part 2).

52 Finally, the Court held that art 82(1) GDPR precludes national courts from reducing compensation below the actual damage suffered by the claimant on the basis of factors such as the defendant's public-interest motive, absence of intent to cause harm, or complexity of the relevant legislation. The Court explicitly distinguished the purely compensatory nature of art 82(1) from the punitive objectives underlying art 83 GDPR, which permits consideration of aggravating or mitigating factors. Given that art 82(1) GDPR exclusively aims to ensure full compensation, it would contradict this compensatory objective to allow a reduction of compensation on grounds related to the defendant's attitude or motivation (paras 38–45 and operative part 3).

c) Commentary

53 The judgment addresses the important practical question of adequate forms of redress for non-material harm, affirming that non-financial remedies – specifically, apologies – can constitute sufficient compensation, provided such remedies fully compensate the claimant for the actual harm suffered. The Court emphasises the principle of procedural autonomy of Member States in deciding the specific form of compensation, subject to ensuring the effectiveness and equivalence of EU law. Thus, national courts are tasked with carefully evaluating whether an apology genuinely offers complete and effective satisfaction for non-material harm in each individual case. This approach provides valuable flexibility but simultaneously imposes significant responsibility on national judges, whose assessment

must remain aligned with GDPR's overarching goal of effective protection of personal data.

Significantly, the Court rejects the notion that a controller's motivation or subjective factors – such as good intentions, public-interest objectives, or complexity of legislation – can mitigate liability by reducing the compensation owed to below the actual damage. The Court stresses that the compensatory purpose of art 82(1) GDPR strictly limits the criteria applicable to determining compensation, distinguishing it clearly from art 83 GDPR, which explicitly allows subjective factors to influence administrative fines. 54

6. CJEU 19 December 2024 – C-65/23, *MK v K GmbH,* ECLI:EU:C:2024:1051

a) Brief Summary of the Facts

The claimant is employed by the defendant, a company governed by German law, 55 and serves as chairman of its works council. Initially, the defendant processed certain personal data of its employees, including the claimant, using SAP software, and had entered into multiple works agreements governing this data processing.

In 2017, the defendant's parent group introduced a new cloud-based human 56 resources software, 'Workday' across all its subsidiaries. Consequently, the defendant transferred various employee personal data, including those of the claimant, from the SAP system to servers belonging to the parent company located in the United States. This transfer of data was initially governed by a works agreement concluded in 2017, which explicitly prohibited the use of Workday for human resources management purposes, such as employee appraisals, during its test phase. This agreement specified a limited set of permissible personal data for transfer. Its provisions remained effective until replaced by a final works agreement concluded in 2019.

The claimant brought proceedings before the German labour courts, alleging 57 that the defendant had unlawfully processed personal data exceeding the categories explicitly permitted by the works agreement, including private contact details, contractual and remuneration details, tax and national insurance numbers, nationality, and marital status. Following partial dismissals by the lower courts, the claimant lodged an appeal on a point of law with the German Federal Labour Court. Only the claimant's demand for compensation for non-material damage due to allegedly unlawful processing under the GDPR remained pending.

In this context, the Federal Labour Court referred several questions to the 58 Court of Justice of the European Union. Specifically, it asked whether national provisions adopted pursuant to art 88(1) GDPR concerning personal data processing in employment relationships must comply not only with art 88(2) but also with general GDPR requirements under arts 5, 6(1), and 9(1) and (2); whether parties to a collective agreement (such as the defendant's works agreement) enjoy a margin of discretion in determining the 'necessity' of data processing subject only to limited judicial review; and, if so, what the scope of such judicial review should be. Additional questions concerning the right to compensation under art 82(1) GDPR were initially submitted but subsequently withdrawn (paras 13–26).

b) Judgment of the Court

59 The Court held that art 88(1) and (2) GDPR must be interpreted as meaning that national provisions adopted under art 88(1) GDPR concerning the processing of personal data within employment relationships must ensure compliance not only with the specific conditions set out in art 88(2) GDPR, but also with the general requirements established by arts 5, 6(1), and 9(1) and (2) GDPR. The Court explicitly clarified that the introduction of 'more specific rules' under art 88 GDPR by national law or collective agreements (including works agreements) cannot derogate from these fundamental GDPR principles. Particularly, the Court emphasised that compliance with the necessity criterion laid down by these articles remains mandatory, irrespective of any national specific provisions or agreements concluded between employer and employee representatives (paras 34–43 and operative part 1).

60 Further, the Court stated that the margin of discretion enjoyed by the parties to a collective agreement (such as a works agreement), permitted by art 88(1) GDPR, does not restrict the national courts from performing a full judicial review concerning whether the data processing at issue is genuinely necessary within the meaning of arts 5, 6(1), and 9(1) and (2) GDPR. While acknowledging that the parties involved in collective agreements typically have specialised knowledge and insight into operational and practical requirements of employment relationships, the Court emphasised that their decisions must still strictly comply with GDPR principles. Thus, judicial review must fully evaluate whether the parties' assessment of necessity is correct, without being limited by considerations of economic or practical convenience (paras 51–60 and operative part 2).

61 Consequently, given the comprehensive scope of judicial review affirmed in its response to the preceding question, the Court deemed it unnecessary to address the referring court's subsequent query regarding specific limits to such review (para 24).

c) Commentary

This judgment makes a valuable contribution to clarifying the interplay between art 88 GDPR and other key provisions of the Regulation, particularly emphasising the boundaries within which Member States and social partners may establish 'more specific rules' for processing employees' personal data. The Court explicitly confirms that these more specific rules, whether introduced by national legislation or collective agreements such as works agreements, must always comply not only with the procedural safeguards laid down in art 88(2) GDPR but also with the foundational principles outlined in arts 5 (data minimisation, purpose limitation), 6(1) (lawfulness of processing), and 9(1) and (2) (processing special categories of personal data). This ruling underscores that any national or collectively negotiated provisions cannot undermine fundamental GDPR standards, effectively restricting Member States' discretion. 62

The practical implication of this finding is substantial, particularly in employment contexts, where collective agreements are common instruments to regulate workplace practices. The judgment makes clear that although art 88 GDPR explicitly accommodates collective bargaining, this does not grant collective parties a carte blanche to deviate from GDPR's general principles such as necessity, data minimisation, and the prohibition of processing special categories of data without proper justification. This highlights the necessity for careful scrutiny by negotiating parties when drafting collective agreements to ensure that such provisions do not conflict with GDPR standards, especially concerning the transfer and use of sensitive personal data, as illustrated in this case. 63

Moreover, the Court reinforces the role and responsibility of national courts, explicitly clarifying that they must exercise full judicial review of the necessity of processing stipulated by collective agreements. The Court explicitly rejects the idea that parties to a collective agreement could benefit from a limited judicial oversight justified by their proximity to practical or economic workplace considerations. Such a thorough judicial oversight requirement ensures GDPR compliance is rigorously enforced in practice and that fundamental rights and freedoms of employees are not compromised by pragmatic or economic trade-offs negotiated between employers and employee representatives. Consequently, national courts must thoroughly examine the factual and legal justification for data processing outlined in collective agreements, disregarding any elements of such agreements found incompatible with GDPR obligations. 64

Thus, controllers – in particular employers using personal data processing based on collective agreements – must take proactive steps to document and justify the necessity of all employee-data processing operations, mindful of potential judicial scrutiny and the overarching GDPR compliance framework. This ruling, 65 therefore, reinforces the critical intersection between labour law and data protection law, highlighting a heightened scrutiny standard that both employers and employee representatives must observe when negotiating workplace data practices.

C. Other Cases

1. CJEU 11 January 2024 – C-122/22 P, *Dyson Ltd v European Commission*, ECLI:EU:C:2024:11

a) Brief Summary of the Facts

66 The claimant, Dyson Ltd, a manufacturer of household appliances, particularly vacuum cleaners, sought damages under art 340 Treaty on the Functioning of the European Union (TFEU). The basis of the claim was the Commission's alleged wrongful adoption of Delegated Regulation (EU) No 665/2013[10], which supplemented Directive 2010/30/EU regarding energy labelling requirements for vacuum cleaners. Dyson argued that the regulation had placed its bagless vacuum cleaners at an unfair disadvantage, resulting in economic damage.

67 Specifically, Dyson argued that the Regulation's energy performance testing method was misleading and inadequate, as it tested vacuum cleaners only with empty bags, thus favouring traditional vacuum cleaners over bagless vacuum cleaners like those produced by Dyson. Dyson contended that this misleading approach harmed its commercial interests by inaccurately representing product performance, causing financial and reputational damage.

68 The General Court dismissed Dyson's action for damages.[11] Dyson subsequently lodged an appeal before the Court of Justice, maintaining that the General Court had erred in law in interpreting the conditions necessary to establish the non-contractual liability of the European Union under art 340 TFEU, particularly regarding the existence of a sufficiently serious breach and causation.

10 Delegated Regulation (EU) No 665/2013 of 3 May 2013 supplementing Directive 2010/30/EU of the European Parliament and of the Council with regard to energy labelling of vacuum cleaners [2013] OJ L 192/1.

11 CJEU 8.12.2021, T-127/19, *Dyson and Others v Commission*, ECLI:EU:T:2021:870.

b) Judgment of the Court

The CJEU dismissed Dyson's appeal against the General Court's earlier dismissal of its action for damages. 69

The Court reaffirmed that, under settled EU law, non-contractual liability of the Union pursuant to art 340 TFEU arises only where three cumulative conditions are satisfied: the existence of a sufficiently serious breach of a rule of law intended to confer rights on individuals, actual damage, and a direct causal link between the breach and the damage suffered (paras 52–54). 70

Specifically, the Court held that Dyson failed to demonstrate that the Commission had manifestly and gravely disregarded the limits on its discretion when adopting Delegated Regulation (EU) No 665/2013. The choice of testing methods adopted by the Commission fell within a broad discretion area afforded to the institution, particularly concerning complex economic and technical assessments (paras 72–74). 71

Moreover, the Court found Dyson had not sufficiently substantiated a direct causal link between the Commission's conduct and the alleged financial and reputational damage. In particular, the Court emphasised that Dyson had not adequately demonstrated that the alleged misleading representation of energy efficiency on labels directly led to identifiable economic harm to Dyson's market position or brand reputation (paras 65–69). 72

Consequently, the Court confirmed the General Court's finding that the conditions for non-contractual liability under art 340 TFEU had not been satisfied, and thus Dyson's appeal was dismissed in its entirety (para 73). 73

c) Commentary

The judgment provides valuable clarification regarding the stringent conditions applicable to the EU's non-contractual liability under art 340 TFEU, reaffirming that the threshold remains notably high for claimants. Consistent with established jurisprudence, the Court underlines the cumulative conditions required: the existence of a sufficiently serious breach of a rule of law intended to confer rights on individuals, actual damage, and a direct causal link between the breach and damage suffered. In dismissing Dyson's appeal, the Court emphasises the discretionary scope available to the Commission, especially concerning technically or economically complex policy choices. 74

Notably, the Court provides clarity on the standard necessary to establish a 'sufficiently serious breach', reiterating that only a manifest and grave disregard of the limits placed upon institutional discretion would trigger liability. Here, 75

Dyson failed precisely on this critical condition. The contested choice by the Commission to test vacuum cleaners with empty dust containers, although disadvantageous to bagless technologies, did not constitute a clear excess of the Commission's discretionary powers, given that regulatory choices involving highly technical assessments are subject to limited judicial review.

76 Equally significant, the judgment highlights the evidentiary threshold required to substantiate claims of damage and causation in non-contractual liability actions against EU institutions. Dyson did not adequately establish how the allegedly flawed testing methodology directly caused measurable economic harm or loss of reputation. The judgment thus underscores the importance for claimants of clearly substantiating the direct and concrete effects resulting from an alleged infringement. General assertions concerning damage or abstract allegations of market disadvantage remain insufficient.

77 From a practical perspective, this ruling clarifies that claimants seeking damages from EU institutions must navigate stringent judicial scrutiny, particularly where the contested measures involve complex technical and regulatory considerations. The judgment signals caution for businesses contemplating damages claims under art 340 TFEU, reinforcing the principle that the EU judiciary will intervene only in instances of manifest and grave misconduct by Union institutions. Consequently, businesses operating within heavily regulated markets should anticipate limited scope for success when challenging regulatory measures through claims based on non-contractual liability, absent clear evidence of manifest error or serious misconduct.

2. CJEU 11 January 2024 – C-473/22, *Mylan AB v Gilead Sciences,* ECLI:EU:C:2024:8

a) Brief Summary of the Facts

78 The dispute in the main proceedings arose from provisional measures granted at the request of Gilead Sciences Finland Oy, Gilead Biopharmaceutics Ireland UC, and Gilead Sciences Inc. against Mylan AB.

79 The case related to a supplementary protection certificate (SPC) issued by the Finnish Patent and Registration Office, based on a European Patent held by Gilead, covering the antiretroviral medicinal product 'Tenofovir disoproxil' in combination with 'emtricitabine', indicated for treating HIV infection. In early 2017, Mylan successfully tendered to supply Finnish health districts with a generic version of this medicinal product. Gilead subsequently initiated infringement proceedings in Finland, alleging violation of their SPC rights. Concurrently, Gilead re-

quested provisional measures to stop Mylan from marketing, importing, manufacturing, or otherwise handling the generic medicine, pending final judgment.

The Finnish Market Court (*Markkinaoikeus*) granted these provisional measures in December 2017, imposing significant restrictions on Mylan, subject to a fine of € 500,000 in case of non-compliance. However, upon Mylan's challenge, the Supreme Court of Finland revoked the provisional measures in April 2019. Subsequently, the Finnish Market Court declared the SPC invalid in September 2019, a decision which became final after the Supreme Court denied Gilead leave to appeal in November 2020. 80

Following the revocation of the provisional measures and the invalidation of the SPC, Mylan initiated proceedings to recover € 2,367,855 in damages from Gilead, relying on Finnish national law, specifically para 11 of ch 7 of the Finnish Code of Judicial Procedure. Under Finnish law, the party obtaining provisional measures is strictly liable to compensate the other party for losses caused if the measures later prove unnecessary or unjustified. Gilead contested this claim, arguing, based on the earlier CJEU judgment in *Bayer Pharma*,[12] that strict liability was incompatible with art 9(7) of Directive 2004/48/EC[13]. 81

In these circumstances, the Finnish court suspended proceedings and referred questions to the CJEU whether art 9(7) of Directive 2004/48 precluded national legislation imposing strict liability on the applicant for provisional measures that subsequently prove unjustified or invalid, or whether liability required proof of fault or abuse of rights. 82

b) Judgment of the Court

The Court held that art 9(7) of Directive 2004/48/EC on the enforcement of intellectual property rights does not preclude national legislation from imposing strict liability on an applicant who obtains provisional measures that are later revoked, lapse, or are otherwise found unjustified, such as where the intellectual property right relied upon (here, an SPC) is subsequently declared invalid (para 51). 83

In reaching this conclusion, the Court emphasised that art 9(7) sets a minimum standard derived from art 50(7) of the TRIPS Agreement,[14] granting Member 84

12 CJEU 12.9.2019, C-688/17, *Bayer Pharma AG v Richter Gedeon Vegyészeti Gyár Nyrt. and Exeltis Magyarország Gyógyszerkereskedelmi Kft*, ECLI:EU:C:2019:722.

13 Directive 2004/48/EC of the European Parliament and of the Council of 29 April 2004 on the enforcement of intellectual property rights [2004] OJ L 157/45.

14 Agreement on Trade-Related Aspects of Intellectual Property Rights (TRIPS Agreement, <https://www.wto.org/english/docs_e/legal_e/31bis_trips_01_e.htm>).

States considerable discretion in choosing between fault-based or strict liability regimes. The Court further clarified that this discretion allows Member States to adopt a strict liability approach, provided courts retain authority to adjust compensation by considering all circumstances of the case, including the conduct of both parties, particularly if the defendant contributed to the injury (paras 36, 40, 43).

85 The Court considered such a strict liability regime proportionate and equitable, reasoning that Directive 2004/48 ensures a balance between effective protection of intellectual property rights and the avoidance of unjustified barriers to legitimate trade. The risk allocation inherent in strict liability was seen as acceptable, as it corresponds to the nature of provisional measures, which may be ordered quickly and without conclusive proof of infringement. Any deterrent effect on right holders seeking provisional protection is mitigated by allowing courts discretion to adjust compensation amounts based on the circumstances of each individual case (paras 44–48).

86 The Court thus confirmed the compatibility of the Finnish strict liability regime with the EU Directive, provided that compensation awards could reflect the nuances of each case and the defendant's potential contribution to their own losses (para 50 f).

c) Commentary

87 The judgment strikes a sound and balanced approach by affirming the compatibility of strict liability regimes for unjustified provisional measures under art 9(7) of Directive 2004/48. Its reasoning is consistent with the protective intent underlying the Enforcement Directive, ensuring both effective provisional protection of intellectual property rights and safeguarding against potential abuses. By explicitly acknowledging national discretion, the Court respects Member States' varied legal traditions and practices, yet clearly delineates the Directive's outer limits to preserve fairness and proportionality.

88 Notably, the judgment clarifies the balance of risks between intellectual property right holders and alleged infringers. By placing the risk of unjustified provisional measures squarely on applicants, the ruling incentivises prudent use of provisional remedies, discouraging overly aggressive litigation tactics. This also aligns with international standards, notably those under the TRIPS Agreement, enhancing legal certainty and predictability across jurisdictions.

89 However, the judgment raises questions concerning potential chilling effects on legitimate rights enforcement actions, as applicants must bear significant economic risks even if acting diligently and in good faith. Nevertheless, the Court ad-

dresses this concern by emphasising that national courts must evaluate all circumstances, particularly the behaviour of both parties, thus allowing flexibility in awarding damages. This pragmatic approach effectively mitigates the harshness inherent in strict liability.

3. CJEU 20 June 2024 – C-236/23, *Matmut v TN, MAAF assurances SA*, ECLI:EU:C:2024:761

a) Brief Summary of the Facts

The dispute arose from a motor vehicle insurance contract concluded between the claimant, *Mutuelle assurance des travailleurs mutualistes* (Matmut), and PQ, the policyholder. At the time of contracting, PQ falsely declared himself as the vehicle's usual driver, whereas the actual regular driver was TN, who had prior convictions for driving under the influence of alcohol. Subsequently, while TN was driving and PQ was travelling as a passenger, the vehicle was involved in a road accident, injuring PQ. 90

Matmut contested liability, claiming the insurance contract was void due to PQ's intentional false declaration regarding the usual driver. French courts initially accepted Matmut's argument and declared the insurance contract void, absolving Matmut of liability. However, the Lyon Court of Appeal subsequently held that, based on EU law, the contract's nullity could not be invoked against PQ in his capacity as a passenger-victim, even though he was the policyholder responsible for the false statement. 91

Upon further appeal, the French *Cour de cassation* referred the issue to the CJEU for clarification. The central legal question was whether Directive 2009/103/EC[15] precluded national legislation from allowing insurers to invoke the nullity of a motor insurance contract against a policyholder-victim who intentionally provided false information at the contract's inception, and whether insurers could subsequently reclaim payments from such a policyholder based on intentional misconduct. 92

15 Directive 2009/103/EC of the European Parliament and of the Council of 16 September 2009 relating to insurance against civil liability in respect of the use of motor vehicles, and the enforcement of the obligation to insure against such liability [2009] OJ L 263/11.

b) Judgment of the Court

93 The Court ruled that arts 3 and 13(1) of Directive 2009/103/EC preclude national legislation from allowing insurers to invoke contract nullity against a passenger-victim who is also the policyholder responsible for making intentional false statements at the time of contract formation, unless an abuse of rights is established (para 66).

94 The Court reiterated that the Directive's principal purpose is to protect accident victims and guarantee compensation regardless of the victim's concurrent status as the policyholder who had made false declarations (paras 36–40, 42, 47).

95 It further emphasised that allowing insurers to reclaim all payments made to such a policyholder-victim due to the initial false declaration would disproportionately infringe upon the Directive's objectives, effectively negating mandatory insurance protection (para 65).

96 However, the Court acknowledged an exception under EU law's general principle prohibiting abuse of rights. The national court must evaluate whether the policyholder's actions deliberately sought unjust benefits through fraudulent means, considering both objective and subjective criteria (paras 50–56, 60 f).

c) Commentary

97 The Court's decision highlights critical tensions between compulsory motor insurance obligations and contractual autonomy, specifically concerning intentional misrepresentations by policyholders. By significantly restricting the insurer's ability to invoke contract nullity against a policyholder-victim, the ruling risks incentivising intentional misstatements, thus imposing undue financial burdens on insurers. The limited exception recognised by the Court – conditional upon proving an 'abuse of rights' – offers insufficient clarity and practical guidance for insurers. Such restrictive interpretation diminishes legal certainty and undermines the deterrent effect of truthful disclosure in insurance relationships, thereby distorting the contractual risk assessment that underpins motor insurance markets.

4. CJEU 20 June 2024 – C-367/23, *EA v Artemis security SAS*, ECLI:EU:C:2024:529

a) Brief Summary of the Facts

The dispute at hand arose between EA, an employee originally assigned day shifts, and Artemis security SAS, his employer, following Artemis' decision to transfer EA to night work without performing the obligatory health assessments required by art 9(1)(a) of Directive 2003/88/EC[16]. EA subsequently brought proceedings before the French labour courts, seeking judicial termination of his employment contract and damages for the alleged infringement of Artemis' statutory obligations regarding health assessments for night workers. 98

Central to the proceedings was EA's argument that the mere infringement of Artemis' obligations under Directive 2003/88 should entitle him automatically to compensation, without the need for him to establish specific harm resulting from that infringement. Artemis contested this, arguing that compensation could only be granted upon proof of actual harm suffered. 99

Consequently, the *Cour de cassation*, uncertain about the conditions for establishing liability under EU law in such circumstances, referred to the CJEU the question of whether art 9(1)(a) of Directive 2003/88/EC precluded national legislation that required the worker to demonstrate specific harm as a condition for compensation arising from the employer's breach of the obligation to carry out regular health assessments of night workers. 100

b) Judgment of the Court

The Court held that art 9(1)(a) of Directive 2003/88 does not preclude national laws which condition the employer's liability for breaches of obligations regarding health assessments of night workers on the requirement that the affected worker must prove actual harm resulting from such breaches (para 43). 101

In arriving at this conclusion, the Court emphasised that Directive 2003/88 does not contain explicit rules governing liability or establishing automatic compensation rights for breaches of its provisions. Rather, Member States retain broad discretion under their procedural autonomy to determine the conditions 102

16 Directive 2003/88/EC of the European Parliament and of the Council of 4 November 2003 concerning certain aspects of the organisation of working time [2003] OJ L 299/9.

governing liability claims, provided they adhere to the principles of equivalence and effectiveness of EU law (paras 26–29).

103 The Court further reasoned that, unlike other provisions of Directive 2003/88 – such as those limiting maximum working hours, whose breach inherently entails harm – the failure to carry out mandated health assessments does not necessarily result in automatic or presumed damage. Any harm arising from such a failure depends significantly on the individual circumstances of the worker concerned. Accordingly, conditioning liability and thus compensation on proof of actual harm aligns with the Directive's objectives, respecting both the proportionality and fairness principles within national compensation systems (paras 39–42).

c) Commentary

104 Although the Court attempts to strike a balanced approach by distinguishing inherently harmful infringements (such as breaches of working-time limits) from violations of preventative obligations (such as the duty to provide health assessments for night workers), the judgment nonetheless leaves critical questions unanswered regarding the precise boundaries of liability under EU law.

105 The judgment suggests a binary approach – automatic liability for certain breaches and conditional liability for others – but fails to provide clear criteria for national courts to apply in borderline cases. While the Court rightly emphasises the preventive nature of health assessments, it does not sufficiently articulate why the omission of preventive measures should categorically differ in terms of inherent harm from breaches of working-time limits. Arguably, preventive measures are integral precisely because night work inherently poses health risks, implying that their omission might also be intrinsically harmful.

106 By not clearly explaining why some breaches per se inherently justify compensation, while others require proof of concrete harm, the judgment may lead to inconsistent interpretations and arbitrary results in national courts. Workers who are unable to clearly demonstrate individual harm might face unjustified obstacles in securing compensation, thus potentially undermining the protective aims of Directive 2003/88.

5. CJEU 4 July 2024 – C-425/22, *MOL v Mercedes-Benz Group AG*, ECLI:EU:C:2024:578

a) Brief Summary of the Facts

The claimant, MOL, a Hungarian parent company, brought an action against the defendant, Mercedes-Benz Group AG, in Hungary. MOL sought compensation for indirect losses allegedly incurred by its foreign subsidiaries due to a cartel involving several European truck manufacturers, including Mercedes-Benz. Between 1997 and 2011, the cartel participants coordinated prices and timelines related to emission technologies for medium and heavy trucks, contrary to art 101 TFEU[17]. MOL claimed damages solely in its own right for the indirect economic harm suffered through these subsidiaries, invoking the theory of economic unity within corporate groups. 107

The Hungarian courts at first instance dismissed MOL's claims, asserting a lack of international jurisdiction. These courts held that the damage in question had not occurred at MOL's registered office in Hungary but at the subsidiaries' respective locations where the trucks had been purchased at cartelised prices. MOL contested this view, arguing that jurisdiction could be founded at its own registered office under art 7(2) of the Brussels Ia Regulation,[18] on the basis that it indirectly suffered losses through its subsidiaries. 108

Faced with this jurisdictional dispute, the Supreme Court of Hungary referred the matter to the CJEU for a preliminary ruling and asked the CJEU to determine whether the concept of the 'place where the harmful event occurred', as stated in art 7(2) Brussels Ia Regulation, could encompass the claimant's registered office in Hungary when damages were claimed solely on behalf of subsidiaries located elsewhere. The central legal question thus focused on whether indirect economic harm sustained by a parent company through subsidiary companies established jurisdiction at the parent company's seat under the Brussels Ia Regulation. 109

b) Judgment of the Court

The CJEU ruled that the place where indirect damage occurred, within the meaning of art 7(2) Brussels Ia Regulation, does not include the seat of the parent com- 110

17 Treaty on the Functioning of the European Union [2012] OJ C 326/1.

18 Regulation (EU) No 1215/2012 of the European Parliament and of the Council of 12 December 2012 on jurisdiction and the recognition and enforcement of judgments in civil and commercial matters (recast) [2012] OJ L 351/1.

pany claiming compensation solely for indirect damage sustained by its subsidiaries (paras 46–49). The Court emphasised that jurisdiction based on the place where the damage occurred requires a direct and foreseeable link between the harmful event and the claimant's economic loss (para 47).

111 Specifically, the Court reasoned that MOL, as a parent company, did not directly purchase trucks at cartelised prices; rather, its subsidiaries were the direct purchasers. Consequently, the alleged damage was primarily sustained at the subsidiaries' locations, not at MOL's seat. Therefore, the parent company's registered office in Hungary could not be regarded as the place where the harmful event occurred within the meaning of art 7(2) Brussels Ia Regulation (para 48 f).

112 Furthermore, the Court rejected MOL's argument based on the theory of 'economic unity', noting that this theory pertains exclusively to determining which entities within a corporate group may be held liable for antitrust infringements. It cannot, however, be invoked to expand jurisdiction in favour of claimants, especially not to establish the claimant's seat as a jurisdictional forum for purely indirect losses sustained by subsidiaries abroad (paras 50–52).

c) Commentary

113 The present judgment deserves approval as it reaffirms established principles on the interpretation of art 7(2) Brussels Ia Regulation. The Court rightly emphasises the importance of clearly delineating the 'place where the harmful event occurred', highlighting that indirect damage sustained by a parent company through foreign subsidiaries does not establish jurisdiction at the parent's seat. This clarification aligns closely with fundamental considerations underpinning EU private international law, notably foreseeability and predictability of jurisdiction, essential to uphold legal certainty.

114 Central to the Court's reasoning is the requirement that jurisdiction at the place where damage occurs must be limited to situations involving direct and foreseeable harm. MOL's attempt to ground jurisdiction at its Hungarian registered office failed because it had not directly participated in the transactions giving rise to the damage. Instead, MOL had only subsequently become the parent of companies that had acquired trucks at cartelised prices. Thus, any damage it suffered was indirect and unforeseeable from the perspective of Mercedes-Benz at the time of the infringement. Jurisdiction under art 7(2) Brussels Ia Regulation cannot extend to damage that is remote, indirect, and not reasonably foreseeable from the perspective of the infringing party.

115 Equally significant is the Court's rejection of MOL's reliance on the theory of 'economic unity'. While this theory legitimately addresses questions of liability

within corporate groups, it cannot extend to determining jurisdiction at the claimant's registered office. Indeed, MOL's reliance on economic unity to support its position appears contradictory. As the theory's sole purpose is to prevent strategic corporate structures that evade liability, it cannot be turned on its head to benefit a claimant seeking to establish jurisdiction at a forum more convenient for itself but disconnected from the direct damage.

Moreover, the ruling aligns with established case law, notably the judgments 116 in *Kronhofer*[19] and *Tibor-Trans*[20], which consistently restrict jurisdiction at the claimant's domicile to situations involving clear, direct economic loss. Although these precedents concerned investor-related damage rather than cartel damage, their logic applies equally here. Extending jurisdiction to indirect damage occurring at the claimant's seat would undermine the essential clarity required in jurisdictional rules, compromising their function of guiding parties in identifying appropriate fora for litigation.

6. CJEU 11 July 2024 – C-632/22, *Volvo AB v Transsaqui SL*, ECLI: EU:C:2024:601

a) Brief Summary of the Facts

The claimant, Transsaqui SL, a Spanish transport company, initiated proceedings 117 against the defendant, Volvo AB, before the Spanish courts. Like the preceding *MOL* decision (no 107 above), this case arose from the European trucks' cartel, in which several truck manufacturers, including Volvo, were involved. Transsaqui sought compensation for losses allegedly incurred due to cartelised pricing practices when purchasing trucks from Volvo.

Volvo challenged the jurisdiction of the Spanish courts, arguing that Trans- 118 saqui had failed to correctly serve judicial documents initiating the proceedings in compliance with Regulation (EC) No 1393/2007[21]. Specifically, Volvo alleged

19 CJEU 10.6.2004, C-168/02, *Kronhofer v Maier et al*, ECLI ECLI:EU:C:2004:364.

20 CJEU 29.7.2019, C-451/18, *Tibor-Trans Fuvarozó és Kereskedelmi Kft v DAF Trucks NV*, ECLI:EU:C:2019:635. On this case, see *BA Koch/T Thiede*, European Union, in: E Karner/BC Steininger (eds), ETL 2019 (2020) 684, no 45 ff.

21 Regulation (EC) No 1393/2007 of the European Parliament and of the Council of 13 November 2007 on the service in the Member States of judicial and extrajudicial documents in civil or commercial matters (service of documents), and repealing Council Regulation (EC) No 1348/2000 [2007] OJ L 324/79.

that procedural requirements governing the cross-border service of documents had been breached, adversely affecting Volvo's right of defence.

119 The key issue submitted to the CJEU concerned whether improper service of judicial documents under Regulation (EC) No 1393/2007 would preclude the Spanish court's jurisdiction under the Brussels Ia Regulation in this cartel damages action.

b) Judgment of the Court

120 The Court held that the improper service of judicial documents under Regulation (EC) No 1393/2007 does not automatically negate the jurisdiction of the court seized under the Brussels Ia Regulation, provided the defendant's rights of defence are not substantially impaired (paras 39–42). It emphasised that while compliance with service requirements is critical to safeguard procedural fairness, minor procedural irregularities do not invalidate jurisdiction if the defendant was able to prepare an adequate defence (para 43).

121 Specifically, the Court noted that Volvo had become aware of the proceedings in sufficient time to effectively organise its defence and respond appropriately. Consequently, the alleged irregularity concerning the service of judicial documents did not, in itself, invalidate the jurisdiction of the Spanish courts under art 7(2) Brussels Ia Regulation (paras 44–46).

c) Commentary

122 The Court's approach reinforces procedural efficiency and fairness in cross-border cartel litigation. By clarifying that minor irregularities in the service of judicial documents under Regulation (EC) No 1393/2007 do not automatically undermine jurisdiction under the Brussels Ia Regulation, the Court ensures that technical procedural deficiencies do not impede substantive claims, provided fundamental rights of defence remain intact. The threshold set – namely, whether the defendant was actually able to prepare its defence – strikes an appropriate balance, protecting defendants from serious procedural prejudice without enabling strategic procedural challenges to frustrate justified claims.

123 This decision importantly refines the interplay between Regulation 1393/2007 and the Brussels Ia Regulation, highlighting that jurisdictional rules serve substantive justice rather than purely procedural formality. Volvo's awareness and ability to effectively defend itself became decisive, rather than strict compliance with procedural technicalities. Thus, the Court affirms the principle that procedural

rules should facilitate, not obstruct, genuine cross-border access to justice in EU competition law damages actions.

7. CJEU 5 September 2024 – C-86/23, *E.N.I., Y.K.I. v HUK-COBURG-Allgemeine Versicherung AG*, ECLI:EU:C:2024:689

a) Brief Summary of the Facts

The Bulgarian parents of a person killed in a road traffic accident in Germany in 2014[22] seek compensation before the Sofia City Court (Bulgaria) for the immaterial harm resulting from losing their child. The person liable for the accident was insured with defendant HUK Coburg. While the first-instance court granted compensation to the claimants, the Bulgarian appellate court dismissed their claims altogether, arguing that the applicable German law at the time[23] only foresaw compensation for (secondary) immaterial harm to surviving relatives if the latter had themselves incurred damage to their psychological health (which had neither been claimed nor proven). The appellate court also refused to apply the more favourable rules of Bulgarian law (allowing compensation on the basis of fairness, irrespective of any pathological harm of the claimants themselves) as 'overriding mandatory provisions' within the meaning of art 16 Rome II.[24] The Bulgarian Supreme Court therefore asked the CJEU whether art 16 Rome II could be applied in the instant case nevertheless. 124

22 The same accident had already triggered a case before the CJEU (concerning the claims of the two surviving children of the direct victim in this case, ie of the grandchildren of the current claimants): CJEU 15.12.2022, C-577/ 21, *LM et NO représentées par CD v HUK-COBURG-Allgemeine Versicherung AG*, ECLI:EU:C:2022:992. On this case, see *BA Koch/T Thiede*, European Union, in: E Karner/BC Steininger (eds), ETL 2022 (2023) 695, no 104 ff.

23 On the new statutory rules on damages for (mere) bereavement in Germany, see *J Fedtke*, Germany, in: E Karner/BC Steininger (eds), ETL 2016 (2017) 214, no 1 ff; *W Wurmnest/M Gömann*, Germany, in: Karner/Steininger (eds), ETL 2017 (2018) 207, no 1 ff.

24 Regulation (EC) No 864/2007 of the European Parliament and of the Council of 11 July 2007 on the law applicable to non-contractual obligations (Rome II) [2007] OJ L 199/40.

b) Judgment of the Court

125 The Court first pointed to the exceptional nature of art 16 Rome II, hence warranting a restrictive interpretation (para 30). If at all, the case would, as a minimum, require 'sufficiently close links with the Member State of the forum'.

126 In the instant case, the applicants were Bulgarian nationals suing before a Bulgarian court, whereas the immediate victim – while also being a Bulgarian national – had taken residence in Germany, which was also the residence of the liable person and of the defendant insurer, as well as the place of the accident.

127 Furthermore, in order to apply art 16 Rome II, the national court must certify 'on the basis of a detailed analysis of the wording, general scheme, objectives and the context in which the national provision concerned was adopted, that it is of such importance in the national legal order that it justifies a departure from the law designated pursuant to art 4 of that regulation' (para 40). The Bulgarian rule, based on the notion of fairness, could override the otherwise applicable German law 'only if its application were justified by particularly important reasons reflecting public interests judged to be essential in the Bulgarian legal order'. While the German law – unlike the Bulgarian rule – required pathological harm to the claimants themselves at the time, both are based on the notion of fairness, albeit leading to substantially different (monetary) outcomes. The latter in and of itself cannot justify the application of art 16 Rome II, however.[25]

c) Commentary

128 The CJEU did not have to give a definitive answer to the question posed and could therefore pass the ball back to the referring court to determine whether the requirements given in this ruling for applying the Bulgarian rules via art 16 Rome II

25 The Court thereby followed the reasoning of Advocate General Szpunar in his opinion on this case, who had argued 'that it goes without saying that the mere fact that, by applying the *lex fori*, there would be a different outcome with regard to the amount of compensation from that which would have been reached by applying the *lex causae* is not sufficient to conclude that the Bulgarian provision at issue may be classified as an "overriding mandatory provision" within the meaning of art 16 of the Rome II Regulation, provided that the application of the *lex causae* is compatible with considerations of justice. In other words, that difference – namely the fact that the amount of compensation for damage suffered by the parents is lower simply because their daughter died in a road traffic accident in Germany and not in Bulgaria – does not allow such a classification to be made unless that difference arises from the protection, in particular, of a fundamental right justifying the application of the *lex fori*.' (no 32).

were actually met in the instant case. Advocate General Szpunar at least seemed to have had doubts in this regard.[26]

It is indeed doubtful whether art 16 Rome II should ever be (ab)used to circumvent the clear and conscious decision of the EU legislator at the time to resolve all aspects of tort law claims (including in particular the determination of the extent of compensation) according to the law identified as applicable under the provisions of this Regulation (see in particular art 15 Rome II). Attempts to apply the laws of the victims to determining the award of damages arising out of an accident otherwise governed by the laws of the place where the accident occurred were rightly rejected by the EU legislator at the time.[27] 129

8. CJEU 4 October 2024 – C-546/22, *GF v Schauinsland-Reisen GmbH*, ECLI:EU:C:2024:847

a) Brief Summary of the Facts

GF booked a package holiday to the Maldives through Schauinsland-Reisen GmbH, scheduled from 26 December 2020. Before departure, the Austrian Ministry of Foreign Affairs issued a high-level travel warning against all non-essential travel to the Maldives due to the COVID-19 pandemic. As a result, Schauinsland-Reisen terminated the package travel contract, refunded GF's deposit, but did not provide additional compensation. 130

GF subsequently sought damages from Schauinsland-Reisen, arguing that the official travel warning did not constitute unavoidable and extraordinary circumstances preventing performance of the trip, as defined by art 12(3)(b) of Directive 2015/2302[28]. GF argued that he and his wife wished to proceed with the holiday despite the official warning, asserting it was objectively possible to perform the trip safely. 131

---

26 'The fact that the case-law of the Bulgarian courts is contradictory, as the referring court notes, leads me, at first sight to doubt the fact that the principle of fairness is a fundamental principle of the Bulgarian legal order. It is nevertheless for that court to verify it.' Opinion of AG Szpunar, no 65.

27 See *BA Koch*, European Union, in: H Koziol/BC Steininger (eds), ETL 2006 (2008) 487, no 4.

28 Directive (EU) 2015/2302 of the European Parliament and of the Council of 25 November 2015 on package travel and linked travel arrangements, amending Regulation (EC) No 2006/2004 and Directive 2011/83/EU of the European Parliament and of the Council and repealing Council Directive 90/314/EEC [2015] OJ L 326/1.

132 The Austrian courts at first instance and on appeal dismissed GF's claim. The Austrian Supreme Court then referred questions to the CJEU, seeking clarification on whether an official travel warning alone could suffice to establish 'unavoidable and extraordinary circumstances', allowing an organiser to terminate a package travel contract without additional compensation, even if travel was not objectively impossible and the traveller expressed willingness to proceed.

b) Judgment of the Court

133 The Court held that art 12(3)(b) of Directive 2015/2302 must be interpreted as meaning that a travel organiser may terminate a package travel contract due to 'unavoidable and extraordinary circumstances', relying upon an official recommendation issued by national authorities advising against travel to the destination concerned, even if the traveller explicitly insists on proceeding with the journey and even though performance of the trip would not have been objectively impossible (para 57).

134 However, the Court emphasised that such an official recommendation does not constitute compelling evidence in itself. National courts must independently assess, based on all relevant circumstances at the time of termination, whether the organiser was genuinely prevented from performing the contract. This evaluation does not require demonstrating absolute impossibility of performance but only that the circumstances cited significantly affect the conditions under which the contract could reasonably be performed, without disproportionate costs to the organiser (paras 33, 36–39, 49–52).

135 Therefore, while an official travel warning holds considerable evidential value, national courts retain the final responsibility to verify whether the organiser's reliance on such a recommendation to justify contract termination was objectively justified under the conditions prevailing at the relevant time (para 56 f).

c) Commentary

136 Although the Court appropriately affirms the relevance of official travel warnings as valuable evidence for travel organisers, it introduces considerable uncertainty by insisting that such warnings do not constitute compelling evidence automatically justifying termination. This judgment places travel organisers in a precarious position, leaving them uncertain as to precisely when reliance on official advice is sufficient. Without more explicit guidelines, organisers may face unpredictable outcomes in litigation and must weigh difficult commercial risks when deciding

whether to terminate contracts, potentially leading to inconsistent practices across the Member States.

Moreover, requiring national courts to evaluate independently whether circumstances significantly affect contractual performance creates additional uncertainty, as it opens the door to subjective and varying interpretations. This uncertainty risks undermining the Directive's objective of providing uniform protection and clear standards for consumers and travel organisers alike. 137

Thus, while intended to balance fairness for both parties, the judgment inadequately addresses the practical consequences of shifting significant assessment burdens onto national courts and commercial actors, potentially compromising the Directive's objectives of uniformity, predictability, and effective consumer protection. 138

9. CJEU 4 October 2024 – C-633/22, *Real Madrid Club de Fútbol, AE v EE, Société Éditrice du Monde SA,* ECLI:EU:C:2024:843

a) Brief Summary of the Facts

In 2006, the French newspaper Le Monde published an article authored by its employee EE, which alleged that the football clubs Real Madrid and Fútbol Club Barcelona had retained the services of a doctor who was suspected of assisting cyclists and other professional athletes with doping. In 2007, Real Madrid and a member of its medical team sued Le Monde and its journalist for compensation of their alleged immaterial harm caused by the infringement of their honour through said article. The claimants were awarded € 300,000 and € 30,000 respectively, which was ultimately confirmed by the Spanish Supreme Court. 139

The claimants subsequently sought enforcement of this ruling against Le Monde and its staff member in France. While the French first-instance court issued two declarations of enforceability to the Spanish judgment, the appellate court overturned this ruling, bringing the matter before the *Cour de cassation.* This court stayed proceedings and asked the CJEU for a preliminary ruling essentially on the question whether enforcement could be denied if it amounted to a violation of French public policy, in particular the freedom of expression guaranteed both by the Charter of Fundamental Rights of the European Union (CFR) and the European Convention for the Protection of Human Rights and Fundamental Freedoms (ECHR). 140

b) Judgment of the Court

141 The Court, in essence, had to examine whether the enforcement of the Spanish award in France falls within the scope of art 34 no 1 of the Brussels I Regulation[29] (now art 45 para 1 lit a Brussels Ia[30]). This provision allows Member States to deny enforcement of judgments of another Member State if they were 'manifestly contrary to public policy in the Member State in which recognition is sought'. The Court acknowledged that this exception must be applied narrowly, and that it does not suffice 'that there is a discrepancy between the legal rule applied by the court of the Member State of origin and that which would have been applied by the court of the Member State in which enforcement is sought' (para 36). Instead, enforcing the foreign ruling must clash with the legal system of the jurisdiction where enforcement is sought 'to an unacceptable degree', which can be given if it amounts to an infringement of fundamental rights, in particular those guaranteed by the CFR and the ECHR (para 40).

142 The Court pointed to art 11 CFR, which guarantees the freedom of expression and information. Its para 2 in particular postulates that '[t]he freedom and pluralism of the media shall be respected'. While this does not amount to an absolute right, allowing certain limitations, these must nevertheless respect 'the essence of those rights and freedoms', considering that they contribute to the 'essential foundations of a pluralist, democratic society' (para 49). Any interpretation of art 11 CFR must also consider 'the corresponding rights guaranteed by art 10 ECHR, as interpreted by the European Court of Human Rights, as the minimum threshold of protection' (para 52). Particularly when it comes to the freedom of the press, their 'vital role of "public watchdog"' must be preserved (para 55), leaving 'little scope for restrictions on freedom of expression in the fields of political speech and matters of public interest' (para 53), to which professional sports belong.

143 While the Court conceded that victims of defamatory statements should be able to seek compensation, 'any judgment awarding damages for harm to reputation must comprise a reasonable relationship of proportionality between the amount awarded and the harm in question' (para 57). Large awards would have a 'chilling effect on the exercise of the freedom of the press' (para 62). 'Such a deterrent effect may even result from an award of a relatively modest

29 Council Regulation (EC) No 44/2001 of 22 December2000 on jurisdiction and the recognition and enforcement of judgments in civil and commercial matters [2001] OJ L 12/1.

30 Regulation (EU) No 1215/2012 of the European Parliament and of the Council of 12 December 2012 on jurisdiction and the recognition and enforcement of judgments in civil and commercial matters (recast) [2012] OJ L 351/1.

amount, in the light of the standards applied in comparable defamation cases.' (para 64).

c) Commentary

While the Court could obviously not render a final decision in the matter referred 144
to it, it is clear from the tone and overall wording that it considered the Spanish awards in violation of the freedoms of the press guaranteed by the CFR and the ECHR. The Court thereby set an important marker when it comes to determining the boundaries of the principle of full compensation of victims, on the one hand, and fundamental freedoms of those causing the harm for which such compensation is sought, on the other.

10. CJEU 4 October 2024 – C-650/22, *FIFA v BZ*, ECLI:EU:C:2024:824

a) Brief Summary of the Facts

The case concerns a claim for damages brought by BZ, a professional football play- 145
er, against FIFA arising from alleged harm caused by FIFA regulations purportedly incompatible with EU law. Following termination of his employment contract with his previous club, Lokomotiv Moscow, BZ sought to enter into an employment relationship with Sporting du Pays de Charleroi, a Belgian football club. However, FIFA regulations – specifically art 17 of its Regulations on the Status and Transfer of Players (RSTP) – imposed joint and several liability on any new club employing a player who had terminated his previous contract without just cause. FIFA regulations also presumed that the new club induced the player's breach and, as a result, refused to issue the necessary International Transfer Certificate (ITC) to enable the player to register with the new club until compensation issues were resolved.

Due to these restrictions, BZ alleged that he suffered significant financial and 146
professional harm, being unable to secure new employment promptly. Consequently, BZ initiated civil proceedings in Belgium against FIFA, seeking damages for infringement of his freedom of movement under art 45 TFEU and for breach of EU competition rules under art 101 TFEU. The national court referred questions to the CJEU, specifically asking whether FIFA's regulatory framework imposing joint liability and restrictions on player transfers violates EU provisions protecting the free movement of workers and prohibiting restrictive practices under compe-

tition law, thus potentially giving rise to civil liability and damages claims under EU law.

147 BZ initiated proceedings before the Belgian courts, claiming damages from FIFA and the URBSFA for the harm allegedly suffered due to these restrictions, arguing that the FIFA rules breached arts 45 and 101 TFEU by restricting his freedom of movement as a worker and competition between football clubs.

148 The Belgian courts declared themselves competent and found his claims prima facie valid, prompting FIFA's appeal and the referral to the CJEU seeking clarification on whether arts 45 and 101 TFEU preclude FIFA's rules regarding joint liability, presumption of inducement, and restrictions on player registrations under the ITC regime.

b) Judgment of the Court

149 The Court held that arts 45 and 101 TFEU must be interpreted as precluding rules adopted by sports associations – such as FIFA's regulations imposing joint and several liability on a player's new club for compensation owed to a former club due to a contract breach presumed induced by the new club – if those rules disproportionately restrict a player's freedom of movement and competition between clubs (paras 61–63, 76).

150 Addressing the liability issue specifically, the Court emphasised that individuals harmed by infringements of directly applicable EU Treaty provisions, such as art 45 TFEU on the free movement of workers or art 101 TFEU on competition, are entitled to seek compensation for damage from entities responsible for such breaches under conditions provided by national law, subject to the principles of equivalence and effectiveness (paras 81–83). The Court clarified that if FIFA's regulations indeed infringe arts 45 and 101 TFEU, this infringement may give rise to civil liability claims against FIFA, provided that the conditions for liability under national law – interpreted consistently with EU law principles of equivalence and effectiveness – are met (para 84 f).

151 Thus, while leaving it ultimately to national courts to determine the existence and extent of damage and causal connection, the Court clearly opened the door for affected players to seek compensation from sports governing bodies for harm resulting from rules incompatible with fundamental freedoms guaranteed by EU law, reinforcing the direct horizontal enforceability of Treaty rights (para 86 f).

c) Commentary

The judgment builds significantly upon the Court's prior landmark decisions in football-related cases, particularly *Bosman* (C-415/93) and *Bernard* (C-325/08), by explicitly extending the principles established in these cases into the domain of civil liability. While *Bosman* and *Bernard* clarified substantive issues regarding freedom of movement restrictions in football, the present ruling explicitly highlights the conditions under which such infringements of arts 45 and 101 TFEU may give rise to actionable civil liability claims against governing bodies like FIFA. 152

This explicit recognition of potential liability broadens the practical impact of fundamental freedoms and competition law within professional sport, making sports federations directly accountable for harm caused by rules incompatible with EU law. The judgment notably emphasises the necessity for national courts to ensure that claims remain practically effective and accessible, aligning with the principles of equivalence and effectiveness central to EU law. 153

11. CJEU 19 December 2024 – C-157/23, *Ford Italia SpA v ZP, Stracciari SpA*, ECLI:EU:C:2024:1045

a) Brief Summary of the Facts

On 4 July 2001, ZP purchased a Ford vehicle from Stracciari, an Italian car dealership. The vehicle was manufactured by Ford-Werke AG (Ford WAG), a German manufacturer, and distributed in Italy by Ford Italia SpA (Ford Italia), both entities being part of the Ford corporate group. On 27 December 2001, ZP was involved in a traffic accident in which an airbag installed in the vehicle failed to deploy, allegedly due to a defect. Consequently, ZP initiated legal proceedings before the *Tribunale di Bologna* against Ford Italia and Stracciari, seeking compensation under Italian legislation transposing Directive 85/374/EEC[31]. 154

Ford Italia argued that it was merely a supplier, not the actual manufacturer, since the vehicle had been produced by Ford WAG. It asserted that it could not be considered a 'producer' under art 3(1) of Directive 85/374/EEC, as it had not physically affixed its name or trademark to the vehicle – rather, these had been affixed by Ford WAG. The Italian courts initially rejected Ford Italia's argument, concluding that Ford Italia was liable as a supplier who had effectively presented itself as 155

31 See fn 2.

a producer due to the partial identity between its corporate name and the manufacturer's trade mark placed on the vehicle.

156 Upon appeal, the Italian *Corte Suprema di Cassazione* referred the issue to the CJEU, asking whether art 3(1) of Directive 85/374/EEC must be interpreted as including, under the concept of 'producer', a supplier whose name partially matches both the manufacturer's name and the trade mark affixed to the product, even though the supplier itself did not physically place its name or mark on the product.

b) Judgment of the Court

157 The Court ruled that art 3(1) of Directive 85/374/EEC must be interpreted as meaning that a supplier of a defective product qualifies as a 'producer' if the supplier's name or a distinctive element thereof is identical to the trade mark or name placed on the product by the actual manufacturer, even if the supplier has not actively placed that mark or name on the product (para 49).

158 The Court emphasised that Directive 85/374 seeks comprehensive harmonisation regarding liability for defective products, aiming to provide strong consumer protection. Thus, it extends liability not only to the actual manufacturer but also to any party presenting itself as the producer by placing or associating its name, trade mark, or distinguishing feature with the product, irrespective of whether the supplier physically placed such markings on the product itself (paras 30–34, 40 f).

159 Accordingly, the Court found that in circumstances where the product bears a trade mark identical or very similar to the supplier's name, thereby creating the reasonable impression that the supplier is closely associated with, or responsible for, the production, the supplier must be regarded as a 'producer' within the meaning of art 3(1) of Directive 85/374. This interpretation ensures that the consumer's right to compensation is effectively safeguarded by making liability jointly and severally applicable to all identifiable parties who present themselves as producers, thus facilitating the consumer's access to redress (paras 43–48).

c) Commentary

160 The judgment provides a clear and justified application of art 3(1) of Directive 85/374/EEC, reinforcing consumer protection without unnecessarily broadening the scope of liability. By treating a supplier whose corporate identity overlaps significantly with that of the manufacturer as a 'producer', the Court correctly ad-

dresses situations in which corporate structures could obscure responsibility. In substance, the judgment is merely piercing the corporate veil, clarifying that suppliers closely associated by branding or corporate identity with manufacturers cannot escape liability simply due to formal separation. This approach maintains the Directive's objective to ensure that consumers have direct and effective access to remedies without artificially expanding the scope of liability or burdening unrelated suppliers.

Ronen Perry

XXXII. Israel

A. Legislation

1. Compensation to Victims of Terror Act (Exemplary Damages) 2024 Sefer HaHukim (SH) 594

Under Israeli law, individuals affected by acts of terror, and their families in cases of fatality, have two primary options for seeking redress. Firstly, they may receive certain benefits from the State under secs 4 and 7 of the Benefits to Victims of Hostile Actions Act,[1] which is administered by the National Insurance Institute. Alternatively, they may file tort claims against the perpetrators and their aides. Historically, victims had to choose between these two legal routes – pursuing tort claims against responsible parties or seeking benefits from the State.[2] Opting for the latter might weaken the deterrent effect of tort liability, to the extent that liability can truly deter terrorist activities. 1

In the 2022 case of *John Doe v The Palestinian Authority*,[3] the Supreme Court held that by offering special rewards (allowances and grants) to Palestinians convicted of security offences in Israel and to families of terrorists killed in action, the Palestinian Authority 'ratified' these acts. As a result, it was liable in torts under sec 12 of the Civil Wrongs Ordinance (CWO) as a 'ratifier.'[4] However, the Court determined by a 2:1 majority that punitive damages could not be imposed on entities liable solely as 'ratifiers.' The reason was that two exceptional doctrines, deviating from general tort principles, should not be combined. Liability for ratification is deemed an exception because there can be no causal link between the ratification, which applies to past conduct, and either the wrongdoer's conduct or the victim's harm. Similarly, punitive damages are an exception to the 2

1 1970 Sefer Hahukim (SH) 126.

2 Benefits to Victims of Hostile Actions Act, 1970 SH 126, § 17(b). But see below no 4, Section A.2 (discussing Amendment No 43).

3 Civ App 2362/19 *John Doe v The Palestinian Authority* (Supreme Court, 10.4.2022), reported in *R Perry*, Israel, in: E Karner/BC Steininger (eds), European Tort Law (ETL) 2022 (2023) 729, nos 9–20.

4 1968 Nosah Hadash (NH) 266.

https://doi.org/10.1515/9783111389271-033

general principles because they do not aim to restore the plaintiff to the state they would have been in but for the defendant's misconduct.[5]

3 In 2023, before the Israel-Hamas war, the Knesset proposed to change this reality through the Compensation to Victims of Terror Bill (Exemplary Damages).[6] The proposal passed the second and third readings in 2024 and is now in force.[7] The Act provides that if a person is killed by a terrorist act, the court shall award the estate NIS 10 million (approx € 2.5 million) in punitive damages against the perpetrators, any entities that reward the perpetrators or their beneficiaries, and any entities liable under secs 12–14 of the CWO (whether directly like ratifiers or vicariously like employers and principals).[8] If a person is injured by a terrorist act, the court shall award NIS 5 million in punitive damages against the same parties.[9] Moreover, a person claiming punitive damages under the Act is not required to give up the statutory State benefits under the Benefits to Victims of Hostile Actions Act.[10] If the direct victim or the relatives obtain State benefits, the punitive award is not deducted therefrom.[11] The Act also enables the victim (or the estate in the case of death) to obtain the award from a defendant's assets seized or frozen by the State.[12]

2. Benefits to Victims of Hostile Actions Act (Amendment No 43) 2024 SH 738

4 The Benefits to Victims of Hostile Actions (Amendment No 43) allows victims of terror to receive partial tort damages in addition to statutory State benefits. Recall that, historically, victims of terror and their families had to choose between tort damages and State benefits. The Amendment added sec 17(b1) to the main Act, allowing victims of terror or their families, who are entitled to statutory State benefits, to also bring an action in torts against the perpetrators of the hostile action, the entities that reward the perpetrators, and any entities liable under secs 12–14 of the CWO. In such a case, the claimants can recover tort damages in the amount of *either* the difference between full compensatory tort damages and the capi-

5 *R Perry*, It's a Wonderful Life, 93 Cornell Law Review 329, 381 (2008).
6 2023 Hazaot Hok (HH) 142.
7 2024 SH 594.
8 Ibid § 2(a).
9 Ibid § 2(b).
10 Ibid § 3.
11 Ibid § 2(c).
12 Ibid § 2(d).

talised value of the statutory State benefits *or* 25 % of full compensatory tort damages, whichever is greater. The State can then claim reimbursement for the capitalised value of the statutory benefits from those liable in torts (up to their liability minus the amount paid to the victims). In addition, the amendment reiterates that the victim (or the estate) can recover punitive damages in a tort action.[13]

3. Aviation Services Bill (Compensation and Assistance Following the Cancellation of a Flight or a Change in its Conditions) (Amendment No 3 and a Temporary Provision – Iron Swords) 2024 Hazaot Hok (HH) 1008

Prior to the enactment (in 2012) of the Aviation Services Act (Compensation and 5
Assistance Following the Cancellation of a Flight or a Change in its Conditions),[14] Israeli law did not provide a satisfactory solution for harms caused to passengers who were prevented, without their fault, from flying in accordance with the terms of their tickets. The Act was inspired by, and in many respects followed, the European Air Passengers Rights Regulation (Regulation (EC) No 261/2004), which established common European rules on compensation and assistance to airline passengers in cases of denied boarding, flight cancellations, and delays.[15]

A passenger for whom an airline ticket was issued, and who arrived on time 6
for check-in at the airport (unless the flight was cancelled), is entitled to various benefits in five cases: (1) If the flight operator refuses to carry the passenger, inter alia on account of overbooking, then the passenger is entitled to 'assistance' and compensation, in addition to a refund of the ticket's value or an alternative ticket, unless security, health or flight safety issues or inadequate travel documentation justify such refusal.[16] (2) If the flight is cancelled (or delayed for more than eight hours), the passenger is similarly entitled to 'assistance' and compensation in addition to a refund or an alternative ticket.[17] (3) If a flight is delayed for two hours or more, the passenger is entitled to food and beverages, and communication services; if the flight is delayed for five to eight hours, the passenger is entitled, in addition, to a refund or an alternative ticket.[18] (4) If the flight departs more

13 Benefits to Victims of Hostile Actions Act § 17(b2).
14 2012 SH 414.
15 2011 HH 6, 7.
16 Aviation Services Act (fn 14) § 5.
17 Ibid § 6.
18 Ibid § 7.

than eight hours earlier than planned, the passenger is entitled to compensation, in addition to a refund or an alternative ticket.[19] (5) If the passenger is downgraded to a cheaper cabin, he or she is entitled to compensation.[20]

7 'Assistance' may include complimentary food and beverages, communication services, and, if necessary, accommodation and transportation to and from the airport.[21] 'Compensation' is determined based on flight distance. For all cases but downgrades, the award is fixed, based on the flight's distance: NIS 1,250 (approx € 310) for flights up to 2,000 kilometres, NIS 2,000 for flights up to 4,500 kilometres, and NIS 3,000 for longer distances.[22] In cases of refusal to carry or flight cancellation, compensation may be reduced if the passenger accepts an alternative ticket and the delay is not substantial.[23] In cases of downgrade, the passenger is entitled to compensation in the amount of 60 % of the ticket price if downgraded from first to business class, 80 % if downgraded from business class to coach, 90 % if downgraded from first class to coach, and 100 % for any downgrade to coach in flight distances greater than 4,500 kilometres.[24] If a flight operator knowingly refrains from conferring the above benefits on an entitled passenger, the court may award up to NIS 10,000 without proof of harm, in addition to the benefits themselves.[25] This Act applies without prejudice to a passenger's rights to further compensation,[26] although it excludes liability if the passenger has already obtained similar benefits under foreign law.[27]

8 The Covid-19 pandemic, and to an even greater extent the Israel-Hamas war (which started in October 2023), had a considerable impact on the aviation market, with airlines cancelling or reducing service to and from Israel. Many airlines withheld flights for long periods of time, fearing inter alia that the need to cancel flights on short notice due to special circumstances would give rise to obligations under the Act. The reduced supply has led to an intolerable spike in airfare, and the government has considered various steps to bring back foreign airlines and increase supply. One of the major steps was the proposed amendment to the Aviation Services Act, aimed at reducing the burden borne by airlines in cases of

19 Ibid § 8.
20 Ibid § 9.
21 Ibid § 3.
22 Ibid Appendix 1.
23 Ibid § 5 f.
24 Ibid Appendix 2.
25 Ibid § 11.
26 Ibid § 16.
27 Ibid § 20.

flight cancellations and delays. The Bill, introduced in 2024, proposed three key changes, of which only two passed the second and third readings in 2025.[28]

First, under sec 6(e)(1) of the main Act, the operator is not obliged to pay compensation when a flight is cancelled under extraordinary circumstances beyond its control if it could not have prevented the cancellation by doing everything in its power. The Bill aimed to align the exception with the language of art 5(3) of the European Air Passengers Rights Regulation, stating that an operator would not be obliged to pay compensation if the cancellation was caused by extraordinary circumstances, and it took all reasonable measures to prevent that cancellation. Note, however, that this change was abandoned in the second and third readings and not included in the final version in 2025. 9

Second, the amendment added sec 9 A, whereby if the Minister of Transportation declares a Special Condition for a period longer than 14 days, the Minister can, after consultation with the Minister of Economy and with the approval of the Economy Committee of the Knesset, limit the 'assistance' and deny compensation available to passengers under the Act. Special Conditions may be declared in response to threats of attack on the civil population, civil emergencies (involving physical risk to a sizeable group of people or to a large area, like natural disasters, hostile chemical or biological activities, and radiation accidents), or dangerous contagious disease. This part of the amendment is prospective.[29] 10

Third, the amending legislation retroactively denied or limited passengers' rights to compensation for flight cancellations, considerable delays, and early departures, from October 2023, following the Hamas attack on Israel, and throughout certain stages of the war, depending on their relative intensity and impact on air travel. This change was introduced as a special temporary provision in the amending legislation, without modifying the Aviation Services Act itself.[30] 11

---

28 Aviation Services Act (Compensation and Assistance Following the Cancellation of a Flight or a Change in its Conditions) (Amendment No 2 and a Temporary Provision – Iron Swords), 2025 SH 304.

29 Ibid § 3.

30 Ibid § 2.

B. Cases

1. Leave Civ App 7265/23 *Amidar – The National Company for Housing in Israel Ltd v John Doe* (Supreme Court, 4.3.2024): Negligent Misrepresentation; Interrelation Between Contract and Tort Law

a) Brief Summary of the Facts

12 R1 and R2 were interested in purchasing an apartment from R4, and hired a lawyer, R3, to advance the deal. The lawyer contacted Amidar, the national housing company, to verify R4's rights in the apartment. Amidar certified that R4 had full property rights, and even though the lawyer R3 encountered some discrepancies in the documentation, R1 and R2 ended up buying the apartment.[31] Two years later, when the buyers decided to sell the apartment, it transpired that R4 owned only 50 % of the property, so the buyers received this share despite having paid for full ownership.[32] R1 and R2 sued the seller R4 for breach of contract, the lawyer R3 for malpractice, and Amidar for negligent misrepresentation. The trial court decided that there was no breach of contract by R4, imposed tort liability on the lawyer (R3), and rejected the claim against Amidar for lack of a causal link between the misrepresentation and the economic harm.[33] The court of appeal (District Court of Jerusalem) reversed in part, finding that R4 breached the contract and that Amidar was liable for negligent misrepresentation.[34]

b) Judgment of the Court

13 Amidar argued that there was no causal link between its negligence and the economic harm, due to the lawyer's negligence.[35] The lawyer argued that there was no causal link between her negligence and the economic harm, due to Amidar's negligence.[36] Justice Sohlberg found that these conflicting allegations relate to

31 Leave Civ App 7265/23 *Amidar – The National Company for Housing in Israel Ltd v John Doe* (Supreme Court, 4.3.2024) paras 2–6.
32 Ibid para 7.
33 Ibid para 8.
34 Ibid para 10 f.
35 Ibid para 13.
36 Ibid para 15.

the application of undisputed law and therefore do not merit discussion by a third instance.[37]

Amidar and the lawyer also argued that finding them liable in tort for harm caused by the materialisation of a contractual risk would circumvent a carefully crafted contractual allocation of risks (between R4 and R1-R2) and that the need for judicial prudence with respect to tort liability in contractual environments is particularly pressing in cases of purely economic loss.[38] 14

Justice Sohlberg rejected this argument. He explained first that liability for negligent misrepresentation is a routine matter and that negligent misrepresentation typically involves purely economic loss.[39] He observed that prior case law qualified liability for negligent misrepresentation in order to control the spectre of indeterminate liability and avoid the cooling effect of liability on transfer of information.[40] Inter alia, a plaintiff must demonstrate that the information provider had special skills in the field in which the information was provided, that the information was provided in the ordinary course of business (and not randomly and inattentively), that the information provider intended for the victim to rely on the information, and that there is a practical way to limit the scope of liability.[41] These conditions are met in the case at bar.[42] 15

Next, Justice Sohlberg held that many cases of purely economic loss arise against a backdrop of contractual relationships. Israeli case law has been consistent in allowing a claimant to choose between, or simultaneously pursue, causes of action in torts and in contracts, when they can establish the elements of both, subject to the prohibition on double-recovery.[43] 16

In Justice Sohlberg's opinion (which has not yet been generally accepted), a tort action should not be allowed to circumvent and hence undermine the contractual allocation of risks between the same parties. But in the current case, the tort defendant was not a party to any contract with the plaintiffs, so no contractual relationship was circumvented.[44] 17

Some argue that tort law should not be used to exempt a person liable for breach of contract, unjust enrichment, or other kinds of wrongdoing from liability by seeking to shift the burden through an action in negligence to another. Without 18

37 Ibid para 19 f.
38 Ibid paras 12, 15, 21, 26.
39 Ibid para 23 f.
40 Ibid para 24.
41 Ibid.
42 Ibid para 25.
43 Ibid paras 26–28.
44 Ibid paras 29, 31.

expressing an opinion on this kind of argument, Justice Sohlberg explained that it would be inapplicable here because the tort action is not brought by a person liable for wrongdoing. In the current case the victims bring an action in contract against one party and tort actions against others.[45]

19 There is some scholarly debate on whether A can sue C for the materialisation of risk that A assumed through (and that was priced into) a contract with B. For example, if the buyer in a sales contract assumes the risk of damage to the purchased item upon delivery to the carrier and before the transfer of ownership, one may argue that the buyer should be prevented from bringing a tort action against a third party who injures the item in transit. This question must await future discussion, because in the current case, the buyers (R1 and R2) did not assume the risk of receiving only partial ownership in the sales contract.[46]

c) Commentary

20 The Supreme Court discussed two important matters in *Amidar v John Doe*. The first is the scope of liability for purely economic loss caused by negligent misrepresentation. The Court held that liability can be imposed when certain conditions are met. Inter alia, the plaintiff must establish that the information provider had special skills in the area in which the information or advice was given, that the information was provided in the ordinary course of business, that the provider intended the victim to rely on the information, and that the scope of liability could be reasonably limited. However, the Court did not provide any reference in support of these conditions and ignored relevant changes in the law of negligent misrepresentation. In fact, these conditions were laid down in a seminal 1954 decision and have eroded in subsequent case law.

21 In *Weinstein v Kadima*,[47] ten years before the universally renowned *Hedley Byrne v Heller*,[48] the Supreme Court of Israel departed from the traditional rule of English law barring liability for negligently caused economic loss. It held that in certain circumstances, economic loss arising from reliance on negligent misrepresentation was compensable. A contractor had built a water tank for a cooperative society in accordance with the design of an engineer, who was also employed by the same society. The latter refused to pay the contractor's wages because of

45 Ibid para 30.

46 Ibid para 32.

47 Motion 106/54 *Weinstein v Kadima*, 8 PD 1317 (1954).

48 *Hedley Byrne & Co Ltd v Heller & Partners Ltd* [1964] Appeal Cases (AC) 465, [1963] United Kingdom House of Lords (UKHL) 4 (HL).

the defects discovered in the tank, so the contractor claimed damages for his losses from the engineer. The claim was based on the tort of negligence since there had never been a contractual privity between the contractor and the engineer. The District Court dismissed the claim, relying on the English law in force at the time. The Supreme Court reversed, holding that the nature of the harm caused should not be seen as a basis for not imposing liability in negligence. Still, there are important practical reasons for a distinction between cases of negligent misrepresentation and cases of negligent conduct and between economic and physical harms. Therefore, the rule established in *Weinstein* was very narrow. Eligibility was conditioned on the defendant being a professional who provided the statement in the course of his work. The statement should have been made for the purpose of a specific transaction as a result of which the harm was caused. The provider owes a duty of care to the receiver only if the former intends the latter (as an identified individual or a prospective party to the specific transaction) to rely on the statement, and if the provider had no reasonable basis to assume that his statement would be subject to further, independent scrutiny before being relied on. Another condition for imposing liability is that the extent of the economic harm was foreseeable. Ultimately, the claim was dismissed, since the defendant could not have foreseen that the plaintiff would not independently examine the building plans. *Weinstein*, though not referenced in *Amidar v John Doe*, is the source of the conditions for liability mentioned therein.

However, the *Weinstein* conditions have eroded since the 1950s. For instance, 22
in 1978, the Supreme Court extended liability for negligent misrepresentation to cases where the statement was made by a non-professional, who gave advice that required professional skill, pretending to have such skill.[49] In 1984, the Court held that a duty to avoid false misrepresentation arises if the provider could have reasonably foreseen the receiver's reliance on the statement and the resulting harm, regardless of whether or not the provider was a professional, and whether or not the statement was made in the course of a specific transaction.[50] In 1985 and in subsequent cases, the Court held that liability for negligent misrepresentation is conditional merely on the defendant's foreseeability of the plaintiff's reliance on the false statement.[51] Thus, the factors enumerated in

---

49 Civ App 86/76 *Amidar – The National Company for Housing of Newcomers in Israel Ltd v Aharoni*, 32(2) Judgments from the Supreme Court of Israel (Piskei Din, PD) 337 (1978).

50 Civ App 783/83 *Kaplan v Novogrozki*, 38(3) PD 477 (1984).

51 Civ App 790/81 *American Microsystems Inc v Elbit Computers Ltd*, 39(2) PD 785 (1985); Civ App 209/85 *Kyriat Ata Municipality v Ilanco Ltd*, 42(1) PD 190, 203–204 (1988); Civ App 7440/19 *Emblaze Co Ltd v Double U Trading Fund Inc* (Supreme Court, 27.4.2021) para 17. Courts sometimes state

Weinstein are considered indicia of such foreseeability rather than strict conditions for liability.[52] The *Amidar v John Doe* decision misses this development in treating the *Weinstein* factors as conditions.

23 The second fundamental topic discussed in *Amidar v John Doe* is the interrelation between contract and tort law. In particular, the Court was interested in the possible impact of the contractual background of the interaction on possible causes of action in tort. The initial question in this regard is whether and to what extent a contract between two parties may affect a cause of action in tort that one may have against the other. In the common law (as opposed to some continental jurisdictions), the existence of a contract does not in itself negate the victim's cause of action in tort. It seems undisputed that victims of wrongdoing can choose their cause of action from the full private law menu – including contract, tort, and unjust enrichment, and invoke several causes of action simultaneously.[53] One does not bar the other.

24 However, the victim cannot file a tort claim if this is inconsistent with valid provisions of the contract. In other words, the parties can, within the framework of the agreement, negate or limit their liability in tort, subject to relevant limits on the freedom of contracts. This principle reflects the priority of the contract, which expresses the parties' voluntary allocation of risks, opportunities, benefits, and burdens, over non-contractual arrangements. Of course, a contractual disclaimer of tort liability will be given effect only if the victim was, or should have been, aware of it.[54] More importantly, in the case of risk to life and limb, where there is an asymmetry of power between the parties, a disclaimer may be contrary to public policy and hence invalid.[55] While there is some support to the view that even in the case of physical risk and asymmetry of power a disclaimer should be invalidated only if the risky goods or services provided by the defendant were essential for the plaintiff,[56] the dominant view is that essentiality is not required for invalidation.[57]

---

that the plaintiff's reliance should be reasonable, but this too may be one of the indicia of foreseeability rather than an additional requirement.

52 Civ App 790/81 *American Microsystems Inc v Elbit Computers Ltd*, 39(2) PD 785, 796–797 (1985).

53 *JG Fleming*, Tort in a Contractual Matrix, 3 Tort Law Review 12, 13–14 (1995); *MD Lieder*, Constructing a New Action for Negligent Infliction of Economic Loss: Building on Cardozo and Coase, 66 Washington Law Review 937, 945 (1991); *JM Thomson*, Delictual Liability for Pure Economic Loss: Recent Developments, 1995 Scots Law Times (SLT) 139, 143.

54 Civ App 285/73 *Lagil Trampoline & Sports Equipment Ltd v Nahmias*, 29(1) PD 63 (1974).

55 Ibid.

56 Justice Witkon in a concurring opinion in *Lagil Trampoline v Nahmias*, ibid.

57 Civ Case 10148/97 *Nagler v Pearl* (District Court Haifa, 2.1.2006).

A related question, which was mentioned but not resolved in *Amidar v John Doe*, is whether and to what extent a contract between two parties may affect a cause of action in tort that one may have against a third (non-contracting) party or a cause of action that a third party may have against one of the contracting parties. Consider, for example, the following case. An agreement for the sale of goods stipulates that the risk of damage passes to the buyer upon loading onto the cargo ship and that ownership passes upon delivery to the buyer at the port of destination. Under the bill of lading, signed by the shipowner and the seller of the goods, the former is exempted from liability for any damage caused to the cargo during transport. The goods are damaged in transportation, and the buyer files a negligence action against the shipowner. On the one hand, it seems unfair to dismiss the buyer's claim based on a disclaimer it was unaware of in a contract to which it was not a party. On the other hand, it seems unfair to subject the shipowner to liability exceeding what it contractually agreed to assume in this venture. 25

According to one approach, adopted by the House of Lords in *The Aliakmon*,[58] the shipowner cannot owe a duty of care to the buyer before the transfer of ownership. If a duty of care existed, it would not be governed by the terms of the shipping contract, because a contract between A and B does not affect the rights and duties that either of them may have in a legal relationship with C. Thus, the shipowner's tort liability could exceed what it voluntarily assumed under the shipping contract. To avoid the possible injustice to the shipowner, a duty of care to a third party (the buyer) must not be recognised at all. 26

Under an alternative approach, the existence of a contract between the shipowner and the seller cannot negate the duty of care that the shipowner owes to the buyer, and the contractual limits on the shipowner's obligations to the seller (in contracts and in torts) cannot limit the shipowner's tort liability to the buyer. The tort is independent of the contractual background. This avoids injustice to the buyer. 27

According to a middle-ground approach, the fact that the shipowner has a contract with the seller should not in itself negate the duty of care that the shipowner may owe to the buyer, because tort actions are generally independent of the contractual background. But if the contract explicitly limits the shipowner's liability to the seller, the limitations must also apply, with the necessary changes, to the shipowner's duty of care towards the buyer, because the sales contract is 28

58 *Leigh & Sillavan Ltd v Aliakmon Shipping Co Ltd (The Aliakmon)* [1986] 2 All England Law Reports (All Eng Rep) 145, 153, 155–156, 157 (HL).

intended to ultimately put the buyer in the seller's shoes.[59] While this approach seems to do justice to all parties involved, it is applicable only to a limited type of cases in which A transfers a risk to B while contractually exempting C from liability for its materialisation.

2. Leave Fam App 4181/22 *John Doe v Jane Doe* (Supreme Court, 19.5.2024): Liability for Paternity Fraud

a) Brief Summary of the Facts

29 The petitioner and the respondent got married in 2011, gave birth to a child in 2014, and separated in 2019. At this point the respondent revealed that the petitioner was not the child's biological father. The petitioner filed a lawsuit against the respondent seeking damages for pecuniary losses – the costs of upbringing the child, and non-pecuniary losses arising inter alia from breach of the petitioner's autonomy and dignity and the dissociation from the child. He based his claim on the torts of negligence, deceit, and breach of statutory duty, as well as on a contractual cause of action (breach of the duty to perform a contract in good faith).[60] The Family Court allowed the claim in torts and in contracts.[61] The appellate court (the District Court of Jerusalem) reversed, holding that there can be no cause of action for paternity fraud for reasons rooted in the child's interests, the legal obstacles to establishing biological paternity, and the similarity between claims for paternity fraud and claims for adultery, which are not recognised under Israeli law.[62] The petitioner sought leave for appeal to the Supreme Court.

b) Judgment of the Court

30 The question which has never been decided by the Supreme Court is whether Israeli law recognises a cause of action for 'paternity fraud,' that is, whether a woman is legally obliged to disclose to her spouse that he is not the biological father of her newborn.

---

59 *BS Markesinis*, An Expanding Tort Law – The Price of a Rigid Contract Law (1987) 103 Law Quarterly Review (LQR) 354, 359.
60 Leave Fam App 4181/22 *John Doe v Jane Doe* (Supreme Court, 19.5.2024) paras 1–3.
61 Ibid paras 4–6.
62 Ibid paras 7–10.

Justice Willner explained that the limits of judicial intervention in the marital and family sphere have undergone changes over the years, with the last decade making it clear that there are weighty reasons to limit the application of tort and contract law to spousal relationships. The law now distinguishes between (1) cases of physical and psychological abuse and violence, including instances of refusal to grant a Jewish divorce (*Gett*), in which the law protects victims through civil remedies,[63] and (2) cases arising within the intimate and emotional sphere of the relationship, in which the law is reluctant to impose legal duties, particularly if such duties might impact other important interests.[64] A key milestone with respect to the second category was Justice Amit's rejection, in a 2013 case, of the cause of action for adultery (both between spouses and against third parties) for reasons of policy. In the same spirit, the Court refused to recognise the duty of spouses to disclose their sexual orientation or degree of religious commitment. Justice Willner opined that claims for paternity fraud belong to the second category and should not be allowed.[65] 31

In her view, this conclusion is supported by several policy reasons.[66] First, the legal system is not the proper venue for investigating, analysing, and regulating intimate, complex, dynamic, emotionally-charged, intensive, long-lasting relationships.[67] Second, even if the legal system had the appropriate tools to investigate such relationships, courts should not interfere with matters that lie deep in the most private and intimate realms of the marital unit. Doing otherwise might violate not only the spouses' privacy and autonomy but also the rights of third parties, including the minor child and the biological father.[68] Third, recognition of a cause of action for paternity fraud is inconsistent with the denial of the cause of action for adultery.[69] Fourth, the best interests of the child constitute an important consideration supporting the denial of the cause of action for paternity fraud. Paternity fraud claims subject children to anguishing uncertainties throughout the process, make them feel unwanted, and destabilise their familial unit; a genetic test is rarely decreed in Israel due to the dreaded classification of the child as a *Mamzer*, making proof of paternity fraud complicated and distressing 32

---

63 Ibid paras 18, 22.
64 Ibid paras 19–21.
65 Ibid para 23.
66 Ibid para 16.
67 Ibid para 24.
68 Ibid para 25.
69 Ibid para 26.

for the child with little chance of success.[70] Refusing to recognise a cause of action in tort does not diminish the moral objection to paternity fraud.

33 Justice Canfy-Steinitz commented in a concurring opinion that paternity fraud is different from cases in which the Supreme Court refused to subject the intimate and emotional relationship between spouses to tort law, because it also involves the legal relation between the defrauded spouse and the child. Thus, one cannot directly apply the Court's rulings in the abovementioned cases to paternity fraud.[71]

34 Justice Canfy-Steinitz opined that policy concerns pull in opposing directions, making the decision difficult, but that the scales tip towards denial of liability. Some considerations support the recognition of a cause of action for paternity fraud.[72] Firstly, a woman who misleads her partner about parentage deeply harms the partner's dignity and autonomy, by forcing him to become a parent to a non-biological child and holding the power to deny such parenthood at any stage. Furthermore, 'forced paternity' caused by such misrepresentation spawns a fundamental change in the defrauded spouse's legal status, which carries with it a wide range of burdens with pecuniary and non-pecuniary components that he should not have borne. The late realisation of the truth might also cause the defrauded spouse severe mental and emotional harm. In addition, the child has a right to know their origins. The child might suffer from the late disclosure of their father's identity and from being disowned by the person they believed to be the father. Finally, the biological father has a right to know about the existence of his child and to serve as a parent.

35 However, stronger policy considerations support the opposite conclusion.[73] To begin with, a duty to disclose extramarital pregnancy might have unwarranted consequences for the woman (social and familial reprimand or even violence, and inability to remarry), the child (illegitimacy, mental instability) and other children in the family (suffering from family breakdown). A key concern is the best interests of the child. Although a child has the right to know the identity of their biological father and not to be an indirect victim of a paternity fraud, pursuing an action for paternity fraud may cause the child considerable mental harm, particularly because the person they considered a father now claims the relationship caused them harm. The claim might also affect the child's ability to marry under Jewish law (due to being a *Mamzer*). Moreover, tort and contract law are inadequate for handling such cases. For instance, it is impractical to determine

70 Ibid paras 27–31.
71 Justice Canfy-Steinitz, paras 1–4.
72 Justice Canfy-Steinitz, paras 5–9.
73 Justice Canfy-Steinitz, paras 10–12.

the extent of harm caused to the defrauded spouse by having to raise a non-biological child, because he believed he was raising a biological child. Also, the benefits of fatherhood must somehow be deducted from any harm caused. Other complexities involve the possible contributory negligence of the claimant (who might have had a suspicion or treated his wife in a way that discouraged disclosure) and the possible liability of the biological father. In her view, these policy considerations do not apply to (and may not negate liability in) a different type of paternity fraud, where an unmarried woman misled a man to believe he was the biological parent of her child to obtain economic benefits.

In a concurring opinion, Justice Grosskopf agreed that actions for paternity 36 fraud should not be generally allowed under the tort of negligence, because policy considerations negate the duty of care. However, in his view, a cause of action may be available under the tort of deceit. This will happen in exceptional cases where the mother made a false representation regarding paternity, knowing that this representation was false, with an intent to mislead the husband, causing him *special* pecuniary damage, namely an extraordinary expense that he would have avoided had he known that the child was not biologically his. Justice Grosskopf further explained that ordinary costs of raising a child are not a special pecuniary damage. Using a limited legal framework, such as the tort of deceit causing special pecuniary loss, reduces the disadvantages associated with the legal adjudication of paternity frauds and does not leave the problem without any legal response.

c) Commentary

Historically, Israeli tort law was disinclined to regulate spousal relationships. 37 Thus, sec 18(a) of the Civil Wrongs Ordinance, which was abolished in 1969, granted each spouse immunity from tort actions by the other. In addition, sec 62(b) of the CWO, which is still in force, provides that the relationship created by marriage cannot be deemed a contract for the purposes of the tort of intentional interference with contractual relations (so third parties cannot be sued for breaking a marriage). Courts then gradually allowed claims for violent, abusive, or otherwise agonising conduct within a relationship.[74] According to the analysis in *Jane Doe v John Doe*, courts ultimately realised that the expansion of liability must be curbed for policy reasons and refused to recognise duties concerning the intimate and

74 See eg, Civ App 245/81 *Sultan v Sultan*, 38(3) PD 169 (1984); Leave Fam App 7073/13 *John Doe v Jane Doe* (Supreme Court, 31.12.2013).

emotional sphere of a relationship with possible impact on other important interests.

38 The most important development in the last (reactionary) phase was probably a 2013 case, mentioned by Justices Willner and Canfy-Steinitz, in which the Court held that there can be no cause of action for adultery, either against an unfaithful spouse or against a third party.[75] In that case, two friends married two sisters. Each couple had children, and the two families used to spend their free time together. At a certain point, one of the friends and the other friend's wife became romantically involved. The betrayed friend brought an action in negligence against the betraying friend arguing that upon learning about the adulterous relationship, he became depressed. The Court explained that D owes a duty of care to P if D ought to have foreseen that their conduct would cause harm to P. Under the interpretation of this rule in *Gordon v Municipality of Jerusalem*,[76] where the harm is technically foreseeable, a conceptual duty arises, unless policy considerations support its negation. In cases of adultery, policy considerations negate the conceptual duty. First, Israeli law does not consider adultery a tort by one spouse against the other, and the legislature explicitly expressed its view in sec 62(b) that adultery should not give rise to an action against the adulterous spouse's lover. This legislative decree must not be circumvented by using a different tort (here negligence). Second, the mutual commitment to faithfulness arises on the social, moral, and religious levels, and should not be imported into the law. Tort law must not intervene in intimate personal relations. Third, because adultery is currently very common, imposing liability may open the floodgates of litigation. Fourth, tort actions for adultery might prevent reconciliation between the spouses (which actually began in the 2013 case) or aggravate a divorce dispute. Fifth, allowing liability would reintroduce fault into the property relations between spouses, contrary to recent trends in Israeli law.

39 Justices Willner and Canfy-Steinitz also mentioned a 2021 decision that validates the more restrictive approach.[77] The Court held there that one spouse owes no duty to disclose their sexual orientation or degree of religious commitment to the other, as such a duty would violate the former's privacy and autonomy. In another case, the Supreme Court declined to recognise a cause of action for concealing a pre-marital relationship.[78]

---

75 Civ App 8489/12 *John Doe v Richard Roe* (Supreme Court, 29.10.2013), reported in *R Perry*, Israel, in: E Karner/BC Steininger (eds), European Tort Law (ETL) 2013 (2014) 731, nos 29–36.
76 Civ App 243/83 *Gordon v Municipality of Jerusalem*, 39(1) PD 113 (1985).
77 Leave Fam App 5827/19 *John Doe v Jane Doe* (Supreme Court, 16.8.2021).
78 Leave Fam App 7939/17 *John Doe v Jane Doe* (Supreme Court, 9.11.2017).

Still, this analysis of the case law is incomplete as Israeli courts have allowed claims involving the intimate and emotional sphere of personal relationships. For example, the Supreme Court upheld actions for misrepresentation underlying an insincere promise to marry (primarily misrepresentation of the promisor's status).[79] Similarly, some courts allowed claims for misrepresentation concerning a person's fertility or use of contraceptives, when resulting in unwarranted pregnancy.[80] 40

At any rate, the judges differed in their classification of paternity fraud cases. Justice Willner believed they were similar to recent cases involving the intimate interaction and trust between spouses, in which the Supreme Court denied liability. Justice Canfy-Steinitz held a more compelling view, whereby paternity fraud is distinguishable from the reactionary cases because it involves an important external interest, that of the child. This controversy was not crucial in the case on hand because both judges reached the same conclusion based on policy analysis. Moreover, even though the two used different policy analyses, they reached the same conclusion (of no liability). Justice Willner opined that policy considerations require denial of paternity fraud claims, whereas Justice Canfy-Steinitz thought that legitimate policy considerations pulled in opposing directions, with those supporting denial of liability ultimately having the upper hand. 41

The main problem with the Court's analysis is the underlying assumption that judges can subject all causes of action invoked by the plaintiff to a general policy screening. The general torts (negligence, breach of statutory duty) consist of elements that provide conceptual frameworks for a policy analysis of the merits and demerits of liability. The prime example is the duty of care in negligence, which has been interpreted and applied as a means for delineating the proper boundaries of liability. In contrast, specific torts, such as battery, conversion, malicious prosecution, defamation, and deceit do not have equivalent elements. A specific tort is structured as a list of concrete mostly factual elements capable of being established through evidence. They do not contain general legal elements that can serve as conceptual frameworks for a policy analysis, so liability under the specific torts cannot be conditional on the results of such analysis. Thus, the fact that policy considerations call for non-recognition of a cause of action for paternity fraud (as per Justice Willner) or that considerations supporting non-recognition overcome those supporting recognition (as per Canfy-Steinitz) can bar an action in negligence but not an action in deceit. 42

79 Civ App 386/74 *John Doe v Jane Doe*, 30(1) PD 383 (1975).

80 Civ App 4438-01-14 *HH v DG* (District Court Tel Aviv, 26.2.2015).

43 Even Justice Grosskopf's less restrictive approach reads into sec 56 of the CWO a restriction that has no basis in its language. According to sec 56, deceit is a false representation of fact, made with the knowledge that it is false or without belief in its truth or recklessly, not caring whether it be true or false, with intent that it will be acted upon by the person deceived; provided that no action will be brought for such representation unless it was intended to, and did, deceive the plaintiff and they acted upon it and thereby suffered pecuniary damage. Section 56 requires proof of pecuniary damage. Justice Grosskopf's requirement of *special* pecuniary damage is baseless.

44 Lastly, some of the policy concerns enumerated by the judges are patently unconvincing. For example, Justice Canfy-Steinitz argued that assessing the defrauded spouse's harm raises considerable difficulties. Yet such difficulties are not unique to the case of paternity fraud and have been routinely handled by the courts in other contexts. Specifically, assessing the burden of unwanted parenthood is the very essence of wrongful birth claims which have been recognised in Israel for decades. Similarly, Justice Canfy-Steinitz emphasised the possible complexities associated with the claimant's contributory negligence or the biological father's liability for the fraud. Again, none of these concerns, though admittedly real, is unique to paternity fraud and all are regularly addressed by the judiciary.

3. Leave Civ App 8153/23 *State of Israel v Shay* (Supreme Court, 16.6.2024): State Liability for Negligent Investigation of Crime/Failure to Prosecute

a) Brief Summary of the Facts

45 A pedestrian was killed in a car accident while crossing the street. The driver was the Deputy State Attorney, so to avoid any appearance of bias, the evidence collected about the accident by the police was transferred to the Military Prosecution. After examining the material, the Military Prosecution decided to close the criminal case against the driver on the grounds of lack of evidence. The victim's family members filed an appeal, but the Military Advocate General rejected it.

46 The family members brought an action in tort against the State, arguing that the investigation of the accident was negligent, biased, and affected by extraneous considerations, due to the driver's position as a senior official in the State Attorney's Office. The claimants alleged that during the investigation, the investigators ignored various pieces of evidence and deviated from police practice in cases of

fatal road accidents. They emphasised that the action was brought for the negligent investigation, not for the decision not to bring an indictment against the driver. The court of first instance (Haifa Magistrate Court) decided not to dismiss the claim and the court of appeals (District Court of Haifa) affirmed. The State sought leave for appeal to the Supreme Court.

b) Judgment of the Court

Justice Kasher, with whom Justices Amit and Willner concurred, explained that although the issue of attacking an administrative act through a tort action has been discussed in prior decisions, there is still some ambiguity that calls for clarification about the difference between 'collateral attack' and 'direct attack in disguise,' and the implications of this distinction on the power of civil courts. In addition, the case raises a question that has never been decided before: does the State owe a duty of care to a victim of a crime or his family with respect to the mental harm they incur as a result of a decision not to prosecute a suspect?[81] 47

Concerning the attack on administrative acts, Justice Kasher clarified the fundamental distinction: If the requested remedy is the invalidation of an administrative decision – through a direct attack – the competent administrative court has jurisdiction. If the requested remedy is genuinely monetary, the competent civil court has jurisdiction, and the plaintiff can contest the legality of administrative acts or the validity of administrative decisions through collateral attack. Justice Kasher added that sometimes what appears to be a monetary claim is not genuinely monetary but a disguised direct attack on an administrative act or decision, and in such a case the civil court has no jurisdiction. The question therefore is whether the attack on the administrative act or decision is at the heart of the claim (hence direct and in the administrative court's jurisdiction) or incidental to a genuine monetary dispute (hence collateral and in the civil court's jurisdiction). Still, even when the monetary dispute is genuine and the attack on the administrative act or decision is collateral, the civil court can dismiss the claim despite having jurisdiction if it concludes that a direct attack in the administrative court is more appropriate as a matter of policy.[82] In the case at bar, the claimants essentially contested the decision not to prosecute the driver, which is a direct at- 48

81 Leave Civ App 8153/23 *State of Israel v Shay* (Supreme Court, 16.6.2024) para 10.
82 Ibid paras 12–18.

tack in disguise, so the civil court has no jurisdiction over the case.[83] This in itself justifies dismissal.

49 Next, Justice Kasher held that there was no cause of action because the State owed no duty of care to the claimants. The existence of a conceptual duty of care entails two conclusions: the defendant could reasonably foresee that their conduct would cause the damage in question as a factual matter, and ought to have foreseen the damage as a normative matter. Normative foreseeability is determined based on policy analysis, and the relevant policy considerations can be classified into two groups: (1) traditional tort considerations, such as proximity, the type of harm (economic, emotional), and the type of conduct (act, omission), and (2) broader considerations determining whether it is fair, just, and reasonable to impose liability.

50 In the present case, policy considerations lead to the conclusion that the State owes no duty of care to a crime victim or his family with respect to the mental harm they incur as a result of a decision not to prosecute a suspect.[84] First, the criminal process focuses on the relation between the offender and the State, representing society, not between the offender or the State and the victim. The State's power to prosecute is aimed at the offender, the victim has a very limited role in the process, and the legislature explicitly stipulated that the victim has no redress for being denied such role. Therefore, there is no juridical link sufficient to establish a duty of care between the State and the victim. Second, a duty of care to the victim, and the expected liability for breach, might undermine the professional independent prosecutorial discretion. Prosecutorial discretion should be regulated only when the suspect's liberty is put at risk. Liability for non-prosecution might induce undesirable prosecution, particularly when the alleged victim has the resources and determination to fight the State in court. Third, the harm that victims and their family members might sustain following a decision not to prosecute the offender is primarily emotional. Liability for emotional harm, particularly when indirect, should be restricted due to verification and assessment problems, the risk of fabrication, and the fear of indeterminate liability.

c) Commentary

51 The decision has two important components. The first is the systematic discussion of the use of tort actions as a tool for challenging the validity of administrative

83 Ibid paras 19–26.
84 Ibid paras 27–37.

decisions and the legality of administrative conduct. The Supreme Court explained that the analysis entails two steps. First, the court must determine whether the essence of the tort claim is the invalidation of the administrative decision or a monetary remedy. In the former case, that of direct attack, the civil court has no jurisdiction at all. In the latter case, the civil court has jurisdiction, and it can address the validity of the administrative decision indirectly when necessary to resolve the civil dispute (collateral attack). The Supreme Court emphasised that what seems to be a monetary claim might sometimes be a disguised direct attack on the administrative act or decision and that in such a case, the civil court has no jurisdiction. Second, even if the civil court has jurisdiction, because the claim is genuinely monetary and the attack on the administrative act or decision is collateral, the court can dismiss the claim if it concludes that a direct attack in the administrative court is more appropriate as a matter of policy. In other words, an attack on an administrative act or decision within the tort process goes through two sieves: jurisdiction and policy.

The Supreme Court did not explain how judicial discretion is exercised in the 52
second stage. In *Zanlakol Ltd v Haifa Tax Assessor*,[85] the Supreme Court provided a non-exhaustive list of relevant considerations: (1) the scope of the arguments made under the collateral attack and their cumulative weight compared to other arguments; (2) the nature of the administrative body and the specific conduct in question (eg, the higher the body's or the norm's rank and the greater the exercise of government powers, the less appropriate collateral attack is); (3) the nature of the flaw and its consequences (eg, less severe administrative flaws should be attacked only directly); (4) the importance, sensitivity, complexity, and breadth of impact of the required decision; (5) the existence of relevant guidelines concerning the proper way to attack the particular administrative conduct; (6) the plaintiff's conduct (eg, failure to resort to direct attack when reasonable or to comply with the administrative decision should prevent collateral attack).

The second component of the decision is the analytical framework for estab- 53
lishing a duty of care in negligence and its concrete application to the relationship between State prosecution and victims of criminal activity. The traditional structure of the tort of negligence comprises four elements: (1) duty of care, (2) breach of duty through unreasonable conduct (fault), (3) harm, and (4) a causal relation between the breach and the harm. According to the so-called *Gordon* model, the duty of care is examined and tested on two levels: conceptual or notional (taking into account general categories of injurers, victims, activities, and harms) and concrete (taking into account the specific injurer, victim, activity, and harm). On each

85 Civ App 3129/19 *Zanlakol Ltd v Haifa Tax Assessor* (Supreme Court, 25.8.2022).

level, if the harm (or category of harms) is foreseeable as a factual matter, then a duty arises unless policy considerations call for its negation or limitation as a normative matter.[86] Causation is also tested on two levels: factual (determined by the *causa sine qua non* test) and legal (determined by the foreseeability, scope of risk, or common sense tests).

54 In *State of Israel v Levi*,[87] Chief Justice Shamgar opined that the policy considerations that may limit or negate the duty of care on the normative level can be classified into two main categories: (1) Considerations that originate in the law of torts itself, that can be reduced to the requirement of proximity. A duty of care does not exist when the parties are remote from each other. Proximity analysis considers, eg, the nature of the conduct (act, omission), the directness of the link between the conduct and harm, and the type of harm (physical, economic, emotional). (2) Considerations that can be reduced to the question of whether it is fair, just, and reasonable to impose liability. These are general policy considerations that are not necessarily attached or unique to tort law, which derive from the interrelation between tort law and other branches of law and from the normative roles of tort law. In conclusion, according to Chief Justice Shamgar, the establishment of a duty of care requires foreseeability, proximity, and a conclusion that liability would be fair, just, and reasonable.

55 It is unclear whether the *Levi* case was intended to replace the *Gordon* model, which examines foreseeability and policy on two levels (conceptual-notional and concrete), with a three-prong test, or to complement it by adding precision to the examination of policy on both levels. But Justice Kasher's analysis mixed up the prior case law in at least two respects. First, he argued that policy considerations of the first kind, namely traditional tort considerations, 'include, inter alia, proximity, the type of harm caused (physical, purely emotional, purely economic), and the nature of the defendant's conduct (act, omission, or failure to prevent an act).'[88] Put differently, he considered proximity, the type of harm, and the nature of the conduct as separate items on the list of traditional tort considerations. This is quite different from the *Levi* case and the vast body of case law to which it relates. Chief Justice Shamgar considered proximity as the overarching principle, the second requirement in a three-prong analysis, while the type of harm and the nature of the conduct are merely characteristics that courts consider in the proximity analysis.

86 Civ App 243/83 *Gordon v Municipality of Jerusalem*, 39(1) PD 113 (1985).
87 Civ App 915/91 *State of Israel v Levi*, 48(3) PD 45 (1994).
88 Leave Civ App 8153/23 *State of Israel v Shay* (Supreme Court, 16.6.2024) para 28.

Second, Justice Kasher repeatedly stated that the question under discussion was whether a conceptual duty of care existed.[89] Yet in explaining why past recognition of a duty of care of investigative and prosecutorial bodies did not necessarily apply to the case at bar, he stated that the recognition of a duty of care 'is not done at a general level of abstraction, but in relation to a specific injurer, a specific victim, specific conduct, and specific harm.'[90] Alas, the latter statement, referring to specific injurer, victim, conduct, and harm is the exact definition of the concrete duty of care in *Gordon* and its progeny. The accurate explanation should have been that a conceptual duty of care is not one that exists between two abstract classes of people with respect to all kinds of conduct and harm, but one defined with respect to carefully defined, and casuistically evolving (expanding or contracting) categories of injurers, victims, conduct, and harm. 56

The Court's analysis of policy considerations within the framework of the duty of care seems overreaching. Justice Kasher offered three policy justifications for denying negligence actions by crime victims and their families against the State prosecution for mental harm resulting from a decision not to prosecute the respective offenders. Each may justify some restraint but not necessarily negation of the duty of care. To begin with, Justice Kasher argued that the criminal process focuses on the relation between the State and the offender, not between the State (or the offender) and the victim, who has a very limited role in the process and – under explicit legislation – no redress for being denied that role. He concluded, therefore, that the relation between the State and the victim is insufficient to support a duty of care. Yet the fact that the relation between D and P1 is weaker or more 'distant' than the relation between D and P2, to whom D may owe a duty of care, does not mean that D cannot also owe a duty to P1. Tort law often generates the juridical link where no such link existed under other branches or segments of law. Although the role of victims in the criminal process is limited, their potential harm in the case of prosecutorial failure is highly foreseeable and direct. 57

Next, Justice Kasher opined that a duty of care to the victim, and the expected liability for breach, might undermine the prosecutorial discretion and induce undesirable prosecution. However, courts in Israel recognise the prosecution's duty (towards suspects) to avoid undesirable prosecution which foreseeably ends up in acquittal. Fairness may require recognition of an equivalent duty (to victims) not to avoid desirable prosecution. From an economic perspective, a duty not to avoid desirable prosecution, which might induce undesirable prosecution, may balance 58

89 Ibid paras 27–39.

90 Ibid para 29.

the duty to avoid undesirable prosecution, which might induce avoidance of desirable prosecution.

59 Lastly, Justice Kasher argued that the harm that victims and their family members might sustain following a decision not to prosecute the offender is mostly emotional and that liability for such loss must be restrictive due to verification and assessment problems, the risk of fabrication, and the fear of indeterminate liability. This analysis ignores a fundamental development in Israeli tort law. In *Gordon v Municipality of Jerusalem*,[91] the Supreme Court famously recognised a duty to avoid negligent infliction of emotional harm. The Court in *Gordon* opined that verification, assessment, and fabrication problems were not sufficiently acute to deny recovery and that the fear of indeterminacy should be resolved through limitation rather than negation of liability. In fact, the plaintiff in *Gordon* itself incurred and ultimately recovered damages for non-pecuniary loss resulting from negligent prosecution. It would seem peculiar if non-pecuniary loss would be irrecoverable in the analogous case of negligent non-prosecution.

4. Civ App 3619/23 *John Doe v The Palestinian Authority* (Supreme Court, 20.8.2024): Relational Emotional Harm

a) Brief Summary of the Facts

60 Family members of victims of a terrorist attack brought tort actions against the perpetrators and the Palestinian Authority. The Supreme Court, in a prior decision in this case, held that the conditions for awarding punitive damages were met, that plaintiffs entitled to punitive damages can recover them in addition to statutory State benefits under the Benefits to Victims of Hostile Actions Act,[92] and that those entitled to punitive damages are the same parties entitled to ordinary damages. The Court held that some of the conditions for the claimants' entitlement to compensation for negligent infliction of relational (indirect, secondary) emotional harm were satisfied and returned the case to the court of first instance to decide whether the other conditions were also met.[93] The District Court of Jerusalem decided that some family members were entitled to compensation for emotional harm, and therefore to punitive damages, while others were not. Those found ineligible as well as the Palestinian Authority appealed.

---

91 Civ App 243/83 *Gordon v Municipality of Jerusalem*, 39(1) PD 113 (1985).
92 1970 SH 126, § 3.
93 Civ App 71/18 *The Palestinian Authority v Estate of Sharon Ben Shalom* (Supreme Court, 10.3.2021).

b) Judgment of the Court

Justice Amit explained that under *Alssouha v Dahan*,[94] liability for secondary emotional harm is limited to cases that satisfy four conditions: (1) the plaintiff must be a first-degree relative of the direct victim; (2) the secondary victim must have incurred the harm through direct exposure to the event and its consequences, although liability for foreseeable harm caused by indirect exposure may also be considered; (3) proximity in time and place between the occurrence of the secondary harm and the occurrence of the primary injury (including extended exposure to the primary victim's suffering); and (4) the plaintiff's emotional harm must be severe, amounting to mental illness or a mental disorder with substantial disability.[95] These conditions balance between the need to protect people from negligently caused harm and policy considerations supporting restraint, such as the fear of over-deterrence, the possibility of false and inflated claims, verification and assessment problems, the possible exacerbation of emotional harm due to prolonged litigation, the benefits of loss spreading, and others.[96] 61

While the second and third *Alssouha* conditions are somewhat flexible, the fourth is very strict (with only one exception to be discussed in the commentary).[97] Still, the Court in *Alssouha* did not provide clear guidelines for determining whether a specific harm is sufficiently severe. According to subsequent case law, severity must be established through medical opinion, and a medical disability of 5%–15% with limited impact on daily life and functioning is not sufficiently severe. Legal literature demonstrates that a disability of less than 10% is deemed insufficient, a disability of more than 20% is deemed sufficient, and the range between these yardsticks is a 'grey area.' Apart from the medical disability, courts assessing the severity of the harm may consider the duration of the suffering, the chances of recovery, the likelihood of aggravation, the need for ongoing psychiatric or psychological treatment, the need for medication, impairment of functioning, impairment of work capacity, integration in daily life, etc.[98] 62

Justice Amit then applied these guidelines to the various claims. Thus, two claimants who sustained a medical disability of 30% with a considerable impact on social functioning (one of whom was treated by a professional and received medication) were entitled to damages for emotional harm.[99] Two other claimants, 63

94 Leave Civ App 444/87 *Alssouha v Estate of Dahan*, 44 (3) PD 397 (1990).
95 Civ App 3619/23 *John Doe v The Palestinian Authority* (Supreme Court, 20.8.2024) para 10.
96 Ibid para 11.
97 Ibid para 12.
98 Ibid para 13.
99 Ibid para 16.

who had already passed away before their medical disability could be determined, suffered from major depression with serious impairment of functioning following severe chronic bereavement, and were also entitled to recover.[100] Two of the claims raised doubts because the claimants suffered from a medical disability of 20 % but there was no evidence of impairment of functioning or work capacity. Given the uncertainties, Justice Amit decided to affirm the conclusion of the court of first instance that their emotional harm was sufficiently severe.[101] In contrast, three claimants with medical disabilities of 15 %, 20 %, and 25 % and a very limited impact on functioning did not meet the *Alssouha* condition.[102]

64 Justice Amit concluded that the court of first instance should assess the punitive award to each of the parties entitled to compensation in accordance with the new Compensation to Victims of Terror Act (Exemplary Damages).[103]

c) Commentary

65 Relational emotional harm is emotional distress consequent upon a wrongful infliction of injury to another. It may result from witnessing the occurrence in which the other person is injured or imperilled, from learning about the ensuing injury after its occurrence, or from sympathising with the mental anguish of another relational victim. Historically, the common law did not allow recovery for relational emotional harm. Thus, liability for negligent infliction of emotional harm was recognised in the United States only if that harm culminated in the plaintiff's illness or bodily impact.[104] Purely emotional harm was irrecoverable.[105] Moreover, the conventional view was that even when emotional distress culminated in physical injury, it was irrecoverable if caused by the fear of injury to another.[106]

66 With time, most jurisdictions have recognised at least a limited exception to the traditional rule. The most restrictive approach allows a plaintiff to recover for emotional harm that was suffered from witnessing another person being injured in a certain incident only if the plaintiff was physically injured in the same incident.[107] A more liberal approach, once considered the majority view

---

100 Ibid para 17.
101 Ibid para 19.
102 Ibid para 18.
103 See nos 1–3 of this report.
104 Restatement (Second) of Torts § 313(1) (1965).
105 Ibid § 436 A.
106 See eg, *Southern Railway Co v Jackson*, 91 South Eastern Reporter (SE) 28, 29 (Georgia 1916).
107 See eg, *Lee v State Farm Mutual Insurance Co*, 533 SE 82, 86 (Georgia 2000).

in the United States,[108] enables a person to recover for relational emotional harm if that person was among those physically endangered by the conduct that caused the physical injury to the third party.[109] Some jurisdictions require physical manifestation, whereas others allow recovery for serious emotional harm.

In many common law jurisdictions, liability for relational emotional harm 67
was expanded even further. In *Dillon v Legg*,[110] the Supreme Court of California held that liability for relational emotional harm should depend on its foreseeability, and that in determining whether the harm was reasonably foreseeable, courts should consider whether (1) the plaintiff was located near the scene of the accident or a distance away from it; (2) the plaintiff's shock resulted from the sensory and contemporaneous observance of the accident; and (3) the plaintiff and the victim were closely related. The court stated that the evaluation of these factors would indicate the degree of foreseeability. It confined its ruling to cases in which the plaintiff's fear was manifested in physical consequences. This requirement was eventually replaced by the need to show that the plaintiff's emotional distress was serious.[111] More than half of the US states have adopted *Dillon's* holding that recovery for relational emotional harm is not limited to those who suffer a physical impact in the same incident or are in the zone of danger.[112] However, most require more than mere foreseeability to allow recovery. In many jurisdictions, the *Dillon* guidelines have been practically converted – sometimes with variations or additions – into substantive limitations on recovery.[113] For example, it is generally necessary that the plaintiff have a close relationship with the injured victim.[114] Additionally, in most states, recovery is allowed only where the harm

108 Restatement (Second) of Torts §§ 313(2), 436(3) (1965).

109 See eg, *Keck v Jackson*, 122 Arizona Reports (Ariz) 114, 116 (1979); *Rickey v Chicago Transit Authority*, 98 Illinois Reports, Second Series (Ill 2d) 546, 555 (1983); *KAC v Benson*, 527 North Western Reporter, Second Series (NW 2d) 553, 557–58 (Minnesota 1995); *Asaro v Cardinal Glennon Memorial Hospital*, 799 South Western Reporter, Second Series (SW 2d) 595, 599–600 (Missouri 1990); *Bovsun v Sanperi*, 61 New York Reports, Second Series (NY 2d) 219, 228–31 (1984); *Kloepfel v Bokor*, 149 Washington Reports, Second Series (Wash 2d) 192, 200–01 (2003).

110 68 California Reports, Second Series (Cal 2d) 728 (1968).

111 See *Molien v Kaiser Foundation Hospitals*, 27 Cal 3d 916, 930 (1980).

112 *DJ Gilsinger*, Annotation, Recovery under State Law for Negligent Infliction of Emotional Distress under Rule of Dillon v Legg, 68 Cal 2d 728, 69 California Reporter (Cal Rptr) 72, 441 P 2d 912 (1968), or refinements thereof, 96 American Law Reports (ALR) 5th 107 (2002).

113 See *RS Miller*, The Scope of Liability for Negligent Infliction of Emotional Distress: Making the Punishment Fit the Crime, 1 University of Hawaii Law Review 1, 5 (1979).

114 See *DJ Gilsinger*, Annotation, Relationship between Victim and Plaintiff-Witness as Affecting Right to Recover under State Law for Negligent Infliction of Emotional Distress Due to Witnessing Injury to Another where Bystander Plaintiff Is Not Member of Victim's Immediate Family, 98 ALR 5th 609 (2002).

culminates in physical manifestation,[115] or is at least serious or severe.[116] The Israeli Supreme Court in *Alssouha v Dahan* took this path.

68 The Court in *Alssouha* held that liability for relational emotional harm is subject to four guidelines: (1) the plaintiff must be the direct victim's spouse, child or parent; (2) the plaintiff's direct exposure to the event and its consequences is an indicator of the foreseeability of the secondary harm (though not a strict condition to liability); (3) the proximity in time and place between the occurrence of the secondary harm and the occurrence of the primary injury is also an indicator of foreseeability; and (4) the plaintiff's emotional harm must be severe, amounting to psychosis or neurosis, as established by expert opinion. Subsequent cases, including the one under discussion, have misinterpreted the four guidelines as four preconditions for liability,[117] even though the Court in *Alssouha* was quite clear that only the nature of the relationship and the severity of the harm were intended to be conditions, while direct exposure and proximity were merely signals for foreseeability.

69 Attempts to relax the fourth and most rigid requirement have generally failed. The Supreme Court recognised only a single exception in *Levi v Shaare Zedek*.[118] In that case, medical malpractice resulted in the death of a fetus, and the parents were allowed to recover for emotional harm which did not meet the severity requirement. The Court explained that the fetus itself can have no cause of action for its unintentional killing, because legal personhood crystallises only upon live birth, so without granting the parents a right of action, there would be no legal-economic incentive to avoid the non-intentional killing of fetuses.[119]

70 Therefore, the most critical question in cases of relational emotional harm is whether the plaintiff's harm satisfies the severity requirement. In *Alssouha*, the Court stated that severity should be established through professional medical opinion but did not explain which criteria would be considered. Subsequent decisions have identified various criteria and the Court in *John Doe v The Palestinian Authority* summarised and implemented them. These include medical disability (20 % is usually, but not necessarily, sufficient), the duration of the suffering, the chances of recovery, the likelihood of aggravation, the need for ongoing psychiatric or psychological treatment, the need for medication, impairment of func-

115 Eg *Zell v Meek*, 665 Southern Reporter, Second Series (So 2d) 1048, 1054 (Fla 1995).
116 Eg *Clohessy v Bachelor*, 237 Connecticut Reports (Conn) 31, 56 (1996).
117 See eg, Civ App 9466/05 *Shweki v State of Israel*, 62(3) PD 806, 831–832 (2008).
118 Civ App 754/05 *Levi v Shaare Zedek Medical Centre*, 62(2) PD 218 (2007)
119 The Court relied on *R Perry/Y Adar*, Wrongful Abortion: A Wrong in Search of a Remedy, 5 Yale Journal of Health Policy Law & Ethics 507 (2005).

tioning, impairment of work capacity, and the plaintiff's integration in daily life.[120]

5. Personal Injury

Since its enactment, the Road Accident Victims' Compensation Act (RAVCA)[121] has been subject to continuous interpretation. According to the basic definition in sec 1, a 'road accident' is an incident in which someone sustains bodily injury as a result of the use of a motor vehicle for transportation purposes. Section 1 expands the scope of what qualifies as a road accident through the so-called 'inclusion presumptions', whereby the term also encompasses: (1) Incidents involving explosion or combustion of the vehicle, originating from either its components or another substance essential for its mobility, even when triggered by an external factor; (2) Incidents caused by collision with an illegally parked vehicle; and (3) Incidents resulting from the use of the vehicle's mechanical power, provided that its original function remains unchanged. Lastly, sec 1 excludes from the definition any incident caused by an act intended to inflict harm to the victim's body or property, as long as the injury stemmed from the act itself and not from its interference with the use of the vehicle. 71

The same section also clarifies the meaning of terms included in the basic definition, such as 'bodily injury,' 'use of a motor vehicle,' and 'motor vehicle.' The term 'use of a motor vehicle' is broadly defined to include activities like driving, entering or exiting the vehicle, parking, pushing or towing it, and conducting roadside repairs not in one's professional capacity. It also covers the sliding down or overturning of the vehicle and the falling or disengagement of the vehicle's parts or cargo, whether the vehicle was moving or stationary, so long as it was not under professional maintenance. Notably, the definition excludes cargo loading or unloading while the vehicle is at rest. 72

In a recent case, the Supreme Court discussed incidents in which a person sustains personal injury when *exiting or entering* a vehicle for the purpose of *loading or unloading* cargo.[122] The question, which has been controversial among the lower courts, was whether such an incident constitutes a road accident under RAVCA. On the one hand, entering and exiting is included in 'use of a motor vehicle.' On the other hand, loading and unloading is excluded. In overruling a two- 73

120 Ibid para 13.

121 1975 SH 234.

122 Leave Civ App 4393/22 *John Doe v Harel Insurance Co Ltd* (Supreme Court, 31.7.2024) para 1.

decade-old interpretation,[123] the Supreme Court held that since the legislature excluded 'cargo loading or unloading' from the definition of 'use of a motor vehicle,' exiting or entering in carrying out these activities (as opposed to entering and exiting associated with driving) cannot be deemed 'use of a motor vehicle.'[124] The legislature clearly opined that risks associated with loading and unloading are not covered by RAVCA.[125] The exclusion of loading and unloading from the definition of 'use of a motor vehicle' would be pointless if entering and exiting in carrying out such activities were still deemed 'use of a motor vehicle', because loading/unloading typically entails exiting and entering.[126] Also, allowing claims for injuries sustained in entering or exiting for the purpose of loading or unloading while denying claims for injuries caused by other aspects of loading and unloading might require very fine distinctions that courts should not be required to make.[127] Entering and exiting constitute 'use of a motor vehicle' only if there was driving immediately after the entering or before the exiting.[128]

74 In another recent case, the Supreme Court had to decide whether the crash of a construction site crane on a vehicle whose driver stopped at an on-street parking spot to take a phone call (without unbuckling or turning off the engine) is a road accident involving that vehicle under RAVCA.[129] The Supreme Court restated that only acts that are essential for the driving and constitute a natural and integral part of the driving can be deemed 'driving' within the definition of 'use of a motor vehicle.'[130] It then compared the current case with a 2023 decision discussed in last year's report,[131] whereby a driver was injured when he pulled over at a bus bay to use a navigation app, staying buckled and leaving the engine running. In the 2023 case, the Court concluded that the short stop at the bus bay to use the navigation app (without unbuckling or turning off the engine) did not end the driving, so the driver was still using the vehicle at the time of the accident. In the 2024 case, the Court distinguished the earlier decision, explaining that taking a friendly phone call, as opposed to using a navigation app, is not a natural and in-

123 Leave Civ App 418/03 *Osem Food Industries Ltd v Smadja*, 59(3) PD 541 (2004).
124 Leave Civ App 4393/22 *John Doe v Harel Insurance Co Ltd* (Supreme Court, 31.7.2024) para 9.
125 Ibid.
126 Ibid para 10.
127 Ibid para 11.
128 Ibid paras 6, 12.
129 Leave Civ App 8995/23 *Buildings and Paths (Mivnim U'Netivim) Co Ltd v John Doe* (Supreme Court, 19.9.2024).
130 Ibid para 12.
131 Civ App 5903/22 *Clal Insurance Co v Jane Doe* (Supreme Court, 30.10.2023); *R Perry*, Israel, in: E Karner/BC Steininger (eds), European Tort Law (ETL) 2023 (2024) 753, no 57.

tegral part of driving.[132] Still, the Court opined that the policy of incentivising safe driving, in this case by encouraging drivers without handsfree mobile phones to stop for taking calls, could support the opposite view that the driving was not discontinued by such a stop.[133] The Court concluded that the incident was not a road accident either way given the lack of a causal link between the use of the vehicle and the injury.[134]

132 Leave Civ App 8995/23 *Buildings and Paths (Mivnim U'Netivim) Co Ltd v John Doe* (Supreme Court, 19.9.2024) paras 14–16.
133 Ibid para 16.
134 Ibid paras 17–23.

Filip Melzer

XXXIII. Comparative Remarks

A. Introduction

It is a great honour to contribute to this year's European Tort Law Yearbook by offering some comparative remarks. 1

While many interesting cases were presented in the national reports, the aim of this contribution is to provide a selection of those decisions. Where appropriate, I will seek to draw connections between them, highlight similarities, or point out contrasts. 2

This selection gives rise to two challenges. 3

First, it requires a degree of familiarity with foreign legal systems. I ask for the reader's indulgence should any of my interpretations of national laws prove inaccurate. 4

Second, any such selection is necessarily subjective. My choices have inevitably been shaped by my own legal background. As Czech law belongs – broadly speaking – to the Germanic legal tradition, I invite the reader to consider these remarks as those of a lawyer writing from that particular perspective. I would like to focus in particular on developments in the following areas: 5

1. Legislation
2. Causation
3. Personal Injury
4. Secondary Victims
5. Liability for Increased Danger
6. Product Liability
7. Protection of Personality Rights
8. Liability for Auxiliaries
9. Impact of Contractual Arrangements on Tort Liability

B. Developments in Tort Law in Europe 2024

1. Legislation

To begin with, I would like to briefly address the legislative developments. 6

https://doi.org/10.1515/9783111389271-034

7 Of particular importance is the new EU Directive on Liability for Defective Products.[1] The transposition deadline is 9 December 2026, so we can expect to observe the national implementation of its provisions in the coming years.

8 Among national reforms, Belgium stands out, as it has adopted a completely new tort law framework. Our Belgian colleagues will certainly have their hands full, and I am sure they will keep us informed about how legal practice is adjusting to this new regime. Based on experience from my own jurisdiction, we know that key judgments interpreting new laws often begin to emerge only five or six years after enactment.

9 Some Member States were still completing the transposition of the Motor Insurance Directive[2] in the course of last year. The deadline expired by the end of December 2023, so these jurisdictions were already slightly overdue. Among them were Germany, Ireland, Estonia, Latvia, Slovenia and the Czech Republic.

10 Some partial legislative changes were also adopted. For example, Germany introduced the Guideline Decision Procedure; Austria adopted new rules on liability for damage caused by trees; Estonia enacted mandatory liability insurance for health care providers; France codified the doctrine of private nuisance, and so forth.

11 We will now turn to the cases. The first set of issues I have selected concerns causality.

2. Causation

12 One of the fundamental elements of tort liability is the existence of a causal link between the harmful act and the damage for which compensation is sought. At the same time, this is one of the most challenging issues in practice. Therefore, it comes as no surprise that no fewer than 14 decisions from the country reports addressed this issue.

13 The most problematic cases typically involve establishing causation in relation to harm to human health. Physiological and psychological effects are often

1 Directive (EU) 2024/2853 of the European Parliament and of the Council of 23 October 2024 on liability for defective products and repealing Council Directive 85/374/EEC [1985] Official Journal (OJ) L 210/29.

2 Directive (EU) 2021/2118 of the European Parliament and of the Council of 24 November 2021 amending Directive 2009/103/EC relating to insurance against civil liability in respect of the use of motor vehicles, and the enforcement of the obligation to insure against such liability [2021] OJ L 430/1.

difficult to trace back to a specific cause. This is particularly true in medical malpractice cases, which I will address first.

There is a general trend towards easing the burden of proving causation in such cases. However, jurisdictions differ in their approaches – some reduce the standard of proof, others reverse the burden of proof. 14

A typical method of easing the proof of causation is to lower the standard of proof. But there is no consistent rule regarding how low the threshold should be. For example, we heard that in Sweden, a balance of probabilities is sufficient.[3] Similarly, a Danish court[4] addressed whether a traffic accident caused psychological deterioration. The Medical Board concluded that there was a greater than 50 % probability of a causal link. Based on additional factors, the court accepted the existence of causation. From the decision presented, it is not entirely clear whether the court considered the medically established predominant probability alone to be sufficient, or whether additional circumstances led it to the conclusion that there was, in fact, a higher degree of probability – or even practical certainty – regarding the existence of a causal link. 15

The Swiss Federal Supreme Court[5] also accepted predominant probability. It did not specify an exact threshold, but referred to academic opinion stating that a simple 51 % is not enough, and that a substantially higher level of certainty is required – around 75 %. I would note that this threshold aligns well with my own view under Czech law. 16

A Slovak court[6] also showed a tendency to ease the burden of proof in a medical case. However, the ruling reflects some of the same problems seen in earlier Czech case law. It is not entirely clear whether the court relied on the concept of loss of a chance or whether it simply lowered the standard of proof. The distinction between these two approaches is not merely academic. It has a direct impact on the amount of compensation awarded. Under the loss of a chance doctrine, only partial compensation is awarded. That is, the claimant does not receive full damages for the harm suffered, but rather a proportion of the total, corresponding to the value of the lost opportunity. 17

3 Supreme Court (Högsta domstolen) 8 May 2024, Nytt Juridiskt Arkiv (NJA) 2024, 277: Patient compensation and the issue of proof requirements in cases of injury in the course of treatment.
4 Østre Landsret (High Court, Eastern Division) 15 August 2024, UfR (Ugeskrift for Retsvæsen, Weekly Law Report) U 2024.5043 Ø: Causation between a car collision and the physical and mental harm suffered by the claimant was established.
5 Swiss Federal Supreme Court, 15 May 2024, BGE 4 A_401/2023: Proof of the preponderance of probability of causality in medical malpractice cases.
6 Judgment of the Regional (Appeal) Court in Prešov, 10 December 2024, Case No 5Co/29/2024: Causality in medical cases; loss of a chance.

18 In contrast, where the court lowers the standard of proof – for example, from a high threshold like 'certainty' to a lower one such as 'balance of probabilities' – and then finds causation on that basis, full compensation may be awarded. In this Slovak case, it seems more accurate to say that the court relaxed the standard of proof rather than applying the loss of a chance doctrine in its strict sense.

19 By comparison, if I understood the presentation correctly, Lithuanian courts[7] award partial compensation based on the loss of a chance doctrine.

20 A different and very interesting approach comes from the Latvian Supreme Court,[8] which addressed harm caused by the late diagnosis of cancer. As I understand it, under Latvian law, it is not necessary to prove causation in such cases. The mere delay in treatment constitutes a compensable harm. This is notable because the Czech Supreme Court has taken a similar position: in such cases, the harm lies not in the deterioration of health per se, but in the infringement of a still undefined aspect of the personality protected under the general right of personality.[9]

21 A special situation was considered by the French *Cour de cassation*,[10] which dealt with cases where not even the quality of care could be evaluated due to missing medical records. The Court ruled that if a hospital fails to maintain sufficient documentation, the burden to prove that proper care was given shifts to the health care provider. If this cannot be done, the provider is liable. This approach is convincing: the obligation to keep medical records lies with the provider. If this duty is breached, the provider should not benefit from their own misconduct. The Czech Constitutional Court reached the same conclusion a few years ago.[11]

22 Beyond medical cases, I would like to highlight two decisions dealing with general causation issues, and one decision that, in my view, is highly problematic.

23 The first is an Austrian case dealing with liability for the consequences of a 'shitstorm'.[12]

24 I fully agree that the appropriate concept for addressing this type of case is that of minimal causation. However, under Austrian law (unlike, for example,

7 LSC decision of 25 September 2024, case no e3K-3 – 162 – 1120/2024.
8 Judgment of the Senate of the Republic of Latvia, Department of Administrative Cases, X 2024, no SKA-[C]/2024 X ECLI:LV:AT:2024 X: Compensation insurance indemnity as compensation for late diagnosis of oncological disease.
9 Judgment of the Supreme Court of the Czech Republic, 9 February 2022, Case No 31 Cdo 2376/2021.
10 Cour de cassation, Première chambre civile (Cass Civ 1) 16 October 2024, no 22 – 23433: Liability of health professionals; presumption of fault in the case of insufficient medical documentation.
11 Judgment of the Constitutional Court of the Czech Republic, 9 May 2018, Case No IV. ÚS 14/17.
12 OGH 26 April 2024, 6 Ob 210/23k: Shitstorm; causation; non-pecuniary loss.

Czech law), there is a potential issue that only partial liability might be attributed to each individual participant. Still, according to the commentary on the case presented, it appears that even within the Austrian legal framework, it is possible to conclude that joint and several liability may apply in this situation.

A practically important and elegant decision comes from the German Federal Court of Justice (BGH) concerning the so-called 'garage risk'.[13] This refers to the risk that a repair shop (a garage) may overcharge for repairs to a damaged car, charging for services not performed or inflating costs. The question is whether these costs are attributable to the tortfeasor. More broadly, one may ask whether they constitute a causal consequence of the traffic accident. 25

Since 1974, the BGH has followed the garage risk doctrine, under which the injured party must only exercise due care in selecting the repair shop. If they do so, and are not negligent, the risk of overpricing shifts to the tortfeasor. The injured party is compensated in full, but must assign any claims against the repair shop to the tortfeasor (eg for unjust enrichment). This system is, in my view, well balanced. 26

The BGH also acknowledged that this system works only if the injured party has already paid the repair bill. Otherwise, they could recover the full inflated amount from the tortfeasor, then pay a lower, correct amount to the repair shop, resulting in unjust enrichment on the side of the injured party. The BGH resolved this issue by requiring the tortfeasor to pay directly to the repair shop in such cases. This is a pragmatic and fair solution, and may serve as inspiration for other jurisdictions, including Czech law. 27

Finally, the decision I consider very problematic comes from the Slovak Supreme Court,[14] in a case involving a pedestrian hit by a car at night while wearing dark clothing and no reflectors. The Court found no fault on the part of the driver, who was driving in a sober state, at a safe speed, and with lights on. Under Slovak (and Czech) law, strict liability applies to vehicle operators where the harm results from the inherent risk of operation. The operator may nevertheless be released from liability if they can prove that the damage was caused by circumstances unrelated to the operation itself and that they acted with due care. The contributory fault of the victim is also a relevant consideration. 28

Surprisingly, the Court ruled that there was no causation between the operation of the vehicle and the harm. In truth, the vehicle's movement was clearly a *conditio sine qua non.* A pedestrian being hit is a direct materialisation of the spe- 29

---

13 BGH 16 January 2024, VI ZR 253/22: Garage risk.

14 Judgment of the Supreme Court of the Slovak Republic, 22 February 2024, Case No 4Cdo/197/2022, published in Collection 69/2024: Release of liability for damage caused by the operation of motor vehicles.

cific risk associated with the operation of a vehicle. The only real issue here was contributory negligence. Thus, this was clearly not a question of causation. This flawed reasoning appears to rely on similarly questionable Czech case law, which treats contributory fault as the absence of causation. In this decision, that logic was taken to an absurd extreme.

3. Personal Injury

30 Personal injury cases are among the classic subjects of tort law. One of the most difficult issues is determining the appropriate level of compensation for non-pecuniary damage. Here, we are trying to assign a monetary value to something that is, by its nature, not measurable in money. There is no objectively correct amount. Instead, the amount of compensation reflects a form of social consensus about what is fair and this consensus varies between countries. Interestingly, it does not always correspond to the level of economic prosperity.

31 Personal injury often results not only in non-pecuniary harm but also in significant pecuniary loss and that is what I would like to focus on.

32 Aside from the cost of medical treatment, one of the most important categories is loss of income. This issue was addressed in several national reports.

33 One particularly interesting question is whether compensation for loss of income should be calculated on a gross or net basis. Two cases dealt with this question and came to different conclusions.

34 In a Dutch decision[15] dealing with the loss of income from illegal work, the Court held that the relevant measure is the net income, ie the earnings the claimant would have received after taxes and social security contributions.

35 In contrast, in the Slovenian case,[16] the Court ruled that compensation must place the claimant in the same financial position they would have been in had the harm not occurred. Since the claimant had previously received a gross salary, that amount was the proper measure of damages. The fact that the employer was legally obliged to make deductions on behalf of the employee did not alter this conclusion. According to the Slovenian court, it is irrelevant that the claimant might pay taxes on the compensation received – the loss suffered relates to the gross salary.

15 HR 12 April 2024, ECLI:NL:HR:2024:568: Estimating the extent of damage and undeclared work (Achmea c.s./defendant).

16 Judgment of the Supreme Court II Ips 70/2023, 13 February 2024: Determination of the amount of full compensation.

In my view, this issue may be approached through the lens of *compensatio lucri cum damno* – the principle that the benefit obtained as a result of the damaging event should be deducted from the compensation. In the first step, I agree with the Slovenian court: the injured person has lost the right to a gross salary. What happens next depends on whether or not compensation for loss of income is itself subject to taxation under the relevant national law. 36

If it is subject to tax, then full compensation must reflect the gross amount, since the tax will be deducted anyway. However, if compensation is not taxable – whereas the hypothetical salary would have been – then the non-payment of tax represents a benefit for the injured party. If the conditions for *compensatio lucri cum damno* are met, then this tax advantage should be deducted. In that case, the Dutch approach makes good sense. 37

The Dutch decision is also notable for addressing the issue of earnings from undeclared (illegal) work. The contractor was injured in an accident while working for a school, having fallen from a ladder that had been provided by the school. Liability for the accident was accepted on the school's behalf. However, during the settlement of the claim, it emerged that the contractor had received a significant portion of income from undeclared work – that is, income on which no income tax had been paid. The school's insurer took the position that such income should not be taken into account when assessing the loss of earning capacity. 38

The question arises: should a tortfeasor be liable to compensate income that was generated through illegal work, for which no taxes were paid? The answer of the Dutch court was: yes. 39

And I agree. If the work could have been performed legally, there seems to be no reason to deny compensation. 40

The Czech Supreme Court recently dealt with a similar situation involving work in the United States performed on a tourist visa.[17] The Czech Court used as its criterion whether the claimant could have successfully asserted their right to that income in the relevant country. In my view, the Court should also have considered whether it would have been realistically possible to legalise the work arrangement going forward. 41

An important issue relating to personal injury was addressed by the Hungarian Supreme Court.[18] Specifically, the Court considered the loss of earnings of an individual who provided long-term care to their spouse, who had sustained serious injuries in a traffic accident. The caregiving spouse gave up their employment 42

17 Judgment of the Supreme Court of the Czech Republic, 14 March 2025, Case No 30 Cdo 477/2024.

18 Supreme Court, BG 2024 no 39, Kúria Pfv III.20.223/2023/5, 2024 January: Annuity to compensate the lost income of the victim's relative.

in order to care for the injured partner. In this context, the Hungarian Supreme Court recognised the caregiver's standing (*locus standi*) to bring a claim in their own right. From a comparative perspective, there is also a fundamentally different approach according to which, the caregiver suffers only a pure economic loss, which is generally not compensable. Under this alternative approach, it is instead the injured person who holds the right to claim monetary compensation that enables them to obtain the necessary care services.[19] The divergence between these approaches affects not only standing to sue but also the criteria for assessing the amount of compensation (a point also highlighted by the author of the Hungarian report).

4. Secondary Victims

43 A significant number of decisions discussed at the Annual Conference on European Tort Law relate to the compensation of secondary victims.

44 Let me remind you of the case heard by the Czech Constitutional Court,[20] which brought an end to a long-standing and somewhat absurd practice in Czech case law regarding shock damage (*Schockschaden*). The key question was whether a surviving relative who develops a medically diagnosable mental illness following the death of a loved one can claim compensation for personal injury or only for the pure emotional damage. It is worth highlighting that this shift in case law was prompted by strong doctrinal criticism, which the Constitutional Court ultimately accepted.

45 A particularly interesting issue was addressed by a Scottish court,[21] which considered whether a general settlement with the primary victim excludes any later claims by secondary victims. Under Scottish law, if I understood it correctly, the answer is generally yes, although there is an exception in cases involving mesothelioma.

46 The case is especially noteworthy because secondary victims hold their own independent claims, not merely claims inherited from the primary victim. From

19 Cf eg, the judgment of the Grand Chamber of the Civil and Commercial Division of the Czech Supreme Court, 10 November 2021, Case No 31 Cdo 1904/2021.

20 Constitutional Court of the Czech Republic (Ústavní soud České republiky) 28 May 2024, Constitutional Court Pl. ÚS 14/24: Causation; interruption of causal nexus; theory of adequacy; secondary and primary victims.

21 *Crozier v Scottish Power UK Ltd*, Court of Session (Inner House) 4 June 2024, [2024] CSIH 14, 2024 SC 373: Whether family of deceased man, who had claimed for risk of developing mesothelioma, could also claim damages in respect of his death from mesothelioma.

this perspective, it seems problematic for another person – the primary victim – to decide the fate of those claims.

On the other hand, the primary victim is not a complete stranger to those rights. The damage suffered by the secondary victim relates to the loss of a personal relationship with the deceased primary victim. And the primary victim had control over that relationship during their lifetime – they could have ended it at any time. If someone ends their life through negligence or suicide, we do not say they unlawfully interfered with the rights of their loved ones who mourn them. Likewise, contributory negligence on the part of the deceased must be taken into account. A close relative cannot claim compensation from the deceased's estate simply because the deceased, through their own actions, terminated the relationship. If this relationship – the protected interest – was under the control of the primary victim, we should ask why the right to compensation for harm to that interest should not also be within their control. From this perspective, I find the Scottish legislative approach not unreasonable. However, I believe that Czech courts would not recognise such a possibility for the primary victim. 47

This also shows that, when compensating secondary victims, it is essential to define what interest is protected and what the legal basis of the claim is. Legal systems differ here. In the Czech Republic and Slovakia, courts treat these cases as infringements of personality rights, especially the right to privacy, which they understand in light of the case law of the European Court of Human Rights under art 8 of the European Convention on Human Rights. The right to respect for private life within the meaning of this article of the European Convention includes the right to form and maintain relationships with close persons. 48

In cases involving psychiatric injury, the issue is not merely one of greater intensity of non-pecuniary damage compared to pure emotional harm. Rather, these two forms of harm are grounded in the violation of different legally protected interests. Accordingly, where psychiatric injury is inflicted, the victim is entitled both to compensation for the personal injury itself and to damages for emotional suffering resulting from the loss of a close person. 49

If it is assumed that pure emotional harm and shock harm differ only in intensity, then compensation can only be awarded for one type of harm. 50

Among the cases dealing with compensation for secondary victims, I would like to mention the English *Paul* case.[22] The English approach stands out for its 51

22 *Paul and another v Royal Wolverhampton NHS Trust*; *Polmear and another v Royal Cornwall Hospitals NHS Trust*; *Purchase v Ahmed*, United Kingdom Supreme Court (UKSC) 2 [2024] Weekly Law Reports (WLR) 417: Negligence; psychiatric harm; secondary victims; medical negligence.

strict limitations. Not only is emotional distress generally not compensable, but even compensation for shock damage is narrowly confined. The *Paul* case limits compensation to instances of fatal accidents, with the notion of 'accident' being construed in a relatively narrow sense.

52 Another notable decision comes from Croatia, where a court denied compensation for the death of a pet.[23] The commentary accompanying this case shows that there is growing debate about whether pets should be considered part of a household, and whether harm caused by their death might be treated similarly to claims of secondary victims. Some jurisdictions do provide such compensation. In Czech law, I am also aware of one minority decision that follows this line.

53 Importantly, these claims are not for *pretium affectionis* – ie loss of sentimental value – as recognised in Austrian (§ 1331 ABGB) or Czech law (§ 2969 Civil Code). However, these would be the right of the owner. If a case concerned the rights of a secondary victim, then the right to compensation would not belong to the owner, but to the person for whom the animal was a companion.

54 Like the Croatian case, the prevailing view is still largely dismissive of such claims. Recognising them would raise complex issues, such as foreseeability of harm and standing to sue.

5. Liability for Increased Danger

55 Another fundamental issue in tort law is the question of what type of liability should apply to particularly dangerous activities. These are typically operations where a high level of danger cannot be fully eliminated, even with the exercise of due care. Should such activities be governed by fault-based liability, or is strict (objective) liability more appropriate? When liability arises without fault due to permitted risk, we speak of liability for danger, or risk-based liability.

56 If the legislator opts for a concept of strict liability, two legislative approaches can be distinguished: legal systems either provide for a general clause of strict liability or rely on specific statutory provisions covering particularly dangerous activities.

57 When a general clause exists, it is necessary to assess whether a given activity qualifies as sufficiently dangerous. This is not always straightforward. For exam-

23 Presuda Županijskog suda u Slavonskom Brodu (Judgment of the County Court in Slavonski Brod) No Gž-161/2023–2, 30 August 2024: No compensation of non-material damage for deceased pet.

ple, the Czech Supreme Court[24] addressed whether organising a motocross race – not just an individual rider's actions – constituted a particularly dangerous activity. The Court concluded that it did. It is remarkable that practically the same case with the same outcome was also heard by Hungarian courts.[25] Although both legal frameworks are very similar, which would suggest an identical outcome in both cases, the differing legislative definitions of the notion of 'operator' merit attention. While Czech law defines the operator as the person who has actual control over the source of increased danger, ie the party who exercises certain qualified supervision over it, Hungarian law considers the operator to be the person in whose interest the activity is carried out.

The Polish Supreme Court[26] examined whether operating a petrol station qualifies as a dangerous enterprise. Interestingly, the damage in that case was caused not by flammable substances, but by an armed robbery. The Court found that a petrol station only stores fuel, without processing it, and therefore does not qualify as a dangerous enterprise under art 435 of the Polish Civil Code. 58

Strict liability requires that the specific risk inherent in the dangerous nature of the activity actually materialises. This is the 'risk nexus' (*Gefährdungszusammenhang*). In the Polish case, the harm did not result from the inherent risk of storing flammable substances but from a criminal act. It is noteworthy that the Polish Supreme Court did not examine this connection. 59

This notion of materialisation of risk also appeared in other judgments. For instance, the German Federal Court of Justice[27] ruled on liability for damage caused by a dog acting under a human's command. The Court held that even when an animal follows instructions, it can still act with its own energy and autonomy, especially if it is not under immediate human control. This behaviour thus reflects the inherent risk of keeping an animal, justifying strict liability. 60

In systems relying on specific statutory grounds for strict liability, the question often arises whether such rules can be applied by analogy to similar but uncovered situations. Legal systems differ on this point, as shown in two contrasting cases. 61

24 Supreme Court of the Czech Republic (Nejvyšší soud České republiky) 20 August 2024, 25 Cdo 3108/2023: Motocross race, particularly dangerous operation.

25 Supreme Court, BH 2024 38, Kúria Pfv.III.20.239/2023/5, 2024 January: Liability for accident at a sports event.

26 SN, Izba Pracy i Ubezpieczeń Społecznych (Chamber of Labour and Social Insurance) 22 May 2024, III PSKP 17/23 (OSNP 2024 no 10 item 98): Liability of a petrol station operator for an employee's injury caused by a robbery attack.

27 BGH 11 June 2024, VI ZR 381/23: Animal keeper's liability for a dog under human direction.

62 The Swedish Supreme Court[28] considered damage caused by the overheating of a connector in a high-voltage cable. Since the case involved damage to another electrical device, it fell under an exception to strict liability under electricity law. The Court concluded that the statutory regime exclusively governs risks related to electricity, and broader principles of strict liability could not be applied in parallel.

63 In Greece, the Athens court[29] also dealt with a case in which damage was caused by a fire resulting from the transmission of electricity within the distribution network. The court held the electricity company liable without requiring proof of fault. It based liability on the risk principle (liability for danger), which applies to activities involving a high level of danger that cannot be controlled through ordinary care. According to the court, the fire that occurred in connection with the operation of the distribution infrastructure fell within the scope of strict liability for risk.

64 The court also relied on classical arguments related to evidentiary difficulties – arguments that were already brought in the late 19th century by my compatriot and Vienna-based professor, Adolf Exner.

65 Greek law recognises specific statutory provisions for strict liability, but electricity distribution networks are not explicitly included among them. The court therefore concluded that in such cases, liability must be derived directly from constitutional principles – specifically from art 25(1) of the Constitution, which enshrines the horizontal effect of fundamental rights in relationships between private individuals.

66 The court explicitly addressed the idea of a conscious legislative gap – where the legislature deliberately limits the scope of strict liability to certain cases. It found, however, that this was not the case. The exclusion of power grids from statutory liability rules was not intentional but merely the result of incomplete regulation. Denying liability in this case, while imposing it for, say, animal owners, would be illogical and inconsistent with the principle of legal equality.

67 Another interesting approach appears in a decision of the Dutch Supreme Court[30] concerning damage caused by construction work involving an 'immersion pit'. This approach also comes close to liability for risk. During construction work, damage was caused to a neighbouring property. The liability in this case was classified as liability for a wrongful act. However, art 6:162 of the Dutch Civil Code – if

28 Supreme Court (Högsta domstolen) 23 December 2024. NJA 2024, 911: No strict liability outside of electricity legislation.

29 Three-Member Court of Appeal of Athens, 12 July 2024, no 3095: Risk liability.

30 HR 12 January 2024, ECLI:NL:HR:2024:17: Standard of care towards third parties (immersion pit).

I have understood it correctly – considers an act to be unlawful even where it merely constitutes an infringement of another person's right, provided that the cause of the infringement can be attributed to the defendant's sphere of risk, according to prevailing legal understanding. There is, therefore, no need for fault or defective conduct on the part of the defendant.

In the case at hand, the Court indeed found that even properly executed construction work may constitute an unlawful act vis-à-vis third parties if it causes them serious harm and there is no justification for requiring them to tolerate it. This approach, in substance, is very close to the concept of strict liability for permitted danger. 68

6. Product Liability

In the important field of product liability, we should begin by mentioning the recent CJEU judgment in Ford Italia.[31] The key issue was whether Ford Italia could be considered the 'producer' of the vehicle in question. The car had not been manufactured by Ford Italia, but by Ford-Werke AG, the German entity. Ford Italia argued that it did not meet the definition of a 'producer' under art 3(1) of the 1985 Product Liability Directive, since it had not physically affixed its name or trademark to the vehicle. That had been done by Ford-Werke AG. 69

However, the name 'Ford' was also part of Ford Italia's company name. The CJEU held that a supplier of a defective product may be considered a producer under the Directive if the name or distinctive sign under which it operates is identical, or very similar, to the brand or name affixed to the product, even if the supplier did not physically apply it. This condition was met in the case of Ford Italia. 70

In another case relating to product liability, the Austrian Supreme Court[32] addressed whether anxiety about potential health damage can be classified as compensable harm. In this case, the anxiety did not reach the level of a diagnosable health disorder or any equivalent interference with physical integrity. Under Austrian law, mere fear or discomfort does not qualify as damage. Moreover, European product liability law does not itself provide for compensation for pure non-material harm. 71

By contrast, French law adopts a more open approach to compensating distress or anxiety. Two cases were discussed in which the French *Cour de cassa-* 72

31 CJEU 19.12.2024, C-157/23, *Ford Italia SpA v ZP, Stracciari SpA*, ECLI:EU:C:2024:1045.

32 OGH 22 October 2024, 4 Ob 109/24v: Fear of injury; product liability.

tion[33] considered whether fear of future harm could justify compensation. Although French law does recognise such claims, the court has moved toward a more restrictive standard. While in 2023 it accepted that mere exposure to risk could be enough, it now requires anxiety resulting from exposure to a high risk of developing a serious pathology.

7. Protection of Personality Rights

73 The most controversial decision in the area of personality rights comes from Poland. It concerned the question of whether the right to reproduction constitutes an autonomous personality right protected under general civil law personality rights. The issue arose in a case where a hospital's medical negligence resulted in the permanent infertility of a female patient. Both the patient and her husband sought compensation.

74 The Polish Supreme Court answered this question in the negative. This does not mean, of course, that such a consequence of negligent medical treatment is without legal effect. However, the Court considered the harm to be a matter of serious personal injury, rather than a violation of a separate personality right.

75 This approach had practical implications, particularly for the patient's husband. He was not entitled to bring a claim for personal injury in his own right, and, since no independent personality right had been infringed, he lacked a legal basis for compensation.

76 The Polish Supreme Court rejected the view that the scope of personality rights under civil law is automatically determined by the protection provided under art 8 of the European Convention on Human Rights or art 47 of the Polish Constitution. Rights such as the right to private life, family life, honour, and dignity are not identical to the personal rights protected under civil law.

77 It is important to emphasise that art 8 of the ECHR protects 'private life', not 'privacy' in the narrow sense. In contrast to the Universal Declaration of Human Rights, the drafters of the Convention intentionally opted for the concept of 'private life', which they intended to be interpreted more broadly.

78 This Polish decision represents a fundamentally different approach from that followed in Czech case law. I would expect a different outcome if the same case were to be decided under Czech law.

---

33 Cass Civ 1, 11 July 2024, no 23–10068 and 18 December 2024, no 24–14750: Redefining the outlines of 'prejudice of anxiety' ('préjudice d'anxiété').

Closely related to the protection of personality rights is an interesting Israeli case concerning liability for paternity fraud.[34] In 2019, the claimant discovered that he was not the biological father of a child born to his wife in 2014. The petitioner brought an action against the respondent seeking compensation for pecuniary loss, namely the costs of raising the child, and for non-pecuniary damage resulting, among others, from a violation of the petitioner's autonomy and dignity, as well as from the separation from the child. The key legal question was whether a woman is under a legal duty to inform her spouse that he is not the biological father of her newborn child. Policy considerations played a decisive role in the Court's reasoning. Based on such considerations, the Court rejected the father's claim. However, the reasoning among the individual judges was not entirely uniform. The use of openly acknowledged legal policy reasoning is characteristic of judges in common law jurisdictions.[35] I believe, however, that such reasoning is also employed – albeit often implicitly – by judges in other legal systems. This raises the important question of how such reasoning should be positioned within the legal dogmatics of other jurisdictions. From the perspective of Czech law (and similarly, for example, German, Austrian, or Swiss law), such considerations can be integrated into the assessment of whether a given legal rule constitutes a protective norm, or when determining the scope of its protective purpose, in this case, for example, in relation to the statutory rule that spouses owe each other fidelity (sec 687(2) of the Czech Civil Code). 79

8. Liability for Auxiliaries

Several of the decisions presented also addressed the important issue of vicarious liability, that is, liability for damage caused by auxiliaries or subordinates. 80

At first glance, a decision by the Austrian Supreme Court[36] may seem surprising. The case concerned a municipality's liability for sexual abuse committed by its mayor. While this was technically addressed as a case of liability for the exercise of public power, as rightly noted in the accompanying commentary, the core issue arises in any hierarchical organisation. The key question is whether the may- 81

34 Leave Fam App 4181/22 *John Doe v Jane Doe* (Supreme Court, 19.5.2024): Liability for paternity fraud.

35 Cf also this line of reasoning in another Israeli decision: Leave Civ App 8153/23 *State of Israel v Shay* (Supreme Court, 16.6.2024): State liability for negligent investigation of crime/failure to prosecute.

36 OGH 19 November 2024, 1 Ob 167/24a: Liability of a town for a mayor's sexual abuse.

or's conduct can be regarded as an act of so-called excess, for which the principal (in this case, the municipality) is not liable.

82 Generally, to attribute the conduct of an auxiliary to the principal, three elements are required: temporal, locational, and functional (or substantive) connection with the tasks performed for the principal. In this case, both the temporal and locational criteria were clearly met. The controversial question was whether the functional connection was present. This is usually denied if the auxiliary acted purely for their own personal interest and sexual abuse typically falls under this category.

83 However, the Court emphasised that the mayor had a duty of care toward his subordinates, and that he abused the power of his office to commit the act. His position as a representative of the municipality allowed him to exploit structural power. Therefore, the municipality was held liable.

84 I agree with the outcome, but find the reasoning problematic. If we were to accept the Court's reasoning in full, then any tortious act – even one committed exclusively for personal reasons – by someone owing a duty of care would never be considered an 'excess', as long as there was a physical and temporal connection. That seems overly broad.

85 In my view, the proper starting point is to ask whether the auxiliary acted for the principal or solely in their own personal interest. However, this test should allow for exceptions. There may be circumstances where, even if the auxiliary acted in their own interest, liability should still be attributed to the principal, namely, when the harm results from the misuse of a specific opportunity that was made available by the principal.

86 By 'specific opportunity', I mean a situation that enabled the harm in a particular way, not merely a *conditio sine qua non*. An example would be where an employee gains access to a private space because of their job – say, a plumber stealing from a customer's home. Another example is the so-called *'heparin murderer'* case in the Czech Republic, where a nurse intentionally killed patients by injecting them with heparin. This was only possible because patients trusted the hospital and allowed medical staff to inject substances into their bodies.[37] The specific opportunity created by the hospital was thus a crucial enabling factor.

87 On the other hand, if the act could have been practically committed anywhere and under any circumstances, with no such special link within the principal's

37 However, according to Czech courts, the conduct in question constituted an excess for which the principal is not liable; cf Judgment of the Supreme Court of the Czech Republic, 31 March 2009, Case No 6 Tdo 1334/2008.

sphere, then the conduct should be treated as an 'excess' and not attributed to the principal.

88 Returning to the Austrian case, the decisive question is whether the mayor's authority, attributable to the municipality, enabled the commission of the act. If so – and this seems to be the case – then the municipality should be held liable.

89 A contrasting example can be found in a Greek case.[38] The claimant, a truck driver, was hired by a transport company. On his second day at work, while on company premises during working hours, a dispute between colleagues escalated into a shooting, and the claimant was seriously injured. He sued the employer on the basis of vicarious liability.

90 The Greek Supreme Court rejected the claim. Although the temporal and locational requirements were satisfied, the Court found no functional link between the violent act and the employee's professional duties. The attack stemmed from a personal motive, unrelated to the employer's interests. I fully agree with this assessment. When an employee acts exclusively in their own interest, vicarious liability is generally excluded, unless they exploited a specific opportunity created by the employer. That was not the case here. The incident could have occurred anywhere: the fact that it happened at work was, in this context, coincidental.

91 From the perspective of a Central European lawyer within the Germanic legal tradition, I find a Scottish decision particularly difficult to understand. It concerned the State's liability for the conduct of a judge. Judicial conduct is a typical example of the exercise of public power. In the Czech Republic, such liability has been recognised since 1867. It is therefore difficult to comprehend that the State could be exempt from liability on the basis of separation of powers and the idea that liability could threaten judicial independence. This reflects a very different legal tradition.

9. The Impact of Contractual Arrangements on Tort Liability

92 Some court decisions addressed one of the classic (and still highly controversial) issues of tort law, namely, the impact of contractual limitations on tort liability, particularly in cases involving liability towards third parties. A French decision[39] dealt with a situation where a French branch of a packaging company hired a transport company to handle and unload machines owned by its Italian parent

38 Areios Pagos (Greek Supreme Court) 24 February 2024, no 433: Liability for assistants.

39 Cour de cassation, Chambre commerciale (Cass Com) 3 July 2024, no 21–14947: Liability of contracting parties towards third parties; extension of contractual provisions to extra-contractual liability.

company. One of the machines was damaged. The parent company's insurer paid compensation and, acting in its place, sued the transport company for both contractual and tort liability. The question was whether a limitation clause provided in the contract could be enforced against the claimant, even though the parent company was a third party. The Court of Cassation held that a third party relying on a contractual breach in tort can be subject to the same liability limits as those agreed between the contracting parties, so as not to confer greater rights on the third party other than those held by the original creditor.

93 A similar issue arose before the Israeli court in *Amidar v John Doe:*[40] whether and to what extent a contract between two parties may affect a cause of action in tort that one may have against a third (non-contracting) party, or that a third party may have against one of the contracting parties. Unfortunately, the Court did not resolve this general question. However, with regard to the parties to the case, it concluded that the victim cannot file a tort claim if this is inconsistent with valid provisions of a contract.

C. Conclusion

94 In conclusion, this contribution has sought to select and highlight a number of tort law decisions from 2024, with particular attention to cases addressing comparable issues, at times leading to similar outcomes, at others diverging in significant ways.

95 Naturally, such an overview cannot cover all the decisions contained in the national reports. Readers are therefore encouraged to examine the remaining noteworthy cases included in this Yearbook, which, for various reasons, could not be addressed within the scope of these Comparative Remarks.

40 Leave Civ App 7265/23 Amidar – *The National Company for Housing in Israel Ltd v John Doe* (Supreme Court, 4.3.2024): Negligent misrepresentation; interrelation between contract and tort law).

Contributors

Ewa BAGIŃSKA

Faculty of Law and
Administration
Gdańsk University
Jana Bażyńskiego 6
80 – 309 Gdańsk, Poland
Tel: (+48) 58 523 2851
baginska@fulbrightmail.org

Ewa Bagińska (Prof Dr hab) holds the Chair of Civil Law at the School of Law and Administration of the University of Gdańsk. She was a Fulbright Visiting Scholar (1998/1999) and NATO Science Fellowship grantee (2000/2001) at the CUA Columbus School of Law, Washington, DC. She has authored a number of books on product liability, public liability and medical law, as well as over 200 other contributions in the area of civil law. She is the editor of 'Damages for Violations of Human Rights. A Comparative Study of Domestic Legal Systems', Springer Verlag (2016). Ewa Bagińska is a member of the Commission for the Codification of Civil Law. She is a member of the European Group on Tort Law, the International Academy of Comparative Law (of which she is currently vice-president) and the European Law Institute. She is also a member of several advisory boards of law journals in the field of comparative law (incl European Review of Private Law) and is editor of two national journals (State and Law and the Insurance Quarterly Review). She acts as a National Correspondent for the Journal of Civil Law Studies (Louisiana, US).

Marko BARETIĆ

University of Zagreb, Faculty of Law
Trg Republike Hrvatske 3
10000 Zagreb, Croatia
Tel: (+385) 1 4597 561
mbaretic@pravo.hr

Marko Baretić is a tenured Professor of Civil Law and Consumer Protection Law at the Faculty of Law of the University of Zagreb. He obtained his LLM (Pre-Contractual Liability) and PhD (Liability for Defective Products) degrees from the University of Zagreb. He also studied at the Asser College Europe, Asser Institute, The Hague, The Netherlands. He publishes on various topics in the fields of civil law, predominantly the law of obligations (contract law and tort law) and consumer protection law. Baretić was active in negotiations of the Republic of Croatia for accession to the EU as a member of the working group 28 (consumer protection and health). As a member of various legislative working groups, he actively

https://doi.org/10.1515/9783111389271-035

participated in drafting the Croatian Obligations Act and the Consumer Protection Act. He was the representative of the Republic of Croatia in the working group III of UNCITRAL (online dispute resolution). Baretić is also active in commercial arbitration.

Elena BARGELLI

Faculty of Political Science
Pisa University
Via Serafini 3
56126 Pisa, Italy
Tel: (+39) 50 2212458
bargelli@sp.unipi.it

Elena Bargelli is currently a full Professor of Private Law at the University of Pisa, Law Department. She was a Research Fellow of the Alexander von Humboldt Stiftung at the Max Planck Institut für ausländisches und internationales Privatrecht in Hamburg (2008 – 2009). She is a member of ECTIL, the International Academy of Comparative Law (IACL) and the European Law Institute. She is on the editorial board of several journals and book series. She has authored a number of books as well as numerous contributions in various fields of civil law. Her areas of interest are contract law, tort law and family law from a national, comparative and EU perspective.

Søren BERGENSER

Bergenser Advokatfirma
Ostre Kanalgade 4
9000 Aalborg, Denmark
Tel: (+45) 21177472
sb@bergenserlaw.dk

Søren Bergenser is an Assistant Professor at the University of Aalborg, Institute of Private Law, where he deals with professional and product liability and the liability of public authorities. Bergenser holds a PhD from the University of Copenhagen and he was a research fellow at Duke University School of Law and at the Max Planck Institute of Private Law in Hamburg. In 1999, Bergenser graduated from Aarhus University, where he also worked as an Assistant Professor from 1997 – 1999. He is also a practising lawyer and liability and insurance law, litigation and arbitration are his areas of expertise.

Agris BITĀNS

University of Latvia, Faculty of Law
Raina bulvaris 19
Riga, LV 1586, Latvia
Tel: (+371) 67280102
agris.bitans@eversheds-sutherland.lv

Agris Bitāns graduated from the Faculty of Law at the University of Latvia with a Bachelor's degree in law in 1993 and with a Master's degree in law in 1995. As well as practising as an attorney-at-law, he continues his academic studies at the

University of Latvia for a doctorate degree. He also lectures at the Civil Law Department, Faculty of Law, University of Latvia. His area of expertise is the law of obligations, with a focus on civil liability, contract law, tort law, intellectual property law and Roman law. Bitāns is a co-author of the commentaries on Obligation Law of the Latvian Civil Law and co-author of the commentaries on Sections 2 and 8 of the Latvian Constitution. He is the author of the book 'Civil liability and its kinds' ('Civiltiesiskā atbildība un tās veidi') and of many articles relating to law issues, as well as co-author of the book 'Problems of Contract Law and Tort Law in the European Union and Latvia' ('Līgumu un deliktu problēmas Eiropas Savienībā un Latvijā'). He is a member of the Latvian Bar, International Bar Association and AIPPI (International Association for the Protection of Industrial Property). From 2008 until 2014, Bitāns was the Council's member of the Latvian Bar and since 2005 he has been the President of AIPPI Latvian National Group. Since his admittance to the Latvian Bar in 1998, he has been practising mostly in civil (contracts and tort), intellectual property, commercial and administrative matters. Bitāns is a managing partner of the law office 'Eversheds Sutherland Bitāns'. His fields of legal research include contract and tort law, personality law, medical law and media law. He is also a regular participant at international conferences and workshops dealing with civil law, intellectual property law, litigation and arbitration.

Lucian BOJIN

West University of Timisoara, Faculty of Law
Bd Eroilor de la Tisa no 9/A
300557 Timisoara, Romania
Tel: (+40) 256 592400
lucian.bojin@e-uvt.ro

Lucian Bojin was born in 1975 in Timisoara. He graduated from the University of Timisoara in 1998 and pursued postgraduate and PhD studies in Business Law. He is an Associate Professor at the West University of Timisoara where he teaches International Law and Human Rights. Bojin is also a practising barrister and partner in the law firm 'Valentin & Asociatii'. He has authored three books and published over 40 papers on European Law, International Law, Business Law, Private Law and Human Rights.

Sergiu CĂILEANU

West University of Timisoara
Faculty of Law
Bd Eroilor de la Tisa no 9/A
300557 Timisoara, Romania
Tel: (+40) 256 592400
sergiu.caileanu@e-uvt.ro

Sergiu Căileanu graduated from the University of Timişoara in 2017 and obtained a Master's degree in Business Law in 2018. He is a PhD candidate in Civil Law, with a thesis on the relation between property and contract law in the field of securities. He has also been a practising barrister in the Timis Bar Association since 2017 and has published several papers in the field of contract law.

Giannino CARUANA DEMAJO

Judges' Chambers, Courts of Justice
Republic Street
Valletta VLT 2000, Malta
Tel: (+35) 6 2590 2281
giannino.caruanademajo@gov.mt

Giannino Caruana Demajo was born in Malta in 1958. He graduated in law (LLD) from the University of Malta in 1982 and was awarded a warrant to practise as Advocate in the Superior Courts in April of that year, after which he exercised the profession in private practice until 1994. Caruana Demajo was appointed lecturer in Civil Law at the University of Malta in 1989 and Head of the Department of Civil Law in 1993. Between 1992 and 1994, he also served as Chairman of the Board of a commercial reinsurance company. In 1997, Caruana Demajo was appointed Chairman of the Committee of Experts on Efficiency of Justice of the Council of Europe, a post he held until 1999, during which time he also served on the Committee of Experts advising on the drafting of the Enforcement Code of Bosnia-Herzegovina, the Code of Procedure of Moldova and the Civil Code of Ukraine. In December 1994, he was appointed Judge of the Superior Courts, where he is Senior Administrative Judge since 2007 and Vice-Chairman of the Judicial Studies Board since 2009.

Rui CASCÃO

Lusófona University of Porto, Faculty of Law and Political Science
Rua Augusto Rosa, nº 24
4000 – 098 Porto, Portugal
Tel: (+351) 22 2 073 230
Rui.cascao@ulusofona.pt

Rui Cascão (LLB Coimbra, PhD Tilburg, ECPC-B DPO Cert Maastricht) is a Professor of EU Law and Law of Succession at the Lusófona University of Porto and researcher at the Centre for Advanced Legal Studies Francisco Suárez (CEAD). He is also Adjunct Professor at the Higher School of Management and Technology of the Polytechnic Institute of Leiria, Portugal. Cascão has taught and conducted research in several higher education institutions: Centre for Biomedical Law of the University of Coimbra (since 2001); ISIT-University of Paris 2 Panthéon-Assas (since 2021); Legal and Judicial Training Centre of Macau, China (2009 – 2016); Karl-Franzens-University of Graz, Austria (2006 – 2008); and Tilburg University, The Netherlands (2000 – 2005). Between 2008 and 2021, he was Senior Legal Advisor to the Government of Macau, China, responsible for legislative production, legal reform, and international law matters. Cascão is a member of the board of the Portuguese Association of Health Law (ALDIS), as well as a member of the European Law Institute (ELI) and the World Association for Medical Law (WAML). He is the author of several scientific productions in the area of private, European and healthcare law and has participated in high-impact international research projects, such as the Draft Common Frame of Reference (DCFR) and Shifts in Compensation between Private and Public Systems (Tort and Insurance Law vol 22). Cascão is currently developing research on international and European health law, medical liability, European law of successions, law and technology, and fundamental rights and private law.

Orcid: 0000 – 0001 – 9783 – 2337.

Michael CHATZIPANAGIOTIS

University of Cyprus, Department of Law
1 Panepistimiou Ave OED 02, office B126
2109 Aglantzia, Nicosia, Cyprus
Tel: (+357) 22892937
chatzipanagiotis.michael@ucy.ac.cy

Michael Chatzipanagiotis is an Assistant Professor in Private Law at the Department of Law of the University of Cyprus. He teaches Tort Law, Insurance Law, Consumer Protection, Banking Law, European Private Law and Air Law. His main research interests are Legal aspects of Artificial Intelligence (AI), Torts, Air and Space Law, Insurance Law, Consumer Protection, Intellectual Property Rights (IPR), Banking Law and Alternative Dispute Resolution (ADR). He has also participated in various research and consulting projects of the European Commission on the digitalisation of justice, air law, space law and consumer protection. Before joining the University of Cyprus, he worked as a lawyer and a legal advisor in Cyprus, Greece and Germany.

Sébastien DE REY

UC Louvain, Faculté de droit et de criminologie
Centre de droit privé
Place Montesquieu 2 bte L.2.07.01
1348 Louvain-la-Neuve, Belgium
Tel: (+32) 10 47 47 35
sebastien.derey@uclouvain.be

Sébastien De Rey is Visiting Professor at UC Louvain (Belgium) and Associate Professor at the University of Amsterdam (the Netherlands) and the Royal Military Academy of Belgium, where he teaches tort law, contract law, and specific contracts. His research covers comparative contract law and torts, with a focus on sanctions and private law remedies. He obtained his Master's degree from KU Leuven (2014) and completed a PhD on non-monetary relief at the same institution (2018). He held postdoctoral positions at the City University of Hong Kong (2019–2020) and KU Leuven (2021–2022), and has been a visiting scholar at Leiden University, the Max Planck Institute for Comparative and International Private Law, the University of Zurich, and the University of Paris 2 Panthéon-Assas. He is also a member of the Commission responsible for reforming the Belgian Civil Code, serving on the subcommittee for Book 7 on Specific Contracts.

Emanuel GD VAN DONGEN

Utrecht Centre for Accountability and Liabilty Law
Molengraaff Institute for Private Law
Utrecht Law School
Achter Sint Pieter 200
3512 HT Utrecht, The Netherlands
e.g.d.vandongen@uu.nl

Emanuel van Dongen is an Associate Professor at the Molengraaff Institute for Private Law, Utrecht University, the Netherlands, and a Research Fellow at the Utrecht Centre for Accountability and Liability Law. He is also a deputy judge at the Court of Appeal, Arnhem-Leeuwarden. He studied law at Tilburg University and, partly, at the Catholic University of Nijmegen. He obtained his PhD at Maastricht University. In 2017 and 2019, he was a visiting scholar and professor at UISS Universita di Guido Carli, Rome. From 2018–2024, he was a visiting professor at Universita degli Studi di Torino. In 2019, he was a visiting fellow at Universita degli studi Roma Tre. In 2021–2022, he was a visiting professor at Ghent University.

Anton DULAK

Pan-European University, Law Faculty
Tomašikova 20
820 09 Bratislava, Slovakia

After graduating in law in 1985, Anton Dulak started to work at the Department of Civil Law at Comenius University, Bratislava as an assistant. In

Tel: (+421) 2 4820 8834
anton.dulak@gmail.com

2001, he obtained his PhD degree. In 2003, Dulak habilitated with a thesis on Product Liability Law and was promoted to an associate professor. He has attended courses at Cambridge University, the University of Oslo and University Louvain la Neuve. He is a member of the Slovak Bar Association. From 2007 until 2015, Dulak was a member of the Ministry of Justice Recodification Commission for a new Civil Code. From 2013–2015, he was the Chairman of this Commission. Since 2018, he has been a full professor at the Law Faculty of the Pan-European University in Bratislava.

Andreas BLOCH EHLERS

Copenhagen University
Studiegaarden
Studiestraede 6
1455 Copenhagen, Denmark
Tel: (+45) 353 – 23103
andreas.ehlers@jur.ku.dk

Andreas Ehlers is a Professor of Tort Law at the University of Copenhagen. He obtained his Master's degree from the University of Copenhagen in 2004 and subsequently worked for the law firm 'Kromann Reumert' in Copenhagen. In 2006, Andreas Ehlers was awarded the Sir Gerrard Brennan Scholarship at the University of Queensland (Australia) from where he obtained an LLM degree in 2007. In 2011, he published his PhD thesis, which deals with the doctrine of adequacy in tort law. In 2017, Andreas Ehlers published an LLD thesis on causation and personal injury.

Sandra FRIBERG

Juridiska institutionen Uppsala universitet
Riddartorget, Trädgårdsgatan 1
751 20 Uppsala, Sweden
Tel: (+46) 18 – 471 71 44
sandra.friberg@jur.uu.se

Sandra Friberg is an Associate Professor of Tort Law at the faculty of law, University of Uppsala. She obtained her doctorate in law (LLD) at the end of 2010 after defending her thesis on Non-Pecuniary Damages to Victims of Crime. The thesis rendered her the Karnov prize (Thomson-Reuters Professional) and the Benzelius award (the Royal Society of Sciences at Uppsala). Her main research and teaching areas are tort law, civil law and criminal law. Friberg is a board member of the Centre for Multidisciplinary Studies on Racism (Faculty of Theology, Uppsala University) and a part-time guest researcher at the Uppsala Religion and Society Research Centre.

Lukas GLÖCKNER

Trier University
Fachbereich V – Rechtswissenschaft
Universitätsring 15
54296 Trier, Germany
sekipr@uni-trier.de

Lukas Glöckner was born in Trier (Germany) in 1999. He studied law at Trier University and graduated in 2025. In addition to German law, he studied French law as part of the International Legal Studies Programme at Trier University. During his studies, he was supported by the German Academic Scholarship Foundation. Since 2021 he has been working as a (student) research assistant at the chair of Prof Dr Jens Kleinschmidt LLM (Berkeley). Additionally, he works for the Centre for Legal Exam Preparation at Trier University.

Martin HOGG

Head of the School of Law and Established Professor
University of Galway
Galway H91 TK 33, Ireland
Tel: (+35) 3 91 524411
martin.hogg@universityofgalway.ie

Martin Hogg is Head of School and Established Professor at the Law School of the University of Galway, having previously held a Chair at the University of Edinburgh. He has written and published extensively in the obligations field since 1992, from both a national and comparative legal perspective. Hogg is a contributor to the Digest of European Tort Law, as well as to the European Tort Law Yearbook, and is a Member of the European Centre of Tort and Insurance Law (ECTIL). He is a non-practising member of the Scottish Bar (the Faculty of Advocates).

Jiří HRÁDEK

Charles University, Faculty of Law, Department of Civil Law
Nám.Curieových 901/7
116 40 Praha, Czech Republic
Tel: (+420) 728 228224
hradek@prf.cuni.cz

Jiří Hrádek is an Assistant Professor at the Department of Civil Law at the Faculty of Law of Charles University and a lawyer at Zeppelin CZ. He graduated in law from the Faculty of Law of Charles University (2002). Jiří Hrádek studied at the University of Hamburg (2000–2001), in the LLM programme at the Eberhard Karls University in Tübingen (2002–2003) and in the post-graduate programme of the Charles University (2002–2009). In 2002 and 2003, he completed research stays at the European Centre of Tort and Insurance Law (ECTIL) in Vienna; in 2007, Hrádek received an internship at the European Commission, DG Health and Consumer Protection. Jiří Hrádek is a member of the editorial board of the Czech journal, Jurisprudence. He specialises in civil and procedural law, with a special focus on tort law. He is the author of a book on pre-contractual liability, co-author of a book on delict law as well as commentaries on the Czech Civil Code and the Czech Civil Procedure Code.

Zoé JACQUEMIN

University Toulouse Capitole
2 rue du Doyen Gabriel Marty
31000 Toulouse, France
zoe.jacquemin@ut-capitole.fr

After completing a double-degree (Master's in Law in Paris and LLM at Humboldt University in Berlin), Zoé Jacquemin engaged in a PhD under the supervision of Benedicte Fauvarque-Cosson (co-founder and Chair of the ELI French Hub) and Gerhard Dannemann (founding member of the Acquis Group). In September 2016, she became a permanent lecturer at the University Sorbonne Paris Nord. In January 2022, Jacquemin joined the University Toulouse Capitole as a full Professor of Law. Her work focuses on contract law and civil liability, mostly from a European and/or comparative perspective. Her thesis on contractual liability in French, English and German law has been awarded several prizes. She has served as the President of Trans Europe Experts since 2022 and as the Head of the European School of Law Toulouse since 2023.

Ernst KARNER

Institute for European Tort Law/ European Centre of Tort and Insurance Law
Reichsratsstraße 17/2
1010 Vienna, Austria
Tel: (+43) 1 4277 34880
ernst.karner@oeaw.ac.at

Ernst Karner is the Director of the Institute for European Tort Law, Austrian Academy of Sciences and University of Graz, and of the European Centre of Tort and Insurance Law. He holds a chair in civil law at the University of Vienna. Born in 1969, he studied law in Vienna (Dr jur 1997 with distinction) and completed his habilitation in 2004 with a thesis on bona fide acquisition. Karner is co-editor of the Journal of European Tort Law (JETL) and a member of the European Group on Tort Law (EGTL) and the World Tort Law Society (WTLS). Furthermore, he was a member of the commission for the reform of Austrian tort law established by the Ministry of Justice in 2000. Karner has written extensively in the fields of Austrian and European tort law and has been granted several prizes including the Figdor-Preis of the Austrian Academy of Sciences and the Kardinal-Innitzer-Förderungspreis.

Anne LM KEIRSE

Utrecht Centre for Accountability and Liabilty Law
Molengraaff Institute for Private Law, Utrecht Law School
Achter Sint Pieter 200
3512 HT Utrecht, The Netherlands
a.l.m.keirse@uu.nl

Anne Keirse is a judge at the Court of Appeal in Amsterdam and a professor of Private Law at the Utrecht Centre for Accountability and Liability Law (UCALL) of Utrecht University. She is a member of the European Group on Tort Law. Born in 1975 in Oxford, she studied law at the University of Groningen (1993 – 1997), where she also obtained her doctorate and became a (senior) lecturer (1997 – 2006). Before becoming a professor in Utrecht (2008), Keirse was appointed senior lecturer at the Radboud University of Nijmegen (2006 – 2008). In 2013 – 2104, she was a visiting professor at the University of the Free State, Bloemfontein, South Africa. The teaching and research activities of Keirse are primarily focused on the law of obligations, with an emphasis on the field of (national and European) contract law, tort law, law of damages, prevention and mitigation of damage.
Alongside her academic work, she has been engaged in judicial work, first as a registrar at the District Court in Assen, subsequently as a judge at the District Court in Groningen, thereafter as a judge at the Court of Appeal in Arnhem. Keirse presently works as a justice at the Court of Appeal in Amsterdam and handles cases regarding commercial law and civil law, especially in the field of contract law, tort law, law of damages, and international and European private law.

Jens KLEINSCHMIDT

Trier University
Fachbereich V – Rechtswissenschaft
Universitätsring 15
54296 Trier, Germany
Tel: (+49) 651 201 2508
kleinschmidt@uni-trier.de

Jens Kleinschmidt is a Professor of Private Law, Private International Law and Comparative Law at Trier University. He studied law at the universities of Cologne, Geneva, and Freiburg, obtained an LLM from the University of California at Berkeley and a doctorate from Regensburg University. Before joining the law faculty in Trier, he was a senior research fellow at the Max Planck Institute for Comparative and International Private Law in Hamburg and a part-time lecturer at Bucerius

Law School in Hamburg, where he also completed his 'habilitation' at the interface between substantive private law and procedural law. Kleinschmidt publishes and lectures on private law (national, European and comparative), private international law and international procedural law. He has contributed to the Digest of European Tort Law. He is a member of ECTIL, a fellow of the European Law Institute as well as a member of the editorial committee of the Rabel Journal of Comparative and International Private Law.

Jonas KNETSCH

University Paris 1
Panthéon-Sorbonne
Sorbonne Law School
12, place du Panthéon
75231 Paris Cédex 05, France
Tel: (+33) 628 78 12 61
jonas.knetsch@univ-paris1.fr

Jonas Knetsch is a Professor of Civil and Comparative Law at the Sorbonne Law School (University Paris 1 Panthéon- Sorbonne). Before his PhD in Comparative Tort Law, he graduated from the University Panthéon-Assas and from the University of Cologne (Germany). He was a senior lecturer at the University Panthéon-Assas before being appointed full professor in 2013 following his success in the concours d'agrégation in private law. From 2013 to 2021, he held professorships at the University of Réunion Island and Jean Monnet University of Saint-Étienne. Jonas Knetsch has published extensively in tort and insurance law as well as in comparative law. Lately, he has conducted research projects on tort law and insurance law issues related to data protection and on the interplay of social security, private insurance and tort law compensation.

Bernhard A KOCH

University of Innsbruck
Innrain 52
6020 Innsbruck, Austria
Tel: (+43) 512 507 – 81210
bernhard.a.koch@uibk.ac.at
<www.zivilrechts.info>

Bernhard A Koch was born in 1966 in Feldkirch (Austria). He studied law in Innsbruck (Mag iur 1989), Tübingen (Germany, Dr iur summa cum laude 1992), and Michigan (USA, LLM 1993). He completed his habilitation for private law and comparative law in 1998. Koch started to work as an assistant at the University of Innsbruck in 1985, where he was awarded tenure in 1999. After two years on leave for work at the European Centre of Tort and Insurance Law (ECTIL) and the Austrian Academy of Sciences, he returned to Innsbruck in 2003, where he since holds a chair in civil law. Koch is currently the Dean of Studies of the Law Faculty and serves as the academic director of the faculty's medical law programme. From 2004 to 2010, Koch was also the Vice Director of the Austrian Academy of Sciences' Institute for European Tort Law (ETL). He was a member of the EU Expert Group on Liability for New Technologies. Koch's main fields of research are tort, contract, real property and family law. He is part of the European Group on Tort Law.

Päivi KORPISAARI

Professor in Communication Law
University of Helsinki
PO Box 4 (Yliopistonkatu 3)
00014 Helsinki, Finland
Tel: (+358) 50 4482617
paivi.korpisaari@helsinki.fi

Päivi Korpisaari is a Professor in Communication Law at the Faculty of Law of the University of Helsinki. Before her career at the university, she worked (1993 – 2003) as a lawyer at a law firm, as a younger judge at the District Court of Riihimäki, as a presenting officer at the Court of Appeal of Helsinki and as a legal counsel at the Finnish Soil Mechanics Association. Korpisaari has worked at the university since 2003 and has published many books and articles in the fields of media and communication law, information law, tort law, criminal law and constitutional law. Her main fields of research are media and communication law, tort law, personal data protection law, constitutional law, human rights law, and criminal law in respect of 'freedom of expression offences'. Korpisaari has been a national expert in studies in the field of media and communications.

Irene KULL

University of Tartu, Faculty of Law
Naituse 20
50409 Tartu, Estonia
Tel: (+372) 737 5060
irene.kull@ut.ee

Irene Kul is a Professor of Civil Law and holds the position of the head of the Private Law Department of the Tartu University Law School. She has participated in a number of international research groups. She lectures on contract law, the law of obligations and European contract and commercial law. Kull is a member of the group of authors of comments on the Estonian Civil Code Acts. Her main interests include the general principles of contract and tort law, the harmonisation of European private law and comparative contract law.

Janno LAHE

University of Tartu
Faculty of Law
Näituse 20
50409 Tartu, Estonia
Tel: (+372) 737 5992
www.oigus.ut.ee
www.ut.ee
Janno.Lahe@ut.ee

Janno Lahe is a Professor of Tort Law at the University of Tartu (since 2016). He obtained his PhD in Civil Law in 2005. Among his publications there are a variety of journal articles on issues in tort and insurance law. He lectures on insurance law and non-contractual obligations. His main interests include the law of obligations, insurance law and harmonisation of European tort law.

Peter LOSER

University of Basel, Faculty of Law
4002 Basel
St Galler Kantonalbank AG Legal & Compliance
St Leonhardstrasse 25
9000 St Gallen, Switzerland
Tel: (+41) 71 231 3131
peter.loser@sgkb.ch

Peter Loser, born in 1964, is a Professor at the University of Basel (Adjunct professor 'Titularprofessor' for Private, Commercial and Comparative Law), where he habilitated in 2006 with a comprehensive work on 'liability based on reliance', after studies in St Gallen and Lausanne, Switzerland (University of St Gallen HSG, lic iur 1990; Dr iur summa cum laude 1994). He was a visiting scholar at Yale University in 1992/93 and did research at the UNIDROIT in Rome and at the University of Oxford. Currently Loser teaches private, tort and banking law at the Universities of Basel and St Gallen HSG. He is a Fellow of the European Law Institute (ELI, Brussels), a Member of the European Centre of Tort and Insurance Law (ECTIL, Vienna) and has been an active participant of the project 'The Common Core of European Private Law' (University of Torino, Italy). From 2006 to 2009, he was a Member of the Board of the Swiss Society of Lawyers. Loser has worked as a Lawyer in a large law firm and as a Legal Advisor, Deputy Head Legal and Member of Senior Management of a bank in Switzerland.

Inês OLIVEIRA MARTINS

University of Coimbra, Faculty of Law
Pátio da Universidade
3004 – 528 Coimbra, Portugal
Tel: (+351) 239 859 801
mivom@fd.uc.pt

Inês de Oliveira Martins is a Professor of Civil and Commercial Law at the Faculty of Law of the University of Coimbra and a private legal consultant in Portugal and Brazil. She was a visiting scholar at the Max-Planck Institut für ausländisches und internationales Privatrecht, Hamburg (2011, 2014/15, 2017/18), at Faculdade de Direito da Universidade de São Paulo (2016), and at the

Centre de Droit Privé, Faculté de droit et de criminologie de l'Université Catholique de Louvain (2015/2016), and a speaker at conferences and post-graduate courses in the fields of insurance law, personal data and medical law in several countries. She is a member of the Supervisory Board of the Institute for Banking, Insurance and Capital Market Law of the Faculty of Law of the University of Coimbra (BBS), of the board of the general meeting of the Portuguese Chapter of the Association Internationale de Droit des Assurances (AIDA), of the Brazilian Institute for Insurance Law (IBDS), and of the German-Portuguese Legal Association (DLJV). De Oliveira Martins is also responsible for the Section of European Insurance Contract Law of the Institute of Iberian-American Law (IDIBE). She has conducted research on contract and liability law and devoted a great amount of attention to insurance law, which she has always approached as a part of the general system of private law. She is also very interested in legal methodology, in the questions raised by big data and technology and, more recently, in company law, examining these fields through the lenses of comparative law.

Colm Peter McGRATH

The Dickson Poon School of Law, King's College London
Strand
London WC2R 2LS, United Kingdom
Tel: (+44 20) 7848 5013
colm.mcgrath@kcl.ac.uk

Colm Peter McGrath is a Reader in Comparative Law at the Dickson Poon School of Law, King's College London, an Academic Fellow of the Middle Temple, and a Global Associate Professor of Law at The University of Notre Dame's London programme. Previously he was the WYNG Research Fellow in Medical Law and Ethics at Trinity Hall in the University of Cambridge. He studied law as an undergraduate and as a doctoral student at the University of Cambridge. His research focuses on comparative private law and professional liability, particularly liability and regulation in the healthcare context in both the modern and historical common law and civilian legal traditions. His monograph, The Development of Medical Liability in Germany 1800 – 1945, (Klostermann, 2019) was selected by jury as one of the '2019 Legal Books of the Year' in the Neue Juristische Wochenschrift. McGrath is joint General

Editor of the long-running Journal of Professional Negligence, Book Review Editor for the Journal of European Tort Law, and a Fellow and Member of the European Centre of Tort and Insurance Law.

Filip MELZER

Palacký University, Faculty of Law
tř. 17. listopadu 8
779 00 Olomouc, Czech Republic
Tel: (+420) 585 63 7686
filip.melzer@upol.cz

Filip Melzer is an associate professor at the Department of Private Law and Civil Procedure at the Faculty of Law of Palacký University in Olomouc and at the Department of Civil Law at Masaryk University.
He obtained his Master's and Doctoral degrees at the Faculty of Law of Masaryk University. Melzer completed his postgraduate Master's studies (Magister legum, LLM) at the University of Passau, Germany. He also studied at the law faculties of the Europa-Universität Viadrina in Germany, the University of Vienna in Austria, and the Collegium Polonicum in Poland. He achieved his habilitation in civil law at Palacký University in Olomouc.
In legal practice, Melzer worked as an assistant to a judge of the Constitutional Court and the Supreme Administrative Court and, since 2013, he has been practising as an attorney.
He was a member of the codification commission for the new Civil Code. He is the president of the professional association Czech and Slovak Association for Tort Law and Related Fields. Melzer is a member of the working commission for private law of the Government Legislative Council, a member of the commission for the recodification of private law in Slovakia, and a lecturer at the Judicial Academy in the Czech Republic and in the Slovak Republic. He has also served as Deputy Minister of Justice, Vice-Chairman of the Judicial Academy Council, and Vice-Dean of the Faculty of Law of Palacký University responsible for curriculum reform.
Among other honours, he was awarded the Antonín Randa Bronze Medal by the Union of Czech Lawyers (2018), the Václav Mandák Prize for the best scholarly article in the Bulletin advokacie (2020), the Pacta sunt servanda Medal from the Faculty of Law of Trnava University, and twice received the Author's Award for the best Czech

legal publication, presented by the Karlovy Vary Legal Days Society.
Melzer is the author of Methodology of Legal Reasoning, an introduction to legal argumentation, and one of the two main editors of the Grand Commentary on the Civil Code. He is also co-author of the expert podcast, Judikatúra.

Attila MENYHÁRD

ELTE Faculty of Law, Civil Law Department
Egyetem ter 1 – 3
1364 Budapest, Hungary
Tel: (+36) 1 411 6510
menyhard@ajk.elte.hu

Attila Menyhárd works at the University of Eötvös Loránd, Faculty of Law, Civil Law Department (Budapest) as a full professor. He was the Dean of the Faculty from 2016 – 2019. He is also affiliated with the Institute of the Information Society of Ludovika University of Public Services (Budapest) as a Research Professor. His special research fields are: contract law, tort law and property law, company law, commercial law, law and economics, law and literature and human rights in private law as well as international commercial contracts, European business law, European company law and law and technology issues. Upon the invitation of the Ministry of Justice, Menyhárd contributed to the project on a new Hungarian Civil Code, being responsible for the provisions on property law and rent law. He is a registered member of the Arbitration Court of the Hungarian Chamber of Commerce and Industry, Budapest and the ICSID Panel of Arbitrators. He is a member of the Centre for Social Sciences, the Institute for Legal Studies, the Hungarian Academy of Sciences Centre of Excellence, a fellow of ECTIL, a member of the UNIDROIT Governing Council and Head of the New Civil Code Advisory Board to the Supreme Court. Menyhárd is also the counsel to the Oppenheim Law Firm (Budapest).

David MESSNER-KREUZBAUER

Institute for European Tort Law of the Austrian Academy of Sciences and the University of Graz
Reichsratsstraße 17/2
1010 Vienna, Austria
Tel: (+43) 1 4277 29660
david.messner@oeaw.ac.at

David Messner-Kreuzbauer is a postdoctoral researcher at the Institute for European Tort Law of the Austrian Academy of Sciences and the University of Graz, which he joined in 2015. He studied law at the University of Vienna and Shanghai Jiao Tong University from 2011 – 2021

(Mag iur 2015, Dr iur 2021). During this time, he successfully defended and published his thesis on 'Permitted Acts of Necessity and Civil Liability' (Erlaubte Notstandshandlungen und zivilrechtliche Ausgleichsansprüche), published articles on various topics of civil law in highly regarded journals, and presented papers in Austria and abroad. He was a guest researcher at Harvard Law School (USA), Université Paris I Panthéon-Sorbonne (France) and Keble College, University of Oxford (UK).

Barbara NOVAK

University of Ljubljana
Faculty of Law
Poljanski nasip 2
SI – 1000 Ljubljana, Slovenia
Tel: (+386) 1 42 03 141
Fax: (+386) 1 42 03 115
barbara.novak@pf.uni-lj.si

Barbara Novak is full Professor of Civil and Commercial Law at the Faculty of Law at the University of Ljubljana. Her teaching and research work is focused on tort law, family law, comparative family law, personality rights law and introduction to the civil law. Barbara Novak received her doctorate in 1999 and in 2009 became a full professor. Well over two hundred bachelor, master and doctoral degree candidates have so far graduated under her mentorship. Barbara Novak fulfilled numerous duties at the faculty and university level: she was head of the Department of Civil Law, member of the faculty senate and served in the University of Ljubljana Habilitation Commission. Barbara Novak has long served as a member of the Council for Children and on the Expert Council for Family at the Ministry of Labour, Family, Social Affairs and Equal Opportunities. She held the position of advisor to the Constitutional Court of the Republic of Slovenia, was head of the State research project 'Codification of Civil Law' (Kodifikacija civilnega prava), head of the State project 'Comparative analysis of special educational forms for students with disabilities' (Primerjalnopravna analiza posebnih organizacijskih oblik v vzgoji in izobraževanju za otroke z motnjo v duševnem razvoju) and has authored numerous monographs, textbooks, papers and commentaries. Barbara Novak is active as a member of the following: the expert group at the CEFL Contributors 791 (Commission on European Family Law), ECTIL (European Centre of Tort and Insurance Law, Vienna), the Cambridge Family

Law Centre, the Royal Society of Edinburgh-founded Multi-Disciplinary Research Network by Edinburgh Napier University, the international editorial board of the Zeitschrift für das gesamte Familienrecht, the editorial board of Der Familien-Rechtsberater; the editorial board of Family & Law; the Wissenschaftliche Vereinigung für Familienrecht e V, Bonn; the working group of the Ministry of Labour, Family, Social Affairs and Equal Opportunities in drafting the revised Marriage and Family Relations Act 2004; the working group drafting the new Family Code. In 2015: appointment by the Ministry of Labour, Family, Social Affairs and Equal Opportunities to update the draft of the new Family Code. Barbara Novak maintains close academic ties with numerous European institutions, such as the University of Regensburg, the Katholieke Universiteit Leuven, the Ludwig-Maximilians-Universität München, the Vrije Universiteit Amsterdam, the Union Internationale du Notariat Latin (UINL) – Commission des Affaires Europeennes et de la Mediterranee (CAEM), the University of Osnabrück, Deutsches Jugendinstitut e V. (DJI), the University of Zagreb. In 2018, Barbara Novak received an excellence award for her scientific work at the Faculty of Law. Barbara Novak is a member of the Academia Europaea and held the position of the Vice-Rector of the University of Ljubljana (2018 – 2021).

André PEREIRA

University of Coimbra
Faculty of Law
3004 – 545 Coimbra, Portugal
Tel: (+351) 239 051725
andreper@fd.uc.pt

André Pereira is a Professor of Law at the University of Coimbra (Portugal), Director of the Centre for Biomedical Law and Researcher at the University of Coimbra Institute for Legal Research. Pereira is a Vice-President of the National Council of Ethics for Life Sciences, President of the Institutional Review Board of AIBILI and a member of the Ethics Committee of the National Institute of Legal Medicine and Forensic Sciences. At the international level, Pereira is Chair of the Educational Committtee of the World Association for Medical Law and he is a fellow of the European Centre of Tort and Insurance Law (Austria), member of the Brazilian Institute for Tort Law (IBERC), member of the Iberoamerican Law In-

stitute (IDIBE), Founder of the Portuguese Speaking Association for Health Law (ALDIS), member of the Luso-Brazilian Institute for Comparative Law and he is member of the International Academy of Comparative Law.
Orcid: 0000 - 0001 - 9871 - 5298.

Ronen PERRY

University of Haifa
Faculty of Law
31905 Haifa, Israel
Tel: (+97) 2 4 828 - 8487
rperry@law.haifa.ac.il

Ronen Perry is a Professor of Law and Director of the Aptowizer Center for Risk, Liability, and Insurance at the University of Haifa, former President of the Israeli Private Law Association, and member of the World Tort Law Society, the European Centre of Tort and Insurance Law, and the Global Young Academy. Ronen Perry received his LLB magna cum laude from the Tel Aviv University (1996), where he studied in the special programme for excellent students (admitting 0.5% of undergraduate students). He completed with distinction his LLM studies, as part of the direct doctoral track requirements (1997), and received his LLD summa cum laude from the Hebrew University (2001). Ronen Perry has been a visiting researcher at New York University, University of Oxford, Pompeu Fabra University, and the University of Vienna. He is one of the founding editors, and a senior editor of the Journal of Tort Law, the editor-in-chief of the Haifa Law Review, and member of the editorial board of the Asian Journal of Law & Economics and Law & Social Inquiry. Ronen Perry has published sixty articles on tort law, contract law, insurance, remedies, jurisprudence, and the legal process, and his book, Economic Ricochets, discusses relational economic loss from historical, comparative, and theoretical perspectives.

Giulia PULEIO

Pisa University, Faculty of Law
Via del Collegio Ricci 10
56126 Pisa, Italy
Tel: (+39) 340259 3765
giulia.puleio@unipi.it

Giulia Puleio is a Research Fellow in Private law at the University of Pisa, where she teaches IT Law and Private Law. She obtained her PhD in Private Law at the University of Pisa and the University of Bremen. Her work focuses on European non-contractual liability, in particular on European antitrust damages actions, on which she wrote her first monograph, and on Climate Change litigation. Puleio graduated from the University of Catania in 2015, and was a visiting fellow at the Max Planck Institute in 2018 and 2021. She is a member of the Doctoral Committee in Law at the University of Pisa.

Eoin QUILL

University of Limerick, School of Law
Limerick, Ireland
Tel: (+35) 3 61 20 2220
eoin.quill@ul.ie

Eoin Quill was born in Limerick in 1965. He studied law at University College Cork, a constituent college of the National University of Ireland, between 1982 and 1988 obtaining two bachelors and a master's degree – BCL; LLB; LLM. He lectured at the School of Professional and Management Studies in Limerick from 1988–1990 and has been lecturing in the University of Limerick since 1991 in a variety of subjects including Tort, Commercial Law and International Tort Law & Business. Quill's publications include Torts in Ireland (Gill& Macmillan 1999, 4th edn 2014), Tort Law in Ireland (Kluwer 2015), Damages and Compensation Culture: Comparative Perspectives (2016, co-edited with Raymond J Friel) and a variety of journal articles and chapters in edited books on issues in tort. He is currently an examiner in Tort for the Law Society of Ireland, a member of the International Commercial & Economic Law Group, University of Limerick and a member of ECTIL.

Lawrence QUINTANO

19 Gulio Cauchi Street
Balzan BZN 1130, Malta
lawrence.quintano@gov.mt

Lawrence Quintano is a retired judge. He is now chairman of the Permanent Commission Against Corruption. He also teaches Civil Law at the University of Malta with his areas of specialisation being Contract Law and the Law of Marriage and Betrothal. He also teaches that part in the Law of Obligations which is entitled 'Extinction of Obligations' and he also deals with the Law of Evidence in Civil Procedure. He has been selected as an examiner in the board which discusses the merits of dissertations or MA theses dealing with themes from the Civil Code. For a long time, he served as an advocate with the Attorney General's Office where his main areas were Constitutional

Law, Human Rights, EU Law and International Law. He also served as an ad hoc judge in the European Court of Human Rights.

Albert RUDA

University of Girona, Facultat de Dret
Campus de Montilivi C/ de la UdG 12
17003 Girona, Spain
Tel: (+34) 972 41 97 68
albert.ruda@udg.edu

Albert Ruda is an Associate Professor in Private Law and Former Dean (2016–2024) at the Faculty of Law of the University of Girona. He is also a member of the Institute of European and Comparative Private Law of the same University, the European Centre of Tort and Insurance Law (ECTIL, Vienna), the Instituto Brasileiro de Estudos de Responsabilidade Civil (IBERC) and the Institute of Iberoamerican Law (IDIBE); research fellow of the Utrecht Centre for Accountability and Liability Law (UCALL), founding member and chair of the European Law Institute (ELI) Spanish Hub, chair of the ELI Special Interest Group on Global Private Law and member of the Commission of Codification of Catalonia. Ruda is also a former scholar of the Japan Foundation and former van Calker scholar of the Swiss Institute of Comparative Law.

Loreta ŠALTINYTĖ

Mykolas Romeris University, Faculty of Law, Institute of International and European Union Law
Ateities g 20
08303 Vilnius, Lithuania
Tel: (+370) 5 271 4512
Fax: (+370) 5 271 4561
losal@mruni.eu

Loreta Šaltinytė has been a reporter on Lithuanian tort law developments for the European Tort Law Yearbook since 2008. She is also a Fellow of the European Law Institute. Being an Associate Professor of EU law at the law school of Mykolas Romeris University in Vilnius, Šaltinytė offers EU law courses. She holds a doctoral degree from Mykolas Romeris University (2009), a master in law degree from Vilnius University (2002), an LLM from Riga Graduate School of Law (2003) and an LLM in natural resources law and policy (with distinction) from Dundee University, CEPMLP (2008), where she studied as a Chevening scholar. Since 2013, Šaltinytė has been practising as an individual legal consultant offering expert advice to courts and assisting clients with EU law and tort law as well as human rights law issues. Her research interests also include international investment law and tort law.

Barbara C STEININGER

University of Graz, Centre of European Private Law
Universitätsstraße 15 Bauteil D/IV
8010 Graz, Austria
Tel: (+43) 316 380 3585
barbara.steininger@uni-graz.at
Institute for European Tort Law/European Centre of Tort and Insurance Law
Reichsratsstraße 17/2
1010 Vienna, Austria

Barbara C Steininger studied law and Dutch in Vienna and Leiden, obtaining Master degrees from the University of Vienna in both areas as well as a doctoral degree in law from the same university. During her studies, she was employed as a student assistant at the Institute of Roman Law of the University of Vienna. She worked as a researcher at the European Centre of Tort and Insurance Law, the Institute for European Tort Law, the University of Geneva and at the University of Graz, where she completed her habilitation in 2019. Since April 2020, Steininger has been Associate Professor (tenured) in Civil and Comparative Law at the University of Graz. For her habilitation thesis, she was awarded the Kardinal-Innitzer-Förderungspreis, the VKB-Wissenschaftspreis and the Alois Mock-Wissenschaftspreis. In October 2020, Steininger was appointed Vice-Director of ECTIL and since October 2023 she has been Director of the Centre of European Private Law of the University of Graz and Vice-Director of ETL. While (comparative) tort law remains her favourite, the law of obligations, property law and family law are also among her areas of interest. Steininger is a Fellow of the European Law Institute.

Hristina TANCHEVA

Sofia University 'St. Kliment Ohridski'
Faculty of Law
15 Tsar Osvoboditel blvd
1504 Sofia, Bulgaria
Tel: (+359) 889954546,
hr.tancheva@gmail.com

Hristina Tancheva is a head assistant professor at Sofia University 'St. Kliment Ohridski', Department of Civil Law Sciences. She was born in 1988 in Ruse, Bulgaria. In 2012, she graduated with a master's degree in law from Sofia University 'St. Kliment Ohridski'. Since 2014, she has been an assistant professor in 'Obligations Law' and as, of 2022, also of civil law – general part. She is also a lecturer in commercial and tax law and foundations of civil law in English at the Faculty of Economics of Sofia University. In 2018, Hristina Tancheva acquired her PhD in civil law with a thesis on product liability, which was published in 2019. She has been a member of the editorial board of the science magazine 'Commercial Law' (ISSN 0861 – 6892) since 2018. As of 2019, she is a member of the Union of scientists in Bulgaria. Since 2014, she has been registered as a lawyer at the Sofia Bar Association specialising in civil and commercial law, including corporate law, contract law, tort law and bankruptcy. She is the author of a dozen articles dedicated to contract and tort law issues. She is also a judge at the disciplinary court of Sofia Bar Association.

Knut Martin TANDE

University of Bergen, Faculty of Law
Magnus Lagabotesplass 1
Bergen, Norway
Tel: (+47) 5 55589551
knut.tande@uib.no

Knut Tande is an Associate Professor and Vice Dean at the Faculty of Law of the University of Bergen. His main topics for teaching and research are copyright law, legal methodology and tort law. He has been the Vice Dean of Education and the Vice Dean of Digitalisation at the faculty and is now the head of the Learning and Communication Center. For several years Tande was a member of the National Committee for Research Ethics in the Social Sciences and the Humanities (NESH), and is now a member of the Research Ethics Committee of the Faculty of Medicine at the University of Bergen.

Thomas THIEDE

SPIEKER & JAEGER
Phoenixseestraße 24
44263 Dortmund, Germany
Tel: (+49) 231 95858 0
thomas.thiede@spieker-jaeger.de
<www.spieker-jaeger.de>

Thomas Thiede studied Law, Economics, and Political Sciences in Germany, earning a Bachelor of Laws in 2003 and later completing a Master of Laws (Comparative and EU Law). He subsequently joined the Institute for European Tort Law at the Austrian Academy of Sciences in Vienna, where he completed his doctorate with distinction. For his dissertation, he received the 2011 Franz-Gschnitzer Award and was promoted to Junior Scientist at the Academy. Since 2013, Thomas Thiede has taught at the Institute for Civil Law, Foreign and Private International Law at the University of Graz, where he was appointed Honorary Professor in 2023. He has also lectured at Ruhr University Bochum since 2016. He is the author of numerous publications and contributes to leading commentaries such as Soergel (BGB) and Schwimann/Kodek (ABGB). He regularly publishes in NZG (Neue Zeitschrift für Gesellschaftsrecht) and serves on the editorial advisory board of EuZW (Europäische Zeitschrift für Wirtschaftsrecht), both published by C.H. Beck. Admitted to the German bar in 2017, he has practised at SPIEKER & JAEGER, a commercial law firm based in Dortmund, since 2022 as a partner. His legal practice focuses on German and European competition law as well as commercial and corporate law. He advises clients in merger control proceedings, cartel fine procedures, and antitrust damages claims, and manages complex cross-border corporate transactions.

Viktor TOKUSHEV

University of Sofia, Faculty of Law
15 Tsar Osvoboditel blvd
1504 Sofia, Bulgaria
Tel: (+359) 888 603 090
v.tokushev@law.uni-sofia.bg

Viktor Tokushev is an Assistant Professor in Civil and Commercial Law at the Law Faculty of Sofia University. He was born in Sofia (Bulgaria) in 1978. He studied law at Sofia University and graduated with honours in 2002. In the following year, Tokushev specialised in 'Legal English and Writing for Global Lawyers' at the Boston University, London Center (London). He further developed his interest in private law by participating in the development of more than 50 legislation projects for the 39th National Assembly of Bulgaria. Since 2005, he has been running a law office, 'Tokushev and Partners' in which he is a managing partner. Tokushev acquired his doctorate degree in 2012 with a thesis on Special Purpose Investment Companies, which was published in the same year. From 2012, he has been a lecturer on Capital Markets Law at Sofia University. He is a fellow of the European Centre of Tort and Insurance Law (ECTIL, Vienna).

Zafeirios TSOLAKIDIS

Associate Professor of Civil Law
National & Kapodistrian University of Athens, Law School
8, Vissarionos Str.
106 72 Athens, Greece
Tel: (+30) 210 3647397
zatsolak@law.uoa.gr

Zafeirios Tsolakidis was born in Athens in 1977. He graduated and received his doctorate with merits from the Law School of the National & Kapodistrian University of Athens. He is an Associate Professor of Civil Law at the National & Kapodistrian University of Athens Law School, where he teaches General Principles of Civil Law, Law of Obligations (General and Special Part), Family Law, Applications of Civil Law, as well as Banking Law, Land Register Law and Methodology of Law (in postgraduate courses). Tsolakidis is the author of six books (among which 'Compensation in Pre-Contractual Liability', 'Bank Transactions Law Pt I' and 'Contractual and Delictual Liability for Assistants') and more than 30 articles in legal journals and essays' collections. He is also a Member of the Parliamentary Committee of the Hellenic Republic for the Scrutiny of the Quality of the Legislative Process. He is a Fellow of the European Centre of Tort and Insurance Law. Tsolakidis practises law in Athens, issues legal opinions and serves as an arbitrator.

Paulina WYSZYŃSKA-ŚLUFIŃSKA

Faculty of Law and
Administration
Gdańsk University
Jana Bażyńskiego 6
80 – 309 Gdańsk, Poland
Tel: (+48) 58 523 28 51
paulina.wyszynska-slufinska@ug.edu.pl

Paulina Wyszyńska-Ślufińska is an Assistant Professor in the Department of Civil Law at the Gdańsk University Law School. In 2014, she received her law degree from the University of Gdańsk. From September 2013 to February 2014, she attended the University of Sheffield, Law School. In July 2012, she took part in the Sommerschule Internationales Sportrecht und Schiedsgerichtsbarkeit, organised by Salzburg University. In the summer of 2013, she participated in the Catholic University of America's International Business and Trade Law Programme in Cracow, Poland. Since 2018, she has been a licensed attorney-at-law. She is an author and co-author of publications in the following areas of law: civil law, torts and insurance law. Wyszyńska-Ślufińska serves as a content supervisor of Wiadomości Ubezpieczeniowe (Insurance Review).

Index

The numbers given refer to marginal numbers, the letters refer to the reports. A stands for Austria, B for Belgium, BU for Bulgaria, CH for Switzerland, CR for the Comparative Report, CRO for Croatia, CY for Cyprus, CZ for the Czech Republic, D for Germany, DK for Denmark, E for Spain, EST for Estonia, EU for European Union, EW for England and Wales, F for France, FIN for Finland, GR for Greece, H for Hungary, I for Italy, IRL for Ireland, ISR for Israel, LT for Lithuania, LV for Latvia, MT for Malta, N for Norway, NL for the Netherlands, P for Portugal, PL for Poland, RO for Romania, S for Sweden, SCO for Scotland, SK for Slovakia, SLO for Slovenia.

https://doi.org/10.1515/9783111389271-036

Publications

Principles of European Tort Law Series

Volume 1: *The Limits of Liability: Keeping the Floodgates Shut*
Edited by Jaap Spier
Kluwer Law International, The Hague
Hardcover. ISBN 90 – 411 – 0169 – 1
1996, 162 pp

Volume 2: *The Limits of Expanding Liability: Eight Fundamental Cases in a Comparative Perspective*
Edited by Jaap Spier
Kluwer Law International, The Hague
Hardcover. ISBN 90 – 411 – 0581 – 6
1998, 244 pp

Volume 3: *Unification of Tort Law: Wrongfulness*
Edited by Helmut Koziol
Kluwer Law International, The Hague
Hardcover. ISBN 90 – 411 – 1019 – 4
1998, 144 pp

Volume 4: *Unification of Tort Law: Causation*
Edited by Jaap Spier
Kluwer Law International, The Hague
Hardcover. ISBN 90 – 411 – 1325 – 8
2000, 161 pp

Volume 5: *Unification of Tort Law: Damages*
Edited by Ulrich Magnus
Kluwer Law International, The Hague
Hardcover. ISBN 90 – 411 – 1481 – 5
2001, 225 pp

Volume 6: *Unification of Tort Law: Strict Liability*
Edited by Bernhard A Koch and Helmut Koziol
Kluwer Law International, The Hague
Hardcover. ISBN 90 – 411 – 1705 – 9
2002, 444 pp

Volume 7: *Unification of Tort Law: Liability for Damage Caused by Others*
Edited by Jaap Spier
Kluwer Law International, The Hague
Hardcover. ISBN 90 – 411 – 2185 – 4
2003, 335 pp

Volume 8: *Unification of Tort Law: Contributory Negligence*
Edited by Ulrich Magnus and Miquel Martín-Casals
Kluwer Law International, The Hague
Hardcover. ISBN 90 – 411 – 2220 – 6
2004, 300 pp

https://doi.org/10.1515/9783111389271-037

Volume 9: *Unification of Tort Law: Multiple Tortfeasors*
Edited by WV Horton Rogers
Kluwer Law International, The Hague
Hardcover. ISBN 90-411-2319-9
2004, 313 pp

Volume 10: *Unification of Tort Law: Fault*
Edited by Pierre Widmer
Kluwer Law International, The Hague
Hardcover. ISBN 90-411-2098-4
2005, 391 pp

Tort and Insurance Law Series

Volume 1: *Cases on Medical Malpractice in a Comparative Perspective*
Edited by Michael Faure and Helmut Koziol
Verlag Österreich, Vienna
Softcover. ISBN 978-3-7046-6056-5
2001, 331 pp

Volume 2: *Damages for Non-Pecuniary Loss in a Comparative Perspective*
Edited by WV Horton Rogers
Verlag Österreich, Vienna
Softcover. ISBN 978-3-7046-6057-2
2001, 318 pp

Volume 3: *The Impact of Social Security Law on Tort Law*
Edited by Ulrich Magnus
Verlag Österreich, Vienna
Softcover. ISBN 978-3-7046-6083-1
2003, 312 pp

Volume 4: *Compensation for Personal Injury in a Comparative Perspective*
Edited by Bernhard A Koch and Helmut Koziol
Verlag Österreich, Vienna
Softcover. ISBN 978-3-7046-6082-4
2003, 501 pp

Volume 5: *Deterrence, Insurability and Compensation in Environmental Liability. Future Developments in the European Union*
Edited by Michael Faure
Verlag Österreich, Vienna
Softcover. ISBN 978-3-7046-6891-2
2003, 408 pp

Volume 6: *Der Ersatz frustrierter Aufwendungen. Vermögens- und Nichtvermögensschaden im österreichischen und deutschen Recht*
by Thomas Schobel
Verlag Österreich, Vienna

Softcover. ISBN 978-3-7046-6093-0
2003, 342 pp

Volume 7: *Liability for and Insurability of Biomedical Research with Human Subjects in a Comparative Perspective*
Edited by Jos Dute, Michael G Faure and Helmut Koziol
Verlag Österreich, Vienna
Softcover. ISBN 978-3-7046-5812-8
2004, 445 pp

Volume 8: *No-Fault Compensation in the Health Care Sector*
Edited by Jos Dute, Michael G Faure and Helmut Koziol
Verlag Österreich, Vienna
Softcover. ISBN 978-3-7046-5821-0
2004, 492 pp

Volume 9: *Pure Economic Loss*
Edited by Willem H van Boom, Helmut Koziol and Christian A Witting
Verlag Österreich, Vienna
Softcover. ISBN 978-3-7046-5790-9
2004, 214 pp

Volume 10: *Liber Amicorum Pierre Widmer*
Edited by Helmut Koziol and Jaap Spier
Verlag Österreich, Vienna
Softcover. ISBN 978-3-7046-5792-3
2003, 376 pp

Volume 11: *Terrorism, Tort Law and Insurance. A Comparative Survey*
Edited by Bernhard A Koch
Verlag Österreich, Vienna
Softcover. ISBN 978-3-7046-5795-4
2004, 313 pp

Volume 12: *Abschlussprüfer. Haftung und Versicherung*
Edited by Helmut Koziol and Walter Doralt
Verlag Österreich, Vienna
Softcover. ISBN 978-3-7046-5822-7
2004, 180 pp

Volume 13: *Persönlichkeitsschutz gegenüber Massenmedien/The Protection of Personality Rights against Invasions by Mass Media*
Edited by Helmut Koziol and Alexander Warzilek
Verlag Österreich, Vienna
Softcover. ISBN 978-3-7046-5841-8
2005, 713 pp

Volume 14: *Financial Compensation for Victims of Catastrophes. A Comparative Legal Approach*
Edited by Michael Faure and Ton Hartlief
Verlag Österreich, Vienna
Softcover. ISBN 978-3-7046-5849-4
2006, 466 pp

Volume 15: *Entwurf eines neuen österreichischen Schadenersatzrechts*
Edited by Irmgard Griss, Georg Kathrein and Helmut Koziol

Verlag Österreich, Vienna
Softcover. ISBN 978-3-7046-5865-4
2006, 146 pp

Volume 16: *Tort Law and Liability Insurance*
Edited by Gerhard Wagner
Verlag Österreich, Vienna
Softcover. ISBN 978-3-7046-5850-0
2005, 361 pp

Volume 17: *Children in Tort Law. Part I: Children as Tortfeasors*
Edited by Miquel Martín-Casals
Verlag Österreich, Vienna
Softcover. ISBN 978-3-7046-5848-7
2006, 476 pp

Volume 18: *Children in Tort Law. Part II: Children as Victims*
Edited by Miquel Martín-Casals
Verlag Österreich, Vienna
Softcover. ISBN 978-3-7046-5869-2
2007, 320 pp

Volume 19: *Tort and Regulatory Law*
Edited by Willem H van Boom, Meinhard Lukas and Christa Kissling
Verlag Österreich, Vienna
Hardcover. ISBN 978-3-7046-5870-8
2007, 477 pp

Volume 20: *Shifts in Compensating Work-Related Injuries and Diseases*
Edited by Saskia Klosse and Ton Hartlief
Verlag Österreich, Vienna
Hardcover. ISBN 978-3-7046-5913-2
2007, 236 pp

Volume 21: *Shifts in Compensation for Environmental Damage*
Edited by Michael Faure and Albert Verheij
Verlag Österreich, Vienna
Hardcover. ISBN 978-3-7046-5911-8
2007, 338 pp

Volume 22: *Shifts in Compensation between Private and Public Systems*
Edited by Willem H van Boom and Michael Faure
Verlag Österreich, Vienna
Hardcover. ISBN 978-3-7046-5912-5
2007, 246 pp

Volume 23: *Tort Law of the European Community*
Edited by Helmut Koziol and Reiner Schulze
Verlag Österreich, Vienna
Hardcover. ISBN 978-3-7046-5935-4
2008, 693 pp

Volume 24: *Economic Loss Caused by Genetically Modified Organisms. Liability and Redress for the Adventitious Presence of GMOs in Non-GM Crops*
Edited by Bernhard A Koch

Verlag Österreich, Vienna
Hardcover. ISBN 978-3-7046-5937-8
2008, 747 pp

Volume 25: *Punitive Damages. Common Law and Civil Law Perspectives*
Edited by Helmut Koziol and Vanessa Wilcox
Verlag Österreich, Vienna
Hardcover. ISBN 978-3-7046-6117-3
2009, 335 pp

Volume 26: *Aggregation and Divisibility of Damage*
Edited by Ken Oliphant
Verlag Österreich, Vienna
Hardcover. ISBN 978-3-7046-6116-6
2009, 568 pp

Volume 27: *Damage Caused by Genetically Modified Organisms. Comparative Survey of Redress Options for Harm to Persons, Property or the Environment*
Edited by Bernhard A Koch
de Gruyter, Berlin/New York
Hardcover. ISBN 978-3-89949-811-0
eBook. ISBN 978-3-89949-812-7
2010, 954 pp

Volume 28: *Loss of Housekeeping Capacity*
Edited by Ernst Karner and Ken Oliphant
de Gruyter, Berlin/Boston
Hardcover. ISBN 978-3-89949-813-4
eBook. ISBN 978-3-89949-814-1
2012, 339 pp

Volume 29: *Medical Liability in Europe. A Comparison of Selected Jurisdictions*
Edited by Bernhard A Koch
de Gruyter, Berlin/Boston
Hardcover. ISBN 978-3-11-026010-6
eBook. ISBN 978-3-11-026016-8
2011, 701 pp

Volume 30: *Tort Law in the Jurisprudence of the European Court of Human Rights*
Edited by Attila Fenyves, Ernst Karner, Helmut Koziol and Elisabeth Steiner
de Gruyter, Berlin/Boston
Hardcover. ISBN 978-3-11-025966-7
eBook. ISBN 978-3-11-026000-7
2011, 906 pp

Volume 31: *Employers' Liability and Workers' Compensation*
Edited by Ken Oliphant and Gerhard Wagner
de Gruyter, Berlin/Boston
Hardcover. ISBN 978-3-11-026996-3
eBook. ISBN 978-3-11-027021-1
2012, 619 pp

Volume 32: *Medical Malpractice and Compensation in Global Perspective*
Edited by Ken Oliphant and Richard W Wright

de Gruyter, Berlin/Boston
Hardcover. ISBN 978-3-11-026997-0
eBook. ISBN 978-3-11-027023-5
2013, 573 pp

Volume 33: *Proportional Liability: Analytical and Comparative Perspectives*
Edited by Israel Gilead, Michael D Green and Bernhard A Koch
de Gruyter, Berlin/Boston
Hardcover. ISBN 978-3-11-028253-5
eBook. ISBN 978-3-11-028258-0
2013, 376 pp

Volume 34: *Mass Torts in Europe: Cases and Reflections*
Edited by Willem H van Boom and Gerhard Wagner
de Gruyter, Berlin/Boston
Hardcover. ISBN 978-3-11-034945-0
eBook. ISBN 978-3-11-034946-7
2014, 311 pp

Volume 35: *Compulsory Liability Insurance from a European Perspective*
Edited by Attila Fenyves, Christa Kissling, Stefan Perner and Daniel Rubin
de Gruyter, Berlin/Boston
Hardcover. ISBN 978-3-11-048469-4
eBook. ISBN 978-3-11-048617-9
2016, 564 pp

Volume 36: *Directors' & Officers' (D & O) Liability*
Edited by Simon Deakin, Helmut Koziol and Olaf Riss
de Gruyter, Berlin/Boston
Hardcover. ISBN 978-3-11-048971-2
eBook. ISBN 978-3-11-049149-4
2018, 1008 pp

Volume 37: Civil Liability for Artificial Intelligence and Software
Edited by Ernst Karner, Bernhard A Koch, Mark A Geistfeld and Christiane Wendehorst
de Gruyter, Berlin/Boston
Hardcover. ISBN 978-3-11-077534-1
eBook. ISBN 978-3-11-077540-2
2023, 407 pp

European Tort Law Yearbook

European Tort Law 2001
Edited by Helmut Koziol and Barbara C Steininger
Verlag Österreich, Vienna
Softcover. ISBN 978-3-7046-6085-5
2002, 571 pp

European Tort Law 2002
Edited by Helmut Koziol and Barbara C Steininger
Verlag Österreich, Vienna

Softcover. ISBN 3-211-00486-6
2003, 596 pp

European Tort Law 2003
Edited by Helmut Koziol and Barbara C Steininger
Verlag Österreich, Vienna
Softcover. ISBN 978-3-7046-5825-8
2004, 493 pp

European Tort Law 2004
Edited by Helmut Koziol and Barbara C Steininger
Verlag Österreich, Vienna
Softcover. ISBN 978-3-7046-5847-0
2005, 674 pp

European Tort Law 2005
Edited by Helmut Koziol and Barbara C Steininger
Verlag Österreich, Vienna
Softcover. ISBN 978-3-7046-5871-5
2006, 711 pp

European Tort Law 2006
Edited by Helmut Koziol and Barbara C Steininger
Verlag Österreich, Vienna
Hardcover. ISBN 978-3-7046-5908-8
2008, 576 pp

European Tort Law 2007
Edited by Helmut Koziol and Barbara C Steininger
Verlag Österreich, Vienna
Hardcover. ISBN 978-3-7046-5938-5
2008, 661 pp

European Tort Law 2008
Edited by Helmut Koziol and Barbara C Steininger
Verlag Österreich, Vienna
Hardcover. ISBN 978-3-7046-6120-3
2009, 708 pp

European Tort Law 2009
Edited by Helmut Koziol and Barbara C Steininger
de Gruyter, Berlin/New York
Hardcover. ISBN 978-3-11-024606-3
eBook. ISBN 978-3-11-024607-0
2010, 735 pp

European Tort Law 2010
Edited by Helmut Koziol and Barbara C Steininger
de Gruyter, Berlin/Boston
Hardcover. ISBN 978-3-11-023941-6
eBook. ISBN 978-3-11-023942-3
2011, 706 pp

European Tort Law 2011
Edited by Ken Oliphant and Barbara C Steininger

de Gruyter, Berlin/Boston
Hardcover. ISSN 2190 – 7773
eBook. ISSN 2190 – 7781
2012, 789 pp

European Tort Law 2012
Edited by Ken Oliphant and Barbara C Steininger
de Gruyter, Berlin/Boston
Hardcover. ISSN 2190 – 7773
eBook. ISSN 2190 – 7781
2013, 816 pp

European Tort Law 2013
Edited by Ernst Karner and Barbara C Steininger
de Gruyter, Berlin/Boston
Hardcover. ISSN 2190 – 7773
eBook. ISSN 2190 – 7781
2014, 824 pp

European Tort Law 2014
Edited by Ernst Karner and Barbara C Steininger
de Gruyter, Berlin/Boston
Hardcover. ISSN 2190 – 7773
eBook. ISSN 2190 – 7791
2015, 758 pp

European Tort Law 2015
Edited by Ernst Karner and Barbara C Steininger
de Gruyter, Berlin/Boston
Hardcover. ISSN 2190 – 7773
eBook. ISSN 2190 – 7791
2016, 764 pp

European Tort Law 2016
Edited by Ernst Karner and Barbara C Steininger
de Gruyter, Berlin/Boston
Hardcover. ISSN 2190 – 7773
eBook. ISSN 2190 – 7781
2017, 747 pp

European Tort Law 2017
Edited by Ernst Karner and Barbara C Steininger
de Gruyter, Berlin/Boston
Hardcover. ISSN 2190 – 7773
eBook. ISSN 2190 – 7781
2018, 762 pp

European Tort Law 2018
Edited by Ernst Karner and Barbara C Steininger
de Gruyter, Berlin/Boston
Hardcover. ISSN 2190 – 7773
eBook. ISSN 2190 – 7781
2019, 803 pp

European Tort Law 2019
Edited by Ernst Karner and Barbara C Steininger
de Gruyter, Berlin/Boston
Hardcover. ISSN 2190 – 7773
eBook. ISSN 2190 – 7781
2020, 797 pp

European Tort Law 2020
Edited by Ernst Karner and Barbara C Steininger
de Gruyter, Berlin/Boston
Hardcover. ISSN 2190 – 7773
eBook. ISSN 2190 – 7781
2021, 778 pp

European Tort Law 2021
Edited by Ernst Karner and Barbara C Steininger
de Gruyter, Berlin/Boston
Hardcover. ISSN 2190 – 7773
eBook. ISSN 2190 – 7781
2022, 785 pp

European Tort Law 2022
Edited by Ernst Karner and Barbara C Steininger
de Gruyter, Berlin/Boston
Hardcover. ISBN 978-3-11-124019-0
eBook. ISBN 978-3-11-124124-1
2023, 817 pp

European Tort Law 2023
Edited by Ernst Karner and Barbara C Steininger
de Gruyter, Berlin/Boston
Hardcover. ISBN 978-3-11-137612-7
E-book: 978-3-11-137672-1
2024, 841

European Group on Tort Law

Principles of European Tort Law. Text and Commentary
Edited by the European Group on Tort Law
Verlag Österreich, Vienna
Softcover. ISBN 978-3-7046-5837-1
2005, 282 pp

The Liability of Public Authorities in Comparative Perspective
Edited by Ken Oliphant
Intersentia, Cambridge/Antwerp/Portland
Softcover. ISBN 978-1-78068-238-9
2016, 887 pp

The Borderlines of Tort Law: Interactions with Contract Law
Edited by Miquel Martín-Casals
Intersentia, Cambridge/Antwerp/Portland
Softcover. ISBN 978-1-78068-248-8
2019, 846 pp

Prescription in Tort Law. Analytical and Comparative Perspectives
Edited by Israel Gilead and Bjarte Askeland
Intersentia, Cambridge/Antwerp/Portland
Softcover. ISBN 978-1-78068-963-0
2020, 746 pp

Digest of European Tort Law

Volume 1: *Essential Cases on Natural Causation*
Edited by Bénédict Winiger, Helmut Koziol, Bernhard A Koch and Reinhard Zimmermann
Verlag Österreich, Vienna
Hardcover. ISBN 978-3-7046-5885-2
2007, 632 pp

Volume 2: *Essential Cases on Damage*
Edited by Bénédict Winiger, Helmut Koziol, Bernhard A Koch and Reinhard Zimmermann
de Gruyter, Berlin/Boston
Hardcover. ISBN 978-3-11-024848-7
eBook. ISBN 978-3-11-024849-4
2011, 1175 pp

Volume 3: *Essential Cases on Misconduct*
Edited by Bénédict Winiger, Ernst Karner and Ken Oliphant
de Gruyter, Berlin/Boston
Hardcover. ISBN 978-3-11-053434-4
eBook. ISBN 978-3-11-053567-9
2018, 1286 pp

Volume 4: *Essential Cases on the Limits of Liability*
Edited by Bénédict Winiger, Bjarte Askeland, Elena Bargelli , Martin Hogg and Ernst Karner
de Gruyter, Berlin/Boston
Hardcover. ISBN 978-3-11-100121-0
e-ISBN (PDF) 978-3-11-100127-2
e-ISBN (EPUB) 978-3-11-100152-4
DOI https://doi.org/10.1515/9783111001272
2024, 829 pp

Sino-European Legal Studies

The Aims of Tort Law. Chinese and European Perspectives
Edited by Helmut Koziol
Jan Sramek Verlag, Vienna
Hardcover. ISBN 978-3-7097-0127-0
2017, 230 pp

The Legal Protection of Personality Rights. Chinese and European Perspectives
Edited by Ken Oliphant, Zhang Pinghua and Chen Lei
Brill | Nijhoff, Leiden/Boston
Hardcover. ISBN 978-9-0042-7629-1
eBook. ISBN 978-9-0043-5171-4
2018, 227 pp

Tortious and Contractual Liability. Chinese and European Perspectives
Edited by Ernst Karner
Jan Sramek Verlag, Vienna
Hardcover. ISBN 978-3-7097-0275-8
2021, 263 pp

Fault-Based and Strict Liability. Chinese and European Perspectives
Edited by Ernst Karner and David Messner-Kreuzbauer
Jan Sramek Verlag, Vienna
Hardcover. ISBN 978-3-7097-0291-8
2024, 307 pp

World Tort Law Society

Product Liability. Fundamental Questions in a Comparative Perspective
Edited by Helmut Koziol, Michael D Green, Mark Lunney, Ken Oliphant and Yang Lixin
de Gruyter, Berlin/Boston
Hardcover. ISBN 978-3-11-054600-2
eBook. ISBN 978-3-11-054581-4
2017, 610 pp

Others

European Tort Law. Basic Texts
Edited by Ernst Karner, Ken Oliphant and Barbara C Steininger
Jan Sramek Verlag, Vienna
Softcover. ISBN 978-3-7097-0170-6
2018, 2nd Edition, 466 pp

Grundfragen des Schadenersatzrechts
by Helmut Koziol
Jan Sramek Verlag, Vienna
Hardcover. ISBN 978-3-902638-28-1
2010, 371 pp

Grundfragen des Schadenersatzrechts aus rechtsvergleichender Sicht
Edited by Helmut Koziol
Jan Sramek Verlag, Vienna
Hardcover. ISBN 978-3-7097-48-8
2014, 941 pp

Basic Questions of Tort Law from a Germanic Perspective
by Helmut Koziol
Jan Sramek Verlag, Vienna
Hardcover. ISBN 978-3-902638-85-4
2012, 380 pp

Basic Questions of Tort Law from a Comparative Perspective
Edited by Helmut Koziol
Jan Sramek Verlag, Vienna
Hardcover. ISBN 978-3-7097-0040-2
2015, 867 pp

Comparative Stimulations for Developing Tort Law
Edited by Helmut Koziol
Jan Sramek Verlag, Vienna
Hardcover. ISBN 978-3-7097-0060-0
2015, 273 pp

Harmonisation and Fundamental Questions of European Tort Law
by Helmut Koziol
Jan Sramek Verlag, Vienna
Hardcover. ISBN 978-3-7097-0128-7
2017, 168 pp

Austrian Private Law. An Overview in Comparison with German Law and with References to English and French Law
by Gabriele Koziol and Helmut Koziol, in cooperation with Andrew Bell and Samuel Fulli-Lemaire
Jan Sramek Verlag, Vienna
Softcover. ISBN 978-3-7097-0156-0
2017, 119 pp

Grundzüge des japanischen Schadenersatzrechts
by Keizo Yamamoto
Jan Sramek Verlag, Vienna
Softcover. ISBN 978-3-7097-0102-7
2018, 220 pp

Basic Features of Japanese Tort Law
by Keizo Yamamoto
Jan Sramek Verlag, Vienna

Softcover. ISBN 978-3-7097-0188-1
2019, 202 pp

Tort Liability Law of China
by Lixin Yang
Jan Sramek Verlag, Vienna
Softcover. ISBN 978-3-7097-0088-4
2018, 384 pp

Essays in Honour of Helmut Koziol
Edited by Ernst Karner, Ulrich Magnus, Jaap Spier and Pierre Widmer
Jan Sramek Verlag, Vienna
Hardcover. ISBN 978-3-7097-0228-4
2020, 262 pp

Essays in Honour of Jaap Spier
Edited by Helmut Koziol and Ulrich Magnus
Jan Sramek Verlag, Vienna
Hardcover. ISBN 978-3-7097-0101-0
2016, 325 pp

Politikerhaftung. The Liabilities of Politicians
Edited by Helmut Koziol
Jan Sramek Verlag, Vienna
Hardcover. ISBN 978-3-7097-0242-0
2020, 487 pp

Die Haftung von Eisenbahnverkehrs- und Infrastrukturunternehmen im Rechtsvergleich
Edited by Helmut Koziol
Jan Sramek Verlag, Vienna
Softcover. ISBN 978-3-7097-0191-1
2019, 318 pp

Schadenersatzrechtliche Verantwortlichkeit im internationalen Eisenbahnverkehr
by Gregor Christandl and Olaf Riss
Jan Sramek Verlag, Vienna
Softcover. ISBN 978-3-7097-0273-4
2021, 161 pp

Die Vereinheitlichung der Haftung von Eisenbahnunternehmen in der Europäischen Union
by Helmut Koziol
Jan Sramek Verlag, Vienna
Softcover. ISBN 978-3-7097-0274-1
2021, 229 pp

Medienpolitik und Recht. Media Governance, Wahrhaftigkeitspflicht und sachgerechte Haftung
Edited by Helmut Koziol, Josef Seethaler and Thomas Thiede
Jan Sramek Verlag, Vienna
Hardcover. ISBN 978-3-902638-36-6
2010, 214 pp

Medienpolitik und Recht II. Presserat, WikiLeaks und Redaktionsgeheimnis
Edited by Helmut Koziol, Josef Seethaler and Thomas Thiede
Jan Sramek Verlag, Vienna

Hardcover. ISBN 978-3-902638-63-2
2013, 216 pp

Tatsachenmitteilungen und Werturteile. Freiheit und Verantwortung
Edited by Helmut Koziol
Jan Sramek Verlag, Vienna
Hardcover. ISBN 978-3-7097-0171-3
2018, 197 pp

Österreichisches Haftpflichtrecht Band I. Allgemeiner Teil
by Helmut Koziol
Jan Sramek Verlag, Vienna
Hardcover. ISBN 978-3-7097-0225-3
2020, 4th Edition, 1002 pp

Österreichisches Haftpflichtrecht Band II. Haftung für eigenes und fremdes Fehlverhalten
by Helmut Koziol
Jan Sramek Verlag, Vienna
Hardcover. ISBN 978-3-7097-0173-7
2018, 3rd Edition, 1074 pp

Österreichisches Haftpflichtrecht Band III. Gefährdungs-, Produkt- und Eingriffshaftung
by Helmut Koziol, Peter Apathy and Bernhard A Koch
Jan Sramek Verlag, Vienna
Hardcover. ISBN 978-3-7097-0022-8
2014, 3rd Edition, 596 pp

Mangelfolgeschäden in Veräußerungsketten. Am Beispiel der Aus- und Einbaukosten
by Ernst Karner and Helmut Koziol
Jan Sramek Verlag, Vienna
Softcover. ISBN 978-3-902638-84-7
2012, 96 pp

Zur Anwendbarkeit des UN-Kaufrechts bei Werk- und Dienstleistungen. Am Beispiel der Maschinen- und Industrieanlagenlieferungsverträge
by Ernst Karner and Helmut Koziol
Jan Sramek Verlag, Vienna
Softcover. ISBN 978-3-7097-0052-5
2015, 91 pp

Obsoleszenzen im österreichischen Recht. Geltendes Recht, Schutzlücken und Reformbedarf
by Helmut Koziol
Jan Sramek Verlag, Vienna
Softcover. ISBN 978-3-7097-0108-9
2016, 137 pp

Vertragsstrafe und Schadenspauschalierung
by Ernst Karner and Alexander Longin
Jan Sramek Verlag, Vienna
Softcover. ISBN 978-3-7097-0234-5
2020, 240 pp

Haftungsfreizeichnungen zulasten Dritter. Im Zwischenbereich von Vertrag und Delikt
by Johannes Angyan
Jan Sramek Verlag, Vienna

Hardcover. ISBN 978-3-7097-0257-4
2021, 351 pp

Recht auf Anpassung des Werkvertrags
by Alexander Longin
Jan Sramek Verlag, Vienna
Hardcover. ISBN 978-3-7097-0258-1
2021, 396 pp

Mehrstufiger Warenverkehr. Spezifische Probleme bei Vertragsketten
by Helmut Koziol
Jan Sramek Verlag, Vienna
Hardcover. ISBN 978-3-7097-0284-0
2021, 317 pp

Rechtsunkenntnis und Schadenszurechnung
by Helmut Koziol
Jan Sramek Verlag, Vienna
Hardcover. ISBN 978-3-7097-0309-0
2022, 189 pp

Erlaubte Notstandshandlungen und zivilrechtliche Ausgleichsansprüche
by David Messner-Kreuzbauer
Jan Sramek Verlag, Vienna
Hardcover. ISBN 978-3-7097-0314-4
2022, 448 pp

Baumgefahren-Management in Österreichs Nationalparks. Zugleich ein Beitrag zu den Grundlagen der Baum- und Forsthaftung samt Entscheidungsübersicht
by Ernst Karner and Karoline Zsak
Jan Sramek Verlag, Vienna
Hardcover. ISBN 978-3-7097-0322-9
2023, 159 pp

Rechtszuweisung, Güterzuordnung und deren Schutz
by Helmut Koziol
Jan Sramek Verlag, Vienna
Hardcover. ISBN 978-3-7097-0367-0
2024, 314 pp

Die Ehre Verstorbener und ihr Schutz
by Helmut Koziol
Jan Sramek Verlag, Vienna
Softcover. ISBN 978-3-7097-0374-8
2024, 108 pp

Journal of European Tort Law

The Journal of European Tort Law (JETL) is published three times a year. The General Editor is Professor Ken Oliphant, University of Bristol.

Further information, including subscription details and instructions for authors, is available on the JETL website <http://www.degruyter.com/view/j/jetl>.

Queries may be addressed to <information@jetl.eu>. Articles, comments and reviews should be submitted for consideration to <submissions@jetl.eu>. The Journal applies a policy of double-blind peer review.